P9-CAF-416

Accounting: an introduction

Second edition

Charles J. Woelfel

PhD, CPA

Professor of Accountancy
Southern Illinois University
Carbondale, Illinois

Goodyear Publishing Company, Inc.
Santa Monica, California

Library of Congress Cataloging in Publication Data

Woelfel, Charles J.
Accounting: An Introduction.

Includes index.
1. Accounting I. Title.
HF5635.W8445 1977 657 76–17204
ISBN 0–87620–025–0

Current printing (last digit):

10 9 8 7 6 5 4 3 2 1

Y–0250–4

Printed in the United States of America

To my wife
Colette

Preface to second edition

Accounting: An Introduction, Second Edition, is a major development of the first edition of this text. In this revision, the strong balance between (1) the conceptual and the procedural approaches to accounting and (2) the financial and managerial content of accountancy has been maintained. The text includes the most recent pronouncements of authoritative accounting bodies available (at the date of publication) that are relevant to an introductory text in accountancy. The text also updates material related to payroll tax legislation and similar legislative changes.

In the revised edition, additional questions, exercises, and problems have been added to give instructors greater flexibility in assigning problems and in selecting material for classroom demonstrations. The material on the accounting cycle has been rearranged (see Exhibit P-1) to provide a more measured development of this topic. The major part of a new chapter (Chapter 21) has been devoted to Financial Statement Analysis and inserted at the end of the financial accounting section of the book. This modification reinforces the chapter-by-chapter introduction of financial statement analysis throughout the preceding chapters. The chapter on Manufacturing Operations has been developed into two chapters for the convenience of instructors who prefer to treat either job-order and process costs (Chapter 30) or standard costs (Chapter 31).

The revised text retains its challenging material on impact analysis which has proven itself to be a valuable tool for developing an understanding of what accounting is all about. Impact analysis provides accounting and nonaccounting majors with a real insight into the accounting process.

This Second Edition of *Accounting: An Introduction* is user oriented. Students and instructors are the primary users of accounting texts and this book is custom-made to meet their needs. It is my expectation that students using this text will have a unique opportunity to obtain a solid foundation in a discipline that has proven itself to be indispensable to the business world.

Exhibit P-1
Topical outline of accounting: an introduction

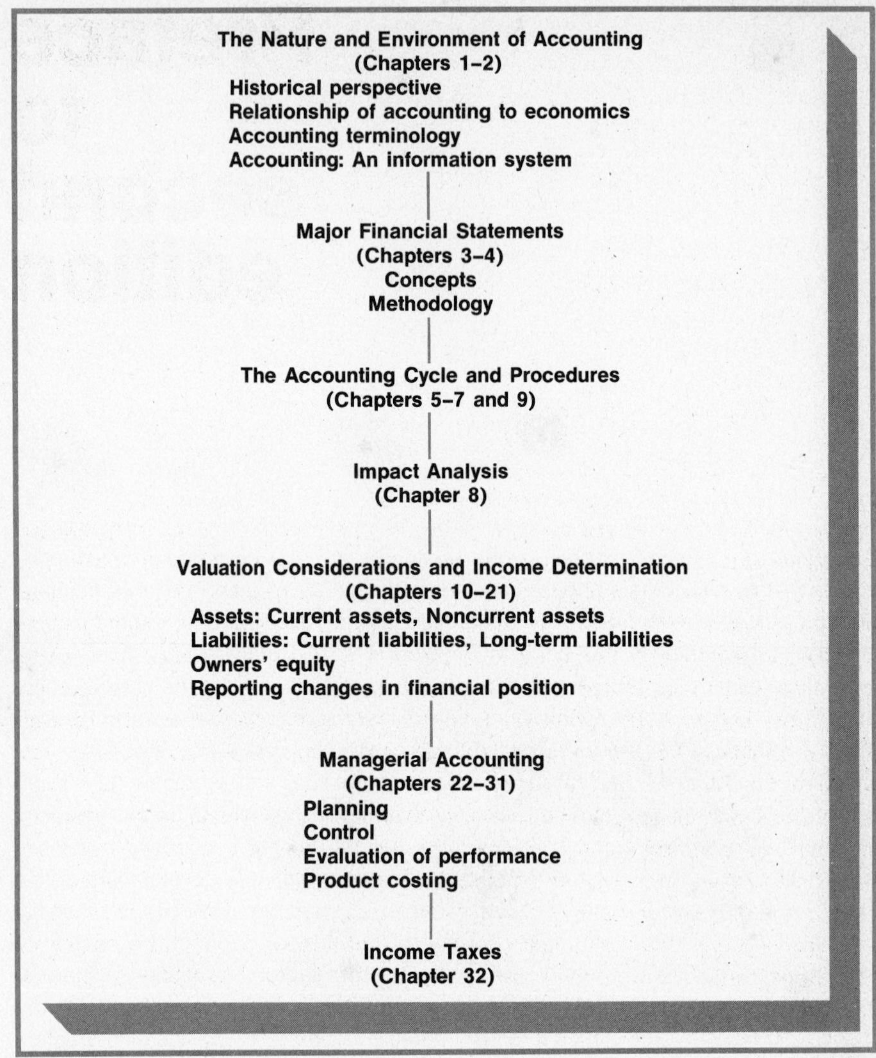

Sincere appreciations to the editors and staff of the Goodyear Publishing Company who worked diligently in getting the revision through the production stages—especially to Colette Conboy, Supervising Editor. Without the expert counsel of Sally Kostal, Production Editor, the revision of this text would not have been possible. Above all, thanks to Steven Lock, Editor. Finally, thanks to my patient counselor, friend, and wife—Colette Woelfel.

Charles J. Woelfel
Carbondale, Illinois
October 1976

Preface to first edition

This accounting text is intended primarily for use in introductory accounting courses for college students. It is designed to cover financial and managerial accounting as a first college-level course in accounting for undergraduates with no previous exposure to accounting. It can also be used as a survey text at the graduate level.

The basic objective of this book is to present a comprehensive coverage of financial and managerial topics in accounting in a clear and concise format. The topics covered in this book are those with which all students of business should be familiar. Textual material is adequately supplemented by numerous examples and diagrams, which facilitate the learning and teaching processes.

The book can be divided conveniently to accommodate college or university calendar and scheduling. As a full-year accounting course, it can be divided to fit into two semesters, two quarters, or three quarters. As a sequence of courses, it can be divided into courses in financial accounting and managerial accounting.

In planning this text, the author has taken care to develop a balanced approach to what he considers to be the needs of students. This built-in balance is reflected in the following ways.

1. Users:
   a. accounting majors,
   b. nonaccounting majors.
2. Instruction:
   a. conceptual approach,
   b. procedural approach.
3. Content:
   a. financial accounting.
   b. managerial accounting.

The book places proper emphasis upon—

1. theory of accounting (concepts, principles, and standards);

2. administrative and managerial uses of accounting for planning, controlling, evaluating, and decision making;
3. practices and procedures.

A study of both financial and managerial accounting is basic to an understanding of accounting as the language of business and as a tool of management. Approximately 60 percent of this text is devoted to financial accounting and 40 percent to managerial accounting. Because of the flexibility of the subject matter and the comprehensiveness of the coverage, these two major areas can be divided by an instructor to suit his preferences, his experience, and the needs of his students.

The chapters on financial accounting are externally oriented. They deal mainly with the major financial statements that report on financial position, results of operations, and changes in financial position. These topics are covered extensively in Chapters 1 through 16 and 26 and 27, where the following areas are developed:

1. fundamental accounting concepts and terminology;
2. accumulation, measurement, and communication of economic data in and through the accounting system;
3. interpretation and use of financial statements;
4. decision-making implications of accounting information.

Managerial accounting is concerned primarily with internal reporting. It relates essentially to planning, controlling, evaluating performance, and product costing for inventory valuation and income determination. Chapters 17 through 25 treat this material in a concise and relevant manner.

This book is thoroughly current. It contains references to the most recent opinions and statements of the American Institute of Certified Public Accountants and the American Accounting Association. Early in their education, students should learn the necessity of keeping currently informed about developments in their career fields. The author considers it imperative that students be taught accounting theory and practice from an updated text. No substitute for this information is acceptable.

A major innovative feature of this text is the development of *impact analysis* as an aid to understanding the nature, scope, and significance of accounting. Through an appreciation of impact analysis, the student develops insights into and an awareness of the importance of economic transactions and events on major sets and subsets of the accounting system. For example, a sales transaction has a direct impact on net assets, owners' equity, working capital, net income per share of stock, rate of return on investment, and other major accounting categories. Impact accounting stresses the reality that managerial decisions must be designed not as isolated events but rather as parts of the whole. With a knowledge of the ripple effect of transactions and events on other elements in the accounting system, management can devise ways of improving performance and facilitating control and decision-making processes. An impact approach to accounting makes the study of accounting a serious and rewarding experience. It transforms the apprentice into the professional. Impact analysis evokes total involvement.

This book incorporates certain special topics that the author believes should be covered in a basic manner in an introductory accounting text:

1. earnings-per-share computations (primary and fully diluted earnings per share),
2. consolidated statements,
3. investments in unconsolidated subsidiaries,
4. price-level adjustments,
5. allocation of income taxes,
6. income tax planning,
7. quantitative techniques,
8. behavioral-sciences applications to accounting.

An instructor may not have time to cover all of these topics, but the material is here and the choice is his to make.

Each chapter of this book contains study materials:

1. questions, which review chapter highlights and evoke insights into and awarenesses of the intricacies of accounting;
2. exercises, which stress fundamental concepts and techniques; and
3. problems, which challenge the student by expanding and developing basic concepts and techniques.

Achievement tests and comprehensive examinations are available. Practice sets have been prepared for the professor who prefers to use this tool to reinforce the learning process. Transparencies with solutions to many exercises and problems accompany the text. Working papers, key solution figures, and special Student Aids have been designed for students. A detailed solutions manual is provided for instructors. A Study Guide for students is also available.

This book provides a broad perspective of accountancy for the future accountant, manager, or economist, and for other persons interested in the business scene. Hopefully, when this book has been read, digested, and mastered, the student will be in a position to pursue his studies and his career with the realization that he now possesses a firm foundation in the fundamentals of accounting.

Charles J. Woelfel
Carbondale, Illinois
June 1974

Contents

The nature and environment of accounting

Part One

1

The environment of accounting

You probably approach the study of accounting with enthusiasm and awe. These mixed emotions are reasonable. Accounting involves a body of knowledge that has grown over many years in size, complexity, and importance. However, you should not hesitate to undertake this study. If you approach it with some joy in ideas and in practical efforts, the study of accounting can be an exciting and rewarding experience.

We begin with a brief history of accountancy.[1] After our look at the overall subject in this chapter, you will soon be immersed in many different concepts related to accounting. In these early chapters, you need not worry too much about mastering all the details. But an early introduction to these critical ideas will help give more meaning to the routine study of procedures. We refer to these concepts again and again throughout the text. In this way, we hope that you will better understand and appreciate accountancy as an art and a profession.

Accounting: an historical viewpoint

History began when people learned to record their activities. The ancient scribes made their marks on stone, papyrus, or wax tablets. These ways of keeping records were invented to meet a need for gathering, processing, and preserving information. The growth of empires and commerce made some form of written records necessary.

As early as 5000 B.C. in the Babylonian empire, clay tablets were used to record facts. The tablets describe the business of the empire and of its traders. Similar records are found in documents from ancient Egypt, Greece, and Rome. Many of the early records simply list events in the order that they happened. Others describe inventories of grains, precious metals, and the like. These records are in words and sentences, unlike the columns of numbers we might use today. Business and household records often are mixed together.

1. ***Accounting*** refers to the process or system of accounting. ***Accountancy*** is the art, occupation, or profession of the accountant.

The earliest business records merely list the goods belonging to some person or temple. Later records begin to show concern about profit and loss on ventures. Income and expenses are recorded, and even rough budgets are planned. Further advances in accounting were made by government and church officials during the Middle Ages.

During the Renaissance of art, literature, and philosophy, a major breakthrough was made in Venice. In 1494—two years after the discovery of America—Luca Pacioli published a book on mathematics called ***Summa Mathematica.*** In it he gave the first complete description of a way of keeping business records that had developed gradually over the past few centuries. This double-entry form of bookkeeping was to become the basis of modern accounting procedures. An interesting side note: Pacioli's book also contained drawings and sketches by a renowned Italian artist, Leonardo da Vinci.

With the Industrial Revolution in England and on the Continent, there was a great expansion of business activity. Large industrial and commercial enterprises emerged. Many of these companies were owned by shareholders rather than by those who managed the business. Accounting then began to serve as a communicating process rather than just a way of keeping records. When the owners no longer managed the business, they began to demand from their managers accurate and detailed reports. They judged the business and the managers in terms of the profit earned. Profitability became a major concern of accountants.

Through the nineteenth and twentieth centuries, corporations have become more important, larger, and more complex. Large-scale business operations involving mass production, distribution, and consumption processes have become common. Owners have demanded that the accounting system provide better information to use in evaluating these operations. Income tax legislation has become ever more complex. Government has assumed a role in regulating such areas as the security markets, public utilities, railroads, and price and cost controls. These government activities brought innovations in financial reporting practices and stimulated the evolution of accounting theory.

In the twentieth century, accountants and theoreticians have paid increasing attention to specialized accounting procedures and applications such as budgeting, cost accounting, and electronic data processing. Also in this century, accountants organized themselves into vigorous professional associations such as the American Institute of Certified Public Accountants (AICPA),[2] the American Accounting Association (AAA),[3] and the National Association of Accountants (NAA).[4]

2. The American Institute of Certified Public Accountants is a major association of Certified Public Accountants (CPAs). The membership of the AICPA consists mainly of accounting practitioners and educators. Among the purposes of the AICPA are the following: (1) to assist in maintaining high standards for the profession; (2) to develop accountancy education, research, and the interests of the profession. The AICPA publishes ***The Journal of Accountancy.***

A CPA is an accountant who has passed certain examinations related to accounting, business law, and auditing, and who has met other educational and character requirements set forth in state laws governing the practice of public accounting. The CPA designation indicates that the person having this title has a certain capability to provide competent service to the public in the areas of accounting and auditing.

3. The American Accounting Association is an organization of individuals interested in the development of accounting. Although most of the AAA members are educators, many practitioners of accounting also belong

In recent years, accountants have become interested in such areas as quantitative methods used in operations research, the behavioral sciences, and environmental problems. As the twentieth century enters its final quarter, accountancy has achieved the status of a profession. Its practice has major social and economic significance.

The environment of accounting

Fish live in water; birds fly through the air. Each thing lives in a natural environment. So it is with man. Humans respond to the environment in which they live; they also act upon it. They discover, create, and have imposed upon them the human condition.

To survive and then thrive in an economic environment, men developed economic systems. In these systems they produce goods and services, distribute income, and exchange and consume the outputs of the system. No matter what political system we live in, we depend on the processes of production, distribution, exchange, and consumption. They form a major part of our everyday activity. Clearly, economic tasks are central human tasks.

In any economic system—except perhaps the most primitive—we see that we must account for the inputs and outputs of the system. The art of accounting sprang from this need for accountability. Accounting operates within the confines of an economic system. If it is to meet the needs and desires of the users of the system, it must reflect that system. Thus a study of accounting must begin with a look at the nature and scope of the economic system we have devised to cope with our economic environment. So we turn to a ***brief*** overview of economic activity in our society.

We begin by noting that an economic system should meet man's physical needs without unduly restricting his personal freedom. However, the goals of the economic system must not necessarily be seen as the only—or even as the primary—goal of man. Life has other and larger purposes.

Any economic system exists to deal with certain basic environmental conditions. Whether the system is developing or mature, it must meet four basic economic problems that we can express as questions.

1. What kinds and amounts of goods and services shall be produced? In economics, this question deals with the ***production process.***
2. For whom are goods and services to be produced? Here we deal with the ***distribution of income.*** This is the process of assigning the outputs of the production process among the four factors of production.
   a. ***land*** with its return called ***rents;***
   b. ***labor*** with its remuneration called ***wages;***
   c. ***capital*** with its payment called ***interest;***
   d. ***ownership*** with its reward for risk-taking and innovating called ***profit.***

to the AAA. The objectives of the AAA include the following: (1) to encourage and sponsor research in accounting; (2) to develop accounting principles and standards; and (3) to improve methods of accounting instruction. The AAA publishes ***The Accounting Review.***

4. The National Association of Accountants is an organization of industrial accountants and educators whose interests are in cost and managerial accounting. The NAA published ***Management Accounting.***

3. How are goods and services traded for other economic resources? This process of transforming one good into another through a price and market system is called the ***exchange process.***
4. How is the output of the production process to be used? As the goods and services are used, their utility is lessened. This process is called ***consumption.***

In an economic system, people also ***save*** and ***invest.*** These activities become major elements in the economic environment. Saving occurs when an individual or group postpones the consumption of goods and services. If some of today's income is not consumed, the individual or group can divert productive resources away from production of more consumer goods. These diverted resources can be invested in creation of new factories and machines. In other words, saving is a process that adds to the stock of economic resources through the creation of capital goods—goods that are not consumed directly, but are used to expand the production facilities. With increased savings and intelligent investments, the wealth of the nation grows as more machines, factories, and tools are produced. Savings and investments are the keys to the growth of a nation's economy. Accounting for the national economy is a specialized facet of accounting; it is a major concern of economists and statisticians.

In a simple economic system, the consumer-citizen makes many of the decisions about the four problems just listed. As industry and commerce evolve, the system becomes more complex. Modern economic theory holds that the consumer then loses much of his power. Giant industrial and commercial enterprises take over economic and political power. As power is concentrated in the hands of the giant businesses, they establish favored working relationships with government. Some theorists are bold enough to argue that this must lead to lowered quality of life and the loss of personality. As industry and government merge, they create forces that regulate the whole economy, from the first step of production to the final swallow of consumption. The behavior and attitudes of individuals and groups often reflect this merger.

The future of the economic system seems to hinge more and more on a fusion of big business and big government. In this bureaucratic marriage, economic survival and progress depend ever more on planning, control, and accommodation. The size and complexity of economic activities increase. Administration and control of prices, the marketplace, and the consumer become more commonplace. The free world and the free enterprise system are being socialized—for better or for worse, depending on your political viewpoint. We must take care that the individual does not become as obsolete as a breath of fresh air.

Economic events

We have viewed the economic system from a wide perspective. Now we look at individual parts of the economic environment, especially as they relate to accounting. A modern economic system is made up of a wide variety of complex arrangements. This variety of structures and processes has been developed to produce, exchange, distribute, consume, save, and invest within the system. Over the centuries institutions, laws, customs, habits, and codes have been established that make economic activities more stable, predictable, and continuous. We have learned to cope with our economic environment.

In the learning process, men found it useful to concentrate their energies into highly organized structures called ***business enterprises.*** These structures provide two major advantages. First, they permit each worker to specialize in a certain job; this division of labor increases the productivity of the worker. Second, they make possible mass production, exchange, distribution, and consumption of goods and services; this reduces the costs of these activities. All businesses are not the same in structure. Again, different circumstances have led to a wide variety of arrangements. Some businesses are single proprietorships—that is, they are owned by one person. Others are set up as partnerships, cooperatives, corporations, or other structures. These business entities engage in economic activities that increase or decrease their economic resources and their owners' claims to these resources.

When economic activities occur, accounting enters the picture. The accountant codes these ***events*** in financial terms. He or she can then process and communicate these data so that they can be interpreted by those who have an interest in the economic activities of the enterprise. To cope with events, accountants found that they had to distinguish between external events and internal events. ***External events*** are those that affect both the enterprise itself and other parties. For example, if a firm borrows money from a bank, buys a building from a realtor, or sells a boat to a customer—these are external events. ***Internal events*** are those economic activities that involve only the enterprise itself. If the business transforms lumber into furniture or sugar into candy, destroys outdated goods that had been stored in its warehouse, or loses a building in a fire—these are internal events. Internal and external events are the ***inputs*** of the accounting system. The term ***transaction*** is used in accounting to refer to events that require accounting recognition.

Before these inputs can be processed by the accounting system, the activities must be ***measured.*** In a modern economy, economic activities are measured primarily by ***prices*** expressed in terms of ***money.*** A laborer's wage is so many dollars; a pound of steak costs so much. In a barter economy, each producer must trade his or her output for goods and services produced by others. If he produces sandals, he must barter with the butcher to find out how many pounds of meat he can get for a pair of sandals. In a money economy, each item or service has a price. Money serves as (1) a medium of exchange, (2) a standard unit of value, and (3) a store of value. First, money helps smooth the exchange process. A good or service is traded for money; the money then is used to buy other goods or services. Second, money gives a common denominator of value. Using money we can compare the worth of such diverse items as a sirloin steak and a ticket to a football game. Third, money is a convenient way of holding personal wealth for future use.

Money is the yardstick that the accountant uses to measure economic activity. With this measure of economic value, he can devote his attention to the task of recording and interpreting economic events. He can develop principles and procedures that make it possible to translate economic events into data on financial reports.

Accounting defined

Accounting provides the eyes and ears of management. Each business entity must know what it is doing and where it is going financially. Accounting keeps the financial score for a business. It calls attention to the problems and the opportunities that confront the enterprise. Where action is needed, it suggests possible courses of action.

Because accounting is an intellectual discipline, we need a working definition of accounting as a background for our study. The American Accounting Association has defined accounting as

> the process of identifying, measuring, and communicating economic information to permit informed judgments and decisions by users of the information. . . . [The] objectives of accounting are to provide information for the following purposes:
>
> *1.* Making decisions concerning the use of limited resources, including the identification of crucial decision areas, and determination of objectives and goals.
> *2.* Effectively directing and controlling an organization's human and material resources.
> *3.* Maintaining and reporting on the custodianship of resources.
> *4.* Facilitating social functions and controls.[5]

In this definition, the AAA committee emphasizes that the major job of accounting is to provide information for the *judgments* and *decisions* of those who use the information. The definition specifies three major functions of accounting: *identifying, measuring,* and *communicating* economic information. Throughout this text we examine and use all three functions to shed light upon the accounting process. In listing the major purposes of accounting, the AAA put its main emphasis on the activities of *decision making, control,* and *custodianship.* The definition also suggests that accounting has certain broad social functions that carry with them a responsibility to those who use the outputs of the accounting system.

Another definition of accounting was set forth in 1970 by the Accounting Principles Board (APB) of the American Institute of Certified Public Accountants.

> Accounting is a service activity. Its function is to provide quantitative information, primarily financial in nature, about economic entities that is intended to be useful in making economic decisions—in making reasoned choices among alternative courses of action.[6]

The APB definition of accounting is *goal oriented* rather than process oriented. It emphasizes economic *decision-making activities* rather than the recording, classifying, summarizing, and interpreting processes of accounting. This interpretation emphasizes the true role of accounting in its modern setting.

5. AAA Committee to Prepare a Statement of Basic Accounting Theory, *A Statement of Basic Accounting Theory* (Evanston, Ill.: American Accounting Association, 1966), p. 1.

6. Accounting Principles Board, *Statement No. 4: Basic Concepts and Accounting Principles Underlying Financial Statements of Business Enterprises* (New York: American Institute of Certified Public Accountants, 1970), para. 40. Copyright 1970 by the American Institute of Certified Public Accountants, Inc. This and other quotes from this publication cited in this text are used with the permission of the AICPA. Hereafter this document is referred to as *APB Statement No. 4.*

The users of accounting information

As we have seen, accounting is essentially a system for gathering and disseminating information. It gathers, processes, communicates, and interprets data about the economic activity of the enterprise. For whom does the accounting system prepare its outputs? Individuals and groups with a variety of different needs look to the outputs of the system to meet their desires for information. Some users of accounting have a direct interest in financial accounting information; other users have only an indirect interest. The function of those who have an indirect interest in financial statements is to assist or protect those who have a direct interest in the statements. Those who have a ***direct*** interest in the statements include owners, creditors, potential investors, managers, taxing authorities, employees, customers, and others. Those who have an ***indirect*** interest include financial analysts and advisors, lawyers, regulatory authorities, trade associations, labor unions, and others.

Owners of business enterprises need periodic reports on their economic resources and obligations. They are directly and vitally interested in the performance of their managers and the profitability of their investments. They need information for the many decisions they must make as owners, risk takers, and innovators.

Managers of business entities also have a direct interest in accounting information. They face many problems in determining company policy, establishing objectives for the organization, evaluating the performance of the units of the company and its employees, and making other decisions about the businesses they manage. Accounting and management cannot be separated without doing violence to both.

Potential investors in a business learn a great deal about a company from its financial reports. They are assisted by ***financial analysts*** and ***advisors*** in the study of this information. These individuals and groups are interested in such things as the growth potential of the firm, its earning trends, and comparative analyses of companies and industries. Accounting helps in assembling and interpreting such data for these parties.

Creditors of an enterprise supply goods, services, and financial resources to the firm. They need to evaluate the risks involved in extending credit. An informed interpretation of financial statements gives them information about the credit rating of a business.

Customers and ***clients*** also have an interest in the financial position and operations of the firm with which they are dealing. A careful reading of financial statements can sometimes provide information about prices and potential price changes. From financial reports these parties can estimate the viability of a firm as a continuing source of supplies.

Employees and ***unions*** are interested in the financial position and operations of a firm. From financial reports they often gain information about such things as fringe benefits, salary determination, and working conditions. Employees and unions look to financial statements for insights into matters affecting their economic and social interests.

Federal, state, and local ***governmental units*** have become increasingly interested in the internal operations of business enterprises. The Internal Revenue Service has a vested interest in the taxable income of business. Other governmental agencies look to the outputs of the accounting system to help them administer legislative directives. These agencies include the Securities and Exchange Commission, Federal Trade Commission, Interstate Commerce Commission, and many others.

Accounting statements have evolved over the years to meet the needs of these various interests. In some situations, the interests of the different users of financial statements conflict. In such cases, the accountant must decide which interests have priority. It can be argued that the interests of owners and creditors must be given first priority when information conflicts arise.[7]

For most businesses, there exists a variety of users for the output of the accounting system. As you might expect, this makes the task of accounting more complex. Reports that meet the needs of one group may be irrelevant for others. The preparation of reports that meet the needs of all the users may be a practical impossibility. However, accountants must persevere in the attempt to develop and practice their art so that what they produce is ***user oriented.*** This is the real challenge to the accounting profession.

Careers in accounting

The trained accountant is a professional. As a group, accountants are highly respected members of the business community. The accounting profession has grown in size and importance at a promising rate over the years. Accountants are providing an increasingly broad range of counsel and services to society. The accountant can find a career in education or in private, public, or governmental accounting.

In ***private accounting,*** the accountant is employed by a single enterprise such as General Motors or IBM. In most private firms, the chief accountant is called the ***controller.*** This title refers to his major function of using accounting to assist in the control of business operations. The private accountant has major responsibilities in such areas as designing and operating accounting systems, budgeting future operations, tax planning, internal auditing, and so on.

The ***public accountant*** is an independent professional who offers his accounting services to the public for a fee. Most public accountants are Certified Public Accountants (CPAs). The public accountant provides assistance to his clients in three major areas: auditing and accounting, tax, and management consulting. As an ***auditor,*** the accountant examines financial statements prepared by others (his clients). He then gives an opinion about the fairness of the statements and their conformity with generally accepted accounting principles. The public accountant often provides ***tax services*** for his clients. He makes available to them his knowledge, research capabilities, and experience in this increasingly complex area of business. As a ***management consultant,*** the public accountant provides knowledge about

7. "Financial accounting presents general-purpose financial information that is designed to serve the common needs of owners, creditors, managers, and other users, with primary emphasis on the needs of present and potential owners and creditors." ***APB Statement No. 4,*** para. 125.

such areas as information processing, management sciences, budgeting, accounting systems, and so on.

Governmental accountants are employed by federal, state, and local governmental units. Their duties include maintenance of government accounting records, preparation of budgets, audit operations, review of income tax returns, and a variety of other services.

As an ***educator,*** the accountant uses his extensive knowledge of accounting to prepare others for careers in accounting or in other areas of business. Most accounting educators have had experience as private, public, or governmental accountants. They bring their practical experience into the classroom to make accounting theory more meaningful. As in public accounting, educators often specialize in certain areas of accounting such as financial or managerial accounting, taxes, auditing, or systems. They often serve as consultants to business or government. Some write textbooks.

Careers in accounting have much to offer the individual. There is a genuine challenge, job satisfaction, and an opportunity for personal development and service to others. Also, the accountant may obtain generous rewards, professional and social contacts, and special chances to move into top positions in management. Those who have the ability and the desire can find a vital place for themselves in the accounting profession.

Summary

Chapter 1 is an overview of accounting. It begins with a broad and sweeping historical look at accounting and its origins. Although accounting began with the earliest written records, it evolved slowly. It was greatly influenced by external forces, slowly developed a theoretical structure, and finally achieved the status of a profession.

Accounting operates in an economic environment. Economic processes of production, distribution, exchange, and consumption provide the major events that are recorded by accounting. Economic events are measured in dollars, which become the reporting symbols of accounting.

The chapter includes definitions of accounting set forth by major professional associations. The student should be familiar with the content and scope of these definitions. Most accounting terms have precise, technical meanings; the student must master these concepts. Attention should be focused on three major functions of accounting: decision making, control, and custodianship.

Accounting is a practical study. It gathers, processes, and reports information about financial events. The users of its output include owners, creditors, and managers. To justify its existence, accounting must provide relevant information to those who rely on it. In the final analysis, accounting is a service function.

Accountants are professionals. They practice in areas of private, public, or governmental accounting, or in education. Careers in each of these areas offer rewarding opportunities to qualified men and women.

Questions

1. The roots of accounting reach back into history. Briefly trace the development of accounting from its early stages to modern times.
2. In a barter economy, goods are exchanged directly for other goods without using money as a medium of exchange. Would some form of accounting be necessary in a barter economy? Would it be possible? Discuss.
3. Why did the development of large-scale business increase the need for accounting?
4. Briefly describe the membership and goals of the following professional organizations: the American Institute of Certified Public Accountants; the American Accounting Association; the National Association of Accountants.
5. What is meant by the economic environment of accounting?
6. What is the major objective of an economic system?
7. State the four fundamental economic problems that must be met by any economic system.
8. What is meant by saving and investing activities in an economic system? What is their importance in economic growth?
9. Why does man organize his economic activities in structures called business enterprises?
10. What is meant by an economic event? Distinguish between external and internal events. Give several examples of each kind of event.
11. What are the three major functions served by money?
12. Define accounting. Compare the definitions of accounting proposed by the AAA and the AICPA.
13. Distinguish between accounting and accountancy.
14. List several major users of accounting information and discuss why each is interested in the output of the accounting system.

2 Accounting: an information system

Human societies have always relied upon ***systems,*** whether they were called by that name or not. Early men planted crops according to a system; they used a system to organize the hunt; they waged wars under a system. As societies evolved, business emerged as a major human activity. There was an increasing need for information about business activities, and business information systems were soon evolved to meet that need. As businesses became bigger and more complex, they demanded more sophisticated approaches to the collecting, processing, and reporting of information. Accounting systems were among the earliest systems designed to control the financial affairs of business. The first accounting systems were mainly recording systems. Over the centuries, they evolved into complete information systems. Production systems were developed to control men and machines. Marketing systems were used to increase sales productivity. In the modern economy, systems are becoming an ever more important fact of life.

Information is the raw material for decision making. There is a direct relationship between the quality of information available and the appropriateness of the decisions that are made. The quality of the information depends on the nature of the system used to gather, process, and communicate that information. The computer has made it possible to process vast amounts of information at incredible speeds. Information itself has become a prime economic resource.

Business information systems have always been ***functionally oriented.*** That is, they are designed to provide information for production, marketing, and financial operations. They were developed mainly for use within the business.

A business information system consists of all the activities, forms, and procedures that regulate the systematic flow of information within an organization. Obviously, control of the information system can lead to better control of the processes that the system reports on. Those who design and run information systems have long dreamed of integrating all of a firm's information sources into a ***total system.*** Today this dream is close to reality. In a total information system, a number of independent systems are plugged into a master system that has as its inputs the outputs of the subsystems. At one time accounting was the number one business system. Today it is assuming a role as only one subsystem in a total information system.

Accounting as an information system

By thinking of accounting as an ***information system*** or ***process,*** we can add a new dimension to our basic understanding of accounting. This system has its own resources, activities, and objectives as a separate system. Or we can view it as a subsystem of a larger information system. Either viewpoint puts a proper emphasis on the role that accounting plays in the drama of the business world.

We can think of an information system—in its most general outline—in terms of inputs, processing, and outputs. ***Inputs*** into the system are made by individuals and by the environment in which the business operates. The inputs then are ***processed*** by the system. This processing is based on assumptions, principles, and procedures that have been set up to achieve a particular objective. Finally, the ***outputs*** of processing are communicated to the users of the information. Exhibit 2-1 broadly visualizes accounting as an information system.

The accounting system supplies information to management for use in planning and operating the business. It also serves parties who have rights and interests in the company. To be effective, the system must supply ***the kind*** of information needed and must make it available ***when*** it is needed.

There is a very important relationship between an information system and the goal-setting and goal-attaining activities of the firm. If it is designed and used effectively, an accounting system will provide owners, managers, and others with information useful in (1) establishing goals for the organization, (2) selecting means to achieve established goals, (3) controlling operations, and (4) measuring and evaluating performance. The designer of an accounting system must specify the

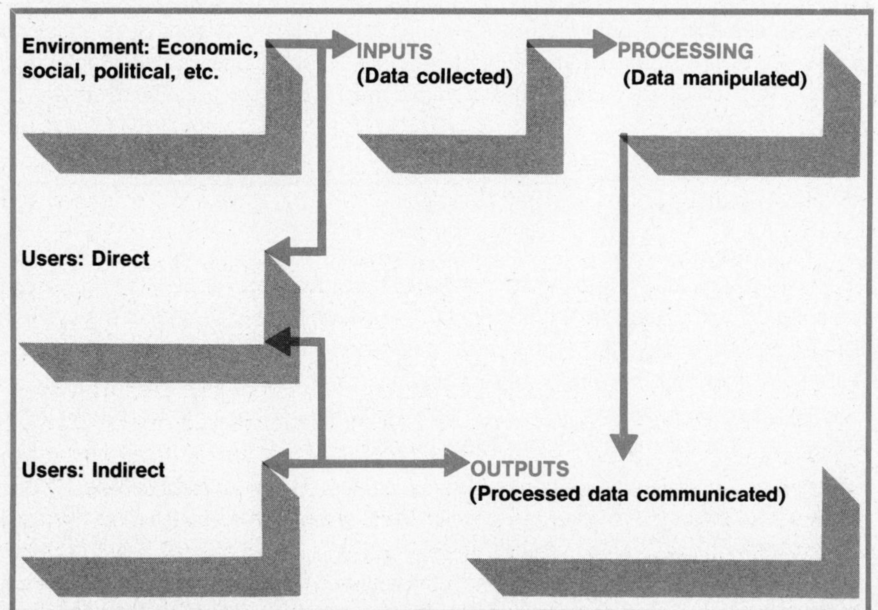

Exhibit 2-1
Accounting as an information system (condensed)

Exhibit 2-2
A financial information system (condensed)

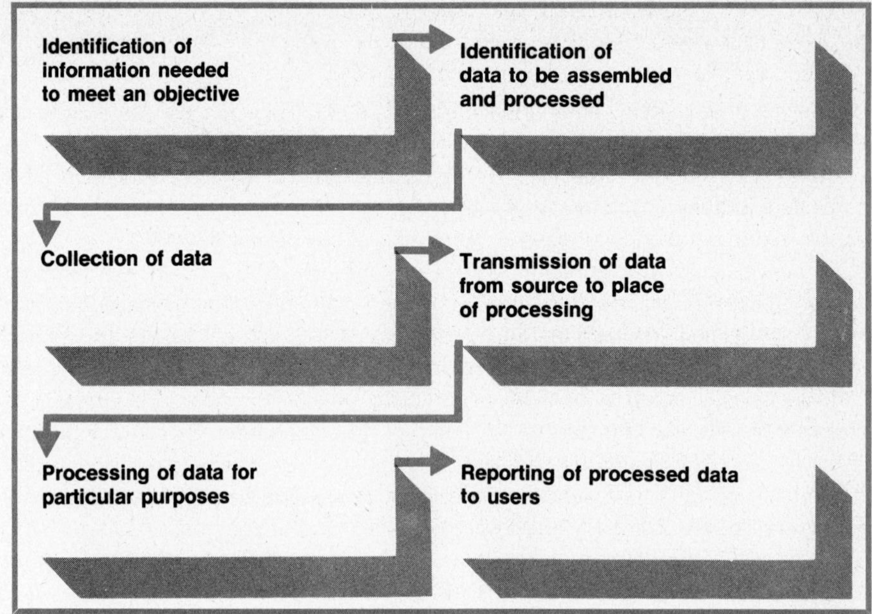

outputs expected from the system. Once this is known, he can develop procedures to provide the flow of inputs and to manipulate the data within the system. Exhibit 2-2 is a flowchart for a financial information system.

The designer of an information system must respond to developments in information sciences and computer technologies. Information management is emerging as a new and exciting profession. Accountancy must keep abreast of developments in this new field and share in the insights and discoveries that flow from these advances.

Criteria for accounting information

The basic reason for accounting is the need of individuals and groups to know about the activities and prospects of a business. These people are the users of the system. It must provide a flow of information that can serve as a basis for their decision making. A study by the American Accounting Association[1] recommends that accounting data be judged by four information criteria. These criteria are relevance, verifiability, freedom from bias, and quantifiability.

1. American Accounting Association, ***A Statement of Basic Accounting Theory*** (Evanston, Ill.: AAA, 1966), pp. 3–13. The Accounting Principles Board of the AICPA in ***APB Statement No. 4*** (paragraphs 87–92) lists seven qualitative objectives of financial accounting: relevance (the primary qualitative objective), understandability, verifiability, neutrality (information directed toward the common needs of users), timeliness (information communicated in time to be used for decision-making purposes), comparability, and completeness.

RELEVANCE. Students often talk about relevance, saying that classes cannot be meaningful unless they are relevant to students' needs. Relevance is also a part of the accountant's vocabulary. Accounting information must be relevant to the user. That is, the outputs of the accounting system must be useful to the persons who can reasonably be expected to be users of the system. Information is relevant if it meets the ***common needs*** of users in establishing policies, maintaining controls, and making decisions.

VERIFIABILITY. In Missouri, a doubter is apt to insist that you "show me." Accountants don't like to take things for granted either. The standard of verifiability requires that the accounting system operate under consistent, well-defined, established procedures of processing. Any qualified accountant using the same inputs should reach similar conclusions or outputs. Recall that the users of the outputs may have conflicting interests. Also they may have varying degrees of access to the original data that went into the system. Therefore, they must be able to rely on the outputs and to verify those outputs if necessary.

FREEDOM FROM BIAS. Parents often are biased about the skills or charms of their children. It is impossible to make valid decisions if you have only biased information. The accounting system must give its users information free from bias. It must record, measure, and report economic events in an impartial and objective manner. If the system is to be useful and trustworthy, it must take an ***independent*** stance in dealing with the inputs, processing, and outputs. Although the users may "pay its salary," the system would ill serve their needs if it gave them information slanted toward "what they'd like to hear."

QUANTIFIABILITY. After your first test in this course, you will probably receive a grade that measures your performance. That letter or number will be processed and eventually will become part of a report on your ability in accounting. Accounting is something of a numbers game too. Quantifiability as a standard of information requires that the data processed by the accounting system be such that they can be expressed in numbers. The accounting system reports on economic events. These events must be translated into numerals before the system can accept, process, and communicate them. In the United States, the accounting system generally converts all information into ***dollars***.

The standard of quantifiability has caused the accounting system to ignore certain kinds of events. For example, it is hard to put a dollar value on clear air or clean water. Therefore, until recently, the accounting system has largely ignored the firm's effect on its physical environment. Today many people worry about the effects of business on the "quality of life" of its employees and customers. At present, there is no precise way to give a dollar valuation to such effects, so they are generally ignored by the accounting system.

Functions of the accounting system

Accounting is a quantitative system. That is, it deals with numbers and measurable quantities. In its operation, the system performs three major functions: the accumulation, measurement, and communication of economic data.

Accumulation ⟶ Measurement ⟶ Communication.

We next discuss each of these functions, stressing the operations of accounting as a custodial, control, and decision-making system.

THE ACCUMULATION FUNCTION. Squirrels collect nuts. The accounting system collects data.[2] The system provides procedures for gathering and processing masses of data. This accumulative process mainly involves the recording and analysis of events. These records are essentially ***historical*** in nature; that is, they record events that have already occurred. The records designed for this accumulation function are called journals, ledgers, and summaries. As an accumulator of economic data, the accounting system identifies, classifies, and summarizes the financial activities of the firm.

THE MEASUREMENT FUNCTION. You may be very interested in certain measurements that describe you—your height and weight, the distance you have travelled, your IQ or grades. Accounting also is concerned with measurement. The accounting system must establish guidelines that allow it to assign numerals (dollar values) to economic events. In this measurement function, it must act according to ***principles*** and ***procedures.*** The measuring process provides a system of valuation that is applied to the data the system has accumulated. In many cases, accounting does not produce exact measurements. Some economic events must be measured through ***estimates*** and ***judgments.*** Such approximations must be verifiable, however. The guidelines for measurement form the underlying theory of accounting. Internal ***consistency*** in forming and applying these guidelines is as necessary to the accounting process as logic is to reasoning.

THE COMMUNICATION FUNCTION. Accounting is the language of business. The accounting system must periodically transfer and communicate its outputs to interested parties. If they are to be useful, the outputs must mean what informed users think they mean. Management has the main responsibility to be sure that the financial statements of the firm are reliable and accurate. Ideally, accounting reports would be prepared separately to meet the special needs of each kind of user. However, in practice, reports must go to multiple users with various needs and goals. In communicating information to these many users, the system must follow certain criteria that standardize the way economic data are reported. Five criteria or stan-

2. In general, a ***datum*** is a single fact or figure. The accounting system gathers large numbers of ***data,*** processes them to produce more general ***information,*** and communicates the information to the users. However, in many cases, the terms data and information are used interchangeably.

dards of reporting are relevant for this purpose: full disclosure, materiality, consistency, conservatism, and fairness. We discuss these standards later in this chapter. First we take a look at typical accounting reports.

Typical accounting reports

The outputs of the accounting system are the reports that it gives to the users of the system. A study group of the AICPA concluded in 1973 that the basic objective of financial statements is to aid in economic decision making.[3] This study states that financial statements should contain (among other things) information for predicting, comparing, and evaluating the earning power of enterprises. It also stipulates that financial statements should serve the needs of the users who rely on such reports as their principal source of information for economic decisions.[4]

Four major reports or statements are used by profit-making entities for ***external*** reporting to owners, potential investors, creditors, and others. These are (1) the balance sheet, or statement of financial position, (2) the income statement, (3) the statement of owner's equity (or owners' capital), and (4) the statement of changes in financial position. A broad overview of these major statements will be helpful at this stage of our study. However, we postpone a detailed discussion of many of the significant accounting terms appearing in these statements to later chapters.

THE BALANCE SHEET. The balance sheet is more formally called the ***statement of financial position.*** This financial statement reports the ***financial condition*** of an accounting entity ***at a particular moment in time.*** In its most general format, this statement follows the basic accounting model,[5]

Economic resources − Economic obligations = Residual interest,
or Assets − Liabilities = Owners' equity.

Assets are things of value that are owned by the business entity. That is, assets are economic resources. ***Liabilities*** are debts owed to creditors—in other words, economic obligations. ***Owners' equity*** represents the investment of the owners in the firm. It also includes the accumulated earnings of the firm. Thus the owners' equity can also be called the residual interest of the owners in the firm. The balance sheet can be shown in the simplified and generalized format of Exhibit 2-3.

3. ***Objectives of Financial Statements*** (New York: AICPA, 1973). This study group is sometimes called the Trueblood Committee, because its chairman is Robert M. Trueblood.

4. In ***APB Statement No. 4*** (paragraphs 76–84), the Accounting Principles Board lists the following general objectives of financial statements: (1) "to provide reliable financial information about economic resources and obligations of a business enterprise"; (2) "to provide reliable information about changes in net resources (resources less obligations) of an enterprise that result from its profit-directed activities"; (3) "to provide financial information that assists in estimating the earning potential of the enterprise"; (4) "to provide other needed information about changes in economic resources and obligations"; and (5) "to disclose, to the extent possible, other information related to the financial statements that is relevant to statement users' needs."

5. This model is expressed in the form and terminology used by the AICPA.

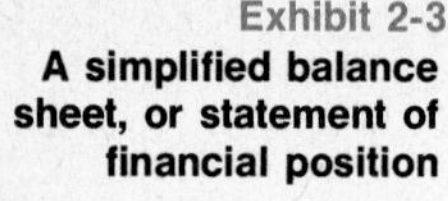

Exhibit 2-3
A simplified balance sheet, or statement of financial position

Exhibit 2-4
A simplified income statement

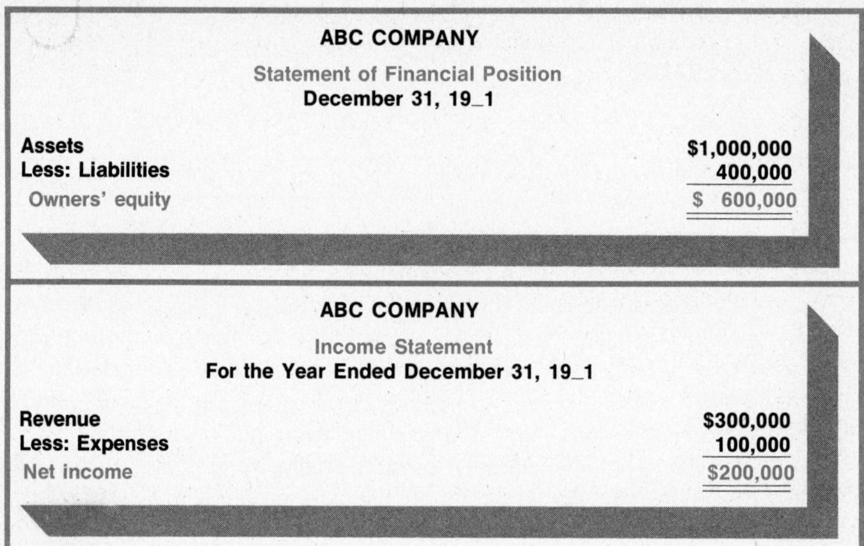

ABC COMPANY
Statement of Financial Position
December 31, 19_1

Assets	$1,000,000
Less: Liabilities	400,000
Owners' equity	$ 600,000

ABC COMPANY
Income Statement
For the Year Ended December 31, 19_1

Revenue	$300,000
Less: Expenses	100,000
Net income	$200,000

THE INCOME STATEMENT. The income statement is a financial report or statement that matches revenue earned by the firm against the expenses incurred in producing that revenue. ***Revenue*** describes the source of the inflow of assets from customers or clients. It is received in exchange for merchandise or services. Among the sources of revenue may be sales of goods, rent received from tenants, interest income on bonds, dividends from stock, and so on. ***Expenses*** are the costs of the materials and services that were used to produce the revenue. Among the expenses may be salaries of employees, premiums on insurance policies, and property taxes. The excess of revenue over expenses is called ***net income.*** In contrast to the balance sheet (which represents a moment in time), the income statement covers ***a period of time.*** This period may be a month, a year, or some other convenient time period. The income statement can be represented by the following basic model:

Revenue − Expenses = Net income.

A simplified and generalized income statement is shown in Exhibit 2-4.

The income statement is related to the balance sheet. For example, revenue increases the owners' equity, while expenses decrease the equity. This relationship is discussed more fully in Chapter 4.

STATEMENT OF OWNERS' EQUITY. A statement of owners' equity (or capital) shows the changes that have occurred in the owners' equity during the accounting period. It reports the owners' equity (capital balance) at the beginning of the period. It shows the net income (or loss) for the period as reported on the income statement. It also shows any additional investments or withdrawals by the owners during the period. Finally, it reports the capital balance at the end of the period. The ending balance of owners' equity on the statement of owners' equity agrees with the owners' equity shown on the balance sheet for the end of the period. The following model represents the statement of owners' equity:

Owners' equity at beginning of period	+	Net income	+	[Investments by owners during period	−	Withdrawals by owners during period]	=	Owners' equity at end of period.

For a corporation, withdrawals take the form of dividends distributed to stockholders. Exhibit 2-5 shows a simplified statement of owners' equity.

STATEMENT OF CHANGES IN FINANCIAL POSITION. The statement of changes in owners' equity provides information about the inflow and outflow of cash (or working capital) during a period of time. It describes the major investing and financing activities of the period engaged in by the company. As the name of the statement suggests, it explains why the balance sheet (the statement of financial position) changed from the beginning of the period to the end of the period. In its most general form, this statement reports

Cash inflows − Cash outflows = Changes in cash.

Exhibit 2-6 shows a simplified statement of changes in financial position.

Standards of reporting

In our discussion of the communication function of accounting, we mentioned that there are five major standards of reporting. This section discusses the five standards.

FULL DISCLOSURE. Full disclosure is "telling it like it is." Any accounting report should disclose all significant facts that an informed user of the report would need in a decision-making situation. If the users of financial statements are to rely on the statements, the accounting system must provide ***understandable, complete, and***

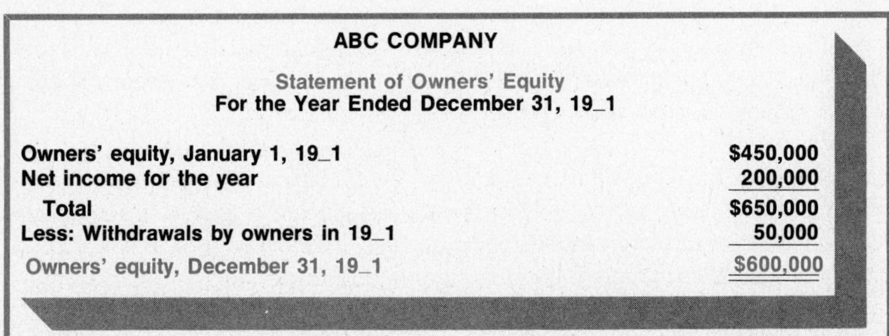

ABC COMPANY

Statement of Owners' Equity
For the Year Ended December 31, 19_1

Owners' equity, January 1, 19_1	$450,000
Net income for the year	200,000
Total	$650,000
Less: Withdrawals by owners in 19_1	50,000
Owners' equity, December 31, 19_1	$600,000

Exhibit 2-5
A simplified statement of owners' equity

Exhibit 2-6
A simplified statement of changes in financial position

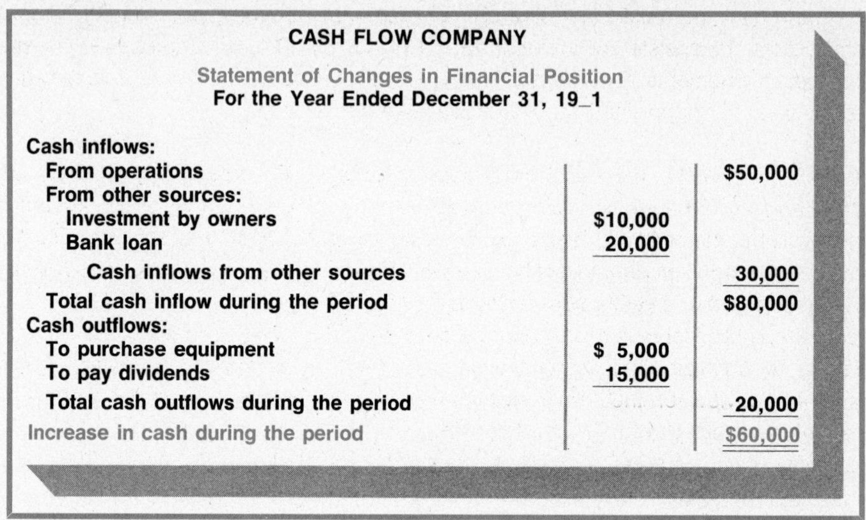

CASH FLOW COMPANY

Statement of Changes in Financial Position
For the Year Ended December 31, 19_1

Cash inflows:		
From operations		**$50,000**
From other sources:		
Investment by owners	**$10,000**	
Bank loan	**20,000**	
Cash inflows from other sources		**30,000**
Total cash inflow during the period		**$80,000**
Cash outflows:		
To purchase equipment	**$ 5,000**	
To pay dividends	**15,000**	
Total cash outflows during the period		**20,000**
Increase in cash during the period		$60,000

neutral disclosure of all *relevant* information. Of course, the terms used in financial reports often are technical in nature: they have specific meanings to accountants. The accountant does assume that the users of his reports are somewhat familiar with business terminology, practices, and characteristics—and with the limitations of financial accounting.

MATERIALITY. Suppose you trip and fall down a flight of stairs. When you report the event to someone later, he asks if you were hurt. You might answer no, even though you did get a slight scratch or bruise. He probably would consider your answer an honest one. However, if you broke your arm, he would expect to hear about it. A broken arm would be a material part of the story; a scratch would not. In accounting, the concept of materiality deals with the relative importance of economic data. In the accounting sense, an item is material if it would be useful or important to an informed user of a financial statement in a decision-making situation. Matters that are material should be fully disclosed in the reports. Of course, it is sometimes difficult to decide what is material and what is not. This decision usually is a matter of professional judgment by the accountant. As a rule of thumb, an item would usually be considered material if it were as large as 5 to 15 percent of net income. Thus an item involving $10,000 might be material for a small company, but it could be immaterial for a company as large as General Motors.

CONSISTENCY. Accountants use a variety of principles and procedures as they accumulate, measure, and communicate data about financial events. In some cases, two or more contradictory methods could be used in treating a given event. It is very important that the accountant be consistent in applying principles and procedures to similar situations. The user must be sure that data on one statement is *comparable* to that on another. For example, if he compares net income from one year with that from the next, he must know that similar rules were followed in preparing the two statements. Inconsistency in reporting can cause misleading interpretations and erroneous judgments about facts, trends, or the fairness of the reports. Consistency is essential to sound financial and managerial accounting.

CONSERVATISM. We describe political parties as conservative or liberal. Accountants try to be conservative, but the meaning of conservatism in accounting is not similar to the political meaning of the word. In accounting, conservatism refers to the early recognition of unfavorable events. The accountant draws attention to events that result in the lowest value or income. He underplays favorable prospects. The principle of conservatism has been expressed in the warning that an accountant should "recognize all losses and anticipate no gains." He gives the user the most pessimistic view of the firm's position. This conservative approach to financial reporting is a result of the uncertainty of events and historical experience.[6] Caustically speaking, "if a catastrophe can happen, it will."

FAIRNESS. Everyone likes to be treated fairly and tends to think of himself as a fair person. Fairness in dealing with others is essential to an harmonious existence. In accounting, fairness requires that accounting reports give a fair presentation or summary of the events that were the inputs for the reports. Fairness implies that the reporting process does not favor certain ones of the individuals and groups who use the reports. It implies that the financial reports are substantially correct and that they follow generally accepted accounting principles. Fairness is rooted in the ethical concepts of ***justice*** and ***equity.***

Audited financial statements

Some of the reports produced by a firm's accounting system are used only by management within the firm. Other financial statements are prepared for stockholders, prospective investors, bankers, and other outside groups. In most cases, the reports for outside users are audited (examined) by Certified Public Accountants. The CPAs give an independent professional opinion about the extent to which the statements are presented fairly. The management of a business assumes primary responsibility for the accounts and statements of the firm.

If the CPA gives an ***unqualified opinion,*** the reader of the reports is assured that the audit was made in accordance with ***generally accepted standards*** for such examinations. The auditor assures the user that his examination ***included all procedures*** that the CPA thought necessary in order to get ***enough evidence*** to form an opinion about the fairness of the statements. He reports that the statements ***fairly present*** all ***material*** matters, and that the statements are prepared ***in conformity***

6. The author of this text is not happy with the conservatism convention in accounting. Conservative reports often tend to be inconsistent and unrealistic accounts of economic events. Always choosing conservative accounting practices gives an improper bias to accounting statements.

with accounting principles that have substantial support in the accounting profession. Finally, the auditor assures the user that the statements have been prepared using accounting principles that are the same as (***consistent*** with) those used in the preceding reports. An unqualified opinion from a CPA takes the following standard form:

> We have examined the balance sheet of XYZ Company as of December 31, 19__, and the related statements of income, retained earnings, and changes in financial position for the year then ended. Our examination was made in accordance with generally accepted auditing standards, and accordingly included such tests of the accounting records and such other auditing procedures as we considered necessary in the circumstances.
>
> In our opinion, the statements mentioned above present fairly the financial position of XYZ Company at December 31, 19__, and the results of its operations and changes in its financial position for the year then ended, in conformity with generally accepted accounting principles applied on a basis consistent with that of the preceding year.

If the CPA feels that his audit does not justify such an unqualified opinion, he will offer either a qualified opinion, an adverse opinion, or a disclaimer of opinion.

CPAs are voluntarily bound by Rules of Professional Conduct. These rules are intended to benefit and protect their clients, the public, and the accounting profession. The behavior expected of a CPA is suggested by the following sampling of general precepts of conduct.

1. The CPA is expected to be independent in thought and action with respect to his examinations.
2. The CPA is expected to keep his clients' affairs in strict confidence.
3. The CPA is expected to maintain high personal and professional standards.
4. The CPA is prohibited from advertising his services, soliciting business, accepting contingent fees, and similar acts deemed unprofessional.

Summary

Chapter 1 sketched the historical background of accounting, from its birth through evolutionary stages to its modern position as a profession. Chapter 2 describes accounting as an information system that provides the basis for accumulating, measuring, and communicating the results of economic events. As a system, accounting serves its direct and indirect users by giving them significant and meaningful information about a business. The reports or statements that are the outputs of the system should be relevant, verifiable, free from bias, and quantifiable. The accounting system has three major functions: accumulation, measurement, and communication (reporting). The communication function of the accounting system must meet five criteria or standards of reporting: full disclosure, materiality, consistency, conservatism, and fairness.

In this chapter, four major accounting statements are described in general terms. The balance sheet follows the model,

Assets − Liabilities = Owners' equity.

The income statement follows the model,

Revenue − Expenses = Net income.

The statement of owners' equity follows the model,

Owners' equity at beginning of period	+ Net income	+ Investments by owners during period	− Withdrawals by owners during period	= Owners' equity at end of period.

The statement of changes in financial position provides information concerning the investing and financing activities of the business. This statement follows the model,

Cash inflow − Cash outflow = Change in cash.

An efficient accounting system must provide routine reports for management, giving them the information they need for adequate planning and for control over current operations. The system also must provide periodic and timely reports of financial conditions and the results of operations for external parties, especially owners and creditors. Such external reports usually are examined or audited by a CPA, who checks to be sure that they meet accepted standards of the profession.

This chapter completes our introduction to accounting. We now turn in Chapter 3 to a study of the balance sheet.

Questions

1. List several "systems" with which you are familiar.
2. Distinguish between ***data*** and ***information***.
3. Distinguish between a total information system and a subsystem.
4. Discuss an information system in terms of inputs, processing, and outputs.
5. List four major areas where an accounting system can provide information and assistance to owners, managers, and others.
6. State four important information criteria for accounting data. Briefly discuss each criterion.
7. List and discuss the three major functions of the accounting system.
8. List and discuss five criteria or standards of reporting for economic data.
9. List and briefly describe four major financial statements that are outputs of the accounting system.
10. Which financial statement shows assets, liabilities, and owners' equity? Define assets, liabilities, and owners' equity.
11. Which financial statement reports revenue and expenses? Define revenue and expenses. What is meant by net income?
12. Which statement shows the dividends distributed by a corporation?
13. The various users of financial statements have special and sometimes conflicting interests. What problems does this situation create when the accounting system prepares and communicates identical financial statements to all users? How do accountants deal with these problems?
14. If you were a creditor of a business, what general information would you wish to have about the financial position and operating results of the firm? What would you wish to know if you were a stockholder?

Exercises

E2-1 The Post Company has assets of $625,000 and liabilities of $375,000 as of December 31, 19_1. Prepare a balance sheet for the Post Company on this date.

E2-2 During the year 19_1, the Post Company (see Exercise E2-1) had revenue of $160,000 and expenses of $115,000. Prepare an income statement for the Post Company for the year ended December 31, 19_1.

E2-3 The capital of the Post Company (see Exercises E2-1 and E2-2) at the beginning of 19_1 was $85,000. Withdrawals by the firm during the year amounted to $30,000. Prepare a statement of owners' equity for the Post Company for the year ended December 31, 19_1.

E2-4 On December 31, 19_1, the R-Own Company has liabilities of $65,000 and owners' equity of $125,000. Compute the amount of assets owned by the firm on that date.

E2-5 At the end of 19_1, the R-Own Company has owners' equity (capital) of $125,000. During the year, it paid dividends of $60,000. The net income of the company for the year was $35,000. What was the amount of owners' equity at the beginning of 19_1? Show your computations.

E2-6 The accounting records of the Disco Company show the following data on December 31, 19_1:

Withdrawal	$ 22,000
Assets	225,000
Expenses	180,000
Owners' equity, January 1, 19_1	45,000
Liabilities	167,000
Revenue	215,000

Prepare for this company (a) a balance sheet, (b) an income statement, and (c) a statement of owners' equity.

E2-7 Prepare an income statement for the Another Company for the year ending December 31, 19_1, using the following data:

Revenue	$85,000
Expenses	92,000

E2-8 You are an independent auditor. You have just completed the examination of a set of financial statements issued by the Bee Fine Company and have written your opinion. You visit the president of the Bee Fine Company and explain that your opinion is an unqualified opinion. After reading the opinion, the president asks you to explain the extent of confidence he should have in the financial statements. He also asks you to explain to him the significance of the phrase "applied on a basis consistent with that of the preceding year." Give your answers to the president's questions.

E2-9 Criticize the financial statement shown in Exhibit 2-7. This statement was prepared and released by the New Company. NOTE: In financial statements, a negative amount is indicated by enclosing the amount in parentheses. For example, $(200,000) means a negative amount of $200,000. Accountants *do not* write such a number as −$200,000. Parentheses also may be used to indicate amounts being subtracted in a column of numbers to be summed.

E2-10 The records of the Bean Company provide the following information about the operations of the company during 19_1.

Statement of Financial Position

For the Year Ended December 31, 19_1

Assets	500,000
Revenue	300,000
Expenses	(200,000)
Liabilities	(100,000)
Owners' equity	$(500,000)

Exhibit 2-7
Financial statement for Exercise E2-9

	Case 1	Case 2	Case 3	Case 4	Case 5
Owners' capital, January 1, 19_1	$15	$?	$ 85	$100	$195
Net income during 19_1	75	50	?	190	415
Investments by owners during 19_1	10	25	55	?	90
Withdrawals by owners during 19_1	30	10	15	30	?
Owners' capital, December 31, 19_1	?	90	200	340	640

Exhibit 2-8 **Table for Exercise E2-11**

Owners' equity at beginning of year	$27,000
Net income for the year	45,500
Investments by owners during the year	1,500
Withdrawals by owners during the year	30,000

Compute the owners' equity for the Bean Company at the end of 19_1.

E2-11 Exhibit 2-8 shows various elements of statements of owners' equity for five independent cases. In each case, compute the missing item indicated by a question mark.

E2-12 Prepare a statement of changes in financial position for the year for the External Reporting Company from the following information:

Cash from operations	$100,000
Cash paid for dividends	50,000
Cash borrowed from a bank	10,000
Cash from sale of land	45,000
Cash paid for an investment	15,000

E2-13 Prepare a statement of financial position, income statement, and statement of changes in owners' equity from the following data and by supplying any additional required data:

Assets	$900
Owners' equity, December 31, 19_0	500
Revenue	800
Withdrawal by owner	100
Owners' equity, January 1, 19_0	350

Major financial statements

Part Two

3 The statement of financial position

Nobody likes to grope through unknown territory in the dark. It's nice to have some idea of where you're going. So, before we look at various financial statements in detail, we'll take a look at a few basic principles and assumptions of accounting theory. With this background, you'll be able to see how the details fit into the big picture. After our look at principles and assumptions, we'll turn to the basic accounting report, the statement of financial position, or balance sheet.

Generally accepted accounting principles

The younger generation gets lots of lectures about the right and wrong of things. Those who do the lecturing view this as a process of instilling principles. The accounting profession has not been reluctant to speak about principles either. If there are such things as accounting principles, we should know something about them as we begin our study.

Broadly speaking, ***accounting principles*** are guidelines that establish standards for sound accounting practices and procedures. These standards seek to achieve fair presentation of statements that report the financial position and results of operations of a business. Accounting principles have been developed over the years from experience, reason, usage, and necessity. They have been set forth by various accounting associations, governmental agencies, practitioners, and others. Certain principles are generally recognized by the accounting profession as being preferable to others. The term ***generally accepted accounting principles*** is a technical concept that describes the conventions, rules, and procedures that represent accepted accounting practice at a particular time. They represent a consensus view by the profession of good accounting practices and procedures. Currently, the ***Opinions*** issued by the Accounting Principles Board and the ***Statements*** of the Financial

Accounting Standards Board[1] of the AICPA are major sources of generally accepted accounting principles.

In discussing generally accepted accounting principles in ***APB Statement No. 4,*** the AICPA Accounting Principles Board says that

> **generally accepted accounting principles incorporate the consensus at any time as to which economic resources and obligations should be recorded as assets and liabilities, which changes in them should be recorded, when these changes should be recorded, how the recorded assets and liabilities and changes in them should be measured, what information should be disclosed and how it should be disclosed, and which financial statements should be prepared.**[2]

Exhibit 3-1 summarizes the relationship of generally accepted accounting principles to economic events and financial statements.

Basic accounting assumptions

A teacher makes certain assumptions about his or her students. The teacher assumes that they have an adequate background for the course, and that they are taking the course in order to learn something about the subject. The students at least begin the course with the assumption that the teacher knows something and can teach it to them. Sometimes these assumptions prove valid, sometimes not. Yet we all must operate under assumptions that we accept as being reasonably realistic. The accountant also makes certain assumptions when he or she accumulates, measures, and communicates data. We need to examine these assumptions.

In developing accounting theory, the profession has agreed to take for granted certain basic concepts. That is, certain ideas are assumed or accepted in order to develop the structure of accounting theory and to relate the theory to accounting practice. Accounting assumptions are basic concepts that underlie the accounting

1. The Accounting Principles Board (APB) was organized by the AICPA on September 1, 1959, to supersede its former Committee on Accounting Procedure. The APB studied difficult and often controversial problem areas in accounting. It issued ***Opinions*** and ***Statements*** dealing with these problems, after soliciting the views of members of the AICPA. The ***Opinions*** of the APB are a substantial authoritative source of accounting principles. There are other primary sources for accounting principles. (A ***primary*** source is one that by itself is considered sufficient to establish evidence of substantial authoritative support for the principle.) The other primary sources for principles include the ***Accounting Research Bulletins*** of the AICPA Committee on Accounting Procedure, AICPA audit guides, Regulations S–X of the SEC, and releases in the SEC accounting series. Predominant practice within an industry also establishes authoritative support for a principle. ***Secondary*** sources of substantial authoritative support include statements of industry regulatory authorities, ***Accounting Trends and Techniques,*** accounting research studies of professional societies, court decisions, textbooks, distinguished individuals in the profession, and others. No single secondary source is sufficient evidence that a particular principle is generally accepted.

In 1972 the AICPA established the Financial Accounting Standards Board (FASB) to replace the APB. The FASB has seven members, each salaried and serving full-time on the board for a term of five years. A financial accounting standard must be approved by the affirmative vote of five of the seven board members before the standard is issued by the FASB. Standards announced by the FASB are considered primary sources of generally accepted accounting principles.

2. ***APB Statement No. 4,*** para. 27. Copyright 1970 by the AICPA.

Exhibit 3-1
Generally accepted accounting principles and the accounting system

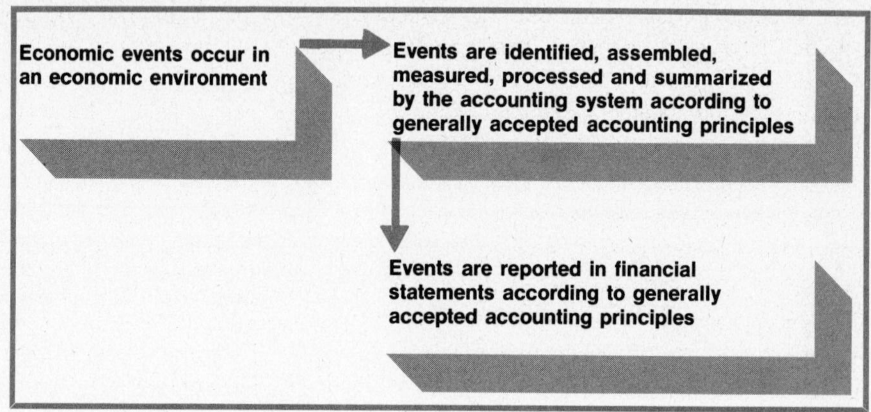

system. They provide its unifying theoretical structure and its internal logic. Among the more important accounting assumptions are the business-entity assumption, the going-concern assumption, the dollar-measurement assumption, and the periodic-and-timely-reporting assumption.

BUSINESS-ENTITY ASSUMPTION. You are a person distinct from the individual next to you. Each of you is distinct from the entity called the class. Similarly, the president of a company or an owner of a company is an individual distinct from the business entity. As a group, accountants are very concerned with logic. They prefer to know exactly for whom they are accounting. Thus they talk about the business-entity assumption.

A ***business entity*** is an organization of persons and properties joined to accomplish an economic goal. In most cases, the goal is the maximization of profit within the constraints or limits imposed upon the entity by the owners, managers, and society. The entity acquires, controls, and transforms economic resources, produces and exchanges goods and services, and performs other tasks. ***The entity that represents this union of persons and properties is separate and distinct from the owners of the enterprise.*** The business-entity assumption states that the accounting system accumulates, measures, and communicates economic inputs and outputs that relate to the enterprise; the system does not deal with the economic data associated with the owners as individuals. For example, the personal assets of owners or stockholders are not considered when listing the assets of the firm. A corporation is an entity separate and distinct from the stockholders who own the corporation. The corporation has an existence and accountability separate from that of the stockholders. This basic business- (or accounting-) entity assumption establishes the range and the boundaries of information to be included in the records and the reports of an enterprise.

Among the major forms of business entities are the corporation, partnership, and single proprietorship. We discuss these forms of enterprises throughout this text, particularly in Chapters 16 and 18. The business-entity assumption is the most basic accounting assumption because it requires that the organization to be accounted for must be identified; this assumption also sets the boundaries of what is to be accounted for. When financial statements are prepared, this assumption requires that the statements clearly identify the business entity to which the statements relate.

GOING-CONCERN ASSUMPTION. You and I know that we could die at any time. Yet we keep on acting as if we will be here tomorrow. Accountants make a similar assumption about business entities. ***Accounting for a business entity assumes that the business will continue in operation and will not be dissolved in the immediate future.*** Unless there is evidence to the contrary, the accounting system assumes that the entity will continue to exist indefinitely. This concept of ***indefinite continuance*** implies that the business will exist at least as long as needed to complete its present contractual obligations and to follow through on its existing plans for using the resources it holds. In special cases, the going-concern assumption may not apply to a particular business entity. For example, it might seem likely that a particular firm will be liquidated, or closed out, in the near future. In such a case, the accounting system changes its procedures for accumulation, measurement, and communication to reflect this departure from the normal case.

DOLLAR-MEASUREMENT ASSUMPTION. Fortunately or not, we tend to put a price on everything. We speak of the "almighty dollar." We accumulate dollars; we spend dollars. The dollar is the common unit of measurement in the world of business. The accountant deals with dollars. In fact, he accepts the dollar as the basic unit of accounting. He accounts for dollars.

Many business events could be measured or expressed in terms of other units—for example, pounds, acres, gallons, man-hours, or kilowatt-hours. However, ***money*** has been adopted by the accounting system as its basic unit of measurement. The dollar-measurement assumption states that ***economic events are accumulated, measured, and reported in terms of money that is the medium of exchange and the standard of economic value.*** The ***dollar*** is the monetary expression of economic events. The dollar is accepted as the measuring unit for accounting in the United States. Accountants in other nations may use other monetary units. The unit of measure always is identified on a financial statement.

Note that the unit used is the dollar—not the purchasing power of a dollar, which varies. The justification for the dollar-measurement assumption is that accounting should communicate data that have been assembled and processed by an ***inelastic*** measuring unit. The dollar is one hundred cents yesterday, today, and tomorrow. Unfortunately, this means that financial statements currently are not adjusted for changes in the price level. The dollar of last year does not have the same value as the dollar of this year, when measured against the amount of resources it will buy. Because dollars are used without adjustment for changing price levels, the accounting outputs are seriously distorted. This price-level problem is discussed in a later chapter.

PERIODIC-AND-TIMELY-REPORTING ASSUMPTION. A student usually attends classes throughout the school term. At some point, examinations are required and reporting occurs. Educators assume that periodic reports on student performance are desirable. They also assume that these reports will have maximum benefit if they are not unduly delayed after the time of examination. Accountants make similar assumptions about their reports.

To improve their usefulness, ***accounting statements are prepared periodically and to cover relatively short time periods.*** The ultimate economic success or failure of the firm will not be known until it is dissolved. However, reports at that time covering the entire life of the firm will be of little use to managers, owners, or investors —except in a post mortem to see what happened. Users of the accounting system need frequent reports. The accounting statements that reflect the results of operations and the financial position of the business entity usually are prepared either for a specific date or for a period of time such as a year, a quarter (three months), or a month.

To be relevant, accounting reports must be timely. In general, a financial statement is most useful when the data it presents are current. The accounting system must use procedures that allow it to issue reports very soon after the close of the time period the reports cover.

The time period selected for reports on the financial position and results of operations of a firm is usually one year. A firm that selects the ***calendar year*** as a basis of reporting assembles its financial data for the period from January 1 through December 31. Any 12-month period selected by a firm for its annual reporting is called its ***fiscal year.*** In many cases, the fiscal year is not the calendar year. In most cases, ***interim statements*** are issued to summarize information for shorter periods during the fiscal year. Public statements may be issued on a quarterly or a monthly basis. Statements for internal use by management may be issued much more frequently— sometimes daily. Any statement must carry a clear identification of the time period or specific date that it covers.

The statement of financial position

The statement of financial position is one of the oldest and most significant financial statements produced by the accounting system. This statement is often called the ***balance sheet.***[3] This statement communicates information about the resources and obligations of an entity and about its owners' residual interests in the business at a specific point in time. For example, a particular balance sheet might show the financial condition of a firm at the close of business on December 31, 1978. The balance sheet carries only the date; it is assumed that the statement is prepared for the close of business on that date. In its broadest scope, the statement of financial position

3. This author prefers the title ***statement of financial position,*** because it is more meaningful as a description of the statement. However, the older term ***balance sheet*** is still in common use and is generally accepted. In order to simplify sentences and to make reading easier, the statement is often called a balance sheet throughout this text. Both terms are used interchangeably, and the student should be familiar with both.

presents the assets, liabilities, and owners' equity for the business entity as of a specific point in time. This statement is a static document that shows dollar residuals assigned to assets, liabilities, and owners' equity.

ASSETS (ECONOMIC RESOURCES). Assets are things of value owned—wealth and rights to wealth. Assets reflect economic resources that will be of benefit to the entity in ***future*** periods. Assets represent (1) stored purchasing power (for example, cash), (2) money claims to rights (such as accounts receivable, stocks, and bonds), and (3) tangible and intangible items that can be sold or used in the business. Tangible items are those that have physical substance, such as buildings, land, equipment, or stocks of materials. Intangible items are things whose value does not lie in their physical nature—for example, patents, trade names, or good standing with customers. In ***APB Statement No. 4,*** the Accounting Principles Board defines assets as "economic resources of an enterprise that are recognized and measured in conformity with generally accepted accounting principles." Economic resources represent scarce means that are available to the firm for use in carrying on its business activities. (Resources such as air and sunlight are not scarce in most cases, so no value is assigned to them as assets.)

LIABILITIES (ECONOMIC OBLIGATIONS). Liabilities are debts that the business owes to its creditors. Liabilities represent obligations to provide cash, goods, or services at some future date. Most liabilities are created by borrowing money or by purchasing goods and services on credit. Typical liabilities include accounts payable, notes payable, wages payable, interest payable, and taxes payable. In ***APB Statement No. 4,*** the APB defines liabilities as "economic obligations of an enterprise that are measured in conformity with generally accepted accounting principles."

OWNERS' EQUITY (RESIDUAL INTEREST). Owners' equity is a measure of the ownership group's interest in the economic resources of the firm. The excess of assets (economic resources) over liabilities (economic obligations) reflects the owners' equity in the business. In this sense, owners' equity is the residual interest that would remain after all liabilities were settled. Owners' equity arises mainly from investments in the firm by the owners and from the accumulated earnings that result from the enterprise's profit-making activities.

THE ACCOUNTING EQUATION. The accounting equation expresses the relationship that exists between assets, liabilities, and owners' equity, as presented in the statement of financial position. In its simplest form, the accounting equation reads as follows:

Assets − Liabilities = Owners' equity.

To illustrate this equation, assume that a business has assets of $100,000, liabilities of $60,000, and owners' equity of $40,000. In equation format, this information takes the form

$100,000 − $60,000 = $40,000.

Obviously, the accounting equation ($A - L = OE$) states an *equality* and establishes a relationship among the three major accounting categories. Owners' equity is shown as the residual of assets over liabilities. This format emphasizes the proprietorship (ownership) role of the owners of the enterprise. The owners' equity is what remains of the firm's resources after its liabilities have been taken care of.

Using a simple arithmetic procedure, we can rewrite the accounting equation in this form:

Assets = Liabilities + Owners' equity.

Using the values from the example just given, we see that this form of the equality does hold true:

$100,000 = $60,000 + $40,000.

When written in this form ($A = L + OE$) the accounting equation emphasizes that the assets of the firm can be divided between the claims of creditors and owners against the firm.

CONTENT AND FORM OF THE STATEMENT

Sometimes it seems that American consumers care only about the form of the things they buy. Vast amounts of attention and money go into the choice of package shapes, colors, and designs for supermarket products. Detroit worries about the styling and image that will sell the most cars. Yet the growing consumer movement shows that many people also worry about the content of the things they purchase. The accountant also must be concerned with both the form and the content of his statements. The contents of the statement (the financial information) must be accurate, relevant, and complete. The form in which they are presented must be useful and clear to those who use the statements.

The balance sheet contains information about the financial position of an enterprise. The statement may assume various forms. Like most financial statements, the statement of financial position must contain a ***heading.*** The heading includes the ***name of the business entity*** being accounted for, the ***type of statement*** being presented, and the ***date*** to which the statement applies. A balance sheet must carry in its heading a specific date, such as December 31, 1978. The statement presents the assets, liabilities, and owners' equity as of the close of business on this date.

The body of the statement, containing the financial information, may take one of three generally accepted forms: the account form, the modified account form, or the report form. The ***account form*** (Exhibit 3-2) reflects the accounting equation expressed in terms of $A = L + OE$. Assets are listed in the left column. Liabilities and owners' equity are listed in the right column. As the equation indicates, the sums of these two columns must be equal.

The ***modified account form*** (Exhibits 3-3 and 3-12) presents the same listings in a single column, with the assets appearing above the liabilities and owners' equity. Notice the use of single and double underlining in this form. This usage follows a general practice in accounting statements. The number just below the single underline represents the result of some arithmetic operation (usually addition or subtraction) on the numbers above the line. A double underline usually indicates the end of a section of the presentation. In this form, the numbers just above the double under-

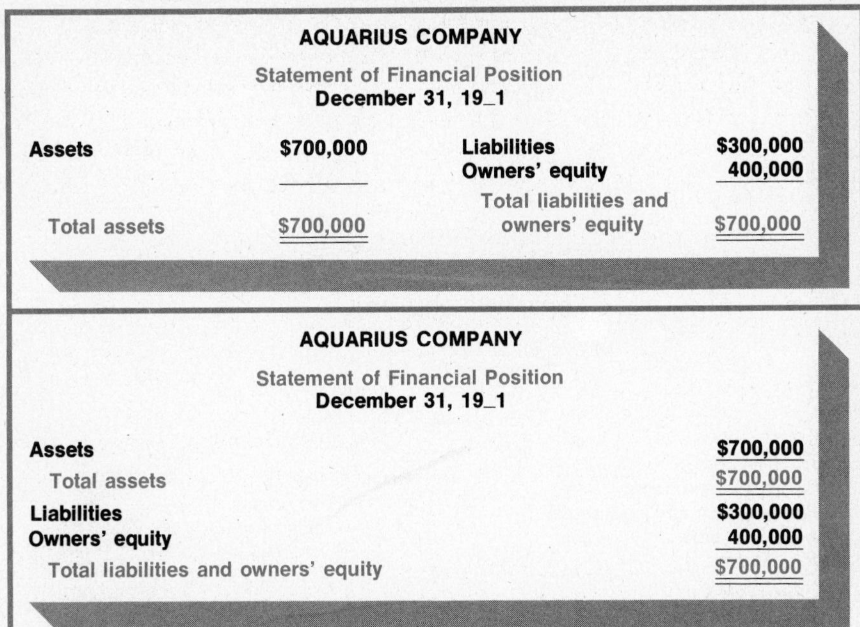

AQUARIUS COMPANY

Statement of Financial Position
December 31, 19_1

Assets	**$700,000**	**Liabilities**	**$300,000**
		Owners' equity	**400,000**
Total assets	$700,000	Total liabilities and owners' equity	$700,000

Exhibit 3-2
The account form of a balance sheet (condensed)

AQUARIUS COMPANY

Statement of Financial Position
December 31, 19_1

Assets	**$700,000**
Total assets	$700,000
Liabilities	**$300,000**
Owners' equity	**400,000**
Total liabilities and owners' equity	$700,000

Exhibit 3-3
The modified account form of a balance sheet (condensed)

lines are the same as those at the bottoms of the two columns in the account form. These two numbers must be equal.

The ***report form*** (Exhibits 3-4, 3-5) also uses a single column, but the information is arranged to reflect the accounting equation in the form of $A - L = OE$. Assets are listed first. Liabilities are listed next. The liabilities then are subtracted from the assets to give the owners' equity. The modified account form of the statement sometimes is called the "report form of $A = L + OE$."

Another important part of any form of a statement is the identification of the unit used for measurement. A dollar sign appears before the first amount in any column and before the first amount following an underline. The dollar signs usually are omitted on other amounts shown.

CLASSIFICATIONS

Up to this point, we have used general terms such as assets and liabilities to represent the basic accounting classifications. Now we can expand these general classifications in terms of major subsets that appear on a ***classified statement*** of financial position (see Exhibit 3-5).[4] A classified balance sheet arranges the major categories of assets, liabilities, and owners' equity into significant groups and subgroups. A detailed classified statement of financial position is shown in Exhibit 3-12 in the appendix to this chapter. The appendix also defines the items that appear on the statement. This material should be carefully studied as an integral part of this chapter.

4. The AICPA periodically publishes ***Accounting Trends and Techniques,*** a study that illustrates current usage in financial statements. The accountant can refer to these studies for examples of current practice in statement presentation.

Exhibit 3-4
The report form of a balance sheet (condensed)

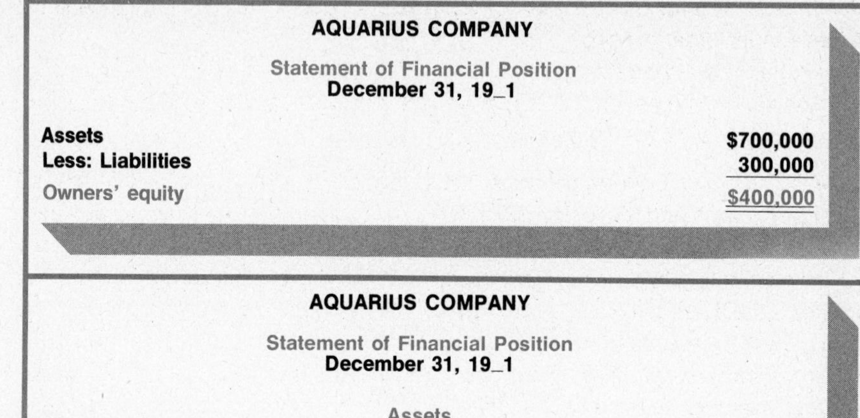

AQUARIUS COMPANY
Statement of Financial Position
December 31, 19_1

Assets	$700,000
Less: Liabilities	300,000
Owners' equity	$400,000

Exhibit 3-5
A classified balance sheet in the report form (condensed)

AQUARIUS COMPANY
Statement of Financial Position
December 31, 19_1

Assets

Current assets		$200,000
Long-term investments		50,000
Property, plant, and equipment		340,000
Intangible assets		80,000
Other assets		30,000
Total assets		$700,000
Liabilities and Owners' Equity		
Current liabilities	$100,000	
Long-term liabilities	200,000	
Total liabilities		300,000
Owners' equity		$400,000

1. Assets
   a. Current assets
   b. Long-term investments (or Investments)
   c. Property, plant, and equipment
   d. Intangible assets
   e. Other assets (or Deferred charges)
2. Liabilities
   a. Current liabilities
   b. Long-term liabilities
3. Owners' equity (or capital) [for a corporation]
   a. Paid-in (or contributed) capital
   b. Retained earnings

Because the corporation is the dominant form of business organization in the United States, this text concentrates on accounting for the corporation. The text does adequately treat single proprietorships and partnerships in cases where accounting for these organizations differs from that for a corporation. Chapter 16 describes in detail the major items that appear in the owners' equity section of a balance sheet for these other organizations.

To expand our understanding of the terms that appear on a balance sheet, we now examine the major items that appear on a classified statement of a corporation (refer to Exhibit 3-12 for illustrations).

CURRENT ASSETS. Current assets include those resources of the firm that are in the form of cash and those that are reasonably expected to be sold, consumed, or converted into cash during the normal operating cycle of the business (or within one year if the operating cycle is shorter than one year). The ***normal operating cycle*** of a business is the average time it takes to convert cash into inventory, sell the inventory, and collect the amounts due that result from the sales (Exhibit 3-6). Among typical items included in current assets are cash, temporary investments, accounts receivable, and inventory. In the statement of financial position, current assets usually are listed in the order of their ***liquidity***—that is, the ease and speed with which they could be converted into cash.

The most liquid (readily spent) current asset is cash. *Cash* includes actual money on hand and balances in checking accounts. *Marketable securities* are short-term investments in stocks, bonds, and similar securities that are readily marketable and are to be converted into cash within the operating cycle. *Accounts receivable* are the amounts due to the business from customers as a result of sales or services performed. *Notes receivable* are unconditional promises in writing to pay definite sums of money at certain or determinable dates, usually with a specified interest rate. *Inventory* includes the merchandise, materials, or stock that the business normally uses in its manufacturing and selling operations. *Prepaid expenses* also are included as current assets. These are expenses of a future period that have been paid in advance—for example, prepaid rent or insurance.

INVESTMENTS. The second major group of assets is long-term investments. Here the accountant lists the firm's holdings of stocks, bonds, and similar commitments of funds for profit or control, where the securities are to be held for a period of time greater than the operating cycle. Investments reported in this section are investments by the business in other firms, governmental bodies, and so on. These investments should not be confused with investments in the company by owners, which are capital, from the company's viewpoint. (Recall that short-term investments are listed as current assets.)

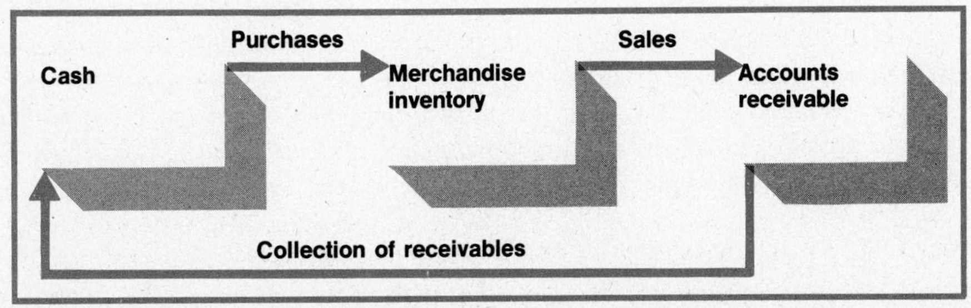

Exhibit 3-6
The operating cycle of a business

PROPERTY, PLANT, AND EQUIPMENT. The third major group of assets is called property, plant, and equipment. Here the accountant lists tangible, long-lived assets that are held for use in the business, not primarily for resale. This group includes land, buildings, machinery, tools, and so on. Other terms used to describe this group on some statements include ***fixed assets*** and ***long-term assets.*** If this group is further classified on the statement of financial position, the subgroups with the longest lives are usually listed first—thus, land, buildings, equipment.

INTANGIBLE ASSETS. In the group of intangible assets the accountant lists long-lived, nonphysical rights, values, and privileges other than receivables and investments. Among the subgroups included here are patents, copyrights, franchises, trademarks, trade names, and goodwill.

OTHER ASSETS. Assets not adequately classified in other sections of the statement can be reported as "other assets." The final group of assets includes long-term prepayments for services or other benefits, called deferred charges. Examples of deferred charges would be long-term prepayments for insurance, and rent. If the benefits are to be received within the operating cycle, prepayments would be listed as prepaid expenses under current assets.

CURRENT LIABILITIES. The first group of liabilities, current liabilities, includes debts that are to be paid, liquidated, or settled during the normal operating cycle of the business. The payment of liquidation may involve use of current assets or the substitution of another current liability. *APB Statement No. 4* defines current liabilities as those liabilities "expected to be satisfied by either the use of assets listed as current in the same balance sheet or the creation of other current liabilities, or those [liabilities] expected to be satisfied within a relatively short period of time, usually one year."[5] Liabilities are listed in the balance sheet in the order in which they are to be settled. Liabilities with shorter lifetimes are listed first.

WORKING CAPITAL. Working capital is the ***excess of current assets over current liabilities.*** In effect, the working capital represents the cash that the company could make available for various uses during the operating cycle of the business. Adequate working capital is necessary for the business if it is to pay its short-term and long-term debts as they mature. Working capital is not one of the groups of assets and liabilities shown on the usual statement of financial position; it is a value computed by subtracting current liabilities from current assets. On the forms of the balance sheet examined thus far, current assets and current liabilities are listed separately; the user must make the subtraction to determine working capital. However, accountants sometimes use the ***working-capital form*** of the statement of financial position (Exhibit 3-7), in which the assets and liabilities are rearranged to disclose this amount explicitly.

5. ***APB Statement No. 4,*** para. 198. Copyright 1970 by the AICPA.

LONG-TERM LIABILITIES. Long-term liabilities include obligations or debts due to be met in a period of time greater than the operating cycle. Such liabilities sometimes are called ***fixed liabilities.*** The current liabilities and long-term liabilities are the two major classifications in the category of liabilities on the balance sheet.

OWNERS' EQUITY. As we have seen, owners' equity represents the financial interest of the owners in the enterprise. It is a ***residual interest*** that reflects the excess of the firm's economic resources over its economic obligations. Owners take risks when they invest their resources in the enterprise; in return they benefit if the firm's operations are successful. The owners' equity arises initially from their investment of resources in the enterprise. Any increases or decreases in the resources of the enterprise that are not associated with obligations to creditors cause increases or decreases in the owners' equity. Most changes in owners' equity are caused by ***earnings*** of the firm and the ***distribution*** of these earnings to owners. In the balance sheet of a corporation, owners' equity is usually divided into two groups: ***paid-in*** (or contributed) ***capital*** and ***retained earnings.*** As the names imply, these two groups reflect the initial and later investments by the owners and the increases in owners' equity caused by the firm's operations. In statements of single proprietorships and partnerships, owners' equity is usually called ***owners' capital.*** (See Exhibits 3-13 and 3-14.)

Initial recording principle

We have seen that each resource and obligation of the business is listed on the balance sheet with a money value. Where did these values come from? How does the accountant decide what dollar value to give to a particular item? We begin our discussion of the valuation or measuring process with a few introductory comments about the nature of wealth.

The accounting system is designed to account for ***quantities*** of wealth and for ***changes*** in the inventory of wealth. In most cases, an accountant is concerned with

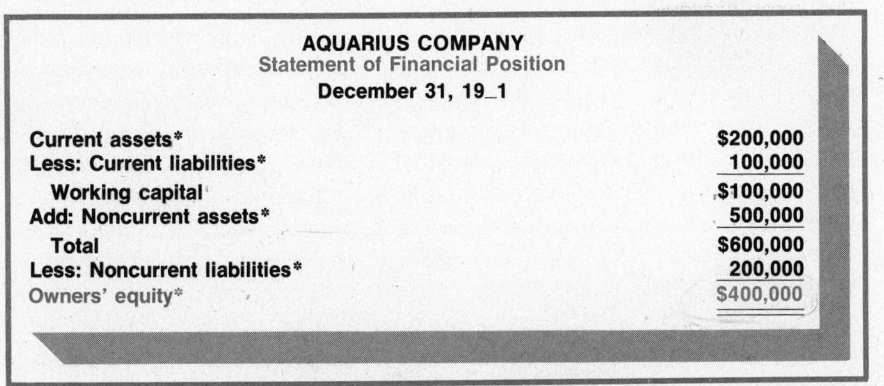

AQUARIUS COMPANY
Statement of Financial Position
December 31, 19_1

Current assets*	$200,000
Less: Current liabilities*	100,000
Working capital	$100,000
Add: Noncurrent assets*	500,000
Total	$600,000
Less: Noncurrent liabilities*	200,000
Owners' equity*	$400,000

Exhibit 3-7
The working-capital form of a balance sheet (condensed)

*In a classified statement, these major categories would be broken down into groups and subgroups.

the valuation of the wealth of a single entity—a business firm, a person, or an institution. He must also account for the changes that occur in the wealth of that entity. Financial statements are the major tools used by the accounting system in reporting on the stock of wealth and on its flow.

In coding, processing, and reporting wealth and its flow, accountants rely upon a generally accepted accounting principle called the ***initial recording principle.*** This principle states that the ***acquisition*** (or historical) ***cost*** is the proper amount at which events involving assets, liabilities, or owners' equity should be recorded in the accounting system. These events are measured by the exchange price at which a transfer takes place—a transfer involving the acquisition of resources from other entities or the incurring of obligations to creditors or owners.

Cost is the exchange price in an arm's length transaction—that is, a transaction in which each of the parties involved is seeking to serve his own best interest. In most cases, acquisition cost is the appropriate measure of value. Some specific cases will help to illustrate the principle.

Case 1: Acquisition of an asset through a cash purchase. The firm purchases land for a cash price of $16,000. The acquisition cost of the land is $16,000. In the balance sheet, this land will be listed as an asset with a value of $16,000.

The initial recording principle applies to the assumption of liabilities as well as to the acquisition of assets.

Case 2: Assumption of Liability. A firm purchases merchandise on account for $10,000 from a supplier. At some future date, the firm promises to pay for the merchandise. The liability is recorded in the accounting statements at the cost that the firm has agreed to pay, $10,000.

The initial recording principle also applies to economic events involving owners' equity.

Case 3: Increase of owners' equity. One of the owners invests an additional $100,000 of capital in the firm. The owners' equity on statements is increased by $100,000, the acquisition cost of the capital to the firm.

Although many items appearing on the statement of financial position are valued at their initial cost, departures from cost are allowed under certain circumstances. Financial statements often reflect the accountants' estimates, judgments, and approximations. For example, the accountant may list the value of accounts receivable as a sum somewhat smaller than the total of the separate amounts owed to the firm. This allows for the fact that some of the accounts probably will never be collected. He may adjust downward the value of marketable securities and inventories if the current market price of these items decreases from the acquisition cost. He may modify the values of plant and equipment for statement purposes, reflecting the decreasing value of these items as they are used or become obsolete. Exhibit 3-12 in the appendix shows how various items might actually be reported on the balance sheet.

Functions of the statement

The statement of financial position has several major functions. The position statement serves as (1) a summary of economic resources and claims to resources, (2) a measure of liquidity, and (3) a measure of solvency.

In the first function, the balance sheet fills a custodial or stewardship role. It reports to the owners and others on the assets owned and the debts owed by the firm, and indicates the resulting equity of the owners in the firm. In effect it is a report on the economic results of the actions taken by the managers of the firm. In its second function, the position statement reports on the liquidity of the firm. ***Liquidity*** refers to the ability of the enterprise to pay its debts as they mature. The working capital—reported explicitly or implicitly in the balance sheet—is a basic measure of the firm's liquidity. This information is of particular importance to the creditors of the firm. In its third function, the position statement indicates the solvency of the firm. ***Solvency*** refers to the firm's ability to meet eventually all of its long-term and short-term debts. The relationship of total assets to total liabilities is one important measure of a firm's solvency.

The statement of financial position presents a balance or equality that we have summarized in the equation $A - L = OE$. This statement thus serves as a check on the balance between assets minus claims against those assets (liabilities) on the one hand and owners' equity on the other. The common name, balance sheet, often given to this statement reflects this basic nature of the statement.

In terms of accounting functions, the statement of financial position (1) ***accumulates*** financial data in accordance with the basic accounting model, $A - L = OE$; (2) ***measures*** resources and claims to resources according to the initial recognition principle (although many exceptions to this generality exist); and (3) ***communicates*** information about the resources, obligations, and residual interest of the firm.

Analysis and interpretation of the statement

Newscasters and reporters try to distinguish between their roles as reporters of facts and as interpreters of those facts. An accounting statement is—as nearly as the accountant can make it so—simply a report of facts. Yet the value of the statement to a user does not lie in the columns of numbers on the page. The user must analyze and interpret the information in the statement in order to get the story behind the facts—to read between the lines.

In and of itself, a financial statement does not explain anything. It merely gives some information about financial events. The user gains meaningful insights and conclusions about the firm only through his own analysis and interpretation of the information in the statement.

Accountants and business analysts have developed various techniques to assist in the interpretation and analysis of financial statements. Two major techniques are (1) comparative financial statements, and (2) ratio analysis.

Comparative statements

The user can learn more about the firm if he is able to compare financial statements covering several time periods. The ***nature*** of current changes and the ***trends*** in these changes that affect the enterprise are disclosed when two or more similar statements for different periods are presented together in a ***comparative statement.*** A single financial statement is but one chapter in the continuous history of a business. Thus the analyst can learn far more from a series of statements than he can from a single statement. A comparative statement usually gives similar reports for the current year and for one or more preceding years.

When preparing a comparative statement, the accountant must be sure that the principles and procedures used in compiling the data for the statements are in fact comparable. Otherwise the comparison of the statements could seriously mislead the user about trends or changes. Any exceptions to this rule of comparable procedures must be clearly disclosed to the user. Exhibit 3-8 shows a condensed comparative statement of financial position. Note that the statement for the most recent year is placed closest to the listing of items, in order to emphasize its relative importance as the most recent information about the firm.

RATIO ANALYSIS

Ratio analysis is a major tool of analysis and interpretation for financial statements. In many accounting courses and textbooks, this is considered an advanced topic, and it is not mentioned until late in the study of accounting. However, ratios are easy to understand. The use of ratio analysis will help us throughout our study to see what information users can get from the accounting system output.

In mathematics, a ***ratio*** is the quotient formed when one magnitude is divided by another measured in the same units. Thus the ratio is a pure quantity or number, independent of the measurement units being used. In this section we look at four major ratios that use the information found on the balance sheet. As a specific example, we apply these ratios to the analysis of data from the statement in Exhibit 3-5.

CURRENT RATIO. The current ratio is a measure of a firm's ability to pay its debts as they mature—in other words, a measure of its liquidity. This ratio serves as

Exhibit 3-8
A comparative balance sheet (condensed)

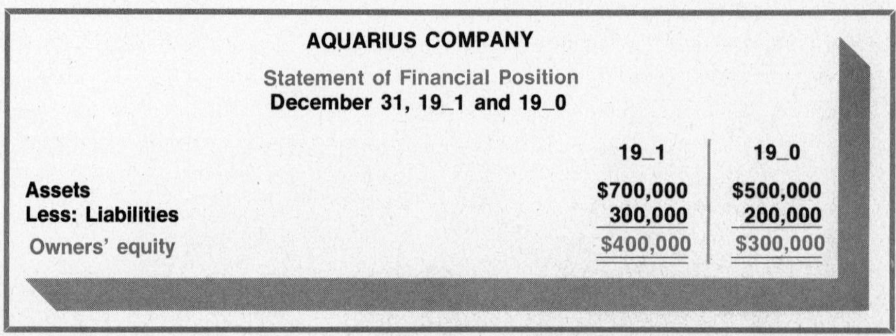

AQUARIUS COMPANY
Statement of Financial Position
December 31, 19_1 and 19_0

	19_1	19_0
Assets	**$700,000**	**$500,000**
Less: Liabilities	**300,000**	**200,000**
Owners' equity	**$400,000**	**$300,000**

a check on the adequacy of the working capital (current assets minus current liabilities) of the firm. The current ratio is formed by dividing current assets by current liabilities. Exhibit 3-5 shows that the Aquarius Company (on December 31, 19_1) had current assets of $200,000 and current liabilities of $100,000. Thus, the Aquarius Company had working capital of $100,000 ($200,000 − $100,000). Its current ratio is "two to one" as calculated here:

$$\frac{\text{Current assets}}{\text{Current liabilities}} = \frac{\$200{,}000}{\$100{,}000} = \frac{2}{1} = 2 \text{ to } 1.$$

This value of the current ratio shows that the firm has current assets twice as large as the amount needed to pay current liabilities. Depending upon circumstances, this may be enough to assure the liquidity of the firm.

ACID-TEST (QUICK) RATIO. The acid-test ratio is a more severe measure of a company's liquidity than the current ratio. The acid-test ratio compares quick assets (cash, marketable securities, and receivables) with current liabilities to test the ability of a company to pay its debts as they mature. The ratio is

$$\frac{\text{Cash, marketable securities, receivables}}{\text{Current liabilities}}$$

In Exhibit 3-12, the Aquarius Company has $165,000 of quick assets and $100,000 of current liabilities. The acid-test ratio is computed as follows:

$$\frac{\text{Quick assets}}{\text{Current liabilities}} = \frac{\$165{,}000}{\$100{,}000} = 1.65 \text{ to } 1.$$

RATIO OF OWNERS' EQUITY TO TOTAL ASSETS. The ratio of owners' equity to total assets measures the proportion of the firm's assets that are provided or claimed by the owners. This ratio is a measure of the financial strength or weakness of the firm. Recall that the owners' equity is the residual interest in the firm's assets after allowance has been made for the claims of creditors against the assets. If the owners' equity is a small proportion of the total assets, the firm may be considered financially weak, because the owners have a relatively small investment in the firm as compared to the creditors. On the other hand, a higher ratio of owners' equity to assets can represent a relatively larger degree of security for the firm. This ratio is important to creditors in deciding how safe it is to advance credit to the firm. From Exhibit 3-5, we see that the Aquarius Company has owners' equity of $400,000 and total assets of $700,000. Thus, the ratio is

$$\frac{\text{Owners' equity}}{\text{Total assets}} = \frac{\$400{,}000}{\$700{,}000} = 0.57 \text{ to } 1.$$

This is a relatively high value for this ratio. It suggests that the Aquarius Company is a relatively safe credit risk.

RATIO OF TOTAL LIABILITIES TO TOTAL ASSETS. The ratio of total liabilities to total assets measures the proportion of the firm's assets that are financed by creditors. This ratio is a measure of the solvency of the firm. To the creditor, a low value of this ratio represents a relatively large degree of security for extending credit to the firm. On the other hand, if the value of this ratio is too low, the owners may conclude that the company is not using its credit most advantageously. From Exhibit 3-5, we see that the Aquarius Company has total liabilities of \$300,000 and total assets of \$700,000. The value of the ratio therefore is

$$\frac{\text{Total liabilities}}{\text{Total assets}} = \frac{\$300{,}000}{\$700{,}000} = 0.43 \text{ to } 1.$$

This value is low enough to suggest that the firm is a good credit risk, but the value is not excessively low. Note that this ratio is closely related to the ratio of owners' equity to total assets, because of the basic accounting model ($A - L = OE$).[6]

RATIO OF OWNERS' EQUITY TO TOTAL LIABILITIES. The ratio of owners' equity to total liabilities is a measure of the relative claims of the owners and the creditors against the resources of the firm. A high value of this ratio shows that the claims of the owners are greater than those of the creditors. Thus a high value of this ratio is viewed by creditors as a favorable sign that the firm has a high degree of security. From Exhibit 3-5, we see that the value of this ratio for the Aquarius Company is

$$\frac{\text{Owners' equity}}{\text{Total liabilities}} = \frac{\$400{,}000}{\$300{,}000} = 1.33 \text{ to } 1.$$

This is a relatively high value, so it confirms the relative safety of this business as a credit risk. Again, this ratio can be shown to be related mathematically to the other ratios involving *A, L,* and *OE.* Thus the three ratios OE/A, L/A, and OE/L are not independent measures. Rather, they give three different ways of looking at the same basic facts about the solvency of the firm.

USING RATIO ANALYSIS

The user must not undertake the interpretation and analysis of financial ratios in isolation from other information. He must relate his interpretation to such matters as the general economic condition of the country, expectations about the future, the availability of opportunities, the acceptance of risk, comparisons with similar ratios for other firms in the industry, and so forth. Experience and judgment are involved in the interpretation of such relative terms as "high" or "low." A ratio that is high for one business at one time may be low for another business or for the same business at a different time.

Two basic sources are available for interpreting ratios. ***Historical standards*** are provided by the past record of the firm. ***Industry standards*** involve comparisons of similar ratios for a number of different companies in the same industry. Dun and Bradstreet publishes major ratios for many industries. Robert Morris Associates, National Cash Register Company, and others also publish industry ratios.

6. Because OE must equal $(A - L)$, the ratio OE/A must equal $(A - L)/A$, or $(OE/A) = 1 - (L/A)$. In the example, note that $0.57 = 1 - 0.43$.

Impact analysis

Every stimulus provokes a response. Economic events have an impact on financial statements. To understand accounting, we must know something about the stimuli that evoke responses in the outputs of the accounting system. This kind of study is called impact analysis.

In our study of the significance of the statement of financial position, it is important that we understand the impact that ***changes*** in assets, liabilities, and owners' equity have upon one another. Let us pursue this thought for a moment.

We have already stated that $A - L = OE$ (or, equivalently, $A = L + OE$). We can now develop this formula more fully by adding some additional concepts. The first new concept is that of net assets. ***Net assets*** are defined as total assets minus total liabilities or

$$NA = A - L.$$

However, we know that $A - L = OE$ (the basic accounting model), so

$$NA = A - L = OE,$$
$$\text{or} \quad NA = OE.$$

This equality states that net assets are always equal to the owners' equity. However, this relationship is an equality of values, ***not*** an identity of concepts. The owners' equity represents the amount of claims that the owners have against the resources (assets) of the firm. This amount is computed by calculating the net assets of the firm, which is the result obtained when total liabilities are subtracted from total assets. The value of the net assets must be equal to the value of the owners' equity. The fact that these two values must be equal is a result of the basic model chosen by accounting theoreticians.

Exhibit 3-9 is a condensed statement of financial position that emphasizes the relationship between owners' equity and net assets. The subtraction determines the net assets of the firm. The owners' equity then is declared to have a value equal to the net assets.

Now let us explore the way that impact analysis can be applied to the statement of financial position. We use the following two basic equations for our analysis: $NA = OE$, and $A - L = OE$. Exhibit 3-10 shows a table that summarizes the impact of changes in the basic accounting categories. In this table, a plus sign (+) indicates

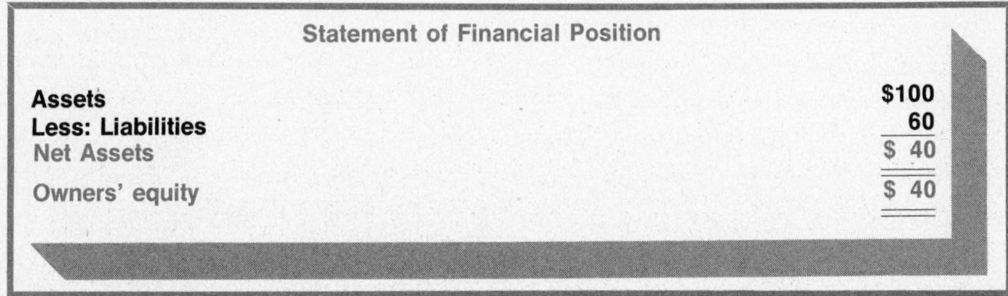

Statement of Financial Position

Assets	**$100**
Less: Liabilities	**60**
Net Assets	$ 40
Owners' equity	$ 40

Exhibit 3-9
A condensed statement illustrating net assets and owners' equity

Exhibit 3-10
Impact analysis of categories in the balance sheet

Assets	−	Liabilities	=	Owners' Equity	=	Net Assets
+		0		+		+
+		−		+		+
+		+ but less than increase in assets		+		+
+		+ greater than increase in assets		−		−
−		0		−		−
−		+		−		−
−		− but less than decrease in assets		−		−
−		− greater than decrease in assets		+		+
0		0		0		0
0		+		−		−
0		−		+		+

NOTE: The impact analysis presented in this table can be summarized in words as follows.

1. An increase in net assets will result in an increase in owners' equity. Net assets will increase (a) if assets increase while liabilities remain unchanged, decrease, or increase less than assets increase; (b) if assets decrease while liabilities decrease more than assets do; or (c) if assets remain unchanged while liabilities decrease.

2. A decrease in net assets will result in a decrease in owners' equity. Net assets will decrease (a) if assets decrease while liabilities remain unchanged, increase, or decrease less than assets decrease; (b) if assets increase while liabilities increase more than assets do; or (c) if assets remain unchanged while liabilities increase.

3. If net assets remain unchanged, owners' equity will also remain unchanged. Net assets will remain unchanged (a) if both assets and liabilities remain unchanged; (b) if both assets and liabilities increase by the same amount; or (c) if both assets and liabilities decrease by the same amount. (The latter two situations are not included in the table.)

an increase, a minus sign (−) indicates a decrease, and a zero (0) indicates no change. As an illustration of the way the table is read, consider the first line of the table. It indicates that, if assets increase and liabilities remain unchanged, then net assets and owners' equity must increase. Or, if owners' equity increases while liabilities remain unchanged, then assets and net assets must increase.

In studying Exhibit 3-10, you may find it useful to replace the plus or minus signs by specific dollar values (say $5), then use the equations to determine the impact on other values in the table. For example, if assets increase by $5 while liabilities remain unchanged, it is clear that owners' equity and net assets must each increase by $5. Do not neglect the footnote to the table, which you may find helpful in learning to read the table.

This impact analysis of the items in the statement of financial position provides a way to ask and answer some key managerial questions. How can the firm increase its net assets and its owners' equity? What may cause decreases in net assets and owners' equity? What happens to net assets and owners' equity if assets and liabilities both increase? An understanding of Exhibit 3-10 will provide answers to these and many similar questions. Impact analysis provides insights into the meaning and content of financial statements. It helps in a close and perceptive examination of statement items, major categories, and the relationships that are implied in accounting reports. We use impact analysis throughout this book to clarify the meanings of accounting statements.

An examination of the ***change*** in net assets and owners' equity from one period in time to another indicates that the change in net assets (ΔNA) equals the change in owners' equity (ΔOE), or $\Delta NA = \Delta OE$. Exhibit 3-11 illustrates this relationship in a comparative statement of financial position.

An increase in owners' equity can be caused only by an increase in net assets. Or, to make the statement more general, owners' equity increases or decreases from period to period in direct correspondence with changes in net assets. An explanation of a change in owners' equity from one period to another must be based on an explanation of changes in net assets. For example, an increase in owners' equity can be caused by an increase in assets or a decrease in liabilities, but a firm cannot increase its owners' equity simply by issuing more shares of ownership without any changes in its net assets.

Impact analysis can help in understanding ***why*** changes occur from period to period in financial statements. The separate statements of financial position do not reflect changes in financial position; they present static information relating to a specific date. Users of the statements must use impact analysis and other tools to interpret the changes between statements. The income statement, which we discuss in the next chapter, is one of the tools that helps indicate what has happened between one balance sheet and the next.

Summary

Chapter 3 deals with the statement of financial position, or balance sheet. Before discussing this important financial statement, the chapter pauses to reflect upon the accounting principles and assumptions that form the underpinning of financial reports. Of special importance to the accountant are the initial recording principle and the business-entity, going-concern, dollar-measurement, and periodic-and-timely-reporting assumptions.

The statement of financial position (or balance sheet) summarizes information associated with the economic resources and liabilities and the owners' equity at a

Exhibit 3-11
Interperiod changes in the balance sheet

	Dec. 31, 19_1	Dec. 31, 19_0	Changes
Assets	$200	$100	+$100
Less: Liabilities	150	60	+ 90
Net assets	$ 50	$ 40	+$ 10
Owners' equity	$ 50	$ 40	+$ 10

specific point in time. The balance sheet is prepared according to various accounting assumptions and principles. This statement can be structured in the account form, the modified account form, the report form, or the working-capital form.

The major categories appearing on the statement of financial position are assets, liabilities, and owners' equities. Each of these sets can be further classified into subsets. For example, the set of assets includes the subsets of current assets; investments; property, plant, and equipment; intangible assets; and deferred charges. These subsets can be further classified into smaller subsets.

Among its various functions, the balance sheet serves as (1) a summary of resources and claims to resources, (2) a measure of liquidity, and (3) a measure of solvency.

The user of financial statements makes use of a variety of techniques and tools in order to analyze and interpret the information in the statements. Among the more important tools of analysis are comparative financial statements and ratios. Several important ratios useful in analyzing a balance sheet are discussed in the chapter. In particular, ratio analysis and other tools use the position statement to gain insight into the firm's ability to meet its debts as they mature.

Certain basic relationships should now be clearly established. These relationships can be summarized in formulas:

$$A - L = OE \text{ (the accounting equation);}$$
$$A = L + OE;$$
$$A - L = NA;$$
$$OE = NA;$$
$$\Delta OE = \Delta NA.$$

An understanding of these formulas provides a foundation for an intelligent approach to the study of accounting.

The appendix to Chapter 3 describes in detail the various items that appear in the statement of financial position.

Appendix

TERMINOLOGY USED IN THE STATEMENT OF FINANCIAL POSITION

Many different items may appear on a fully classified statement of financial position. Exhibit 3-12 shows an example of such a statement. This appendix gives a brief description of each of the items. These items are discussed in great detail in following chapters. For the moment, a general understanding of these items is sufficient. The full listing is given here primarily to serve as a convenient reference during study of the chapters that follow.

ASSETS. Economic resources of the firm; wealth and rights to wealth.

Current assets. Cash and other assets that are expected to be converted into cash, sold, or consumed within one year or during the normal operating cycle of the business, whichever is longer.

Exhibit 3-12 **A classified balance sheet in the modified account form**

AQUARIUS COMPANY

Statement of Financial Position
December 31, 19_1

Assets

Current assets:			
Cash		$ 30,000	
Marketable securities—at the lower of cost or market (cost $22,000)		20,000	
Accounts receivable	$100,000		
Less allowance for doubtful accounts	5,000	95,000	
Notes receivable		20,000	
Inventories—at cost		30,000	
Prepaid insurance		5,000	
Total current assets			$200,000
Investments:			
Stock of the XYC Co.—at cost (market $7,000)		$ 5,000	
Bonds of the CDE Co.—at cost (market $12,000)		15,000	
Real estate—at cost (market $35,000)		30,000	
Total investments			50,000
Property, plant, and equipment:			
Land		$150,000	
Factory building	$500,000		
Less accumulated depreciation	400,000	100,000	
Machinery and equipment	$140,000		
Less accumulated depreciation	60,000	80,000	
Office equipment	$ 20,000		
Less accumulated depreciation	10,000	10,000	
Total property, plant, and equipment			340,000
Intangible assets:			
Patents		$ 50,000	
Franchise		30,000	
Total intangible assets			80,000
Other assets:			
Long-term loan to officers			30,000
Total assets			$700,000

Liabilities and Stockholders' Equity

Current liabilities:			
Accounts payable		$ 30,000	
Notes payable		10,000	
Federal income tax payable		60,000	
Total current liabilities			$100,000
Long-term liabilities:			
Bonds payable—6%, due June 30, 19_9			200,000
Total liabilities			$300,000
Stockholders' equity:			
Common stock, $3 par value, authorized and issued 50,000 shares		$150,000	
Paid-in capital in excess of par value		50,000	
Total paid-in capital		$200,000	
Retained earnings		200,000	
Total stockholders' equity			400,000
Total liabilities and stockholders' equity			$700,000

Cash. Money on hand and balances of checking accounts at banks. Cash on hand includes any item acceptable to a bank for deposit—such as currency, coins, checks, money orders, bank drafts, and so on.

Marketable securities. Stocks, bonds, and similar securities that are to be converted into cash within the operating cycle of the business and that are readily marketable; also called temporary or short-term investments. Accountants list marketable securities at the lower value of their original cost or their current market value; this is a conservative valuation.

Accounts receivable. Amounts due from customers (debtors) arising from sales or from services performed.

Allowance for doubtful accounts. A reduction of the accounts receivable that is established to adjust this item to an estimate of the amount actually realizable—that is, to take into consideration the fact that some accounts may never be collected.

Notes receivable. Unconditional promises in writing to pay definite sums of money at certain or determinable dates, usually with a specified interest rate.

Inventories. Merchandise, materials, or stock that a business normally uses in its manufacturing and selling operations. Inventories usually are carried in the statements at cost or at the lower of cost or market value.

Prepaid expenses. Expenses of a future period that have been paid in advance, such as prepaid rent, prepaid insurance, or prepaid advertising fees.

Long-term investments. Stocks, bonds, and other investments owned by the company that are to be held for a period of time exceeding the normal operating cycle of the business. Long-term investments in bonds are reported on the statement at their original cost; current market values may be disclosed in parentheses. Long-term investments in stock are reported at the lower of the original cost of the stock or the current market value.

Property, plant, and equipment. Tangible, long-lived assets such as land, buildings, machinery, and tools acquired for use in normal business operations (not primarily for sale) during a period of time greater than the normal operating cycle; sometimes called fixed or long-term assets.

Land. Natural resources owned and used for the operations of a business. (Land held as an investment is listed as a long-term investment.) Unless otherwise disclosed, land is valued at its acquisition cost.

Buildings. Structures owned and used in the operations of a business. Normally listed at cost.

Machinery. Devices owned and used in the business—devices that perform prescribed tasks, such as lathes, turbines, and so on. Normally listed at cost.

Equipment. Physical property other than land, buildings, and machinery (and improvements of a somewhat permanent nature on these)—property that is ordinarily useful in carrying on business operations, including such items as tools, trucks, typewriters, desks, and so on. This group is often subdivided into such categories as office equipment, delivery equipment, or shop equipment. Normally listed at cost.

Accumulated depreciation. After each listing of buildings, machinery, and equipment at the value determined by cost, the accountant normally deducts an item called accumulated depreciation. This represents the accumulation of charges resulting from allocating the cost of an asset over its life. The cost of the asset is decreased each year to reflect the effect of use, wear and tear, and obsolescence.

Intangible assets. Long-lived assets representing nonphysical rights, values, privileges, and so on—exclusive of receivables and investments.

Patents. Exclusive rights granted by the government enabling the holder thereof to control the use of an invention for 17 years.

Copyrights. Exclusive rights to reproduce and sell literary, musical, and artistic works for a period covering the life of the author plus an additional 50 years.

Franchises. Contracts giving exclusive rights to perform certain functions or to sell certain services or products.

Trademarks and trade names. Exclusive rights granted by the government to use certain names, symbols, labels, designs, and so forth. The life of a trademark or trade name is unlimited.

Goodwill. Excess earning power of a business due to special advantages that it possesses.

Other assets. Assets that cannot be classified elsewhere on the balance sheet, including prepayments for services or benefits that will affect the company over a future period greater than the operating cycle—for example, prepayment of several years' rent.

Liabilities. Economic obligations; claims against the assets by creditors.

Current liabilities. Debts that are to be paid, liquidated, or settled out of current assets or through the substitution of another current liability.

Accounts payable. Amounts owed to creditors through purchase of goods or services on account.

Notes payable. Unconditional promises in writing to pay certain sums in money at fixed or determinable future times.

Long-term liabilities. Debts to be paid during a period of time that exceeds the normal operating cycle of the business. Sometimes called fixed liabilities.

Bonds payable. Long-term promises to repay loans represented by bonds issued by the firm.

OWNERS' EQUITY (OR CAPITAL). Residual interests of owners in the assets.

For a corporation. A corporation is a legal entity created by a charter received from the state and owned by stockholders.

Paid-in (or contributed) capital. Amount invested by stockholders.

Common (or capital) stock. Capital paid into the corporation by owners of common stock, usually listed at the par value of par-value stock. Par value is a value per share assigned to the stock in the charter of the corporation and printed on the face of each stock certificate. Par value does not establish the market value of the stock.

Paid-in capital in excess of par value—common stock. The amount contributed by owners of common stock in excess of the par value of the stock.

Retained earnings. Accumulated net income of the corporation resulting from profitable operations less dividend distributions to shareholders.

For a single proprietorship. A business owned by one individual. Exhibit 3-13 shows a condensed balance sheet for a single proprietorship.

Proprietor, Capital. Capital contributed by the owner and retained in the business; also may include accumulated earnings.

Proprietor, Drawing. A temporary capital account in which such items as proprietor's salary, withdrawals, and income of the business are recorded before transferral to the Capital account.

For a partnership. A business owned by two or more partners. Exhibit 3-14 shows a condensed balance sheet for a partnership.

Partners, Capital, and Partners, Drawing. The Capital and Drawing accounts for a partnership are similar to the Capital and Drawing accounts for a single proprietorship, except that they refer to the individual partners in the partnership.

Exhibit 3-13
A condensed balance sheet for a single proprietorship

JOHN JONES STORE

Balance Sheet
December 31, 19_1

Assets	**$100,000**	**Liabilities**	**$ 60,000**
		John Jones, Capital	**40,000**
Total assets	$100,000	Total liabilities and owners' equity	$100,000

Exhibit 3-14
A condensed balance sheet for a partnership

RED AND BLUE FURNITURE STORE

Balance Sheet
December 31, 19_1

Assets	**$100,000**	**Liabilities**	**$ 60,000**
		Frank Red, Capital	**30,000**
		Joe Blue, Capital	**10,000**
Total assets	$100,000	Total liabilities and owners' equity	$100,000

NOTES TO FINANCIAL STATEMENTS. Notes to financial statements are an integral part of the statements. They are used to disclose information that cannot be disclosed in the captions and headings of the financial statements, but that are required for a fair presentation of financial position and results of operations. Notes should be concise, clear, and exact. The sample financial statements presented in the appendix to this text contain notes.

Questions

1. Define the technical term "generally accepted accounting principles."
2. List several sources of generally accepted accounting principles.
3. What are accounting assumptions?
4. Name and describe four basic accounting assumptions.
5. What is the unit of measurement used in accounting? What does the accountant assume about this unit of measurement?
6. Distinguish between the calendar year and the fiscal year.
7. What are interim statements?
8. What is the statement of financial position? Does this statement show the value of the assets owned by a company? List other names that are used to describe the statement of financial position.
9. Define assets, liabilities, and owners' equity.
10. State the accounting equation in words and in symbols.
11. The statement of financial position can be prepared in various forms. Name and describe four forms used in the preparation of this statement.
12. Explain the conventions of use of dollar signs and underlining in financial reports. What information should appear in the heading of a financial report?
13. List the major categories of assets, liabilities, and owners' equity that appear in a classified statement of financial position.
14. What is meant by the normal operating cycle of a business?
15. What are current assets? List the major subgroups of current assets.
16. What items are included in each of the following sections of a statement of financial position: (a) investments; (b) property, plant, and equipment; (c) intangible assets; (d) other assets; (e) current liabilities; (f) long-term liabilities?
17. In the statement of financial position, what order should be used in listing assets? liabilities?
18. What is meant by working capital? Why is working capital an important financial concept? How is working capital shown in a statement of financial position?
19. List some significant kinds of information that might require disclosure in a statement of financial position, either in the body of the statement by comments in parentheses or in footnotes to the statement.
20. What is the initial recording principle of accounting?
21. Distinguish between a "stock of wealth" and a "flow of wealth."
22. List the major functions of the statement of financial position.
23. What is meant by "analysis of a financial statement"?
24. What is a comparative financial statement?
25. What is a ratio? What is ratio analysis?
26. What is the current ratio? How is it used in analysis of a statement?

27. On December 31, 19_1, the AAA Company had a current ratio of 5 to 1, and the BBB Company had a current ratio of 2 to 1. Assume that both companies are in the same industry and that the companies are similar in other important financial conditions. Which firm is in a better position to pay its current liabilities as they mature? Discuss.

28. Indicate whether each of the following statements is true or false.
   a. $A - L = OE$.
   b. $OE = A + L$.
   c. $A - OE = L$.
   d. $A + OE = L$.
   e. $OE = NA$.
   f. $OE = NA = A - L$.
   g. $\Delta NA = \Delta OE$.
   h. $\Delta NA = \Delta A - \Delta L$.
   i. Owners' equity can increase only if there is an increase in net assets.

29. How might a creditor's interest in a statement of financial position differ from that of an investor (a potential owner)?

30. Why are the claims of owners against the firm's assets segregated from the claims of creditors on a statement of financial position?

31. In the stockholders' equity section of the statement of financial position for a corporation, a distinction is made between contributed capital and retained earnings. Discuss.

Exercises

E3-1 The following listings give some financial information about three companies as of December 31, 19_1. Prepare a statement of financial position for each company, classifying the statement as far as possible. Use the account form of the statement.

AZ Company:	Assets	$150
	Liabilities	95
BZ Company:	Current assets	$205
	Noncurrent assets	360
	Current liabilities	55
	Noncurrent liabilities	220
CZ Company:	Current liabilities	$485
	Intangible assets	100
	Current assets	310
	Investments	485
	Long-term liabilities	430
	Property, plant, and equipment	915
	Other assets	115

E3-2 Prepare a statement of financial position in the account form for the Stuart Company, using the following data (as of December 31, 19_1):

Intangible assets	$ 45,000
Current liabilities	120,000
Investments	190,000
Retained earnings	?

Current assets	$265,000
Other assets	60,000
Capital stock	450,000
Long-term liabilities	130,000
Property, plant, and equipment	490,000

E3-3 Using the same data from Exercise E3-2, prepare a statement of financial position in the modified account form for the Stuart Company.

E3-4 Using the same data from Exercise E3-2, prepare a statement of financial position in the working-capital form for the Stuart Company.

E3-5 Using the same data from Exercise E3-2, prepare a statement of financial position in the report form for the Stuart Company.

E3-6 Prepare a statement of financial position in the report form for the OZ Company, using the following data (as of the end of 19_1):

Prepaid insurance	$ 5,000
Inventory (at the lower of cost or market)	125,000
Patents	2,000
Cash	55,000
Accounts payable	35,000
Accounts receivable	45,000
Allowance for doubtful accounts	15,000
Notes payable	15,000
Common stock	280,000
Marketable securities	15,000
Retained earnings	?
Land	120,000
Bonds payable—7%, due June 30, 1999	85,000
Bonds of the MN Co. (market $900); the bonds are to be held for several years	950
Factory building	150,000
Accumulated depreciation—factory	35,000
Paid-in capital in excess of par value	20,000

E3-7 Using the same data from Exercise E3-6, compute the following ratios:

a. current ratio;
b. ratio of owners' equity to total assets;
c. ratio of owners' equity to total liabilities;
d. ratio of total liabilities to total assets.

Assume that ratios a, b, and c are significantly higher than the corresponding ratios computed for the end of 19_0, but ratio d is significantly lower than the corresponding ratio for the end of 19_0. What interpretations would you draw from this analysis?

E3-8 Prepare a properly classified statement of financial position in the modified account form for the AX Company, using the following data (as of December 31, 19_1):

Accounts payable	$ 48,000
Investments in stock	105,000
Merchandise inventory	41,000
Land	87,000
Machinery	100,000
Prepaid expenses	7,000
Wages payable	12,000
Taxes payable	9,000
Common stock	81,000

Cash	$ 35,000
Accounts receivable	28,000
5% bonds payable, due 19_5	87,000
Marketable securities	17,000
Patents	16,000
Accumulated depreciation—machinery	35,000
Allowance for doubtful receivables	3,000
Retained earnings (to be computed)	?

E3-9 The following information relates to the books of the Firm Co.:

	19_1	19_2
Assets	$180	$235
Liabilities	90	120

Compute the following:

a. net assets at the end of 19_1;
b. net assets at the end of 19_2;
c. owners' equity at the end of 19_1;
d. owners' equity at the end of 19_2;
e. change in net assets from 19_1 to 19_2;
f. change in owners' equity from 19_1 to 19_2.

What relationships do you observe as a result of these computations?

E3-10 A comparison of statements for two successive years for the same company yields the observations shown below for changes in total assets and total liabilities in each of several cases. For each case, indicate the changes that must occur in net assets and in owners' equity.

	Assets	Liabilities
Case 1	+$ 250	−$ 50
Case 2	−$1,200	−$700
Case 3	+$ 500	+$200
Case 4	+$ 600	no change
Case 5	no change	+$250
Case 6	+$ 800	+$350
Case 7	no change	no change
Case 8	no change	unknown
Case 9	−$ 350	+$350
Case 10	+$ 500	no change

E3-11 The B Company has current assets of $335,000; investments of $55,000; property, plant, and equipment of $60,000; current liabilities of $35,000; and stockholders' equity of $325,000.

a. Compute the long-term liabilities of the B Company.
b. Compute the current ratio.

E3-12 The Z Company has assets of $750,000; shareholders' equity of $500,000; current liabilities of $100,000. Compute the ratio of stockholders' equity to total liabilities.

Problems

P3-1 The following is a list of the assets, liabilities, and owners' equity accounts of the Dusty Road Company as of December 31, 19_1.

Cash	$ 17,000
Marketable securities	4,500

Accounts payable	$ 23,000
Notes payable	6,000
Accounts receivable	63,000
Notes receivable	9,500
Allowance for doubtful accounts receivable	8,000
Bonds payable (due June 30, 19_9)	105,000
Mortgage payable (due December 31, 19_8)	45,000
Merchandise inventory	47,000
Prepaid insurance	1,500
Land	43,000
Building	92,000
Investment in bonds	55,500
Capital stock	90,000
Equipment	54,500
Retained earnings	20,500
Accumulated depreciation—building	61,000
Accumulated depreciation—equipment	29,000

Required:

a. Prepare a statement of financial position in the modified account form.

b. Compute the following ratios: current ratio; ratio of owners' equity to total assets; ratio of total liabilities to total assets; and ratio of owners' equity to total liabilities.

c. Compute the working capital of the Dusty Road Company.

d. Give your analysis of the financial position, liquidity, and solvency of the Dusty Road Company.

P3-2 Criticize the statement of financial position shown in Exhibit 3-15.

P3-3 You are the chief accountant of the BC Company. A major stockholder of the company is in your office questioning the dollar values assigned to various items on the statement of financial position you have just issued. Among other things, she questions the fact that the statement shows the value of the company's land as $1,000,000—the amount that the company paid for the land some 20 years ago. In the current real estate market, the land could be sold for a considerably larger amount. The stockholder feels that this asset is undervalued on the statement, and that the net assets and therefore the stockholders' equity should in fact be larger than the statement shows. In terms of basic accounting assumptions and/or principles, how would you explain the statement treatment of this item?

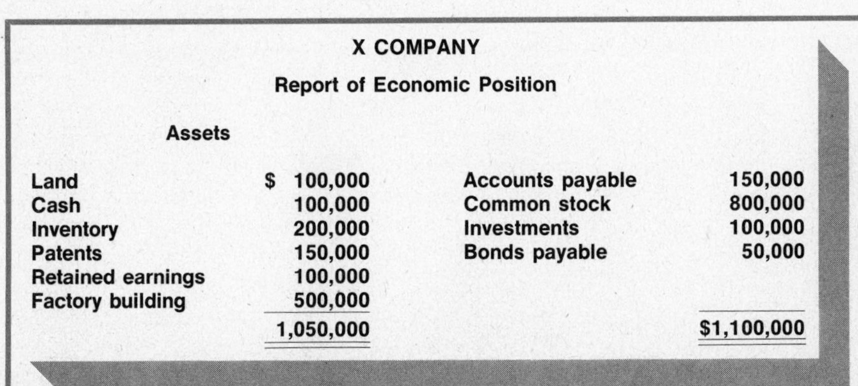

X COMPANY

Report of Economic Position

Assets			
Land	**$ 100,000**	**Accounts payable**	**150,000**
Cash	**100,000**	**Common stock**	**800,000**
Inventory	**200,000**	**Investments**	**100,000**
Patents	**150,000**	**Bonds payable**	**50,000**
Retained earnings	**100,000**		
Factory building	**500,000**		
	1,050,000		**$1,100,000**

Exhibit 3-15
An incorrect statement for Problem P3-2

P3-4 As a public accountant, you are asked to evaluate the comparative statement of financial position of a client for the past two years. You discover that the current ratio has changed from 4/1 to 2/1, and that the ratio of owners' equity to total assets has changed from 3/1 to 2/1. Suggest some possible causes for these changes and the possible significance of the changes. Also suggest some ways in which these ratios might possibly be improved in the following year.

P3-5 Prepare a detailed statement of financial position in the account form from the following information for the Equity Company as of December 31, 19_1:

Cash	$ 30,000
Marketable securities ($25,000 cost; $24,000 market)	
Accounts receivable	15,000
Allowance for doubtful accounts	2,000
Notes receivable	5,000
Inventories (cost)	50,000
Prepaid insurance	12,000
Long-term investments:	
Stock of GTM Co. ($5,000 cost; $4,500 market)	
Bonds of MTG Co. ($9,000 cost; $10,000 market)	
Land	100,000
Factory Building	250,000
Accumulated depreciation—Factory	50,000
Patent	25,000
Franchise	35,000
Common stock, $10 par value, authorized and issued 10,000 shares	100,000
Paid-in capital in excess of par value	10,000
Retained earnings (to be computed by student)	?
Accounts payable	20,000
Wages payable	50,000
Bonds payable—6%, due September 30, 19_9	100,000

P3-6 A company engaged in the following activities in its first year of operations:

a. Issued $100,000 of common stock for cash.
b. Purchased a building for $60,000 cash.
c. Borrowed $20,000 from a bank at the end of the year.
d. Purchased office euqipment for $5,000 cash.
e. Purchased $10,000 of inventory on account.
f. Paid $6,000 on account for inventory purchased in item e.
g. Sold 50% of its inventory purchased in item e for $25,000. The sale was on account.
h. Collected $10,000 on the account sale in item g.
i. Expenses of $15,000 were paid in cash.

Required: Prepare a statement of financial position from the data provided above for the U.S. Company on December 31, 19_6. Depreciation on office equipment and building for the year were $1,000 and $2,000 respectively.

The income statement

4

The income statement is the official scoreboard for a business. It shows the outcome of last year's game. The bottom line of the statement gives the final score. The rest of the statement provides further details about how the game was played; from these the user can evaluate the performance of the team.

In the past, most users regarded the statement of financial position as the most significant financial statement. This was particularly true of bankers and other extenders of credit, who were interested mainly in a firm's financial strength, as measured by its resources and the claims against those resources. More recently, business analysts have given increasing attention to the earning capacity of a firm as a test of its financial strength and potential. Earning capacity is reflected mainly on the income statement. Thus the income statement is becoming an ever more important tool of financial and managerial accounting. Before turning to a study of the income statement, we discuss briefly the matching concept that underlies the presentation of this statement.

The matching concept

A football team scores a touchdown and wins the game. The victory is the reward for the effort spent in weeks of conditioning and practice, as well as for the action on the day of the game. Was the effort worthwhile? To answer such a question, we must somehow match the value of the victory against the value of the effort needed to get the victory. As we try to judge our lives, we constantly match rewards against punishments, pleasure against pain, and accomplishment against effort. Accounting inherited much of this philosophy. Periodically the accounting system matches revenue earned against expenses incurred. The result of this matching is net income or loss.

The users of the accounting system want to know whether the business entity is operating profitably—that is, have the operations of the firm caused an increase in its net assets and owners' equity? To meet this need for information, the accounting system periodically prepares a summary of the firm's net income (or net loss) during the period. To determine the net income, the system matches the revenue earned during the accounting period against the expenses that were incurred in the process of earning this revenue. Accountants call this attempt to match revenue against the appropriate expenses the ***matching concept.*** The procedures and principles used to accomplish this matching form a basic part of our study of the income statement.

To help visualize the matching process, think of revenue as a stream of rewards coming in to the firm, and think of expenses as a stream of efforts flowing out from the firm. Which part of the stream of efforts should be matched in an accounting period against a given part of the stream of rewards? As we examine the income statement, we will see what principles the accountant follows in performing this matching process.

Content and format of the statement

The income statement is a financial statement that reports the revenue, expenses, and net income (or net loss) of a business entity, showing the results of its profit-directed activities during the accounting period (usually one year). The income statement reflects the ***changes*** in owners' equity that have resulted from the firm's profit-directed activities during the period. It summarizes the inflows and outflows of assets during the period. The income statement sometimes is called the statement of profit and loss, or the operating statement.

Exhibit 4-1 shows an income statement in its most elementary form. The heading of the statement names the entity, the statement, and the time period for which net income is being computed. The body of the statement shows the net income as the excess of revenue over expenses.

The identification, recognition, and measurement of revenue and expenses are processes that involve a number of accounting principles. As we study the nature of revenue, expenses, and net income, we will also learn about the principles used in preparing the income statement.

NATURE AND SOURCES OF REVENUE

Revenue is the gross inflow of assets or the gross decrease in liabilities that results from certain profit-directed activities of the enterprise that can change owners' equity.[1] Revenue can result from (1) the sale of products to customers, (2) the rendering of services or the "loan" of the firm's economic resources to others, resulting in the receipt of rent, interest, royalties, fees, dividends, and so on, and (3)

Exhibit 4-1
The income statement in its simplest form

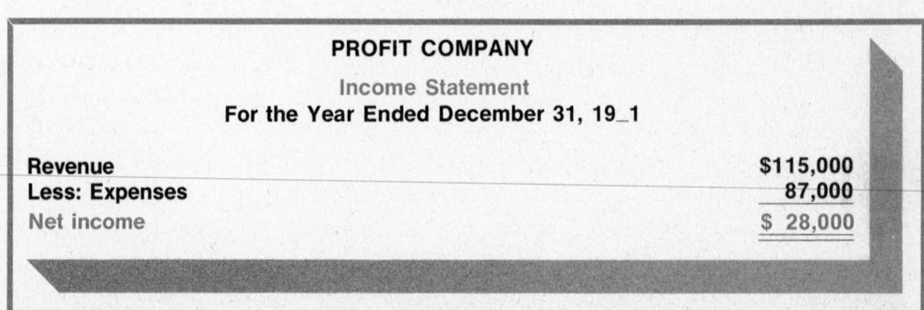

PROFIT COMPANY
Income Statement
For the Year Ended December 31, 19_1

Revenue	**$115,000**
Less: Expenses	**87,000**
Net income	$ 28,000

1. ***APB Statement No. 4,*** para. 148. Transactions between the enterprise and its owners are excluded from the kinds of activities that can lead to realization of revenue.

the disposal of assets of the firm other than those held as stock in trade (for example, land, buildings, or investments).

In order to understand this definition, let us look first at the phrase "the gross inflow of assets or the gross decrease in liabilities." Suppose that a furniture company sells a bedroom suite for $790 in cash. This event is a part of the normal profit-directed activity of the firm. The company realizes revenue. An ***inflow of assets*** in the form of cash results from the sale. Think this through in terms of the accounting equation,

$A - L = OE.$

Suppose that before the sale the company has assets of $100,000 and liabilities of $60,000:

$100,000 − $60,000 = $40,000.

After the sale, the asset of cash has increased. The realization of revenue has increased the owners' equity:

$100,790 − $60,000 = $40,790.

Now suppose that another customer of the firm orders some special furniture built to his specifications. He pays the full $1,000 price in advance at the time he places the order. Again, assume that the assets and liabilities before this transaction are $100,000 and $60,000, respectively:

$100,000 − $60,000 = $40,000.

The company receives $1,000 cash and incurs a liability to deliver $1,000 worth of furniture in the future:

$101,000 − $61,000 = $40,000.

No revenue is realized at this point. The increase of liabilities offsets the inflow of assets; there is no change in net assets and no change in owners' equity. When the company actually delivers the finished furniture, the $1,000 liability is settled:

$101,000 − $60,000 = $41,000.

The delivery of the furniture decreases liabilities, thereby increasing net assets and owners' equity. Revenue is realized at the time the furniture is delivered.

In both cases—the cash sale and the delivery of prepaid goods—the revenue is realized at the point when net assets (and therefore owners' equity) increase. In both cases, revenue is realized from the first of the three sources listed at the beginning of this section: the sale of goods. The second source of revenue involves the rendering of services, or letting someone else use the firm's resources in return for some payment. For example, a doctor performs a service for a patient and then bills the patient for $500. The doctor has rendered a service, and her accountant recognizes revenue in the amount of $500. In this case, the doctor has an inflow of assets in the form of a claim against her patient—that is, an increase in her accounts receivable.

As an example of the "loan" of resources that results in revenue, suppose that the ABC Company owns a building that it rents as a part of its normal profit-directed activity. The tenant pays his rent annually. At the beginning of the year, he pays $10,000 for a year's use of the building. The ABC Company now has an obligation to let the tenant use the building for a year. That is, the ABC Company has a $10,000 liability offsetting the inflow of cash. At the end of the year, the obligation has been fulfilled—the tenant has gotten his year of use of the building. Now the ABC Company can remove the liability from its books. The company has realized revenue in the amount of $10,000 through the decrease in its liabilities.

The third source of revenue involves the sale of assets of the enterprise that are not held for sale as part of the normal business activities. For example, the ABC Company some years ago purchased for $1,000 some stock of the XYZ Company as an investment. It now sells that stock for $1,200. Revenue is recognized in the amount of $1,200. The $1,200 inflow of cash increases net assets and owners' equity by $1,200. (The $1,000 cost of the asset is treated as an expense associated with the transaction. Similarly, the cost of the furniture sold in the earlier examples is treated as an expense. The way of accounting for expenses is discussed later in the chapter.) The net gain of $200 is reported in the income statement.

Not all inflows of assets into the enterprise create revenue. Similarly, revenue does not result from all decreases in liabilities. Although assets increase, revenue does not result from borrowing money, from sale of the company's own stock, or from several other kinds of transactions. The reasons for this are discussed later. For now, we need simply to get a general idea of the nature of revenue.

As we have said before, revenue increases net assets and owners' equity. For most enterprises, such increases are the main reason for the existence of the business. The accountant tries to be sure that the revenue reported on the income statement accurately reflects the increase in net assets caused by the firm's profit-making activities. He must also be sure that the revenue is recognized at the proper time to give an accurate picture of the changes in the financial position of the firm. We turn next to the question of when revenue should be recognized.

THE REALIZATION PRINCIPLE

As we have seen, it is not always easy to decide exactly ***when*** revenue should be recognized in the accounting records and on the income statement. To decide when revenue is realized, the accountant makes use of a major generally accepted accounting principle called the ***realization principle.*** In its most concise form, this principle can be stated as follows:

Revenue is generally recognized when both of the following conditions are met: (1) the earning process is complete or virtually complete, and (2) an exchange has taken place.[2]

In general, revenue is recognized at the point of a sale or at the performance of a service. That is, the revenue is realized when the activity that produces the revenue has been performed. At the time of sale or the performance of a service, the earning

2. ***APB Statement No. 4,*** para. 150. Copyright 1970 by the AICPA. There are other bases for recognizing revenue. Construction companies often use the percentage-of-completion method, in which revenue is recognized as construction progresses. Companies that sell expensive items on installment plans may choose to use the installment method, in which revenue is recognized as payments are received. In some other cases, revenue is recognized when production is completed and before a sale is made. These alternative methods are discussed in advanced accounting courses.

process is complete. An exchange has occurred. The enterprise has given up a product or performed a service. In exchange it has received an inflow of assets (or a decrease in liabilities) in the form of cash, accounts receivable, or some other asset. With this exchange completed, revenue can be recorded at the value of the assets obtained (or the decrease in liabilities). It is possible to objectively determine or estimate the exchange price of the product sold or the service performed, so that a value can be assigned to the transaction. Furthermore, at this point in time the accountant usually is able to determine or estimate the expenses associated with production of the revenue, so that revenue and expenses can be properly matched on the income statement.

From a legal viewpoint, ***a sale occurs when title to*** (ownership of) ***the goods passes from seller to buyer.*** For reasons of ease in keeping records, the accounting system usually assumes that title passes when the products that have been sold are shipped to the customer—that is, when the goods leave the premises of the seller.

CASH AND ACCRUAL METHODS OF ACCOUNTING

We have seen that the realization principle calls for the recognition of revenue on the income statement during the period when the sale is made or when the service is performed. This method of recognition is called the ***accrual method of accounting.*** This method is generally preferred to other methods of recognizing revenue, but other methods do exist. The most common other method is called the ***cash method of accounting.*** Using the cash method, the accounting system recognizes revenue whenever cash or some other asset is received for the sale or service, regardless of when the sale is made or the service performed.

Suppose that the XYZ Company sells some goods in December 19_1. The agreement for the sale is completed in that month, and the goods are shipped from the XYZ Company warehouse. However, the customer does not send a check in payment for the goods until January 19_2. If the accountant for the XYZ Company is using the accrual method, he will recognize the revenue in 19_1 when the sale is made. If he is using the cash method, he will recognize the revenue in 19_2 when the check (considered a form of cash) is received.

Accountants prefer the accrual method because it usually results in a more realistic matching of expenses and revenue. The costs of the goods or services are incurred near the time of the sale or performance in most cases, regardless of when the firm gets its payment. For most large businesses, accounting systems use the cash method only when the accrual method would be misleading—for example, if there is considerable uncertainty about the probability of collecting a receivable resulting from a sale or a service performed. However, individuals and small service or professional enterprises (such as doctors and lawyers) sometimes use the cash method.

To summarize, the accrual method of accounting recognizes revenue as being earned at the point of sale or with the performance of a service, regardless of when cash is received in payment for the goods or service. The cash method of accounting recognizes revenue as being earned at the time when cash is received, regardless of the point of sale or when the service was performed. In general, accountants prefer use of the accrual method.

NATURE AND SOURCES OF EXPENSES

Expense is the cost of producing revenue. Expenses arise when assets are used up or liabilities are increased in order to produce revenue. To put it more formally, expenses represent a gross decrease in assets or gross increase in liabilities that results from profit-directed activities that change owners' equity.

When a furniture company pays the salaries of its salesmen, the company incurs an expense. The company used the services of the employees in selling its furniture —that is, in activities directed toward production of revenue. If the salaries are paid in cash, there is a ***decrease in the assets*** of the company. Even if the salesmen are not paid immediately, an expense still is incurred. Suppose that the salesmen are not due to get their paychecks until sometime in the next accounting period. Nonetheless, the company has an obligation to pay them for the services they have rendered, so there is an ***increase in the liabilities*** of the company. In either case, the net assets of the company decrease and so does the owners' equity.

To understand the nature of expenses, we must examine the broader concept of cost. ***Cost*** is the price paid or the consideration given to acquire an asset. In an economic sense, cost is the sacrifice that results from economic activities.

Accounting principles make a distinction between unexpired costs and expired costs. ***Unexpired costs*** are those costs that will help produce revenue in a future period—for example, prepaid rent, buildings, land or investments. Unexpired costs are reported on the statement of financial position as assets.

Expired costs are those costs that will not help produce revenue in future periods. Expired costs are reported on the income statement as expenses. In other words, an expense is a cost that has used up its status as an asset (its ability to benefit the company in future periods). Expenses can be divided into two groups. First, some expenses are expired costs that have assisted in the production of revenue reported on the same income statement. This group includes such costs as salesmen's salaries, rent expenses, costs of goods sold, and portions of the costs of buildings or equipment that are gradually being "worn out." The second group of expenses includes expired costs that have not assisted in the production of revenue. This group includes such costs as the cost of buildings that burn down or are destroyed by flood, or the cost incurred when marketable securities are sold for less than their acquisition price. Expenses in this second group are sometimes called ***losses.***

In our discussion of the cost concept, we have seen that expenses are defined as expired costs. Assets (unexpired costs) become expenses (expired costs) as they lose their ability to benefit the company in future periods (Exhibit 4-2). We have also seen that expenses reduce net assets and owners' equity.

Exhibit 4-2
Expiration of costs and the financial statements

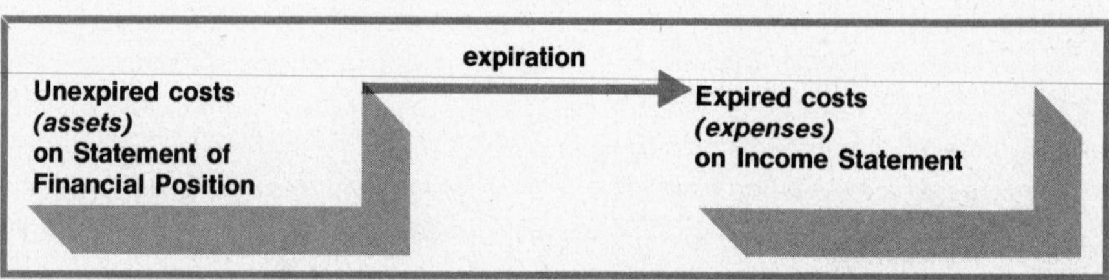

Next we must ask ***when*** costs expire. That is, when does a cost lose its status as an asset (reported on the statement of financial position) and become an expense (matched against revenue on the income statement)?

The accounting profession has accepted three major ***expense recognition principles*** as standards for reporting expense in income determinations. These principles identify the basis for recognizing expenses that should be deducted from revenue to determine the net income (or loss) during an accounting period.

The first expense recognition principle is the principle of ***associating cause and effect.***[3] It states that certain costs expire in a particular accounting period because they can be associated ***directly*** with specific revenue recognized during that period. Among the costs covered by this principle are such items as sales commissions, costs incurred in performing specific services, and costs specifically related to producing certain goods that are sold.

The second principle is the principle of ***systematic and rational allocation.***[4] It deals with the expiration of costs that do benefit revenue but cannot be associated directly with specific revenue. The principle says that such costs should be allocated in a systematic and rational manner among the accounting periods in which they benefit revenue. Among the costs covered by this principle are depreciation expenses for property, plant, and equipment.

The third principle, the ***immediate recognition principle,***[5] applies to costs that provide no discernible future benefits. These costs are to be recognized as expenses during the period in which they are incurred. Examples of such costs include most selling and administrative expenses, as well as most losses.

CASH AND ACCRUAL METHODS APPLIED TO EXPENSES

We have seen that the accounting system can recognize revenue according to either the accrual method or the cash method of accounting. The two methods also can be applied to expenses. Under the accrual method, expenses are recorded and reported in the period during which the costs expire (under the three principles discussed in the preceding section). In general, the expense is recognized at the time when the company acquires an obligation. For example, suppose that salesmen are to be paid in January 19_2 for the work that they did during December 19_1. Using the accrual method, the accounting system would report the salesmen's salaries as an expense on the 19_1 income statement, matched against the revenue of that period. The obligation to pay the salesmen would appear as a liability (wages payable) on the position statement for the end of 19_1.

Under the cash method, expenses are recognized at the point when cash or other assets are paid out. Under the cash method, the accounting system would report the salesmen's salaries on the 19_2 income statement, matched against the revenue (cash received) of that period.

As we have said, the accounting profession prefers the accrual method of accounting. Use of the cash method can result in a mismatching of revenue and expenses.

3. ***APB Statement No. 4,*** paras. 157–158.

4. ***APB Statement No. 4,*** para. 159.

5. ***APB Statement No. 4,*** para. 160.

For example, suppose that the company offered high bonuses to the salesmen for extra efforts in December 19_1. In order to earn those bonuses, the salesmen made unusually large amounts of cash sales during that month. Under the cash method of accounting, the revenue from the sales appears on the 19_1 income statement, but the expense of the bonuses (paid in January) appears on the 19_2 statement. Thus the net income for 19_1 may appear quite high, while that for 19_2 appears low. The net income for both years has been distorted by a mismatching of expenses and revenues.

In general, the accounting profession accepts the accrual method as the most preferable way of matching revenue and expenses.[6]

MEASUREMENT OF REVENUE AND EXPENSES

In its measurement process, the accounting system must assign dollar values to revenue and expenses. In general, the ***exchange price*** agreed upon by the parties to the transaction represents the inflow or outflow of assets and is generally accepted as the proper measure of the revenue or expense involved in a transaction.

For example, suppose that the firm sells some goods for $140 and pays the salesman a commission of $10 on the sale. This transaction results in revenue of $140 for the firm (the exchange price of the goods) and an expense of $10 for the firm (the exchange price of the commission). (Note that this expense can be associated directly with particular revenue, so the principle of associating cause and effect requires that the expense and the revenue be matched in the same accounting period.)

The initial recording principle (Chapter 3) applies to revenue and expense transactions as well as to assets and liabilities. As you recall, this principle states that the ***acquisition*** (or historical) ***cost*** is the proper accounting basis for initially recording transactions in the accounting system.

NET INCOME (OR NET LOSS)

If the revenue of a business entity exceeds the expenses incurred in producing that revenue, net income results; net assets and owners' equity increase. If expenses exceed revenue, a net loss results; net assets and owners' equity decrease.

For another way of looking at it, think of revenue as the gross inflow of assets from profit-directed activities, and expenses as the gross outflow of assets from those activities. Then net income may be regarded as the ***net*** inflow (excess of inflow over outflow) of assets as a result of profit-making activities.

A net inflow of assets causes an increase in net assets, and therefore an increase in owners' equity. Thus we see that there is a relationship between the income statement and the balance sheet (Exhibit 4-3).

6. The cash method of accounting is discussed in the AICPA's ***Statement on Auditing Procedure No. 28.*** This ***Statement*** indicates that it is inappropriate to use the names "balance sheet" or "income statement" for statements prepared using the cash method, because such statements do not present financial position and results of operations according to generally accepted accounting principles. The AICPA suggests that a statement showing revenue and expenses determined on a cash basis might appropriately be titled "cash flow from operations."

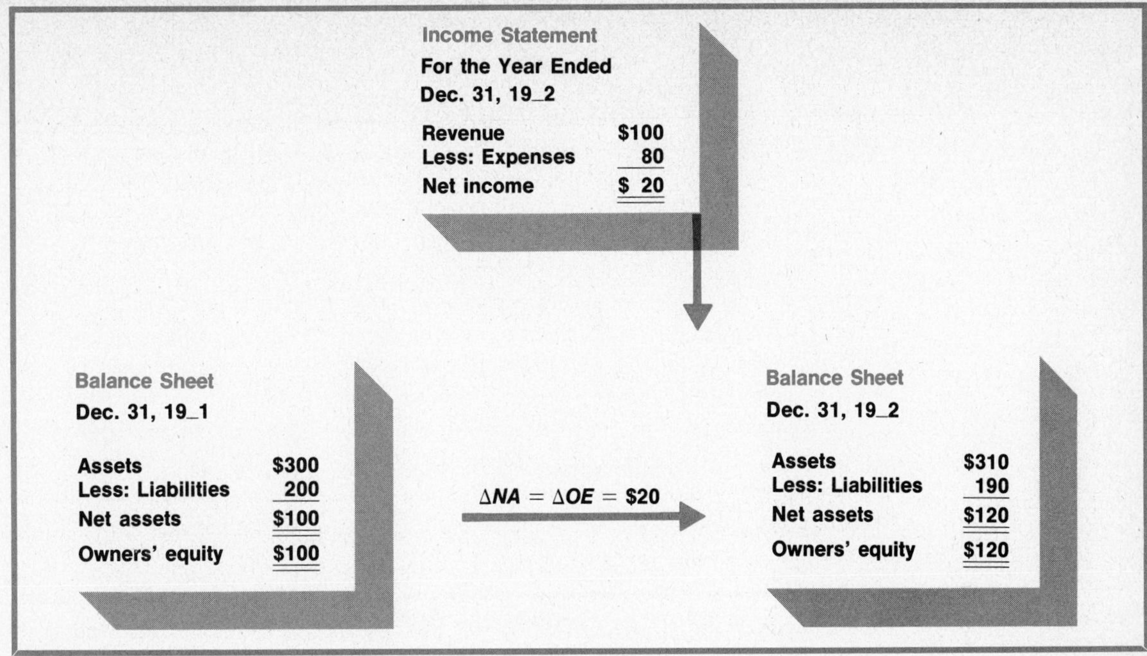

Exhibit 4-3 **A net inflow of assets and the financial statements**

FORMS OF THE INCOME STATEMENT

The income statement contains information about the earnings of an enterprise. The *heading* of the income statement identifies the entity being reported on, the title of the statement, and the *period of time* (such as "the year ended December 31, 1978") to which the statement relates. The income statement shows the revenue and expenses accumulated during the period, rather than the revenue and expenses of a particular day.

Like the balance sheet, the income statement may be presented in several formats. Two popular forms of this statement are the single-step income statement and the multiple-step income statement.

The *single-step income statement* (Exhibit 4-4) lists and totals all revenue items at the beginning of the statement. All expense items are then listed, and the total of the expenses is deducted from the total revenue to give the net income. A more fully classified example of the single-step income statement is shown in Exhibit 4-12. The appendix to this chapter explains the major terms that appear on the income statement.

The Accounting Principles Board has issued an opinion stating that the income statement of a corporation must report earnings per share on outstanding common stock.[7] In Exhibit 4-4, the Aquarius Company states that it had 50,000 shares of its common stock outstanding during the year. With net income of $125,000 for the year, the Aquarius Company earned $2.50 for each of these shares. In more complex

7. Accounting Principles Board, ***Opinion No. 15: Earnings per Share*** (New York: American Institute of Certified Public Accountants, 1969), para. 12.

cases, generally accepted accounting principles specify extremely complicated rules for calculating the earnings per share.

The *multiple-step income statement* (Exhibit 4-5) presents operating revenue at the beginning of the statement, and nonoperating revenue and expenses near the end of the statement. However, various items of revenue and expenses are added and deducted throughout the statement at intermediate levels. The statement is arranged in an order that shows explicitly several important amounts such as gross margin on sales, operating income, income before taxes, as well as net income.

The advantage of the multiple-step income statement is that it does explicitly display important financial and managerial information that the user must calculate from a single-step form. However, the disadvantage of the multiple-step form is that it seems to rank expenses in the order of their importance as deductions from revenue. For example, suppose that the firm has a net loss for the period. An unsophisticated user glancing down the statement might assume that the company had net

Exhibit 4-4
An income statement in the single-step form

AQUARIUS COMPANY
Income Statement
For the Year Ended December 31, 19_1

Sales		$600,000
Other revenue		50,000
Total revenue		$650,000
Cost of goods sold	$150,000	
Selling expenses	250,000	
General and administrative expenses	100,000	
Other expenses	25,000	525,000
Net income		$125,000
Earnings per common share (50,000 shares outstanding)		$2.50

Exhibit 4-5
An income statement in the multiple-step form

AQUARIUS COMPANY
Income Statement
For the Year Ended December 31, 19_1

Sales		$600,000
Cost of goods sold		150,000
Gross margin		$450,000
Operating expenses:		
Selling expenses	$250,000	
General and administrative expenses	100,000	350,000
Net income from operations		$100,000
Other income	$ 50,000	
Other expenses	25,000	25,000
Net income		$125,000
Earnings per common share (50,000 shares outstanding)		$2.50

income until the last few expense items were deducted. Therefore he would feel that the company could achieve net income in future periods simply by eliminating those few expenses. Such an interpretation, of course, is very misleading. All expenses and losses contribute to the net loss. Such an unsophisticated user also is unlikely to understand the significance of the intermediate amounts such as gross margin and operating income.

The single-step form has the advantage of being relatively simple to prepare and to understand, as well as avoiding the dangers of misinterpretation just discussed. The popularity of the single-step income statement is increasing.

On the income statement, ***sales*** consists of the total dollar amount of merchandise sold during the year. This represents the revenue for the period. ***Cost of goods sold*** refers to the cost to the Aquarius Company of the merchandise that was sold in the period. ***Gross margin*** is the difference between sales and cost of goods sold. It is the "profit" before operating expenses are deducted. ***Operating expenses*** represent the cost of doing business as reflected by selling, general and administrative expenses. ***Selling expenses*** represent expenses associated with the sales function, that is, with selling goods and services. Expenses incurred in performing the selling function include expenses related to preparing goods for sale, advertising expenses, salespersons' salaries, delivery expenses, and others. ***General and administrative expenses*** include expenses related to the administrative offices (e.g., the president's salary), accounting and legal activities, personnel, credits and collections. Expenses associated with both the selling and administrative functions, such as rent, utilities, insurance, supplies, usually can be divided (prorated; allocated) to selling expenses and to general and administrative expenses. Terms used on income statements are explained in greater detail in the appendix to this chapter. This material should be considered an integral part of your study of the income statement.

Characteristics of the income statement

The income statement represents a flow of economic data—that is, the accumulations of revenue and expenses through a period of time. This statement reflects the ***changes*** in various critical areas of the firm's operations. The statement matches revenue and expenses to give an estimate of net income or net loss. This statement also helps to account for the major changes between the statement of financial position at the end of one period and that at the end of the next period.

In terms of an information system, the income statement ***accumulates*** economic data according to the basic model.

Revenue − Expenses = Net income,
or $R - E = NI.$

The income statement also ***measures*** net income by matching revenues and expenses according to accounting principles discussed in this chapter. Further, the income statement ***communicates*** information about the efforts and accomplishments involved in the profit-making activities of the firm, as reflected in the inflow and outflow of the firm's net assets.

Analysis and interpretation

A careful study of the income statement gives the user information about the quality of a firm's management, the credit and investment worthiness of the enterprise, and similar matters. In his study, the user can employ special tools designed to help in analysis and interpretation of the income statement. As we have seen in Chapter 2, comparative statements and ratio analysis are important tools for the study of accounting statements.

COMPARATIVE INCOME STATEMENTS

A comparative income statement shows income statements for two or more periods (usually two or more years), arranged in side-by-side columns for easy comparison. These comparative statements are important financial and managerial tools of analysis and interpretation. They help to identify ***trends*** and ***relationships*** in the operations of the business. Comparative statements provide information about completed earning cycles of a business—past and current. This information makes the income statement more useful for predicting, comparing, and evaluating the earning power of an enterprise.[8] Exhibit 4-6 shows a comparative income statement in condensed and conceptualized form.

RATIO ANALYSIS

As in the case of the balance sheet, ratio analysis of the income statement provides important insights into the financial situation of a company. After ratios are computed, the values can be compared with similar computations for prior years, to see whether the company is improving. Ratios of a particular company can be compared with ratios of other companies in the same industry, or with industry averages, to evaluate the relative position of the firm. Because not all companies use comparable accounting procedures, the comparison of ratios for different companies is not always meaningful.

Here we discuss five of the more important income-statement ratios. As examples, we use information from the income statement in Exhibit 4-5.

Exhibit 4-6
A simplified comparative income statement

AQUARIUS COMPANY
Income Statement
For the Years Ended December 31, 19_1 and 19_0

	19_1	19_0
Revenue [*normally classified*]	**$650,000**	**$600,000**
Less: Expenses [*normally classified*]	**525,000**	**500,000**
Net Income	**$125,000**	**$100,000**

8. See *Objectives of Financial Statements* (New York: American Institute of Certified Public Accountants, 1973), pp. 61–66.

RATIO OF NET INCOME TO NET SALES. The ratio of net income to net sales gives a measure of the profit margin per dollar of sales. In other words, this ratio measures the amount of earnings for each dollar taken in through sales. The higher the value of the ratio, the more favorable the interpretation of the profit-making operations of the company. Exhibit 4-5 indicates that the Aquarius Company had net income of $125,000 on net sales of $600,000.

$$\frac{\text{Net income}}{\text{Net sales}} = \frac{\$125{,}000}{\$600{,}000} = 0.21 \text{ to } 1.$$

RATIO OF NET INCOME TO OWNERS' EQUITY. The ratio of net income to average owners' equity gives a measure of the rate of earnings on the resources provided by the investments of the owners of the firm. Because owners' equity can change during the year, this ratio is computed using the average of the values of owners' equity at the beginning and at the end of the period. This ratio measures the amount of earnings for each dollar that the owners have invested in the firm. The higher the ratio, the more favorable the interpretation of the firm's use of its resources contributed by the owners. From Exhibit 3-8, we see that the Aquarius Company had owners' equity of $300,000 at the end of 19_0 and $400,000 at the end of 19_1. Therefore we take the average of these two values as the denominator value for the ratio.

$$\frac{\text{Net income}}{\text{Average owners' equity}} = \frac{\$125{,}000}{(\$300{,}000 + \$400{,}000)/2} = \frac{\$125{,}000}{\$350{,}000} = 0.36 \text{ to } 1.$$

NET INCOME PER SHARE OF COMMON STOCK. In the simple case of a firm whose ownership is represented only by a certain number of shares of common stock, the net income per share of common stock can be calculated as a simple ratio:

$$\frac{\text{Net income}}{\text{Average number of shares of common stock outstanding}}$$

Where the owners' equity is divided among several kinds of stock, more complex calculations are needed. In any case, generally accepted accounting principles require that the value of this factor be listed explicitly on the income statement. In effect, this value measures the share of the firm's earnings that is represented by a single share of common stock. The higher the value, the more favorable the interpretation of the firm's potential as a profitable investment. From Exhibit 4-5, we see that the net income per share of common stock of the Aquarius Company has been computed as the simple ratio,

$$\frac{\$125{,}000}{50{,}000 \text{ shares}} = \$2.50 \text{ per share.}$$

PRICE-EARNINGS RATIO. The price-earnings ratio for a firm is another important measure used by potential investors. This ratio is determined by the following formula:

$$\frac{\text{Market price per share of common stock}}{\text{Net income per share of common stock}}$$

It expresses the market price of the stock as a multiple of its annual earnings. In effect, this ratio gives the number of dollars paid for one dollar of a company's annual net income. Let us assume that the common stock of the Aquarius Company is currently selling for $25. Using the value of $2.50 for net income per share of common stock (Exhibit 4-5), we find the value of the ratio to be

$$\frac{\$25}{\$2.50} = 10 \text{ to } 1.$$

RETURN ON INVESTMENT. The ratio of net income to total assets is called the return on investment. It is a measure of the annual earnings per dollar of total assets of the firm. Therefore it measures how well the firm is using all of its assets—both those provided by its owners and those provided by its creditors. The higher the ratio, the more favorable the interpretation of the firm's use of its total economic resources. From Exhibit 3-5, we see that the Aquarius Company had total assets of $700,000 at the end of 19_1. Therefore, the return on investment for the company is

$$\frac{\text{Net income}}{\text{Total assets}} = \frac{\$125{,}000}{\$700{,}000} = 0.178 \text{ to } 1.$$

The value of this ratio usually is expressed as a percentage:

$$0.178 \times 100\% = 17.8\%.$$

Impact analysis

The statement of financial position (balance sheet) and the income statement are *related* financial statements. ***The income statement is a link between the balance sheet at the beginning of the period and the balance sheet at the end of the period.*** Throughout the analysis in this section, keep in mind that revenue is an inflow of assets, and that expenses are an outflow of assets. From that viewpoint, it is easy to see that the revenue and expense events summarized on the income statement must have an impact on the balance sheet, which lists the assets at the end of the period.

Although net income normally is computed according to the principles set forth in this chapter, you can also compute net income indirectly from the statements of financial position for the beginning and end of the period (see Exhibit 4-3). This fact is important because it emphasizes the role of the income statement as a ***link*** between consecutive statements of financial position. The income and position statements are not separate and independent reports about a firm; they are related reports.

In Exhibit 4-3, the net income for the period is equal to the change in net assets (and owners' equity) during the period. However, this is a simplified situation. In fact, there is another change that can affect owners' equity, as discussed in Chapter 2. Any additional investments or withdrawals by owners during the period will cause changes in the owners' equity. In Chapter 2 this relationship is summarized by the following formula:

$$\begin{matrix}\text{Owners' equity} \\ \text{at beginning} \\ \text{of period}\end{matrix} + \begin{matrix}\text{Net} \\ \text{income}\end{matrix} \quad \left[\begin{matrix}\text{Investments} \\ \text{by owners} \\ \text{during period}\end{matrix} - \begin{matrix}\text{Withdrawals} \\ \text{by owners} \\ \text{during period}\end{matrix}\right] = \begin{matrix}\text{Owners' equity} \\ \text{at end} \\ \text{of period}\end{matrix}$$

Let us rearrange this formula so that we can use it to compute net income.

$$\begin{matrix}\text{Net} \\ \text{income}\end{matrix} = \begin{matrix}\text{Owners' equity} \\ \text{at end} \\ \text{of period}\end{matrix} - \left[\begin{matrix}\text{Investments} \\ \text{by owners} \\ \text{during period}\end{matrix} - \begin{matrix}\text{Withdrawals} \\ \text{by owners} \\ \text{during period}\end{matrix}\right] - \begin{matrix}\text{Owners' equity} \\ \text{at beginning} \\ \text{of period}\end{matrix}$$

Using symbols, we can write the equation in this form:

$$NI = OE_e - (OI - OW) - OE_b$$

Of course, if net income is computed to be a negative amount, it is called a net loss.

Now let us apply this formula to some examples. Exhibit 4-7 shows a condensed comparative statement of financial position for the Change Company. To examine the effects of owners' investments and withdrawals we apply the equation to five different cases.

Case 1. There are no additional investments or withdrawals by the owners during 19_1.

Case 2. The owners invested an additional $6 and withdrew nothing during 19_1.

Case 3. The owners invested an additional $6 and withdrew $2 during 19_1.

Case 4. The owners invested an additional $14 and withdrew nothing during 19_1.

Case 5. The owners withdrew $5 during 19_1.

Putting these values for *OI* and *OW* into the formula, we get the following results for *NI* (net income).

Case 1. $NI = \$50 - (\$0 - \$0) - \$40 = \$10.$

Case 2. $NI = \$50 - (\$6 - \$0) - \$40 = \$4.$

Case 3. $NI = \$50 - (\$6 - \$2) - \$40 = \$6.$

Case 4. $NI = \$50 - (\$14 - \$0) - \$40 = -\$4$ [a net loss of $4].

Case 5. $NI = \$50 - (-\$5) - \$40 = \$15.$

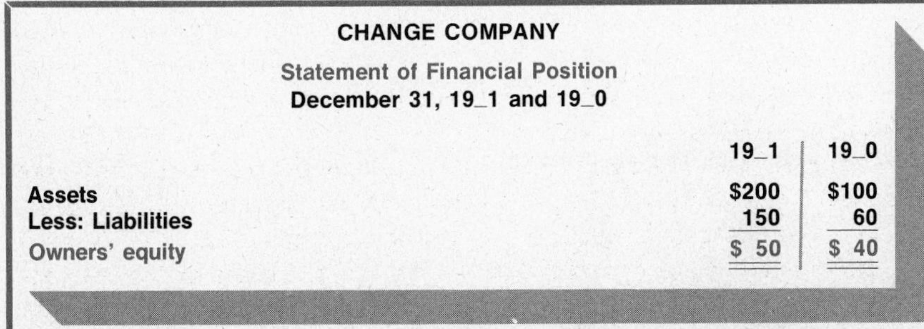

CHANGE COMPANY

Statement of Financial Position
December 31, 19_1 and 19_0

	19_1	19_0
Assets	$200	$100
Less: Liabilities	150	60
Owners' equity	$ 50	$ 40

Exhibit 4-7
A condensed comparative balance sheet

At first it may seem confusing that an increase in owners' investments during the period seems to cause a smaller net income, or even a net loss. However, remember that in this example we have kept the ***change*** in owners' equity during the period constant. In effect, what is happening is that a larger investment by the owners simply means that more of the change in owners' equity is due to the additional investment, while less of the change is due to net income.

This relationship may be more obvious if we rewrite the equation in this form:

$$OE_e - OE_b = NI + (OI - OW).$$

In words, the change in owners' equity during the period is equal to the sum of the net income and the net additional investment by the owners. Therefore, the larger the net additional investment, the less of the change in owners' equity that will be due to net income. Or—to put it the other way around—the income statement helps the user to see whether an increase in owners' equity is actually due to earnings by the firm (net income) or is simply due to the fact that the owners have put more capital into the enterprise.

From this impact analysis, we see that revenue and expense transactions resulting in net income (or net loss) have an identifiable impact on the statements of financial position. In fact, revenue and expense events are major causes of changes in owners' equity. Recall that owners' equity is equal to net assets (assets minus liabilities) and that changes in owners' equity equal changes in net assets. It follows that, when revenue and expense transactions change owners' equity, they also change net assets in the same direction and amount. The relationships among the three major financial statements are illustrated in Exhibit 4-10.

Statement of retained earnings

Another significant financial statement is a statement that accounts for certain changes in owners' equity from period to period. For a corporation, the statement of retained earnings explains the changes in retained (or undistributed) earnings from one period to the next. ***Retained earnings*** are the earnings of the enterprise that are kept in the business, rather than being distributed to the owners. Exhibit 4-8 shows a typical retained earnings statement.

Exhibit 4-8
A typical statement of retained earnings

AQUARIUS COMPANY
Statement of Retained Earnings
For the Year Ended December 31, 19_1

Retained earnings, January 1, 19_1	**$100,000**
Add: Net income per income statement	**125,000**
Total	**$225,000**
Less: Dividends	**25,000**
Retained earnings, December 31, 19_1	**$200,000**

The dividends declared by a corporation are not expenses of the enterprise, because they are not paid for the purpose of producing revenue. Rather, dividends represent a *distribution* of part of the accumulated earnings of the firm to its stockholders. For this reason, dividends do not appear as expenses on the income statement.

Some firms prepare a combined income and retained earnings statement. Such a statement is shown in condensed form in Exhibit 4-9. A combined statement of income and retained earnings shows in one statement all relevant information about changes in owners' equity during the year arising from profit-directed activities. A problem with this format is that net income—a key figure—appears within the statement rather than as a bottom-line figure, and thus is not given the emphasis that it should receive.

Relationships among major financial statements

Exhibit 4-10 illustrates the relationships among the three major financial statements. Note that net income for the period is computed on the income statement. Net income is then transferred to the retained earnings statement. Retained earnings for the beginning of the period (the end of the preceding period) also are transferred to the retained earnings statement from the preceding balance sheet. Retained earnings for the end of the period are then computed on the retained earnings statement and transferred to the balance sheet for the end of the period.

In Exhibit 4-10, a statement of owners' equity (see Chapter 2) could be substituted for the statement of retained earnings. The analysis then would show how owners' equity of \$300,000 on December 31, 19_0, increased to \$400,000 on December 31, 19_1. The equation discussed in the preceding section helps to show what happened:

$$OE_e - OE_b = NI + (OI - OW);$$
$$\$400{,}000 - \$300{,}000 = \$125{,}000 + (OI - \$25{,}000);$$
$$\$100{,}000 = \$125{,}000 - \$25{,}000.$$

The \$100,000 change in owners' equity was due to the \$125,000 net income, less the \$25,000 withdrawn by the owners in the form of dividends.

AQUARIUS COMPANY
Statement of Income and Retained Earnings
For the Year Ended December 31, 19_1

Revenue	**$650,000**
Less: Expenses	**525,000**
Net income	**$125,000**
Retained earnings, January 1, 19_1	**100,000**
Total	**$225,000**
Less: Dividends	**25,000**
Retained earnings, December 31, 19_1	**$200,000**

Exhibit 4-9
A condensed statement of income and retained earnings

Summary

Net income is the excess of revenue over expenses ($R - E = NI$). The determination of net income is essential to business planning and control, and to the evaluation of a firm's efficiency and effectiveness.

To understand the concept of net income, you must know something about the concepts of revenue and expenses.

Exhibit 4–10 **Relationships among major financial statements**

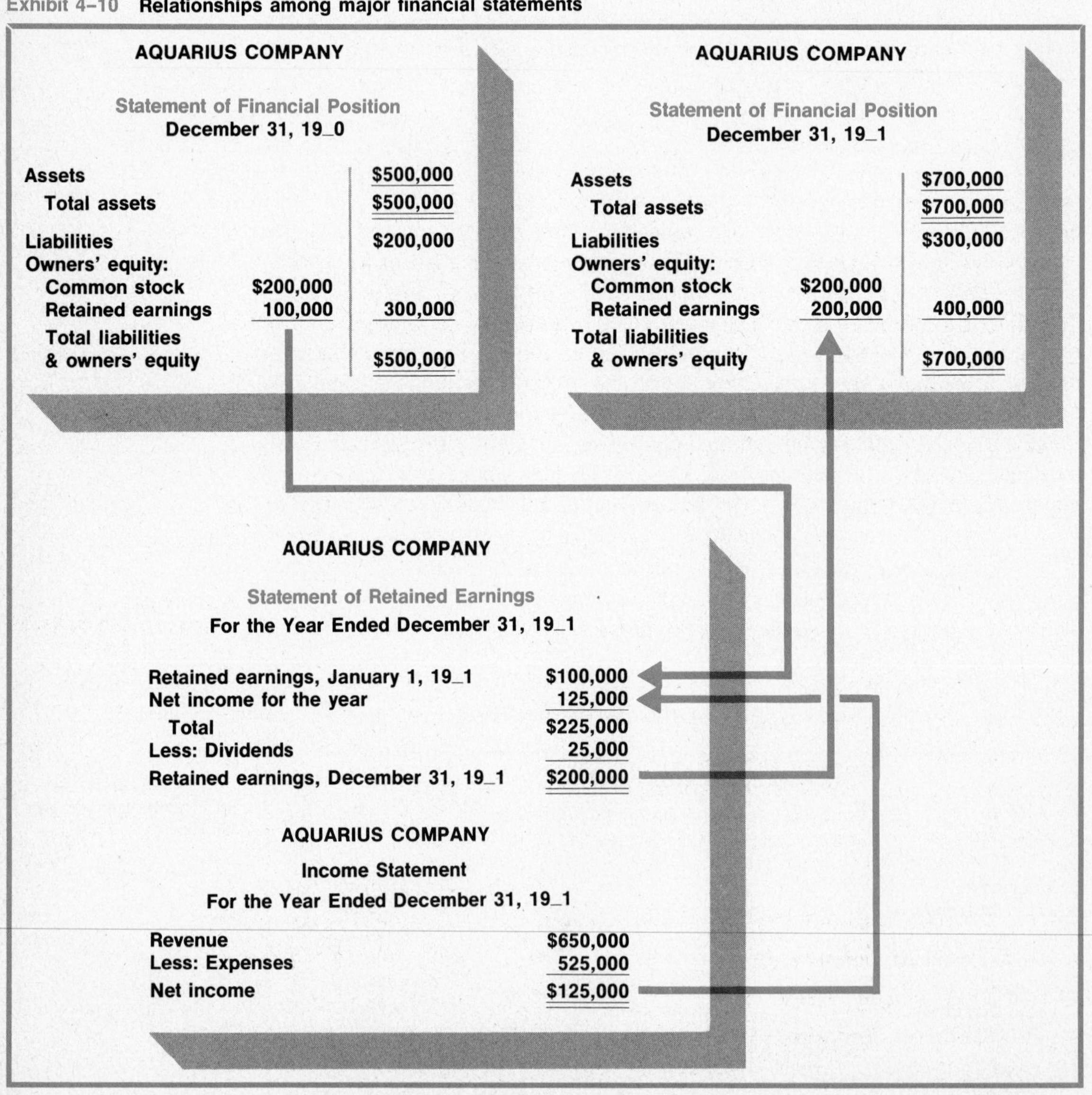

AQUARIUS COMPANY
Statement of Financial Position
December 31, 19_0

Assets		$500,000
Total assets		$500,000
Liabilities		$200,000
Owners' equity:		
Common stock	$200,000	
Retained earnings	100,000	300,000
Total liabilities & owners' equity		$500,000

AQUARIUS COMPANY
Statement of Financial Position
December 31, 19_1

Assets		$700,000
Total assets		$700,000
Liabilities		$300,000
Owners' equity:		
Common stock	$200,000	
Retained earnings	200,000	400,000
Total liabilities & owners' equity		$700,000

AQUARIUS COMPANY
Statement of Retained Earnings
For the Year Ended December 31, 19_1

Retained earnings, January 1, 19_1	$100,000
Net income for the year	125,000
Total	$225,000
Less: Dividends	25,000
Retained earnings, December 31, 19_1	$200,000

AQUARIUS COMPANY
Income Statement
For the Year Ended December 31, 19_1

Revenue	$650,000
Less: Expenses	525,000
Net income	$125,000

Revenue is the gross inflow of assets (or the gross decrease in liabilities) that results from certain profit-directed activities of the enterprise. The three major sources of revenue are (1) the sale of goods, (2) the rendering of services or the "loan" of the firm's economic resources to others, and (3) the disposal of assets other than those held as stock in trade. In general, revenue is recognized at the time when a sale is made (goods are shipped to the customer) or a service is rendered. In general, revenue is measured by the exchange price of the transaction.

An expense is a gross outflow of assets (or a gross increase in liabilities) that is incurred in order to produce revenue. An expense may also be defined as an expired cost. An unexpired cost is one that will benefit the revenue of the firm in future periods; an unexpired cost is treated by the accounting system as an asset. When a cost expires (loses its ability to benefit future periods), it becomes an expense. The time at which expenses are recognized (at which a cost expires) is determined according to three expense recognition principles: the principle of associating cause and effect, the principle of systematic and rational allocation, and the immediate recognition principle. In general, an expense is measured by the exchange price of the transaction.

Accounting for revenue and expenses according to the principles just described is called the accrual method of accounting. In the cash method of accounting, revenue and expenses are recognized at the time when cash is received or paid out by the firm. The cash method is not generally accepted for the accounting systems of most businesses.

There are two major formats for the income statement: the single-step income statement and the multiple-step income statement.

The income statement and the statement of financial position are related statements. The income statement is a link between successive balance sheets. The

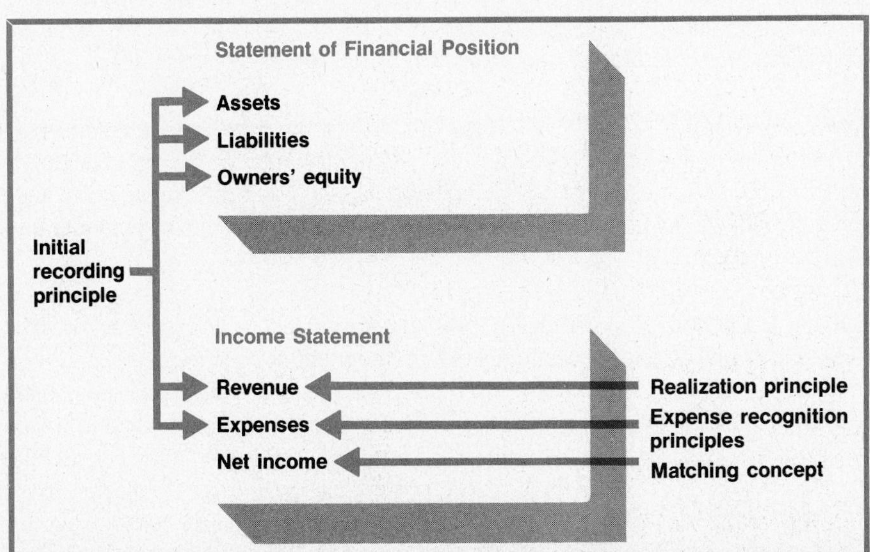

Exhibit 4-11
Relationships of accounting principles to major categories

change in owners' equity from one period to the next is a result of two factors: (1) the net income (or net loss) for the period, and (2) owners' investments or withdrawals during the period. Exhibit 4-11 summarizes the relationships of accounting principles to the two major financial statements.

The statement of retained earnings shows changes in the portion of stockholders' equity called retained earnings—the portion of the owners' equity that has accumulated as a result of the net income of the enterprise over past periods. This statement also shows the dividends declared during the period.

The appendix to this chapter gives detailed descriptions of the various items that appear on a classified income statement.

In Chapters 1 through 4 we have established the basis for an understanding of complex accounting concepts and practices. As we move into more detailed and advanced studies in the field, you must not lose sight of these broad, basic principles and relationships. We refer to them or assume that you understand them constantly throughout this text.

Appendix

TERMINOLOGY USED IN THE INCOME STATEMENT

This appendix gives a brief description of each of the items that appears on the income statement. These concepts are discussed in greater detail later in the text. For now, you should try to get a general picture of their meaning; complete mastery of these concepts will come later. Exhibit 4-12 shows a typical classified single-step income statement; Exhibit 4-13 shows the same information in the multiple-step form of the statement.

SALES. The total (or gross) amount charged to customers as the sales prices of products sold during the accounting period. Sales discounts and sales returns (or allowances for such returns) may be shown as adjustments to total sales.

COST OF GOODS SOLD. Cost to the business of the merchandise sold to customers during the period. For example, if merchandise purchased for $100,000 is sold for $150,000, the cost of goods sold is $100,000. The cost of goods sold is an expense; it is deducted from net sales in the multiple-step income statement to give the gross margin.

GROSS MARGIN. Gross margin (or gross profit on sales) is the excess of net sales over cost of goods sold. Gross margin is an important accounting and managerial concept. It represents the gross profit from sales operations; from this gross profit the firm must cover its operating and other expenses—what is left after that will be net income.

OPERATING EXPENSES. Operating expenses are those costs incurred in normal profit-directed operations.

Exhibit 4-12 **A typical classified single-step income statement**

STYLE COMPANY

Income Statement

For the Year Ended December 31, 19_1

Revenues:		
Net sales (Gross sales $1,000,000 less sales adjustments)		$980,000
Gain on sale of equipment		2,000
Interest income		8,000
Dividend income		8,000
Total revenue		$998,000
Cost and expenses:		
Cost of goods sold	$500,000	
Selling expenses	100,000	
General and administrative expenses	110,000	
Other expenses	4,000	
Income taxes	102,400	
Total cost and expenses		816,400
Income before extraordinary item		$181,600
Extraordinary item:		
Earthquake loss, less applicable income taxes		53,600
Net income		$128,000
Earnings per common share (10,000 shares outstanding):		
Income before extraordinary item		$18.16
Extraordinary item (loss)		(5.36)
Net income		$12.80

Selling expenses. Selling expenses are those operating expenses associated with the selling function. They include such items as salaries of salesmen, advertising expenses, depreciation of store equipment, and delivery expenses.

General and administrative expenses. Those operating expenses associated with the general operations of the firm, exclusive of selling expenses. Included here are such items as officers' salaries, depreciation of office equipment, postage, telephone, insurance, property taxes, accounting, and similar expenses not directly related to the selling function.

OPERATING INCOME. Operating income is the excess of gross margin over operating expenses; it is shown explicitly on the multiple-step form. Operating income represents the income arising from normal operations of the business.

OTHER REVENUE AND EXPENSES. Other revenue and expenses arise from transactions not directly related to normal business operations. Items listed as other revenue include dividends and interest received from stocks or bonds owned, income from such things as rents and royalties, gains and losses on sale of assets, and so

Exhibit 4-13 **A typical classified multiple-step income statement**

STYLE COMPANY
Income Statement
For the Year Ended December 31, 19_1

Sales			$1,000,000
Less: Sales discounts		$ 10,000	
Sales returns and allowances		10,000	20,000
Net sales			$ 980,000
Cost of goods sold			500,000
Gross margin			$ 480,000
Operating expenses:			
Selling expenses:			
Sales salaries	$50,000		
Advertising	10,000		
Depreciation of store equipment	40,000	$100,000	
General and administrative expenses:			
Officers and office salaries	$50,000		
Depreciation of office equipment	10,000		
Property taxes	30,000		
Insurance	20,000	$110,000	210,000
Operating income			$ 270,000
Other revenue and expense:			
Gain on sale of equipment		$ 2,000	
Interest income		8,000	
Dividend income		8,000	
Total other revenue		$ 18,000	
Interest expense		4,000	14,000
Income before income taxes and extraordinary item			$ 284,000
Income taxes			102,400
Income before extraordinary item			$ 181,600
Extraordinary item:			
Earthquake loss		75,000	
Less: Applicable income taxes		21,400	53,600
Net income			$ 128,000
Earnings per common share (10,000 shares outstanding):			
Income before extraordinary item			$18.16
Extraordinary item (loss)			(5.36)
Net income			$12.80

on. Items listed as other expenses include costs related to financial transactions, and costs related to certain "other revenue" items—for example, interest expenses.

INCOME BEFORE INCOME TAXES AND EXTRAORDINARY ITEMS. The sum of operating income and other revenue, less other expenses. This item reports the earnings of the firm before income taxes and extraordinary items have been considered.

INCOME TAXES. Taxes on earnings that are payable to federal, state, and local governmental units.

INCOME AFTER TAXES. The excess of "income before income taxes and extraordinary items" over income taxes. This item represents the net earnings of the enterprise after all revenue and expense items except extraordinary items have been considered.

EXTRAORDINARY ITEMS. An *Opinion* of the APB issued in 1973 defines extraordinary items in the following way: "Extraordinary items are events and transactions that are distinguished by their unusual nature ***and*** by the infrequency of their occurrence." An event of an unusual nature is one that is "of a type clearly unrelated to, or only incidentally related to, the ordinary and typical activities of the entity." Infrequency of occurrence refers to situations "that would not reasonably be expected to recur in the foreseeable future."[9] An event should be reported as an extraordinary item only if it meets *both* of these criteria. An event may be unusual in nature for one company, but not for another. The environment in which a company operates often is significant in determining whether a particular event is unusual in nature and infrequent in occurrence. Extraordinary items would usually include any losses that are a direct result of a major calamity, such as an earthquake. An extraordinary item alerts the user of the statement to the fact that the net income for this period has been affected significantly by events that should not be expected to recur in future periods. If an extraordinary gain or loss has a tax consequence, the tax effect of the transaction is associated with the item. The taxes shown in the main body of the statement are computed to reflect the taxes that would have been paid if the extraordinary item had not occurred. This procedure improves the matching of revenue and expenses. In Exhibits 4-12 and 4-13, "earthquake loss" is an extraordinary item and is assumed to be material.

NET INCOME. The excess of total revenue of a given accounting period over total expenses and losses of the period.

EARNINGS PER SHARE. The amount of earnings attributable to each share of common stock. Further discussed in the section on "Ratio Analysis" in this chapter.

Questions

1. Distinguish between the types of information provided on the income statement and those that appear on the statement of financial position.
2. What is the matching process?
3. Name and describe three forms of the income statement. Explain the advantages and disadvantages of each form.
4. Define revenue.
5. What are the sources of revenue?
6. When should revenue be recognized in the income statement?
7. Explain the realization principle.

9. Accounting Principles Board, ***Opinion No. 30: Reporting the Results of Operations—Reporting the Effects of Disposal of a Segment of a Business, and Extraordinary, Unusual and Infrequently Occurring Events and Transactions*** (New York: American Institute of Certified Public Accountants, 1973), para. 20.

8. Define expense.
9. Distinguish between expired costs and unexpired costs.
10. What are losses?
11. When do costs expire? Give your answer in terms of the expense recognition principles.
12. How are revenue and expenses measured?
13. Give the formulas for the following ratios:
    a. net income to net sales;
    b. net income to owners' equity;
    c. net income per share of common stock;
    d. price-earnings ratio.
14. Discuss the interpretation of the four ratios listed in Question 13.
15. What information is presented on a statement of retained earnings? How does this statement supplement the information on the position and income statements?
16. Discuss the relationships between the income statement, the statement of financial position, and the statement of retained earnings.
17. Explain the cash and accrual methods of accounting. Evaluate the advantages, disadvantages, and general acceptance of these two methods.
18. Does the receipt of cash by a business always occur at the same time as realization of revenue? Explain.
19. Does the payment of cash by a business always occur at the same time as realization of expense? Explain.
20. What is the difference between a dividend and an expense?

Exercises

E4-1 Three companies show the following information in their records for the year ended December 31, 19_6. Prepare a single-step income statement for each company, classifying the items as far as possible. The Singles Company had 100 shares of common stock outstanding; the Doubles and Triples Companies each had 10,000 shares of common stock outstanding.

Singles Company:	Expenses	$ 275
	Revenue	650
Doubles Company:	Revenue	$200,000
	Selling expenses	18,000
	Cost of goods sold	27,000
	General expenses	7,500
Triples Company:	Flood loss (an unusual and nonrecurring event)	$ 9,000
	Applicable income tax reduction associated with flood loss	4,500
	Dividend income	600
	Sales (gross)	310,000
	Interest expense	2,100
	Interest income	3,200
	Insurance expense	1,200
	Officers' salaries	12,000
	Sales discounts	8,000
	Sales returns and allowances	3,000

Salesmen's salaries	$31,000
Advertising expenses	16,000
Cost of goods sold	34,000
Income taxes	45,000

E4-2 Using the information given in Exercise E4-1, prepare a multiple-step income statement for the Triples Company.

E4-3 Using information from the income statement you prepare in Exercise E4-2, compute the following ratios:

a. net income to net sales (use net income before extraordinary items);
b. income before extraordinary items per share of common stock;
c. net income per share of common stock;
d. price-earnings ratio (assume that the market price of the stock is $100 per share);
e. return on investment (assume that the average total assets of the firm amount to $220,000).

NOTE: When extraordinary items appear on financial statements, ratios using "income before extraordinary items" are usually more relevant than those based on "net income." This is especially true when the user is interested in evaluating the normal trends of the enterprise.

E4-4 Prepare a statement of retained earnings for the Lo Company for the year ended December 31, 19_6, using the following information from the company's records.

Net income for 19_6	$125,000
Retained earnings, December 31, 19_5	450,000
Dividends declared during 19_6	100,000

E4-5 For the year 19_6, the Lomax Company reported total revenue of $875,000 total cost and expenses of $525,000, and an average of 35,000 shares of common stock outstanding.

a. Compute the net income for the year.
b. Compute the earnings per share on the common stock for the year.

E4-6 In its accounting records for the year, the Star Corporation has total amounts for each of the following items:

a. land owned but not used in the profit-directed activities of the firm;
b. rental income from the land listed as item 1;
c. sales discounts;
d. deferred pension cost;
e. bonds payable;
f. gain on land sold (an unusual and nonrecurring transaction);
g. interest expense on six-month note payable;
h. common stock;
i. notes payable due in five years;
j. accumulated depreciation on delivery truck;
k. allowance for bad debts;
l. dividend income on marketable securities;
m. merchandise inventory;
n. copyright;
o. accounts payable;

p. services;
q. salesmen's salaries;
r. rent expense;
s. interest income.

In its statement of financial position and its income statement, the Star Corporation includes the following classifications:

A. current assets;
B. investments;
C. property, plant, and equipment;
D. deferred charges and intangible assets;
E. current liabilities;
F. long-term liabilities;
G. paid-in (contributed) capital;
H. retained earnings;
I. footnote on statement of financial position;
J. revenues;
K. sales adjustment;
L. cost of goods sold;
M. operating expenses;
N. other income;
O. other expense;
P. extraordinary gains and losses;
Q. line for income taxes before items and net income.

Required: For each of the items (a through s), indicate the financial statement categories (A through Q) under which that item should be included.

E4-7 Indicate the category of a multiple-step income statement in which each of the following items would appear. Use the categories (A through Q) listed in Exercise E4-6.

a. Sales discount.
b. Insurance expense.
c. Fire loss (an unusual and nonrecurring event).
d. Sales
e. Salesmen's salaries.
f. Interest income.
g. Income taxes.
h. Depreciation of office equipment.
i. Sales returns and allowances.
j. Property taxes.
k. Gain on sale of equipment (a recurring transaction).
l. Loss from a strike (a usual and recurring event).
m. Bad debts expense.
n. Dividends received on investments.

E4-8 For each of the following economic events, indicate whether or not the firm realizes revenue. Explain your answers.

a. Stock acquired several years ago at a cost of $8,500 has a current market value of $11,000.
b. The company built equipment for its own use at a cost of $42,500. Similar equipment purchased elsewhere would have cost $52,000.
c. The city in which the company is located gave the firm (without charge)

land valued at $85,000 to encourage the firm to expand its operations and thus provide jobs for individuals living in the area.

d. The firm rented one floor of its office building to a lawyer.

e. Merchandise costing $11,000 was sold to a customer for $14,500 in cash.

f. Merchandise costing $9,500 was sold to a customer on account for $17,000.

g. The firm owns timberland on which it grows trees for its sawmill operations. New growth of trees on the land increases the value of the forest by $200,000.

E4-9 The Sarah Company is engaged in a service business. During 19_5, the company billed its customers for $1,200,000 in charges for services that the company performed during 19_5. These billings resulted in cash payments to the company of $850,000 during 19_5 and $350,000 during 19_6. The company incurred expenses of $760,000 while carrying out these services during 19_5. The company paid out $440,000 in cash on these expenses during 19_5, and paid out another $320,000 in cash on these expenses during 19_6.

a. What revenue and expense amounts would be reported in each of the years 19_5 and 19_6 if the company uses the cash method of accounting?

b. What revenue and expense amounts would be reported in each year if the company uses the accrual method of accounting?

c. Assume that the company carried out no other transactions during 19_5 and 19_6. What net income would be reported for each year using the cash method? using the accrual method?

d. Which of the two methods provides the most reasonable matching of revenue and expense? Explain your answer.

E4-10 The condensed statement of financial position of a company at the beginning of the year is shown here:

HOLD COMPANY

Statement of Financial Position
January 1, 19_0

Assets		$100,000
Liabilities		$ 30,000
Stockholders' equity:		
Capital stock	$50,000	
Retained earnings	20,000	70,000
Total		$100,000

Additional information resulting from transactions during the year 19_1:	
Assets increased by	$14,000
Liabilities decreased by	15,000
Revenue earned	30,000
Expenses incurred	8,000
Dividends paid	5,000
Additional investment in capital stock by shareholders	12,000

Required:

a. Prepare a statement of financial position, income statement, and statement of retained earnings for the year 19_1.

b. Explain the interrelationship of the three statements.

Problems

P4-1 You work for a CPA firm. One of your firm's client companies had a ratio of net income to net credit sales of 0.05 to 1 in its most recent accounting period. The management of the client company has asked for advice on how to improve this ratio. Suggest various possibilities that you might point out to the client.

P4-2 The net income per share of common stock for the Camco Company was $5 per share in the most recent accounting period. As president of the company, you feel that this value is too low. In what portions of the company's activities would you look for the causes of this situation?

P4-3 You work as an accountant for a business. Your accounting department prepares monthly income and position statements for the use of management. A clerk in the department suggests that considerable time and effort could be saved if the annual statements were prepared simply by combining the data on the monthly statements. How would you respond to this suggestion?

P4-4 The Blue Ribbon Corporation had a totally inadequate accounting system. The president of the corporation acquires the services of your accounting firm to help him determine what net income or net loss his corporation made during the year just ended. Your firm assigns you as the accountant for this client. Suggest a possible approach that might provide the president with the information he seeks.

P4-5 For each of the following cases, compute the unknown item indicated by a question mark.

	Case 1	Case 2	Case 3	Case 4	Case 5
Owners' equity at beginning of period	$150	?	$150	$400	$410
Net income	?	$400	100	150	115
Investment	75	200	?	0	75
Withdrawal	25	100	25	?	45
Owners' equity at end of period	200	600	375	500	?

P4-6 A friend of yours owns and manages her own business. In January 19_7, she comes to your office and asks you to help her find out whether she operated at a profit during 19_6. After examining the records that she has available, you are able to determine the following information.

Total assets, December 31, 19_5	$ 95,000
Total liabilities, December 31, 19_5	55,000
Total assets, December 31, 19_6	190,000
Total liabilities, December 31, 19_6	105,000

Your friend also tells you that she withdrew from the business for her own use during the year $4,500 in cash, and merchandise costing $1,700. Can you compute the profit or loss for your friend's business during 19_6?

P4-7 You operate a bookkeeping service for local doctors and merchants. At the local country club, you play a game of golf with two of your clients, Doctor A and Merchant B. During the game, your clients insist on keeping up a conversation about the finances of their respective businesses. You play the worst round of golf in your life. In the dining room after the game, the clients compare the annual statements you have recently prepared for them. In the course of explaining some differences between the two statements, you mention that Doctor A's statement was prepared using the cash method of accounting, while Merchant B's statement was prepared using the accrual method. The two clients are very interested in this comment. They ask you to explain the difference between the two methods. Each wants to know why you chose the method used for his accounts, and each wonders if he might not come out better (in lower taxes or increased earnings) if you used the other method for his accounts. How do you explain this matter to your clients in the few minutes remaining before your dinners arrive?

P4-8 Using the following information, prepare a multiple-step income statement for the Doall Company for the year ended December 31, 19_6. During the year, the company had an average of 5,000 shares of common stock outstanding.

Sales	$615,000
Cost of goods sold	126,000
Insurance expense	10,500
Sales salaries	235,000
Interest expense	7,000
Depreciation on store equipment	25,000
Depreciation on office equipment	7,500
Property taxes	4,000
Advertising	65,000
Flood loss, less applicable income tax reduction	14,000
Interest income	62,000
Dividend income	27,000
Sales discounts	8,000
Sales returns and allowances	11,000
Officers' and office salaries	85,000
Income taxes	55,000

P4-9 Using the information given in Problem P4-8, prepare a single-step income statement for the Doall Company for the year ended December 31, 19_6.

P4-10 From the following information, prepare an income statement in the multiple-step form for the Equity Company. Refer to Problem P3-5 (Chapter 3) for any information required from a statement of financial position.

Sales	$800,000
Sales discounts	50,000
Sales salaries	100,000
Advertising	200,000
Rent expense—salesroom	50,000
Rent expense—office	10,000
Officers' and office salaries	100,000
Property taxes	10,000
Insurance expense	20,000
Interest income	15,000
Dividend income	10,000
Income taxes	40,000
Extraordinary loss (net of taxes)	25,000
Cost of goods sold	150,000

P4-11 *a.* Compute owners' equity at the beginning of a period from the following data:

Owners' equity at the end of the year	$200,000
Expenses	30,000

Investments during the year	$ 25,000
Withdrawals during the year	5,000
Revenues	100,000

b. Compute net income on the accrual basis and on the cash basis for the months of December 19_0 and January 19_1 from the following information for a business that began operations on December 1, 19_0:

	December	January
Credit sales	$100,000	$150,000
Cash collected on credit sales	70,000	90,000
Cash sales	20,000	30,000
Expenses incurred	55,000	75,000
Cash paid for expenses	30,000	50,000

The accounting cycle and procedures

Part Three

5

The accounting cycle—analyzing transactions

Chapters 1 through 4 focused mainly on the statement of financial position and the income statement. These statements are important ***outputs*** of the accounting system. Now we turn to the procedures of accumulating and processing data—the first steps in the accounting system.

The accounting system provides procedures and forms used to record, classify, and summarize economic events. The summarized information ultimately appears in the financial statements. In Chapters 5 and 6 we discuss the basic accounting procedures and forms used as data is gathered, processed, and summarized. In this electronic age, most large accounting systems use punch cards and magnetic tapes to record data. Accountants design flowcharts and programs that tell a computer how to store, manipulate, and retrieve the data in the desired form. However, a written system of record-keeping is used in this chapter because it is much easier to see and understand the accounting concepts involved in the processing of written forms.

The accounting cycle

Economic events are activities that cause changes in the assets, liabilities, or owners' equity of a business. The ***accounting cycle*** is a sequence of activities that involve the recording, summarizing, and reporting of economic events.[1] As an information system, the accounting cycle starts with the recording of events and ends with the presentation of summary information in formal financial statements.

1. In ***APB Statement No. 4*** (para. 176), the Accounting Principles Board describes the accounting process in terms of eight operations: (1) ***selecting*** the events to be accounted for, (2) ***analyzing*** the events to determine their effects on the financial position of an enterprise, (3) ***measuring*** the effects and representing them by money amounts, (4) ***classifying*** the measured effects in terms of the accounts affected, (5) ***recording*** the measured effects according to the accounts affected, (6) ***summarizing*** the recorded effects for each account and classification, (7) ***adjusting*** the records, and (8) ***communicating*** the processed information.

In Chapters 5 and 6, we view the accounting cycle in terms of the written records and the computations that the accountant uses in the accounting cycle. From this point of view, the accounting cycle contains the following sequence of activities:

1. the general journal;
2. the general ledger;
3. the trial balance;
4. the adjusting entries;
5. the work sheet;
6. the financial statements,
   a. the statement of financial position,
   b. the income statement,
   c. the statement of retained earnings,
   d. the statement of changes in financial position;
7. the closing entries;
8. the post-closing trial balance.

ACCOUNTING PROCEDURES

Most of the economic events that the accounting system must record are business transactions. In most cases, the accounting system gathers data about these transactions in the form of copies of business documents such as purchase orders, sales invoices, payroll time cards, cash receipts. memoranda of cash disbursements, and so on. Using these source documents, the accountant records the transactions in a ***book of original entry*** called a ***journal.*** In the journal, he lists the transactions in chronological order—that is, in the order of their occurrence in time. As the accountant records the items in the journal, he analyzes each transaction to decide which assets, liabilities, revenue, or expenses are affected by it. From the journal, the accountant then transfers each item to a ***book of accounts*** called a ***ledger.*** Exhibit 5-1 summarizes the flow of data through the accounting system.

Ledger accounts

We begin our study of the accounting cycle by examining the accounts that appear in the general ledger. These accounts play the central role in the accumulation and processing of financial data.

A ledger ***account*** is a form used to assemble information that affects one specific item of assets, liabilities, owners' equity, revenue, or expense. In its simplest form,

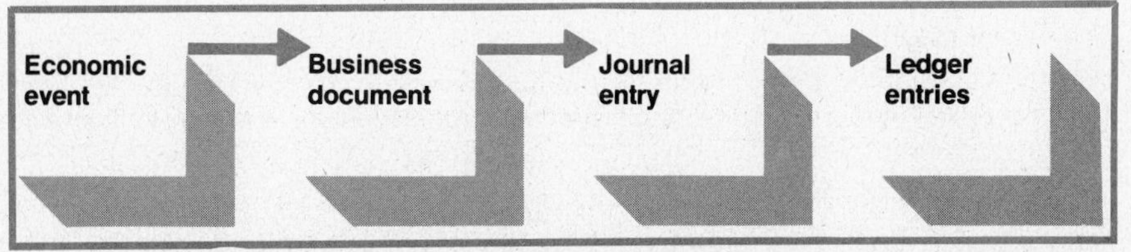

Exhibit 5-1
Flow of data into the accounting system

a ledger account can be represented in the form of a T as shown in Exhibit 5-2(a). The title of the account appears across the top of the T. The stem of the T divides the account into two columns or sides in which amounts are recorded. Because the ledger is a working document normally used only by the accountants, dollar signs usually are omitted on entries.

The left side of an account is called the ***debit side*** of the account; an entry recorded on the left side is called a ***debit entry,*** or a ***debit.*** The right side of an account is called the ***credit side;*** an entry recorded on the right side is called a ***credit entry,*** or a ***credit.*** The dollar difference between the total debits and the total credits in an account is called the ***account balance.*** If the total debits are larger than the total credits, the account has a debit balance; if the total credits are larger, the account has a credit balance. For example, the Cash account shown in Exhibit 5-2(b) has a $500 debit balance, because the total of the entries on the debit side is $500 larger than the total of the entries on the credit side. Some accounts may have no balance (a zero balance).

To understand how an accounting system operates, you must master the rules for recording increases (+) and decreases (−) in accounts. These rules are summarized as follows.

Debit an account to record:	*Credit an account to record:*
1. an *increase* in an *asset;*	**1.** a *decrease* in an *asset:*
2. a *decrease* in a *liability;*	**2.** an *increase* in a *liability;*
3. a *decrease* in *owners' equity,*	**3.** an *increase* in *owners' equity,*
a. a *decrease* in *revenue,*	*a.* an *increase* in *revenue,*
b. an *increase* in *expenses.*	*b.* a *decrease* in *expenses.*

Revenue and expense accounts are subsets of the owners' equity accounts. Because expenses reduce owners' equity, an increase in an expense is recorded on the debit side of the expense account. Because revenue increases owners' equity, an increase in a revenue account is recorded on the credit side of the revenue account.

Exhibit 5-3 shows how these rules affect the recording of increases or decreases in each of the five basic classifications of accounts. The appendix to this chapter explains why the rules for debits and credits operate as they do.

Analyzing accounting transactions

Each accounting transaction has an impact on at least two accounts in the ledger. The basic assumptions of the accounting system require that each transaction result in both a debit entry and an offsetting credit entry. By "offsetting," we mean that the dollar amounts of the debit and the credit must be the same. The rules discussed in the preceding section ensure that the information recorded in the accounting system will always agree with the basic accounting model, $A - L = OE$. Because each event must be recorded by two ledger entries—a debit entry and a

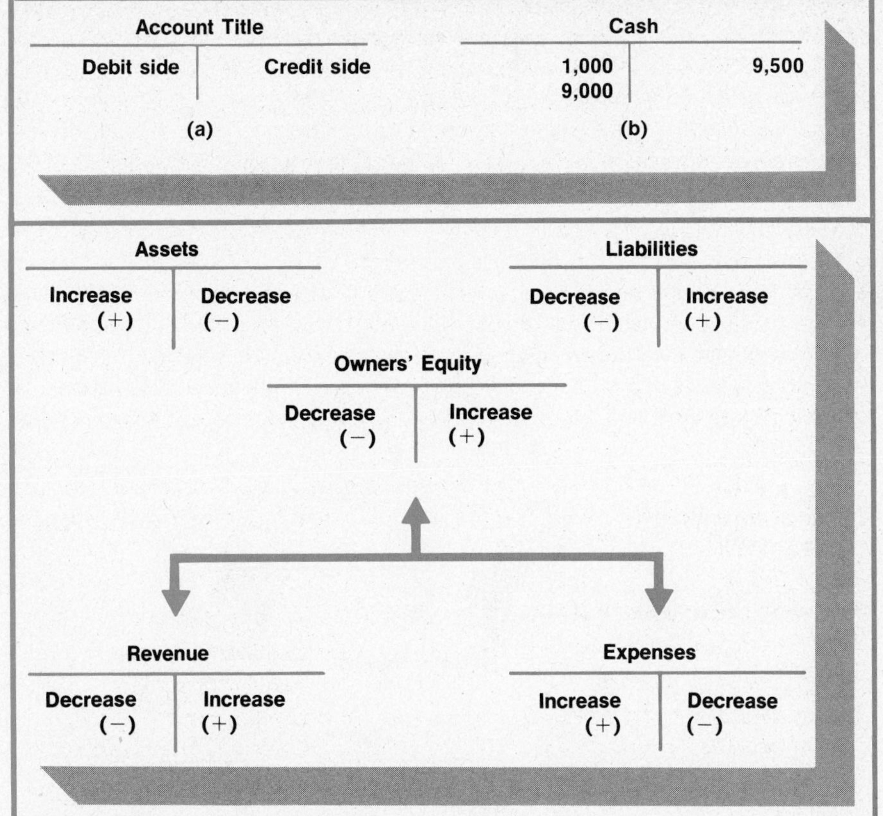

Exhibit 5-2
The ledger account in its simplest form

Exhibit 5-3
Recording increases and decreases in ledger accounts

credit entry—the accounting system is called the *double-entry system of accounting.*

Before the accountant can record an event in the accounting system, he must analyze each event to decide how it affects the ledger accounts. This process of *analyzing a transaction* involves several steps.

1. The accountant must determine the specific ledger accounts (for example, Cash, Accounts Receivable, Land, or Income Tax Expense) that are involved in the transaction.
2. He must determine the nature of the accounts involved. Is each account involved an asset, liability, owners' equity, revenue, or expense account?
3. He must determine the effect of the transaction on each of the accounts involved. Is the account balance to be increased or decreased? What is the dollar amount involved in each account change?
4. He must apply the rules to determine whether each account should be debited or credited.
5. He must check to make sure that his ledger entries for the transaction show equal debit and credit amounts.

Exhibit 5-4 summarizes this process of transaction analysis. Note that steps 2, 3, and 4 must be carried out for each of the accounts involved.

If the process of transaction analysis is carried out correctly, the overall balance of the ledger accounts must at all times give equal dollar amounts for total debits and total credits. This guarantees that the totals of the accounts comply with the basic accounting model, $A - L = OE$. Although the totals in individual accounts and in each major category change as events occur and are recorded, the basic equality remains.

TRANSACTION ANALYSIS: AN ILLUSTRATIVE CASE

At first, the process of transaction analysis seems complex. However, with a little practice, it soon becomes straightforward and logical to the accountant. In order to help you see how the process is carried out, we now examine selected transactions of the XYZ Company and follow their analysis by the firm's accounting system. At this point we assume that information about these transactions has been gathered

Exhibit 5-4
The process of transaction analysis

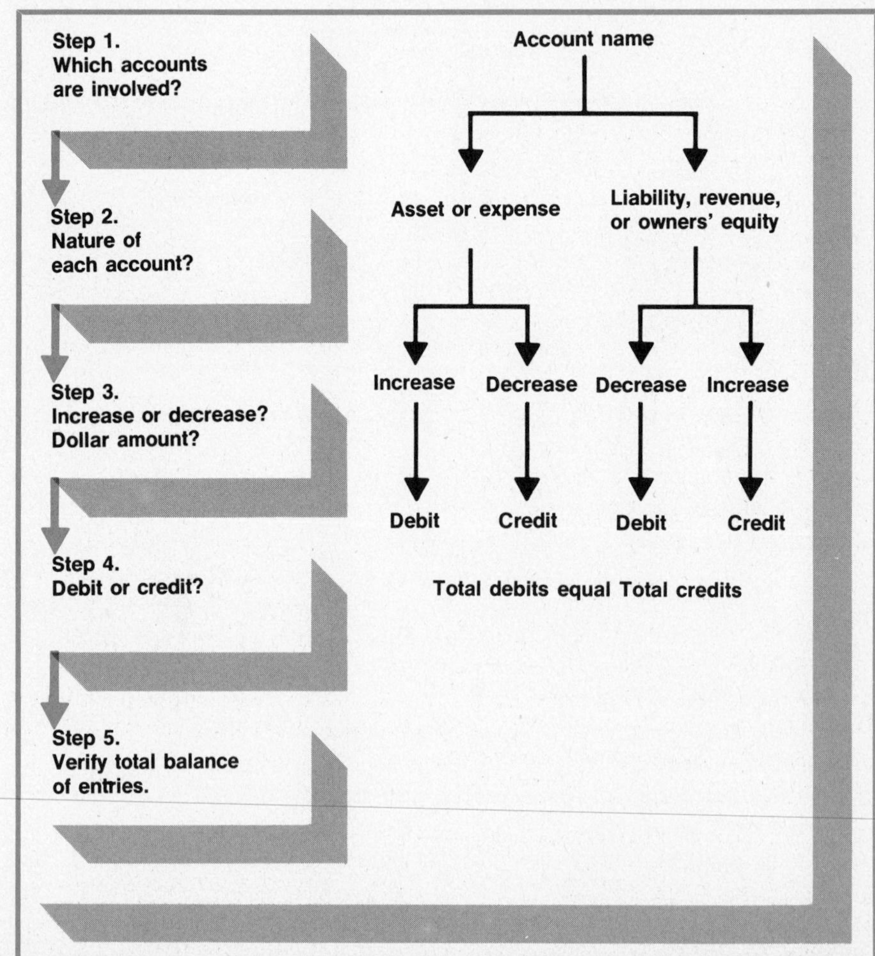

Asset accounts:	Owners' equity accounts:
Cash	Dividends
Accounts receivable	Retained earnings
Land	Common stock
Building	
Office equipment	**Revenue account:**
	Sale of services
Liability accounts:	**Expense accounts:**
Notes payable	Salesmen's salaries
Accounts payable	Rent expense
Dividends payable	Utilities expense
Income taxes payable	Income tax expense

Exhibit 5-5
Ledger accounts of the XYZ Company used in examples

in the form of business documents and transferred into the journal. We are looking at the process of transferring the information from the journal into the ledger accounts. (The nature of journal entries is discussed in a later section.)

To illustrate basic concepts in a logical order, our example is greatly simplified.[2] The first five transactions deal only with accounts that are summarized in the balance sheet: asset, liability, and owners' equity (other than revenue or expense) accounts. The remaining transactions introduce the revenue and expense accounts. The specific accounts of the XYZ Company involved in the transactions are listed in Exhibit 5-5.

ISSUANCE OF STOCK. The ownership interest in a corporation is divided into shares of stock. *Common stock* is a term applied to corporate shares that represent basic ownership interests in the corporation. Owners of common stock have a right to vote at stockholders' meetings. In this way they have a voice in determining the major policies to be followed by the management of the firm. They also have a right to share in the earnings of the corporation—that is, the right to receive dividends distributed by the corporation.

Transaction 1. The XYZ Company was organized in January 19_1. On January 5, 19_1, the company issued common stock to various individuals in return for cash payments totaling $100,000. The company's accounting system analyzed this transaction as follows (using the five steps shown in Exhibit 5-4).

Step 1. Cash was received. Common stock was issued.
Step 2. Cash is an asset account. Common Stock is an owners' equity account.

2. We have postponed to later chapters discussion of certain basic concepts such as depreciation that make this example somewhat incomplete. Also, this case involves relatively few transactions spread out over an entire year. This enables us to demonstrate major elements of the accounting cycle before introducing complexities.

Step 3. The Cash account is increased by $100,000. The owners' equity account is increased by $100,000.
Step 4. Debit Cash account $100,000. Credit Common Stock account $100,000.
Step 5. Total debits ($100,000) = Total credits ($100,000).

Exhibit 5-6 shows the entries made in the ledger accounts. The numbers in parentheses are the transaction number. In terms of the accounting equation, $NA = OE$, we see that net assets have been increased by $100,000 (Cash account) and that there has been an equal increase of $100,000 in owners' equity (Common Stock account).

PURCHASE OF ASSETS FOR CASH. The purchase of an asset for cash is one of the most frequently encountered transactions in accounting. In effect, one asset is exchanged for another.

Transaction 2. On January 31, 19_1, the company purchased land and a building for $70,000 in cash. The bill of sale specified that $50,000 of the payment was for the building.

Step 1. Land was acquired. Building was acquired. Cash was paid.
Step 2. Land, Building, and Cash are all asset accounts.
Step 3. The Land account is increased by $20,000. The Building account is increased by $50,000. The Cash account is decreased by $70,000.
Step 4. Debit Land account $20,000. Debit Building account $50,000. Credit Cash account $70,000.
Step 5. Total debits ($20,000 + $50,000) = Total credits ($70,000).

Exhibit 5-7 shows the entries made in the ledger accounts. In terms of $NA = OE$, we see that both net assets and owners' equity are unchanged by this transaction. The $70,000 increase and $70,000 decrease in assets balance each other. Also note that the Cash account now has two entries; the account shows a debit balance of $30,000 ($100,000 − $70,000). Color item represents a previous transaction.

Exhibit 5-6
Entries in ledger accounts for transaction 1

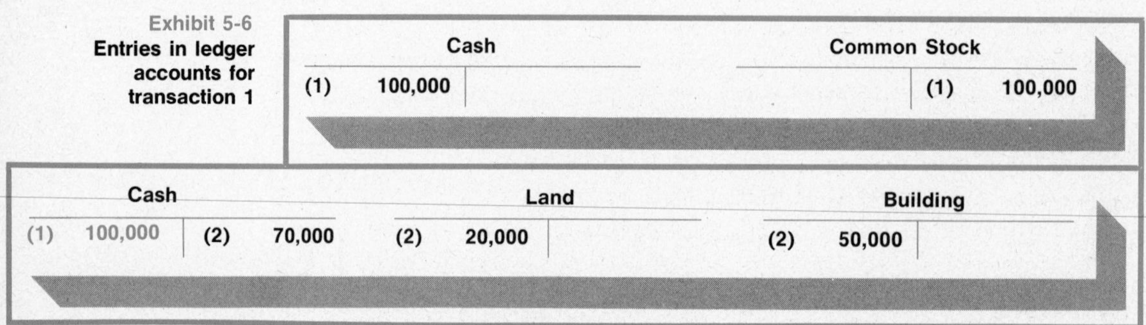

Exhibit 5-7 Entries in ledger accounts for transaction 2

Exhibit 5-8
Entries in ledger accounts for transaction 3

PURCHASE OF ASSETS ON ACCOUNT. When a firm purchases something on account (that is, for credit), the company acquires a liability in order to acquire the asset.

Transaction 3. On March 15, 19_1, the company purchases office equipment on account for $10,000 from the Supplier Company.

Step 1. Office equipment was acquired. A debt was incurred in the form of an account payable to a specific company, the Supplier Company.
Step 2. Office Equipment is an asset account. Accounts Payable is a liability account.
Step 3. The Office Equipment account is increased by $10,000. The Accounts Payable account is increased by $10,000.
Step 4. Debit Office Equipment account $10,000. Credit Accounts Payable account $10,000.
Step 5. Total debits ($10,000) = Total credits ($10,000).

Exhibit 5-8 shows the entries made in the ledger accounts. Normally the Accounts Payable account is divided into a number of subaccounts—one for each entity to which the firm owes money. In terms of $NA = OE$, we see that both net assets and owners' equity remained unchanged; an increase of $10,000 in assets was offset by an increase of $10,000 in liabilities.

INTERIM FINANCIAL STATEMENTS. The accountant may be required at times other than at the end of a fiscal year to prepare financial statements, either for use by management or for release to outside users. Such statements are called *interim financial statements.* The ledger accounts can be used to prepare interim statements when needed. The balances of the various accounts give the amounts that should appear on the statements.

Interim statement of financial position. The management of the XYZ Company asks the accountant to prepare a balance sheet for the company as of the end of March. The accountant uses the balances of the ledger accounts to prepare the statement shown in Exhibit 5-9. Note that net assets equal owners' equity in this statement, as required. The double-entry system of accounting maintains an equality of debits and credits in the ledger accounts, and this equality carries through to the equality of net assets and owners' equity on the statement of financial position.

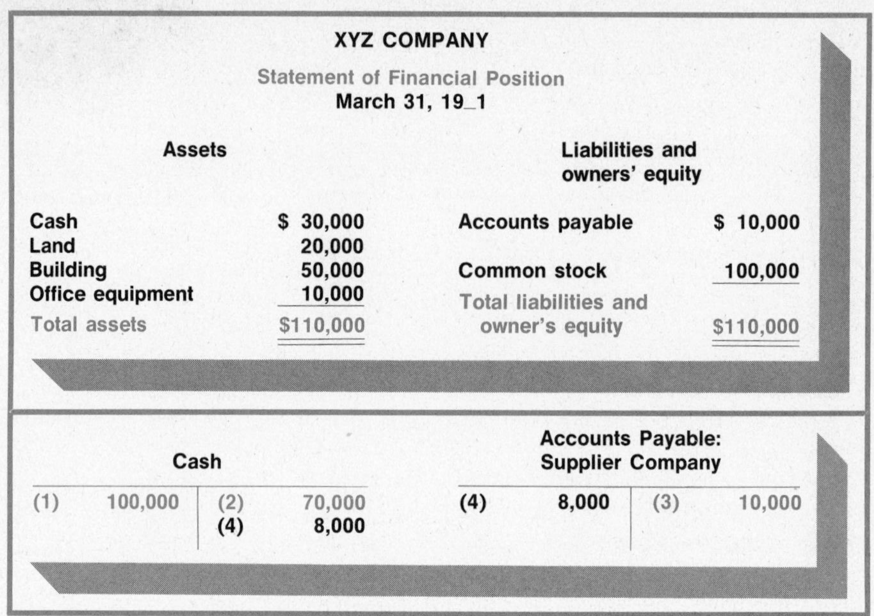

Exhibit 5-9
An interim balance sheet after transaction 3

XYZ COMPANY
Statement of Financial Position
March 31, 19_1

Assets		**Liabilities and owners' equity**	
Cash	$ 30,000	Accounts payable	$ 10,000
Land	20,000		
Building	50,000	Common stock	100,000
Office equipment	10,000		
Total assets	$110,000	Total liabilities and owner's equity	$110,000

Exhibit 5-10
Entries in ledger accounts for transaction 4

Cash

(1)	100,000	(2)	70,000
		(4)	**8,000**

Accounts Payable: Supplier Company

(4)	**8,000**	(3)	10,000

PAYMENTS ON ACCOUNT. When the firm makes a payment on an account payable, it decreases a liability (accounts payable) by giving up an asset (cash).

Transaction 4. On April 17, 19_1, the company prepares a check for $8,000 and mails it to the Supplier Company as a partial payment for the office equipment purchased in transaction 3.

Step 1. A payment was made on an account payable. Cash was paid out.
Step 2. Accounts Payable is a liability account. Cash is an asset account.
Step 3. The Accounts Payable account is decreased by $8,000. The Cash account is decreased by $8,000.
Step 4. Debit Accounts Payable account $8,000. Credit Cash account $8,000.
Step 5. Total debits ($8,000) = Total credits ($8,000).

Exhibit 5-10 shows the entries made in the ledger accounts; note that both accounts contain entries from earlier transactions. Again, the entry in the Accounts Payable account is made in the specific subaccount reserved for dealings with the Supplier Company. This account now shows a credit balance of $2,000, the amount still owed on the furniture. Similarly, the cash account shows a debit balance of $22,000, the amount of cash the firm still has on hand.

BORROWING MONEY. Companies frequently need to borrow money to help finance their operations. The accounting system records borrowing transactions by recognizing the receipt of cash and the acceptance of a liability to repay the loan.

Transaction 5. On July 15, 19_1, the XYZ Company obtains a $50,000 short-term, non-interest-bearing loan from one of its stockholders. On this date the company signs a note for the loan and receives cash in the amount of $50,000.

Step 1. Cash was received. A debt was incurred in the form of a note payable.
Step 2. Cash is an asset account. Notes Payable is a liability account.
Step 3. The Cash account is increased by $50,000. The Notes Payable account is increased by $50,000.
Step 4. Debit Cash account $50,000. Credit Notes Payable account $50,000.
Step 5. Total debits ($50,000) = Total credits ($50,000).

Exhibit 5-11 shows the ledger accounts after these entries are made. Note that the Cash account now shows a debit balance of $72,000, the amount of cash on hand.

REVENUE AND EXPENSE TRANSACTIONS. In transactions 1 through 5, we have dealt only with asset, liability, and owners' equity accounts. In each case where the company has purchased something, the cost has been for the benefit of future periods (land, building, office equipment—all to be used in producing revenue over many years). Therefore, these have been unexpired costs, treated as assets. Now we look at several transactions that involve revenue and expenses. Recall that revenue is recognized when the firm has a net inflow of assets as a result of sale of products, rendering of services, or "loan" of its resources to others for a fee. Expense is recognized when a cost expires—that is, when the cost has no benefit to future earnings. For convenience, some costs are recorded as expenses when they are incurred.

Before looking at these transactions, you may find it useful to review the rules for debiting and crediting revenue and expense accounts (Exhibits 5-3 and 5-4).

Transaction 6. On July 15, 19_1, the XYZ Company (which is an advertising agency) makes a cash sale of advertising services for $60,000.

Step 1. Cash was received. Revenue was earned through a sale of services.
Step 2. Cash is an asset account. Sale of Services (or Services) is a revenue account.
Step 3. The Cash account is increased by $60,000. The Sale of Services account is increased by $60,000.
Step 4. Debit Cash account $60,000. Credit Sale of Services account $60,000.
Step 5. Total debits ($60,000) = Total credits ($60,000).

Exhibit 5-12 shows the ledger accounts after these entries are made. In terms of *NA* = *OE*, the effect of this revenue transaction has been to increase net assets by $60,000 (increase in assets) and to increase owners' equity by $60,000 (revenue). For now, the increase in owners' equity is recorded in a revenue account. (Remember that revenue and expense accounts are regarded as subcategories of the owners' equity accounts.)

Cash				Notes Payable			
(1)	100,000	(2)	70,000			(5)	**50,000**
(5)	**50,000**	(4)	8,000				

Exhibit 5-11
Entries in ledger accounts for transaction 5

Exhibit 5-12
Entries in ledger accounts for transaction 6

Exhibit 5-13
Entries in ledger accounts for transaction 7

Exhibit 5-14
Entries in ledger accounts for transaction 8

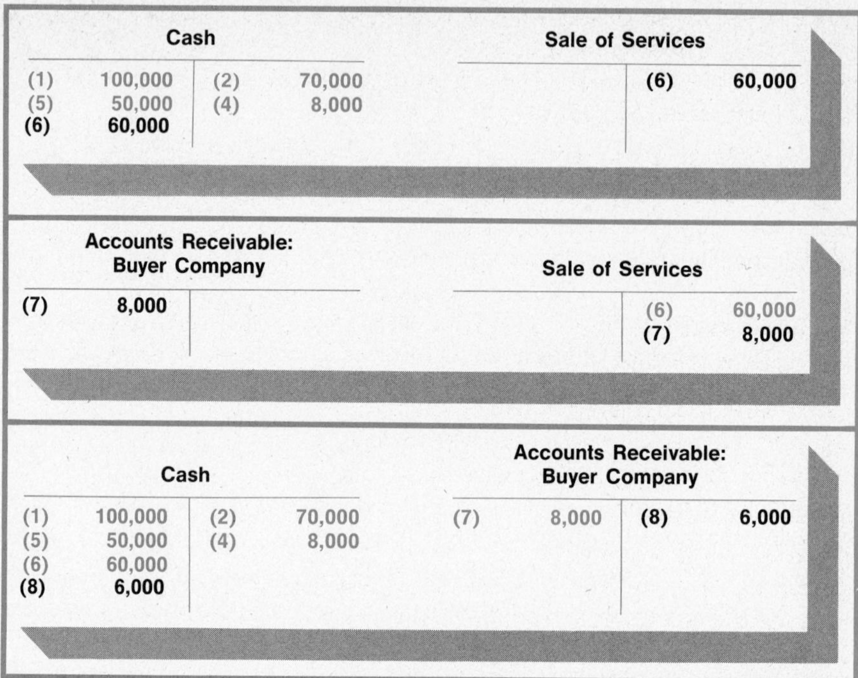

Cash

(1)	100,000	(2)	70,000
(5)	50,000	(4)	8,000
(6)	**60,000**		

Sale of Services

		(6)	**60,000**

Accounts Receivable: Buyer Company

(7)	**8,000**		

Sale of Services

		(6)	60,000
		(7)	**8,000**

Cash

(1)	100,000	(2)	70,000
(5)	50,000	(4)	8,000
(6)	60,000		
(8)	**6,000**		

Accounts Receivable: Buyer Company

(7)	8,000	**(8)**	**6,000**

Transaction 7. On August 10, 19_1, the XYZ Company renders advertising service to the Buyer Company. The Buyer Company agrees to pay $8,000 for this service, but puts the charge on account rather than paying cash for it.

Step 1. An account receivable claim arose from a credit sale. Revenue was earned through a sale of services.

Step 2. Accounts Receivable is an asset account. Sale of Services is a revenue account.

Step 3. The Accounts Receivable account is increased by $8,000. The Sale of Services account is increased by $8,000.

Step 4. Debit Accounts Receivable account $8,000. Credit Sale of Services account $8,000.

Step 5. Total debits ($8,000) = Total credits ($8,000).

Exhibit 5-13 shows the ledger accounts after these entries are made. Note that revenue is recognized at the time that the service is rendered, although cash will not be received until later. As with accounts payable, the Accounts Receivable account is usually divided into subaccounts for the various entities who owe the firm money.

Transaction 8. On September 15, 19_1, the XYZ Company receives a check in the amount of $6,000 from the Buyer Company, in partial payment of the balance due on its account.

Step 1. Cash was received. An account receivable balance was reduced.

Step 2. Cash is an asset account. Accounts Receivable is an asset account.

Step 3. The Cash account is increased by $6,000. The Accounts Receivable account is decreased by $6,000.
Step 4. Debit Cash account $6,000. Credit Accounts Receivable account $6,000.
Step 5. Total debits ($6,000) = Total credits ($6,000).

Exhibit 5-14 shows the ledger accounts after these entries are made. Note that the Buyer Company's Accounts Receivable account shows a debit balance of $2,000, indicating that the XYZ Company still has a $2,000 claim arising from the sale of services to this client in transaction 7.

Transaction 9. On December 31, 19_1, the XYZ Company pays its salesmen for their work during the year. The total amount paid to the salesmen is $30,000.

Step 1. An expense was incurred in paying salesmen's salaries. Cash was paid.
Step 2. Salesmen's Salaries is an expense account. Cash is an asset account.
Step 3. The Salesmen's Salaries account is increased by $30,000. The Cash account is decreased by $30,000.
Step 4. Debit Salesmen's Salaries account $30,000. Credit Cash account $30,000.
Step 5. Total debits ($30,000) = Total credits ($30,000).

Exhibit 5-15 shows the ledger accounts after these entries are made. In terms of *NA* = *OE*, the effect of this expense transaction has been to reduce net assets by $30,000 (decrease in assets) and to reduce owners' equity by $30,000 (expense).

Transaction 10. On December 31, 19_1, the XYZ Company pays $20,000 in rent for some office space that it has occupied during the year.

Step 1. A rent expense was incurred. Cash was paid.
Step 2. Rent Expense is an expense account. Cash is an asset account.
Step 3. The Rent Expense account is increased by $20,000. The Cash account is decreased by $20,000.
Step 4. Debit Rent Expense account $20,000. Credit Cash account $20,000.
Step 5. Total debits ($20,000) = Total credits ($20,000).

Exhibit 5-16 shows the ledger accounts after these entries have been made.

Transaction 11. On December 31, 19_1, the XYZ Company receives a bill from the Utilities Company in the amount of $5,000, for gas and electricity used by the XYZ Company during 19_1. This bill will not be paid until January 19_2.

Cash

	Debit		Credit
(1)	100,000	(2)	70,000
(5)	50,000	(4)	8,000
(6)	60,000	**(9)**	**30,000**
(8)	6,000		

Salesmen's Salaries

	Debit		Credit
(9)	**30,000**		

Exhibit 5-15
Entries in ledger accounts for transaction 9

Exhibit 5-16
Entries in ledger accounts for transaction 10

Exhibit 5-17
Entries in ledger accounts for transaction 11

Exhibit 5-18
Entries in ledger accounts for transaction 12

Exhibit 5-19
Entries in ledger accounts for transaction 13

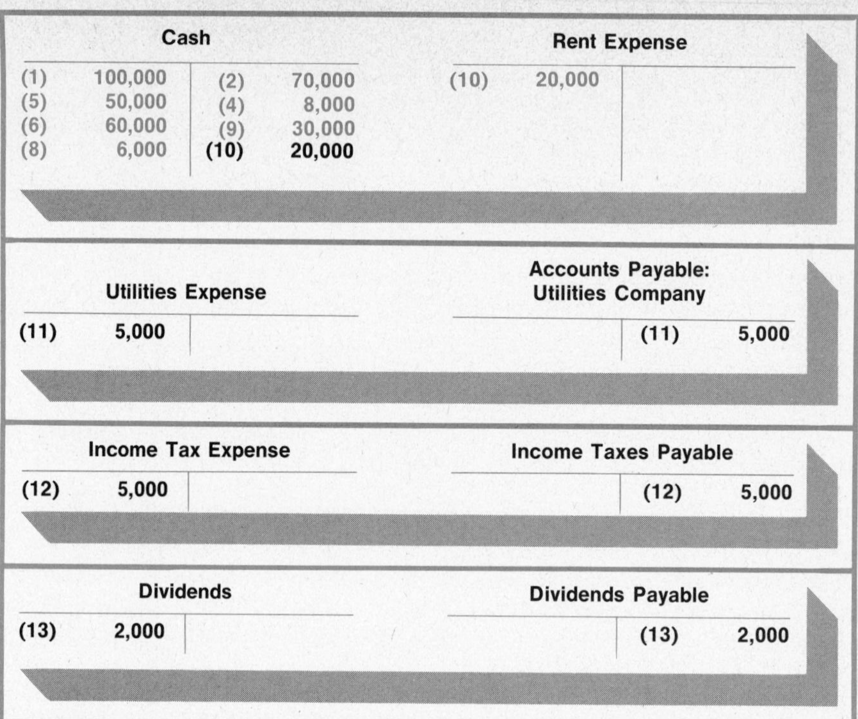

Cash

(1)	100,000	(2)	70,000
(5)	50,000	(4)	8,000
(6)	60,000	(9)	30,000
(8)	6,000	**(10)**	**20,000**

Rent Expense

(10)	20,000		

Utilities Expense

(11)	**5,000**		

Accounts Payable: Utilities Company

		(11)	**5,000**

Income Tax Expense

(12)	**5,000**		

Income Taxes Payable

		(12)	**5,000**

Dividends

(13)	**2,000**		

Dividends Payable

		(13)	**2,000**

Step 1. A utilities expense was incurred. A debt was incurred in the form of an account payable to the Utilities Company.

Step 2. Utilities Expense is an expense account. Accounts Payable is a liability account.

Step 3. The Utilities Expense account is increased by $5,000. The Accounts Payable account is increased by $5,000.

Step 4. Debit Utilities Expense account $5,000. Credit Accounts Payable account $5,000.

Step 5. Total debits ($5,000) = Total credits ($5,000).

Exhibit 5-17 shows the ledger accounts after these entries have been made.

Transaction 12. On December 31, 19_1, the accountant computes that the XYZ Company will owe $5,000 in income taxes on its earnings during the year 19_1. This tax will not be paid until March 15, 19_2. Again, we record the expense for now on the date that it is computed.

Step 1. An income tax expense was incurred. A debt was incurred in the form of income taxes payable.

Step 2. Income Tax Expense is an expense account. Income Taxes Payable is a liability account.

Step 3. The Income Tax Expense account is increased by $5,000. The Income Taxes Payable account is increased by $5,000.

Step 4. Debit Income Tax Expense account $5,000. Credit Income Taxes Payable account $5,000.

Step 5. Total debits ($5,000) = Total credits ($5,000).

Exhibit 5-18 shows the ledger accounts after these entries are made.

Transaction 13. On December 31, 19_1, the board of directors of the XYZ Company declares a $2,000 dividend to its stockholders, to be paid on February 15, 19_2. Dividends represent the distribution of the corporation's earnings to its stockholders (owners). Therefore, dividends are not an expense, but are treated as an owners' withdrawal (an owners' equity account). A detailed discussion of dividends is given in Chapters 10 and 15.

Step 1. A dividend was declared. A debt was incurred in the form of dividends payable.
Step 2. The Dividends account is an owners' equity account. The Dividends Payable account is a liability account.
Step 3. The Dividends account is increased by $2,000 to show a decrease in owners' equity. The Dividends Payable account is increased by $2,000.
Step 4. Debit Dividends account $2,000. Credit Dividends Payable account $2,000.
Step 5. Total debits ($2,000) = Total credits ($2,000).

Exhibit 5-19 shows the ledger accounts after these entries are made. Note that the payment of dividends is treated as a decrease in owners' equity because it represents a distribution to the owners of a part of their interest in the firm's resources. In terms of $NA = OE$, we see that net assets have been decreased by $2,000 (increase in liabilities), and that owners' equity has been decreased by the same amount.

LEDGER SUMMARY OF TRANSACTIONS. For purposes of our illustration, we assume that the thirteen transactions just discussed are the only economic events affecting the assets, liabilities, and owners' equity of the XYZ Company during the year 19_1. Exhibit 5-20 shows the entries in all of the company's ledger accounts at the close of business on December 31, 19_1.

In the ledger, the accounts are usually arranged in the same order as that in which these items will appear on financial statements. Asset, liability, and owners' equity accounts are arranged in the order in which the corresponding items appear on the statement of financial position. Revenue and expense accounts then follow, usually in the order in which the corresponding items appear on a multiple-step income statement.

After all transactions for an accounting period have been recorded in the ledger accounts, the accountant foots (totals) the accounts in order to determine the account balances. The debit and credit sides of each account are footed. The debit or credit balance, if it exists, is inserted in the appropriate side and circled. Exhibit 5-21 shows the cash account after it has been footed and balanced. This account shows a debit balance of $88,000.

THE TRIAL BALANCE

A trial balance is a list of account balances taken from the ledger to test the mathematical accuracy of the ledger as indicated by an equality of debits and credits. If the accountant has properly maintained the balance of debits and credits with each transaction entered, the trial balance will show an equality between the total of debit balances and the total of credit balances in the ledger. Exhibit 5-22 shows the trial

Exhibit 5-20 Ledger accounts after entries for transactions 1 through 13

Cash

	Debit		Credit
(1)	100,000	(2)	70,000
(5)	50,000	(4)	8,000
(6)	60,000	(9)	30,000
(8)	6,000	(10)	20,000

Accounts Receivable: Buyer Company

	Debit		Credit
(7)	8,000	(8)	6,000

Land

	Debit		Credit
(2)	20,000		

Building

	Debit		Credit
(2)	50,000		

Office Equipment

	Debit		Credit
(3)	10,000		

Notes Payable

	Debit		Credit
		(5)	50,000

Accounts Payable: Supplier Company

	Debit		Credit
(4)	8,000	(3)	10,000

Accounts Payable: Utilities Company

	Debit		Credit
		(11)	5,000

Dividends Payable

	Debit		Credit
		(13)	2,000

Income Taxes Payable

	Debit		Credit
		(12)	5,000

Dividends

	Debit		Credit
(13)	2,000		

Common Stock

	Debit		Credit
		(1)	100,000

Sale of Services

	Debit		Credit
		(6)	60,000
		(7)	8,000

Salesmen's Salaries

	Debit		Credit
(9)	30,000		

Rent Expense

	Debit		Credit
(10)	20,000		

Utilities Expense

	Debit		Credit
(11)	5,000		

Income Tax Expense

	Debit		Credit
(12)	5,000		

balance drawn up by the accountant for the XYZ Company (taken from Exhibit 5-20) to check his ledger entries for 19_1. A trial balance does not prove that the correct accounts were debited or credited.

Note that asset and expense accounts usually have debit balances, but revenue, liability, and owners' equity accounts usually have credit balances. This is a result of the basic rules for double-entry accounting. For most ledger accounts, increases during a period exceed decreases. Because an increase in an asset or expense account is recorded as a debit, the account normally shows a debit balance. Because an increase in a revenue, liability, or owners' equity account is recorded as a credit, these accounts normally show credit balances.

Summary

In Chapter 5 we began a discussion of the accounting cycle. In this chapter we gave the rules for recording changes in ledger accounts. These rules can be summarized as follows:

Assets		−	Liabilities		=	Owners' Equity	
Debit for increases	Credit for decreases		Debit for decreases	Credit for increases		Debit for decreases	Credit for increases

Expenses		Revenue	
Debit for increases	Credit for decreases	Debit for decreases	Credit for increases

Exhibit 5-21
Cash account in ledger after footing and balancing

	Cash		
(1)	100,000	(2)	70,000
(5)	50,000	(4)	8,000
(6)	60,000	(9)	30,000
(8)	6,000	(10)	20,000
(88,000)	216,000		128,000

Exhibit 5-22
Trial balance taken from ledger accounts

XYZ COMPANY
Trial Balance
December 31, 19_1

	Debits	Credits
Cash	88,000	
Accounts Receivable: Buyer Co.	2,000	
Land	20,000	
Building	50,000	
Office Equipment	10,000	
Notes Payable		50,000
Accounts Payable: Supplier Co.		2,000
Utilities Co.		5,000
Dividends Payable		2,000
Income Taxes Payable		5,000
Dividends	2,000	
Common Stock		100,000
Sale of Services		68,000
Salesmen's Salaries	30,000	
Rent Expense	20,000	
Utilities Expense	5,000	
Income Tax Expense	5,000	
	232,000	232,000

Ledger accounts were used to illustrate how transactions can be analyzed and recorded. The trial balance, consisting of a list of ledger account balances, was used to test the mathematical accuracy of the ledger. An interim statement of financial position was drawn up to show the statement prepared at a time other than at the end of a fiscal year.

Questions

1. What is a transaction?
2. What are accounting procedures?
3. What is the accounting cycle?
4. What is a ledger?
5. Explain the process of transaction analysis.
6. What is a "debit" and a "credit"? Give the rules used to determine whether an account should be debited or credited in a particular entry.

7. Fill in the following table with the words "debit" and "credit" to show how an increase or decrease in each kind of account should be recorded.

	Increase	Decrease
Asset account	—	—
Liability Account	—	—
Owners' equity account	—	—
Revenue account	—	—
Expense account	—	—

8. Explain why expense accounts are debited and revenue accounts credited to record increases in such accounts in a double-entry accounting system.
9. Explain why an increase in dividends is recorded as a debit entry in the Dividends account.
10. For each of the following kinds of accounts, indicate whether such an account ***normally*** shows a ***debit balance*** or a ***credit balance.***
    a. An asset account.
    b. A liability account.
    c. An owners' equity account.
    d. An expense account.
    e. A revenue account.
    Explain the reasons for each of your answers.
11. What is a trial balance?
12. Are the totals of debits and credits shown on the trial balance equal to the totals of assets and of liabilities and owners' equity shown on the corresponding statement of financial position? Why, or why not?

Exercises

E5-1 Using the ledger accounts in Exhibit 5-23, record the following transactions.

a. The company issued $50,000 of its common stock to investors.
b. The company acquired a section of land for $15,000.
c. The company performed $20,000 services for a client on account.
d. The company collected $5,000 from its client.
e. The company purchased $7,000 of office equipment from the Zero Company on account.
f. The company paid $5,000 to the Zero Company in partial payment of its account.
g. The company paid the following bills in cash:

Rent	$2,000
Utilities	5,000

h. The accountant estimated the company's income tax to be $9,000.

E5-2 Record the following transactions of the Learning Company in T-accounts.

a. The company issued $75,000 common stock when it was organized.
b. The company paid $5,000 for the first month's rent on its office.
c. The company sold $8,000 of services to a customer.
d. The company purchased office supplies in the amount of $7,000 for cash. The company recorded the supplies in an asset account called Office Supplies.
e. The company sold $15,000 of services on account to Assignment Company.

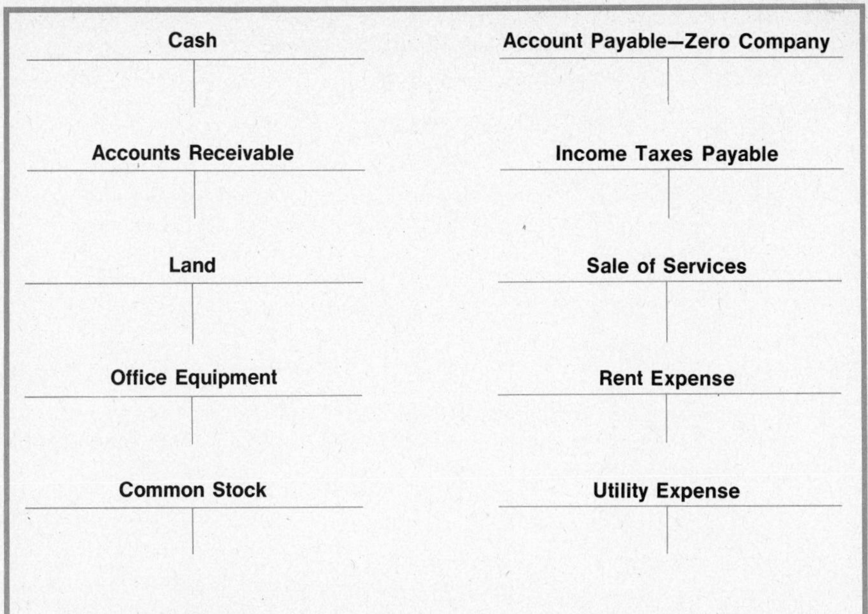

Exhibit 5-23
Ledger accounts for Exercise E5-1

f. The company borrowed $25,000 from the First National Bank and signed a note for this amount.
g. The company paid salaries of $10,000.
h. The company declared a $10,000 dividend.
i. The company paid miscellaneous expenses of $1,000.
j. The company repaid the bank loan and the interest expense on the note. The interest expense amounted to $2,000.

E5-3 Refer to Exercise E5-1. Prepare a trial balance from the ledger for December 31, 19_1, for the company.

E5-4 Refer to Exercise E5-2. Prepare a trial balance from the ledger for December 31, 19_1, for the company.

E5-5 The general ledger of the Zero Company shows the following account balances on December 31, 19_1. Prepare a trial balance for the company's accounts. Be sure to arrange the accounts in proper order.

Cash	$120,000
Retained Earnings	368,000
Notes Payable	70,000
Land	295,000
Common Stock	425,000
Merchandise Inventory	235,000
Accounts Payable	55,000
Rent Expense	35,000
Salaries Expense	195,000
Sale of Services	775,000
Accounts Receivable	410,000
Factory Building	540,000
Patents	80,000
Dividends Payable	12,000
Bonds Payable	205,000

E5-6 Refer to Exercise E5-1. For each of the transactions, indicate the effect on the accounting equation in terms of increases, decreases, or no effect.

Example for transaction a:

	Assets	− Liabilities	= Owners' equity
a.	+$50,000		+$50,000

E5-7 Refer to Exercise E5-2. For each of the transactions, indicate the effect on the accounting equation in terms of increases, decreases, or no effect.

Problems

P5-1 Exhibit 5-24 shows a chart in which transactions are to be recorded. The chart also shows beginning balances in certain accounts.

Required: Record the transactions in the chart. After the transactions have been recorded, total the columns.

a. What is the amount of total assets?
b. What is the amount of total liabilities?
c. What is the amount of owners' equity?

P5-2 Seven individuals organize the Big Seven Company on July 1, 19_1. During July the following transactions took place.

1. The company issued $70,000 of common stock to the seven stockholders.
2. Rented office space in a downtown office building for $10,000.

Exhibit 5-24 **Chart for Problem P5-1**

	Assets			Liabilities		Owners' Equity
	Cash	**Account Receivable**	**Equip-ment**	**Account Payable**	**Dividend Payable**	
Balances, Jan. 1	**$10,000**	**$20,000**	**$50,000**	**$15,000**		**$65,000**
1. Collected $15,000 on account receivable						
2. Purchased $10,000 equipment for cash						
3. Paid $10,000 on account payable						
4. Issued $25,000 common stock						
5. Paid $5,000 rent expense						
6. Sold services on account in amount of $10,000						
7. Collected $5,000 on its account						
8. Declared a $10,000 dividend						

3. Purchased office equipment for the office and paid $10,000 for it.
4. Purchased office supplies on account for $3,000 from the Office Supply Company.
5. Billed a client for $25,000 of services performed.
6. Paid insurance expense totalling $1,000.
7. Paid salaries totalling $5,000.
8. Paid Office Supply Company $2,000 on account.
9. Collected $20,000 from client on account (see transaction 5).
10. Borrowed $10,000 from a bank.
11. Received the utility bill for the month from the Utility Company in the amount of $1,000. The transaction was recorded. The bill will be paid next month.
12. Paid $1,000 interest expense on the note.

Required:

a. Record the transactions in T-accounts.
b. Prepare a trial balance from the ledger at the end of July.
c. Prepare an income statement for the company from the data available.
d. Prepare a statement of financial position from the data available.

P5-3 The following notes describe transactions of the Fundamental Company:

1. Three stockholders invested the following assets in the company in exchange for common stock:

Cash	$10,000
Truck	10,000
Office equipment	15,000
Office supplies	5,000

2. Paid the rent for the month, $2,000.
3. Performed $10,000 services for cash.
4. Performed $20,000 services on account.
5. Collected $15,000 for services performed on account.
6. Purchased $8,000 office equipment on account.
7. Paid $6,000 on account for office equipment purchased in transaction 6.
8. Recorded but did not pay $10,000 in salaries. The company uses a Salaries Payable account.
9. Paid the salaries recorded in transaction 8.
10. Paid repair expense, $2,000.
11. Paid the utility bill, $5,000.

Required:

a. Record the transactions in T-accounts. Use appropriate account titles for ledger accounts that describe the item, e.g., Truck, Repair Expense, Salaries Expense.
b. Prepare a trial balance as of December 31, 19_1, from the ledger accounts for the Fundamental Company.

P5-4 The Burr Company began operations when stockholders invested $50,000 for the common stock. During the year the company had the following cash receipts:

From clients for cash sales	$60,000
From clients on account	40,000
Bank loan	30,000

Exhibit 5-25
Problem material for P5-5

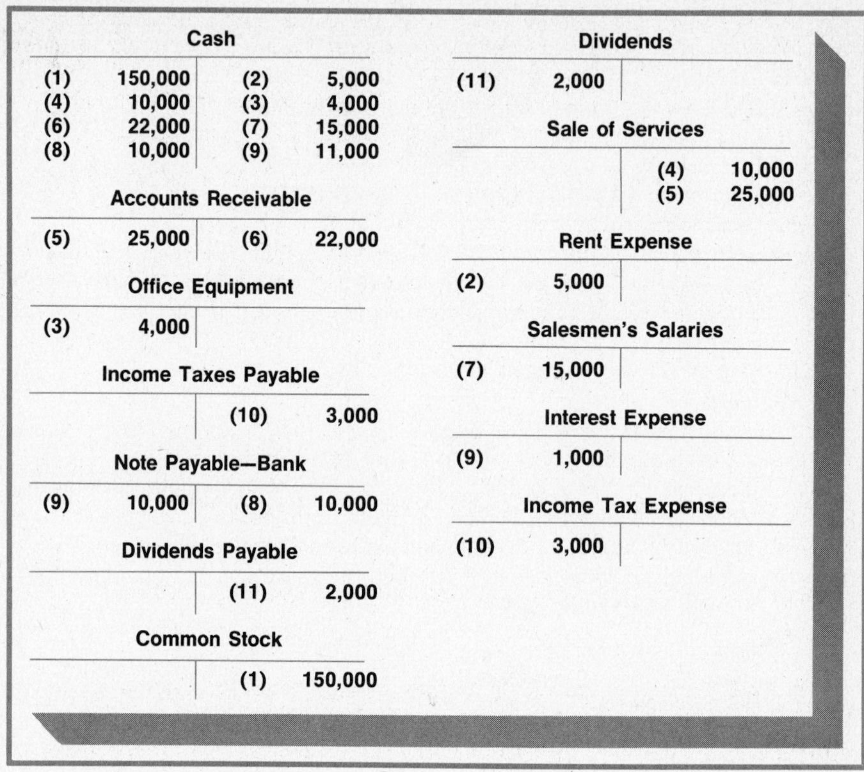

Cash

(1)	150,000	(2)	5,000
(4)	10,000	(3)	4,000
(6)	22,000	(7)	15,000
(8)	10,000	(9)	11,000

Accounts Receivable

(5)	25,000	(6)	22,000

Office Equipment

(3)	4,000		

Income Taxes Payable

		(10)	3,000

Note Payable—Bank

(9)	10,000	(8)	10,000

Dividends Payable

		(11)	2,000

Common Stock

		(1)	150,000

Dividends

(11)	2,000		

Sale of Services

		(4)	10,000
		(5)	25,000

Rent Expense

(2)	5,000		

Salesmen's Salaries

(7)	15,000		

Interest Expense

(9)	1,000		

Income Tax Expense

(10)	3,000		

Credit sales to customers amounted to $50,000. The following cash expenditures occurred during the year:

Property taxes	$ 3,000
Land acquired	25,000
Salaries	10,000
Rent	5,000
Utilities	10,000
Dividends	10,000
Bank loan repaid with interest	32,000

Required:

a. Record the transactions of the company in T-accounts.

b. Prepare a trial balance for the Burr Company on June 30, 19_1.

c. Prepare a statement of owners' equity for the company.

d. Prepare a statement of financial position for the company.

P5-5 Exhibit 5-25 shows ledger accounts with entries. These entries reflect transactions entered into by a company during the year. Give an explanation of the transaction that resulted in each entry.

The accounting cycle-continued

6

In Chapter 5 we began a discussion of the accounting cycle and procedures. In this chapter we continue this discussion, beginning with a description of the general journal.

The general journal

As we have seen, the accounting system becomes aware of economic events through the business documents that it gathers. The ***journal*** is the ***book of original entry*** for the data taken from these documents. The journal is an accounting record that lists in chronological order the economic events that affect the firm. The journal records the date of each transaction, the basic information about the nature of the transaction, and the dollar amounts involved. Thus it provides a record of all the transactions gathered by the accounting system and a continuous financial history of the business.

The process of recording a transaction in the journal is called ***journalizing.*** The entry that records the transaction is called a ***journal entry.***

The ***general journal*** is a basic accounting journal. Other journals may be used for special purposes; these special journals are discussed in later chapters. A typical general journal has (1) a column in which the date of the transaction is recorded, (2) an explanation column in which the accountant lists the accounts to be debited and credited and a brief explanation of the major facts about the transaction, (3) a reference column in which the accountant notes the ledger pages to which the transaction is posted, and (4) debit and credit money columns. Exhibit 6-1 shows a typical general journal entry.

The procedure for journalizing a transaction involves the following steps.

1. The date of the transaction is recorded. The year is written once at the top of the Date column on each page. The month is written once in the month column at the top of the page and then only for the first entry in a new month. The day is written in the day column for each entry.

Exhibit 6-1 A typical general journal entry

GENERAL JOURNAL					Page 1
Date		Explanation	Ref.	Debit	Credit
19_1					
Jan.	5	Cash	1101	100,000	
		Common Stock	3110		100,000
		To record the issuance of 1,000 shares of no-par			
		common stock.			

2. The title of the account debited is written in the Explanation column near the left edge of the column.
3. The amount of the debit is placed on the same line in the Debit money column. (As in the ledger, trial balance, and other internal working documents, dollar signs are omitted.)
4. The title of the account credited is written on the line beneath the debit information and is indented.
5. The amount of the credit is entered on the same line in the Credit money column.
6. An explanation of the transaction is written on the line(s) beneath the credit information, indented more than the title of the account credited. This explanation records important information about the entry and provides a reference about the source of the transaction data.

After one or more entries have been journalized, the accountant must *post* (transfer) the entries to the ledger. As he does so, he records the ledger pages to which the debit and credit amounts are posted in the Reference column of the journal. The entries in the Reference column serve two purposes. First, they indicate that the journal entry has been posted to the ledger. Second, they provide a way of tracing the information from the journal to the ledger if it becomes necessary to look for errors in the accounting records.

Exhibit 6-2 shows the general journal of the XYZ Company after the journalization of transactions 1 through 13 discussed earlier. A journal entry that contains more than one debit or more than one credit item (such as the entry for January 31 in Exhibit 6-2) is called a ***compound entry.*** Exhibit 6-2 shows the journal before the entries have been posted, so there are no notations in the Reference column.

Posting to the general ledger

After the accountant has journalized the transactions, he must *post* (transfer) the data from the journal to the ledger. Earlier in this chapter, we discussed the posting process in general terms, using a simplified T-form for the ledger accounts. In practice, the ledger accounts are recorded on a more detailed form (Exhibit 6-3). The form provides Date, Explanation, Reference, and money columns for debit entries on the left side of the page and a similar set of columns for credit entries on the right side of the page.

Exhibit 6-2 **The general journal of the XYZ Company for 19_1**

Date		Explanation	Ref	Debit	Credit
19_1					
Jan.	5	Cash		100,000	
		Common Stock			100,000
		To record the issuance of 1,000 shares of no-par			
		common stock.			
	31	Land		20,000	
		Building		50,000	
		Cash			70,000
		To record the purchase of land and building for $70,000.			
Mar.	15	Office Equipment		10,000	
		Accounts Payable: Supplier Co.			10,000
		To record the purchase of equipment on account from			
		Supplier Co.			
Apr.	17	Accounts Payable: Supplier Co.		8,000	
		Cash			8,000
		To record payment of $8,000 on account for equipment			
		purchased Mar. 15, 19_1, from Supplier Co.			
July	15	Cash		50,000	
		Notes Payable			50,000
		To record a 6-month, noninterest loan from A.			
		Stockholder.			
	15	Cash		60,000	
		Sales of Services			60,000
		To record sale of services for cash.			
Aug.	10	Accounts Receivable: Buyer Co.		8,000	
		Sale of Services			8,000
		To record sale of services on account to Buyer Co.			
Sept.	15	Cash		6,000	
		Accounts Receivable: Buyer Co.			6,000
		To record receipt of $6,000 from Buyer Co. on account.			
Dec.	31	Salesmen's Salaries		30,000	
		Cash			30,000
		To record payment of salesmen's salaries for 19_1.			
	31	Rent Expense		20,000	
		Cash			20,000
		To record payment of rent expense for 19_1.			
	31	Utilities Expense		5,000	
		Accounts Payable: Utilities Co.			5,000
		To record utilities expense for 19_1.			
	31	Income Tax Expense		5,000	
		Income Taxes Payable			5,000
		To record income tax expense for 19_1.			
	31	Dividends		2,000	
		Dividends Payable			2,000
		To record dividend declared Dec. 31, 19_1, and payable			
		Feb. 15, 19_2.			

Exhibit 6-3 **Cash account for XYZ Company recorded in T-form**

				Cash				Account No. 1101	
Date		**Explanation**	**Ref.**	**Debit**	**Date**		**Explanation**	**Ref.**	**Credit**
19_1					19_1				
Jan.	5		J1	100,000	Jan.	31		J1	70,000
July	15		J1	50,000	Apr.	17		J1	8,000
	15		J1	60,000	Dec.	31		J1	30,000
Sep.	15		J1	6,000		31		J1	20,000

The posting procedure involves the following steps.

1. Locate in the ledger the account for the debit or credit item in the journal that is to be posted.
2. Record the date of the entry in the Date column, the amount of the debit or credit in the money column, and the journal page number from which the item is being posted in the Reference column. All these entries are made on the appropriate debit or credit side of the page.
3. Enter the number of the ledger account in the Reference column of the journal to show that the item has been posted.

Exhibit 6-4 illustrates the posting of the first journal entry from Exhibit 6-2. The cash debit item of $100,000 in the journal is debited to the Cash account in the ledger; this happens to be account number 1101 in the general ledger. The date of the transaction is recorded in a manner similar to that used in the journal. The debit amount is entered in the Debit money column. Finally, the journal page (J1) from which this item was posted is entered in the Reference column of the ledger, and the ledger page number (1101) is recorded in the Reference column of the general journal. The posting procedure for the credit item in this journal entry is handled in similar fashion, but the ledger entry is posted on the credit side of the account.

Exhibits 6-3 and 6-4 show ledger accounts recorded in the common T-form, where debits and credits are entered on opposite sides of the page. Various other ledger account forms are used. Exhibit 6-5 shows the Cash account from the XYZ Company ledger in the popular ***balance form.*** In this form, a single set of Date, Explanation, and Reference columns is used for both debit and credit entries. Separate columns are provided for the debit and credit amounts, and a third money column provides space to compute the account balance after each entry. If this form is used, the procedure of footing and balancing the accounts need not be carried out separately at the end of an accounting period.

In most cases, the accountant need not use the Explanation column in the ledger. A full explanation of the transaction can be found in the journal on the page indicated in the ledger Reference column.

Work sheet

At the end of an accounting period, after all transactions for the period have been journalized and posted to the ledger, the accountant checks his work by preparing a trial balance of the ledger accounts—a procedure discussed earlier in this chapter.

Exhibit 6-4 **Posting of the first journal entry from Exhibit 6-2**

GENERAL JOURNAL — Page 1

Date		Explanation	Ref.	Debit	Credit
19_1 Jan.	5	Cash	1101	100,000	
		Common Stock	3110		100,000
		To record the issuance of 1,000 shares of no-par common stock.			

Cash — Account No. 1101

Date		Explanation	Ref.	Debit	Date		Explanation	Ref.	Credit
19_1 Jan.	5		J1	100,000					

Common Stock — Account No. 3110

Date		Explanation	Ref.	Debit	Date		Explanation	Ref.	Credit
					19_1 Jan.	5		J1	100,000

After confirming the balance of his ledger accounts, the accountant prepares a work sheet. The *work sheet* is a working document used to help in the preparation of financial statements. It also is used in handling certain technical problems associated with the end of an accounting period.

Exhibit 6-6 shows the work sheet prepared by the XYZ Company's accountant at the end of 19_1. The heading of a work sheet is similar to that of a financial statement, but this is still considered a working document for use by the accounting system, so dollar signs are omitted. In the form used for the work sheet, columns are provided for the trial balance. The accountant might actually prepare his trial balance on this form, or he might copy the amounts onto the work sheet from a trial balance prepared earlier. The Debit and Credit columns of the trial balance are footed to prove the balance of the accounts, and a double rule is drawn below the totals.

Exhibit 6-5 **Cash account for YXZ Company recorded in balance form**

Cash — Account No. 1101

Date		Explanation	Ref.	Debit	Credit	Balance
19_1						
Jan.	5		J1	100,000		100,000
	31		J1		70,000	30,000
Apr.	17		J1		8,000	22,000
July	15		J1	50,000		72,000
	15		J1	60,000		132,000
Sept.	15		J1	6,000		138,000
Dec.	31		J1		30,000	108,000
	31		J1		20,000	88,000

Exhibit 6-6 Work sheet for XYZ Company at end of 19_1

XYZ COMPANY
Work Sheet
For the Year Ended December 31, 19_1

Account Title	Trial Balance		Income Statement		Balance Sheet	
	Debit	Credit	Debit	Credit	Debit	Credit
Cash	88,000				88,000	
Accounts Receivable	2,000				2,000	
Land	20,000				20,000	
Building	50,000				50,000	
Office Equipment	10,000				10,000	
Notes Payable		50,000				50,000
Accounts Payable:						
Supplier Co.		2,000				2,000
Utilities Co.		5,000				5,000
Dividends Payable		2,000				2,000
Income Taxes Payable		5,000				5,000
Common Stock		100,000				100,000
Retained Earnings		0				0
Dividends	2,000				2,000	
Sale of Services		68,000		68,000		
Salesmen's Salaries	30,000		30,000			
Rent Expense	20,000		20,000			
Utilities Expense	5,000		5,000			
Income Tax Expense	5,000		5,000			
	232,000	232,000	60,000	68,000	172,000	164,000
Net income for the year			8,000			8,000
			68,000	68,000	172,000	172,000

The next pair of columns is labeled Income Statement. Debit and credit amounts for revenue and expense accounts are transferred directly from the Trial Balance columns to the Income Statement columns.

The final pair of columns is labeled Balance Sheet. Debit and credit amounts for asset, liability, and owners' equity accounts are transferred directly from the Trial Balance columns to the Balance Sheet columns.

After the amounts from the Trial Balance columns have been transferred to the Income Statement and Balance Sheet columns, the following steps are taken to complete the work sheet.

1. Foot the Income Statement and Balance Sheet columns.
2. If the credit total exceeds the debit total for the Income Statement columns, there is a net income for the period because revenue exceeds expenses. The net income is equal to the credit balance of the Income Statement columns. Enter the amount of net income in the ***Debit*** column under the column total. Enter the same amount under the ***Credit*** total in the Balance Sheet section. Write "Net income for the period" in the Account Title column on this line.

   (If the Income Statement columns show a debit balance when they are footed, expenses exceed revenue, and there is a net loss for the period. In this case, enter the amount of the net loss in the ***Credit*** column of the Income Statement section and in the ***Debit*** column of the Balance Sheet section under the column totals, and write "Net loss for the period" in the Account Title column on this line.)

   The Retained Earnings account balance that appears in the trial balance represents the retained earnings at the beginning of the period. (In our example, this balance was zero because the XYZ Company did not exist prior to 19_1.) The insertion of the net income (or net loss) for the period in the Balance Sheet columns updates this amount so that the retained earnings at the end of the period can be determined.
3. Draw a single line across the last four columns, under the net income amounts just entered. Foot these four columns and draw double lines under the totals. The debit and credit totals for the Income Statement columns should now be equal. The debit and credit totals for the Balance Sheet columns should also be equal.

Exhibit 6-7 visualizes the steps involved in preparing the work sheet. You should study Exhibits 6-6 and 6-7 carefully until the steps in the procedure are clear to you.

PREPARING FINANCIAL STATEMENTS

After the work sheet is completed, the accountant is ready to prepare the financial statements from the information on the work sheet. All of the amounts that should appear in the income statement and the balance sheet are found in the appropriate columns of the work sheet. The work sheet also contains the information needed to prepare the statement of retained earnings, although the information for this statement is not transferred into a special set of columns on the work sheet. Exhibit 6-8 shows the financial statements prepared by the accounting system of the XYZ Company, using the work sheet of Exhibit 6-6.

Closing the books

After the financial statements have been completed, the accountant is ready to ***close the books*** for the period. The closing procedure prepares the ledger accounts for the start of another accounting cycle. To accomplish this objective, ***closing entries***

Exhibit 6-7 **Preparation of the work sheet**

NAME OF COMPANY Work Sheet For the Year Ended December 31, 19__						
	Trial Balance		Income Statement		Balance Sheet	
Account Title	**Debit**	**Credit**	**Debit**	**Credit**	**Debit**	**Credit**
Assets	*A* →				→ *A*	
Liabilities		*L* →				→ *L*
Owners' equity		*OE* →				→ *OE*
Revenue		*R* →		→ *R*		
Expenses	*E* →		→ *E*			
	XXX	XXX	XXX	XXX	XXX	XXX
Net income			*NI* ←			→ *NI*
			XXX	XXX	XXX	XXX

are made in the journal and posted to the ledger.[1] The closing entries are designed to close out the revenue and expense accounts, leaving these accounts with zero balances. Usually the revenue and expense accounts are closed by transferring their balances to a temporary owners' equity account called *Income Summary.* (This account sometimes is called the Revenue and Expense account, or the Profit and Loss account.) In the case of a corporation, the Income Summary account is then closed by transferring its balance to the Retained Earnings account, a permanent owners' equity account. In addition to the revenue and expense accounts, the Dividends account also is closed by transferring its balance to the Retained Earnings account.

The process of closing the books at the end of the period clears the balances of the revenue, expense, and Dividends accounts so that their balances at the end of the next accounting period will properly reflect the transactions carried out during that period. In other words, these accounts are used to summarize the revenue, expense, and dividend transactions for one period only. They are then reset to zero to begin accumulating the totals for the next period. On the other hand, the asset, liability, and permanent owners' equity accounts always show cumulative balances over the life of the firm, as required for the statement of financial position. When the temporary accounts are closed out, their balances are transferred into the Retained Earnings account, which is used to keep track of the cumulative results of revenue, expenses, and withdrawals (dividends) over the lifetime of the firm.

Each of the revenue and expense accounts that is to be closed appears in the Income Statement columns of the work sheet (Exhibit 6-6). Therefore, the following procedure can be used to close these accounts.

1. The revenue and expense accounts that appear on the income statement are sometimes called ***nominal accounts.*** Nominal accounts are temporary capital accounts and are closed at the end of the accounting period. The asset, liability, and owners' equity accounts that appear on the statement of financial position are carried forward from period to period without closing; these are sometimes called ***real accounts.*** Real accounts are more permanent in nature than are nominal accounts.

Exhibit 6-8

Financial statements for the XYZ Company at the end of 19_1

XYZ COMPANY

Income Statement

For the Year Ended December 31, 19_1

Sale of services		$68,000
Expenses:		
Salesmen's salaries	$30,000	
Rent expense	20,000	
Utilities expense	5,000	
Income tax expense	5,000	60,000
Net income		$ 8,000

XYZ COMPANY

Statement of Financial Position

December 31, 19_1

Assets

Current assets:		
Cash	$ 88,000	
Accounts receivable	2,000	$ 90,000
Property, plant, and equipment:		
Land	$ 20,000	
Building	50,000	
Office equipment	10,000	80,000
Total assets		$170,000

Liabilities

Current liabilities:		
Notes payable	$ 50,000	
Accounts payable	7,000	
Dividends payable	2,000	
Income taxes payable	5,000	$ 64,000

Owners' Equity

Common stock	$100,000	
Retained earnings	6,000	106,000
Total liabilities and owners' equity		$170,000

XYZ COMPANY

Statement of Retained Earnings

For the Year Ended December 31, 19_1

Retained earnings, January 1, 19_1	—
Net income for the year	$8,000
Total	$8,000
Less: Dividends	2,000
Retained earnings, December 31, 19_1	$6,000

1. *a.* Debit each of the accounts that appears in the Credit column of the Income Statement section of the work sheet by an amount equal to the balance shown in the work sheet.
   b. Credit each of the accounts that appears in the Debit column of the Income Statement section of the work sheet by an amount equal to the balance shown in the work sheet.
   c. Credit (or debit) the net income (or net loss) to an account called Income Summary. Verify that this item balances the compound entry.
2. If you are closing the books of a corporation, close the Income Summary account to the Retained Earnings account.

As indicated by the alternatives in parentheses in step 1c, a net loss for the period is debited to the Income Summary account, rather than being credited as net income is.

Exhibit 6-9 shows the closing entries made in the journal of the XYZ Company at the end of 19_1. Note that the balance of the Income Summary account, just before it is closed, equals the net income ($8,000) shown on the work sheet and the income statement. The closing of this account has the effect of transferring the net income for the year into the Retained Earnings account. Similarly, the closing of the Dividends account has the effect of deducting the dividends from the retained earnings.

Exhibit 6-10 shows the ledger accounts of the XYZ Company after the closing entries have been posted to the ledger. For simplicity of illustration, the accounts are shown in the simplified T-form used earlier in this chapter. In the illustration, the compound journal entry used to close the revenue and expense accounts to the Income Summary account is called transaction A. This single compound journal entry accomplishes the same thing as a series of separate entries, each closing one

Exhibit 6-9 **Closing entries in the XYZ Company journal at the end of 19_1**

Dec.	**31**	**Sales**		**68,000**	
		Salesmen's Salaries			**30,000**
		Rent Expense			**20,000**
		Utilities Expense			**5,000**
		Income Tax Expense			**5,000**
		Income Summary			8,000
		To close the revenue and expense accounts to Income Summary.			
	31	Income Summary		8,000	
		Retained Earnings			**8,000**
		To close the Income Summary account to Retained Earnings.			
	31	**Retained Earnings**		**2,000**	
		Dividends			**2,000**
		To close the Dividends account to Retained Earnings.			

Exhibit 6-10 Ledger accounts of the XYZ Company after closing entries

Cash

(1)	100,000	(2)	70,000
(5)	50,000	(4)	8,000
(6)	60,000	(9)	30,000
(8)	6,000	(10)	20,000

Accounts Receivable: Buyer Company

(7)	8,000	(8)	6,000

Land

(2)	20,000		

Building

(2)	50,000		

Office Equipment

(3)	10,000		

Notes Payable

		(5)	50,000

Accounts Payable: Supplier Company

(4)	8,000	(3)	10,000

Accounts Payable: Utilities Company

		(11)	5,000

Dividends Payable

		(13)	2,000

Income Taxes Payable

		(12)	5,000

Dividends

(13)	2,000	(C)	2,000

Common Stock

		(1)	100,000

Retained Earnings

(C)	2,000	(B)	8,000

Sale of Services

(A)	68,000	(6)	60,000
		(7)	8,000
	68,000		68,000

Salesmen's Salaries

(9)	30,000	(A)	30,000

Rent Expense

(10)	20,000	(A)	20,000

Utilities Expense

(11)	5,000	(A)	5,000

Income Tax Expense

(12)	5,000	(A)	5,000

Income Summary

(B)	8,000	(A)	8,000

account to Income Summary. The journal entry that closes the Income Summary account to Retained Earnings is called transaction B; the final entry that closes the Dividends account to Retained Earnings is called transaction C. Exhibit 6-11 gives a graphic presentation of the closing process.

THE POST-CLOSING TRIAL BALANCE

After the closing entries have been journalized and posted to the ledger, the revenue, expense, and Dividends accounts have zero balances. The only accounts in the ledger that show debit or credit balances after the closing process are the asset, liability, and permanent owners' equity accounts.

Because additional postings have been made to the ledger in the closing process, it is a good idea to take another trial balance (a ***post-closing trial balance***) to make sure that the balance between debits and credits in the ledger has not been disturbed by some error in the posting. Exhibit 6-12 shows the post-closing trial balance for the XYZ Company.

RULING ACCOUNTS

The ledger is now almost ready for the beginning of a new accounting cycle. The only step that remains is to prepare the accounts for a fresh start on the new year. This process is called ***ruling*** the accounts.

Exhibit 6-11
The closing process in a graphic representation

Exhibit 6-12
Post-closing trial balance for the XYZ Company ledger

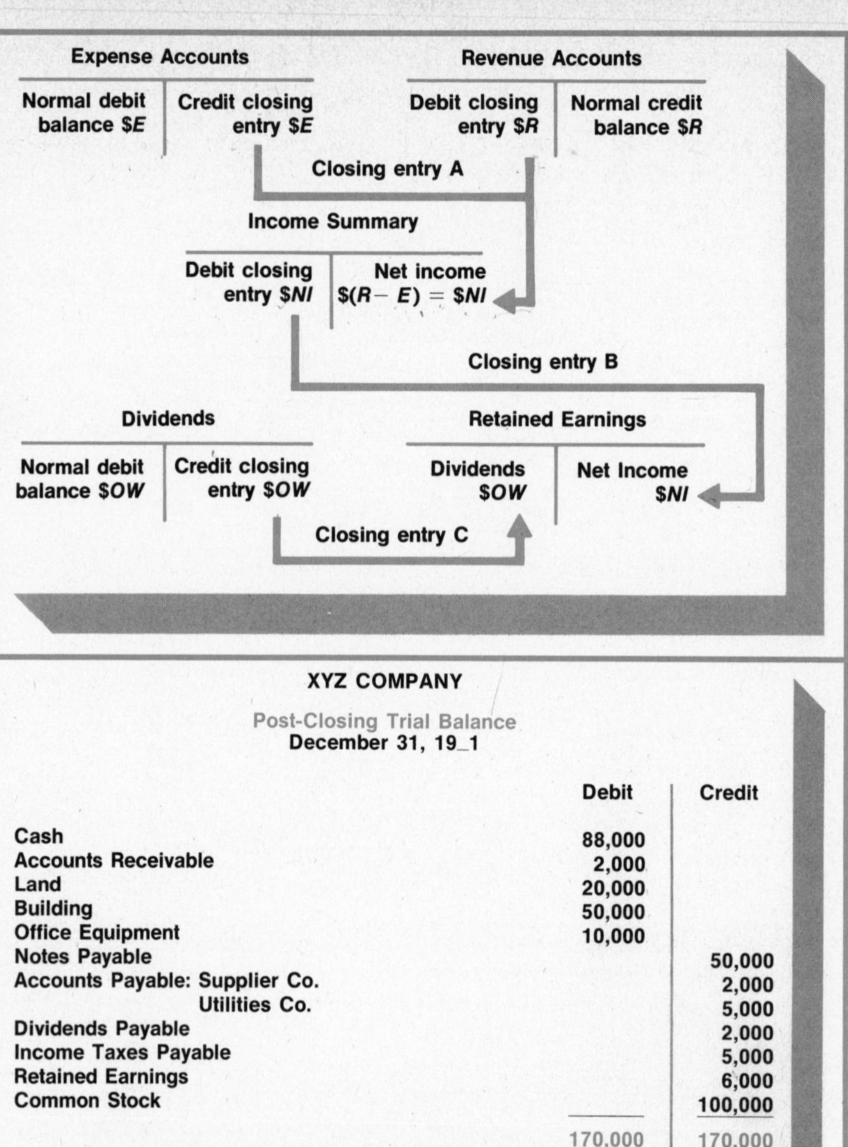

XYZ COMPANY
Post-Closing Trial Balance
December 31, 19_1

	Debit	Credit
Cash	88,000	
Accounts Receivable	2,000	
Land	20,000	
Building	50,000	
Office Equipment	10,000	
Notes Payable		50,000
Accounts Payable: Supplier Co.		2,000
Utilities Co.		5,000
Dividends Payable		2,000
Income Taxes Payable		5,000
Retained Earnings		6,000
Common Stock		100,000
	170,000	170,000

Exhibit 6-13 shows two of the XYZ Company ledger accounts after ruling. When the Cash account was footed (in the process of getting ready for the first trial balance), the debit balance of $88,000 was noted in the margin of the account (see Exhibit 5-21). In the process of ruling, the balance is entered in the *credit* money column, and the column is footed again to show that this does balance the account. A double line is drawn across all columns except the Explanation columns. The account balance is then entered in the *debit* side of the account as the beginning balance for the new year. A check mark (√) is placed in the reference columns of the balance entries to show that these entries are not posted from a journal. An explanation is written for each balance entry.

In the case of the Rent Expense account, there is only one entry on each side of the page, so no footing is needed. The account has no balance, so all that is done in ruling is to draw the double lines.

Chart of accounts

As we have seen, each of the ledger accounts is kept on a separate page in the ledger. The accounts are usually arranged in the order in which they appear on the financial statements. First, asset, liability, and permanent owners' equity accounts appear in the order of their listing on the statement of financial position. Then revenue and expense accounts appear in the order of their listing on the income statement.

The account-numbering system is designed as a code that indicates classifications and relationships of accounts. For example, each account might be given a four-digit number. In the system used by the XYZ Company accountants, the first digit of the account number indicates the major classification of the account:

1___ asset accounts,
2___ liability accounts,
3___ owners' equity accounts,
4___ revenue accounts,
5___ expense accounts.

The second digit is used to indicate the subclassification of the account. For example, current asset accounts are numbered 11__; investment accounts are numbered 12__; plant, property, and equipment accounts are numbered 13__; and so

Exhibit 6-13 Two ledger accounts after ruling

Cash — Account No. 1101

Date		Explanation	Ref.	Debit	Date		Explanation	Ref.	Credit
19_1					19_1				
Jan.	5		J1	100,000	Jan.	31		J1	70,000
July	15		J1	50,000	Apr.	17		J1	8,000
	15		J1	60,000	Dec.	31		J1	30,000
Sep.	15		J1	6,000		31		J1	20,000
							Balance	✓	88,000
				216,000					216,000
19_2									
Jan.	1	Balance	✓	88,000					

on. The third and fourth digits refer to the order in which the accounts of a particular subclassification appear on the financial statements. For example, the account that appears first on the balance sheet—Cash, a current assets account—is account number 1101.

For easy reference to the contents of the ledger, an index or ***chart of accounts*** usually is kept in the front of the ledger. Exhibit 6-14 shows the chart of accounts for the XYZ Company ledger.

Single proprietorships and partnerships

In this chapter we have concentrated on accounting for a corporation. The corporation is the dominant type of business organization today and must be given considerable attention. Your advanced accounting courses will concentrate primarily upon accounting for the corporation. Nevertheless, we must not ignore other forms of business enterprises, such as the single (or sole) proprietorship or the partnership.

Fortunately, the accounting principles and procedures developed for corporations apply to other forms of business enterprises as well. If we modify several transactions illustrated in this chapter for the corporation, we can learn quickly how to account for the single proprietorship and the partnership.

In our first illustration, stockholders acquired $100,000 of stock in the corporation. If we assume that an owner invested $100,000 in a single proprietorship, the entry to record the investment would be the following.

Jan. 5	Cash	100,000	
	John Smith, Capital		100,000

Exhibit 6-14
Chart of accounts for the XYZ Company

Account Number	Account Name
1101	Cash
1102	Accounts Receivable
1303	Land
1304	Building
1305	Office Equipment
2106	Notes Payable
2107	Accounts Payable
2108	Dividends Payable
2109	Taxes Payable
3010	Common Stock
3011	Retained Earnings
3012	Dividends
4001	Sale of Services
5002	Salesmen's Salaries
5003	Rent Expense
5004	Utilities Expense
5005	Income Tax Expense
6000	Income Summary

The John Smith, Capital account is an owner's equity account. It replaces the Common Stock account of a corporation. It is used to record investments by the owner. In transaction 13, the corporation declared $2,000 dividends, which represented a distribution of the corporation's earnings to its stockholders. If we now assume that the owner of the single proprietorship withdrew $2,000 from the business, we would record the reduction in owner's equity in a temporary owner's equity account called John Smith, Drawings.

Dec. 31	John Smith, Drawings	2,000	
	Cash		2,000

When the closing entries for a single proprietorship are made, the Income Summary account is closed to the Drawings account (instead of to the Retained Earnings account that is used for a corporation).

Dec. 31	Income Summary	8,000	
	John Smith, Drawings		8,000

Finally, the Drawings account (a temporary capital account) is closed to the permanent Capital account. In our illustration, the Drawings account has a credit balance of $6,000, so it is closed as follows:

Dec. 31	John Smith, Drawings	6,000	
	John Smith, Capital		6,000

All of the other entries illustrated in this chapter would be made in the same form for any business organization.

If we were accounting for a partnership instead of a single proprietorship, we would have two or more Capital accounts and two or more Drawing accounts. Each partner has a Capital account and a Drawings account to record his dealings with the partnership. The sole proprietorship and the partnership forms of business organization are discussed more fully in a later chapter.

Locating errors

The trial balance is a working document, used by the accountant to make sure that he has not made any mathematical errors in recording ledger entries or in footing and balancing the accounts. If the trial balance does not show a balance between debits and credits, some error does exist in his work. In such a case, the accountant will probably use a procedure such as the following to find the error(s):

1. Refoot the trial balance (error in adding up figures on the trial balance?).
2. Compare the balances listed in the trial balance with those written in the ledger when accounts were balanced (error in transferring balances to the trial balance?).
3. Refoot and balance the ledger accounts (error in adding up entries in accounts or in computing account balances?).

4. Compare the ledger entries with the journal entries (error in transferring entries from journal to ledger?).
5. Make sure that each journal entry results in equal debit and credit entries in the ledger (error in deciding how to post transactions as debits or credits?).

Any error(s) leading to imbalance in the trial balance should be located by this procedure. Note that the trial balance only checks on the equality of debits and credits in the ledger accounts. The trial balance will not reveal any errors made by entering transactions in the wrong accounts.

Summary

The accounting cycle is a sequence of activities that begins with the recording of events and ends with the presentation of summary information in the formal financial statements. For the accountant, the accounting cycle involves the following procedures.

1. Journalize the economic events that affect the business in chronological order in a book of original entry called the journal. Analyze and record the transactions using double-entry procedures.
2. Post the transactions from the journal to the ledger.
3. At the close of the accounting period, prepare a trial balance of the ledger accounts to test the equality of debits and credits and to begin the preparation of the work sheet.
4. Adjust the books. (This process is discussed in Chapter 7.)
5. Prepare a work sheet to help in preparation of the financial statements and in making the closing entries.
6. Prepare the financial statements from the work sheet.
7. Close the books by making journal entries based on information in the Income Statement columns of the work sheet. Post the closing entries to the ledger. Rule the accounts to prepare for the beginning of the next cycle.
8. Prepare a post-closing trial balance.

Exhibit 6-15 visualizes the accounting cycle in terms of these steps.

In reviewing the accounting procedures described in Chapters 5 and 6, note how they embody the major accounting concepts discussed in earlier chapters. The accounting cycle involves procedures consistent with the four accounting assumptions discussed in Chapter 3: the assumptions of a business entity, a going concern, dollar measurement, and periodic and timely reporting.

Accumulation of data is a major function of the accounting cycle. First, data about all events affecting the firm are accumulated and journalized in chronological order. Then, in the process of posting, the data are accumulated into accounts that group data of similar nature. The process of balancing tests the accumulation of data into the two categories of debits and credits. The adjusting and closing entries accumulate further data about the firm's economic condition and activities.

Measurement is also involved in the accounting cycle. The guides or rules that govern the cycle include the initial recording principle, the realization principle, the concept of matching revenue against expenses, and the three expense recognition principles. The system measures economic events as it journalizes them and as it properly classifies them into accounts. The adjustment procedure discussed in Chapter 6 also involves measurement.

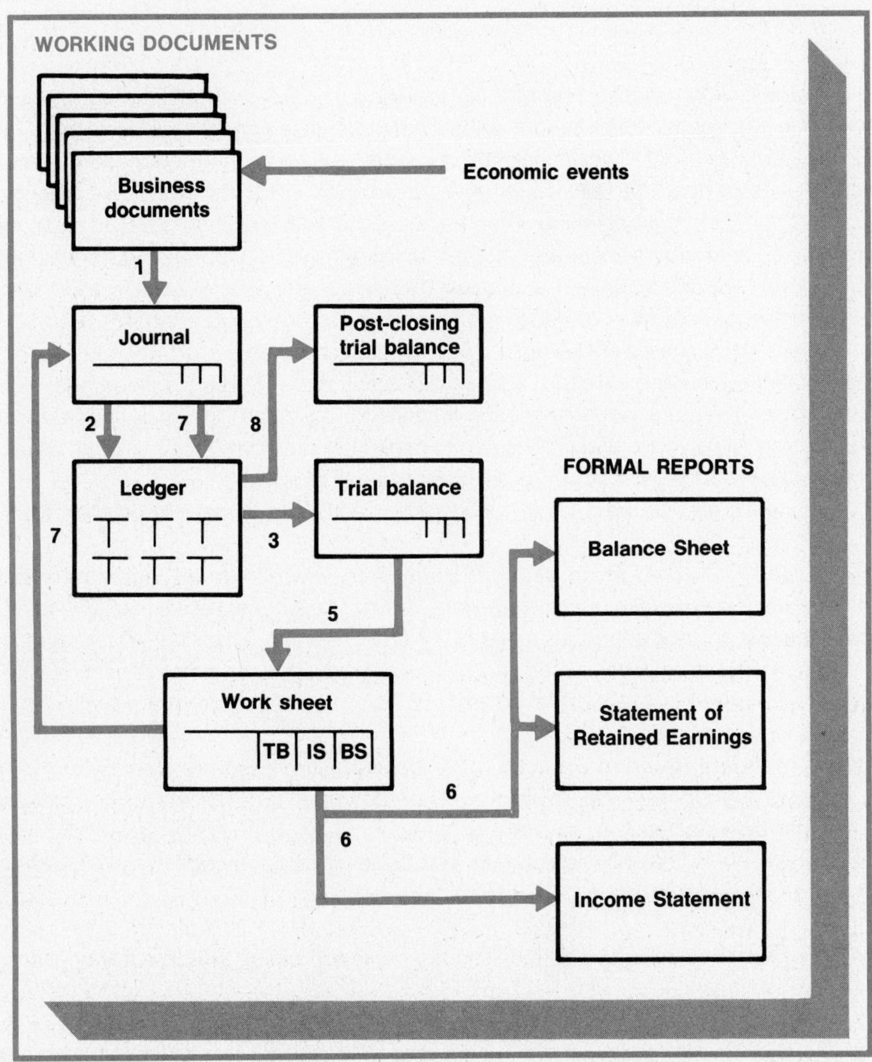

Exhibit 6-15
A visualization of the accounting cycle

Communication is the function that ultimately justifies the existence of the accounting system, and this function is carried out mainly through the preparation and release of the financial statements. However, in order to properly communicate information about economic events, the entire accounting cycle must be governed by such guides as full disclosure, materiality, consistency, conservatism, and fairness.

Chapter 5 omits one very important step in the accounting cycle. The process of adjusting the accounts in order to properly match revenue against expenses is discussed in Chapter 6.

Appendix

DOUBLE-ENTRY SYSTEM OF RECORDING

Each event or transaction recorded by the accounting system must affect at least two ledger accounts. Every journal entry involves at least one debit to some account and at least one credit to some other account. As mentioned in Chapter 1, this double-entry system of bookkeeping was developed in Italy with the rise of commercial activity at the beginning of the Renaissance. Although books based on some form of double-entry system are known from as early as 1340, the system was not fully developed and explained until about 150 years later. Luca Pacioli set forth the first complete discussion of debits and credits in his book published in 1494.

In this chapter, we listed simple rules for deciding whether an account should be debited or credited to record a particular event. Here we restate those rules in a more theoretical form and discuss the reasons for the rules. You may find that this discussion helps you to understand and to remember the rules. If not, you can simply memorize the rules in the form given earlier in the chapter.

First, let us restate the rules for debits and credits in a somewhat different form.

1. ***A debit is entered in an account if the entry represents an increase in net assets or a decrease in owners' equity.*** An increase in net assets may be caused either by an increase in an asset or by a decrease in a liability. A decrease in owners' equity may be caused by a decrease in revenue, an increase in expenses, or a decrease in the owners' investment (usually in the form of a withdrawal or dividend distribution).
2. ***A credit is entered in an account if the entry represents a decrease in net assets or an increase in owners' equity.*** A decrease in net assets may be caused either by a decrease in an asset or by an increase in a liability. An increase in owners' equity may be caused by an increase in revenue, a decrease in expenses, or an increase in the owners' investment.

These rules for debiting and crediting accounts are based on three assumptions:

1. the basic accounting model, $A - L = OE$, or $NA = OE$;
2. the total credits entered in the system shall always equal the total debits entered in the system;

3. an increase in owners' equity shall be recorded as a credit, while an increase in net assets shall be recorded as a debit.

Notice that each transaction will result in entries in two accounts in the system. If the transaction causes an increase in owners' equity, there will be a credit entry in an owners' equity account and a debit entry in a net assets account. If the transaction causes a decrease in owners' equity, there will be a debit entry in an owners' equity account and a credit entry in a net assets account. In either case, the total credits in the system will remain equal to the total debits in the system (assumption 2).

So far, things are fairly simple. Now they get more complicated. In fact, the ledger contains two classifications of accounts that represent net assets: asset accounts and liability accounts. Remember that $NA = A - L$. From this equation we know that an increase in assets causes an increase in net assets, while a decrease in assets causes a decrease in net assets. Therefore, the rules for an asset account are the same as those for net assets: ***an increase in an asset is recorded as a debit,*** while ***a decrease in an asset is recorded as a credit.***

On the other hand, an increase in liabilities causes a decrease in net assets, while a decrease in liabilities causes an increase in net assets. So the rules for a liability account are the opposite of those for net assets: ***an increase in a liability is recorded as a credit,*** while ***a decrease in a liability is recorded as a debit.***

Things get even more complicated on the owners' equity side of the equation. From Chapter 4, recall that changes in owners' equity are caused by revenue, expenses, and owners' withdrawals or additional investments during the period:

$$OE_e - OE_b = \Delta OE = NI + (OI - OW) = (R - E) + (OI - OW).$$

From this equation we see that an increase in revenue causes an increase in owners' equity. Therefore, ***an increase in revenue is recorded as a credit,*** while ***a decrease in revenue is recorded as a debit.*** However, an increase in expenses causes a decrease in owners' equity. Therefore, the rule for expense accounts is reversed: ***an increase in expenses is recorded as a debit,*** while ***a decrease in expenses is recorded as a credit.***

Total debits = Total credits

$$\underset{\begin{pmatrix}+\ \text{debit}\\-\ \text{credit}\end{pmatrix}}{\Delta NA} = \underset{\begin{pmatrix}+\ \text{credit}\\-\ \text{debit}\end{pmatrix}}{\Delta OE}$$

$$\underset{\begin{pmatrix}+\ \text{debit}\\-\ \text{credit}\end{pmatrix}}{\Delta A} - \underset{\begin{pmatrix}+\ \text{credit}\\-\ \text{debit}\end{pmatrix}}{\Delta L} = \underset{\begin{pmatrix}+\ \text{credit}\\-\ \text{debit}\end{pmatrix}}{R} - \underset{\begin{pmatrix}+\ \text{debit}\\-\ \text{credit}\end{pmatrix}}{E} + \underset{\begin{pmatrix}+\ \text{credit}\\-\ \text{debit}\end{pmatrix}}{OI} - \underset{\begin{pmatrix}+\ \text{debit}\\-\ \text{credit}\end{pmatrix}}{OW}$$

Exhibit 6-16
Debits and credits for basic accounting categories

An increase in owners' investments during the period causes an increase in owners' equity. Therefore, ***an increase in an account representing owners' investment or capital is recorded as a credit,*** while ***a decrease in owners' investment is recorded as a debit.*** However, an increase in owners' withdrawals causes a decrease in owners' equity. Therefore, ***an increase in an account representing owners' withdrawals (or dividend distributions) is recorded as a debit,*** while ***a decrease in owners' withdrawals or dividends is recorded as a credit.***

At first, all of this probably seems confusing. However, once you understand the three basic assumptions, you should be able to work out all the special rules and see how they follow from the assumptions. Exhibit 6-16 summarizes the rules in a form that may prove helpful.

Questions

1. List the steps in the accounting cycle.

2. Review the accounting cycle:

a. What is a journal?
b. What is journalization?
c. What is a ledger?
d. What is posting?
e. What is an account?
f. Describe the steps involved in analyzing a transaction for double-entry accounting.
g. What is a work sheet? Describe its use.
h. What are closing entries? Describe the process by which closing entries can be made directly from the work sheet.
i. What is a trial balance? a post-closing trial balance?
j. Describe the process of ruling ledger accounts.
k. What is a chart of accounts?

3. What is meant by double-entry accounting? Explain the relationship between double-entry accounting and the basic accounting model or equation.

4. Suppose that you prepare a trial balance and find that the totals of debits and credits do not balance. What might be the cause(s) of this situation? What steps would you take to locate the problem?

5. After the books have been closed, which accounts should show no balance? Which accounts may show a balance?

Exercises

E6-1 Journalize the following transactions of the Tucker Company, for the month of April, 19_1.

April	1	Common stock of the Tucker Company was issued for $200,000.
	4	A $75,000 office building was purchased for $30,000 cash; a note was signed for $45,000 to complete the purchase.
	7	The company paid $2,400 for advertising in the local newspaper. (The ledger contains an account called Advertising Expenses.)

April 9 The company disbursed $100 in cash to pay miscellaneous expenses. (The ledger contains an account called Miscellaneous Expenses.)
16 The company paid wages of $1,200 for the first two weeks of August.
16 The company rendered a service for John Jones, a client, and billed him for $6,500.
21 The company received a $2,500 check from Jones for services rendered on April 16.
30 The company received a bill from the Gas Company for April in the amount of $275.
30 The company paid wages of $1,200 for the second two weeks of April.

E6-2 Journalize the December 19_1 transactions of the Watson Company from the following notes.

December 1 Received $12,000 cash for services rendered today.
5 Paid office rent for December, $750.
5 Purchased land for $6,250 cash. (Land is to be held for speculative purposes.)
6 Paid traveling expenses incurred by salesmen, $875.
15 Paid salaries for first half of December, $6,200.
21 Paid repair expenses, $15.
27 Purchased $4,400 office equipment on account from Typewriter City.
31 Paid dividend of $1,000 to stockholders. (The dividend was declared in November, and the liability was recorded at that time.)
31 Paid $2,900 to Typewriter City on account.

E6-3 The Bermor Company was organized on July 1, 19_1. The company was involved in the following transactions during July. Journalize these transactions for the company in chronological order.

On July 1, the company issued common stock for $30,000 cash.

On July 3, the company rendered a service for a client and collected a $900 cash payment for a service.

On July 5, the company rendered a service for the Little Company and sent a bill for $1,200 for the service. The Little Company made a partial payment of $700 on July 12.

On July 7, the company purchased $500 of office supplies on account from the Jaxx Company. The Bermor Company sent a check for $400 in partial payment on this purchase on July 17. (Use an asset account called Office Supplies.)

On July 20, the directors declared a $1,200 dividend to stockholders. The dividend was paid on July 31.

On July 30, the company purchased office equipment for $1,700 in cash.

On July 11, the company paid $1,100 in salaries to its employees.

On July 2, the company paid $600 for the use of office facilities that it rented during the month.

On July 13, the company borrowed $2,000. The company signed a non-interest-bearing note agreeing to repay the loan in one month.

E6-4 After closing of the books at the end of September, 19_6, the general ledger of the Sallee Company shows the following account balances at the start of business on October 1, 19_6.

Cash	$ 40,000
Accounts Receivable: Benji Company	48,000
Land	150,000

Office Equipment	$ 6,400
Accounts Payable: Office Supplies Co.	1,100
Accounts Payable: Jamie Company	10,200
Common Stock	90,000
Retained Earnings	75,000

Required:

a. Set up general ledger accounts for the Sallee Company in the T-form and enter the balances for October 1, 19_6.

During October 19_6, the Sallee Company is involved in the following transactions.

Oct.	1	Paid $400 for October rent.
	2	Collected $27,000 from the Benji Company for services rendered and billed on account in September 19_6.
	5	Paid $1,200 to the Office Supplies Company for office supplies purchased on account in September 19_6.
	7	Paid $6,000 to the Dex Company on account.
	8	Purchased office supplies for $900 cash.
	9	Rendered services to Patsie Company for $13,500 on account.
	16	Rendered services to Jamie Company for $25,000 cash.
	20	Collected $8,500 on account from Patsie Company for services rendered on October 9.
	21	Purchased an office desk on account from the Office Supplies Company, $475.
	23	Paid $200 cash for advertising in the local newspaper.
	29	Paid October salaries of employees, $6,500.
	30	Purchased marketable securities for $3,500 cash.

b. Journalize the October transactions. Create new accounts as needed. Assign page numbers to your journal and ledger accounts.

c. Post the journal entries to the ledger accounts.

d. Prepare a trial balance as of October 31, 19_6.

E6-5 The following list shows the balance of the ledger accounts for the Unit Company at the close of business on December 31, 19_1. Prepare a six-column work sheet using this information.

Cash	$ 15,000
Marketable Securities	17,000
Accounts Receivable	31,000
Allowance for Doubtful Receivables	7,000
Prepaid Insurance	2,000
Land	98,000
Building	505,000
Accumulated Depreciation: Building	110,000
Notes Payable	8,000
Accounts Payable	9,000
Common Stock	91,000
Retained Earnings, December 31, 19_0	399,000
Sale of Services	350,000
Salaries Expense	102,000
Utilities Expense	47,000
Insurance Expense	87,000
Advertising Expense	41,000
Miscellaneous Expense	29,000

E6-6 From the work sheet prepared for Exercise E6-5, prepare an income statement and a statement of financial position for the Unit Company.

E6-7 From the work sheet prepared for Exercise E6-5, journalize the closing entries for the Unit Company.

E6-8 The Arrow Company uses the following ledger accounts.

Account Number	Account Name
1	Cash
2	Accounts Receivable
3	Land
4	Office Equipment
5	Accounts Payable
6	Notes Payable
7	Common Stock
8	Retained Earnings
9	Sale of Services
10	Rent Expense
11	Salaries Expense
12	Power Expense

Required: For each of the following transactions, indicate the numbers of the account to be debited and the account to be credited. List only the ***account numbers,*** not the amounts of the debits and credits.

x. *Example:* Sold common stock for $10,000 cash. ***Answer:*** Debit account 1; credit account 7.

a. Land costing $42,000 is purchased for $11,000 cash, and a note is signed for the balance.

b. Services are sold on account for $300 to the Fox Company.

c. A utility bill is received for electricity used during this month; the bill will be paid next month.

d. Fox Company pays for the services received in transaction b.

e. Employees are paid their monthly salaries.

f. Rent expense is paid.

g. Office equipment is purchased on account.

E6-9 The following list shows selected account balances from the ledger of the Foto Company at the close of business on December 31, 19_6. Journalize the entries needed to close the books.

Sale of Services	$575,000
Utility Expense	70,000
Insurance Expense	65,000
Retained Earnings	117,000
Dividends	140,000

E6-10 Selected ledger account balances of the Moto Company at the close of business on December 31, 19_6, are shown in the following list. Journalize the entries needed to close the books.

Sale of Services	$210,000
Salaries Expense	115,000
Advertising Expense	48,000
Miscellaneous Expenses	17,000

E6-11 From the trial balance shown in Exhibit 6-17,

a. prepare the post-closing trial balance;

b. prepare a statement of retained earnings.

Unfortunately, the accountant omitted one figure in the credit column of his trial balance. You will have to compute the balance of the Retained Earnings account.

E6-12 Exhibit 6-18 shows a trial balance. Using this trial balance, journalize the entries needed to close the books.

E6-13 Give an explanation for the transaction recorded by each of the following journal entries.

	Account	Debit	Credit
a.	Cash	150,000	
	Common Stock		150,000
b.	Accounts Receivable: A Co.	145,000	
	Sale of Services		145,000
c.	Rent Expense	60,000	
	Cash		60,000
d.	Cash	90,000	
	Sale of Services		90,000
e.	Cash	85,000	
	Accounts Receivable: A Co.		85,000
f.	Office Equipment	7,000	
	Accounts Payable: Office Co.		7,000
g.	Cash	85,000	
	Notes Payable		85,000
h.	Land	200,000	
	Cash		75,000
	Notes Payable: Land		125,000
i.	Notes Payable: Land	125,000	
	Cash		125,000
j.	Inventory	60,000	
	Accounts Payable: B Co.		60,000
k.	Accounts Payable: B Co.	40,000	
	Cash		40,000
l.	Dividends	35,000	
	Dividends Payable		35,000
m.	Dividends Payable	35,000	
	Cash		35,000
n.	Sale of Services	100,000	
	Rent Expense		60,000
	Income Summary		40,000
o.	Income Summary	40,000	
	Retained Earnings		40,000
p.	Retained Earnings	35,000	
	Dividends		35,000

Problems

P6-1 The following set of notes describes the transactions of the Big Dealer Company during December 19_6.

The Big Dealer Company was organized on December 1, 19_6. On this date, common stock was sold for $400,000.

On December 3, the company purchased land for $150,000 cash.

On December 4, the company paid $6,000 for advertising done in December.

On December 6, the company purchased $65,000 of office equipment. It paid $30,000 cash and signed a 60-day, non-interest-bearing note for the balance.

On December 9, the company rendered services to the Cardo Company, a client, and received a cash payment of $70,000.

On December 14, the company paid $40,000 salaries to its salesmen.

On December 17, the company rendered further services to the Cardo Company and billed them for $85,000.

Exhibit 6-17
Trial balance for Exercise E6-11

BELL COMPANY
Trial Balance
December 31, 19_6

Cash	92,000	
Accounts Receivable	41,000	
Equipment	37,000	
Accumulated Depreciation		18,000
Accounts Payable		21,000
Notes Payable		27,000
Common Stock		45,000
Retained Earnings, December 31, 19_5		?
Dividends	8,000	
Sale of Services		90,000
Salaries Expense	17,000	
Rent Expense	9,000	
Depreciation Expense	6,000	
	210,000	210,000

Exhibit 6-18
Trial balance for Exercise E6-12

BIG SKY COMPANY
Trial Balance
December 31, 19_1

Cash	127,000	
Merchandise Inventory	113,000	
Land	272,000	
Factory Building	410,000	
Accounts Payable		220,000
Common Stock		400,000
Retained Earnings		240,000
Dividends	78,000	
Sale of Services		550,000
Rent Expense	140,000	
Salaries Expense	270,000	
	1,410,000	1,410,000

On December 29, the company received a bill from the Gas Company for utilities used in December. The bill for $4,500 was not paid during December.
On December 29, the company collected $70,000 from the Cardo Company in payment on the services rendered December 17.
On December 30, the board of directors of the company declared dividends in the amount of $15,000, payable in January 19_7.
On December 31, the income tax expense for 19_6 was computed to be $50,000.

Required:

a. Journalize the transactions in a general journal.
b. Prepare a general ledger and post the journal entries to the ledger.
c. Prepare a trial balance from the general ledger.
d. Prepare a work sheet.
e. Prepare an income statement.
f. Prepare a statement of financial position.
g. Prepare a statement of retained earnings.
h. Prepare closing entries and journalize them.
i. Post the closing entries; rule the accounts.
j. Prepare a post-closing trial balance.

P6-2 For each of the transactions journalized in Problem P6-1, indicate the impact, if any, of the transaction in terms of increases and decreases on asset, liability, and permanent owners' equity accounts. Use a table like the following, indicating increases or decreases by + or − for each of the categories of accounts. If there is no increase or decrease for a category, put a zero in the column.

Transaction	Assets =	Liabilities +	Owners' Equity
Dec. 1	+	0	+

P6-3 Journalize the following 19_1 transactions of the Golden Company.

August	1	Issued $350,000 common stock for cash.
	2	A building costing $70,000 purchased for cash.
	4	100 shares of stock in Texas Oil Company purchased for $12,000 cash, to be held as a long-term investment.
	9	Equipment acquired for $7,000 cash and a $23,000 non-interest-bearing note.
	17	Borrowed $20,000 from the Western Bank.
	20	Performed a service for the Goods Company, a client, and billed the Goods Company for $60,000.
	21	Received $25,000 from the Western Lumber Company in partial payment of its account.
	30	Paid the monthly salaries in the amount of $11,000.
	31	Paid the monthly utilities in the amount of $6,000.
	31	Paid the note given on August 9 in partial payment for the land.

P6-4 Exhibit 6-19 shows in simplified T-form the ledger accounts of the Gordon Company as of the close of business on May 31, 19_6. You are the company accountant, and you have just gotten an urgent message from the company president, asking to have interim financial statements for January ready for a meeting of the board of directors tomorrow. She also mentions that one of the directors has been very critical of the company's performance lately, and has been asking for more detailed information about the company's activities. So,

Exhibit 6-19 **Ledger accounts of the Gordon Company for Problem P6-4**

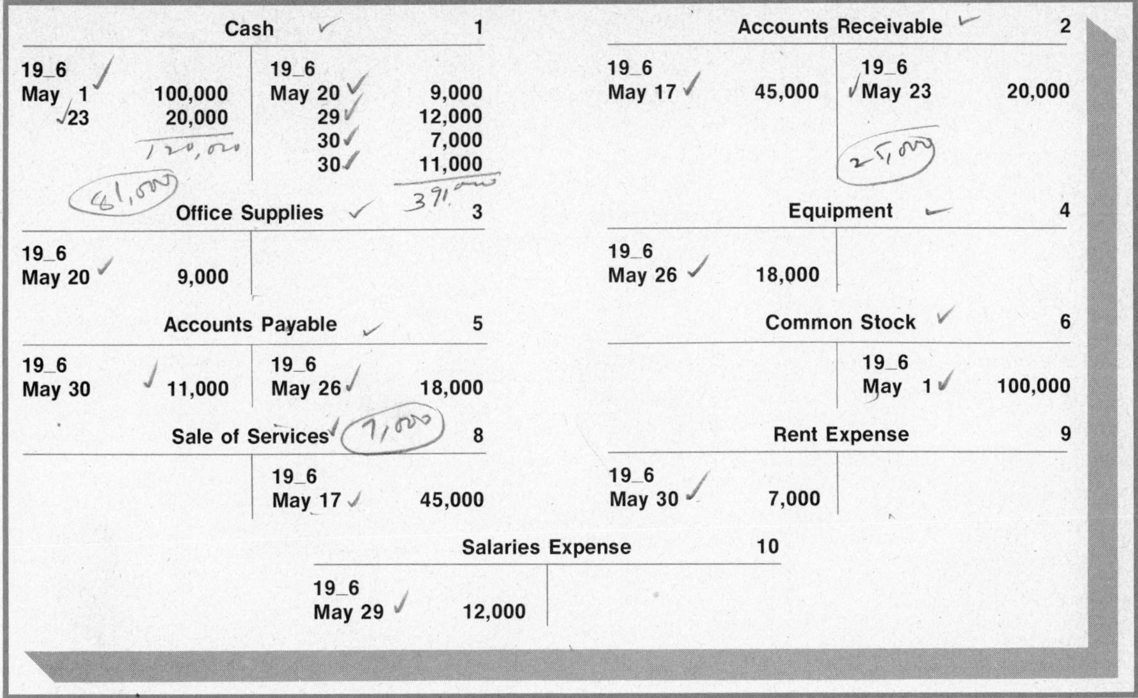

Cash — 1

19_6		19_6	
May 1	100,000	May 20	9,000
23	20,000	29	12,000
		30	7,000
		30	11,000

Accounts Receivable — 2

19_6		19_6	
May 17	45,000	May 23	20,000

Office Supplies — 3

19_6			
May 20	9,000		

Equipment — 4

19_6			
May 26	18,000		

Accounts Payable — 5

19_6		19_6	
May 30	11,000	May 26	18,000

Common Stock — 6

		19_6	
		May 1	100,000

Sale of Services — 8

		19_6	
		May 17	45,000

Rent Expense — 9

19_6			
May 30	7,000		

Salaries Expense — 10

19_6			
May 29	12,000		

the president asks you to bring your accounting books to the meeting and be prepared to answer questions in detail about the statements.

a. To your horror, you discover that the general journal for May has somehow disappeared. Reconstruct the journal entries from the information in the ledger.

b. Prepare a trial balance.

c. Prepare a statement of financial position in account form, as of May 31, 19_6.

d. Prepare an income statement in the single-step form for the month of May.

e. Close the books. (Show your closing entries in the journal only.)

f. Prepare a post-closing trial balance.

P6-5 Reconstruct the journal entries that are reflected in the following general ledger accounts.

Cash

50,000	15,000
20,000	6,000
7,000	13,000

Sales

	80,000

Accounts Receivable

60,000	7,000

Rent Expense

10,000	

Accounts Payable	
13,000	45,000

Power Expense	
15,000	

Dividends Payable	
6,000	6,000

Miscellaneous Expense	
5,000	

Dividends	
6,000	

Salaries	
30,000	

Common Stock	
	50,000

Adjusting entries

Financial statements must go beyond a simple account of cash inflow and outflow if they are to give a fair picture of the financial situation of a firm. We have seen in Chapter 6 that the financial statements prepared at the end of an accounting cycle should contain the account balances of *all* asset, liability, owners' equity, revenue, and expense accounts. If any accounts were left out of the statements, the reports would not *fairly* present the financial position of the firm and the results of its operations.

However, it is not enough merely to include all the accounts. The accounts themselves must reflect accurately and completely the impact of economic events that affect the firm. If the information in the accounts is incomplete or incorrect, the statements will simply summarize that information. Such statements will be deficient and misleading. In most cases, the normal process of journalizing events from business documents does not result in fully accurate or complete accounts. The accountant usually must make adjusting entries at the end of the accounting period to bring the accounts up to date.

If the statements are to be fair and complete, they must meet certain standards. The income statement should reflect a proper matching of revenue and expenses for the period. The balance sheet should show a complete picture of the assets and liabilities of the firm, as of the date of the statement.

We can state these requirements more explicitly in terms of the principles discussed in Chapters 3 and 4.

1. The income statement must:
   a. include revenue earned during the period and exclude revenue associated with other periods; and
   b. include expenses representing costs that expire during the period and exclude unexpired costs that will benefit the future.

2. The balance sheet must:
   a. include all assets that are unexpired costs on the date of the statement and exclude all costs that have expired on or before that day; and
   b. include all liabilities that represent obligations to be met in future periods and exclude any obligations that have already been met on or before the statement date.

Adjusting entries are procedures designed to meet these standards by recording items that have not yet been entered in the system through the usual journalization of transactions, or by apportioning among accounting periods items that have already been recorded.

In the most general terms, the following three steps are involved in adjusting a ledger account.

1. Foot and balance the account to see what its present balance is.
2. Determine the balance that the account should show for a fair representation of the situation.
3. Make adjusting entries to bring the recorded balance into agreement with the correct balance.

It is obvious that the second and third steps can involve estimates and judgments by the accountant. Yet the process of adjusting the accounts is governed by definite principles and procedures that help to protect the user of the accounting system's output. He must be able to know that adjustments have been made fairly and consistently, so that the financial statements are a reliable guide to the financial information about a business.

The easiest way to understand the process of adjusting the accounts is to look at some typical examples of adjusting entries. Most of the problems that require adjustments of accounts fall into one of six categories: accrued expenses, prepaid expenses, depreciation expense, bad debt expense, accrued revenue, or revenue received in advance. In the following sections we look at examples of each of these problems and see how they are handled through adjusting entries.

The study of adjusting entries is one of the more challenging areas in accounting. One measure of a good accountant is his skill in using adjusting entries to make his accounts and statements give the most complete and accurate picture of the firm's economic condition and operations, no matter how difficult the problems facing him. Therefore, it is important to give considerable attention to this topic, and to master as thoroughly as possible the procedure of adjusting accounts.

Accruals

The verb ***to accrue*** means to increase, to grow, to accumulate. Certain expenses and revenue accrue during the accounting period but are not systematically journalized during the period through the procedures discussed in Chapter 5. Adjusting entries are needed to recognize these unrecorded increases ***(accruals)*** in revenue and expense accounts.

ACCRUED EXPENSES

An ***accrued expense*** is an expense incurred during the accounting period but not recognized in the accounts. Accrued expenses often include accrued salaries, interest, rent, taxes, and other expenses. In the case of an accrued expense, both an expense and a liability exist at the end of the accounting period without having been recorded in the books. The nature of the problem becomes clear when we look at some examples.

Transaction 1. The salesmen of the Circle Company are paid on the 15th of each month. When the annual statements are prepared as of December 31, 19_1, the salesmen's salaries account shows a balance of $30,000. This represents the amount earned by and paid to the salesmen up through December 15. However, the salesmen have earned an additional $1,000 of salaries from December 16 through December 31; they will receive this money in their January 15, 19_2, paychecks. This is an expense incurred in December 19_1 because the men have done their work and the company has promised to pay them. The expense should be matched with the revenue earned through the salesmen's work during December. The salaries expense and liability for salaries payable have not been journalized, however, because the accounting system normally records salaries at the time paychecks are issued.

When the Circle Company's accountant examines the salesmen's salaries account at the end of the period, he should notice that something is wrong. He sees that the salesmen have been paid for their work up through December 15, but not for their work in the last half of December [Exhibit 7-1(a)]. He knows that the salesmen are still working. A liability exists for the accrued salaries. He checks the appropriate liability account, accrued salaries payable, and finds no liability recorded there [Exhibit 7-1(a)].

Next he must find out the amount of the accrued expense. If possible, he will find out exactly what salaries the salesmen have earned in the last half of December. If that information is not available, he will make the best estimate he can from what he knows about past salaries and any changes in current work conditions or wages. In this case, we assume that he is able to find out that the salesmen have earned $1,000 during the second half of December.

The final step is to make an adjusting entry that will record the accrued expense

Exhibit 7-1 **Ledger accounts for transaction 1**

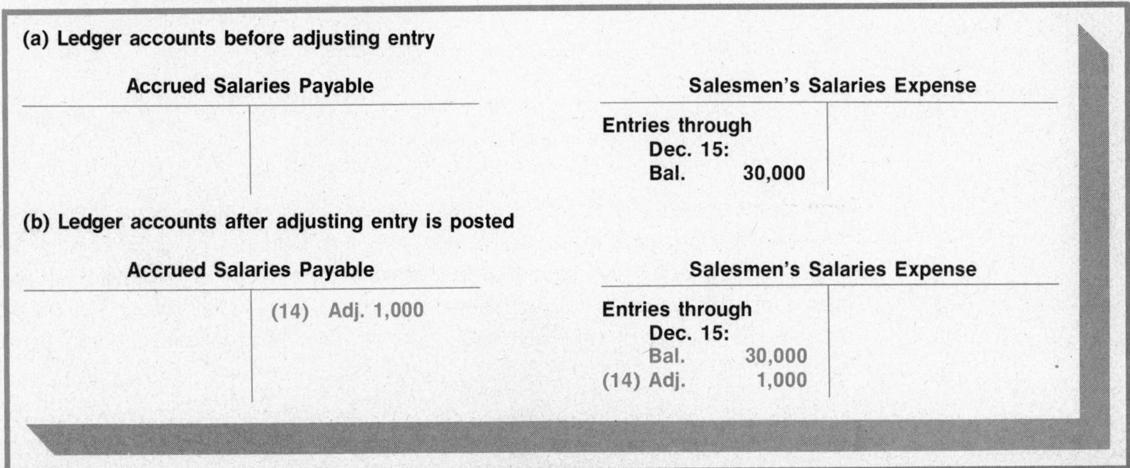

(a) Ledger accounts before adjusting entry

Accrued Salaries Payable	

Salesmen's Salaries Expense	
Entries through Dec. 15: Bal. 30,000	

(b) Ledger accounts after adjusting entry is posted

Accrued Salaries Payable	
	(14) Adj. 1,000

Salesmen's Salaries Expense	
Entries through Dec. 15: Bal. 30,000	
(14) Adj. 1,000	

(Salesmen's Salaries) and liability (Accrued Salaries Payable). The necessary adjusting entry is journalized as follows.

Dec. 31	Salesmen's Salaries Expense	1,000	
	Accrued Salaries Payable		1,000
	To record salaries earned Dec. 16 through Dec. 31		

Note that an adjusting entry for accrued expense requires a debit to an expense account and a credit to a liability account. Exhibit 7-1(b) shows the accounts after the adjusting entry is posted to the ledger.

On January 15, 19_2, the salesmen will be paid, and the liability will be removed. In this case, the salesmen earn an additional $1,000 during the first half of January, so on January 15 they are paid a total of $2,000. The following journal entry is made at that time.[1]

19_2			
Jan. 15	Salesmen's Salaries Expense	1,000	
	Accrued Salaries Payable	1,000	
	Cash		2,000
	To record payment of salaries payable (earned in Dec. 19_1) and salaries earned Jan. 1 through Jan. 15.		

This entry settles the accrued liability and properly records the January salary expense in the 19_2 period.

Transaction 2. On November 1, 19_1, the Circle Company borrows $12,000 from a bank. It signs a note, agreeing to repay the $12,000 to the bank in six months and to pay interest of 6 percent on the borrowed money. According to the terms of the note, the interest is to be paid at the time the loan is repaid. When the company's books are being closed on December 31, 19_1, the company has incurred an unrecorded liability because it has an obligation to pay interest for the two months (November and December) during which it has had the use of the bank's money. An interest expense has accrued. This expense should be recognized in 19_1 although it will not be paid until 19_2.

When the note was signed for the loan, the $12,000 obligation to repay the principal amount and the $12,000 cash inflow were journalized.

Nov. 1	Cash	12,000	
	Notes Payable		12,000
	To record $12,000 loan from Friendly Bank, to be repaid May 1, 19_2, with 6% interest.		

When he examines the accounts at the close of the year, the accountant notices the entry for the loan in the Notes Payable account [Exhibit 7-2(a)]. He checks the original journal entry and finds that the company does have an obligation to pay interest of 6 percent on the loan. However, he finds no entry in the accounts to record this interest expense or the liability of interest payable. He must adjust the accounts to bring them up to date.

1. The need for a compound entry in a subsequent period can be avoided through the use of reversing entries. Because reversing entries are not necessary (although they are useful), a discussion of this refinement in the accounting cycle is left to the intermediate accounting course.

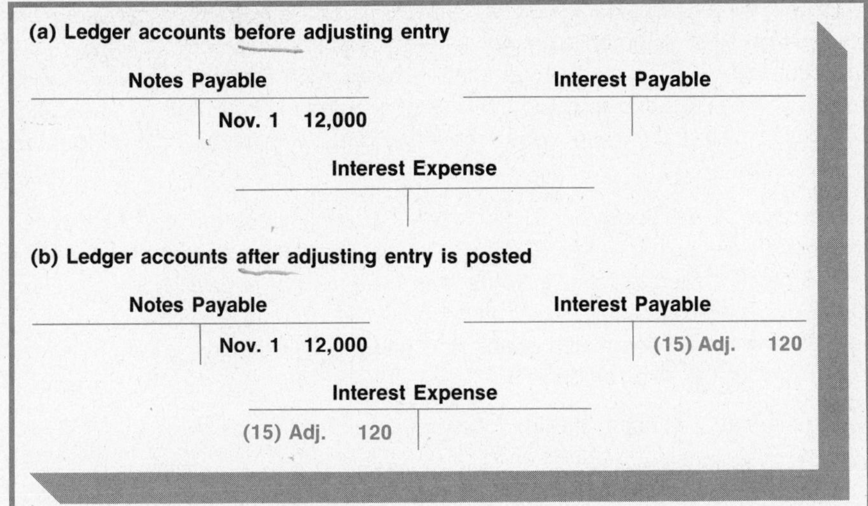

Exhibit 7-2
Ledger accounts for transaction 2

First, he must determine the amount of the obligation. He uses a simple formula.[2]

Principal × Interest rate × Time = Interest;
$12,000 × 6%/year × 2/12 year = $120.

He makes the following adjusting entry in the journal.

Dec. 31	Interest Expense	120	
	Interest Payable		120
	To record accrued interest on Nov. 1 loan from Friendly Bank: $12,000 at 6% for 2 months, $12,000 × 0.06 × 2/12 = $120.		

Exhibit 7-2(b) shows the ledger accounts after the adjustment is posted.

When the company repays the note with interest on May 1, 19_2, the journal entry made then records payment of the principal and interest payable (liabilities) and the interest expense incurred during the first four months of 19_2. The interest expense for January through April is computed as $12,000 at 6 percent per year for 4/12 year, or $240.

19_2			
May 1	Notes Payable	12,000	
	Interest Payable	120	
	Interest Expense	240	
	Cash		12,360
	To record payment of Nov. 1 loan from Friendly Bank: $12,000 at 6% for 6 months, $12,000 × 0.06 × 6/12 = $360 (120 interest accrued in 19_1).		

2. Banks and other creditors often use more complex formulas to compute the amount of interest due as of a particular date, particularly if the loan is to be repaid in installments. The adjustment will give the most fair picture of the present obligation if it represents the amount of interest that would be due if the loan were repaid immediately. Therefore the accountant should try to compute the interest expense according to the same formula as that used by the creditor.

ACCRUED REVENUE

Accrued revenue represents revenue earned during the current accounting period that has not been recorded in the accounts through normal procedures of journalizing transactions. Accrued revenue often includes such items as accrued interest, rent, royalties, fees, and so on. In the case of accrued revenue, both an asset and a revenue item exist at the end of the accounting period without having been recorded in the books.

Transaction 3. On December 1, 19_1, the Circle Company renders services to a client and accepts in payment a $100,000 note. This note is payable in 12 months, with 6 percent interest payable at the time the principal is paid. When the Circle Company's books are being closed on December 31, 19_1, the company has earned interest revenue for one month on the note and has an asset in the form of interest receivable for the same amount.

When the note was accepted, the following journal entry was made.

Dec. 1	Notes Receivable	100,000	
	Sale of Services		100,000
	To record services rendered to Later Co. for 12-month, $100,000 note receivable Dec. 1, 19_2, with 6% interest.		

Exhibit 7-3(a) shows the relevant ledger accounts at the close of the year. An adjusting entry is needed.

Dec. 31	Interest Receivable	500	
	Interest Revenue		500
	To record accrued interest earned on Dec. 1 note from Later Co.: $100,000, at 6% for 1 month, $100,000 × 0.06 × 1/12 = $500.		

Note that the adjusting entry needed for accrued revenue involves a debit to an asset account and a credit to a revenue account.

Exhibit 7-3
Ledger accounts for transaction 3

(a) Ledger accounts before adjusting entry

Notes Receivable

Debit	Credit
Dec. 1 100,000	

Interest Receivable

Debit	Credit

Interest Revenue

Debit	Credit

(b) Ledger accounts after adjusting entry is posted

Notes Receivable

Debit	Credit
Dec. 1 100,000	

Interest Receivable

Debit	Credit
(16) Adj. 500	

Interest Revenue

Debit	Credit
	(16) Adj. 500

Exhibit 7-4 **Ledger accounts for transaction 4**

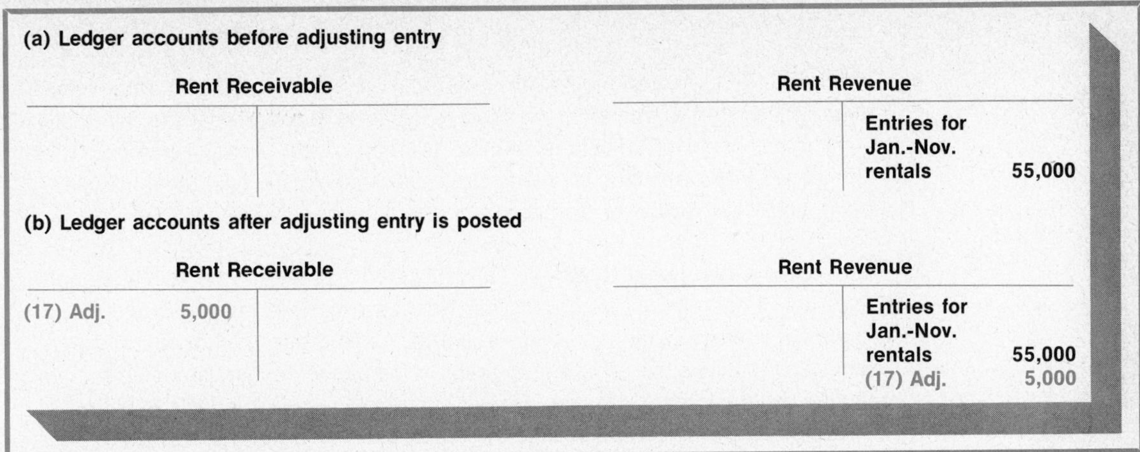

(a) Ledger accounts before adjusting entry

Rent Receivable			

Rent Revenue			
		Entries for Jan.-Nov. rentals	55,000

(b) Ledger accounts after adjusting entry is posted

Rent Receivable			
(17) Adj.	5,000		

Rent Revenue			
		Entries for Jan.-Nov. rentals	55,000
		(17) Adj.	5,000

When the principal and interest are collected from the Later Company, the following journal entry will be made.

19_2			
Dec. 1	Cash	106,000	
	Interest Receivable		500
	Notes Receivable		100,000
	Interest Revenue		5,500
	To record collection of Dec. 1, 19_1, note from Later Co. with interest: $100,000 at 6% for one year, $100,000 × 0.06 × 1 = $6,000 ($500 interest accrued in 19_1).		

Transaction 4. The Circle Company leases trucks to various clients. The clients are billed on the 5th of each month for the preceding month's rent. When the books are being closed on December 31, 19_1, the company has earned $5,000 of rental income for December, but this revenue has not been recorded because the customers will not be billed for December rents until January 5, 19_2. There is accrued revenue and a corresponding asset (rent receivable).

Exhibit 7-4(a) shows the relevant ledger accounts at the close of the year. The necessary adjustment is recorded by the following entry.

Dec. 31	Rent Receivable	5,000	
	Rent Revenue		5,000
	To record rent accrued on trucks for Dec.		

Exhibit 7-4(b) shows the ledger accounts after this entry is posted.

Deferrals

Deferrals are adjusting entries required when a payment is received in a period before the revenue is recognized, or a payment is made in a period before the expense is recognized. The prepayment of rent, insurance, or other expenses is recorded as an outflow of cash and an increase in an asset (prepaid rent or insurance). The prepaid expense is listed as an asset because it is an unexpired cost, one that will benefit a future period. However, as the cost expires, adjusting entries must be made to record the change from asset to expense in the proper period.

A similar need for adjustments arises in dealing with prepayments made to the company by its clients or customers. These adjustments are called ***deferrals*** because recognition of revenue or expense is deferred until a later period.

PREPAID EXPENSES

A ***prepaid expense*** is an asset—it is an unexpired cost that will benefit future periods, although it has already been paid for. Prepaid expenses include prepaid rent, insurance, interest, taxes, and office supplies. As time passes, the cost expires. The company receives the benefit of the rent or insurance payments, incurs the obligation to pay the interest or taxes, or uses up the office supplies. As this happens, the prepaid expense account no longer represents only an asset. Part (or all) of the asset has become an expense that should be recognized in the current period. Such an account that has both asset and expense elements is called a ***mixed account.*** At the end of the period, an adjusting entry is needed to transfer the expense element to an expense account, while leaving the remaining asset element in the asset account.

Transaction 5. On January 2, 19_1, the Circle Company purchases a three-year insurance policy for $900. The cost is recorded as an asset, Prepaid Insurance. When the books are being closed on December 31, 19_1, the company has received the benefit of one year of protection under this policy. The cost of this year of protection should be recognized as an insurance expense during 19_1.

The following journal entry was made at the time the policy was purchased.

Jan. 2	Prepaid Insurance	900	
	Cash		900
	To record purchase of 3-year insurance policy.		

Exhibit 7-5(a) shows the ledger accounts before the adjusting entry is made. The necessary adjustment is the following.

Exhibit 7-5 Ledger accounts for transaction 5

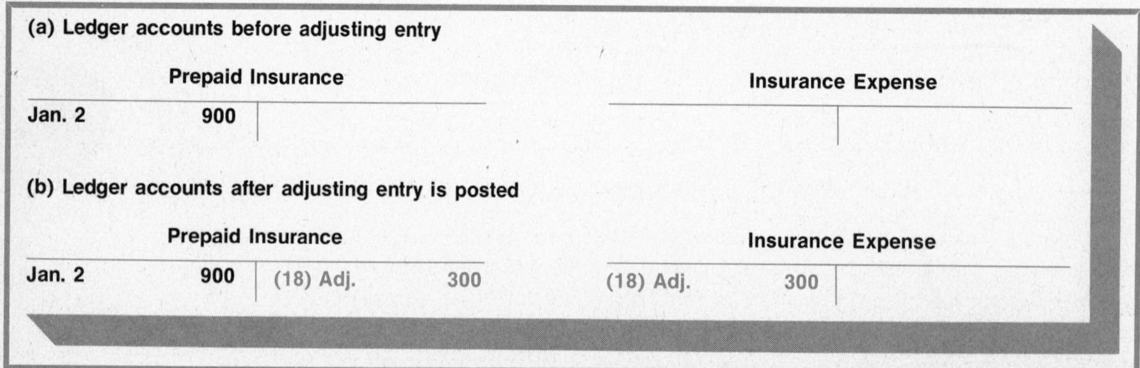

Dec. 31	Insurance Expense	300	
	Prepaid Insurance		300
	To record insurance expense for 19_1 from 3-year policy prepaid on Jan. 2, 19_1: $900/3 years = $300/year.		

Note that the adjusting entry required for a prepaid expense involves a debit to an expense account and a credit to an asset account (the prepaid expense)—if the prepaid expense was originally recorded as an asset.[3]

At the close of the 19_2 and 19_3 periods, similar adjusting entries will be made. Thus, when the policy expires at the end of 19_3, all of its cost will have been recognized as expenses spread evenly over the three years, as required by the expense recognition principle of systematic and rational allocation.

Transaction 6. On November 1, 19_1, the Circle Company rents a building and pays in advance for the first six months of rent, a cash prepayment of $6,000. This cost is recorded as an asset, Prepaid Rent. When the books are being closed at the end of 19_1, an expense has been incurred for two months of rent. An adjustment is needed to transfer part of the asset to the Rent Expense account.

The following journal entry was made when the rent was prepaid.

Nov. 1	Prepaid Rent	6,000	
	Cash		6,000
	To record prepayment of 6 months' rent.		

The adjusting entry made at the end of the year is the following.

Dec. 31	Rent Expense	2,000	
	Prepaid Rent		2,000
	To record rent expense for Nov.-Dec. from Nov. 1 prepayment of 6 months' rent: $6,000/6 months = $1,000/month.		

Exhibit 7-6 shows the ledger accounts before and after the adjusting entry is posted. When the books are closed at the end of 19_2, a similar adjusting entry will be made to allocate the balance of the rent as an expense for that year.

3. It would be possible to record the payment for the insurance policy as an expense (Insurance Expense) in the original journal entry. In that case, an adjusting entry would be needed at the close of the year to account for the fact that part of the cost is not yet expired. Part of the recorded insurance expense would be transferred to an asset account (Prepaid Insurance) by the adjusting entry. The original entry (on January 2) would debit Insurance Expense $900 and credit Cash $900. The adjusting entry (on December 31) would debit Prepaid Insurance $600 and credit Insurance Expense $600.

For most transactions, this alternative approach is not recommended. It is more appropriate to view the purchase of the insurance policy as acquisition of an asset than as an expense. Furthermore, the accountant is more likely to notice the need for an adjustment if the amount has been entered in a prepaid expense (asset) account. However, if a transaction involves a prepaid expense that will expire completely during the same accounting period, it is desirable to record the initial transaction as an expense, thus avoiding the need for an adjusting entry at the close of the period. For example, if the monthly rent is paid on December 1, it can be recorded by a debit to Rent Expense because it will become an expense before the books are closed on December 31.

Exhibit 7-6 **Ledger accounts for transaction 6**

(a) Ledger accounts before adjusting entry

Prepaid Rent

Nov. 1	6,000		

Rent Expense

(b) Ledger accounts after adjusting entry is posted

Prepaid Rent

Nov. 1	6,000	(19) Adj.	2,000

Rent Expense

(19) Adj.	2,000		

REVENUE RECEIVED IN ADVANCE

Revenue received in advance (sometimes called deferred revenue or unearned revenue) is an inflow of assets (or decrease of liabilities) that will be earned by the firm at a later time. Revenue may be received in advance for such items as rent income, interest income, and subscription income. At the time the payment is received, the firm has not yet earned the revenue. The revenue should be recognized in the future when it is earned.

We can think of the revenue received in advance as a deposit made by the customer. The company receives cash (an asset) and also acquires an offsetting liability (the obligation to earn the cash in the future). Therefore, there is no revenue at the time of the prepayment. When the service is performed, the liability is liquidated (that is, settled) and the revenue is recognized. Again, the details can best be made clear through examples.

Transaction 7. On September 1, 19_1, the Circle Company leases one of its buildings to the Square Company for one year. The Square Company pays $12,000 rent for the year in advance at the time the lease is signed. The accountant offsets the $12,000 increase in assets (Cash) by a $12,000 increase in liabilities (Rent Received in Advance). No revenue is recognized at this time. When the books are being closed on December 31, 19_1, the Circle Company has earned four months' rent because the Square Company has now had the use of the building for four months. An adjustment to the accounts is needed to recognize the revenue.

The following journal entry was made at the time the prepayment of rent was received.

Sep. 1	Cash	12,000	
	Rent Received in Advance		12,000
	To record receipt of one year's rent from Square Co.		

Be sure to remember that Rent Received in Advance is the title of a liability account. This might be more clear if the account were called something like Rental Obligation, but accountants often use the title given here or a title such as Deferred Rent Revenue or Unearned Rental Revenue. The adjusting entry needed at the end of the year accounts for the actual revenue earned during the year and also adjusts the liability account to show the extent of the remaining obligation.

Dec. 31	Rent Received in Advance	4,000	
	Rent Revenue		4,000
	To record four months' rent earned in 19_1 of year's rent prepaid by Square Co. Sep. 1: $12,000/year × 4/12 yr. = $4,000.		

Exhibit 7-7 shows the ledger accounts after the adjusting entry is posted. Note that the adjusting entry needed for revenue received in advance involves a debit to a liability account and a credit to a revenue account—if the original entry recorded the prepayment in a liability account.[4]

Transaction 8. The Circle Company sells magazine subscriptions. On January 2, 19_1, it receives a total of $36,000 in cash from various customers as prepayment for three-year subscriptions. The accountant offsets the increase in assets (Cash) by an equal increase in liabilities (Unearned Subscription Revenue). When the books are being closed on December 31, 19_1, the company has earned part of this revenue by supplying magazines to the customers for one year. An adjusting entry is needed to recognize the earned revenue and to decrease the liability.

The following journal entry was made at the time the subscription prepayments were received.

Jan. 2	Cash	36,000	
	Unearned Subscription Revenue		36,000
	To record sale of 3-year magazine subscriptions.		

The adjusting entry needed at the end of the year is the following.

Dec. 31	Unearned Subscription Revenue	12,000	
	Subscription Revenue		12,000
	To recognize revenue earned in 19_1 from 3-year subscriptions sold Jan. 2: $36,000/3 years = $12,000/year.		

Exhibit 7-7 **Ledger accounts for transaction 7**

Rent Received in Advance			
(20) Adj.	4,000	Sep. 1	12,000

Rent Revenue			
		(20) Adj.	4,000

4. As with prepaid expenses, it is possible to reverse the procedure described here. That is, the receipt of the prepayment could be recorded by a credit of $12,000 to the Rent Revenue account. In that case, the adjusting entry at the end of the year would be needed to transfer the unearned portion of the revenue to the Rent Received in Advance account. This procedure is not recommended, because it is more realistic to recognize the prepayment as a liability rather than revenue initially, and because the need for an adjustment is more obvious if the amount is recorded in a liability account.

However, if a transaction involves revenue received in advance that is to be fully earned during the same accounting period, the accountant usually records the initial transaction as receipt of revenue in order to avoid the need for an adjustment.

Exhibit 7-8 Ledger accounts for transaction 8

Unearned Subscription Revenue				Subscription Revenue			
(21) Adj.	12,000	Jan. 2	36,000			(21) Adj.	12,000

Exhibit 7-8 shows the ledger accounts after the adjustment is posted. Similar adjusting entries will be made at the end of 19_2 and 19_3. Thus, when the subscriptions end, all of the revenue will have been recognized and all of the liability will have been liquidated.

Depreciation

Depreciation is the process of allocating the cost of a tangible fixed asset over its estimated life in a rational and systematic manner. Depreciation is applied to such assets as buildings, machinery, tools, equipment, and other items that benefit the company over a number of accounting periods. The cost of the item is recorded initially as an asset, an unexpired cost. In each accounting period, a portion of the cost expires and is transferred to an expense account. This procedure reflects the fact that the utility of the item to the company (for future periods) decreases with time, as the item wears out or becomes obsolete. Land is not depreciated because land does not wear out.

Depreciation is discussed in detail in Chapter 14. However, it is useful to discuss the subject briefly at this point, because an adjusting entry usually is required (1) to record the depreciation expense for the period, and (2) to adjust the recorded value of the fixed asset. For our example here, we use the simplest form of depreciation, which is called straight-line depreciation. Under this system, the cost of the fixed asset (less the expected salvage value of the asset when it is discarded) is allocated in equal amounts to the periods during which the asset is expected to benefit the company.

Transaction 9. On January 2, 19_1, the Circle Company purchases machinery for $10,500 in cash. The machinery is expected to be used for ten years. At the end of the ten years, the company expects to sell the machinery as scrap for $500. The initial journal entry records the machinery as an asset with a value of $10,500 (its acquisition cost). When the books are being closed on December 31, 19_1, the machinery has been in use for one year (one-tenth of its estimated life). An adjustment is needed to allocate a portion of the cost of the asset to expense for this period.

At the end of the ten years, the machinery is expected to have a scrap value of $500. Therefore, the other $10,000 of its cost must be allocated among the ten years during which it benefits the company. Using straight-line depreciation, we divide the cost evenly over the ten years:

Depreciation per year = (Cost − Scrap value)/Estimated life
= ($10,500 − $500)/10
= $1,000.

The purchase of the machinery was recorded by the following entry, debiting the acquisition cost of the machinery to an asset account.

Jan. 2	Machinery	10,500	
	Cash		10,500
	To record purchase of machinery for cash.		

The following adjusting entry is made at the end of the first year.

Dec. 31	Depreciation Expense	1,000	
	Accumulated Depreciation		1,000
	To record 19_1 depreciation expense for machinery purchased Jan. 2 19_1: straight-line, 10-year life, $500 scrap value.		

Exhibit 7-9 shows the ledger accounts after the adjustment is posted. The adjusting entry records the depreciation expense for the accounting period in the Depreciation Expense account. This is the portion of the asset cost that has expired during the period. The Depreciation Expense account appears on the income statement as an expense for the period. When the books are closed, the Depreciation Expense account is closed to the Income Summary account, so that it shows a zero balance at the beginning of the new period.

The adjusting entry for depreciation credits an Accumulated Depreciation account instead of reducing the balance in the asset account. The Accumulated Depreciation account is a *contra* (or *negative*) asset account. This account balance is deducted from the asset account on the balance sheet.

Property, plant, and equipment:		
Machinery	$10,500	
Less: Accumulated depreciation	1,000	$9,500

Similar adjusting entries for depreciation will be made yearly, until the asset is fully depreciated. Because the Accumulated Depreciation account is not closed at the end of the period, the balance in this contra asset account increases from year to year. In our illustration, at the end of the ten-year estimated life of the machinery, the Accumulated Depreciation account will have a $10,000 credit balance. When this point is reached, the asset cost of $10,500 will have been written off to expense, except for the expected salvage value of $500.

Exhibit 7-9 **Ledger accounts for transaction 9**

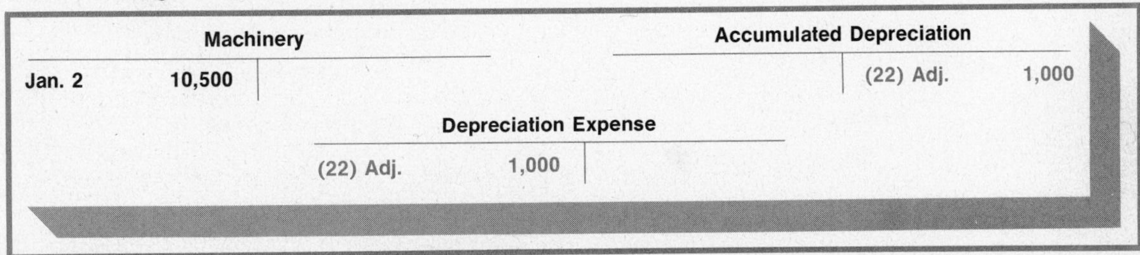

Bad debts expense

When sales are made on account (for credit), the accountant knows that it is likely that some of those accounts will turn out to be uncollectible. He cannot know which accounts will prove to be valueless assets, but he knows that the total revenue recorded for credit sales during the period probably will prove to be an overestimate of the amount the firm does finally receive. In other words, an adjustment is needed to account for the fact that the asset of Accounts Receivable is probably of less value than indicated by the account balance. The adjustment also must record an expense for bad debts for the period. The treatment of bad debts expense is discussed more fully in Chapter 12, but we look at one example here to see how adjusting entries are used in this procedure.

Transaction 10. During 19_1, the Circle Company made sales on account of $1,000,000. From past experience, the accountant estimates that 2 percent of the total credit sales recorded will be uncollectible. At the close of 19_1, the normal journalizing procedures have increased the balances of both the Accounts Receivable (asset) and the Sales (revenue) accounts by $1,000,000 to record the credit sales. An adjustment is needed before closing the books to indicate the estimate of the true value of the asset, and to offset the revenue by an expense for the estimated bad debts.

The necessary adjustment is made by the following entry.

Dec. 31	Bad Debts Expense	20,000	
	Allowance for Doubtful Receivables		20,000
	To record bad debts expense estimated for 19_1 credit sales: $1,000,000 × 2% = $20,000.		

Exhibit 7-10 shows the ledger accounts after the adjustment is posted. As in the case of depreciation of a fixed asset, the adjustment of the Accounts Receivable account is not made directly to the asset account. Instead, the full balance of Accounts Receivable is listed on the statement, and then an allowance for doubtful receivables is subtracted from it. This practice discloses more fully to the user the estimates being made by the accounting system. A contra asset account called Allowance for Doubtful Receivables is used to record the adjustment that will be

Exhibit 7-10 Ledger accounts for transaction 10

Accounts Receivable

Bal.	800,000		

Allowance for Doubtful Receivables

		(23) Adj.	20,000

Sales

		Bal.	1,000,000

Bad Debts Expense

(23) Adj.	20,000		

subtracted from the balance of the Accounts Receivable account on the balance sheet.

Current assets:		
Accounts receivable	$800,000	
Less: Allowance for doubtful receivables	20,000	$780,000

The Bad Debts Expense account is an expense account. Its balance appears on the income statement, and it is closed to Income Summary when the books are closed.

In this example, some of the credit sales had already been collected by the end of the year, so the balance of the Accounts Receivable account was $800,000 when the books were closed. In our example, the allowance is computed on the total credit sales for the year, not on the balance of accounts receivable.

Adjusting entries: a review

The topic of adjusting entries is complex, but very important. You should review the preceding sections of this chapter carefully to be sure that you understand the procedures for adjusting the books in each of the six kinds of cases discussed. Exhibit 7-11 presents a summary and outline that may help in your review. As you review, keep firmly in mind the basic purpose of adjusting entries—to ensure that financial statements prepared at the end of an accounting period correctly report (1) the revenue realized and expenses incurred during the period, and (2) the assets, liabilities, and owners' equity at the end of the period. The normal recording of transactions during the accounting period may not fully accomplish these objectives; adjusting entries may be needed to complete the job.

Adjusting entries and the work sheet

The procedures described in Chapters 5 and 6 for the accounting cycle move directly from the footing and balancing of accounts to the preparation of a trial balance and a work sheet. Now we know that adjusting entries usually are needed before proper statements can be prepared. How should the procedures described in Chapters 5 and 6 be modified to allow for adjusting entries?

Usually it is desirable to take a trial balance of the accounts before making adjusting entries. This procedure tests to ensure that the balance of debits and credits has been maintained through the normal journalization and posting activity of the period. Some of the account balances shown on the trial balance also are useful in preparing the adjusting entries. The six-column work sheet used in Chapter 6 (Exhibit 6-6) can be modified to accommodate adjusting entries, as shown in Exhibit 7-12. The following steps are involved in preparing this kind of work sheet.

1. Copy the ***unadjusted*** account balances from the general ledger (or from a trial balance already prepared) into the Trial Balance columns of the work sheet. Foot

Exhibit 7-11 **Procedures for making six kinds of adjusting entries**

ACCRUALS	**Accrued revenue.** Revenue earned but not recorded.	a. Recognize asset (debit). b. Recognize revenue (credit).
	Accrued expense. Expense incurred but not recorded.	**Typical accrued expense.** a. Recognize expense (debit). b. Recognize liability (credit).
		Bad debt expense. a. Recognize estimated bad debt expense (debit). b. Establish allowance for estimated uncollectible receivables (credit).
DEFERRALS	**Revenue apportionment.** Payment received in period before full revenue is earned. (Initially recorded as liability.)	**Revenue received in advance.** a. Decrease liability that shows unearned revenue (debit). b. Recognize revenue earned during period (credit).
	Cost apportionment. Payment made in period before full expense is incurred. (Initially recorded as asset.)	**Prepaid expense.** a. Recognize expired portion of cost as expense (debit). b. Decrease asset account that shows unexpired cost (credit).
		Depreciation. a. Recognize depreciation expense allocated to period (debit). b. Establish allowance for expired portion of cost (credit).

these Debit and Credit columns; they should balance. Double rule the columns. This completes the initial trial balance.

2. Record the adjusting entries in the Adjustments columns of the work sheet. Foot these Debit and Credit columns; they should balance. Double rule the columns.

In Exhibit 7-12, five adjusting entries are shown in the Adjustments columns. Exhibit 7-13 shows the journal entries for these adjustments, as well as the closing journal entries. The first adjusting entry accounts for the fact that part of a prepaid insurance expense has been used up during the year. The second entry accounts for depreciation on equipment, which is being depreciated on a straight-line basis over ten years. The third entry accounts for accrued interest expense on the notes payable. The fourth entry accounts for accrued salaries that have not yet been paid. The fifth entry establishes a bad debts expense, estimated at 2 percent of total sales for the period.

3. Combine the Trial Balance columns and the Adjustments columns to reach an adjusted balance for each account. Record the adjusted balances in the columns

Exhibit 7-12 **An example of a work sheet with adjusting entries**

Z COMPANY
Work Sheet
For the Year Ended December 31, 19_1

Account Title	Trial Balance		Adjustments		Adjusted Trial Balance		Income Statement		Balance Sheet	
	DEBIT	CREDIT	DEBIT	CREDIT	DEBIT	CREDIT	DEBIT	CREDIT	DEBIT	CREDIT
Cash	9,000				9,000				9,000	
Accounts Receivable	80,000				80,000				80,000	
Allowance for Doubtful Receivables		1,000		(e) 2,000		3,000				3,000
Prepaid Insurance	1,000			(a) 750	250				250	
Equipment	100,000				100,000				100,000	
Accumulated Depreciation		30,000		(b) 10,000		40,000				40,000
Notes Payable		10,000				10,000				10,000
Accounts Payable		20,000				20,000				20,000
Income Taxes Payable		2,000				2,000				2,000
Common Stock		60,000				60,000				60,000
Retained Earnings		40,000				40,000				40,000
Dividends	1,000				1,000				1,000	
Sale of Services		100,000				100,000		100,000		
Salaries Expense	60,000		(d) 5,000		65,000		65,000			
Rent Expense	10,000				10,000		10,000			
Income Tax Expense	2,000				2,000		2,000			
	263,000	263,000								
Insurance Expense			(a) 750		750		750			
Depreciation Expense			(b) 10,000		10,000		10,000			
Interest Expense			(c) 100		100		100			
Interest Payable				(c) 100		100				100
Accrued Salaries Payable				(d) 5,000		5,000				5,000
Bad Debts Expense			(e) 2,000		2,000		2,000			
			17,850	17,850	180,000	180,100	89,850	100,000	190,250	180,100
Net Income for Year							10,150			10,150
							100,000	100,000	190,250	190,250

Exhibit 7-13 **Adjusting and closing entries associated with Exhibit 7-12**

19_1		ADJUSTING ENTRIES			
Dec.	31	Insurance expense		750	
		Prepaid insurance			750
		To record insurance expense for 19_1.			
	31	Depreciation expense		10,000	
		Accumulated depreciation			10,000
		To record depreciation expense on equipment for 19_1.			
	31	Interest expense		100	
		Interest payable			100
		To record interest expense for 19_1 on notes payable.			
	31	Salaries expense		5,000	
		Accrued salaries payable			5,000
		To record accured salaries for last week of			
		December 19_1.			
	31	Bad debts expense		2,000	
		Allowance for doubtful receivables			2,000
		To record estimated bad debts expense for			
		19_1 at 2% of sales.			
		CLOSING ENTRIES			
	31	Sale of services		100,000	
		Salaries expense			65,000
		Rent expense			10,000
		Depreciation expense			10,000
		Insurance expense			750
		Interest expense			100
		Bad debts expense			2,000
		Income tax expense			2,000
		Income summary			10,150
		To close revenue and expense accounts to			
		income summary account.			
	31	Income summary		10,150	
		Retained earnings			10,150
		To close income summary account to retained earnings.			
		earnings.			
	31	Retained earnings		1,000	
		Dividends			1,000
		To close dividends account to retained			
		earnings.			

labeled Adjusted Trial Balance. Foot these Debit and Credit columns; they should balance. Double rule the columns. This completes the adjusted trial balance. The balances shown in these columns should agree with the ledger account balances after adjusting entries have been posted.

4. Transfer balances of revenue and expense accounts from the adjusted trial balance to the Income Statement columns. Foot these columns. Determine the net income (or net loss) as the difference between the debit and credit totals. Insert the net income (or net loss) as a balancing figure in the Income Statement columns *and* also in the Balance Sheet columns. Foot the Income Statement columns and double rule them.
5. Transfer balances of asset, liability, and owners' equity accounts from the adjusted trial balance to the Balance Sheet columns. Foot these Debit and Credit columns just above the net income (or net loss) line. Then foot them again, including the net income (or net loss). The columns should balance. Double rule the columns.

The work sheet is now complete, and the preparation of the financial statements can proceed as described in Chapter 6. The adjustments worked out on the work sheet can now be journalized and posted. The closing entries can be journalized from the work sheet and posted, as discussed in Chapter 6. Note that any revenue or expense accounts created during the adjustments should also be closed. Finally, a post-closing trial balance can be taken to ensure that the balance of the ledger has been maintained through the adjusting and closing entries. This completes the accounting cycle; the ledger is now ready to begin receiving data from the next accounting period.

Summary

Adjusting entries usually are needed at the close of an accounting period in order (1) to ensure proper matching of revenue and expenses for the period, and (2) to see that all assets and liabilities are recorded properly.

Adjustments are needed at the close of an accounting period if (1) a single ledger account contains both asset and expense elements, such as a Prepaid Insurance account whose cost has partly expired; (2) a single ledger account contains both liability and revenue elements, such as an Unearned Rent account containing some rent that has now been earned; or (3) expenses or revenue have accrued during the period without being recorded in the journal or ledger. Examples of unrecorded data include accrued interest payable and interest expense on a note payable, salary expense and accrued salaries payable, bad debts expense and allowance for bad debts, and depreciation expense and accumulated depreciation.

Most adjusting entries fall into one of six categories: accrued expenses, prepaid expenses, depreciation expenses, bad debts expense, accrued revenue, or revenue received in advance.

Questions

1. What is an adjusting entry? Why are adjusting entries usually required at the end of the accounting cycle?

2. Explain the meanings of the following terms:
a. accrued expenses,
b. prepaid expenses,
c. depreciation expense,
d. bad debts expense,
e. accrued revenue,
f. revenue received in advance.
Give two examples of each of these items.

3. Distinguish between revenue apportionment and cost apportionment.

4. Explain the procedure for using a ten-column work sheet with provision for adjustments.

5. Why is a post-closing trial balance required after the adjusting and closing entries have been journalized and posted?

6. Under what conditions may it be preferable to record a prepaid expense as an expense rather than as an asset (prepaid expense)? When may it be preferable to record revenue received in advance as revenue rather than as a liability (unearned revenue)?

7. What is a contra account? Name two contra accounts involved in adjusting entries.

8. On a balance sheet, where do you classify prepaid expenses? unearned revenue? allowance for doubtful receivables? accumulated depreciation?

9. What is a mixed account?

Exercises

E7-1 The trial balance of the Dill Company on April 30, 19_6, included the following unadjusted account balances.

Unearned Rent Revenue	$ 48,000
Prepaid Advertising	800
Prepaid Insurance	1,800
Prepaid Rent	30,000
Office Supplies	600
Salaries	50,000
Building	47,500
Interest Expense	6,000
Accumulated Depreciation: Building	14,250
Sales	105,000

Journalize the necessary adjusting entries, taking into consideration the following information.

a. The balance of the Prepaid Insurance account represents a one-year fire insurance policy on the building; the policy was purchased on April 1, 19_6.

b. The balance of the Prepaid Rent account represents payment in advance for one year's rent of an office building, paid on January 1, 19_6.

c. The advertising manager reports that only $150 worth of advertisements has been used with the local newspaper.

d. An inventory of office supplies on hand at the end of the year showed a total value of $360.

e. The company's factory building was purchased on July 1, 19_2, and is being depreciated on a straight-line basis with an estimated life of ten years and a salvage value of $2,500.

f. It is estimated that 2 percent of the sales during the year will be uncollectible accounts receivable. The Sales account is a revenue account.

g. Accrued interest payable is $3,500.

h. Estimated income taxes for the year are $14,000.

i. Accrued property taxes are $1,050.

j. Three-fourths of the unearned revenue recorded during the period had been earned as of April 30, 19_6. The Unearned Rent Revenue account shows a credit balance.

k. Accrued April salaries amount to $1,200.

E7-2 When preparing to close your accounts on December 31, 19_6, you find that the Prepaid Insurance account has a debit balance of $4,200. Checking the journal entries, you find that this balance represents three policies purchased during the year. Policy number P1660 was purchased on January 1 for $1,500 and has a life of three years. Policy H772 was purchased on September 1 for $3,000 and has a life of two years. Policy B1131 was purchased on April 1 for $1,200 and has a life of one year. Prepare the necessary adjusting entries.

E7-3 In February 19_6, the Long List Magazine Company received advance payments of $18,000 for one-year subscriptions to its monthly magazine. This amount was credited to the Subscription Revenue account. These subscribers were mailed their first issue in April. Journalize the adjusting entry required on August 31, 19_6.

E7-4 At the close of the accounting period on June 30, 19_6, you find the following two notes receivable on hand.

Date	Principal	Life of Note	Interest Rate
March 1	$12,000	12 months	6%
January 1	50,000	2 years	9%

Journalize the required adjusting entry.

E7-5 On December 31, 19_6, you find the following two notes payable outstanding.

Date	Principal	Life of Note	Interest Rate
September 1	$15,000	4 months	8%
October 1	20,000	3 months	10%

Journalize the required adjusting entry.

E7-6 On December 31, 19_6, the Prepaid Insurance account shows an unadjusted balance of $8,700. Journalize the required year-end adjusting entry in the following two cases:

a. an examination of the policies shows that $4,700 of insurance has expired;

b. an examination of the policies shows $4,700 of unexpired insurance.

E7-7 At the end of 19_6, the Office Supplies account contains the entries shown in Exhibit 7-14. An inventory of office supplies on December 31, 19_6, shows

Exhibit 7-14
Ledger account for Exercise E7-7

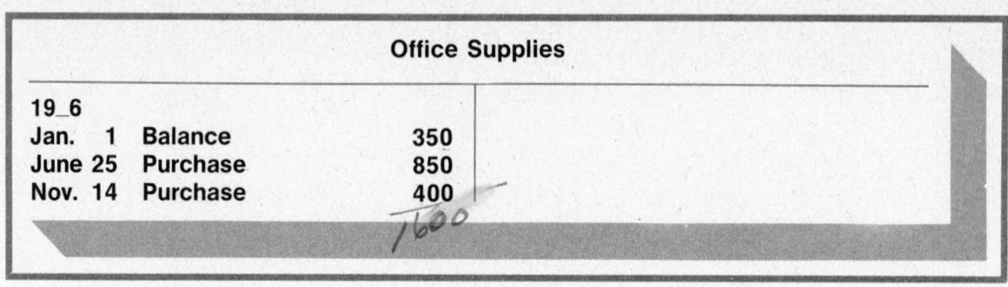

Office Supplies			
19_6			
Jan. 1	Balance	350	
June 25	Purchase	850	
Nov. 14	Purchase	400	

$600 of unused supplies on hand. Journalize any adjusting entry that you think is needed before preparing the year-end statements.

E7-8 Journalize the adjusting entries required by each of the following items.

a. Depreciation on factory building is estimated at $8,200 for the year.

b. Bad debts expense for the year is estimated to be $3,600.

c. The balance of the Office Supplies account on January 1 was $150. During the year, $600 worth of supplies were purchased. An inventory of office supplies at the end of the year shows $350 of supplies on hand.

d. At the end of the year, employees have not been paid for their work during the last three days of the year. The wages earned during these three days total $3,750.

e. Property taxes estimated at $1,220 have accrued at the end of the year; they have not been recorded.

f. During the year, $14,000 of rental income was received and was journalized as follows.

Cash	14,000	
Rent Received in Advance		14,000

At the end of the year, $13,000 of this rent has been earned.

E7-9 On May 1, 19_6, a two-year insurance policy was purchased for $6,600. The purchase was recorded by debiting the Insurance Expense account. Journalize the adjusting entry needed on June 30, 19_6.

E7-10 On August 1, 19_6, $14,400 was received as prepayment for 12 months of rent beginning on November 1. The receipt of the rent was recorded in a liability account. Journalize the adjusting entry needed on December 31, 19_6.

E7-11 You are a public accountant, and one of your clients is Dr. Molar, a dentist. You prepare monthly financial statements for him. The following transactions were reported to you during July 19_6.

July	1	Paid $750 office rent for July.
	7	Billed patients $2,100 for services rendered in July.
	11	Purchased $650 of dental supplies ($300 of these supplies were still on hand unused at the end of the month) for cash.
	17	Received $800 from patients billed on July 7.
	30	Paid $750 office rent for the month of August. Additional space was rented.

Required:

a. What is the net income for Dr. Molar in July on a cash basis?

b. What is the net income for Dr. Molar on an accrual basis?

E7-12 Using a table similar to that prepared for Problem P6-2, explain the impact on the elements of the accounting equation ($A - L = OE$) of the following adjusting entries. Indicate increase, decrease, or no change for each factor in the equation by +, −, or 0.

a. The adjusting entry to record bad debt expense.
b. The adjusting entry to record accrued interest receivable.
c. The adjusting entry to record adjustment of an unearned revenue account to report revenue earned during the period.
d. The adjusting entry to record depreciation expense.
e. The adjusting entry to record accrued interest payable.
f. The adjusting entry to record adjustment of a prepaid expense account to report expense incurred during the period.

E7-13 Exhibit 7-15 shows the unadjusted trial balance of the Infacto Company on December 31, 19_5. Seven transactions requiring adjusting entries are listed below. Prepare a nine-column table showing the dollar impact of each transaction on each of the following summaries: net sales, operating expenses, net operating income, net income, retained earnings, current assets, working capital, net assets, and owners' equity.

Transaction 1 Accrued salaries at the year's end total $700.
2 Accrued interest receivable at the year's end totals $1,400.
3 Rent earned during the year totals $650.
4 Depreciation expense for the year amounts to 15 percent of the cost of the asset.
5 Bad debts expense (considered an operating expense) for the year amounts to 2 percent of net sales.
6 Accrued interest expense on notes payable totals $635.
7 Insurance expense for the period totals $400.

Exhibit 7-15
Trial balance for Exercise E7-13

THE IMPACT SERVICE COMPANY
Unadjusted Trial Balance
December 31, 19_5

Cash	**9,000**	
Marketable Securities	**11,500**	
Accounts Receivable	**17,000**	
Allowance for Doubtful Receivables		**600**
Prepaid Insurance	**1,200**	
Building	**65,000**	
Accumulated Depreciation		**19,500**
Notes Payable		**12,000**
Accounts Payable		**16,000**
Unearned Rent Revenue		**2,400**
Common Stock		**20,000**
Retained Earnings		**23,300**
Sale of Services		**18,000**
Sales Discounts	**2,100**	
Salaries Expense	**6,000**	
	111,800	**111,800**

Problems

P7-1 Journalize adjusting entries (without explanations) for the Swenson Company on June 30, 19_6, from the following information.

a. A total of $120,000 of wages and salaries was earned by employees during June. By June 30, $90,000 of June salaries had been paid and recorded.

b. A machine was purchased on April 1, 19_6, for $26,000. It is estimated to have a useful life of five years and a scrap value of $1,000.

c. Sales during the year totaled $1,400,000. From past experience it is expected that uncollectible receivables will equal 1 percent of total sales.

d. A two-year fire insurance policy was purchased on January 1, 19_6. At the time the policy was purchased, the following entry was made.

Jan. 1	Prepaid Insurance	2,200	
	Cash		2,200

e. On May 1, 19_6, the company received $12,000 in prepayment of a two-year rental contract. The transaction was recorded by the following entry. (See footnote 4.)

May 1	Cash	12,000	
	Rent Revenue		12,000

f. The balance of the Office Supplies account on June 30, 19_6, is $11,500. An inventory of office supplies on the same date shows a total of $3,500 worth of supplies on hand.

g. On February 1, 19_6, the company loaned $30,000 to a customer at 8% interest, with principal and interest payable in six months.

h. On June 1, 19_6, the company borrowed $40,000 from a bank for six months at 6% interest. At that time, the following entry was made.

June 1	Cash	40,000	
	Notes Payable		40,000

i. On June 30, 19_6, the federal income tax for the fiscal year is computed to be $47,000.

In addition, journalize the adjusting entries that would be required if the original entries for transactions d and e had been the following.

Jan. 1	Insurance Expense	2,200	
	Cash		2,200
May 1	Cash	12,000	
	Unearned Rent Revenue		12,000

P7-2 The unadjusted trial balance of the Rowbo Company on December 31, 19_6, shows the following account balances.

	Debit	Credit
Accounts Receivable	87,000	
Allowance for Doubtful Receivables		7,000
Merchandise Inventory	21,000	
Office Supplies Expense	92,000	
Prepaid Insurance	8,000	
Salaries Expense	447,000	

Journalize the adjusting entries needed for the end of the year on the basis of the following information.

a. Sales for the year were $400,000. Past experience indicates that 4 percent of sales will be uncollectible.
b. One-half of the balance in the Prepaid Insurance Account applies to future years.
c. Salaries earned by employees during the last week of December and not yet paid amount to $3,500.
d. The utility bill for the month of December was $410; no entry has been made for this item.
e. An inventory of office supplies on hand shows a total of $600.

P7-3 Exhibit 7-16 shows the account balances of the Rocky Road Company on December 31, 19_6. The following additional information is available.

1. Past experience suggests that 2 percent of Services (sale of services) will not be collected.
2. An inventory of office supplies on hand indicates that the storeroom contains $700 of such supplies.
3. Accrued salaries amount to $40,000.
4. The building is being depreciated at a rate of 10 percent per year and has no salvage value.
5. There is one note payable: a six-month, 9% note dated September 1, 19_6.
6. The notes receivable are one-year, 8% notes dated October 1, 19_6.
7. Of the rent received in advance, $800 has been earned in 19_6.

Required:

a. Prepare a ten-column work sheet for the year ended December 31, 19_6.
b. Prepare a single-step income statement for the year ended December 31, 19_6.
c. Prepare a balance sheet for December 31, 19_6, in modified account form.

Exhibit 7-16
Trial balance for Problem P7-3

ROCKY ROAD COMPANY
Unadjusted Trial Balance
December 31, 19_6

Cash	**12,000**	
Accounts Receivable	**110,000**	
Allowance for Doubtful Receivables		**1,200**
Notes Receivable	**15,000**	
Office Supplies	**3,100**	
Land	**150,000**	
Factory Building	**240,000**	
Accumulated Depreciation: Factory		**72,000**
Accounts Payable		**45,000**
Notes Payable		**50,000**
Rent Received in Advance		**6,000**
Capital Stock		**100,000**
Retained Earnings		**147,800**
Services		**360,000**
Utilities	**19,900**	
Salaries Expense	**125,000**	
Advertising Expense	**107,000**	
	782,000	782,000

d. Journalize the adjusting entries.
e. Journalize the closing entries.

P7-4 Explain the impact of the following situations on net income and on total assets.

a. Depreciation expense was overstated in the amount of $25,000.
b. The Prepaid Rent account was not adjusted at the close of the fiscal year to reflect rent expense incurred during the year.
c. The Allowance for Doubtful Receivables was erroneously credited for $30,000 instead of the correct $50,000 when the adjusting entry was made.
d. Accrued utilities expense of $15,000 were not recorded.
e. Accrued interest receivable was not recorded.
f. The Unearned Interest account was not adjusted to reflect $7,000 interest income earned during the year.
g. The Office Expense account was not adjusted to show an office supplies inventory of $21,000.

P7-5 A two-year fire insurance policy was purchased for $4,800 on July 1, 19_5. At the end of 19_6, a question arose about the proper amount of prepaid insurance that should be reflected in the balance sheet. The following three proposals were made.

1. List the policy as $800 of prepaid insurance, the short-rate cancellation value of the policy at the end of the year.
2. List it at $1,200, one-fourth of the original cost.
3. List it at $1,800, the current cost of the premium for a similar six-month policy.

Discuss the three proposals and state reasons for or against each.

P7-6 In studying the financial statements of the MIT Company, you compare the balance sheets as of December 31, 19_5, and December 31, 19_6. The statements show prepaid insurance of $1,800 in 19_5 and $3,100 in 19_6. The income statement for 19_6 shows insurance expense of $2,000. How much money did the company actually pay out for insurance premiums during 19_6?

P7-7 The Ra Ra Fraternity publishes a quarterly magazine. A one-year subscription (four issues) costs $6; a two-year subscription costs $10. During 19_6, the fraternity made the following subscription sales.

	One-year subscriptions	Two-year subscriptions
1st quarter	400	200
2nd quarter	800	600
3rd quarter	1,600	1,000
4th quarter	2,000	1,000

Magazines are mailed to each subscriber starting with the issue for the quarter during which the subscription is received. The fraternity closes its books on December 31. Compute the correct amount of revenue earned and the amount of unearned revenue for 19_6.

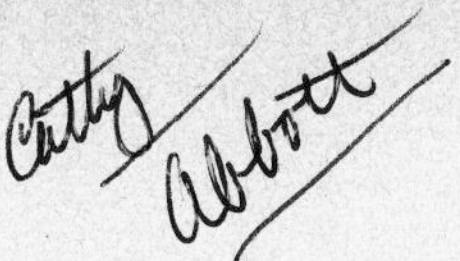

P7-8 Exhibit 7-17 shows financial statements for the Match Company. The accountant who prepared these statements failed to take into account the following information.

a. Accrued salaries on December 31, 19_6, were $3,000.
b. Depreciation expense for the year was $12,000.
c. Interest receivable at the end of the year was $800.
d. Insurance expense for the year was $1,500.
e. Rental income earned but not collected was $1,800.

Required: Prepare corrected financial statements.

HINT: Set up a work sheet and use it to reconstruct the unadjusted trial balance. Then begin from there and complete corrected statements.

P7-9 The balance sheet shown in Exhibit 7-18 is forwarded to you for evaluation. Your investigation of the company's records reveals the following information.

a. It is estimated that $1,700 of the accounts receivable will not be collected.
b. The plant and equipment is considered to be 20 percent depreciated as of the statement date.
c. No adjustment was made for accrued salaries of $650.
d. Prepaid insurance in the amount of $1,100 was ignored when the adjusting entries were made.
e. Interest expense of $700 on the loan payable had accrued as of the statement date.

Required: Prepare a corrected balance sheet.

SUGGESTION: Try to adjust the statement of financial position without the help of a work sheet.

P7-10 Prepare any required adjusting entries on December 31, 19_9, for the following items. Assume that in prior years, correct adjusting entries were made where required.

a. A company purchased the following insurance policies and debited Insurance Expense account when the policies were purchased:

19_7 Jan. 1	2-year policy	$24,000
19_8 Jan. 1	2-year policy	24,000
19_8 July 1	2-year policy	24,000
19_9 Jan. 1	2-year policy	24,000
19_9 July 1	2-year policy	24,000

b. A company sells magazine subscriptions to its monthly magazine. When the magazines are sold, the company credits a Subscriptions Revenue account.

	One-year subscriptions	Two-year subscriptions
19_7 July 1	$29,000	$24,000
19_8 July 1	40,000	48,000
19_9 July 1	12,000	24,000

P7-11 *a.* The Award Company's accountant did not record accruals and prepayments for the year. Information regarding reported net income, accruals and prepayments at the end of the year are shown here:

Reported net income for the year	$10,000
Accrued expenses	5,000

Exhibit 7-17 **Financial statements for Problem P7-8**

MATCH COMPANY

Income Statement
For the Year Ended December 31, 19_6

Revenue:		
Services	$210,000	
Rent Income	60,000	$270,000
Less expenses:		
Salaries expense	$ 81,000	
Rent expense	12,000	
Utilities expense	7,000	100,000
Net income		$170,000

MATCH COMPANY

Statement of Financial Position
December 31, 19_6

Assets

Current assets:		
Cash	$ 8,500	
Marketable securities	21,000	
Accounts receivable (net)	27,000	
Notes receivable	3,000	
Inventory	42,000	
Prepaid insurance	3,500	$105,000
Property and equipment:		
Land	$ 60,000	
Building (net)	160,000	220,000
Total Assets		$325,000

Liabilities and Owners' Equity

Current liabilities:			
Accounts payable		$ 65,000	
Notes payable		15,000	$ 80,000
Owners' equity:			
Common stock	$160,000		
Additional paid-in capital	20,000	$180,000	
Retained earnings		65,000	245,000
Total liabilities and owners' equity			$325,000

MATCH COMPANY

Statement of Retained Earnings
For the Year Ended December 31, 19_6

Retained earnings, January 1, 19_6	$ 10,000
Net income for the year	170,000
	$180,000
Less dividends	115,000
Retained earnings, December 31, 19_6	$ 65,000

Exhibit 7-18
Balance sheet for Problem P7-9

STIKY TAPE COMPANY
Statement of Financial Position
December 31, 19_6

Assets		**Liabilities and Owners' Equity**	
Cash	**$ 40,000**	**Accounts payable**	**$ 15,000**
Accounts receivable	**30,000**	**Loan payable**	**31,000**
Inventories	**100,000**	**Common stock**	**240,000**
Plant and equipment	**105,000**	**Retained earnings**	**30,000**
Patents	**19,000**		
Goodwill	**22,000**		
Total assets	$316,000	Total liabilities and owners' equity	$316,000

Prepaid expenses	$7,000
Accrued income	3,000
Unearned income	4,000

Required: Compute the correct net income for the year according to generally accepted accounting principles.

b. The following account balances were taken from the records of a company:

	Beginning Balance	Ending Balance
Prepaid salary expense	$500	$800
Accrued salary expense	200	400

Cash paid for salaries during the year totalled $15,000.

Required: Compute the salary expense for the year to be reported on this year's income statement.

8 Impact analysis

In the last three chapters, we have concentrated on the details of accounting procedure, as reflected in journal entries and ledger accounts. We have seen how to record, analyze, and process data about many kinds of transactions. But our focus on practical matters of procedure tends to confuse and conceal the broader impact of transactions on the accounting system as a whole. Such narrow vision impedes or limits the managerial and administrative uses of accounting. To avoid distortion in our image of the accounting system, it's a good idea to take another look at the forest (the overall picture) after spending some time examining the trees (the details).

In this chapter we examine the ***impact*** of events on the major sets and subsets of data in the accounting system. A student of business must understand the ***ripple effect*** by which a specific transaction causes changes throughout the system. It is not enough to be skillful at paperwork—knowing just the right way to process data for a particular event such as a sale on account. Such mastery of procedures by itself gives a narrow and inadequate view of accounting. It must be combined with an understanding of the impact of the specific event on other sets, categories, and classifications in the system—on working capital, net assets, owners' equity, and so on.

When you understand the impact of events on all the parts of the accounting system, you can begin to understand their impact on the system as a whole. Then you can suggest ways to improve or correct the whole system by recommending and carrying out changes in specific parts of the system. For example, what can be done to improve the rate of return on investment of a firm (its net income divided by total assets)? The value of the ratio will be increased if net income is increased. Net income is a function of revenue and expense; net income will be increased if revenue is increased or if expenses are decreased. On the other hand, the rate of return also will increase if the investment in total assets can be decreased without reducing net income. In order to improve the rate of return, we need certain patterns of change in various parts of the system. What kinds of transactions tend to bring about those particular patterns of change? What kinds of transactions tend to produce patterns of change that decrease the rate of return? Which of the company's activities should be encouraged and which discouraged? Impact analysis of this sort is central to managerial accounting. We return to it again and again throughout this text.

Impact of events on basic classifications

To demonstrate impact analysis of events on basic accounting classifications, we use the thirteen transactions of the XYZ Company introduced in Chapter 5. We examine the impact of these events on a number of basic categories: owners' equity, net assets, assets, liabilities, working capital, and some important ratios. The discussion in the text is brief. You will come to understand the impact of the events best through careful study of the exhibits and through study of other examples on your own.

Implicit in the exhibits of this chapter are certain ***key*** concepts of impact analysis and the ripple effect that are basic to an understanding of accounting. Exhibit 8-1 shows the impact of the thirteen transactions on the elements of the basic accounting

Exhibit 8-1 Impact analysis and the accounting equation

	ASSETS		− LIABILITIES		= OWNERS' EQUITY	
TRANSACTION	**Increase Debit**	**Decrease Credit**	**Decrease Debit**	**Increase Credit**	**Decrease Debit**	**Increase Credit**
1. Common stock sold for cash.	+100,000					+100,000
2. Land & building purchased for cash.	+20,000 +50,000	−70,000				
3. Office equipment purchased on account.	+10,000			+10,000		
4. Cash payment on account payable.		−8,000	−8,000			
5. Cash borrowed.	+50,000			+50,000		
6. Services sold for cash.	+60,000					+60,000
7. Services sold on account.	+8,000					+8,000
8. Cash collected on an account receivable.	+6,000	−6,000				
9. Salaries paid in cash.		−30,000			−30,000	
10. Rent paid in cash.		−20,000			−20,000	
11. Utilities bill received (not paid).				+5,000	−5,000	
12. Income tax expense & tax liability recorded.				+5,000	−5,000	
13. Dividends declared (not paid).				+2,000	−2,000	
Total	+304,000	−134,000	−8,000	+72,000	−62,000	+168,000

NOTE: Plus and minus signs only emphasize effect of each transaction in increasing or decreasing a particular category balance. Each entry in a debit column, for example, is a debit entry regardless of the + or − shown.

equation, $A - L = OE$. The table shows the changes in each element caused by each transaction, both in terms of increases and decreases (+ and −) and in terms of debits and credits (separate columns).

The column totals demonstrate that the accounting system maintains the basic equality as events are recorded:

$$\text{Total debits} = \text{Total credits};$$
$$\$304{,}000 + \$8{,}000 + \$62{,}000 = \$134{,}000 + \$72{,}000 + \$168{,}000;$$
$$\$374{,}000 = \$374{,}000.$$

(Notice that similar totals of increases and decreases do ***not*** balance.)

Study Exhibit 8-1 carefully to see how each transaction affects assets, liabilities, and owners' equity. For example, note that transaction 2 has no effect on the total assets. One asset (cash) is exchanged for two other assets (land and building). A $70,000 credit is offset by debits of $50,000 and $20,000, all three entries being in asset accounts. Total assets, total liabilities, and owners' equity remain unchanged by this transaction. Is this true for any cash purchase? Is it true for a purchase on account? Is it true whenever cash is paid out? This exhibit contains a wealth of information that can help you understand the impact of events on the accounting system, but the understanding will come only as you work out carefully for yourself the effects of each transaction and think about the implications.

Total assets represent the economic resources of the firm. How can these resources be increased? An increase in assets can occur only when there is a corresponding increase in liabilities (economic obligations) or in owners' equity (residual interest of the owners). Which kinds of transactions involve each of these situations?

Try thinking of the accounting equation in its other form, $A = L + OE$. This emphasizes that the assets are divided between the claims of the creditors and the residual interest of the owners. This viewpoint may lead to new insights about the relationships implied in the exhibit.

Exhibit 8-2 summarizes the same basic equation in its most compact form, $NA = OE$. (Remember that net assets represent the excess of assets over liabilities, $NA = A - L$.) This table emphasizes the fact that the residual interest (owners' equity) in a business entity changes directly with changes in net assets. That is, when one increases, so must the other; when one decreases, so must the other. One of the major reasons that anyone invests money in a business—becomes an owner—is to increase his residual interest in the business. That is, he wants to make a profit on his investment. If a business is to survive and grow, it must have owners willing to invest in it. Therefore, the increase in owners' equity must be one very important goal of management, if not the most important goal. The ability of the accounting system to reveal just how certain kinds of events—or certain specific events—affect net assets is the major reason that management and owners rely on the outputs of the system as powerful tools to help in their decision making. For, as net assets go, so goes owners' equity.

Exhibit 8-3 demonstrates the impact of the thirteen transactions on working capital, a key concept in accounting. Working capital (current assets less current liabilities) focuses attention on the short-term financial position of the firm. If working capital

Exhibit 8-2 **Impact analysis and net assets**

TRANSACTION	NET ASSETS Increase Debit	NET ASSETS Decrease Credit	= OWNERS' EQUITY Decrease Debit	OWNERS' EQUITY Increase Credit
1. Common stock sold for cash.	+100,000			+100,000
2. Land & building purchased for cash.				
3. Office equipment purchased on account.				
4. Cash payment on account payable.				
5. Cash borrowed.				
6. Services sold for cash.	+60,000			+60,000
7. Services sold on account.	+8,000			+8,000
8. Cash collected on account receivable.				
9. Salaries paid in cash.		−30,000	−30,000	
10. Rent paid in cash.		−20,000	−20,000	
11. Utilities bill received (not paid).		−5,000	−5,000	
12. Income tax expense & tax liability recorded.		−5,000	−5,000	
13. Dividends declared (not paid).		−2,000	−2,000	
Total	+168,000	−62,000	−62,000	+168,000

NOTE: This table shows only the *net* effect of each transaction on the net assets columns. For example, in transaction 2 net assets are debited $70,000 and credited $70,000; the net effect shown here is to leave net assets unchanged. Observe that total debits ($168,000 + $62,000) equal total credits ($62,000 + $168,000). Observe also that increases in net assets equal increases in owners' equity, while decreases in net assets equal decreases in owners' equity. This is the basic equality maintained in the accounting system through the continual balance of debits and credits.

is too small, the firm has a constant struggle to come up with the cash to pay its bills as they fall due. It may find that suppliers and banks are no longer willing to advance credit. Many problems associated with liquidity and growth can be traced directly to the need for adequate working capital. Therefore, it is very important to understand the impact of various kinds of events upon working capital. For example, if the firm is having a liquidity problem due to a shortage of working capital, which kinds of transactions should be postponed and which speeded up to help ease the difficulty? Again, spend a lot of time studying the exhibit to absorb the many implications that it contains. Note that transaction 2, which has no effect upon total assets and liabilities, has a very heavy impact on the working capital.

Impact of events on ratios

Exhibit 8-4 further demonstrates the ripple effect of events on the accounting system. Here we move beyond the basic categories themselves to look at the effects of events on ratios of those categories. The exhibit summarizes the effects of the thirteen transactions on the current ratio, the net income per share of common stock, and the return on investment. In fact, the example of the XYZ Company is not very well suited to this study of ratios because some important categories (such as net income) have a zero balance through the first five transactions. The entries in the table show the effects that would occur from a similar transaction under more normal circumstances.

For example, rate of return on investment is the ratio of net income to total assets. In the case of the XYZ Company, there is no net income until transaction 6, so the

Exhibit 8-3 Impact analysis and working capital

TRANSACTION	CURRENT ASSETS		−	CURRENT LIABILITIES		=	WORKING CAPITAL	
	Increase	Decrease		Decrease	Increase		Increase	Decrease
1. Common stock sold for cash.	+100,000						+100,000	
2. Land & building purchased for cash.		−70,000						−70,000
3. Office equipment purchased on account.					+10,000			−10,000
4. Cash payment on account payable.		−8,000		−8,000			no effect	
5. Cash borrowed (short-term loan).	+50,000				+50,000		no effect	
6. Services sold for cash.	+60,000						+60,000	
7. Services sold on account.	+8,000						+8,000	
8. Cash collected on account receivable.	+6,000	−6,000					no effect	
9. Salaries paid in cash.		−30,000						−30,000
10. Rent paid in cash.		−20,000						−20,000
11. Utilities bill received (not paid).					+5,000			−5,000
12. Income tax expense & tax liability recorded.					+5,000			−5,000
13. Dividends declared (not paid).					+2,000			−2,000
	+224,000	−134,000		−8,000	+72,000		+168,000	−142,000

NOTE: Debits and credits in this table do not balance because the transactions involve other entries in the system that are not included here. In fact, working capital can change only when a transaction involves both a current account (current assets or current liabilities) *and* a noncurrent account (any other account). The first transaction increases working capital because it involves an increase in current assets (cash) that is balanced by an increase in a noncurrent account (common stock). Transaction 4 does not affect the working capital because it involves offsetting decreases in current accounts.

Observe that the net effect of the thirteen transactions is to increase current assets by $90,000 and to increase current liabilities by $64,000. Thus the net effect is to increase working capital by $26,000. This value can be computed either from the net changes in current assets and current liabilities ($90,000 − $64,000) or from the totals of the changes in working capital ($168,000 − $142,000). An understanding of the impact of the events on current assets, current liabilities, and working capital is of value in the study of Chapter 20, which deals with the statement of changes in financial position.

Exhibit 8-4 **Impact analysis and ratios**

Transaction	CURRENT RATIO	NET INCOME PER SHARE ON COMMON STOCK	RETURN ON INVESTMENT
1. Common stock sold for cash.	Increase*	Decrease*	Decrease*
2. Land & building purchased for cash.	Decrease*	No effect	No effect
3. Office equipment purchased on account.	Decrease	No effect	Decrease*
4. Cash payment on account payable.	Increase	No effect	Increase*
5. Cash borrowed (short-term loan).	Decrease	No effect	Decrease*
6. Services sold for cash.	Increase	Increase	Increase
7. Services sold on account.	Increase	Increase	Increase
8. Cash collected on account receivable.	No effect	No effect	No effect
9. Salaries paid in cash.	Decrease	Decrease	Decrease
10. Rent paid in cash.	Decrease	Decrease	Decrease
11. Utilities bill received (not paid).	Decrease	Decrease	Decrease
12. Income tax expense & tax liability recorded.	Decrease	Decrease	Decrease
13. Dividends declared (not paid).	Decrease	No effect	No effect

NOTE: The entries marked with an asterisk (*) represent the normal effects of similar transactions on these ratios. In the particular example being used, current liabilities are zero until the third transaction and net income is zero until the sixth transaction. Therefore, the values of these ratios are infinite or zero in these cases and the normal changes in values cannot be observed. In the case of transaction 1, for example, the issuance of additional stock would normally (1) increase current assets without changing current liabilities, thus increasing the current ratio, (2) increase the number of shares of common stock without changing net income, thus decreasing the net income per share, and (3) increase the total assets without changing net income, thus decreasing the return on investment. However, when one of the categories in a ratio has a zero balance, the value of the ratio will always be either zero ($0/x$) or infinite ($x/0$), so changes in the category represented by x will not change the ratio. In transactions 1 through 5 we assume that there are current liabilities and net income.

As a general rule, if the value of a ratio is less than 1.00, equal increases in both quantities in the ratio cause the value of the ratio to increase. For example, $3/4 = 0.75$ and $(3 + 1)/(4 + 1) = 4/5 = 0.80$. Similarly, equal decreases in both numerator, and denominator cause the value of the ratio to decrease. (In Exhibit 8-4, the return on investment ratio is $1 < 1$.)

On the other hand, if the value of the ratio is greater than 1.00, equal increases in both quantities in the ratio cause the value of the ratio to decrease. For example, $4/3 = 1.33$ and $(4 + 1)/(3 + 1) = 5/4 = 1.25$. Equal decreases in both numerator and denominator cause the value of the ratio to increase. The analysis of the effect of events on the current ratio in our illustration assumes that current assets exceed current liabilities. (In Exhibit 8-4, the current ratio is $1 < 1$.)

Finally, if the value of the ratio is exactly 1.00 (numerator equal to denominator), equal changes in numerator and denominator will have no effect on the value of the ratio, which will remain 1.00.

rate of return in this case remains zero through the first five transactions. This conceals the fact that the changes in total assets in some of these transactions would normally affect the rate of return of the firm. The table shows the more general impact of such transactions on the ratios.

Compare the impact of the transactions on the current ratio (current assets divided by current liabilities) with their impact on working capital (Exhibit 8-3). Both the current ratio and the working capital are measures of the firm's liquidity, but not all events have the same impact on the two measures. Note the impacts of transactions 4 and 5 on these two measures, for example.

Impact of adjusting entries

We can extend impact analysis even farther to look at the impact on various categories and ratios of the kinds of events that are usually recorded by adjustments to the books at the end of a period. These adjusting entries are discussed in Chapter 7. Exhibit 8-5 summarizes some of the impact felt throughout the system if the appropriate adjustments are ***not*** made at the end of the accounting period.

Review the nature of the entries made for each of these adjustments and the other exhibits in this chapter. You should be able to understand why the ripple effect from an omitted adjustment has these effects on the various categories and ratios.

Another word about this chapter

It would be easy to glance over these exhibits and pass quickly on, feeling that you have grasped the main points mentioned in the text. We want to emphasize again that these few exhibits illustrate many of the key concepts of accounting. An awareness of the relationships implied in these exhibits will improve your understanding of accounting. It will give you a much deeper appreciation of the services that the accounting system offers to its users. This will be the beginning of your growth as a student of financial and managerial accounting.

Exhibit 8-5 **Impact analysis and adjusting entries**

ADJUSTMENT NOT RECORDED (See Note)	NET ASSETS	OWNERS' EQUITY	NET INCOME	WORKING CAPITAL	CURRENT RATIO	EARNINGS PER SHARE ON COMMON STOCK
Accrued expense	High	High	High	High	High	High
Accrued revenue	Low	Low	Low	Low	Low	Low
Prepaid expense	High	High	High	High	High	High
Unearned revenue	Low	Low	Low	Low	Low	Low
Depreciation	High	High	High	Correct	Correct	High
Bad debts expense	High	High	High	High	High	High

NOTE: This table shows the impact of a failure to record a needed adjustment. "High" means that the value of this cateogry is overstated without the adjustment; that is, the value computed will be larger than the true value that would be obtained with the required adjustment. Similarly, "Low" means that the value of the category is understated without the adjustment. "Correct" means that the value of the category is unaffected by the failure to make the adjustment.

How does one explain the impact of unrecorded adjustments on these major accounting categories? If an accrued expense is not recorded, an expense and a liability are omitted. If accrued revenue is not recorded, an asset and revenue are omitted. If the prepaid expense adjustment is not made, an expense is omitted, and the prepaid expense is overstated, because it was not adjusted. If unearned revenue is not adjusted, revenue is unrecorded, and a liability is overstated. If depreciation expense is omitted, an expense is unrecorded, and fixed assets are overstated, because the Accumulated Depreciation account (a ***contra*** asset account) is understated. Recall that fixed assets are noncurrent accounts and do not affect working capital or the current ratio. If the bad debts expense adjustment is omitted, an expense is unrecorded and the Allowance for Uncollectable Receivables (a ***contra*** asset account) is understated, which overstates the current Accounts Receivable account.

As you review the exhibits and work on the examples in the exercises and problems for this chapter, you will begin to see the many kinds of relationships that exist among elements in the accounting system. Study these relationships carefully now and keep them in mind as you go on. Don't let yourself get lost in detailed procedures as the course progresses. Keep the larger picture constantly in mind. It provides the reason for the existence of all the details.

Summary

Chapter 8 illustrates the concept of impact analysis through a study of the effect of specific transactions on various elements of the accounting system. Impact analysis requires that the analyst consider the effect of a business event or transaction on all major sets and subsets of the accounting system, as well as on the specific accounts involved.

Impact analysis helps accountants, managers, and others to penetrate the mysteries of the double-entry accounting system. It provides an invaluable tool for analysis and interpretation of financial statements. Throughout this text, we direct our emphasis toward a comprehensive view of accounting as an information system. Impact analysis plays a major role in this approach.

Questions

1. What is impact analysis?
2. Why is it important for anyone concerned with accounting outputs to be aware of the impact of
   a. transactions that are properly recorded, classified, and reported?
   b. events that are incorrectly recorded, classified, or reported due to errors, fraud, omission, or other causes?
3. In general terms, explain how each of the following items can be increased and decreased.
   a. Working capital.
   b. Current ratio.
   c. Return on investment.
   d. Net income per share.
   e. Ratio of owners' equity to total assets.
4. Describe the impact of each of the following transactions on (A) net assets, (B) owners' equity, (C) working capital, (D) current ratio, and (E) the ratio of owners' equity to total assets.
   a. The investment of cash, land, and inventory in a firm by its shareholders; additional shares of stock are issued by the firm and given in exchange for the investments.
   b. The purchase of land and machinery with cash.
   c. The purchase of land and machinery with a short-term note payable.
   d. The purchase of land and machinery with the issuance of common stock.
   e. The sale of services for cash.
   f. The sale of services on account.

g. The collection of a long-term debt owed to the firm.
h. The payment in cash of such expenses as salaries, rent, and utilities.
i. The payment in cash of a short-term debt.

5. Describe a transaction that will
a. increase an asset and increase owners' equity.
b. decrease an asset and decrease owners' equity.
c. increase an asset and increase a liability.
d. increase an asset and decrease a liability.
e. decrease an asset and decrease a liability.

Exercises

E8-1 You are the chief accountant of the Mac Company. The president of the company calls you in and expresses her concern about the net assets and the owners' equity of the business. She asks you to meet with the board of directors and explain to them what kinds of steps the firm could take that would have impact on the net assets and owners' equity of the company. Summarize the suggestions you would make to the board of directors.

E8-2 You are the controller of the Sand Company. You get a memo from the chairman of the board. He explains that the directors have been concerned about the need to raise funds to meet the firm's current liabilities and long-term debts. One of the directors feels that the company should issue additional shares of common stock to get money to retire the debts owed to creditors. In the last board meeting, there was a heated discussion about the effect this action would have on the financial position and operations of the firm. The chairman would like you to give a brief talk at the next board meeting, explaining the impact of the issuance of additional stock on (a) working capital, (b) current ratio, and (c) the ratio of owners' equity to total assets. Give a summary of the remarks you would make to the board. (For current ratio, assume 1 > 1.)

E8-3 Working capital and the current ratio are two measures used to check on a firm's liquidity—its ability to come up with the cash it needs for its day-to-day operations. Another commonly used measure of liquidity is called the ***acid-test ratio***. This is the ratio of "quick assets" to current liabilities. Quick assets include cash, receivables, and marketable securities, but ***do not*** include the current assets of inventories and prepaid expenses. Prepare a table similar to Exhibit 8-3 showing the impact of the following transactions on (A) working capital, (B) current ratio, and (C) acid-test ratio. (For the ratios, simply indicate "increase" or "decrease." Assume 1 > 1.)
a. Janitorial supplies are purchased for $600 on account.
b. Parts to be used in producing goods for sale are purchased for $2,000 cash.
c. Land is sold for $6,000 cash.
d. A building is sold and a long-term note for $100,000 accepted in payment.
e. A year's rent ($18,000) is prepaid.
f. Money is borrowed by signing a long-term note for $20,000.
g. The company sells its fleet of trucks for $80,000 and pays $20,000 as prepayment of a year's lease on a similar fleet of trucks owned by a truck rental company.

E8-4 One of the junior accountants working under you asks you to explain the impact of converting a long-term liability into a current liability. For example, a bond payable listed as a long-term liability becomes a current liability when it matures and is to be paid during the current period (from current assets). Explain the impact of such an event on the following items.

a. Current ratio (1 > 1).
b. Assets, liabilities, and owners' equity.
c. Ratio of total liabilities to owners' equity.
d. Revenue, expenses, and net income.
e. Acid-test ratio.
f. Ratio of long-term liabilities to total assets.

E8-5 Explain the impact of each of the following transactions on (A) net income per share on common stock, and (B) the current ratio (1 > 1).

a. A building is purchased with a long-term note.
b. An account payable is paid in cash.
c. Cash is borrowed from a local bank, to be repaid in two years.
d. Services are rendered to a client on account.
e. Services are rendered to a client for cash.
f. Expenses are paid in cash.
g. The following adjusting entries are made at the end of the year.

Dec. 31	Depreciation expense	XX	
	Accrued depreciation		XX
31	Rent received in advance	XX	
	Rent income		XX
31	Bad debts expense	XX	
	Allowance for doubtful receivables		XX
31	Salaries expense	XX	
	Accrued salaries payable		XX
31	Insurance expense	XX	
	Prepaid insurance		XX

E8-6 Prepare a table similar to the exhibits in this chapter, showing the effect of each of the following transactions on (A) current assets, (B) noncurrent assets, (C) liabilities, (D) owners' equity, (E) revenue, and (F) expenses. In the table entries, use +, − , and 0 to indicate increase, decrease, and no effect. Fill in all spaces in the table.

a. Owner contributes a truck to the business.
b. Equipment is purchased for cash.
c. Services are sold on account.
d. Rent is paid in cash.
e. A building is purchased with a long-term note.
f. A payment is received on an account receivable.

Problems

P8-1 Prepare a table showing the impact of the following transactions on working capital and net income.

a. Federal income taxes in the amount of $30,000 are paid; the transaction is journalized as follows.

Income Tax Expense	30,000	
Cash		30,000

b. Taxes are paid as in transaction a, but the journal entry is the following.

Income Taxes Payable	30,000	
Cash		30,000

c. A payment of $2,000 on an account receivable is made by a customer.
d. The company sells for $12,000 a product that cost it $15,000.
e. Land held as an investment (acquisition cost $15,000) is sold for $21,000.
f. The company declares and pays a dividend in the amount of $1,000.

Retained Earnings	1,000	
Cash		1,000

g. Accrued salaries at the end of the year amount to $17,100; the required adjusting entry is made.
h. On the last day of the fiscal year, the company borrows $31,000 from the bank on a six-month note; the bank gives the company $30,000 in cash and holds the remaining $1,000 as interest paid in advance.
i. Accrued interest payable amounting to $1,600 is recorded by an adjusting entry.
j. Prepaid insurance in the amount of $1,200 expired during the year; the required adjusting entry is made.
k. Accrued interest receivable amounting to $1,700 is recorded by an adjusting entry.
l. At the beginning of the year, the company purchased equipment for $16,000.
m. The equipment purchased in transaction l has a ten-year life and no scrap value; at the end of the year, the depreciation expense for the year is recorded in an adjusting entry.
n. The company receives $6,000 rental income on February 1 and this is journalized as rent received in advance.
o. The rent received in transaction n represents full payment on a two-year lease; the required adjusting entry is made at the end of the year.

P8-2 Prepare a table showing the impact of each of the following transactions on assets, liabilities, and owners' equity. Arrange the headings of the columns of the table to show the accounting equation in the form $A = L + OE$. For entries, use +, −, and 0 to indicate increase, decrease, and no effect.

a. Stockholders invest $60,000 in the company.
b. Rent is paid in cash.
c. A service is performed for a client and he is billed for the work completed.
d. A check is received in payment for the services rendered in transaction c.
e. Wages are paid in cash.
f. Money is borrowed from a bank.
g. The company purchases a building on long-term credit.
h. The bank loan is repaid with interest.

P8-3 The following are certain 19_5 transactions.

a. Advance payment for a one-year service contract was received at the beginning of 19_5 and recorded as unearned revenue. No adjustment was made.
b. Employees' wages for December were unpaid at the end of the year, and the books were closed without any adjusting entry to record this.

c. No depreciation expense on office equipment was recorded for 19_5.
d. Rent for January 19_6 was paid in December 19_5 and recorded as an expense in 19_5.
e. Interest earned on a note receivable was not recognized in 19_5.
f. Interest on a note payable was not recognized in 19_5.
g. A three-year insurance policy purchased at the beginning of 19_5 was recorded as insurance expense. No adjustment was made.
h. Advance payment for services to be rendered in 19_7 was received and recorded in 19_5 as revenue.

Each of these transactions represents a failure to make a necessary adjustment at the end of the year.

Required:

1. For each of the transactions, indicate whether the indicated errors affected the income statement, the balance sheet, or both statements.
2. Indicate the impact of each transaction on assets, liabilities, and owners' equity in a table, using ''overstated,'' ''understated,'' or ''no effect'' as the entries in the table.

9 Data processing systems

In Chapters 5 through 8, we learned how to record and analyze the transactions of the XYZ Company during a year. If companies were involved in only a few dozen transactions each year, a very simple accounting system would be all they would need. But businesses tend to grow in size and complexity. They are engaged in hundreds or thousands of transactions each day. At first, a new company may have relatively simple accounting records. But very soon the firm acquires hundreds of different accounts in its ledger, and its accounting system must deal with large numbers of transactions every day.

As the business becomes larger and more complex, the problem of processing data becomes increasingly important. A single manager can no longer keep track of all the things that are happening in the company each day. Systems must be established to enable management to control the many activities that are carried out for the firm by its various employees. Control requires a steady flow of current information summarizing the activities, so that the top management can keep in touch with what is happening. It requires procedures that prevent lower-level employees from exceeding desirable limits on their activities.

Along with the need for control comes a need to bring order into the complexity of the daily input to the accounting system. The firm is involved in numerous transactions each day, but most of these fall into certain repetitious patterns. In most businesses, daily transactions fall into groups: cash purchases and cash payments for expenses; purchases on account and payments on account; receipts of cash for sales and as payments on customers' accounts; sales on account. This means that the general journal and ledger soon fill up with page after page of entries that are almost the same. The accountant finds himself writing down the same information again and again with minor variations. With everything having to go into the same general journal and ledger, he finds it difficult to split up the work so that several clerks can handle the load of entries to be made.

In order to deal with these problems, accountants have devised shortcuts and special methods that speed up and simplify the accumulation and processing of data in the accounting system. These approaches also help in dividing the labor so that various parts of the accounting process can be assigned to different persons or teams. In this chapter we discuss certain of the procedures and controls designed to deal with complexity in a firm's acitivities. We learn how to use control accounts, subsidiary ledgers, and special journals to bring order into the complexity. In Chapter 10 we add one other similar tool to our accounting system—the voucher system.

Another tool that helps the accounting system deal with complexity is the computer. The advantage of a computer is that it has a perfect memory for a very large number of data and that it is very fast at processing those data in various ways. The disadvantage of a computer is that it has no intelligence—it does only and exactly what it is told to do with the data. An accountant (we hope) would stop and ask some questions before blindly posting a $1,000 charge to the account of a customer who just bought a garden rake. The computer will post the amount without a second (or first) thought. Everyone has heard stories of computers that dutifully sent out bills for $0.00 to all the customers with zero balances in their accounts because the programmer forgot to tell the computer what to do in such a case.

The computer can be a valuable tool in the complex accounting system, but its value depends on the skill with which accountants and programmers can tell it exactly what needs to be done. At any rate, most accountants these days will have to deal with computers, so we need to learn something about them and about how they are used by accounting systems.

Before we look at computers, though, we review some of the ways to modify the basic written accounting procedure (Chapters 5 and 6) to deal with complexity and repetition.

Control accounts and subsidiary ledgers

Thus far, we have been recording a credit sale in the general journal and general ledger in the fashion shown in Exhibit 9-1. A separate and complete entry in the journal is needed for each sale. The ledger must contain a separate subaccount for each customer.

Exhibit 9-1
General journal and general ledger entries for a credit sale

GENERAL JOURNAL **Page 531**

Date		Explanation	Ref	Debit	Credit
19_1					
Apr.	17	Accounts Receivable: X Co.	1109	100,000	
		Sale of Services	4001		100,000
		To record sale of			
		services on account			
		to X Co.			

GENERAL LEDGER

Accounts Receivable: X Company **1109**

19_1 Apr. 17	J531 100,000		

Sale of Services **4001**

		19_1 Apr. 17	J531 100,000

This procedure is adequate if the firm has only a few accounts receivable and if it makes only a few credit sales each day. But even a fairly small business may have thousands of customers with charge accounts. If each is represented by a separate page in the general ledger, it becomes hard to find the other important accounts of the company—the ledger is nearly all accounts receivable. Furthermore, the chances of error in posting to the wrong account are quite high.

To simplify the procedure, accountants often use a single Accounts Receivable account (called a ***control account***) in the general ledger. The subaccounts for specific customers are kept in a separate ledger called a ***subsidiary ledger.*** The control account shows only the overall balance of accounts receivable. The balances of individual subaccounts can be found in the subsidiary ledger. A sum of all the subaccount balances in the subsidiary ledger should equal the control account balance in the general ledger. Each time that an entry is made in the individual subaccount (subsidiary ledger), a corresponding entry is made in the control account (general ledger). Periodically, the equality of the subsidiary ledger with the control account is tested by taking a trial balance of the subsidiary ledger and comparing it to the total balance of the control account.

Note that this procedure does not disturb the overall equality of debits and credits in the general ledger. All debits and credits to any accounts receivable appear in the control account. On the other hand, the subsidiary ledger does not normally contain an equality of debits and credits. Think of the subsidiary ledger as an expanded explanation of the control account, in which Accounts Receivable entries are re-grouped by customers. The entries in the subsidiary ledger are extra entries, duplicating those in the general ledger, and they would not be included in a trial balance of the general ledger.

Exhibit 9-2 illustrates the use of a subsidiary ledger for accounts receivable. In this illustration, the company made credit sales to the X, Y, and Z Companies in the amounts of $5,000, $3,000 and $2,000, respectively. Credit sales total $10,000. During the same time period, cash payments on account were received from the X and Y Companies in the amounts of $3,000 and $2,000, respectively—a total of $5,000 in payments on accounts. Note that each entry in the control account is duplicated in the subsidiary ledger.

The control account in the general ledger summarizes all of the activity related to Accounts Receivable. From this control account, it is easy to take a balance of Accounts Receivable at any time. For example, the accounting system can readily supply management with weekly or daily reports on the balance of Accounts Receivable. At intervals (perhaps monthly), a trial balance (or schedule) of the subsidiary ledger can be prepared to make sure that the information in the control account and the subsidiary ledger are the same (Exhibit 9-3). In this case, the trial balance agrees with the control account balance ($10,000 − $5,000 = $5,000).

Exhibit 9-4 shows another illustration in which all journal and ledger entries are included. These entries record the following transactions.

January	15	Credit sale of merchandise to M Company, $2,500.
	30	Credit sale of merchandise to N Company, $1,000.
	30	Collection of $500 on account from M Company.

Exhibit 9-2
General and subsidiary ledger entries for accounts receivable

GENERAL LEDGER

Accounts Receivable **1100**

19_1				19_1			
Apr. 5	Credit sale	J53	5,000	Apr. 10	Cash collect.	J61	3,000
13	Credit sale	J64	3,000	19	Cash collect.	J72	2,000
25	Credit sale	J79	2,000				

SUBSIDIARY LEDGER

X Company

19_1				19_1			
Apr. 5	Sale	J53	5,000	Apr. 10	Cash collect.	J61	3,000

Y Company

19_1				19_1			
Apr. 13	Sale	J64	3,000	Apr. 19	Cash collect.	J72	2,000

Z Company

19_1							
Apr. 25	Sale	J79	2,000				

Exhibit 9-3
Trial balance of subsidiary ledger in Exhibit 9-2

CONTROL COMPANY
Trial Balance of Accounts Receivable Ledger
April 30, 19_1

X Company	$2,000
Y Company	1,000
Z Company	2,000
Total	$5,000

As you study the exhibit, note the following points.

1. For each transaction, two postings are made from the journal for the accounts receivable item (one for the control account in the general ledger and one for the subsidiary ledger). The two postings are both noted in the reference column of the journal. The posting to the control account is recorded by giving the account number; the posting to the subsidiary ledger is recorded by a check mark. (In this example, as is often the case, the accounts in the subsidiary ledger are arranged in alphabetical order and are not given separate account numbers.)
2. Each of the entries in the control account for Accounts Receivable is duplicated by an entry in the subsidiary ledger. A trial balance of the subsidiary ledger would agree with the balance of the control account in the general ledger.
3. A trial balance of the general ledger (*not* including the subsidiary ledger) would show total debits equal to total credits.

Exhibit 9-4
Journal and ledger entries when subsidiary ledger is used

GENERAL JOURNAL — Page 3

Date		Explanation	Ref	Debit	Credit
19_1					
Jan.	15	Accounts Receivable: M Co.	1102/√	2,500	
		Sales	4001		2,500
	30	Accounts Receivable: N Co.	1102/√	1,000	
		Sales	4001		1,000
	30	Cash	1101	500	
		Accounts Receivable: M Co.	1102/√		500

GENERAL LEDGER

Cash — 1101

Date	Ref	Amount	Date	Ref	Amount
19_1					
Jan. 30	J3	500			

Accounts Receivable — 1102

Date	Ref	Amount	Date	Ref	Amount
19_1			19_1		
Jan. 15	J3	2,500	Jan. 30	J3	500
30	J3	1,000			

Sales — 4001

Date	Ref	Amount	Date	Ref	Amount
			19_1		
			Jan. 15	J3	2,500
			30	J3	1,000

SUBSIDIARY LEDGER:
ACCOUNTS RECEIVABLE

M Company

Date	Ref	Amount	Date	Ref	Amount
19_1			19_1		
Jan. 15	J3	2,500	Jan. 30	J3	500

N Company

Date	Ref	Amount	Date	Ref	Amount
19_1					
Jan. 30	J3	1,000			

Similar control accounts and subsidiary ledgers can be set up for any category in the general ledger that is very active or contains many subaccounts. Control accounts and subsidiary ledgers often are used for Notes Receivable, Accounts Payable, Notes Payable, Common Stock, and Property, Plant, and Equipment. The use of control accounts and subsidiary ledgers offers chances to improve efficiency and control in business operations. The use of a control account and subsidiary ledger has the following advantages over the use of only a general ledger.

1. The size of the general ledger is reduced, because the individual subaccounts are replaced by a single control account.
2. The probability of errors in the general ledger is reduced, because there are fewer general ledger accounts, and there is less chance of posting an entry to the wrong account. If an error does occur, it can be localized more easily. For example, if the general ledger is off balance by $1,000, and the control account

balance disagrees with the subsidiary ledger balance by the same amount, the error probably is related to the posting of entries into the particular account using the subsidiary ledger.

3. Clerical work can be divided. The subsidiary ledger can be assigned to one person with responsibility for posting the entries in that ledger. Controls can be established over his activities. The same or another person can be given responsibility for preparing monthly bills from the balances in the subsidiary ledger for accounts receivable, for example. Work such as this can be carried out independently, while other persons are using the general ledger for normal accumulation and processing of data.
4. The control account provides an easy check on the total balance of the category for frequent reports or control checks.

Special journals

The use of subsidiary ledgers provides some advantages for the accounting system that must deal with large numbers of transactions. However, as you probably noticed, this procedure alone does not reduce the amount of paperwork needed. In fact, it greatly increases the number of ledger entries that must be made. There is a way to dramatically reduce the number of repetitious entries in the system. This involves the use of special journals along with the subsidiary ledgers.

Recall that we have discussed the general journal as the basic book of original entry for the accounting system (Chapters 5 and 6). However, many transactions are repetitive in nature; they require constant repetition of similar entries in the general journal. To meet this problem, accountants have devised ***special journals*** to record transactions that are similar and can be treated in the same manner. For example, all transactions involving cash receipts (or cash disbursements) involve a debit (or credit) to the Cash account. Each credit sale transaction requires a debit to Accounts Receivable and a credit to Sales. Each time one of these transactions is recorded in the general journal, the same account titles and reference numbers must be written out again.

Special journals are designed to permit the accountant to record all transactions of a similar nature with a maximum of efficiency. For example, one special journal might be used to record all cash receipts, another to record all cash payments, a third to record all credit sales, and a fourth to record all purchases of merchandise on account acquired for resale. The general journal then is used to record all other transactions that do not fall into one of the special categories. The entries made in the special journals are not duplicated in the general journal. All of the journals together—general and special journals—are needed to give the complete journalization of the company's transactions.

With the use of special journals, it becomes possible to divide the labor of journalization smoothly among several clerks. All business documents showing cash receipts, for example, can be routed to the clerk who keeps the special journal for cash receipts. He has responsibility for journalizing these transactions, controls can be established over his work, and he can specialize in mastering all the details involved in properly handling such journal entries. Furthermore, the design of the special journals not only reduces the amount of writing needed to record a transaction, but also permits a great reduction in the number of entries that must be posted to the general ledger control accounts. Because of these advantages, the use of special journals usually results in cost savings and improved control opportunities for a business involved in many transactions each day.

The basic idea in the design of a special journal is the use of special columns to record items of information that appear over and over again in the individual entries. For example, in a special journal for cash receipts, a special column for entering the amount of debit to the Cash account saves the need for writing the name of this account over and over again. When an accounting system is designed for a business, the special journals should be designed to meet the specific needs of that individual business. In this chapter we look at some generalized examples of commonly used special journals.

Exhibit 9-5 shows the general flow of data in an accounting system using special journals and subsidiary ledgers. Note again that the general journal serves as only one of the books of original entry for transactions, whereas the general ledger serves as a summary of all the information contained in the subsidiary ledgers, as well as containing other accounts not covered by subsidiary ledgers.

In this chapter, we look at four examples of special journals, in order to illustrate the techniques involved in the use of special journals.

1. Sales journal (SJ): journalization of sales on account.
2. Purchases journal (PJ): journalization of purchases on account.
3. Cash receipts journal (CR): journalization of cash collections.
4. Cash disbursements journal (CD): journalization of cash payments.

Remember that the exact form of special journals normally varies from one business to the next, in keeping with the differences in the kinds of transactions that recur frequently in their activities.

SALES JOURNAL

A special sales journal can be used to record sales of merchandise on account. (Cash sales are recorded in the cash receipts journal.) All credit sales tickets are routed to the clerk who keeps the sales journal; these are the source documents for entries in this special journal.

Exhibit 9-6 shows an example of a sales journal and the postings made from it to the ledgers. In this illustration, two credit sales were made during the month to the M Company and the N Company, in amounts of $2,500 and $1,000, respectively. The sales journal used here provides a column in which to note the number of the sales ticket or invoice that is the source document for the entry. Only the name of the subaccount (customer's account) being debited is written in the explanation column; it is assumed that each transaction recorded here will involve a debit to a particular account receivable and a credit to Sales. Only a single money column is provided, because the amounts of the debit and credit are the same.

After the entries are journalized, posting to the ledgers proceeds in the following steps.

1. At the end of the day, post all of that day's entries to the debit side of the individual accounts in the accounts receivable subsidiary ledger. Place a check mark

Exhibit 9-5 **Flow of information in a complex accounting system**

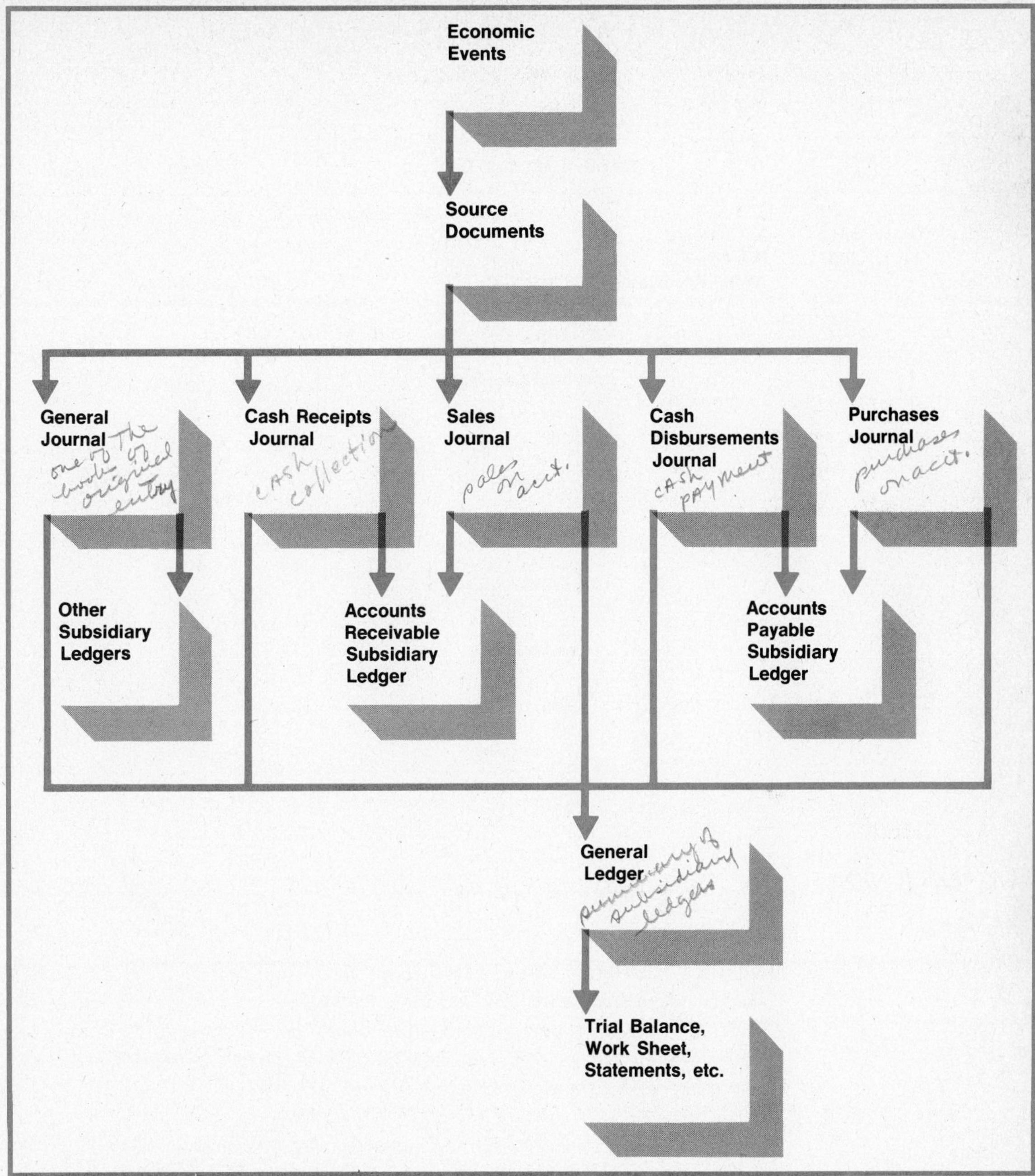

in the Reference column of the sales journal to indicate that each entry has been posted. (If the individual accounts are numbered, enter the account number here.) Enter the page number of the special journal in the Reference column of the subsidiary ledger entries. This daily posting to the subsidiary ledger keeps the customers' accounts current, so that credit status can be checked, bills sent, or inquiries answered with current information.

Exhibit 9-6 Entries in sales journal and in ledgers to record credit sales

SALES JOURNAL — Page SJ15

Date		Invoice No.	Name of Account Debited	Ref.	Amount
19_1					
Jan.	15	1512	M Company	✓	2,500
	30	1513	N Company	✓	1,000
			Accts. Receivable, Dr./Sales, Cr.	1102/4001	3,500

GENERAL LEDGER

Accounts Receivable — 1102

Date	Explanation	Ref.	Debit	Date	Explanation	Ref.	Credit
19_1							
Jan. 31	Jan. credit sales	SJ15	3,500				

Sales — 4001

Date	Explanation	Ref.	Debit	Date	Explanation	Ref.	Credit
				19_1			
				Jan. 31	Jan. credit sales	SJ15	3,500

SUBSIDIARY LEDGER:
ACCOUNTS RECEIVABLE

M Company

Date	Explanation	Ref.	Debit	Date	Explanation	Ref.	Credit
19_1							
Jan. 15		SJ15	2,500				

N Company

Date	Explanation	Ref.	Debit	Date	Explanation	Ref.	Credit
19_1							
Jan. 30		SJ15	1,000				

2. At the end of the month, post the *total* of the Amount column to the general ledger. Debit this amount to Accounts Receivable, and credit the same total amount to Sales. The general ledger account numbers are entered in the sales journal to reference the posting, and the page of the sales journal is entered as the reference for the general ledger entries.

Note that a single posting to the Accounts Receivable control account and to the Sales account in the general ledger is used to summarize a large number of individual journal entries.

As you will have noted, the use of the special journal reduces the amount of information to be written out for each entry in the journal and also reduces the number of postings to the general ledger. Furthermore, it makes possible the division of labor, with one or more clerks assigned to handle the sales journal and the accounts receivable ledger. These clerks can carry on their daily work without needing access to the general ledger. Yet the control account in the general ledger provides at least a monthly summary of the activity being recorded by the special sales journal clerks.

PURCHASES JOURNAL

If a company sells goods to its customers, it must make frequent purchases of merchandise for eventual resale. It may purchase materials that it uses in manufacturing goods for sale, or it may purchase goods at wholesale and resell them to retail customers. In either case, most of the purchases are made on account. If these transactions are journalized in a general journal, each entry involves a debit to a Purchases (or Inventory) account, and a credit of the same amount to an account payable for the specific company involved. The Purchases (or Inventory) account is used to record the cost of merchandise acquired for resale. Accounts Payable is a liability account. In earlier chapters, we used subaccounts in the general ledger for the different suppliers.

With a subsidiary ledger for accounts payable—in which each account with a supplier is kept separately—the general ledger will contain only an Accounts Payable control account, similar to that used for accounts receivable in the preceding section. A special purchases journal can be used to simplify the journalizing and posting procedures for these transactions.

Purchase transactions are discussed extensively in Chapter 13, in relation to ways of accounting for inventory. Here we simply examine the purchases journal briefly as another example of a special journal. The purchases journal (Exhibit 9-7) is designed to simplify the listing of information about purchases of merchandise on account. (Cash purchases are recorded in the cash disbursements journal.)

The source document for entries in the purchases journal is the invoice received from the seller (along with any supporting documents such as copies of purchase orders and receiving documents). These documents are routed to the clerk in charge of the purchases journal. The illustration shows entries for three purchases on account made by the company during January. The purchase order number is recorded in the journal column provided for this purpose. The explanation column contains only the name of the account payable being credited. Again, as in the sales journal, a single Amount column is used because each entry represents equal amounts debited to Purchases and credited to Accounts Payable.

After transactions are journalized in the purchases journal, posting to the ledgers involves the following steps.

1. At the end of the day, each entry is posted to the credit side of the appropriate individual account in the accounts payable subsidiary ledger, to keep these accounts current. Individual accounts payable are rarely numbered, so a check mark is used in the Reference column to show that the posting has been done. The page number from the journal is entered in the reference column for the subsidiary ledger entry.
2. At the end of the month the *total* of the Amount column is posted to the general ledger: as a debit to the Purchases account, and as a credit to Accounts Payable (the control account). The account numbers are listed as references in the journal; the journal page is listed as reference in the ledger entries.

Exhibit 9-7 **Entries in purchases journal and in ledgers to record credit purchases**

PURCHASES JOURNAL — Page PJ15

Date		Purch. Order No.	Name of Account Credited	Ref.	Amount
19_1					
Jan.	15	105	Rex Co.	✓	5,000
	20	106	Prince Co.	✓	10,000
	25	107	Pawn Co.	✓	15,000
			Purchases, Dr./Accounts Payable, Cr.	4005/2107	30,000

GENERAL LEDGER

Purchases — 4005

Date		Ref.	Amount	Date		Ref.	Amount
19_1							
Jan. 31	Jan. purchases	PJ15	30,000				

Accounts Payable — 2107

Date		Ref.	Amount	Date		Ref.	Amount
				19_1			
				Jan. 31	Jan. purchases	PJ15	30,000

SUBSIDIARY LEDGER: ACCOUNTS PAYABLE

Pawn Company

Date		Ref.	Amount	Date		Ref.	Amount
				19_1			
				Jan. 25		PJ15	15,000

Prince Company

Date		Ref.	Amount	Date		Ref.	Amount
				19_1			
				Jan. 20		PJ15	10,000

Rex Company

Date		Ref.	Amount	Date		Ref.	Amount
				19_1			
				Jan 15		PJ15	5,000

Control of purchasing is an important problem for management. The purchasing department of the firm should have the exclusive authority to make purchases of merchandise. The purchasing department should issue purchase orders (serially numbered and signed by a person with the proper authority) only after the need for the item has been verified, competitive bids obtained, and approval for the purchase documented. The receiving department should examine the merchandise when it arrives to determine the quantities and quality of goods received. The merchandise received should be compared with the purchase order to make sure that what was ordered has been received. The receiving department transfers the merchandise to the stores department, where it again is counted and inspected before it is accepted. The stores department then notifies the accounting department that the merchandise ordered has been received. The accounting department now can make payment on account to the supplier.

The storekeeper is responsible for the merchandise in inventory. He should issue merchandise from stores only when he is given a prenumbered requisition form, properly authorized. In a merchandising business, the requisition form will usually be an order from the sales department.

All of these procedures are designed to ensure that complete records are kept of all transfers of merchandise and all transactions. They also ensure that control can be maintained over purchases charged to the company's accounts with suppliers and over the use of merchandise once it has arrived. Good purchase control practices require that the purchasing, receiving, storing, and accounting functions be clearly separated.

CASH RECEIPTS JOURNAL

Accounting systems often use a special journal to record all receipts of cash, including cash sales. (Remember that cash includes currency, coins, checks, money orders, bank drafts, or any other items that can be deposited in a checking account.) Because this journal is used to record many different kinds of transactions (all involving a debit to the Cash account), the special journal form usually provides a large number of columns to simplify the recording of the most common kinds of transactions.

Exhibit 9-8 shows a typical cash receipts journal. It includes the usual columns for date and explanations, as well as the following special columns.

1. Cash column. The amount of each cash receipt is entered here. This is the amount of the debit to the Cash account.
2. Sales Discounts column. The amount of any cash discount granted on a sale to a customer is entered here. The discounts are debited to a contra revenue (negative sales) account called Sales Discounts.

When a company sells merchandise on credit, it often offers the buyer a discount for prompt payment, to encourage quick collection of the accounts receivable. This discount usually is expressed as a percentage that can be deducted from the gross amount of the invoice. For example, the seller's invoice may state that the credit terms are "2/10, n/30." The phrase "2/10" means that the buyer may deduct 2 percent of the gross amount of the invoice if he makes payment within 10 days from the date of the invoice. If he does not pay within 10 days, he must pay the full amount of the invoice within 30 days ("n/30" means "net thirty days"). Because discounts represent attractive savings to a purchaser, he often gives priority to the payment of invoices that offer discounts. Thus the seller gets quick settlement of his accounts receivable in return for the cost of the discount. In a general journal, the collection of an account receivable involving a sales discount would require a compound entry debiting Cash and Sales Discounts and crediting the account receivable of the individual customer.

3. Reference column. This column is used to record the posting of cash collections on accounts receivable to the appropriate subsidiary ledger.
4. Accounts Receivable column. This column is used to record the amount of a credit to an account receivable (when a cash payment on account is received).

Exhibit 9-8 Entries in cash receipts journal and in ledgers

CASH RECEIPTS JOURNAL

Page CR5

Date		Explanation	Cash Dr.	Sales Discounts Dr.	Ref.	Accounts Receivable Cr.	Sales Cr.	Sundry Accounts			
								Ref.	✓	Dr.	Cr.
19_1											
Jan.	15	Issued common stock	100,000					3001	✓		100,000
	17	Cash sale	5,000				5,000				
	22	B.B. Smith Co.	500		✓	500					
	24	A.C. Blue Co.	980	20	✓	1,000					
	25	Mktbl. Sec.	950					1104			1,000
								5006	✓	50	
			107,430	20		1,500	5,000			50	101,000
			[1101]	[4002]		[1102]	[4001]			[✓]	[✓]

GENERAL LEDGER

Cash 1101

Date	Explanation	Ref.	Amount	Date	Explanation	Ref.	Amount
19_1							
Jan. 31	Jan. Rcpts.	CR5	107,430				

Accounts Receivable 1102

Date	Explanation	Ref.	Amount	Date	Explanation	Ref.	Amount
19_1				19_1			
Jan. 1	Balance	✓	2,500	Jan. 31	Jan. pmts.	CR5	1,500
31	Jan. sales	SJ8	1,000				

Marketable Securities 1104

Date	Explanation	Ref.	Amount	Date	Explanation	Ref.	Amount
19_1				19_1			
Jan. 1	Balance	✓	5,000	Jan. 25	Sale of sec.	CR5	1,000

Common Stock 3001

19_1				19_1			
				Jan. 1	Balance	✓	500,000
				15	Issue	CR5	100,000

Sales 4001

				19_1			
				Jan. 31	Cash sales	CR5	5,000
				31	Acct. sales	SJ8	1,000

Sales Discounts 4002

19_1							
Jan. 31	Jan. Dscnts.	CR5	20				

Loss on Sale of Marketable Securities 5006

19_1							
Jan. 25		CR5	50				

SUBSIDIARY LEDGER: ACCOUNTS RECEIVABLE

B.B. Smith Company

19_1				19_1			
Jan. 1	Balance	✓	1,000	Jan. 22		CR5	500

A.C. Blue Company

19_1				19_1			
Jan. 1	Balance	✓	1,500	Jan. 24		CR5	1,000
	Credit sale	SJ8	1,000				

The name of the individual account to be credited is shown in the explanation column.

When a customer takes a sales discount, the ***gross*** (total) amount of the account being settled is listed in the Accounts Receivable column (and credited to the appropriate ledger account). For example, in the transaction recorded on January 24, the A.C. Blue Company had been billed for $1,000. This is the amount that has been posted as a debit in their account receivable for some earlier transaction. When they receive the bill (invoice), they send payment within ten days and take the 2 percent sales discount. Therefore they send a payment of $1,000 − $20 = $980. The cash receipt of $980 is recorded in the Cash column and the $20 discount in the Sales Discounts column. This payment does fully settle what they owe, so we must credit their account with $1,000 to balance the debit entered earlier. This is why the discount is treated as a debit and recorded in a special contra revenue account. To summarize the analysis of this transaction, we note again that Cash is debited $980 and Sales Discounts is debited $20; these debits are balanced by a $1,000 credit to Accounts Receivable.

5. Sales column. The amounts of all cash sales are entered here. These amounts will be credited to the Sales account.
6. Sundry Accounts columns. These columns provide a shortened version of the general journal form. They are used to record debit or credit items on unusual cash transactions, where all debits and credits cannot be recorded in the other columns.

The example illustrated in Exhibit 9-8 records the following transactions.

January 15 **Common stock issued for $100,000 cash.**
17 **Cash sale for $5,000.**
22 **Collection of $500 from B.B. Smith Company for a sale made in December.**
24 **Collection of $1,000 account receivable from A.C. Blue Company after a 2 percent cash discount was taken on a sale made on January 18. Cash in the amount of $980 was received.**
25 **Marketable securities purchased in November for $1,000 were sold at a loss for $950.**

In the transaction recorded on January 25, the securities have been shown as a $1,000 debit in the Marketable Securities (asset) account, because this was the acquisition cost of the asset. So, that account must be credited $1,000 to show that these particular securities no longer are held as an asset. The cash receipt of $950 is recorded as a debit to Cash. An additional debit of $50 is needed to balance the entry. This debit is entered in an expense account called Loss on Sale of Marketable Securities. Note that both the credit to Marketable Securities and the $50 debit to the expense account are recorded in the Sundry Accounts columns.

After the cash receipt transactions have been journalized in the special journal, the following steps are involved in posting the entries to the ledgers.

1. At the end of the day, post entries in the Accounts Receivable column to the credit side of the individual accounts in the accounts receivable subsidiary ledger,

in order to keep the customers' accounts current for reasons discussed earlier. Indicate the posting by a check mark in the Reference column next to the Accounts Receivable column. Cross-reference the special journal page in the ledger entries.

2. At the end of the month (or as often as required by control and reporting procedures),
   a. post entries in the Sundry Accounts columns to the appropriate general ledger accounts; and
   b. total the columns and post these amounts (except the sundry accounts) to the appropriate general ledger accounts. Cross-reference these postings.

The reference numbers for the entries in the Sundry Accounts columns are entered at the time of journalization to identify the accounts involved. Therefore, a separate column is provided for check marks to show that the posting has been done. In this example, the account numbers to which the column totals are posted have been written in the columns below the totals. The amounts in the Sundry Accounts columns have already been posted, so those totals are not posted again; the check marks simply show that no errors have been found and that all items in the columns have been posted. Note that the total of the Accounts Receivable column *is* posted to the control account in the general ledger; the individual entries have already been posted to the subsidiary ledger.

It is a good practice to total the debit and credit columns in the special journal, to make sure that there is a balance between total debits and total credits for the month's entries. In this case, total debits do equal total credits:

$107,430 + $20 + $50 = $107,500 = $1,500 + $5,000 + $101,000.

The check marks beneath the Sundry Accounts totals are used in this case to show that all entries in the columns have been posted and that the totals are not to be posted.

The source documents for entries in the cash receipts journal may vary widely in nature. Cash sales probably will be documented by sales tickets, payments on account by checks and / or invoices with notations of payments received, and other transactions by various appropriate documents or checks.

CASH DISBURSEMENTS JOURNAL

A cash disbursements journal often is used to record all transactions that involve cash disbursements (credits to the Cash account). Like the cash receipts journal, the cash disbursements journal (Exhibit 9-9) contains columns for transactions that occur frequently and Sundry Accounts columns to record unusual transactions. The journal illustrated here provides the following columns.

1. Cash column. The amount of each cash disbursement; the total of this column is entered as a credit to the Cash account.
2. Purchase Discounts column. Cash discounts are discussed in the section on the cash receipts journal. When the company takes a cash discount on an invoice that it is paying, the discount is listed here and credited to a Purchase Discounts (contra Purchases) account.

Exhibit 9-9 Entries in cash disbursements journal and in ledgers

CASH DISBURSEMENTS JOURNAL

Page CD9

Date		Explanation	Cash Cr.	Purchase Discounts Cr.	Ref.	Accounts Payable Dr.	Purchases Dr.	Sundry Accounts			
								Ref.	√	Dr.	Cr.
19_1											
Jan.	15	Cash Purchase	5,000				5,000				
	20	Green & Smith	1,000		√	1,000					
	29	Salaries	10,000					5002	√	10,000	
	30	Rent	5,000					5003	√	5,000	
	31	Red Co.	980	20	√	1,000					
			21,980	20		2,000	5,000			15,000	
			[1101]	[4006]		[2107]	[4005]			[√]	

GENERAL LEDGER

Cash — 1101

Date	Explanation	Ref.	Dr.	Date	Explanation	Ref.	Cr.
				19_1			
				Jan. 31	Jan. disbursements	CD9	21,980

Accounts Payable — 2107

Date	Explanation	Ref.	Dr.	Date	Explanation	Ref.	Cr.
19_1				19_1			
Jan. 31	Jan. disbursements	CD9	2,000	Jan. 1	Balance	√	1,500
				31	Jan. purchases	PJ7	1,000

Purchases — 4005

Date	Explanation	Ref.	Dr.	Date	Explanation	Ref.	Cr.
19_1							
Jan. 31	Jan. cash purchases	CD9	5,000				
31	Jan. acct. purchases	PJ7	1,000				

Purchase Discounts 4006

Date	Item	Ref.	Amount	Date	Item	Ref.	Amount
				19_1 Jan. 31	Jan. discounts	CD9	20

Salary Expense 5002

Date	Item	Ref.	Amount	Date	Item	Ref.	Amount
19_1 Jan. 29	Jan. salaries	CD9	10,000				

Rent Expense 5003

Date	Item	Ref.	Amount	Date	Item	Ref.	Amount
19_1 Jan. 30	Jan. rent	CD9	5,000				

SUBSIDIARY LEDGER: ACCOUNTS PAYABLE

Green & Smith Company

Date	Item	Ref.	Amount	Date	Item	Ref.	Amount
19_1 Jan. 20		CD9	1,000	19_1 Jan. 1	Balance	✓	1,000

Red Company

Date	Item	Ref.	Amount	Date	Item	Ref.	Amount
19_1 Jan. 31		CD9	1,000	19_1 Jan. 1	Balance	✓	500
				25		PJ7	1,000

3. Reference column. Notation of posting to accounts payable subsidiary ledger.
4. Accounts Payable column. Records amount to be debited to Accounts Payable control account (general ledger) and to accounts for individual creditors (subsidiary ledger).
5. Purchases column. Records amount to be debited to Purchases account for cash purchases.
6. Sundry Accounts columns. Used in the same way as the Sundry Accounts columns in the cash receipts journal, to record any items posted to accounts not covered by the other columns.

The illustration in Exhibit 9-9 shows entries for the following transactions. The source documents for this journal are the check stubs that indicate the disbursement of cash.

January 15	Check No. 7001. Cash purchase, $5,000.
20	Check No. 7002. Payment to Green & Smith Co. on account, $1,000.
29	Check Nos. 7003–7015. Payment of January salaries, total $10,000.
30	Check No. 7016. Payment of January rent, $5,000.
31	Check No. 7017. Payment to Red Company on account of $980 after taking a 2 percent cash discount on a $1,000 invoice.

If a general journal had been used to record the last transaction, it would have been recorded by a compound entry, debiting the account payable for the Red Company by $1,000, and crediting Purchase Discounts by $20 and Cash by $980. In preparing the income statement, Purchase Discounts will be subtracted from Purchases to give the total of net purchases of merchandise for resale. The debit to Accounts Payable properly indicates that the full $1,000 listed as a liability has been settled.

After the cash disbursement transactions have been journalized in the special journal, the following steps are involved in posting the entries to the ledgers.

1. At the end of the day, post entries in the Accounts Payable column to the debit side of the individual accounts in the accounts payable subsidiary ledger, in order to keep these creditors' accounts current. Indicate the posting by a check mark in the Reference column next to the Accounts Payable column. Cross-reference the special journal page in the subsidiary ledger entries.
2. At the end of the month (or as often as required by control and reporting procedures),
   a. post entries in the Sundry Accounts columns to the appropriate general ledger accounts; and
   b. total the columns and post these amounts (except the Sundry Accounts columns) to the appropriate general ledger accounts. Cross-reference these postings.

The reference numbers and markings used in this journal are similar to those used in the cash receipts journal. Again, the total of debits and credits in the journal entries should be checked to make sure that the proper equality of debits and credits has been maintained.

Electronic data processing

Computers are influencing the private and public lives of individuals in many different ways. They can be used to compare the poetry of Shakespeare and Milton, or to assist an architect in planning a shopping center or model city. We are in the age of the Computer Revolution.

Computing devices have a long and honorable history. The early prototypes of computing devices include the abacus used in ancient China and the slide rule developed by the Arabs. The French philosopher Blaise Pascal invented a calculating machine in 1642 (when he was nineteen). In 1671, Gottfried Wilhelm Leibniz developed the first machine to multiply and divide directly. Joseph Marie Jacquard in 1804 used holes punched in paper to direct the operations of weaving looms in France. In 1822, Charles Babbage designed the Difference Engine that could produce logarithmic and astronomical tables. Electronic computers of the twentieth century use several basic principles that were devised for the Difference Engine.

In the 1880s, Dr. Herman Hollerith developed a practical procedure for storing data on punched paper cards that could be read by computing and printing machines. Hollerith designed this system for the U.S. Census Office, which used it to complete the 1890 census in one-third the time that had been needed for the 1880 census. Now masses of data could be processed quickly and accurately. In 1937, Dr. Howard H. Aiken of Harvard University published general plans for a large-scale, automatic digital calculator. Seven years later—after a lot of work by graduate students at Harvard and engineers of the International Business Machines Corporation (IBM)—the Mark I based on Aiken's design was completed. It accepted instructions and data on punched paper tape, then performed the arithmetic and logical operations on the data as instructed. The Mark I used electromagnetic relays and mechanical counters, but the first electronic digital computer (called ENIAC) was developed about the same time at the University of Pennsylvania for the U.S. Army.

This was the beginning of a series of advances in computer technology that assumed the proportions of a scientific and technological explosion. The first commercially available computer went on sale in 1951, and it was not long before a computer was put to work by General Electric Company to process business data. The resulting revolution is still underway, as businesses try to modify their old procedures to take full advantage of the capabilities of computers.

ELECTRONIC DATA PROCESSING SYSTEMS

Electronic data processing (EDP) is perhaps the major technological development affecting business in recent years. With the aid of computers, payrolls can be prepared quickly and accurately, inventory records can be maintained on a daily basis, and managerial problems can be simulated through the use of complicated mathematical formulas. EDP systems provide high-speed operations, accuracy, reliability, and versatility unattainable through any other existing means.

The businessman must learn to relate the computer's capabilities to the resources and functions for which he is responsible. He must acquaint himself with the role that computers play in the world of business. He must learn to communicate with the professionals who design and operate EDP systems—the computer analysts, programmers, and system designers. He must keep abreast of developments in computer applications and EDP systems.

An EDP system is a network of machine components. A wide range of components is available, making it possible to design a system that meets the particular needs of each business. The system accepts data, processes it according to instructions provided by programmers and operators, and prints out or displays the results for those who use the system. The various interconnected devices that are the components of the system each handle particular functions such as receiving data, processing data, storing data and instructions, and providing output in various forms. Exhibit 9-10 shows the five basic components of an EDP system. In this exhibit, solid arrows indicate the flow of data to and from various units; dashed arrows indicate commands that control the timing of input and output.

An EDP system can accept data in a variety of forms, depending on the particular *input devices* in the system. Punched paper cards (Exhibit 9-11) are commonly used as a form of input for both data and instructions. The holes punched in the cards form a code that a card-reader device can read at very high speed. Other input devices accept data from punched paper tape, magnetic tape, documents printed in special characters with magnetic ink (Exhibit 9-12), and some forms of specially prepared documents that the computer can read visually. Keyboards on the console or at remote terminals also provide direct access to the computer (Exhibit 9-13). Although a lot of experimentation has been done and is continuing, input devices that read ordinary handwritten, typed, or printed documents or understand the human voice are not yet practical for commercial uses.

Exhibit 9-10
Basic components of an EDP system

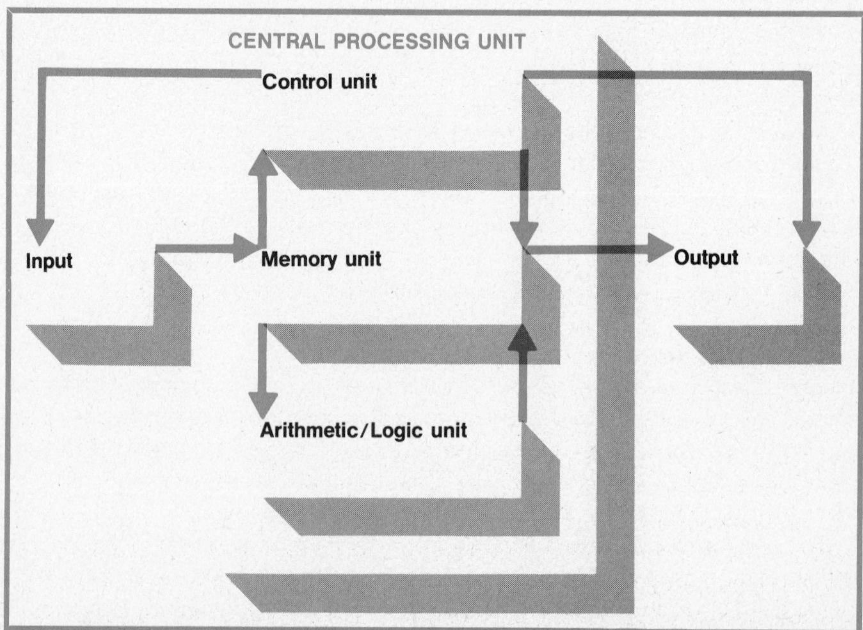

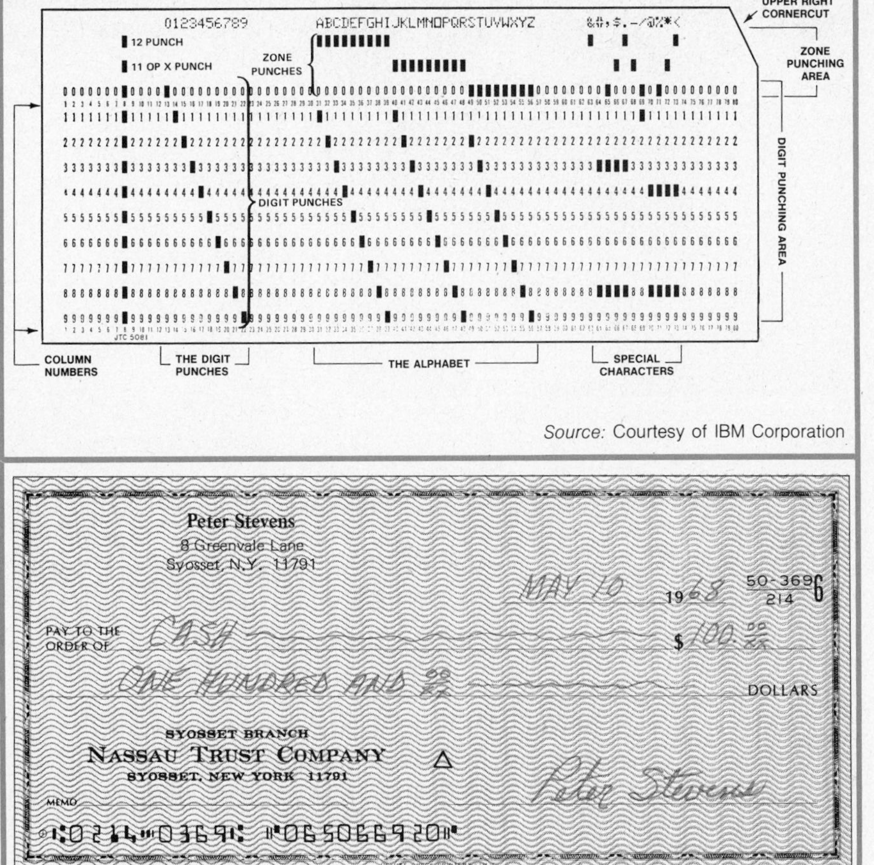

Source: Courtesy of IBM Corporation

Exhibit 9-11
Eighty-column punched card showing Hollerith code of punches

Exhibit 9-12
Bank check imprinted with numerals in magnetic ink for machine input

The *central processing unit* (CPU) of the system contains a *memory unit* that stores instructions and data for transferral and use as needed. This main storage (or core storage) unit is the central memory of the system, containing up to several million data that can be rapidly located and processed. Extra memory units (often using magnetic tape) may be used to give slower, sequential access to very large tables of data such as account balances for a company with many thousands of customer accounts.

The CPU also contains a *control unit,* which coordinates and directs the computer process. Circuits in the control unit and *programs* (instructions) supplied by the designers or users of the system control the flow of information through the CPU and specify the operations to be performed on the data.

The *arithmetic/logic unit* of the CPU performs all the calculations and logical operations needed to carry out the processing. The time needed for a single operation in modern computers is measured in hundreds of nanoseconds (1 nanosecond = 0.00000001 second). This means that tens of millions of data are pulled out of

Exhibit 9-13
Remote terminal with keyboard input and visual display output

Source: Courtesy of IBM Corporation

memory, processed, and returned to memory each second as the CPU carries out its instructions.

The ***output devices*** included in the EDP system can also take a variety of forms. High-speed printers capable of printing 1,000 or more lines per minute are commonly used to convert computer data to conventional words and numbers. If the output is to be used as input for some other EDP operation, rather than being read directly by humans, other output devices may be used to reproduce the data on punched cards, punched tape, or magnetic tape. Visual display screens sometimes are used at remote terminals for direct access to computer output.

Exhibit 9-14 shows a typical EDP system.[1] The numbers in the photograph identify the following components of the system.

1. The control console, from which the operator can start or shut down the system and can keep a running check on machine operation.
2. The console terminal, which can be used by the operator to type instructions and enter them into the system. This terminal may also be used to type out preprogrammed messages to the operator—for example, to warn him to prepare a magnetic-tape memory unit for an upcoming job.
3. The central processing unit, containing the control, core memory, and arithmetic/logic units.
4. Magnetic-tape units, which may be used for output, input, or auxiliary storage (memory) during an operation. The data on the tape can be searched or accessed only by going through the whole sequence of data in the order in which they were stored.

1. The author expresses his thanks to IBM for its permission (1) to reproduce the photographs in Exhibits 9-11, 9-12, 9-13 and 9-14, and (2) to adapt the definitions of computer terminology and some other descriptions of EDP systems used in this section. Reprinted by permission from "More About Computers" 505-0020-1. © by International Business Machines Corporation.

5. Magnetic-disk units, which may be used in the same way as the tape units, but which are able to access any datum in storage directly without searching through the whole storage in order.
6. Card reader/punch units, which read input or produce output in the form of punched cards.
7. High-speed printers used to prepare reports, analyses, business documents, and other forms of printed output.

We communicate with the computer through instructions, or programs. Computer languages bridge the communication gap between man and machine. Only a trained specialist can communicate with the computer in "its own language"—the code that it uses for data and instructions in its internal operations. ***Computer languages*** are special codes that can be learned fairly quickly by nonspecialists. The computer is able to translate these codes into its own language.

Major computer languages in use for business applications today include FORTRAN (FORmula TRANslator), COBOL (COmmon Business Oriented Language), ALGOL (ALGOrithmic Language), and BASIC (Beginner's All-purpose Symbolic Instruction Code).

COBOL is a popular computer language designed particularly to handle the kinds of instructions needed for business data processing. It enables the programmer to

Exhibit 9-14 **A typical EDP system installation**

Source: Courtesy of IBM Corporation

give his commands in a language very similar to English. For example, to find the value of inventory on hand, he writes a COBOL statement that appears as follows (the asterisk means "multiply"):

```
COMPUTE STOCK-VALUE = UNIT PRICE
*(STOCK-ON-HAND + RECEIPTS − SHIPMENTS).
```

In using computer languages that look like English, it is important to remember that the computer does not understand English. It understands only a simplified code that ***looks*** like English. If you tell the computer to "CALCULATE VALUE-OF-STOCK," it will either misinterpret the instruction or be unable to understand you at all.

COMPUTER USE: AN ILLUSTRATION

One major use of computers in business today is the processing and control of inventory. An EDP system can be set up to store and process current information about the stock of merchandise in the inventory. As orders are placed, shipments received, and requisitions filled from stock, the information is supplied immediately to the computer (in the form of punched cards, for example). The computer keeps its inventory records in auxiliary magnetic-disk storage (memory) units. These records can be updated daily. The speed with which the computer performs computations and processes data makes it possible to know from day to day just what the status of inventory is. Furthermore, the computer can handle many of the routine chores of producing business documents and reports.

With the proper program of instructions, the EDP system can perform the necessary arithmetic and logical processes to produce the following output useful in inventory processing and control.

1. A report on the items currently in inventory, their cost, their storage locations, and the time the stock of each item is expected to last.
2. Statements showing the current status of customers' accounts and accounts payable.
3. Reports identifying best-selling and slow-moving merchandise; sales analyses comparing current sales to those of last week, last month, or last year, or projecting current trends into the future.
4. Printed purchase orders for items needed to replenish the stock, along with reports on suppliers, costs, and so on.
5. Printed invoices to be sent to customers for items shipped.
6. Printed shipping notices showing the purchaser's name, order number, address, items purchased, prices, discounts, and similar information.

If a computer is to be used for this kind of work, the programmers must prepare a detailed set of instructions telling the computer just exactly what to do in every conceivable possibility. Before trying to write a program, the programmer usually prepares a flowchart that summarizes the nature of the processing that is to be done, and that shows the order in which various operations are to be carried out. Exhibit 9-15 shows a flowchart of an inventory problem for an airline. Seat reservations are

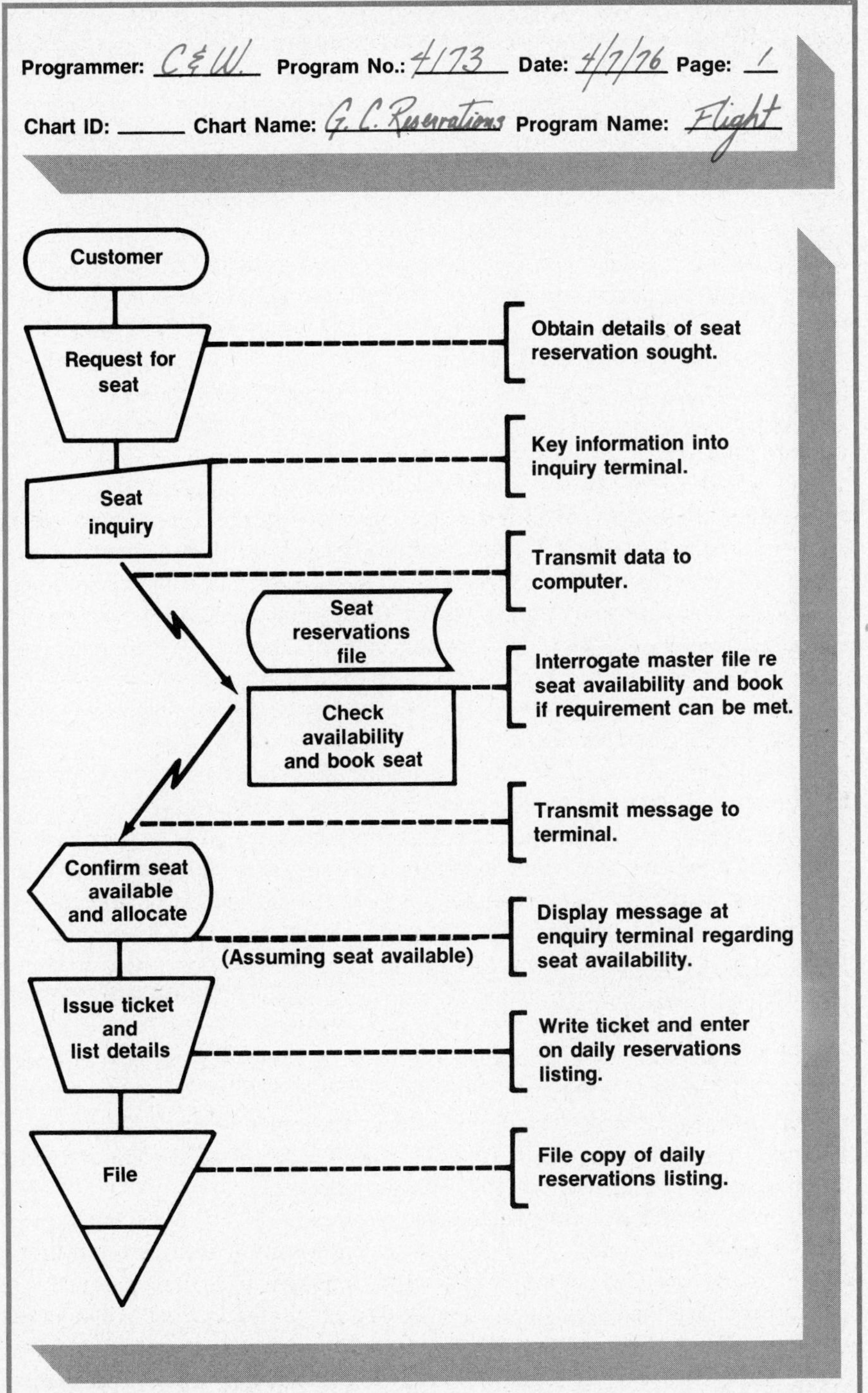

Exhibit 9-15
Flowchart showing an airline inventory-control system

the items in the airline's inventory. Reservations are constantly being made and cancelled by customers at a great many locations (offices). Thus, the availability of seats changes from minute to minute. Yet each of the airline's widely scattered ticket agents and telephone information operators must be able to give current information about seat reservations. Every major airline now uses computer systems to maintain this kind of minute-by-minute control and reporting on its inventory of seat reservations. Remote terminals are used to give the agents and operators direct access to computer input and output.

After a general flowchart like this one has been prepared and studied to be sure that the general needs for the system are understood, more detailed flowcharts will be prepared for each step in the system. For example, such flowcharts would show just what items of information are to be transmitted at each step, and just how any processing steps are to be carried out. The process continues until very detailed flowcharts are prepared for each individual operation that the computer is to carry out. Then the flowcharts will be translated into programs.

BASIC COMPUTER CONCEPTS

The modern businessman—and the business student—must be familiar with certain basic terms associated with electronic data processing. If he does not deal with computers directly himself, he must supervise and communicate with those who do. EDP systems cost a great deal to purchase and to operate; decisions about computer use and details of the company's EDP system and its operation are among the most important managerial decisions. The computer vocabulary is expanding with each new generation of computers that comes upon the scene. This section defines some of the more fundamental concepts.

Hardware refers to the mechanical, magnetic, electrical, and electronic devices that are the components of the EDP system. ***Software*** is the collection of programs (computer instructions) needed to solve problems with a computer, as well as all of the documents needed to guide its operation (manuals, flowcharts, and so on).

A computer ***programming language*** is a precisely defined set of symbols that the computer (using certain programs) can translate into its own ***machine language*** (the code used for internal operations of the computer). ***ALGOL,*** or Algorithmic Language, is a programming language that uses algebraic symbols to express problem-solving formulas for machine solution. ***COBOL,*** or Common Business Oriented Language, is a programming language designed to resemble business English and to provide easy instructions for common business-related problems. ***FORTRAN*** and ***BASIC*** are programming languages designed for all-purpose use in giving instructions to computers; they closely resemble algebraic notation with some "pseudo-English" words used for additional instructions.

A ***program*** is the basic set of instructions needed to tell a computer what operations it is supposed to perform in processing input, storing data, and producing output. It is the ability to store a program and to follow its instructions (including making logical decisions) through a complex data-processing operation that makes a computer different from a calculating machine. The ***source program*** is a program written in a programming language. When this source program is input to the computer, the computer follows the instructions of another stored program (called an assembler or a compiler) to translate the source program into an object program. The ***object program*** is the program machine-language stored inside the computer's memory in the form of electrical pulses; it is this pattern of pulses that actually guides the operation of the computer.

A ***flowchart*** is a graphic representation used to define, analyze, or solve a problem. In the flowchart, symbols are used to represent operations, data flow, and equipment (Exhibit 9-16). A *system flowchart* is a flowchart that shows the overall flow of data and operations to be performed at each step in the solution of a particular problem. The flowchart must be translated into a program before it can be used to instruct a computer.

A *file* is a collection of related records, stored in some form that can be read by the computer's input devices. In inventory control, for example, one line of an invoice forms an *item,* a completed invoice forms a *record,* and the complete set of invoices forms a *file.* Other files contain purchase orders, accounts receivable, accounts payable, and so on.

Sequential access is a technique for storing and retrieving data in the order in which the data appear in a file. For example, if the computer is to get certain data from (or write certain data into) invoice number 53867, it must scan through the preceding 53,866 invoices in the file before it finds the one it is looking for. The *random* access technique allows the computer to go directly to a certain record without scanning through the rest of the file. As an analogy, think of the index as a random access device that lets you find an item without searching through the whole book page by page for what you need (a sequential access technique).

Turn-around time is the time that elapses from the moment when the program and data are fed into the computer until the results are output. In many cases, program and data are prepared on punched cards or on tape, which are saved until a large number of such inputs can be fed into the computer at one time; this is called *batch processing.* The input is prepared *offline* and is given to the computer input devices by the operator when he is ready to run the particular job(s). The user usually delivers the punched cards or tapes to the computer operator and then returns later to pick up the output.

If the user has an *online* terminal that is itself a direct input to the computer, he can give input directly to the computer and can receive output as soon as the processing is completed. This makes it possible to write programs in which the computer does some processing and reports some results, then waits for further instructions before continuing. In other words, the user can interact with the computer program, making decisions about the operation at preprogrammed points. This, in turn, makes it possible to design *real-time* computer systems, in which results of computer processing are made available quickly enough that they can be used in guiding the event that provides the input. For example, the airline ticket clerk has an online terminal and gets information about current seat availability quickly enough to guide him in selling tickets to a particular customer. This is a real-time system. Even if an inventory control system only provides daily summary reports as a result of batch processing, this may be fast enough to provide real-time control of the inventory procedures for most companies.

Exhibit 9-16
Symbols used in flowcharts

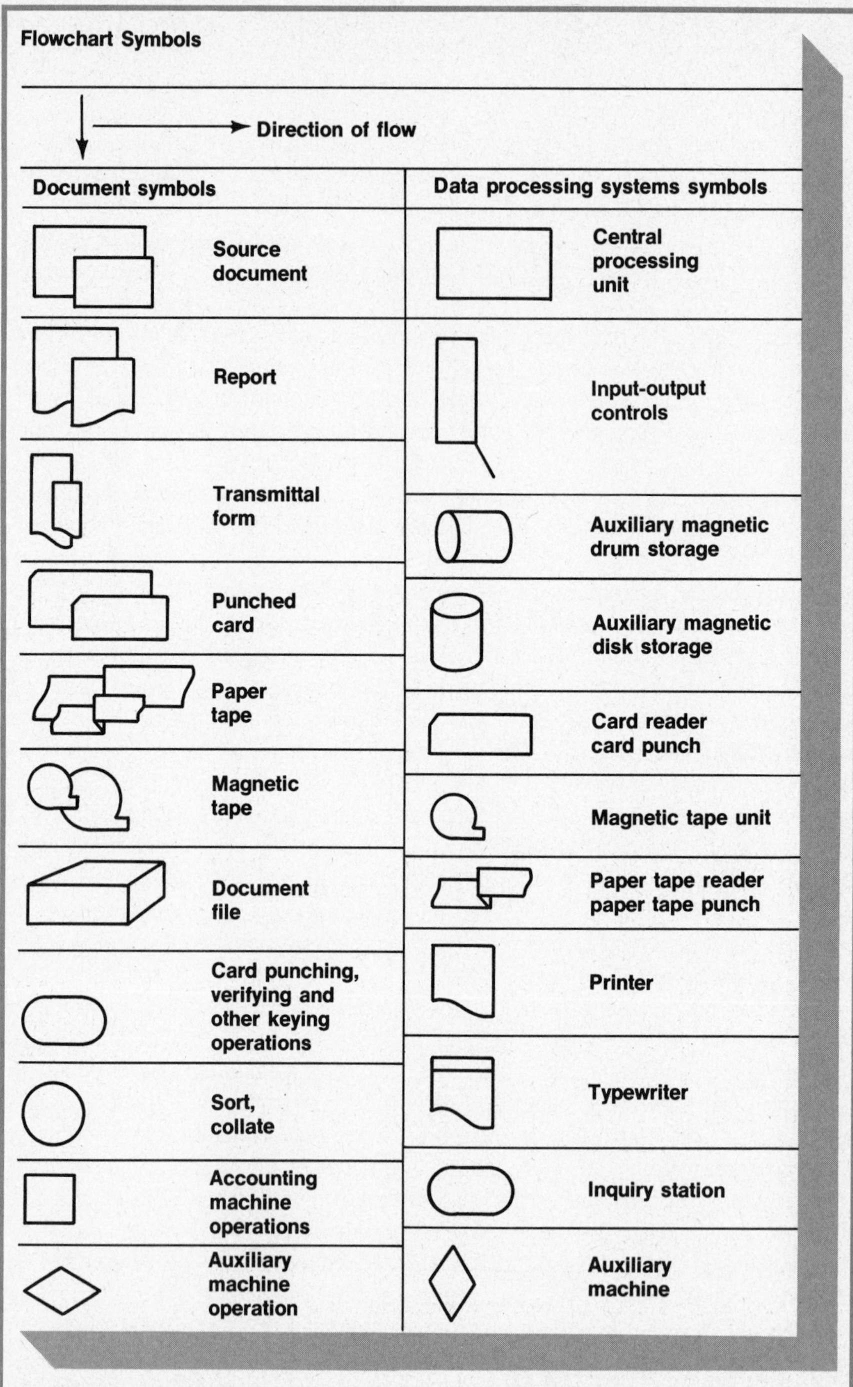

In order for a single computer to service many online terminals, most such systems use ***shared time.*** This is a scheduling arrangement that allows the computer to divide its time among all the online users in a scheduled sequence. The computer carries out any processing requested at the first terminal and outputs its results. It then turns its attention to the second terminal and carries out any instructions that have been entered there, and so on. Because the computer is so much faster than the humans with whom it is interacting, it can handle dozens of terminals at once and still give each user the impression that the computer is responding immediately to his inputs. Such time-sharing systems are coming into common use as a way for a small company to purchase only the amount of computer time that it needs. It leases a terminal from the company that owns the time-sharing system, and then is billed only for the actual computer time that it uses. Such systems also are used within a large company to allow many departments to simultaneously use a large computer for many different programs.

Summary

Accountants have devised procedures to ease the processing of huge numbers of transactions, many of them repetitious in nature. These procedures also are designed to help management in the difficult task of controlling the economic activities of a large company, where many employees must be involved in day-to-day decisions about large sums of money.

Special journals are designed to speed and simplify the recording of certain kinds of transactions that recur frequently—for example, cash receipts and disbursements, credit sales, and credit purchases. Special columns in these journals reduce the amount of writing needed to record each transaction. They also provide economies in posting, because the column totals (representing a group of transactions) can be posted to certain very active accounts, eliminating the need to post each individual item into the general ledger.

Subsidiary ledgers are used to keep records of individual customer's accounts (Accounts Receivable) or accounts with individual creditors (Accounts Payable). These ledgers can be posted daily, and they can be used for purposes of billing, reporting, or preparing checks for payments. Control accounts in the general ledger provide ready information about the overall balance of Accounts Receivable or Accounts Payable, without requiring posting of individual entries. The use of control accounts and subsidiary ledgers simplifies the division of labor in a large accounting system and makes it possible to maintain control over the activities of the various accountants and clerks.

The use of computers in data processing has vastly increased the capacity of a firm to process quantities of data with great speed, efficiency, accuracy, and economy. Computer technology is evolving rapidly, and businesses are continually modifying their procedures to take advantage of the growing capabilities of computers. Thus far, computers have been put to work mainly in the processing of data from repetitive, high-volume operations such as receivables, payables, inventories, and payrolls. They are used mainly to carry out data processing operations at high speed, and to print out various business documents and summary reports. These reports are of great value to management. For the first time, it is now possible for management of a large business to have a current report each day on the exact situation of the company's inventories or accounts. However, it also seems clear that computers can offer much greater help in decision-making situations; much remains to be undertaken in this area.

Questions

1. What special tools and techniques have been developed to process large numbers of transactions more efficiently through the accounting system?
2. What is a control account? What is a subsidiary ledger? How are control accounts related to subsidiary ledgers? In which ledger is a control account recorded?
3. What is a special journal? Name four special journals and describe the kinds of transactions that are recorded in each. What advantages are obtained from the use of special journals? Why are special journals and subsidiary ledgers usually used together?
4. In general terms, describe the posting process required when special journals and subsidiary ledgers are used.
5. What are the major components of an electronic data processing system?
6. Distinguish among the concepts included in each of the following groups:
   a. computer hardware, computer software;
   b. ALGOL, COBOL, FORTRAN;
   c. programming language, machine language;
   d. sequential access, random access;
   e. real time, turn-around time, shared time;
   f. online, offline, batch processing.

Exercises

E9-1 The Mift Company makes about 12,800 purchases on account during each month. If the company uses a two-column general journal, how many postings to the Purchases account would be required each month? If the company uses a purchases journal, how many postings would be required?

E9-2 Exhibit 9-17 shows postings made during one month in certain general ledger accounts of the Sleepy Company. The company uses the four special journals described in this chapter. Describe the probable source of each entry in the accounts.

E9-3 Your accounting system uses the four special journals described in this chapter and a two-column general journal. Indicate the journal in which each of the following transactions should be recorded.
a. Payment is made on an account payable.
b. Merchandise is purchased on account.
c. Owner contributes land to the company.

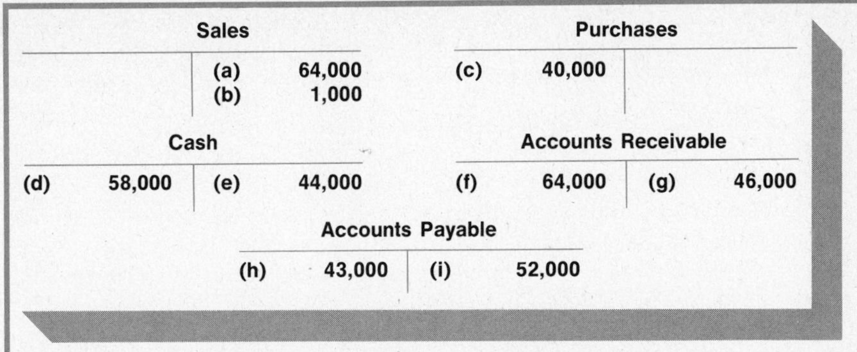

Exhibit 9-17
General ledger accounts for Exercise E9-2

d. Money is borrowed from a bank.
e. Merchandise is sold on account.
f. Merchandise is purchased for cash.
g. Rent expense is paid.
h. A collection is made on an account receivable.
i. Adjusting and closing entries are made.

E9-4 The Brown company was involved in the following transactions during August 19_6.

Aug.	12	Sold merchandise on account to Spottie Co., Invoice No. 1, $700.
	14	Sold merchandise on account to Rover Co., Invoice No. 2, $900.
	15	Purchased merchandise on account from Blackie Co., $200.
	20	Sold merchandise on account to Spottie Co., Invoice No. 3, $1,100.
	22	Purchased merchandise on account from Bowzer Co., $350.

Required:

a. Open the following general ledger accounts, using the account numbers indicated: Accounts Receivable 1015; Sales 4075; Accounts Payable 3015; Purchases 4085.
b. Open accounts in an accounts receivable subsidiary ledger for the Spottie Co. and the Rover Co.
c. Open accounts in an accounts payable subsidiary ledger for the Blackie Co. and the Bowzer Co.
d. Using appropriate special journals, journalize the August transactions of the Brown Company. Post each journal entry immediately to the subsidiary ledgers. Post to the general ledger at the end of August.
e. Take a trial balance of the accounts receivable subsidiary ledger at the end of August and compare this balance with the proper control account.
f. Repeat part e for the accounts payable subsidiary ledger.

E9-5 The Ice Company engaged in the following transactions during May 19_6.

May	4	Issued additional common stock to stockholders for $45,000.
	5	Purchased land for $18,000 cash.
	9	Purchased a building for $42,000 cash.
	11	Cash sale, $12,000.
	12	Cash purchase, $3,200.
	12	Collected $800 on account from the Soda Company for a sale in April.
	15	Collected $870 on account from the Ski Company, for a $900 sale in April; the Ski Company took a $30 discount for prompt payment of the $900 bill.

May 15 Paid utilities for the month, $700.
16 Paid salaries for the first two weeks of May, $12,500.
19 Paid the Water Company $1,600 on account for a purchase made in April.
19 Paid the Snow Company $700, the full balance of the amount owed to that company.
31 Paid salaries for the second half of the month, $12,500.

Required:

a. Open the following accounts in the general ledger, using the account numbers shown in parentheses and inserting the opening balances (May 1) indicated: Cash (1) $94,000; Accounts Receivable (2) $1,700; Accounts Payable (10) $2,300; Common Stock (30) $93,400. Open any additional accounts required and assign appropriate account numbers to them.

b. Open the following accounts in an accounts receivable subsidiary ledger with the opening balances indicated: Soda Company $800; Ski Company $900.

c. Open the following accounts in an accounts payable subsidiary ledger with the opening balances indicated: Water Company $1,600; Snow Company $700.

d. Using cash receipts and cash disbursements journals, journalize the May transactions. Make daily postings of entries to the subsidiary ledgers; post entries to the general ledger at the end of the month.

e. Prepare a trial balance of the general ledger at the end of the month.

E9-6 The Balloon Company uses the four special journals described in this chapter (SJ, PJ, CR, CD). It also uses subsidiary ledgers for accounts receivable (ARSL) and accounts payable (APSL), as well as a general ledger (GL) with control accounts for the subsidiary ledgers. The following column headings appear in the special journals.

a. Accounts Payable debit
b. Cash debit
c. Sales credit
d. Sundry credit
e. Purchases debit
f. Accounts Payable credit
g. Sundry debit
h. Accounts Receivable credit
i. Accounts Receivable debit
j. Cash credit

Required: For each of these column headings,

1. list the abbreviation(s) for the special journal(s) in which this heading would be found;
2. list the abbreviation of the ledger (if any) into which individual entries in this column would be posted;
3. list the abbreviation of the ledger (if any) into which the total of this column would be posted.

E9-7 Describe some of the impacts of computers on

a. corporate planning,
b. control,
c. individual employees,
d. management.

Problems

P9-1 The Drill Company began operations on November 1, 19_6. The following data are taken from the firm's sales journal for November 19_6.

Date	Debtor	Amount	Date	Debtor	Amount
Nov. 2	P. Plan	$9,000	Nov. 14	H. Host	$ 5,500
7	M. Mora	2,000	17	G. Greb	11,000
9	A. Arva	1,000	24	S. Sten	6,000
10	O. Osti	3,000			

The total amount of sales on account during November is $37,500. A total of $19,500 is received during the month in payments by debtors on their accounts. The cash receipts journal contains the following data about those collections.

Date	Debtor	Amount
Nov. 8	P. Plan	$4,000
15	O. Osti	3,000
21	G. Greb	7,000
23	H. Host	5,500

Required:

a. Post the amounts to the subsidiary ledger for accounts receivable, and post the total for the month to the control account.

b. Prove (test the correctness of) the subsidiary ledger by taking a trial balance of the subsidiary ledger and comparing it with the balance of the control account.

P9-2 Exhibit 9-18 shows a post-closing trial balance of the general ledger of the Thompson Tank Company. On October 1, 19_6, the subsidiary ledgers of the company show the following account balances.

Exhibit 9-18
Trial balance for Problem P9-2

THOMPSON TANK COMPANY
Trial Balance
October 1, 19_6

Cash	**12,000**	
Accounts Receivable	**27,000**	
Prepaid Insurance	**4,000**	
Investments	**31,000**	
Land	**19,000**	
Buildings	**120,000**	
Accumulated Depreciation		**50,000**
Accounts Payable		**32,000**
Salaries Payable		**10,000**
Taxes Payable		**4,000**
Common Stock		**106,000**
Retained Earnings		**11,000**
	213,000	213,000

estab. accts from this.

Accounts Receivable: Sellers Co. $9,000; Given Co. $18,000.
Accounts Payable: Nuts Co. $12,000; Bolts Co. $20,000.

The following transactions took place during October 19_6.

Oct. 1 Issued additional shares of common stock for cash, $20,000.
2 Sold merchandise to Jones Co. on account, $3,000: Invoice No. 23.
5 Purchased merchandise on account from Nuts Co., $6,000.
8 Sold merchandise to Sellers Co. on account, $8,000; Invoice No. 24.
8 Given Co. remitted a check on account, $12,000.
9 Made cash sales amounting to $14,000.
9 Paid biweekly salaries in amount of $22,000.
11 Administrative expenses paid in cash, $11,000.
12 Selling expenses paid in cash, $23,000.
16 Sold merchandise on account to Wolk Co., $17,000: Invoice No. 25.
17 Sellers Co. remitted a check in the amount of $6,000.
18 Paid Bolts Co. $3,000 on account.
19 Purchased merchandise on account from Bolts Co., $9,000.
22 Received payment from Wolk Co. on account; Wolk Co. settled $15,000 of the amount billed on Invoice No. 25, taking a 3 percent cash discount; actual cash received was $14,550.
22 Sold merchandise on account to Castor Co., $16,000: Invoice No. 26.
24 Paid biweekly payroll, $22,000.
25 Sold investments for $31,000.
29 Received a 60-day note from Wolk Co. in settlement of its account, $2,000.
30 Purchased an insurance policy for cash, $4,400.
31 Cash purchase of merchandise, $1,600.

Required:

a. The Thompson Tank Company uses the four special journals described in this chapter and a two-column general journal. Record each October transaction in the appropriate journal.

b. The company's accounting system prepares for management a summary of current balances in the general ledger at the close of business on the last day of each month. It keeps all accounts in the subsidiary ledgers current as of the close of the previous day's business. Keeping in mind these requirements, post all journals to the ledger accounts.

c. Prepare trial balances of the general ledger and of the two subsidiary ledgers as of the end of the month.

d. If the accounting system were to prepare interim financial statements at the end of the month, indicate in general terms the kinds of adjusting entries that would be required before closing the books.

P9-3 The accounting system of the Clouds Company receives the following source documents during the month of July 19_6, relating to the company's transactions during the month.

Invoice No. 120, dated July 2. Merchandise sold to Bumber Co. on account, $16,000; terms 2/10, n/30.

Invoice No. 121, dated July 6. Merchandise sold to Trulu Co. on account, $18,000; terms 2/10, n/30.

Purchase Order No. 75, dated July 8. Merchandise purchased from the Limbo Co. on account, $6,000; terms 2/30, n/90.

Purchase Order No. 76, dated July 10. Merchandise purchased from the Neeto Co. on account, $14,000; terms 2/30, n/90.

Purchase Order No. 77, dated July 11. Merchandise purchased from the Boxer Co. on account, $27,000; terms 2/10, n/30.

Check from Bumber Co., received July 11, for $15,680; accompanying letter states this is in full payment of Invoice No. 120.
Stub for Check No. 500, issued July 12, for $20,000; explanation on stub says "cash payment for land."
Stub for Check No. 501, issued July 14, for $9,000; explanation says "payment to Sons Co. on account."
Receipts and other documents showing that on July 15 additional common stock was issued for $30,000 in cash.
Check from Daughters Co., received July 15, for $6,000; notation says check is in payment of Invoice No. 118.
Check from Roses Co., received July 16, for $9,000; notation says check is in payment on account.
Sales tickets turned in by sales department on July 17, show cash sales amounting to $40,000 for the first two weeks of the month.
Check from Trulu Co., received July 18, for $7,000; accompanying letter states this is in payment on Invoice No. 121.
Stub for Check No. 502, issued July 19, for $400; explanation says "advance payment of premium for 2-year fire-insurance policy"; accompanying copy of policy shows that it went into effect on July 1.
Stub for Check No. 503, issued July 20, for $26,190; explanation says "payment to Boxer Co. for our Purchase Order No. 77."
Copies of receipts and invoices turned in by the purchasing department on July 21, show that the Clouds Co. made cash purchases totalling $12,000 during July.
Sales tickets turned in July 21, show cash sales of $30,000 for past week.
Stub for Check No. 504, issued July 22, for $1,000; explanation says "purchase of office supplies."
Stub for Check No. 505, issued July 24, for $10,000; explanation says "payment of July rent."
Stubs for Checks Nos. 506–515, issued July 25, totaling $45,000; explanations say "payment of July salaries."
Bill from the Utilities Co., received July 31, showing amount due of $10,000 for utilities used during July.

The Clouds Company uses the four special journals described in this chapter as well as a two-column general journal; it uses subsidiary ledgers for accounts receivable and accounts payable in addition to its general ledger. Exhibit 9-19 shows the post-closing trial balance of the general ledger after the books were closed at the end of June 19_6. The trial balances of the subsidiary ledgers also are shown in the exhibit.

Required:

a. Set up the general and subsidiary ledgers using the data provided in Exhibit 9-19. Enter the opening balances in the accounts for July 1, 19_6.
b. Journalize the July transactions in the appropriate journals.
c. Make the necessary postings for the month of July. (Column totals from the special journals are posted only at the end of the month.)
d. Prove the balances of the accounts receivable and accounts payable subsidiary ledgers by comparing them to the control accounts.
e. Prepare a trial balance of the general ledger for the end of July.

Exhibit 9-19
Trial balance for Problem P9-3

CLOUDS COMPANY
Post-Closing Trial Balance
June 30, 19_6

Acct. No.	Account Name	Debit	Credit
111	Cash	42,000	
112	Accounts Receivable	21,000	
113	Inventory	87,000	
114	Office Supplies	12,000	
116	Land	60,000	
117	Equipment	40,000	
211	Accounts Payable		18,000
311	Common Stock		220,000
312	Retained Earnings		24,000
411	Sales		0
412	Sales Discounts	0	
511	Purchases	0	
512	Purchases Discounts		0
611	Rent Expense	0	
612	Salaries Expense	0	
613	Utilities Expense	0	
		262,000	262,000

Accounts Receivable Subsidiary Ledger:

	Debit	Credit
Cousins Company	6,000	
Daughters Company	6,000	
Roses Company	9,000	
	21,000	

Accounts Payable Subsidiary Ledger:

	Debit	Credit
Sons Company		9,000
Turk Company		9,000
		18,000

P9-4 The following transactions of the Journal Company occurred in January, 19_0. The numbers preceding the transaction refer to dates in January.

1. The Journal Company issued $100,000 of common stock for cash.
2. The company purchased $50,000 merchandise on account from Co. Y.
3. The company had cash sales of $30,000.
4. The company had credit sales of $75,000 to Company X.
5. The company had cash sales of $20,000.
6. The company purchased $30,000 merchandise on account from Co. Z.
7. The company paid Co. Y in full for its purchase on January 2.
8. The company purchased office equipment for $10,000 cash.
9. The company paid the office rent for January in the amount of $5,000.
10. The company purchased a three-year fire insurance policy for $2,000.

11. The company paid the utility bill of $5,000 which it received this morning.
12. The company purchased marketable securities for $15,000.
13. The company collected the amount due from Company X resulting from the sale on January 4.
14. The company sold merchandise in the amount of $10,000 to Company A.
15. The company received a check from Company A in the amount of $9,800 in full settlement of its account. Company A took a sales discount that was allowed them.
16. The company sold the marketable securities it purchased on January 12, for $18,000.
17. The company purchased $10,000 merchandise for cash.
18. The company purchased $10,000 of merchandise on account from Co. M.
19. The company paid Co. M in full after a cash discount of $200.

Required:

a. Journalize the transactions of the Journal Company in a cash receipts journal and a cash disbursements journal. Transactions involving other journals are to be ignored.

b. Post the two cash journals. The company uses control accounts for accounts receivable and accounts payable. Assign page numbers to accounts in the general ledger.

P9-5 The Reff Company has an accounting system that uses a general, sales, purchases, cash receipts, and cash disbursements journal to record all transactions. Indicate in which journal(s) each of the following transactions would be recorded.

1. Cash purchases.
2. Credit purchases.
3. Cash sales.
4. Credit sales.
5. Payment of accounts payable.
6. Receipts from customers.
7. Purchase of office equipment for cash.
8. Purchase of factory equipment on account.
9. Payment of salaries.
10. Sale of capital stock for cash.
11. Purchase of marketable securities.
12. Sale of marketable securities at a loss.
13. Recording depreciation for the year.
14. Adjusting entries at the end of the year.
15. Closing entries at the end of the year.
16. Purchased office supplies on account.

Valuation considerations and income determination

10 Effective control and use of cash

The preceding chapters describe the general accounting model and the basic procedures used by the accounting system. Now we turn to a study of specific accounts in considerable detail. The topics discussed in this part of the book can be grouped as follows.

1. Short-term business financing
   a. Cash (Chapter 10)
   b. Marketable securities (Chapter 11)
   c. Accounts receivable and notes receivable (Chapter 12)
   d. Inventory (Chapter 13)
   e. Current liabilities (Chapter 15)
2. Long-term business financing
   a. Investments (Chapter 11)
   b. Property, plant, and equipment; intangible assets; natural resources (Chapter 14)
   c. Long-term liabilities (Chapter 15)
   d. Capital stock and related accounts (Chapters 16 and 19)
3. Reporting changes in financial position (Chapter 20)

In these chapters we look both at the detailed accounting procedures appropriate to each account and at some of the managerial and financial implications of these accounts for the firm.

Cash

Cash is a current asset. The Cash account balance usually is the first item listed in the asset portion of the statement of financial position. In one sense, cash is just another commodity among the many assets of the firm. However, the Cash account is of special significance for two reasons. First, cash is the most liquid asset—the one most readily available to meet the obligations of the firm and the one most universally accepted by creditors. Second, the Cash account is ultimately affected by almost every business transaction in one way or another. Almost any economic activity of the firm must sooner or later involve the flow of cash to or from the firm.

In the accounting context, ***cash*** includes coins, currency, and negotiable paper such as checks, money orders, traveler's checks, cashier's checks, and similar items that will be accepted by a bank for deposit in a checking account. Time certificates and savings accounts are not classified as cash because there usually are restrictions on their convertibility or withdrawal; such items usually are listed as temporary or long-term investments. Postage stamps (prepaid postage) and IOUs (informal cash-due memoranda, treated as receivables) are not cash.

Management of cash

The management of cash is of vital importance for most businesses. The company that manages its cash properly obtains the advantages of adequate liquidity, higher return on investments, and greater profitability. Cash management involves two problems: (1) the determination of the most desirable balance for the Cash account; and (2) the safeguarding of cash.

HOW MUCH CASH? Cash is an unproductive asset. The firm's holdings of cash produce no revenue for the company. To maximize profits and return on investments, any unneeded cash should ordinarily be invested in some asset that will produce revenue. On the other hand, it is important to keep enough cash on hand to assure the liquidity of the firm—that is, to make sure that the firm will have enough cash to pay its obligations as they mature. The firm can decrease its expenses if it is able to take advantage of discounts for prompt payments of its bills. It wants to avoid fees and interest that would be charged for late payments. Furthermore, it wants to protect its credit rating and its reputation among investors.

SAFEGUARDING CASH. Being a highly liquid and greatly desired asset, cash is especially in danger of misappropriation. Adequate safeguards must be established to control the access to and the use of the firm's cash. Among the more important techniques developed for this purpose are (1) internal control procedures for cash receipts and cash disbursements,[1] (2) establishment of an imprest petty cash fund, (3) periodic bank reconciliations, (4) cash forecasts, and (5) a voucher system. This chapter discusses each of these control procedures.

INTERNAL CONTROL PROCEDURES

The AICPA's Committee on Auditing Procedure gives the following definition of ***internal control.***

Internal control comprises the plan of organization and all of the coordinate methods and measures within a business to safeguard its assets, check the accuracy and reliability of

1. The cash receipts and disbursements statement is an important financial statement. This statement is discussed in Chapter 20, where the concept of cash flow is examined.

its accounting data, promote operational efficiency, and encourage adherence to prescribed managerial policies.[2]

The major objectives of a good system of internal control are information, protection, and control.

The Committee on Auditing Procedure goes on to state that good internal control requires

> A plan of organization which provides appropriate segregation of functional responsibilities;
>
> A system of authorization and record procedures adequate to provide reasonable accounting control over assets, liabilities, revenues, and expenses;
>
> Sound practices to be followed in performance of duties and functions of each of the organizational departments; and
>
> Personnel of a quality commensurate with responsibilities.[3]

The internal control procedures for handling and accounting for cash have special importance because of the special risks associated with the receipt and disbursement of cash. Certain basic procedures are generally recognized as desirable to achieve control of cash.

PROCEDURES FOR CONTROL OF CASH RECEIPTS. The following procedures are designed to provide internal control over cash received by the firm.

1. All cash receipts should be recorded immediately upon receipt by the firm, both to provide a record and to discourage misappropriations of cash.
2. Total cash receipts should be deposited daily in a bank account. This procedure reduces the possibility of misappropriation. It also requires that the daily cash receipts recorded in the books correspond with the cash recorded as a deposit on the books of the bank. This creates a double record of the cash received—one record in the company accounts and one in the books of the bank.
3. The custody of cash should be entrusted only to a person who (a) is not entitled to authorize cash transactions and (b) is not involved in recording cash transactions. In other words, the accounting, custodial, and authorization functions should be kept separate and in the hands of different persons.

PROCEDURES FOR CONTROL OF CASH DISBURSEMENTS. The following procedures are designed to provide internal control over the process of spending the firm's cash.

1. All disbursements of cash should be made by check (except for small disbursements of cash controlled by the imprest petty cash system discussed later). This

2. AICPA Committee on Auditing Procedure, ***Internal Control—Elements of a Coordinate System and Its Importance to Management and the Independent Public Accountant*** (New York: American Institute of Certified Public Accountants, 1949), p. 6.

3. Ibid.

procedure provides a clear record of the recipients of any cash disbursements (with the endorsed check returned by the bank serving as a proof that the money was received). It again creates a double record of cash transactions in the books of the company and in those of the bank.

a. A check should be issued only when the request is supported by evidence relating to the expenditure and is duly authorized. The supporting evidence should be cancelled when the check is written, to prevent reuse of the evidence.

b. Checks should be preprinted with sequential numbers to control their use and to establish a procedure of accountability for all check blanks.

2. The person authorized to sign checks should (a) not have the authority to approve check requests and (b) not be involved in recording cash transactions.

3. The signature of two persons should be required to make a check valid. Other procedures such as the use of a mechanical check-writing machine or preprinting of maximum amounts on check blanks may be used to control alteration of checks after they are written.

OTHER PROCEDURES FOR CONTROL OF CASH. The preceding two lists summarize the basic internal control procedures for cash receipts and disbursements. In addition, it is advisable to adopt the following procedures.

1. The bank statement should be periodically reconciled to the company's books by a person not involved in the receipt or disbursement of cash and not involved in the authorizing or recording of cash transactions.
2. An internal audit or count of cash on a surprise basis should be conducted at irregular intervals.
3. A fidelity bond should be required for individuals who have custody of cash.
4. A cash forecast should be prepared to control the use of cash.
5. The voucher system should be considered for adoption in the accounting system as an effective procedure for controlling cash disbursements.

IMPREST SYSTEM OF PETTY CASH

For purposes of internal control, cash disbursements ordinarily should be made by check after due authorization and processing of a check request. However, this procedure often is inconvenient or unduly expensive when very small disbursements are to be made. In a typical company, it might cost a few dollars in salaries and forms to process a check request. If the amount to be disbursed is only a few dollars, the cost becomes excessive when weighed against the need for tight control over such petty amounts. Or suppose that a postman arrives at the front desk with an important special delivery letter for the president, but will not surrender the letter until he is paid 10 cents postage due. The normal check-issuing procedure obviously is not practical in such a situation.

To handle such situations (if they are likely to occur in a particular firm), a petty cash fund can be established. Small cash disbursements can be made from this fund without elaborate authorization procedures.

The imprest (advance payment) system usually is used to maintain systematic control over the disbursements from the petty cash fund. The custodian of the fund is given a certain amount of cash (usually in the form of currency and coins) to establish the fund. At any time, the custodian is responsible for that amount. He must be able to produce signed receipts to represent any approved disbursements from the fund, and he is personally responsible for the cash balance not accounted for by such receipts.

To establish a petty cash fund, a check drawn to petty cash is cashed for the amount of the fund. The currency and coins in the amount of the fund are given to the custodian of the fund, who signs a receipt for the money. When the fund is established, an entry is made in the cash disbursements journal crediting the Cash account by the amount of the petty cash fund and debiting a current asset account called Petty Cash by the same amount.

To control the use of the fund, a limit is established on the maximum amount allowed for a single disbursement. Other regulations usually are established to control the kinds of expenses that can be used as justification for a petty cash disbursement.

Each time the custodian of the fund disburses cash from the fund, he obtains a signed receipt for the amount. To improve control, forms with preprinted sequential numbers should be used for such receipts. When the cash in the fund is almost exhausted, the custodian applies for more cash by submitting a check request through the normal control procedures, attaching as evidence for his request the receipts for the disbursements he has made from the fund. A check is then written to petty cash for the amount that has been disbursed from the fund. The evidence supporting the check request is cancelled at this time to prevent reuse. The check is cashed and the money is given to the custodian of the fund, who again signs a receipt for the amount.

As an example, suppose that a petty cash fund is established on January 2 in the amount of $500.

Jan. 2	Petty Cash	500	
	Cash		500
	To record establishment of petty cash fund.		

On January 31, the custodian of the fund submits a check request showing that disbursements from the fund during January totaled $125 for postage, $175 for office supplies, and $25 for miscellaneous expenses. The request is properly documented by receipts, so a check is written for $325. This cash disbursement represents certain expenses that have not been recognized in the accounts as yet. Therefore, the entry in the cash disbursements journal contains the following information.[4]

Jan. 31	Postage Expense	125	
	Office Supplies	175	
	Miscellaneous Expenses	25	
	Cash		325
	To record petty cash disbursements during January.		

4. Throughout this text, we show journal entries in the general journal form for clarity and simplicity, although many of these entries normally would be made in the special journals.

Note that the credit of $325 is posted to the Cash account (*not* to the Petty Cash account). Unless the petty cash fund is to be increased or decreased, the balance of the Petty Cash account remains unchanged at $500, the amount for which the custodian is responsible.

If an audit were made of the petty cash fund while the replenishment check is being processed, the custodian should be able to produce (1) the copy of his check request for $325 representing January disbursements from the fund (documenting receipts were attached to the original of the request), (2) receipts for any disbursements made since the request was submitted, and (3) the balance of the $500 in cash.

When the $325 replenishment check is ready, it is cashed at the bank, and the custodian receives (and signs for) $325 in currency and coins.

BANK RECONCILIATION

If each day's cash receipts are deposited intact and immediately in a bank account, the bank's record of deposits in the account will be identical with the daily total of the Cash Debit column in the cash receipts journal. If all payments are made by check, the bank's record of payments from the company's account will contain all the same items as the entries in the Cash Credit column of the cash disbursements journal. Hence, these two procedures result in the independent maintenance of two separate records of the company's cash receipts and cash payments.

As an illustration, suppose that the XYZ Company follows these procedures, depositing all cash receipts daily in its checking account at Bank A, and making all cash disbursements through checks written on that account. Suppose further that all of the deposits of January cash receipts were credited by the bank to the XYZ Company account during January, and that all checks written by the XYZ Company during January were debited to the checking account by the bank before the end of the month. In that case, the balance of the Cash account in the XYZ Company ledger at the end of January should equal the balance of the XYZ Company checking account at the end of January in the books of Bank A. In the simplified example shown in Exhibit 10-1, the company's Cash account has a debit balance of $20,000, and the bank's XYZ Company checking account has a credit balance of $20,000. Note the matching of the various entries in the two accounts.

For a variety of reasons, the bank balance and the Cash account balance usually do not agree at any particular moment. Hence, the two accounts must be reconciled in order to make sure that the double records of cash transactions are consistent with each other.

Exhibit 10-1
Cash account in company books and checking account in bank books

Cash [in books of the XYZ Company]

Opening balance (Jan. 1)	**10,000**	**Cash disbursed in Jan.**	**40,000**
Cash received in Jan.	**50,000**		

XYZ Company [checking account in books of Bank A]

Checks cleared in Jan.	**40,000**	**Opening balance (Jan. 1)**	**10,000**
		Deposits received in Jan.	**50,000**

Each entry in the bank's records for the checking account should correspond to an entry in the books of the company. Therefore, a careful comparison of the bank and company account records should isolate and identify any discrepancies between the two account balances.

Differences between the two account balances may arise for any of the following reasons.

1. An entry appears in the bank's records with no corresponding entry in the company's books.
   a. The bank debited the depositor's account for a bank service charge, interest on a loan, an overdraft, a returned check that had been deposited, or some other similar fee.
   b. The bank credited the depositor's account for collection of a note plus interest; the depositor had left the note with the bank for collection.
2. An entry appears in the company's books with no corresponding entry in the bank's records.
   a. Cash receipts were recorded on the company's books and forwarded for deposit, but not received for deposit by the bank; that is, a deposit was in transit at the time the two balances were taken.
   b. Checks written and recorded in the company's books had not yet been presented to the bank for payment (that is, had not yet cleared); in other words, some checks were outstanding at the time the two balances were taken.
3. Errors were made in one or both of the accounts.
   a. Mathematical errors were made in either account; for example, a check written for $91 was misrecorded as $19 in the company's books.
   b. Errors were made in posting to either account; for example, the bank charged the XYZ Company with a check that should have been debited to the account of the XYC Company.
   c. Fraudulent entries were made in either account.

To understand the bank reconciliation process, it is important that you first be familiar with the bank statement that is sent to a depositor to summarize his relationship with the bank. A typical monthly bank statement for a checking account contains the following information (see Exhibit 10-2):

1. the balance of the account at the beginning of the period;
2. an itemization of deposits received during the period;
3. an itemization of checks paid (cleared) during the period;
4. an itemization of other bank charges and credits to the account.

The *bank reconciliation* is a process of bringing into agreement the balance of the depositor's account in the bank's records and the balance of the Cash account in the company's books. The objective of the reconciliation is to disclose any errors or irregularities in either the bank's or the company's records. For internal control

Exhibit 10-2 **A typical bank statement**

BANK A

Central City, Illinois

Statement of Checking Account for:	Par Company 512 Main Street Central City, Ill.	Period Ending: December 31, 19_1 Checking Account No.: 04312-5-75186

Date	Checks and Other Debits			Deposits	Balance
Nov. 31					5,000
Dec. 5				4,000	9,000
Dec. 8	1,500			1,000	8,500
Dec. 10	1,000	250		700	7,950
Dec. 12	500	1,750		1,300	7,000
Dec. 15	2,000			5,000	10,000
Dec. 17	1,500	100	1,400	4,500	11,500
Dec. 19	200			500	11,800
Dec. 21	800			6,060CM	17,060
Dec. 22	1,050			1,200	17,210
Dec. 26	2,000	1,500		800	14,510
Dec. 28				1,000	15,510
Dec. 30	500	10SC			15,000

Previous Balance	No. Checks	Debits	No. Deposits	Credits	New Balance
5,000	15	16,060	11	26,060	15,000

SC—Service Charge
NSF—Not Sufficient Funds
M—Miscellaneous

DM—Debit Memo
CM—Credit Memo
OD—Overdraft

purposes, the reconciliation should be made by an individual who does not handle cash or have access to the books of the company.

To illustrate the process of reconciliation,[5] assume that the Par Company received a statement from its bank indicating that the balance of its checking account on December 31, 19_1, was $15,000. The first step in the reconciliation is to compare this balance with the balance of the company's Cash account on the same date. The Cash account balance on December 31, 19_1, was $6,950. The two balances do not agree (the usual situation).

The next step is to carefully compare the items on the bank statement with the entries in the Cash account. This comparison involves the following:

1. comparing the list of deposits on the bank statement with the daily totals of cash receipts in the company journal;
2. comparing the list of checks cleared on the bank statement with the cash disbursements recorded in the company journal;
3. comparing any other items on the bank statement with any other debits or credits to the Cash account in the company books.

5. This illustration summarizes the major steps in the process of bank reconciliation. A more detailed description of the procedure is given in the appendix to this chapter.

In our example, this comparison revealed the following discrepancies between the entries in the two accounts.

1. The $5,000 total of cash receipts for December 31 recorded in the company journal was not listed as a deposit on the bank statement. This was not unusual. The deposit was placed in the bank's night-deposit box after the close of business on December 31 and would not be recorded as a deposit until the next business day.
2. A total of $7,000 in checks recorded in the company journal as cash disbursements during December did not appear on the statement; apparently these checks had not yet cleared.
3. A credit for $6,060 was recorded on the bank statement as a credit memo. This amount represented a note receivable for $6,000 left with the bank for collection and collected by the bank with $60 interest. The note is recorded in the Notes Receivable account of the company, and its collection has not yet been reflected in the Cash account.
4. A debit for $10 appears on the bank statement as a service charge for the checking account; no corresponding entry has been made in the company's books.

To determine whether these discrepancies account for the differences between the two balances, a bank reconciliation is now prepared. Two forms are widely used for the reconciliation. The form shown in Exhibit 10-3 begins with the balance on the bank statement, makes all appropriate adjustments for discrepancies found, and ends with a balance that should be equal to the balance of the Cash account in the company books.

The form shown in Exhibit 10-4 adjusts or corrects each of the balances, to show the adjusted balance that each account would have if all missing entries were made. That is, the bank statement balance is adjusted for items not yet recorded by the bank and for any errors made by the bank; the Cash account balance is adjusted for items not yet recorded in the journal account and for any errors in the company's books. The adjusted balances should be equal.

Exhibit 10-3
Bank reconciliation in form that adjusts bank balance to match book balance

PAR COMPANY

Bank Reconciliation
December 31, 19_1

Balance per bank statement		**$15,000**
Add: Deposit in transit	**$5,000**	
Bank service charge	**10**	**5,010**
		$20,010
Deduct: Outstanding checks	**$7,000**	
Note collected by bank	**6,000**	
Interest on note	**60**	**13,060**
Balance per books		**$ 6,950**

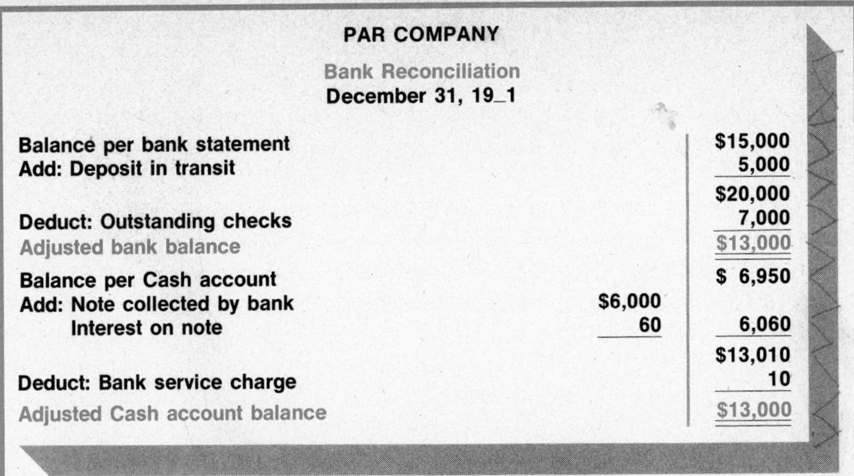

PAR COMPANY

Bank Reconciliation

December 31, 19_1

Balance per bank statement		**$15,000**
Add: Deposit in transit		**5,000**
		$20,000
Deduct: Outstanding checks		**7,000**
Adjusted bank balance		$13,000
Balance per Cash account		**$ 6,950**
Add: Note collected by bank	**$6,000**	
Interest on note	**60**	**6,060**
		$13,010
Deduct: Bank service charge		**10**
Adjusted Cash account balance		$13,000

Exhibit 10-4
Bank reconciliation in form that adjusts bank and book balances separately

In our example, the reconciliation is complete; all discrepancies between the bank statement and the Cash account have been explained. The reconciliation often discloses information that must be recorded by one or more journal entries to bring the company books up to date. In the example, two entries are required.

1. The collection of the note receivable and interest must be recorded.

Dec. 21	Cash	6,060	
	Notes Receivable		6,000
	Interest Earned		60

2. The payment of the bank service charge must be recorded.

Dec. 30	Bank Service Charge Expense	10	
	Cash		10

These two entries would be made in the special cash journals. After the entries are journalized and posted, the Cash account balance has been adjusted to $13,000 (balance of $6,950 + $6,060 note and interest − $10 service charge), as indicated in Exhibit 10-4.

Both forms of the bank reconciliation are satisfactory, but the form shown in Exhibit 10-4 is somewhat preferable because (1) it shows clearly which discrepancies require adjustments in the company's books (through journal entries); (2) the adjusted Cash balance shown in the reconcilliation is the amount reflected in the Cash account after adjustments and therefore is the amount to be listed as cash balance in the balance sheet; and (3) the adjusted bank balance indicates the balance in the bank account actually available for future check writing by the firm.

CASH FORECAST

The cash forecast is a basic managerial tool for control and utilization of cash resources. Cash inflows and outflows are a constant concern of management. Cash usage must be coordinated with the basic objectives of the business—especially with profitability, liquidity, and solvency. If it is to make efficient and effective decisions, management must know in advance what its cash requirements will be. A forecast or budget of anticipated cash receipts and disbursements therefore is essential to sound management.

A forecast of cash requires projection into the future of the plans and estimates of activities that cause cash flow—for example, sales, inventory acquisitions, and operational expenses. The forecast of cash must be coordinated with available information about accounts receivable, investments, accounts payable, and so on. To prepare a cash forecast, the accountant must assemble data that will explain or support the forecast.

The steps involved in preparing a cash forecast for a given future period include the following.

1. Estimate cash receipts for the period. This requires estimates of such items as cash sales of merchandise, collections of receivables, and so on.
2. Estimate cash disbursements for the period. This requires estimates of cash purchases of merchandise, payments of expenses, and so on.
3. Estimate cash balance at the end of the period. This amount is obtained by taking the beginning cash balance, adding estimated cash receipts, and subtracting estimated cash disbursements.
4. Forecast the financing that will be required to maintain a desired minimum cash balance, or forecast the amount of excess cash that will be available for investment or other uses.

We illustrate the procedure of assembling the necessary data and preparing the cash forecast with a simplified example. At the beginning of 19_1, the accountant for the Scorpio Company is to prepare a cash forecast for the first quarter (three months) of the year.

He begins by gathering data about estimated cash receipts. The sales department provides an estimate of sales for the three months. This estimate is based upon past years' sales in the first quarter, overall trends from year to year in sales, and any information that the sales department has about new products, the state of the economy, and so on. The sales department estimates the following sales.

January 19_1:	Credit sales $100,000;	Cash sales $ 5,000.
February 19_1:	Credit sales $120,000;	Cash sales $26,000.
March 19_1:	Credit sales $130,000;	Cash sales $10,000.

The Scorpio Company allows no cash discounts. Past experience indicates that the firm collects about 10 percent of the amount due for that month's credit sales before the end of the month; the remaining 90 percent is collected in the following month. Credit sales in December 19_0 were $90,000, and the amount still to be collected in January is $81,000.

From the data gathered so far, the accountant prepares a schedule of estimated cash receipts (Exhibit 10-5). Next he gathers data about estimated cash disbursements during the first quarter of the year.

Exhibit 10-5 **Schedule 1 for cash forecast**

Schedule 1

Estimated Cash Receipts from Sales
For Three Months Ended March 31, 19_1

	January	February	March
Cash sales	**$ 5,000**	**$26,000**	**$ 10,000**
Cash collections on accounts receivable:			
On December 19_0 sales ($90,000 actual)	**81,000**		
On January sales ($100,000 estimated)	**10,000**	**90,000**	
On February sales ($120,000 estimated)		**12,000**	**108,000**
On March sales ($130,000 estimated)			**13,000**
Estimated cash receipts	$96,000	$128,000	$131,000

All purchases of merchandise for resale are made on credit, and the purchasing department provides the following estimates of credit purchases, based upon past experience and the forecasts of sales.

January 19_1:	Credit purchases $30,000.
February 19_1:	Credit purchases $40,000.
March 19_1:	Credit purchases $50,000.

Past experience shows that payment of about 50 percent of a month's credit purchases is made during that month; the remaining 50 percent is paid in the following month. Credit purchases during December 19_0 were $45,000, and half of that amount remains to be paid during January.

The accountant also gathers information about the normal expenses to be paid during the quarter. He summarizes the information thus far collected in a schedule of estimated normal cash disbursements (Exhibit 10-6).

Exhibit 10-6 **Schedule 2 for cash forecast**

Schedule 2

Estimated Normal Cash Disbursements
For Three Months Ended March 31, 19_1

	January	February	March
Estimated cash payments on accounts payable:			
On December 19_0 purchases ($45,000 act.)	**$22,500**		
On January purchases ($30,000 est.)	**15,000**	**$ 15,000**	
On February purchases ($40,000 est.)		**20,000**	**$ 20,000**
On March purchases ($50,000 est.)			**25,000**
	$37,500	**$ 35,000**	**$ 45,000**
Estimated salaries expense	**20,000**	**20,000**	**20,000**
Estimated rent expense	**10,000**	**10,000**	**10,000**
Other estimated normal expenses	**25,000**	**36,000**	**50,000**
Estimated cash disbursements	$92,500	$101,000	$125,000

He also gathers the best available information about unusual cash receipts or disbursements expected during the quarter. He learns of two events:

1. In February 19_1, new equipment is to be purchased for $50,000 in cash.
2. In March 19_1, marketable securities are to be sold for an estimated $50,000 in cash.

Now that the accountant has all available data about estimated cash receipts and disbursements for the period, he needs to learn about plans for maintaining an adequate cash balance. From discussions with management, the following plans emerge.

1. The company desires to maintain a minimum cash balance of $10,000.
2. If the cash balance at the end of any month is less than $10,000, the company plans to borrow (from a local bank at 6% interest) enough cash on the first of the month to restore the $10,000 minimum cash balance by the end of the month.
3. If the cash balance at the end of any month is more than $10,000, the company plans to repay with interest any outstanding loans from the bank.

After the books were closed on December 31, 19_0, the balance in the Cash account was $5,000. This is the beginning cash balance for 19_1.

The accountant now has all of the data he needs to prepare the cash budget (Exhibit 10-7). Note that the schedules showing details of his forecast are attached as explanations to the cash budget. This budgeted statement of cash receipts and disbursements (or cash forecast, or cash budget) reflects management's plans and expectations for cash accumulation and utilization within the budget period.

Note that the budget predicts that the cash balance at the end of January will fall $1,500 short of the desired $10,000 minimum. Therefore, the company will borrow $1,500 on January 1. With this financing, the cash balance on February 1 will be $10,000. However, the budget then predicts that the balance by the end of February without additional financing would fall $23,000 short of the desired minimum. So, an additional $23,000 is to be borrowed on the first of February. With this financing, the cash balance on March 1 should be $10,000. At the end of March, however, the budget predicts a cash balance $46,000 in excess of the desired minimum. Therefore, no money need be borrowed on March 1, and at the end of March the company will be able to repay its bank loans with interest and still have an excess of $31,247 above the desired minimum in its Cash account.

The financing procedure used in this example does not guarantee that the balance of the Cash account will never fall below $10,000. It only guarantees that the balance will be at least $10,000 at the first of each month (if the estimates and predictions prove valid). For example, if many cash disbursements had to be made early in a month while many of the cash receipts did not come in until late in the month, it would be possible for the company to run out of cash during the middle of the month. In other words, the company might have a problem of liquidity. However, in this case, management feels that the $10,000 minimum balance at the beginning of the month is sufficient to allow for any likely problems of this sort.

Exhibit 10-7 **Cash forecast, or cash budget**

SCORPIO COMPANY
Budgeted Statement of
Cash Receipts and Disbursements
For Three Months Ended March 31, 19_1

	January	February	March
Cash balance, beginning of period	$ 5,000	$ 10,000	$ 10,000
Cash receipts:			
Collections on customers' accounts (Schedule 1)	91,000	102,000	121,000
Cash sales	5,000	26,000	10,000
Other: Sale of marketable securities			50,000
Available cash, before financing (*a*)	$101,000	$138,000	$191,000
Cash disbursements:			
Payments on accounts payable (Schedule 2)	$ 37,500	$ 35,000	$ 45,000
Normal expenses (Schedule 2)	55,000	66,000	80,000
Purchase of equipment		50,000	
Total cash disbursements (*b*)	$ 92,500	$151,000	$125,000
Cash balance required	10,000	10,000	10,000
Total cash needed (*d*)	$102,500	$161,000	$135,000
Excess (or deficiency) (*a* − *d*)	($ 1,500)	($ 23,000)	$ 56,000
Financing:			
Borrowing	$ 1,500	$ 23,000	
Repayment			($ 24,500)
Interest at 6% per year			(253)
Total effect of financing (*c*)	$ 1,500	$ 23,000	($ 24,753)
Cash balance, end of period (*a* + *c* − *b*)	$ 10,000	$ 10,000	$ 41,247

Of course, the cash budget is only an estimate or prediction. It is a good idea to redo the cash budget at the end of each month—or more often if there is any reason to think that conditions have changed significantly since the forecast was made. The importance of accurate cash predictions can hardly be overstated—the entire financial program of an institution depends to a great extent upon the coordination of the inflow and outflow of cash.

THE VOUCHER SYSTEM

Accountants have developed a special system (as a part of the accounting system) to control cash payments and promote efficiency by eliminating the special purchases journal and the accounts payable subsidiary ledger. This special system is called the voucher system.

In the *voucher system,* each cash disbursement must be authorized by a voucher. The *voucher* (Exhibit 10-8) is a serially numbered document that includes all pertinent information about the requested disbursement. The voucher must be signed by those authorized to approve cash disbursements. Supporting documents (such as purchase invoices, freight bills, or receiving documents) for the expenditure must be attached to the voucher.

Exhibit 10-8 A typical voucher form

XYZ COMPANY

Voucher

Payable to: ____________________

Voucher No. __________ **Date Due** __________

Purchase Order No. __________ **Date Paid** __________

Vendor's Invoice No. __________ **Check No.** __________

Terms: __________

Date	Account No.	Description	Quantity	Unit Price	Total

Approved __________

Entered __________

Date Entered __________

After a voucher is authorized, it is filed according to its due date in an *unpaid voucher file.* This file replaces the accounts payable subsidiary ledger.

The voucher is the authorization for an accounting entry in the voucher register. The *voucher register* is a special journal used to record all liabilities approved for payment. Entries in this register include liabilities arising from purchases of merchandise, services, supplies, payroll, and so on. An entry is made in the register when an approved voucher is received; the voucher provides the information needed for the entry. Each authorized voucher is recorded in the voucher register by a debit to the appropriate account (usually an expense account) and a credit to Vouchers Payable. Vouchers Payable is a liability account similar to Accounts Payable. It also is a control account; the credit balance of the Vouchers Payable account represents the total amount of the unpaid vouchers in the unpaid voucher file.

Each day, the unpaid vouchers falling due for payment on that day are removed from the front of the unpaid voucher file. A check is written to pay each of the vouchers. The checks are recorded in the *check register,* a special journal that replaces the cash disbursements journal. Each check is recorded in this register as a debit to Vouchers Payable and a credit to Cash. At the time the check is written and recorded in the check register, a notation is made in the Payment column of the voucher register to show that the voucher has been paid. The voucher itself is cancelled (usually marked "Paid") so that it cannot be used again as authorization for another cash disbursement. The paid vouchers are filed by voucher number in a *paid voucher file.*

Exhibit 10-9 illustrates the entries made in the voucher and check registers and the general ledger of the XYZ Company during June 19_1. During June, the accounting system received the following approved vouchers.

June	1	Voucher No. 1. Payable June 15. Payment for purchase of $10,000 of merchandise on account from the Supplier Co.
	3	Voucher No. 2. Payable July 10. Payment for purchase of $20,000 of equipment on account from the Equipment Co.
	5	Voucher No. 3. Payable June 27. Payment for purchase of $25,000 of merchandise on account from the Newproduct Co.
	10	Voucher No. 4. Payable June 17. Payment for purchase of $1,000 of merchandise on account from Replier Co. Invoice dated June 8; terms 2/10, n/30.
	30	Voucher No. 5. Payable July 5. Monthly payroll in the amount of $50,000.

As each of these approved vouchers was received, it was recorded in the voucher register. The vouchers were then filed in the unpaid vouchers file, with those to be paid first in the front of the file. For example, on June 15 the file contained four vouchers in this order: Voucher No. 1, Voucher No. 4, Voucher No. 3, Voucher No. 2. On June 15, the first voucher in the file was payable, so a check was written to the Supplier Company. The check was recorded in the check register, and the voucher was cancelled and moved to the paid vouchers file. Similarly, checks were written on June 17 and on June 27 as Vouchers No. 4 and No. 3 became payable. On June 30, Voucher No. 5 was received, recorded in the voucher register, and filed in front of Voucher No. 2 in the unpaid voucher file (because it is to be paid first).

The entries in the voucher and check registers are posted to the general ledger in a fashion similar to that described in Chapter 9 for special journals. Column totals usually are posted to the appropriate accounts at the end of the month; individual entries in the Sundry Accounts columns must be posted separately. Note the way that the purchase discount on the Replier Company payment is recorded.

At the end of June, the Vouchers Payable account in the general ledger (after posting) shows a balance of $70,000. This equals the total of the two unpaid vouchers in the unpaid voucher file. They can be located in the voucher register by looking for those vouchers for which no payment has been recorded. The Vouchers Payable account is a control account that replaces the Accounts Payable account used in earlier chapters. The unpaid voucher file replaces the accounts payable subsidiary ledger, and it acts in effect as a subsidiary ledger for the Vouchers Payable control account.

The preceding brief description of a voucher system demonstrates the control procedures associated with this system. A cash disbursement is made only after a voucher (request for disbursement) has been *verified* by supporting documents and *approved* by an appropriate authority. Each approved voucher is *promptly recorded* in a particular journal, the voucher register. Unpaid vouchers are filed in order of their due dates, assuring that *no obligation will be overlooked when due,* especially if a discount is available for payment within a specified time period. Paid vouchers are filed to provide *evidence of payment authorization and supporting docu-*

Exhibit 10-9 **Register and ledger entries for approved and paid vouchers**

VOUCHER REGISTER

Page VR8

Date		Vouch. No.	Name	Payment		Vouchers Payable Cr.	Purchases Dr.	Sundry Account			
				Date	Ch. No.			Ref.	✓	Dr.	Cr.
19_1											
June	1	1	Supplier Co.	6/15	1	10,000	10,000				
	3	2	Equipment Co.			20,000		1306	✓	20,000	
	5	3	Newproduct Co.	6/27	3	25,000	25,000				
	10	4	Replier Co.	6/17	2	1,000	1,000				
	30	5	Payroll			50,000		5002	✓	50,000	
						106,000	36,000			70,000	
						[2107]	[4005]			[✓]	

CHECK REGISTER

Page CR4

Date		Voucher No.	Name	Check No.	Vouchers Payable Dr.	Purchases Discounts Cr.	Cash Cr.
19_1							
June	15	1	Supplier Co.	1	10,000		10,000
	17	4	Replier Co.	2	1,000	20	980
	27	3	Newproduct Co.	3	25,000		25,000
					36,000	20	35,980
					[2107]	[4006]	[1101]

GENERAL LEDGER

Cash 1101

Date	Item	Ref.	Debit	Date	Item	Ref.	Credit
				19_1 June 30	Disburs.	CR4	35,980

Equipment 1306

Date	Item	Ref.	Debit	Date	Item	Ref.	Credit
19_1 June 3		VR8	20,000				

Vouchers Payable 2107

Date	Item	Ref.	Debit	Date	Item	Ref.	Credit
19_1 June 30	Disburs.	CR4	36,000	19_1 June 30		VR8	106,000

Purchases 4005

Date	Item	Ref.	Debit	Date	Item	Ref.	Credit
19_1 June 30	Vouchers	VR8	36,000				

Purchases Discounts 4006

Date	Item	Ref.	Debit	Date	Item	Ref.	Credit
				19_1 June 30	Disburs.	CR4	20

Payroll 5002

Date	Item	Ref.	Debit	Date	Item	Ref.	Credit
19_1 June 30		VR8	50,000				

mentation. The check register provides a convenient record of checks issued for comparison with the bank statement in the process of reconciliation.

In the voucher system, individuals who are authorized to approve vouchers do not prepare or sign checks or have access to the voucher and cash registers. The individual who signs checks is allowed to do so only when a voucher for the payment has been authorized.

Impact analysis

The cash balance of a firm is a very important element of its financial condition. Analysts and investors look closely at the cash balance, working capital, current ratio, and acid-test ratio as they evaluate a company. All of these measures depend heavily on the cash position of the firm.

Because the cash balance is so important, accountants sometimes are tempted to handle the records improperly in order to make the cash position of the firm look better on statements. For example, if the cash balance is low at the end of a period, the books might be kept open into the next period—so that cash from sales or other sources actually received in the following period can be reported as cash on the current statements. Similarly, if there is an excess of cash, liabilities might be reduced by keeping the records of payments on account open for a few days longer and recording next year's payments in the current period.

Such practices obviously are improper and misleading. The cash balance reported on the statement of financial position should reflect the cash on hand and in the bank account on the date of the statement. All books should be closed at the same moment (usually the close of business on the last day of the accounting period). Any cash received or paid after the date of the statement should not be reflected in the cash balance on the statement.

We have seen that cash normally is classified as a current asset. However, there are some situations where items included in the Cash account should properly be classified elsewhere on the statement of financial position. For example, some funds may be deposited in foreign banks or closed banks where they cannot be readily withdrawn. Sometimes special funds are established to reserve certain amounts of cash for a particular future use—such as payment of the principal of a long-term debt or retirement of common stock. Such cash is not fully liquid in the sense usually attached to the cash item on the financial statement. Therefore, including these amounts in the cash balance will give misleading values for working capital, the current and acid-test ratios, and other indicators. Such funds should be removed from the Cash account and recorded in some other asset account that more properly reflects their liquidity as assets of the firm.

Summary

Cash includes any item that customarily is accepted by a bank for deposit. The control and use of cash to assure the firm's liquidity while getting maximum profit from the firm's assets are prime managerial considerations.

Procedures associated with the control and use of cash include:

1. Internal control, the means by which the firm obtains information, protection, and control needed for successful operations.
2. The imprest system of petty cash, which provides procedures to control disbursement of minor sums while minimizing inconvenience and expense.
3. Bank reconciliation, a procedure required to prove that the balance of the firm's checking account in the bank's records is in agreement with the balance of the Cash account in the company's books.
4. Cash forecast, a budgetary procedure used to predict and control the amount of cash available for business purposes.
5. The voucher system, which provides procedures for controlling all cash disbursements.

Appendix

STEPS IN BANK RECONCILIATION

This chapter outlines the process of bank reconciliation in general terms. The detailed steps involved in the procedure can be outlined as follows.

1. Examine cancelled checks and other memoranda received from the bank (such as bank service charge slips, notices for the collection of notes plus interest left with the bank for collection, memoranda of charges for overdrafts, or checks returned unpaid for various reasons). Verify that each item is genuine and properly recorded in this account. Compare the items with the bank statement to be sure that each amount has been correctly entered on the statement.
2. Arrange the cancelled checks returned by the bank in numerical order. When arranged in this manner, they will correspond to the order of entry in the check book and in the cash disbursements journal or check register. Compare each cancelled check with the check stub to be sure that the name of the payee and the amount are properly recorded on the stub. Signatures and endorsements also may be examined at this time.
3. Compare the debits and credits in the bank statement with the related entries in the company's books.
   a. Compare the date and amount of deposits shown on the bank statement with the date and amount shown in the cash receipts records of the company.
      (1) Any deposit in transit at the beginning of the period (shown on the bank reconciliation at the end of the prior period) should appear as a deposit on the bank statement for the current period. Tick mark (√) the item on the prior period's bank reconciliation form and on the bank statement.
      (2) Compare the unticked deposits on the bank statement with the record of cash receipts during the current period. Tick each deposit on the bank statement and the corresponding entry in the books. Any unticked item remaining in the books is a deposit in transit for the current period.
      (3) Note any errors or omissions on the bank statement or in the books.
   b. Compare the date and amount of cancelled checks returned by the bank with

(1) checks outstanding at the beginning of the period, as shown on the previous period's bank reconciliation form, and (2) the cash disbursements records in the company books for checks written during the period. As each item is located, tick the debit on the bank statement, the entry in the cash disbursements records, and (if appropriate) the item on the previous period's bank reconciliation form. Any entries in the cash disbursements record not ticked are outstanding at the end of the period; so are any checks outstanding at the beginning of the period and not ticked on the previous period's reconciliation form. Note any errors or omissions on the bank statement or in the books.

c. Examine the bank statement for any unticked items. Such items may require an entry in the company's books and a listing on the reconciliation form.

4. Prepare the bank reconciliation (Exhibits 10-3 and 10-4).

5. If the reconciliation is not achieved (the accounts do not match after adjustments),

a. prove the calculations on the bank statements;

b. prove the footings in the company's cash receipts and cash disbursements records and in the Cash account in the general ledger.

Questions

1. Indicate whether or not each of the following items should be classified as cash, and explain your answer in each case.

a. The balance in a checking account at a bank.

b. The balance in a savings account at a bank.

c. Postage stamps.

d. An IOU from an officer of the corporation.

e. Checks received from customers.

f. A post-dated check received from a customer.

g. A traveler's check received from a customer.

h. The balance of a special bank account containing funds being reserved to pay a legal judgment against the company if the pending court appeal is rejected.

2. What is meant by internal control? List some sound procedures for the control of cash receipts and disbursements. What is the responsibility of management in respect to internal control?

3. Explain the operation of an imprest petty cash fund. List some ways in which such a fund might be misused by employees or others. Describe control procedures that protect against each possible abuse of the fund.

4. Why is it necessary to periodically reconcile the Cash account and the bank statement? Describe and explain the two forms for this reconciliation shown in this chapter. Which do you prefer? Why?

5. Discuss the need for a cash forecast. Summarize the procedure by which such a forecast is prepared.

6. Does each of the following procedures strengthen or weaken internal control? Explain your answers. If internal control is weak, describe the nature of possible abuses and suggest corrective procedures.

a. The operator of a theater requires that each ticket presented for admission be torn in two and one portion given to the patron.

b. The purchasing department of the X Company prepares six copies of each purchase order. One copy is forwarded to the receiving department, which records on this copy the merchandise received. The quantity of items ordered is omitted on the copy sent to the receiving department.
c. The treasurer (who controls cash) of a company is also its comptroller (chief accountant).
d. The check-out clerk at a supermarket is required to give the customer a cash register tape receipt along with the correct change at the time of a purchase.
e. The Small Company has a single accountant responsible for handling and recording cash receipts, making bank deposits, writing checks, recording cash disbursements, and preparing bank reconciliations.
f. The head of the Small Company's accounting department (who can authorize cash disbursements for expenses of his department) also is authorized to sign checks whenever the treasurer of the company is out of town.

7. What is the voucher system? Describe the major forms, procedures, and journals used in a voucher system.

8. What accounting entry is required if a check received from a customer is returned by the bank marked "Not Sufficient Funds"?

Exercises

E10-1 (Petty cash)

The Deft Company uses an imprest petty cash fund. Journalize the following transactions if necessary.

a. On November 1, a check for $150 is cashed to establish the petty cash fund.
b. Disbursements from the fund (supported by approved receipts) during the month include the following.

Nov.	3	Meals (advertising expense)	$24
	5	Office supplies	69
	11	Delivery expense	11
	17	Advertising	17
	21	Charitable contributions	20

c. The fund is replenished on November 30. Prior to reimbursement, $9 of cash remains in the fund.
d. On December 2, the fund is increased to $200.

E10-2 (Petty cash)

Assume the same facts as in Exercise E10-1, except that the cash on hand in the fund on November 30 amounted to $4 instead of $9. Give the necessary journal entry for the replenishment of the fund on November 30.

E10-3 (Petty cash)

The Petty Parts Company uses an imprest petty cash fund. Journalize the following transactions if necessary.

a. On April 1, a check for $600 is cashed to establish the petty cash fund.
b. Authorized disbursements from the fund during April include:

Office supplies	$310
Advertising expense	40
Telephone expense	35
Travel expense	60

c. The company closes its books on April 30. The petty cash fund is not replenished at this time. However, an entry is required.

d. The petty cash fund is replenished on May 5.

E10-4 (Bank reconciliation)

The Drafty Company has a checking account with the Windy National Bank. On August 31, 19_6, the Cash account in the ledger of the company shows a balance of $32,015. The bank statement received from the bank shows a balance on August 31 in the checking account of $27,400. In the reconciliation process, it is discovered that checks amounting to $2,600 were outstanding on August 31, and that a deposit of $7,200 was in transit on that date. A bank service charge of $15 was shown on the statement.

Required:

a. Prepare the bank reconciliation in each of the two forms shown in this chapter.

b. Journalize any entries required on August 31, 19_6.

E10-5 (Cash forecast)

Prepare a cash forecast for the Miser Company for the period from October 1, 19_6, to January 31, 19_7. Consider the following facts, predictions, and estimates:

The balance of Cash on October 1, 19_6, is $27,000, and management wants to maintain a minimum balance of $1,000. If additional cash is required in any month, it can be borrowed at the beginning of the month from a local bank at 6% interest. Borrowed funds are to be repaid with interest at the end of any month when excess cash is available. All sales are on account and are collected in full during the month following the sale. The sales forecast is as follows: September $12,000; October $10,000; November $20,000; December $25,000; January $15,000; February $14,000.

The Miser Company buys merchandise at wholesale for 60 percent of the price for which it sells the merchandise. Merchandise is purchased one month before it is sold. Purchases are made on account, with 80 percent of the accounts payable being paid in the month of purchase and the balance in the following month.

Operating expenses are $3,400 per month, of which $300 is depreciation. A dividend of $2,500 will be declared in October and paid in November. A second dividend of $15,000 will be paid in January.

E10-6 (Cash budget)

The Automate Company prepares a budgeted statement of cash receipts and disbursements. The accountant for the company compiles the following actual data for July and predictions for August and September.

	Sales	Purchases	Expenses (including depreciation)
July (actual)	$ 90,000	$140,000	$25,000
August (forecast)	110,000	50,000	35,000
September (forecast)	130,000	70,000	40,000

a. All sales are on credit; 50 percent of sales total is collected in the month of sale and the balance in the following month. The company gives a 1 percent cash discount for payments made during the month of the sale.

b. The Automate Company makes all purchases on account. It pays 50 percent of the total purchases amount in the month of the purchase (taking a 2 percent discount on these payments) and pays the balance in the following month.
c. Depreciation expense is $8,000 per month. The company pays all of its expenses in the month following the month in which they were incurred.
d. The company will pay a cash dividend of $4,000 in September.
e. The cash balance of the firm on August 1 is $14,000.

Required:

1. Compute the estimated cash receipts for August and for September.
2. Compute the estimated cash disbursements in August and in September, related to payments on accounts payable.
3. Compute the estimated cash payments for expenses in August and in September.
4. Prepare a cash budget for August and September, assuming that the firm will not borrow any cash.

E10-7 (Cash balance)

In each of the following independent cases, indicate the proper cash balance that should be shown on the statement of financial position. Explain your answers.

a. The Moe Company has a $12,000 balance in its checking account at First Bank. It has another account at Second Bank, which shows an overdraft of $8,000.
b. The Flo Company has a $17,000 balance in its checking account at Jinx Bank. In the office safe it holds a check for $6,000 written to the company by its vice-president in payment for some merchandise he has purchased from the company. The chief secretary in the office is custodian of a $300 imprest petty cash fund; she also holds $100 in postage stamps belonging to the company. Advances of $2,000 cash have been given to salesmen to cover their expenses; they will later be required to provide documentation of their expenses and return any unspent cash. The company has a $600 balance in a checking account in a foreign bank; checks written on this account will not be accepted by American banks.

E10-8 (Impact analysis)

Prepare a table showing the impact of each of the following transactions on working capital, current ratio (value of 3.0 to 1 before first transaction), net assets, net income, and owners' equity.

a. The petty cash fund is replenished in the amount of $300 for disbursements of $200 in advertising expenses and a $100 advance given to an officer of the firm (due to be repaid in two weeks).
b. A cash account in a foreign bank with a balance of $9,000 is reclassified from the Current Assets to the Other Assets classification.
c. The company borrows $15,000 from the bank at 8% interest for 90 days.
d. The company repays the bank loan, with interest.
e. An employee defrauds the company of $600 cash. The loss is not insured, and the funds cannot be recovered from the employee.
f. The company establishes a $400 petty cash fund.

Problems

P10-1 (Bank reconciliation)

The following information relates to the banking activities of the Broken Drum Company with the County Bank during the month of June 19_6.

a. The company's ledger shows a balance in the Cash account of $17,000 on June 1, and a balance of $12,651 on June 30.

b. The bank statement shows a balance in the company's checking account of $14,000 on June 30.

c. An examination of the cancelled checks and the check register shows that the following checks are outstanding on June 30: No. 13, $600; No. 19, $2,300.

d. A deposit of $3,000 is in transit on June 30.

e. The bank service charge for the month is $15.

f. Along with the returned cancelled checks received from the bank is a debit memo indicating that a $100 check of the Gong Company (which the Broken Drum Company had deposited as part of its cash receipts) is being returned marked NSF.

g. Examination of the returned cancelled checks reveals that the bank erroneously debited a $200 check written by the Bobo Company to the Broken Drum Company's account.

h. A credit memo enclosed with the statement shows that the bank has collected an $1,800 note receivable plus interest of $18 for the Broken Drum Company; this transaction has not yet been recorded in the company books.

i. Comparison of the cancelled checks and the check stubs reveals that a check written to the Coho Company in the amount of $82 was recorded erroneously as a $28 payment in the company's books.

Required:

1. Prepare bank reconciliation forms for the end of June in each of the two forms shown in this chapter (Exhibits 10-3 and 10-4).

2. Prepare any journal entries that are required on June 30, 19_6.

P10-2 (Bank reconciliation)

The ledger of the Vase Company shows a balance of $110 in the Cash account at the end of 19_6. The company's bank statement shows a balance of $79 in the firm's checking account on December 31, 19_6. Cash receipts of $48 received on December 31 were not deposited on that day. A check for $17 was outstanding at the end of the year.

On January 6, 19_7, a firm of public accountants audits the accounts of the Vase Company. One of the auditors assembles from bank and company records the information shown in Exhibit 10-10 in preparation for a reconciliation of the firm's Cash account and its checking account. The detailed debits and credits on the bank statement are found to be correct. The $3 charge on January 2 is for bank service charges. All other charges on the bank statement are verified by valid cancelled checks in the amounts shown. Each bank deposit represents the firm's total cash receipts for the preceding business day.

The charge of $41 on the bank statement for January 5 is a correct representation of Check No. 4, written to a creditor as a payment on an account payable.

Exhibit 10-10 Auditor's working paper for Problem P10-2

	Check No.	Cash Receipts Journal	Cash Payments Journal	Bank Statement Charge	Bank Statement Deposit	Bank Statement Balance
19_6						
Dec. 31 Balance		110				79
19_7						
Jan. 2	1		4	17	48	110
2	2		8	3SC		107
3		50				
3	3		11	8		99
3	4		14			
4		80			50	149
4	5		17	4		145
4	6		6	11		134
5		40			80	214
5	7		67	41		173
5	8		7	7		166
5 Balance			146			
		280	280			
6 Balance		146				

Required:

a. Prepare a reconciliation of the bank account and Cash account as of the close of business on January 5, 19_7.

b. Journalize any entries arising from the bank reconciliation.

c. What cash balance should the auditors show on a statement of financial position they are preparing for the firm, as of January 5, 19_7?

P10-3 (Cash forecast)

Prepare a budgeted statement of estimated cash receipts and disbursements for April 19_6 for the Tryon Company. A trial balance of the books gives the following opening balances at the beginning of April for selected accounts: Cash $44,000; Accounts Receivable $15,000; Merchandise Inventory $23,333; Accounts Payable $8,000. The firm's credit purchases are paid within ten days. One-fourth of the purchases of a given month are paid in the following month.

The firm buys merchandise for $10 per unit and sells it for $15 per unit. Management policy requires that inventory at the end of the month equal at least 75 percent of the following month's estimated sales requirements. Selling terms allow a 2 percent discount if payment is made by the end of the month of the sale. Past experience shows that 50 percent of a month's sales are collected in the month of the sales; 25 percent are collected in the following month; 20 percent are collected in the second month following the sales; the remaining 5 percent are uncollectible.

Sales forecasts call for total sales of $80,000 in April and $100,000 in May. Actual sales were $60,000 in February and $64,000 in March. Operating expenses for April are estimated at $18,000, including depreciation expense of $4,000. Operating expenses are paid during the month in which they are incurred.

P10-4 (Accrual accounting)

During 19_6, the Tosser Company collected $140,000 for rent from clients and paid out $180,000 in wages. The ledger of the company showed an opening balance of $6,000 and a closing balance of $12,000 for the year in the Unearned Rent account, and an opening balance of $21,000 and a closing balance of $15,000 in the Accrued Salaries account. The company does its accounting on an accrual basis. Compute the correct amounts of rent income and salaries expense that the company should report on its 19_6 income statement.

P10-5 (Cash budget)

The Howe Company reports the following data concerning its 19_6 operations. No other data are available.

	Opening Balance	Closing Balance
Accounts Receivable	$ 7,000	$ 18,000
Purchases of Merchandise	0	91,000 on account
Sales	0	116,000 on account
Accounts Payable	12,000	16,000

Required:

a. Compute the amount of cash collected on accounts receivable in 19_6.
b. Compute the amount paid to creditors for purchases in 19_6.

P10-6 (Voucher system)

The Balsam Company uses the voucher system to record transactions that involve cash disbursements. During March 19_6, the following approved vouchers were received and checks issued by the accounting system.

Mar. 1 Voucher No. 101 for $1,200 payable April 10 to Suds Company for merchandise purchased today.
3 Voucher No. 102 for $800 payable immediately to Croner Company for March rent expense.
4 Check No. 510 issued in payment of Voucher No. 102
4 Voucher No. 103 for $4,000 payable March 7 to News Company for advertising expense.
5 Voucher No. 104 for $200 payable April 1 to Typo Company for office supplies.
8 Voucher No. 105 for $5,000 payable April 5 to Popper Company for office equipment.
10 Check No. 511 issued in payment of Voucher No. 103.
12 Voucher No. 106 for $2,000 payable April 12 to Dutch Company for merchandise purchased on account.
30 Voucher No. 107 for $15,000 payable immediately to company paymaster for March salaries.
30 Voucher No. 108 for $7,000 payable April 10 to Gas Company for March utilities expenses.
31 Check No. 512 issued in payment of Voucher No. 107.

Required:

a. Set up a voucher register and a check register as illustrated in this chapter.
b. Journalize the March transactions and post to general ledger accounts.
c. Prepare a Vouchers Payable account and post those items that involve Vouchers Payable.
d. Prepare a schedule showing the contents (in proper order) of the unpaid voucher file at the end of March. Compare the total of the amounts of unpaid vouchers with the balance of the Vouchers Payable account.

P10-7 (Voucher system)

On June 30, 19_6, the voucher register of the Rogers Company showed the following unpaid vouchers as of that date.

Voucher No. 450, recorded June 15, for $400 payable to Booker Co.
Voucher No. 490, recorded June 28, for $1,300 payable to Hooks Co.
Voucher No. 499, recorded June 30, for $300 payable to Club Co.

The following transactions occurred during July.

July 1 Check No. 440 issued in payment of Voucher No. 499.
5 Received approved Voucher No. 510, payable July 12 to John Joseph for $2,700 worth of merchandise purchased today; terms 1/10, n/30.
8 Returned a portion of the merchandise purchased on Voucher No. 450 to the Booker Co. because it was damaged. Received credit of $150 for the returned merchandise. Voucher No. 450 is cancelled and Voucher No. 511 is issued and approved for the proper amount due. In the voucher register, Vouchers Payable is debited $400 for the cancelled voucher and credited $250 for the new voucher; the remaining $150 is credited to an account called Purchase Returns and Allowances.
12 Check No. 441 issued in payment of Voucher No. 510, taking the appropriate purchases discount.
15 Received approved Voucher No. 512 payable to Tommy Co. for $6,000 merchandise purchased today on account; terms 2/10, n/30.
20 Issued check in partial payment of $700 on Voucher No. 490; no discount is taken. The old voucher is cancelled and a new voucher issued and approved for the balance due.
28 Rent in amount of $12,000 for July falls due. A voucher is prepared and approved, and a check is issued to the Rents Company.
29 A credit sale is made to the Sparks Co. for $30,000; terms n/30.
30 A check for $5,000 in payment on account is received from the Sparks Co.

Required:

a. Prepare a voucher register similar to the one illustrated in this chapter. Enter the unpaid vouchers from June. Draw double rules under the last of these entries.

b. Record the July transactions in the voucher register. Prepare a check register and make the entries needed for the July transactions. Ignore the July transactions that do not involve the voucher register or the check register.

c. Enter the total of unpaid vouchers as of June 30 ($2,000) as a credit balance in a Vouchers Payable account in the general ledger.

d. Rule the voucher and check registers. Post the July transactions from the registers to the general ledger, creating accounts as needed.

e. From the voucher register, prepare a schedule of unpaid vouchers.

P10-8 (Cash forecast)

The following information is available for the Excelsior Company regarding its cash requirements.

Beginning cash balance, Jan. 1, 19_6	$10,000
Cash sales:	
January	10,000
February	20,000
Credit sales;	
December	10,000
January	10,000
February	10,000

No discounts are allowed on credit sales. Cash is collected from credit sales as follows:

20% in the month of the sale;
80% in the month following the sale.

Cash expenses:

December	$ 5,000

January	7,000
February	10,000
March	12,000

Purchases (all credit purchases payable 50% in month of purchase and 50% in the following month):

December	$ 5,000
January	5,000
February	5,000
March	10,000

Required: Prepare a cash forecast for the Excelsior Company for the months of January and February.

P10-9 (Voucher system)

The Better Company uses the voucher system to record various transactions. The system employs a voucher register and a check register. The following transactions occurred during the month of January. Numbers assigned each transaction refer to the day of the month.

1. Purchased merchandise on account from the A Company in the amount of $100,000. Purchases are subject to a discount of 2/10; n/30. Voucher No. 101. Vouchers are numbered consecutively.
2. Purchased a three-year fire insurance policy for $10,000 and paid this amount today. Check No. 17.
3. Purchased office equipment for $10,000 from the Mart Company on account.
4. Sold merchandise to the Redford Company on account in the amount of $50,000.
5. Collected the amount due from the Redford Company in full.
6. Purchased merchandise on account from the B Company in the amount of $50,000. Credit terms: 2/10; n/30.
7. Paid the monthly rent in the amount of $30,000.
8. Paid week's salaries in the amount of $50,000.
9. Paid the Mart Company the amount due. No discount is allowed.
10. Cash sales amounted to $75,000.
11. Paid the A Company for the purchase of January 1. The discount was allowed.
12. Purchased merchandise from the Bedford Company on account in the amount of $25,000. Credit terms are 2/10; n/30.
13. Made the adjusting entries for the month. Depreciation was $10,000 and $2,000 of the credit sales are estimated to be uncollectible.
14. Made the closing entries for the month.

Required:

a. Record the above transactions in the voucher system where required.
b. Post the voucher register and the check register.
c. Prepare a trial balance of unpaid vouchers. Compare this total with the balance in the vouchers payable account.

Temporary and permanent investments

In our discussion of cash in Chapter 10, we mentioned that a firm with excess cash funds should find a productive use for these resources. In this chapter, we explore certain possible uses for excess cash. One such use is the acquisition of stocks or bonds. We now turn to a discussion of the accounting problems associated with the acquisition, holding, and disposal of such securities. The appendix to this chapter describes various types of securities and the market facilities in which they are bought and sold. If you are not already familiar with these concepts, you should read the appendix in order to have the background information needed for a fuller understanding of the accounting problems discussed in this chapter. In Chapter 16 we discuss the corporation and its financing operations; in that chapter we look at stocks and bonds from the point of view of the issuer.

INVESTMENT RISKS

Most students are curious about the mysteries of the stock market. The idiom (or jargon, if you prefer) of the securities market has found its way into everyday language, in the use of terms such as ticker tape, Dow-Jones average, short selling, price-earnings ratios, and the Big Board. The accounting student has a very practical need to be familiar with the promises and the problems of investments.

An ***investment*** is defined as an asset or property right acquired and kept to earn an income or to conserve or increase capital. The objectives of the investor include one or more of the following: a liberal income, safety of the principal amount, or long-term growth of the principal amount. Investments include a wide range of economic resources such as savings accounts, stocks, bonds, mortgages, commodities, insurance, and real estate.

The risks involved in an investment are related to the objectives of investing. To a greater or a lesser extent, any investment of resources involves the assumption of four fundamental risks: a business risk, a market risk, a money-rate risk, and a price-level risk.

BUSINESS RISK. An investment in a business or other property involves the risk that the value of the investment may decline because the asset loses utility or the business loses earning power. Such business declines can occur as a result of managerial errors, governmental action, competitive forces, technological changes, or other factors. In general, the business risk is so low as to be almost absent in such investments as bonds and notes issued by state and federal governments.

MARKET RISK. Most investments are subject to the possibility that the price or value of the asset may fluctuate on the market—in a downward as well as an upward direction. In most cases, investments such as savings accounts and government bonds are not subject to the market risk.

MONEY-RATE RISK. An investment in an asset producing a fixed income (for example, a $1,000 corporate bond with a contractual rate of 6% interest) involves a risk that the interest rate on new issues of similar securities may be higher. For example, the 6% corporate bond will be worth less if new bonds issued by corporations pay 7% interest. On the other hand, the bond will be worth more if new issues of bonds pay 5% interest. High-grade bonds, preferred stock, mortgages, and similar securities with fixed incomes and relatively long lives are vulnerable to the money-rate risk. This risk is somewhat mitigated in the purchase of short-maturity investments—usually at the cost of accepting a somewhat lower income rate.

PRICE-LEVEL RISK. During a period of rising prices (that is, a period of inflation), the purchasing power of a dollar diminishes. With only minor exceptions, prices have been rising continuously in the United States since the early 1930s. If an investment is made today in an asset that is to be payable in a definite dollar amount at some future time (for example, a ten-year bond), the purchasing power of the dollars received at maturity will almost certainly be less than that of the dollars invested today. Bonds and other securities with a fixed maturity date and value (in dollars) are most vulnerable to the price-level risk. Common stock and real estate offer some reduction in this risk, because their market prices tend to rise and fall proportionately with the general price level.

REASONS FOR INVESTING IN SECURITIES. There are two basic ways to put excess cash to work earning revenue for the owners. The firm can become an owner or a lender. One business may invest in the stock (ownership) or bonds (loans) of another company for many reasons. The most important are:

1. to obtain dividends, interest income, or capital gains (that is, increases in the market value of the investment principal) through the use of excess cash resources; and
2. to obtain control of another company
   a. to reduce competition or to obtain a business advantage,
   b. to assure a steady supply of a needed product at a reasonable price, or
   c. to expand its own operations, thereby increasing sales, profits, earnings per share, and so on.

TEMPORARY AND PERMANENT INVESTMENTS

Because businesses do make investments in other enterprises, the accounting system must accumulate, measure, and report data about the value of these assets and about the income that they generate. In accounting for securities, the accounting system may report investments in stocks or bonds either as temporary or as long-term investments.

A ***temporary investment*** is a security that meets two requirements:

1. the security is readily marketable; and
2. management intends to dispose of the security to meet cash requirements during the current operating cycle of the business.

Temporary investments often are called ***marketable securities*** and are classified as current assets. In the statement of financial position, the value of any marketable securities owned by the company appears as a classification under current assets. In keeping with the initial recording principle, the value of the securities is initially determined by their acquisition cost. ***Long-term*** or ***permanent investments*** are those investments that do not meet the two requirements given for temporary investments. Permanent investments are classified in the statement of financial position under the category of investments.

Investment in stock

The acquisition of stock is recognized initially in the accounts according to the initial recording principle (see Chapter 3): an asset is recorded initially at an amount measured by the exchange price at which the transfer takes place. The cost of an investment in stock includes its purchase price and any brokerage fees, taxes, or similar expenditures associated with the acquisition of the security. The details of accounting for purchases and sales of stock can best be illustrated through a series of examples.

Transaction 1. Stocks acquired for cash. One hundred shares of the Get-Rich-Quick Company's stock are purchased on the market at a price of $25 per share. Brokerage fees and taxes on the purchase are $37. The stock is to be held as a permanent investment.

This ***purchase of stock for cash*** is recorded by a debit to an Investment in Stock account and a credit to the Cash account. Observe in the following journal entry that the cost of the stock is its market price plus the incidental costs.

Investment in Stock	2,537	
Cash		2,537
To record purchase of 100 shares of Get-Rich-Quick Co. stock at $25 per share, plus brokerage fee and tax of $37.		

If the stock were to be held as a temporary investment (to be sold within the current operating cycle or within a year if shorter), it would be listed as a marketable security (current asset).

Marketable Securities	2,537	
Cash		2,537

In either case, the acquisition cost of the stock is readily and objectively determined by the cash exchange price.

Transaction 2. Stock acquired in an exchange. One hundred shares of Blue Chip Company's stock are acquired in exchange for property consisting of land acquired ten years ago for a cost of $100,000. The land has been carried on the books at the value of its acquisition cost. Its current appraised value is $115,000. The current fair market value of the stock is $120,000.

When ***stock is acquired in exchange for another asset,*** the initial recording principle requires that the exchange price be determined by the fair market value of the property or service given up or the fair market value of the security acquired, whichever is more objectively determinable. In transaction 2, the market value of the stock is considered to be more realistic than the appraised value of the land (dependent on many estimates and comparisons) or the original cost of the land (not a good measure of its current value). Therefore, the following journal entry would be used to record this transaction.

Investment in Stock	120,000	
Land		100,000
Gain on Exchange of Land		20,000
To record exchange of land (cost $100,000) for stock with fair market value of $120,000.		

Again, if the stock were to be held as a temporary investment, the debit would be recorded in the Marketable Securities account.

Transaction 3. Sale of stock at a gain. One hundred shares of Long-Short Company stock acquired for $9,000 several years ago are sold for $10,000.

This ***sale of stock at a gain*** is reported by a debit to the Cash account, a credit of $9,000 to the Investment in Stock account (to offset the balance carried there for the value of the stock at cost), and a credit of $1,000 to an income account.

Cash	10,000	
Investment in Stock		9,000
Gain on Sale of Stock		1,000
To record the sale of 100 shares of Long-Short Co. stock at $100 per share.		

If the stock were recorded as a temporary investment, the $9,000 would be credited to Marketable Securities.

Transaction 4. Sale of stock at a loss. Another one hundred shares of the same stock described in transaction 3 are sold for $8,000.

In this case of the ***sale of stock at a loss,*** the loss is debited to an expense account.

Cash	8,000	
Loss on Sale of Stock	1,000	
Investment in Stock		9,000

On the income statement, any gains or losses from sale of securities are reported in the categories of other income or other expenses.

Transaction 5. Sale of stock acquired at different prices. On February 1, a temporary investment is made by the purchase of 500 shares of Hot-Tip Company's stock at $10 per share. On March 15, an additional 1,000 shares are purchased at $12 per share. On June 10, 750 shares of the Hot-Tip Company stock are sold for $9 per share.

This case involves the ***sale of securities acquired at different prices.*** To determine the gain or loss on the sale, the accountant must decide which securities are being sold. Two methods are generally accepted for identifying the shares sold: (1) the specific identification method, and (2) the first-in, first-out (FIFO) method.

SPECIFIC IDENTIFICATION METHOD. If the shares sold can be specifically identified as coming from a particular purchase, the acquisition cost of each share can be determined. Such identification is sometimes possible if records have been kept of the serial numbers of the shares purchased in each lot at a particular price. Suppose that such records were kept for the stock described in transaction 5. Study of the shares sold and the records of the purchases shows that 500 of the shares sold were purchased on March 15 and 250 were purchased on February 1. The acquisition cost of the stock sold can then be determined:

$$
\begin{aligned}
(250 \text{ shares} \times \$10/\text{share}) + (500 \text{ shares} \times \$12/\text{share}) &= \$2{,}500 + \$6{,}000 \\
&= \$8{,}500.
\end{aligned}
$$

The journal entry to record the sale would then be the following.

Cash	6,750	
Loss on Sale of Stock	1,750	
Marketable Securities		8,500

The explanation for the journal entry should show how the cost was computed.

Many accountants prefer the specific identification method for recording the sale of securities because it gives the most objective and clearly determined value for the acquisition cost.

FIRST-IN, FIRST-OUT (FIFO) METHOD. Under the FIFO method of determining the acquisition cost of shares sold, the shares sold are assumed to be those that were purchased first among the shares held. Applying this method to transaction 5, we assume that the 750 shares sold include all 500 purchased on February 1 and 250 of those purchased on March 15. This assumption gives the following acquisition cost:

(500 shares × \$10/share) + (250 shares × \$12/share) = \$5,000 + \$3,000
= \$8,000.

This leads to the following journal entry to record the sale.

Cash	6,750	
Loss on Sale of Stock	1,250	
Marketable Securities		8,000

Again, the explanation for the entry should show the way in which the cost was computed.

The FIFO method does not require the specific identification of shares when stock is purchased or sold; therefore it simplifies the record-keeping needed. Furthermore, there may be some cases in which it is not possible to match shares sold with shares purchased.

Stock valuation

The Financial Accounting Standards Board issued ***Statement 12,*** "Marketable Equity Securities," that dealt with accounting for these securities. "Marketable" means readily tradeable. "Equity" means capital stock and rights to capital stock (e.g., stock options). It excludes bonds. ***Statement 12*** provides for the following treatment of marketable equity securities:

1. All marketable equity securities must be grouped in two separate portfolios—current and noncurrent. The noncurrent classification is usually determined by the ability of the holder to hold the securities for longer than one year.
2. At the balance sheet date, the total cost and total market values of each portfolio are compared.
   a. For the current portfolio, a loss is recorded if the total cost exceeds the total market value.
   b. For the noncurrent portfolio, the excess of cost over market value is deducted in the equity section of the balance sheet.
3. When a portfolio is written down to market, a subsequent write-up may be made for market value recoveries, but not in excess of original cost.

When the accountant adopts the *lower-of-cost-or-market method* to account for temporary investments in stock, he makes an adjusting entry before closing the books at the end of each period, if the market value is lower than the acquisition cost. This method of valuing stock recognizes the decline in value of the asset as an expense in the period in which the market value declines. The lower-of-cost-or-market method presents the most conservative value for temporary investments. The following example will clarify this method of valuing stock.

Transaction 6. Lower-of-cost-or-market valuation for temporary investments. During 19_1, several investments are made in stock. Because the company expects to sell this stock within the next year, it is recorded as a current asset (marketable securities). The total cost of the stock was $7,000. At the end of 19_1, when the books are being closed, it is necessary to decide on the value that should be listed for marketable securities on the statement of financial position. Exhibit 11-1 shows the cost and current market value of the stock holdings.

Each purchase of stock was recorded by a credit to the Cash account and a debit to the Marketable Securities account for the purchase price of the stock. Therefore, the Marketable Securities account at the end of the year shows a balance of $7,000. When we use the lower-of-cost-or-market method of value the stock, we must make an adjustment before closing the books. The balance of the Marketable Securities account must be adjusted downward from the $7,000 acquisition cost to the $6,700 total of the lower market shown in the last column in Exhibit 11-1. A contra asset account is recommended for this purpose. The decline in market value is recognized as an expense by a debit to an expense account. The adjusting entry in the journal appears as follows.

Dec. 31	Market Loss on Securities	300	
	Allowance for Decline in Value of Marketable Securities		300
	To recognize securities at lower-of-cost-or-market value.		

After this entry is posted, the Marketable Securities account retains its balance of $7,000. In the ledger, it is followed immediately by a contra asset account (Allowance for Decline in Value of Marketable Securities) with a credit balance of $300. On the statement of financial position, the marketable securities item could be presented in either of the following two ways.

1. Current assets:		
Marketable securities	$7,000	
Less: Allowance for decline in market value	300	$6,700
2. Current assets:		
Marketable securities, at lower-of-cost-or-market (cost $7,000)		$6,700

The expense account, Market Loss on Securities, is closed to the Income Summary account in the closing process. On the income statement, this item appears under

Exhibit 11-1
Schedule of marketable securities for transaction 6

Company Issuing Stock	No. of Shares	Cost per Share	Total Cost	Current Market Value per Share	Total Market
E Company	100	$ 10	$1,000	$12	$1,200
F Company	50	100	5,000	90	4,500
G Company	50	20	1,000	10	1,000
Total values			$7,000		$6,700

the category of "other expenses." Note that the effect of this valuation method is to recognize the expense in the period during which the market price falls, regardless of when the stock is sold.

Transaction 7. Sale of stock valued at lower-of-cost-or-market. On June 15, 19_2, one-half of the stock holdings in Companies E, F, and G described in transaction 6 are sold for a total of $4,500. Exhibit 11-2 shows the details of the sale.

The journal entry to record this sale must report the cash receipt of $4,500 and must decrease the balance of the Marketable Securities account by the value shown there for the stock sold. Any gain or loss on the sale will be recorded as revenue or expense. The sale can be recorded by the following entry in the journal.

June 15	Cash	4,500	
	Marketable Securities		3,500
	Gain on Sale of Marketable Securities		1,000
	To record sale of securities with a cost of $3,500.		

The balance of the contra asset account can be adjusted at the end of the period to reflect properly the market values of the stock then held.[1]

Transaction 8. At the end of 19_2, as a result of additional transactions in stock during the year, the Marketable Securities account shows a balance of $12,000. The contra asset account still shows the $300 balance established by the closing entry for the previous year. At this time, the market value of the shares held is $15,000.

The most conservative approach in this case is to retain the $300 allowance, listing the lower-of-cost-or-market value of the stock on the balance sheet as $11,700. However, if it is desired to increase the recorded lower-of-cost-or-market value back to original cost of $12,000 (but *not* to the current market price of $15,000,

Exhibit 11-2
Schedule of marketable securities sold in transaction 7

Company Issuing Stock	No. of Shares Sold	Cost per Share	Total Cost	Selling Price per Share	Total Selling Price
E Company	50	$ 10	$ 500	$30	$1,500
F Company	25	100	2,500	80	2,000
G Company	25	20	500	40	1,000
Total values			$3,500		$4,500

1. Some accountants would adjust the contra asset account at the time the sale is recorded. They would do this by considering the gain on the sale to be the difference between the *net* value of the stock shown in the books and the sale price, $4,500 − $3,350 ($3,500 − $150) = $1,150. The balance of the contra asset account accordingly is reduced $150. The journal entry for the sale using this approach would be the following:

June 15	Cash	4,500	
	Allowance for Decline in Value of Marketable Securities	150	
	Marketable Securities		3,500
	Gain on Sale of Stock		1,150

which is above cost), this can be done by recognizing "other income" analogous to the "other expense" reported in 19_1 when the allowance was established. The adjusting entry at the end of 19_2 would be the following.[2]

Dec. 31	Allowance for Decline in Value of Marketable Securities	300	
	Market Gain on Securities		300
	To recognize current lower-of-cost-or-market value of securities.		

The same general procedures used to apply the lower-of-cost-or-market method to short-term investments in equity securities is used for long-term investments in such securities (see Exhibit 11-1). However, the loss resulting from the write-down is an unrealized loss and is not closed periodically to the Income Summary account. The cumulative amount in the valuation allowance is deducted in the equity section of the balance sheet. Excerpts from a balance sheet show how long-term equity securities are disclosed when cost exceeds market by $600,000 and an entry was made to record the write-down to the lower market:

Investments:		
Marketable equity securities	$6,600,000	
Less: Allowance for decline in market value	600,000	$6,000,000
Stockholders' equity:		
Capital stock		XXX
Paid-in capital in excess of par value		XXX
Retained earnings		XXX
Net unrealized loss on noncurrent marketable equity securities		(600,000)

DIVIDENDS

A dictionary defines a ***dividend*** as a number or quantity, usually of money, to be divided among stockholders. In another sense, a dividend is the reward received by shareholders for their investment in a corporation.

To understand the accounting treatment of dividends, you must know something of the mechanics of dividend declaration and payment. In theory, a corporation set forth a well-defined policy of dividend payment, so that investors will have a clear understanding of the return to be expected from their investments. In practice, many corporations pay out a fixed percentage of their earnings as dividends, usually in the form of cash or in additional shares of their own stock.

As a procedural matter, dividends on stock usually are declared on a certain day, to be paid to the stockholders of record on a later day, and actually to be payable on a still later day. For example, the dividend announcement by the board of directors might read as follows.

The Board of Directors at its annual meeting on November 15, 19_1, declared an annual dividend on outstanding common stock at $1 per share payable on January 15, 19_2, to stockholders of record at the close of business on December 15, 19_1.

2. If the sale were recorded by the entry shown in footnote 1, the balance of the contra asset account at the end of the year would be only $150. The amount of the debit and credit in the adjusting entry would then be $150.

The dividend is declared on November 15, but the list of stockholders to be paid will not be made up until December 15. The dividend checks will actually be distributed on January 15. If a shareholder at the time of the declaration (November 15) holds his stock until the date of record (December 15), he will receive the dividend when it is distributed (even if he sells the stock after the date of record). However, if he sells the stock before the date of record, the dividend will go to the person who owns the share on December 15. (On the New York Stock Exchange, stock goes ex-dividend five trading days before the date of record, because it takes five days to deliver stock and record the transfer of ownership on the company's list of stockholders.)

If a company owns stock of another company, its accounting system must recognize dividends received on that stock as income. The dividends can be recognized and recorded as income at the date of record.[3] As of this date, there is a firm obligation for the dividends to be paid to the company that owns the stock. For the example given in the declaration above, the following entry could be made to record dividend income by a company that owns 1,000 shares of the stock.

19_1			
Dec. 15	Dividends Receivable	1,000	
	Dividends Earned		1,000
	To record dividend declared by Company X.		

The Dividends Receivable account is a current asset account; the Dividends Earned account is a revenue account (classified on the income statement as "other income"). The effect of this entry is to recognize the income on the date of record for the dividend. When the actual payment is received, the following entry is made.

19_2			
Jan. 15	Cash	1,000	
	Dividends Receivable		1,000
	To record receipt of stock dividend from Company X.		

Transaction 9. Purchase of stock with dividend. The Hope Company purchases 100 shares of No Company stock on March 1, 19_1, at $95 per share. On February 15, 19_1, the No Company had declared a dividend of $1 per share, payable to stockholders of record on March 15, 19_1, and payable on April 1, 19_1. The Hope Company pays brokerage fee and tax of $50 on the purchase.

In practice, the total cash paid including brokerage fees and taxes would be considered the cost of the investment and would be recorded in the Investment in Stock account. No part of the cash expenditure would be assigned the dividend which was also acquired in the purchase.

3. In theory, the dividend should be recognized as income to the shareholder on the date of declaration. On this date, the stock-issuing company assumes a legal obligation to pay the dividends and enters in its books a liability for dividends payable. Therefore, the stock-holding corporation becomes the beneficiary of this obligation on the date of declaration. However, there is always the possibility that the investor will see his stock before the date of record, so it seems reasonable to wait and recognize the income on the date of record. In practice, many companies do not record the income until the dividend is actually received.

Mar. 1	Investment in Stock	9,550	
	Cash		9,550
	To record purchase of 100 shares of No Co. stock with $1 per share dividend receivable.		

When the dividend is actually received on April 1, the following entry is made.

Apr. 1	Cash	100	
	Dividends Earned		100
	To record receipt of $100 dividend on No Co. stock.		

TYPES OF DIVIDENDS

Dividends may be declared payable in the form of (1) cash, (2) property (such as marketable securities), (3) script (such as notes payable), or (4) stock of the company declaring the dividends. Exhibit 11-3 shows the journal entries required to record the earning and the receipt of the dividends in each of the first three cases. Dividends in property or script are rarely declared.

When a dividend in stock is declared, the stockholder receives no income because no assets of the corporation are being distributed. A dividend in stock results merely in an increase in the number of shares of the company's stock that are outstanding. After the dividend is received, the shareholder still has the same claim against the same proportion of the company's net assets. Therefore, a dividend in stock requires no entry in the journal. However, a memorandum entry is made in the ledger account (and in the journal if desired for completeness of the journal record) to record the increase in the number of shares held. This will affect the price per share to be used in computing the cost of shares sold later.

Transaction 10. Stock dividend. On January 1, the Up Company buys 100 shares of stock in the TAT Company at $5 per share. On January 30, it buys another 100 shares at $10 per share. On February 15, the board of directors of the TAT Company declares a 25 percent dividend in stock, payable on March 15 to stockholders of record on March 1.

At the date of record of the dividend, the Up Company owns 200 shares of TAT Company's stock. Therefore, it will receive 25 percent of this number, or 50 additional

Exhibit 11-3 Journal entries needed to record stock dividends paid in assets

Type of Dividend	Journal Entry On Date of Record			Journal Entry On Date of Payment		
Cash	Dividends Receivable	XXX		Cash	XXX	
	Dividends Earned		XXX	Dividends Receivable		XXX
Property (in marketable securities)	Property Dividends Receivable	XXX		Marketable Securities	XXX	
	Dividends Earned		XXX	Property Dividends Receivable		XXX
Script (in notes payable)	Script Dividends Receivable	XXX		Notes Receivable	XXX	
	Dividends Earned		XXX	Script Dividends Receivable		XXX

shares in the dividend distribution. When the dividend is received, the following memorandum can be entered in the journal and/or the ledger account.

Mar. 15 Memorandum entry: receipt of 50 shares of TAT stock as stock dividend. After dividend is received, 250 shares are owned.

The Up Company now owns more shares of TAT stock, but it has not paid any more money to get them. It would be misleading to consider the dividend shares to have a value (acquisition cost) of $0. Therefore, the most fair adjustment is one that spreads the purchase price of the shares over both the original shares bought and the shares later received as dividends (see Exhibit 11-4). This information can be recorded as a memorandum in the ledger account, so that the appropriate price per share will be used when any of these shares are sold at a later date.

A ***stock split*** is similar to a dividend in stock. When a company splits its stock, it recalls the outstanding shares and issues a larger number of new shares in exchange. In most cases, a company declares a dividend in stock or splits its stock to reduce the market price per share. This is desirable if the price per share becomes so high that investors are reluctant to purchase the company's stock. A corporation may also declare a dividend in stock because it wishes to distribute dividends, but does not want to weaken its cash position by distributing cash.

A stock split is accounted for in the same manner as a stock dividend, through the use of a memorandum entry. As with a dividend in stock, the recorded cost per share is adjusted to a lower value after a stock split.

To repeat the reason for this procedure, we emphasize again that a dividend in stock or a stock split leaves the stockholder with the same share of the pie (share of the net assets of the stock-issuing firm); it simply is cut into smaller pieces.

Investment in bonds

A ***bond*** is a formal promise to pay a specified amount of money at a designated date in the future and to pay interest at a specified rate at periodic intervals. A bond is similar to a note in that it represents an obligation to repay a principal amount of money (a loan) with interest. However, bonds normally are issued in large numbers at one time to raise a substantial sum of money. The bonds are printed and numbered in a fashion similar to stock certificates and are offered for sale. Those who purchase

Exhibit 11-4
Schedule showing adjusted cost per share after dividend in stock for transaction 10

Date of Purchase	No. of Shares Purchased	(A) Purchase Cost	(B) No. of Shares Owned After 25% Dividend in Stock	Adjusted Cost per Share (A ÷ B)
Jan. 1	100	$ 500	125	$4
30	100	1,000	125	8

the bonds can sell them through a stock exchange or dealer before the maturity date. These tradings establish current market prices for bonds similar to those for stock.

Bonds usually are issued in denominations of $1,000 and pay interest semiannually. The bond interest rate is stated on the face of the bond as an ***annual*** rate of interest. The bond matures at a specific date listed on the face of the bond.

The market price of a bond is usually given as a percentage of the par value (face value) of the bond. For example, a $1,000 par value bond quoted at 99 would sell for $990—that is, at 99 percent of its face value.

Bonds may be purchased at par, at a premium, or at a discount. A bond purchased ***at par*** is purchased at a price equal to its face value. A bond purchased ***at a premium*** is purchased at a price above the amount stated on the face of the bond. A bond purchased ***at a discount*** is purchased at a price below the face value. A bond will sell at a premium if the interest rate being paid on that bond is more than the average interest rate being paid for similar bonds on the market. The interest rate on the face of the bond is called the ***contract rate*** (or nominal rate, or stated rate). The typical rate being paid for bonds on the market is called the ***market rate.***

Obviously, a bond with a contract rate higher than the market rate is a more attractive investment for the given amount of money to be invested, so the demand for these bonds causes their market prices to rise. On the other hand, there is less demand for bonds with contract rates lower than the market rate, so the market price of these bonds falls until investors are willing to purchase them.

If the bonds are registered, the issuing company keeps a list of the bondholders (similar to its list of stockholders). At the date of record for each interest payment, it prepares the interest checks from the list of bondholders. If the bonds are not registered, a set of coupons is printed as part of the bond. At the time of each interest payment, the holder of the bond sends in the appropriate coupon giving his name and address, and the company sends him the interest payment.

At the maturity date of the bond, the company that issued the bond pays the full amount of the face value to the holder of the bond. Unregistered bonds are payable to the bearer; registered bonds are payable only to the owner of record in the company list.

TEMPORARY INVESTMENTS IN BONDS

Like stocks, bonds are recorded initially at their acquisition cost, including the price of the bond, brokerage fee, taxes, and related costs. If a bond is purchased between interest payment dates, interest is accrued from the last interest payment date to the date of purchase and this accrued interest is purchased along with the bond.

Transaction 11. Bonds purchased. On January 2, 19_1, the Try-It Company purchases 100 bonds of the Investment Company at 102. The face value of the bonds is $1,000 and the contract rate is 6%. Interest is paid on January 1 and July 1. The brokerage fee and other costs related to the purchase amount to $60. The bonds are to be held as temporary investments.

Exhibit 11-5 shows the journal entries related to these bonds during the first year that they are held by the Try-It Company. (The Try-It Company closes its books on December 31.)

Exhibit 11-5 **Try-It Company journal entries related to transaction 11**

Date		Debit	Credit
19_1			
Jan. 2	**Marketable Securities: Bonds**	**102,060**	
	Cash		**102,060**
	To record purchase of bonds of the Investment Co. at 102, plus related costs of $60.		
July 1	**Cash**	**3,000**	
	Bond Interest Earned		**3,000**
	To record receipt of semiannual interest on bonds of Investment Co.: $100,000 × 0.06 × 6/12 = $3,000.		
Dec. 31	**Accrued Interest Receivable**	**3,000**	
	Bond Interest Earned		**3,000**
	To record bond interest accrued on Investment Co. bonds July 1 to Dec. 31.		
31	**Bond Interest Earned**	**6,000**	
	Income Summary		**6,000**
	To close Bond Interest Earned account to Income Summary account.		
19_2			
Jan. 1	**Cash**	**3,000**	
	Accrued Interest Receivable		**3,000**
	To record receipt of semiannual interest on bonds of Investment Co. accrued on Dec. 31, 19_1.		

Transaction 12. Bonds purchased between interest payment dates at a premium. On March 1, 19_1, the Like-It Company purchases 100 bonds of the Investment Company identical to the bonds described in transaction 11. Because this purchase is made between interest dates, the bonds are purchased at 102 *plus* accrued interest.

In addition to the $102,000 purchase price of the bonds, the Like-It Company must purchase the interest that has accrued between the last interest payment date (January 1) and the date of the bond purchase (March 1). The Like-It Company will receive this accrued interest purchased (along with the interest it has earned by owning the bonds from March 1 through July 1) when it receives the full six-month interest payment on July 1. This practice of selling bonds at market price plus accrued interest eliminates the need for the issuing company to compute special interest payments for bonds held by two or more different owners during the interest period.

Exhibit 11-6 shows the first two journal entries related to these bonds in the books of the Like-It Company.[4] Observe that the six-month interest payment received on July 1 is not entirely interest earned by the company. Two months' interest was

4. The initial entry in the journal could also be made in the following form.

Mar. 1	Marketable Securities: Bonds	102,060	
	Bond Interest Earned	1,000	
	Cash		103,060

Then when the interest payment is received, the following entry is made.

July 1	Cash	3,000	
	Bond Interest Earned		3,000

This leaves $3,000 − $1,000 = $2,000 credit balance in the Bond Interest Earned account, correctly reflecting the portion of the interest that has been earned.

Exhibit 11-6 Like-It Company journal entries related to transaction 12

19_1			
Mar. 1	**Marketable Securities: Bonds**	102,060	
	Accrued Bond Interest Receivable	1,000	
	Cash		103,060
	To record purchase of bonds of the Investment Co. at 102 plus accrued interest, and related costs of $60. $100,000 × 0.06 × 2/12 = $1,000.		
July 1	**Cash**	3,000	
	Accrued Bond Interest Receivable		1,000
	Bond Interest Earned		2,000
	To record receipt of semiannual interest on bonds of Investment Co.; two months' interest accrued on Mar. 1.		

purchased along with the bond. The accrued interest purchased is an asset purchased for cash, not revenue earned by the company's investment.

Transaction 13. Sale of bonds between interest dates. On September 1, 19_2, the Try-It Company sells the bonds purchased in transaction 11 for 101½ plus accrued interest.

The Try-It Company sells the bonds themselves for $101,500. The cost of the bonds was $102,060. Therefore, there is a loss on the sale of $102,060 − $101,500 = $560. In addition to the $101,500 for the bonds, the company receives $1,000 for the accrued interest from July 1 through August 31. This amount represents the income the company has earned on its investment during the two months. The journal entry for the sale is the following.

Sept. 1	Cash	102,500	
	Loss on Sale of Bonds	560	
	Marketable Securities: Bonds		102,060
	Bond Interest Earned		1,000
	To record sale of bonds with cost of $102,060, plus two months' accrued interest: $100,000 × 0.06 × 2/12 = $1,000.		

The Loss on Sale of Bonds account is an expense account categorized under "other expenses" on the income statement.

Transaction 14. Bonds valued at lower-of-cost-or-market. The Like-It Company values its temporary investments in stocks and bonds using the lower-of-cost-or-market method. On December 31, 19_1, the only marketable securities that it holds are the bonds purchased in transaction 12 at $102,060. The current market value of these bonds is 101.

Bonds held as temporary investments may be valued either (1) at cost, or (2) at the lower-of-cost-or-market value. If the bonds are reported at cost, no adjusting entry is required at the close of the accounting period, regardless of the current market price of the bonds. Full disclosure of the current market price should, however, be made in the balance sheet, usually by a parenthetical insertion.

If the bonds are valued at the lower of cost or market, an adjusting entry is needed at the end of the period if the market price of the bonds has fallen below their cost. The necessary entry for transaction 14 is the following.

Dec. 31	Market Loss on Securities	1,060	
	Allowance for Decline in Value of Marketable Securities		1,060
	To adjust bond values to lower of cost or market, i.e., a reduction from $102,060 to $101,000.		

Note that the accrued interest purchased along with the bonds does not affect their value as recorded in the Marketable Securities account. The cost of the bonds was $102,060. The current market value is $101,000. Therefore, the market loss (an "other expense" account) is debited $1,060 and a similar amount is established as a contra asset to be subtracted from the value of the securities. The other details of accounting using this valuation method are the same as those described earlier for stocks.

LONG-TERM INVESTMENTS IN BONDS

We have seen that bonds—like stocks—held as short-term investments can be valued at the lower of cost or market. However, bonds held as long-term investments are valued at an adjusted cost and not at the lower of cost or market.

Bonds are often purchased at a premium or a discount, depending on the comparison between their contract rate and the market rate of interest paid. A premium represents an extra price paid for a bond that will earn higher interest than the prevailing market rate; a discount represents a price cut on a bond that will earn lower interest. However, as the maturity date approaches, the differences in interest rates become less and less significant. On the maturity date, each bond can be exchanged for its face value in cash. Therefore, any bond obviously is worth exactly its face value on its maturity date.

The proper matching of revenue and expense requires that the cost of any premium paid for a bond be amortized (that is, written off as a reduction of interest earned) over the periods during which the bond is earning the higher interest for which the premium was paid. Similarly, any discount obtained should be accumulated (that is, recognized as income) over the period during which the bond is earning the lower interest that was the reason for the discount. These periodic adjustments in value should be systematic and rational, and they should bring the recorded value of the bond to its face value at the maturity date.

Transaction 15. The Amortization Company purchases a $1,000 bond on January 1, 19_1, for a cost of $1,064. The bond matures on January 1, 19_5, and has a contract rate of 6%. The company intends to hold the bond until its maturity date. Interest on the bond is paid on January 1 and July 1.

Each interest payment on this bond will be

$1,000 × 0.06 × 6/12 = $30.

Over the remaining life of the bond, the Amortization Company will receive eight interest payments, or a total of $240 interest (see Exhibit 11-7). At the maturity date,

Exhibit 11-7 **Schedule of straight-line premium amortization for bond purchased in transaction 15**

Date		Cash Dr.	Interest Earned Cr.	Investment in Bonds Cr.	Carrying Value of Bond
19_1	Jan. 1	—	—	—	$1,064
	July 1	$ 30	$ 22	$ 8	1,056
19_2	Jan. 1	30	22	8	1,048
	July 1	30	22	8	1,040
19_3	Jan. 1	30	22	8	1,032
	July 1	30	22	8	1,024
19_4	Jan. 1	30	22	8	1,016
	July 1	30	22	8	1,008
19_5	Jan. 1	30	22	8	1,000
		$240	$176	$64	

the company will cash in the bond for $1,000 (its face value). Therefore, the $64 premium paid for the bond should be amortized as a reduction of interest earned in even amounts over the four years. At the same time, the value of the bond should be adjusted downward by the same amounts to systematically reduce its value to the face value on the maturity date. Exhibit 11-7 shows how this is done using a straight-line (equal-amounts) method of amortizing the bond premium.

As each interest payment is received, the accountant refers to the schedule of premium amortization (Exhibit 11-7) and makes the entry indicated there. For example, the entry to record the receipt of $30 interest and the amortization of the premium on July 1, 19_1, would be the following.[5]

July 1	Cash	30	
	Investment in Bonds		8
	Interest Earned		22
	To record the receipt of semiannual bond interest and amortization of bond premium.		

Observe that the amortization of the premium reduces the value of the bond in the Investment in Bonds account to face value at the maturity date. Each bond interest payment received is also reduced systematically to reflect a systematic allocation of the premium expense against the income earned. If the company holds the bond until its maturity date, the transaction of receiving cash for the face value of the bond on that date will be recorded by the following journal entry.

19_5			
Jan. 1	Cash	1,000	
	Investment in Bonds		1,000
	To record receipt of $1,000 for face value of mature bond.		

5. This compound entry has the same effect as the following two entries, which could be used instead.

July 1	Cash	30	
	Interest Earned		30
	To record receipt of bond interest.		
1	Interest Earned	8	
	Investment in Bonds		8
	To record amortization of bond premium.		

After this entry is posted, the Investment in Bonds account would appear as shown in Exhibit 11-8.

Transaction 16. The Allocation Company purchases a $1,000 bond on January 1, 19_1, for a cost of $936. The bond matures on January 1, 19_5, and has a contract rate of 6%. Interest on the bond is paid on January 1 and July 1. The company intends to hold the bond until the maturity date.

In this example, the bond is purchased at a discount of $64. This discount is accumulated as income over the life of the bonds in a fashion similar to the amortization of the premium in transaction 15. Using a straight-line schedule of discount accumulation (Exhibit 11-9), the discount is recognized in equal installments with each interest receipt. At the maturity date, the full $64 discount has been recognized as income, and the book value of the bond has been increased to the $1,000 that will be received on the maturity date.

The schedule of discount accumulation provides the necessary information for the periodic journal entries that record the receipt of interest income and the accumulation of the discount. For example, the entry required on July 1, 19_1, is the following.[6]

July 1	Cash	30	
	Investment in Bonds	8	
	Interest Earned		38
	To record receipt of semiannual interest and accumulation of bond discount.		

Exhibit 11-8
Bond investment account after maturation of bond purchased in transaction 15

Investment in Bonds

19_1			**19_1**		
Jan. 1	**Purchase**	**1,064**	**July 1**	**Amortization**	**8**
			19_2		
			Jan. 1	"	**8**
			July 1	"	**8**
			19_3		
			Jan. 1	"	**8**
			July 1	"	**8**
			19_4		
			Jan. 1	"	**8**
			July 1	"	**8**
			19_5		
			Jan. 1	"	**8**
			1	**At maturity**	**1,000**
		1,064			1,064

6. This compound entry has the same effect as the following two entries, which could be used instead.

July 1	Cash	30	
	Interest Earned		30
	To record receipt of bond interest.		
1	Investment in Bonds	8	
	Interest Earned		8
	To record accumulation of discount.		

Exhibit 11-9 **Schedule of straight-line discount accumulation for bond purchased in transaction 16**

Date		Cash Dr.	Investment in Bonds Dr.	Interest Earned Cr.	Carrying Value of Bond
19_1	Jan. 1	—	—	—	$ 936
	July 1	$ 30	$ 8	$ 38	944
19_2	Jan. 1	30	8	38	952
	July 1	30	8	38	960
19_3	Jan. 1	30	8	38	968
	July 1	30	8	38	976
19_4	Jan. 1	30	8	38	984
	July 1	30	8	38	992
19_5	Jan. 1	30	8	38	1,000
		$240	$64	$304	

Investment in Bonds

Date			Date		
19_1			19_5		
Jan. 1	Purchase	936	Jan. 1	At maturity	1,000
July 1	Accumulation	8			
19_2					
Jan. 1	"	8			
July 1	"	8			
19_3					
Jan. 1	"	8			
July 1	"	8			
19_4					
Jan. 1	"	8			
July 1	"	8			
19_5					
Jan. 1	"	8			
		1,000			1,000

Exhibit 11-10
Bond investment account after maturity of bond purchased in transaction 16

When the bonds mature, an entry is made debiting Cash by $1,000 and crediting Investment in Bonds by $1,000. Exhibit 11-10 shows the entries in the Investment in Bonds account after the face value of the bond has been received in cash.

Transaction 17. Purchase of bonds at a premium with accrued interest; premium amortization. On March 1, 1976, the Premium Company purchases 100 bonds at 105 plus accrued interest. Brokerage fees and taxes on the purchase amount to $310. The bonds each have a face value of $1,000, a contract rate of 6% and mature on January 1, 1986. Interest is paid on January 1 and July 1. The Premium Company plans to hold the bonds for at least a few years. It closes its books on December 31.

Exhibit 11-11 shows the journal entries relating to this transaction in the books of the Premium Company during 1976. Note that the total cost of the bonds is $105,310, a premium of $5,310. The bonds will be outstanding over a period of 118 months from the date of purchase to the date of maturity. Therefore, the premium is amortized over this 118-month period. Again, the cost of the accrued interest at the time of purchase does not affect the cost of the bonds.

Exhibit 11-11 Premium Company journal entries related to transaction 17

Date	Account / Explanation	Debit	Credit
1976			
Mar. 1	Investment in Bonds	105,310	
	Accrued Bond Interest Receivable	1,000	
	Cash		106,310
	To record purchase of $100,000 of 6% bonds at 105 plus accrued interest, and brokerage fees of $310. $100,000 × 0.06 × 2/12 = $1,000.		
July 1	Cash	3,000	
	Accrued Bond Interest Receivable		1,000
	Bond Interest Earned		2,000
	To record receipt of semiannual interest on bonds; $1,000 accrued at purchase.		
1	Bond Interest Earned	180	
	Investment in Bonds		180
	To record premium amortization for four months from Mar. 1 to July 1: $5,310 × 4/118 = $180.		
Dec. 31	Accrued Bond Interest Receivable	3,000	
	Bond Interest Earned		3,000
	To record accrual of semiannual interest from July 1 to Dec. 31.		
31	Bond Interest Earned	270	
	Investment in Bonds		270
	To record premium amortization for six months from July 1 to Dec. 31: $5,310 × 6/118 = $270.		
31	Bond Interest Earned	4,550	
	Income Summary		4,550
	To close Bond Interest Earned account to Income Summary account.		
1977			
Jan. 1	Cash	3,000	
	Accrued Bond Interest Receivable		3,000
	To record receipt of semiannual interest accrued on Dec. 31, 1976		

Transaction 18. Purchase of bonds at a discount; accumulation of discount. On March 1, 1976, the Discount Company purchases bonds at 94½ plus accrued interest. The bonds have a total face value of $100,000, a contract rate of 6% payable on January 1 and July 1, and mature on January 1, 1986. Brokerage fees and taxes on the purchase are $190. The Discount Company plans to hold the bonds for the full 118 months until maturity. The company closes its books on December 31.

Exhibit 11-12 shows the journal entries relating to this transaction in the books of the Discount Company during 1976. The cost of the bonds is $94,690, a discount of $5,310. The discount is accumulated on a straight-line basis over the 118 months from purchase to maturity.

At maturity, the Investment in Bonds account will contain a debit balance of $100,000. The receipt of the maturity value of the bonds will be recorded by an entry like the following.

Date	Account / Explanation	Debit	Credit
1986			
Jan. 1	Cash	100,000	
	Investment in Bonds		100,000
	To record collection of maturity value of bonds purchased March 1, 1976.		

Ratio analysis

Many of the financial ratios discussed in Chapters 3, 4, and 8 are especially useful in evaluating investments in stocks and bonds. This is a good point in our study for you to review these ratios and to see how they relate to investment decisions.

An investor purchasing corporate bonds is concerned with the safety of his investment and of his interest income. That is, he wants to be sure that the bond-issuing company will be able to pay the maturity value of the bonds and also will be able to meet its interest payments during the life of the bonds.

Security analysts have developed a special ratio to give some insight into the ability of the company to meet its interest obligations. This ratio shows how many times the company's earnings exceed the bond interest to be paid. In its simplest form, this ratio can be written as

$$\text{Number of times bond interest is earned} = \frac{\text{Net income} + \text{Annual bond interest} + \text{Income taxes}}{\text{Annual bond interest}}$$

Exhibit 11-12 Discount Company journal entries related to transaction 18

Date	Account and explanation	Debit	Credit
1976			
Mar. 1	**Investment in Bonds**	**94,690**	
	Accrued Bond Interest Receivable	**1,000**	
	Cash		**95,690**
	To record purchase of 6% bonds at 94½ plus fees and tax of $190 and accrued interest for Jan. and Feb.: $100,000 × 0.06 × 2/12 = $1,000.		
July 1	**Cash**	**3,000**	
	Accrued Bond Interest Receivable		**1,000**
	Bond Interest Earned		**2,000**
	To record receipt of semiannual interest (two months accrued at purchase).		
1	**Investment in Bonds**	**180**	
	Bond Interest Earned		**180**
	To record discount accumulation for four months (Mar. 1 to July 1): $5,310 × 4/118 = $180.		
Dec. 31	**Accrued Bond Interest Receivable**	**3,000**	
	Bond Interest Earned		**3,000**
	To record accrual of semiannual bond interest from July 1 to Dec. 31.		
31	**Investment in Bonds**	**270**	
	Bond Interest Earned		**270**
	To record discount accumulation for six months (July 1 to Dec. 31): $5,310 × 6/118 = $270.		
31	**Bond Interest Earned**	**5,450**	
	Income Summary		**5,450**
	To close Bond Interest Earned account to Income Summary.		
1977			
Jan. 1	**Cash**	**3,000**	
	Accrued Bond Interest Receivable		**3,000**
	To record collection of semiannual interest accrued on Dec. 31, 1976.		

Net income ***before*** the bond interest expense is used in order to see how many times the interest expense fits into the earnings. If the company earned just enough to pay the bond interest, its net income would be zero (because the bond interest is deducted as an expense), but the value of this ratio would be 1, indicating that the company did earn the bond expense. Similarly, net income ***before*** income taxes is used because the bond interest expense is deductible from income before computing the taxes. Therefore, no taxes would have to be paid if interest expenses used up all the earnings. In other words, the ratio shows how many multiples of the current bond interest expense could be absorbed by the company's current earnings.

Transaction 19. Ratio of number of times bond interest is earned. The Investing Company is considering the purchase of some 6% bonds issued by the Issuing Company. The most recent financial statements of the Issuing Company show that it has bonds outstanding with total face value of $1,000,000. Its income statement for the preceding year shows net income after taxes of $300,000, bond interest expense of $60,000, and income taxes of $140,000. The Investing Company wants to be sure that the Issuing Company is in a good financial position to meet the interest payments on the bonds before going ahead with the purchase of the bonds.

Using the formula for the ratio just discussed,

$$\text{Number of times bond interest is earned} = \frac{\$300{,}000 + \$60{,}000 + \$140{,}000}{\$60{,}000} = \frac{\$500{,}000}{\$60{,}000} = 8.3.$$

This value is relatively high for this ratio, indicating a relatively safe investment in the bonds. Of course, the investor should not rely entirely upon the value of any single indicator. He must use other analysis techniques to make a careful study of the financial statements of the bond-issuing company, to learn as much as possible about the firm's ability to meet its obligations. The various measures of liquidity are important, for example.

In evaluating the company's ability to pay the maturity value of the bonds, the investor will be interested in ratios and other measures of the company's solvency. If the maturity date is several years in the future, he will be interested in any available information about the company's long-range plans and projected earnings.

Similar factors are involved in the analysis of an investment in stock. In this case the investor is interested in the company's dividend policy and projected earnings, in order to evaluate the income he will receive. In terms of the long-range safety of his investment, he must try to evaluate the probable future market price of the stock. Obviously, many kinds of information—including many of the ratios thus far discussed—are needed to analyze the desirability of an investment in stock.

Impact analysis

To maximize income, the enterprise wants to put all of its resources to productive use. Excess cash (beyond the amount needed to meet day-to-day obligations) earns no income. One major outlet for idle cash resources is investments in stocks and bonds. The impact of these investments on income depends to a great extent upon the availability of resources, current market conditions, the experience of management, and a great deal of luck.

Because temporary investments are current assets, these investments have an impact on the working capital, current ratio, and acid-test ratio, among other measures of the firm's liquidity. These measures are considered key indicators of management's ability to keep the firm in a sound position to pay its debts as they mature. Because these measures of working capital are so important to financial analysts, it is essential that the items having strong impact on these measures be reported accurately. Of particular importance in this regard is the proper classification of short-term and long-term investments. A failure to classify securities properly on the statement of financial position can have very serious consequences in causing misinterpretation of the firm's financial condition.

Summary

Chapter 11 deals with investments in stocks and bonds. A basic distinction is made between temporary and permanent investments. Temporary investments (marketable securities) are current assets; they represent securities that the firm expects to dispose of during the current operating cycle (if it is longer than a year) and that have a ready market. Permanent (long-term) investments represent securities that do not meet these conditions.

The acquisition of securities is recorded in the accounts at their acquisition cost. Investments in stocks are carried at the lower of cost or market. Where the lower-of-cost-or-market method of valuation is used, a contra asset account can be set up to reflect declines in market value below acquisition cost. The credit entries to this account are balanced by debit entries to an "other expense" account. Short-term investments in bonds can be carried (1) at cost, or (2) at the lower of cost or market.

Permanent investments in bonds are carried in the accounts at cost adjusted to amortize any premium or accumulate any discount over the remaining life of the bonds. These adjustments bring the value of the bonds in the accounts to face value on the maturity date. The adjustment process adds discounts to or deducts premiums from the interest income over the life of the bond.

The appendix to this chapter describes various types of securities and the markets in which they are bought and sold.

Appendix

AN INVESTMENT PRIMER

COMMON STOCK. The ownership of stock represents an equity or owners' interest in a corporation. Every stock corporation must issue common stock. Chapter 16 describes in detail the nature of the corporation and the various kinds of stock it can issue.

An investment in common stock carries with it a strong business risk. Common stock represents a residual ownership. That is, it entitles the common stockholders to ownership of any earnings and assets of the corporation that remain after paying the claims of creditors and of preferred stockholders, if any.

PREFERRED STOCK. Many corporations issue stock in addition to common stock. The owner of preferred stock has a prior claim to dividends and to corporate assets (on dissolution) over the claims of common stockholders. Although the claims of the preferred stockholders have priority over those of the common stockholders, the preferred stockholders' claims rank below those of bondholders and other creditors. The holder of preferred stock is entitled to a fixed dividend (usually expressed as a percentage of the par value of the stock or as a fixed number of dollars per share). However, he has no legal right to enforce dividend payment by the board of directors.

BONDS. Unlike stock, which represents a share of ownership, a bond is a debt instrument. The bondholder is a creditor of the corporation. A bond is an obligation of the corporation to pay a certain sum of money at a fixed date in the future, with specified interest payments to be made over the life of the bond.

Exhibit 11-13 summarizes typical investment characteristics of bonds, preferred stock, and common stock.

THE STOCK EXCHANGE. A stock exchange is an auction market in which securities are sold to the highest bidder and bought from the lowest seller. In the United States, the New York Stock Exchange (the Big Board) and the American Stock Exchange are the two national marketplaces for transactions in stocks and bonds. In addition to these national exchanges, there are regional exchanges located in principal cities throughout the country.

Trading in securities takes place on the floor of the exchange from 10 A.M. to 4:00 P.M. on business days. Admission to the floor of the exchange is restricted to members or their representatives; only these parties can execute orders on the exchange. Trading is conducted by brokers and dealers. A broker executes orders for his customers and receives a commission for his services. A dealer acts largely for his own account, making his profit through his own purchases and sales on the exchange and through transactions with his customers outside the exchange.

LISTED STOCK. A listed security is one that has been accepted by the exchange as being qualified for trading on the exchange. Corporations that meet the standards of the exchange file registration statements with the Securities and Exchange Commission. Basic standards for listing on the Big Board at the present time include the following: a going concern, national investors' interest in the firm, good standing in the industry, net assets and earnings above a specified amount, and a minimum of 500,000 shares outstanding and owned by no fewer than 1,500 individuals owning at least 100 shares each. Approximately 1,200 corporations are listed on the New York Stock Exchange (NYSE). Over 4,000 other corporations are listed on the other U.S. exchanges.

Exhibit 11-13
Comparative evaluation of stocks and bonds as investments

Type of Security	Safety of Principal	Income	Growth
Bonds	Best	Very stable	Very limited
Preferred Stock	Good	Stable	Variable
Common Stock	Least	Variable	Considerable

TRADING ON THE EXCHANGE. Trading on the NYSE is done in standard numbers of shares, called round lots. A round lot is usually 100 shares or a multiple thereof. For bonds, the standard unit is one $1,000 bond. Lots smaller than round lots are called odd lots. In an odd-lot transaction, one-eighth of a point is added to (or deducted from) the price of each share purchased (or sold). (Market prices are listed in points; a point is equal to a market price of $1 per share. Listings normally are given to the nearest one-eighth of a point.) The execution price for an odd lot includes the price differential charged for handling the odd lot.

For example, suppose that you place an order with an odd-lot dealer to buy 10 shares of XYZ stock. On the next round-lot transaction after your order is placed, XYZ stock is selling at 25. Your odd-lot purchase will be made at a cost to you of 25⅛ per share. If you were selling 10 shares, the odd-lot price would be 24⅞. The odd-lot dealer makes up round lots from the orders he receives from customers, brokers, and other dealers and trades the round lots on the exchange. He earns his profit from the differentials charged on the odd-lot transactions.

The delivery and settlement of securities traded on the exchange are closely regulated. In most cases, a transaction is settled "regular way"—that is, payment for and delivery of the securities on the fifth full business day following the transaction.

OVER-THE-COUNTER MARKET. The over-the-counter or unlisted market consists of a network of dealers in cities throughout the country, linked together by telephone and teletype. In this market, securities not listed on the exchanges are bought and sold. In the unlisted market, transactions are arranged by "negotiation" rather than by auction. The National Association of Securities Dealers, established in 1939 by an Act of Congress, promotes ethical standards and regulates practices and procedures in the over-the-counter market.

Some over-the-counter dealers act as agents or brokers for investors, charging commissions for the services they render. However, most unlisted transactions are arranged by dealers who act as principals, buying and selling for their own accounts and then trading with customers on a net price basis that includes an element of profit.

COMMISSIONS. A commission is imposed on both buyers and sellers of stock on an exchange. Exhibit 11-14 shows the minimum commission schedule for the New York Stock Exchange as of March 24, 1973. To illustrate the application of this schedule, assume that you purchase 100 shares of stock at 13⅞ per share. The cost of 100 shares at this price is $1,387.50. The commission on this sale is 1.3% of the price plus $12:

Exhibit 11-14 Minimum commission schedule for New York Stock Exchange as of March 24, 1973

Single Round-lot Orders

Money Involved in the Order	Minimum Commission
$ 100 – $ 799	2.0% + $ 6.40
800 – 2,499	1.3% + 12.00
2,500 – 19,999	0.9% + 22.00
20,000 – 29,999	0.6% + 82.00
30,000 – 500,000	0.4% + 142.00

Multiple Round-lot Orders

Money Involved in the Order	Minimum Commission
$ 100 – $ 2,499	1.3% + $ 12.00
2,500 – 19,999	0.9% + 22.00
20,000 – 29,999	0.6% + 82.00
30,000 – 500,000	0.4% + 142.00

PLUS:
First to tenth round lot:
$6 per round lot.
Eleventh round lot & over:
$4 per round lot.

Odd-lot Orders

Same as single round-lot rate less $2.00, subject to the provision that the minimum commission on an odd-lot order is not to exceed $65.

$$(\$1{,}387.50 \times 0.013) + \$12.00 = \$30.04.$$

You will pay the broker $1,417.54 for the stock. Since 1975, negotiated commissions have been allowed.

MUTUAL FUNDS. A mutual fund is a company that combines the investment resources of many investors who purchase shares in a large investment pool. This pool is managed by the directors or trustees of the fund who use the funds to acquire stocks or bonds of other companies. Mutual funds provide investors an opportunity to diversify their investments and to obtain some benefit from professional management and supervision of their investments, while still making only a single investment decision.

The price of mutual fund shares is calculated twice daily by taking the net value of securities and cash owned by the fund and dividing by the number of fund shares outstanding. This calculation yields a "net asset value," which is the "bid" price used in the negotiation process to arrive at an "asked" price. Mutual funds redeem shares for cash at a single price on any business day; this price is the net asset value of the shares at the time of redemption. Mutual fund shares are sold by "distributors," who usually are established securities firms. There is a limited market for mutual shares in the over-the-counter market.

FINANCIAL INFORMATION. The market price of stock of a particular corporation is influenced by many factors. These include the quality and stability of its earning power, its policies as to dividends, the caliber of corporate management, the general business outlook, prospective future growth, popularity of the stock among investors, and similar considerations.

The most popular stock-price index is probably the Dow-Jones average, which is compiled as a composite (containing 65 representative stocks) and as three separate averages: industrial (30 industrial stocks), transportation (20 transportation stocks), and utilities (15 utility stocks). The stocks included in the Dow-Jones averages are "blue-chip" stocks—that is, stocks considered to represent relatively safe investments with potential for steady if limited growth and dividends. Other popular stock-price indexes are published by Standard and Poor's Corporation, Moody's Investors Service, and Barron's. These firms also compute bond and preferred stock averages, usually on a price and yield basis.

A list of the leading financial publishers in the United States would include Standard and Poor's, Moody's, and Fitch. The ***Wall Street Journal, Barron's, Forbes, Business Week, Magazine of Wall Street, Financial World, Commercial*** and ***Financial Chronicle,*** and ***Fortune*** are reputable financial journals that publish comprehensive information on stocks, bonds, and the market.

All corporations with securities listed on the NYSE are required to publish annual reports including financial statements, and to supplement these reports with quarterly interim statements. When a new issue of stock is offered for sale, the corporation must publish a prospectus disclosing many facts about the financial position and management of the corporation. These reports, statements, and prospectuses are usually available on request from the corporations issuing them. The requirements for publication of this information are based on the premise that full disclosure is needed to keep investors adequately informed.

FINANCIAL PAGE. The financial pages of many newspapers carry information about stock market activity. The extent of the information and details of the presentation vary from paper to paper. Exhibit 11-15 shows a line from a rather complete listing of stock-market information. Reading from left to right, this listing notes first that the highest and lowest prices paid for XYZ stock in the current year to date were $22 and $15, respectively. The XYZ Company is currently paying an annual dividend of $3 per share. During the day of this listing, 3,200 shares of XYZ stock were traded. The price-earnings ratio was 12 to 1. The highest price paid today was $19 per share, the lowest was $18 per share, and the last sale of the day was at $18.25, which was $0.50 per share lower than the closing price on the last previous day when this stock was traded.

Transactions in corporate bonds are reported similarly.

SPECIALIZED TRADING PRACTICES. The securities markets involve many complex trading practices and procedures. The investor who intends to make major investments in securities should be familiar with such terms as market orders, limited

19_1 High	Low	Stk, Div	Sales 100s	P–E Ratio	High	Low	Close	Net Change
22	15	XYZ 3	32	12	19	18	18¼	– ½

Exhibit 11-15
A line from a newspaper listing of stock-market information

orders, stop-loss orders, buy-stop orders, specialists, quotations, time limits, dollar averaging, bonds sold flat, call and put options, long holdings, short sales, trading on margin, and so on. Without a detailed knowledge of the market procedures, no investor can expect to make the best profit on his investments.

In this brief primer, we cannot begin to provide the necessary background for a potential investor. However, as examples, we describe in general terms two of these specialized practices: short sales and margin trading.

SHORT SALES. When an investor sells short, he sells a security that he does not own, intending to purchase the security before the time when he must deliver it to the buyer. A short sale is practically the reverse of a normal securities transaction. The only reason for an investor to sell short is that he expects the price of the securities to decline. For example, suppose that XYZ stock is currently selling at 60, and the investor expects the market price of this stock to fall sharply in the future. If he can sell the stock now at 60 and later purchase stock at a lower price—say 50—for delivery to the buyer, he will make a profit of $10 per share on the transaction. On the other hand, if the price of the stock should rise, he would have to buy the stock at a higher price than he is getting from the buyer, and he would lose money on the transaction.

When an investor sells short, the buyer expects to receive the securities he has purchased within five business days after the sale is made. Therefore, the investor's broker borrows the necessary stock from some other stockholder and delivers it to the buyer. The broker holds the cash received for the sale as collateral for the borrowed stock. At a later date, if the price of the stock does fall, the short seller buys stock at the lower price to repay the loan of stock, pays interest for the loan of the stock, pays a commission on the transaction, and then may have a profit remaining from the short sale. If the price of the stock should rise instead of falling, the broker will ask the investor either to put up additional collateral to cover the increased value of the borrowed stock or to come up with the funds needed to buy stock to repay the loan.

Obviously, short selling involves the assumption of risks greater than those related to normal market transactions. Short selling is for the professionals.

MARGIN TRADING. In a transaction on margin, the investor purchases securities and pays only a percentage of their cost; the balance of the cost is paid by the broker and is treated as a loan to the investor. The Federal Reserve System sets margin requirements.

For example, suppose that an investor purchases on margin 100 shares of stock at a price of 90. The investor might be asked to maintain a 60 percent margin—that is, he must pay 60 percent of the cost, or $5,400. This amount is his equity in the stock. The broker pays the remaining $3,600 as a loan to the investor, keeping the stock as collateral. The investor thus is able to purchase stock worth $9,000 while putting forth only $5,400 of his own funds. The broker charges a commission on the full $9,000 purchase price, and he also collects monthly interest on his loan to the investor.

The investor who buys on margin obviously expects the price of the stock to rise. If it does, he will be able to sell the stock at a profit, repay the loan from the broker, and still earn money on his investment. The use of margin trading permits him to increase his profit potential by buying more stock than he could finance through his own funds alone.

If the price of the stock should decline, the investor could sell the stock at a loss. In addition to the loss caused by the fall in market price, he would also have to pay the interest expense on the broker's loan. If the investor does not sell the stock and the price declines significantly, the buyer will receive a margin call from his broker, asking him to put up additional cash or collateral to keep the investor's equity up to a required level. If the additional resources are not forthcoming, the broker will sell the stock to recover the amount of his loan and any interest due to him.

Like short selling, trading on the margin is not for amateurs.

PROTECTING THE INVESTOR. The federal and state governments and the securities industry have taken steps to protect investors through detailed regulations and supervision. In general, these activities seek to enforce honesty and fair practices in securities trading, rather than seeking to evaluate the quality or pricing of the securities offered for sale.

Every state has "blue-sky" laws that require securities firms and salesmen to be licensed. These laws set forth requirements for pertinent information that must be disclosed when new securities are offered for sale within the state. State statutes are administered by securities commissions or agencies.

The principal federal securities acts were passed during the period from 1933 to 1940. The truth-in-securities laws administered by the Securities and Exchange Commission seek to protect the investing public by providing for (1) disclosures of pertinent financial information and other facts about securities offered for public sale, (2) current reporting of financial data and corporate matters that an informed investor would want to know about, and (3) the establishment of penalties for fraudulent practices in the sale of securities and for market manipulation.

CONCLUSION. It would be bordering on the miraculous to discover an investment opportunity that was perfectly safe, paid liberal dividends or interest, and appreciated in value over the years. The investor who hopes to find such a combination of virtues in a single investment is naive.

It is a real talent to be able to estimate the true worth of things. True worth is the heart of the investment enigma. Perhaps the best advice that can be given about investing is this: investigate—then invest or do not invest. The value of stocks or bonds is related primarily to the earning power, assets, and management of the issuing company. Successful investing requires a correct appraisal of these factors.

The whole matter of investments can be put into focus through an insight expressed by the seventeenth-century French moralist, Jean de La Bruyère.

> It takes a kind of genius to make a fortune and especially a large fortune. It is neither goodness nor wit, nor talent, nor strength, nor delicacy. I don't know precisely what it is. I am waiting for someone to tell me.

Questions

1. Name and discuss four major risks associated with investments.
2. What are two basic ways to put excess money to work?
3. Why might a business invest in the stock or bonds of another company?
4. What is a temporary investment? a permanent investment?
5. What is the cost of an investment?
6. How should gains and losses resulting from the sale of securities be reported on the income statement? How would they be reported on the income statement of a securities dealer?
7. When selling securities that have been purchased at different prices, what procedures can be used to determine the gain or loss on the sale?
8. For the statement of financial position, what valuation basis should be used to report stock held as a temporary investment? stock held as a permanent investment?
9. Explain the procedure used to calculate the lower-of-cost-or-market value of securities. Explain the accounting procedure that can be used to reflect the reduction of value of a marketable security from cost to a lower market value.
10. What are dividends? Explain the significance in relation to dividends of the date of declaration, date of record, and date of payment.
11. Distinguish among dividends in cash, property, script, and stock. Give journal entries to record the declaration and payment of each of these four types of dividends.
12. What are bonds? What is meant by the purchase of bonds at par, at a premium, and at a discount? What is meant by the contract rate, the market rate, the par value, and the maturity date of a bond?
13. How should temporary and long-term investments in bonds be valued in the asset accounts?
14. Give an illustration of the journal entry required to record the purchase of bonds between interest payment dates.
15. Explain bond premium amortization and bond discount accumulation.
16. Give the formula for the ratio called "number of times bond interest is earned." Explain the significance of this ratio.
17. Describe some major impacts that could result if permanent investments are misclassified as temporary investments; if temporary investments are misclassified as permanent investments.

Exercises

E11-1 (Basic entries for stocks and bonds)
Prepare journal entries to record the following transactions of the Rice Company during 19_6. All of these transactions involve temporary investments.

a. Purchased 200 shares of Able Corporation stock at $25 per share, plus brokerage cost and taxes of $70.

b. Purchased a $5,000 bond of Baker Corporation at par, plus accrued interest of $50.

c. Received a cash dividend of $2.50 per share from the Able Corporation's stock. (No entry had been made on the declaration date or date of record.)

d. Received interest of $150 on the Baker Corporation bond.

e. Purchased 100 shares of Able Corporation stock at $30 per share, plus brokerage commissions and taxes of $80.

f. Sold 100 shares of the Able Corporation stock at $35 per share. (Use the FIFO method.)

g. Received interest of $150 on the Baker Corporation bond.

h. At the end of the year, interest receivable on the Baker Corporation bond amounts to $100. (An adjusting entry is needed.)

i. The books are closed at the end of the year.

E11-2 (Acquisition of bonds at premium and discount)

The Bond Company purchases 8% bonds of the Golden Corporation with a face value of $120,000 plus accrued interest on March 1, 19_6. Interest is paid on May 1 and November 1. The bonds mature 200 months after the date of purchase. The Bond Company closes its books on December 31.

Required: Prepare all 19_6 journal entries relating to this bond purchase, under each of the following assumptions:

a. the bonds were purchased at 104;

b. the bonds were purchased at 96.

E11-3 (Marketable securities at lower-of-cost-or-market valuation)

The Lo Ball Company holds the following temporary investments as of December 31, 19_6.

	Cost	Current Market Price
Stock of the Smith Company	$21,000	$25,000
Stock of the Jones Company	60,000	54,000
Bonds of the White Company	24,000	18,000

Required: Assume that the Lo Ball Company values its temporary investments at the lower of cost or market. Record the adjusting entry needed on December 31, 19_6, to give the proper valuation in the accounts. (All of these securities are currently carried in the books at cost.)

E11-4 (Adjusting entry for marketable securities)

At the end of 19_7, the Marketable Securities account of the Lo Ball Company (see Exercise E11-3) contains the following securities.

	Cost	Current Market Price
Stock of the Red Company	$37,000	$32,000
Stock of the Green Company	55,000	51,000

Required: No adjusting entries have been made since the books were closed at the end of 19_6 (Exercise E11-3). Prepare any adjusting entry needed to reflect the proper valuation of the securities at the end of 19_7.

E11-5 (Adjusting entry for marketable securities)

On December 31, 19_8, the Marketable Securities account of the Lo Ball Company (see Exercises E11-3 and E11-4) contains the following securities.

	Cost	Current Market Price
Stock of the Peter Company	$12,000	$18,000
Stock of the Paul Company	11,000	20,000

Required: No adjusting entries have been made since the books were closed at the end of 19_7 (Exercise E11-4). Prepare any adjusting entry needed to give the proper valuation of the securities at the end of 19_8.

E11-6 (Bond ratio)

Exhibit 11-16 shows a condensed income statement of the Penn Company. Compute the number of times bond interest expense has been earned by the Penn Company.

E11-7 (Impact analysis)

Prepare a table showing the impact (in dollars) of each of the following transactions on (a) current assets, (b) working capital, (c) net income, and (d) net assets.

1. Marketable securities costing $47,000 are sold for $53,000 on November 15, 19_6.
2. A cash dividend is received on stock held as marketable securities. The transaction is recorded by a $2,000 debit to Cash and a $2,000 credit to Dividend Income.
3. The company's bond portfolio, with a cost of $150,000, has a lower-of-cost-or-market value of $145,000 on December 31, 19_6. The company adjusts its accounts to change the value of the Marketable Securities to the lower amount.
4. An adjusting entry is made on December 31, 19_6, to record $300 accrued interest receivable.
5. The company purchases $80,000 par value bonds for $90,000; the bonds are to be held as marketable securities.
6. The company receives a 25 percent stock dividend on 400 shares of stock (value $80,000) held as temporary investments.

Exhibit 11-16
Condensed income statement for Exercise E11-6

PENN COMPANY
Income Statement
For the Year Ended December 31, 19_6

Sales	**$1,400,000**
Expenses (including $150,000 bond interest expense)	**750,000**
Net income before taxes	**$ 650,000**
Income taxes	**200,000**
Net income	$ 450,000

E11-8 (Bonds acquired at interim date)
The Star Company acquires twenty $1,000, 8% bonds on July 1, 19_6, for $25,000 plus accrued interest. Interest on the bonds is payable semiannually on April 1 and October 1. The bonds mature in ten years from the date of purchase.
Required: Make all general journal entries relating to these bonds needed in the books of the Star Company during 19_6. (The Star Company uses no special journals.) The company amortizes the bond premium on December 31, when it closes its books.

E11-9 (Bond acquisition and amortization)
On July 1, 19_6, the Investor Company purchases $200,000-face-value, 6% bonds for $192,800 plus $200 brokerage fees. The bonds mature in five years and pay interest semiannually on July 1 and December 31.
Required: Prepare all 19_6 journal entries (in general journal form) relating to these bonds in the books of the Investor Company. The company accumulates the bond discount on December 31, when it closes its books.

E11-10 Refer to Exercises E11-3, E11-4, and E11-5. What entries would be required if there were long-term investments in stock?

Problems

P11-1 (Amortization of bond premium)
Prepare a schedule of straight-line premium amortization for 9% bonds purchased on January 1, 19_6, for $106,000. The bonds mature on January 1, 19_8, and have a par value of $100,000. Interest is paid on January 1 and July 1.

P11-2 (Amortization of bond discount)
Prepare a schedule of straight-line discount accumulation using the data given in Problem P11-1, except that the bonds were purchased at 92.

P11-3 (Basic entries for stocks and dividends)
Journalize the following 19_1 transactions of the Final Company involving its long-term investments in stocks.

Jan. 7	Purchased 1,000 shares of Quarter Company's stock at 17.
Feb. 4	The Quarter Company declared a cash dividend of $2 per share. Date of record is February 15. Dividend payment date is March 15.
Mar. 15	Dividend check received from Quarter Company.
Apr. 30	The Quarter Company split its stock five for one. The Final Company exchanged 1,000 shares of Quarter Company $10-par-value stock for 5,000 shares of Quarter Company no-par-value stock.
May 30	The Quarter Company declared a $1 cash dividend.
June 15	Dividend check received from Quarter Company.
Oct. 15	Stock received from Quarter Company in payment of a 10 percent stock dividend declared by the Quarter Company on September 1.

Nov. 1 The Quarter Company declared a property dividend payable in stock of the Dime Company. The Final Company will receive shares of Dime Company stock with a current market value of $3,000.

Nov. 30 The Final Company received the Dime Company stock distributed by the Quarter Company in payment of the dividend declared on November 1.

Dec. 31 The Final Company closes its books on December 31.

P11-4 (Bond amortization)

The Pulver Company purchases 20 $1,000, 8% bonds dated January 1, 19_6, as a long-term investment. The bonds mature in ten years from the issue date. Interest is paid annually on January 1. The Pulver Company purchases the bonds on April 1, 19_6, for $20,711 plus accrued interest.

Required:

a. Record the purchase of the ten bonds on April 1, 19_6.

b. Record any entries needed at the end of the year (December 31, 19_6), when the company closes its books.

c. Record any entries needed on January 1, 19_7.

P11-5 (Balance sheet valuation of securities)

You are the chief accountant for the Dry Gulch Company. The company has invested $200,000 in stock as a long-term investment. This stock currently has a market value of $420,000. One of the directors of the company calls you over after a board meeting and points out this item on the statement of financial position. He feels that the listing of the stock at cost seriously understates the assets of the company, and therefore understates the owners' equity. He points out that the company could sell the stock at any time if it needed cash, and that the stock is issued by reputable companies whose stock is unlikely to decrease significantly in market value in the foreseeable future. He asks why you can't adjust the value to reflect the increased worth of the stock. How do you explain it to him?

P11-6 A company purchased $100,000 of X Company's 6% bonds at $104 on January 1. The bonds mature in five years. Interest is paid semiannually on June 30 and December 31.

Required:

a. Record all transactions relating to the bonds for the year. The company amortized any bond premium once a year.

b. At what valuation would the bonds be presented in the statement of financial position at the end of the year?

c. What would be the amount of interest earned reported on the income statement for the year?

P11-7 Refer to Problem P11-6. Assume the same information as in Problem P11-6 except that the bonds were purchased at a discount at $96.

Required:

a. Record all transactions relating to the bonds for the year. The company amortized any bond discount once a year.

b. At what valuation would the bonds be presented in the statement of financial position at the end of the year?

c. What would be the amount of interest earned reported on the income statement for the year?

P11-8 (Comprehensive problem)

The following marketable securities were owned by the Rett Company on January 1.

10 Sol Company 6% bonds, $1,000 par value; interest is paid on April 1 and October 1	$9,800
100 Moon Company common stock, par value $10 per share, cost:	
50 shares at $10	500
50 shares at $12	600

The following transactions occurred during the year.

1. Received a $1 per share dividend on the common stock.
2. Collected the semiannual interest on the Sol Company bonds.
3. Sold five of the Sol Company bonds for $5,500, including $100 interest accrued since April 1.
4. Sold 75 shares of Moon Company stock at $20 a share. The company uses a first-in, first-out assumption to identify shares sold. Brokerage fees were $50 on the sale.
5. Received a 100% stock dividend on the common stock.
6. Sold 10 shares of Moon Company stock at $9 a share. Brokerage fee was $6.
7. Collected the semiannual interest on the 6% bonds on October 1.
8. The books of the company were adjusted on December 1. At that date, the market value of the securities were as follows:

Bonds—Sol Company	$4,800
Stock—Moon Company	230

Required:

a. Journalize the transactions that occurred during the year.

b. Refer to item 8. If the stocks and bonds were to be held as long-term investments instead of as temporary investments, what accounting differences would have to be considered?

If long-Term - valued at adjusted cost

12

Valuation and control of receivables

The sale of merchandise on account (that is, for credit) is a typical business activity. When sales are made on credit, receivables are created. In an accounting sense, receivables are assets that represent claims against other parties. Normally, such claims are settled through the payment of money by the debtor. In our economy today, credit is the lifeblood of the exchange system; the creation and settlement of receivables is a common occurrence. Hence, it is important that the accounting system fairly record and report receivables arising from credit transactions.

Receivables assume many forms. The most common are:

1. Accounts receivable (trade): claims against customers or clients arising through regular trade transactions.
2. Notes receivable (trade): claims against customers or clients arising through regular trade transactions and represented by a note.
3. Accrued receivables: claims arising through the accumulation of unrecorded revenue, such as interest receivable on a note receivable or rent receivable on property rented to others.
4. Receivables from officers, stockholders, and so on: claims against officers, stockholders, or others arising through trade transactions or otherwise.

Accounts receivable

Accounts receivable are claims against customers or clients arising from sales made or services rendered on open account. The basic record of the debt is the account receivable in the ledgers of the company selling for credit. Each addition to the debt should be documented by a sales ticket, purchase order, or similar document signed by the debtor. If large amounts of money are involved, the customer or client often is asked to sign a contract before opening a charge account. This contract sets forth details of procedures to be used in making charges, billing the account, sending payments on the account, charging of fees or interest for overdue balances, and so on.

Accounts receivable that will be collected during the current operating cycle of the business (or within a year, if longer) are classified as current assets on the statement of financial position (balance sheet).

A company selling for credit often offers a cash discount to debtors to encourage them to pay their accounts at an early date. Good business practice requires that the debtor take advantage of the discount, because it represents a substantial savings to him if taken. If the seller offers discount terms of 2/10, n/30, the purchaser can save 2 percent of the gross amount owed by paying within 10 days rather than waiting the full 30 days allowed for payment on the account. If the purchaser keeps his cash for the additional 20 days, how much interest or other income would it have to earn for him in order to justify not taking the discount? A rate of 2 percent for 20 days is approximately 36 percent per year (360 days × 2%/20 days). This is a very high rate, and it is most unlikely that the purchaser will have any other use for his cash that will earn him more profits than his savings by paying the account early. Therefore, competent management will take advantage of cash discounts whenever they are available.

Typical accounting procedures related to creation and collection of accounts receivable can best be illustrated through some examples. To give the clearest picture of the accounts being debited and credited, we show all journal entries in the general journal form.

Transaction 1. Sale on account. On January 10, the Seller Company makes a sale in the amount of $1,000 to the Buyer Company subject to credit terms of 2/10, n/30.

This sale is recorded in the journal by the following entry.

Jan. 10	Accounts Receivable: Buyer Co.	1,000	
	Sales		1,000
	To record sale on account to Buyer Co.		

Transaction 2. Payment received within discount period. On January 16, the Seller Company collects payment from the Buyer Company for the sale made on January 10. Because it is paying within 10 days, the Buyer Company deducts the 2% cash discount from the $1,000 gross amount due and sends a check for $980.

Because the account is settled by the payment, the account receivable must be credited for the gross amount due, $1,000. Cash is debited for the $980 received. The sales discount is recorded by a debit to a contra revenue account. (Discounts will be subtracted from sales on the income statement.)

Jan. 16	Cash	980	
	Sales Discounts	20	
	Accounts Receivable: Buyer Co.		1,000
	To record settlement of account within the discount period.		

If the Buyer Company did not send in its payment until after the discount period had expired, it would be required to pay the full $1,000 gross amount. In that case, the entry to record the collection would be the following.

Jan. 30	Cash	1,000	
	Accounts Receivable: Buyer Co.		1,000
	To record settlement of account after expiration of discount period.		

If the Buyer Company sent only $980 on January 30, this would be treated as a partial payment on the account. The account receivable would still show a balance of $20. The Seller Company would notify the Buyer Company that its payment was received too late to qualify for the discount, and that a balance of $20 was still owed on its account.

Transaction 3. Sales returns and allowances. On February 10, the Seller Company makes a sale in the amount of $1,000 to the Purchaser Company on account. On February 15, the Purchaser Company returns $400 worth of defective merchandise and asks for credit on this return.

The entry to record the sales transaction is similar to the entry shown for transaction 1. The entry to record the return of merchandise must remove $400 from the amount owed by the Purchaser Company. The amount also is debited to a contra revenue account. The transaction should be documented by a credit memo showing the details of the merchandise returned and the reasons for the return.

Feb. 15	Sales Returns and Allowances	400	
	Accounts Receivable: Purchaser Co.		400
	To record return of damaged merchandise (see Credit Memo No. 105).		

In the income statement, the Sales Returns and Allowances account—like the Sales Discount account—is deducted from the Sales account. These items are treated as adjustments to sales revenue, *not* as expenses. The relevant lines of the income statement are shown in the following form.

Sales		$500,000
Less: Sales discount	$30,000	
Sales returns and allowances	20,000	50,000
Net sales		$450,000

ALLOWANCE FOR DOUBTFUL RECEIVABLES AND BAD DEBTS EXPENSE

Because credit sales are recognized as revenue at the time of the sale (regardless of when collection is made), any expense or loss resulting from difficulties in collecting the accounts receivable should be recognized as an expense during the period in which the sales were made. Some estimate of the bad debts expense must be matched against the reported income from the credit sales in the current period. Furthermore, the value of the accounts receivable reported on the balance sheet should represent the expected realizable value—that is, the amount that actually is expected to be collected from the customers. To accomplish these objectives, the accounting system must

1. record an estimated expense in the income statement in the period of sale for accounts that are expected to be uncollectible, and
2. report the value of accounts receivable in the balance sheet by deducting from the gross amount of accounts receivable an estimated amount for accounts that are expected to be uncollectible.

The journal entry used to record these estimates is an adjusting entry made at the close of an accounting period.

Dec. 31	Bad Debts Expense	2,000	
	Allowance for Doubtful Receivables		2,000

The Bad Debts Expense account is disclosed in the income statement as a selling expense or as a general and administrative expense (depending upon whether the responsibility for credit approval and collection is assigned to the selling or the administrative departments of the company). The Allowance for Doubtful Receivables account is a contra asset account; it appears on the balance sheet as a deduction from Accounts Receivable.

Current assets:		
Accounts receivable	$30,000	
Less: Allowance for doubtful receivables	2,000	28,000

The contra asset account is sometimes called Allowance for Bad Debts, Allowance for Uncollectibles, or Provision for Estimated Losses.

Accountants have developed three different methods for estimating the amount of bad debts expense to be recorded in the adjusting entry.

1. *Percentage of sales.* From past experience, estimate the percentage of credit sales that will prove to be uncollectible. *Increase* the Allowance for Doubtful Receivables by this percentage of the credit sales made during the period. This is an income statement method, because bad debts expense is determined in relation to the amount of credit sales income during the period.
2. *Percentage of accounts receivable.* From past experience, estimate the percentage of open accounts receivable at the end of the period that will prove eventually to be uncollectible. *Adjust* the Allowance account balance to match this percentage of the Accounts Receivable balance at the end of the period. This is a balance sheet method, because bad debts expense is determined in relation to the asset accounts receivable.
3. *Aging of accounts receivable.* At the end of the period, prepare a schedule showing the amounts due in accounts receivable that have remained unpaid for various lengths of time. On the basis of past experience, estimate the percentage of each age group that will prove uncollectible. From this information, estimate the total amount of the Accounts Receivable balance that will prove uncollectible. *Adjust* the Allowance account balance to match this amount. This is another balance sheet method.

To illustrate these three methods, we apply them to one particular example. At the end of 19_5, the Collector Company has a balance in its Accounts Receivable account of $200,000. The credit balance of the Allowance for Doubtful Receivables account (remaining from the preceding year) is $2,050. The total credit sales for the year were $1,000,000.

PERCENTAGE-OF-SALES METHOD. An examination of the ledgers from past years yields information about the collections that have been made on accounts in the past. This information is summarized in the schedule shown as Exhibit 12-1. From this information, we conclude that the company can expect about 1.0 percent of its credit sales to result in uncollectible accounts receivable. Therefore, we wish to *increase* the balance of the Allowance for Doubtful Receivables account by 1.0 percent of the $1,000,000 credit sales in 19_5.

19_5			
Dec. 31	Bad Debts Expense	10,000	
	Allowance for Doubtful Receivables		10,000
	To increase allowance for doubtful accounts by 1% of year's credit sales: $1,000,000 × 0.01 = $10,000.		

After this entry is posted, the balance of Accounts Receivable remains unchanged at $200,000. A Bad Debts Expense account has been established with a balance of $10,000. On the income statement, this expense will be matched against the sales revenue of the period. The balance of the Allowance for Doubtful Receivables account has been increased from $2,050 to $12,050. The $2,050 balance from the previous year presumably represents some of the accounts considered uncollectible from last year's sales. The $10,000 allowance added now represents the portion of this year's sales that will never be collected. On the balance sheet, the value of accounts receivable will be adjusted by subtracting the allowance from the receivables balance, giving a carrying value of $187,950 for accounts receivable.

The percentage-of-sales method provides a good matching of revenue and expenses for the period, because the expected bad debts expense is based directly upon the amount of credit sales producing income for the period. It is preferable to compute the loss percentage on the basis of credit sales as we have done here. However, in practice, total net sales are often used because these figures are more readily available than figures for credit sales alone. (Of course, if total sales are used to compute the historical percentage, total sales for the year should be used in computing the allowance.) The use of total sales is less preferable because no losses result from cash sales; therefore the relationship of losses to total sales can vary considerably if the relationship of credit sales to total sales varies.

A disadvantage of the percentage-of-sales method is that it makes no correction for poor estimates in past years. We have not checked to see whether the $2,050 balance in the allowance account before this year's adjustment is a fair estimate of

Exhibit 12-1
Schedule of collections on credit sales in past years

Year	Credit Sales	Amount Collected	Bad Debts Loss	Loss as % of Sales
19_1	$900,000	$891,900	$ 8,100	0.9%
19_2	950,000	939,550	10,450	1.1%
19_3	975,000	965,250	9,750	1.0%
19_4	990,000	Collections still in progress		—
				3.0%

Average percentage of losses = 3.0%/3 years = 1.0% per year.

the accounts remaining uncollected from previous years. If last year's actual loss was much lower than usual, this balance might overstate the amount that should be subtracted from the current receivables balance.

PERCENTAGE-OF-OPEN-ACCOUNTS METHOD. We begin by examining ledgers from past years and preparing a schedule similar to Exhibit 12-1. This time, however, we look at the amount eventually collected from the balance of Accounts Receivable at the end of each year. In this case, such a study shows that an average of 2 percent of the accounts receivable uncollected at the close of the year will prove uncollectible. The balance of Accounts Receivable at the close of 19_5 was $200,000, so we estimate that 2 percent of this amount, or $4,000, will prove uncollectible.

The Allowance for Doubtful Receivables already has a credit balance of $2,050, so we need to add another $1,950 to bring the balance up to the estimated $4,000.

Dec. 31	Bad Debts Expense	1,950	
	Allowance for Doubtful Receivables		1,950
	To adjust $2,050 balance of allowance to 2% of Accounts Receivable balance: $200,000 × 0.02 = $4,000; $4,000 − $2,050 = $1,950.		

After this entry is posted, the Allowance for Doubtful Receivables has the desired balance of 2% of open accounts receivable, or $4,000. The bad debts expense to be charged against income in this year is $1,950.

In some cases, the Allowance account may show a ***debit*** balance at the close of the period. (We will see later how this situation can arise if estimates of bad debts in previous years have been too low.) If the Allowance account showed a ***debit*** balance of $1,000 before the adjusting entry, it would be necessary to credit the account $5,000 in order to bring it up to the desired ***credit*** balance of $4,000. Therefore, the bad debts expense for the year would be $5,000.

The advantages of the percentage-of-open-accounts method are (1) that it is relatively simple to use, and (2) that it results in an adjustment of the bad debts estimate each year to give a realistic estimate of the bad debts likely to be included in the present receivables. That is, it gives a good estimate of the proper adjustment in value of the current accounts receivable for the balance sheet. On the other hand, it does not consider the amount of credit sales in the current period, so it may not result in the best possible matching of bad debts expense to the corresponding revenue.

AGING-OF-ACCOUNTS-RECEIVABLE METHOD. This method is a more complex and reliable version of the percentage-of-open-accounts method. In using this method we must analyze each uncollected account to determine how long the balance has remained unpaid. For example, assume that the Collector Company sells on credit terms of 2/10, n/30. On December 31, 19_5, the account of the X Company in the accounts receivable subsidiary ledger appears as shown in Exhibit 12-2. The account shows a balance of $2,800. Of this amount, $1,300 was debited on December 15 and therefore will not be due for another 14 days. The remaining

Exhibit 12-2
A typical account receivable in the subsidiary ledger

X Company					
19_5			19_5		
June 15	Sale	1,000	July 16	Collection	1,000
Sep. 10	Sale	3,000	Oct. 9	Collection	1,500
Dec. 15	Sale	1,300			

Customer	Debit Balance	Amount Not Due	Number of Days Past Due 1–30	31–60	61–90	Over 90
X Co.	2,800	1,300			1,500	
Y Co.	1,800	1,800				
Z Co.	500	400	100			
Others	498,500	450,000	20,000	15,000	8,500	5,000
Totals Dec. 31, 19_5	503,600	453,500	20,100	15,000	10,000	5,000
Estimated percentage uncollectible from past experience		1%	5%	10%	25%	50%
Estimated uncollectible accounts as of Dec. 31, 19_5		$4,535	$1,005	$1,500	$2,500	$2,500
Total estimated uncollectible accounts as of Dec. 31, 19_5: $12,040						

Exhibit 12-3 **Aging schedule of accounts receivable**

$1,500 is due on a sale made September 10, and therefore was due for payment before October 10. At the end of the year, this amount is 82 days past due.

Exhibit 12-3 shows a schedule of the accounts receivable, with the balances aged by the number of days past due. (Only three accounts have been shown in detail in this example; totals are given for the other accounts.) A study of ledgers from past years is made to determine the percentage of bad debts eventually arising from accounts of various ages. The results of the study are shown in Exhibit 12-3. In this example, the company finds that in the past it has collected 99 percent of the amount owed on accounts not yet due. However, the longer an account goes uncollected, the more chance there is that it will never be collected. The company collects only 50 percent of the amounts more than 90 days past due. These percentages are then applied to the current balances of various ages, as shown in the exhibit, yielding a total estimate of $12,040 for uncollectible accounts among the present accounts receivable.

Again, this method requires that the Allowance account balance be adjusted to equal the estimate of bad debts among the current accounts receivable. The Allowance account has a present credit balance of $2,050, so this account must be credited by $9,990 to bring it to the desired balance. This credit is balanced by a $9,990 debit to Bad Debts Expense.

The aging-of-accounts-receivable method provides the best possible estimation of the realizable value of the current accounts receivable. It is generally considered the most preferable method to use for this reason. Like the percentage-of-open-accounts method, however, it does not necessarily relate the bad debts expense for the period to the credit sales of the period.

WRITE-OFF OF UNCOLLECTIBLE ACCOUNTS

As we have seen, it is necessary to estimate an allowance for uncollectible accounts receivable in order to match bad debts expense against the corresponding sales revenue, and to assign a realistic value to the balance of accounts receivable as an asset. At the time this estimate is made, there is no way to know exactly which accounts will not be collected.

However, when it is determined that a particular account receivable will not be collected, this information should be recorded in the accounts. First, it is no longer realistic to assign any value to this account as an asset. Second, it should be recognized that a part of the allowance for doubtful receivables has been "used up" by an actual uncollectible receivable.

Transaction 4. Write-off of an account receivable. On May 15, 19_2, the Write-Off Company learns that the X Company has declared bankruptcy. The Write-Off Company made a credit sale to the X Company in 19_1, and the X Company's account receivable in the ledger shows a debit balance of $500 at this time. It is now clear that the Write-Off Company will never be able to collect the $500 owed to it by the X Company.

Two steps are needed to record this information in the accounts. First, the X Company account receivable should be written off—that is, removed from the accounts receivable. Second, the Allowance for Doubtful Receivables should be reduced by $500 to show that this amount of the allowance has been used in writing off a specific uncollectible account. These steps are accomplished by the following journal entry.

May 15	Allowance for Doubtful Receivables	500	
	Accounts Receivable: X Co.		500
	To write off X Co. account.		

After this entry is posted, the accounts appear as shown in Exhibit 12-4.

Note that the write-off of an account receivable involves a debit entry to the Allowance for Doubtful Receivables account—*not* to the Bad Debts Expense account. The expense was recognized when the allowance was established, in the period of the credit sale. If bad debts actually prove to be greater than the allowance established,

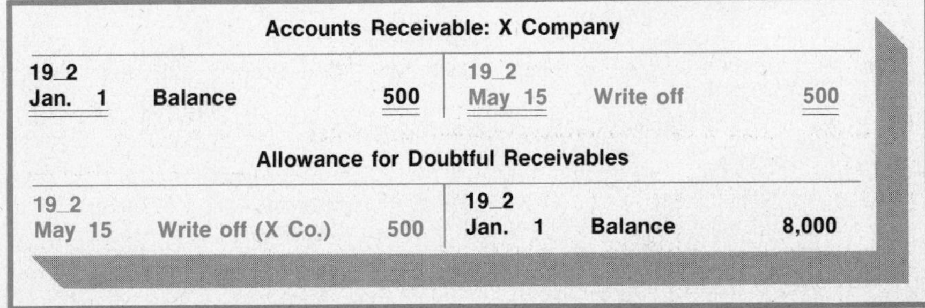

Accounts Receivable: X Company

19_2 Jan. 1	Balance	500	19_2 May 15	Write off	500

Allowance for Doubtful Receivables

19_2 May 15	Write off (X Co.)	500	19_2 Jan. 1	Balance	8,000

Exhibit 12-4
Ledger accounts after write-off entry is posted

the Allowance account will have a debit balance at the end of the period. As noted earlier, this will result in the recording of a larger bad debts expense for the current year if a balance sheet method is being used to estimate the allowance.

In most cases, an account is written off after all reasonable efforts to collect it have failed. In only a few cases, such as transaction 4, is it unquestionably clear that collection will never be made. More often, the decision to write off an account is a matter of judgment.

COLLECTION OF AN ACCOUNT PREVIOUSLY WRITTEN OFF. In some cases, an account is written off as uncollectible, but the debtor later does make a payment on the account.

Transaction 5. Recovery of an account written off. In transaction 4, the Write-Off Company wrote off the account receivable of the X Company. However, on December 13, 19_2, a $500 check from the X Company arrives in the mail as a payment on the written-off account. Apparently the X Company has recovered from its financial woes.

Two journal entries are needed to record this transaction. First, the account receivable must be restored to the ledger—in other words, the write-off entry must be reversed. Second, the collection of cash must be recorded and the balance due on the account receivable must be reduced.

Dec. 13	Accounts Receivable: X Co.	500	
	Allowance for Doubtful Receivables		500
	To reverse write-off of X Co. account (May 15) by restoring receivable claim against debtor.		
13	Cash	500	
	Accounts Receivable: X Co.		500
	To record collection of balance due on the X Co. account.		

Exhibit 12-5 shows the ledger accounts after these entries have been posted. The reason for making the two separate entries is that the receivable account now shows a complete record of dealings with the X Company. From the ledger, anyone interested can see that a sale was made on account, the account was written off as uncollectible, and finally the account was restored and a collection was made.

Exhibit 12-5
Ledger accounts after posting reversal of write-off and collection

Accounts Receivable: X Company

19_2 Jan. 1	**Balance**	**500**	**19_2 May 15**	**Write off**	**500**
19_2 Dec. 13	**Restore acct.**	**500**	**19_2 Dec. 13**	**Collection**	**500**

Allowance for Doubtful Receivables

19_2 May 15	**Write off (X Co.)**	**500**	**19_2 Jan. 1**	**Balance**	**8,000**
			Dec. 13	**Recovery (X Co.)**	**500**

RATIO ANALYSIS

The analysis of accounts receivable by aging provides management with valuable information about the collectibility of individual accounts. In addition to the procedure of aging, the use of various financial ratios related to receivables can provide insights into the effectiveness of the firm's use of its receivables as a significant current asset.

The ***receivables turnover*** is a useful ratio that measures the average number of times the accounts receivable were converted into cash during the period. It is computed by the formula

$$\text{Receivables turnover} = \frac{\text{Net credit sales}}{\text{Average trade receivables}}$$

where Average Trade Receivables can be computed as one-half the sum of the opening and closing balances of Accounts Receivable. This ratio measures the average frequency with which the firm is able to collect the amount due on its credit sales. It is a measure of the liquidity of the accounts receivable. A high value of this ratio indicates that the firm collects quickly on its receivables, and therefore that the balance of accounts receivable should be considered a very liquid current asset.

Another important ratio measuring the liquidity of the accounts receivable is the ***average number of days' sales uncollected.*** This ratio measures the average number of days required to collect a receivable, or—looked at another way—the average number of days of credit sales represented by accounts receivable at any moment. The ratio is computed as

$$\begin{array}{c}\text{Average number of days'} \\ \text{sales uncollected}\end{array} = \frac{\text{365 days}}{\text{Receivables turnover}}$$

The value of this ratio is most meaningful when compared with the firm's credit terms, as an indication of the success or failure of the collection process. For example, if the firm makes credit sales of terms of n/30, the value of this ratio should be considerably less than 30. A value of more than 30 would indicate that the average account is not collected until it is past due.

IMPACT ANALYSIS

Accounts receivable make up a very significant part of the current assets of most firms. Any material overstatement or understatement of the Accounts Receivable account can distort the financial statements and certain financial ratios derived from the statements.

Exhibit 12-6 illustrates the impact of receivables transactions on some important accounting categories and ratios. In this exhibit, the impact of each transaction is indicated as an increase, a decrease, or no effect in the category by a +, −, or 0, respectively.

Notes receivable

Most sales are made or services rendered on a cash basis or for credit through an open account. In many cases, the open account may be handled on an installment basis, with payments to be made at regular intervals and for specified portions of the

Exhibit 12-6 Impact of some receivables transactions

Transaction (see Note)	Impact On					
	Current assets	Net assets	Gross margin	Net income	Earnings per share	Owners' equity
1. Sale of goods or services on credit	+	+	+	+	+	+
2. Adjustment to record bad debts expense	–	–	0	–	–	–
3. Write off of an account receivable	0	0	0	0	0	0
4. Recovery of account previously written off	0	0	0	0	0	0
5. Failure to record bad debts adjusting entry when closing books	+	+	0	+	+	+

NOTE: These transactions involve the following entries in ledger accounts:
1. debit Accounts Receivable, credit Sales;
2. debit Bad Debts Expense, credit Allowance for Doubtful Receivables;
3. debit Allowance for Doubtful Receivables, credit Accounts Receivable;
4. debit Accounts Receivable and Cash, credit Allowance for Doubtful Receivables and Accounts Receivable;
5. failure to debit Bad Debts Expense, failure to credit Allowance for Doubtful Receivables.

amount due. The company offers credit to make a sale or service more attractive to customers. The extension of credit accommodates the terms of the transaction to the customer's ability to pay.

On the other hand, the extension of credit involves additional expense and risk for the selling company. As we have seen, open accounts are debts created without formal debt instruments (such as signed notes for the loan). If a firm is unwilling to extend credit on open account to a customer or client, it may decide to finance such a transaction through the use of notes. Financing through notes can have certain advantages over open account financing.

1. A note is easier to enforce in court if the debtor defaults, because the note is a formal, written acknowledgment of the obligation to pay.
2. A note is relatively easy to discount (that is, sell to a bank or collection agency) in order to obtain cash; it also is relatively easy to use as security for a loan or other debt.
3. A note may be interest-bearing, and therefore may be a source of revenue.
4. A note is especially attractive if the credit period is relatively long, because it improves the collectibility of the debt.

The Uniform Negotiable Instruments Law defines a *note* as follows.

A negotiable promissory note within the meaning of this act is an unconditional promise in writing made by one person to another, signed by the maker, engaging to pay on demand or at a fixed or determinable future time a sum certain in money to order or to bearer.

The party who signs the note and promises to pay is called the ***maker*** of the note; the person who is to receive payment is called the ***payee.*** The term ***negotiable*** means that the note can be transferred from one person to another. The note is negotiated, or transferred, when it is delivered by one party to another party, with the intention of giving the first party's rights in the instrument to the other party. The instrument is first negotiated when the maker transfers the note to a payee, with the intention of making the payee a ***holder*** of the note—that is, a person who possesses an instrument issued or delivered to him. The note may be negotiated at any time that the current holder chooses to deliver the note to a new holder with the intention of transferring his rights in the note to the new holder.

Negotiation can be made (1) by endorsement and delivery, or (2) by delivery alone. An ***endorsement*** is the signature of the current holder of the note. ***Delivery*** refers to the physical transfer of possession of the note from one party to another.

A note ***payable on demand*** must be paid immediately whenever the current holder of the note presents it to the maker for payment. A note payable at a fixed or determinable future time cannot be presented for payment until the date that is specified on the note or is determinable from the conditions specified on the note.

A ***bearer*** instrument is one that specifies on its face that the note is payable to bearer, or one that uses terms indicating such an intention—for example, "Pay bearer thirty dollars." The bearer is the person who has physical possession of the instrument. A bearer instrument can be transferred by mere physical delivery; no endorsement is required to negotiate the instrument.

An ***order*** instrument is one that specifies on its face the payee of the note—for example, "Pay to the order of John Smith thirty dollars." Negotiation of an order instrument is not complete until the current holder of the note has endorsed the note.

Exhibit 12-7 shows a typical note. This example is an order instrument payable on a specific date. The maker of the note is the Maker Company, which signs the note. The Maker Company promises to give the Payee Company (the payee) $1,000 plus 6% interest 60 days after the date of the note, or on August 14, 19_1.

This example is an ***interest-bearing note.*** At the maturity date of the note, the maker must pay both the face value of the note and the specified interest on this amount for the time that the note has been outstanding. (Unless otherwise specified, the interest rate given on the note is assumed to be an annual interest rate.) It is also possible to issue a ***non-interest-bearing note,*** which requires the maker to pay only the face value of the note at maturity.

If the maker fails to pay the note at maturity, the note is said to be ***dishonored.*** The holder of the note may then go to court to attempt to force the maker to honor the note—that is, to pay the amount promised.

The holder of a note may choose to ***discount*** the note before maturity. That is, in order to convert the note into cash, the holder sells the note to a bank or other note buyer before the maturity date of the note. The buyer of the note usually pays the holder the face value and interest value of the note, less a discount to allow for interest he earns from lending money on the note. At the maturity of the note, the maker is expected to pay the bank or other party who bought the discounted note.

Exhibit 12-7 A typical note

$ 1,000 Chicago, Illinois June 15, 19_1

Sixty days after date I promise to pay

to the order of Payee Company

One Thousand and NO/100 Dollars

Payable at First National Bank, Chicago, Illinois

With interest at 6 %

Due August 14, 19_1

MAKER COMPANY

Larry G. Gibson

Treasurer

In most cases, the buyer of the discounted note buys the note "with recourse." This means that the seller of the note retains a *contingent liability* on the discounted note. If the maker of the note dishonors it at maturity, the buyer of the note will return it to the seller and will charge the seller the face and interest value of the note plus a protest fee. The seller of the note then has a legal claim against the maker who dishonored the note—both for the original value of the note, the unpaid interest, and for the protest fee that he was required to pay to the note buyer.

The maturity date of a note may be expressed in various ways. If the note specifies a term until maturity in months or years, the note is normally considered to fall due on the same day of the appropriate month or year. For example, a three-year note issued June 1, 19_1, is due on June 1, 19_4. A two-month note issued on June 1 is due August 1. On the other hand, if the term is expressed in calendar days, the actual number of days must be counted to determine the maturity date. (The date of issue is not included; the date of maturity is included.) For example, a 60-day note issued on June 1 is due on July 31 because there are 29 days remaining in June after the date of issue and an additional 31 days in July, including the 31st: 29 + 31 = 60.

Interest is the price of credit—that is, it is the charge made for the use of money. The rate specified is normally the charge made if the money is kept for one year. If the money is kept for less than one year, the interest usually is computed at the rate specified on the note for an appropriate fraction of a 360-day year. For example, suppose a $1,000 note matures in 30 days and bears an interest rate of 6 percent. The interest due on the note at maturity is computed as follows:

$$\text{Principal} = \text{Interest} \times \text{Rate} \times \text{Time (in years)}$$
$$= \$1{,}000 \times 0.06 \times (30/360).$$

ACCOUNTING FOR THE RECEIPT AND COLLECTION OF NOTES

The journal entries needed to account for the receipt and collection of notes can best be explained through examples.

Transaction 6. Receipt of a note receivable. On June 1, 19_1, the Payee Company accepts a $1,000, 60-day, non-interest-bearing note (issued that day) from a stockholder of the company in exchange for a loan of $1,000.

Because this note pays no interest, the maturity value of the note is the same as its face value, or principal. The receipt of the note is recorded by a $1,000 increase in the Notes Receivable account; the loan is recorded by a $1,000 decrease in the Cash account.

June 1	Notes Receivable	1,000	
	Cash		1,000
	To record receipt of note in exchange for advance of $1,000.		

When the maturity value of the note is collected, the collection is recorded as a decrease in Notes Receivable and an increase in Cash.

July 31	Cash	1,000	
	Notes Receivable		1,000
	To record collection of note at maturity:		

Transaction 7. Note issued to settle past-due account On June 1, 19_1, the Merchant Company receives a $1,000, 6%, 60-day note from the Maker Company to settle a past-due account. The note is settled on July 31.

At the time of receipt, an interest-bearing note is recorded at the exchange price, or acquisition cost, which normally is the principal amount of the note. Interest income is recognized at the time that the interest is collected. (As we discuss later, an adjusting entry would be needed if the books are closed before the interest is collected, in order to recognize accrued interest earned during the current period.)

June 1	Notes Receivable	1,000	
	Accounts Receivable: Maker Co.		1,000
	To record receipt of 60-day note to settle past-due account.		
July 31	Cash	1,010	
	Notes Receivable		1,000
	Interest Earned		10
	To record collection of $1,000, 60-day, 6% note at maturity: $\$1,000 \times 0.06 \times 60/360 = \$10$.		

Transaction 8. Note receivable received when sale is made. On June 1, 19_1, the Sales Company receives a $1,000, 6%, 60-day note from the Buyer Company for a sale of merchandise on credit.

The simplest way to record this transaction is to regard the note as payment for the sale.

June 1	Notes Receivable	1,000	
	Sales		1,000
	To record note received on sale.		

However, if the Sales Company uses the entries in the Accounts Receivable account as a measure of its credit sales, two entries are needed to record the transaction. This approach also ensures that the ledger account for the Buyer Company will contain a complete record of all credit transactions with that customer.

June 1	Accounts Receivable: Buyer Co.	1,000	
	Sales		1,000
	To record sale on account.		
1	Notes Receivable	1,000	
	Accounts Receivable: Buyer Co.		1,000
	To record receipt of note to settle open account.		

In either case, collection of the note will be recorded by the following entry.

July 31	Cash	1,010	
	Notes Receivable		1,000
	Interest Earned		10
	To record collection of $1,000, 60-day, 6% note at maturity: $\$1,000 \times 0.06 \times 60/360 = \$10$.		

Transaction 9. Settlement of note with interest. On June 1, 19_1, the Merchant Company receives a 60-day note for $1,010 from the Debtor Company in settlement of a $1,000 account.

In effect, this transaction is the same as transaction 7. However, instead of issuing a 6% interest-bearing note for $1,000, the Debtor Company has decided to issue a non-interest-bearing note for $1,010 to settle the $1,000 account. Because it is customary to record the note at face value when it is received, the note would normally be recorded at the value of $1,010. The extra $10 is treated as interest received in advance.

June 1	Notes Receivable	1,010	
	Accounts Receivable: Debtor Co.		1,000
	Interest Received in Advance		10
	To record receipt of note in settlement of open account.		
July 31	Cash	1,010	
	Notes Receivable		1,010
	To record collection of note.		
31	Interest Received in Advance	10	
	Interest Earned		10
	To record earning of interest received in advance.		

In a case like this, where the note is to be collected within the current period, the interest could be recorded as Interest Earned in the original entry.

NOTES DISHONORED AT MATURITY

When the maker fails to pay a note at maturity, the claim against the maker is transferred to an account receivable classification and the note receivable is removed from the records.

Suppose that the stockholder dishonors the note accepted in transaction 6. When the note is not paid at maturity, an entry is made in the journal to reclassify the non-interest-bearing note receivable as an account receivable.

July 31	Accounts Receivable: A. Stockholder	1,000	
	Notes Receivable		1,000
	To record dishonoring of note.		

This debt is reclassified because it loses most of the advantages of a note when it is dishonored: it is no longer more likely to be collected, more readily convertible into cash, or more acceptable as collateral. Its only distinction from other past-due accounts is that the formal note may be more readily collected through court action because the company holds more compelling evidence of the promise to pay.

The dishonoring of an interest-bearing note is recorded in a similar fashion, with the amount of interest due being recorded as earned income and added to the account receivable. For example, if the Maker Company dishonors the note issued in transaction 7, the following journal entry would be made.

July 31	Accounts Receivable: Maker Co.	1,010	
	Notes Receivable		1,000
	Interest Earned		10
	To record dishonoring of note.		

If the note issued in transaction 9 were dishonored, two entries would be needed: one to transfer the $1,010 from Notes Receivable to Accounts Receivable, and one to transfer the $10 from Interest Received in Advance to Interest Earned.

DISCOUNTING OF NOTES RECEIVABLE

When a negotiable promissory note is discounted prior to the maturity of the note, the current holder (usually the original payee) endorses the note and delivers it to a new holder. The new holder in exchange pays the maturity value of the note less a discount (interest he charges for the loan). When a company discounts its notes receivable, the proceeds must be calculated and an entry made to account for the transaction.

Transaction 10. Discounting a note receivable. The Payee Company holds a 90-day, 4% note for $1,000 from the Maker Company, dated September 3, 19_1. In order to obtain cash needed for its day-to-day operations, the Payee Company discounts the note on October 3, 19_1, at the First National Bank. The bank buys the note at 8% discount.

The calculation of the proceeds from the discounted note is made in three steps.

1. Calculate the maturity value of the note. The face value of the note is $1,000. In addition, the maker will pay 4% interest for 90 days, or

   $\$1,000 \times 0.04 \times 90/360 = \$10.$

   Therefore the total maturity value of the note is $1,010.

2. Calculate the discount expense charge by the note buyer on the maturity value of the note for the number of days from the date of discount to the date of maturity:

   $\$1,010 \times 0.08 \times 60/360 = \$13.47.$

3. Calculate the proceeds that the company receives from the discounted note, by subtracting the discount charge from the maturity value:

$1,010 - $13.47 = $996.53.

When the Payee Company accepted the note on September 3 in payment for a sale, it made the following journal entry.

Sep. 3	Notes Receivable	1,000	
	Sales		1,000
	To record receipt of note in payment for sale.		

When it discounts the note at the First National Bank, it makes the following journal entry.

Oct. 3	Cash	996.53	
	Interest Expense	3.47	
	Notes Receivable Discounted		1,000
	To record discounting of note receivable (matures Dec. 1).		

Observe that this entry does not remove the $1,000 from Notes Receivable. Instead, it credits $1,000 to a contingent liability account called Notes Receivable Discounted. This recognizes the fact that the company still has some liability for the note until the maker pays it. On the balance sheet, Notes Receivable and Notes Receivable Discounted can be reported in several ways. Suppose that the balances of these accounts at the end of the year are $100,000 and $9,000, respectively. (All of the notes involved are classified as current assets.) The relevant item on the balance sheet could take any one of the following three forms.

1. Current assets:		
Notes receivable	$100,000	
Less: Notes receivable discounted	9,000	$91,000
2. Current assets:		
Notes receivable (less notes receivable discounted of $9,000)		$91,000
3. Current assets:		
Notes receivable*		$91,000

*The company is contingently liable on December 31, 19_1, for notes receivable discounted in the amount of $9,000.

To continue the illustration, assume that the maker of the discounted note pays the bank at maturity. The entry on the payee's books would be the following.

Dec. 1	Notes Receivable Discounted	1,000	
	Notes Receivable		1,000

This entry removes the contingent liability from the records because the note has been paid by the maker. Also, the Notes Receivable account is credited, to indicate that this asset is removed from the accounts.

DISCOUNTED NOTES DISHONORED AT MATURITY

After a note has been discounted, the original holder still has a contingent liability for the note in case the maker dishonors it.

Transaction 11. A discounted note receivable is dishonored. When the note described in transaction 10 matures, the Maker Company dishonors the note. That is, the Maker Company fails to pay the principal and interest due to the bank that has purchased the note at discount. The bank charges the Payee Company the full $1,010 maturity value of the note, plus a $6 protest fee to cover certain legal expenses associated with certifying the dishonoring of the note. The Payee Company now has a legal right to recover the full $1,016 from the Maker Company.

Two entries are needed to recognize this transaction in the books of the Payee Company. First, the cash payment of $1,016 to the bank must be recorded and an account receivable established to show the $1,016 owed to the company by the Maker Company.

Accounts Receivable: Maker Co.		1,016	
Cash			1,016
To record payment of Sept. 3 note of Maker Co. dishonored by maker:			
Face of note	$1,000		
4% interest for 90 days	10		
Protest fee	6		

Second, the contingent liability for the note must be cancelled by removing the $1,000 carried in Notes Receivable Discounted (this liability has just been paid), and the $1,000 entry in Notes Receivable must be reversed because the note no longer has status as an asset.

Notes Receivable Discounted	1,000	
Notes Receivable		1,000
To remove contingent liability on dishonored note and remove note from receivables.		

If the Payee Company eventually collects from the Maker Company, the collection will be treated in the books as a normal collection on account. If it fails to collect, even after legal action, the account will be written off in the same fashion as other uncollectible accounts.

ENTRIES IN MAKER'S BOOKS

The maker of a note records his liability on the note when the note is issued. Payment of the note eliminates the liability. If the note is interest-bearing, interest expense is recorded when paid. If the maker dishonors the note at maturity, he makes no entry since his liability on the note is not eliminated. If the payee discounts the maker's note, the maker of the note makes no entry since his liability on the note is not eliminated. The parallel entries in the books of the payee and the maker of notes are summarized in Exhibit 12-8.

INTEREST RECEIVABLE

If an interest-bearing note is outstanding at the close of an accounting period, interest has been accrued from the date of the last interest receipt or the date of issuance of the note to the close of the period. An adjusting entry is needed to recognize the interest earned and the interest receivable when the books are closed.

Transaction 12. Adjusting entries for interest earned. The Payee Company receives a 6%, 60-day note for $1,000 on December 1, 19_1. The receipt of the note is recorded by a $1,000 debit to Notes Receivable. The company closes its books on December 31.

Exhibit 12-8 Short-term note transactions in books of payee and of maker

Transaction	Payee's Books			Maker's Books		
1a. Maker pays Payee for sale with $100 non-interest-bearing note.	Notes Receivable	100		Purchases	100	
	Sales		100	Notes Payable		100
1b. Payee collects note (1a) from Maker at maturity.	Cash	100		Notes Payable	100	
	Notes Receivable		100	Cash		100
2a. Maker pays Payee for sale with 6%, 60-day, $400 note.	Notes Receivable	400		Purchases	400	
	Sales		400	Notes Payable		400
2b. Payee collects note (2a) from Maker at maturity.	Cash	404		Notes Payable	400	
	Notes Receivable		400	Interest Expense	4	
	Interest Earned		4	Cash		404
2c. Maker dishonors note (2a) at maturity.	Accounts Receivable	404		No Entry		
	Notes Receivable		400			
	Interest Earned		4			
2d. Payee discounts note (2a) 30 days before maturity at 6% discount	Cash	402		No Entry		
	Notes Receivable Discounted		400			
	Interest Earned		2			
2e. Maker dishonors discounted note (2d) at maturity; $5 protest fee and maturity value paid by Payee.	Accounts Receivable	409		No Entry		
	Cash		409			
	Notes Receivable Discounted	400				
	Notes Receivable		400			
2f. Maker pays discounted note (2d) at maturity.	Notes Receivable Discounted	400		Notes Payable	400	
	Notes Receivable		400	Interest Expense	4	
				Cash		404

The required adjusting entry is the following.

19_1			
Dec. 31	Accrued Interest Receivable	5	
	Interest Earned		5
	To accrue interest for 30 days: $\$1,000 \times 0.06 \times 30/360 = \$5$.		

When the Payee Company collects the note on January 30, 19_2, the following entry is made.

19_2			
Jan. 30	Cash	1,010	
	Accrued Interest Receivable		5
	Interest Earned		5
	Notes Receivable		1,000
	To record collection of note, accrued interest, and earned interest.		

The effect of the adjusting entry is to allocate the interest income systematically between the two periods during which it is earned.

Summary

For most business, receivables represent major current assets. They arise primarily from credit transactions associated with the sale of goods and services.

The proper valuation of receivables requires that an allowance be provided for uncertainties associated with the ultimate collection of the receivables. An adjustment is made to set up an Allowance for Doubtful Receivables as a contra asset account (reducing the carrying value of the receivables to the estimated amount realizable); this credit is balanced by an equal debit to a Bad Debts Expense account (that will be matched against the revenue from credit sales during the period). Three methods are available for computing the amount of this adjustment at the close of a period.

1. Percentage-of-sales method (an income statement method, and the most accurate method for estimating bad debts expense).
2. Percentage-of-open-accounts method (a balance sheet method that is easy to use).
3. Aging-of-accounts-receivable method (another balance sheet method, and the most accurate method for estimating the allowance for doubtful receivables).

The first method gives a direct estimate of the bad debts expense that will ultimately arise as a result of the period's credit sales; it only indirectly results in an estimate of the uncollectible receivables and normally makes no provision for correcting poor estimates made in earlier periods. The second and third methods give direct estimates of the uncollectible receivables and provide for adjustment of the allowance from year to year; they only indirectly result in an estimate of bad debts expense for the current period.

An account that is determined to be uncollectible is written off by a debit to the Allowance for Doubtful Receivables account and a credit to Accounts Receivable. If the written-off account is later collected, two entries are required: one to reverse the write-off, and one to record the collection of the receivable.

Notes receivable represent a form of short-term financing that may be used when cash is not available and the firm does not wish to advance credit on an open account basis. Most notes receivable are interest-bearing notes. Interest is the expense to the borrower (income to the loaner) charged for the use of money.

If a note receivable is not paid by the maker at maturity, the note is said to be dishonored. A dishonored note is transferred from the category of notes receivable to the category of accounts receivable.

The holder of a note may discount it before maturity at a bank or elsewhere to receive cash. The discounter of the note is contingently liable for the note until it is paid by the maker at maturity. If the maker dishonors the note at maturity, the discounter of the note must pay the bank the maturity value of the note plus a protest fee. He then has a legal right to collect this full amount from the maker of the note.

This chapter illustrates many of the specific accounting procedures used to record transactions involving accounts and notes receivable.

Questions

1. Describe various types of receivables.
2. Identify the classification and use of each of the following accounts:
   a. Sales Returns and Allowances;
   b. Sales Discounts;
   c. Bad Debts Expense;
   d. Allowance for Doubtful Receivables.
3. Describe three methods of estimating bad debts expense and evaluate each.
4. What is the purpose of the adjusting entry for bad debts expense?
5. Explain how to write off an account receivable that is determined to be uncollectible. Explain how to account for a later collection on a written-off account receivable.
6. Explain how each of the following ratios is computed and comment on its significance:
   a. Receivables turnover;
   b. Average number of days' sales uncollected.
7. What is a note receivable?
8. What is meant by dishonoring a note?
9. What is meant by "discounting a note receivable"? Explain the steps involved in calculating the proceeds received from discounting a note.
10. What is the nature of the Notes Receivable Discounted account? How is this account presented on a statement of financial position?
11. A company has the following account balances in its ledger:

Accounts Receivable	$100,000
Allowance for Doubtful Receivables	5,000 (credit balance)

The company writes off a $3,000 account. Describe the impact of the write-off on net income for the period and on total current assets. What is the net accounts receivable balance before and after the write-off?

Exercises

E12-1 (Basic entries of accounts receivable)

Record the following transactions in a two-column general journal.

a. May 1 Sale of merchandise on account to Tic Company for $8,000 terms 2/10, n/30.
b. May 6 Collection of Tic Company's account.
c. May 10 Sale of merchandise on account to Tac Company for $4,000; terms 2/10, n/30. Sale of merchandise on account to Toe Company for $12,000; terms 2/10, n/30.
d. May 13 The Tac Company returns $1,000 of damaged goods and is given an allowance for this amount on the account.
e. June 7 Collection of Toe Company's account.
f. June 8 Collection of Tac Company's account.

E12-2 (Adjustment for estimated uncollectibles)

The general ledger of the Mini Company shows the following selected account balances on December 31, 19_1.

Accounts Receivable	$200,000
Sales	600,000
Allowance for Doubtful Receivables (credit balance)	1,500

Required: Prepare the necessary adjusting entries at the end of the year under each of the following assumptions.

a. The Mini Company estimates its bad debts to be 4 percent of sales.

b. The Mini Company estimates its bad debts expense to be 8 percent of accounts receivable.

c. The Mini Company ages its accounts and estimates that $11,500 of its receivables will be uncollectible.

E12-3 (Aging accounts receivable)

The Brewer Company ages its accounts receivable to estimate their collectibility. Credit terms of the Brewer Company are 2/10, n/30. Exhibit 12-9 shows the account receivable of the Donz Company in the ledger of the Brewer Company. Prepare an aging schedule similar to the one in Exhibit 12-3 to age the Donz Company's account as of June 30.

E12-4 (Write-off of account receivable)

Journalize the following transactions.

a. Sale of services to Lastee Company, $12,000 on July 2, 19_6; terms 2/10, n/30.

b. Collection of $2,000 from Lastee Company on August 30.

c. The Lastee Company files for bankruptcy. The seller writes off this account on October 30, 19_6.

d. The Lastee Company eventually recovers. On May 1, 19_7, it pays the balance due on its account.

E12-5 (Ratios)

Exhibit 12-10 shows two ledger accounts from the books of the Patio Company. Using the information in the accounts, compute the following ratios:

a. the receivables turnover;

b. the average number of days' sales uncollected.

Donz Company

Feb. 15	20,000	Feb. 20	20,000
Mar. 15	7,000	Mar. 20	4,000
May 15	8,000		
June 15	5,000		

Exhibit 12-9
Account receivable for Exercise E12-3

Accounts Receivable

19_6			19_6		
Jan. 1	Balance	12,000	Dec. 31	Collections during year	174,000
Dec. 31	Sales during year	210,000			

Sales

			19_6		
			Dec. 31	Sales during year	210,000

Exhibit 12-10
Ledger accounts for Exercise E12-5

E12-6 (Maturity date calculations for notes)
Give the maturity date of each of the following notes:
a. a 6-month note dated February 20;
b. a 60-day note dated April 15.

E12-7 (Basic entries for notes)
Record the following transactions on the books of the Grill Company.
a. On September 2, 19_6, the Grill Company sold merchandise to the Bar Company and received a 9%, 3-month note for $2,100. (The Grill Company wishes its accounts receivable to include records of all credit sales to customers.)
b. On December 2, 19_6, the Grill Company collects the Bar Company's note.
c. Assume that the Bar Company dishonored its note on December 2 instead of paying it.

E12-8 (Note payable)
Record the transactions listed in Exercise E12-7 on the books of the Bar Company.

E12-9 (Discounting and dishonoring a note)
On June 15, 19_6, the Discounting Company receives an 8%, 90-day note for $2,000 from the Maker Company in settlement of a past-due open account. On July 31, 19_6, the Discounting Company discounts the Maker Company's note at the First National Bank; the bank discount rate is 6%.
Required:
a. Journalize the receipt of the Maker Company's note by the Discounting Company on June 15.
b. Compute the cash proceeds resulting from discounting the note on July 31.
c. Record the receipt of cash resulting from the discounting of the note receivable.
d. Assume that the Maker Company pays its note at maturity on September 13; journalize this transaction.
e. Assume that the Maker Company dishonors its note (instead of paying it as in part d). On June 20, the Discounting Company pays the bank the maturity value of the note plus a protest fee of $20; journalize this transaction.

E12-10 (Note payable)
Journalize the entries required on the Maker Company's books for each of the transactions in Exercise E12-9.

E12-11 (Adjusting entry for interest)
On November 1, 19_6, the Benz Company receives from the Menz Company a $3,000, 9%, 90-day note. Record the adjusting entry required when the Adjust Company closes its books at the end of the calendar year.

E12-12 (Impact analysis)
The following items deal with impact analysis. For each item, select the appropriate completion for the statement.
a. A dishonored non-interest-bearing note receivable is reclassified as an account receivable. The effect of this transaction on current assets, total assets, working capital, net assets, net income, and owners' equity is that
(A) all increase; (B) all decrease; (C) none is affected.

b. On December 31, 19_1, the aging of accounts receivable leads to an estimate that $4,500 of open accounts will be uncollectible. On this date, the Allowance for Doubtful Receivables has a debit balance of $200. The amount of the December 31 adjusting entry is
(A) $4,500; (B) $4,700; (C) $4,300.

c. An interest-bearing note is discounted for cash. The proceeds from the discounted note are less than the carrying value of the Note Receivable in the books. The effect of this transaction on current assets, total assets, working capital, net income, and owners' equity is that
(A) all increase; (B) all decrease; (C) none is affected.

d. The write-off of an uncollectible account receivable causes the value of the current ratio to
(A) increase; (B) decrease; (C) remain unchanged.

e. A non-interest-bearing note receivable is discounted for cash. The effect of this transaction on current assets, total assets, and working capital is that
(A) all increase; (B) all decrease; (C) none is affected.

f. The write-off of an uncollectible account receivable causes the carrying value of accounts receivable to
(A) increase; (B) decrease; (B) remain unchanged.

g. A non-interest-bearing note is received in payment of a past-due open account. The effect of this transaction on current assets, total assets, working capital, net assets, net income, and owners' equity is that
(A) all increase: (B) all decrease; (C) none is affected.

h. On December 31, 19_1, the balance of Sales is $400,000. The Allowance for Doubtful Receivables has a debit balance of $100. The company estimates that 3 percent of its sales will be uncollectible. The amount used in the December 31 adjusting entry is
(A) $12,000; (B) $12,100; (C) $11,900.

i. On December 31, 19_1, the balance of Accounts Receivable is $100,000. The Allowance for Doubtful Receivables has a credit balance of $300. The company estimates that its uncollectible accounts will be 2 percent of Accounts Receivable. The amount of the December 31 adjusting entry is
(A) $2,000; (B) $2,300; (C) $1,700.

j. On December 31, 19_1, the balance of Accounts Receivable is $100,000. The Allowance for Doubtful Receivables has a debit balance of $300. The company estimates that its uncollectible accounts will be 2 percent of Accounts Receivable. The amount used in the December 31 adjusting entry is
(A) $2,000; (B) $2,300; (C) $1,700.

E12-13 (Account analysis)
Exhibit 12-11 shows a general ledger account. Explain each of the four entries in the account.

E12-14 (Impact analysis)
Prepare a table showing the dollar impact of each of the following transactions on current assets, working capital, net income, and net assets.

a. A $2,000 note receivable is discounted at a local bank for $1,900; Interest Expense is debited $100.

b. The company writes off a $751 account as uncollectible.

Exhibit 12-11
Ledger account for Exercise E12-13

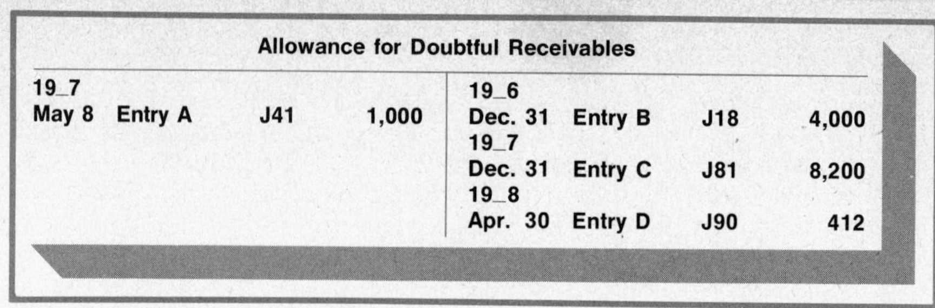

Allowance for Doubtful Receivables

19_7				19_6			
May 8	Entry A	J41	1,000	Dec. 31	Entry B	J18	4,000
				19_7			
				Dec. 31	Entry C	J81	8,200
				19_8			
				Apr. 30	Entry D	J90	412

c. The company collects a $300 account previously written off.
d. A $1,200 interest-bearing note is collected for the face value plus $75 interest.
e. A $3,000 discounted note is paid at maturity by the maker.
f. The company collects $15,000 from a client it had billed 60 days ago.
g. A $1,400 note receivable with interest of $80 is dishonored at maturity.
h. The company bills a client for $20,000 for services rendered today.
i. In an adjusting entry, the company records $2,100 as a bad debts expense.
j. A $1,200 note receivable is accepted to settle an account receivable.

E12-15 (Discounting of notes receivable)

a. Compute the interest on a $750 note bearing 6% interest for 96 days.
b. A company received a 90-day, 6%, $4,000 note dated June 1. The note was discounted at a bank on July 1. The bank discount rate was 6%. Compute the proceeds of the note. Record the discounting of the note.
c. A company received a $3,000, 90-day, 7% note on May 1. The note was discounted at a bank on May 31. The bank discount rate was 6%. Compute the proceeds of the note and record the discounting. What entry is made by the discounter of the note if the note was paid at maturity by the maker?

Problems

P12-1 (Basic entries for accounts and notes)
The Block Company is involved in the following transactions during December 19_6. All sales are made on account and carry terms of 2/10, n/30. Record the transactions in a general journal.

Dec.	2	Sold merchandise to Sun Company for $600.
	3	Sold merchandise to Bond Company for $1,300.
	4	Gave credit to Sun Company for defective merchandise, $200.
	7	Bond Company paid its account.
	8	Sold merchandise to Brue Company for $950.
	10	Sold merchandise to Temp Company for $2,000.
	19	Sun Company paid its account in full.
	22	Accepted a 120-day 10% note receivable from Temp Company for $2,000 in settlement of its account.
	25	Brue Company declared bankruptcy. The account of the Brue Company is considered uncollectible.
	31	The books are closed. The estimated bad debts expense for the year is 3 percent of credit sales, which amounted to $200,000. The Allowance for Doubtful Receivables account has a debit balance on this date of $950.

P12-2 (Bad debts expense adjustment)

Some of the accounts on the trial balance of the Valet Company on December 31, 19_6, show the following balances before adjustments.

	Debit	Credit
Accounts Receivable	300,000	
Allowance for Doubtful Receivables		500
Sales		620,000
Sales Discounts	15,000	
Sales Returns and Allowances	5,000	

Required:

a. Prepare the adjusting entry for bad debts expense, where estimated bad debts expense is 1 percent of accounts receivable.

b. Prepare the adjusting entry for bad debts expense, where estimated bad debts expense is 3 percent of net sales.

c. Prepare the adjusting entry for bad debts expense, where accounts receivable are aged to arrive at an estimated bad debts expense of $6,500.

P12-3 (Discounting and dishonoring a note)

The Helena Company holds a $2,400, 8%, 90-day note dated September 10, which it received from a customer. On September 30, the Helena Company discounts the note at its bank; the bank discount rate is 10%.

Required:

a. Compute the cash proceeds from the discounting of the note.

b. Prepare the journal entry on September 30 to record the discounting of the note.

c. Assume that the maker of the note dishonors the note at maturity, and the Helena Company pays the bank the maturity value of the note plus a $10 protest fee. Prepare any necessary journal entries.

P12-4 (Analyses of allowance for doubtful receivables)

During each of the years 19_6, 19_7, and 19_8, the Buyers Stores have annual sales of $150,000 (all on credit). Expenses ***other than*** bad debts expense amount to $110,000 per year.

a. At the beginning of 19_6, the firm begins its business with the estimate based on industry averages that its bad debts will amount to 3 percent of sales. How much does the firm expect to collect from customers as a result of its first year's business?

b. What is the bad debts expense reported for 19_6?

c. Journalize the December 31, 19_6, adjusting entry for bad debts.

d. What is the net income for 19_6?

e. During 19_6, the company collects $130,000 from customers and identifies and writes off $2,600 of uncollectible accounts. What is the balance of the Accounts Receivable account at the end of 19_6?

f. What is the balance of the Allowance for Doubtful Receivables account on January 1, 19_7?

g. What is the carrying value of accounts receivable on the balance sheet for December 31, 19_6?

h. In 19_7, the company collects $140,000 from customers and writes off $2,000 of uncollectible accounts. What is the balance of the Accounts Receivable account at the end of this year? What is the carrying value of accounts receivable on the balance sheet for December 31, 19_7?

i. In 19_8, the company collects $146,000 from customers and writes off $5,000 of uncollectible accounts. What are the balances of the Accounts Receivable and the Allowance for Doubtful Receivables accounts on January 1, 19_9?

j. In 19_9, an account of $400 that was written off in 19_7 is collected. Journalize the necessary entries. Does this transaction have any impact on the net income for 19_9?

k. On the basis of the company's experience thus far, is its estimate of bad debts expense as 3 percent of sales a realistic one?

P12-5 (Analysis of allowance for doubtful receivables)

Suppose that the Buyers Stores begin business with the estimate that bad debts expense will equal 5 percent of the year-end balance of Accounts Receivable. All other information remains the same as that given in Problem P12-4.

a. Using this method of estimating bad debts, answer parts e through j of Problem P12-4.

b. Compare the validity of the two methods and the two specific estimates against the actual results of operations for the three years.

P12-6 (Note receivable)

On May 1, 19_6, a $2,000, 90-day, 9% note is received in settlement of an account receivable from the Pearl Company.

a. Journalize the receipt of the note.

b. When will the note become due?

c. How much cash should the firm expect to collect when the note is due?

d. If the firm holds the note to maturity, what will be the dollar impact of this transaction on net income?

e. On May 31, 19_6, the note is discounted at the bank at a discount rate of 6%. Calculate the proceeds of the note.

f. Journalize the discounting of the note.

g. At the maturity date, the maker of the note pays. Journalize the necessary entry.

h. How much interest expense will the ***maker*** of the note show on his income statement as a result of this note?

i. How much interest income will the bank show on its books as a result of this note?

j. How much interest income will the firm that discounted the note show on its books as a result of this note?

k. Suppose that the maker had failed to pay the note at maturity. The bank charges the discounting firm a protest fee of $10 in addition to the maturity value of the note. Journalize the payment to the bank.

l. Journalize the entries needed to write off the receivable if it is decided that the maker of the note will never pay the debt.

P12-7 (Note receivable)

When it is closing its books on December 31, 19_6, the Cook Company holds two notes receivable. One is a $2,000, 3-month, 9% note that was received and dated November 1, 19_6. The second is a 6-month, non-interest-bearing note for $4,060 that was received for the sale of merchandise on December 1, 19_6. The merchandise was priced at $4,000, and the second note was recorded by the following journal entry.

Dec. 1	Notes Receivable	4,060	
	Sales		4,000
	Interest Received in Advance		60

Required:

a. Journalize the adjusting entry needed for the first note.
b. Journalize the adjusting entry needed for the second note.
c. How much interest income should be reported on the income statement of the Cook Company for the year 19_6? $402
d. Show the items related to these notes as they should appear on the balance sheet of December 31, 19_6. Include amounts.

P12-8 (Analysis of bad debts expense adjustments)

The following account balances are taken from the general ledger at the end of the year:

Accounts Receivable	$ 50,000
Sales	500,000
Allowance for Doubtful Receivables (debit)	1,000
Sales Discounts	40,000
Sales Returns and Allowances	60,000

Required:

a. Prepare the adjusting entry for bad debts expense where estimated bad debts expense is 10 percent of accounts receivable.
b. Prepare the adjusting entry for bad debts expense where estimated bad debts expense is 2 percent of net sales.
c. Prepare the adjusting entry for bad debts expense where accounts receivable are aged to arrive at an estimated bad debts expense of $10,000.

P12-9 (Accounts receivable analysis)

Record the following transactions in a general journal:

1. Sold merchandise on account to the Bend Company for $10,000, subject to 2/10; n/30.
2. Five days later, gave credit to the Bend Company for $1,000 of merchandise that was defective.
3. Bend Company paid its account within the discount period.
4. Refer to item 3. Assume that Bend Company paid its account after the discount period.

13 Valuation and control of inventory

When you shop for a new car, stereo, or pair of pants, you come into direct contact with perhaps the most critical business problem—the acquisition and disposition of inventory. Problems of inventory valuation and control have perplexed the business community and the accounting profession. This chapter examines many of these problems and describes some of the solutions that have been adopted.

The problems and procedures involved in accounting for inventory are very complex. At this introductory state in your study of accounting, you should avoid getting bogged down in excessive detail. Rather, concentrate on getting an understanding of the range of the inventory problem. Hopefully, an intelligent study of this chapter will help you to attain that objective.

Basic inventory costs and relationships

Inventory is a term used to identify material or merchandise owned by the firm that eventually will be sold to customers in one form or another. Inventory includes three basic categories:

1. items held for sale in the normal course of business (merchandise inventory, or finished goods);
2. goods in the process of production (work in process awaiting completion);
3. material not yet entered into production (raw material).

The inventory of a manufacturing firm normally includes all three of these categories. Generally, only the first category appears in the inventory of a retail or wholesale merchandising firm. A firm that sells only services normally has a limited inventory of items that it consumes or distributes as a part of the services that it renders.

For the typical manufacturing or merchandising firm, inventory represents a major commitment of the firm's resources. Therefore, problems of inventory merit considerable attention in accounting theory and practice. Inventory plays an important role in financial and managerial accounting. It is essential that you understand certain basic inventory concepts and relationships at the outset of our discussion.

The *ending inventory* (or end-of-the-period inventory) is the total carrying value of the material and merchandise in the inventory at the close of an accounting period. This value appears as a current asset on the balance sheet. For many firms, it is the largest item among the current assets. Therefore, it has major impact upon the balance sheet. The ending inventory represents the merchandise available for sale in future accounting periods.

The ending inventory of one period becomes the ***beginning inventory*** (or beginning-of-the-period inventory) for the next period. The ***goods available for sale*** during a period include the beginning inventory and any goods purchased during the period.

Subtraction of the ending inventory (goods left for future sale) from the goods available for sale during the period gives the *cost of goods sold* during the period. Finally, subtraction of the cost of goods sold from the net sales for the period gives the firm's *gross margin* on sales.

Because gross margin normally is the major contribution to income on the income statement of a manufacturing or merchandising firm, we see that beginning and ending inventory have major impact on the income statement. Exhibit 13-1 shows an example of the appearance of items related to inventory on a partial income statement. In this example, purchases are shown at *net* value. This value represents the delivered cost of purchases made during the period, less any purchase discounts and purchase returns and allowances.

Exhibit 13-2 represents the relationship of inventories to the income statement in another form. Observe that

$$\text{Beginning inventory} + \text{Net purchases} = \text{Goods available for sale} = \text{Cost of goods sold} + \text{Ending inventory}$$

The goods available for sale come from two sources: beginning inventory and net purchases. The goods available for sale during the period become cost of goods sold during the period and the ending inventory. In this example, the beginning inventory is known to be $50,000 and the net purchases during the period amount to $300,000. Therefore, the goods available for sale are determined to have a value

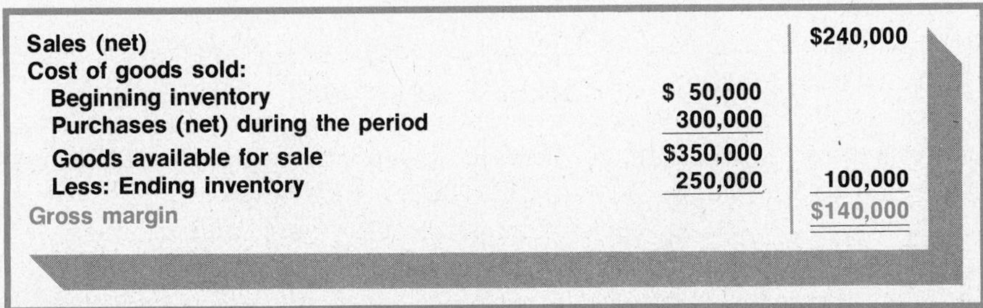

Sales (net)		**$240,000**
Cost of goods sold:		
Beginning inventory	**$ 50,000**	
Purchases (net) during the period	**300,000**	
Goods available for sale	**$350,000**	
Less: Ending inventory	**250,000**	**100,000**
Gross margin		**$140,000**

Exhibit 13-1
Partial income statement showing items related to inventory

Exhibit 13-2 **Relationship of inventories to the income statement**

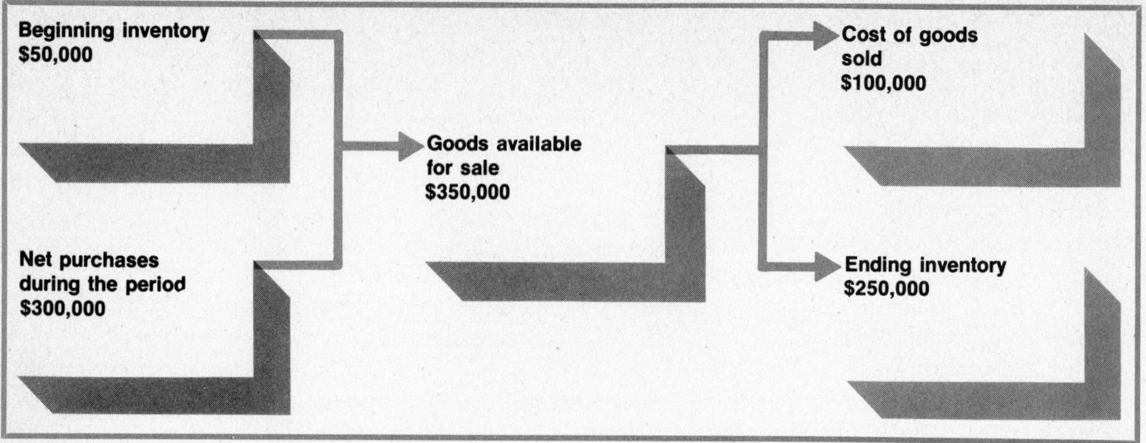

of $350,000. The value of the ending inventory is known to be $250,000. Therefore, the cost of goods sold during the period must be $100,000.

Keep this basic relationship in mind throughout this chapter. Most of the problems that arise in accounting for inventory have to do with the methods used to measure the inventory—ways of counting the items on hand, purchased, or sold, and ways of assigning values to those items. As we discuss these problems, you should be able to see how each fits in the basic relationship and therefore what the impact will be of each method on the financial statements.

ITEMS INCLUDED IN INVENTORY

A company includes in its inventory all merchandise or material intended for sale in the normal course of business and to which it has legal title at the time the inventory is measured. As a general rule, title to inventory passes from seller to buyer when the goods are delivered to the buyer or his agent. If merchandise is in transit from seller to buyer at the inventory date, the merchandise should be included in the inventory of the entity that has legal title to it at that time.

If the seller pays for the transportation of the goods, the carrier is an agent of the seller; the seller retains title to the goods until they are turned over to the buyer. On the other hand, if the buyer pays for the transportation, the carrier acts as an agent of the buyer; the buyer takes title to the goods as soon as they are turned over to the carrier by the seller. The terms of payment for transportation are normally stated on purchase orders, sales tickets, invoices, or other sales documents. The goods are sold F.O.B. ("free on board") a certain location. This means that the seller pays for transportation (and retains title to the goods) only to that point.

Suppose that a company in Los Angeles buys goods from a supplier in Chicago. If the sale is "F.O.B. Chicago," the buyer pays transportation across the country. Title to the goods passes to the buyer as soon as the supplier delivers the goods to a carrier in Chicago. If the goods are in transit across the country on December 31, when the two firms take inventory, the goods in transit will be included in the inventory of the buyer and excluded from the inventory of the seller.

If the sale is "F.O.B. Los Angeles," the supplier pays transportation to the buyer's place of business in Los Angeles. Title passes when the carrier delivers the goods to the buyer. If inventory is taken while the goods are in transit, they are included in the inventory of the seller. The point at which title to the goods changes hands is important, not only for purposes of inventory, but also to determine who is responsible for the goods if they are damaged or destroyed in transit.

To summarize again, items are included in inventory if the firm has legal title to them. When items are bought or sold, title to the goods changes hands from seller to buyer at the point where the seller turns the goods over to the buyer. This point is determined by the location specified after the letters F.O.B. on the sales documents.

Valuation of inventory

The valuation, or costing, of inventory is the first major problem we encounter in our study of inventory. Like other assets, inventory is initially recorded in keeping with the initial recording principle. That is, inventory is recorded at cost in the accounts when it is acquired. Inventory cost includes all expenditures needed to bring the inventory to its present location and condition. Therefore, inventory costs include

1. the invoice cost of the item (less any purchase discounts);
2. transportation charges (that is, freight charges to bring the merchandise to its present location);
3. insurance charges while merchandise is in transit or in storage;
4. import duties and other miscellaneous charges.

NET AND GROSS METHODS OF RECORDING TRANSACTIONS

The accounting system can record purchases of merchandise either at the gross or at the net purchase price. ***Gross*** price is the full invoice cost of the merchandise. ***Net*** price is the gross price less any applicable cash discount.[1] As we have seen, efficient management requires that purchase discounts be taken if available, because they represent substantial savings.

Exhibit 13-3 illustrates the two methods of recording purchase transactions in a case where $1,000 of merchandise is purchased on terms of 2/10, n/30. In this case, the gross price of the merchandise is $1,000. The net price is $1,000 less the 2 percent discount, or $980. The Purchases account accumulates the cost of merchandise bought for resale during the current accounting period.

The net price method of recording purchases has certain advantages over the gross price method. The net method records the purchase at its cost (that is, at the cash-equivalent exchange price when it is acquired). If the company has to pay the full $1,000, the extra $20 above the net price of $980 is a cost of financing the late

1. Purchases often involve ***trade discounts*** as well as cash discounts. A trade discount is a reduction from list price that is offered to purchasers who fit in certain categories—for example, to wholesalers, retailers, libraries, schools, and so on. The gross purchase price is the price ***after*** any applicable trade discounts, but ***before*** any cash discounts. For example, suppose that merchandise with a list price of $1,000 is purchased at $1,000 less trade discounts of 30%–10% and a cash discount of 2%. In this case, the gross and net purchase prices are computed as follows:

$1,000 less 30% = $1,000 − $300 = $700.00;
700 less 10% = 700 − 70 = 630.00 (gross purchase price);
630 less 2% = 630 − 12.60 = 617.40 (net purchase price).

Exhibit 13-3 **Purchase transactions under gross and net methods (Periodic)**

Transaction	Accounts Debited/Credited	Net Method		Gross Method	
Purchase is made on account.	Purchases	980		1,000	
	Accounts Payable		980		1,000
Invoice is paid within the discount period.	Accounts Payable	980		1,000	
	Cash		980		980
	Purchase Discounts		—		20
Invoice is paid after the discount period.	Accounts Payable	980		1,000	
	Purchase Discounts Lost	20		—	
	Cash		1,000		1,000
Adjusting entry at end of period if invoice has not been paid and discount period has lapsed.	Purchase Discounts Lost	20		No Entry	
	Accounts Payable		20		

payment of the bill, not really a part of the cash price of the merchandise. The usefulness of the asset to the firm is not increased by the payment of this sum, which is really a penalty for late payment. Furthermore, since purchase discounts usually are taken, the net price more commonly represents the actual cash expenditure for the merchandise.

With the net method, data about *purchase discounts lost* are recorded in a special expense account. This account gives management attention-getting and control information of some importance; it represents the discounts that were available, but were not taken. Discounts lost should be investigated to determine their cause and to avoid their recurrence. On the income statement, purchase discounts lost appears as a financial administrative expense item. The gross method recognizes purchase discounts if taken. Purchase discounts usually are deducted from purchases on the income statement. Whichever method of recording inventory transactions is used, it should be applied consistently from period to period.

Periodic and perpetual inventory systems

There are two generally accepted methods of accounting for and controlling the quantities of inventory on hand.

1. The *periodic inventory method* requires a count of all the inventory on hand at specific times. This method also is called the *physical inventory* method, because it is based on a physical count of the merchandise or materials at periodic intervals, usually to determine the ending inventory at the close of each accounting period. This method provides a periodic stewardship of the inventory. Little is known about the exact content of the inventory between counts. Items in the beginning inventory or purchased during the period, but not found on hand in the physical count at the end of the period, are presumed to have been sold. (Exhibit 13-3 shows basic accounting entries when the periodic inventory method is used.)
2. The *perpetual inventory method* requires continuous record keeping of all inflows and outflows of inventory items. Under this method, the inventory account is continuously updated with each purchase or sale transaction. This method pro-

vides a continuous stewardship of the inventory. This method is sometimes called the ***continuous inventory,*** or ***book inventory*** method. When this method is used, a physical count of the entire inventory (or of a sample of it) usually is undertaken at least once each year to see whether the book inventory equals the physical inventory. If a discrepancy appears, the books are adjusted. The perpetual method of controlling and accounting for inventory is generally considered superior to the periodic inventory method, because it maintains a continuous record of inventory acquisitions, disposals, and balances throughout the year.

The journal entries needed to record purchases and sales of inventory depend on

1. whether purchases are recorded at their gross or net cost; and
2. whether the periodic or perpetual inventory method is used.

In the preceding section we looked at the differences between gross and net methods. Now we look at differences between periodic and perpetual inventory methods. For the time being, we use the gross method of recording purchases, so that we can concentrate upon the differences between periodic and perpetual inventory methods.

PERIODIC INVENTORY METHOD

Under the periodic inventory method, the balance in the Inventory account remains unchanged throughout the accounting period. This balance shows the beginning inventory, as determined by the physical count at the close of the preceding period. Acquisitions and disposals of inventory during the period are not processed through the Inventory account. The account is adjusted only at the end of the period when a new physical count is made.

When merchandise is purchased, the addition to inventory is recorded in a Purchases account. Any transportation charges paid to bring the inventory purchased F.O.B. shipping point to the firm's premises are recorded in a Transportation-In (or Freight-In) account. The following are some typical journal entries recording purchases of merchandise for inventory when the periodic inventory method is used (see also Exhibit 13-3).

Purchases	10,000	
Accounts Payable: Supplier Co.		10,000
To record purchase of merchandise on account.		
Purchases	10,000	
Cash		10,000
To record purchase of merchandise for cash.		
Transportation-In	500	
Accounts Payable: Freight Co.		500
To record freight charge on merchandise shipped F.O.B. shipping point; on account.		
Transportation-In	500	
Cash		500
To record freight charges on merchandise shipped F.O.B. shipping point; cash paid.		
Accounts Payable: Supplier Co.	500	
Cash		500
To record cash payment of freight charges on merchandise shipped F.O.B. our warehouse; liability to supplier reduced.		

In the last transaction, the firm paid some freight charges that were the responsibility of the supplier. The amount is debited against the liability to the supplier, because these freight charges were included in the invoice price for the merchandise.

As discussed in the preceding section (see Exhibit 13-3), purchase discounts are recorded in a Purchase Discounts account at the time when payment is made on account within the discount period.

If the firm receives defective, damaged, or unwanted merchandise, it applies to the supplier for authorization to return the merchandise for credit against its debt to the supplier. When authorization is received and the merchandise shipped back, a journal entry must be made.

Accounts Payable: Supplier Co.	35,000	
Purchase Returns and Allowances		35,000
To record authorized return of $35,000 merchandise damaged in transit.		

The Purchase Returns and Allowances account is used to keep track of (and hopefully minimize) these costly and inconvenient problems. This account is a contra Purchases account.

When a sale is made and merchandise leaves the inventory, an entry is made to record the revenue. However, no entry is made at this time to recognize the disposal of merchandise from the inventory.

Accounts Receivable: Customer Co. [or Cash]	15,000	
Sales		15,000
To record sale of merchandise on account [or for cash].		

The cost of goods sold is computed and recorded at the end of the period (when the physical inventory is taken) through adjusting entries. This procedure is discussed in a later section of this chapter.

If a customer applies for authorization to return defective, damaged, or unwanted merchandise, an entry must be made when the authorization is granted.

Sales Returns and Allowances	5,000	
Accounts Receivable: Customer Co.		5,000
To record authorization of sales return and allowance.		

The Sales Returns and Allowances is a contra Sales account, used for management information and control purposes.

To summarize, the periodic inventory method (used with the gross pricing method for purchases) provides the following items of merchandise costs during the period for managerial information, control, and analysis:

1. invoice cost of purchases (Purchases account);
2. freight cost of purchases (Transportation-In account);
3. amount of purchase discounts taken (Purchase Discounts account);
4. amount of purchase returns and allowances (Purchase Returns and Allowances account).

Exhibit 13-4 shows a partial income statement prepared using the periodic inventory and gross pricing methods.

Exhibit 13-4 Partial income statement prepared using gross pricing and periodic inventory methods

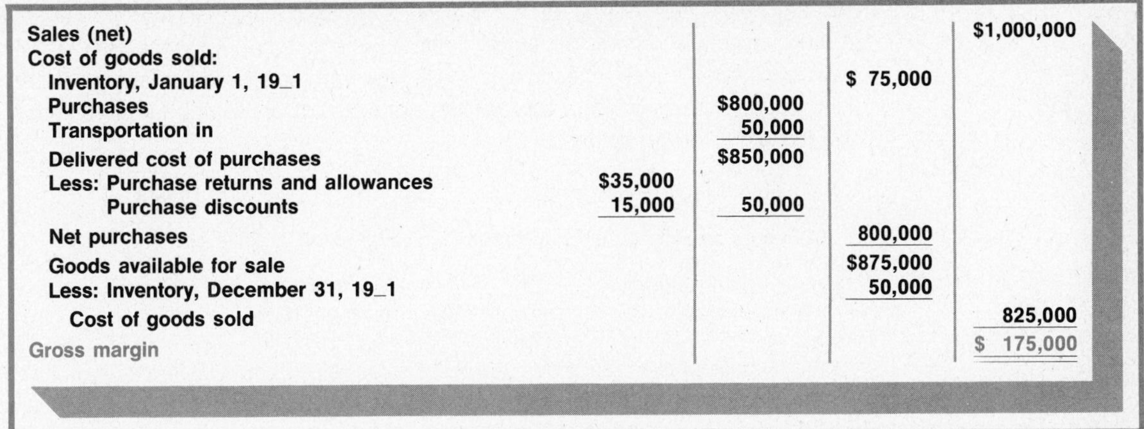

Sales (net)				**$1,000,000**
Cost of goods sold:				
Inventory, January 1, 19_1			**$ 75,000**	
Purchases		**$800,000**		
Transportation in		**50,000**		
Delivered cost of purchases		**$850,000**		
Less: Purchase returns and allowances	**$35,000**			
Purchase discounts	**15,000**	**50,000**		
Net purchases			**800,000**	
Goods available for sale			**$875,000**	
Less: Inventory, December 31, 19_1			**50,000**	
Cost of goods sold				**825,000**
Gross margin				**$ 175,000**

PERPETUAL INVENTORY METHOD

Under the perpetual inventory method, each purchase of merchandise is recorded as an increase in the Merchandise Inventory (or Inventory) account. Transportation-in costs are recorded as additions to inventory.

Merchandise Inventory	10,000	
Accounts Payable: Supplier Co.		10,000
To record purchase of merchandise on account.		
Merchandise Inventory	500	
Cash		500
To record payment of freight-in on merchandise shipped F.O.B. shipping point.		

When the gross method of recording purchases is used with the perpetual inventory method, purchase discounts taken are credited to the Inventory account rather than to a separate Purchase Discounts account. For example, suppose that the $10,000 owed to the Supplier Company for the purchase just recorded is paid with a 2 percent cash discount. The payment is recorded by the following entry.

Accounts Payable: Supplier Co.	10,000	
Cash		9,800
Merchandise Inventory		200
To record payment of account with 2% cash discount.		

The effect of this entry is to reduce the value added to the Inventory account at the time of purchase to correspond to the cash actually paid. (If the net pricing method were used, the Purchase Discounts Lost account would be ***debited*** whenever a purchase discount is ***not*** taken.)

Similarly an authorized purchase return and allowance is recorded by a direct credit to the Inventory account when the perpetual inventory method is used.

Accounts Payable: Supplier Co.	35,000	
Merchandise Inventory		35,000
To record an authorized purchase return.		

Under the perpetual inventory method, no separate account is kept for purchase returns and allowances.

When goods are sold, the inventory value can be reduced by the cost of the goods sold. The cost of goods sold can be readily determined under this method from the perpetual inventory records (illustrated later in the chapter). Two entries are needed under this method to record each sale: (1) a sales entry to record the revenue aspect of the transaction; and (2) a cost expiration entry to transfer the value of merchandise from inventory to cost of goods sold.

Accounts Receivable: Customer Co.	15,000	
Sales		15,000
To record sale of 100 units @ $150/unit selling price.		
Cost of Goods Sold	7,000	
Merchandise Inventory		7,000
To record cost of 100 units sold @ $70/unit cost price.		

If a customer applies for and is granted a sales return and allowance, two entries again are needed: (1) a sales entry to record the allowance in a contra Sales account; and (2) an entry to transfer the cost of the merchandise from cost of goods sold back into inventory.

Sales Returns and Allowances	4,500	
Accounts Receivable: Customer Co.		4,500
To record authorization of sales return and allowance (30 units @ $150/unit selling price).		
Merchandise Inventory	2,100	
Cost of Goods Sold		2,100
To return to inventory merchandise returned by Customer Co. and reduce cost of goods sold recorded at time of sale (30 units @ $70/unit cost price).		

Under the perpetual inventory method, all information about costs assigned to inventory is accumulated in the Merchandise Inventory account. Invoice and freight costs are debited to this account; purchase discounts taken (when the gross method was used) and purchase returns and allowances are credited to the Merchandise Inventory account, as are the costs of goods sold. Therefore, the balance of the Merchandise Inventory account throughout the period represents the cost of the inventory on hand at any particular moment.

Under this system, the cost of goods sold is shown by the balance of the Cost of Goods Sold account, so this item is measured directly and can be reported on the income statement rather than computed there. A partial income statement prepared using the perpetual inventory method can take the following form.

Sales (net)	$1,000,000
Less: Cost of goods sold	825,000
Gross margin	$ 175,000

Note that the value of inventory on hand is shown continuously by the balance of the Merchandise Inventory account under this method. The only reason for taking a physical count of the inventory is to make sure that the records are accurate. For example, such a count would detect any unauthorized removals of merchandise from the inventory and any damaged or obsolete inventory items.

Assigning cost to inventory items

The net and gross pricing methods provide ways of accounting for the value of merchandise purchased and added to the inventory. The periodic and perpetual inventory systems provide techniques for controlling the quantities of inventory. However, a very important valuation problem still remains. Some method must be used to assign dollar costs to particular items of the inventory for accounting purposes at the close of each period or at the time of a sale.

If prices never changed, no problem would arise. When 10 units of item A are sold, we would know the unchanging acquisition price of a unit of item A and could easily determine the cost of goods sold. Or if we are using the periodic inventory method, we could easily determine the value of 100 units of item A in the inventory. However, in practice, prices are constantly changing. Purchases of item A may have been made several times during the period at different prices. How do we decide what cost to assign to the units of item A that were sold and what cost to assign to the units that remain in inventory?

The method of valuation selected should be that method that provides the best measure of net income. Several different methods are generally accepted for assigning costs to inventory items. Each method involves an assumption about the ***flow of goods*** through the inventory. Whichever method is adopted, it must be applied consistently both within a period and from one period to the next.

The more common methods of assigning cost to inventory include the following.

1. *Specific identification method.* Each item is individually identified and a record kept of its actual cost; the actual flow of goods is monitored and recorded exactly.
2. *First-in, first-out (FIFO) method.* The flow of goods is assumed to be such that the oldest items in the inventory are sold or used first.
3. *Last-in, first-out (LIFO) method.* The flow of goods is assumed to be such that the items most recently purchased are sold or used first.
4. *Weighted average method.* The flow of goods is assumed to be such that all items available for sale during the period are intermingled randomly, and items sold or used are picked randomly from this intermingled inventory.
5. *Moving average method.* The flow of goods is assumed to be such that the items in the inventory are intermingled randomly after each addition to the inventory; items sold or used are picked randomly from those items in the inventory at the time.

The choice of which method to use may be made because there is reason to believe that the flow of goods through a particular firm's inventory closely matches one of these assumptions. More importantly, however, the chosen method should be the one that gives the fairest presentation of the firm's net income. The advantages and disadvantages of each method are discussed in the following pages.

To illustrate these five cost-assigning inventory procedures, we will apply each of them to the same example. The Merchandising Company is involved in the following transactions during 19_1 that affect its inventory.

Jan. 1 Inventory on hand of 1,000 units that cost $1 per unit.
Mar. 7 Purchase of 6,000 units for cost of $9,000.
Apr. 2 Sale of 2,000 units.
July 4 Purchase of 3,500 units for cost of $7,000.
Oct. 8 Sale of 500 units.

Exhibit 13-5 shows a schedule summarizing the effects of these transactions on the inventory. The problem is that of dividing the $17,000 cost of the units available for sale between the 2,500 units sold and the 8,000 units on hand in the ending inventory.

SPECIFIC IDENTIFICATION METHOD

If sales of merchandise can be identified with (or traced to) specific purchase transactions, the specific identification method can be used to provide satisfactory cost data for the ending inventory and cost of goods sold.

For example, assume that the Merchandising Company keeps careful records of each unit in its inventory. These records show that the 2,000 units sold on April 2 came from the group of units purchased on March 7, and that the 500 units sold on October 8 came from the group of units on hand in the beginning inventory.

If the company is using the perpetual inventory method, the cost of goods sold can be determined from these records at the time of sale. Subtract cost of goods sold ($3,500) from goods available for sale ($17,000) to get ending inventory ($13,500).

2,000 units sold April 2 @ cost of $1.50/unit	$3,000
500 units sold October 8 @ cost of $1/unit	500
2,500 units sold at cost of	$3,500

If the company is using the periodic inventory method, the value of the ending inventory can be determined from these records when the count is taken at the end of the year.

500 units on hand from beginning inventory @ cost of $1/unit	$ 500
4,000 units on hand from March 7 purchase @ cost of $1.50/unit	6,000
3,500 units on hand from July 4 purchase @ cost of $2/unit	7,000
8,000 units on hand at cost of	$13,500

The cost assigned to ending inventory and to cost of goods sold is the same, whether the company uses the periodic or the perpetual inventory method. With the perpetual method, the $3,500 cost of goods sold is deducted from the Merchandise

Exhibit 13-5
Schedule of Merchandising Company's inventory transactions

Opening inventory	**1,000 units @ $1 per unit**	**$ 1,000**
March 7 purchase	**6,000 units @ $1.50 per unit**	**9,000**
July 4 purchase	**3,500 units @ $2 per unit**	**7,000**
Units available for sale	10,500 units	$17,000
Units sold:		
April 2 sale	**2,000 units**	
October 8 sale	**500 units**	
Units sold	2,500 units	
Units available for sale	**10,500 units**	
Less: Units sold	**2,500 units**	
Ending inventory	8,000 units	

Inventory account during the year, and the account shows a final balance of $13,500. With the periodic method, the computed $13,500 ending inventory is subtracted from the $17,000 cost of goods available for sale (Exhibit 13-5), giving a value for cost of goods sold for $3,500.

The advantage of the specific identification method is that it does measure accurately and fairly the actual acquisition cost of each item that is sold or remaining in inventory. On the other hand, strange as it may seem at first, this accurate reporting may not give the fairest picture of the firm's income for the year. For example, suppose that the warehouse staff had happened to fill the October 8 sale with units that came from the July 4 purchase. In this case, the cost of goods sold would be increased by $500, and the net income of the firm for the year would be correspondingly decreased. Is it fair to use a method of accounting in which a decision about which specific item is being sold can significantly affect the net income reported for the year?

The specific identification method has another disadvantage. It requires detailed records that may not be practical or even possible for some businesses. For example, when a gasoline station purchases more gasoline for its inventory, the new fuel is pumped into a storage tank and mixes with the fuel already on hand. There is no way to identify the particular source of the fuel being pumped into a customer's automobile.

This method is most commonly used by firms handling expensive items of merchandise (television sets, automobiles, and so on) that are identified normally by serial numbers on purchase and sales records. In these cases, there usually is a systematic policy that associates purchases with sales, so that random choices from the inventory do not significantly affect the net income.

FIRST-IN, FIRST-OUT (FIFO) METHOD

FIFO costing assumes that the first item purchased is the first item sold. That is, the oldest merchandise in the inventory is sold first, and all goods are sold in the order in which they were acquired. Therefore, the units on hand in inventory at the end of the period are assumed to have been acquired in the most recent purchases. And the cost of goods sold represents the cost of items acquired in the earliest purchases. These assumptions correspond to the actual physical flow of merchandise through the inventories of many firms. For example, a grocery store makes every effort to see that it sells its oldest merchandise first.

FIFO PERIODIC METHOD. Under the FIFO periodic method, the inventory on hand at the end of the year is priced as follows.

3,500 units from purchase of July 4 @ cost of $2/unit	$ 7,000
4,500 units from purchase of March 7 @ cost of $1.50/unit	6,750
8,000 units on hand at cost of	$13,750

Because goods available for sale totalled $17,000, the cost of goods sold is computed to be $17,000 − $13,750 = $3,250.

FIFO PERPETUAL METHOD. Under the FIFO perpetual method, a detailed record of the inflow and outflow of merchandise is maintained in a subsidiary record.

Exhibit 13-6 **FIFO perpetual inventory record for the Merchandising Company**

DATE	RECEIVED			SOLD			INVENTORY BALANCE		
19_1	Quantity	Unit Cost	Total Cost	Quantity	Unit Cost	Total Cost	Quantity	Unit Cost	Total Cost
Jan. 2							1,000	1.00	1,000
Mar. 7	6,000	1.50	9,000				1,000 6,000	1.00 1.50	1,000 9,000
Apr. 2				1,000 1,000	1.00 1.50	1,000 1,500	5,000	1.50	7,500
July 4	3,500	2.00	7,000				5,000 3,500	1.50 2.00	7,500 7,000
Oct. 1				500	1.50	750	4,500 3,500	1.50 2.00	6,750 7,000

This record shows quantities, unit costs, and total costs of merchandise for each purchase or sale. Exhibit 13-6 shows the inventory record for our example. (In practice, a record of this kind would be kept for each different kind of item that the company buys and sells.)

The record shows that the inventory on hand at the end of the year consists of 4,500 units @ $1.50/unit and 3,500 units @ $2/unit. Therefore, the valuation of the ending inventory ($13,750) is the same as that computed by the FIFO periodic method. From the sales entries in this record, you can see that costs of $3,250 were charged to the cost of goods sold during the period. This would be the ending balance of the Cost of Goods Sold account.

ADVANTAGES AND DISADVANTAGES. The FIFO method does correspond to actual flow of goods in many firms. However, when prices are constantly rising, it has the effect of giving the lowest possible value to the cost of goods sold (inventory acquired at the early, lower prices) and the highest possible value to the ending inventory (inventory acquired at later, higher prices). This has the effect of giving the highest possible net income (an inventory profit!) for the period and the greatest possible value for the current asset of inventory. This may result in a picture of the firm's financial position that is somewhat more favorable than is really justified. Similarly, in a period of falling prices the effects of deflation are exaggerated by this method to give the lowest possible values for net income and inventory on hand.

One advantage of this method is that the value given for inventory does represent the most recent prices paid, so that it is a fair estimate of the cost of replacing the inventory at current market prices as it is used up in future operations.

LAST-IN, FIRST-OUT (LIFO) METHOD

Under LIFO costing, the most recent units purchased are assumed to be the first units sold. Therefore, the goods sold are assumed to come from the most recent purchases, and the ending inventory is assumed to have come from the earliest purchases.

LIFO PERIODIC METHOD. Using LIFO periodic method, we assume that the 8,000 units in the ending inventory came from the earliest purchases.

1,000 units from opening inventory @ $1/unit	$ 1,000
6,000 units from purchase of March 7 @ $1.50/unit	9,000
1,000 units from purchase of July 4 @ $2/unit	2,000
8,000 units on hand at a cost of	$12,000

Because goods available for sale totaled $17,000, the cost of goods sold is computed to be $17,000 − $12,000 = $5,000.

LIFO PERPETUAL METHOD. Under the LIFO perpetual method, a detailed record is kept of the inflow and outflow of merchandise (Exhibit 13-7). This is similar to the record kept with the FIFO perpetual method, but this time each sale is considered to come from the most recently purchased items in the inventory. From this record, we compute the value of the ending inventory to be

1,000 units from opening inventory @ $1/unit	$ 1,000
4,000 units from purchase of March 7 @ $1.50/unit	6,000
3,000 units from purchase of July 4 @ $2/unit	6,000
8,000 units on hand at a cost of	$13,000

The total cost of goods sold (recorded at the time of each sale) is $4,000.

Note that the LIFO periodic and LIFO perpetual methods give different results in this example. This is because the April 2 sale must be filled in the perpetual method from units actually in the inventory at that time. Under the periodic method, we were able to assume that the April 2 sale was filled from the July 4 purchase.

ADVANTAGES AND DISADVANTAGES. The impact of the LIFO method on many accounting problems is the opposite of that of the FIFO method. In times of rising prices, LIFO costing tends to give the lowest possible values for net income

Exhibit 13-7 **LIFO perpetual inventory record for the Merchandising Company**

DATE	RECEIVED			SOLD			INVENTORY BALANCE		
19_1	Quantity	Unit Cost	Total Cost	Quantity	Unit Cost	Total Cost	Quantity	Unit Cost	Total Cost
Jan. 2							1,000	1.00	1,000
Mar. 7	6,000	1.50	9,000				1,000 6,000	1.00 1.50	1,000 9,000
Apr. 2				2,000	1.50	3,000	1,000 4,000	1.00 1.50	1,000 6,000
July 4	3,500	2.00	7,000				1,000 4,000 3,500	1.00 1.50 2.00	1,000 6,000 7,000
Oct. 8				500	2.00	1,000	1,000 4,000 3,000	1.00 1.50 2.00	1,000 6,000 6,000

and for inventory on hand. This method is often used because it minimizes the reported income, and therefore the income taxes to be paid. It can be argued that this method effectively minimizes the distortions caused by inflation and deflation, giving a more consistent long-run picture of the firm's operations. Also, this method matches the income from each sale with the cost of the most recent inventory purchases—in effect, regarding the cost of a sale as the current cost of replacing the item sold. On the other hand, it can result in a serious understatement of the current market value of the inventory on hand as reported in the balance sheet.

WEIGHTED AVERAGE METHOD

The weighted average method of costing inventory is used only with the periodic inventory method. The weighted average cost per unit is computed according to the following formula:

$$\frac{\text{Beginning inventory} + \text{Purchases}}{\text{Units in beginning inventory} + \text{Units purchased}} = \text{Average cost per unit}$$

The value of the ending inventory is computed by multiplying the number of units on hand (from the physical count) by the weighted average cost per unit.

From Exhibit 13-5, we obtain the data needed to compute the average cost per unit in our example:

$$\text{Average cost per unit} = \frac{\$1{,}000 + \$16{,}000}{1{,}000 + 9{,}500} = \frac{\$17{,}000}{10{,}500} = \$1.619.$$

Therefore, the 8,000 units in the ending inventory have a value of

$$8{,}000 \text{ units} \times \$1.619 \text{ per unit} = \$12{,}952.$$

Subtracting this value of ending inventory from the $17,000 value of goods available for sale, we obtain $4,048 as the cost of goods sold during the year.

In effect, the weighted average method assumes that all items available for sale during the year were acquired at an average price, and that all items sold had this same average cost. Because this weighted average is computed from the totals of the information at the end of the period, it is not a suitable method for use with perpetual inventory procedures. (There is no way under this method to compute the cost of goods sold at the time of the sale, as required for the journal entries under the perpetual method.)

In its general effect, the weighted average gives a middle course between the effects of FIFO periodic and LIFO periodic methods. Therefore, this method has neither the strong advantages nor the strong disadvantages of those methods.

MOVING AVERAGE METHOD

The moving average method of costing inventory is used only with the perpetual inventory method. Under this method, an average cost per unit for the items in the inventory is computed after each purchase. This computation is made according to the following formula:

$$\frac{\text{Total cost of inventory on hand after each purchase}}{\text{Total number of units in inventory on hand after each purchase}} = \text{Average cost per unit.}$$

Exhibit 13-8 **Moving average perpetual inventory record for the Merchandising Company**

DATE	RECEIVED			SOLD			INVENTORY BALANCE		
19_1	Quantity	Unit Cost	Total Cost	Quantity	Unit Cost	Total Cost	Quantity	Unit Cost	Total Cost
Jan. 2							1,000	1.000	1,000.00
Mar. 7	6,000	1.50	9,000.00				7,000	1.4287	10,000.00
Apr. 2				2,000	1.4287	2,857.40	5,000	1.4287	7,142.60
July 4	3,500	2.00	7,000.00				8,500	1.6636	14,142.60
Oct. 8				500	1.6636	831.80	8,000	1.6636	13,310.80

Exhibit 13-8 shows the perpetual inventory record for the example, with the balance of the inventory valued according to this method. Note that the cost of sale is computed according to the current average cost per unit for the inventory on hand at that time.

As an example of the computations needed, consider the purchase on March 7. After this purchase, the inventory balance contains 7,000 units acquired at a total cost of $10,000. Therefore, the moving average cost per unit is

$10,000/7,000 units = $1.4287/unit.

When the sale is made on April 2, the cost of the goods sold is computed from this average unit cost:

2,000 units × $1.4287/unit = $2,857.40.

At the end of the year, the balance columns of the record show a value for the ending inventory of $13,310.80. The total of the sales columns shows a cost of goods sold of $3,689.20. The accuracy of the computations is confirmed by summing these two numbers and showing that they do agree with the value of goods available for sale:

$13,310.80 + $3,689.20 = $17,000.00.

The moving average method gives a middle course between the extremes of FIFO perpetual and LIFO perpetual methods. Therefore, this method avoids both the strong disadvantages and the strong advantages of those two methods.

IMPACT OF COSTING METHODS

Exhibit 13-9 summarizes the results of applying each of the five costing methods to the example of the Merchandising Company. Note that in each case, the sum of Cost of Goods Sold and Ending Inventory is equal to $17,000, or Goods Available for Sale. In other words, the effect of using the different methods is to give different distributions of the total cost of goods available for sale between the values of the goods sold and of the goods on hand in ending inventory.

The impact of the specific identification, weighted average, and moving average methods varies with the details of the particular example to which they are applied. However, it is possible to make some general statements about the impact of the FIFO and LIFO methods, which tend to give extreme results for the division of cost

Exhibit 13-9
Results of using different inventory costing methods on 19_1 transactions of the Merchandising Company

Inventory Costing Method	Cost of Goods Sold	Ending Inventory
Specific identification method	$3,500	$13,500
FIFO periodic method	3,250	13,750
FIFO perpetual method	3,250	13,750
LIFO periodic method	5,000	12,000
LIFO perpetual method	4,000	13,000
Weighted average method	4,048	12,952
Moving average method	3,689.20	13,310.80

between goods sold and goods on hand. In studying the following summary, pay special attention to the statement on which costs approximate current market costs.

1. Effects of FIFO and LIFO methods on the income statement:
   a. *Sales* under both FIFO and LIFO are presented at current market prices.
   b. *Cost of sales:*
      (1) under LIFO is shown at current market prices if the inventory is being frequently replenished;
      (2) under FIFO is shown at oldest market prices among items in inventory, so that costs tend to fluctuate widely depending on how often inventory is replenished; in times of rising prices, cost is shown at values lower than current market prices.
   c. *Conclusion:* LIFO on the income statement tends to give a better matching of current sales with current cost of replacing the items sold than does FIFO.
2. Effect on balance sheet:
   a. *Inventory,* a current asset:
      (1) under LIFO is shown at an earlier or older market price;
      (2) under FIFO is shown at current market price, if the inventory is being frequently replenished.
   b. *Conclusion:* FIFO tends to give a more current balance sheet than does LIFO, because the current asset of inventory is carried at a more realistic current valuation.
3. In a period of rising prices (inflation), the use of FIFO or LIFO methods tends to have the impacts shown in Exhibit 13-10. In a period of falling prices (deflation), the reverse of these impacts would be reflected in the financial statements.

Exhibit 13-10
Impact of FIFO and LIFO inventory costing methods on financial statement items in times of rising prices

Classification	Inventory Costing Method	
	FIFO	LIFO
Ending inventory	Higher	Lower
Current assets	Higher	Lower
Working capital	Higher	Lower
Total assets	Higher	Lower
Cost of sales	Lower	Higher
Gross margin	Higher	Lower
Net income	Higher	Lower
Taxable income	Higher	Lower
Income taxes payable	Higher	Lower

Lower-of-cost-or-market inventory costing

The costing procedures discussed thus far (specific identification, FIFO, LIFO, weighted average, and moving average) are ***cost methods*** of valuing inventory. Their effect is simply to vary the distribution of acquisition cost among the units sold and the units on hand. However, if the ***utility*** of the inventory (its current value to the company) is less than its acquisition cost, it is usually considered proper to price the inventory at its lower market value. The American Institute of Certified Public Accountants recommends that there be

> a departure from the cost basis of pricing the inventory when the utility of the goods is no longer as great as its cost. When there is evidence that the utility of goods, in their disposal in the ordinary course of business, will be less than cost, whether due to physical deterioration, obsolescence, change in price levels, or other causes, the difference should be recognized as a loss of the current period. This is generally accomplished by stating such goods at a lower level commonly designated as *market*.[2]

In the phrase "lower of cost or market," the term ***market*** means current replacement cost (by purchase or by reproduction).

When the lower-of-cost-or-market method is applied to the valuation of inventory, the application of this method can follow any one of three different procedures, or methods:

1. the item-by-item method (the most conservative method);
2. the inventory category method;
3. the total inventory method.

Exhibit 13-11 shows the application of these three procedures or methods to a specific inventory example.

Exhibit 13-11 Three different methods of applying the lower-of-cost-or-market valuation method to an inventory example

Item	Quantity	Unit Cost	Unit Market	Total Cost	Total Market	Lower of Cost or Market: Item-by-Item	Lower of Cost or Market: by Category	Lower of Cost or Market: Total Inventory
A	10	$50	$80	$ 500	$ 800	$ 500		
B	20	60	50	1,200	1,000	1,000		
C	30	70	70	2,100	2,100	2,100		
Men's Clothing Category				$ 3,800	$ 3,900		$ 3,800	
X	40	80	80	$ 3,200	$ 3,200	3,200		
Y	50	90	80	4,500	4,000	4,000		
Women's Clothing Category				$ 7,700	$ 7,200		7,200	
Total Inventory				$11,500	$11,100	$10,800	$11,000	$11,100

2. *Accounting Research Bulletin No. 43* (New York: American Institute of Certified Public Accountants, Accounting Research and Terminology Bulletins, 1961), p. 30.

When each item is valued at lower of cost or market, the total value for the inventory is $10,800. When cost and market are totalled for each category, and then the lower of those two totals is taken as the value of the category, the total value of the inventory is $11,000. When cost and market are totalled for the whole inventory, and then the lower of those totals is taken as the value of inventory, the value obtained is $11,100.

The item-by-item method will give the lowest and most conservative value for the inventory, because the lowest appropriate value is assigned to each item. The total inventory method usually gives the highest value for the inventory, because some items usually will be priced at the higher of market or cost. The category method gives results that fall between these two extremes.

The lower-of-cost-or-market method of costing inventory is a departure from the principle of carrying assets at cost value. The use of this method is justified by the argument that, where the market value of inventory items has decreased, the later selling price of the items also will decrease. Therefore, the most conservative picture of financial condition is given by carrying the inventory items at their current market values if these are lower than cost. The lower-of-cost-or-market method recognizes the loss in the period during which the value of the inventory falls, by writing down the value of the inventory to the lower market value.

However, the assumption that lower market value will mean lower selling prices is not always valid. It is not uncommon for retail prices to remain high for some time after a decline in wholesale prices. In such cases, the use of lower-of-cost-or-market costing for inventory may have the effect of shifting income from the period in which it is earned (because an expense for loss in value of inventory is deducted) to the following period (when sales prices do not decline as expected).

Various accounting procedures can be used to adjust the value of the inventory on the books from cost to a lower market. To illustrate one method, assume that an inventory with a cost of $90,000 declines to a lower-of-cost-or-market value of $80,000 at the close of an accounting period. To recognize the loss and to write down the value of the inventory, the following adjusting entry can be made (using a contra Inventory account).

Dec. 31	Loss in Reduction of Inventory to Lower of Cost or Market	10,000	
	Reduction of Inventory to Lower of Cost or Market		10,000

The debit is to an operating expense account; the credit is to the contra Inventory account. On the balance sheet, the inventory would be listed as follows.

Current assets:		
Inventory, at cost	$90,000	
Less: Reduction of inventory to lower of cost or market	10,000	$80,000

On the income statement, the loss in reduction of inventory is disclosed as an adjustment of the gross margin.

Sales	$500,000
Cost of goods sold	300,000
Gross margin	$200,000
Loss on reduction of inventory to lower of cost or market	10,000
Gross margin less inventory loss	$190,000
Operating expenses and income taxes	160,000
Net income	$30,000

Estimating inventory costs

Accountants have developed various methods of ***estimating*** inventory costs. Estimating methods can be used:

1. when inventory has been destroyed partially or wholly by fire, flood, or other calamity, and it is necessary to estimate inventory and cost of goods sold for the financial statement (and for purposes of claiming insurance benefits on the lost merchandise);
2. when inventory cost data is needed for interim financial statements, and a physical inventory count would be too expensive or inconvenient;
3. when there is some reason to use an independent means to test the inventory valuation of management (for example, when an independent auditor is evaluating the reasonableness of the procedures used by the accounting system).

GROSS PROFIT METHOD

The gross profit method of estimating inventory can be used only if the company's gross profit rate (gross margin/sales) is known or obtainable and if this percentage is relatively stable from period to period. The following steps are used in this method of estimation.

1. Obtain the firm's gross profit rate from past (historical) experience. Obtain information about sales and gross margin for at least the three preceding years. Compute the gross profit rate for each year and for the totals over the three-year period. If the rate for each year is relatively close to the rate for the total period, this method can be used with confidence. If the rates vary significantly from the rate for the total period, this method should not be used.
2. Apply the gross profit rate to current sales to obtain the estimated gross profit for the current period.
3. Deduct the estimated gross profit derived in step 2 from sales to obtain estimated cost of goods sold.
4. Deduct the cost of goods sold derived in step 3 from goods available for sale (that is, opening inventory plus net purchases) to obtain an estimate of the ending inventory.

An example should help clarify this method.

Example. Historical records show that the gross profit rate of the Estimation Company is relatively stable and averages 30 percent of sales. Sales for January 19_1 were $500,000; beginning inventory for 19_1 was $180,000; net purchases during January total $420,000. The company accountant wishes to compute an estimate of the inventory on hand at the end of January.

The computation of the estimated ending inventory can be carried out according to the steps just described.

1. The historical gross profit rate is 30 percent and is stable.
2. Estimated gross profit for January is $500,000 × 0.30 = $150,000.
3. Estimated cost of goods sold in January is $500,000 − $150,000 = $350,000.
4. Goods available for sale in January total $180,000 + $420,000 = $600,000. Estimated ending inventory is $600,000 − $350,000 = $250,000.

In schedule form, we can present the computation in this way.

Inventory, January 1, 19_1		$180,000
Purchases (net)		420,000
Goods available for sale		$600,000
Less: Estimated cost of goods sold:		
Sales	$500,000	
Less: Estimated gross profit	150,000	350,000
Estimated inventory, January 31, 19_1		$250,000

Exhibit 13-12 shows another presentation of the same calculation, using the conventional income-statement format.

If the gross profit rate is given as a percentage of cost (instead of sales), the rate can be converted to a percentage of sales by the following formula:

$$\frac{\text{Rate as a percentage of cost}}{100\% + \text{Rate as a percentage of cost}}$$

RETAIL INVENTORY METHOD

The ***retail inventory*** method is another procedure that can be used to estimate inventory on a specific date. If can be used

1. to estimate inventory without taking a physical count; or
2. to estimate inventory from a physical count in which the merchandise is valued at listed retail prices marked on the merchandise.

The second situation often arises in a retail sales operation. It is easiest to take the physical count of goods on hand in a store in terms of the retail selling prices marked on the goods. In such a case, the inventory value expressed in selling prices must be converted to an inventory at cost (or at lower of cost or market). Many businesses such as grocery and department stores routinely use the retail inventory method to determine the inventory on the shelves in their stores.

In order to estimate ending inventory by the retail inventory method, the following information must be available: (1) beginning inventory at cost and at retail; (2) net purchases during the period at cost and at retail; and (3) sales for the period (at retail, of course). The computation for the estimate can be summarized in the following steps.

Exhibit 13-12 **Solution of estimated inventory problem in income-statement format**

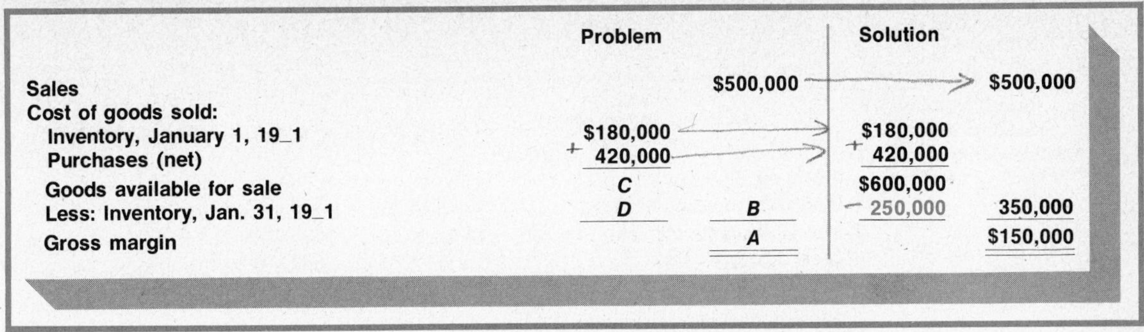

	Problem		Solution	
Sales		$500,000		$500,000
Cost of goods sold:				
Inventory, January 1, 19_1	$180,000		$180,000	
Purchases (net)	+ 420,000		+ 420,000	
Goods available for sale	C		$600,000	
Less: Inventory, Jan. 31, 19_1	D	B	− 250,000	350,000
Gross margin		A		$150,000

NOTE: The solution proceeds as follows. First, compute *A* (estimated gross margin) by taking 30 percent (gross profit rate) of sales. Then, compute *B* (estimated cost of goods sold) by subtracting *A* from sales. Next, compute *C* (goods available for sale) by adding beginning inventory and purchases. Finally, compute *D* (estimated ending inventory) by subtracting *B* from *C*.

1. Add beginning inventory and net purchases to determine the goods available for sale, both at cost and at retail.
2. Compute the ratio of cost to retail (cost value of goods available for sale divided by retail value of goods available for sale).
3. Compute the ending inventory at retail by subtracting sales from the beginning inventory at retail.
4. Compute the ending inventory at cost by multiplying the ending inventory at retail times the ratio of cost to retail.

The schedule shown in Exhibit 13-13 illustrates this computation for a particular example.

Costing methods and the balance sheet

The costing procedures used in valuing the inventory should be disclosed in the statement of financial position, because this information will be of interest to an informed user of the statement. The following examples show how the pertinent information may be disclosed.

Current assets:	
Inventory (at cost, on a first-in, first-out basis)	$100,000
Current assets:	
Inventory (at lower of cost or market, on a first-in, first-out basis)	$ 75,000
Current assets:	
Inventory (see note)	$ 90,000

NOTE. Merchandise inventory is valued at the lower of cost (first-in, first-out basis) or market.

Inventory and the work sheet

The work sheet illustrated in Chapter 6 is that of a service firm; merchandise inventory is not involved in that example. In this section we develop a work sheet that can be used for a manufacturing or merchandising firm.

The work sheet shown in Exhibit 13-14 is that of a firm that keeps its inventory on the perpetual inventory method. Note that Cost of Goods Sold and ending inventory

Exhibit 13-13
Computation of estimated ending inventory using retail method

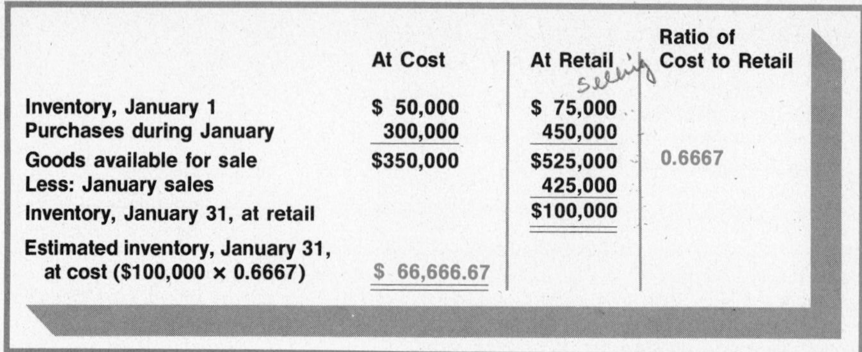

	At Cost	At Retail	Ratio of Cost to Retail
Inventory, January 1	$ 50,000	$ 75,000	
Purchases during January	300,000	450,000	
Goods available for sale	$350,000	$525,000	0.6667
Less: January sales		425,000	
Inventory, January 31, at retail		$100,000	
Estimated inventory, January 31, at cost ($100,000 × 0.6667)	$ 66,666.67		

appear as account balances on the trial balance, and that there is no Purchases account. In this example, adjusting entries have been made for bad debts expense ($1,000) and depreciation expense ($10,000).

Exhibit 13-15 shows a work sheet for a firm using the periodic inventory method. The trial balance shows the Inventory account balance before adjustments, which is the beginning balance of inventory for the period. The ending inventory was determined by count and costing to total $40,000. This amount is entered directly in the Balance Sheet columns as a debit (because it is the asset value to be shown on the statement of financial position on December 31, 19_1) and in the Income Statement columns as a credit (because it is required to compute net income for the period and serves as a deduction from goods available for sale). The beginning inventory from the trial balance is transferred directly to the Income Statement columns, where it is required to compute net income for the period. Again, adjusting entries have been made for bad debts expense ($4,000) and depreciation expense ($10,000).

An accounting system that uses the periodic inventory method must make certain adjustments: (1) to remove the beginning inventory from the Inventory account; and (2) to place the ending inventory in the Inventory account. The closing entries shown in Exhibit 13-16 accomplish these transfers. Observe that the data needed for the closing entries can be obtained directly from the Income Statement columns of the work sheet. Also, observe that the adjustment of the inventory[3] produces the correct Inventory account balance of $40,000 on December 31, 19_1 (see Exhibit 13-17).

If it is desired to record cost of goods sold separately, the accounts used to compute cost of goods sold can be closed into a Cost of Goods Sold account. In the following closing entry, the amount debited to Cost of Goods Sold is the amount needed to balance the entry.

Dec. 31	Inventory [ending]	40,000	
	Purchase Returns and Allowances	10,000	
	Purchase Discounts	10,000	
	Cost of Goods Sold	340,000	
	Inventory [beginning]		50,000
	Purchases		300,000
	Transportation-In		50,000

3. It would be possible to adjust the Inventory account through a single debit (or credit) item equal to the net increase (or net decrease) in inventory during the year. In the example, the Inventory account would be credited for the $10,000 decrease in inventory.

Exhibit 13-14 Work sheet including inventory kept by perpetual method

ABC COMPANY

Work Sheet (Perpetual Inventory)

For the Year Ended December 31, 19_1

Account Titles	Trial Balance		Adjustments		Adjusted Trial Balance		Income Statement		Balance Sheet	
	Dr.	Cr.	Dr.	Cr.	Dr.	Cr.	Dr.	Cr.	Dr.	Cr.
Cash	100,000				100,000				100,000	
Accounts Receivable	10,000				10,000				10,000	
Allowance for Doubtful Receivables		1,000		(*a*) 1,000		2,000				2,000
Inventory, Dec. 31, 19_1	50,000				50,000				50,000	
Land	300,000				300,000				300,000	
Buildings	300,000				300,000				300,000	
Accumulated Depreciation		50,000		(*b*) 10,000		60,000				60,000
Accounts Payable		10,000				10,000				10,000
Common Stock		500,000				500,000				500,000
Retained Earnings		109,000				109,000				109,000
Sales		200,000				200,000		200,000		
Sales Returns and Allowances	5,000				5,000		5,000			
Sales Discounts	5,000				5,000		5,000			
Cost of Goods Sold	50,000				50,000		50,000			
Expenses (various)	50,000				50,000		50,000			
	870,000	870,000								
Bad Debts Expense			(*a*) 1,000		1,000		1,000			
Depreciation Expense			(*b*) 10,000		10,000		10,000			
			11,000	11,000	881,000	881,000	121,000	200,000	760,000	681,000
Net Income							79,000			79,000
							200,000	200,000	760,000	760,000

Exhibit 13-15 **Work sheet including inventory kept by periodic method**

XYZ COMPANY

Work Sheet (Periodic Inventory)

For the Year Ended December 31, 19_1

Account Titles	Trial Balance		Adjustments		Adjusted Trial Balance		Income Statement		Balance Sheet	
	Dr.	Cr.	Dr.	Cr.	Dr.	Cr.	Dr.	Cr.	Dr.	Cr.
Cash	40,000				40,000				40,000	
Accounts Receivable	60,000				60,000				60,000	
Allowance for Doubtful Receivables		5,000		(*a*) 4,000		9,000				9,000
Inventory, Jan. 1, 19_1	50,000				50,000		50,000	(*c*) 40,000	(*c*) 40,000	
Land	100,000				100,000				100,000	
Buildings	200,000				200,000				200,000	
Accumulated Depreciation		50,000		(*b*) 10,000		60,000				60,000
Accounts Payable		50,000				50,000				50,000
Common Stock		100,000				100,000				100,000
Retained Earnings		175,000				175,000				175,000
Sales		510,000				510,000		510,000		
Sales Returns and Allowances	2,000				2,000		2,000			
Sales Discounts	8,000				8,000		8,000			
Purchases	300,000				300,000		300,000			
Purchase Returns and Allowances		10,000				10,000		10,000		
Purchase Discounts		10,000				10,000		10,000		
Transportation-In	50,000				50,000		50,000			
Expenses (various)	100,000				100,000		100,000			
	910,000	910,000								
Bad Debts Expense			(*a*) 4,000				4,000			
Depreciation Expense			(*b*) 10,000				10,000			
			14,000	14,000	924,000	924,000	524,000	570,000	440,000	394,000
Net Income							46,000			46,000
							570,000	570,000	570,000	570,000

NOTE (*c*): Ending inventory of $40,000 is inserted in the work sheet as a debit in the Balance Sheet columns and as a credit in the Income Statement columns.

Exhibit 13-16 Closing entries for example shown in Exhibit 13-17

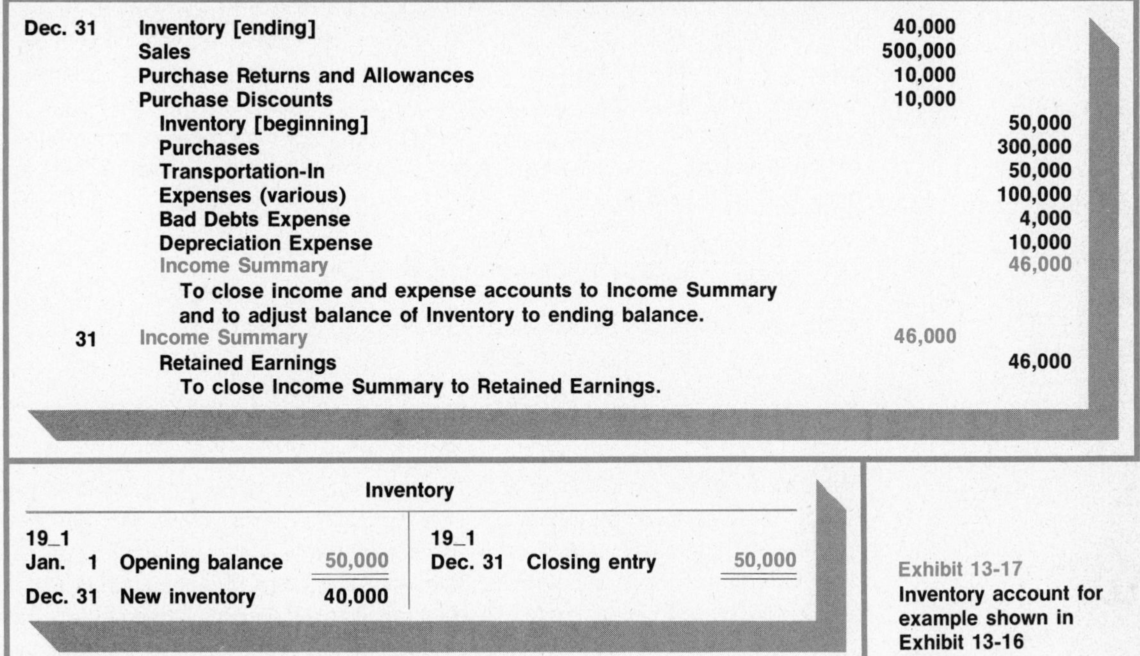

Dec. 31	Inventory [ending]	40,000	
	Sales	500,000	
	Purchase Returns and Allowances	10,000	
	Purchase Discounts	10,000	
	Inventory [beginning]		50,000
	Purchases		300,000
	Transportation-In		50,000
	Expenses (various)		100,000
	Bad Debts Expense		4,000
	Depreciation Expense		10,000
	Income Summary		46,000
	To close income and expense accounts to Income Summary and to adjust balance of Inventory to ending balance.		
31	Income Summary	46,000	
	Retained Earnings		46,000
	To close Income Summary to Retained Earnings.		

Inventory

19_1			19_1		
Jan. 1	Opening balance	50,000	Dec. 31	Closing entry	50,000
Dec. 31	New inventory	40,000			

Exhibit 13-17 Inventory account for example shown in Exhibit 13-16 after closing

The Cost of Goods Sold and the remaining expense and income accounts can then be closed to Income Summary in another entry.

Dec. 31	Sales	500,000	
	Costs of Goods Sold		340,000
	Expenses (various)		100,000
	Bad Debts Expense		4,000
	Depreciation Expense		10,000
	Income Summary		46,000

Ratio analysis

Accountants and financial analysts have developed financial ratios that are helpful in evaluating a firm's investment in and utilization of merchandise inventory. Two such ratios are (1) merchandise inventory turnover, and (2) average number of days per turnover of merchandise inventory.

Merchandise inventory turnover is a ratio showing the average number of times the inventory was replaced during the accounting period. It is computed according to the formula

$$\text{Merchandise inventory turnover} = \frac{\text{Cost of goods sold}}{\text{Average merchandise inventory}}$$

where average merchandise inventory is one-half the sum of the beginning and ending inventories. This ratio is a measure of the liquidity of inventory, when compared to ratios of previous periods and to ratios of the industry. A rapid turnover (high value) is considered favorable, because profit is made through the sale of inventory. A low value of this ratio may indicate either that the firm has too large an inventory (a nonproductive use of resources) or that sales are unusually slow.

Average number of days per turnover of merchandise inventory is a related ratio that measures the average number of days required to replace the inventory once. It is computed as

$$\frac{\text{365 days}}{\text{Merchandise inventory turnover}}$$

A low value of this ratio indicates a rapid turnover of inventory.

Impact analysis

Inventories have a significant impact on those financial ratios that involve current assets, because inventory often is a very significant current asset. Current ratio, for example, is strongly influenced by inventory in the typical manufacturing or merchandising firm. Accountants and managers who are aware of the managerial impact of inventory on various ratios can use these ratios as a measure of their performance in utilizing inventory effectively. As they strive to improve the ratios, hopefully they will also improve the financial position of the firm and the results of its operations.

In the discussion of inventory methods in this chapter, we have said that a firm should select the method that best measures net income. When prices are relatively stable, the various costing methods provide approximately the same results. (In fact, if prices were unchanging, all of the methods would give exactly the same results.) However, when prices fluctuate significantly, the choice of an inventory costing procedure will have a measurable impact on the financial statements and on income taxes. An awareness of the impact of inventory procedures on financial data is of great importance to the accountant and to the decision makers who rely on financial statements. The impact of FIFO and LIFO procedures on financial statements is discussed earlier in this chapter.

It also is obvious that consistency in the use of inventory procedures, statement presentations, and so on from year to year is necessary to give meaningful financial and managerial data. If a firm changes its inventory costing procedures from one year to the next (for example, changing from FIFO to LIFO), it should disclose in the financial statements the nature of the change, the reason for the change, and the effect of the change on net income. The Internal Revenue Service requires that a company planning such a change in inventory costing procedures apply for permission to make the change in its tax computation methods during the first half of the fiscal year in which it plans to begin using the new procedure.

An error in computing the dollar value of inventory can have very serious impact in distorting the information in the financial statements. Furthermore, because the ending inventory of one year becomes the beginning inventory of the next year, such an error can distort the statements for at least two years.

As an illustration of the effect of an error in computing inventory, Exhibit 13-18 shows the income statement for 19_1 of a company that overstates its ending inventory by $10,000. Both the erroneous and the correct statements are shown. Note that overstatement of the ending inventory results in understatement of the cost of goods sold and overstatement of gross margin and net income. In this example, the $10,000 overstatement of ending inventory causes a $10,000 overstatement of net income. In the corresponding statement of financial position, the value of inventory will also be overstated by $10,000, causing a $10,000 overstatement of current assets, total assets, and owners' equity. An understatement of ending inventory would have the opposite impacts.

If the statements for 19_2 are computed without detecting and correcting the error, the overstatement of 19_1 ending inventory (19_2 beginning inventory) will distort these statements as well. Exhibit 13-19 shows that the $10,000 overstatement of the

Exhibit 13-18 **Impact of overstatement of ending inventory on income statement**

Income Statement
For the Year Ended December 31, 19_1

	Inventory Correctly Stated		Inventory Incorrectly Stated	
Sales		$800,000		$800,000
Beginning inventory	$100,000		$100,000	
Purchases	500,000		500,000	
Goods available for sale	$600,000		$600,000	
Less: Ending inventory	100,000		110,000	
Cost of goods sold		500,000		490,000
Gross margin		$300,000		$310,000
Operating expenses		200,000		200,000
Net income		$100,000		$110,000

Income Statement
For the Year Ended December 31, 19_2

	Inventory Correctly Stated		Inventory Incorrectly Stated	
Sales		$1,000,000		$1,000,000
Beginning inventory	$100,000		$110,000	
Purchases	700,000		700,000	
Goods available for sale	$800,000		$810,000	
Less: Ending inventory	150,000		150,000	
Cost of goods sold		650,000		660,000
Gross margin		$ 350,000		$ 340,000
Operating expenses		225,000		225,000
Net income		$ 125,000		$ 115,000

Exhibit 13-19 **Impact of overstatement of beginning inventory on income statement**

beginning inventory causes a $10,000 understatement of gross margin and net income and a $10,000 overstatement of cost of goods sold. In this example, the ending inventory for 19_2 has been computed correctly, so the corresponding balance sheet gives a correct picture of the financial position. The combined net income for 19_1 and 19_2 is $225,000, and the incorrect statements give this same total for the two years. The effect of the error in inventory was to shift $10,000 of income from 19_2 to 19_1. By the end of 19_2, the errors have balanced out, and future income statements should be correct.

Overstatement or understatement of purchases will have impacts similar to those of errors in beginning inventory. Errors in reporting discounts, allowances, freight-in, and so on can have an impact on financial statements, but the impact is usually much less serious because these amounts are relatively less important on the financial statements.

Summary

Inventory consists of all items of merchandise and material intended for eventual sale and to which a firm has legal title. Title usually passes from seller to buyer when the goods are handed over from the seller (or his agent) to the buyer (or his agent). The title to goods in transit is determined by the question of who is paying the carrier (whose agent he is). Items shipped F.O.B. destination remain the property of the seller while in transit; items shipped F.O.B. shipping point belong to the buyer while in transit.

Inventory is priced according to the initial recording principle—that is, its cost is initially recorded at the cost needed to bring the merchandise to its present location and condition. Purchases may be recorded at net or at gross invoice price; the net method of pricing is theoretically preferable. Exhibit 13-3 illustrates basic entries for purchase transactions for the net and gross methods when the periodic inventory system is used. Exhibit 13-20 summarizes basic entries for purchase transactions when the perpetual inventory system is used.

Inventory control may be handled by either the periodic or the perpetual system. The periodic method involves physical count of the inventory at regular intervals, with no detailed record kept of the outflow of inventory items between counts. The perpetual method involves detailed records of all inventory inflow and outflow, resulting in continuous updating of the Inventory and Cost of Goods Sold accounts.

Methods of assigning cost to inventory (and to goods sold) include specific identification, FIFO, LIFO, weighted average, and moving average. The method chosen should be the one that best measures periodic income for the particular firm.

The lower-of-cost-or-market method of pricing inventory is a departure from the cost method. It should be used where the utility of merchandise has decreased from its cost value, especially if this decrease is expected to cause (or be accompanied by) a reduction of the sales price of the merchandise. It is a conservative method of pricing inventory.

To summarize, the accountant must make the following decisions in deciding how to record, control, and price inventory. The methods chosen should be applied consistently from accounting period to period.

Exhibit 13-20 **Purchase transactions under gross and net methods (perpetual)**

Transaction	Accounts	Net Method		Gross Method	
Purchase is made on account.	Mdse. Inventory	980		1,000	
	Accounts Payable		980		1,000
Invoice is paid within the discount period.	Accounts Payable	980		1,000	
	Cash		980		980
	Mdse. Inventory				20
Invoice is paid after the discount period.	Accounts Payable	980		1,000	
	Purchase Discounts Lost	20			
	Cash		1,000		1,000
Freight bill is paid on goods shipped F.O.B. shipping point.	Mdse. Inventory	100		100	
	Cash		100		100
Merchandise is returned and an allowance is received.	Accounts Payable	98		100	
	Mdse. Inventory		98		100
A sale on account is made for $250 on merchandise costing $100 gross.	Accounts Receivable	250		250	
	Sales		250		250
	Cost of Goods Sold	98		100	
	Mdse. Inventory		98		100

1. Should purchases be recorded at net or at gross invoice price?
2. Should inventory be controlled by the periodic or by the perpetual method?
3. Should cost be assigned to individual items by specific identification, FIFO, LIFO, weighted average, or moving average?
4. Should items be valued at cost or should the value be adjusted to a lower market value?

The gross profit method and the retail inventory method of estimating inventory are useful in certain situations. The gross profit method is used to estimate inventory when an inventory count is not taken, or as a test of other inventory methods. The retail inventory method can be used to approximate a lower-of-cost-or-market inventory through a procedure using retail prices. It may be used as an independent check on inventory, or for situations where the physical count of inventory is most easily accomplished at retail prices.

The appendix to this chapter discusses inventory models that can be used to compute the most economical order size of inventory and the replacement point (the time when the order should be placed). These quantitative techniques for controlling and managing inventory are being intensively developed by management.

Appendix

INVENTORY MODELS

The control of inventory involves two major managerial decisions.

1. What is the optimal size for a purchase order?
2. When should the order be placed?

When considering the optimal order size, a manager knows that

1. certain expenses tend to increase with an increase in order size (for example, storage-space cost, insurance, taxes, risk of spoilage or theft, interest on money invested in insurance, risk of obsolescence); but
2. certain expenses tend to decrease with an increase in order size (for example, cost of clerical work associated with purchasing and receiving and paying bills, freight expenses per item—also, quantity discounts on larger purchases may decrease the cost of merchandise).

As order size increases, the cost of ordering inventory decreases while the cost of carrying inventory increases. Exhibit 13-21 illustrates the relationship between order size and inventory-handling costs. Observe that carrying costs increase as order size increases, while ordering costs decrease as order size increases. The sum of these two costs, the total cost, reaches a minimum at a certain order size—the optimal order. This optimal order size is also the order size at which the ordering-cost and carrying-cost curves intersect.

Standard formulas are available to compute optimal order size. Each formula is based upon a different inventory model. To illustrate the use of an inventory model, we demonstrate a very simple one. Much more complex models are available, and these more closely approximate realistic business situations.

For our formula, let Q equal order size (number of units per order) and let D equal the demand for inventory items (number of units sold per year). Then D/Q is the number of orders that must be placed each year. If K is the cost of placing an order, then

ordering cost/year $= KD/Q$.

Exhibit 13-21 Relationship of inventory carrying and ordering costs to order size

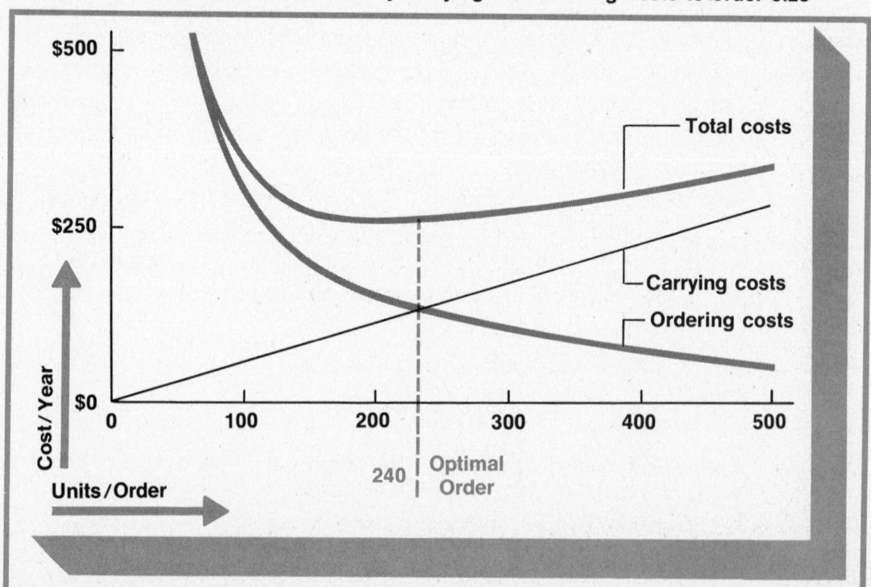

Suppose that we can measure carrying cost by k_c, the cost of carrying one unit of inventory for one year. Then carrying cost will be equal to k_c multiplied by the average number of units in inventory during the year. To make our model very simple, we assume that orders will be placed so that a new order arrives just as the last unit is being taken out of inventory. That is, the inventory will have a size of Q units just after an order arrives, and the size of the inventory will decrease steadily to zero, at which point a new order of Q units will arrive. (As you may have already noticed, our simple model assumes that demand for inventory is evenly spread through the year and is unchanging.) Under these assumptions, the average size of the inventory will be $Q/2$. Therefore,

$$\text{carrying cost/year} = k_cQ/2.$$

Combining the expressions for ordering cost and carrying cost, we arrive at the following expression for total cost:

$$\text{total cost/year} = (KD/Q) + (k_cQ/2).$$

As an example, suppose that a particular company uses 3,600 units from inventory each year ($D = 3{,}600$). The cost of placing an order is \$8 ($K = 8$), and it costs \$1 to carry one unit in inventory for one year ($k_c = 1$). The graph of Exhibit 13-21 was computed from these figures and using this simple model. For example, suppose that the company orders 100 units in each order ($Q = 100$). Then total cost/year equals

$$\begin{aligned}(KD/Q) + (k_cQ/2) &= ([8 \times 3{,}600]/100) + ([1 \times 100]/2)\\ &= 288 + 50 = 338.\end{aligned}$$

Thus, if the company orders 100 units at a time, its ordering costs will be \$288/year and its carrying costs will be \$50/year, for a total inventory-handling cost of \$338/year.

You could keep trying different order sizes until you happen to find the one that gives the smallest total cost. However, there are mathematical tricks that give a formula for the smallest value of an expression. (With this model, you can get such a formula fairly easily by noting that carrying cost equals ordering cost at the optimal order size. Therefore, set $KD/Q = k_cQ/2$ and solve for Q to find the optimal value of Q.) For this model, the optimal order size (Q_{opt}) is given by the following formula:

$$Q_{opt} = \sqrt{2KD/k_c}.$$

For the example shown in Exhibit 13-21,

$$Q_{opt} = \sqrt{(2 \times 8 = 3{,}600)/1} = \sqrt{57{,}600} = 240.$$

Therefore, this company will have the lowest inventory-handling costs if it orders 240 units in each purchase for inventory.

In the formula for optimal order size, note that Q_{opt} becomes larger if demand (D) or ordering cost/order (K) increases, while it becomes smaller if carrying cost/unit (k_c) increases.

How often should the orders be placed? The demand is 3,600 units/year, or approximately 10 units/day. Therefore, one order of 240 units will last for about 24 days. The time between orders will have to be 24 days, and the orders should be placed so that the new order will arrive just as the last one is used up. For example, suppose that it takes 14 days from the time an order is placed until the goods arrive. In that case, each order should be placed 10 days after the last one has arrived, so that the new goods will arrive on the 24th day after the arrival of the previous order.

Questions

1. Define inventory. Mention three major inventory classifications.
2. Prepare the section of an income statement that shows computation of cost of goods sold.
3. What is meant by the terms "F.O.B. shipping point" and "F.O.B. destination"? In general, when does title to goods pass from the seller to the buyer?
4. Inventory acquisitions are recorded at cost. Mention various items that are included in inventory cost.
5. Distinguish between the net and gross methods of recording purchases. Which one is theoretically preferable? Why?
6. Distinguish between the periodic and the perpetual inventory methods.
7. For each of the following accounts, indicate whether such an account would normally be found in the books of an accounting system that uses the periodic inventory method, a system that uses the perpetual method, or both systems. (Assume that both systems use the gross method of recording purchases.)
   a. Purchases.
   b. Purchase Discounts.
   c. Transportation-In.
   d. Purchase Returns and Allowances.
   e. An Inventory account that has a balance equal to the beginning inventory throughout the accounting period.
   f. An Inventory account that changes balance with purchases and sales during the accounting period.
   g. A Cost of Goods Sold account that accumulates the cost of inventory sold during the period.
8. Explain the following inventory costing methods.
   a. Specific identification.
   b. FIFO.
   c. LIFO.
   d. Moving average.
   e. Weighted average.
9. Describe the retail inventory method, and mention several situations where its use would be advisable.
10. Describe the lower-of-cost-or-market inventory costing procedure, and explain when it would be used. What has "conservatism" to do with this inventory method?
11. Describe the gross profit method of estimating inventory, and explain when it could be used.

12. What are two major inventory problems that involve managerial decisions?
13. How does an understatement of ending inventory affect net income in the period of the error? in the following period?
14. Suppose that a company chooses to use FIFO costing procedures instead of LIFO procedures during a period of rising prices. What is the impact of this decision on the statement of financial position? on the income statement? on income taxes payable?
15. The net income of a company in years 1 and 2 was $100,000 and $150,000 respectively. At the end of year 1, the ending inventory of the company was overstated by $10,000. What is the impact of the error on cost of goods sold, net income, total assets, and owners' equity for years 1, 2, and 3? (Assume that the error is not discovered but that the ending inventory is properly taken at the end of year 2.)
16. A company is filling an order for a customer on December 31. The order is packaged and ready for shipment but is not shipped until January of the following year. The company closes its books on December 31. In what year should the sale be recognized? Should the packaged merchandise be included in the December inventory of the seller?
17. Two companies have the same operating data. However, one company uses FIFO inventory and the other company uses LIFO. Prices have been rising during the year. If the companies sold more merchandise than they purchased during the year, which company would have the smaller net income? Explain.

Exercises

E13-1 (Inventory on the income statement)
Prepare a partial income statement, using the following data.

Inventory, January 1, 19_6	$ 80,000
Inventory, December 31, 19_6	65,000
Sales during year	300,000
Purchases (net) during year	150,000

E13-2 (Inventory methods)
The Sand Company records its purchases under the gross method. During February 19_6, it is involved in the following transactions.

Feb. 2	Purchased $20,000 of merchandise from Good Company, on terms of 3/10, n/30, F.O.B. shipping point.
7	Paid $70 freight bill on merchandise from Good Company.
9	Paid the Good Company account.
27	Assume that, instead of settling its account with the Good Company on February 9, the Gross Company paid the account in full on February 27.

Required: Prepare journal entries to record these transactions, assuming that the Sand Company uses

a. the perpetual inventory method;

b. the periodic inventory method.

E13-3 (Inventory methods—net recording of payable)

Repeat Exercise E13-2, this time assuming that the Sand Company uses the net method to record its purchases.

E13-4 (Inventory on income statement)

Prepare a partial income statement using the following 19_6 data.

Inventory, December 31, 19_6	$ 54,000
Inventory, January 1, 19_6	300,000
Transportation-in	15,000
Purchase discounts	8,000
Purchase returns and allowances	27,000
Sales	710,000
Purchases	285,000
Sales returns and allowances	17,600
Sales discounts	6,400

E13-5 (Inventory methods)

On May 31, the Nova Company sold $165,000 of merchandise subject to terms of 3/10, n/30. The merchandise cost the Nova Company $125,000. Record the necessary May 31 journal entries, assuming the Nova Company uses

a. the perpetual inventory method;
b. the periodic inventory method.

E13-6 (Inventory costing methods)

The records of the Colors Company disclose the following data.

Feb.	1	20,000 units on hand in inventory @ $3 cost per unit.
	16	Purchase: 40,000 items @ $4 per unit.
	21	Purchase: 60,000 items @ $5 per unit.
	27	Sale: 80,000 units.

Required:

a. Calculate the number of units in the ending inventory.
b. Compute the ending inventory value using the periodic inventory method and each of the following inventory costing methods:
  (1) specific identification (all units on hand at end of month came from the February 16 purchase);
  (2) FIFO;
  (3) LIFO;
  (4) weighted average;
  (5) moving average.
c. Compute the ending inventory value using the perpetual inventory method and each of the following inventory costing methods:
  (1) FIFO;
  (2) LIFO;
  (3) weighted average;
  (4) moving average.

E13-7 (Lower-of-cost-or-market method)

The Best Company uses the lower-of-cost-or-market method of valuing its inventory. Exhibit 13-22 shows data gathered about the value of five different items in the firm's inventory. Give the correct inventory carrying value for each item.

Exhibit 13-22
Inventory data for Exercise E13-7

Item	Cost	Market
A	$47	$51
B	47	60
C	47	47
D	47	37
E	47	40

Exhibit 13-23
Inventory data for Exercise E13-8

Category	Item	Quantity	Unit Cost	Unit Market
Commodity X	A	150	$25	$27
	B	290	10	8
	C	400	12	14
Commodity Y	D	200	40	40
	E	50	66	70

E13-8 (Lower-of-cost-or-market method)
The Lizzy Company uses the lower-of-cost-or-market method of valuing its inventory. Exhibit 13-23 shows data gathered about the five different items in the firm's inventory. Compare the value of the total inventory using
a. the item-by-item method;
b. the category method;
c. the total inventory method.

E13-9 (Adjusting entry for lower-of-cost-or-market method)
The Lizzy Company (Exercise E13-8) decides to use the item-by-item method to value its inventory. Give the journal entry that is needed to reduce the inventory from cost to lower-of-cost-or-market value.

E13-10 (Gross profit method)
From past experience, a firm knows that its gross profit rate is 25 percent of sales. From the following 19_6 data, compute the ending inventory for the year.

Merchandise inventory, January 1, 19_6	$ 18,000
Purchases (net)	157,000
Sales (net)	200,000

E13-11 (Retail method)
The Fresh Fruit Grocery Company uses the retail inventory method to estimate inventory values for monthly statements. From the following data, estimate the ending inventory for July.

	Cost	Retail
Merchandise inventory, July 1, 19_6	$140,000	$ 240,000
Purchases (net) during July	560,000	1,160,000
Sales (net) during July		1,260,000

E13-12 (Inventory acquisition)
Bone Company sold Rock Company $1,600 of goods, terms 1/10, n/30, F.O.B. shipping point. Bone prepaid $120 of freight charges on the shipment. Prepare a journal entry recording this transaction for the books of the Rock Company. (The Rock Company uses the periodic inventory system and records its purchases gross.)

E13-13 (Inventory acquisition)
The Rock Company (see Exercise E13-12) pays its bill within the discount period. Prepare a journal entry recording this transaction for the books of the Rock Company.

E13-14 (Purchase discounts)
The Bone Company sold the Rock Company (see Exercise E13-12) $1,600 of goods, terms 1/10, n/30, F.O.B. destination. When the goods arrive, the Rock Company pays the freight bill of $120. Rock Company pays its account with Bone Company within the discount period. Prepare journal entries recording these transactions for the books of the Rock Company.

E13-15 (Account identification)
The following is a list of classifications for ledger accounts.

A. Current assets
B. Fixed assets
C. Current liabilities
D. Long-term liabilities
E. Shareowners' equity
F. Revenue (including contra revenue)
G. Cost of goods sold
H. Operating expenses

Required: For each of the following accounts, indicate the classification under which its balance should appear on the financial statements. Also indicate for each account whether its normal balance is a debit or a credit balance.

a. Sales.
b. Sales Discounts.
c. Sales Returns and Allowances.
d. Cost of Goods Sold.
e. Merchandise Inventory [ending balance].
f. Purchases.
g. Transportation-In.
h. Purchase Returns and Allowances.
i. Purchase Discounts.
j. Purchase Discounts Lost.
k. Income Summary [when revenues exceed expenses].

E13-16 (Gross profit method)
On September 20, the warehouse of the Aero Company is badly damaged in a fire, and much of the firm's merchandise inventory is destroyed. The following information about the inventory is available in the company's accounting records.

Inventory, January 1	$ 24,000
Purchases to September 20	132,000
Net sales to September 20	160,000
Average gross margin rate on sales	12.5%

Required:

a. Compute the value of the inventory on September 20, before the fire.
b. Goods salvaged from the inventory after the fire amounted to $8,000. What was the amount of the fire loss?

c. If the gross margin rate had been 20% on cost, what value would have been computed for the inventory on September 20?

E13-17 (Comparison of inventory methods)
Indicate whether each of the following objectives is better met by FIFO or by LIFO inventory procedures.

a. Provide higher net income when prices are rising.
b. Cause inventory to be reported on the balance sheet at approximate current replacement cost.
c. Match current costs with current sales revenue on income statement.
d. Stress the importance of the income statement.
e. Match older inventory costs with current sales prices on the income statement.
f. Provide lower net income when prices are decreasing.
g. Cause net income to increase with increase in selling prices.

E13-18 (Inventory content)
Which of the following items should be included in inventory?

a. Merchandise ordered and in the firm's receiving department; invoice from vendor has not been received.
b. Merchandise returned by a customer with prior approval from the firm.
c. Merchandise held on consignment for a manufacturer.
d. Merchandise on store shelves.
e. Merchandise shipped today F.O.B. destination to a firm in a distant city; invoice not yet mailed.
f. Merchandise in warehouse.
g. Merchandise in warehouse for shipment to a customer next period; the customer has been billed for the sale.
h. Merchandise at a branch store.

E13-19 (Relationships on income statement)
Exhibit 13-24 shows portions of two unrelated income statements. Supply the amounts that should appear in the spaces designated by the letters (a) through (j).

	First Statement	Second Statement
Sales	**$180,000**	**$ — (f)**
Sales returns and allowances	**4,000**	**7,000**
Sales discounts	**2,000**	**3,000**
Net sales	**(a) —**	**— (g)**
Beginning inventory	**$ 8,000**	**$ 40,000**
Purchases	**(b) —**	**210,000**
Purchase returns and allowances	**$ 800**	**15,000**
Purchase discounts	**1,200**	**10,000**
Transportation-in	**1,000**	**20,000**
Net purchases	**41,000**	**— (h)**
Goods available for sale	**(c) —**	**— (i)**
Ending inventory	**(d) —**	**$ 55,000**
Cost of goods sold	**(e) —**	**— (j)**
Gross margin	**$130,000**	**$110,000**

Exhibit 13-24
Partial income statements for Exercise E13-19

Exhibit 13-25
Partial chart of accounts for Exercise E13-20

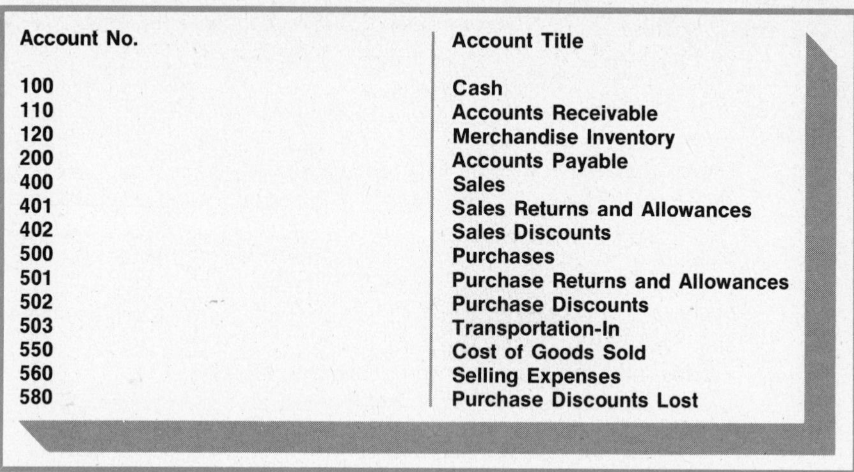

Account No.	Account Title
100	Cash
110	Accounts Receivable
120	Merchandise Inventory
200	Accounts Payable
400	Sales
401	Sales Returns and Allowances
402	Sales Discounts
500	Purchases
501	Purchase Returns and Allowances
502	Purchase Discounts
503	Transportation-In
550	Cost of Goods Sold
560	Selling Expenses
580	Purchase Discounts Lost

E13-20 (Journalizing purchases)

Exhibit 13-25 shows a partial chart of accounts for the Max Company. For each of the following transactions of the corporation, indicate the proper accounts that should be debited and credited in journalizing the events. Indicate the account number(s) to be debited and the account number(s) to be credited. The corporation uses a periodic inventory system and records purchases under the net price method.

a. The Max Co. sells merchandise to a customer on terms of 2/10, n/60 F.O.B. shipping point.

b. The customer in transaction a pays for the merchandise within the discount period.

c. Purchased merchandise on account from the Gaily Company; terms 1/10, n/30, F.O.B. destination.

d. Merchandise purchased in transaction c arrives by truck; driver demands payment of freight bill on delivery; Max Co. pays freight bill.

e. Merchandise purchased in transaction c is not what was ordered; Max Co. contacts Gaily Co. and requests and is granted a reduction in the purchase price on the merchandise.

f. The Max Co. pays for the merchandise purchased in transaction c, after the discount period is over.

E13-21 (Impact analysis)

Indicate the dollar impact of each of the following transactions on current assets, working capital, cost of sales, gross margin, operating expenses, net income, net assets, and retained earnings. Prepare your answers in the form of a table.

a. Merchandise was sold for $2,000; cost of the merchandise sold was $1,100; terms $300 cash, balance in 30 days; perpetual inventory method used.

b. Merchandise was purchased on account in the amount of $350; terms net cash in 60 days; perpetual inventory method used.

c. Freight-in paid ($13) on purchases shipped F.O.B. shipping point; perpetual inventory method used.

d. An account receivable in the amount of $125 is written off as worthless.
e. An account receivable of $16, formerly written off, is ultimately collected.

Problems

P13-1 (Inventory systems and entries)
The following represent major merchandising transactions of the Sophomore Company during November 19_6.

Nov. 2 Purchased merchandise from the Cody Company in the amount of $30,000; terms 2/10, n/30, F.O.B. destination.
4 Returned $4,000 of the merchandise purchased from the Cody Company.
6 Paid the amount owed the Cody Company.
7 Purchased $6,000 merchandise from the Wilder Company; terms 3/10, n/30, F.O.B. shipping point.
9 Sold merchandise costing $1,200 (gross) to the Danz Company for $1,800; terms 1/10, n/30, F.O.B. destination.
11 Received merchandise from Wilder Company; paid $200 freight bill.
13 Granted permission to the Danz Company to return $300 of the merchandise sold on account June 6; this returned merchandise had a cost (gross) of $200; merchandise received.
17 Sold merchandise costing $3,000 (gross) to the Belzer Company for $4,000; terms 2/10, n/30, F.O.B. shipping point.
20 Collected cash from the Danz Company for amount owed on account.
21 Received a freight bill from a trucking company for $60 for delivery of the Danz Company sale; paid the bill in cash.
24 Paid the amount owed the Wilder Company.
28 Collected cash from the Belzer Company for amount due on their account.

Required: Journalize all of the preceding transactions in four parallel journals, one prepared under each of the following procedures:
a. perpetual inventory system, gross method of recording purchases;
b. periodic inventory system, gross method of recording purchases;
c. perpetual inventory system, net method of recording purchases;
d. periodic inventory system, net method of recording purchases.

P13-2 (Retail method)
Using the following data from books of the Absent Company, estimate the October 31 inventory.

Sales	$875,000
Sales discounts	50,000
Sales returns and allowances	25,000
Purchases (cost)	560,000
Purchases (at retail)	850,000
Purchase discounts	30,000
Transportation-in	100,000
Inventory, October 1 (cost)	70,000
Inventory, October 1 (at retail)	100,000

P13-3 (Work sheet)
The Skyler Company uses the periodic inventory system. From the following list of account balances (and the additional information given after the list), prepare a work sheet for the Skyler Company.

Cash	150,000	
Accounts Receivable	250,000	
Allowance for Doubtful Accounts		44,000
Inventory, January 1, 19_1	80,000	
Building	300,000	
Accumulated Depreciation		45,000
Accounts Payable		120,000
Common Stock		200,000
Retained Earnings		60,000
Sales		961,000
Sales Returns and Allowances	25,000	
Sales Discounts	35,000	
Purchases	400,000	
Purchase Discounts		50,000
Purchase Returns and Allowances		30,000
Transportation-In	30,000	
Expenses	240,000	
	1,510,000	1,510,000

Additional information:

a. Inventory on December 31, 19_6, was $160,000.
b. Estimated bad debts expense is $6,000.
c. Depreciation expense on building for the year is 5 percent.
d. Accrued salaries expense amounts to $20,000.

P13-4 (Work sheet)

The True Company uses the perpetual inventory system. From the following list of account balances (and the additional information given after the list), prepare a work sheet for the True Company.

Cash	120,000	
Accounts Receivable	210,000	
Allowance for Doubtful Receivables		40,000
Inventory, December 31, 19_1	180,000	
Building	220,000	
Accumulated Depreciation		44,000
Accounts Payable		160,000
Common Stock		150,000
Retained Earnings		40,000
Sales		761,000
Sales Returns and Allowances	15,000	
Sales Discounts	30,000	
Cost of Goods Sold	180,000	
Expenses	240,000	
	1,195,000	1,195,000

Additional information:

a. Estimated bad debts expense is $4,000.
b. Depreciation expense on building for the year is 10 percent.
c. Accrued salaries expense amounted to $20,000.

P13-5 (Impact analysis)

Prepare a table showing the dollar impact of each of the following errors on (1) cost of goods sold 19_6; (2) cost of goods sold 19_7; (3) gross profit 19_6; (4) gross profit 19_7; (5) net income 19_6; (6) net income 19_7; (7) retained earnings 19_6; (8) retained earnings 19_7.

a. Ending inventory in 19_6 was overstated $3,000.

b. Beginning inventory in 19_6 was understated $2,000 as a result of an error in 19_5.

c. Purchases in 19_6 were understated $4,000 when a 19_6 purchase was not recorded. All other accounts were correct. The error was discovered and the 19_6 purchase was recorded as a purchase in 19_7.

P13-6 (Impact analysis)

Indicate the dollar impact of each of the following transactions on (1) net assets and (2) owners' equity.

a. Merchandise is sold on account for $1,200 subject to terms of 2/10, n/30 and the sale is recorded at gross. Invoice cost of the merchandise sold was $600; purchase terms 1/10, n/30; the purchase was recorded net and the company uses the perpetual inventory system.

b. Merchandise is purchased on account for $2,000, subject to terms of 3/10, n/30, F.O.B. shipping point. Transportation-in amounts to $100 and is paid in cash. The company uses the perpetual inventory system.

c. An account payable recorded $1,560 net is settled after discount date for $1,600 cash.

d. An account receivable recorded at $1,400 is settled in full for $1,372 after a 2 percent sales discount is taken.

P13-7 (Inventory methods)

The Tiger Company purchased 40,000 units at $6 per unit during the year. It sold 90,000 units; 20,000 units were contained in the final inventory. The opening inventory was carried at $560,000.

Required:

a. Compute the number of units in the opening inventory.

b. Compute the final inventory valuation assuming use of each of the following methods:

1. FIFO;

2. LIFO;

3. weighted average.

c. If the firm made a net income of $220,000 using FIFO, what net income would the firm have reported if it were using

1. LIFO?

2. Weighted average?

P13-8 (Inventory methods)

The inventory records of the Pandora Company show the following data.

Balance, January 1	20,000 units @ $1/unit
First purchase	60,000 units @ $2
First sale	40,000 units
Second purchase	30,000 units @ $3
Second sale	50,000 units
Third purchase	30,000 units @ $4

Required:

a. Compute the number of units in final inventory.

b. Compute the final inventory value using FIFO and a periodic inventory system.

c. Compute the final inventory using FIFO and a perpetual inventory system.

d. Compute the final inventory using LIFO and a periodic inventory system.

e. Compute the final inventory using LIFO and a perpetual inventory system.

P13-9 (Gross profit method)

A company's beginning inventory was $20,000. During the year the company purchased $185,000 of merchandise. Freight-in charges were $5,000. Sales and sales returns were $205,000 and $5,000, respectively. Estimate the inventory at the end of the year if the gross profit margin was

a. 40% of sales; and

b. 40% of cost of merchandise.

P13-10 (Gross profit method)

Fire destroyed a company's inventory on June 1. Records indicate that the January 1 inventory was $10,000. Purchases from January 1 to June 1 were $50,000. Sales were $80,000. The company's gross profit margin was 60% of sales. Compute the value of the inventory destroyed by the fire.

P13-11 (Optimal order size)

An accountant accumulates the following statistics about inventory.

1. Cost of placing an order is $19.44.
2. Demand during one year is 20,000 units.
3. Cost of carrying one unit of inventory for one year is $6.

Required:

a. Using the model given in the appendix to this chapter, compute the optimal order size.

b. Using this optimal order size, what is the total cost associated with ordering and handling inventory for one year?

P13-12 (Optimal order size)

Compute the optimal order size based on the following statistics.

1. Cost of placing an order is $5.
2. Demand during one year is $1,250 of inventory.
3. Carrying cost is 20 percent of the average annual inventory.

P13-13 (Optimal order size)

To maintain a desired inventory level, a firm knows that it would like to have at least 300 units on hand at all times as a safety factor. During the time between placing an order and delivery of the order, the firm uses 500 units from inventory. At what inventory level (in units) should the firm place an order for more units?

P13-14 (Inventory valuation)

A company had a beginning inventory of 10,000 units at $10 per unit. During the period it purchased $80,000 at $12 per unit. It sold 85,000 units at $20 per unit. Expenses other than cost of goods sold totalled $50,000. Income tax rate is 50% of income before taxes.

Required:

a. Compute the net income of the company assuming the company uses FIFO inventory procedures.

b. Compute the net income of the company assuming the company uses LIFO inventory procedures.

P13-15 (Optimal order size)

Determine the economic order quantity for a company that provides the following data:

Setup cost per setup in the factory	$600
Requirements per year	2,400 units
Carrying cost for inventory	15%
Factory cost per unit	$10

Long-lived assets 14

To operate a business successfully, a company normally needs the use of land, plant, building, and equipment. For certain types of businesses, such natural resources as oil, minerals, and timber are basic to operations. Other enterprises need patents, copyrights, formulas, franchises, and similar intangible assets for their business activities.

The acquisition of these tangible and intangible assets involves the utilization of major economic resources of the firm—it represents a significant commitment of capital. As a result, accounting for long-lived assets becomes deeply involved in problems related to

1. the acquisition of the asset;
2. the allocation of the cost of the asset to expenses over its estimated life in a rational and systematic manner (through depreciation, amortization, or depletion); and
3. the disposal of the asset by sale, discard, or exchange for another asset.

In this chapter we deal first at some length with the problems of accounting for property, plant, and equipment. Natural resources and intangible assets are treated in the later sections of the chapter.

Property, plant, and equipment

Property, plant, and equipment are tangible assets (that is, assets having physical substance) that are

1. relatively long-lived (their use will extend over more than one accounting period, so they are noncurrent or fixed assets);
2. used in the operations of the business; and
3. not acquired primarily for resale.

The assets that normally meet these qualifications include such items as land, buildings, machinery, store and office equipment, furniture and fixtures, tools, and similar tangible property. These assets are sometimes called ***permanent assets, capital***

assets, noncurrent assets, or ***tangible fixed assets.*** When reported on the balance sheet, these items are most fully described by the title "Property, plant, and equipment." This caption for the category is widely used and is adopted in this text.

ACQUISITION OF PROPERTY, PLANT, AND EQUIPMENT

Property, plant, and equipment usually are recognized in the accounts according to the initial recording principle. This accounting principle states that the cost of an asset is the exchange price required to obtain the asset. At the date of acquisition, the asset is recorded in the accounts at acquisition cost—that is, at the cash price of the asset (regardless of whether the purchase actually was made for cash or on account).

If the asset is acquired in exchange for noncash assets, the acquisition cost of the asset acquired is considered to be equal to the fair market value of the asset acquired or the fair market value of the asset given up, whichever is more clearly (objectively) determined.

The acquisition cost of property, plant, and equipment includes the purchase price (less cash discount) of the asset and all necessary expenditures required to get the asset ready for use in the operations of the business.

For example, consider the purchase of land that is to be used in the operations of the business. When the land is purchased, a Land account is set up, and the purchase price of the land (less cash discount) is debited to this account. Also debited to the Land account are the real estate broker's commission, any delinquent property taxes paid by the purchaser, legal fees for examining title, title insurance, surveying costs, draining and clearing costs, landscaping outlays, and any other expenditures involved in getting the land ready for use in the business.

If the land is to be used as a building site, it may be necessary to tear down an old building already present on the site and purchased as part of the land acquisition. In that case, the entire purchase price paid for the land and the old building is debited to the Land account. Costs incurred in removing the old building (less any salvage proceeds) are debited to the Land account.

If the land is purchased as an investment (and not for use in the normal business operations), the costs associated with the acquisition are debited to an Investment in Land account. This account is reported in the investments section of the balance sheet; it is not considered part of property, plant, and equipment.

If the land is purchased to be held as a future building site, but is not currently being used in the business operations, its costs are debited to an account called Land: Future Building Site. This account is reported in the "other assets" section of the balance sheet. It will not be considered a part of property, plant, and equipment until the firm begins to make use of it in its business operations.

Land is an unusual asset because there is normally no limit to its useful lifetime. Land does not wear out or become obsolete. The company can continue to use the land indefinitely. Therefore, the cost of land normally is retained as an unexpired cost (an asset) indefinitely. None of the cost is written off as an expense.

However, some expenditures associated with the land do involve costs that expire with time. For example, costs of installing sidewalks, parking lots, driveways, lawn sprinkler systems, and so on should be allocated as expenses over the expected lifetimes of these improvements. Therefore, these costs are debited to a separate account called Land Improvements, rather than being treated as part of the cost of the land itself.

As another example, consider the purchase or construction of a building. Expenditures debited to the Building account would include the purchase price or construction cost of the building, the cost of building permits, architect and engineering fees, the broker's commissions, and any interest or insurance on the building during its construction period.

Similarly, the cost of a machine (debited to a Machinery account) would include the purchase price of the machine (less cash discount), sales taxes, freight charges involved in bringing the machine to the place where it is to be used, and installation and testing costs required to get the machine ready and in place for its use.

Case 1. Asset acquired in a cash transaction. On June 15, a company acquires machinery priced at $1,000, subject to terms of 2/10, n/30. The company pays cash for the machinery, so it pays $980. On June 22, the company pays a freight charge of $100 cash for delivery of the machine. On June 25, it pays in cash a charge of $200 for installation of the machine in its factory and another charge of $50 for costs of testing the machine prior to putting it into regular use.

The transactions related to the acquisition of this machinery are recorded by the following journal entries.

June 15	Machinery	980	
	Cash		980
	To record the invoice cost of machine, less 2% cash discount.		
22	Machinery	100	
	Cash		100
	To record freight charge on machine.		
25	Machinery	250	
	Cash		250
	To record installation costs of $200 and testing costs of $50 on machine.		

In the general ledger, a single control account (called Machinery) could be used to accumulate costs associated with the acquisition of all machines. Similar control accounts could be used for buildings, equipment, and other categories of tangible fixed assets. In subsidiary ledgers, details associated with specific assets could be accumulated. Exhibit 14-1 shows an example of a subsidiary record for equipment; in this case the subsidiary ledger for the Equipment control account is kept in the form of a card file.

Case 2. Asset acquired in a credit transaction. Assume that the machinery described in case 1 is acquired on June 15 on account.

The machine should be recorded at its cash price, whether or not the cash discount is taken.

June 15	Machinery	980	
	Interest [or Financing] Expense	20	
	Accounts Payable		1,000
	To record acquisition of machine on credit terms of 2/10, n/30.		

Exhibit 14-1 **Equipment ledger card**

Item Name ______	Location ______
Identification No. ______	Control Account No. ______
Manufacturer ______	Date Acquired ______
Service Life ______	Date Disposed ______
Estimated Scrap Value ______	

Date		Description	Ref.	Total Cost	Depreciation Current Year	Accumulated Depreciation

Freight, installation, and testing costs should be debited to the Machinery account, as in case 1.

Case 3. Asset acquired in an exchange transaction. The machinery described in case 1 is acquired on June 15 in an exchange transaction. The company exchanges for the machine some marketable securities carried in the books at their original cost of $700. A recent quotation on the New York Stock Exchange indicates that the securities have a current market value of $950.

Should the machine be recorded at its cash price ($980), at the fair market value of the marketable securities ($950), or at the original cost of the marketable securities ($700)? The market quotation for the securities (adjusted daily in accordance with supply and demand on the securities market) appears to be more objectively determined than does the price quoted for the machine. The original cost of the marketable securities is not relevant to the value of the machinery. Therefore, the transaction could be recorded as follows.

June 15	Machinery	950	
	Marketable Securities		700
	Gain on Exchange		250
	To record acquisition of machine in exchange for marketable securities with quoted price of $950.		

Case 4. Two assets acquired for a lump sum. The company acquires land and a building for $90,000 in cash. An appraisal indicates that the land has an appraised value of $20,000 and the building an appraised value of $80,000.

When two assets are purchased for a lump sum, the purchase price is apportioned between them in proportion to their relative sales (or appraisal) values. In this case, the total appraised value of the land and building is $100,000. Of that total appraised value, 20 percent represents the value of the land and 80 percent represents the value of the building. Therefore, the total cash price for land and building should be allocated as follows:

	Appraisal	Allocated	Cost allocated
Land	$ 20,000	20/100 × $90,000 =	$18,000
Building	80,000	80/100 × $90,000 =	72,000
	$100,000		$90,000

The transaction is recorded as follows.

July 15	Land	18,000	
	Building	72,000	
	Cash		90,000
	To record purchase of land (appraised value $20,000) and building, (appraised value $80,000).		

Case 5. Asset is constructed. The company obtains a bid from the Supplier Company in the amount of $50,000 for a machine that it needs. Instead of buying the machine for this price, the company decides to build the machine in its own plant. It does so at a total cost of $48,000.

When an asset is constructed by a company, the acquisition cost of the asset is the expenditure for material, labor, and factory expenses associated with its construction. The purchase price of a similar asset that could be obtained from others is not a factor in determining the cost of the asset. In this case, the machine is recorded at its actual cost of $48,000.

Aug. 15	Machinery	48,000	
	[Various accounts]		48,000

It would be incorrect to record the asset at $50,000 (the bid price for a similar asset purchased from the Supplier Company). If the asset were recorded at this price, the accounts would show a $2,000 gain on the construction of the asset. A company does not earn income by constructing assets for its own use. The company ***saved*** $2,000 by constructing the asset instead of purchasing it; such savings are not revenue.

In the same way, the company might save money by finding a lower price for a particular asset from one certain supplier. No matter what the situation, the cost recorded for the asset is the actual cash price paid (so long as the transaction is an "arm's length" exchange, where each party is seeking to serve his own best interests).

DEPRECIATION OF PLANT AND EQUIPMENT

Most long-lived assets have a limited useful life. The asset will benefit the company only during its useful life. Therefore, the acquisition cost of the asset (initially recorded as an unexpired cost—a cost that will benefit future periods) should be written off as an expense during the useful life of the asset. At the end of its useful life, the asset may still have some salvage value. The total cost to the company of having and using the asset will be the acquisition cost less the salvage value. Although the expenditures usually are made early in the life of the asset, it will help produce revenue for the company throughout its useful life. Therefore, the cost should be recognized (written off) against revenue in a systematic manner over the lifetime of the asset.

By definition, ***depreciation*** is the process of allocating the cost less salvage value of a tangible fixed asset over its estimated useful life in a rational and systematic manner.

The decline in value during the life of the asset is the result of

1. decay and deterioration from wear and tear of use, time, and the elements;

2. ordinary obsolescence arising from technological improvements and the inadequacy of the asset for its intended purpose.

The accounting entry to record depreciation is made as an adjusting entry at the close of each accounting period. The entry recognizes as an expense (to be matched against revenue for the period) the portion of the cost less salvage value of the asset that is to be allocated to this particular period. The entry takes the following form.

Dec. 31	Depreciation Expense: Building	XXX	
	Accumulated Depreciation: Building		XXX

Depreciation expense appears in the income statement as an operating expense. The Accumulated Depreciation account is a contra asset account. It is deducted from the related asset account in the balance sheet:

Equipment	$1,000,000	
Less: Accumulated depreciation	600,000	$400,000

The ***carrying value*** (or ***book value***) of an asset is its cost less its accumulated depreciation. In the preceding illustration, the carrying value of the equipment is $400,000. This carrying value may or may not happen to be equal to the current market value of the equipment. The market value of the equipment is irrelevant, because the company intends to keep the fixed asset for use. Depreciation is a process of allocating cost over several periods, ***not*** a way of determining the current market value of the asset.

If the company should decide to sell the fixed asset (for example, because it is closing a particular factory), the carrying value at the time of the sale would represent the unexpired portion of the cost of the asset. If the asset were sold at a price higher than the carrying value, the company would recognize a gain (revenue) on the sale. If the asset were sold at a price lower than the carrying value, the company would recognize a loss on the sale.

To explain depreciation more fully, we wish to emphasize the following points.

1. Depreciation is the accounting process of allocating the cost of the asset over its useful life. It does ***not*** necessarily follow that the depreciation charge calculated for accounting purposes corresponds to
   a. the rate of physical decay or deterioration of the asset; or
   b. the decline in market value of the asset.
2. Depreciation is an ***expense*** that is to be reported on the income statement in good years and in bad years; the amount to be allocated to each year is determined systematically and rationally in advance. Depreciation assigns the cost of the asset to expenses over its useful life. The amount debited to Depreciation Expense each year is not affected by changes in the market value of the asset, or by maintenance practices of the firm which may be keeping the plant and equipment in excellent condition.
3. Depreciation does not provide funds for replacing the asset when its useful life ends. Depreciation writes off the cost of an asset—that is, a cost already incurred is charged to expense. This procedure does have the effect of reducing the carrying value of the asset during its life, but the amount shown on the balance sheet as "accumulated depreciation" is ***not*** an amount of assets being hoarded by the

company to replace the plant or equipment at the end of its life. The accumulated depreciation is simply the portion of the cost that has already been written off as an expense, and therefore is no longer reported as an unexpired cost or asset. Disclosing the amount of accumulated depreciation provides information about the extent to which the asset has been depreciated.

4. Land is not subject to depreciation because its useful life is considered to be unlimited.

METHODS OF DEPRECIATION

Computation of the periodic depreciation charge involves consideration of the following items.

1. The ***depreciation base.*** Usually, this base is the cost of the asset, including those expenditures needed to get the asset ready for use.
2. The ***scrap (salvage) value of the asset.*** The scrap value represents the amount that can be recovered when the asset is removed from service. In practice, the scrap value of an asset is often ignored because its estimate is a matter of many uncertainties and imponderables.
3. The ***estimated life of the asset.*** The estimated useful life may be expressed in terms of
   a. time (for example, a certain number of years),
   b. operating periods (for example, a certain number of working hours), or
   c. units of output.

   The accounting system should adopt for each asset the estimate of useful life that provides the best matching of revenue and expense. The Internal Revenue Service publishes useful-life guidelines for broad classes of assets.

The process of depreciation should allocate the depreciation base less scrap value over the estimated life in a systematic and rational manner. Many methods are available for computing the expense to be allocated to each period. In the following pages, we discuss certain methods commonly used by business:

1. straight-line depreciation method;
2. working-hour method;
3. unit-of-production method;
4. accelerated depreciation methods,
   a. double-declining-balance method,
   b. sum-of-years'-digits method.

STRAIGHT-LINE DEPRECIATION. Straight-line depreciation allocates equal portions of the asset's cost less salvage value to equal amounts of time in the life of the asset. That is, this method assumes that the cost of the asset expires as a steady (straight-line) function of time. The depreciation charge for each year can be computed by the following formula:

$$\text{Depreciation} = \frac{\text{Cost} - \text{Salvage value}}{\text{Estimated number of years of service life}}$$

Case 6. Straight-line depreciation. On January 2, 19_1, the company acquires a machine for $1,100. The machine has an estimated salvage value of $100 at the end of its estimated life of five years.

The annual depreciation expense for the machine is computed as follows, using the formula given just before the case:

$$\text{Depreciation} = \frac{\$1{,}100 - \$100}{5 \text{ years}}$$
$$= \$200.$$

Exhibit 14-2 is a depreciation schedule showing the periodic adjusting entries to be made for depreciation on this machine.

Case 7. Depreciation for partial accounting periods. Assume that the machine described in case 6 was purchased on May 1, 19_1, instead of at the beginning of the year.

The depreciation expense to be recorded at the end of 19_1 in this case would be computed for eight months (8/12 year) instead of a full year.

Dec. 31	Depreciation Expense: Machine	133.33	
	Accumulated Depreciation: Machine		133.33
	To record 8 months' depreciation for machine purchased May 1: $200 × 8/12 = $133.33.		

Because the depreciation expense is only an estimate, it is usually considered sufficient to compute the charge to the nearest month. In this case, the expenses allocated to the years 19_2 through 19_5 would be the same as those computed for case 6 (Exhibit 14-2). The final four months' depreciation expense would be recognized in 19_6.

In both case 6 and case 7, the carrying value of the machine is reduced to the estimated salvage value at the end of the estimated life. If the machine is still in use at that time, it will be carried on the books at its estimated salvage value until it actually is removed from service.

WORKING-HOUR METHOD. The working-hour method of calculating depreciation assumes that the life of the asset is best estimated in terms of the time that it is

Exhibit 14-2
Depreciation schedule for case 6 using straight-line method

Date of Entry	Depreciation Expense Dr.	Accumulated Depreciation Cr.	Accumulated Depreciation Balance	Carrying Value
Jan. 1, 19_1	—	—	—	1,100
Dec. 31, 19_1	200	200	200	900
Dec. 31, 19_2	200	200	400	700
Dec. 31, 19_3	200	200	600	500
Dec. 31, 19_4	200	200	800	300
Dec. 31, 19_5	200	200	1,000	100

in actual use, rather than in terms of the time that has passed since its acquisition. The more (or less) hours that the asset is actually in use during a particular year, the more (or less) the depreciation expense to be recognized in that year. The ***depreciation rate per working hour*** is computed as follows:

$$\text{Depreciation } rate = \frac{\text{Cost} - \text{Salvage value}}{\text{Estimated life of asset in working hours}}$$

Depreciation expense for a year is computed by multiplying the depreciation rate (per working hour) by the number of hours worked during the year.

The working-hour method may be the most appropriate method for computing depreciation on an asset that is in use for significantly different amounts of time in different years, and on an asset whose decline in value over the years is mainly due to the wear and tear resulting from use.

Case 8. Working-hour method. The company acquires a machine for $1,000 early in 19_1. It is estimated that the machine will have no scrap value at its disposal; its estimated useful service life is 500 working hours. The machine was used for 75 hours during 19_1.

The depreciation rate for this machine is computed as follows:

$$\text{Depreciation rate} = \frac{\$1{,}000 - \$0}{500 \text{ working hours}} = \$2 \text{ per hour.}$$

Therefore, the depreciation expense to be recognized for 19_1 is

$$\text{Depreciation expense} = \$2 \text{ per hour} \times 75 \text{ hours} = \$150.$$

UNIT-OF-PRODUCTION METHOD. The unit-of-production method assumes that the useful life of the asset is best measured in terms of the number of units produced by the asset. Under this method, the ***depreciation rate per unit produced*** is computed as follows:

$$\text{Depreciation } rate = \frac{\text{Cost} - \text{Salvage value}}{\text{Estimated units of production during life}}$$

Depreciation expense for a year is computed by multiplying the depreciation rate (per unit of production) by the number of units produced during the year.

Case 9. Unit-of-production method. The company early in 19_1 acquires a machine for $1,200. The machine is expected to produce 1,000 widgets during its useful life. At the end of its life, it is estimated that the machine will have a scrap value of $200. In 19_1, the machine produces 300 widgets.

The depreciation rate for this machine is

$$\frac{\$1{,}200 - \$200}{1{,}000 \text{ widgets produced}} = \$1 \text{ per widget produced.}$$

Therefore, the depreciation expense to be recognized for 19_1 is

$$\$1 \text{ per widget produced} \times 300 \text{ widgets produced} = \$300.$$

ACCELERATED (REDUCING-CHARGE) DEPRECIATION. Some depreciation methods are available that match larger portions of the cost of the asset against revenue during the early years of its life. This procedure of writing off the cost of the asset at an accelerated pace can be justified if the case can be made that the asset is more effective and productive in its earlier life than it is later.

Another justification has been suggested for the use of accelerated depreciation methods. The cost of using a fixed asset includes both depreciation expense and repairs expense. Repair expenses are usually smaller during the early years of the life of an asset than they are during the later years of its life. Therefore, it is desirable to use a depreciation method that gives a uniform distribution of the total cost of using the asset over its life. Exhibit 14-3 shows a schedule illustrating this concept.

Accelerated depreciation methods sometimes are adopted to reflect the fact that the market value of many assets undergoes relatively large reductions during the early years of their lives. Therefore, the accelerated depreciation method is said to reflect more nearly the current market value of the asset at any given time during its life. However, you should keep in mind that depreciation is essentially a process of allocating expense—not a valuation process. The market values of assets are ***not*** a primary consideration in choosing depreciation procedures.

Here we illustrate two accelerated depreciation methods: (1) the double-declining-balance method, and (2) the sum-of-years'-digits method.

DOUBLE-DECLINING-BALANCE METHOD. Under the double-declining-balance method of depreciation, depreciation expense for each year is computed as follows.

1. The ***rate*** of depreciation is computed as $(1/n) \times 2$, where n is the estimated life of the asset in years.
2. The first year's depreciation expense is computed by multiplying the depreciation rate by the cost (***not*** cost minus salvage value) of the asset.
3. For each following year, the depreciation expense is computed by multiplying the depreciation rate by the carrying value of the asset at the beginning of the year. (Recall that the carrying value is equal to the cost less the accumulated depreciation.)
4. When the carrying value of the asset declines to its estimated salvage value, no further depreciation expense is recognized. That is, the carrying value of the asset is not reduced below its estimated salvage value.

Exhibit 14-3
Illustration of one justification for accelerated depreciation

Year	Accelerated Depreciation Expense	Repairs Expense	Total Expense of Using Fixed Asset
1	$500	$ 0	$500
2	400	100	500
3	300	200	500
4	200	300	500
5	100	400	500

Case 10. Double-declining balance method. On January 2, 19_1, the company purchases equipment with an estimated life of five years and an estimated salvage value of $50. The equipment is purchased for $1,000.

If the company chooses to use the double-declining-balance method of computing depreciation expense for this equipment, the accountant must first compute the depreciation rate:

Depreciation rate = (1/5 years) × 2 = 40% per year.

Exhibit 14-4 shows a schedule of depreciation for the equipment. Note that the depreciation expense written off during the final year of the estimated life is adjusted in order to bring the carrying value to the salvage value at the end of the estimated life.

The adjusting entry made at the end of the first year in this case is the following.

Dec. 31	Depreciation Expense: Equipment	400	
	Accumulated Depreciation: Equipment		400

SUM-OF-YEARS'-DIGITS METHODS. Under the sum-of-years'-digits method of computing depreciation expense, the depreciation charge for each year is computed as follows.

1. Compute the sum of the digits from one through the number of years of the asset's estimated life. For example, if the estimated life of the asset is six years, the sum of years' digits is

$$1 + 2 + 3 + 4 + 5 + 6 = 21.$$

This sum can be computed by using the following formula, where N is the number of years in the life of the asset:

$$\text{Sum of years' digits} = N\left(\frac{N+1}{2}\right);$$

$$\text{Sum for 6 years} = 6\left(\frac{6+1}{2}\right) = 21.$$

Exhibit 14-4 **Depreciation schedule for case 10 using double-declining-balance method**

Year	Computation	Annual Depreciation	Accumulated Depreciation	Carrying Value
1	40% × $1,000	$400	$400	$600
2	40% × 600	240	640	360
3	40% × 360	144	784	216
4	40% × 216	86*	870	130
5	40% × 130 = $52	80†	950	50

*Rounded to nearest dollar.

†In the last year of the estimated life of the asset, the annual depreciation charge is adjusted to the amount needed to bring the carrying value of the asset to its salvage value.

2. For each year, the depreciation rate is expressed as a fraction. The denominator of the fraction is the sum computed in step 1. The numerator of the fraction for each year is determined by taking the digits in reverse order. For example, if the life is 6 years, the numerator of the fraction for the first year is 6. The rates for the years are 6/21, 5/21, 4/21, and so on.
3. Compute the depreciation expense for each year by multiplying the depreciation rate for that year by the ***cost minus salvage value.***

Exhibit 14-5 shows a depreciation schedule for the equipment described in case 10, this time using the sum-of-years'-digits method. The dollar amounts for the annual depreciation entries can be read from the annual depreciation column of the exhibit.

Case 11. Sum-of-years'-digits method of depreciation. On July 1, 19_1, the company purchases an $800 asset with a salvage value of $50 and a five-year estimated life. The company wishes to use the sum-of-years'-digits method to compute depreciation expense for this asset.

To compute depreciation for a part of a year, the depreciation for the full year is computed first. This annual depreciation is then multiplied by the appropriate fraction representing the portion of the year being considered.

The first year of the asset's life (in case 11) extends from July 1, 19_1, to June 30, 19_2. Half of this year falls in the calendar year 19_1 and half of it in the calendar year 19_2. The depreciation expense for the full year is:

5/15 × $750 = $250.

Half (6/12) of this expense should be recognized in 19_1:

Depreciation expense (July 1 to Dec. 31, 19_1) = 6/12 × $250 = $125.

The depreciation expense for 19_2 includes half of the first year's depreciation and half of the second year's depreciation:

Depreciation (Jan. 1 to June 30, 19_1) = 6/12 × 5/15 × $750 = $125;

Depreciation (July 1 to Dec. 31, 19_2) = 6/12 × 4/15 × $750 = $100;

Depreciation (Jan. 1 to Dec. 31, 19_2) = $125 + $100 = $225.

Exhibit 14-5
Depreciation schedule for case 10 using sum-of-years'-digits method

Year	Computation	Annual Depreciation	Accumulated Depreciation	Carrying Value
1	5/15 × $950	$317	$317	$683
2	4/15 × 950	253	570	430
3	3/15 × 950	190	760	240
4	2/15 × 950	127	887	113
5	1/15 × 950	63	950	50

*Values for annual depreciation expense are rounded to the nearest dollar.

EXPENDITURES: CAPITAL AND REVENUE

An expenditure is the payment—or the incurring of an obligation to pay at a future date—for a benefit received. During the life of a tangible fixed asset, various expenditures may be incurred in connection with the use of the assets. Questions arise as to whether such expenditures should be treated as revenue expenditures or as capital expenditures.

1. ***Revenue expenditures*** are expensed—that is, charged as expense in the year they are incurred.
2. ***Capital expenditures*** are capitalized—that is, charged to an asset account.

A revenue expenditure is assumed to benefit only the current year. Hence it is recognized as an expense during the current year. Capital expenditures are assumed to represent costs that will benefit future years. Hence these expenditures are recorded as unexpired costs in asset accounts. Exhibit 14-6 conceptualizes the differences between capital and revenue expenditures.

The schedule shown in Exhibit 14-7 summarizes the accounting treatment of difficult problems associated with distinguishing capital expenditures from revenue expenditures. The following cases illustrate these problems.

Case 12. Ordinary repair. The company spends $75 to replace broken windows in its factory. Such replacement of windows is a regular reconditioning process, and management considers this to be an ordinary repair.

The ordinary repair is treated as a revenue expenditure and is recorded by the following entry.

June 15	Repairs Expense	75	
	Cash		75

Case 13. Extraordinary repair. A machine costing $10,000 and having a ten-year estimated life is completely reconditioned at the end of eight years, at a cost of $2,400.

This extraordinary repair is treated as a capital expenditure because it extends the estimated useful life of the machine.

July 15	Accumulated Depreciation	2,400	
	Cash		2,400

The debit to Accumulated Depreciation cancels some of the previous charges and increases the book value of the asset by the cost of the extraordinary repair. In this case, if the straight-line method were being used to compute depreciation expense on the machine, the book value before the repair would be $2,000 ($10,000 cost less $8,000 depreciation for eight years). The effect of the repair is to increase the book value to $4,400. Assuming that the effect of the repair is to extend the estimated life of the machine another two years beyond the original estimated life of ten years, the depreciation expense would then be $1,100 per year ($4,400 ÷ 4 years).

Exhibit 14-6
Accounting treatment of revenue and capital expenditures

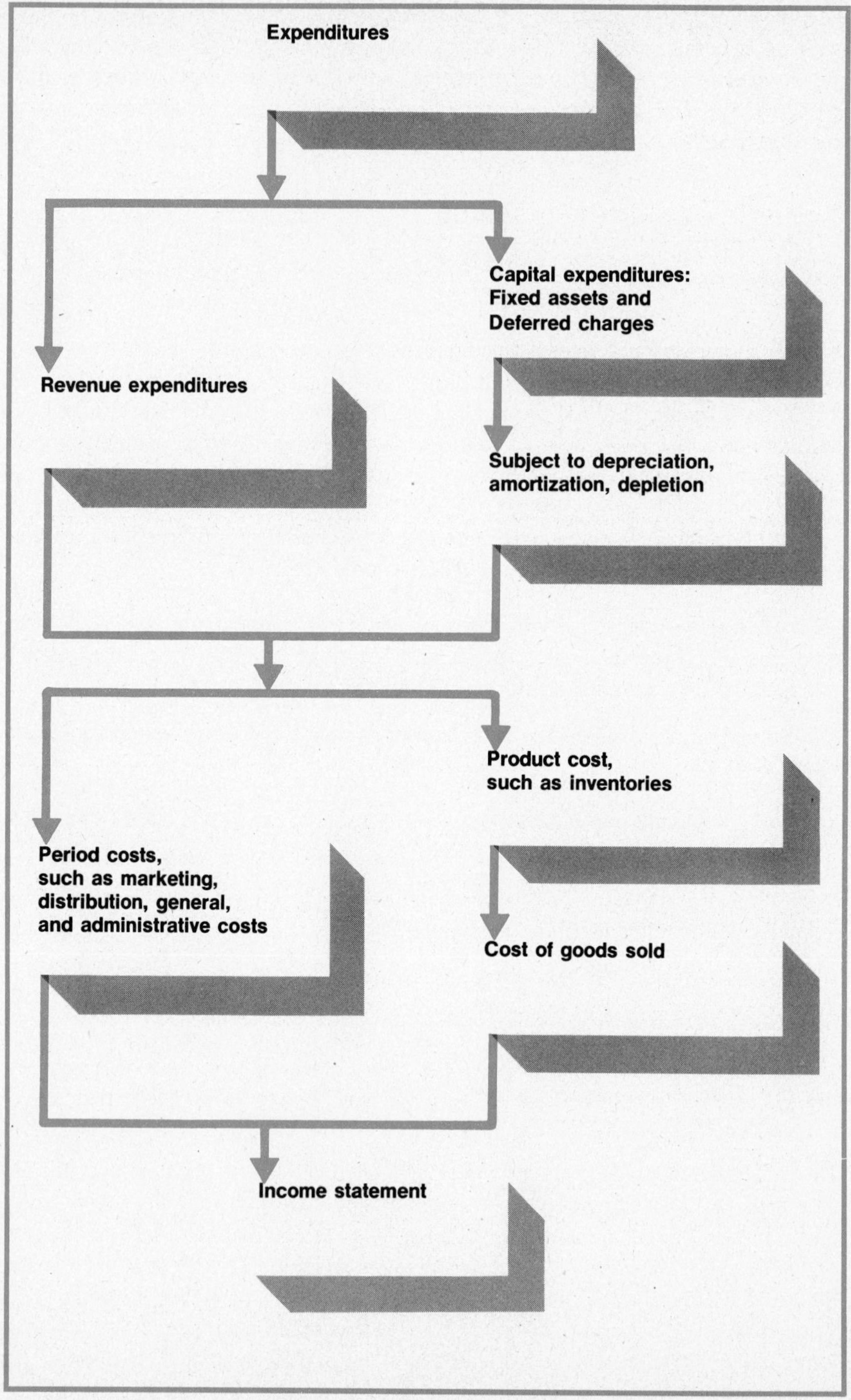

Exhibit 14-7 **Account debited for various kinds of expenditures associated with the use of tangible fixed assets**

	REVENUE EXPENDITURES	CAPITAL EXPENDITURES	
EXPENDITURE	**Expense Account Dr.**	**Asset Account Dr.**	**Accumulated Depreciation Dr.**
1. *Repairs* (reconditioning, overhaul):			
a. Ordinary repair	X		
b. Extraordinary repair (extends life of the asset)			X
2. *Additions:* new units; extensions; expansions; enlargements		X	
3. *Improvements* (betterments); substitutions involving an increase in *quality:*			
a. Minor (lack of materiality)	X		
b. Major (material)		X	
4. *Replacement* of entire units (as distinguished from ordinary and extraordinary repairs)		X	

Case 14. Additions. The company constructs a new wing on its factory building at a cost of $100,000.

This expenditure will benefit revenue in future periods, so it is treated as a capital expenditure and charged to an asset account.

Aug. 12	Factory Building	100,000	
	Cash		100,000

Case 15. Major improvements. The company has a factory building that was constructed four years ago at a cost of $500,000, including $10,000 for plain glass windows. The company now replaces these windows with high-quality, safety-glass windows at a cost of $20,000. The depreciation expense for the building is being computed by the straight-line method over an estimated life of twenty years.

Major improvements and betterments are capital expenditures and are charged to an asset account. In recording improvements, betterments, and replacement of entire units, the accountant must first remove from the asset account the cost of the item being replaced. He must also remove from the Accumulated Depreciation account the accumulated depreciation associated with the item being replaced. Then the cost of the improvement or betterment can be recorded in the asset account without a duplication of costs.

In this case, the Building account contains the $10,000 original cost of the windows. The depreciation on the windows is $500 per year, so the Accumulated Depreciation account contains $2,000 of depreciation charges recorded for the windows during the four years. These old windows are now being taken out of service, so they are no longer an asset that will benefit future periods. The part of their cost that has not been recognized as expense during the four years of their use must now be recognized as an expense (a loss) in this period.

Oct. 20	Loss on Undepreciated Windows	8,000	
	Accumulated Depreciation: Building	2,000	
	Building		10,000
	To remove recorded cost of old windows and related accumulated depreciation from the accounts.		

Now that the amounts related to the discarded windows have been removed from the asset and contra asset accounts, the cost of the new windows can be recorded.

Oct. 20	Building	20,000	
	Cash		20,000
	To record $20,000 cost of new safety-glass windows.		

Accounting for the replacement of entire units is similar to accounting for major improvements and betterments. Accounting for minor improvements and betterments is similar to accounting for ordinary repairs.

DISPOSAL OF TANGIBLE FIXED ASSETS

The company may dispose of assets in various ways—for example, by sale, by discarding, or by trading an asset for another asset. Certain problems arise in any case where an asset is disposed of.

1. Depreciation Expense and Accumulated Depreciation accounts associated with the asset must be updated to record depreciation expense accrued since the last adjusting entry for depreciation.
2. The cost of the disposed asset must be removed from the asset account; the updated accumulated depreciation associated with the asset must be removed from the Accumulated Depreciation account.
3. Any gain or loss on the disposal transaction must be recorded.

Case 16. Sale of depreciable asset. On July 1, 19_3, the company sells some equipment for $600. This equipment was purchased for $1,000 on January 1, 19_1. Depreciation expense for the equipment has been computed by the straight-line method, with an estimated life of five years and no salvage value.

Exhibit 14-8 shows the relevant ledger accounts as they appear at the time the equipment is sold. The following entries are needed to record the sale of the equipment.

19_3			
July 1	Depreciation Expense: Equipment	100	
	Accumulated Depreciation: Equipment		100
	To record depreciation on equipment for 6 months (Jan. 1 to June 30, 19_3): $1,000 × 1/5 × 6/12 = $100.		
1	Cash	600	
	Accumulated Depreciation: Equipment	500	
	Equipment		1,000
	Gain on Sale of Equipment		100
	To record sale of equipment at a gain.		

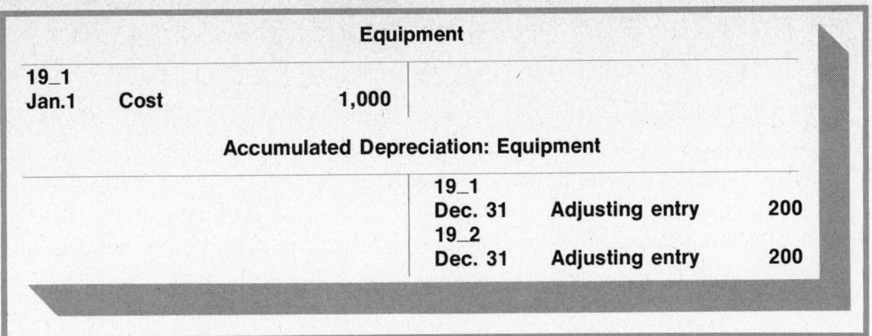

Equipment

19_1 Jan. 1	Cost	1,000			

Accumulated Depreciation: Equipment

			19_1 Dec. 31	Adjusting entry	200
			19_2 Dec. 31	Adjusting entry	200

Exhibit 14-8
Ledger accounts at time of sale in case 16

Note that the carrying value of the equipment at the time of the sale was $500 (cost of $1,000 less accumulated depreciation of $500). Because the company received $600 for an asset with a book value of $500, the company must recognize a gain of $100. This gain should be listed as "other income" on the income statement.

If the asset were sold for less than its carrying value, a loss on the sale would be recognized. If sold for the carrying value, neither gain nor loss would result.

Case 17. Fully depreciated asset discarded. On January 3, 19_6, the company discards some equipment that it had acquired five years ago for $10,000. The complete cost of the equipment has been recognized as depreciation expense over the five years.

Exhibit 14-9 shows the relevant ledger accounts as they appear at the time of the discard. Note that there is no gain or loss on this discard, because the carrying value of the equipment has been reduced to zero by writing off the cost of the equipment to depreciation. Therefore, the only entry needed to record the discard is one that removes the cost from the asset account and removes the related accumulated depreciation from the contra asset account.

19_6 Jan. 3	Accumulated Depreciation: Equipment	10,000	
	Equipment		10,000
	To record discard of fully depreciated equipment.		

Equipment

19_1 Jan. 2	Acquisition cost	10,000			

Accumulated Depreciation: Equipment

			19_1 Dec. 31	Adjusting entry	2,000
			19_2 Dec. 31	Adjusting entry	2,000
			19_3 Dec. 31	Adjusting entry	2,000
			19_4 Dec. 31	Adjusting entry	2,000
			19_5 Dec. 31	Adjusting entry	2,000

Exhibit 14-9
Ledger accounts at time of discard in case 17

If this equipment were not discarded at this time, but remained in use for one or more accounting periods, the cost and accumulated depreciation would be carried in the accounts (and reported on the balance sheet) even though the carrying value of the equipment has been reduced to zero. This practice discloses to the user the existence of the equipment, its acquisition cost, and the fact that the full cost has been recognized as depreciation expense.

If a tangible fixed asset being depreciated individually (not as part of a group) is discarded before the end of its estimated life, a loss on the disposal must be recognized to account for the carrying value being removed from the books.

COMPOSITE DEPRECIATION. To expedite depreciation calculations, a composite depreciation rate can be applied to a major group of assets, or to all assets owned. Composite depreciation provides a more uniform depreciation charge over the useful life of the group of assets than would be the case if depreciation of individual assets were used. It also eliminates much clerical work required when assets are depreciated individually.

Exhibit 14-10 illustrates a group of three assets for which a composite depreciation rate is to be computed. The average life of the group of assets is computed as follows:

$$\text{Average life} = \frac{\text{Depreciable cost}}{\text{Annual depreciation}} = \frac{\$17{,}000}{\$3{,}400 \text{ per year}} = 5 \text{ years.}$$

The annual rate of depreciation (rounded value) is computed as follows:

$$\text{Annual rate} = \frac{\text{Annual depreciation}}{\text{Total cost}} = \frac{\$3{,}400 \text{ per year}}{\$17{,}700} = 19.21\% \text{ per year.}$$

Depreciation per year at the average rate of 19.21% (rounded) applied to total cost of $17,700 is $3,400 (rounded). At the end of the five-year average life, the accumulated depreciation will be $17,000, which is the depreciable cost of the assets. Assuming that the three assets were acquired on January 1 and that the company closes its books on December 31, the adjusting entry to record annual depreciation in each of the following five years would be as follows.

Dec. 31	Depreciation Expense	3,400	
	Accumulated Depreciation		3,400

Exhibit 14-10 Schedule of depreciation information for a group of three assets

Asset	Cost	Estimated Salvage Value	Depreciable Cost	Estimated Useful Life (in years)	Annual Straight-Line Depreciation
1	$10,000	$ 0	$10,000	10	$1,000
2	5,500	500	5,000	2½	2,000
3	2,200	200	2,000	5	400
	$17,700	$700	$17,000		$3,400

If the company is using a form of composite depreciation and discards one asset in a group, no gain or loss is recognized on the disposal. Instead, it is assumed that the discarded asset has been fully depreciated. For example, consider the group of assets shown in Exhibit 14-10. If asset number 2 is discarded at the end of the second year of its life, the disposal is recorded by the following entry.

Jan. 1	Accumulated Depreciation	5,500	
	[asset account]		5,500

Underdepreciation of asset number 2 used less than its estimated useful life is assumed to be offset by overestimations on other items in the group. Composite depreciation assumes that assets are replaced with similar assets on a regular basis. If asset number 2 is replaced with a similar asset at a cost of $6,000, the depreciation expense for the assets in the group will be recognized at the rate originally computed (19.21%), calculated on the balance in the asset account, excluding the original cost of the asset retired and including the cost of the asset acquired. The balance in the asset account is now $18,200 (i.e., $17,700 − $5,500 + $6,000).

TRADE-IN OF A TANGIBLE FIXED ASSET. When a fixed asset is traded in for another asset, certain accounting questions arise. At what dollar amount shall the new asset be recorded? Was there a gain or a loss on the exchange? The answers to these questions depend upon (1) whether the assets exchanged were similar or dissimilar assets, and (2) whether any cash (boot) was involved in the exchange.[1] Similar assets are productive assets that are of the same general type, that perform the same function, or that are employed in the same line of business.

Case 18. Exchange of dissimilar assets. On January 2, 19_1, a company purchased equipment for $1,000. This equipment is being depreciated on a straight-line basis with an estimated useful life of five years and no estimated salvage value. On July 1, 19_3, the company acquires another asset of a dissimilar nature (e.g., real estate or securities) with a price of $1,300, when it exchanges the old equipment. The company is also required to give $400 cash in the trade. The company trades in the old equipment and is given a trade-in allowance of $900 for the old equipment (which has a current market value of $800). Therefore, the company gets the new asset in exchange for $400 cash (boot) and the old (dissimilar) equipment.

Exhibit 14-11 shows the relevant ledger accounts at the time of the exchange: Before the exchange can be recorded, the accrued depreciation on the old equipment (since the last adjusting entry for depreciation on December 31) must be recognized.

19_3			
July 1	Depreciation Expense: Equipment	100	
	Accumulated Depreciation: Equipment		100
	To record 6 months' depreciation on old equipment (Jan. 1–July 1): $1,000 × 1/5 × 6/12 = $100.		

1. These problems are examined in *APB Opinion No. 29.* Accounting Principles Board, *Opinion No. 29: Accounting for Nonmonetary Transactions* (New York: American Institute of Certified Public Accountants, 1973), paras. 18–22.

Exhibit 14-11
Ledger accounts at time of exchange in case 18

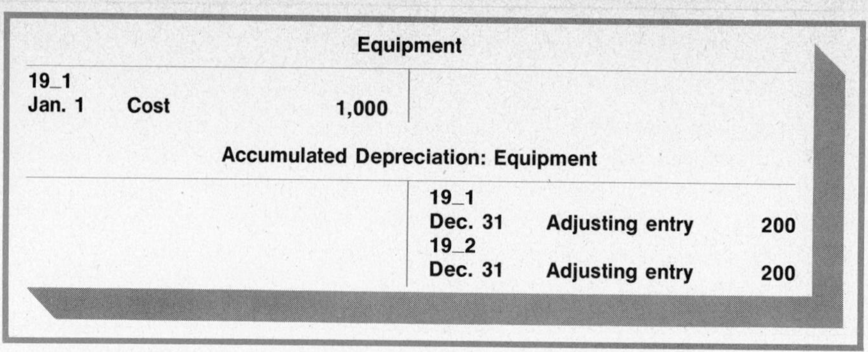

Equipment

19_1 Jan. 1	Cost	1,000			

Accumulated Depreciation: Equipment

			19_1 Dec. 31	Adjusting entry	200
			19_2 Dec. 31	Adjusting entry	200

Now that the accumulated depreciation has been updated to the time of the trade-in, we see that the old equipment has a book value of $500 (cost of $1,000 less accumulated depreciation of $500). The acquisition cost of the new equipment is equal to the value of the old equipment traded in plus the $400 boot. But which value should be used for the old equipment: the $500 carrying value, the $800 current market value, or the $900 trade-in allowance?

In a case like this that involves exchange of dissimilar assets, the current market value of the old equipment plus the boot is regarded as the most objective measure of the exchange price for the trade-in.[2]

19_3 July 1	New asset	1,200	
	Accumulated Depreciation: Equipment	500	
	Equipment [old asset]		1,000
	Cash		400
	Gain on Exchange of Equipment		300
	To record acquisition of new equipment by trade-in of old equipment with market value of $800, plus $400 boot.		

Note that this entry removes from the accounts the $1,000 cost and $500 accumulated depreciation carried for the old equipment. It records the new equipment at a cost of $1,200 (boot of $400 plus $800 market value of old equipment traded in). The $1,300 list price of the new equipment is ignored because list prices of many assets are quite arbitrary, with little relation to actual exchange prices. A $300 gain results from the transaction because the $500 carrying value of the old equipment was less than its $800 market value.

Case 19. Exchange of similar assets (no boot). The company owns machine A that cost $1,000. On August 1, the company exchanges machine A for a similar machine B that was owned by another company; no cash is involved in the transaction. Accumulated depreciation of $300 has been recognized for machine A as of the date of the exchange, so the book value of machine A at the time of the exchange is $700.

2. The APB makes the following comments about the current market value or fair value of the asset being exchanged. "Fair value of a nonmonetary asset transferred to or from an enterprise in a nonmonetary transaction should be determined by referring to estimated realizable values in cash transactions of the same or similar assets, quoted market prices, independent appraisals, estimated fair values of assets or services received in exchange, and other available evidence. If one of the parties in a nonmonetary transaction could have elected to receive cash instead of the nonmonetary asset, the amount of cash that could have been received may be evidence of the fair value of the nonmonetary assets exchanged." *APB Opinion No. 29,* para. 25.

When the assets exchanged are similar and no boot is involved, the asset acquired is recorded at the book value of the asset given up. The transaction is recorded by the following entry.

Aug. 1	Machinery [new asset, machine B]	700	
	Accumulated Depreciation: Machinery	300	
	Machinery [old asset, machine A]		1,000

Note that this entry removes the cost and accumulated depreciation for the old machine from the accounts, and then records the new machine at the same book value as the old machine.

Case 20. Exchange of similar assets (boot involved). The Boot Company owns machine C, which was purchased for $10,000 several years ago. The accumulated depreciation on machine C is $4,000, as of September 1. On this date, the Boot Company exchanges machine C plus $2,000 cash for a similar machine D owned by the Receiver Company.

Again, when the exchange involves similar assets, the value of the old machine is assumed to be its book value. The cost of the new machine is the book value of the machine traded in ($6,000) plus the cash boot given ($2,000).

Sep. 1	Machinery [new asset, machine D]	8,000	
	Accumulated Depreciation: Machinery	4,000	
	Machinery [old asset, machine C]		10,000
	Cash		2,000

This entry in the books of the Boot Company (the giver of the boot) removes the cost and accumulated depreciation related to the old asset from the accounts, and records the new asset at a cost equal to the sum of the book value of the old asset ($6,000) and the $2,000 boot. No gain or loss is recognized on the exchange of similar assets by the company that pays the boot. The party who receives the boot could have a recognized gain or loss. Because of its complexities, the accounting treatment for the party who receives the boot in an exchange of similar assets is not covered in this introductory course.

Natural resources (wasting assets)

Natural resources such as oil properties, mines, and timberlands are a form of tangible fixed assets classified separately from property, plant, and equipment. Accounting for natural resources involves many complex principles and procedures. Here we treat the topic very briefly to illustrate general procedures. Because the objective of acquiring natural resources usually is to convert them into inventory, to process the material, and then to sell the output, these assets are sometimes called wasting assets.

Natural resources are recorded at cost when acquired. The conversion of the natural resource into inventory (barrels of oil, tons of coal, feet of lumber, and so on) exhausts the cost or other value of the wasting asset. The process of writing off the cost of the asset to expense over the life of the asset is called ***depletion.*** The depletion charge recorded in a particular period is computed as follows.

1. Compute the ***unit depletion charge*** as

$$\frac{\text{Cost (or appraised value) of wasting asset}}{\text{Estimated number of units in natural resource}}$$

2. Compute the ***depletion charge for the period*** as

Unit depletion charge × Number of units converted from resource during period.

Case 21. ***Depletion.*** The company purchases an oil well for $1,000,000. Engineers estimate that this well will produce 500,000 barrels of oil. During the first year of operation, 100,000 barrels of oil are removed from the well.

The unit depletion charge (or depletion rate) for this well is

$$\frac{\$1{,}000{,}000}{500{,}000 \text{ barrels}} = \$2 \text{ per barrel.}$$

The depletion expense for the first year of operation is

$2 per barrel × 100,000 barrels recovered = $200,000.

The depletion charge is recorded in an adjusting entry made at the end of the accounting period.

Dec. 31	**Depletion Expense [for Inventory]**	**200,000**	
	Accumulated Depletion: Oil Well		**200,000**

The Accumulated Depletion account is a contra asset account; in the balance sheet, this amount is deducted from the cost of the asset being depleted.

Intangible fixed assets

Intangible fixed assets represent immaterial rights, privileges, and competitive advantages owned by a business. Among items classified as intangible fixed assets are patents, copyrights, franchises, trademarks, trade names, goodwill, organization costs, leases, and leasehold improvements.

A ***patent*** is an exclusive right granted by the federal government, enabling the holder of the patent to control the use of an invention for seventeen years. A patent protects an inventor against the unauthorized use of his creation by another person for a limited period of time.

A ***copyright*** is an exclusive right granted by the federal government to reproduce and sell literary matter or works of art and music. Copyrights are issued for the life of the author and an additional fifty years.

A ***franchise*** is a contract giving exclusive rights to perform certain functions or to sell certain services or products. The terms of the franchise contract establish the life of the franchise.

Trademarks and ***trade names*** are exclusive rights to use certain names, symbols, labels, designs, and so on. The life of a trademark or trade name is not limited by law.

Goodwill is the excess earning power of a business due to some special advantage(s) it possesses.

Organization costs are those expenditures incurred in starting a business. Organization costs include attorneys' fees and fees paid to the state in connection with the process of getting the business ready for operation.

A *lease* is a contract entitling a lessee (the tenant) to use property of another for a period of time, in exchange for the payment of rent to the lessor (the landlord). If a lessee constructs a building or other improvements on the leased property, such items are accounted for as *leasehold improvements.*

Intangible assets usually are acquired through purchase or are developed by the business. Accounting for intangible assets involves problems associated with

1. determining the initial value to be recorded in the accounts when the intangible asset is acquired or developed; and
2. deciding how to amortize (that is, write off) the cost of the intangible asset over its estimated useful life by systematic charges to expense.

The initial recording principle indicates that intangible assets should be recorded at their acquisition cost. If a patent, copyright, or other intangible asset is acquired by purchase, the purchase price and costs associated with the acquisition would be capitalized. If the patent, copyright, trade name, or similar intangible asset were developed by the business, all costs associated with the development of the asset would be capitalized.

Case 22. The question of intangible asset. On January 1, the company purchases a patent for $28,000 from an inventor who held the patent.

The acquisition of the patent is recorded by the following entry.

Jan. 1	Patent	28,000	
	Cash		28,000

If the company developed a patent itself, the acquisition of the patent would be recorded in a similar asset account, but the credit portion of the entry would remove appropriate amounts from the various expense and asset accounts where the costs of developing the patent had been initially recorded.

After acquisition, an intangible asset is subject to amortization. The cost of the asset should be written off over its estimated useful life (see *APB Opinion No. 17*).[3] The life of an intangible asset may be limited by law, regulations, or agreement. *APB Opinion No. 17* specifies that an intangible asset is to be amortized over its estimated useful life, but ***not to exceed*** forty years. ***Amortization*** is the process of systematically allocating the cost of an intangible asset to expense over its useful life. *APB Opinion No. 17* also specifies that the ***straight-line method*** of amortization should be used to write off an intangible asset, unless it can be shown that another method is more appropriate under the circumstances. If the useful life of an intangible asset is shorter than its legal life, the asset should be amortized over the shorter period.

3. Accounting Principles Board, ***Opinion No. 17: Intangible Assets*** (New York: American Institute of Certified Public Accountants, 1970).

The amortization of an intangible asset is recorded by an adjusting entry made when the books of the company are closed at the end of an accounting period. For example, suppose that the patent acquired in case 22 is estimated to have a useful life of ten years. (That is, the company expects its ownership of the patent to benefit its revenue for only ten years, even though the legal life of the patent may be longer. The amortization period of an intangible asset is the shorter of the economic or legal life.) Using straight-line amortization, one-tenth of the cost of the patent should be written off as an expense in each year of the patent's useful life. The adjusting entry at the end of each year would be the following.

Dec. 31	Patent Expense	2,800	
	Patent		2,800

When an intangible asset is amortized, the credit entry is usually made directly to the asset account rather than to a contra asset account.

Research and development costs were often treated as intangible assets or deferred charges. FASB's ***Standard No. 2,*** "Accounting for Research and Development Costs," now requires that all R&D costs be charged to expense when incurred.

GOODWILL

We give special attention here to the intangible asset of goodwill, because special problems are associated with this intangible asset. ***Goodwill is the excess earning power of a business*** beyond the earning power that would be expected for a firm in a similar business and with a similar amount of other assets. Goodwill includes excess power that can be attributed to such factors as the location of the business, good relations with customers and employees, and managerial efficiency.

Goodwill is recorded only if it has been paid for. For example, suppose that a business with tangible assets of $100,000 is purchased for $120,000. Assuming that the tangible assets are properly priced and that there are no other intangible assets, the $20,000 extra cost (or value) of the firm must be attributed to goodwill. In this case, goodwill can be recorded as an intangible asset with value of $20,000 because it has been purchased.

Many businesses have built up excess earning power over the years and undoubtedly have developed a valuable intangible asset. However, it would be improper to recognize this goodwill in the accounts, because it has not been purchased and therefore its value cannot be objectively determined.[4]

Various methods can be used to estimate goodwill. We demonstrate one method as an example of a procedure that might be used to estimate the value of a company's goodwill. Suppose that the business has had average earnings of $50,000 over the past five years. The normal earnings of similar businesses are estimated to be approximately $40,000. Therefore, the goodwill of the company is resulting in excess earnings of $10,000 per year. If we assume that the asset of goodwill pro-

4. "The Board concludes that a company should record as assets the costs of intangible assets acquired from other enterprises or individuals. Costs of developing, maintaining, or restoring intangible assets which are not specifically identifiable, have indeterminate lives, or are inherent in a continuing business and related to an enterprise as a whole—such as goodwill—should be deducted from income when incurred." ***APB Opinion No. 17*** para. 24.

duces a return of 10 percent on its value each year, we can estimate the value of the goodwill as follows:

$$\text{Estimated goodwill} = \frac{\text{Estimated excess earnings}}{\text{Estimated rate of return on goodwill}}$$

$$= \$10{,}000/0.10 = \$100{,}000.$$

This estimated value for goodwill might be used in setting a price for the company, but it should not be reported as an intangible asset unless it is paid for when a business is purchased.

Ratio analysis

Owners and creditors of a firm can derive important information by evaluating relationships that exist between property, plant, equipment, and various other accounting categories. In this section we sample some of the ratios associated with property, plant, and equipment.

The ***ratio of stockholders' equity to fixed assets*** measures the relationship between owners' residual interest and the investment in fixed assets. This ratio is a measure of over- or underinvestment in fixed assets. In general, a low value of this ratio suggests that the firm may be overinvested in fixed assets and may be in danger of having liquidity problems. The ratio is computed by the following formula:

$$\text{Ratio of stockholders' equity to fixed assets} = \frac{\text{Stockholders' equity}}{\text{Fixed assets less accumulated depreciation}}$$

The ***ratio of sales to fixed assets*** indicates the effectiveness of the firm's utilization of its fixed assets. This ratio also may be used as a measure of over- or underinvestment in fixed assets. In general, a higher value of this ratio indicates a better utilization of the fixed assets. The ratio is computed as

$$\text{Ratio of sales to fixed assets} = \frac{\text{Net sales for the year}}{\text{Fixed assets less accumulated depreciation}}$$

The ***ratio of net income to total assets*** (or rate earned on total assets) is a measure of the profitability of the firm's investment in assets. This ratio is computed as

$$\text{Ratio of net income to total assets} = \frac{\text{Net income for the year}}{\text{Total assets at end of the year}}$$

In order to obtain a more objective view of the normal business operations of the firm, this ratio is often computed on the basis of the income and assets directly related to business operations. Extraordinary gains or losses, gains or losses on investments, and expenses and revenue related to investments are excluded from net income. Assets held for possible future use or as investments are excluded from the total assets. In this case, the ratio is usually called ***rate earned on total productive assets.***

Impact analysis

Impact analysis can focus attention on a variety of managerial problems associated with the acquisition, use, and disposal of fixed assets. For management, each decision about fixed assets is usually a decision of major importance. Most fixed assets come in expensive units—a decision about the treatment of fixed assets is likely to involve very large sums of money.

If a fixed asset is acquired for cash or through short-term financing, the large drain upon working capital may cause serious liquidity problems. If the fixed asset is financed through long-term debt, the firm's solvency risk is increased and significant interest expense may be added to the expenses of many future years. If the fixed asset is financed through issuance of additional capital stock, the owners' equity in the firm may be diluted without a corresponding increase in net income.

In addition to these problems of acquisition, the investment in fixed assets has other impacts on the financial statements of the firm in future years. Large depreciation expenses may have significant impact on the net income. So may expenses for property taxes, insurance, maintenance, and repair. To a large extent, these expenses will be fixed by the level of investment in fixed assets, regardless of the level of use of those assets or the level of income in a particular year. A large investment in a fixed asset (such as a building or equipment for a major new plant) usually represents a claim against a major part of the firm's income for many years to come.

For these reasons, overinvestment in fixed assets can have a very serious impact on both the liquidity and the solvency of a company. A slump in sales after a large investment in property, plant, and equipment can have disastrous effects on the firm's financial position. On the other hand, underinvestment in fixed assets may make it impossible for the firm to expand its operations and grow to produce proper return on its owners' investments.

The firm's choice of a depreciation method will be of considerable importance, because depreciation methods may have different impacts on the financial statements and on income. For example, suppose that a firm acquires an asset for $9,000 cash. The asset has an estimated life of three years and is expected to have no scrap (salvage) value. Exhibit 14-12 compares depreciation expenses for the three years under the straight-line method and the sum-of-years'-digits method.

Exhibit 14-12
Comparison of straight-line and accelerated depreciation charges

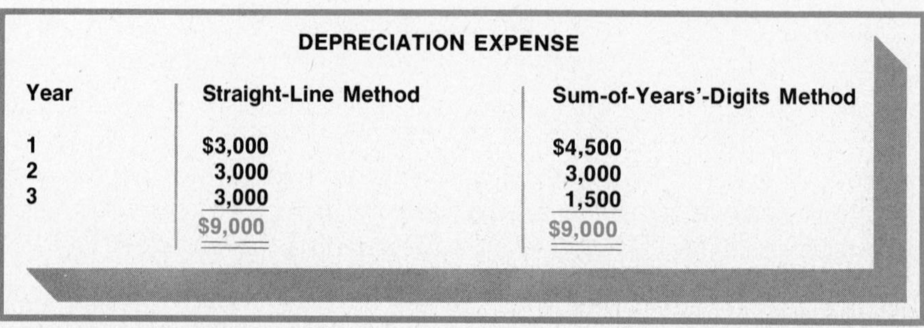

DEPRECIATION EXPENSE

Year	Straight-Line Method	Sum-of-Years'-Digits Method
1	$3,000	$4,500
2	3,000	3,000
3	3,000	1,500
	$9,000	$9,000

The actual cash flow involved in paying for the asset is unaffected by the choice of depreciation method. In this case, the expenditure was made at the time of acquisition. The choice of depreciation method has impact only on the amount of expense to be recognized and matched against income in each year of the asset's estimated life. Choice of the sum-of-years'-digits method results in larger depreciation expense in the early years of the life of the asset, and smaller depreciation expense in later years. Therefore, income taxes are reduced in early years and increased in later years by the choice of the accelerated depreciation method. The use of accelerated depreciation reduces the net income reported in early years and *increases* the net cash inflow in those early years (by reducing the income tax expenditures). This means that the company actually recovers its cash expenditure on the asset more quickly when it uses accelerated depreciation for tax purposes, and therefore is able to invest that working capital in other ways that earn money for the firm.[5]

Another major impact on the financial statements can result from improper classification of expenditure that should have expensed instead of capitalized, or vice versa. To appreciate the importance of properly classifying the expenditures associated with tangible fixed assets, consider the following possibilities.

1. If an expenditure is capitalized when it should have been expensed:
   a. assets are overstated until the capitalized asset is disposed of or fully depreciated;
   b. expenses in the current period are understated because, although depreciation expense is recorded for the asset capitalized, this expense is not as large as the expenditure that should have been expensed;
   c. expenses in subsequent periods (until the asset is disposed of or is fully depreciated) are overstated as a result of depreciation expense being recorded on the capitalized asset;
   d. net income in the current period is overstated, and net income in subsequent periods is understated by the depreciation for the period;
   e. retained earnings will be overstated in the current period and throughout the life of the asset.

2. If an expenditure is expensed when it should have been capitalized:
   a. assets are understated throughout the period when the expenditure is benefiting the firm's earnings;
   b. expenses in the current period are overstated by the amount that the charge to expense exceeds the depreciation expense that should have been recorded for the period on the capitalized asset;

5. The Internal Revenue Service permits use of accelerated depreciation on most fixed assets. Generally accepted accounting principles require that the method of depreciation be chosen that will give the best matching of revenue and expenses. Therefore, in some cases, a company may choose to use accelerated depreciation for its income tax computations and reports, when it is required to use a nonaccelerated depreciation method in its financial statements. This procedure has the effect of deferring to a later period payment of some of the income taxes on income reported on a particular income statement. This situation may require special accounting procedures to recognize the deferred taxes. Such problems are discussed in *APB Opinion No. 11: Accounting for Income Taxes* (New York: American Institute of Certified Public Accountants, 1967) and in Chapter 32 of this text.

c. expenses in subsequent periods (throughout the time when the expenditure is benefiting the firm's earnings) are understated because no depreciation is being recorded—an omission resulting from the failure to capitalize the expenditure;
d. net income is understated in the current period and overstated in subsequent periods because of the misstatement of expenses described in *b* and *c;*
e. retained earnings are understated throughout the period when the expenditure is benefiting the firm's earnings.

Summary

Fixed assets are economic resources that have relatively long lives (longer than one year) and that are used in the operations of the business (rather than being primarily intended for resale). These long-lived, or fixed, assets are classified as follows.

1. Tangible fixed assets:
   a. assets not subject to depreciation (land);
   b. assets subject to depreciation (such as property, plant, and equipment);
   c. assets subject to depletion (natural resources such as oil wells, mines, or timber tracts).
2. Intangible fixed assets: assets subject to amortization (such as patents, copyrights, franchises, and goodwill).

Accounting for tangible or intangible fixed assets involves similar accounting problems associated with the acquisition, use, and disposal of the asset. Tangible and intangible assets are recognized in the accounts according to the initial recording principle. Expenditures that provide benefits for future periods are capitalized and subsequently allocated as expenses to the periods benefited. Expenditures that benefit only the current period are expensed.

With the exception of land, tangible fixed assets are subject to depreciation or depletion. Depreciation is the process of allocating the cost of a tangible fixed asset over its useful life in a rational and systematic manner. Depreciation accounting is required for a proper matching of revenue and expense in accounting for expenditures on property, plant, and equipment.

In computing depreciation, the accountant must consider three factors: (1) the cost of the asset, (2) the estimated salvage value of the asset at the time of its disposal, and (3) the estimated useful life of the asset. Major methods of computing depreciation for property, plant, and equipment include the following:

1. straight-line depreciation;
2. working-hour method;
3. unit-of-production method;
4. accelerated depreciation:
   a. sum-of-years'-digits method,
   b. double-declining-balance method.

The group depreciation method is an approach in which depreciation charges are computed in a single calculation for a number of similar assets. If this approach is applied to major nonhomogeneous groups of assets or to all assets owned, the approach is called composite depreciation.

A second major group of tangible fixed assets includes natural resources, or wasting assets. As natural resources are extracted for use, depletion expense is recognized. Depletion is the process of allocating the cost of a natural resource to expense (or inventory) as quantities of the resource are removed.

The third major grouping of assets discussed in this chapter is intangible fixed assets, representing noncurrent and nonphysical assets. Intangible assets represent certain rights and privileges that are valuable to the business. Intangible assets are recorded initially at their acquisition cost (exchange price). Generally, an intangible asset should be amortized over its estimated useful life (or over forty years if the estimated life is longer than that). Amortization is the process of allocating the cost of the intangible asset to expense over the estimated life of the asset. The straight-line method of amortization is preferred.

Goodwill is an intangible asset that poses certain accounting and managerial problems of particular interest. Goodwill is the capability of a firm to realize earnings that are above the normal amount to be expected on the basis of the firm's type of business operations and its other assets. In other words, goodwill represents a way of accounting for the value that a business may have in excess of the total value of its other assets. Only purchased goodwill is recognized in the accounts.

Questions

1. What items are included in the accounting classification of property, plant, and equipment?
2. What items are included in the acquisition cost of property, plant, and equipment?
3. Distinguish between capital and revenue expenditures.
4. Which of the following items are usually expensed, and which are considered to be capital expenditures?
   a. Ordinary repair.
   b. Extraordinary repair.
   c. Additions.
   d. Major improvements.
5. Define depreciation. What are the reasons for depreciation accounting?
6. What is meant by the book value (or carrying value) of a tangible fixed asset?
7. Define the following terms as related to depreciation:
   a. the depreciation base;
   b. the scrap or salvage value of the asset;
   c. the estimated life of the asset.
8. List five methods of depreciation. Explain how depreciation is computed by each method.
9. What is composite depreciation? group depreciation? Distinguish composite and group depreciation from unit depreciation.
10. What accounting problems arise when tangible fixed assets are disposed of by sale or discard?

11. Explain the accounting treatment for the trade-in of one tangible fixed asset for another. In your answer, distinguish between exchanges of similar and of dissimilar assets.
12. What is meant by a wasting asset? Give four illustrations of wasting assets.
13. What is depletion and how is it computed?
14. What is an intangible fixed asset? What is meant by amortization as applied to intangible fixed assets?
15. What is goodwill? Explain one method of estimating the amount of goodwill.
16. Describe some ratios that are useful in evaluating investments in fixed assets.
17. The Rebuild Company purchased an old plant for $500,000. To prepare the plant for use, the Rebuild Company spent $50,000 to recondition the building (for repairs, painting, and so on). Should the additional $50,000 cost be capitalized or expensed?
18. The Excel Company purchased equipment priced at $10,300 for its store on January 1, 19_1. Terms of the purchase were as follows: $4,000 on delivery of the equipment; seven $1,000 annual installment notes, the first note to be due on December 31, 19_1. The seller retains title to the equipment until the final installment note is paid. The accountant for the Excel Company made the following entries relating to the purchase.

19_1			
Jan. 1	Equipment	10,300	
	Deferred Financing Cost	700	
	Cash		4,000
	Notes Payable		7,000
Dec. 31	Notes Payable	1,000	
	Cash		1,000
31	Depreciation Expense	500	
	Accumulated Depreciation		500
31	Interest Expense	100	
	Deferred Financing Cost		100

Required: Explain each of the journal entries made by the Excel Company's accountant.

19. True or false:
    a. The market value of a machine used in the manufacturing process exceeds its cost. The accountant should cease depreciation on the machine.
    b. An asset held for sale in the normal course of business is subject to depreciation and depreciation should be provided when adjusting entries are made at the end of the fiscal period.
    c. A company purchases a delivery truck. Sales tax and freight-in charges on the truck should be added to the cost of the truck and depreciated.
    d. Depreciation is a process that attempts to reflect the decline in physical efficiency of an asset in the accounts.
    e. A car acquired by a car dealer for sale to his customers should be depreciated by the accountant.
    f. A company should include in the Property, Plant, and Equipment section of its balance sheet a machine that is in workable condition but which will not be used by the company in the future.
    g. A company spent $50,000 to pave a road leading to its new plant. The expenditure should be reported as a capital expenditure subject to depreciation and disclosed in the Property, Plant, and Equipment section of the balance sheet.

h. After a machine has been installed and used in operations, the cost of maintaining the machine should be added to the cost of the machine and depreciated.

i. The financial statement of a company shows the following:

Building	$1,000,000
Less accumulated depreciation	900,000

This means that the company has $900,000 cash available to replace the building when it requires replacement.

j. Goodwill is an unidentifiable intangible asset. It can be sold separately from the business as can an identifiable intangible asset such as a patent.

Exercises

E14-1 (Entries for asset acquisitions)

Journalize the following transactions.

a. Equipment was purchased on May 1, 19_6, for $20,000, subject to terms of 1/10, n/30. The account was paid on May 8, 19_6.

b. Equipment was purchased on June 1, 19_6, for $15,000, subject to terms of 2/10, n/30. The account was paid on June 15, 19_6.

c. A machine was purchased for $15,000 on July 15, 19_6. Terms of the purchase were $10,000 cash plus five equal annual payments of $1,000; five $1,000 notes were given by the purchaser. Interest of 8 percent is to be paid on the outstanding notes. Record the purchase of the machine and the payment of the first note one year after the date of purchase.

d. Land was acquired at a cost of $200,000 on October 15, 19_6. On October 15, 19_9, this land is exchanged for a new bookkeeping machine (office equipment). The machine regularly sells for $240,000. The appraisal value of the land is $250,000. Record the exchange.

E14-2 (Account analysis for long-lived assets)

For each of the following expenditures, indicate the account(s) to be debited when the transaction is recorded.

a. Expenditure to pay the freight-in on the machine.

b. Expenditure to pay for an additional room added to the factory building.

c. Expenditure to pay for delinquent property taxes on land purchased on this date.

d. Expenditure to pay for sales tax on the machine.

e. Expenditure to pay for a new electrical system in an apartment building rented out as part of normal business operations. Management considers this to be a repair that will significantly extend the useful life of the building.

f. Expenditure to pay for the installation of the machine in the factory.

g. Expenditure to acquire a machine.

h. Expenditure to acquire land to be held for speculative purposes.

i. Expenditure to acquire land to be held as a future building site for a new factory.

j. Expenditure to pay for the testing of the machine before it is put into operation.

k. Expenditure to remove old building described in transaction o from the property.
l. Expenditure to paint the apartment building five years after purchase. The building is repainted every five years to maintain the building in good condition.
m. Expenditure to acquire land and building; the building is to be used as an apartment building, and the purchasing company is a real estate and rental company.
n. Expenditure to pay for replacement of a part on the machine that broke two weeks after the machine was put into operation.
o. Expenditure to acquire land and building; the old building is to be torn down immediately and a new building is to be built on the property.
p. Expenditure to pay for sidewalks and fencing around the factory.
q. Expenditure to acquire land.

E14-3 (Entries for asset acquisitions)
Journalize the following transactions.

a. The Next Company acquires an old building for $60,000 on March 15, 19_6. During March, it spends an additional $30,000 to prepare the building for occupancy on April 1. In March 19_7 the Next Company spends $2,000 to repair the electrical and plumbing systems.
b. After obtaining a bid of $45,000 on a new machine that is needed in its factory, the Next Company decides to build the machine itself, making use of some unused factory capacity currently available. The new machine is completed and put into operation on December 1, 19_6. During the preceding two months, $41,500 of expenditures related to the construction of the machine have been debited to an expense account called Machine Construction Expense.
c. On December 15, 19_6, the Next Company acquires land with a building on it for $300,000. The land is appraised at a value of $150,000; the building is appraised at a value of $450,000. The building is to be used as a factory.

E14-4 (Account analysis for long-lived assets)
For each of the following transactions, state which account(s) should be debited and the amount of the debit.

a. The firm purchases for $60,000 land with a building on it. The land has an appraisal value of $16,000 and the building of $48,000. The firm plans to use the building.
b. The firm purchases for $70,000 land with a building on it. The building is to be torn down immediately to prepare the site for construction of a new factory. The old building is demolished at a cost of $8,000. The old bricks from the building are sold for $4,000.
c. The firm constructs a new building for a cost of $120,000. Costs of excavation amount to an additional $6,000. Attorneys' fees associated with the new building construction amount to $12,000.
d. The firm paves its parking lot for a cost of $5,700.

E14-5 (Asset construction and depreciation)
During May and June of 19_6, the MFG Company constructs an additional wing to its factory. Expenditures of $30,000 during May and $20,000 during June are made in relation to the construction of the new wing; these expenditures are paid in cash. The original factory building was constructed 10

years previously at a cost of $400,000. It was estimated to have a life of 40 years and no salvage value. The factory has been depreciated according to the straight-line depreciation method. The additional wing has an estimated life of 20 years and no salvage value.

Required:

a. Record the construction of the addition.

b. Record the depreciation when the books are closed on December 31, 19_6.

E14-6 (Trade-in of asset)

The Lamont Company owns equipment with an original cost of $10,000 and a current carrying value of $7,000. On February 20, 19_6, it trades the equipment to the Likert Company for a truck with a current market value of $12,000. (The assets are dissimilar.) The trade-in allowance on the old machine is $6,600; the Lamont Company makes an additional cash payment of $5,400 as a part of the trade. The current market value of the old machine is $4,500.

Required:

a. Record the exchange on the books of the Lamont Company.

b. Record the exchange on the books of the Likert Company. The truck was purchased at a cost of $14,000 and has a current book value of $10,000.

c. Suppose that the asset traded in by the Lamont Company had been an old truck instead of an old machine. In this case, the assets traded are similar. All other facts about the exchange remain the same as given above. Record this exchange on the books of the Lamont Company.

E14-7 (Impact analysis)

Describe the impacts of the transaction described in Exercise E14-6 (exchange of dissimilar assets) on the following items in the accounts and statements of the Lamont Company and in the accounts of the Likert Company:

a. ratio of stockholders' equity to fixed assets ($1 > 1$);

b. earnings per share on common stock;

c. current ratio;

d. ratio of sales to fixed assets ($1 > 1$);

e. working capital;

f. owners' equity.

E14-8 (Double-declining-balance method)

A machine with a cost of $8,000, an estimated life of five years, and estimated salvage value of $1,100 is purchased on January 1, 19_6. Prepare a schedule showing depreciation per year over the life of the asset, using the double-declining-balance method of depreciation.

E14-9 (Depreciation methods)

The Dogs Company purchases equipment for $6,100 on January 1, 19_6. The company spends $550 to install the equipment and $850 for special guidance tools that become a part of the equipment. The salvage value of the equipment is estimated to be $300 at the end of an estimated useful life of three years.

Required:

a. Compute the cost of the machine.

b. Compute the annual depreciation expense by the following methods:

(1) straight-line method for 19_6;
(2) sum-of-years'-digits method for 19_6, 19_7, and 19_8;
(3) double-declining-balance method for 19_6.

E14-10 (Depreciation methods)

On January 1, 19_6, the Worn Company purchases a machine for $22,000. The machine has an estimated eight-year life. At the end of the seven years, the machine is expected to have a scrap value of $1,000. The machine is expected to produce 7,000 units during its lifetime and to be capable of 7,000 working hours of operation before it is discarded. During 19_6, the machine is operated for 4,500 hours and produces 3,200 units.

Required: Compute the depreciation expense for 19_6 using

a. straight-line method;
b. unit-of-production method;
c. working-hour method;
d. sum-of-years'-digits method;
e. double-declining-balance method.

E14-11 (Composite depreciation)

A firm uses a composite depreciation system for the following three assets.

Asset	Original Cost	Salvage Value	Estimated Service Life
A	$200,000	$ 0	10 years
B	62,000	2,000	12 years
C	34,000	4,000	15 years

Required:

a. Compute the composite depreciation rate.
b. Prepare the entry to record depreciation for the first accounting period.

E14-12 (Depletion)

An oil company purchases oil property for $1,700,000. After the oil is withdrawn, the land will have a residual value of $100,000. The company estimates that its oil property has potential production of 8 million barrels of crude oil. During the first year of production, 2 million barrels of crude oil are produced.

Required:

a. Record the acquisition of the oil land.
b. Compute the depletion rate per barrel of oil.
c. Record the depletion expense for the first year.

E14-13 (Intangible assets)

A company acquires a patent for $51,000. The company plans to amortize the cost of the patent over its full legal life. The firm also acquires a trademark for $80,000. The useful life of the trademark is expected to extend indefinitely into the future.

Required: Prepare the amortization entry or entries for the first year in the lives of these intangible assets. (If necessary, assume an appropriate estimated life for the assets.)

E14-14 (Goodwill)

A firm has accumulated the following net-income data for the past three years: 19_6 $41,000; 19_7 $43,000; 19_8 $42,000. In bargaining to purchase the firm, a potential buyer has agreed to capitalize average excess earnings at a .05 percent rate. (That is, it will be assumed that the average excess earnings represent .05 percent of the firm's goodwill.) The normal earnings of similar businesses are estimated at $40,000 per year.

Required:

a. Compute average excess earnings of the firm.

b. Compute the estimated goodwill.

E14-15 (Depreciation analysis)

The diagram in Exhibit 14-13 shows annual depreciation expense for an asset computed by each of the following three methods:

a. straight-line method;

b. double-declining-balance method;

c. sum-of-years'-digits method.

Identify the line (A, B, or C) that reflects each of the three depreciation methods.

E14-16 (Impact analysis)

Prepare a table showing the dollar impact of each of the following transactions on working capital, net income, net assets, and owners' equity.

a. A machine is acquired on January 1, 19_6, for $20,000 cash; the machine has an estimated salvage value of $2,000 and an estimated useful life of three years.

b. Appropriate adjusting entries related to the machine acquired in transaction a are made when the company closes its books on December 31, 19_6.

c. On July 1, 19_1, the company acquires a patent in exchange for a short-term, non-interest-bearing, $25,000 note. The useful life of the patent is estimated to be five years.

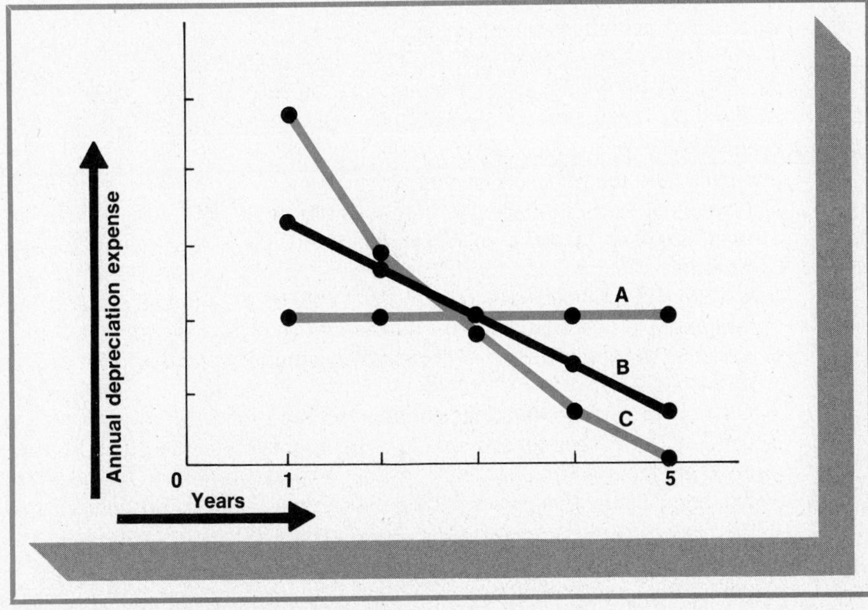

Exhibit 14-13

Exhibit 14-13
Graph of depreciation expense for Exercise E14-15

d. Appropriate adjusting entries related to the patent acquired in transaction c are made when the company closes its books on December 31, 19_6.

E14-17 (Balance sheet presentation)
Indicate the items and sections of the balance sheet where each of the following assets would appear, indicating the amount to be shown for each item.

a. A building with a cost of $450,000 and accumulated depreciation of $150,000.
b. A patent with a cost of $12,000 and amortization of date of $8,000.
c. Goodwill less amortization to date, $60,000.
d. Land held for speculative purposes, $14,700 cost.
e. Land acquired for a future plant site, $44,000 cost.

Problems

P14-1 (Entries for long-lived assets)
The Riva Company purchased land and constructed a building on it. The following expenditures were incurred in relation to this project. For each expenditure, indicate the amounts that should be debited or credited to the Land account, to the Building account, and to other accounts.

a. Purchase of factory site, $210,000; title fee, $3,000.
b. Grading of land prior to building, $700.
c. Sidewalks and curbs constructed at cost of $9,500; basement for building excavated at cost of $4,800.
d. Attorney fees amounting to $2,200. Of this amount, $800 was for legal services related to the land purchase; the remainder was for legal services related to the construction of the building.
e. Building permits acquired for $600.
f. An old building on the land demolished a cost of $750.
g. Materials from demolished building sold as salvage for $1,100.
h. Property taxes paid on building during construction period, $1,200.

P14-2 (Entries for long-lived assets)
Journalize the following transactions.

a. On July 5, 19_6, a building is purchased for $120,000. A cash payment of $30,000 is made; a five-year, $90,000, 9% note is given for the balance.
b. On July 10, the building is repaired at a cost of $9,000 after the building is already in use. Management considers this a major repair.
c. On July 15, a wire fence is constructed around the property at a cost of $4,100.
d. On July 16, two broken windows are replaced for $35.
e. On July 20, a secondhand machine is purchased for $6,200. Costs of $800 are incurred on July 21 for inspection and overhaul of the machine. On July 22, the machine is installed at a cost of $500. On July 23, the machine is tested at a cost of $2,100. On July 24, a bill is received from a moving company for removal of an old machine to make room for the new machine; the charge is $900.

P14-3 (Impact analysis)

Prepare a table showing the impact of each of the transactions in Problem P14-2 on net assets, owners' equity, working capital, and current ratio ($1 > 1$).

P14-4 (Trade-in)

Given the following data concerning the trade-in of a machine for a truck, record the exchange. The assets are dissimilar.

List price of truck acquired	$20,000
Cash payment for truck	17,000
Cost of old machine given up (16-year life)	20,000
Accumulated depreciation to date on machine	15,000
Secondhand value of old machine	6,000

P14-5 (Sale of asset)

A machine that cost $9,200 on February 1, 19_5, is sold on July 1, 19_9, for $4,200. The asset was depreciated using the straight-line method of depreciation. The machine was estimated to have a service life of ten years and an estimated residual value of $200. The company closes its books on December 31. Record the entries needed at the time the machine is sold.

P14-6 (Acquisition of assets)

The Farmer Company acquires land, building, and equipment for a total payment of $200,000 in a lump-sum transaction. The accountant decides to allocate the cost among the three assets in proportion to their appraised values, which are $125,000 for the land, $50,000 for the building, and $75,000 for the equipment. Record the acquisition of the assets.

P14-7 (Content of long-lived asset accounts)

For each of the following independent cases, state the proper cost to use for recording the acquisition of the assets.

a. Ten acres of land with an appraised value of $60,000 is acquired in exchange for the issuance of 1,000 shares of $10-par-value stock, which is currently selling at $52 per share.

b. Land is acquired for $8,000, and taxes in arrears are assumed in the amount of $3,000.

c. Machinery with a list price of $15,000 is purchased subject to terms of 3/10, n/30. Payment is made six days after the purchase.

d. Machinery with a list price of $16,000 is purchased subject to terms of 2/10, n/30. Payment is made twenty days after the purchase.

e. A truck acquired years ago at a cost of $11,000 (and having a current book value of $4,000) is exchanged for a new truck with a list price of $10,000. In addition to the old truck, $9,000 cash is given in exchange for the new truck. The fair market value of the old truck is $6,000.

f. Land and building are acquired for a lump sum of $1,500,000. The appraised value of the land is $800,000; of the building is $200,000.

g. A building is constructed by the firm. The following costs are incurred in the construction: (1) direct labor on this project, $200,000; (2) direct material used for this project, $350,000; (3) other costs attributable to this project, $150,000. The company had received a bid from an independent contractor to construct the building for $650,000.

h. All conditions are the same as in case g, except that the bid from the independent contractor was $750,000.

P14-8 (Asset acquisitions)

The Big Spender Corporation incurred the following expenditures in connection with the construction of a factory building. Identify the account(s) affected by each transaction and show the amount to be debited to each account.

a. Purchase of site, $60,000.
b. Closing fees for purchase of land, $3,000.
c. Building permit, $450.
d. Payment to a former tenant to terminate his lease and vacate the land, $4,700.
e. Cost of removing an old building on the site, $7,000; salvage value received for old bricks from building, $1,500.
f. Excavation for basement of new building, $3,250.
g. Construction of sidewalks, $2,700.
h. Property taxes on the site during the construction period, $1,600.
i. Property taxes on the site for the six months following occupation of the building, $1,800.

P14-9 (Trade-in)

Company A owns asset A that cost $14,000 and has accumulated depreciation of $12,000 recorded. Company B owns asset B that cost $18,000 and has accumulated depreciation of $10,000 recorded. It is estimated that the fair value of asset A is $12,000. The assets are similar. A and B exchange assets and Company A pays Company B $4,000 as a part of the transaction. Record the transaction on the books of Company A.

P14-10 (Intangible assets)

At the beginning of the year, the Mainstream Company developed a patent at a cost of $35,000. The economic life of the patent is 10 years. The legal life of the patent is 17 years. At the beginning of the third year, the company paid $16,000 to defend the patent successfully against a claim of patent infringement. At the beginning of the fourth year, the company spent $21,000 to acquire another patent that would have made the original patent worthless. This patent had a useful life of 12 years.

Required:

a. Prepare entries to record expenditures related to the patents.
b. Prepare amortization entries for the first, third, and fourth years as related to the patents.

P14-11 (Goodwill)

A company has pre-tax earnings of $400,000. The following items were deducted in computing the earnings:

Depreciation of plant	$50,000
Loss on sale of equipment	50,000
Income tax refund for prior years	60,000
Bonus to officers (not expected to recur)	50,000

In negotiating the selling price of the business, the plant is estimated to have a value of 50% above its original cost.

Required:

a. Compute the normal earnings that should be used when computing goodwill that might exist.

b. Compute the goodwill if normal earnings are to be capitalized at 10%.

c. Assume that the normal earnings for the industry in which the company operates is 8% of total assets and that the company has $3,000,000 of assets. Compute goodwill if goodwill is defined as excess (superior) earnings of the company capitalized at 5%.

15 Liabilities

In a credit economy, the creation and retirement of debt is a common experience for most businesses. The firm buys goods and services on account; it borrows short-term funds from banks; it issues bonds and signs mortgage notes to finance the acquisition of property, plant, and equipment. Debts are a fact of life. For this reason, accounting courses give considerable attention to the study of liabilities.

Liabilities arise when a firm receives assets or services, and in exchange gives a commitment to repay assets or services at a future date. Liabilities are obligations that the firm has accepted by acquiring assets or incurring expenses.

The AICPA defines ***liabilities*** as "economic obligations of an enterprise that are recognized and measured in conformity with generally accepted principles."[1]

The major accounting problems associated with liabilities are

1. proper classification of liabilities in the financial statements; and
2. the inclusion of *all* liabilities in the financial statements.

We begin with a discussion of the first problem, then turn later in the chapter to the second.

Classification of liabilities

The proper classification of liabilities in the financial statement requires a distinction between debts that are currently maturing and those debts that involve long-term obligations. Therefore, the basic categories of liabilities are

1. *current liabilities*—debts that will be paid from current assets or through the creation of other current liabilities during the normal operating cycle of the business or within a year, whichever period is longer,[2] and

1. ***APB Statement No. 4,*** para. 132. A committee of the American Accounting Association described accounting for liabilities in the following way: "Equities should be accorded accounting recognition in the period in which money, goods, or services are received or obligations are incurred, and should be measured initially by the agreed cash consideration or its equivalent." In this context, ***equities*** include owners' equity transactions and liabilities (creditors' equity transactions). The APB definition excludes owners' equity transactions from the liabilities classification.

2. ***APB Statement No. 4*** (para. 198) states that "current liabilities include those expected to be satisfied by either the use of assets classified as current in the same balance sheet or the creation of other current liabilities, or those expected to be satisfied within a relatively short period of time, usually one year."

2. *long-term* (or *fixed*) *liabilities,* which include all debts that are not current liabilities.

In the statement of financial position, liabilities are listed in the order of their maturity. For example, current liabilities usually are listed before long-term liabilities. The current liabilities, in turn, are arranged with the most current (most immediately payable) liabilities first. Ordinarily, accounts payable and notes payable appear first in the list of current liabilities because they result from normal business operations and are relatively large current liabilities. If a bank overdraft exists, however, it must be listed first because it would have to be settled immediately.

MEASUREMENT OF LIABILITIES. In keeping with the initial recording principle, liabilities are measured initially by the exchange price at which the transaction takes place. For short-term liabilities, this amount usually represents the amount of cash to be paid upon settlement of the debt. For example, a company borrows $10,000 from its bank for 90 days, the principal and interest to be paid at maturity. The liability is recognized at the exchange price of the transaction, $10,000.

Cash	10,000	
Notes Payable		10,000

The interest charge is an expense incurred over the life of the debt, representing a payment for the use of the bank's cash resources. At maturity, the obligation to pay the loan and interest is settled with a cash payment.

Notes Payable	10,000	
Interest Expense	150	
Cash		10,150

A firm sometimes records a long-term obligation at the present value of future outlays of assets required to pay the obligation. Discussion of discounting of liabilities is usually reserved for advanced accounting courses. However, to demonstrate the concept briefly, assume that a firm leases property for eight years at an annual rental of $4,000. The present value of the eight payments of $4,000 can be computed from present value tables. If we assume the company uses a 4.5 percent rate to determine the present value of the $4,000 annual payments, the table would show the present value as $27,570.80. The obligation on the lease can be recorded at this value. When the firm assumes the lease obligation, it also obtains rights in the leased property, which are recorded at the same time.

Lease Rights	27,570.80	
Lease Obligations		27,570.80

Each rental payment when made is considered part interest expense and part payment of lease obligation. At the date of the first rental payment, the following entry would be made.

Interest Expense	1,241	
Lease Obligation	2,759	
Cash		4,000

Interest: $27,570.80 × 4.5% = $1,241.

The reduction in the Lease Obligation account is computed as the balance of the $4,000 payment that is not debited to Interest Expense.

The Lease Rights account is an intangible asset and should be amortized over the life of the lease. If the company uses the straight-line method of amortizing intangible assets, the following entry would be made.

Expense: Amortization of Lease Rights	3,446	
Lease Rights		3,446
$27,570.80/8 years = $3,446.		

Current liabilities

We have defined current liabilities as those debts that will mature within the current operating cycle of the business, and therefore those debts that will have to be paid out of current assets or through the creation of other current liabilities. Among the current liabilities frequently incurred by businesses are the following.

1. ***Accounts payable:*** liabilities that result from the purchase of goods and services on open account. Accounts payable play an important part in the discussion of inventory in Chapter 13.
2. ***Notes payable:*** liabilities that arise from the signing of notes promising to pay determinable amounts at definite future dates. Notes are discussed in Chapter 12.
3. ***Accrued liabilities:*** debts that result from the recognition of an expense that has been incurred but has not been paid. Accounting procedures for dealing with accruals are discussed in Chapter 7; accrued taxes payable are discussed in this chapter.
4. ***Unearned revenue:*** recognition of debts arising from the receipt of revenue that has not been earned during the current accounting period, thus creating an obligation to provide goods or services in a future period. These liabilities are discussed in Chapter 7.
5. ***Dividends payable:*** amounts payable to stockholders because the firm's board of directors has declared (authorized) a dividend distribution, but the dividends have not been disbursed at the date of the financial statement. Dividends are discussed in Chapter 17.
6. ***Currently maturing long-term obligations.*** Certain bonds are payable in a series of annual installments. Normally, bonds payable are classified as long-term liabilities. However, if a maturing series of a bond issue is payable from current assets, the maturing portion of the debt is classified as a current liability. For example, suppose that on December 31, 19_0, serial bonds in the amount of $400,000 are outstanding, and that one series amounting to $50,000 of bonds is to mature in 19_1. This debt will have to be paid from assets listed as current assets on the statement of financial position at the end of 19_0. This information could be disclosed in the position statement as follows.

Current liabilities:		
6% Serial bonds payable, due March 1, 19_1		$ 50,000
Long-term liabilities:		
6% Serial bonds payable	$400,000	
Less bonds due March 1, 19_1	50,000	$350,000

As noted in this list, most current liabilities are discussed in some detail elsewhere in this book. However, liabilities for certain kinds of tax payments do not fall conveniently into topics covered in other chapters, so we discuss those here before turning to a discussion of long-term liabilities.

SALES AND EXCISE TAXES

Various governmental units impose taxes on sales of food, clothing, gasoline, and other necessities, as well as on luxury items. For the most part, the seller passes these sales and excise taxes on to the purchaser, by adding the cost of the taxes onto the price of the merchandise. The seller is liable to the taxing authority for the taxes collected; periodically he must file reports and make payment.

Two accounting procedures commonly are used to account for sales and excise taxes. In the first procedure, the tax liability is recorded at the time of each sale. In the second procedure, tax liability is computed and recorded only at the time when the tax return is to be filed. The sales tax and the amount of sales are not separated at the time of sale.

The first procedure requires that money paid for taxes be kept separate in the records from revenue. For example, suppose that a retailer makes sales totaling \$10,500 (including the tax charges of \$500 to the customers). He records the day's sales transactions by the following entry.

Accounts Receivable [or Cash]	10,500	
Sales		10,000
Sales Taxes Payable		500

At the end of the month, the retailer is required to report his sales and remit the taxes on those sales to the state government.

Sales Taxes Payable	XXX	
Cash		XXX
To record payment of state tax on month's sales.		

If the amount of taxes collected during the month differs from the amount computed by the governmental formula to be due when the tax return is prepared, the difference can be recorded as a miscellaneous expense or income, and the liability account can be adjusted accordingly.

If the second method of recording sales tax is used, the taxes are not separated from sales at the time of the sale. Both sales and sales tax are credited to the Sales account. For example, suppose that a furniture dealer makes sales (including customers' tax payments) of \$105,000 during a month. The tax rate is 5 percent of sales. As the sales are recorded during the month, no record is kept of the taxes owed.

Accounts Receivable [for Cash]	105,000	
Sales		105,000

The amount of the tax is computed as follows. Let x = sales (not including taxes); then the amount of tax due is $0.05x$. The \$105,000 collected during the month includes both the basic sales and the tax. Therefore,

$$x + 0.05x = \$105{,}000;$$

$$1.05x = \$105{,}000;$$

$$x = \$105{,}000/1.05 = \$100{,}000;$$

$$0.05x = 0.05 \times \$100{,}000 = \$5{,}000.$$

Certain states also have state unemployment taxes and/or income taxes that must be withheld from employees' wages.

The employer must maintain accurate personnel records for each employee on the company's payroll. Such records should show the employee's name, address, social security number, earnings, and payroll deductions. An example will help to illustrate the journal entries involved in accounting for payroll deductions.

Transaction 1. Withholding employees' taxes. During February, the Withholding Company pays $10,000 in gross salaries. None of the employees has yet reached the $12,000 limitation for the year, so all of these salaries are subject to F.I.C.A. taxes of 5.85%. Computation of income tax to be withheld for each employee gives a total of $1,800 to be deducted from the paychecks for income tax.

The payroll is recorded by the following journal entry.

Feb. 28	Salaries Expense	10,000	
	Income Tax Withholding Payable		1,800
	F.I.C.A. Taxes Payable		585
	Salaries Payable		7,615
	To record payroll for February.		

When the paychecks are issued to the employees, another entry is needed.

Mar. 5	Salaries Payable	7,615	
	Cash		7,615

The taxes withheld will be paid to the government at the end of the quarter.

EMPLOYER'S PAYROLL TAXES. In addition to the taxes withheld from the employees' wages, the federal and state governments impose payroll taxes on the employer.

1. F.I.C.A. taxes at the same rate as the tax on employees, imposed on the first $12,000 of each employee's yearly earnings.
2. Federal unemployment tax of 3.2% of the first $4,200 of each employee's yearly earnings.
3. State unemployment tax of a designated percent, usually 2.7% of the first $4,200 of each employee's yearly wages. State unemployment taxes up to 2.7% of taxable wages may be taken as a credit against the federal unemployment tax. State laws usually provide merit ratings that reduce the state contribution rate for employers who have given steady employment.

To illustrate the computation and recording of the employer's payroll taxes, we continue the example of the Withholding Company (transaction 1).

Transaction 2. Employer's payroll taxes recorded. The state in which the Withholding Company operates has a state unemployment tax of 2.7% on the first $4,200 of each employee's yearly gross wages. Payment of the February salaries does not bring any employee's total for the year over $4,200, so all of the February salaries paid are subject to the unemployment tax. The federal unemployment tax is 0.5% (the basic 3.2% federal tax, reduced by the credit for the 2.7% payment on the state tax). In addition, the Withholding Company must match from its own funds the F.I.C.A. taxes withheld from the employees' salaries.

The payroll taxes and related liabilities of the company for the February payroll are recorded by the following entry.

Feb. 28	Payroll Tax Expense	905	
	F.I.C.A. Taxes Payable		585
	State Unemployment Taxes Payable		270
	Federal Unemployment Taxes Payable		50
	To record payroll taxes for Feb. F.I.C.A.: $10,000 × 0.0585 = $585. State: $10,000 × 0.027 = $270. Fed.: $10,000 × 0.005 = $50.		

The computations involved in computing withholding and payroll taxes become more complex later in the year, when various employees begin to accumulate salaries for the year that exceed the ceilings for computation of some of the taxes.

Transaction 3. Employees' earnings in excess of amounts subject to tax. The Withholding Company pays $25,000 in gross salaries for the month of September. Of this amount, $5,000 goes to employees who have previously earned $12,000 or more during the year. Another $10,000 goes to employees who have previously earned $4,200 or more, but have not yet earned $12,000. The final $10,000 goes to employees who have not yet earned $4,200 for the year. Federal income tax withholding on the September salaries is $4,000.

The tax computations can be summarized as follows.

Gross earnings	$25,000
Wages in excess of $12,000 (not subject to F.I.C.A. taxes)	5,000
Wages subject to 5.85% F.I.C.A. withholding and employer's taxes	$20,000
Wages in excess of $4,200 but less than $12,000 (not subject to unemployment taxes)	$10,000
Wages subject to 0.5% federal and 2.7% state unemployment payroll taxes	$10,000
Income taxes to be withheld	$ 4,000

The following journal entries record the payroll, the payroll taxes, and the payment of the salaries.

Sep. 30	Salaries Expense	25,000	
	Income Tax Withholding Payable		4,000
	F.I.C.A. Taxes Payable		1,170
	Salaries Payable		19,830
	To record September payroll. F.I.C.A.: $20,000 × 0.0585 = $1,170.		
30	Payroll Tax Expense	1,490	
	F.I.C.A. Taxes Payable		1,170
	State Unemployment Taxes Payable		270
	Federal Unemployment Taxes Payable		50
	To record September payroll taxes. F.I.C.A.: $20,000 × 0.0585 = $1,170. State: $10,000 × 0.027 = $270. Fed.: $10,000 × 0.005 = $50.		
Oct. 5	Salaries Payable	19,830	
	Cash		19,830
	To record payment of September wages.		

At various times during the year, the company must submit tax returns and payments to the various governmental units for the payroll taxes and the taxes withheld from employees' salaries. These payments normally would be made at various times and covering some months' taxes, but for simplicity we combine all the payments for the September taxes in a single journal entry.

Oct. 31	Income Tax Withholding Payable	4,000	
	F.I.C.A. Taxes Payable	2,340	
	State Unemployment Taxes Payable	270	
	Federal Unemployment Taxes Payable	50	
	Cash		6,660
	To record payment of Sep. payroll and withholding tax liabilities.		

REPORTING AND PAYING WITHHOLDING AND PAYROLL TAXES. Every employer who is required to withhold income taxes and F.I.C.A. taxes from wages, or to pay F.I.C.A. taxes on his payroll, must file a quarterly tax return (Form 941) with the Internal Revenue Service. For these taxes, the calendar year is divided into quarters ending on March 31, June 30, September 30, and December 31. Returns and payments for taxes on salaries of each quarter are due by the end of the month after the quarter. For example, by April 30, the employer must file a return and submit payment for withholding and payroll taxes on January, February, and March salaries.

However, if the employer makes timely deposits of the full amount of taxes due during the quarter, he need not file his return until the tenth day of the second month following the quarter. Generally, the taxes must be deposited with an authorized commercial bank or a Federal Reserve Bank.

On or before January 31, the employer must give each employee a statement (Form W-2) reporting the gross wages and payroll deductions for that employee during the preceding calendar year. The employee is required to submit a copy of this W-2 form with his personal income tax return. The employer also submits copies of all W-2 forms to the Internal Revenue Service for cross-checking.

On or before January 31, each employer must file a federal unemployment tax return (Form 940) and deposit or pay the tax in full. If timely deposits of the full amount of tax due are made during the year, ten additional days are allowed to file the return. Federal unemployment tax must be deposited with an authorized commercial bank or a Federal Reserve Bank.

Similar requirements exist for the reporting, deposit, and payment of state unemployment taxes.

OTHER PAYROLL DEDUCTIONS. Employees and employers may make arrangements for payroll deductions in addition to those required for taxes. Such deductions may include optional withholdings for the purchase of U.S. Savings Bonds, health and accident insurance, union dues, and so on. Such deductions are recorded in a fashion similar to the recording of the tax deductions.

Jan. 31	Salaries Expense	9,570	
	Income Tax Withholding Payable		1,210
	F.I.C.A. Taxes Payable		590
	Union Dues Payable		360
	Bond Deductions Payable		500
	Salaries Payable		6,910

At the appropriate times, the amounts withheld can be paid to the various entities specified by the withholding agreements between employer and employees.

PAYROLL RECORDS. A payroll register (Exhibit 15-2) is used to summarize earnings of employees. This register provides money columns for gross (total) earnings, various deductions from gross earnings, and net pay. Data for the general journal entry recording the payroll is compiled in this register. In the column for "Other Deductions," the nature of each deduction is indicated by a letter symbol. For example, *A* might represent Community Chest contributions, *B* a payment on a group insurance plan, *C* a payment on a hospital insurance plan, *D* a payment for purchase of U.S. Savings Bonds, *E* a payment on union dues, *F* a payment on a purchase of merchandise made from the company, and so on.

The journalization of the payroll shown in Exhibit 15-2 would have the following form.

Apr. 13	Salaries Expense	1,030.40	
	Income Tax Withholding Payable		105.08
	F.I.C.A. Taxes Payable		45.00
	[Various payables]		40.92
	Salaries Payable		839.40
	To record payroll for week ending April 13.		

The payroll register summarizes the information about each payroll. In addition, the company must maintain an individual earnings record for each employee (Exhibit 15-3). This record shows a period-by-period summary of the employee's gross earnings, deductions, and net pay. The Cumulative Pay column of this record enables the accountant to know when an employee's earnings have reached the tax-exempt

Exhibit 15-2 **A payroll register**

PAYROLL REGISTER

Week Ended April 13, 19_1

Employee					Deductions				Net Pay	
No.	Name	Marital Status	No. of Exemptions	Total Earnings	FICA Tax	Income Tax	Other	Total	Amount	Check No.
8	Patrick Maher	S	1	110.00	5.50	13.20	A 7.25	25.95	84.05	207
17	George Higgins	M	4	147.00	6.17	13.50	B 5.00	23.67	123.33	208
	Other names	.	.	.	.	.	.	.	.	.
		.	.	.	.	.	.	.	.	.
		.	.	.	.	.	.	.	.	.
				1,030.40	45.00	105.08	40.92	190.00	839.40	

Exhibit 15-3 **An employee's individual earnings record**

EMPLOYEE'S EARNINGS RECORD

NAME Patrick Maher
ADDRESS 102 Park Lane
Dale, Illinois 62901
TELEPHONE NO. 555-1212
SOC. SEC. NO 207-27-549 **EMPLOYEE NO.** 8
MARITAL STATUS S **EXEMPTIONS** 1 **PAY RATE** $2.75/hr.
DATE EMPLOYED 12 Sept. 19_0 **BIRTH DATE** 3 May 1939
TERMINATION DATE **OCCUPATION** Clerk
TERMINATION REASON

Pay Period			Deductions						
Week No.	Week Ended	Total Earnings	FICA Tax	Income Tax	Other	Total	Net Pay	Check No.	Cumulative Pay
1	4/6	110.00	5.50	13.20		18.70	91.30	96	1,430.00
2	4/13	110.00	5.50	13.20	A 7.25	25.95	84.05	207	1,540.00

point for payroll taxes. The totals on this record also are used in preparing the employee's withholding statement (Form W-2) at the end of the year. In most cases, the deductions are computed and entered on the individual earnings record for each employee; information then is transferred from this record to the payroll register. Checks are prepared from the payroll register; the check numbers for each employee then are entered from the register into the individual records.

Long-term liabilities: bonds payable

Bonds payable and mortgages payable are typical long-term liabilities. A *bond* is a written, unconditional promise made under seal in which the borrower promises to pay a specific sum at a determinable future date, together with interest at a fixed rate and at fixed dates. Corporate bonds usually are issued in denominations of $1,000.

Transaction 4. Bond concepts. On July 1, 19_1, the Liable Corporation issues 1,000 bonds, each with face value (maturity value, or principal) of $1,000, for $1,000,000. The bonds mature at the end of ten years; at this time the Liable Corporation will repay the principal amount of the bonds to the holders of the bonds. Interest at 6 percent per year is to be paid to the holders semiannually on July 1 and December 31.

Chapter 11 discusses bonds such as these from the viewpoint of the bondholders. For the company issuing the bonds, the sale of the bonds represents acquisition of a long-term liability (for repayment of the bond principal) in exchange for the receipt of cash. On each July 1 and December 31 from the issuance of the bonds until their maturity date, the Liable Corporation is obligated to pay interest of $30,000 ($\$1,000,000 \times 0.06 \times 6/12$). This will be recorded as an interest expense for the appropriate period. At the end of the ten years, the Liable Corporation is obliged to pay the $1,000,000 principal of the bonds.

If the bonds offer unusually high interest rates, the issuing corporation may be able to sell them at a premium (that is, at a price above the face value). If the interest rate is lower than the current market average for similar bonds, the company may have to sell the bonds at a discount (at a price below the face value). As discussed in Chapter 11, the price of bonds usually is quoted in terms of a percentage of face value. A $1,000 bond selling at 98 is selling for 98 percent of its face value, or $980. A $1,000 bond selling for 102 brings a price of $1,020.

The issuance of long-term bonds is one way for a company to increase its capital. Capital can be defined as the wealth owned by a company. The statement of financial position is a statement of the company's capital. This capital can be expressed either in terms of assets (things of value owned by the company) or in terms of liabilities and owners' equity (claims of creditors and owners against the assets).

In terms of assets, the capital consists of current assets, long-term investments, and fixed assets. In terms of liabilities and owners' equity, the capital consists of current liabilities, long-term liabilities (capital debts), capital stock, and retained earnings. In thinking about capital, it is convenient to subtract current liabilities from both sides of the basic equation. On the left side of the equation, subtraction of current liabilities from current assets leaves working capital. On the right side, subtraction of current liabilities leaves only capital debts, capital stock, and retained earnings. Thus we can express the basic accounting model as follows:

Working Capital + Long-Term Investments + Fixed Assets = Capital Debts + Capital Stock + Retained Earnings

The left side of this equation is sometimes called ***gross capital;*** the right side is called ***capital structure.*** Any increase in the company's capital must involve both an increase in gross capital (wealth owned by the company) and an increase in the capital structure (claims against the wealth). When bonds are issued, the current asset of cash (and therefore the working capital) is increased. This is balanced on the other side of the equation by an increase in capital debts (the long-term liability for repayment of the bond principal). The firm also could increase its capital by selling additional capital stock for cash (or in exchange for other assets), or by earning money that is reinvested in the firm (retained earnings).

Why does a firm wish to increase its capital? Among the more common reasons for seeking additional capital are the following.

1. The firm wants to increase its working capital. This might be done in order to meet an existing liquidity problem, or to prepare for a greater volume of business operations expected in the future.
2. The firm wants to increase its long-term investments. In other words, it wants to obtain capital funds that it can invest in some securities to gain income from interest, dividends, or control over another company.
3. The firm may wish to increase its fixed assets. Purchase of additional plant, property, and equipment can help the firm to expand its operations and increase its earnings. Again, the firm hopes to come out of the deal with a permanent increase in its capital structure.

Given these reasons for seeking capital funds, why might a firm choose to issue bonds rather than selling additional stock?

1. Bond interest expense is deductible from taxable income, but dividend payments on stock are not deductible. Therefore, part of the cost of obtaining capital funds through bonds is offset by a decrease in income taxes payable.
2. Bondholders are creditors rather than owners. Normally, they obtain no formal voice in the control of the corporation through their ownership of bonds. On the other hand, issuance of additional stock might dilute control of the company, giving additional stockholders' votes to persons or groups seeking to take over the company or to change its basic operating plans.
3. The bond market is another source of capital that a company might wish to use to raise capital funds.

On the other hand, the issuance of bonds does have certain disadvantages. For example, the company must meet its interest payments and the payment of the maturity value of the bonds on the specified dates. If interest payments are not made when due, the bondholders may take legal action to enforce their claim against the company, thereby creating a financial and legal crisis for the bond-issuing company. On the other hand, dividends to stockholders can be postponed or eliminated if financial difficulties require it. Furthermore, the bond-issuing firm is committed to pay the fixed rate of interest specified on the bond. If financial conditions in the economy change, the firm may find itself in a position of earning a smaller rate of return on the borrowed funds than the interest that it must pay.

BOND CHARACTERISTICS

Bonds assume a variety of forms. Bonds may be classified according to (1) security characteristics, (2) interest payment procedures, and (3) special features associated with certain bonds.

SECURITY CHARACTERISTICS. In terms of security, bonds fall into two general categories: (1) secured bonds, and (2) unsecured bonds.

The holder of a secured bond has a claim against specific assets of the corporation if the corporation fails to make its interest payments or the maturity repayment. The holder of a ***real-estate mortgage bond*** has a claim against specified real property such as land or a building.[5] The holder of a ***chattel mortgage bond*** has a claim against personal property such as machinery or equipment. The holder of a ***collateral trust bond*** has a claim against negotiable securities such as stocks or bonds.

When the secured bonds are issued, the issuing company gives a lien (or claim) against the property used as security over to the bondholders or to a trustee who

5. Bonds may be secured by first, second, or third mortgage bonds on the same property. If foreclosing proceedings develop and the mortgaged property is sold to pay the bondholders, the proceeds of the sale are first used to satisfy the claims of the first-mortgage bondholders; what remains is used to pay off the second-mortgage bonds; and so on. The terms of the contract associated with a mortgage bond normally specify that any future mortgages issued against the same property must have claims secondary (junior) to the claims of the present mortgage holders.

represents them. The lien is removed after the company has met all of its obligations on the bonds.

The holder of an unsecured bond (or ***debenture***) does not have a claim against any specific assets of the corporation, but relies on the general credit of the issuer for security.

INTEREST PAYMENT PROCEDURES. A ***registered bond*** is one issued in the name of the bondholder and payable only to the registered holder. The corporation or its transfer agent who represents the company records the number of each bond and the name of its holder in the company books. Ownership of a registered bond may be transferred only by endorsement of the bond and presentation of the endorsed bond (or a written statement of the transfer from the registered holder) at the office of record for the bond issuer. The issuer of the bond is responsible to make interest payments and maturity payment to the registered holder of the bond, regardless of who may have physical possession of the certificate.

Some bonds are registered as to principal only. They are called ***coupon bonds,*** because interest coupons are attached to the bonds. As each coupon matures on an interest payment date, the holder can detach the coupon and deposit it with a bank for collection.

Bearer bonds are bonds that are completely unregistered. The person with physical possession of the bond is entitled to receive interest and maturity payments. No endorsement is needed to transfer the bearer bond from one holder to another. Interest payments are made on bearer bonds by the same procedure as that used for coupon bonds.

SPECIAL FEATURES OF CERTAIN BONDS. Many long-term corporate bonds are ***callable*** (or redeemable) ***bonds.*** This means that the issuer of the bonds can choose to retire or redeem the bonds at any time by paying the par value, any accrued interest, and a small call premium to the holder. Usually, the issuer must give some advance notice of his intention to redeem the bonds. The call premium usually is set initially at a value somewhat above par value, and it declines steadily over the life of the bond, so that the bond is redeemable at face value on its maturity date. For the issuer, the advantage of the callable bond is that the company can choose to pay off part of its debt whenever it finds that it has excess working capital on hand.

Some bonds are ***convertible bonds;*** the holder of a convertible bond has the option of exchanging the bond for other securities (usually common stock in the issuing corporation) according to conditions specified on the bond.

The issuing company may choose to repay its debt over a number of years rather than at one maturity date. In that case, it issues ***serial bonds.*** The bond-issue is divided into series of bonds, each series having a different maturity date. For example, the company might borrow $500,000 by issuing $100,000 of bonds due to mature in sixteen years, $100,000 due to mature in seventeen years, and so on.

A similar effect can be achieved by issuing ***sinking-fund bonds.*** In this case, the company is required to make regular payments into a ''sinking fund'' that will be used to redeem the bonds at maturity. The sinking fund often is handled by a trustee in much the same fashion as security for a secured bond.

MORTGAGE NOTES. Mortgage notes payable make up a second major classification of long-term liabilities. These notes are similar to mortgage bonds, but the loan is made in a private transaction (rather than offering an issue of bonds for sale), and the note is not issued formally under the company's seal as is a bond. The mortgage involves the pledge of property to a creditor as security for the payment of the debt; this is the mortgage claim against the securing property. The mortgage serves as security for the long-term note that is the liability against the company.

BOND INTEREST

Interest is the price paid for the use of borrowed funds. The annual interest rate stated on the face of a bond is called the ***nominal*** (or contract, or stated) rate. For example, a $1,000 bond may carry a 6 percent nominal interest rate. The yearly interest on the bond is calculated by multiplying the nominal rate by the face value (or maturity value, or principal) of the bond. Thus, a $1,000, 6% bond requires an annual interest payment of $60.

The ***yield*** (or ***effective interest rate***) on a bond is the true rate of interest paid on the bond after consideration is given to any bond premium or discount. If a bond is issued at a premium, the yield on the bond is less than the nominal rate. For example, a $1,000, 6% bond will pay interest of $60 per year (nominal rate of 6 percent). However, if the holder paid $1,002 for the bond, he will be receiving less than 6 percent interest on his actual investment. (Six percent of $1,002 is $60.12.) Similarly, if the bond is issued at a discount, the yield is higher than the nominal rate.

Formulas exist for the calculation of bond prices and bond yields. However, bond-yield tables are available and provide the desired information in most cases. Exhibit 15-4 shows a selection from a bond-yield table. To illustrate its use, suppose that a 5-year, $1,000 bond with a contract rate of 5 percent payable semiannually is to be sold at a price that will yield 4.95 percent. Looking in the "5 years" column at the row for 4.95% yield, we see that the bond should be priced at $1,002.19.

The table also can be used to find the yield of a bond purchased at a certain price. For example, suppose that a $1,000, 5-year bond similar to the one just described is issued for $1,044.91. Finding this price in the "5 Years" column, we see that it is in the row for a 4.00% yield. If the particular price or yield in question is not in the table, the information can be approximated by interpolation.

Exhibit 15-4
Selected portions of a bond-yield table

$1,000,000 BOND AT 5% INTEREST, PAYABLE SEMIANNUALLY

Yield	4 Years	4½ Years	5 Years
4.00	1,036,627.41	1,040,811.19	1,044,912.93
4.85	1,005,394.84	1,005,999.36	1,006,589.56
4.90	1,003,592.72	1,003,994.85	1,004,387.36
4.95	1,001,794.45	1,001,995.07	1,002,190.85
5.00	1,000,000.00	1,000,000.00	1,000,000.00
5.25	991,084.91	990,094.92	989,130.25

ACCOUNTING FOR BONDS

Chapter 11 discusses accounting procedures associated with the purchase and holding of bonds. Now we look at the entries that must be made in the books of the company issuing the bonds.

Transaction 5. Bonds authorized and issued. The Borrower Corporation has been authorized by its board of directors to issue up to $150,000 in 5% bonds. The authorization also sets forth the terms and similar matters of a contractual nature associated with the bond. On January 1, 19_1, the firm issues $100,000 of the authorized bonds, due on January 1, 19_9, for $100,000.

At the time of the authorization, a memorandum entry is usually entered in the Bonds Payable account to record the total amount of bonds authorized and other details of the authorization. When the bonds are actually issued, a journal entry is needed.

19_1			
Jan. 1	Cash	100,000	
	Bonds Payable		100,000
	To record issuance of bonds at 100, due Jan. 1, 19_9.		

At the time of issuance, the bonds are recorded ***at face value*** in a liability account properly identified. In the statement of financial position, the long-term liabilities should be described adequately. The rate of interest and due date should be disclosed. If a bond payable has a preferred lien on some asset of the company, this matter also should be disclosed.

Long-term liabilities:	
5% debenture bonds, due January 1, 19_9 (authorized bonds, $150,000)	$100,000

Interest on these bonds is paid semiannually on June 30 and December 31. The entries to record the first two interest payments are made as follows.

19_1			
June 30	Bond Interest Expense	2,500	
	Cash		2,500
Dec. 31	Bond Interest Expense	2,500	
	Cash		2,500

BONDS ISSUED BETWEEN INTEREST DATES. If bonds are issued between interest dates, the purchaser is required to pay for the interest that has accrued from the previous interest-payment date specified on the bonds to the date of the purchase. When the next interest-payment date arrives, the bondholder receives the interest payment for the entire period, so this payment is in effect refunded to him. The purchase of accrued interest simplifies the accounting needed by the issuer when a large number of bonds and bondholders are involved and issue dates differ.

Transaction 6. Bonds issued at an interim date. The Interim Corporation decides to issue $100,000 in 6%, 20-year bonds dated January 1, 19_1, with interest payment dates of June 30 and December 31. However, the company does not sell the bonds until March 1, 19_1. The sale is made for face value plus accrued interest.

The entry to record the sale of the bonds and accrued interest is made as follows.

Mar. 1	Cash	101,000	
	Bonds Payable		100,000
	Bond Interest Payable		1,000
	To record issuance of bonds at 100 plus 2 months' accrued interest: $100,000 × 0.06 × 2/12 = $1,000.		

When the first interest payment is made on June 30, it is recorded in this way.

June 30	Bond Interest Payable	1,000	
	Bond Interest Expense	2,000	
	Cash		3,000
	To record payment of semiannual 100 plus 2 months' accrued interest: $100,000 × 0.06 × 2/12 = $1,000.		

BONDS ISSUED AT A PREMIUM. If the bonds are issued at a premium, the bond issuer receives an amount in excess of the face value for the bonds. A bond premium is paid when the contract (or nominal) interest rate on the bonds exceeds the current market interest rate on similar investments. For example, suppose that similar bonds are paying interest rates of 5 percent. In this case, the purchaser of the bonds is willing to pay a premium that will cause the bonds to have a yield of around 5 percent.

The premium received by the issuing company is not revenue or income, because ***borrowing*** money is not an activity that can be recognized as a source of revenue. The bond premium is instead regarded as a reduction in the interest expense that will be incurred over the life of the bonds. The bond liability is recorded at face value in the Bonds Payable account; the premium is recorded in a Premium on Bonds account. The premium will be systematically amortized to reduce interest expenses over the years.

*Transaction 7. **Bonds issued at a premium.*** The Premium Company issues $100,000 of bonds at a price of 110.

This transaction is recorded by the following entry.

Cash	110,000	
Bonds Payable		100,000
Premium on Bonds		10,000
To record issuance of bonds at 110.		

BONDS ISSUED AT A DISCOUNT. If the bonds are issued at a discount, the bond issuer receives an amount less than the face value of the bonds. This happens when the contract interest rate on the bonds (say 6%) is smaller than the market interest rate on similar investments (say 7%). In such a case, the purchaser is willing to pay only the price that will give him a yield on the bonds of about 7 percent.

The bond discount is not an expense at the time that it arises. Rather, the bond discount is treated as an addition to the interest expense that will be incurred over the life of the bond. It is recorded in a Discount on Bonds account, to be systematically accumulated as an addition to the interest expense over the years.

Transaction 8. Bonds issued at a discount. The Discount Company issues $100,000 of bonds at a price of 90.

This transaction is recorded by the following entry.

Cash	90,000	
Discount on Bonds	10,000	
Bonds Payable		100,000
To record issuance of bonds at 90.		

PERIODIC WRITE-OFF OF BOND PREMIUMS AND DISCOUNTS. Whatever the actual price received for the bonds, the liability in the Bonds Payable account is always recorded at the face value of the bonds. If the bonds were sold at premium or discount, adjusting entries are needed with each interest payment on the bonds.

Transaction 9. Bonds issued at a premium; premium amortized. On January 1, 19_1, the Amortization Company issues $100,000 of 6%, 10-year bonds with interest-payment dates of January 1 and June 30. The bonds are issued at a premium for 110.

The entry to record this issuance is the same as that shown for transaction 7. After the entry is posted, the Bonds Payable account has a credit balance of $100,000, and the Premium on Bonds account has a credit balance of $10,000.

On June 30, 19_1, the first interest payment on the bonds must be made. A portion of the bond premium is to be amortized (that is, written off) as a reduction in the interest expense. If the bond premium is amortized by the straight-line method, it will be divided evenly among the twenty interest payments to be made over the life of the bonds.

June 30	Bond Interest Expense	3,000	
	Cash		3,000
	To record payment of semiannual interest: $100,000 × 0.06 × 6/12 = $3,000.		
30	Premium on Bonds	500	
	Bond Interest Expense		500
	To amortize bond premium by straight-line method (20 payments): $10,000 × 1/20 = $500.		

These two entries could be combined into a single compound entry.

June 30	Bond Interest Expense	2,500	
	Premium on Bonds	500	
	Cash		3,000

After the June 30 entries are posted, the Bond Interest Expense and Premium on Bonds accounts appear as shown in Exhibit 15-5. (If the compound entry were used, the Bond Interest Expense account would show only a $2,500 debit entry on June 30.)

Note that the effect of issuing bonds at a premium is to reduce the interest expense over the life of the bonds. Exhibit 15-6 shows an amortization schedule for these bonds. Note that the issuer company pays out a total of $60,000 in interest payments over the life of the bonds. At maturity, the company repays the $100,000 face value of the bonds. However, when it sold the bonds at a premium, it received $110,000 in

Exhibit 15-5
Bond-related accounts after first interest payment in transaction 9

Bonds Payable

			19_1		
			Jan. 1	Issuance	100,000

Premium on Bonds

19_1			19_1		
June 30	Amortization	500	Jan. 1	Issuance	10,000

Bond Interest Expense

19_1			19_1		
June 30	Cash payment	3,000	June 30	Amortization	500

Exhibit 15-6
Schedule of bond interest and premium amortization for transaction 9

Payment Date	Bond Interest Expense Dr.	Premium on Bonds Dr.	Cash Cr.	Unamortized Bond Premium
Issuance	—	—	—	10,000
June 30, 19_1	2,500	500	3,000	9,500
Jan. 1, 19_2	2,500	500	3,000	9,000
June 30, 19_2	2,500	500	3,000	8,500
•	•	•	•	•
•	•	•	•	•
•	•	•	•	•
June 30, 19_9	2,500	500	3,000	500
Maturity	2,500	500	3,000	0
	50,000	10,000	60,000	

cash. Therefore, it received $110,000 and repaid $160,000, so the total cost of using the money has been only $50,000. This is an interest expense of $5,000 per year or $2,500 per six months over the life of the bonds.

Transaction 10. Bonds issued at a discount; discount accumulated. On January 1, 19_1, the Accumulation Company issues $100,000 of 6%, 10-year bonds with interest-payment dates of January 1 and June 30. The bonds are issued at a discount for $90,000.

This issuance is recorded by an entry like that shown for transaction 8. After the entry is posted, the Bonds Payable account has a credit balance of $100,000, and the Discount on Bonds account has a debit balance of $10,000.

When the first interest payment is made on June 30, two entries are made to record the payment of the semiannual interest and the accumulation of the bond discount.

June 30	Bond Interest Expense	3,000	
	Cash		3,000
	To record payment of semiannual interest: $100,000 × 0.06 × 6/12 = $3,000.		
30	Bond Interest Expense	500	
	Discount on Bonds		500
	To accumulate discount (straight-line, 20 payments): $10,000 × 1/20 = $500.		

As with the bond premium (transaction 9), the two entries can be combined in a compound entry. After the June 30 entries are posted, the relevant accounts appear as shown in Exhibit 15-7.

Note that the effect of issuing bonds at a discount is to increase the interest expense over the life of the bond. The issuer received $90,000 cash in this case. Over the life of the bonds, he pays out $60,000 interest and he repays $100,000 face value at maturity. Therefore the cost of the loan is $160,000 − $90,000 = $70,000. This is an interest cost of $7,000 per year, or $3,500 per semiannual interest payment.

On the statement of financial position, bond premium or bond discount can be presented as adjustments of the long-term debt.

Long-term liabilities:		
Bonds payable, 6% first-mortgage bonds, due 19_9	$100,000	
Add: Unamortized bond premium	10,000	$110,000
Long-term liabilities:		
Bonds payable, 6% first-mortgage bonds, due 19_9	$100,000	
Less: Unaccumulated bond discount	10,000	$90,000

Thus, the bonds are shown initially at the exchange price of their issuance, but over the life of the bonds, the value is gradually adjusted toward the face value that will be the company's liability at maturity. Meanwhile, the amortized premium or accumulated discount appears as a reduction or an increase of the interest expense on the income statement for each period.

END-OF-THE-PERIOD ADJUSTING ENTRIES. If the interest-payment dates on bonds payable do not coincide with the fiscal year of the issuing company, certain adjusting entries are needed at the close of each fiscal year to record the proper amount of interest expense and interest payable on the statements.

Transaction 11. Adjusting entries for interest expense. The Adjustment Corporation issues $100,000 in 6%, 10-year bonds with interest payment dates of March 1 and September 1. The bonds are dated September 1, 19_1. They are sold on November 1 (118 months from date of issue to maturity) for $101,000 plus accrued interest. The company closes its books on December 31.

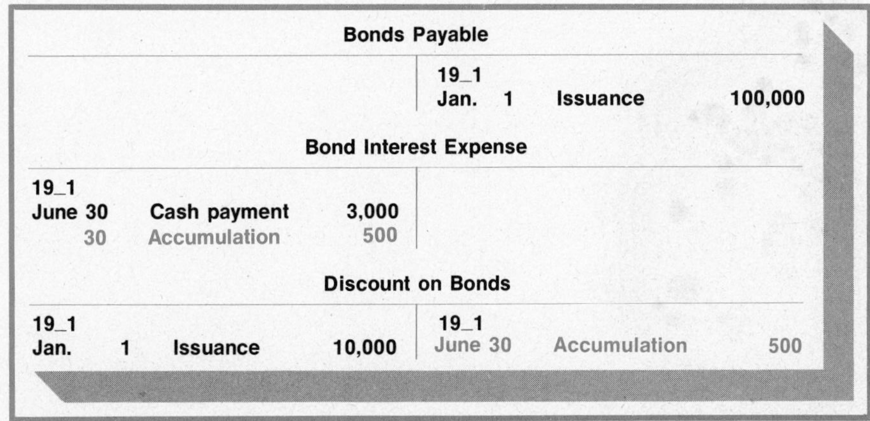

Bonds Payable

			19_1			
			Jan. 1	Issuance	100,000	

Bond Interest Expense

19_1			
June 30	Cash payment	3,000	
30	Accumulation	500	

Discount on Bonds

19_1			19_1		
Jan. 1	Issuance	10,000	June 30	Accumulation	500

Exhibit 15-7
Bond-related accounts after first payment in transaction 10

The entry to record the issue of the bonds involves both accrued interest and a premium.

19_1			
Nov. 1	Cash	102,000	
	Bonds Payable		100,000
	Premium on Bonds		1,000
	Bond Interest Payable		1,000
	To record issuance of bonds at 101 plus accrued interest: $100,000 × 0.06 × 2/12 = $1,000.		

When the books are closed at the end of the year, adjusting entries are needed to record the expense accrued during November and December, and to amortize the bond premium for those 2 months. In this case, the premium is being amortized on a straight-line basis over the 118 months of the bonds' life.

Dec. 31	Bond Interest Expense	1,000	
	Bond Interest Payable		1,000
	To record accrued interest Nov. 1 through Dec. 31: $100,000 × 0.06 × 2/12 = $1,000.		
31	Premium on Bonds	16.95	
	Bond Interest Expense		16.95
	To amortize premium for Nov.–Dec.: $1,000 × 2/118 = $16.95.		

When the first interest payment is made on March 1, 19_2, the $3,000 cash payment to the bondholders is recorded as $1,000 of interest expense (for January and February), $1,000 of interest payable (for the accrued interest purchased by the bondholders at the time of issuance), and another $1,000 of interest payable (for the accrued interest recorded when the books were closed at the end of 19_1).

19_2			
Mar. 1	Bond Interest Payable	2,000	
	Bond Interest Expense	1,000	
	Cash		3,000
	To record payment of semiannual interest: $100,000 × 0.06 × 6/12 = $3,000.		
1	Premium on Bonds	16.95	
	Bond Interest Expense		16.95
	To record amortization of premium for Jan.–Feb.: $1,000 × 2/118 = $16.95.		

After these entries are posted, the liability account for Bond Interest Payable will show a zero balance, clearing the liabilities recorded at issuance and at closing.

RETIREMENT OF BONDS. When bonds are retired at maturity, the entry to record the retirement simply recognizes the payment of cash to remove the liability for the bonds.

Bonds Payable	100,000	
Cash		100,000

If the issuing company recalls or repurchases the bonds before the maturity date, several entries are needed.

1. Any premium or discount related to the bonds redeemed should be amortized from the date of the last write-off to the date of the call or purchase.
2. Any accrued interest on the bonds from the last interest-payment date to the date of the call or purchase should be recognized.
3. The Bonds Payable account should be relieved of the bonds called or repurchased.
4. Gain or loss, if any, on the call or repurchase should be recognized.

Transaction 12. Retirement of bonds. The Buy Back Corporation has a bond issue of $100,000 outstanding. Its books show an unamortized premium of $5,000 related to these bonds on June 30, when it purchases the bonds from the holder at 102. The interest has been paid on June 30, and the premium has been amortized to June 30.

The repurchase of the bonds is recorded by the following entry.

June 30	Bonds Payable	100,000	
	Premium on Bonds	5,000	
	Cash		102,000
	Gain on Repurchase of Bonds		3,000

If adjusting entries are needed to record accrued interest or amortization of premium as of the date of redemption of the bonds, these entries must be made first. Then the gain or loss on the sale can be computed properly. Corporations usually redeem bonds on an interest date.

Recording all liabilities

We turn now to the second of the major problems mentioned at the beginning of this chapter—the problem of recognizing *all* liabilities on the position statement. To be sure that all liabilities are shown in the accounts, the accountant must check all of his records for (1) definite liabilities, (2) estimated liabilities, and (3) contingent liabilities. He must make sure that each liability in any of these categories is properly reflected in the account balances that he will use to prepare the financial statements.

DEFINITE LIABILITIES. Definite liabilities are those debts that have been recorded or negotiated in some form such that a definite obligation exists to pay a certain amount to a certain person or business. Examples of definite liabilities include accounts payable, notes payable, bonds payable, and interest payable. In some cases, the obligation exists without any clear record in the form of a business document that will be journalized. For example, at the close of the year, the company may owe salaries to its employees for work done on which timesheets or payroll records have not yet been turned in. The accountant must be alert to recognize the existence of such accrued expenses and to record them as liabilities through adjusting entries when closing the books.

ESTIMATED LIABILITIES. A definite obligation to pay some debt may exist in cases where there are various uncertainties associated with the amount of the debt, the person to be paid, or the time when the debt is to be paid. For example, suppose that a firm has established a pension program for its employees; the workers are entitled to receive pensions from the company when they retire. It is impossible to predict exactly how much the company will have to pay at any particular time in the future, but it is clear that an obligation exists and should be reflected in the financial statements. Another example would be the case of a firm that guarantees the materials and workmanship on products that it sells. From experience, the firm knows that it will be obligated to recondition a certain percentage of the products that it sells under the terms of this warranty. In such situations, the accountant must recognize the liability and must use any information that is available in order to show a fair and realistic estimate for the amount of the liability.

CONTINGENT LIABILITIES. In some cases, there may be a debt that does not exist at the moment, but that is likely to arise if certain events occur. If the contingency is considered to be material (that is, large enough to affect the statements significantly) but unlikely to occur (i.e., not probable), the contingent liability should be disclosed in the financial statements. If the material contingency is considered probable and the amount of the liability is known, the liability should be recognized in the accounts and financial statements, with a disclosure of the facts about the contingency.[6]

Contingent liabilities may arise through such matters as pending lawsuits, renegotiations of contracts, and disputed taxes. In the discussion of notes receivable in Chapter 12, we noted that a company has a contingent liability for a note that it has discounted for cash. If the maker fails to honor the note, the company will be obligated to pay the buyer of the note. In this instance, the contingent liability is recorded in the accounts as a liability account called Notes Receivable Discounted. It is retained in the books as a liability until the maturity of the note.

As another example, suppose that a company is involved in a lawsuit that could result in a large loss to the company if it loses the case. If the company attorney feels that the case probably will be decided in favor of the company, the accountant may decide to disclose the existence of the lawsuit and the amount of the possible loss only in a footnote to the statements. On the other hand, if the attorney advises that it is probable that the company will lose the case, the accountant should recognize the contingent liability in the accounts. For example, if the amount of the contingent liability is $500,000, it would be entered as follows:

Loss on Lawsuit	500,000	
Provision for Possible Loss on Lawsuit		500,000

This entry recognizes a loss (an expense account) that will appear on the income statement, and will reduce the net income for the current period. The Provision for Possible Loss account is a liability account that will appear in the balance sheet.

The decision of how to account for a contingent liability is a difficult one. The

6. *FASB Statement No. 5,* "Accounting for Contingencies."

accountant must try to give the most realistic picture possible of the company's financial position, as required by the principle of full disclosure. To include or exclude contingent liabilities in financial statements is usually a judgmental problem for the accountant.

Ratio analysis

The liabilities of a firm represent its obligations to creditors. The creditors are interested in the safety of the funds they loan to the firm. Likewise, the owners and managers of the firm are aware of the importance of maintaining a good credit standing, so that they can obtain additional capital when needed. There are several financial ratios that provide insights into the credit position of a firm. Some of these ratios are discussed in Chapters 10, 11, and 12. Here we look at some ratios that measure the firm's long-term solvency, as well as the safety of the firm's bonds as an investment for creditors.

The ***ratio of stockholders' equity to total debt*** is one important measure of a firm's long-term solvency. This ratio is computed as

$$\frac{\text{Stockholders' equity}}{\text{Total liabilities}}$$

This ratio measures the relationship between the claims of owners and those of creditors against the assets of the firm. The larger the value of this ratio, the less risk there is that the firm will fail to be solvent enough to pay off its debts to creditors.

The ***ratio of total liabilities to total assets*** is a related measure of long-term solvency. This ratio expresses the claims of the creditors as a fraction of the firm's total assets. The smaller the value of this ratio, the less the solvency risk in loaning money to the firm. This ratio is computed as

$$\frac{\text{Total liabilities}}{\text{Total assets}}$$

The ***ratio of security to long-term liabilities*** measures the proportion of the firm's specific assets pledged to secure long-term debts to the long-term debt. This ratio is computed as

$$\frac{\text{Assets pledged as security for long-term debts}}{\text{Long-term liabilities}}$$

A high value of this ratio suggests that the firm has sufficient potential security available to meet the demands of long-term creditors.

The ratio showing ***number of times bond interest is earned*** is discussed in Chapter 11. This ratio is computed as

$$\frac{\text{Net income} + \text{Bond interest} + \text{Income tax}}{\text{Bond interest}}$$

It is a measure of the firm's ability to earn the interest required on its bonds payable.

Impact analysis

The accounting treatment of liabilities has impact on the financial statements in various ways. The two major problems discussed in this chapter are areas where this impact may be significant: (1) the classification assigned to liabilities on the position statement; (2) the omission of liabilities from the statement.

Suppose that a current liability is improperly classified as a long-term liability. This might happen, for example, if a currently maturing long-term debt payable out of current assets is reported in the balance sheet as a long-term liability. Such a misclassification has the following impacts.

1. Working capital is overstated, because a current liability has been omitted from the computation of working capital. If the firm has not been accumulating current assets to pay off the debt, it may be in line for serious liquidity problems that won't be reflected in the misstated working capital.
2. Financial ratios involving current liabilities (such as current ratio and acid-test ratio) or long-term liabilities (such as debt to owners' equity and debt to fixed assets) will give misleading conclusions.

The omission of liabilities from the financial statements can have various impacts, depending on whether the omitted liability is a current or a long-term liability. In any case, failure to record a liability (a credit) means that some offsetting debit entry has also been omitted—usually an asset or an expense. For example, failure to adjust the books to record accrued wages, taxes, and interest expense would cause understatement of expenses as well as liabilities. In such a situation, the impact spreads through both the income statement and the balance sheet, along with many of the ratios derived from these statements.

In the discussion of bond issuance in this chapter, we mention briefly the impact of income tax laws on decisions about fund raising. Because bond interest is deductible from taxable income, the issuance of bonds can result in a reduction of taxes and an increase in the earnings per share of common stock. For example, suppose that a company with 1,000,000 outstanding shares of $10 par-value common stock (representing owners' investment of $10 million) is considering the possibility of raising $5 million by issuing either (1) 500,000 additional shares of common stock to be sold at $10 per share, or (2) $5 million of 6% bonds at par. The firm currently earns $400,000 per year before taxes, $200,000 after income taxes. Therefore, current earnings per share on the million outstanding shares are 20 cents per share. If an additional $5 million can be invested in the business, net income before taxes can be increased from $400,000 to $1,000,000.

Exhibit 15-8 illustrates the impact of the two possible kinds of financing. The issuance of the additional shares of stock instead of the 6% bonds will increase net income after taxes (earnings available for common stockholders) by $150,000. The savings of $300,000 in not having to pay bond interest expense is partially offset by the fact that income taxes must be paid on the larger net income. However, note that the earnings per share of common stock are larger if the financing is done

Exhibit 15-8 **Impacts of fund-raising decisions to use bonds or common stock**

	PLAN A	PLAN B
	Issuance of 500,000 additional shares of stock at $10 per share	Issuance of $5 million in 6% bonds
Original common stock (1,000,000 shares)	$10,000,000	$10,000,000
Additional resources gained	5,000,000	5,000,000
Total invested capital after plan	$15,000,000	$15,000,000
Net income before bond interest and taxes	$ 1,000,000	$ 1,000,000
Less: Bond interest expense	0	300,000
Taxable income	$ 1,000,000	$ 700,000
Less: Income taxes (50% rate assumed)	500,000	350,000
Net income after taxes (earnings available for common stockholders)	$ 500,000	$ 350,000
Earnings per share of common stock:		
Plan A ($500,000 ÷ 1.5 million shares)	33.3¢	
Plan B ($350,000 ÷ 1 million shares)		35.0¢

through bonds. The smaller number of shares outstanding in this case more than compensates for the smaller net income. (This would not be true if it were not for the tax advantage of the bond expense.)

If the firm's management uses earnings per share as its major criterion in deciding how to raise the additional funds, the firm would issue the 6% bonds. The firm uses the $5 million borrowed funds to increase its earnings (net income) by $150,000 (from $200,000 before the bond issue to $350,000 after). This means that the firm is paying the 6% interest on the bonds and earning an additional 3% return on the investment for the stockholders through the use of the borrowed funds. This is an example of financial leverage used profitably, because the earnings on funds acquired exceed the cost of obtaining them.

Summary

Liabilities are economic obligations that require a future outlay. Liabilities must be properly classified in the financial statements (for example, as current or longterm liabilities). All liabilities must be reported in the statements. Liabilities are listed in the statements in the order of their maturity dates.

Liabilities are measured initially by the exchange price at which the transaction creating the liability occurs. This amount usually is the amount of cash (principal) to be paid upon settlement of the debt.

Bonds payable represent a major long-term liability. Bonds payable are initially recorded at face value in the accounts. Any difference between the issue price and face value is established as a premium or discount. Bonds sell at par (face value) if interest on the bonds equals the market rate at the time the bonds are issued. If the market rate exceeds the nominal rate, the bonds are issued at a discount. If the market rate is less than the nominal rate, the bonds are issued at a premium. Bond premiums and discounts are amortized from the date of issue of the bonds to the date of maturity. The amortization process allocates the premium or discount as an adjustment to interest expense over the life of the bonds.

An estimated liability exists when the amount of a definite obligation is uncertain. Estimated liabilities should be reported in the financial statements. Contingent liabilities represent obligations that do not exist currently, but may develop if certain events occur. If a contingent liability is material and is likely to develop into a definite liability, it should be disclosed in the financial statements.

Questions

1. Define liabilities.
2. What are the two major classifications of liabilities?
3. Distinguish between current liabilities and noncurrent liabilities.
4. How are liabilities initially measured?
5. Describe two accounting procedures used to account for sales and excise taxes.
6. When does a liability arise for payments due on property taxes?
7. Discuss payroll taxes as they relate to employees and to employers.
8. What is a bond? bond interest?
9. Distinguish among nominal (or contract), market, and effective interest rates.
10. What is a bond premium? a bond discount?
11. Distinguish among definite, estimated, and contingent liabilities.
12. Describe some of the impacts of (a) improperly classifying liabilities on the statement of financial position, and (b) omitting liabilities that should appear on the statement.
13. A $1,000 bond is sold at 101½. Another $1,000 bond is sold at 97¾. What is the price of the two bonds?
14. A company issued $1,000,000 of 5% bonds due in 5 years at $989,130. Another company issued $1,000,000 of 5% bonds due in 4 years at $1,000,000. Which bonds incurred the higher effective rate of interest?

Exercises

E15-1 (Sales tax)
During the month of October, the Toppy Company sold $60,000 of candy (not including sales taxes). The sales tax in the state is 6 percent. Journalize the month's sales (the tax is collected and recorded at the time of sales).

E15-2 (Sales tax)
During the month of January, the Sousa Company sold $41,600 of furniture (including sales taxes collected from customers). The sales tax rate is 4 percent. Sales taxes are not separated from sales at the time of the sale, but are determined when the sales tax return is filed.

Required:

a. Journalize the month's sales.
b. Record the payment of the sales tax.

E15-3 (Property tax)
Sun Beach, California, imposes a property tax on business property. The city assesses taxes on January 1 for the tax year beginning on July 1. Taxes are paid in equal amounts on August 1 and November 1. The Taxie Company is assessed a tax of $60,000

Required: Journalize the entries the Taxie Company will make during the current year in relation to the property tax. The company prepares monthly interim statements.

E15-4 (Payroll)
Exhibit 15-9 shows the payroll register of the Miller Company.

Required:

a. Prepare a journal entry to record the payroll.
b. Journalize the payment of the salaries.
c. Record the employer's portion of social security taxes.

E15-5 (Payroll)
The Radial Company pays $460,000 in salaries for January. Income tax withholdings amount to $50,000. Assume that F.I.C.A. taxes are 8 percent, the Federal Unemployment tax rate is 2 percent, and there are no state unemployment taxes.

Required:

a. Record salaries and employee payroll taxes.
b. Record the employer's payroll taxes.

E15-6 (Bonds payable)
The Bond Company issued $500,000 of 9% bonds at 102. The bonds are dated January 1, 19_6, and mature in ten years. Interest-payment dates January 1 and July 1.

Required: Make the journal entries required in the books of the Bond Company in relation to this bond issue:

a. to record the issuance of the bonds;
b. to record the first interest payment on July 1, 19_6;
c. to record the amortization of the bond premium on July 1;
d. to record the accrual of bond interest expense on December 31;
e. to record the amortization of the bond premium on December 31;
f. to record the payment of interest on January 1, 19_7.

Exhibit 15-9
Payroll register for Exercise E15-4

Employee	Earnings	Deductions			Net Pay
		FICA	Income Tax	Union Dues	
Bill Scot	200.00	10.00	21.00	4.00	165.00
Jack Vallee	80.00	3.75	6.00	4.00	66.25
Ted Toms	130.00	5.25	8.00	4.00	112.75
Others	1,710.00	67.00	71.00	40.00	1,532.00
	2,120.00	86.00	106.00	52.00	1,876.00

E15-7 (Bonds payable)

The Manor Company issues $200,000 of 8% bonds at 104 plus accrued interest on April 1, 19_6. The bonds are dated January 1, 19_6, and mature in eight years. The interest-payment dates are January 1 and July 1.

Required: Make the entries relating to this bond issue that are needed in the books of the Manor Company during 19_6.

E15-8 (Bonds payable)

The England Company issues $800,000 of 10% bonds at 96, dated January 1, 19_6. The bonds mature in 20 years. Interest dates are January 1 and July 1.

Required: Make the entries relating to this bond issue that are needed in the books of the England Company during 19_6.

E15-9 (Bond ratio)

The Freed Company's condensed income statement appears as follows.

Revenue		$190,000
Less: Bond interest expense	$ 15,000	
Other expenses	100,000	115,000
Net income before taxes		$ 75,000
Less income taxes		37,500
Net income		$ 37,500

Required: Compute the number of times bond interest has been earned by the Freed Company.

E15-10 (Retirement of bonds payable)

Bonds of $150,000 that have a related unamortized premium on bonds of $22,500 are retired at $180,000 prior to maturity. Journalize the retirement of the bonds.

E15-11 (Liabilities on the balance sheet)

How should each of the following items be presented on a statement of financial position?

Accounts payable (trade)	17,500
Notes payable	3,500
State and federal income taxes payable	71,000
Bonds payable, 9% debentures, due in 1992	300,000
Unamortized discount on 9% debenture bonds	9,000

E15-12 (Understanding bond discount)

The Peakie Corporation issued $200,000 of 8% bonds, due in ten years. The bonds sold at 95 when issued.

a. Was the market interest rate larger than, smaller than, or equal to the nominal rate of 8% at the time of issuance?

b. What was the ***total*** interest expense incurred by the company during the ten-year period in which the bonds were outstanding?

c. What is the yearly cash interest payment to bondholders?

d. On an income statement, what interest expense would be reported for one year?

E15-13 (Impact analysis)

Prepare a table showing the dollar impact of each of the following transactions on working capital, total assets, net assets, net income, and owners' equity.

a. Merchandise in the amount of $1,600 is purchased on account; terms 1/10, n/30. The company records purchases net and uses the perpetual inventory method.
b. Cash sale of services amounts to $840, including a $40 sales tax.
c. Property tax liability is recorded as follows.

Property Tax Expense	400	
Property Tax Payable		400

d. The payroll for the period is recorded as follows.

Salaries	12,000	
Taxes Withheld		2,500
Salaries Payable		9,500

e. Salaries payable in the amount of $9,500 are paid.
f. Ten-year bonds with a par value of $300,000 are issued at 106.
g. Bond interest expense in the amount of $24,000 is recorded as follows.

Bond Interest Expense	24,000	
Cash		24,000

h. An adjusting entry is made to record the amortization of bond premiums on bonds outstanding in the amount of $900.
i. An adjusting entry is made to record the accrual of bond interest expense in the amount of $2,400.
j. Bonds payable carried at $300,000 are retired in exchange for $300,000 of the company's no-par common stock.

E15-14 (Bonds payable)
On January 1, 19_7, for a cost of $9,784, the Clouds Company purchases ten $1,000, 8% bonds dated January 1, 19_6, as a long-term investment. Interest is payable annually on January 1. The bonds mature on January 1, 19_9.

Required:
a. Record the purchase of the bonds on January 1, 19_7.
b. Record all entries needed at the end of 19_7, when the company adjusts its books.
c. At what value would the bonds be reported on the December 31, 19_7, statement of financial position?
d. The bonds are redeemed on January 1, 19_9, at 105. Record the redemption.

E15-15 (Payroll)
Payroll records of a company disclose the following information:

Employee	Total Earnings	Cumulative Earnings to End of Prior Week	Federal Income Tax	Retirement Deduction
E. Fred	$200	$2,900	$20	$5
F. Electric	250	3,500	22	6
G. Manpower	400	8,900	30	—
H. Wilson	500	9,050	50	8

F.I.C.A. taxes are withheld at a rate of 5% on the first $9,000 of earnings. State and federal unemployment taxes are respectively 2.7% and .8% on the first $3,000 of wages.

Required:

a. Prepare journal entries to record the payroll for the period.

b. Prepare journal entries to record employer's payroll taxes for the period.

E15-16 (Payroll)

The earnings of sales employees of Chat Company for the last week of December amounted to $100,000. The payroll is paid in the first week in January. The company closes its books on December 31. F.I.C.A. taxes on employer and employees were 5%. Of the $100,000 earnings, $80,000 were subject to F.I.C.A. taxes. Unemployment taxes of 2.7% state and .8 of 1% federal were charged against $10,000 of earnings for the week. Federal income tax withholdings amounted to $12,000.

Required: Prepare journal entries for salaries on December 31. Accrue any payroll taxes that should be recorded.

Problems

P15-1 (Bonds payable)

On January 1, 19_1, the Plow Company issues $400,000 of 9%, 10-year bonds at 96. On March 1, an additional $100,000 of bonds are issued at 95 plus accrued interest. Interest is paid on January 1 and July 1.

Required:

a. Make the necessary journal entries in 19_6 relating to the bond issuance. The Plow Company accumulates the discount on bonds annually on December 31.

b. Record the payment of bond interest on January 1, 19_7.

P15-2 (Methods of acquiring funds)

The Pilot Company has 3,000 shares of $100-par-value common stock outstanding. In order to obtain additional funds, the president of the company is considering two alternatives:

(1) issuance of $200,000 of 8% bonds due in ten years (issued at par); or

(2) issuance at par of $200,000 of 8% preferred stock.

The preferred stock would pay dividends of 8% per year on its par value. Note that interest expense is deductible from taxable income, but dividends are not. The company expects in the future to average $80,000 net income before taxes, interest, and dividends. The income tax rate is 50 percent of taxable income.

a. Should the Pilot Company issue the 8% bonds or the 8% preferred stock? The president wants to make the choice that will provide the larger net income available to the common stockholders.

b. How many times does the Pilot Company expect to earn its interest requirements if it issues the bonds?

P15-3 (Bonds payable)

On January 1, 19_6, the Bonds Payable account of the Sunny Company shows a credit balance of $200,000, which is identified as 9% bonds due December 31, 19_8. The Discount on Bonds account shows a debit balance of $7,200. Interest on the bonds is payable on June 30 and December 31. The company closes its books on December 31. On May 31, 19_8, the bonds were repurchased at 104 plus accrued interest and were retired.

Required: Prepare the journal entries needed:
a. to record bond interest payable on May 31, 19_8;
b. to accumulate the bond discount to May 31, 19_8;
c. to record the retirement of the bonds on May 31, 19_8.

P15-4 (Payroll)

The records of the Helper Company provided the following information for the year 19_6.

Total salaries expense	$210,000
Salaries to employees who have already earned more than $12,000 (these are salaries exempt from the F.I.C.A. taxes)	90,000
Salaries to employees with cumulative earning in excess of $4,200 (salaries exempt from unemployment taxes)	160,000
Income taxes withheld	40,000

Required:
a. Record the payroll for the year. Assume that F.I.C.A. tax is 8 percent.
b. Record the payroll tax expense for the period. Assume a federal unemployment tax of 2.7 percent and a state unemployment tax of 0.5 percent.

P15-5 (Bonds payable)

Both of the following cases involve 10-year, 5%, $1,000 bonds, dated January 1, 19_6. Interest is paid annually on January 1. Treat each case separately; round answers to the nearest dollar.

Case 1:
a. Record the sale of 10 bonds at 92 on April 1, 19_6.
b. Record all necessary adjusting entries on December 31, 19_6.

Case 2:
a. Record the sale of 10 bonds on January 1, 19_7, at 103.
b. Record all necessary adjusting entries on December 31, 19_7.
c. Show the bonds as valued on the December 31, 19_7, statement of financial position.
d. Record the redemption of the bonds at 101 on January 1, 19_9.

P15-6 (Payroll)

The employees of a company are paid at an hourly rate with time and one-half for overtime. In October, the payroll data for the company's five employees appear as follows.

Employee	Hours Regular	Hours Overtime	Rate	Cumulative Pay to Date	Federal Income Taxes
Men	160	10	$4	$ 5,500	$50
Newcomer	160		4	6,000	70
Occer	160		6	4,000	40
Peters	160		3	2,000	50
Quirk	160	10	4	12,000	80

Mr. Men and Ms. Newcomer are administrative officers of the company. The other employees are salesmen. F.I.C.A. taxes are 5% on a maximum of $9,000 in earnings. State unemployment taxes are 2.7% to a maximum of $3,000 earnings; federal unemployment taxes are .8% on the first $3,000 of earnings. Employees must contribute 2% of their gross pay to the medical plan. The company also pays 2% to the plan. The company's payroll records appear as follows:

Employee	Gross Earnings	F.I.C.A. Taxes Withholdings	Federal Income Taxes	Medical Plan	Net Pay

Required:

a. Complete the payroll records of the company for October.

b. Prepare a journal entry to record the payroll for the month.

c. Prepare a journal entry to record the employer's taxes for the month and its contribution to the medical plan.

P15-7 (Payroll)

The Payroll Company has a monthly payroll of $100,000 subject to F.I.C.A. taxes at a rate of 3%, a federal unemployment tax of 0.58%, and a state unemployment tax of 2.7%. Income taxes withheld amounted to $20,000 for the month.

Required:

a. Record the payroll and payroll deductions for the month.

b. Record the payment of the payroll.

c. Record the employer's payroll taxes.

P15-8 (Bonds)

A company has bonds outstanding in the amount of $500,000 on which there is an unamortized premium of $50,000. The bonds are called for retirement at 101. Record the retirement assuming that interest has been paid on the bonds to date.

P15-9 (Bonds)

a. A company purchased $1,000,000 of 5% bonds with interest payable semiannually. The bonds have four years to go before maturity. The company paid $1,001,794.45. What was the effective yield on these bonds?

b. There were $1,000,000 par value, 5% bonds with five years to maturity available on the market. The company wanted to earn an effective yield of 5.25% on its investment in bonds. At what price must the bonds be purchased to attain this yield?

c. A company desires to acquire $1,000,000 par value, 5% bonds, to yield 4.85%. The company would spend $1,005,999.36 for the bonds. How many years would the bonds have to be held under these circumstances?

Owners' equity at formation

16

The long-range goal of almost any business entity is to make a profit for its owners. That is, the purpose of the entity's operations is to increase the owners' equity in the business. The owners' equity represents the residual claim of the owners to the firm's assets, after the claims of creditors have been settled.

Accounting for owners' equity transactions involves procedures that vary with the ownership structure of the particular business entity. We begin this chapter with a brief discussion of various forms of business organization. Then we turn to a detailed discussion of accounting procedures used for the corporate form of business organization. After that we look at accounting procedures used for the sole proprietorship and the partnership forms of business.

The preceding chapters describe basic concepts and procedures of accounting for assets, liabilities, revenue, and expense activities. These are essentially the same for all forms of business organization. This chapter deals primarily with accounting matters that relate to owners' equity transactions.

Forms of business organization

In the beginnings of economic history, the household was the main organization involved in economic activity. From the household developed the small enterprise with limited capital requirements and a single owner-manager. Today, the small business enterprise coexists alongside technically proficient, massively financed, and elaborately organized corporate structures.

Businesses have learned to operate within a legal and economic environment of laws, rules, regulations, courts, and similar restraints. In order to survive and prosper in this environment, businesses have organized themselves within the framework of the restraints to pursue their economic activities.

The more popular forms of business organization include the sole (or single) proprietorship, partnership, and corporation. There are more sole proprietorships than any other form of business organization in the United States today. However, the corporation is the dominant form of organization in terms of size, income, and assets (see Exhibit 16-1).

The *sole proprietorship* is a business owned by a single individual. The owner holds title to all assets and has responsibility for all liabilities. The profits or losses of the firm belong to the owner.

A *partnership* is an association of two or more individuals as co-owners to carry on a business for profit. In a general partnership, all partners are liable for the debts of the firm. Profits and losses are divided among the partners according to a formal agreement. If no formal agreement exists, partnership profits and losses are divided equally.

A *corporation* is a form of business organization established by a charter received from the state. The charter grants certain rights, powers, and privileges to the corporation—for example, the right to conduct business as a legal entity distinct from the individual stockholders, the power to sue and to be sued, the right to own property. Exhibit 16-2 summarizes the similarities and differences among these three major forms of business organization.

The corporation

In terms of size, net income, net profits, and public attention, the modern business environment is dominated by corporations. Accounting for the corporation involves a number of complex procedures associated with the equity of stockholders. Therefore, we look first at the corporate form of business organization.

ORGANIZATION OF A CORPORATION

Individuals (the *incorporators*) who want to organize a corporation apply to an official (usually the Secretary of State) of the state in which they want to incorporate. The application or certificate of incorporation usually requires that the incorporators indicate the name of the corporation, the kind of business it will engage in, the amount of capital stock to be authorized, the names and addresses of those involved in organizing the corporation, and similar information.

If the application is approved, the state issues a *charter* that establishes the legal existence of the corporation. This charter is filed with a clerk in the county where the principal office of the corporation is located.

Exhibit 16-1 **Forms of organization of U.S. businesses (1970 data)**

	Proprietorships	**Partnerships**	**Corporations**
Number of businesses	**9,400,000 (78%)**	**936,000 (8%)**	**1,665,000 (14%)**
Business receipts	**$238 billion (11%)**	**$93 billion (4%)**	**$1,751 billion (85%)**
Net profits (less losses)	**$33 billion (30%)**	**$10 billion (9%)**	**$66 billion (61%)**
Number of businesses with receipts of $500,000 or more	**30,000**	**27,000**	**306,000**

NOTE: Data from U.S. Internal Revenue Service, *Statistics of Income, 1970, Business Income Tax Returns.*

Exhibit 16-2 **Comparison of legal forms of business organization**

FEATURE	PROPRIETORSHIP	PARTNERSHIP	CORPORATION
Number of owners	One.	Two or more.	Usually three or more.
Assets owned by	Proprietor.	Partners as co-owners.	Corporation.
Liability	Sole proprietor is personally liable for all business debts. *Unlimited liability.*	Each partner is personally liable for all business debts. *Unlimited liability.*	Stockholder's liability is usually limited to his own investment. *Limited liability.*
Legal existence	Extension of proprietor.	Extension of partners.	Separate entity, distinct from stockholders.
Life	Ends with change in ownership—for example, death or insolvency of proprietor.	Ends with change in ownership—for example, death or insolvency of a partner, withdrawal of a partner.	Perpetual unless limited by charter.
Organization agreement	Unnecessary.	Should have formal Articles of Copartnership setting forth agreement among partners.	Must be chartered by state.
Ownership powers	Complete.	Complete; any partner binds all other partners unless a partner is restricted.	Certain rights given by stock agreement to stockholders—for example, the right to vote, to receive declared dividends, to buy additional issues of stock.
Federal income tax	Proprietor reports income statement data on his personal tax return and is taxed on profit of the business; the business pays no income tax.	Partners report income statement data of partnership and show income distribution among partners on their personal tax returns; each partner is taxed on his share of the business' net income; the partnership pays no income tax.	Corporation pays income tax; shareholders report dividends as income on their personal tax returns (double taxation of corporate income).
Owners' salary	Personal withdrawal from owner's equity.	Division of net income among partners.	Salaries paid as operating expense; net income may be paid out as dividends.
Advantages	a. Relatively easy to start. b. Relatively free from government regulation. c. Profits taxed once to owner.	Approximately the same as those for proprietorship.	a. Ability to raise large sums of money. b. Ownership shares are relatively easy to transfer. c. Limited liability of shareholders. d. Life of corporation can be perpetual.
Disadvantages	a. Unlimited liability of owner. b. Difficulties of raising large amounts of money. c. Lack of permanency as a form of organization.	Approximately the same as those for proprietorship.	a. Double taxation of income distributed to shareholders. b. Subject to government regulation not required of other forms of business organization.

The incorporators or stockholders hold an organizational meeting (1) to elect ***directors*** who will establish major policies for the corporation, and (2) to adopt bylaws for the corporation. The ***bylaws*** are regulations that specify matters dealing with the internal affairs of the corporation. For example, the bylaws usually outline the qualifications and method for selection of directors, the time and place of stockholders' meetings, the procedures for forming committees, and so on. After the election, the directors meet and elect the officers of the corporation. The ***officers*** (the president, secretary, treasurer, and so on) are employees of the corporation. The board of directors (acting as representatives of the stockholders, or owners) delegates to the officers the authority for the routine management of the corporation.

During the life of the corporation, the board of directors exercises most of the rights of ownership control. The stockholders have the right to elect members of the board of directors.[1] Any decision to liquidate the corporation, merge it with another corporation, or amend the charter must be approved by the majority of the stockholders. Other voting rights of stockholders may be set forth in the original charter or provided by particular state laws. For most practical purposes, however, the directors determine the overall policy of the corporation. The activities of the board of directors are recorded in a ***minutes book*** that becomes the official record of policy decisions. The officers of the corporation are chosen by the directors and are responsible to them for making decisions that carry out the prescribed policies. The officers in turn hire the other employees of the corporation and carry out its day-to-day operations. Exhibit 16-3 summarizes the organizational structure of a corporation.

CAPITAL STOCK

The ownership interest in a corporation is divided into shares of capital stock. The individual who holds shares of stock in the corporation is entitled to certain basic rights. The principal types of capital stock that can be issued by a corporation are common stock and preferred stock. Any business corporation must issue common stock. Some corporations are authorized by their charters or by state law to issue preferred stock in addition to the common stock.

COMMON STOCK. Common stock is a term applied to those corporate shares that represent basic ownership interests in the corporation. Among the more important rights associated with common stock are the following:

1. the right to vote at stockholders' meetings;
2. the right to participate in the earnings of the corporation (that is, to receive dividends when declared by the directors of the corporation);
3. the right to participate proportionately in any additional issues of stock by the corporation (the preemptive right);
4. the right to sell or transfer stock;

1. Some corporations are given the right in the charter or in state law to issue shares of nonvoting stock. Federal law restricts the issuance of nonvoting shares in many kinds of corporations. Investment corporations and those being reorganized under federal bankruptcy laws are forbidden to issue nonvoting shares. Issuance of nonvoting shares in many other kinds of businesses is subject to the approval of various regulatory agencies.

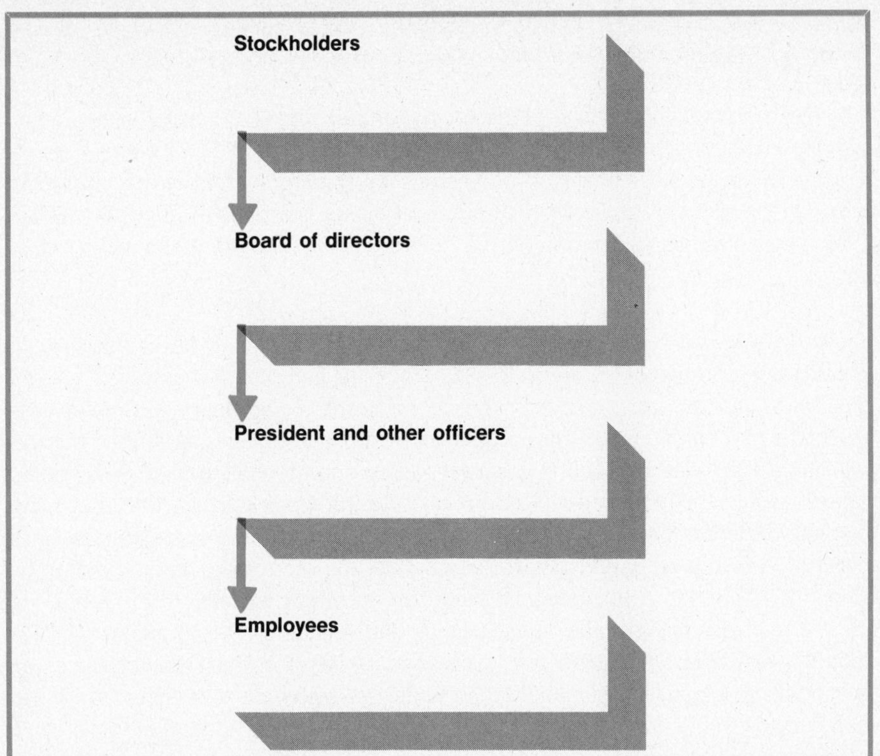

Exhibit 16-3
Organization structure of a corporation

5. the right to share in the distribution of the assets of the corporation if the corporation is dissolved.

AUTHORIZED, ISSUED, AND OUTSTANDING SHARES. The charter of the corporation authorizes it to issue a certain number of shares of stock. The number of ***authorized shares*** may be changed at any time by a vote of two-thirds of the present shareholders. The corporation can issue only the number of shares that has been authorized. A share is ***issued*** when it is acquired by others in an exchange in which the corporation receives cash, property, services, or some other asset and gives out a new stock certificate. The corporation can buy back shares of its own stock (or be given them as a gift), but the shares can be cancelled only by approval of the stockholders. (Shares reacquired by the corporation itself are called ***treasury shares;*** they have no voting rights.) The number of shares issued less the number of treasury shares gives the number of ***shares outstanding.***

RECORD-KEEPING FOR STOCK. When a corporation issues stock, it gives the stockholder a ***stock certificate*** for the number of shares acquired, as evidence of ownership. The corporation maintains a ***shareowners' ledger*** that contains an account for each stockholder, showing the number of shares held by each owner of the corporation. When stock that has been issued is transferred from one owner to another, the transfer is recorded in a ***stock transfer book.*** Entries from the transfer book are posted to the shareowners' ledger, to keep the record of ownership in the ledger current.

Larger corporations often arrange for a ***transfer agent*** to maintain their stock transfer books and shareowners' ledgers. To ensure independent control over the process of issuing stock, many corporations engage a ***stock registrar*** to countersign stock certificates and to ensure that each certificate is properly issued. Banks and trust companies in financial centers serve as stock registrars for most major corporations.

PAR VALUE AND STATED VALUE. Early incorporation laws required the charter of a corporation to state both a number of authorized shares and a dollar amount of capital (cash, property, some other asset, or an equivalent in services) that must be contributed to the corporation in order to obtain one share. This ***par value*** of a share was intended to ensure that each share was equivalent to the others (on a par with them) in terms of contribution to the firm's capital. Most stock was originally required to have $100 par value, and the corporation was expected to receive $100 of capital for each share issued. Over the years, laws gradually changed to permit the issuance of stock with higher or lower par values.

As the stock market grew in importance and volume of trading, the assumption that shares would be handed out to persons investing in the organization of the corporation no longer was valid. Market prices for stock are determined by supply and demand in the auction trading of the stock exchange, and market values have no relationship to par values. Today, when a corporation issues stock, it normally offers shares to its present stockholders (who have a preemptive right to first chance at a proportion of the new issue equivalent to their present proportion of holdings), to investment bankers who will sell the stock on the market, or to institutions or individuals who negotiate to buy the stock for themselves. In any case, the price the corporation receives for the new stock is almost always influenced strongly by the current market price of similar shares (or the expected market price for an issue of a new class of stock). Therefore, the corporation seldom receives exactly the par value for each share issued.

If stock is issued at a price above par value, it is said to be issued at a ***premium;*** if it is issued below par value, it is issued at a ***discount.*** In either case, the ownership rights represented by a single share remain the same as those represented by any other share of the same class—with one exception. Many states still have laws restricting the issuance of stock at discount. (The argument is that creditors of the corporation have a right to expect the corporation to have capital at least equal to the par value of the outstanding shares.) In these cases, the shareholder who buys stock that was issued at a discount may be liable to the creditors for the amount of the discount if the corporation is dissolved.

Early in this century, some states began to authorize the issuance of stock with no par value. Today such ***no-par stock*** is legal in every state, and much of the stock traded on the stock exchanges is no-par stock. In certain cases the directors of the corporation choose a value at which they will carry the outstanding no-par stock in the books of the corporation; this value is called the ***stated value*** of the no-par stock. For all practical accounting purposes, stated value is the same as par value.

LEGAL CAPITAL. Many states have laws that specify a minimum amount of equity capital that must be retained by the corporation. This amount, called the ***legal capital,*** is determined in various ways by the laws of different states. In many states, legal capital is set at the par value of issued stock. In other states (or in cases where no-par stock is issued), legal capital may be determined by the total amount received for issuance of stock, by the total stated value of issued stock, or by some other measure specified in the state's incorporation laws.

In these states, the corporation is not permitted to declare dividends or otherwise distribute its earnings to the shareholders except from owners' equity that exceeds the legal capital. Such a perscription gives some assurance to creditors that the stockholders will absorb losses up to the legal capital requirement before creditors suffer any loss.

PREFERRED STOCK. As the term indicates, the holder of preferred stock has certain preferences or priorities over the holder of common stock. Two major preferences of preferred stockholders are

1. preference as to dividends (that is, preferred stockholders must receive their dividends before any dividends can be paid to common stockholders);
2. preference as to the assets of the corporation if and when it is dissolved (a share of preferred stock usually has a liquidating value, which represents the amount the preferred shareholder is entitled to receive if the corporation is dissolved; preferred shareholders must receive the liquidating value of their shares before any of the assets can be distributed among common shareholders).

On the other hand, preferred stockholders generally do not have a right to vote in the affairs of the corporation. In certain cases, preferred stock is ***convertible.*** That is, the owner of the preferred stock may, at his option, turn in his preferred shares to the corporation in exchange for a stated number of the corporation's common shares. Preferred stock may be (1) cumulative or noncumulative, and (2) participating or nonparticipating.

CUMULATIVE PREFERRED STOCK. If preferred stock is cumulative preferred, the corporation must pay all dividends in arrears (that is, dividends not paid in earlier periods) on the preferred stock before dividends can be paid on common stock. For example, assume the following information about a corporation.

Preferred stock, $100 par value, 6 percent, cumulative;
1,000 shares outstanding; dividends in arrears for 2 years;
total par value $100,000.
Common stock, $10 par value; 20,000 shares outstanding;
total par value $200,000.
Retained earnings of $50,000.

If the directors wish to declare a dividend, they must first pay the dividends in arrears and the current dividends on the preferred cumulative stock. The preferred stockholders would receive $18,000 (6 percent of $100,000 for each of the three years) before any dividends could be paid to common stockholders. Common stock is not cumulative as to dividends.

In this case, suppose that the directors declare a dividend on the preferred stock and also declare a dividend of $1 per share on the common stock. In that case, they would distribute $18,000 to the preferred stockholders and $20,000 to the common stockholders, retaining only $12,000 of the earnings in the equity capital.

NONCUMULATIVE PREFERRED STOCK. If the preferred stock is noncumulative, the stockholder loses all claim to any dividends not declared in a particular year by the board of directors. For example, suppose that the preferred stock in the previous example were noncumulative. In that case, the corporation would have to pay the preferred stockholders only the dividends for the current year ($6,000) before paying dividends to the common stockholders. Most preferred stock is cumulative preferred.

NONPARTICIPATING PREFERRED STOCK. If preferred stock is nonparticipating, the preferred stockholders receive only their specified dividend, but do not participate with the common stockholders in distributions exceeding the specified rate. Most preferred stock is nonparticipating (and is assumed to be so unless otherwise stated).

PARTICIPATING PREFERRED STOCK. If preferred stock is fully participating, it is entitled to receive dividends at the same rate paid on common stock if that rate is higher than the preferred rate. Let us return to our illustration, but this time assume that the preferred stock is noncumulative, fully participating preferred stock and that the dividends are not in arrears. In this case, if the directors declare a dividend, the preferred stockholders are entitled to the specified 6 percent dividend (a total of $6,000). If the directors wish, they may declare a dividend of up to 6 percent on the $200,000 par value, or $12,000, on the common stock without declaring any additional dividend for the preferred stock. (This would be a dividend of 60¢ per share on the common stock, which is 6 percent of the par value of a share.)

If the directors wish to pay the $1 per share dividend on the common stock (a 10 percent dividend on the $10-par-value common shares), they must also pay a 10 percent dividend on the preferred stock. This means that they must distribute $10,000 to the preferred stockholders, as well as the $20,000 to the common stockholders.

Preferred stock is sometimes ***partially participating.*** In such cases, the preferred stockholders participate with the common up to some specified rate (for example, up to 8 percent). Distributions in excess of 8 percent can be made to common stockholders without any further distributions to the preferred stockholders. Other arrangements for partial participation can be made in various cases—for example, dividends beyond the specified rate on preferred stock might be split in a certain ratio between preferred and common stockholders.

ACCOUNTING FOR THE CORPORATION

The corporation is a creation of law. As such, it is a legal entity separate and distinct from its owners, the shareholders. For legal purposes, the corporation has many of the rights and obligations of an individual.

Recall that the business-entity assumption of accounting requires that accounting for a business be kept separate and distinct from accounting for the owners of the business. In the case of a corporation, this distinction is clearly recognized and established in the legal relationship between the corporation and its owners. For that reason, the basic procedures of accounting for owners' equity can be stated most clearly for the corporate form of business organization.

A major accounting problem for the corporation is to distinguish the ***sources of corporate capital*** in the accounts and on the financial statements. The equity capital of a corporation (the shareholders' equity) comes from three primary sources.

1. *Paid-in capital* or *contributed capital* is the amount of capital that has originated from the stockholders' investments in the corporation.
2. *Donated capital* is the amount of capital that has originated from gifts by stockholders or others. For example, a city might give property or plant to a company in order to encourage it to locate there.
3. *Retained earnings* is the amount of capital that has originated from the profit-making activities of the corporation and has been retained in the business.

As we shall see, there are legal and accounting reasons for keeping these categories separate. Keep in mind that we are talking here about the sources of capital, or the claims against the company's wealth. These claims exist against the total wealth (gross capital) of the company. There is no necessary relationship between a particular claim represented in the capital structure and a particular asset represented in the gross capital. In other words, the paid-in capital or the retained earnings does not represent any particular fund of cash or other asset. It represents a claim of a certain amount against the firm's total assets.

With this general introduction to corporations completed, we now turn to a series of transactions that illustrate many of the significant accounting procedures associated with shareholders' equity. A careful study of these cases will provide the framework for an understanding of corporate accounting.

Transaction 1. Common stock authorized and issued. The Example Corporation is organized and is authorized by its charter to issue 100,000 shares of $1-par-value stock. Ninety percent of the authorized stock is issued for cash at par value.

No journal entry is required for the authorization of stock. However, a memorandum entry should be made in the journal to describe the establishment of the corporation and to state the number and classes of stock authorized. A memorandum entry should also be made in the Common Stock account in the ledger: ''100,000 shares of $1-par-value stock authorized.''

The issuance of stock does require a journal entry. The stock account is credited with the par value of the shares issued.

Cash	90,000	
Common Stock		90,000
To record issuance of 90,000 shares of common stock at par ($1/share).		

Transaction 2. Organization Cost. After transaction 1, the corporation issues an additional 1,000 shares of common stock to the organizers of the corporation, as compensation for their efforts in bringing the corporation into existence. The fair value of the shares is estimated from the previous transaction to be $1 per share.

The issuance of these shares is recorded by the following journal entry.

Organization Cost	1,000	
Common Stock		1,000
To record issuance of 1,000 shares of $1-par-value stock in exchange for organizers' efforts.		

In this case, Organization Cost is an asset account. It is an intangible asset, representing the existence that the corporation enjoys as a result of the efforts of the organizers. This cost should be recognized as an expense in some manner allocated systematically over the life of the corporation. Because the corporation is assumed to have an indefinite lifespan, the cost will be amortized over some reasonably long period, but not to exceed 40 years. In this case, the accountant of the Example Corporation decides to amortize the cost over a ten-year period on a straight-line basis. At the end of the first year, he makes the following adjusting entry.

Amortization of Organization Cost	100	
Organization Cost		100
To recognize portion of organization cost as expense (10-year, straight-line amortization of $1,000 cost).		

After transaction 2 (before any amortization of the organization cost), the corporation has $91,000 of capital. In terms of gross capital, this amount is represented by $90,000 of cash and $1,000 of the intangible asset of being organized. In terms of capital structure, the claim against this amount is entirely paid-in capital (owners' equity). The organizers bought their 1,000 shares by paying in the $1,000 intangible asset of the results of their organizational effort. Note how the value of the intangible asset is determined by its exchange price—the cash price of the 1,000 shares of $1-par-value stock, established recently when similar stock was issued for cash.

Transaction 3. Stock issued at a premium. After transaction 2, the Example Corporation issues another 2,000 shares of common stock for $1.50 per share.

Because these shares are issued at a price above par, they are being issued at a premium. The transaction is recorded by the following journal entry.

Cash	3,000	
Common Stock		2,000
Paid-In Capital in Excess of Par Value		1,000
To record issuance of 2,000 shares of $1-par-value stock at a premium.		

The Paid-In Capital in Excess of Par Value account[2] is the excess of the issuance

2. This account is sometimes given other titles, including the following: Excess Over Par Value of Common Stock; Premium on Common Stock; Capital in Excess of Par Value—From Common Stock Issuances.

price over par value. This amount is recorded in a separate account in order to keep the sources of capital separate. This account is an equity capital account, and it represents paid-in capital. It is reported in the stockholders' equity section of the financial statement.

Premium on common stock is not amortized as is premium on bonds payable. One reason for keeping this amount in a separate account is that in many states this amount is not considered a part of legal capital, and therefore it may be available for dividends. Another reason is that investors will be interested in knowing how the actual capital paid in by stockholders compares with the stated or par value of the shares issued.

Transaction 4. Stock issued at a discount. After transaction 3, the Example Corporation issues another 1,000 shares of common stock for 90 cents per share.

Because these shares are issued at a price below par, they are issued at a discount. (Issuances at discount are rare.) The transaction is recorded by the following journal entry.

Cash	900	
Discount on Common Stock	100	
Common Stock		1,000
To record issuance of 1,000 shares of $1-par-value stock at a discount.		

The Discount on Common Stock account represents the excess of par value of stock over its issuance price. This account is a contra equity capital account. On the statement of financial position, this account is deducted from the paid-in capital. In some states, the shareholder may have a contingent liability to the creditors of the corporation for the amount of the discount, in the event of dissolution of the corporation. In certain states, laws forbid a corporation to issue stock at a discount. The discount on stock is not written off as is a discount on bonds payable.

Exhibit 16-4 shows a balance sheet for the Example Corporation after transaction

Exhibit 16-4 **Balance sheet summarizing transactions 1 through 4**

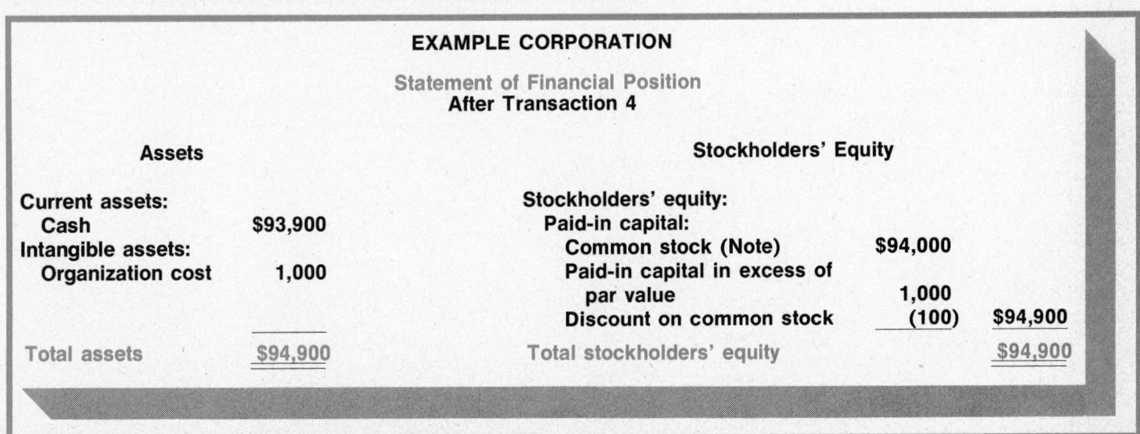

EXAMPLE CORPORATION

Statement of Financial Position
After Transaction 4

Assets		**Stockholders' Equity**		
Current assets:		**Stockholders' equity:**		
Cash	**$93,900**	**Paid-in capital:**		
Intangible assets:		**Common stock (Note)**	**$94,000**	
Organization cost	**1,000**	**Paid-in capital in excess of par value**	**1,000**	
		Discount on common stock	**(100)**	**$94,900**
Total assets	$94,900	Total stockholders' equity		$94,900

NOTE: Common stock, $1 par value: authorized 100,000 shares; issued 9,400 shares.

4 (before amortization of any of the organization cost). The capital of the corporation at this point is $94,900. As gross capital, this is represented by $93,900 cash (current assets) and $1,000 of intangible assets. As capital structure, it is represented by $94,900 of paid-in capital.

Transaction 5. Stock issued for property. The Property Corporation acquires land in exchange for 10,000 shares of its $10-par-value stock. At this time, the stock is selling on the New York Stock Exchange for $12 per share. No reliable information is available about the market value or worth of the land.

When stock is issued for assets other than cash, the transaction should be recorded at the exchange price. The amount used to value the property and the paid-in capital should be the fair market value of the property acquired or the fair market value of the shares issued, whichever is more objectively determinable. Because stock is traded daily in the auction market of the stock exchange, its market price is usually the more objectively determinable. The entry to record this transaction is the following.

Land	120,000	
Common Stock		100,000
Paid-In Capital in Excess of Par Value		20,000
To record acquisition of land in exchange for 10,000 shares of common stock at premium ($12/share market).		

In many states, it is illegal to issue stock at a discount. In those states where it is not illegal to do so, the state law usually establishes a contingent liability on the shareholders for the amount of the discount. No-par stock (that is, stock without any par value) was introduced in order to avoid the necessity of having to record a discount on stock.

If no-par stock is assigned no stated value by the corporation, its issuance must be recorded at the exchange price of the transaction. If the stock is issued for cash, the Common Stock account is credited for the amount of cash received for the stock. For example, if transactions 1 through 5 had involved no-par stock, they could have been recorded by the following journal entries.

1. Cash	90,000	
Common Stock—no par		90,000
2. Organization Cost	1,000	
Common Stock—no par		1,000
3. Cash	3,000	
Common Stock—no par		3,000
4. Cash	900	
Common Stock—no par		900
5. Land	120,000	
Common Stock—no par		120,000

In most cases when no-par stock is issued, the directors of the corporation assign a stated value to each share of stock. For accounting purposes, this stated value is treated similarly to par value. For example, if 100 shares of no-par common stock with a stated value of $10 per share are issued for $12 per share, the following journal entry is made.[3]

Cash	1,200	
Common Stock		1,000
Paid-In Capital in Excess of Stated Value		200
To record issuance of 100 shares no-par stock (stated value $10/share).		

STOCK SUBSCRIPTIONS. In many cases, a purchaser does not fully pay for his stock at the time that the agreement to issue stock is made. In such a case, the purchaser is required to sign a subscription contract stating his agreement to buy a specified number of shares at a stipulated price. (Subscription contracts for a substantial number of shares normally are required before the charter is issued for a corporation. The corporation cannot issue the shares until after it is chartered.) The corporation does not issue stock certificates to the purchaser until he completes the full payment for his stock.

Two new accounts are required to record transactions involving stock subscriptions.

1. Subscriptions Receivable: a current asset account representing a claim by the corporation against the subscriber to the stock.
2. Capital (or Common) Stock Subscribed: a temporary capital stock account appearing in the equity capital (owners' equity) section of the balance sheet.

Transaction 6. Stock subscriptions. The Subscription Company receives subscriptions for 10,000 shares of $10-par-value stock on March 1, 19_1. The subscription price of the stock is $12 per share. A 50 percent down payment is required at the time the subscription is received; the balance is to be paid in one installment on June 1, 19_1.

The stock certificates are not issued until the final installment payment is received by the corporation. The following entries record the subscription transactions on March 1 and June. 1.

Mar. 1	Subscriptions Receivable	120,000	
	Common Stock Subscribed		100,000
	Paid-In Capital in Excess of Par Value		20,000
	To record subscription for 10,000 shares of $10-par-value stock at $12/share.		
1	Cash	60,000	
	Subscriptions Receivable		60,000
	To record receipt of 40% down payment on stock subscription received this date.		

3. Instead of the account title Paid-In Capital in Excess of Stated Value, this account is sometimes given other titles such as Excess of Stated Value of Common Stock; Paid-In Capital—Excess of Stated Value; Capital in Excess of Stated Value—From Stock Issuances.

		Debit	Credit
June 1	Cash	60,000	
	Subscriptions Receivable		60,000
	To record receipt of balance due on stock subscription of Mar. 1.		
1	Common Stock Subscribed	100,000	
	Common Stock		100,000
	To record issuance of stock certificates for 10,000 shares of stock subscribed Mar. 1 and paid for June 1.		

PREFERRED STOCK. Preferred stock has certain things in common with common stock. For example, both preferred stock and common stock represent ownership in the corporation. Neither security requires the payment of a fixed return on the investment or a repayment of the investment at a maturity date.

However, there also exist major differences between the two kinds of stock. Preferred stockholders have priority over common stockholders if dividends are declared. Dividends on preferred stock usually are limited to a specified percentage of par value. Usually, preferred stock is cumulative preferred, meaning that missed dividends on the preferred stock from prior years must be paid before dividends can be distributed to common stockholders. Preferred stockholders have a priority claim to the assets of the corporation on dissolution—that is, a priority over common stockholders, but creditors have a priority over even the preferred stockholders. In most cases, preferred stockholders are denied the right to vote. In short, the properties of preferred stock as an investment are somewhere between those of bonds and those of common stock.

A corporation may issue preferred stock for a variety of reasons. It may turn to preferred stock as another source of capital, to tap a market of more cautious investors who prefer the smaller risks (and are willing to accept smaller growth opportunities) of preferred stock. It may wish to obtain additional capital without diluting voting rights (as would be the case if additional common shares were issued). At the same time, it may wish to avoid the required payment of interest and the future return of principal that would occur if bonds were issued.

The issuance of preferred stock may give the corporation financial leverage that can prove beneficial to the common stockholders. For example, suppose that 6 percent nonparticipating preferred stock can be issued at par. If the firm can use these funds in the business to produce more than a 6 percent return in earnings, the extra earnings can be distributed among the common stockholders. This can produce a greater increase in earnings per common share than would be the case if the funds had been raised through issuance of more common shares.

In recent years, convertible preferred stock has been widely used in business combinations and mergers. In such cases, common shareholders in the acquired corporation may demand preferred (or convertible preferred) stock in the surviving company. This provides greater safety for the value of their investment in the uncertain future of the merged companies. At the same time, convertible preferred stock offers them the option of changing to common stock if the merger proves successful.

Because the holders of convertible preferred stock will tend to switch to common stock if the company is earning high profits, the leverage effect of such preferred stock is greatly reduced.

Accounting for the issuance of preferred stock is essentially the same as for par-value common shares. The accounts used to record the transactions should be properly identified as belonging to preferred stock.

Transaction 7. Preferred stock issued. The Issuance Corporation issues 10,000 shares of 6 percent, $10-par-value preferred stock for $10.50 per share.

The issuance is recorded by the following journal entry.

Cash	105,000	
Preferred Stock		100,000
Paid-in Capital in Excess of Par Value— From Preferred Stock Issuance		5,000
To record issuance of 10,000 shares of $10-par-value preferred stock at a premium.		

Exhibit 16-5 shows the presentation of information about these shares in the owners' equity section of a balance sheet (also see Exhibit 16-8). If dividends on cumulative preferred stock are in arrears (that is, unpaid), the statement of financial position should disclose this fact. Disclosure can be made by a footnote to the statement: "Dividends on preferred stock are in arrears since [date]." The liquidating value of preferred stock should be disclosed in the financial statements if it is different from the par value of the stock. The liquidating value represents the amount that is to be paid per share of preferred stock if the corporation is dissolved. The preferred stockholders would have a priority claim to this amount before the common stockholders could receive any of the assets.

CONVERTIBLE PREFERRED STOCK. As mentioned earlier, a corporation sometimes authorizes issuance of preferred stock with a conversion feature that gives the stockholder the right to exchange his preferred shares for a specified number of common shares in the same corporation. The conversion can be made at the option of the shareholder. The statement of financial position should disclose pertinent data about convertible preferred stock—for example, terms of the conversion, number of shares of common stock available for conversion.

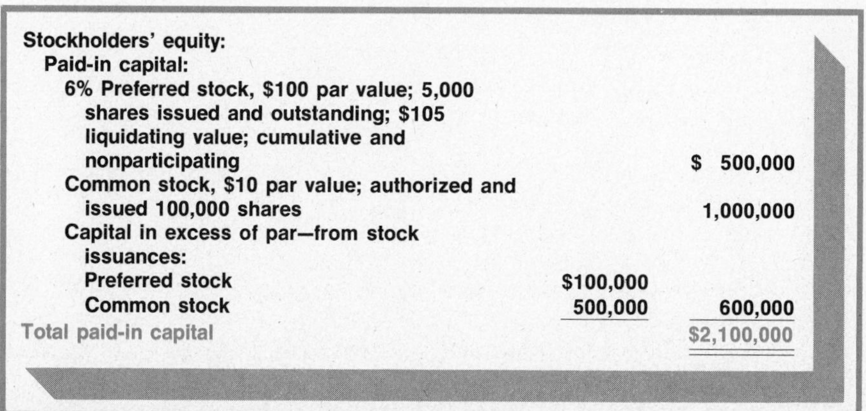

Stockholders' equity:		
Paid-in capital:		
6% Preferred stock, $100 par value; 5,000 shares issued and outstanding; $105 liquidating value; cumulative and nonparticipating		**$ 500,000**
Common stock, $10 par value; authorized and issued 100,000 shares		**1,000,000**
Capital in excess of par—from stock issuances:		
Preferred stock	**$100,000**	
Common stock	**500,000**	**600,000**
Total paid-in capital		**$2,100,000**

Exhibit 16-5
Partial balance sheet showing preferred stock

Transaction 8. Convertible preferred stock converted into common stock. The Conversion Company has 10,000 shares of $10-par-value, 6 percent, convertible preferred stock outstanding, which was issued originally at $102,000. These shares are convertible into 40,000 shares of $2-par-value common stock. The holders of these shares choose to convert them to the common stock.

The entry to record the conversion must cancel the preferred stock and any premium on the preferred, and must assign the total amount of equity capital to the proper common stock accounts.

Preferred Stock	100,000	
Premium on Preferred Stock	2,000	
Common Stock		80,000
Contributed Capital—Excess of Par on Conversion		22,000
To record conversion of 10,000 shares of preferred stock into 40,000 shares of $2-par-value common stock.		

Summary

Owners' equity for a corporation, partnership, or proprietorship is a residual amount, representing the excess of assets over liabilities (that is, $OE = A - L$). On the balance sheet, the owners' equity is divided into categories according to the ***sources*** of the equity capital. It is essential that the amounts derived from these various sources be kept separate in the accounts, because various legal and managerial decisions require different treatments of the equity capital from different sources.

Many users of financial statements need detailed information about the capital stock of a corporation. Therefore, the stockholders' equity section of a balance sheet should provide a description of each class of stock outstanding, including the par or stated value of each share, the special features associated with preferred stock, the existence of any convertible securities, and the status of any dividends in arrears on cumulative preferred stock. The par or stated value of the stock issued must be shown, with the amounts of any discounts or premiums arising through the issuance of the shares, and any other changes in the equity capital arising through other capital transactions.

Questions

1. Define the following terms: corporation, charter, bylaws, board of directors, minutes book, officers, incorporators.
2. What are the more important rights of common stockholders?
3. What are two major preferences of preferred stock?
4. Distinguish between par value stock and no-par stock.
5. What is meant by legal capital?
6. Distinguish between cumulative and noncumulative preferred stock; between participating and nonparticipating preferred stock.

7. Distinguish among authorized capital stock, issued capital stock, and outstanding capital stock.
8. What is a stock subscription?
9. What is convertible stock?
10. The Q Corporation has $100,000 of 6% cumulative preferred stock outstanding. The directors of the corporation have not declared dividends on the preferred stock in 19_0, nor in the current year 19_1.
    a. Does a liability exist to pay the dividend this year on the preferred stock?
    b. Would such a liability exist for noncumulative stock?
    c. How are dividends in arrears shown on a balance sheet?
11. A stockholder owns 100 shares of common stock in a corporation that has 1,000 shares of common stock outstanding. The corporation decides to issue an additional 500 shares of common stock. How many of the additional shares would the stockholder be entitled to receive, assuming that his shares owned had a preemptive right to stock?

Exercises

E16-1 (Issuance of stock)
Make the necessary journal entries to record the following transactions. The Jam Corporation is organized and issued 300,000 shares of no-par stock at $1 per share. Fifty thousand shares of $10-par-value preferred stock are issued for $15 per share. Costs of organizing the corporation amount to $8,000, which is paid from funds contributed for stock. At the end of the first year of operations, the corporation decides to amortize the organization costs over a period of ten years.

E16-2 (Issuance of stock)
The Jerral Company issues $10-par-value common stock as follows:
a. 2,000 shares at $10 per share;
b. 3,000 shares at $12 per share;
c. 4,000 shares at $9 per share.
Required: Journalize these issuances of stock.

E16-3 (Issuance of stock)
The Pitcher Company issues 2,000 shares of its $10-par-value common stock in exchange for some used machinery. The stock is currently selling on a national stock exchange for $18 per share. The used machinery is estimated to be worth approximately $40,000.
Required: Record the acquisition of machinery in exchange for stock.

E16-4 (Stock subscriptions)
The Mission Company is organized on February 15, 19_6. Subscriptions for 6,000 shares of $5-par-value stock are received on February 20, 19_6. The subscription price of the stock is $8 per share; a 50 percent down payment is required at the time the subscription is received. The balance due on the subscription is received in two equal installments on May 1, 19_6, and June 1, 19_6.
Required: Record the transactions relating to the subscription of stock.

E16-5 (Preferred stock conversion)

On May 1, 19_1, the Swinger Company issues 3,000 shares of $15-par-value preferred stock at $15 per share. Each share of preferred stock can be converted into three shares of $5-par-value common stock at the option of the preferred stockholder. On December 15, 19_6, a preferred stockholder chooses to convert 800 shares of the preferred stock into common stock.

Required:

a. Record the issuance of the preferred stock and the conversion of the 800 shares into common stock.

b. Assume that the preferred stock is originally issued at $20 per share. Record the issuance and conversion described above under this revised assumption.

E16-6 (Concepts)

The following accounts appear in the ledger of the Catnip Company.

Common Stock—$10 par value	$200,000
Premium on Common Stock	20,000
Preferred Stock—$50 par value	250,000
Premium on Preferred Stock	15,000
Common Stock Subscribed	80,000
Bonds Payable	100,000
Premium on Bonds Payable	5,000
Retained Earnings	90,000

Required:

a. How many shares of each class of stock have been issued?

b. How many shares of common stock have been subscribed?

c. What is the amount of the legal capital?

d. What is the amount of contributed capital?

e. What is the amount of total owners' equity?

f. The Catnip Company reacquires 300 shares of its common stock at $10 per share and holds this as treasury stock. How many shares of common stock are now outstanding?

g. What is the amount of total owners' equity after part f?

h. If a 5 percent common stock dividend is declared after part f, how many additional shares of common stock are to be issued?

E16-7 (Dividends on preferred stock)

The board of directors of the Preferred Corporation declares a $200,000 cash dividend. No dividends were paid in the preceding year. The company ledger shows the following account balances.

Preferred Stock—8%, $100 par value	$500,000
Premium on Preferred Stock	50,000
Common Stock—$100 par value	600,000
Premium on Common Stock	200,000

Required: Compute (to the nearest dollar) the total amount of dividends to be paid to preferred stockholders and the total amount to be paid to common stockholders if:

a. the preferred stock is noncumulative and nonparticipating;

b. the preferred stock is cumulative and nonparticipating;

c. the preferred stock is noncumulative and participating;

d. the preferred stock is cumulative and fully participating.

Problems

P16-1 (Issuance of stock)

The Dent Corporation is authorized to issue 20,000 shares of $10-par-value common stock. On Setpember 1, 19_6, 8,000 shares are issued at $10.50 per share for cash. Subscriptions are received by the Dent Corporation for 4,000 shares of stock at a subscription price of $10.50 per share. A 50 percent down payment is received at the time the subscriptions are taken (September 1). The balance on the subscriptions is paid in two equal installments on October 1 and November 1. The stock subscribed is issued when fully paid for.

Required: Record these transactions on the books of the Dent Corporation.

P16-2 (Issuance of stock)

The Chapter Company obtained a charter from the state in June. The charter authorized the following capital stocks: Preferred stock, 6%, par $10, authorized 10,000 shares; Common stock, par $5, authorized 50,000 shares. The following transactions occurred during the year:

1. The company issued 20,000 shares of common stock at $7 a share. The stock was paid for and the shares were issued.
2. The company issued 5,000 shares of preferred stock at $12 a share. The stock was paid for and the shares were issued.
3. The company issued 10,000 shares of common stock to the organizers of the company. The stock was given in exchange for services rendered. The directors of the company declared that the stock was to be recorded at $6 a share. Organization Cost will be amortized over ten years.
4. Revenues for the year totalled $200,000 and expenses were $175,000 (excluding the amortization of Organization Cost).

Required:

a. Prepare all entries for the company. Closing entries must also be made.

b. Prepare the stockholders' equity section of the balance sheet on December 31.

P16-3 (Issuance of stock)

The Winter Company was granted a charter from the state. The charter authorized the issuance of 300,000 shares of no-par common stock with a stated value of $2 per share. The charter also authorized the issuance of 50,000 shares of $10 par value, 5% preferred stock. The Winter Company issued 100,000 shares of no-par common stock to one of the organizers of the company. At a later date, the company sold another 100,000 shares of common stock at $3 a share. The company also issued 10,000 shares of $10 par value, 5% preferred stock at $15 a share. The company issued 10,000 shares of common stock in exchange for land with a fair market value of $28,000. Revenues for the year totalled $500,000 and expenses, including the amortization of the Organization Cost, totalled $450,000.

Required:

a. Prepare all entries required from the information given in the problem, including the closing entries.

b. Prepare the stockholders' equity section of the balance sheet on December 31, 19__.

P16-4 (Issuance of stock)

The Avert Company is authorized by charter to issue 100,000 shares of $10-par-value common stock.

1. The company issued 10,000 shares of common stock at $12 a share. The shares were paid for in full.
2. The company received subscriptions for 10,000 shares of common stock at $12 a share. No cash was received at this time.
3. Subscribers to common stock paid in 50 percent of the amount due.
4. Subscribers to 5,000 shares of common stock paid in the remaining 50 percent of the amount due on their subscriptions. The company issued 5,000 shares of common stock.

Required:

a. Prepare all entries required by the information given in the problem.
b. Prepare the stockholders' equity section for the balance sheet.

P16-5 (Stock subscriptions)

The No-Fault Company received subscriptions for 10,000 shares of its $10-par-value common stock at $12 a share. When the subscriptions were received, the subscribers paid in half the subscription price. Later, 90 percent of the subscribers paid in the balance due on their subscriptions. The company issued 9,000 shares of common stock to these subscribers. The remaining subscribers did not make the final payment on their subscriptions. The law of this state says that payments made on defaulted subscriptions remain with the company and no refund is required. Therefore, the amount paid in by the subscribers who defaulted will become Paid-in Capital from Forfeited Stock Subscriptions. The Subscriptions Receivable account will be closed out since no additional collections are to be received. The remaining balance in the Common Stock Subscribed account must also be removed from the records.

Required: Prepare all entries required by the problem.

P16-6 (Dividend distribution)

A company has the following classes of stock outstanding:

6% cumulative preferred stock, $100 par value, issued and outstanding 10,000 shares	$1,000,000
8% noncumulative preferred stock, $100 par value, issued and outstanding 10,000 shares	1,000,000
Common stock, $10 par value, issued and outstanding 100,000 shares	1,000,000

No dividends have been paid for the current year or for the preceding year. At the close of the current year, the company decides to distribute $500,000 as dividends. The preferred shares are nonparticipating preferred.

Required: Prepare a schedule to show how the $500,000 of dividends should be distributed.

P16-7 (Dividend distribution)

A company has 10,000 shares of $10-par-value, 6% preferred stock outstanding. The preferred stock is cumulative. The company has 20,000 shares of $10 par value common stock outstanding.

Required:

a. If the company declared a $3,000 dividend, how would this be shared between the common and the preferred?

b. If the dividend were $6,000, how would this dividend be shared between the common and the preferred?

c. If the dividend were $9,000, how would the dividend be shared?

d. If dividends were in arrears on the preferred for one year and the current dividends were also unpaid, how would a $20,000 dividend be shared between the common and the preferred?

Retained earnings, dividends, treasury stock, book value, earnings per share

Retained earnings represent the undistributed earnings accumulated by the corporation during its existence. Retained earnings are an important source of corporate capital. Retained earnings are sometimes called ***accumulated earnings, earnings retained in the business,*** or ***accumulated income.*** The directors of a corporation may choose to distribute all or part of the current income and retained earnings as dividends to shareholders (assuming that cash or some other distributable asset is available to make the distribution possible), or they may choose to retain all of the earnings for use as capital in the business.

So long as earnings exceed losses and dividend distributions, the Retained Earnings account has a credit balance. If losses and dividend distributions exceed earnings, the Retained Earnings account has a debit balance that is called a ***deficit.*** As noted earlier, most state laws forbid distribution of dividends by a corporation with a deficit. The fact of a deficit means that the stockholders' residual claims against the assets of the corporation have fallen to a value lower than the capital paid in by the stockholders.

DIVIDENDS

Dividends are distributions of capital by a corporation to its stockholders. Normally, dividends represent a distribution to the owners of a part of the earnings of the corporation. The board of directors has the right to declare dividends (restricted in many states by the requirement that the legal capital be retained in the corporation). The directors have no legal obligation to declare dividends, so long as the earnings are being retained for legitimate use in the business for the long-range benefit of the stockholders. Dividends become a liability for the corporation when they are declared by the directors.

Distribution of dividends

As a general rule, cash, property, and debt-instrument dividends represent a distribution of retained earnings. In a few states, dividend distributions may be made from other capital accounts (Paid-In Capital in Excess of Par Value, Donated Capital). Dividends payable in stock of the corporation declaring the dividend represent a special situation that is discussed after the following examples of the more typical kinds of dividends.

Dividends may be distributed in various forms.

1. Dividends payable in cash: the most common form of dividend; taxable as income for the stockholder.
2. Dividends payable in property other than cash. The corporation may hold stocks or bonds in another corporation and distribute these to its stockholders as a property dividend. During World War II, some corporations found themselves with an excess of inventory and a shortage of cash, and made distributions of property dividends in the form of inventory. Property dividends are taxable as income for the stockholder.
3. Dividends payable in a debt instrument. The corporation may distribute its own bonds, notes payable, or other form of debt instrument to its stockholders as a dividend; such dividends are taxable income for the stockholder.
4. Dividends in stock. The corporation may distribute additional shares of its own stock to its stockholders. This may be either an issue of new shares or a distribution of shares from treasury stock. The dividend in stock is not taxable income to the stockholder, so long as the shares received are of the same form as the shares on which the dividend is paid. For this reason and others discussed later in this chapter, the distribution of stock dividends has become increasingly popular.

When the board of directors declares a dividend, an announcement is made to the stockholders that a dividend has been declared on a certain date (say, December 15, 19_0). As of the ***date of declaration,*** the corporation has a legal commitment to pay the dividend. The dividend announcement also states a ***date of payment*** (say, February 15, 19_1) and a ***date of record*** (say, January 15, 19_1). On the date of payment, checks will be distributed to those stockholders who were listed in the shareowners' ledger as of the date of record. A purchaser of stock who buys stock after the date of record but before the date of payment buys the stock ***ex-dividend*** (that is, without the dividend). In such a case, the dividend will go to the person who was registered as owner of the stock on the date of record.

Dividends on common stock usually are stated in terms of a specific amount of money per share of stock (for example, $1.50 per share). Dividends on preferred stock are stated as a percentage of the par value of the preferred shares (for example, a 6 percent dividend). The dividends to be paid on preferred stock are stated as part of the basic properties of the stock when it is issued. For example, if a corporation has 6 percent preferred stock outstanding with a par value of $100,000 and the directors declare a dividend on the preferred, a total of $6,000 ($100,000 × 0.06) will be distributed to the preferred stockholders.

Transaction 1. Declaration and distribution of a dividend. On April 15, 19_1, the Dividend Company declares a quarterly dividend of 25 cents per share on its 1,000,000 shares of outstanding common stock. The dividend is to be paid on May 15, 19_1, to stockholders of record as of May 1, 19_1.

The following journal entries record these events.

Apr. 15	Dividends—Cash	250,000	
	Dividends Payable		250,000
	To record declaration of 25¢ per share dividend on common stock payable May 15 to stockholders of record on May 1.		
May 15	Dividends Payable	250,000	
	Cash		250,000
	To record payment of cash dividend declared Apr. 15; payment to stockholders of record on May 1.		

Dividends Payable is a current liability account. The Dividends—Cash account is a contra owners' equity account. After the declaration of the dividends, the Dividends account has a debit balance, indicating a reduction in owners' equity. When the books are closed at the end of the period, the Dividends account is closed to Retained Earnings.

Dec. 31	Retained Earnings	250,000	
	Dividends—Cash		250,000
	To close Dividends account to Retained Earnings.		

Transaction 2. Declaration and distribution of a property dividend. Although it has been earning healthy profits, the Property Company finds itself short of cash when it comes time to declare its quarterly dividend. On the other hand, the Company holds a large number of marketable securities, carried in the accounts at $250,000, which also is their fair market value. The board of directors decides to declare a dividend payable in the marketable securities. The dates and other details of the declaration and distribution are the same as those for transaction 1.

The declaration and payment of this distribution of property dividends are recorded in the following journal entries.

Apr. 15	Dividends—Marketable Securities	250,000	
	Dividends Payable		250,000
May 15	Dividends Payable	250,000	
	Marketable Securities		250,000

Transaction 3. Declaration and distribution of a dividend in the form of a debt. The Young Company has had a very encouraging quarter. Its sales have increased dramatically and net income has risen also. However, in order to meet the increasing demand for its products, it has had to tie up all its liquid current assets in paying salaries, purchasing inventory, and so on. The board of directors decides to declare a dividend payable in non-interest-bearing notes that will be payable a month after the distribution. (By that time, the company expects to collect on some large sales

and have cash on hand.) Other details of the declaration and distribution are the same as those for transaction 1.

Apr. 15	Dividends—Notes Payable	250,000	
	Dividends Payable		250,000
May 15	Dividends Payable	250,000	
	Notes Payable		250,000
June 15	Notes Payable	250,000	
	Cash		250,000

STOCK DIVIDENDS. Dividends payable in stock of the corporation are not dividends in the same sense as that applied to other dividends—such a transaction does not involve any distribution of corporate assets. Rather, a stock dividend is a distribution of corporate shares to stockholders in proportion to their current holdings. For example, suppose that you hold 100 shares of common stock in the XYZ Corporation, and you learn that the corporation has declared a 10 percent stock dividend. You will eventually receive ten additional shares of common stock without cost to you.

Of course, every other stockholder also has increased his number of shares by 10 percent. Therefore, you still have a claim to the same percentage of the assets and earnings of the XYZ Corporation as you did before the distribution, and the distribution has not changed those assets and earnings.

Companies issue stock dividends for many reasons. For example, such a dividend may be distributed if the corporation wants to preserve its assets for business purposes, but wants to give something to the stockholders on a dividend date. Another common reason is that the company wants to lower the market price of its stock. If the market price becomes too high, trading may slow down because smaller investors do not want or are unable to tie up the funds needed to buy a round lot of the expensive stock. A drop in the market price is likely to stimulate demand for the stock, and therefore to lead to a further increase in market values.

Distribution of a dividend in stock results in a permanent transfer of part of the retained earnings to paid-in capital. The stockholders pay nothing for the new shares. Instead, the paid-in capital for the new shares is drawn from the Retained Earnings account. Thus, the effect of the stock dividend is to plow part of the earnings back into the business in a permanent fashion. They have now become part of the legal capital. For this reason, the company improves its standing with creditors. Encouraged by the larger reserve of safe legal capital, they may be more willing to invest in the company's bonds or to advance credit to it. At the same time, the effect of the dividend will cause retained earnings to appear at a smaller value on the balance sheet; this may reduce criticism otherwise expected from stockholders for failure to pay a cash dividend.

Transaction 4. Declaration and distribution of a stock dividend. The outstanding stock of the Generous Company consists of 10,000 shares of $10-par-value common stock. Issuance of another 10,000 shares is authorized in the charter. At the end of the first half of 19_1, the corporation has $60,000 retained earnings. The directors on June 30,19_1, declare a 50-percent stock dividend payable on September 1, 19_1. The directors state that the new stock is to be issued at par value, with the paid-in capital for the dividend issue to be transferred from retained earnings.

The following journal entries record the declaration and the distribution of this stock dividend.

June 30	Retained Earnings	50,000	
	Stock Dividends Distributable		50,000
	To record declaration of a 50% stock dividend (par value of $10 per share is transferred from Retained Earnings).		
Sep. 1	Stock Dividends Distributable	50,000	
	Common Stock		50,000
	To record distribution of stock dividend declared on June 30.		

The Stock Dividends Distributable account is an owners' equity account (***not*** a liability account). It appears in the owners' equity section of a balance sheet if the stock dividend has not been paid as of the date of the statement.

When the stock dividend is declared, retained earnings are transferred to another capital account. The effect is to reduce retained earnings, increase a capital account, but leave total owners' equity and total assets unchanged. Furthermore, the percentage of ownership held by each stockholder remains unchanged because each shareholder receives additional shares in proportion to his holdings prior to the distribution.

In transaction 4, the directors arranged to transfer from Retained Earnings the par value of the stock to be issued in the form of the stock dividend. In most states, this is the minimum amount that must be transferred. Accounting principles require that an amount equal to the ***fair market value*** of the additional shares issued be capitalized (that is, transferred to a capital stock account) ***if the stock dividend is a small one.*** The market value rather than the par value normally is used if the stock dividend is less than 20 to 25 percent of the total number of shares of stock outstanding before the dividend. In such cases, the market value will not be greatly affected by the stock dividend, and this value gives the most objective exchange price for the transaction. When the dividend is larger than 20 or 25 percent, however, the market price is likely to be affected strongly enough that stockholders are aware that they are not receiving dividend income.

Transaction 5. Small stock dividend. The Stingy Corporation declares a 10 percent stock dividend on its 10,000 shares of $10-par-value common stock outstanding. On the date of declaration, the stock is selling at $12 per share on the market.

The following journal entries show the declaration and distribution of this small stock dividend, with the amount transferred from Retained Earnings determined by the market value of the shares distributed.

Retained Earnings	12,000	
Stock Dividends Distributable		10,000
Contributed Capital—Excess of Par on Stock Dividend		2,000
To record declaration of stock dividend; 1,000 shares at $12 per share market value.		
Stock Dividends Distributable	10,000	
Common Stock		10,000
To record distribution of stock dividend.		

STOCK SPLIT. A stock split occurs when a corporation calls in its outstanding shares (cancels them) and replaces them with a larger number of shares. For example, a corporation having 10,000 shares of stock outstanding announces a 2-for-1 stock split. The 10,000 outstanding shares are cancelled and are replaced by 20,000 newly issued shares. Each shareholder receives two of the new shares for each of the old shares that he held. (Instead of recalling the old shares, the company may merely issue additional shares to shareholders.)

For the shareholder, the effect of a 2-for-1 stock split is the same as that of a 100-percent stock dividend. (In fact, in stock market reports, any stock dividend of more than 25 percent usually is expressed as a stock split.) However, for the accounting system of the company making the split, the effect is different. The stock split involves no transfer of capital funds from retained earnings to paid-in capital. The same paid-in capital is simply redistributed among a larger number of shares.

In most cases, a company undertakes a stock split when it feels that the market price for its shares is too high, so that market trading in the stock is discouraged. In general, the effect of a stock split is to reduce the market price proportionately to the split, because more shares of stock are outstanding after the split. For example, if a stock is selling on the market for $90 per share just before a 2-for-1 stock split, the market price of the stock would be expected to drop to $45 per share just after the split. However, at this lower price, demand for the shares probably would increase, and the price would be expected to rise.

A stock split is popular with investors because it is usually a good indication that the company is prospering. On the market, a stock's price tends to rise prior to the declaration of a stock split, as investors anticipate the decision to undertake a stock split. When the split is proposed, those who bought in preparation for this announcement begin to sell their stock to realize the profit accrued during the pre-split price rise. In response to this profit-taking, the market price of the stock tends to drop soon after the declaration of the split. In most cases, if market conditions are favorable, the stock will rally to another peak at the time of the split, and prices are likely to continue to climb after the split.

Transaction 6. Stock split. The Split Corporation has 50,000 outstanding shares of $10-par-value common stock. The prevailing market price is $150 per share. To reduce the market price to a more attractive level, the corporation decides to make a 2-for-1 stock split—thus reducing the par value from $10 to $5 per share and increasing the number of shares outstanding from 50,000 to 100,000. Because the charter must be amended to permit this change in the authorized stock of the corporation, the proposal is submitted to the stockholders for a vote of approval. After the stockholders approve the proposal and the amendment of the charter, the directors declare the split. On the date of the split, outstanding $10-par-value certificates are called in and cancelled, and new $5-par-value certificates are issued in the ratio of 2 for 1. (In practice, a corporation often merely issues additional shares without calling in outstanding shares.)

The stock split could be recorded by a simple memorandum notation in the Common Stock account, indicating the change in par value. If the par value is a part of the account title, the following journal entry could be used to record the split.

Common Stock—$10 par value	500,000	
Common Stock—$5 par value		500,000
To record 2-for-1 stock split; 50,000 outstanding shares at $10 par value cancelled; 100,000 shares issued at $5 par value.		

Note that this entry simply shifts equity capital from one common stock account to another. There is no change in paid-in capital or retained earnings (as there is in the case of a stock dividend).

TREASURY STOCK. Treasury stock is a corporation's own stock that it has issued (receiving full payment) and later reacquired, but not cancelled. Treasury stock usually is reacquired by purchase, donation, or in settlement of a debt. Treasury stock has no voting right, does not receive dividends, has no preemptive right, and is not counted as a part of the shares outstanding. A corporation may decide to reacquire shares of its own stock for many reasons:

1. to create a market demand that will strengthen the current market for its stock;
2. to acquire shares for distribution to its officers or employees under stock option, bonus, and similar plans;
3. to acquire shares to be sold in the market (without first offering shares to existing stockholders, as would be required for a new issue because of the preemptive right of the stockholders);
4. to acquire shares that can be resold at a discount without creating a contingent liability to creditors for the purchaser (as would be the case if newly issued shares were sold at a discount);
5. to acquire shares for use in a merger with another company.

Treasury stock is considered a reduction or contraction of capital. The cost of the treasury stock is deducted in the shareholder's equity section of the balance sheet.

If a corporation purchases stock of another corporation, the stock is shown as an asset (marketable securities, or investments). Treasury stock, however, is not normally listed as an asset. If the treasury stock has been acquired primarily for purposes of resale or distribution to employees or others, the treasury stock may be shown as an asset. In such an event, the reason for this treatment must be disclosed by footnote or otherwise in the statement of financial position.

Transaction 7. Treasury stock acquired. The A Corporation reacquires 1,000 shares of its own $10-par-value stock at $50 per share. The entry to record the purchase of the stock (valued at cost)[1] is the following.

Treasury Stock—Common	50,000	
Cash		50,000

The impact of this transaction is to reduce cash and shares of stock outstanding.

1. A committee of the American Accounting Association has recommended a different method for dealing with treasury stock transactions. A discussion of this par-value method is left for advanced accounting courses.

The number of shares issued is considered to remain unchanged, because the treasury shares have not been cancelled. Exhibit 17-1 shows the stockholders' equity section of the balance sheet with the treasury stock properly accounted for.

Transaction 8. Treasury stock reissued. After transaction 7, the A Corporation reissues (sells) 500 shares of the reacquired stock for $50 per share (at cost), reissues another 200 shares for $55 per share (above cost), and reissues another 300 shares for $40 per share (below cost).

Again using the cost method of dealing with treasury stock, the entry to record the reissue at cost is straightforward.

	Debit	Credit
Cash	25,000	
Treasury Stock—Common		25,000
To record 500 shares reissued at $50 per share (cost).		

When the treasury stock is reissued at a price above cost, the Treasury Stock account is credited for the cost of the stock; the balance of the amount received is specifically identified in an account properly labeled as a new source of capital.

	Debit	Credit
Cash	11,000	
Treasury Stock—Common		10,000
Contributed Capital from Treasury Stock Transactions		1,000
To record 200 shares reissued at $55 per share (cost $50/share).		

The Contributed Capital from Treasury Stock account appears in the owners' equity section of the balance sheet, along with other sources of contributed (paid-in) capital.

When the treasury stock is reissued at a price below cost, owners' equity must be reduced by transferring an amount equal to the difference from other equity capital accounts. The difference between the cost of the treasury stock and its reissue price can be charged to the Retained Earnings account. (Other treatments are acceptable. These are discussed in advanced accounting courses.)

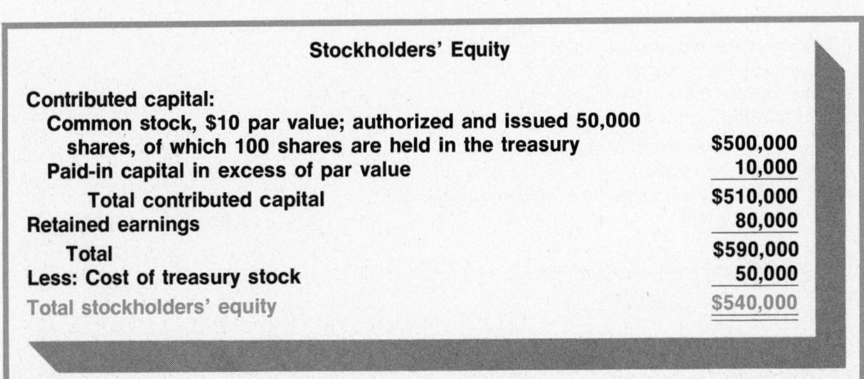

Stockholders' Equity

Contributed capital:	
Common stock, $10 par value; authorized and issued 50,000 shares, of which 100 shares are held in the treasury	**$500,000**
Paid-in capital in excess of par value	**10,000**
Total contributed capital	**$510,000**
Retained earnings	**80,000**
Total	**$590,000**
Less: Cost of treasury stock	**50,000**
Total stockholders' equity	**$540,000**

Exhibit 17-1
Partial balance sheet showing treasury stock

Cash	12,000	
Retained Earnings	3,000	
Treasury Stock—Common		15,000
To record reissuance of 300 shares of treasury stock at $40 per share (cost $50 per share).		

Transaction 9. Donated treasury stock. The B Corporation receives 1,000 shares of its own stock as a donation. It later reissues these treasury shares for $10 per share.

When treasury stock is acquired by donation instead of by purchase, no entry is made in the accounts because no cost is involved. A notation of the number of shares acquired should be made in the Treasury Stock account to provide a record of the number of shares held. When the donated treasury shares are reissued, the entire proceeds can be credited to a contributed capital account.

Cash	10,000	
Contributed Capital—Donation of Stock		10,000
To record reissue of 1,000 shares of treasury stock (donated).		

The Contributed Capital—Donation of Stock account is an owners' equity account and is reported in the owners' equity section of the balance sheet.

When the corporation buys treasury stock, many states impose a restriction on retained earnings to the amount of the cost of the treasury stock. As we have seen, if the company is forced to cancel the treasury stock or to reissue it below cost, the transaction will result in a transfer from retained earnings to paid-in capital. To protect the legal capital (and thereby protect the position of the corporation's creditors), the laws of many states restrict the corporation from distributing as dividends the portion of retained earnings equivalent to the cost of treasury stock on hand. Exhibit 17-2 shows how such a restriction is disclosed in the balance sheet.

RETAINED EARNINGS APPROPRIATIONS. In some cases, restrictions are placed upon retained earnings, making a part of the Retained Earnings account unavailable for dividend distributions. The restriction for the cost of treasury stock on hand is one such legal restriction. Other restrictions may be imposed by law, by

Exhibit 17-2
Partial balance sheet showing restriction on retained earnings

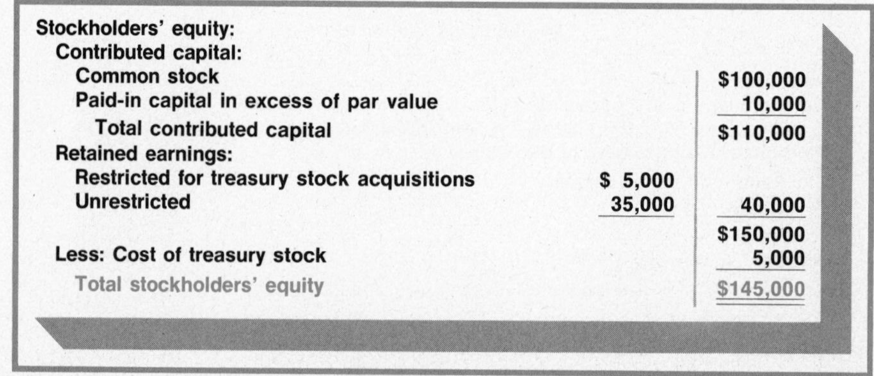

Stockholders' equity:		
Contributed capital:		
Common stock		**$100,000**
Paid-in capital in excess of par value		**10,000**
Total contributed capital		**$110,000**
Retained earnings:		
Restricted for treasury stock acquisitions	**$ 5,000**	
Unrestricted	**35,000**	**40,000**
		$150,000
Less: Cost of treasury stock		**5,000**
Total stockholders' equity		**$145,000**

contractual agreements with bondholders or preferred stockholders, or by resolution of the board of directors. To reflect such a restriction, the portion of retained earnings that is restricted can be transferred to a separate account.

Transaction 10. Retained earnings appropriated. The directors of the LM Corporation resolve that $100,000 of retained earnings be appropriated for general contingencies. This portion of retained earnings is not to be distributed as dividends.

The creation of this reserve is recorded by the following entry.

Retained Earnings	100,000	
Retained Earnings Appropriated for Contingencies		100,000
To appropriate retained earnings per directors' resolution.		

The Retained Earnings Appropriated for Contingencies account does not represent a fund of cash stored for this purpose; it is an owners' equity account, representing a portion of the earned capital that is not available for distribution to stockholders. When the purpose for which the reserve was established no longer exists, the balance in the reserve account can be returned to retained earnings.

Transaction 11. Restrictions on retained earnings removed. A year after transaction 10, the directors of the LM Corporation decide that the reserve for contingencies is no longer needed. They resolve to remove the restriction on retained earnings.

The needed journal entry returns the balance from the reserve to retained earnings.

Retained Earnings Appropriated for Contingencies	100,000	
Retained Earnings		100,000
To return reserve to retained earnings per directors' resolution.		

In other cases, the directors might choose to create an appropriation of retained earnings for plant expansion, for acquisition of treasury stock, for retirement of preferred stock, for redemption of bonds payable, or for other purposes requiring a large reserve of capital not pledged to creditors.

The restriction may be made at the discretion of the directors, because of a contractual agreement, or because of a legal requirement. In any case, the reserve protects a certain portion of the firm's equity capital against distribution in the form of dividends. Again, observe that no particular assets are set aside to make up this reserve. The appropriation merely ensures that a certain amount of capital beyond the liabilities and the paid-in capital will be retained for some future use, rather than being distributed to stockholders. These appropriations are sometimes called reserves.

The existence of any restrictions, reserves, or appropriations should be disclosed in the balance sheet. This may be done as shown in Exhibit 17-2, or through the use of parenthetical comments or footnotes.

EXTRAORDINARY ITEMS. Certain nonoperating gains and losses are classified as extraordinary items on the income statement. Extraordinary items are discussed here because they affect retained earnings. To qualify as an extraordinary item, an event or transaction must meet both of the following conditions.[2]

1. *Unusual in nature*—the event or transaction must be unrelated to the ordinary activities of the enterprise and must be *material* in amount.
2. *Infrequency of occurrence*—the event or transaction must not be expected to recur in the foreseeable future.

The environment in which a firm operates must be considered when deciding whether or not an extraordinary item is involved. A loss due to material storm or frost damage would qualify as an extraordinary item for a firm located in an area where storms or frost are unusual experiences. Major casualties such as earthquakes or the seizure of property by a government would almost always be considered extraordinary items.

Extraordinary items are reported at the bottom of the income statement, with tax consequences of the item included.

Income before extraordinary item		$800,000
Extraordinary item:		
Earthquake loss	$500,000	
Less: Applicable income tax saving	250,000	250,000
Net income		$550,000

PRIOR PERIOD ADJUSTMENTS. The Accounting Principles Board of the AICPA requires that net income should include all items of profit and loss recognized during the period. Prior period adjustments are one exception to this rule. The APB describes prior period adjustments as follows.

> Adjustments related to prior periods—and thus excluded in the determination of net income for the current period—are limited to those material adjustments which (a) can be specifically identified with and directly related to the business activities of particular prior period, *and* (b) are not attributable to economic events occurring subsequent to the date of the financial statements for the prior period, *and* (c) depend primarily on determinations by persons other than management *and* (d) were not susceptible of reasonable estimation prior to such determination. *Such adjustments are rare in modern financial accounting.* They relate to events or transactions which occurred in a prior period, the accounting effects of which could not be determined with reasonable assurance at that time, usually because of some major uncertainty then existing. . . . Treatment as prior period adjustments should *not* be applied to the normal, recurring corrections and adjustments which are the natural result of the use of estimates inherent in the accounting process.[3]

Examples of prior period adjustments include material amounts resulting from (1) tax assessments for prior years, (2) correction of major accounting errors, (3) settlement of lawsuits based on events of a prior period, and (4) settlement by a public utility of a rate dispute.

2. Accounting Principles Board, ***Opinion No. 30: Reporting the Results of Operations*** (New York: American Institute of Certified Public Accountants, 1973).

3. Accounting Principles Board, ***Opinion No. 9: Reporting the Results of Operations*** (New York: American Institute of Certified Public Accountants, 1966), paras. 23–24. (Emphasis added.)

Prior period adjustments can be recorded directly in the Retained Earnings account (rather than in a revenue or expense account). For example, assume that in 19_8 a corporation is assessed for additional income taxes of $150,000 for taxes related to its 19_5 income. The entry to record the transaction in 19_8 would be the following.

Retained Earnings	150,000	
Income Taxes Payable: Prior Period		150,000
To record income taxes payable applicable to fiscal year 19_5.		

Prior period adjustments are reported on the statement of retained earnings as an adjustment of the opening balance of retained earnings.

Retained earnings, January 1, 19_8	$950,000
Prior period adjustment—additional income taxes applicable to 19_5	150,000
Balance as restated	$800,000

When comparative statements are presented, the amounts shown for net income, retained earnings, and other affected balances in the prior years should be adjusted to reflect the retroactive application of the prior period adjustments.

DONATED CAPITAL. Occasionally the firm receives an asset as a donation. We have already mentioned treasury stock donated to the firm. Another example might be the donation of land or other property to the firm by a shareholder. Donated assets can be recorded at their fair market value at the time of the donation. An off-setting credit entry is made to a Donated Capital account.

Transaction 12. Donated property. The city of Pleasant View donates land with a fair market value of $100,000 to the CD Corporation, in order to induce the company to locate its plant in the city.

The transaction is recorded by the following entry.

Land	100,000	
Donated Capital		100,000
To record donation of land with market value of $100,000.		

The Donated Capital account is reported in the stockholders' equity section of the balance sheet. It can be shown above retained earnings as a separate listing.

SOURCES OF CORPORATE CAPITAL

The preceding transactions illustrate various sources of corporate capital. These sources are kept separate in the accounts (1) to provide for the correct application of accounting procedures and legal proscriptions that affect capital from the various sources, and (2) to ensure proper disclosure of information in the financial statements.

Requirements for legal capital differ from state to state. Therefore, the user of the statements needs full information about the sources of capital in order to compare various corporations operating under different restrictions. There is also the possibility that state laws may be changed, or that the corporation may have reason to do business under the laws of another state at some time in the future. Therefore, it is important to keep all the sources of capital separate in the accounts, even if some of this information has no legal significance at the moment.

The major sources of equity capital appear as categories in the stockholders' equity section of the balance sheet. The following outline reviews and summarizes the sources illustrated in the preceding transactions.

1. Contributed (paid-in) capital:
   a. Par or stated value of stock issued or subscribed.
   b. Excess of amounts received over par or stated value of stock.
   c. Reclassified retained earnings resulting from distribution of a stock dividend.
   d. Excess of amount received over cost of reissued treasury stock.
   e. Donated property; any asset given to the corporation without cost.
2. Retained earnings:
   a. Restricted earnings (appropriations).
   b. Unrestricted (unappropriated) earnings.

Exhibit 17-3 shows how these sources of capital (and the accounts introduced for them in the preceding transactions) are reported in the stockholders' equity section of a balance sheet.

BOOK VALUE OF STOCK

Thus far we have discussed the par or stated value and the market value of stock. We have also mentioned the liquidating value of preferred stock. There is another measure of the value of stock that is of importance in estimating the worth of stock as an investment. The ***book value*** of a share of stock is a measure of the amount of wealth (assets) in the corporation's capital owned by the shareholder. Book value per share of stock is the amount of owners' equity assigned to a share of stock.

Exhibit 17-3 Partial balance sheet showing sources of equity capital

Stockholders' Equity			
Contributed capital:			
Preferred stock—6% cumulative, participating; par value $100; authorized and issued 1,000 shares		$100,000	
Common stock—par value $10; authorized and issued 30,000 shares, of which 5,000 shares are in the treasury		300,000	
Common stock subscribed		50,000	
Stock dividend distributable		50,000	
Other contributed capital:			
Paid-in capital in excess of par value:			
Preferred stock	$10,000		
Common stock	20,000		
From treasury stock transactions	5,000	35,000	$ 535,000
Retained earnings:			
Restricted for treasury stock acquisitions		$ 50,000	
Unrestricted		600,000	650,000
Donated capital			15,000
Total			$1,200,000
Less: Cost of treasury stock			50,000
Total stockholders' equity			$1,150,000

Example 1. The Book Value Corporation has only one class of common stock and no preferred stock outstanding. The following information about owners' equity is available from the balance sheet of the corporation.

Total stockholders' equity	$100,000
Number of shares of common stock outstanding	10,000

In this simple case, book value per share is determined by dividing the total stockholders' equity by the number of shares outstanding:

$100,000/10,000 shares = $10 per share.

Example 2. The Complex Corporation has both preferred and common stock outstanding. Exhibit 17-4 shows information from the stockholders' equity section of the balance sheet.

To determine the ***book value of preferred stock,*** it is customary to begin with the liquidating value instead of the par value. To this must be added any dividends in arrears to determine the total equity assigned to preferred stock.

Liquidating value of preferred stock (5,000 shares × $105 per share)	$525,000
Dividends in arrears (0.06 × $500,000 × 2 years)	60,000
Total equity assigned to preferred stock	$585,000

Dividing this total equity by the number of preferred shares outstanding gives the book value per share of preferred stock:

$585,000/5,000 shares = $117 per share.

To determine the ***book value of the common stock,*** we begin by deducting the equity assigned to the preferred stock from the total stockholders' equity. This gives a value for the residual equity of the common stockholders.

Total stockholders' equity	$3,000,000
Less: Preferred stockholders' equity	585,000
Total equity of common stockholders	$2,415,000

Dividing this total equity by the number of common shares outstanding gives the book value per share of common stock:

$2,415,000/100,000 shares = $24.15 per share.

Some caution must be used in interpreting the meaning of book value. First, it must be understood that market value per share is usually different from book value per share. Market value is influenced by a wide variety of factors that may not be reflected in book value.

Second, the particular book value determined from a balance sheet reflects the accounting principles and procedures used in preparing the statement. The amount of equity shown on the balance sheet is influenced by the inventory pricing procedures, depreciation methods, valuation of assets, and other assumptions or estimates used by the accountants. The initial recording principle and the going-concern assumption play important parts in assigning values to assets on the balance sheet. Yet these principles probably do not give the best picture of the amount of

Exhibit 17-4
Partial balance sheet for example 2

Stockholders' equity:		
Contributed capital:		
Preferred stock, 6%, $100 par value; 5,000 shares issued and outstanding; $105 liquidating value; cumulative and nonparticipating; dividends in arrears for current year and preceding year		**$ 500,000**
Common stock, $10 par value; 100,000 shares issued and outstanding		**1,000,000**
Paid-in capital in excess of par value:		
Preferred stock	**$100,000**	
Common stock	**500,000**	**600,000**
Retained earnings		**900,000**
Total stockholders' equity		$3,000,000

cash that could be raised from sale of the assets if the corporation were dissolved.

In a highly theoretical sense, the book value is a figure that represents what the shareholder would receive for his share of ownership if the corporation were liquidated without gain or loss. In other words, if the corporate assets could be sold for exactly the value carried for them in the books, all liabilities settled, and the remaining cash distributed to shareholders, each shareholder should receive the book value of his stock holding. You can appreciate the practical limitations of these assumptions.

EARNINGS PER SHARE

Earnings per share of stock is one of the most significant ratios in financial management and investment analysis. Earnings-per-share data are widely used in judging the operating performance of a business. This ratio appears frequently in financial statements and publications. It is perhaps the one most significant figure appearing on the income statement, because it condenses into a single figure the data reflecting the current net income of the period in relation to the number of shares of stock outstanding. Current accounting practice requires that earnings per share be disclosed prominently on the face of the income statement.

If the capital structure of a corporation contains only common stock, the computation of earnings per share is relatively simple:

$$\text{Earnings per common share} = \frac{\text{Net income}}{\text{Weighted number of common shares outstanding}}$$

The weighted number of common shares outstanding can be determined as the average of the number of shares outstanding each day during the year. In most cases, it can more easily be determined by weighting each additional issue of stock according to the portion of the year that it was outstanding. For example, if 100,000 shares were outstanding on January 1, and 10,000 additional shares were issued on July 1, the weighted number of shares would be 105,000. This represents the 100,000 shares outstanding all year, plus half of the issue that was outstanding for half the year.

Corporations issue a variety of securities that can be converted into common stock—for example, convertible bonds and convertible preferred stock. Stock options and warrants are other securities that can be converted into common stock under specified conditions. If such items were converted, they would increase the number of shares of common stock outstanding and could decrease (dilute) the earnings per share. The user of the statement should be warned of this possible ***dilution*** of the earnings per share in the future. If such convertible securities exist, generally accepted accounting principles require a disclosure of the dilution that would develop if all possible contingencies occurred. That is, what would be the earnings per share if all convertible bonds and convertible preferred stock outstanding were exchanged for common shares?

If the preferred stock is essentially equivalent to common stock (as determined by technical rules) the preferred stock should be included with the common in computing earnings per share. Stock options and warrants are also regarded as "common stock equivalents."

The Accounting Principles Board, in ***Opinion No. 15,*** calls for a dual presentation of earnings per share in cases where the capital structure of the corporation is complex. This dual presentation includes the following parts.

1. *Primary earnings per share:* "The first presentation is based on the outstanding common shares and those securities that are in substance equivalent to common shares and have a dilutive effect."
2. *Fully diluted earnings per share:* "The second is a pro-forma presentation which effects the dilution of earnings per share that would have occurred if *all* contingent issuances of common stock that would individually reduce earnings per share had taken place at the beginning of the period. . . ."[4]

The details of the ***APB Opinion No. 15*** on earnings-per-share procedures are highly technical and are the proper subject for more advanced courses in accounting. The beginning student need only be aware of the basic principle and general procedures involved in computing earnings per share. A simple illustration will demonstrate the presentation recommended by the APB. The following information is available about the outstanding stock of a corporation:

1,000,000 shares of common stock outstanding (par value $10 per share);

100,000 shares of convertible, 6%, preferred stock outstanding (par value $100 per share; assumed not to be a common stock equivalent for primary earnings per share); convertible preferred stock could be exchanged for 500,000 shares of common stock.

The net income of the corporation for the year was $2,000,000.

Exhibit 17-5 outlines the computation of the two presentations of earnings per share. At the bottom of the income statement, the disclosure of this information would be made in the following form.

Net income	$2,000,000
Earnings per common share	**$1.40**
Earnings per common share, assuming full dilution	$1.34

4. Accounting Principles Board, ***Opinion No. 15: Earnings per Share*** (New York: American Institute of Certified Public Accountants, 1969), para. 15.

Exhibit 17-5 **Computation of primary and fully diluted earnings per share**

ASSUMING NO DILUTION:

$$\text{Earnings per common share} = \frac{\text{Net income} - \text{Preferred dividend requirements}}{\text{Weighted average number of common shares}}$$

$$= (\$2{,}000{,}000 - \$600{,}000)/1{,}000{,}000 \text{ shares}$$

$$= \$1.40 \text{ per share.}$$

ASSUMING FULL DILUTION:

Weighted average number of common shares outstanding	**1,000,000**
Additional common shares after conversion of 100,000 shares preferred stock (5-for-1)	**500,000**
Shares outstanding after full dilution	1,500,000

$$\text{Fully diluted earnings per share} = \frac{\text{Net income}}{\text{Shares outstanding after full dilution}}$$

$$= \$2{,}000{,}000/1{,}500{,}000 \text{ shares}$$

$$= \$1.34 \text{ per share.}$$

Impact analysis

The form of business organization chosen by an enterprise will have profound impact on financial and managerial accountability, controls, and decision-making processes. This decision may also have significant impact on the ability of the business to obtain needed capital and on its income after taxes.

For the corporation, the impact of dividend distribution differs with the nature of the dividend distributed: cash, property, or stock. Exhibit 17-6 summarizes the impact of various capital transactions.

In its efforts to raise additional capital, a corporation must consider the impact that the chosen financing method has upon net income, taxes, owners' equity, control, various ratios, risks, and so on. The impact of obtaining funds by issuance of common stock can be significantly different than the impact of borrowing through long-term liabilities or of issuing preferred stock. Exhibit 17-7 suggests some of the differences among the various methods of obtaining capital.

Summary

The gains and losses resulting from the profit-making activities of a corporation are accumulated in the Retained Earnings account. Retained earnings may be reduced by losses, dividend distributions, treasury stock transactions, and other events. Retained earnings is not increased as a result of any transactions involving a corporation's own stock, because the corporation cannot realize revenue on transactions between itself and its owners. For example, if treasury stock is issued at a price in excess of its cost, the increase is credited to contributed capital, not to retained earnings.

After the presentation of the equity capital arising through stockholders' investments, the retained earnings of the business should be set forth separately. Any restrictions on or appropriations of retained earnings should be disclosed. The cost of any treasury stock normally is shown as a deduction from total contributed (paid-in) capital and retained earnings. Any donated capital also is shown as a separate category (usually after contributed capital and before retained earnings).

Dividends may be made in cash, property, debt instruments, and stock. When a dividend in stock is declared, retained earnings is capitalized. Accounting procedures differ for small stock dividends and large stock dividends.

Treasury stock is recorded at cost when acquired. Reissuance of treasury stock at a price above cost results in additional paid-in capital. Reissuance of treasury stock at a price below cost results in a distribution of retained earnings.

Appropriation of retained earnings moves a portion of retained earnings from the Retained Earnings account to an Appropriation account. When the appropriation is no longer needed, the amount in the Appropriation account is returned to the Retained Earnings account.

Extraordinary items are certain events or transactions that are both unusual in nature and nonrecurring. They are shown separately from earnings from continuing operations. Prior period adjustments are disclosed on the statement of retained earnings as an adjustment of the opening balance of retained earnings.

The book value of stock is the amount of owners' equity assigned to a share of stock. Earnings per share is the amount of earnings attributed to a share of common stock. Primary and fully diluted earnings per share disclosure are often required on the income statement.

Exhibit 17-6 Impacts of some corporate capital transactions

	IMPACT ON				
TRANSACTION	**Assets**	**Retained Earnings**	**Total Stockholders' Equity**	**Income to Stockholders**	**Number of Shares Outstanding**
Dividends (Note 1):					
Cash dividend	–	–	–	yes	0
Property dividend	–	–	–	yes	0
Stock dividend	0	–	0	no	+
Stock split	0	0	0	no	+
Treasury stock:					
Acquisition by purchase	–	0	–		–
Reissuance above cost	+	0	+		+
Issuance of new stock	+	0	+		+
Acceptance of donated asset	+	0	+		0
Establishment of an appropriation of retained earnings (Note 2)	0	0	0		0

NOTES: Increase, decrease, and no change are represented by +, –, and 0, respectively.

1. The impacts shown for dividends are the net impacts of declaration and distribution. The declaration of a cash dividend reduces retained earnings and creates a liability. Hence, net assets and stockholders' equity are reduced by the declaration of dividends, and not by the dividend distribution.

2. Although creation of an Appropriation account results in a reduction in the Retained Earnings account, the Appropriation account to which the capital is transferred is also a part of retained earnings.

Exhibit 17-7 Methods of obtaining corporate capital

Method of Capitalization	General Risk Rank for Investor	Net Assets; Owners' Equity	Interest Expense	Income Taxes	Opportunity for Financial Leverage
Issuance of common stock	Highest	Increase	None	—	—
Issuance of preferred stock	Intermediate	Increase	None	—	Possible
Issuance of long-term bonds	Lowest	No change	Increase	Interest deductible	Possible

Questions

1. What is meant by retained earnings?
2. Name four types of dividends. Name three important dates associated with a dividend distribution.
3. What is a stock split?
4. What is treasury stock? What is meant by a treasury stock restriction on retained earnings?
5. What is a reserve or appropriation in regard to retained earnings?
6. What are the major sources of corporate capital?
7. What is meant by the book value of stock? earnings per share? primary earnings per share? fully diluted earnings per share?
8. What are extraordinary items? How are they reported on the income statement?
9. What are prior period adjustments? How are they reported on the statement of retained earnings?
10. Which of the following items are usually treated as an extraordinary item, a prior period adjustment, or a part of earnings before extraordinary items:
a. Write-off of inventory because of obsolescence.
b. Earthquake loss that was not insured.
c. Fire loss that was not insured.
d. Sale of stock investment at a material gain.
e. Write-off of a large account receivable.
f. Large gain resulting from favorable tax negotiations with the Internal Revenue Service resulting from tax return of a former year.
g. Large loss resulting from a lawsuit that was lost. The cause of the suit arose in a prior year, but was not dealt with at that time.
h. Large loss resulting from a lawsuit that was lost. The cause of the suit arose in the current year.
i. Issuance of common stock at a premium.

Exercises

E17-1 (Cash dividends)

The Rollin Company declares cash dividends of $250,000 on May 1, 19_6, to stockholders of record on June 15, 19_6. The dividends are distributed on July 15, 19_6. The company ends its fiscal year and closes its books on September 30.

Required: Record the above transactions on the books of the company.

E17-2 (Stock dividend)

A corporation has 20,000 shares of $10-par-value common stock outstanding. The directors of the corporation declare a 50 percent stock dividend on March 1, 19_6, payable on May 1, 19_6, to stockholders of record on April 15, 19_6. The stock of the corporation is currently selling for $13 per share, and the directors order that the market value of the stock on this date be recorded as the value of the dividend stock by transferring funds from Retained Earnings to the Capital Stock account.

Required: Record the declaration and distribution of the stock dividend.

E17-3 (Stock split)

In 19_1, a corporation issued 10,000 shares of $10-par-value stock at $15 per share. In 19_8, the corporation declares a 3-for-1 stock split. Each share of $10-par-value common stock is to be exchanged for 3 shares of no-par common stock.

Required: Record the issuance of the original common stock and record the stock split.

E17-4 (Impact analysis)

Prepare a table showing the impact of each of the following transactions on net assets, working capital, and owners' equity.

a. A stock split occurs.
b. A reserve for contingencies is established.
c. Treasury stock is reissued at a price above cost.
d. A cash dividend is declared.
e. Treasury stock is acquired with cash.
f. A stock dividend is declared.

E17-5 (Treasury stock)

Record the following transactions.

a. On January 5, 300 shares of $10-par-value stock are issued at $17 per share.
b. One hundred and fifty shares are reacquired at $15 per share on May 1 and are held as treasury stock.
c. On June 1, 20 shares are reacquired at $8 per share and are held as treasury stock.
d. Forty shares of treasury stock acquired on May 1 are reissued on July 1 at $16 per share.
e. Fifty shares of treasury stock acquired on May 1 are reissued on August 1 at $12 per share.

E17-6 (Appropriations of retained earnings)

The Careless Company is involved in a major lawsuit. The outcome of the suit is uncertain. The directors of the corporation establish a $250,000 appropriation for a possible unfavorable decision in the suit.

Required:

a. Record the establishment of the retained earnings appropriation.
b. The lawsuit is settled unfavorably for the corporation. The Careless Company is required to pay $150,000 in judgments and court costs. What disposition should be made of the retained earnings appropriation? Make whatever entry is required.

E17-7 (Book value per share)

The following information is taken from ledger accounts of a corporation.

Common Stock (5,000 shares of $10-par-value stock)	$50,000
Paid-In Capital in Excess of Par Value	8,000
Retained Earnings	17,000

Required: Compute the book value per share of common stock.

E17-8 (Book value per share)

Assume that the following information is available in addition to that presented in Exercise E17-7.

Preferred Stock (8%; $10 par value; $12 liquidating value; 600 shares issued and outstanding; cumulative and nonparticipating; dividend in arrears for the current year)	$6,000

Required:

a. Compute the book value per share of preferred stock.
b. Compute the book value per share of common stock.

E17-9 (Earnings per share)

The following information is taken from ledger accounts and statements of a corporation.

Net income	$300,000
Common shares outstanding	20,000 shares
Convertible, 9% preferred stock outstanding	$100,000
Number of common shares into which convertible preferred stock can be converted	10,000 shares

The preferred stock is not a common stock equivalent.

Required:

a. Compute earnings per common share, assuming no dilution.
b. Compute earnings per common share, assuming full dilution.

E17-10 (Impact analysis)

Indicate the impact on total owners' equity of each of the following transactions.

a. Creation of a reserve for contingencies.
b. Issuance of additional common stock to retire outstanding bonds payable.
c. Operating loss for the year.
d. Payment of a cash dividend.
e. Use of treasury common stock to retire outstanding bonds payable.
f. Issuance of additional common stock in order to convert the company's preferred stock.
g. Use of treasury common stock to convert the company's preferred stock.
h. Declaration of a cash dividend.
i. Issuance of additional common stock for cash.
j. Addition to accumulated depreciation.
k. Declaration of a dividend in stock.
l. Issuance of stock as a stock dividend.
m. Addition to the allowance for doubtful accounts.

E17-11 (Stock-related transactions)

The AA Corporation is authorized to issue 100,000 shares of $5-par-value common stock. Journalize the following transactions that occur during one year.

a. Received subscription for 4,000 shares of stock at $15 per share.

b. Sold 3,000 shares for cash at $10 per share.
c. Received payment of the subscription (part a) and issued the shares.
d. Declared a 10% stock dividend; current market price of the stock is $9 per share.
e. Distributed the stock dividend declared in part d.
f. Repurchased 300 shares of outstanding common stock for $16 per share.
g. Sold the treasury stock acquired in part f for $15 per share.

E17-12 (Treasury stock)

The following transactions occurred during the year.

a. A company issued 10,000 shares of $5-par-value common stock at $6 a share.
b. The company acquired as treasury stock 1,000 shares of its common stock at $8 a share.
c. The company reissued 500 shares of treasury stock at $7 a share.
d. The company reissued 100 shares of treasury stock at $10 a share.
e. At the end of the year, the company appropriated retained earnings for the cost of treasury stock that was not reissued.
f. The net income for the year was $75,000.

Required: Use the following accounts to record the transactions given in the exercise.

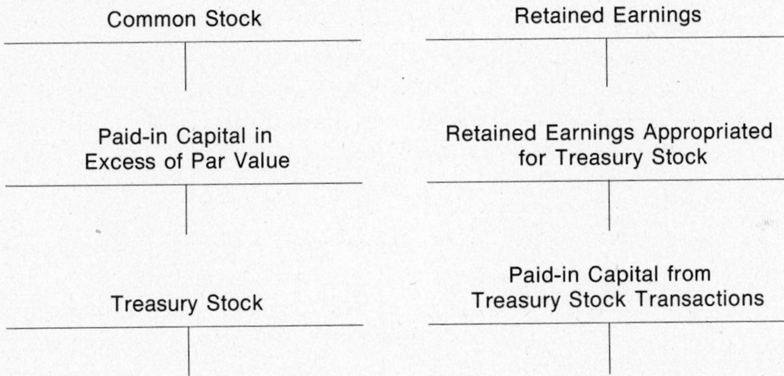

E17-13 (Extraordinary items and prior period adjustments)

a. A company had a fire loss of $50,000 during the year. It also suffered a $75,000 loss from an earthquake. During the year, a serious frost caused $100,000 of damage to the company's orange crop. The company sold some marketable securities at a loss of $60,000.

Required: Discuss how these losses should be treated in the financial statements.

b. The following data are available from the records of a company.

Retained earnings, Jan. 1, 19__	$100,000
Net income for 19__ (exclusive of $10,000 extraordinary gain net of taxes)	50,000
Prior period adjustment (a loss) net of taxes	20,000

Required: Prepare the bottom section of an income statement for the year and a statement of retained earnings.

Problems

P17-1 (Balance sheet disclosure for stock)
Prepare the equity capital (that is, shareholders' equity) section of a balance sheet, using the following information.

Common stock, $10 par value; authorized 100,000 shares; issued and outstanding 80,000 shares	$800,000
Paid-in capital in excess of par value—common stock	60,000
Preferred stock, 5%, par $100, cumulative and nonparticipating; 10,000 shares authorized; 7,000 shares issued	700,000
Paid-in capital in excess of par value—preferred stock	40,000
Retained earnings	75,000
Retained earnings appropriated for contingencies	30,000

P17-2 (Book value; dividends)
The following information is available.

Preferred stock, 6%, $100 par value, $105 liquidating value, cumulative, nonparticipating; 2,000 shares outstanding	$200,000
Common stock, $150 par value; 2,000 shares outstanding	300,000
Retained earnings	100,000

Required:

a. Compute the book value per share of common stock and preferred stock if the dividend is in arrears for two prior years on the preferred stock.

b. Determine how the dividends would be allocated between preferred stock and common stock in the following cases.

(1) Assume the same information as in part a. Dividends declared, $100,000.

(2) Assume the same information as in part a, except that the preferred stock is fully participating. Dividends declared, $100,000.

(3) The preferred stock is noncumulative, partially participating to 10 percent. Dividends declared, $100,000.

P17-3 (Impact analysis)
Prepare a table showing the impact (+ increase, − decrease, 0 no effect) of the following transactions on total assets, total liabilities, working capital, retained earnings, shares of stock issued and outstanding, and total owners' equity.

a. Dividend in stock distributed.
b. Treasury stock reissued at price above cost.
c. Treasury stock acquired for cash.
d. Cash dividend paid.
e. Cash dividend declared.
f. Reserve for Contingencies account established.
g. Dividend in stock declared.

P17-4 (Stock dividend)
A company has 200,000 shares of $5-par-value common stock outstanding. The market value of the stock is $6 a share.

Required:

a. The company declares a 20 percent stock dividend. Record the declaration and distribution of the stock dividend. The dividend is considered to be a small stock dividend.

b. The company declares a 50 percent stock dividend. Record the declaration and distribution of the stock dividend. (Answer part b independently of part a.)

P17-5 (Retained earnings appropriated)
On February 1, 19_6, the directors of the Trouble Corporation resolve to establish a contingency reserve of $300,000 for losses that may result from a damage suit currently in the court. On May 15 of the same year, the damage suit is settled out of court for $240,000. The Trouble Corporation pays the settlement in cash.

Required: Record the following:

a. the establishment of the contingency reserve;
b. the settlement of the claim;
c. any other entry required in relation to the contingency reserve.

P17-6 (Stock dividend)
Selected accounts of the AAA Company appear as follows prior to the declaration of a stock dividend.

Common Stock—no par	$300,000
Retained Earnings	150,000

The AAA Company declares a $40,000 dividend in stock.

Required:

a. Show the effect of the stock dividend on the stockholders' equity section of the balance sheet (1) immediately after the declaration of the dividend in stock, and (2) immediately after the stock issuance.
b. What is total owners' equity before the declaration of the stock dividend, after the declaration, and after the stock issuance?

P17-7 (Earnings per share)
The following cases deal with earnings per share.

a. Company ZYX has 100,000 shares of common stock outstanding at the beginning of the year. An additional 40,000 shares of common stock were issued on April 1. Net income for the year was $260,000. Compute earnings per share for the year.
b. A company had 100,000 shares of common stock outstanding during the year. The company had 12,500 shares of convertible preferred stock outstanding during the year. The preferred stock can be converted into two shares of common stock. The preferred shares are considered to be common stock equivalents. Net income for the year was $100,000. Compute primary earnings per share for the year.
c. A company has $1 million of 6 percent convertible bonds outstanding during the year. The bonds are considered to be common stock equivalents. Each $1,000 bond can be converted into 25 shares of common stock. The company had net income of $250,000 for the year after interest expense and income taxes. The tax rate was 30 percent. The company had 100,000 shares of common stock outstanding during the year. Compute primary earnings per share. (HINT: If the bonds are considered to be common stock, would interest net of taxes have been deducted in computing net income?)

P17-8 (Treasury stock)

During 19_1–19_2, the Treasury Company engaged in the following transactions.

In 19_1:

a. Issued 10,000 shares of its $10 par value common stock at $12 a share.

b. Reacquired 900 shares of its common stock at $10 a share.

c. Established an appropriation account for the cost of the treasury stock.

d. The Income Summary account disclosed a credit balance of $50,000 at the close of the year.

In 19_2:

e. Reissued the 900 shares of treasury stock at the following prices:
300 shares at $10 a share;
300 shares at $9 a share;
300 shares at $11 a share.

f. Removed the restriction on retained earnings.

Required:

1. Prepare journal entries for the two years as required by the problem.

2. Prepare the stockholders' equity section of the balance sheet at the end of the first year.

Single proprietorships and partnerships

In accounting for a corporation, there is seldom much difficulty in applying the business-entity assumption. The corporation is a legal entity distinct from its owners (stockholders). In most cases, the financial affairs of the business and those of its owners are clearly separated.

In accounting for an unincorporated business (such as a single proprietorship or a partnership), the separation of personal and business transactions often is much less distinct. The single proprietorship is legally an extension of the proprietor. He is legal owner of all assets of the business, and he has the legal right to make use of them for his personal purposes. Nonetheless, if the accounting system is to provide a clear statement of the condition of the business, the separation must be made. The personal transactions of the owner must be kept separate from those of the business itself.

The single proprietorship

Accounting for the single proprietorship differs from that for the corporation in the owners' equity accounts. Two owner's equity accounts are used in recording capital transactions:

1. a proprietor's Capital account; and
2. a proprietor's Drawing account.

The ***Capital account*** of a single proprietorship is used to record the original investment by the owner, additional investments, permanent withdrawals of capital, and the balance of the Drawing account at the close of the accounting period.

The ***Drawing account,*** a temporary capital account, is used to record all withdrawals by the proprietor during the year such as "salary of owner," merchandise withdrawn for personal use, and so on. Because withdrawals indicate a decrease in the proprietor's equity, the Drawing account is debited for such transactions. At the end of the accounting period, the Income Summary account is closed to the proprietor's Drawing account. Finally, the Drawing account is closed to the owner's Capital account, which serves as a permanent record of the owner's capital transactions.

Transaction 1. Proprietorship transactions. On January 2, J. T. Jones invests $20,000 to establish a new business. On September 30, Jones withdraws $2,000 for personal use. On December 31, the books are closed for the proprietorship. Revenue amounted to $20,000 for the year; expenses totaled $12,000.

The following journal entries record the transactions affecting owner's equity of J. T. Jones' business.

Jan. 2	Cash	20,000	
	J. T. Jones, Capital		20,000
	To record investment by owner to establish the J. T. Jones Company.		
Sep. 30	J. T. Jones, Drawing	2,000	
	Cash		2,000
	To record withdrawal of cash by owner.		
Dec. 31	Sales	20,000	
	[various expense accounts]		12,000
	Income Summary		8,000
	To close revenue and expense accounts.		
31	Income Summary	8,000	
	J. T. Jones, Drawing		8,000
	To close net income to owner's Drawing account.		
31	J. T. Jones, Drawing	6,000	
	J. T. Jones, Capital		6,000
	To transfer balance of Drawing account to the Capital account.		

Exhibit 18-1 shows the statement of owner's equity for this single proprietorship.

The partnership

A partnership is formed when two or more persons associate as co-owners to carry on a business for profit. The terms of the partnership agreement usually are set forth in a written contract called the Articles of Partnership. However, a partnership can legally be formed simply by the actions of the partners that imply their common intention to carry on a business as co-owners.

The legal status of partnerships was developed in English and American common law. In the United States, a Uniform Partnership Act was proposed in 1914 and has now been adopted in most states. Both the common law and the Uniform Partnership Act are based upon the assumption that a partnership is not a legal entity; the partnership is simply the aggregate (collection) of the partners acting together.

The partnership may carry on a business under the actual names of the partners (such as Smith, Jones & Doe Company; Jones Brothers; or Smith & Co.), or it may use a "fictitious name" (such as Central City Hardware Store; or Max's Trucking

J.T. JONES COMPANY	
Statement of Owner's Equity For the Year Ended December 31, 19_1	
J.T. Jones, Capital, January 1, 19_1	$ 5,000
Add: Net income for the year	8,000
Total	$13,000
Less: Withdrawal	2,000
J.T. Jones, Capital, December 31, 19_1	$11,000

Exhibit 18-1
Statement of owners' equity for a single proprietorship

Company).[1] The partnership can buy, hold, and sell personal property and real estate in the firm name, but the firm name is simply a way of referring to the collection of partners; the partnership has no separate legal existence of its own (as does a corporation).

Each partner is a co-owner of the business. Unless the partnership agreement limits the rights or powers of some partners, each partner has an equal right to inspect the firm's accounting records, make normal business decisions and commitments for the firm, and share in the profits of the firm. Unless otherwise specified in the partnership agreement, each partner is equally liable for any debts or other obligations incurred by any of the partners in the name of the partnership. Even if the agreement states that losses will be shared in certain proportions among the partners, each partner is still personally liable to creditors for all debts of the partnership if the other partners fail to meet their obligations under the agreement.

An individual partner ***does not*** have the power to commit the partnership in transactions that fall outside the course of ordinary business.[2] For example, in a merchandising business, an individual partner could order merchandise from suppliers or make normal sales to customers, but he could not pledge the firm's assets as security on a debt, sell fixed assets, sell the entire stock of inventory, or make a sale on credit terms outside the firm's usual credit policies. Differences that arise in the course of normal business can be resolved by a decision of a majority of the partners. However, unanimous consent of all partners is required to make any changes in the partnership agreement, change the nature of the business, increase or decrease the capital investment of any partner, pledge partnership assets as security for a debt, make a legal concession of rights or claims for the business, dispose of intangible assets, or do anything else that would make it impossible for the business to carry on in a normal fashion.

1. Some states forbid the use of the phrase "& Co." as part of a business name unless the business is a partnership. Some states forbid the use of a person's name as part of a business name unless the person is a partner in the business. The business name is part of the property of the partnership, and the right to its use can be sold or transferred if all of the partners agree to do so (subject to state limitations of the kinds just mentioned).

2. An individual partner also is forbidden to act in ways that do not represent a "good faith" relationship with the other partners. For example, he cannot make secret profits for himself while doing business for the firm, use assets of the partnership for his own gain, or use information obtained through the partnership to benefit his own personal business. On the other hand, if a partner exceeds his powers and makes an unauthorized commitment in the name of the partnership, the other partners may be liable to fulfill that commitment if the other party involved had no reason to doubt the erring partner's authority to act for the partnership.

The life of a partnership may be limited to a fixed time period in the partnership agreement. If there is no agreed term for the partnership, the partnership is dissolved whenever (1) there is any change in the persons making up the partnership (death or bankruptcy or withdrawal of a partner, addition of a new partner); (2) all partners agree to dissolve the partnership; (3) the partnership declares bankruptcy; (4) the business of the firm becomes illegal as a result of a new law; or (5) a court orders the partnership dissolved.

Accounting for a partnership

Accounting for a partnership is similar to accounting for a single proprietorship. However, in a partnership, each partner has his own Drawing and Capital accounts.

Transaction 2. Formation of a partnership. A. B. Smith, B. A. Jones, and J. J. Doe enter into a partnership agreement to operate a business. Smith contributes the following assets to the business and is to receive capital credit for their fair market value as listed: merchandise, $5,000; delivery equipment, $15,000. Jones contributes $10,000 in cash. Doe is made a partner because of his knowledge of the business; he contributes no capital.

The formation of the partnership is recorded by the following journal entry.

Cash	10,000	
Merchandise	5,000	
Delivery Equipment	15,000	
A. B. Smith, Capital		20,000
B. A. Jones, Capital		10,000
To record formation of the Smith, Jones, & Doe partnership (Doe contributes no capital).		

In this case, Doe has been made a full partner (with rights to act as an owner in controlling the business and to share in profits), but has been given no capital credit.

Partnership profits and losses are shared according to the partnership agreement. For example, the partners may agree to divide profits and losses equally. Or, they may decide to share profits and losses in certain proportions if one partner contributes more to the business in the form of an investment, brings more experience and ability to the partnership, devotes more time to partnership affairs, assumes special risks, or for any other reason is agreed to deserve a larger share of the profits.

If the Articles of Partnership say nothing about the distribution of profits, the law provides that they are to be divided equally among the partners. If the Articles say nothing about the distribution of losses, the law provides that they are to be divided in the same proportions as the profits.

Transaction 3. Division of profits. During the first year of the partnership, Smith and Jones make additional investments in the business. Exhibit 18-2 shows the Capital accounts of the partners at the end of the year. The net income of the partnership for the year is $30,000. This amount is shown as the balance of the Income

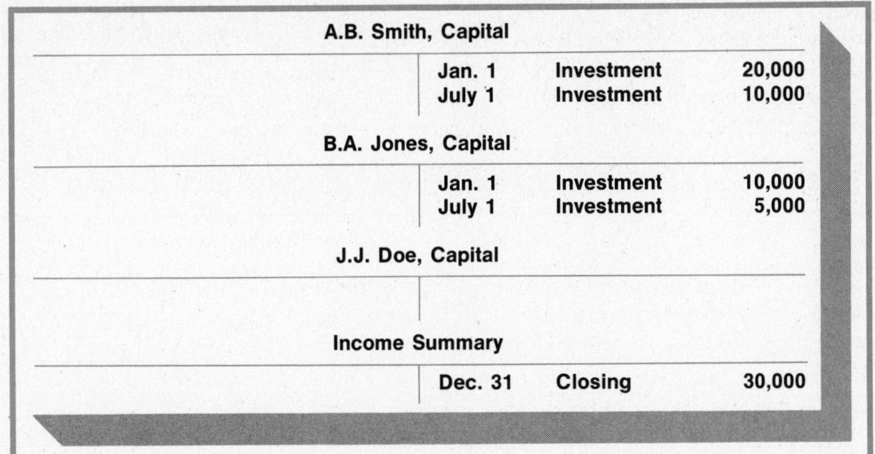

A.B. Smith, Capital

	Jan. 1	Investment	20,000
	July 1	Investment	10,000

B.A. Jones, Capital

	Jan. 1	Investment	10,000
	July 1	Investment	5,000

J.J. Doe, Capital

Income Summary

	Dec. 31	Closing	30,000

Exhibit 18-2
Owners' Capital and Income Summary account balances for transaction 3

Summary account, after the expense and revenue accounts have been closed to Income Summary.

To illustrate some of the ways in which partners can agree to divide the profits or losses of the business, we look at transaction 3 under four different cases, each representing a different agreement among the partners.

Case 1. Profits shared equally. The partnership agreement specifies that Smith, Jones, and Doe will share equally in any profits or losses from the business.

If the $30,000 income is shared equally among the three partners, each receives $10,000. The distribution is recorded by the following entry.

Dec. 31	Income Summary	30,000	
	A. B. Smith, Drawing		10,000
	B. A. Jones, Drawing		10,000
	J. J. Doe, Drawing		10,000

Case 2. Interest on partners' capital allowed. The partnership agreement specifies that each partner is to receive 6 percent interest on his opening capital balance for the year; the remainder of the earnings is to be divided equally among the partners.

This kind of agreement provides extra compensation to the partners who have invested the most capital in the business. Exhibit 18-3 shows the computation of the division of the $30,000 net income for the year. The following journal entry records the distribution.

Dec. 31	Income Summary	30,000	
	A. B. Smith, Drawing		10,600
	B. A. Jones, Drawing		10,000
	J. J. Doe, Drawing		9,400

Although part of this distribution is expressed as an interest rate on capital balance, the transaction still consists of a distribution of earnings, *not* an interest expense for the business.

Exhibit 18-3
Computation of earnings distribution for case 2 (transaction 3)

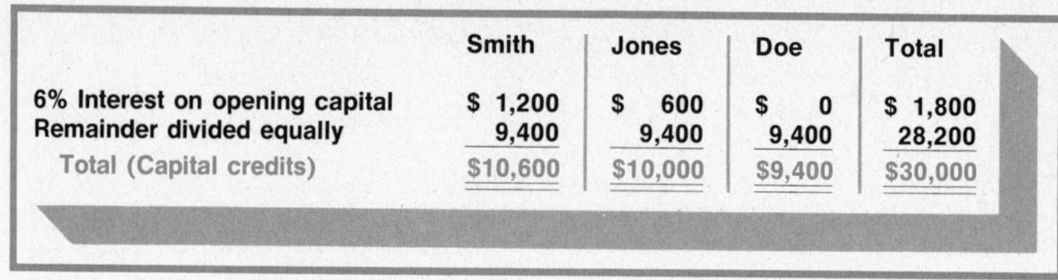

	Smith	Jones	Doe	Total
6% Interest on opening capital	$ 1,200	$ 600	$ 0	$ 1,800
Remainder divided equally	9,400	9,400	9,400	28,200
Total (Capital credits)	$10,600	$10,000	$9,400	$30,000

Case 3. Salaries to partners. Because Doe is to do most of the work of operating the business, the partnership agreement specifies that Doe will receive a salary of $10,000 per year, while Smith and Jones will each receive $8,500 per year. Remaining profits or losses are to be divided equally.

Exhibit 18-4 shows the computation for this distribution. Note that salaries of the partners are *not* salaries expense for the business. These salaries are not the result of an employer–employee relationship. Salaries to partners are simply a way of distributing the partnership profits. They appear on the income statement as a supplementary explanation of the division of the income (below the net income computation).

Case 4. Interest and salaries to partners. The partnership agreement specifies the following distribution for profits and losses. Each partner is to receive 6 percent interest on the closing balance (before closing Drawing accounts) of his Capital account. Smith, Jones, and Doe are to receive salaries of $7,000, $8,000, and $9,000, respectively. Any remaining profit or loss is to be divided 30 percent to Smith, 30 percent to Jones, and 40 percent to Doe.

Exhibit 18-5 shows the computation for this more complex distribution of the income. Such agreements often develop as a compromise, in order to give appropriate rewards both for contribution of capital and for other contributions to the partnership. Exhibit 18-6 shows a simplified income statement for the partnership, using the

Exhibit 18-4
Computation of earnings distribution for case 3 (transaction 3)

	Smith	Jones	Doe	Total
Salaries	$8,500	$8,500	$10,000	$27,000
Remainder divided equally	1,000	1,000	1,000	3,000
Total (Capital credits)	$9,500	$9,500	$11,000	$30,000

	Smith	Jones	Doe	Total
6% Interest on closing capital	$1,800	$ 900	$ 0	$ 2,700
Salaries	7,000	8,000	9,000	24,000
Remainder divided 30%/30%/40%	990	990	1,320	3,300
Total (Capital credits)	$9,790	$9,890	$10,320	$30,000

Exhibit 18-5 Computation of earnings distribution for case 4 (transaction 3)

Exhibit 18-6 **Simplified income statement for the partnership (case 4)**

SMITH, JONES, & DOE COMPANY
Income Statement
For the Year Ended December 31, 19_1

Sales	**$50,000**
Less: Expenses	**20,000**
Net income	$30,000

Division of Net Income

	Smith	Jones	Doe	Total
Interest on partner's closing balance	**$1,800**	**$ 900**	**$ 0**	**$ 2,700**
Salaries	**7,000**	**8,000**	**9,000**	**24,000**
Remainder: 30%/30%/40%	**990**	**990**	**1,320**	**3,300**
	$9,790	$9,890	$10,320	$30,000

distribution of case 4. Observe that the distribution of income among the partners is reported on the income statement, below the net income figure.

Suppose that during the year, Smith, Jones, and Doe withdrew from the business the amounts of $10,000, $8,000, and $7,000, respectively. Using the income distribution of case 4, the partnership's statement of owner's equities would assume the form shown in Exhibit 18-7. In the partnership's balance sheet, the owners' equity section would appear as follows.

Owners' equities:		
A. B. Smith, Capital	$29,790	
B. A. Jones, Capital	16,890	
J. J. Doe, Capital	3,320	$50,000

ADMISSION OF A NEW PARTNER. When a new member is admitted to an existing partnership, the former partnership is dissolved and a new one is created. In such circumstances, the firm need not go through a formal process of dissolution if all of the partners of the new firm agree to accept the liabilities and obligations of the old partnership. In such a case, the new partnership agreement must make very clear the liabilities of the new partner in respect to such obligations of the old partnership.

In accounting for the admission of a new partner, a distinction is drawn between (1) a purchase of an interest, and (2) an investment in a new partnership.

1. *Purchase of an interest.* The new partner purchases all or part of the interest of one or more of the partners in the old partnership. In the transaction, the new partner makes a payment directly to the partner(s) from whom he purchases the interest.
2. *Investment in a new partnership.* The new partner invests assets directly in the new partnership that is being formed. He makes no payments directly to any of the old partners.

Transaction 4. Purchase of an interest. The A & B Partnership has been in existence for some time. A has a capital balance of $10,000 in the partnership, and B has

Exhibit 18-7 **Statement of owners' equities for the partnership (case 4)**

SMITH, JONES, & DOE COMPANY

Statement of Partners' Equities

For the Year Ended December 31, 19_1

	Smith	Jones	Doe	Total
Balance, January 1, 19_1	$20,000	$10,000	$ 0	$30,000
Add: Additional investments	10,000	5,000	0	15,000
Net income	9,790	9,890	10,320	30,000
Total	$39,790	$24,890	$10,320	$75,000
Less: Withdrawals	10,000	8,000	7,000	25,000
Balance, December 31, 19_1	$29,790	$16,890	$ 3,320	$50,000

a capital balance of $20,000. Profits and losses in the business are divided between A and B in the ratio of 60%/40%. At this time, C is to be admitted into the partnership by purchasing a 25 percent interest from each of the former partners for a total of $20,000.

The agreement for C to pay $20,000 to the two existing partners is a private agreement, negotiated between the individuals involved. On the books of the partnership, the only significant part of the transaction is the transfer of 25 percent of each partner's Capital balance to the Capital account of the new partner.

A, Capital	2,500	
B, Capital	5,000	
C, Capital		7,500
To record transfer of 25% of capital interest of A and B to Capital account of new partner C.		

The $20,000 payment by C would be split between A and B in accordance with the negotiated plans; probably it would be split in proportion to the capital interest provided to C—that is, ⅓ to A and ⅔ to B. The proportion in which the three partners are to divide profits and losses of the new partnership would be worked out and specified as part of the new partnership agreement.

Note that C has paid $20,000 to obtain a capital interest of $7,500 in the partnership. Presumably, he does this because he feels that the goodwill of the existing partnership represents an unrecorded, intangible asset of such value that his 25 percent interest in the firm will be worth $20,000 to him. In other words, he is making the private judgment that the owner's equities of the firm are actually worth $80,000, rather than the $30,000 recorded in the books.

Transaction 5. Investment in a partnership. Instead of purchasing a 25 percent interest in the A & B Partnership from the old partners (transaction 4), C agrees to invest $20,000 in the new partnership. In return, C is to receive a 40 percent interest in the new capital equity of $50,000.

In this case, C's payment of $20,000 goes to the partnership and must be recorded in the books.

Cash	20,000	
C, Capital		20,000
To record initial investment by new partner C.		

Note that the $20,000 capital balance does represent 40 percent of the total capital of $50,000 in the new partnership. In this case, C's investment is a transaction that confirms the book value of the assets of the old partnership.

However, in some cases the terms of the new partner's admission to the partnership by investment may indicate that the book values need adjustment. It is useful to set up a schedule in the following form for such a transaction.

Old capital (net assets)	$30,000
New investment	20,000
Balancing amount, if necessary	0
Total new capital	$50,000
New partner's interest (40% of new capital)	$20,000

This schedule is needed in computing the entries needed to record the following transaction.

Transaction 6. Goodwill to former partners. The admission of C to the partnership is made under the same conditions as in transaction 5, except that it is agreed that C is to receive a $20,000 capital credit in the new partnership that represents 25 percent of the total capital equity. Goodwill is to be allowed to the original partners.

In this case, C is agreeing to pay the same amount for a smaller share of the business. This means that he is assigning a higher market value to the firm's net assets than the value shown in the books. An adjustment should be made in the books *before* the new investment is recorded. Using the schedule just described, we can compute the amount of the adjustment needed.

Old capital (net assets)	$30,000
New investment	20,000
Balancing amount, if necessary	30,000
Total new capital	$80,000
New partner's interest (25% of $80,000)	$20,000

The terms of C's admission to the partnership indicate that the market value of the firm's net assets is $30,000 higher than the value shown on the books. Unless some asset shown in the books has been seriously undervalued, this increase normally is regarded as the value of the firm's goodwill. The goodwill is an intangible asset that the old partnership has accumulated over its life. It represents earnings that were not recorded in the books of the old partnership. Therefore, before C's admission is recorded, we should adjust the books of the old partnership to show the additional asset ($30,000 of goodwill) and capital of $30,000 as the balancing credit entry. Because these were earnings of the old partnership, the $30,000 should be divided between the Capital accounts of the old partners according to the 60%/40% ratio of dividing profits set forth in the old partnership agreement.

Goodwill	30,000	
A, Capital		18,000
B, Capital		12,000
To record goodwill earned by old partners at market value established by admission of new partner.		

The entry needed to record C's investment in the business is the following.

Cash	20,000	
C, Capital		20,000
To record investment by new partner.		

Note that the opening capital balances for the new partnership are the following.

A, Capital ($10,000 + $18,000)	$28,000	(35%)
B, Capital ($20,000 + $12,000)	32,000	(40%)
C, Capital ($20,000)	20,000	(25%)
Total equity capital	$80,000	(100%)

Transaction 7. Bonus to former partners. The admission of C to the partnership is made under the same conditions as in transaction 5, except that it is agreed that C's capital balance in the new partnership will be $15,000, with a total equity capital of $50,000. A bonus is to be given to the original partners.

In this case, the value of goodwill is not to be recorded on the books. Instead, C will pay a bonus to the old partners, through a contribution of some of his investment to their capital balances. The bonus should be split according to the 60%/40% terms of profit division under the old agreement.

The schedule for this transaction takes the following form.

Old capital (net assets)	$30,000
New investment	20,000
Balancing amount, if necessary	0
Total new capital	$50,000
New partner's interest (30% of $50,000)	$15,000

C's admission to the partnership is recorded by the following entry.

Cash	20,000	
C, Capital		15,000
A, Capital		3,000
B, Capital		2,000
To record investment by new partner, with $5,000 as bonus split 60%/40% between A and B.		

Transaction 8. Goodwill to new partner. The admission of C to the partnership is made under the same conditions as in transaction 5, except that it is agreed that C's capital balance in the new partnership will be $25,000, with a total equity capital of $55,000. Goodwill is to be allowed to the new partner.

In this case, C is being given a capital credit larger than his investment. Apparently, the old partners regard C as a highly desirable partner, who will bring to the business valuable goodwill in addition to his cash investment. The schedule appears as follows:

Old capital (net assets)	$30,000
New investment	20,000
Balancing amount, if necessary	5,000
Total new capital	$55,000
New partner's interest	$25,000

The $5,000 intangible asset of goodwill is created as a part of the entry recording C's investment. It does not alter the capital balances of the old partners.

Cash	20,000	
Goodwill	5,000	
C, Capital		25,000
To record investment by new partner and recognition of goodwill contributed by new partner.		

Transaction 9. Bonus to new partner. The admission of C to the partnership is made under the same conditions as in transaction 5, except that it is agreed that C's capital balance in the new partnership will be $25,000, with a total equity capital of $50,000. A bonus is to be given to the new partner.

In this case, the old partners agree to transfer a bonus from their capital balances to that of the new partner, rather than recognizing an intangible asset of goodwill. The cost of this bonus should be divided between the old partners according to the 60%/40% division called for in the old agreement.

Old capital (net assets)	$30,000
New investment	20,000
Balancing amount, if necessary	0
New total capital	$50,000
New partner's interest	$25,000

C's admission to the partnership is recorded by the following entry.

Cash	20,000	
A, Capital	3,000	
B, Capital	2,000	
C, Capital		25,000
To record investment by new partner and bonus from old partners ($5,000 split 60%/40%).		

DISSOLUTION OF A PARTNERSHIP. A partnership is dissolved under various conditions listed earlier. If a new partnership is formed and agrees to take over the liabilities of the old partnership, the dissolution is merely a legal formality—the substitution of a new partnership agreement for the old one. However, if the partnership is not being carried on in a new form, the dissolution requires that the business immediately stop carrying out its normal business operations. During the period of "winding up" that follows dissolution, the only operations the firm can carry out are those designed to settle its obligations and liabilities and to convert its assets into cash. Every partner (except one who has caused the dissolution by a wrongful action) is entitled to participate in winding up the business affairs. If dissolution has been caused by the death of a partner, the heirs of the dead partner do not have a right to participate in winding up the affairs of the partnership.

In winding up the partnership, the first obligation is to pay all outside creditors with claims against the business. Then, the assets must be used to repay any loans made to the business by a partner, or any liabilities incurred by a partner acting for the business. Next, any remaining assets must be used to repay the capital investments made in the business by the partners. If any balance remains, this is regarded as profit and is distributed among the partners according to the terms of the agreement. If the assets of the partnership are not enough to settle all the creditors' claims against the business, the firm's creditors have the right to collect the balance due to them from the individual partners.

If the partners also owe money personally, their personal creditors have no claim against the assets of the partnership until the liquidation and distribution of assets is completed. Then the personal creditors have claims against that partner's share of the capital and profits.

When all of the assets of the dissolved partnership have been properly distributed and all claims settled, the partnership is said to be terminated.

Transaction 10. Liquidation of a partnership. The X, Y, and Z partnership is to be liquidated. The noncash assets of the partnership are sold for $65,000. The liabilities of the partnership are paid. The remaining cash is distributed to the partners. The partners share profits and losses equally.

The balance sheet of the X, Y, and Z partnership prior to liquidation is shown as follows.

X, Y, AND Z

Balance Sheet
Date

Cash	$10,000	Liabilities	$20,000
Noncash assets	80,000	X, Capital	10,000
		Y, Capital	20,000
		Z, Capital	40,000
Total	$90,000	Total	$90,000

A schedule can be prepared to show the liquidation of the partnership, as in Schedule 1.

SCHEDULE 1

Statement of Partnership Liquidation
Date

	Cash	Noncash assets	Liabilities	Partners' capital		
				X	Y	Z
Balances	$10,000	$80,000	$20,000	$10,000	$20,000	$40,000
Sale of noncash assets; $15,000 loss shared by X, Y, and Z	65,000	(80,000)		(5,000)	(5,000)	(5,000)
Balances	$75,000		$20,000	$ 5,000	$15,000	$35,000
Payment of debts	(20,000)		(20,000)			
Payment to partners	$55,000			$ 5,000	$15,000	$25,000

Entries that record the liquidation can be obtained from the Statement of Partnership Liquidation (Schedule 1).

Cash	65,000	
X, Capital	5,000	
Y, Capital	5,000	
Z, Capital	5,000	
Noncash Assets		80,000
To record the sale of noncash assets at a $15,000 loss; the loss is shared by the partners in their profit and loss ratios.		
Liabilities	20,000	
Cash		20,000
To record the payment of partnership liabilities.		
X, Capital	5,000	
Y, Capital	15,000	
Z, Capital	35,000	
Cash		55,000
To record the distribution of available cash to the partners.		

If the $80,000 noncash assets had been sold for $35,000 (instead of $65,000), the $45,000 (X's share is $15,000) loss that resulted from the sale would have eliminated X's $10,000 capital balance and would have created a $5,000 deficit (debit) balance in his capital account. This would indicate that X owed the partnership $5,000. If X pays in this amount to the partnership, his capital balance becomes zero. The cash on hand will then be sufficient to pay Y and Z the amounts reflected in their capital accounts. If X is unable to pay the $5,000 that he owes the partnership, the debit balance in X's account means an additional loss to Y and Z and must be shared by these two partners in their profit and loss ratios. Schedule 2 shows a Statement of Partnership Liquidation assuming that X is unable to pay the $5,000 to the partnership.

SCHEDULE 2

Statement of Partnership Liquidation
Date

	Cash	Noncash assets	Liabilities	Partners' capital X	Partners' capital Y	Partners' capital Z
Balances	$10,000	$80,000	$20,000	$10,000	$20,000	$40,000
Sale of noncash assets; $45,000 loss shared by X, Y, and Z	35,000	(80,000)		(15,000)	(15,000)	(15,000)
Balances	$45,000		$20,000	$ (5,000)	$ 5,000	$25,000
Payment of debts	(20,000)		(20,000)			
Balances	$25,000			$ (5,000)	$ 5,000	$25,000
Additional loss from X's deficiency				5,000	(2,500)	(2,500)
Payment to partners	$25,000				$ 2,500	$22,500

Summary

Accounting for a single proprietorship is much the same as that for a corporation, except that only two owner's equity accounts are needed. The owner's withdrawals during the year are recorded in a Drawing account. The Income Summary account is closed to the Drawing account. At the end of the fiscal year, the Drawing account is closed to the owner's Capital account. Because there is only one owner, all contributed capital and earnings can be combined in the single permanent owner's equity account. Legally, the single proprietorship as a business is simply an extension of the personal economic activity of the proprietor.

Accounting for a partnership requires proper recording of the formation of the partnership, divisions of profits and losses, partners' investments and withdrawals after formation, admission of new partners, retirement of old partners, and the dissolution of the partnership. In partnership accounting, separate Drawing and Capital accounts are kept for each of the partners. Although the partnership is an extension of the partners (acting as an aggregate), the legal considerations involved in dissolution require careful separation of the equity claims of each partner against the assets of the business.

Questions

1. What are the major owner's equity accounts for a single proprietorship? What are the major owners' equity accounts for a partnership?
2. How may partnership profits and losses be divided?
3. When a new partner is admitted to a partnership, the new partner may purchase an interest in the partnership or may make an investment in the partnership. Distinguish between these two methods.
4. Describe the disposition of a partnership's assets after dissolution.
5. If the partnership arrangement for interest and salaries to partners results in an amount that exceeds available net income, how should net income be distributed?
6. Gold owns a small retail store. What advantages and disadvantages would be associated with Gold admitting Blue to the business as a partner? If a partnership agreement is reached, should the agreement be in writing? If so, what are some of the major provisions that should be included in the agreement?
7. If you were entering into a partnership arrangement with another person, what factors would you want to consider when it came to arranging the division of profits and losses among the partners?
8. Why might similar business conducted as a partnership and as a corporation have different net incomes?

Exercises

E18-1 (Proprietorship)

On January 1, 19_6, Alan A. Dale organizes a new business as a single proprietorship. He invests $40,000 cash and a truck with a fair market value of $6,000 in the business. The following transactions occur during the year.

A. Cash sales of $80,000.
B. Expenses of $50,000 (paid in cash).
C. Cash withdrawals by Dale totaling $12,000.
D. The firm closes its books on December 31.

Required:

a. Record all transactions affecting Dale's business.
b. Prepare a statement of owner's equity for the year for Alan A. Dale.

E18-2 (Partnership)

On January 1, 19_1, Sarah Lin and Jane Moore organize a partnership. Each partner contributes $60,000 cash to the business. Partnership profits are to be divided 40 percent to Lin and 60 percent ot Moore. During the first year, the partnership has a net income of $90,000.

Required:

a. Record the establishment of the partnership.
b. Record the distribution of partnership profits for the first year. The revenue and expense accounts have already been closed to the Income Summary account.
c. Close the partners' Drawing accounts for the year.

E18-3 (Division of profits)

On December 31, 19_6, the Capital accounts of the Tom & Jerry Partnership show the following balances.

Tom, Capital	$40,000
Jerry, Capital	80,000

For 19_6 the partnership had a net income of $40,000. The partnership agreement specifies that partnership profits and losses are to be distributed as follows:

a. 5% interest on closing balance in each partner's Capital account;
b. salaries of $6,000 and $5,000 to Tom and Jerry, respectively;
c. any remaining profit or loss is to be divided 60% to Tom and 40% to Jerry.

Required: Compute the amounts of partnership net income that should be distributed to Tom and Jerry, and journalize the entries.

E18-4 (Admission of a partner)

The following accounts appear in the ledger of the Ted & Alice Company partnership.

Ted, Capital	$30,000
Alice, Capital	20,000

Joining the partnership is Bob, who is paying $33,000 to Ted to purchase one-half of Ted's interest in the partnership.

Required: Record the admission of Bob to the Ted & Alice partnership.

E18-5 (Admission of a partner)

Record the following independent transactions.

a. A invests $30,000 in the B and C partnership. A is to receive a capital credit of $30,000.
b. M invests $50,000 in the N and O partnership. Prior to A's investment, the capital accounts of N and O are the following.

N, Capital	$80,000
O, Capital	70,000

M is to receive a capital credit of $30,000; total capital after the investment is to be $200,000. N and O share profits equally. (HINT: This transaction involves a bonus to the old partners.)

c. P invests $40,000 in the N and O partnership. P is to receive a capital credit of $50,000. The capital accounts of N and O and the profit-and-loss agreement are the same as in part b of this exercise. Total capital after the investment is to be $200,000. (HINT: This transaction involves recognition of goodwill contributed by the new partner.)

d. Assume the same facts as in part c, except that the total capital after the investment is to be $190,000. (This transaction involves a bonus to the new partner.)

e. Assume the same information as in part c, except that P is to receive a capital credit of $40,000, and total owners' equity is to be $210,000. (This transaction involves recognition of goodwill owned by the old partnership.)

E18-6 (Partnership transactions)

Able and Baker are partners. They have agreed on the following plan for sharing profits: (1) salaries of $10,000 to Able and $15,000 to Baker; (2) interest of 5% on initial capital investments; and (3) remaining profit or loss to be shared equally. (The procedure for carrying out such an agreement is the following. After closing revenue and expense accounts to Income Summary, debit Income Summary for the amounts of the agreed-upon salaries and/or interest and credit these amounts to the appropriate partners' Drawing accounts. Then apportion any remaining debit or credit balance in Income Summary among the Drawing accounts according to the agreed-upon partnership ratio for sharing remaining profit or loss. Finally, close the Drawing accounts to the Capital accounts.) The initial investments of the partners were $30,000 for Able and $50,000 for Baker.

Required:

a. In 19_1, the business has net income of $111,000. Journalize the closing of Income Summary to the Drawing accounts.

b. During 19_1, each partner has withdrawn the amount of his salary in cash. Journalize the closing of the Drawing accounts to the Capital accounts.

c. In 19_2, the business has a net income of $21,000. Again each partner has withdrawn the amount of his salary in cash during the year. Journalize the closing of Income Summary and the Drawing accounts.

d. In 19_3, the business shows a net loss of $29,000. Again each partner has withdrawn the amount of his salary in cash during the year. Journalize the closing of Income Summary and the Drawing accounts.

e. Assume that the business was organized at the beginning of 19_1, and that there have been no additional investments or withdrawals by the partners (except for the cash withdrawals of salaries described for each year). Prepare a comparative statement of owners' equity for the partnership over the three years.

E18-7 (Partnership liquidation)

Prior to liquidation, the balance sheet of a partnership appears as follows.

Cash	$50,000	Liabilities	$20,000
Noncash assets	40,000	A, Capital	40,000
		B, Capital	30,000
Total	$90,000	Total	$90,000

The partners A and B share profits and losses in a 60:40 ratio respectively. The noncash assets are sold for $30,000. The liabilities are paid. Any remaining cash is distributed to the partners.

Required: Prepare a statement of partnership liquidation.

Problems

P18-1 (Proprietorship transactions)

Record the following transactions in general journal form.

a. John Brown invests $10,000 to establish a retail shoe store.

b. During the year Brown withdraws $5,000 in anticipation of earnings from the shoe store.

c. When the books of the shoe store are closed on December 31, the Income Summary account shows a credit balance of $20,000. This account is closed to the Drawing account.

d. The balance in the Drawing account is closed.

P18-2 (Partnership transactions)

William Welch contributes land worth $10,000, a machine worth $20,000, and inventory worth $5,000 to a newly formed Welch and Rabbit partnership. Roberta Rabbit contributes cash of $10,000 and a building worth $30,000 to the partnership. The building has a $16,000 mortgage on it, which the partnership assumes. Partners are to share profits and losses equally. During the year, Welch withdraws $6,000 from the business, and Rabbit withdraws $5,000. The partnership makes a $50,000 profit for the year. This net income currently is the balance of the Income Summary account.

Required: Journalize all transactions just described, including closing the income Summary account and any other accounts to be closed at the end of the year.

P18-3 (Admission of a partner)

C and P are partners who share profits and losses equally. Their Capital account balances are C $50,000 and P $110,000. They agree to accept A as a new partner.

Required (consider the following questions independently):

a. A pays C $80,000 for his interest and pays P $50,000 for one-half of his interest. A's Capital account will be recorded on the partnership books at what dollar amount?

b. A pays the firm $100,000 cash for a 25 percent interest. C and P agree to record goodwill. By what amount will C's Capital account change as a result of the recognition of goodwill and the admission of the new partner?

c. A pays the firm $100,000 cash for a 25 percent interest. Goodwill is ***not*** recorded. What amount will appear in P's Capital account after the new partner is admitted?

P18-4 (Partnership liquidation)

The X, Y, and Z partnership is being liquidated. X, Y, and Z share profits and losses in a ratio of 60:30:10 respectively. The balance sheet of the partnership is as follows prior to liquidation.

Cash	$ 30,000	Liabilities	$ 40,000
Noncash assets	100,000	A, Capital	10,000
		B, Capital	50,000
		C, Capital	30,000
Total assets	$130,000	Total liabilities	$130,000

The noncash assets are sold for $50,000. If any partner develops a debit balance in her capital account as a result of her inability to absorb a loss on the liquidation of noncash assets or her share of a deficit in another partner's capital account, assume that she is unable to make a cash contribution to the partnership to cover the loss.

Required: Prepare a statement of partnership liquidation.

P18-5 (Division of profits)

Partners A, B, and C had average capital balances during the year of $40,000, $50,000, and $10,000 respectively. The partnership agreement provides the following profit-and-loss sharing provisions.

6% interest on average capital balances;

Salaries:	
A	$10,000
B	15,000
C	None

Remaining profits (losses):	
A	20%
B	30%
C	50%

Required:

a. Prepare schedules showing the division of profits or losses to the partners in the following independent cases:
   1. Net income of $41,000 for the year.
   2. Net income of $25,000 for the year.
   3. Net loss of $19,000 for the year.

b. Prepare journal entries to record the division of profits and losses for the three cases.

P18-6 (Division of net profits)

The A, B, and C partnership earned net income of $100,000 for the year. Compute the share of net income that each partner receives under the following independent cases:

1. Profits and losses are shared equally.
2. Partners are allowed a 6% return on their capital invested in the partnership at the end of the year. Remaining profits are shared by A, B, and C in a ratio of 2:3:5 respectively. A, B, and C have $100,000, $200,000, and $300,000 respectively invested at the end of the year.
3. Partners A and B are allowed salaries of $20,000 and $50,000 respectively. Remaining profits are shared equally by A, B, and C.
4. Partners A and B are allowed salaries of $60,000 and $70,000 respectively. Remaining profits and losses are shared equally.

P18-7 (Admission of a partner)

In the A & B Partnership, A and B share profits and losses equally. The capital accounts of partners A and B are $50,000 and $70,000 respectively. C is admitted to the partnership under the following conditions. Consider each case independently of the others.

1. C invests $40,000 for a 25% interest in the firm.
2. C invests $60,000 for a 25% interest in the firm.
   a. Goodwill is to be recorded.
   b. Goodwill is not to be recorded.
3. C invests $60,000 for a 50% interest in the firm.
   a. Goodwill is to be recorded.
   b. Goodwill is not to be recorded.
4. C purchases 50% of A's and B's capital for $100,000.

Required: Record the admission of C to the partnership under the above conditions.

19 Consolidated statements and related topics

The preceding three chapters covered many of the major topics relating to corporations. There remain a few selected topics that we want to examine. In this chapter we discuss consolidated financial statements, the equity method of accounting for investments in common stock, and two methods (purchase versus pooling of interests) of accounting for business combinations. We introduce each of these topics relatively briefly; these subjects receive considerable attention in advanced accounting courses.

Consolidated statements

A consolidation arises when one company acquires a controlling interest in another through common stock ownership. We describe the relationship of the acquiring company to the acquired firm as a parent-and-subsidiary relationship. Exhibit 19-1 visualizes a parent-and-subsidiary relationship for a business combination in which Parent Company owns 90 percent of the voting stock of Subsidiary Company. In this illustration, there exists a minority (outside) interest in Subsidiary Company of 10 percent—the stock of Subsidiary Company owned by someone other than Parent Company.

CONSOLIDATED FINANCIAL STATEMENTS

Consolidated financial statements are prepared to show a summation of the assets, liabilities, revenue, and expenses of the corporations that make up an affiliation. Consolidated statements for a parent company and its subsidiary present information that reflects the results of business transactions with other enterprises that are not members of the affiliation. Transactions between members of the affiliation (parent and subsidiary) are eliminated from the consolidated statements. The assumption of consolidated statements is that the members of the affiliation represent a single economic entity that deals with outsiders. Generally, consolidated statements are

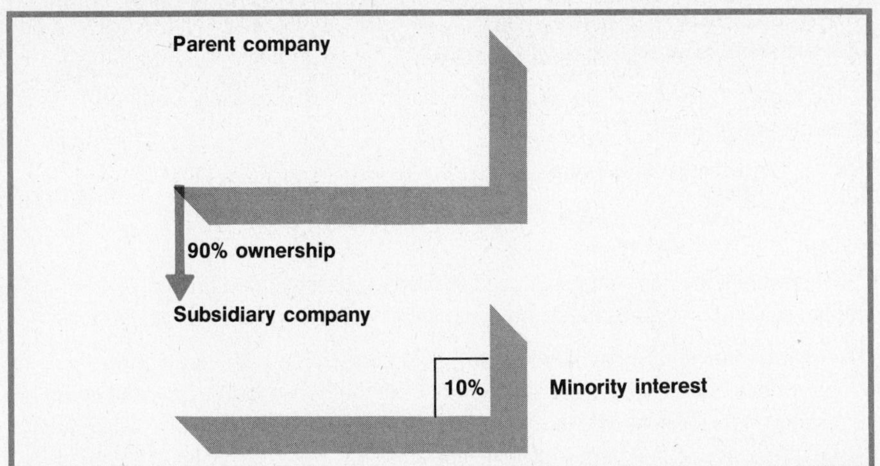

Exhibit 19-1
An example of a parent-and-subsidiary relationship

more useful to shareholders and managers of the parent company than are the parent company's unconsolidated statements.

Consolidated statements are required where management of the parent company needs information about the resources, obligations, and operations of the members of the consolidation that are under the financial control of the parent corporation. *Financial control* of one company by another is usually measured in terms of ownership of a majority voting interest (that is, more than 50 percent of outstanding voting shares), either directly or indirectly. Although voting control of a subsidiary usually is considered basic before the statements of the subsidiary are consolidated with those of the parent, managerial control of the subsidiary by the parent is a second major prerequisite. *Managerial control* implies that the parent corporation governs or regulates the basic business policies of the subsidiary.

A consolidated balance sheet shows the total assets owned and controlled by the parent, as well as the liabilities of all the affiliated companies. Such a statement ignores the legal fact that the consolidation consists of two or more legally distinct corporations. For example, the assets of the subsidiary are not legally available to settle claims of creditors of the parent company. (Recall that the owners of a corporation are not liable for its debts, nor can creditors of the owners lay claim to the assets of the corporation.) Consolidated statements are prepared to reflect the economic reality that the subsidiary is owned and controlled by the parent.

We now present a few cases to demonstrate certain accounting problems associated with the preparation of consolidated financial statements. These cases introduce basic accounting procedures used in preparing consolidated financial statements.

Case 1: Preparation of a consolidated financial statement at date of acquisition; parent company acquires 100 percent interest in a subsidiary. On January 1, 19_0, the Parent Company acquires 100 percent of the voting stock of the Subsidiary Company for $150,000. At the date of purchase, the owners' equity section of the Subsidiary Company's balance sheet shows a Capital Stock account with a balance of $100,000, and a Retained Earnings account with $50,000 balance. A consolidated balance sheet is to be prepared for the affiliation as of the date of purchase.

The Parent Company records the acquisition of the Subsidiary Company's stock at its exchange price.

Jan. 1	Investment in Subsidiary	150,000	
	Cash		150,000
	Purchase of 100% of Subsidiary Company voting stock.		

In the work sheet (Exhibit 19-2) used to prepare consolidated financial statements, certain eliminations are needed before compiling the consolidated statements.

1. The Investment in Subsidiary account appearing in the books of the Parent Company does not exist as a separate entity from the consolidation point of view. The assets and liabilities of the subsidiary will be substituted in the consolidated statements for the Investment in Subsidiary account.
2. The Subsidiary Company's equity accounts should be eliminated, to the extent that they reflect the Parent Company's ownership interest. Again, this ownership is regarded as an internal transaction from the consolidation point of view. Because the Parent Company owns 100 percent of the Subsidiary Company stock, in this case the entire owners' equity section of the Subsidiary Company balance

Exhibit 19-2 Work sheet for consolidated balance sheet (case 1)

PARENT COMPANY AND SUBSIDIARY COMPANY

Consolidated Balance-Sheet Working Paper

January 1, 19_0 (date of acquisition)

	Parent Company	Subsidiary Company	Eliminations Debits	Eliminations Credits	Consolidation
Assets					
Cash	100,000	50,000			150,000
Investment in subsidiary	150,000	—		150,000	—
Other assets	50,000	200,000			250,000
	300,000	250,000			400,000
Liabilities and Stockholders' Equity					
Liabilities	50,000	100,000			150,000
Capital stock:					
Parent Company	175,000	—			175,000
Subsidiary Company	—	100,000	100,000		—
Retained earnings:					
Parent Company	75,000	—			75,000
Subsidiary Company	—	50,000	50,000		—
	300,000	250,000	150,000	150,000	400,000

NOTE: In the Eliminations columns, the Parent Company's Investment in Subsidiary account is eliminated, offset by elimination of the Subsidiary Company's Capital Stock and Retained Earnings accounts.

sheet is eliminated, offsetting the elimination of the Parent Company's Investment in Subsidiary account.

From the Consolidation column of the work sheet, a formal balance sheet can be prepared for the consolidation. Exhibit 19-3 shows such a statement. Note that the capital stock reported in a consolidated balance sheet is the capital stock of the parent company. This treatment emphasizes the point that the consolidated statements are prepared to serve the interests of the stockholders of the parent company. In a statement prepared as of the date of acquisition, the retained earnings shown on the consolidated balance sheet do not contain any of the retained earnings of the subsidiary. Post-acquisition earnings of the subsidiary will be consolidated with those of the parent in the preparation of later consolidated statements.

Case 2: Preparation of consolidated financial statement at date of acquisition; parent company acquires 90 percent of stock of subsidiary company at a cost exceeding book value. On January 1, 19_0, the Parent Company purchases 90 percent of the outstanding capital stock of the Subsidiary Company for $160,000. At this date, the Subsidiary Company's Capital Stock and Retained Earnings accounts showed balances of $100,000 and $50,000, respectively. A minority interest of 10 percent exists in the ownership of the Subsidiary Company.

Again, the Parent Company records the stock purchase in its books at the cash exchange price—$160,000 in this case. Exhibit 19-4 shows the work sheet for preparation of a consolidated balance sheet. The Parent Company has purchased 90 percent interest in the Subsidiary Company's equity accounts, so 90 percent of these account balances are eliminated as "internal" relationships for the consolidation. The amounts not eliminated (10 percent of each account balance) are extended to the Consolidation column; they represent the interest of the minority stockholders in these accounts.

The elimination from the equity accounts is offset by an elimination of an equal amount from the Parent Company's Investment in Subsidiary account. Because the Parent Company paid more than book value for its share of ownership in the subsidiary, this account is not entirely eliminated. The amount not eliminated is extended

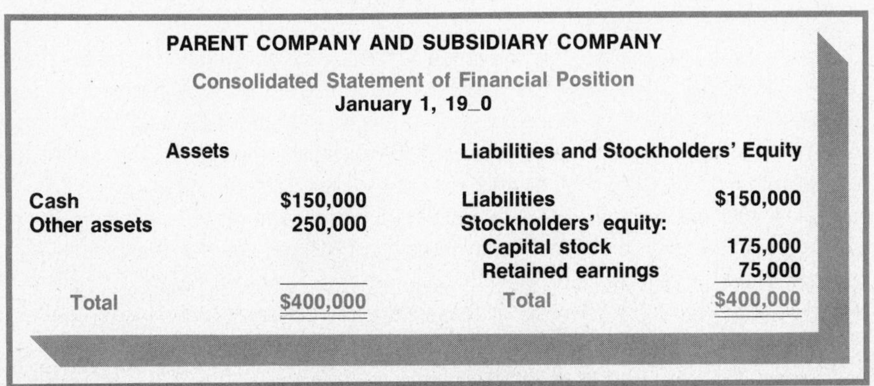

PARENT COMPANY AND SUBSIDIARY COMPANY

Consolidated Statement of Financial Position
January 1, 19_0

Assets		Liabilities and Stockholders' Equity	
Cash	$150,000	Liabilities	$150,000
Other assets	250,000	Stockholders' equity:	
		Capital stock	175,000
		Retained earnings	75,000
Total	$400,000	Total	$400,000

Exhibit 19-3
Consolidated balance sheet for case 1

Exhibit 19-4 **Work sheet for consolidated balance sheet (case 2)**

PARENT COMPANY AND SUBSIDIARY COMPANY

Consolidated Balance-Sheet Working Paper

January 1, 19_0 (date of acquisition)

	Parent Company	Subsidiary Company	Eliminations Debits	Eliminations Credits	Consolidation
Assets					
Cash	100,000	50,000			150,000
Investment in subsidiary	160,000	—		135,000	25,000 Excess
Other assets	40,000	200,000			240,000
	300,000	250,000			415,000
Liabilities and Stockholders' Equity					
Liabilities	50,000	100,000			150,000
Capital stock:					
Parent Company	175,000	—			175,000
Subsidiary Company	—	100,000	90,000		10,000 Minority
Retained earnings:					
Parent Company	75,000	—			75,000
Subsidiary Company	—	50,000	45,000		5,000 Minority
	300,000	250,000	135,000	135,000	415,000

NOTE: In the Eliminations columns, 90 percent of the Subsidiary Company's equity account balances are eliminated, offset by an elimination from the Parent Company's Investment in Subsidiary account. See text for discussion of these eliminations and the significance of the amounts carried over to the consolidated balance sheet.

to the Consolidation column; it represents the excess of cost over book value for the investment. Exhibit 19-5 shows the consolidated balance sheet. In advanced accounting courses, considerable attention is devoted to procedures for dealing with the excess of cost over book value for the Parent Company's investment in the subsidiary. Usually, this differential is assigned to specific assets and, where appropriate, written off.

The minority interest in the Subsidiary Company appears as a liability on the consolidated balance sheet. This item represents the claims of the outside stockholders against the net assets of the subsidiary, which are now included as part of the consolidated net assets.

In both cases 1 and 2, note that the actual impact of the acquisition on the accounts of the Parent Company is simply to exchange a current asset (Cash) for a noncurrent asset (Investment in Subsidiary). There is no change in the total assets, total liabilities, net assets, or owners' equity of the parent company as a result of the acquisition. However, if you look at the consolidated balance sheet drawn up immediately after the acquisition, it appears that the assets and liabilities have increased (although net assets and owners' equity remain unchanged). In fact, the consolidated balance sheet is not comparable with balance sheets of the Parent Company in previous periods. As we have seen, the apparent increase in assets and liabilities is due to the consolidation of statements for two companies—it does not correspond to any actual change in the assets and liabilities of the Parent Company.

The consolidated balance sheet may be useful as a summary of the assets and liabilities under the managerial control of the Parent Company. However, it is not useful as a way of evaluating the claims of owners and creditors against assets of the Parent Company.

Case 3: Preparation of working papers for consolidated financial statements one year after date of acquisition of subsidiary by parent. One year after the acquisition in case 1 (Parent Company acquires 100 percent of Subsidiary Company stock for book value of $150,000), working papers are to be prepared for consolidated statements of income, retained earnings, and financial position. The first two columns of Exhibit 19-6 summarize the statements of the two separate corporations as of the date of the consolidated statements. The following list summarizes transactions between the Parent Company and the Subsidiary Company during 19_0 that require special treatment. (The note to Exhibit 19-6 explains various eliminations.)

1. The Parent Company sold $5,000 of merchandise to the Subsidiary Company during 19_0. From the consolidation point of view, these intercompany purchases and sales are "internal" and must be eliminated from the consolidated income statement.
2. At the end of 19_0, the Subsidiary Company owes the Parent Company $3,000 for purchases made during the year. These intercompany receivables and payables must be eliminated from the consolidated balance sheet.
3. The Subsidiary Company paid a $7,000 dividend during the year. All of this dividend was received by the Parent Company and was recorded as dividend income. The dividend income must be eliminated from the income statement, and the dividend eliminated from dividends paid on the retained earnings statement, to eliminate the effects of the intercompany transaction.
4. The ending inventory of the Subsidiary Company contained inventory purchased from the Parent Company. The Subsidiary Company has listed this inventory at

Exhibit 19-5 Consolidated balance sheet for case 2

PARENT COMPANY AND SUBSIDIARY COMPANY

Consolidated Statement of Financial Position
January 1, 19_0

Assets		Liabilities	
Cash	$150,000	Liabilities	$150,000
Excess of cost over book value	25,000	Minority interest in Subsidiary Company	15,000
Other assets	240,000		
		Stockholders' Equity	
		Capital stock	175,000
		Retained earnings	75,000
Total assets	$415,000	Total liabilities and stockholders' equity	$415,000

Exhibit 19-6 Work sheet for consolidated statements (case 3)

PARENT COMPANY AND SUBSIDIARY COMPANY

Consolidated Working Papers
For the Year Ended December 31, 19_0

	Parent Company	Subsidiary Company	Eliminations Debits	Eliminations Credits	Consolidation
Income Statement					
Sales	30,000	20,000	C 5,000		45,000
Dividend income from S. Co.	7,000	—	B 7,000		—
Inventory, Dec. 31, 19_0	6,000	9,000	D 1,000		14,000
Total credits (*a*)	43,000	29,000			59,000
Inventory, Jan. 1, 19_0	5,000	8,000			13,000
Purchases	5,000	10,000		C 5,000	10,000
Expenses	5,000	4,000			9,000
Total debits (*b*)	15,000	22,000			32,000
Net income (*a* − *b* = *c*)	28,000	7,000	13,000	5,000	27,000
Retained Earnings					
Retained earnings, Jan. 1, 19_0	75,000	50,000	A 50,000		75,000
Net income (*c*)	28,000	7,000	13,000	5,000	27,000
Total credits	103,000	57,000	63,000	5,000	102,000
Less: Dividends paid	3,000	7,000		B 7,000	3,000
Retained earnings, Dec. 31, 19_0 (*d*)	100,000	50,000	63,000	12,000	99,000
Balance Sheet					
Cash	106,000	60,000			166,000
Accounts receivable	20,000	—		E 3,000	17,000
Inventory, Dec. 31, 19_0	6,000	9,000		D 1,000	14,000
Investment in subsidiary	150,000	—		A 150,000	—
Other assets	45,000	192,000			237,000
Total assets	327,000	261,000		154,000	434,000
Accounts payable	8,000	5,000	E 3,000		10,000
Other liabilities	44,000	106,000			150,000
Capital stock	175,000	100,000	A 100,000		175,000
Retained earnings (*d*)	100,000	50,000	63,000	12,000	99,000
Total liabilities and stockholders' equity	327,000	261,000	166,000	166,000	434,000

NOTE: Entries in the Eliminations columns represent the following "internal" interactions.

A Offsetting of subsidiary's Capital Stock and Retained Earnings against parent's Investment in Subsidiary account.

B Intercompany dividends of $1,000.

C Intercompany purchases and sales of $5,000.

D Intercompany profit in ending inventory of $1,000.

E Intercompany receivable and payable of $3,000.

its acquisition cost, which includes $1,000 profit made by the Parent Company on the sale of merchandise to its subsidiary. From the consolidation viewpoint, the ending inventory is overstated by $1,000, because the profit has not been realized by a sale to a firm outside the affiliation. The $1,000 intercompany profit must be eliminated from the ending inventory shown in the income statement and in the balance sheet.

In addition to these eliminations reflecting intercompany transactions during the year, the owners' equity eliminations shown in case 1 also must be made on the new work sheet. Exhibit 19-6 shows work sheets for all three statements. The consolidated statements can now be prepared from the amounts in the Consolidation column.

Compare the consolidated balances with those shown for the separate companies on the work sheet. Note the impacts of the consolidation accounting treatment on the various statements. Because of the consolidated retained earnings for the year, note that the stockholders' equity in the consolidated balance sheet is no longer equal to the stockholders' equity of the Parent Company alone.

LIMITATIONS OF CONSOLIDATED STATEMENTS

The principal limitation of consolidated financial statements is their failure to report distinct information about the assets, liabilities, revenues, and expenses of the separate companies making up the consolidation. The financial positions and results of operations of subsidiaries cannot be read from consolidated financial statements.

The consolidated assets do not represent resources available to satisfy the claims of the consolidated liabilities and stockholders' equity. Only the separate assets of each individual corporation can be used to satisfy the claims of creditors and owners against that particular corporation.

Ratio analyses derived from consolidated statements are of questionable value, because the items included in the ratios reflect the varied resources and activities of a group of companies. Also, the financial position of weak or strong subsidiaries (or the parent) can be concealed when consolidated statements are prepared. A loss operation may be counterbalanced by a profitable one.

In some cases, it may be useful to issue statements for the parent company alone, in addition to the consolidated statements, in order to give adequate information about the position of creditors and stockholders of the parent company. Another possible solution is to issue statements similar to the work sheets shown in this section—with separate columns for the companies making up the consolidation, as well as a column showing the consolidated balances.

Equity method of accounting for investments in common stock

In some cases, a subsidiary company may be excluded from the consolidated financial statements of an affiliated group of corporations—usually because the nature of its operations is very different from that of the remainder of the consolidation. When the parent company has a sizable interest in such a subsidiary, the

Investment in Subsidiary account for the unconsolidated subsidiary should be reported in the consolidated statements according to the equity method of accounting. The equity method provides investors with significant information in that it reflects the underlying nature of their investment in a subsidiary. The equity method is also used when an investor exercises significant influence over an investee even though he does not own a majority of the stock of the investee.

The AICPA Accounting Principles Board made the following comments about the use of the equity method in accounting for investments in common stock.

> The Board concludes that the equity method of accounting for an investment in common stock should also be followed by an investor whose investment in voting stock gives it the ability to exercise significant influence over operating and financial policies of an investee even though the investor holds 50% or less of the voting stock. . . . In order to achieve a reasonable degree of uniformity in application, the Board concludes that an investment (direct or indirect) of 20% or more of the voting stock of an investee should lead to a presumption that in the absence of evidence to the contrary an investor has the ability to exercise significant influence over an investee. . . . When the equity method is appropriate, it should be applied in consolidated financial statements and in parent-company financial statements prepared for issuance to stockholders as the financial statements of the primary reporting entity.[1]

The *equity method* of accounting for investments in common stock of subsidiaries requires that

1. the investor initially record the investment at cost, and
2. the investor adjust the Investment account to recognize the investor's share of earnings, losses, and dividends of the subsidiary after the date of acquisition.

The equity method of accounting for investments in common stock can be contrasted to the *cost method,* under which the investment is recorded at cost and dividends received from the subsidiary are recognized as income. The cost method is used when the equity method is not applicable. Exhibit 19-7 compares the journal entries used under the two methods to record the following transactions.

Exhibit 19-7 Journal entries under equity and cost methods

Transaction	Equity Method			Cost Method		
1	Investment in Subsidiary	100,000		Investment in Subsidiary	100,000	
	Cash		100,000	Cash		100,000
2	Investment in Subsidiary	9,000		*(No Entry)*		
	Subsidiary Income		9,000			
3	Cash	4,500		Cash	4,500	
	Investment in Subsidiary		4,500	Dividend Income		4,500

1. Accounting Principles Board, *Opinion No. 18: The Equity Method of Accounting for Investments in Common Stock* (New York: American Institute of Certified Public Accountants, 1971), para. 17.

1. The Parent Company purchases a 90 percent interest in the Subsidiary Company for $100,000 cash.
2. A year after the acquisition, the Subsidiary Company reports net income for the year of $10,000. The net assets of the subsidiary have increased as a result of the subsidiary's profit-making activities. Under the equity method, the Parent Company's Investment account is increased to reflect this economic reality and to recognize a share of the subsidiary's income.
3. The Subsidiary Company pays a $5,000 dividend. This payment reduces the net assets of the Subsidiary Company by $5,000. Under the equity method, the Parent Company's Investment account is reduced to reflect this economic reality. Under the cost method, the dividend income is recognized.

Exhibit 19-8 compares the relevant accounts on the books of the Parent Company, relating to its investment in the Subsidiary Company, as they appear under the equity method and the cost method after posting of the preceding transactions.

Purchase versus pooling of interests

Business acquisitions, mergers, and consolidations are common occurrences in the modern business world. Basically, a business combination results from efforts to improve the earnings of the enterprise that survives or arises from the combination. Business combinations assume a variety of forms, including mergers, consolidations, and acquisitions (Exhibit 19-9).

1. A *merger* occurs when one company acquires another. The acquired company is dissolved as a separate legal entity; its assets and liabilities become part of the legal assets and liabilities of the acquiring company. The only surviving company is the one that did the acquiring.
2. A *consolidation* occurs when a new corporation is formed for the purpose of acquiring the net assets of two or more existing companies. All of the preexisting companies in the group are dissolved as legal entities; the only surviving company is the one that was newly formed to effect the combination.
3. An *acquisition* is a combination that results from an exchange of ownership securities in the acquiring company for ownership interest in the acquired com-

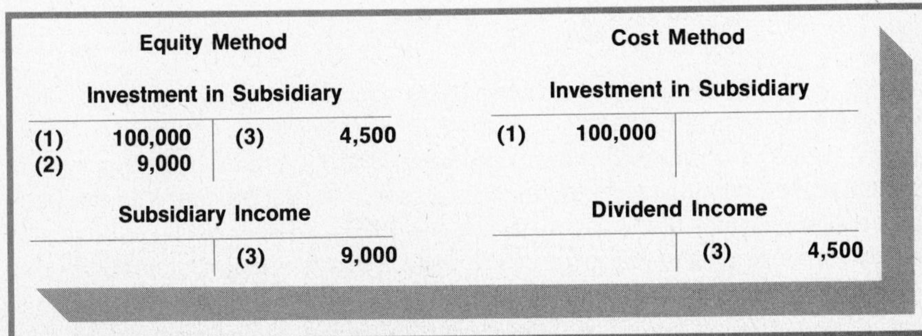

Equity Method

Investment in Subsidiary

	Debit		Credit
(1)	100,000	(3)	4,500
(2)	9,000		

Subsidiary Income

	Debit		Credit
		(3)	9,000

Cost Method

Investment in Subsidiary

	Debit		Credit
(1)	100,000		

Dividend Income

	Debit		Credit
		(3)	4,500

Exhibit 19-8
Ledger accounts under equity and cost methods

Exhibit 19-9
Types of business combinations

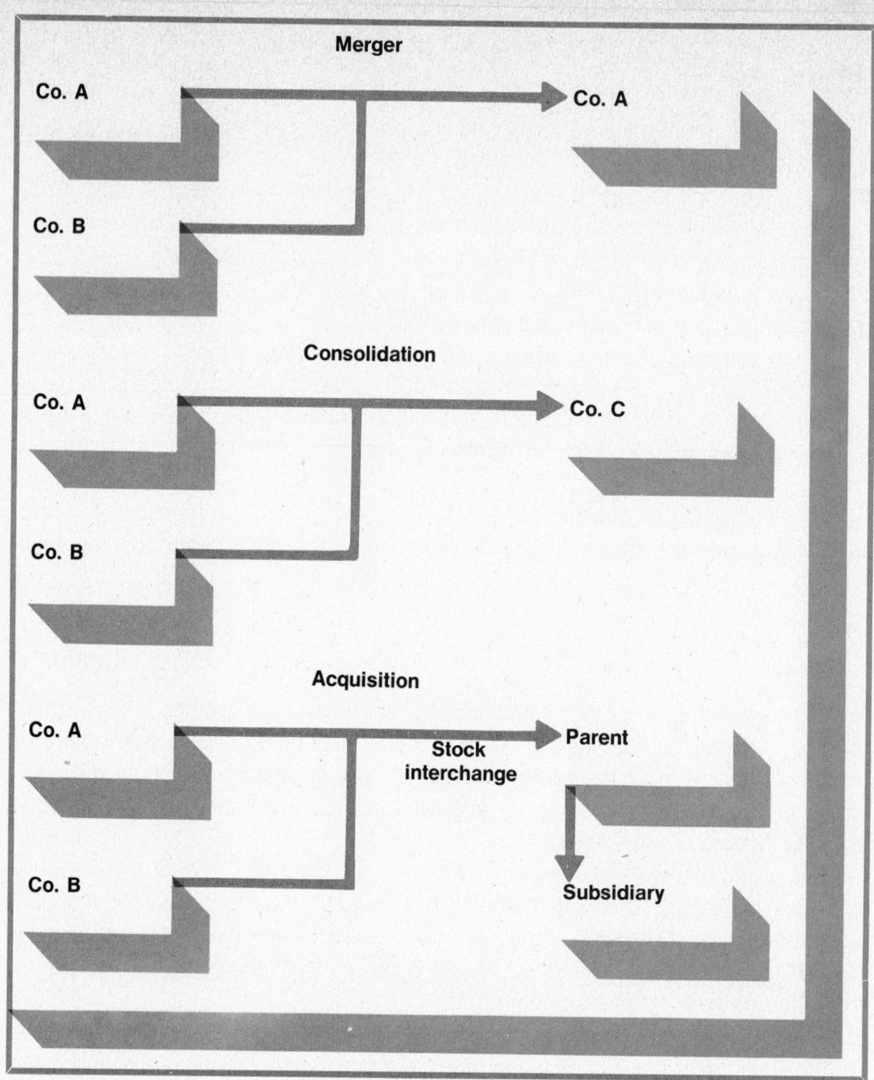

pany. After the acquisition, the acquired company survives as a legal entity, but with most of its voting stock owned by the acquiring (parent) company. The former stockholders of the acquired company have received shares of stock in the parent company as compensation for the purchase of their ownership interest in the acquired company.

In the United States, business combinations occurred in great numbers during three major periods: 1895 to 1908, 1925 to 1929, and 1955 to the early 1970s. During the first period of business combinations, some 5,000 companies were combined into 300, as the great banking houses built gigantic "trusts" to dominate the traditional major industries of the nation. During the 1920s, another period of economic success brought another wave of combinations, this time led by the businesses themselves through stock issues and exchanges. After this period of combinations, almost every significant industry in the United States was dominated by a few large companies that made the great majority of sales in that industry. In recent years, most combinations have involved the affiliation of widely diversified types of businesses having few production or marketing similarities. Such combinations have been popularly called conglomerates.

As an indication of the extent of this trend toward business combinations, we might note, for example, that the 200 largest manufacturing corporations at the end of the 1960s controlled a share of manufacturing assets equal to that controlled by the 1,000 largest thirty years earlier. Or that, by 1973, only twenty corporations accounted for one-fifth of all sales of goods and services in the nation.

ACCOUNTING FOR BUSINESS COMBINATIONS

Much controversy has arisen in the accounting profession about how to account for business combinations. Two major and conflicting approaches have developed: "pooling of interests" and "purchase." The APB has taken the following position about accounting for business combinations.

> The Board concludes that the purchase method and the pooling of interests method are both acceptable in accounting for business combinations, although not as alternatives in accounting for the same business combination. A business combination which meets specified conditions requires accounting by the pooling of interests method. A new basis of accounting is not permitted for a combination that meets the specified conditions, and the assets and liabilities of the combining companies are combined at their recorded amounts. All other business combinations should be accounted for as an acquisition of one or more companies by a corporation. The cost to an acquiring corporation of an entire acquired company should be determined by the principles of accounting for the acquisition of an asset. That cost should then be allocated to the identifiable individual assets acquired and liabilities assumed based on their fair values; the unallocated cost should be recorded as goodwill.[2]

The following two cases illustrate the two methods of accounting for combinations.

Case 4: Business combination treated as a pooling of interests. The Shark Company proposes to issue 2,000 additional shares of its common stock in exchange for the assets and liabilities of the Minnow Corporation, which has 2,000 shares of stock outstanding. The Minnow Corporation will distribute the shares of Shark Company stock to its stockholders, with one share of Shark stock being exchanged for each share of Minnow stock. The Minnow Corporation will then dissolve. This plan of combination meets the criteria for a pooling of interests. Exhibit 19-10 shows the balance sheets of the two corporations immediately prior to the merger on December 31, 19_0.

When the pooling of interests method is used, the acquired assets and liabilities are recorded on the books of the acquiring company at the valuations carried in the books of the acquired firm(s). The Retained Earnings account of the acquired corporation can be carried forward to the books of the acquiring company. The following journal entry summarizes the business combination on the books of the Shark Company.

2. Accounting Principles Board, ***Opinion No. 16: Business Combinations*** (New York: American Institute of Certified Public Accountants, 1970), para. 8.

Exhibit 19-10 **Balance sheets of two companies before combination (case 4)**

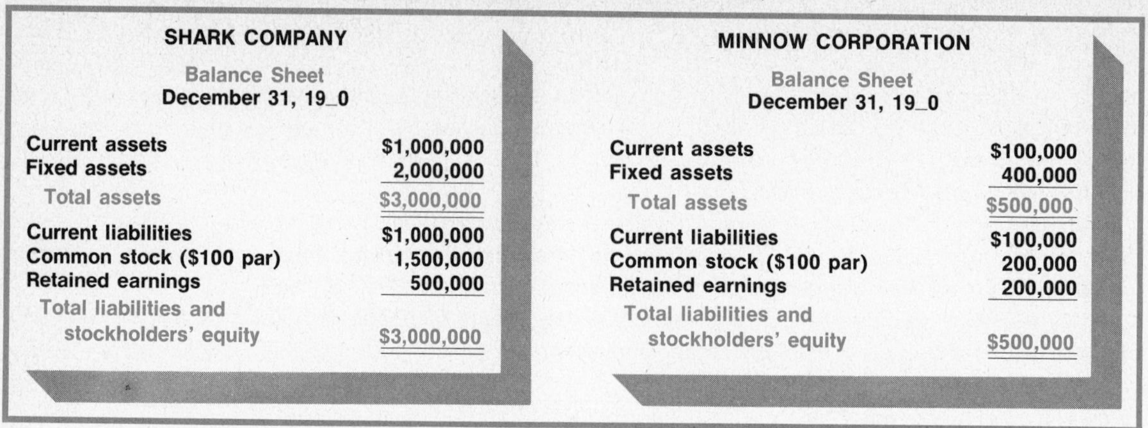

SHARK COMPANY
Balance Sheet
December 31, 19_0

Current assets	$1,000,000
Fixed assets	2,000,000
Total assets	$3,000,000
Current liabilities	$1,000,000
Common stock ($100 par)	1,500,000
Retained earnings	500,000
Total liabilities and stockholders' equity	$3,000,000

MINNOW CORPORATION
Balance Sheet
December 31, 19_0

Current assets	$100,000
Fixed assets	400,000
Total assets	$500,000
Current liabilities	$100,000
Common stock ($100 par)	200,000
Retained earnings	200,000
Total liabilities and stockholders' equity	$500,000

Current Assets	100,000	
Fixed Assets	400,000	
Current Liabilities		100,000
Common Stock [Shark Co.]		200,000
Retained Earnings		200,000

Exhibit 19-11 shows the balance sheet of the Shark Company just after the pooling of interests.

On the income statement of the acquiring company, the revenue and expenses of the acquired company are carried forward in the year of acquisition, even though recognized prior to acquisition. If the combination were treated as a purchase, precombination revenue and expenses of the acquired company could not be carried forward and combined with those of the acquiring entity.

Two major abuses have been attributed to conglomerates using the pooling of interests method of accounting for acquisitions. These abuses were, to some extent, the basis for the issuance of *APB Opinion No. 16* quoted earlier. One of the so-called abuses was the creation of "instant earnings," which result from sale of assets whose carrying value is lower than realizable value. A firm could acquire another firm with assets recorded at their former (historical) costs. If the acquired firm had followed conservative accounting practices, these assets would probably have

Exhibit 19-11 **Balance sheet of acquiring company just after pooling of interests**

SHARK COMPANY
Balance Sheet
December 31, 19_0

Current assets	$1,100,000
Fixed assets	2,400,000
Total assets	$3,500,000
Current liabilities	$1,100,000
Common stock $100 par)	1,700,000
Retained earnings	700,000
Total liabilities and stockholders' equity	$3,500,000

market value higher than their book value. The acquiring firm can then dispose of the assets after acquisition, realizing gains on the sale for the current period, although the "gains" actually represent unrecorded profits earned in earlier periods by the acquired company.

A second abuse is "funny money." This term refers to a firm's equity securities used as consideration for an acquisition. In acquiring businesses, the parent companies have issued strange, new varieties of equity and debt instruments to exchange for the acquired company's stock. When the acquiring company issues new stock to exchange for the ownership interest of the acquired company, the acquiring company is "manufacturing money"; hence the term, "funny money."

Case 5: Business combination treated as a purchase. Suppose that all circumstances are the same as in case 4, except that the transaction cannot be treated as a pooling of interests. Instead, the purchase method is to be used to account for the combination. The current assets and the fixed assets of the Minnow Corporation have fair market values of $90,000 and $350,000, respectively. The current market value of the Shark Company stock being traded for the Minnow stock is $400,000.

In a purchase transaction, the acquired assets and liabilities are recorded at their fair market values. The stock given in exchange for the net assets is recorded at its fair market value. Goodwill may be recorded if the fair market value of the stock given up exceeds the fair market value of the net assets acquired. The following entry summarizes the combination on the books of the Shark Company, using the purchase method.

Current Assets	90,000	
Fixed Assets	350,000	
Goodwill	60,000	
Current Liabilities		100,000
Common Stock [Shark Co.]		200,000
Capital in Excess of Par Value		200,000

Exhibit 19-12 shows the balance sheet of the Shark Company immediately after the purchase. Note the differences between the balance sheets in Exhibits 19-11 and

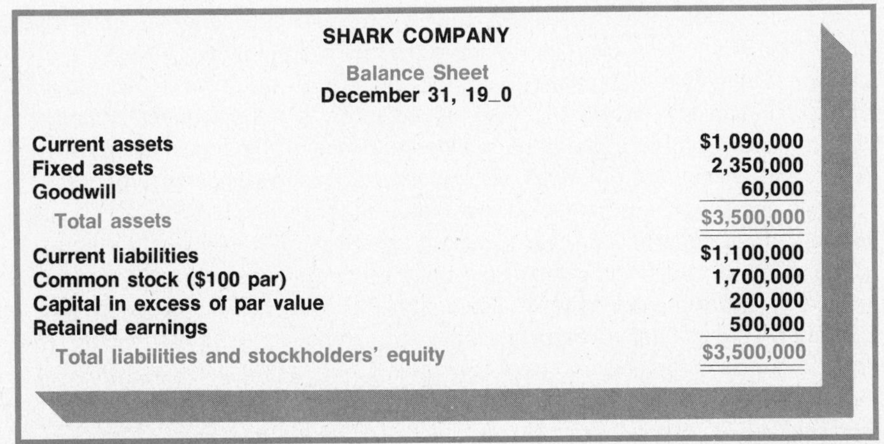

SHARK COMPANY
Balance Sheet
December 31, 19_0

Current assets	**$1,090,000**
Fixed assets	**2,350,000**
Goodwill	**60,000**
Total assets	$3,500,000
Current liabilities	**$1,100,000**
Common stock ($100 par)	**1,700,000**
Capital in excess of par value	**200,000**
Retained earnings	**500,000**
Total liabilities and stockholders' equity	$3,500,000

Exhibit 19-12
Balance sheet of acquiring company just after purchase (case 5)

19-12, showing the different impacts of the two methods of accounting for the combination.

The acquired assets are listed at their current market values, so there is no opportunity to create "instant earnings" through sale of these assets. Goodwill is reported as an intangible asset (the cost in excess of market value paid for the net assets of the Minnow Corporation). This cost will be amortized by the straight-line method over a period of time not to exceed forty years. Because the amortization of goodwill results in an expense reported on future income statements, many businessmen have objected to the purchase method of recording business combinations.

Summary

The first major topic discussed in this chapter is that of consolidated statements. Consolidated statements show a summation of the assets, liabilities, revenue, and expenses of the corporations that make up an affiliation. Consolidated statements show the combined financial position and results of operations of members of the consolidation that are under the financial and managerial control of the parent company. Transactions between members of the affiliation are eliminated from the consolidated statements. The chapter illustrates work sheet procedures for preparing consolidated statements.

The second topic that is discussed is the equity method of accounting for an investment in common stock. This method should be used to account for an investment in a subsidiary company that is excluded from consolidated statements of an affiliated group of corporations, or when a significant investor-investee relationship exists. Under the equity method of accounting, the investment in the subsidiary is recorded initially at cost. Subsequently, the Investment account is adjusted to recognize the investor's share of earnings, losses, and dividends of the subsidiary after the date of acquisition.

The third topic deals with the purchase and the pooling of interests methods of accounting for business combinations. This problem requires a careful analysis of the form of the transaction versus the substance thereof. When a business combination is treated as a purchase, the assets of the acquired company are recorded at their fair market value. None of the retained earnings of the acquired company at date of acquisition are reported as retained earnings of the acquiring or surviving corporation. Also, none of the net income of the acquired company earned prior to the date of acquisition is combined with that of the acquiring or surviving company in the year of combination. In a pooling of interests, the assets of the acquired company are recorded at their historical costs as shown in the books of the acquired company. Retained earnings of the acquired company at date of acquisition can be carried forward as retained earnings of the acquiring or surviving corporation. Also, the net income of the acquired company earned prior to the date of acquisition can be combined with that of the acquiring or surviving company in the year of the combination.

Questions

1. What is a consolidation? What are consolidated statements? When should consolidated statements be prepared?

2. Consolidated statements are prepared primarily for the benefit of what group of users?

3. Give several reasons why one company might acquire the stock of another company.

4. Distinguish between managerial control and financial control as related to consolidations. Are consolidated statements justified whenever one company holds a controlling interest (for example, 90 percent of voting stock) in another company?

5. Why are intercompany transactions (such as purchases, sales, and dividends) eliminated in the preparation of consolidated statements?

6. Company P owns 90 percent of the voting stock of Company S. During the year 19_1, Company P purchases $10,000 of merchandise from Company S; this merchandise cost Company S $8,000. At the end of the year, Company P has in its ending inventory $6,000 of merchandise purchased from Company S.
Required: In preparing consolidated working papers, how much should be eliminated for the following items?
a. Intercompany purchases and sales.
b. Ending inventory of Company P.
c. Intercompany profit in ending inventory.

7. In preparing consolidated statements, what subsidiary accounts are eliminated along with the parent's Investment in Subsidiary account? Explain.

8. What is meant by minority interest? On a consolidated statement of financial position, how is minority interest shown?

9. What is meant by the excess of cost of an investment in a subsidiary over its book value? How does this excess arise? Where is it reported on a consolidated balance sheet?

10. Distinguish between the equity method and the cost method of accounting for investments in subsidiaries. Are the consolidated statements prepared when the equity method is used in accounting for an investment identical with the consolidated statements prepared when the cost method is used?

11. Distinguish between a purchase and a pooling of interests. Explain the accounting treatment used with each method.

12. Should the cost method or the equity method be used for accounting for the investments in the following situations:
a. A company acquired 30 percent of the common stock of an investee company and exercises considerable influence in the operations of the company.
b. A company acquired 60 percent of the common stock of a subsidiary and exercises managerial control over the company.
c. A company acquired 80 percent of the preferred stock of another company.
d. A company acquired 15 percent of the outstanding common stock of another company.

13. A company acquired 90 percent of the common stock of a subsidiary when the retained earnings of the subsidiary were $100,000. At the present time, the retained earnings of the subsidiary are $800,000. What part of the retained earnings of the subsidiary would be considered consolidated retained earnings in a consolidated balance sheet?

14. A Parent Company made a $100,000 sale to a 90 percent-owned subsidiary. The Parent Company's profit on the sale was $10,000. The subsidiary sold one-half of the merchandise purchased from the Parent Company. On a consolidated income statement, how much of the profit made by the Parent Company would be included in consolidated net income? When is intercompany profit considered realized for consolidated statement purposes?

Exercises

E19-1 (Acquisition of a subsidiary)

The Pine Company acquires stock of the Cone Company. Just before the acquisition, the books of the Cone Company show the following account balances: Common Stock $300,000; Paid-In Capital in Excess of Par Value $30,000; Retained Earnings $90,000. For each of the following cases, prepare the journal entry that would be required in the books of the P Company on the date of the acquisition and explain the working paper treatment of any amounts that might not be eliminated by the entry you make.

a. Pine Company acquires 100 percent of Cone Company's stock for $420,000.

b. Pine Company acquires 100 percent of Cone Company's stock for $450,000.

c. Pine Company acquires 100 percent of Cone Company's stock for $400,000.

d. Pine Company acquires 90 percent of Cone Company's stock for $420,000.

E19-2 (Consolidation working papers)

Exhibit 19-13 shows account balances for the Pine Company and the Cone Company just after the Pine Company acquires the Cone Company. The Pine Company has a $12,000 accounts receivable claim against the Cone Company.

Exhibit 19-13
Account balances for Exercise E19-2

	Pine Co.	*Cone Co.*
Cash	$ 30,000	$300,000
Receivables	40,000	20,000
Investment in Subsidiary (90% ownership)	420,000	—
Other assets	20,000	100,000
Total assets	$510,000	$420,000
Liabilities	$ 80,000	$ 40,000
Capital Stock	300,000	250,000
Paid-In Capital in Excess of Par Value	40,000	50,000
Retained Earnings	90,000	80,000
Total liabilities and owners' equity	$510,000	$420,000

Required:

a. Prepare working papers for a consolidated balance sheet.
b. Prepare a consolidated balance sheet.
c. On the consolidated balance sheet, what is shown as consolidated capital stock? (Refer to the working paper.)
d. At date of acquisition, do any of the retained earnings of the subsidiary become a part of the consolidated retained earnings?

E19-3 (Consolidated income statement)

Exhibit 19-14 shows available data on December 31, 19_6, concerning a parent company (Pine Company) and its subsidiary (Cone Company). The Pine Company acquired all of the Cone Company's stock on January 1, 19_6. The following additional information is available.

a. During the year, the Pine Company purchased $8,000 of merchandise from the Cone Company.
b. On the intercompany sale of merchandise, Cone Company made a 10 percent profit. One-fourth of the inventory acquired by Pine Company is still unsold on December 31, 19_6.
c. Intercompany receivables and payables total $9,000.
d. The rent income reported by Pine Company is from the rental of a truck to Cone Company.

Required: Prepare working papers to facilitate preparation of a consolidated income statement.

E19-4 (Equity and cost methods)

The following data are available about Pine Company and its subsidiary, Cone Company.

Jan. 1	Pine Company acquired a 95 percent interest in Cone Company for $200,000.
Dec. 31	Cone Company declared a $30,000 dividend.
31	Cone Company reported a net income of $130,000 for the year.

Required: Journalize the above transactions for the Pine Company, assuming:

Income Statement for 19_6

	Pine Co.	*Cone Co.*
Sales	$200,000	$50,000
Dividend income from subsidiary	30,000	—
Rent income	15,000	—
Inventory, Dec. 31, 19_6	20,000	10,000
Total credits (*a*)	$265,000	$60,000
Inventory, Jan. 1, 19_5	$ 20,000	$ 8,000
Purchases	90,000	22,000
Expenses	80,000	20,000
Total debits (*b*)	$190,000	$50,000
Net income (*a* − *b*)	$ 75,000	$10,000

Exhibit 19-14
Income-statement data for Exercise E19-3

a. that the Pine Company uses the equity method of accounting for its investment in the subsidiary;

b. that the Pine Company uses the cost method of accounting for its investment in the subsidiary.

E19-5 (Pooling of interests; purchase)

The stockholders of two companies agree to a merger plan proposed by the directors of the two companies. The plan provides for the exchange of 1,800 shares of the Into Company's stock for all outstanding stock of the Leaving Company. Exhibit 19-15 shows financial data for the two companies just before the combination. The fair value of the Leaving Company's fixed assets is $200,000. The 1,800 shares of stock issued by the Into Company have a fair market value of $240,000.

Required:

a. Record the acquisition by the Into Company as a pooling of interests.

b. Record the acquisition as a purchase.

Problems

P19-1 (Consolidated statements)

Exhibit 19-16 shows income statements of the Parent Company and its subsidiary. The Parent Company several years ago acquired 90 percent of the stock of the Subsidiary Company. The Subsidiary Company rents a build-

Exhibit 19-15
Financial data for Exercise E19-5

	Into Co.	Leaving Co.
Current assets	$110,000	$ 35,000
Fixed assets	300,000	160,000
Total assets	$410,000	$195,000
Current liabilities	$ 22,000	$ 10,000
Common stock ($100 par value)	200,000	160,000
Retained earnings	188,000	25,000
Total liabilities and owners' equity	$410,000	$195,000

Exhibit 19-16
Income statements for Problem P19-1

	Parent Co.	Subsidiary Co.
Sales	$140,000	$ 80,000
Dividend income	15,000	—
Interest revenue	15,000	—
Rent revenue	—	20,000
Total revenue (*a*)	$170,000	$100,000
Cost of goods sold	$ 50,000	$ 30,000
Expenses	70,000	40,000
Total expenses (*b*)	$120,000	$ 70,000
Net income (*a* − *b*)	$ 50,000	$ 30,000

ing to the Parent Company for $20,000 per year. The Subsidiary Company borrowed money from the Parent Company during the year; the interest payments associated with this loan amounted to $6,000. The Subsidiary Company sold $5,000 of goods to the Parent Company during the year; the Parent Company sold this inventory to another company.

Required:

a. Prepare working papers for a consolidated income statement. Use a format similar to that shown in Exhibit 19-17, but add a column labeled "Minority" after the elimination columns. Use this Minority column to record the minority interest in the net income of the subsidiary.

b. Prepare a formal consolidated income statement.

c. Give a description of the sources of consolidated net income.

P19-2 (Consolidated income statement)

Complete the working papers for the consolidated income statement of the Parent Company and the Subsidiary Company for the year. The following information is available.

a. The Parent Company sold merchandise costing $10,000 to the Subsidiary Company during the year. The sales price was $15,000.

b. The Subsidiary Company paid $5,000 rent to the Parent Company during the year.

c. The Parent Company paid the Subsidiary Company $8,000 interest expense during the year.

d. The Subsidiary Company owed the Parent Company $3,000 on account.

e. The Parent Company owns 90 percent of the common stock of the Subsidiary Company.

Exhibit 19-17 **Working papers for consolidated income statement**

Parent Company and Subsidiary Company
Date

	Parent Company	Subsidiary Company	Eliminations Dr.	Eliminations Cr.	Consolidated Income Statement
Net sales	100,000	75,000			
Other revenues	50,000	10,000			
Total	150,000	85,000			
Expenses:					
Cost of goods sold	40,000	15,000			
Operating expenses	50,000	20,000			
Total	90,000	35,000			
Net income	60,000	50,000			
Less Minority interest in net income of Subsidiary					
Consolidated net income					

P19-3 (Consolidated statements)

The financial statements of the Parent Company and its subsidiary at date of acquisition were as follows.

Assets	Parent	Subsidiary
Cash	$ 10,000	$ 5,000
Accounts receivable	20,000	15,000
Inventory	30,000	20,000
Intercompany receivable	5,000	
Investment in subsidiary	200,000	
Property and equipment	300,000	115,000
Patent		10,000
Total assets	$565,000	$200,000

Liabilities and Stockholders' Equity		
Accounts payable	$ 20,000	$ 10,000
Intercompany payables		5,000
Common stock, $10 par value	400,000	
Common stock, $5 par value		100,000
Paid in capital in excess of par	45,000	10,000
Retained earnings	100,000	40,000
Total	$565,000	$200,000

The Parent Company acquires 100 percent of the capital stock of the subsidiary. The assets of the subsidiary were understated by the following amounts:

Inventory	$10,000
Plant and equipment	30,000

The difference between the cost of the investment and book value of the subsidiary is attributed to the understatement of the two assets on the books of the subsidiary and unrecorded goodwill.

Required:

Prepare a consolidated balance sheet for the Parent Company and Subsidiary at the date of acquisition.

P19-4 (Consolidated statements)

Incomplete working papers for the Pants Company and its Subsidiary Company are shown as follows.

	Pants Company	Subsidiary Company	Eliminations	Consolidated
Income statement:				
Sales	$500,000	$100,000		
Cost of goods sold	200,000	50,000		
Interest expense		20,000		
Interest revenue	15,000			
Balance sheet:				
Accounts receivable	$125,000	$ 30,000		
Accounts payable	40,000	100,000		
Inventories	30,000	20,000		

The interest revenue reported on the Pants Company's income statement was from the Subsidiary Company. The Subsidiary Company owed the Pants Company $20,000 on account. Intercompany purchases and sales for the period totalled $35,000. Intercompany profit in ending inventory totalled $3,000. The Pants Company owned 100 percent of the stock of Subsidiary Company.

Required: Complete the partial consolidated working papers.

P19-5 (Equity and cost methods)

The following transactions relate to a situation where a Parent Company acquires an interest in a Subsidiary Company.

1. The Parent Company acquired 90% of the common stock of the Subsidiary Company for $120,000.
2. The Parent Company had net income of $250,000 for the year and the Subsidiary Company had net income of $100,000 for the year.
3. The Parent Company and the Subsidiary Company declared dividends of $100,000 and $50,000 respectively.
4. In the following year, the Parent Company had net income of $190,000 and the Subsidiary Company had a loss of $10,000.
5. The Parent Company and the Subsidiary Company declared dividends of $50,000 and $10,000 respectively.

Required:

a. Journalize transactions on the records of the Parent Company relating to its acquisition of the Subsidiary Company for the two years, assuming the Parent Company uses the equity method of accounting for its investment in the Subsidiary Company.
b. Refer to item a above. Journalize the transactions, assuming the Parent Company uses the cost method of accounting for its investment in the Subsidiary Company.

20 Reporting changes in financial position

Thus far we have examined three major financial statements: the balance sheet, the income statement, and the statement of owners' equity.

1. The balance sheet (or statement of financial position) presents data showing the economic resources, obligations, and residual interest of a company *as of a certain recent date.*
2. The income statement reports the results of operations *during the preceding accounting period* by summarizing the revenue and expense transactions of the period. It shows how the business transactions of the period created a net income (or net loss) that affect the owners' equity shown on the balance sheet for the end of the period.
3. The statement of owners' equity reports the results of equity capital transactions *during the preceding accounting period* by summarizing the changes in owners' equity that result from earnings (or losses), from dividend distributions or withdrawals by the owners, and from additional investments by the owners.[1]

1. The Accounting Principles Board of the AICPA recommends the presentation of three separate statements to account for changes in owners' equity during the period. "The income statement for a period presents the revenues, expenses, gains, losses, and net income (net loss) recognized during the period and thereby presents an indication in conformity with generally accepted accounting principles of the results of the enterprise's profit-directed activities during the period. . . . A statement of retained earnings presents net income (as shown in the income statement) and items such as dividends and adjustments of the net income of prior periods. A statement of other changes in owners' equity presents additional investments by owners, retirements of owners' interests (except for the part considered to be a distribution of earnings), and similar events." (*APB Accounting Principles* [New York: American Institute of Certified Public Accountants, 1973] paras, 1022.04 and 1022.05.)

The APB goes on to say that the statement of other changes in owners' equity can be replaced by notes to the other statements if such changes are simple and few in number. This is the procedure we have followed, and we have called our statement of retained earnings (combined with the statement of other changes in owners' equity) a "statement of owners' equity."

The statement of owners' equity and the income statement together act as links between the equity capital sections of two successive balance sheets. They show how business transactions and equity capital transactions during the period led to ***changes*** in the owners' equity from the end of one period to the end of the next.

An additional statement is needed to complete the link between successive balance sheets. Changes in the assets and liabilities sections of the balance sheet usually occur as the result of transactions not summarized in the income and owners' equity statements. This statement should summarize

1. changes in the assets and liabilities resulting from financing and investment transactions during the period, as well as those changes that were due to the changes in owners' equity reported on the other statements; and
2. the way in which the firm used its assets during the period (for example, to acquire other assets, to pay debts, to make distributions to owners, and so on).

The statement designed to report this information is called the ***statement of changes in financial position.*** This statement has only recently come to be generally accepted as a necessary part of the financial statements for a company. Therefore, it has existed in the past in a variety of slightly differing forms and under a variety of names:

1. statement of sources and uses (or application) of funds;
2. funds statement, or funds flow statement;
3. statement of funds provided and applied.

Form and content of the statement

The statement of changes in financial position is becoming an increasingly important financial statement. In 1971, the Accounting Principles Board made mandatory the presentation of such a statement along with statements reporting financial position and results of operations.

> The Board concludes that information concerning the financing and investing activities of a business enterprise and the changes in its financial position for a period is essential for financial statement users, particularly owners and creditors, in making economic decisions. When financial statements purporting to present both financial position (balance sheet) and results of operations (statement of income and retained earnings) are issued, a statement summarizing changes in financial position should also be presented as a basic financial statement for each period for which an income statement is presented.[2]

In the past, similar statements reporting the "sources and uses of funds" have interpreted the concept of ***funds*** in various ways:

2. Accounting Principles Board, ***Opinion No. 19: Reporting Changes in Financial Position*** (New York: American Institute of Certified Public Accountants, 1971), para. 7.

1. as cash only (see the Appendix to this chapter);
2. as working capital only (current assets less current liabilities);
3. as all financial resources arising from external business transactions, including funds arising from working capital items and those arising from financing and investing activities that involve only noncurrent items.

The Accounting Principles Board concluded that the third (and broadest) interpretation of funds should be used, and that the statement should be given a title reflecting this broad concept.

> The Board therefore recommends that the title be Statement of Changes in Financial Position (referred to below as "the Statement"). The Statement of each reporting entity should disclose all important aspects of its financing and investing activities regardless of whether cash or other elements of working capital are directly affected. For example, acquisitions of property by issuance of securities or in exchange for other property, and conversions of long-term debt or preferred stock to common stock, should be appropriately reflected in the Statement.[3]

This broad concept of funds provides a more comprehensive view of where the financial resources of the firm come from and how they were used during the period. The statement of changes in financial position may include significant items that would be omitted from a funds statement in which funds are regarded as only cash or only working cpaital.

A typical statement of changes in financial position has two major sections.

1. *Financial resources provided by:*
   Operations
   Extraordinary items
   Other sources
2. *Financial resources applied to:*
   Various items appropriate for the period

Exhibit 20-1 shows a typical statement of changes in financial position, accompanied by a schedule of changes in working capital (Exhibit 20-2) that gives further details about the flow of funds during the year.

Changes in financial resources

The changes during a period in the financial resources of a firm can be analyzed in terms of

1. changes that involve working capital; and
2. changes other than those that involve working capital.

3. *Op. cit.,* para. 8.

Exhibit 20-1 **A typical statement of changes in financial position in balance format**

X COMPANY

Statement of Changes in Financial Position
For the Year Ended December 31, 19_1

Financial resources provided by:		
Operations:		
Income before extraordinary item		$100,000
Extraordinary item:		
Loss from earthquake damage		200,000
Other sources:		
Issuance of bonds	$ 60,000	
Issuance of stock	40,000	100,000
Financial resources provided		$400,000
Financial resources applied to:		
Payment of dividends		$100,000
Purchase of equipment		225,000
Increase in working capital		75,000
Financial resources applied		$400,000

X COMPANY

Schedule of Changes in Working Capital
For Years 19_1 and 19_2

	Dec. 31, 19_1	Dec. 31, 19_2	Working Capital Increase (Decrease)
Cash	$100,000	$170,000	$70,000
Accounts receivable	90,000	50,000	(40,000)
Inventory	130,000	150,000	20,000
Accounts payable	$100,000)	(125,000)	(25,000)
Notes payable	(150,000)	(100,000)	50,000
Working capital	$ 70,000	$145,000	$75,000

Exhibit 20-2
A schedule of changes in working capital accompanying Exhibit 20-1

We now examine the first category of changes in financial position; the second category of changes is discussed later in this chapter.

WORKING CAPITAL

Working capital is defined as the excess of current assets over current liabilities. Because working capital is a basic measure of a firm's liquidity, the business community is interested in knowing the causes of changes in working capital from period to period. Therefore, a statement that reports the flow of working capital and sets forth the changes in working capital represents an important addition to the list of financial statements. The statement of changes in financial position summarizes the changes in working capital (see Exhibit 20-1). A supplementary schedule should be used to give more details about these changes (Exhibit 20-2). Exhibit 20-3 shows an alternate format for a statement of changes in financial position that expresses the change in working capital as the difference between financial resources provided and financial resources applied.

Typical sources and uses of financial resources involving working capital include the following (also see Exhibit 20-4).

Exhibit 20-3 **An alternate format for a statement of changes in financial position**

X COMPANY

Statement of Changes in Financial Position
For the Year Ended December 31, 19_1

Financial resources provided by:		
Operations:		
Net income for the year before extraordinary item		**$100,000**
Extraordinary item:		
Loss from earthquake damage		**200,000**
Other sources:		
Insurance of bonds	**$ 60,000**	
Issuance of stock	**40,000**	**100,000**
Financial resources provided		**$400,000**
Financial resources applied to:		
Payment of dividends	**$100,000**	
Purchase of equipment	**225,000**	
Financial resources applied		**325,000**
Increase in working capital		**$ 75,000**

1. Sources of working capital:
   a. Net income (that is, profitable operations);
   b. Disposal of noncurrent assets:
      (1) sale of long-term investments,
      (2) sale of property, plant, and equipment,
      (3) sale of intangible assets;
   c. Long-term financing:
      (1) long-term borrowing (loans, notes, bonds),
      (2) issuance of common and preferred stock;
2. Uses (application) of working capital:
   a. Net loss from operations;
   b. Acquisition of noncurrent assets:
      (1) purchase of long-term investments,
      (2) purchase of property, plant, and equipment,
      (3) purchase of intangible assets;
   c. Payment of long-term debt;
   d. Reduction in stockholders' equity:
      (1) retirement of common and preferred stock;
      (2) payment of cash dividends.

We now look at some of the changes in financial position that result from working-capital transactions, using as illustrations some specific transactions presented in journal form.

Suppose that a firm issues its common stock for cash. Because cash is a current asset, working capital increases when cash increases. The other part of the transaction involves a noncurrent account. Therefore, working capital has been provided by this transaction.

Cash [a current account]	XXX	
Common Stock [a noncurrent account]		XXX
To record issuance of stock.		

If a firm purchases land for cash, working capital decreases. Cash, a current asset, decreases, while the other part of the transaction involves a noncurrent account. Therefore, working capital has been used in this transaction.

Land [a noncurrent account]	XXX	
Cash [a current account]		XXX
To record purchase of land.		

Not all transactions involving current accounts change the working capital of the firm. For example, the collection of an account receivable represents an increase in cash and a decrease in accounts receivable; this is an exchange of one current asset for another. The net impact of this transaction on working capital is zero.

Cash [a current account]	XXX	
Accounts Receivable [a current account]		XXX
To record collection of an account.		

What about short-term borrowing from a bank? This involves an increase in a

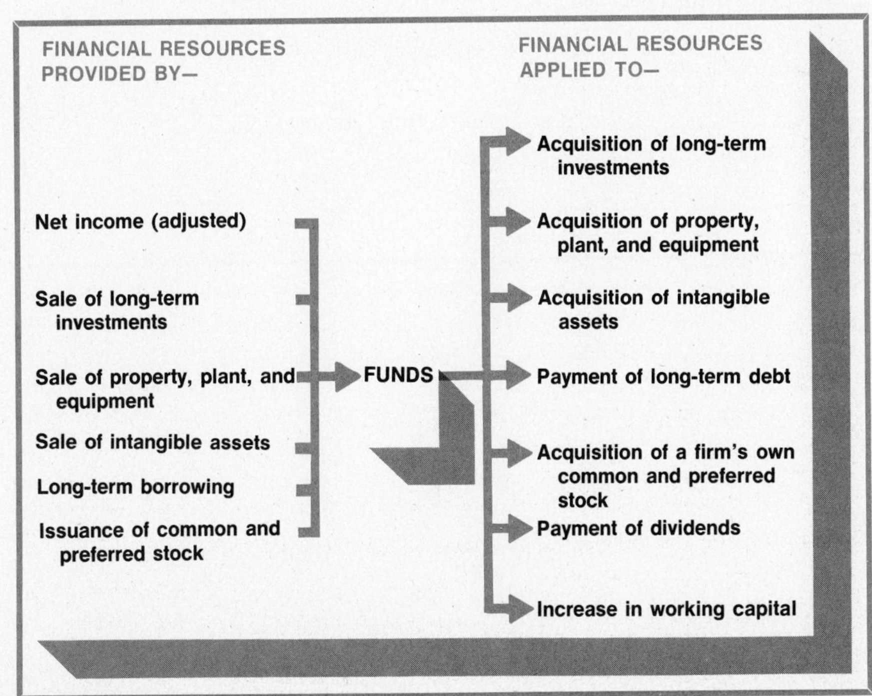

Exhibit 20-4
Visualization of the flow of funds

current asset (cash) and an offsetting increase in a current liability (notes payable). Again, the transaction causes no change in working capital.

Cash [a current account]	XXX	
Notes Payable [a current account]		XXX
To record cash borrowed from bank.		

From the preceding examples, we can derive three basic rules that assist us in preparing a statement of changes in financial position.

Rule 1. A transaction involving a change in working capital will have a combination of a current account and a noncurrent account. For example:

Machinery [a noncurrent account]	XXX	
Cash [a current account]		XXX
To record purchase of machinery.		

Rule 2. A transaction involving only current accounts does not change working capital. For example:

Accounts Payable [a current account]	XXX	
Cash [a current account]		XXX
To record payment of current debt.		

Rule 3. A transaction involving noncurrent accounts only does not involve working capital. (Such a transaction may have impact on total financial resources, and therefore may be reported on the statement of changes in financial position; this matter is discussed later in the chapter.)

Land [a noncurrent account]	XXX	
Mortgage Payable [a noncurrent account]		XXX
To record acquisition of land through assumption of a mortgage.		

Exhibit 20-5 shows a matrix summarizing the rules and indicating whether a particular transaction has impact on working capital.

Working papers for developing the statement

We now develop working-paper techniques that will assist us in preparation of a statement of changes in financial position. To begin this analysis, we need comparative statements of financial position. Exhibit 20-6 shows a comparative statement of the Resource Company indicating its resources at the ends of the years 19_1 and 19_2. This comparative statement shows that the working capital of the firm increased by $40,000 during 19_2.

What caused the change in working capital? The working-capital accounts (current assets and current liabilities) increased by $40,000.[4] Therefore, the noncurrent accounts (intangible and fixed assets, long-term liabilities, and owners' equity) must

4. In Exhibit 20-6, current assets increased by $35,000 and current liabilities decreased by $5,000 during the year. Working capital increased by $40,000. Recall that:
Current assets − Current liabilities = Working capital;
$35,000 − (− $5,000) = $40,000.

DEBIT ENTRY	CREDIT ENTRY	
	Current Account	Noncurrent Account
Current Account	No Impact	Impact
Noncurrent Account	Impact	No Impact

Exhibit 20-5
Summary of rules indicating whether a transaction has an impact on working capital

RESOURCE COMPANY

Statement of Financial Position
For the Years Ended December 31, 19_1 and 19_2

	19_2	19_1	Increase (Decrease)
Current assets:			
Cash	$ 35,000	$ 10,000	$25,000
Accounts receivable	20,000	18,000	2,000
Inventory	40,000	32,000	8,000
Total current assets	$ 95,000	$ 60,000	$35,000
Less: Current liabilities:			
Accounts payable	$ 10,000	$ 15,000	$ (5,000)
Taxes payable	25,000	25,000	—
Total current liabilities	$ 35,000	$ 40,000	$ (5,000)
Working capital (current assets less current liabilities)	$ 60,000	$ 20,000	$40,000
Property, plant, and equipment:			
Land	90,000	80,000	10,000
Building	100,000	100,000	—
Less: Accumulated depreciation	(50,000)	(40,000)	(10,000)
Total gross capital	$200,000	$160,000	$40,000
Less: Long-term liabilities:			
Bonds payable	(60,000)	(40,000)	20,000
Net assets	$140,000	$120,000	$20,000
Owners' equity:			
Common stock, par value $100	$100,000	$ 90,000	$10,000
Capital in excess of par value	15,000	10,000	5,000
Retained earnings	25,000	20,000	5,000
Total owners' equity	$140,000	$120,000	$20,000

Exhibit 20-6 **A comparative statement of financial position**

also have changed by $40,000. Otherwise the statements would not balance. Hence we look to the noncurrent accounts to find an explanation of the changes in the current accounts (in working capital).

To prepare working papers to examine the causes of these changes, we use a T account approach (developed by Professor William J. Vatter). This technique involves the following steps.

Step 1. Obtain a comparative statement of financial position for two consecutive years (or use two successive balance sheets), and calculate the change in each account between the two years (see Exhibit 20-6).

Step 2. Set up a T account for working capital (Exhibit 20-7). In this T account,

Exhibit 20-7
T account for working capital

Working Capital	
40,000	
From operations:	**Uses:**
From extraordinary items:	
From other sources:	

set up three sections on the *debit side,* in which *sources* of working capital will be recorded:

a. from operations;
b. from extraordinary items;
c. from other sources.

On the *credit side* of this account, set up a section called *Uses* in which the applications of working capital will be recorded.

Insert the total change in working capital in the box heading on the appropriate side of the account (an increase in working capital represents an increase in assets, so it is recorded on the debit side of the account).

Step 3. Set up T accounts for the ***noncurrent*** accounts that appear on the comparative statement of financial position, and insert the changes in these accounts in their respective box headings (Exhibit 20-8).

Step 4. Check your work. Total debits entered in the T accounts should equal total credits, including the working capital account. In the example, total debits of $50,000 equal total credits of $50,000. We can proceed with the working papers.

Step 5. Account for all changes in the noncurrent accounts by examining the appropriate ledger accounts (and, if necessary, tracing them back to the corresponding journal entries). Set up a schedule of the transactions causing these changes (expressed in journal form), replacing specific current account names by the general Working Capital account being used in this analysis.

The examination of the records of the Resource Company discloses the following transactions affecting the noncurrent accounts.

1. Land was purchased for $10,000.
2. Bonds were issued at par for $20,000.
3. One hundred shares of $100-par-value stock were sold for $150 per share.
4. Net income for the year was $5,000; details are the following.

Sales		$95,000
Less: Depreciation expense	$10,000	
Other expenses	80,000	90,000
Net income		$ 5,000

Exhibit 20-9 shows the schedule of journal entries related to these transactions. The left column shows the original journal entries; the right column shows the revised entries with the Working Capital account substituted for specific current accounts.

The closing entry (entry d in Exhibit 20-9) summarizes all revenue and expense transactions (which had been closed to the Income Summary account). In this closing entry, the Income Summary account was closed to Retained Earnings. With certain exceptions to be discussed shortly, revenue transactions increase working capital and expense transactions decrease it. Therefore, a net income for the year causes an increase in working capital (from operations); a net loss for the year causes a decrease in working capital.

In the working paper analysis of the closing entry, the total net income of $5,000 is transferred to the Working Capital account. This treatment assumes that all transactions creating net income involves working capital. An analysis of the income statement shows that a depreciation expense was recorded. The journal entry for this expense transaction was the following.

(dd) Depreciation Expense	10,000	
Accumulated Depreciation		10,000

This book entry for depreciation credits a noncurrent account to offset the debit to an expense account. Therefore, this transaction has no impact on working capital, although it does have an impact on net income.

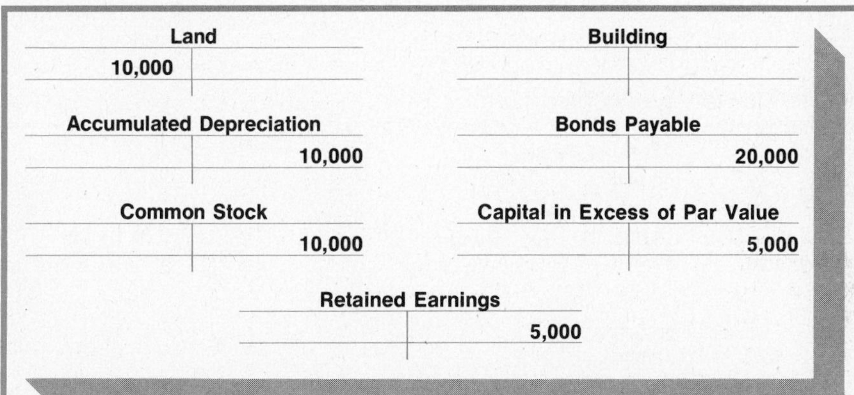

Exhibit 20-8
Noncurrent T accounts drawn from Exhibit 20-6

Original Journal Entries

(a)	Land	10,000	
	Cash		10,000
(b)	Cash	20,000	
	Bonds Payable		20,000
(c)	Cash	15,000	
	Common Stock		10,000
	Capital in excess of Par Value		5,000
(d)	Income Summary	5,000	
	Retained Earnings		5,000

Entries Analyzed in Terms of Working Capital

(a)	Land	10,000	
	Working Capital: Uses		10,000
(b)	Working Capital: Other Sources	20,000	
	Bonds Payable		20,000
(c)	Working Capital: Other Sources	15,000	
	Common Stock		10,000
	Capital in Excess of Par Value		5,000
(d)	Working Capital: From Operations	5,000	
	Retained Earnings		5,000

Exhibit 20-9 **Analysis of journal entries affecting noncurrent accounts**

An adjustment to the entry for net income from operations in the Working Capital T account will therefore be needed. The depreciation expense was ***deducted*** from net income, but the transaction did not involve working capital. Therefore, an adjustment should be made to ***add*** the depreciation expense back into the net income figure in the Working Capital account. Depreciation is not a source or a use of working capital; it is an adjustment to net income needed to arrive at a proper figure for working capital arising from operations. Therefore, one more entry should be added to the right column of Exhibit 20-9, as follows.

	Debit	Credit
(dd) Working Capital: From Operations	10,000	
Accumulated Depreciation		10,000

Step 6. Post the working-paper entries from the right column of Exhibit 20-8 to the T accounts. Exhibit 20-10 shows these accounts as the working papers appear after the posting.

Step 7. Examine each working-paper T account to determine whether the change indicated in the box heading has been explained by the entries in the account. In Exhibit 20-10 we find that the entries account for all the recorded changes. The T accounts can now be balanced and ruled. (If an account showed an unexplained balance, a further investigation of the books would be needed to provide the missing data.)

Exhibit 20-10 T accounts after posting working-paper entries

Working Capital

Debit		Credit	
	40,000		
From Operations:		**Uses:**	
(d) Net income	5,000	(a) Purchase of Land	10,000
(dd) Add back depreciation expense	10,000		
From Other Sources:			
(b) Issuance of bonds	20,000		
(c) Issuance of stock	15,000		

Land

Debit		Credit	
	10,000		
(a)	10,000		

Building

Debit	Credit

Accumulated Depreciation

Debit		Credit	
			10,000
		(dd)	10,000

Bonds Payable

Debit		Credit	
			20,000
		(b)	20,000

Common Stock

Debit		Credit	
			10,000
		(c)	10,000

Capital in Excess of Par Value

Debit		Credit	
			5,000
		(c)	5,000

Retained Earnings

Debit		Credit	
			5,000
		(d)	5,000

Exhibit 20-11 **The statement of changes in financial position**

RESOURCE COMPANY Statement of Changes in Financial Position For the Year Ended December 31, 19_2		
Financial resources provided by:		
Operations:		
Net income for the year	$ 5,000	
Add expenses to operations not requiring working capital in the current period	10,000	$15,000
Other sources:		
Issuance of bonds		20,000
Issuance of stock		15,000
Financial resources provided		$50,000
Financial resources applied to:		
Purchase of land		$10,000
Increase in working capital		40,000
Financial resources applied		$50,000

RESOURCE COMPANY Schedule of Changes in Working Capital For the Year Ended December 31, 19_2	December 31		Working Capital
	19_2	19_1	Increase (Decrease)
Current assets:			
Cash	$35,000	$10,000	$25,000
Accounts receivable	20,000	18,000	2,000
Inventory	40,000	32,000	8,000
Total current assets (*a*)	$95,000	$60,000	$35,000
Current liabilities:			
Accounts payable	$10,000	$15,000	$ 5,000
Notes payable	25,000	25,000	—
Total current liabilities (*b*)	$35,000	$40,000	$ 5,000
Working capital (*a* − *b*)	$60,000	$20,000	$40,000

Exhibit 20-12 **The schedule of changes in working capital**

Step 8. Prepare a formal statement of changes in financial position from the information accumulated in the Working Capital T account (see Exhibit 20-11).

Step 9. Prepare a schedule of changes in working capital (see Exhibit 20-12).

In this example, all changes in financial position involved changes in working capital. This is not always the case. In a later section of this chapter, we examine additional steps needed in this working-paper procedure to account for changes in financial position not involving working capital.

The Resource Company showed an increase in working capital during 19_2 of $40,000. How was this increase brought about? This information can be obtained only partially or in piecemeal form from the comparative balance sheet, income statement, and statement of owners' equity. The statement of changes in financial position provides the relevant information in meaningful, classified, summarized form.

In this example, operations produced $15,000 of working capital. Another $20,000 and $15,000 came from the issuance of bonds and stocks, respectively. Of the total of $50,000 in funds obtained, $10,000 was used to purchase land. The balance of $40,000 in funds was applied to an increase in working capital.

SPECIAL PROBLEMS IN TRANSACTION ANALYSIS

Certain transactions require special analysis in order to compute the change in financial position of the firm from period to period. The following cases present some of the more typical problems that arise.

Case 1: Two or more transactions affecting a noncurrent account. For example, the Equipment account has a change of $80,000. An analysis of the books shows that there were two transactions involving the Equipment account:

1. the purchase of equipment for $100,000 during the year;
2. the sale of equipment for $4,000. (The equipment sold had cost the company $20,000; 80 percent of the acquisition cost had been written off as accumulated depreciation in the accounts.)

Exhibit 20-13 shows the working-paper analysis of the journal entries and the Equipment T account. Note that the two entries do account for the change in the Equipment account during the period.

Case 2: Revenue and expense transactions affecting net income, but not affecting working capital. Certain book entries increase or decrease net income, but have no impact upon working capital or other funds. One such item, depreciation expense, appeared as entry dd in Exhibit 20-10. The following examples typify other revenue and expense transactions that require similar adjustments to "net income from operations" in the working papers.

Example a. Amortization of a patent.
Example b. Gain on sale of a long-term investment in stock. Assume this transaction

Exhibit 20-13 Working-paper analysis for case 1

Original Journal Entries

		Debit	Credit
(1)	Equipment	100,000	
	Cash		100,000
(2)	Cash	4,000	
	Accumulated Depreciation	16,000	
	Equipment		20,000

Entries Analyzed in Terms of Working Capital

		Debit	Credit
(1)	Equipment	100,000	
	Working Capital: Uses		100,000
(2)	Working Capital: Other Sources	4,000	
	Accumulated Depreciation	16,000	
	Equipment		20,000

Equipment

	Debit		Credit
	80,000		
(1)	100,000	(2)	20,000

is an unusual and nonrecurring sale so that it is treated as an extraordinary item.

Example c. Loss on disposal of equipment.

Example d. Amortization of premium on bonds payable.

Exhibit 20-14 shows the working-paper analysis of journal entries for these examples.

OTHER CHANGES IN FINANCIAL POSITION

In its *Opinion No. 19* quoted earlier, the Accounting Principles Board emphasized that the statement of changes in financial position should describe and explain *all* changes between successive statements of financial position. Hence, the statement should disclose all significant financing and investing activities of the firm, regardless of whether cash or working capital was involved.

In the example studied earlier, all changes in noncurrent accounts also involved changes in working capital accounts. In this example, ''changes in financial position'' happens to be synonymous with ''changes in working capital.'' However, there are changes in financial position that result from transactions not involving working capital items. How should we proceed if there were such transactions involving sources or uses of financial resources?

Would the acquisition of land through the issuance of common stock represent a change in financial position, although it does not involve working capital? The APB's opinion would require that this significant transaction be disclosed in the statement of changes in financial position. Exhibit 20-15 shows the working-paper analysis of the journal entry and the working-paper T accounts set up to cover this transaction.

Note that a special T account is set up to summarize the transactions that are to be reported on the statement of changes in financial position, but that do not affect working capital. This account is called Resources Provided and Applied. Each item of the journal entry is posted *both* to the appropriate noncurrent account *and* to the Resources Provided and Applied account. In this example, the acquisition of land

Exhibit 20-14 Working-paper analysis for case 2

Original Journal Entries			Entries Analyzed in Terms of Working Capital		
(a) Amortization of Patent	XXX		(a) Working Capital:		
Patent		XXX	From Operations	XXX	
			Patents		XXX
(b) Cash	XXX		(b) Working Capital: From		
Investment in Stock		XXX	Extraordinary Items	XXX	
Gain in Sale of Stock		XXX	Investment in Stock		XXX
			Retained Earnings		XXX
(c) Cash	XXX		(c) Working Capital:		
Loss on Sale of Equipment	XXX		From Other Sources	XXX	
Accumulated Depreciation	XXX		Working Capital:		
Equipment		XXX	From Operations	XXX	
			Accumulated Depreciation	XXX	
			Equipment		XXX
(d) Premium on Bonds Payable	XXX		(d) Premium on Bonds Payable	XXX	
Interest Expense		XXX	Working Capital:		
			From Operations		XXX

Exhibit 20-15 **Working-paper analysis of transaction not involving working capital**

Original Journal Entries			Entries Analyzed in Terms of Funds Flow		
Land	100,000		Land [Funds Applied]	100,000	
Common Stock		100,000	Common Stock [Funds Provided]		100,000

Land

100,000	
(a) 100,000	

Common Stock

	100,000
	(b) 100,000

Resources Provided and Applied

Provided:		Applied:	
(b) Stocks issued	100,000	(a) Land acquired	100,000

Exhibit 20-16
Non-working-capital transactions on the statement

[STATEMENT HEADING]

Financial resources provided by:	
Operations	$ XXX
Extraordinary items	XXX
Other sources	XXX
Financial resources not affecting working capital:	
Common stock issued for land	100,000
Financial resources provided	$ XXX
Financial resources applied to:	
Purchase of equipment	$ XXX
Financial resources not affecting working capital:	
Land acquired by issuing common stock	100,000
Increased in working capital	XXX
Financial resources applied	$ XXX

was an application of resources; the issuance of common stock provided resource. Because this special Resources account will be used only for transactions that involve two noncurrent accounts, the balance of this account should be zero.

In the statement of changes in financial position, this and similar transactions can be disclosed within the statement as sources and uses of financial resources. Exhibit 20-16 shows a model for such a statement, with the entries for the land-stock transaction in boldface type.

The following examples illustrate the kinds of transactions that cause changes in financial position but do not involve working capital.

1. Conversion of noncurrent debt (or preferred stock) for common stock.

Bonds Payable [Funds Applied]	XXX	
Common Stock [Funds Provided]		XXX

2. Exchange of noncurrent asset for a noncurrent liability.

Building [Funds Applied]	XXX	
Mortgage Payable [Funds Provided]		XXX
To record acquisition of a building and assumption of a mortgage.		

Note that, in these illustrations, all debits and credits involve noncurrent accounts.

Although working capital is not involved, these transactions do represent significant financing and investing activities, and they should be disclosed in the statement of changes in financial position.

There are certain transactions that are mere book entries and that do not require disclosure in the statement. For example, the creation of a reserve for contingencies out of retained earnings involves two noncurrent accounts, but does not represent an external financing or investing transaction. This entry would simply represent a reclassification of part of the retained earnings for purposes of internal reporting and control. It need not be disclosed on the statement of changes in financial position.

Interpretation of the statement

A statement of changes in financial position provides insights into the financial and investing operations of a business. Such statements show specifically where the resources of the firm have been obtained and how they have been used by management. When considered along with the traditional statements made available to owners, creditors, and others, this statement adds significantly to the understanding of what happened to a business during the year.

In examining the details of this statement, analysts can obtain data concerning changes in working capital, the dividend payment capabilities and policies of the firm, the investments made by management in stocks, bonds, property, plant, and equipment. The statement provides information about the long-term-debt financing operations of the firm, as well as about changes in stockholder's equity.

As an illustration of the interpretation of these statements, consider the statements for the Go Company and the No-Go Company in Exhibits 20-17 and 20-18. Assume that both firms are similar in most respects as to size, services offered, and so on. Examine these statements to see what you might be able to conclude from this information about the management of these firms.

1. Where did the financial resources of the companies come from?
2. What is the relationship between the change in financial resources during the period (as reported on these statements) and the net income that would be reported on the income statements of the two companies?
3. Has working capital expanded or contracted during the period?
4. What use was made of the firm's resources during the year?
5. In which of the two companies would you prefer to invest?
6. If you were a creditor of these two companies, which would give you more cause for concern?
7. As a stockholder of both companies, what would be your evaluation of the dividend practices of the firms? Why were dividends not larger than they were?
8. How did the Go Company finance its expansion in equipment? What happened to the proceeds of the sale of property by the No-Go Company?
9. What information can you obtain from these statements that you might not be able to gather from a statement of financial position or an income statement?

Exhibit 20-17
An example of the statement

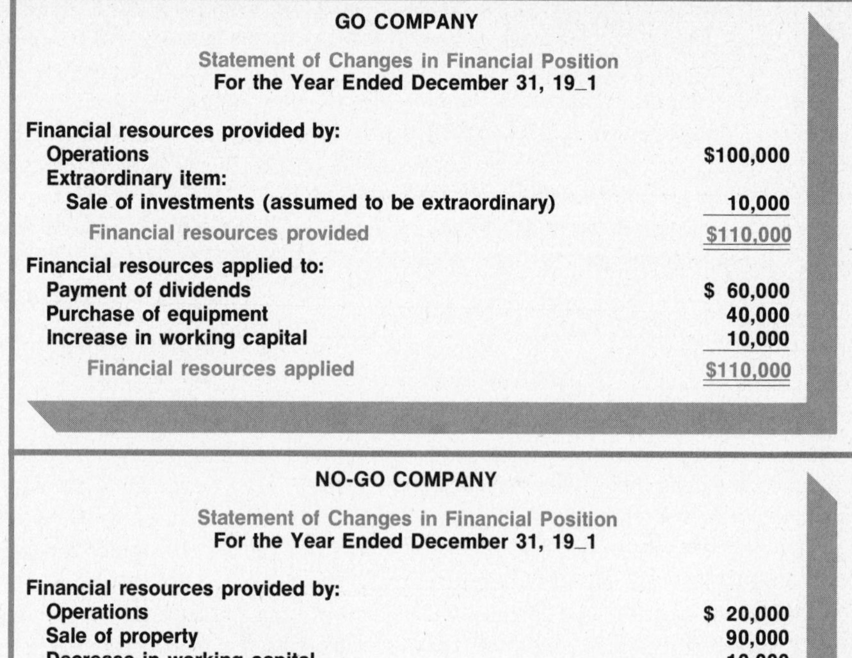

GO COMPANY

Statement of Changes in Financial Position
For the Year Ended December 31, 19_1

Financial resources provided by:	
Operations	$100,000
Extraordinary item:	
Sale of investments (assumed to be extraordinary)	10,000
Financial resources provided	$110,000
Financial resources applied to:	
Payment of dividends	$ 60,000
Purchase of equipment	40,000
Increase in working capital	10,000
Financial resources applied	$110,000

Exhibit 20-18
Another example of the statement

NO-GO COMPANY

Statement of Changes in Financial Position
For the Year Ended December 31, 19_1

Financial resources provided by:	
Operations	$ 20,000
Sale of property	90,000
Decrease in working capital	10,000
Financial resources provided	$120,000
Financial resources applied to:	
Payment of dividends	$ 90,000
Repurchase of outstanding stock	30,000
Financial resources applied	$120,000

The term "cash flow" is often heard in business. *Cash flow* is defined as working capital resulting from operations during the period. In the statement shown in Exhibit 20-11, cash flow is $15,000. The term *cash flow* defined in this way has serious conceptual problems. Working capital from operations, as it appears in the statement of changes in financial position, is not necessarily synonymous with the flow of cash during the period. For example, assume that all the credit sales made during the period have not been collected by the end of the period. Then some receivables arising during the period are still outstanding. However, the total sales would be reported as a source of working capital, because sales increased net income for the period and net income appeared on the statement as a source of working capital. In other words, the statement shows increases in net current assets, which includes receivables and other current assets as well as cash (and decreases in current liabilities). A similar consideration applies to expenses and purchases that involved decreases in current assets other than cash or increases in current liabilities.

About all that can be said for this concept of cash flow is that it represents a *rough* measure of the actual cash flow for the period. The use of this term with this definition probably should be discontinued.[5]

Impact analysis

By now you should be able to explain how various business transactions affect financial resources, which transactions are sources or uses of working capital, and how certain transactions reflect changes in financial resources without affecting working capital.

You should understand that an increase in working capital reflects a flow of resources from a noncurrent to a current classification. Similarly, a decrease in working capital indicates a flow of resources from current to noncurrent accounts.

Typical sources and uses of working capital—and, hence, of financial resources—include the following.

1. Sources of working capital:
   a. increase in long-term debt;
   b. increase in owners' equity from profitable operations or issuance of capital stock;
   c. decrease in long-term investments;
   d. decrease in property, plant, equipment, or intangible assets through sale.
2. Uses of working capital:
   a. decrease in long-term debt;
   b. decrease in owners' equity from net losses on operations or from declaration of cash dividends;
   c. increase in long-term investments;
   d. increase in property, plant, equipment, or intangible assets through purchase.

Recall that the following transactions have no impact on working capital:

1. depreciation of property, plant, and equipment;
2. amortization of discount on bonds payable;
3. amortization of premium on bonds held as long-term investments;
4. write-down of a long-term investment from cost to market value.

These transactions do have impact on net income, so they appear in the working papers and on the formal statement of changes in financial position as adjustments to net income. The adjustments are added back to income to compensate for the impact of these transactions in decreasing the net income reported. The adjusted net

5. There are two useful analytical reports that account for actual changes in cash from period to period. These are the statement of changes in financial position (cash basis), and the cash receipts and cash disbursements statement (see Appendix to this chapter). The criticism expressed in the text here applies to the interpretation of cash flow as measured by "working capital resulting from operations" on the statement of changes in financial position as developed in this chapter.

income more correctly measures working capital provided by operations.

The following transactions also have no impact on working capital:

1. amortization of discounts on bonds acquired as long-term investments;
2. amortization of premiums on bonds payable.

These transactions do increase the net income reported, however. Therefore, they must appear in the working papers and in the formal statement as adjustments deducted from "net income from operations" in order to arrive at working capital provided by operations.

A final question to consider: Does working capital change when (1) cash dividends are declared, or (2) when cash dividends are paid? (See Exhibit 20-19). The dividend-declaration entry results in an application of financial resources. This entry involves a current account (Dividends Payable) and a noncurrent account (Retained Earnings). Working capital decreases as a result of the declaration of cash dividends. Payment of the dividends simply involves a decrease in a current liability and an offsetting decrease in a current asset; there is no impact on working capital.

Summary

Chapter 20 discusses the statement of changes in financial position. This statement (1) accounts for changes in the financial position of a firm (as reflected by the changes from one balance sheet to the next), and (2) summarizes the financing and investing activities of the firm. In a sense, this is a funds statement—summarizing the sources and applications of funds during the year. However, for this statement, the concept of "funds" is given a very broad interpretation to include ***all financial resources*** arising from external business transactions—including funds arising from transactions that involve only noncurrent items as well as funds arising from working-capital transactions.

Exhibit 20-19 Working-paper analysis of cash-dividend transactions

Original Journal Entries				Entries Analyzed in Terms of Working Capital		
19_1						
Dec. 15	Retained Earnings	XXX		Retained Earnings	XXX	
	Dividends Payable		XXX	Working Capital: Uses		XXX
	To record declaration of a cash dividend.					
19_2						
Jan. 15	Dividends Payable	XXX		This transaction involves two current accounts; it has no impact on working capital.		
	Cash		XXX			
	To record payment of the cash dividend.					

The statement of changes in financial position, or funds statement, reports the major sources and uses of funds during the accounting period. The major sources of financial resources include:

1. net income (adjusted);
2. sale of long-term investments, property, plant, equipment, or intangible assets;
3. long-term borrowing;
4. issuance of common or preferred stock.

The major uses of financial resources include:

1. acquisition of long-term investments, property, plant, equipment, or intangible assets;
2. payment of long-term debt;
3. acquisition of a firm's own common or preferred stock;
4. payment of dividends;
5. increase in working capital.

The statement of changes in financial position also provides some insights into the spending, financing, dividend, and operating policies of management. A careful study of this statement can reveal considerable information about the financial strength of a company, especially when this study is correlated with an examination of comparative income statements and balance sheets.

Appendix

STATEMENTS DISCLOSING ACTUAL CASH FLOW

Two supplementary statements can be prepared to account for the change in the cash balance during a period. These statements are (1) a statement of changes in financial position (cash basis), and (2) a cash receipts and disbursements statement (or cash flow statement). Such statements (a) convert the income statement prepared on the accrual basis to a cash basis, and (b) account for other changes in cash balance shown on the statement of financial position.

A work-sheet technique is used to prepare the two statements. (The work-sheet technique described here could be modified and used instead of the T accounts described in this chapter to prepare the formal statement of changes in financial position.) The following steps are involved in preparing the two statements.

Step 1. Obtain a comparative statement of financial position and compute the changes in the accounts during the period. (As an illustration, we use the statements of the Resource Company presented in this chapter.) Copy the year's changes into the Year's Change columns of the work sheet (Exhibit 20-20). Asset increases are placed in the debit column and decreases in the credit column. Liability increases are placed in the credit column and decreases in the debit column. This procedure reflects the basic rules for debiting and crediting accounts.

Exhibit 20-20 **Cash-flow work sheet**

RESOURCE COMPANY
Cash-Flow Work Sheet
For the Year Ended December 31, 19_2

Account	Year's Change		Adjustments to Cash Basis		Cash Flow	
	Dr.	Cr.	Dr.	Cr.	Dr.	Cr.
Cash	37,000				37,000	
Accounts Receivable	2,000			(a) 2,000	—	
Inventory	8,000			(c) 8,000	—	
Accounts Payable	5,000			(b) 5,000	—	
Taxes Payable	—				—	
Land	8,000				8,000	
Building	—				—	
Less: Accumulated Depreciation		8,000	(d) 8,000			—
Bonds Payable		20,000				20,000
Common Stock		10,000				10,000
Paid-in Capital in Excess of Par		5,000				5,000
Retained Earnings		17,000	(e) 17,000			—
	60,000	60,000				
Sales		245,000	(a) 2,000			243,000
Cost of Goods Sold	150,000		(b) 5,000 (c) 8,000		163,000	
Operating Expenses	70,000				70,000	
Depreciation Expense	8,000			(d) 8,000	—	
Net Income	17,000			(e) 17,000	—	
	245,000	245,000	40,000	40,000	278,000	278,000

Step 2. Obtain an income statement for the current period. Copy this statement onto the bottom of the work sheet in the Year's Change columns. Revenue items are placed in the credit column and expenses in the debit column. This procedure reflects the basic rules for debiting and crediting revenue and expense accounts.

Step 3. Examine the changes listed in the Year's Change column. Eliminate all noncash accounts representing accruals, prepayments, inventories, depreciation expense, and so on that appear on the balance sheet that affect net income as reported on the accrual basis in the income statment. These adjustments are indicated by appropriate entries in the Adjustments to Cash Basis columns of the work sheet. If it requires a *debit* to remove the balance sheet item, there will be a corresponding *credit* to an appropriate income statement item, and vice-versa. The following adjustments are required:

1. Eliminate accounts receivable (a).
2. Eliminate inventory (c).
3. Eliminate accounts payable (b).
4. Eliminate depreciation expense (d).

These adjustments eliminate all accrual basis items from the balance sheet and non-cash items from the income statement. The columns are then totalled.

Cash from operations can be conceptualized as follows:

Cash from operations	=	Cash collected from customers	−	Cash paid for inventory purchases	−	Cash paid for expenses

or

Cash from operations	=	Net income	+	Accounting charges not requiring cash outlays	−	Accounting credits not providing cash

The adjustments made in Exhibit 20-20 can be explained as follows:

1. The increase in Accounts Receivable represents sales that were made on credit and uncollected at the end of the period. These sales were reported as income, but they did not produce an inflow of cash. The full $2,000 is removed from Accounts Receivable and from Sales, to convert the sales to a cash basis.
2. The decrease in Accounts Payable represents the payment for some purchases recognized as expenses in an earlier period. This is an outflow of cash that is not included in the expense accounts on the accrual basis. The full $5,000 is removed from Accounts Payable and added to Cost of Goods Sold, to convert the purchases to a cash basis.
3. The increase in Inventory represents purchases that have not yet been recognized as expenses (because the goods in inventory have not yet been sold to produce revenue). The full $8,000 is removed from Inventory and added to Cost of Goods Sold, completing the conversion of purchases to a cash basis.
4. The increase in Accumulated Depreciation does not represent a cash outflow. This change was produced by an adjusting entry that created an offsetting depreciation expense. The full $8,000 is removed from Accumulated Depreciation and from Depreciation Expense, converting the accounting for the value of the building to a cash basis.
5. The increase in Retained Earnings does not represent a cash inflow. This change was produced by a closing entry, transferring net income from the revenue and expense accounts to the Retained Earnings account. The full $17,000 is removed from Retained Earnings and from Net Income because these are duplicate entries. (The closing entry was made after preparation of the income statement, but the effect of the closing entry is included on the balance sheet. The cash inflow portion of net income is reflected in the revenue accounts shown.)

These five adjustments complete the conversion of the statements on the accrual basis into statements on a cash basis. In this illustration, all of the remaining balance sheet accounts shown in the Year's Change columns of the work sheet represent actual inflows or outflows of cash. If any of the balance sheet changes in the Year's Change columns did not reflect cash flow, they would be eliminated in the Adjustments to Cash Basis columns. Exhibit 20-21 shows how accrual-basis accounting can be converted into cash-basis accounting.

Step 4. Transfer any balance for each account to the Cash Flow columns. Foot and balance the Cash Flow columns.

Step 5. Prepare a cash receipts and disbursements statement from the Cash Flow columns (see Exhibit 20-22).

Step 6. Prepare a statement of changes in financial position (cash basis) from the Cash Flow columns (see Exhibit 20-23). Changes in receivables, payables, inventories and other elements of working capital are disclosed in the body of the statement as shown. For this reason, a separate schedule of changes in working capital is not required when the statement is prepared in the cash format.

Questions

1. What information is contained in a statement of changes in financial position?
2. What is meant by the concept of a funds statement in which "funds" refer to "all financial resources"?

Exhibit 20-21
Adjustments to accrual-basis accounts in preparing cash-basis statements

Conversion of Accrual-Basis Income Statement to Cash-Basis Income Statement

Cash receipts from customers:	
Net sales (on accrual basis)	**$245,000**
Decrease (increase) in accounts receivable	**(2,000)**
Cash receipts from customers	$243,000
Cash payments for purchases:	
Cost of goods sold (on accrual basis)	**$150,000**
Increase (decrease) in inventory	**8,000**
Purchases (on accrual basis)	**$158,000**
Decrease (increase) in accounts payable	**5,000**
Cash payments for purchases	$163,000
Cash operating expenses:	
Expenses (on accrual basis)	**$ 78,000**
Decrease (increase) in accrued liabilities	**—**
Increase (decrease) in prepaid expenses	**—**
Less: Depreciation expense	**(8,000)**
Cash payments for expenses	$ 70,000

Exhibit 20-22
Cash receipts and disbursements statement

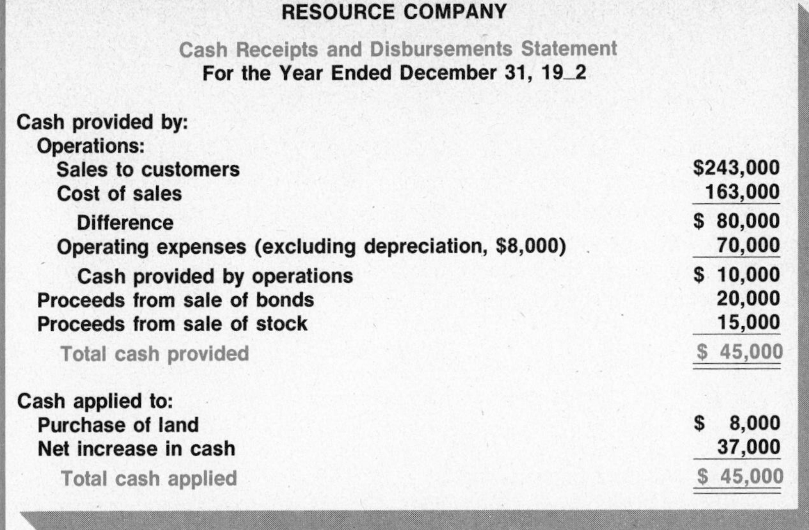

RESOURCE COMPANY

Cash Receipts and Disbursements Statement
For the Year Ended December 31, 19_2

Cash provided by:	
Operations:	
Sales to customers	$243,000
Cost of sales	163,000
Difference	$ 80,000
Operating expenses (excluding depreciation, $8,000)	70,000
Cash provided by operations	$ 10,000
Proceeds from sale of bonds	20,000
Proceeds from sale of stock	15,000
Total cash provided	$ 45,000
Cash applied to:	
Purchase of land	$ 8,000
Net increase in cash	37,000
Total cash applied	$ 45,000

Exhibit 20-23
Statement of changes in financial position (cash basis)

RESOURCE COMPANY

Statement of Changes in Financial Position (Cash Basis)
For the Year Ended December 31, 19_2

Financial resources provided:	
Cash generated:	
Net income	$17,000
Add (deduct) items not requiring cash during the period:	
Trade receivables increase	(2,000)
Inventory increase	(8,000)
Depreciation expense	8,000
Trade payables decrease	(5,000)
Cash generated by operations	$10,000
Other sources of cash:	
Bonds payable sold	20,000
Common stock issued	15,000
Total cash generated	$45,000
Financial resources applied:	
Land purchased	$ 8,000
Increase in cash	37,000
Total cash applied	$45,000

3. What are the major sections of a statement of changes in financial position?
4. Mention several major sources of financial resources. State several applications of financial resources.
5. What is the usual meaning of cash flow? How does this differ from the cash flow reported on the statement of changes in financial position (cash basis)?
6. Explain why such transactions as depreciation expense, amortization of bond premiums and discounts, and similar internal items are neither sources nor applications of financial resources, but rather are treated as adjustments of net income.

7. Is it possible for net income to differ from working capital provided by operations? Explain.

8. The "cash flow" of a business as defined as "net income plus depreciation" can and usually does differ from cash provided by operations as reflected in a statement of cash receipts and disbursements. How is this possible?

9. Why might it be possible for a company with sizeable net income not to be in a position to pay dividends to stockholders? Answer this question by referring to the statement of changes in financial position.

Exercises

E20-1 (Source and application of funds)
For each of the following transactions, indicate whether it represents a source of funds, an application of funds, or an adjustment of net income.
a. Issuance of preferred stock for cash.
b. Depreciation of equipment.
c. Amortization of discount on bonds issued.
d. Increase in intangible fixed assets through cash purchase.
e. Increase in long-term debt (cash borrowed).
f. Decrease in long-term investments through a sale.
g. Decrease in long-term debt through repayment.
h. Issuance of common stock for cash.
i. Increase in property, plant, or equipment for cash.
j. Decrease in equipment through sale.

E20-2 (Source and application of funds)
Identify each of the following as a source or application of financial resources or an adjustment of net income.
a. Depreciation expense.
b. Net income for the year.
c. Purchase of a building.
d. Issuance of stock.
e. Payment of dividends.
f. Purchase of land.
g. Amortization of patent expense and discount on bonds payable.
h. Issuance of bonds.
i. Sale of land.

E20-3 (Preparation of statement of changes in financial position)
Exhibit 20-24 shows the comparative balance sheet of the Ad Lib Corporation. The following information also is available.
A. Net income for the year was $19,000.
B. $35,000 of additional no-par stock was issued during the year.
C. $11,000 of land was purchased for cash during the year.
D. A patent was acquired for cash during the year.
E. A $9,000 cash dividend was declared and paid during the year.

Required:
a. Prepare a statement of changes in financial position, using the T account approach for the working papers.
b. What is the cash flow for the year?

Exhibit 20-24
Comparative balance sheet for Exercise E20-3

AD LIB CORPORATION
Comparative Balance Sheet
December 31, 19_6 and 19_7

	19_7	19_6
Working capital	$ 18,000	$ 11,000
Land	95,000	84,000
Equipment	72,000	72,000
Accumulated depreciation	(12,000)	(9,000)
Patents	27,000	2,000
Total gross capital	$200,000	$160,000
Mortgage payable	$ 40,000	$ 35,000
Common stock	110,000	85,000
Retained earnings	50,000	40,000
Total capital structure	$200,000	$160,000

E20-4 (Preparation of statement)

The following list indicates the changes in account balances for the Drawing Corporation from 19_6 to 19_7.

Working Capital	$ 42,500 increase
Long-Term Investments	15,000 increase
Land	16,000 increase
Buildings (less accumulated depreciation)	30,000 increase
8% Bonds Payable	80,000 increase
Common Stock	200,000 increase
Retained Earnings	66,000 decrease

The following additional information is available.

1. Net income for the year was $52,500.
2. Accumulated depreciation for 19_6 was $22,500; for 19_7, $30,000.
3. A $37,500 building was purchased during the year; depreciation expense for the year was $7,500.
4. A 100% stock dividend was distributed during the year.
5. A $29,000 cash dividend was declared and paid during the year.

Required: Prepare a statement of changes in financial position for the Drawing Corporation.

E20-5 (Cash analysis)

The following information is taken from the records of the Record Company.

Net sales in 19_6	$87,000
Accounts receivable, December 31, 19_5	58,000
Accounts receivable, December 31, 19_6	63,000
Cost of goods sold in 19_6	42,000
Inventory, December 31, 19_5	31,000
Inventory, December 31, 19_6	36,000
Accounts payable, December 31, 19_5	34,000
Accounts payable, December 31, 19_6	40,000
Expenses in 19_6 (including $6,000 depreciation)	22,000
Accrued expenses, December 31, 19_5	9,000
Accrued expenses, December 31, 19_6	14,000
Prepaid expenses, December 31, 19_5	4,500
Prepaid expenses, December 31, 19_6	8,000

Required:
a. Compute cash receipts from customers during 19_6.
b. Compute cash payments for purchases during 19_6.
c. Compute cash operating expenses for 19_6.

E20-6 (Preparation of statement)
A statement of changes in financial position may assume the following form:

Sources:	
From operations:	
Net income	$(1)
Adjustments to net income	(2)
From extraordinary items	(3)
From other sources	(4)
Applications:	(5)
Funds provided and applied other than those requiring working capital	(6)

Required: For each of the following items, indicate by the appropriate number (1 through 6) where this item should be included on the statement. If the item does not belong in any of the categories on the statement, indicate this by the number 7.
a. Declaration of a cash dividend.
b. Issuance of common stock to retire bonds payable.
c. Retirement of bonds payable (a cash transaction).
d. Declaration of a dividend in stock.
e. Purchase of land for cash.
f. Gain on the sale of equipment.
g. Amortization of a patent.
h. Sale of marketable securities.
i. Depreciation for the year.
j. Net income for the period.
k. Issuance of common stock for cash.
l. Proceeds from the sale of a plant.

Problems

P20-1 (Preparation of statement)
The accounts of the Rainy Day Company showed the following net changes during the year 19_6. Changes are shown as credits (debits).

Cash	$(20,000)
Accounts Receivable	(30,000)
Inventory	7,000
Long-term Investments	15,000
Land	(14,000)
Buildings	(70,000)
Accumulated Depreciation	10,000
Accounts Payable	9,000
Wages Payable	4,000
Common Stock	25,000
Retained Earnings	64,000

Exhibit 20-25 shows the company's statement of retained earnings.

Required:

a. Identify current assets and current liabilities.

b. Compute the increase or decrease in working capital.

c. Prepare a statement of changes in financial position.

P20-2 (Preparation of statement)

Exhibit 20-26 shows a comparative statement of financial position for the Misty Blue Company. The following additional information is available from the accounting records for 19_7.

A. Net income for the year, $33,000

B. Equipment depreciated $20,000 during the year; $2,000 of the cost of the patent was amortized during the year.

C. Equipment costing $10,000 was purchased during the year.

D. Common stock of $50,000 par value was issued for $65,000.

Exhibit 20-25
Statement of retained earnings for Problem P20-1

RAINY DAY COMPANY
Statement of Retained Earnings
For the Year Ended December 31, 19_6

January 1, 19_6	$ 61,000
Net income for the year	120,000
Total	$181,000
Dividends	56,000
December 31, 19_6	$125,000

Exhibit 20-26
Comparative statement of financial position for Problem P20-2

MISTY BLUE COMPANY
Comparative Statement of Financial Position
December 31, 19_6 and 19_7

	19_7	19_6
Debits:		
Cash	$ 41,000	$ 11,000
Accounts Receivable	52,000	12,000
Inventory	56,000	30,000
Prepaid Expenses	11,000	7,000
Equipment	190,000	180,000
Allowance for Depreciation	(50,000)	(30,000)
Patents	18,000	20,000
	$318,000	$230,000
Credits:		
Accounts Payable	$ 15,000	$ 7,000
Bonds Payable	51,000	51,000
Premium on Bonds Payable	6,000	9,000
Common Stock	95,000	45,000
Paid-In Capital in Excess of Par Value	15,000	0
Retained Earnings	136,000	118,000
	$318,000	$230,000

E. Bond premium of $3,000 was amortized during the year.
F. Cash dividend of $15,000 was declared and paid.

Required:

a. Using T accounts, prepare working papers to provide data for a formal statement of changes in financial position.
b. Prepare the formal statement of changes in financial position.

P20-3 (Items on statement)

Indicate how each of the following transactions would be shown on a statement of changes in financial position.

a. Sale of land for $200,000; original cost of land was $80,000.
b. Acquisition of a $120,000 building for $75,000 cash and a $45,000 mortgage.
c. Capital stock of $300,000 par value issued to retire $300,000 of long-term notes payable.
d. The creation of a Reserve for Contingencies of $45,000 from Retained Earnings.
e. The conversion of a $20,000 long-term debt into a short-term debt.

P20-4 (Working paper for statement preparation)

Exhibit 20-27 shows some comparative data from the accounts of a company. Using these data, prepare working papers to support a statement of changes in financial position. The following additional data are available: net income $90,000; dividends $30,000. Make whatever assumptions you consider necessary to complete the problem.

P20-5 (Preparation of statement)

The following data are available about changes in the current and noncurrent accounts of the Lovitt Company during 19_6.

Change in current assets	$ 75,000
Change in current liabilities	50,000
Land	70,000
Retained Earnings	20,000
Equipment	95,000
Accumulated Depreciation	30,000
Bonds Payable	100,000
Patent	40,000
Common Stock	80,000

All the changes in the noncurrent accounts were increases. The following additional information is available.

A. Net income for the year was $80,000.
B. A stock dividend in the amount of $60,000 was declared and issued.
C. A machine costing $45,000 was acquired in exchange for preferred stock.
D. Land was acquired by issuing a $70,000 short-term note.
E. Depreciation expense for the year was $30,000.

Required:

a. Prepare working papers in the T account form for a statement of changes in financial position.
b. Prepare the statement of changes in financial position.

P20-6 (Cash analysis)

Exhibit 20-28 shows selections from the accounting records of the Net Company.

Exhibit 20-27
Available accounting data for Problem P20-4

	19_5	19_6
Cash	$ 20,000	$ 30,000
Receivables	15,000	32,000
Land	80,000	100,000
Property, plant	215,000	255,000
Accumulated depreciation	(20,000)	(32,000)
	$310,000	$385,000
Accounts payable	$ 15,000	$ 15,000
Bonds payable	50,000	20,000
Common stock	185,000	230,000
Retained earnings	60,000	120,000
	$310,000	$385,000

Exhibit 20-28
Available accounting data for Problem P20-6

	December 31	
	Year 1	Year 2
Account balances:		
Cash	$ 25,000	$ 30,000
Accounts Receivable [net]	55,000	40,000
Inventory	32,000	17,000
Prepaid Expenses	7,000	3,000
Land	85,000	85,000
Building	320,000	320,000
Allowance for Depreciation: Building	38,000	50,000
Accounts Payable	40,000	50,000
Accrued Liabilities	13,000	9,000
Common Stock	90,000	100,000
Other data:		
Net sales in Year 2		140,000
Cost of goods sold in Year 2		70,000
Expenses in Year 2 (including depreciation)		55,000

Required:

a. Compute cash receipts from customers in Year 2.
b. Compute cash payment for purchases in Year 2.
c. Compute cash operating expenses for Year 2.
d. From parts a, b, and c, compute cash flow from operations.
e. (1) Compute net income for Year 2.
(2) Adjust net income for Year 2 to show cash flow from operations for Year 2.
f. Compute working capital provided by operations (working capital basis) for Year 2.

P20-7 (Cash format for statement)
Refer to Exhibit 20-26. Prepare a statement of changes in financial position using the cash format.

P20-8 (Impact analysis)
Indicate whether the following items will increase, decrease, or have no effect on working capital.

1. Company acquired land for $100,000 cash.
2. Company acquired a factory by issuing a bond payable.

3. Sold long-term investments at a gain.
4. Declared a dividend.
5. Paid a dividend.
6. Recorded depreciation for the year.
7. Amortized the patent for the year.
8. Created a reserve for contingencies.
9. Retired preferred stock by acquiring outstanding shares for cash.
10. Collected on accounts receivable.

P20-9 (Statement of changes in financial position)

The following information concerns changes in account balances from the beginning of the year to the end of the year:

Cash increase	$ 1,000
Accounts receivable decrease	2,000
Inventory increase	4,000
Long-term investment decrease	5,000
Plant and equipment increase	25,000
Accumulated depreciation increase	5,000
Accounts payable increase	5,000
Common stock increase	10,000
Retained earnings increase	3,000

Dividends declared for the year were $1,000.

Required: Prepare a statement of changes in financial position.

Financial statement analysis, price-level changes, and the human element in accounting

21

Like lines in the palm or horoscopes, financial statements can be studied, puzzled over, and scrutinized. When carefully analyzed, financial statements can yield valuable information about a business, especially in terms of trends and relationships. Financial statement analysis is undertaken for a variety of reasons. Ranking high on the list of reasons is the evaluation of the *quality* and *quantity* of the earnings of a business and of the *strength* of its financial position. Earnings should be examined to determine their amount, source, rate, and stability. Earnings characteristics are reflected in such items as sales, operating expenses, net income, economic resources employed, owners' investment commitments, market price of stock, and so on. The financial strength of a business is reflected in the firm's earning capacity and its ability to pay debts and dividends. An examination of the firm's economic resources, liabilities, and owners' equity can shed light on the financial strengths and weaknesses of the company.

Financial statement analysis

In preceding chapters, various aspects of financial statement analysis are treated extensively. Among the ideas related to this topic that are discussed in the earlier chapters are the following:

1. comparative financial statements, which provide information about trends and relationships over two or more years;
2. ratios, which establish relationships between various items appearing on financial statements;
3. special techniques such as gross-margin analysis and break-even analysis.

To broaden the discussion somewhat, we now consider two additional techniques that are used in analyzing and interpreting financial statements: horizontal and vertical analysis.

VERTICAL ANALYSIS. Vertical analysis of financial statements involves the conversion of items appearing in statement *columns* into terms of percentages of a base figure. For example, individual items appearing on the income statement can be expressed as percentages of sales. On the balance sheet, individual assets (such as cash or inventory) can be expressed as a percentage of total assets. Liabilities and owners' equity accounts can be expressed in terms of their relationship to total liabilities and owners' equity. Statements omitting dollar amounts and showing only percentages can be prepared. Such statements are referred to as "common-size statements" since each item in the statement has a common basis for comparison, for example, total assets, net sales. Such statements are especially useful when data for more than one year are used. Exhibits 21-1 and 21-2 illustrate vertical analysis as applied to the income statement and the balance sheet.

HORIZONTAL ANALYSIS. Horizontal analysis spotlights trends and establishes relationships between items that appear on the same *row* of a comparative financial statement. Horizontal analysis discloses changes in items on financial statements over time. Each item (such as cash) on a row for one fiscal period is compared with the same item in a different period. Horizontal analysis may be carried out in terms of changes in dollar amounts, percentages of change, or in a ratio format. Exhibits 21-3 and 21-4 illustrate horizontal analysis as applied to the income statement and the balance sheet. The amount of change is determined by subtracting the amount for the base year from the amount for the current year. For example, on the row for accounts receivable, $5,000 for the current year less $10,000 for the base year gives a change of $(5,000)—a negative change. The percentage of change is also negative—a downward change equal to 50 percent of the amount in the base year

Exhibit 21-1
Vertical analysis of an income statement

VERTICAL COMPANY
Income Statement
For the Year Ended December 31, 19_0

		Percentage of Net Sales
Sales (net)	$200,000	100.0%
Cost of goods sold	50,000	25.0
Gross margin on sales	$150,000	75.0%
Operating expenses	100,000	50.0
Net operating income	$ 50,000	25.0%
Federal income tax	25,000	12.5
Net income	$ 25,000	12.5%

VERTICAL COMPANY		
Balance Sheet		
December 31, 19_0		
		Percentage of Total Assets
Assets:		
Cash	$ 25,000	5%
Accounts receivable	75,000	15
Inventory	50,000	10
Property, plant, and equipment	350,000	70
Total assets	$500,000	100%
Liabilities and owners' equity:		
Accounts payable	$ 25,000	5%
Bonds payable	200,000	40
Common stock	250,000	50
Retained earnings	25,000	5
Total liabilities and owners' equity	$500,000	100%

Exhibit 21-2 **Vertical analysis of a balance sheet**

HORIZONTAL COMPANY					
Income Statement					
For the Years Ended December 31, 19_0 and 19_1					
	19_1	**19_0**	**Amount of Change**	**Percentage of Change**	**Ratio 19_1 to 19_0**
Sales	$150,000	$100,000	$50,000	50.0%	1.50
Cost of goods sold	80,000	50,000	30,000	60.0	1.60
Gross margin on sales	$ 70,000	$ 50,000	$20,000	40.0	1.40
Operating expenses	30,000	20,000	10,000	50.0	1.50
Net operating income	$ 40,000	$ 30,000	$10,000	33.3	1.33
Income tax	20,000	15,000	5,000	33.3	1.33
Net income	$ 20,000	$ 15,000	$ 5,000	33.3	1.33

Exhibit 21-3 **Horizontal analysis of an income statement**

[($5,000)/$10,000 = (50.0)]. The year-to-year ratio is computed by dividing the current year data by the base year data. For example, the year-to-year ratio for accounts receivable is computed as follows: $5,000/$10,000 = 0.50.

Exhibit 21-5 illustrates several examples of the computation of amount, percentage, and ratio of change under various special situations. Study this exhibit until you can see how the various figures are computed in each case, or why they are not computed. Note that percentage of change data and ratio of year-to-year data are computed only when the base figure (19_0) is positive.

RATIOS. Many of the more meaningful financial statement ratios are discussed in earlier chapters dealing with specific asset, liability, and owners' equity accounts. Exhibit 21-6 provides a useful summary of ratios, arranged in groups that relate to disclosure of specific information about a firm. To be especially useful, ratios should

Exhibit 21-4 Horizontal analysis of a balance sheet

HORIZONTAL COMPANY

Statement of Financial Position
December 31, 19_0 and 19_1

	19_1	19_0	Amount of Change	Percentage of Change	Ratio 19_1 to 19_0
Assets					
Cash	$ 15,000	$ 10,000	$ 5,000	50.0%	1.50
Accounts receivable	5,000	10,000	(5,000)	(50.0)	0.50
Inventory	30,000	—	30,000	—	—
Property, plant, and equipment	125,000	150,000	(25,000)	(16.7)	0.83
Total assets	$175,000	$170,000	$ 5,000	2.9	1.03
Liabilities					
Accounts payable	$ 15,000	—	$ 15,000	—	—
Bonds payable	—	$100,000	(100,000)	(100.0)	0.00
Owners' Equity					
Common Stock	155,000	80,000	75,000	93.8	1.94
Retained earnings	5,000	(10,000)	15,000	—	—
Total liabilities and owners' equity	$175,000	$170,000	$ 5,000	2.9	1.03

	19_1	19_0	Amount of Change	Percentage of Change	Ratio 19_1 to 19_0
Group 1: Positive amount in base year 19_0	$2,400	$ 1,600	$ 800	50%	1.50
	1,600	1,600	0	0	1.00
	400	1,600	(1,200)	(75)	0.25
	—	1,600	(1,600)	(100)	0.00
	(400)	1,600	(2,000)	(125)	(0.25)
Group 2: Zero amount in base year	$1,000	—	$1,000	—	—
	—	—	0	—	—
	(1,000)	—	(1,000)	—	—
Group 3: Negative amount in base year	$1,600	$(1,600)	$3,200	—	—
	—	(1,600)	1,600	—	—
	(1,200)	(1,600)	400	—	—
	(1,600)	(1,600)	0	—	—
	(2,000)	(1,600)	(400)	—	—

Exhibit 21-5 Horizontal analysis computations for various situations

be compared with similar data developed for the firm for prior periods. Also, a company's ratios should be compared with similar ratios for the industry to which the firm belongs. Financial strengths and weaknesses of a company can often be identified through ratio analysis.

VALUE OF STATEMENT ANALYSIS. Financial statement analysis has its limitations. Statements represent the past and do not necessarily predict the future. At best, financial statement analysis provides clues. What is found on the statements is the product of accounting conventions and procedures that sometimes distort the economic reality. Statements say little about changes in markets, the business cycle, laws and regulations, management personnel, price-level changes, and other critical concerns. Financial statement analysis is not an end in itself. Rather, it is the beginning of the application of accounting data to the decision-making process.

Price-level changes

Inflation has been an economic fact of life in the United States since World War II. When prices rise in an inflationary period, the value of the dollar (that is, the purchasing power of the dollar) declines.

In the accounting system, economic events are recorded in terms of the number of dollars involved. This procedure reflects the dollar-measurement assumption, which is a basic proposition in the theory of accounting. With some important exceptions, financial statements report historical dollar amounts. When the dollar-measurement assumption and the historical-cost principle are combined, distortions arise in the financial statements. This is particularly true in periods when the price level is changing. We now examine several situations that illustrate the difficulties caused by changing price levels.

Example 1. You purchased land for $100,000 in 19_0. Ten years later, you sell the land for $150,000. If the purchasing power of the dollar has remained unchanged over the ten years, you have made a monetary gain (an increase in number of dollars) and an economic gain (an increase in purchasing power) of $50,000. You have 150 percent of the number of dollars you started with. Each dollar has the same purchasing power now that it had at the time of the land purchase. Therefore, you also have 150 percent of the purchasing power you had then. However, suppose that the price level has doubled during the ten years that you held the land—that is, the purchasing price of the dollar has declined 50 percent. Did you gain from the sale?

Your monetary gain on the sale is still $50,000—the gain in number of dollars. However, each dollar received is worth only half as much as each dollar that you paid for the land. In terms of the purchasing power of the 19_0 dollars, you paid $100,000 for the land but sold it for only $75,000. In terms of purchasing power, you lost. You have more dollars, but these dollars have considerably less purchasing power than the dollars that you invested. To add insult to injury, you must pay income tax on your monetary gain of $50,000. When this "gain" of $50,000 is taxed, are you paying tax on a gain or on part of your capital?

Example 2. A company purchases equipment during three different years when the price level is changing. The company purchases $100,000 of equipment in 19_0, when the price level is 100. It purchases $200,000 of equipment in 19_1, when the price level is 110. It purchases $300,000 of

Exhibit 21-6 **Ratios used for analysis of financial statements**

1. **Measures of a firm's liquidity:**

   a. Current ratio (see Chapter 3) = $\frac{\text{Current assets (net)}}{\text{Current liabilities}}$

   b. Acid-test ratio (see Chapter 3) = $\frac{\text{Quick assets (net)}}{\text{Current liabilities}}$

   c. Cash ratio = $\frac{\text{Cash}}{\text{Current liabilities}}$

2. **Measures of the movement or turnover of current assets:**

   a. Receivables turnover (see Chapter 12) = $\frac{\text{Credit sales (net)}}{\text{Average receivables (net)}}$

   b. Age of receivables (see Chapter 12) = $\frac{365}{\text{Receivables turnover}}$

   c. Merchandise inventory turnover (see Chapter 13) = $\frac{\text{Cost of goods sold}}{\text{Average merchandise inventory}}$

   d. Raw material turnover = $\frac{\text{Cost of raw materials used}}{\text{Average raw materials inventory}}$

   e. Days' supply in inventory (see Chapter 13) = $\frac{365}{\text{Inventory turnover [c or d]}}$

   f. Working capital turnover = $\frac{\text{Net sales}}{\text{Average working capital}}$

3. **Measures of capital structure:**

   a. Owners' equity to total assets (see Chapter 3) = $\frac{\text{Total owners' equity}}{\text{Total assets (net)}}$

   b. Owners' equity to total liabilities (see Chapter 3) = $\frac{\text{Total owners' equity}}{\text{Total liabilities}}$

   c. Fixed assets to total equity (see Chapter 14) = $\frac{\text{Fixed assets (net)}}{\text{Total owners' equity}}$

   d. Book value per share of common stock (see Chapter 17) = $\frac{\text{Common stock equity}}{\text{Number of common shares outstanding}}$

4. **Measures of debt structure:**

   a. Total liabilities to total assets (see Chapter 3) = $\frac{\text{Total liabilities}}{\text{Total assets (net)}}$

   b. Total liabilities to owners' equity (see Chapter 3) = $\frac{\text{Total liabilities}}{\text{Owners' equity}}$

   c. Times bond interest earned (see Chapter 11) = $\frac{\text{Net income} + \text{Bond interest expense} + \text{Income tax}}{\text{Bond interest expense}}$

   d. Bonds payable to fixed assets = $\frac{\text{Bonds payable}}{\text{Fixed assets (net)}}$

5. **Measures of earnings position:**

   a. Net income to sales (see Chapter 4) = $\frac{\text{Net income}}{\text{Sales (net)}}$

   b. Net income to owners' equity (see Chapter 4) = $\frac{\text{Net income}}{\text{Owners' equity}}$

Exhibit 21-6 **(continued)**

c. **Asset turnover** = $\frac{\text{Sales (net)}}{\text{Total assets (net)}}$

d. **Operating ratio** = $\frac{\text{Operating expenses}}{\text{Sales (net)}}$

e. **Net income to total assets** = $\frac{\text{Net income}}{\text{Total assets}}$

f. **Net income per share of common stock (see Chapters 5 and 7)** =

$$\frac{\text{Net income} - \text{Preferred dividend requirements}}{\text{Average number of common shares outstanding}}$$

g. **Current yield of common stock** = $\frac{\text{Annual cash dividends per share}}{\text{Market price of common stock}}$

h. **Price-earnings ratio (see Chapter 4)** = $\frac{\text{Market price per share of common stock}}{\text{Net income per share of common stock}}$

i. **Return on investment (see Chapters 4 and 27)** = $\frac{\text{Net income}}{\text{Total assets (or Owners' equity)}}$

equipment in 19_2, when the price level is 120. (A price level of 120 means that it takes 120 dollars to purchase the same goods as were purchased for 100 dollars in the base year, when the price level was 100.) The company records its purchases in the Equipment account at acquisition cost, so at the end of 19_2 the Equipment account shows a balance of $600,000.

The accountant adds up the different purchases without hesitation. Yet the dollars involved in each purchase have different purchasing powers. The accountant would be horrified at the idea of adding 100,000 dollars, 200,000 francs, and 300,000 yen and calling the result $600,000! Yet, in ignoring the changes in price level, he is doing much the same thing.

In the accounts and financial statements, it appears that this company is following a policy of each year investing $100,000 more in equipment than it had invested in the preceding year. However, can you evaluate management's equipment-investment policy without taking into consideration the changes in purchasing power of dollars from year to year in a period of rising prices? Is the trend in equipment investment properly reflected in financial statements?

What impact does the depreciation of the equipment have on the income statement? Because depreciation expense is computed to reflect the dollars in the asset account (the historical cost of the equipment), this expense is as misleading as the asset account from which it is computed.

Example 3. A company presents to its shareholders the comparative income statement summarized in Exhibit 21-7. If this statement is issued in a time of generally rising price levels, how meaningful is the comparative statement? Have sales, expenses, and net income changed in terms of purchasing power?

Without an analysis in terms of the actual change in price level, such questions cannot be answered. Of what significance is trend analysis derived from financial statements based on historical dollars with no adjustments for changes in the price level?

Exhibit 21-7
Comparative income statement for example 3

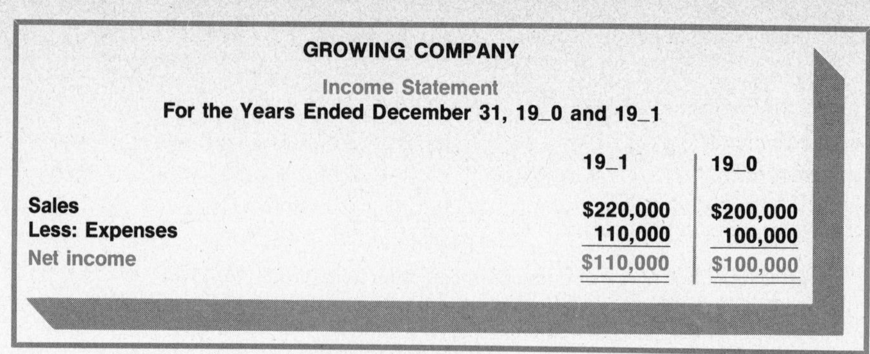

GROWING COMPANY
Income Statement
For the Years Ended December 31, 19_0 and 19_1

	19_1	19_0
Sales	$220,000	$200,000
Less: Expenses	110,000	100,000
Net income	$110,000	$100,000

Do reports to stockholders meet the accounting standards of fairness and full disclosure? It would seem that conventional financial statements leave something to be desired when it comes to these critical areas.

Example 4. A business purchases equipment for $200,000. The equipment has a four-year life and no scrap value. Exhibit 21-8 shows income statements for the company over the four years that the machine is in use. The net income of the firm is distributed to its stockholders each year as a dividend. Exhibit 21-9 shows a statement of changes in financial position for the firm over the four-year period. The working capital of the firm had increased $200,000 from the beginning to the end of the four-year period. Assume that this increase represents an increase in cash (an unlikely assumption). The asset (equipment) is now fully depreciated and needs to be replaced. The price of an identical piece of equipment is now $250,000.

Is the company in a position to replace the equipment without seeking additional funds? Another question—was the income tax paid during the four years a tax on income, or was it a tax on capital? Similarly—were the dividend payments to stockholders a distribution of earnings, or were they in part a return on capital?

Price-level adjustments

Changes in the general purchasing power of money affects business enterprises and financial statements. Such changes are commonly referred to as inflation or deflation. In periods of inflation, the general purchasing power of money declines as reflected in the increase in the general prices of goods and services. In periods of deflation, the general level of prices declines. Changes in the general purchasing power of money are ignored in financial statements prepared according to generally accepted accounting principles. Conventional financial statements generally reflect only the actual number of dollars received or expended while ignoring the purchasing power of these dollars.

Inflation and deflation affect almost every economic decision. Such matters as investing and financing decisions, wage negotiations, and pricing policies are influenced in one way or another by changes in the general price level. Because of their significance, changes in the general price level cannot be ignored.

The change in the general price level can be measured by index numbers. The

Gross National Product Implicit Price Deflator is the best known index of the general price level in the United States. The U.S. Department of Commerce reports the GNP Implicit Price Deflators for 1969–1973 as shown in Exhibit 21-10.

With the use of index numbers, it is possible to restate the historical-dollar financial statements so that all the dollars reported on the statements reflect the same general purchasing power at a specific date. These adjusted statements are called general

Exhibit 21-8 Comparative income statement for example 4

EXAMPLE FOUR COMPANY
Comparative Income Statement
For the Years Ended December 31, 19_1 through 19_4

	19_4	19_3	19_2	19_1
Sales	$500,000	$500,000	$500,000	$500,000
Expenses:				
Depreciation	(50,000)	(50,000)	(50,000)	(50,000)
Other expenses	(350,000)	(350,000)	(350,000)	(350,000)
Net income before taxes	$100,000	$100,000	$100,000	$100,000
Income taxes (50% rate)	(50,000)	(50,000)	(50,000)	(50,000)
Net income	$ 50,000	$ 50,000	$ 50,000	$ 50,000
Dividends paid	$ 50,000	$ 50,000	$ 50,000	$ 50,000

EXAMPLE FOUR COMPANY
Statement of Changes in Financial Position
For the Four Years Ended December 31, 19_4

Sources:	
Net income	$200,000
Add: Depreciation charges	200,000
Financial resources provided	$400,000
Uses:	
Dividends paid	$200,000
Increases in working capital	200,000
Financial resources used	$400,000

Exhibit 21-9 Statement of changes in financial position for example 4

Period	GNP Implicit Price Deflator
1969	128.2
1970	135.2
1971	141.6
1972	146.1
1973	154.3
1974	170.2
1975 (through September)	186.1

Exhibit 21-10 Gross National Product Implicit Price Deflator (1958 = 100)

price-level financial statements. The conversion of historical dollars to current dollars is made by dividing data by the price index of the date on which an event occurred to convert the data to base-year dollars; multiplying the converted data by the current index converts the data to current dollars. An illustration will show the process. Assume that a machine was purchased for $100,000 when the price index was 100. The current value of the index is 150. The conversion is made as follows:

$$\frac{\text{Current index number}}{\text{Index number at time asset acquired}} \times \text{Cost of asset}$$

$$\frac{150}{100} \times \$100{,}000 = \$150{,}000.$$

During periods of inflation, holders of cash and certain contractual claims to fixed amounts of dollars (such as accounts receivables and notes receivables) lose purchasing power since the dollars they hold buy fewer goods and services. This loss in purchasing power is referred to as general price-level loss. The assets that give rise to such losses are referred to as monetary assets. In periods of inflation, debtors repay their obligations with dollars of less purchasing power than the dollars they borrowed in an earlier period. Such gains are called general price-level gains. The liabilities that give rise to such gains are called monetary liabilities. When financial statements are restated to reflect changes in the general purchasing power of the dollar, price-level gains or losses will arise from holding monetary assets and liabilities. All other assets and liabilities are called nonmonetary items. Nonmonetary items include inventory, investments in common stock, plant and equipment, retained earnings, and others. Holding nonmonetary items will not produce general price-level gains and losses.

In 1969, the Accounting Principles Board, in ***Statement No. 3: Financial Statements Restated for General Price-Level Changes,*** recommended that financial statements prepared on an historical cost basis be supplemented by statements that are adjusted for changes in the general price level. This recommendation has not been taken seriously by the business community. The Financial Accounting Standards Board has considered the issuance of a ***Statement*** requiring the preparation of supplementary statements adjusted for price-level changes but has not done so as of the date this book went to press.

RESTATING FINANCIAL STATEMENTS. The procedure for restating conventional financial statements for changes in the general price level is as follows. Assume that a company was organized on January 1, 19_1. Common stock was issued for $10,000 cash. The company acquired equipment on January 1, 19_1 at a cost of $10,000. The equipment has a 10-year life and no salvage value. The company uses straight-line depreciation. Fifty percent of the cost of the building was paid in cash when purchased. The balance is due in the following year. During the year the company performed services for $20,000. Rent expense during the year amounted to $5,000 and was paid in cash. Income taxes were paid at a rate of 50 percent of net income. The historical balance sheets for the beginning and end of the year are presented here:

	Jan. 1, 19_1		Dec. 31, 19_1
Cash	$ 5,000		$13,000
Equipment	10,000	$10,000	
Less accumulated depreciation		1,000	9,000
Total assets	$15,000		$22,000
Accounts payable	$ 5,000		$ 5,000
Common stock	10,000		10,000
Retained earnings			7,000
Total	$15,000		$22,000

The income statement for the year is shown here:

Services		$20,000
Less expenses:		
Depreciation expense	$ 1,000	
Rent expense	5,000	
Income taxes	7,000	13,000
Net income		$ 7,000

General purchasing power index numbers for the year were as follows:

January 1	100
Average during the year	105
December 31	110

The average monetary assets of the company held during the year were $9,000 ($5,000 on January 1 and $13,000 on December 31). The average monetary liabilities of the company during the year were $5,000. Thus the average net monetary assets held during the year were $4,000 ($9,000 assets less $5,000 liabilities). Since there was a 10 percent increase in the general price level, and monetary assets exceeded monetary liabilities, purchasing power loss during the year was $400 ($4,000 multiplied by 10 percent).

The income statement for the year can be restated in terms of purchasing power at the end of the year. It is assumed that the sales and expenses other than depreciation were incurred evenly during the year. Hence an average index number is used to restate these items to reflect purchasing power at the end of the year. Depreciation expense is restated from the date of acquisition of the asset depreciated. The loss in purchasing power is disclosed in the income statement. The historical and restated income statements for the company are shown in Exhibit 21-11.

Exhibit 21-11 Income statement adjusted for price-level changes

	Historical	Conversion Ratio	Restated (Data rounded)
Services	**$20,000**	**110/105**	**$20,900**
Depreciation expense	**(1,000)**	**110/100**	**(1,100)**
Rent expense	**(5,000)**	**110/105**	**(5,200)**
Income taxes	**(7,000)**	**110/105**	**(7,300)**
General price-level loss			**(400)**
Net income	**$ 7,000**		**$ 6,900**

Exhibit 21-12 **Balance sheet adjusted for price-level changes**

	Historical	Conversion Ratio	Restated (Data rounded)
Cash	$13,000		$13,000
Equipment (net)	9,000	110/100	9,900
Total assets	$22,000		$22,900
Accounts payable	$ 5,000		$ 5,000
Common stock	10,000	110/100	11,000
Retained earnings	7,000	From income statement	6,900
Total	$22,000		$22,900

The December 31, 19_1 balance sheet is restated to reflect dollars with year-end purchasing power in Exhibit 21-12. Monetary assets and liabilities have the same purchasing power as reflected on the historical balance sheet and do not require a restatement. Nonmonetary items are restated to indicate the purchasing power invested at current dollars.

Price-level adjustments serve to adjust financial statements for changes in the *general* price level—that is, for the average effects of inflation and deflation. The adjusted data for particular assets does not necessarily correspond to the fair market value or replacement value of these assets. General price-level index numbers are used to convert asset cost into dollars of common purchasing power. Adjusting historical costs does not change the value originally recorded; price-level adjustments simply adjust the size of dollars so that all dollars used in the statements are uniform in terms of purchasing power.

Price-level changes are an economic fact, and accounting statements would be more useful if restated in terms of current prices as a supplement to the conventional, historical-cost statements. The accounting profession has been reluctant to report the impact of price-level changes in the financial statements. This is unfortunate.

The human element in accounting

The behavioral sciences integrate knowledge about the behavior of individuals and groups from many disciplines, including anthropology, biology, economics, history, philosophy, political science, psychiatry, psychology, religion, and sociology.

The language of the behavioral sciences contains such terms as "goals," "perceptions," "aspiration levels," "stimulus-response," "conflict," and "anxiety"—terms that are used to describe individual and group behavior. Empirical evidence made available by behavioral scientists is somewhat inconclusive; the application of these findings to accounting has not been extensively demonstrated. Nevertheless, the behavioral accountant currently is on the frontier of one area of accounting that needs exploring.

Behavioral scientists study the activities of man in relation to his environment, behaviors, and relationships. Accounting must begin to call upon the behavioral sciences for assistance in improving financial and managerial accounting principles, practices, and procedures. The human element in accounting cannot be ignored without the assumption of considerable risks.

A MODEL

Many models and theories of organizational behavior have been proposed. Exhibit 21-13 shows a model for organizational effectiveness. This model depicts relationships that explain or predict organizational effectiveness. This model emphasizes the importance of (1) organizational structure as an influence on behavior of individual employees and groups, and (2) environmental considerations as an influence on organizational structure and functions.

1. The *environment* of a firm includes the economic, legal, political, social, and cultural elements that can influence the firm in its survival and its goal-attainment activities.
2. The *organization* of a firm identifies the structure of the enterprise through which collective action is undertaken to achieve survival and to attain prescribed goals. An organization reflects varying degrees of formal structure, control and information systems, decision-making processes, and leadership perceptions.
3. *Organization behavior* is a composite of individual and group behavior. We turn now to a discussion of some aspects of individual and group behavior, as revealed by behavioral studies.

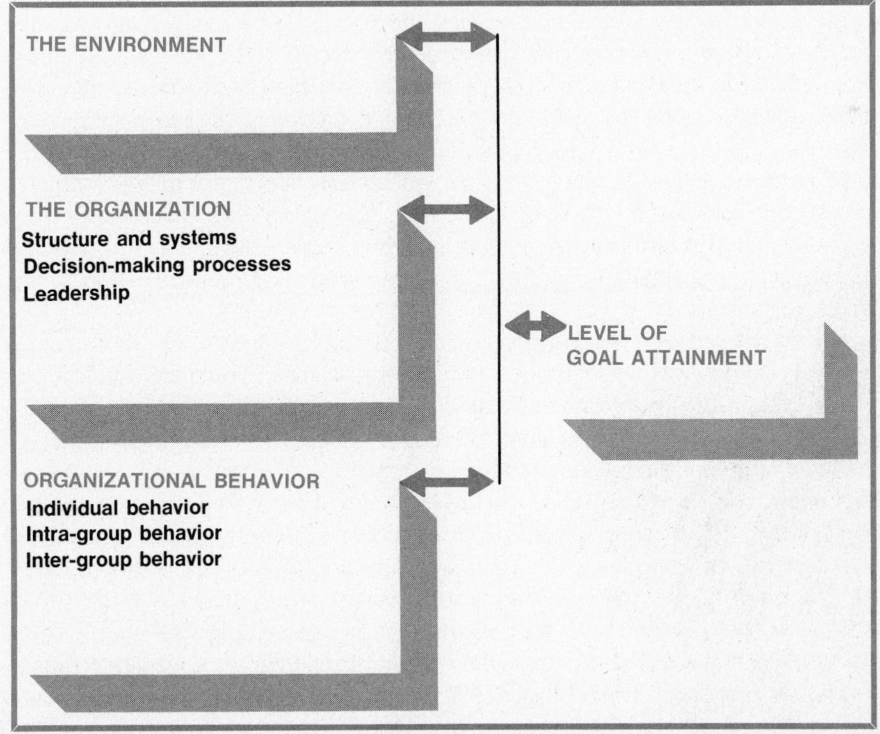

Exhibit 21-13
A behavioral model of organizational effectiveness

HOW GROUPS FUNCTION

A group establishes or adopts behavior norms, standards and patterns that give structure and stability to the group. Through norms, an individual comes to recognize his place in the group and the role he is to play. Violation of norms widely held by the group tends to alienate and isolate the offending party. Such individuals frequently are labeled deviants, delinquents, rebels, or outlaws.

The ability and willingness of individuals to communicate is essential to group activities. In organized societies, complex symbols become the medium through which communication takes place. Group functioning requires the ability of individuals to react to ideas, people, and proposals. As a member of a group, the individual assumes a role that enables him to accept others and to be accepted by them. This process has been expressed in the transactional psychology of interpersonal relationships (popularized in "I'm O.K., you're O.K."). When an individual is unwilling or unable to assume his role in the group, tensions and conflicts arise.

Within a group there exist pressures to conform and pressures to dissolve. These pressures affect communications, acceptances, expectations, and trusts. In groups where members feel that they belong and have a common interest, tensions are at a minimum, and a relaxed atmosphere prevails. Defenses and deceptions are minimized. Group cohesiveness is related to such factors as (1) shared values and common behavior norms, (2) the ability of the group to satisfy needs and achieve goals, (3) morale, rapport, solidarity, and similar vague but real concepts associated with belonging, identification, involvement, and commitment, and (4) leadership.

Group conflict, manifested in tensions and frustrations, arises when individuals within the group feel insecure about their positions within the group, or when the group is prevented from reaching its objective. Factions within a group arise primarily from a failure of the group to cultivate a sense of belonging, from a lack of organization or effective leadership, and from the group's inability to achieve its goal. (Factions also are likely to arise in a group that has achieved its major goal. Once the group's task is accomplished, members turn their attentions again to their individual goals and may set aside the spirit of cooperation adopted while striving toward the group's goal.) Disruptive elements within the group also are associated with personal factors such as personality conflicts, domineering attitudes, sarcasm, and similar faults and failings.

People with common needs and values tend to organize into groups. When people share goals, they tend to develop congenial relationships. Unfortunately, the individual tends to overestimate the aspiration-fulfilling capability of the group with which he associates. He usually joins a group with high hopes, and he may quickly become bitter if the group fails to live up to his expectations.

A small group with an even number of members often is plagued by friction and factions. The group with an odd number of members has more stability and cohesion. An influx of a large number of new members into a group in a short period of time tends to be disruptive. New members tend to feel somewhat inferior to the establishment; old members tend to resent new members who take an active role too soon. Small groups have a built-in potential for (1) high exchange of information, (2) high possibility of deadlock and instability, (3) high differentiation of roles, with one person an active initiator and another a passive controller (perhaps with a veto), and (4) high tension and emotion levels.

Individuals who belong to a group tend to adopt the norms of the group they join or wish to join. The individual tends to find it difficult to resist the established norms of the group, so he usually conforms. Seldom will the group adopt the behavior patterns of a nonconforming member. Occasionally, however, a group will tolerate and even welcome a nonconforming member as a diversion and relief from the tensions and strains of group efforts. This tolerance can easily turn to resentment if the nonconformist is seen as a hindrance to the group's activities.

Group solidarity increases when members of the group are aware of and accept the behavior norms expected by the group. In general, the more an individual conforms to group norms, the better liked he is. The better liked he is, the more he tends to conform. Individuals in a group tend to agree with views expressed by people they like, and to disagree with the opinions of people they dislike. Individuals tend to believe that people they dislike always disagree with them, usually for personal and unreasonable reasons. In many groups, there seems to be a tendency to select one individual as a "scapegoat," with all other members focusing their dislikes on him. Apparently, the members are able to displace all or most of their negative feelings onto the scapegoat, and therefore to minimize their dislikes of the other members with whom they must cooperate in group efforts.

In general, when a group feels that its rewards will come through successful group cooperation, the members tend to suppress unfavorable feelings about one another and to emphasize their good feelings about one another. When the members feel that their relationship in the group is one of competition—with individual rewards and punishments depending on doing or looking better than other group members—there is a tendency for the members of the group to dislike one another, to dislike the group, to pay less attention to what others say in the group, to waste time, and to accomplish less as a group.

The goals of the group tend to correspond to the goals of the dominant group members, to be affected by interpersonal relationships within the group, and to be shaped by the external environment. Business organizations have a variety of goals, two of which are organizational survival and profit maximization. The goals of individuals and those of the firms with which they associate may be similar or may be in conflict. Goal attainment for a firm is related to the degree to which individuals can function within the structure and expectations of the firm and its environment.

BEHAVIORAL IMPACTS ON ACCOUNTING

Humans are adaptive, problem-solving, decision-making creatures motivated by an assortment of differing needs and drives. The activities of individuals and organizations are enhanced or restricted by their environment, the availability of resources, administrative and managerial ability and experience, reward-punishment stimulation, ability to accept responsibility and respond to authority. The behavioral sciences can contribute much to an understanding of individual and group motivation and coordination.

Behavioral concepts have many implications for accounting, and it is hoped that their application will increase in the future. We briefly discuss here several areas where the behavioral sciences can serve accounting.

THE ALLOCATION OF RESOURCES THROUGH BUDGETING. From a behavioral viewpoint, budgeting is a process in which groups compete for a share of available resources. The behavioral scientist would be interested in the budgeting process as a situation in which

1. groups select projects to be submitted to a decision-making committee for approval and funding;
2. a decision-making group evaluates proposed projects after having established priorities and determined restraints;
3. decisions are communicated to project proposers; and
4. approved projects are initiated, controlled, and reviewed.

In studies of budgeting, behavioral scientists have shown that, where conflicts arise over proposals for use of resources, each competing group sees its project as superior to those of competitors. In budgeting, goal achievement is a primary motivating factor. Failure to achieve a goal creates conflicts and influences behavior and attitudes negatively. Goal attainment or failure to attain a goal in one budget period affects behavior, attitude, and motivation in a subsequent period. When a group or individual has experienced success, subsequent action tends to improve; failure tends to lower levels of aspiration and achievement.

CONTROL. Behavioral studies provide some preliminary insights in the area of control, especially with regard to procedures of setting standards.

1. Control systems that encourage responsibility by self-discipline rather than through unbending rules are often more effective within complex business environments.
2. Employees tend to develop their own standards and to manipulate norms established by management, especially when the norms are considered unreasonable or unfair.
3. Feedback on variances from standards tends to emphasize underachievement (unfavorable variances) and punishment, rather than overachievement and reward.

GENERALLY ACCEPTED ACCOUNTING PRINCIPLES. Studies have shown that behavioral and decision-making patterns of management are conditioned to some extent by generally accepted accounting principles. Accounting principles do have an impact on accounting measurement and reporting activities. Generally accepted accounting principles narrow but do not eliminate variations in processing and reporting practices. Alternative accounting principles and procedures are available that require a knowledge of consequences, and eventually a decision. Financial statements do affect the behavior of their users.

Earlier in this book we discussed the continuing debate over treatment of business acquisitions as poolings of interest or as purchases. We suggested that the purchase method is unpopular with many managers because it often involves the creation of a sizable intangible asset on the balance sheet that must be amortized (written off as expense) on future income statements, decreasing the net income and earnings per share in future periods. The general acceptance of the pooling of interest method of accounting for acquisitions was a major stimulation to the merger movement in recent years. Now that generally accepted accounting principles considerably curtail the use of the pooling of interest method, the behavior of management is beginning to change.

Management also reacted to an interpretation of accounting principles that stipulated the write-off of research and development costs in the period during which they were incurred, rather than capitalizing the costs and amortizing them over a period of years. This interpretation seems to have discouraged many firms from undertaking or expanding research and development programs.

The human element in accounting has received insufficient attention from the accounting profession. A few businesses have tried to reflect "human resources" as an asset on their balance sheets. In human-resources accounting, costs of recruiting, familiarizing, and developing personnel are capitalized, in the same way that investments in plant and equipment are capitalized. These costs are then amortized over the working years of the employees. When an employee leaves the firm, the unamortized human investment is written off as a loss. Such accounting for human resources tries to measure more accurately the cost of employee-personnel practices, turnover, and so on. At this writing, human-resource accounting is not accepted as a standard accounting practice.

Financial and managerial accounting as we now know it may change drastically in the future. It is possible that the role of accounting will expand to include a theory and procedures for reporting on the social benefits and social costs of a business entity. Users of financial reports may want to know how well a company is fulfilling its social responsibilities. What impact is the company having on its environment? Do the products it produces and sells improve the quality of life of the consumer? Are the goals and the programs of the business beneficial to society as a whole? How is the firm utilizing its human resources?

If accounting is to move in this social-centered direction, then traditional concepts such as profits, earnings per share, and return on investment must be redefined to accommodate values that do not enter into current computations of these and similar measures of efficiency and effectiveness. Very little has been attempted in this area of expanding the scope and content of accounting. However, this area may very well turn out to be "where the action is" in the accounting profession of the not-too-distant future.

With this brief examination of the relationship of the behavioral sciences to accounting, you should begin to perceive the need for the accountant to consider the human element in his work. Future students will spend more time examining this topic. Hopefully, the accounting profession soon will begin to integrate the findings of the behavioral sciences into the input, processing, and output functions of the accounting system.

Summary

In this chapter, we review and expand our coverage of financial statement analysis. Vertical and horizontal analysis are introduced as tools of financial statement evaluation. Ratios are grouped in a variety of ways to assist in drawing significant information from financial statements.

The impact of price-level changes on financial statements is especially important in periods of serious inflation. A procedure is illustrated whereby financial statements can be adjusted for changes in the price level. We point out significant difficulties associated with the use of financial statements unadjusted for changes in the price level. However, we also note that the accounting profession has not been enthusiastic about the adoption of price-level adjustments as standard accounting procedures.

Finally, the chapter explores the human element in accounting and relates this topic to the behavioral sciences. We discuss individual and group behavior models. We demonstrate the impact of behavioral accounting with regard to budgeting, standard setting, and generally accepted accounting principles.

Questions

1. What are comparative financial statements and what is their significance? Distinguish between vertical and horizontal analysis as applied to financial statement analysis.
2. What is meant by a ratio? Name and discuss at least three ratios associated with the measurement of each of the following: a firm's equity; the turnover of current assets; capital structure; debt structure; earnings.
3. What distortions can arise in interpreting financial statements if major changes occur in the general price level and the financial statements are not adjusted to reflect these changes?
4. Accountants have resisted attempts to depart from the practice of recording and reporting "historical costs" in the records and statements. Several alternatives are available for coping with problems of changes in the purchasing power of the dollar. Discuss the merits and demerits of each of the following approaches.
   a. Continue to report financial data on an historical cost basis.
   b. Report data on a cost basis, but provide additional schedules that show statements converted into dollars with uniform purchasing power through use of price indexes.
   c. Report data only in terms of dollars having a uniform purchasing power.
5. What is meant by the human element in accounting? Why should an accountant be aware of the implications of accounting for human behavior?
6. If the amounts of working capital and the current ratios are the same for two companies, can you conclude that the positions of both firms are equally liquid?
7. As a lender, would you generally consider each of the following conditions to be favorable or unfavorable:
   a. a low current ratio;
   b. high inventory turnover;
   c. a receivable with terms of 2/10, n/30, and age of receivable 36 days;
   d. low ratio (such as 0.2 to 1) of owners' equity to total liabilities;
   e. low ratio of stockholders' equity to assets?

8. Comment on this quotation from the Accounting Principles Board: ". . . that the assumption in accounting that fluctuations in the value of the dollar may be ignored as unrealistic."
9. In 19_1, the Wonder Company purchased equipment with a ten-year life for $100,000. In 19_6, the asset has a book value of $40,000 and is sold for $105,000. The accountant reports a gain on the sale of the equipment at $65,000. To what factors may this "gain" be attributed?
10. Land was purchased in 19_1 for $100,000. By 19_5, the general price level has increased 60 percent. Assuming that no other factors involved in the price of the land have changed, what price would have to be asked in selling the land in 19_5 to avoid a loss in purchasing power on the sale?
11. Explain the following statements. An asset was purchased for $100 when the general price index was 100. The asset was consumed when the general price level was 110, and was replaced by an identical asset costing $112.
12. A company acquires three machines in three different years. Each machine costs $100,000 and is depreciated on a straight-line basis without salvage value over a ten-year life. The first machine is purchased on March 1, 19_0, when the price index is 100. The second machine is purchased on March 2, 19_2, when the price index is 105. The third machine is purchased on March 3, 19_3, when the price index is 120.

    Required:

    a. What depreciation was recorded on the 19_3 income statement?

    b. What is the depreciation expense adjusted by the index number for 19_3? How would you interpret this dollar figure?

    c. If a balance sheet adjusted for changes in the price level were prepared at the end of 19_3, at what gross value would the machines be carried?
13. How does a general price index differ from specific indexes (say, the retail food price index)?
14. Does the adoption of LIFO or FIFO inventory methods adequately account for changes in the purchasing power of the dollar for financial statement reporting?
15. What problems do you perceive with regard to the human element in accounting and

    a. accounting as an information system;

    b. communication in accounting;

    c. materiality as an accounting concept?
16. Cite various examples of ways in which accounting is a social force in our society (for example, in the area of public policy).
17. Comment on the following observations:

    a. Creditors and stockholders usually evaluate ratios as being favorable or unfavorable in the same manner.

    b. It is possible for a company's net income to increase without an increase (or with a decline) in the turnover of inventory and accounts receivable.

Exercises

E21-1 (Statement analysis)

The following are selected data taken from the financial statements of the Analysis Company.

	This Year	Last Year
Sales	$200,000	$150,000
Rent expense	5,000	—
Net income (net loss)	300,000	0
Dividend income	20,000	40,000
Interest income	—	7,000
Operating income (or loss)	(10,000)	15,000
Fire loss	20,000	—
Miscellaneous	(3,000)	—
Extraordinary item	(15,000)	(7,500)

Required: Prepare a schedule to show the dollar amount of change from last year to this year for each item, the percentage of change, and the ratio of this year's amount to last year's amount.

E21-2 (Ratios)

Exhibit 21-14 shows financial statements of the Selfo Company. The company pany paid a $5-per-share cash dividend in 19_6. The average market price of the stock was $25 per share. Compute the following ratios for the company:

a. current ratio;
b. acid-test ratio;
c. cash ratio;
d. receivables turnover;
e. age of receivables;
f. merchandise inventory turnover;
g. days' supply in inventory;
h. working capital turnover;
i. owners' equity to total assets;
j. owners' equity to total liabilities;
k. total liabilities to owner's equity;
l. net income to sales;
m. net income to owners' equity;
n. asset turnover;
o. operating ratio;
p. net income to total assets;
q. net income per share of common stock;
r. current yield of common stock;
s. price-earnings ratio.

E21-3 (Price level)

A firm purchased land in 19_0 for $200,000, when the general price index was 100. In 19_9, the general price index is 150.

a. What is the historical cost of the land?
b. What is the historical cost in terms of current purchasing power?
c. When comparing your answers to the first two parts, do you conclude that the firm had (1) a realized gain, (2) an unrealized gain, or (3) no gain?
d. What dollar value would an accountant report for the land in the 19_0 balance sheet? In the 19_9 balance sheet?
e. The land is sold in 19_9 for $500,000. Prepare condensed income statements for the transaction
(1) on an historical cost basis;
(2) on an historical cost basis adjusted for general price-level change.
Which net income figure best reflects the economic gain or loss?

Exhibit 21-14
Financial statements for Exercise E21-2

SELFO COMPANY

Partial Balance Sheets

	Dec. 31, 19_6	Jan. 1, 19_6
Cash	$ 20,000	
Accounts receivable	30,000	$40,000
Marketable securities	10,000	
Inventory	40,000	20,000
Land	200,000	
Property, plant, and equipment (net)	500,000	
Total assets	$800,000	
Current liabilities	$ 50,000	
Long-term liabilities	150,000	
Common stock (5,000 shares)	500,000	
Retained earnings	100,000	
Total liabilities and owners equity	$800,000	

SELFO COMPANY

Income Statment
For the Year Ended December 31, 19_6

Sales (net; all credit)	$140,000
Cost of goods sold	90,000
Gross margin	$ 50,000
Operating expenses	15,000
Net income	$ 35,000

Problems

P21-1 (Statement analysis)
Exhibit 21-15 shows a comparative income statement for the Trust Company. Prepare a comparative income statement showing (a) the amount of change in each item during the year, and (b) the percentage of change in each item during the year.

P21-2 (Statement analysis)
Exhibit 21-16 shows a comparative balance sheet for the Trust Company. Prepare a comparative balance sheet showing (a) the amount of change in each item over the year, and (b) the percentage of change in each item.

P21-3 (Ratios)
Refer to Exhibits 21-15 and 21-16. Compute the following ratios for the Trust Company for 19_6:

a. current ratio;
b. acid-test ratio;
c. receivables turnover;
d. age of receivables;
e. merchandise inventory turnover;
f. owners' equity to total assets;
g. owners' equity to total liabilities;
h. book value per share of capital stock;
i. times bond interest earned;

Exhibit 21-15
Income statement for Problem P21-1

TRUST COMPANY

Income Statement
For the Years Ended December 31, 19_5 and 19_6

	19_6	19_5
Sales (credit)	$155,000	$123,000
Sales returns and allowances	5,000	3,000
Net sales	$150,000	$120,000
Cost of goods sold	60,000	50,000
Gross margin	$ 90,000	$ 70,000
Operating expenses	50,000	40,000
Net income	$ 40,000	$ 30,000

Exhibit 21-16
Balance sheet for Problem P21-2

TRUST COMPANY

Statement of Financial Position
December 31, 19_5 and 19_6

	19_6	19_5
Cash	$ 35,000	$ 70,000
Accounts receivable	40,000	20,000
Inventory	60,000	30,000
Property, plant, and equipment (net)	165,000	150,000
Total assets	$300,000	$270,000
Current liabilities	$ 40,000	$ 30,000
Long-term liability, 9% bonds	100,000	100,000
Capital stock (1,600 shares)	120,000	120,000
Retained earnings	40,000	20,000
Total liabilities and stockholders' equity	$300,000	$270,000

j. net income to sales;
k. net income to owners' equity;
l. operating ratio;
m. return on investment (total asset approach).

P21-4 (Price-level adjustments)
Exhibit 21-17 shows balance-sheet summaries for two companies as prepared according to conventional accounting principles, and as restated in terms of current dollars (after adjustments for changes in the purchasing power of the dollar). The general price level has increased by 50 percent since the merchandise inventory and fixed assets were acquired and the stock issued. Therefore, each of these three items is multiplied by a factor of 1.50 in preparing the adjusted statements.

Required:

a. Which company held a relatively small amount of monetary assets and relatively large debt? As a result of this combination, did this company gain or lose purchasing power during this period of rising prices? Evaluate the gain or loss in terms of its origins in gains or losses from holding monetary assets and liabilities.

b. Evaluate the change in purchasing power of the other company in terms of its origins in gains or losses from holding monetary assets and liabilities.

c. When a firm holds monetary assets in a period of rising prices, the firm experiences a loss in purchasing power. True or false? Why?

d. When a firm incurs liabilities in a period of rising prices, the firm experiences a gain in purchasing power. True or false? Why?

e. In what sense are the adjusted statements (restated in terms of current dollars) referred to as "common dollar statements"?

f. Do common dollar statements represent a departure from historical costs? Explain.

g. Do common dollar statements report assets at their replacement costs (that is, approximately at their fair market value)?

P21-5 (Price-level adjustments)

Comparative balance sheets for a company formed on January 1 are presented here:

	Jan. 1	Dec. 31
Monetary assets	$1,000	$1,600
Nonmonetary assets	2,000	1,600
Total assets	$3,000	$3,200
Monetary liabilities	$1,000	$1,000
Common stock	2,000	2,000
Retained earnings	0	200
Total	$3,000	$3,200

Exhibit 21-17 **Balance sheets for Problem P21-4**

CONVENTIONAL STATEMENTS

	Company X	Company Y
Cash, receivables, marketable securities	$ 800	$ 100
Merchandise inventory	200	400
Property, plant, and equipment	500	1,000
Total assets	$1,500	$1,500
Liabilities	$ 100	$1,400
Stockholders' equity	1,400	100
Total liabilities and stockholders' equity	$1,500	$1,500

STATEMENTS ADJUSTED TO CURRENT DOLLARS

	Company X	Company Y
Cash, receivables, marketable securities	$ 800	$ 100
Merchandise inventory [conversion ratio 1.50]	300	600
Property, plant, and equipment [conversion ratio 1.50]	750	1,500
Total assets	$1,850	$2,200
Liabilities	$ 100	$1,400
Stockholders' equity [conversion ratio 1.50]	2,100	150
Accumulated gain (or loss) in purchasing power	(350)	650
Total liabilities and stockholders' equity	$1,850	$2,200

The historical-dollar income statement for the year is as follows:

Services	$ 800
Depreciation expense	(400)
Income taxes and other expenses	(200)
Net income	$ 200

Price indexes for the year were as follows:

January 1	100
Average during the year	110
December 31	120

Services were rendered evenly during the year. Taxes and other expenses were paid evenly during the year. The nonmonetary assets were acquired on January 1.

Required: Prepare an income statement and balance sheet restated for changes in the general price level.

P21-6 (Ratio analysis)

The financial statements for a company for two years are as follows.

	Year 2	Year 1
Cash	$ 10,000	$ 5,000
Accounts receivable (net)	20,000	10,000
Inventory	30,000	25,000
Investments in land	65,000	—
Plant and equipment (net)	500,000	400,000
Total	$625,000	$440,000
Accounts payable	$ 5,000	$ 10,000
Taxes payable	10,000	5,000
Bonds payable—6%	100,000	50,000
Premium on bonds payable	10,000	—
Common stock—$10 par value	100,000	100,000
Premium on common stock	10,000	10,000
Retained earnings	390,000	265,000
Total	$625,000	$440,000

The company paid a $10,000 cash dividend in Year 2. The market value of the stock on December 31, Year 1, was $90 per share and $235 per share, Year 2. The income statements of the company for the two years were as follows:

	Year 2	Year 1
Sales (net)	$1,145,000	$800,000
Cost of goods sold	300,000	265,000
Gross margin on sales	$ 845,000	$535,000
Operating expenses	600,000	430,000
Income taxes	10,000	5,000
Net income	$ 235,000	$100,000

In Year 0, the ending inventory was $15,000 and the ending balance in accounts receivable was $2,000.

Required:

a. Compute the following ratios for Year 1 and Year 2.

1. Current ratio.
2. Acid-test ratio.
3. Cash ratio.
4. Receivable turnover.
5. Age of receivables.
6. Inventory turnover.
7. Days' supply in inventory.
8. Owners' equity to total assets.
9. Owners' equity to total liabilities.
10. Book value per share of common stock.
11. Times bond interest earned.
12. Net income to sales.
13. Net income to owners' equity.
14. Net income per share of common stock.
15. Price-earnings ratio.
16. Return on investment.

b. Comment on the change in the following from Year 1 to Year 2:

1. The firm's liquidity.
2. Turnover of current assets.
3. Capital structure.
4. Debt structure.
5. Earning position.

P21-7 (Vertical analysis)
Refer to Problem P21-6. Prepare common-size balance sheets and income statements for Years 1 and 2.

P21-8 (Horizontal analysis)
Refer to Problem P21-6. Prepare schedules for the balance sheets and income statements to show amounts of change and percent of change for the two years.

P21-9 (Price-level statements)
The statements of financial position of two companies are shown:

	Company X	Company Y
Monetary assets:		
Cash and receivables	$100	$200
Nonmonetary items:		
Inventory, plant and equipment	200	100
Total assets	$300	$300
Monetary liabilities:		
Current and noncurrent liabilities	$175	$ 50
Nonmonetary owners' equity	125	250
Total	$300	$300

Required: Assume that the current price index is 150. At the time the nonmonetary items were acquired, the price index was 60.

a. Prepare financial statements for the two companies adjusted for changes in the price level.

b. Comment on how the two companies were affected by inflation.

Managerial accounting

Part Five

22 The comprehensive budget

Thus far in our study of accounting, we have dealt primarily with the problems of accumulation, measurement, and communication that are involved in the preparation of the major financial statements. These statements report ***historical*** data—information about the ***past.*** To a great extent, they are directed toward users of the accounting outputs ***outside*** the business. We now turn our attention to the ways that the accounting system copes with the ***future*** of a business. The planning reports, or budgets, are tools of major importance for the management of the company, which must make daily decisions that will affect the future of the business.

Before turning to the procedures of preparing budgets, we begin with a general discussion of the planning process.

The planning process

Planning gives purpose and direction to a business. Planning is future-oriented. Systematic planning gives a firm some control over its destiny.

It has been said that failure to plan is in itself a plan for the future. The lack of a plan represents a decision to leave the future to the forces of chaos—to abdicate the role of intelligence to chance. Planning recognizes challenges and reveals opportunities.

Speaking broadly, a business succeeds or fails in relation to its knowledge of where it is going and how it will get there. Such knowledge comes from thinking through rational planning processes. The planning must blend with the implementation processes that will turn the plans into reality. The planning and implementation processes can be summarized in the following steps.

1. Define the basic philosophy of the business.
2. Determine and rank the objectives of the firm.
3. Initiate plans and establish programs designed to achieve the firm's objectives.
4. Provide an organization capable of carrying out the company's plans and programs.
5. Staff the organization with qualified personnel.

6. Furnish adequate physical facilities to allow the staff to carry out the plans and programs of the organization.
7. Supply operating and capital funds sufficient to achieve the stated objectives of the firm.

Planning is perhaps the most effective method of obtaining desired results. Some businesses make profits without planning, but these are the exceptions. In general, the successful business manager makes careful plans based on reliable information and reasonable expectations.

Business planning begins with budgeting. Budgeting is perhaps the most basic profit-planning tool available to management. An understanding of budgeting and all that it involves is central to an understanding of managerial accounting. Therefore, this chapter examines the budgeting process, including a review of current budgeting practices, procedures, and problems.

Budgeting

A ***budget*** is an orderly and coordinated plan of financial management. It exists because of the need to plan, motivate, and control business activity to achieve the desired objective(s). A budget may also be viewed as a plan of action that is (1) formulated within a framework of rational assumptions and (2) designed to provide the means for attaining predetermined objectives. Reduced to its essentials, budgeting is a plan, a process, and an evaluation procedure.

THE PLAN. Budgeting requires that the firm determine its objectives, policies, and programs according to a rational design. This clear and explicit plan of action must be prepared before the firm can begin to implement its intentions.

THE PROCESS. Budgeting forces management to develop methods and procedures to coordinate the activities of the enterprise. Successful execution of a plan requires integration of the firm's activities and coordination of its efforts.

THE EVALUATION. Budgeting provides a way to measure performance, control activities, and report progress. Actual accomplishments must be compared with predetermined standards if the company is to know how well it is moving toward completion of its plan. The budget itself must be evaluated and revised as the future becomes the present and as expectations change. Provision for review, evaluation, and enforcement of the budget is the final stage in the budgetary process.

THE PURPOSE OF BUDGETING

The inherent advantages of budgeting arise mainly because budgeting brings a rational approach to problem solving and decision making. The effectiveness of budgeting is increased when the budgeters have the wisdom to think about purpose and the capacity to apply suitable methods to business practices.

In the preparation of a budget, the consolidated judgment of an organization is brought to bear upon specific problems. The strength of systematic budgeting lies in the preventive, remedial, and creative self-evaluation required by the planning and implementing procedures directly associated with the budgeting process. In other words, the budget is a tool for planning, for communicating plans to those responsible for implementing them, for motivating individuals, and for controlling and evaluating performance.

The budget is a purposeful and organized plan of action. In a world where competition is becoming more intense, markets are expanding, and organizations are growing ever more complex, the coordination of a firm's efforts through budgeting becomes a necessity.

THE BUDGET PERIOD

The budget period should be short enough to permit reasonably accurate predictions. Yet it should be long enough to allow time for implementation. For practical purposes, the budget period should coincide with the fiscal period of the business, so that actual results obtained from the accounting records can be compared with budgetary estimates.

Usually, an operating budget is prepared for a year, with supporting schedules in monthly or quarterly terms. A capital-expenditure or project budget usually is developed for a longer time period, because of special conditions associated with the acquisition of long-lived assets.

THE PROCESS

Broadly speaking, the entire organization is responsible for the planning and execution of a budget. In a restricted sense, the board of directors and the chief executive of the company have ultimate responsibility for the development and enforcement of the budget. In practice, an individual (usually a budget director, chief accounting officer, or controller) or a budget committee is specifically charged with the task of developing, coordinating, executing, and enforcing the budget.

BASIC ASSUMPTION. Before developing the details of a budget, the budgeters must accept certain broad assumptions about the philosophy and objectives of the company, prevailing economic conditions, special institutional problems, and similar factors. Decisions related to the following matters usually are made before the preparation of the detailed budget:

1. the products or services to be offered for sale;
2. the capacity of the firm, or the volume of business to be sought;
3. the selling or distribution effort required;
4. the price and credit policies to be adopted;
5. the capital expenditures anticipated.

These primary assumptions and decisions become the rules of the game for those who work out the details of the budget.

THE PROCEDURE. Businessmen and accountants have developed various approaches to the task of setting up and administering a budget. The following budget procedures of planning, controlling, and evaluating are typical of those used where the services of a budget committee and a budget director are involved.

1. The budget committee determines the basic assumptions under which the details of the budget are to be prepared.

2. The board of directors (or other high-level, decision-making group) approves the assumptions set forth by the budget committee.
3. The budget director
   a. defines the policies and procedures under which the budget is to be prepared;
   b. provides the forms and schedules in which budget details are to be accumulated;
   c. establishes timetables for submission of budget estimates;
   d. assists department or division heads in preparing budget estimates for their respective areas;
   e. assembles and publishes the coordinated budget and its supporting schedules;
   f. compares actual data with budgetary estimates;
   g. evaluates, interprets, and reports to the budget committee and to other individuals responsible for performance or for dealing with variances (differences) between budget estimates and actual performance.

BUDGETARY RELATIONSHIPS. Budget construction begins with a forecast of revenue. After revenue is predicted, estimates are made of expenses, collections, and payments. When combined, the revenue, expense, collection, and payment budgets provide the basis for a comprehensive financial plan for the enterprise.

In this chapter, we begin our study of the budgetary process with the preparation of certain supporting budget schedules for a small retail business. These schedules are the basis for (and later the supporting evidence for) the operating budgets, cash budget, and budgeted financial statement.[1] This chapter outlines the preparation of the following schedules and reports.

1. Sales budgets
   a. Units
   b. Dollars
2. Cost-of-goods-sold budget
3. Selling expenses budgets
   a. Selling expenses budget
   b. Selling expenses: Cash requirements
4. Administrative expenses budgets
   a. Administrative expenses budget
   b. Administrative expenses: Cash requirements
5. Budgeted income statement
6. Budget of accounts-receivable collections
7. Purchases budgets
   a. Budget of purchases: Units
   b. Payment-on-purchases budget
8. Budgeted statement of financial position
9. Budgeted statement of changes in financial position

1. Budgeted financial statements sometimes are called ***pro forma*** statements. ***Pro forma*** means "having the form of" or "to give effect to" and is used to indicate forecasts prepared ***in the form of*** the financial statements expected in the future.

The budgeted statements with their supporting schedules make up the ***comprehensive budget*** for the company. We defer until a later chapter the discussion of capital budgeting.

The sales budgets

The sales budget is the starting point for detailed budgeting. The other budgets are based directly or indirectly upon this budget. Sales forecasts involve two intertwined factors: the number of units to be sold, and the dollar amounts of sales to be made. Although each factor influences the other, both are important. Two sales budgets usually are prepared—one expressed in units and the other in prices. The budget expressed in dollar values will be used in preparing the budgeted statements. The budget expressed in units is important for the preparation of certain other budgets. It also plays an important role in evaluating and modifying the budget during the budget period.

The sales forecast is developed by accumulating sales projections from the sales department, market studies, extrapolation of current sales, or statistical analysis involving such factors as gross national product, disposable personal income, and so on—or by a combination of such techniques. Sales projections usually are made by the sales department in consultation with the budget committee or a top-level official of the firm. Periodically, actual sales are compared to budgeted amounts, and differences are evaluated. The performance of the sales manager is evaluated against the sales budget. In this way, the budget serves to motivate the sales force. (On the other hand, it should be recognized that the sales department has a strong incentive to understate its forecasts—so that its later performance will look good in comparison with the budget.)

The sales budget may be categorized according to sales territories, products, salesmen, regions, customers, and so on. Exhibit 22-1 shows the first schedule prepared for our comprehensive budget: a sales forecast in units by territories for the Good Control Company.

The Good Control Company sells a single product. The sales price for this product during the coming year is set at $10 per unit. Using the estimates of sales volume from Schedule 1 and the sales price per unit, the budget director can compile the sales budget in dollars (Exhibit 22-2)[2]

Cost-of-goods-sold budget

From the estimate of sales volume, the budget director can prepare an estimate of the cost of goods to be sold. On the basis of past experience and recent trends, he

2. In practice, preliminary budgets usually are prepared as part of the procedure of setting the sales price per unit. For example, more units might be sold at a price of $8 per unit, or less units sold at a price of $12 per unit. The predicted dollar amount of sales for a given price would be an important factor in the choice of a sales price. Other factors would be considered too: the volume of sales the company is prepared to handle, the price customers feel is ''fair,'' the prices of competitors, and so on.

Exhibit 22-1 **Schedules 4 and 4A, Selling expenses budgets**

Schedule 1

GOOD CONTROL COMPANY

Sales Budget: Units

For the Year Ended December 31, 19_1

Territory	Total	1st Quarter	2nd Quarter	3rd Quarter	4th Quarter
Eastern United States	26,000	5,000	6,000	7,000	8,000
Western United States	11,000	2,000	2,500	3,000	3,500
	37,000	7,000	8,500	10,000	11,500

Schedule 2

GOOD CONTROL COMPANY

Sales Budget: Dollars

For the Year Ended December 31, 19_1

Territory	Total	1st Quarter	2nd Quarter	3rd Quarter	4th Quarter
Eastern United States	$260,000	$50,000	$60,000	$ 70,000	$ 80,000
Western United States	110,000	20,000	25,000	30,000	35,000
	$370,000	$70,000	$85,000	$100,000	$115,000

Exhibit 22-2 **Schedule 2, Sales budget: dollars**

estimates that the cost of the product will be $5 per unit. The cost-of-goods-sold budget (Exhibit 22-3) is prepared by applying this unit cost to the numbers of units to be sold (Schedule 1, Sales Budget: Units).[3]

Selling expenses budgets

The executives in the sales department estimate the expenses that will be incurred in making the sales called for by the sales budget. These estimates are based on past experience, current trends, and plans for future operations. From the data submitted by the sales department, the budget director prepares a selling expenses budget (Exhibit 22-4), showing the estimated expenses for each quarter and for the entire year. Schedule 4A shows the budgeted cash requirements to meet selling expenses. Depreciation expense is excluded from this schedule because depreciation does not require a cash expenditure. In practice, this schedule also might be affected by plans for prepayment or deferred payment of the expenses shown in Schedule 4. The

3. In practice, the purchases budgets might be prepared first. Cost of goods sold may depend upon the volumes of merchandise to be ordered, the costs of handling and storing inventory, and so on. Therefore, the cost per unit would be determined from the computations on the purchases budgets after inventory policies are set. Such factors become particularly important in forecasts for many months in the future, when prices and other factors may change significantly.

Exhibit 22-3 **Schedule 3, Cost-of-goods-sold budget**

Schedule 3

GOOD CONTROL COMPANY

Cost-of-Goods-Sold Budget
For the Year Ended December 31, 19_1

	Total	1st Quarter	2nd Quarter	3rd Quarter	4th Quarter
Units (from Schedule 1)	37,000	7,000	8,500	10,000	11,500
Cost of sales (@ $5/unit)	$185,000	$35,000	$42,500	$50,000	$57,500

Schedule 4

GOOD CONTROL COMPANY

Selling Expenses Budget
For the Year Ended December 31, 19_1

Expenses	Total	1st Quarter	2nd Quarter	3rd Quarter	4th Quarter
Commissions	$46,250	$ 8,750	$10,625	$12,500	$14,375
Rent: Equipment	9,250	1,750	2,125	2,500	2,875
Advertising	9,250	1,750	2,125	2,500	2,875
Telephone	4,625	875	1,062	1,250	1,437
Depreciation	900	225	225	225	225
Other	22,225	4,150	5,088	6,025	6,963
	$92,500	$17,500	$21,250	$25,000	$28,750

Schedule 4A

GOOD CONTROL COMPANY

Selling Expenses Budget: Cash Requirements
For the Year Ended December 31, 19_1

	Total	1st Quarter	2nd Quarter	3rd Quarter	4th Quarter
Total selling expenses	$92,500	$17,500	$21,250	$25,000	$28,750
Less: Depreciation expense	900	225	225	225	225
Cash requirements	$91,600	$17,275	$21,025	$24,775	$28,525

Exhibit 22-4 **Schedules 4 and 4A, Selling expenses budgets**

executives in the sales department will be responsible for keeping their expenses within the amounts budgeted.

Administrative expenses budgets

Executives at the general administrative level provide estimates of the administrative expenses expected during the year. Many of these expenses may be relatively independent of the predicted sales volume, but a general growth of sales volume is likely to have an impact on the general size of the company and the amount of administrative work to be done. From the data submitted, the budget director prepares an administrative expenses budget (Exhibit 22-5). Again, a cash-requirements budget (Schedule 5A) is prepared by subtracting noncash items (such as bad debts expense) from the estimated administrative expenses.

The general executives of the firm will be responsible for implementing this budget. Note that bad debts expense in included in the administrative budget, not in the sales budget. In this company, the administrators have responsibility for overseeing approval of credit and collection of accounts receivable. (This is often the case, because the sales department might be over-generous in extending credit in its eagerness to make a sale.)

Budgeted income statement

From the information summarized in Schedules 1 through 5, the budget director can now prepare a budgeted income statement (Exhibit 22-6). This statement follows the form of an income statement. In effect, it is a prediction of what the income statement prepared at the end of the year will report. It also will serve as a guide or target for all parts of the company in budgeting expenses and profit-making efforts to arrive at the desired net income for the year.

In preparing this budgeted income statement, the budget director has made

Exhibit 22-5 **Schedules 5 and 5A, Administrative expenses budgets**

Schedule 5

GOOD CONTROL COMPANY

Administrative Expenses Budget
For the Year Ended December 31, 19_1

Expense	Total	1st Quarter	2nd Quarter	3rd Quarter	4th Quarter
Salaries	$22,200	$4,200	$5,100	$ 6,000	$ 6,900
Insurance	1,850	350	425	500	575
Telephone	1,850	350	425	500	575
Supplies	5,000	1,000	1,000	1,500	1,500
Bad debts expense	3,700	700	850	1,000	1,150
Other	2,400	400	700	500	800
	$37,000	$7,000	$8,500	$10,000	$11,500

Schedule 5A

GOOD CONTROL COMPANY

Administrative Expenses Budget: Cash Requirements
For the Year Ended December 31, 19_1

	Total	1st Quarter	2nd Quarter	3rd Quarter	4th Quarter
Administrative expenses	$37,000	$7,000	$8,500	$10,000	$11,500
Less: Bad debts expense	3,700	700	850	1,000	1,150
Cash requirements	$33,300	$6,300	$7,650	$ 9,000	$10,350

Exhibit 22-6 **Schedule 6, Budgeted income statement**

Schedule 6

GOOD CONTROL COMPANY

Budgeted Income Statement
For the Year Ended December 31, 19_1

	Total	1st Quarter	2nd Quarter	3rd Quarter	4th Quarter
Sales (Schedule 2)	$370,000	$70,000	$85,000	$100,000	$115,000
Cost of goods sold (Schedule 3)	185,000	35,000	42,500	50,000	57,500
Gross margin (*a*)	$185,000	$35,000	$42,500	$ 50,000	$ 57,500
Operating expense:					
Selling (Schedule 4)	$ 92,500	$17,500	$21,250	$ 25,000	$ 28,750
Administrative (Schedule 5)	37,000	7,000	8,500	10,000	11,500
Total operating expense (*b*)	$129,500	$24,500	$29,750	$ 35,000	$ 40,250
Net income from operations (*a* – *b*)	$ 55,500	$10,500	$12,750	$ 15,000	$ 17,250
Interest expense	450	0	150	150	150
Net income before income taxes	$ 55,050	$10,500	$12,600	$ 14,850	$ 17,100
Income taxes	27,525	5,250	6,300	7,425	8,550
Net income	$ 27,525	$ 5,250	$ 6,300	$ 7,425	$ 8,550

Earnings per common share (1,000 shares outstanding) $27.52

additional assumptions: (1) the federal income tax rate is 50 percent; (2) the company will borrow $10,000 at 6 percent interest at the end of the first quarter from the First National Bank. The interest expense will be accrued on the income statements during the last three quarters of the year, although it is payable at the maturity of the note at the end of the year. (In the appendix to this book we show how Fuqua Industries, Inc., disclosed budgeted data in its annual report.)

Budget of accounts-receivable collections

The accounting department submits data about predicted collections on accounts receivable during the year. From these data, the budget director prepares a budget of accounts-receivable collections (Exhibit 22-7). The Good Control Company makes all of its sales on account. Past experience indicates that 90 percent of sales on account are collected during the quarter in which they are made; 9 percent of the sales are collected in the following quarter; the remaining 1 percent of sales on account are uncollectible. During the first quarter, the company expects to collect $6,000 cash on 19_0 credit sales.

From the sales budget (Schedule 2) and this information about expected collections, the information in Schedule 7 is computed. Information from this schedule also was used to compute the bad debts expense shown in Schedule 6.

Purchases budgets

From the information about expected sales (Schedule 1), the purchasing department makes plans for obtaining and stocking the necessary merchandise. The purchasing department summarizes its plans in a purchases budget expressed in units (Exhibit

22-8). The Good Control Company has 2,000 units on hand in inventory at the beginning of 19_1. The purchasing department decides that it should have the following quantities on hand in inventory at the end of each quarter, to maintain an ample safety margin in relation to the sales volume: 1st quarter, 3,000 units; 2nd quarter, 3,500 units; 3rd quarter, 4,000 units; 4th quarter, 4,500 units.

The purchasing department also supplies information about the estimated costs of the purchases. In practice, this information would include estimates of expected price changes, savings to be achieved by larger-volume purchases, and so on. In our simplified example, the cost of purchases is estimated to be $5 per unit throughout the year. (This information was used in preparing Schedule 3.) With this information about cost per unit and the purchases budget expressed in units (Schedule 8), the purchasing department or the budget director can prepare a purchases budget expressed in dollars (Exhibit 22-9). This budget is prepared by multiplying each quantity of units in Schedule 8 by the $5-per-unit cost. The purchasing department will be responsible for implementing this cost budget.

Exhibit 22-7 **Schedule 7, Budget of accounts-receivable collections**

Schedule 7

GOOD CONTROL COMPANY

Budget of Accounts-Receivable Collections
For the Year Ended December 31, 19_1

On Sales Made During	Total	1st Quarter	2nd Quarter	3rd Quarter	4th Quarter
4th quarter 19_0	$ 6,000	$ 6,000			
1st quarter 19_1	69,300	63,000	$ 6,300		
2nd quarter 19_1	84,150		76,500	$ 7,650	
3rd quarter 19_1	99,000			90,000	$ 9,000
4th quarter 19_1	103,500				103,500
	$361,950	$69,000	$82,800	$97,650	$112,500

Schedule 8

GOOD CONTROL COMPANY

Purchases Budget: Units
For the Year Ended December 31, 19_1

	1st Quarter	2nd Quarter	3rd Quarter	4th Quarter
Sales requirements (Schedule 1)	7,000	8,500	10,000	11,500
Add: Ending inventory requirements	3,000	3,500	4,000	4,500
Total requirements	10,000	12,000	14,000	16,000
Less: Beginning inventory	2,000	3,000	3,500	4,000
Purchase requirements	8,000	9,000	10,500	12,000

Exhibit 22-8 **Schedule 8, Purchases budget: units**

Exhibit 22-9 **Schedule 9, Purchases budget: costs**

Schedule 9

GOOD CONTROL COMPANY

Purchases Budget: Costs
For the Year Ended December 31, 19_1

	1st Quarter	2nd Quarter	3rd Quarter	4th Quarter
Required for sales	$35,000	$42,500	$50,000	$57,500
Required for ending inventory	15,000	17,500	20,000	22,500
Total requirements	$50,000	$60,000	$70,000	$80,000
Less: Beginning inventory	10,000	15,000	17,500	20,000
Required purchases	$40,000	$45,000	$52,500	$60,000

Schedule 10

GOOD CONTROL COMPANY

Payment-on-Purchases Budget
For the Year Ended December 31, 19_1

On Purchases Made During	Total	1st Quarter	2nd Quarter	3rd Quarter	4th Quarter
4th quarter 19_0	$ 5,000	$ 5,000			
1st quarter 19_1	$40,000	20,000	$20,000		
2nd quarter 19_1	45,000		22,500	$22,500	
3rd quarter 19_1	52,500			26,250	$26,250
4th quarter 19_1	60,000				30,000
Payments by quarters	$172,500	$25,000	$42,500	$48,750	$56,250

Exhibit 22-10 **Schedule 10, Payment-on-purchases budget**

From the purchases budget in dollars, the budget director can prepare a budget showing payments to be made on purchases during each quarter (Exhibit 22-10). The Good Control Company pays 50 percent of its accounts during the quarter in which the purchases are made, and pays the remaining 50 percent during the following quarter. Accounts payable of $5,000 from 19_0 are unpaid at the beginning of the year. The Good Control Company always takes available purchase discounts as a matter of good business policy. Therefore, net purchase costs were used in preparing the $5-per-unit cost estimate, and purchase discounts do not appear in these budgets.

Cash budget

From the information in Schedules 4A, 5A, 7, and 10, the company treasurer prepares a cash budget. The beginning cash balance for the year is $15,000. In preparing the cash budget (Exhibit 22-11), the treasurer makes use of other information available to him about plans for the year. Dividends of $20,000 are to be paid in the fourth quarter. Federal income tax of $27,525 is to be paid in the first quarter. Marketable securities in the amount of $15,000 are to be acquired in the first quarter.

Note that the cash budget reveals the probability of a cash deficiency in the first quarter. The company plans to obtain the necessary cash through a bank loan. (This information was reflected in the interest expense included on the budgeted income statement of Schedule 6.)

Budgeted statement of financial position

The accountant for the Good Control Company can now prepare a budgeted statement of financial position Exhibit 22-12). He takes the balance sheet for the end of 19_0 and combines these data with the transactions reflected in the various budgets to obtain an estimate of the balance sheet for the end of 19_1. The accounting department usually has responsibility for the preparation of this statement also.

Budgeted statement of changes in financial position

To complete the comprehensive budget, the accountant prepares a budgeted statement of changes in financial position (Exhibit 22-13). This statement is prepared from the budgeted income statement and statement of financial position in the same way as a normal funds statement (see Chapter 20). Exhibit 22-14 shows the T accounts used in preparing this statement.

Exhibit 22-11 **Schedule 11, Cash budget**

Schedule 11

GOOD CONTROL COMPANY

Cash Budget

For the Year Ended December 31, 19_1

	Total	1st Quarter	2nd Quarter	3rd Quarter	4th Quarter
Beginning cash balance	$ 15,000	$15,000	$ 2,900	$ 14,525	$ 29,650
Cash collections (Schedule 7)	361,950	69,000	82,800	97,650	112,500
Total (*a*)	$376,950	$84,000	$85,700	$112,175	$142,150
Cash payments:					
Purchases (Schedule 10)	$172,500	$25,000	$42,500	$ 48,750	$ 56,250
Selling expenses (Schedule 4A)	91,600	17,275	21,025	24,775	28,525
Administrative expenses (Schedule 5A)	33,300	6,300	7,650	9,000	10,350
Federal income taxes	27,525	27,525	0	0	0
Dividends	20,000	0	0	0	20,000
Marketable securities	15,000	15,000	0	0	0
Interest expense	450	0	0	0	450
Loan repayment	10,000	0	0	0	10,000
Total (*b*)	$370,375	$91,100	$71,175	$ 82,525	$125,575
Cash excess (deficiency) (*a* − *b*)	$ 6,575	$ (7,100)	$14,525	$ 29,650	$ 16,575
Bank loan received	10,000	10,000	0	0	0
Ending cash balance	$ 16,675	$ 2,900	$14,525	$ 29,650	$ 16,575

Exhibit 22-12 **Schedule 12, Budgeted statement of financial position**

Schedule 12

GOOD CONTROL COMPANY

Budgeted Statement of Financial Position
December 31, 19_1

	19_1	19_0
Assets		
Current assets:		
Cash	$ 16,575	$ 15,000
Marketable securities	15,000	0
Accounts receivable	11,500	6,666
Less: Allowance for doubtful accounts	(1,150)	(666)
Merchandise inventory	22,500	10,000
Total current assets (*a*)	$ 64,425	$ 31,000
Property, plant, and equipment:		
Land	$ 50,000	$ 50,000
Building	98,000	98,000
Less: Allowance for depreciation	(34,200)	(33,300)
Total fixed assets (*b*)	$113,800	$114,700
Total assets (*a* + *b*)	$178,225	$145,700
Liabilities and Shareholders' Equity		
Current liabilities:		
Accounts payable (*c*)	$ 30,000	$ 5,000
Shareholders' equity:		
Common stock (1,000 shares outstanding)	$ 50,000	$ 50,000
Retained earnings	98,225	90,700
Total shareholders' equity (*d*)	$148,225	$140,700
Total liabilities and shareholders' equity (*c* + *d*)	$178,225	$145,700

Budget reports

Budgeting requires the development and use of reporting devices for purposes of control and evaluation. Management needs reports on efforts and accomplishments throughout the time span of the budget

1. to determine whether the budget plan is being attained; and
2. to establish and maintain adequate control.

Management achieves control over operations through its comparison of actual performance with budgeted projections.

The budgeters should prepare budget reports in accordance with the organizational structure of the firm. The firm, in turn, must be structured along functional lines, with areas of responsibility and authority clearly identified. Budget reports are informative and evaluative in nature. Therefore they should be carefully constructed, accurately compiled, and promptly communicated. Exhibit 22-15 illustrates two of the many formats that such budget reports and schedules may assume.

Sensitivity analysis

Budgeting reflects the business-forecasting and decision-making activities of the firm. Hence, once the budget has been compiled and tested, profit-minded managers may want to check their planning in the following terms: *what if* some event not built into the budget occurs? For example, what would be the impact on the budget if a competitor introduces a new product? What happens to the budget if assumptions about the state of the economy prove invalid?

Simulation techniques and models are being developed and used in some businesses today to isolate the impact of the dynamic behavior of a wide range of assumptions on budget projections. These models offer a form of laboratory experimentation, where a budget variable can be modified and its impact on the total

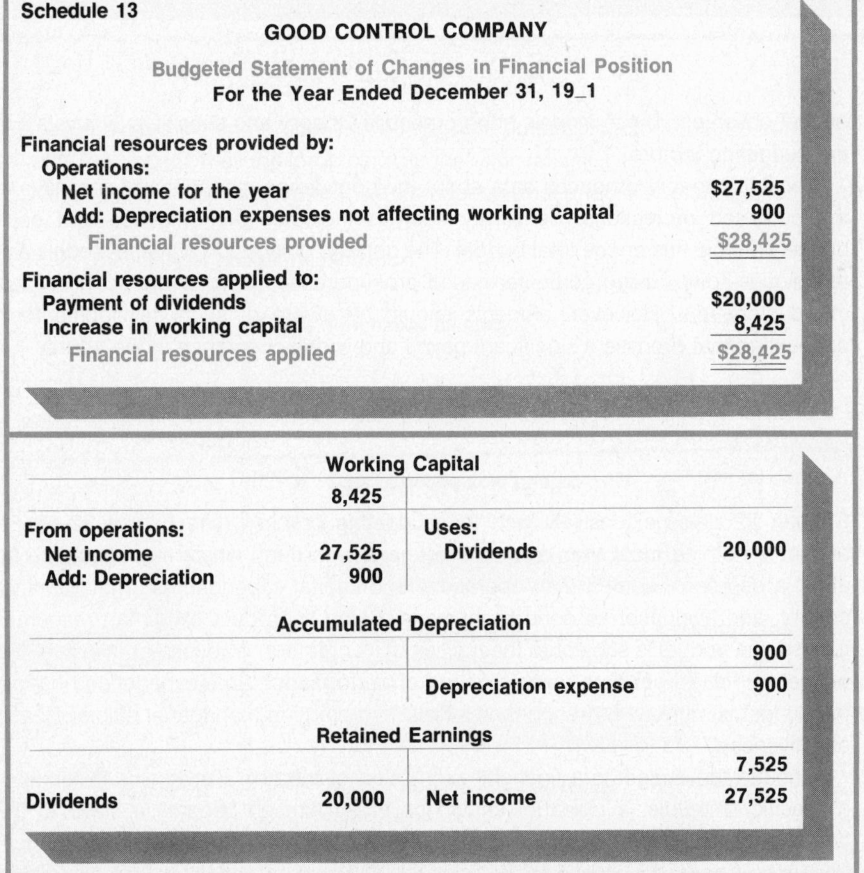

Schedule 13

GOOD CONTROL COMPANY

Budgeted Statement of Changes in Financial Position
For the Year Ended December 31, 19_1

Financial resources provided by:	
Operations:	
Net income for the year	**$27,525**
Add: Depreciation expenses not affecting working capital	**900**
Financial resources provided	$28,425
Financial resources applied to:	
Payment of dividends	**$20,000**
Increase in working capital	**8,425**
Financial resources applied	$28,425

Exhibit 22-13
Schedule 13, Budgeted statement of changes in financial position

Working Capital

	8,425		
From operations:		**Uses:**	
Net income	**27,525**	**Dividends**	**20,000**
Add: Depreciation	**900**		

Accumulated Depreciation

			900
		Depreciation expense	**900**

Retained Earnings

			7,525
Dividends	**20,000**	**Net income**	**27,525**

Exhibit 22-14
Working-paper T accounts for preparation of Schedule 13

that are useful in this evaluation. Because you are not yet familiar with these tools, we suggest that you defer the reading of this appendix until later in the course. This material dealing with the subject of testing the budget is inserted here because it connects logically with the content of this chapter. It will be useful for review at this point, after you have completed the rest of this part of the text.

In evaluating the budget, management will be interested in:

1. the projected break-even point for the business (Chapter 24);
2. an analysis of gross margin by volume/price/cost (Chapter 23);
3. the rate of return on investment (Chapter 27);
4. ratio relationships (current, acid-test, owners' equity to debt, inventory turnover, and so on) and various other financial indicators.

Before approving the budget, management will ascertain whether the results of these tests reflect desirable company objectives.

The following analyses are examples of the kinds of tests that management would be likely to apply before approving the budget.

RETURN ON INVESTMENT (ROI). The ratio of net income to total capital (total assets) is called the ***return on investment*** (ROI). This ratio measures the profit that the company earns in relation to the capital that it employs.

$$\text{ROI} = \frac{\text{Budgeted sales}}{\text{Capital employed}} \times \frac{\text{Budgeted net income}}{\text{Budgeted sales}} = \frac{\text{Budgeted net income}}{\text{Capital employed}}$$

$$= \frac{\text{Budgeted net income}}{\text{Total assets}}$$

In the case of the Good Control Company,

$$\text{ROI} = \frac{\$27{,}525}{\$178{,}225} = 16\%$$

Management would compare this figure with averages for the industry and with historical data for the company to determine whether the budget predicts an acceptable return on investment.

BREAK-EVEN ANALYSIS. The break-even point is that sales volume where no profit is made—that is, where revenue equals expenses. Normally, some expenses of the company are fixed, regardless of sales volume. Others vary directly with the volume of sales. As a result, sales volume below the break-even point results in a net loss. Net income increases as sales volume increases above the break-even point.

In this illustration, we assume that the accountant has made an analysis of expenses into fixed and variable expenses, and that he has found variable expenses to be 60 percent of sales. Fixed expenses amount to $60,000 per year.

Let *S* represent the amount of sales at the break-even point, *VE* represent variable expenses, and *FE* represent fixed expenses.

$$S = VE + FE$$
$$= (0.60 \times S) + \$60{,}000;$$
$$0.40 \times S = \$60{,}000;$$
$$S = \$150{,}000.$$

The budgeted sales figure is well above the break-even point.

RETURN ON STOCKHOLDERS' EQUITY. In this example, the rate of earnings on stockholders' equity is

$$\frac{\text{Net income}}{\text{Common stock equity}} = \frac{\$27{,}525}{\$148{,}225} = 19\%$$

Again, management will compare this ratio with standards for the industry and for the company in the past to determine if the budgeted performance is acceptable.

YIELD ON COMMON STOCK. In this example,

$$\frac{\text{Common stock dividend per share}}{\text{Market value per share of common stock}} = \frac{\$20}{\$200} = 10\%$$

This value also will be interpreted against industry and historical standards.

GROSS MARGIN ANALYSIS. Exhibit 22-17 shows an analysis of the gross margin predicted by the budget.

Exhibit 22-17 Gross margin analysis of Good Control Company budget for 19_1

	Budget year	Last year
Number of units sold	37,000	30,000
Sales price per unit	$10	$9
Cost per unit	$ 5	$4.80

	Sales	Cost of Sales	Gross Margin
Budget year	$370,000	$185,000	$185,000
Last year	270,000	144,000	126,000
	$100,000	$ 41,000	$ 59,000
Changes attributable to:			
Sales-price variance[1]	$ 37,000	—	$ 37,000
Sales-volume variance[2]	63,000	—	63,000
Cost-price variance[3]	—	$ (7,400)	(7,400)
Cost-volume variance[4]	—	(33,600)	(33,600)
	$100,000	$ (41,000)	$ 59,000

1. Budget year's units sold at budget year's sales prices, less Budget year's units sold at last year's sales prices.
2. Budget year's units at last year's prices, less Last year's units at last year's prices.
3. Budget year's units sold at budget year's cost, less Budget year's units sold at last year's cost.
4. Budget year's units sold at last year's cost, less Last year's units sold at last year's cost.

Questions

1. Discuss the reasons that planning is necessary for success in business.
2. What steps usually are required in planning a business operation?
3. What is a budget?
4. What is the purpose of budgeting?
5. What is a comprehensive budget?
6. Why is a sales forecast the starting point for detailed business budgeting?
7. Describe the information that should appear on budget reports.
8. A company plans to sell 50,000 units during the year. It wants to have 5,000 units on hand at the end of the year. There are 7,000 units on hand at the beginning of the year. How many units must be produced during the year?

Exercises

E22-1 (Budgets)

The Sun Company is preparing an estimate of baking powder purchases required for next year's sales (19_6). Sun sells ordinary baking powder and enriched baking powder. Sun's management estimates that its sale of ordinary baking powder will increase 20 percent over last year (19_5), and that its sale of enriched powder will increase 15 percent over last year. The price of ordinary powder will be increased 10 percent, and that of enriched powder by 40 percent. The accountant obtains the following data for 19_5.

Selling price: Ordinary baking powder	$2.50 per pound
Enriched baking powder	$3.50 per pound
Sales: Ordinary	100,000 pounds
Enriched	30,000 pounds
Inventory (Dec. 31): Ordinary	25,000 pounds
Enriched	15,000 pounds
Cost per pound: Ordinary	60 cents
Enriched	90 cents

Sun expects the purchase cost of its baking powder supplies to remain unchanged during the coming year. Sun wants an ending inventory for 19_6 of 20,000 pounds of ordinary baking powder and 5,000 pounds of enriched powder.

Required:

a. Prepare a sales budget in units and another in dollars for Sun's 19_6 baking powder sales.

b. Prepare a purchases budget in units for the coming year.

c. Prepare a purchases budget in dollars for the coming year.

E22-2 (Budgets)

The Kirkwood Company is preparing budgets for 19_6. The company has an inventory policy requiring that the inventory at the end of any month be large enough to meet budgeted customer requirements for the following two months. The Kirkwood Company pays for its purchases as follows:

45 percent in month of purchase;
30 percent in month following month of purchase;
25 percent in second month following month of purchase.

Purchases in November and December 19_5 amounted to $60,000 in each month; ending inventory for 19_5 was $130,000. Cost of goods sold is 75 percent of sales. Sales forecasts for 19_6 are the following: January $120,000; February $140,000; March $220,000; April $300,000.

Required:

a. Calculate the dollar amount of purchases required in January 19_6 (show your calculations).

b. Calculate the cash payments to be made on purchases in January 19_6.

E22-3 (Budgets and receivables)

The Service Company reports actual 19_5 sales of $50,000 in November and $80,000 in December. Budgeted 19_6 sales are the following: January $60,000; February $80,000; March $100,000; April $120,000; May $90,000; June $110,000. The company expects to collect its receivables arising from sales as follows:

50 percent in the month of the sale;
30 percent in the month following the sale;
20 percent in the second month following the sale.

Required: Prepare a schedule showing cash collections from receivables by months for the six months from January through June 19_6.

E22-4 (Budgeted income statement)

The Thomas Company asks that a budgeted income statement be prepared from the following data for the first and second halves of 19_6.

1. Sales forecast:

First half of 19_6	$200,000
Second half of 19_6	300,000

2. Selling expenses are $80,000 and are incurred evenly over the year.

3. Cost of goods sold is 50 percent of sales.

4. Inventory data:

December 31, 19_5	$ 90,000
December 31, 19_6	110,000

5. Administrative expenses are forecast at $20,000 and are incurred evenly over the year.

6. Income taxes are estimated to be 40 percent of net income.

Required:

a. Prepare a budgeted income statement for the first and second halves of 19_6.

b. Compute the purchases for 19_6.

E22-5 (Budgeted cash receipts and payments)

a. From the data given below, prepare a schedule of budgeted cash receipts from sales.

Budgeted sales for 19_6	$260,000
Accounts receivable: January 1, 19_6	30,000
December 31, 19_6	8% of 19_6 sales
Uncollectible accounts	2% of sales

b. From the data given below, prepare a schedule of budgeted payments on purchases for 19_6.

Budgeted sales at selling price	$260,000
Percent of markup on sales price	25%
Accounts payable: January 1, 19_6	$15,000
December 31, 19_6	10,000
Discounts taken: 3% of accounts paid	

There is no beginning inventory and no ending inventory is planned for 19_6.

E22-6 (Cash budget)

The trial balance of the West Company for the first half of 19_6 (ending June 30, 19_6) is the following.

Cash	12,000	
Accounts Receivable	12,000	
Merchandise Inventory	30,000	
Building and Equipment	300,000	
Accumulated Depreciation		75,000
Rent Payable		6,000
Note Payable (9% note due Dec. 31, 19_6)		30,000
Common Stock		100,000
Retained Earnings		82,150
Sales		120,000
Cost of Goods Sold	18,000	
Salaries	20,000	
Rent Expense	6,000	
Depreciation Expense	15,000	
Interest Expense	150	
	413,150	413,150

Additional information:

1. Sales in the second half of 19_6 will be 25 percent larger than sales during the first half of the year.
2. Collections on accounts receivable during the second half of the year will be 100 percent of the receivables outstanding on June 30, 19_6, and 92 percent of the sales made during the second half of the year.
3. Rent expense of $6,000 will be paid in the second half of the year.
4. Salaries during the second half will be 20 percent larger than during the first half of the year.
5. Inventory will decrease $7,500 during the second half of the year.
6. Ten percent of purchases will be unpaid on December 31, 19_6.

Required: Prepare a cash budget for the second half of 19_6. (HINT: In computing cash payment for purchases, examine the trial balance to determine the relationship of cost of goods sold to sales. If you need to compute cost of goods sold during the second half of the year, you will find it useful to know the ratio of cost of goods sold to sales.)

Problems

P22-1 (Master budget)

The Ocean Company is preparing a master budget for the first three months of 19_6. Dollar sales prices are forecast at $20 per unit. Inventories are to be maintained at 150 percent of the following month's sales in units. Merchandise costs $10 per unit, and all purchases are paid during the month following the month of the purchase. All sales are on credit, due in 60 days. Experience shows that 60 percent of a month's sales are collected during the month; the remainder of the receivables are collected in equal installments in the two months following the sale. The following sales data are available: January 1 inventory is 5,000 units; December's credit purchases were $6,000; beginning cash balance was $10,000.

Actual sales: November 19_5	$50,000
December	60,000
Budgeted sales: January 19_6	60,000
February	40,000
March	80,000
April	90,000

Expenses are paid in the month they occur (except for depreciation, which requires no cash outlays). Monthly selling and administrative expenses are estimated as follows.

Salaries	$ 5,200
Advertising	900
Depreciation	1,100
Other expenses	3,800
Total	$11,000

Cash dividends of $8,000 will be paid on February 15, 19_6. The dividends were declared in 19_5 and are reported as dividends payable on the 19_5 balance sheet.

Required:

a. Prepare a sales budget in dollars.
b. Prepare a schedule of cash to be collected from sales.
c. Prepare purchases budgets in units and in dollars.
d. Prepare a budgeted income statement for the first quarter of 19_6, showing budgeted figures for each month.
e. Prepare a cash budget for January, February, and March.

P22-2 (Production budget)

The production manager is considering various production plans for the first quarter of 19_6.

A. Maintain an ending inventory of 2,000 units at the end of each month.
B. Maintain an ending inventory equal to the estimated sales for the following month.
C. Maintain a production schedule that produces 6,000 units per month.

Inventory on hand at the beginning of 19_6 is 1,000 units. Estimated sales are 5,000 units in January, 2,000 units in February, 6,000 units in March, and 4,000 units in April.

Required: Prepare schedules showing the required production for the first quarter under each of the three plans. (HINT: Consider the fact that production for the month is equal to required ending inventory plus estimated sales, less the beginning inventory.)

P22-3 (Budget of cash collections)

The Flame Company has budgeted gross sales of $650,000 for 19_6. Accounts receivable on January 1, 19_6, are budgeted at $100,000. It is estimated that 10 percent of the budgeted sales will be outstanding at the end of the year. The company expects that 5 percent of the average accounts receivable balance during the year will be written off as uncollectible. Sales returns and allowances are estimated to be 3 percent of gross sales. Sales discounts average 2 percent of accounts paid.

Required: Prepare a budget to show collections of cash from customers in 19_6.

P22-4 (Budgeted income statement and balance sheet)

The Olympic Company prepares its budget for three-month periods. At the end of June, the balance sheet of the company shows the following accounts:

Cash	$ 50,000	Accounts payable	$ 75,000
Receivables	100,000	Capital stock	600,000
Inventories	150,000	Retained earnings	125,000
Plant and equipment (net)	500,000		

The following sales forecasts are provided for the accountant:

Estimated sales:	
July	$400,000
August	450,000
September	500,000

All sales are credit sales. They are collected in the month following the sale.

Purchases are estimated to be 80 percent of sales for the period. The company plans to have $450,000 of inventory on hand at the end of September. Purchases are paid for in the month following the purchase. Purchases are subject to a 2 percent discount.

Fixed expenses, except depreciation, total $75,000 per three-month period. Variable expenses are 10 percent of sales. Depreciation expense is $12,500 for the three-month period. Expenses, except for depreciation and income taxes of 30 percent, are paid for in the month incurred.

Required: Prepare a budgeted income statement and a budgeted balance sheet for the quarter ending September 30. Develop supporting schedules where helpful.

P22-5 (Budgeted income statement and balance sheet)

The following account balances are shown in the ledger of the Cash Company on December 31.

Cash	$ 10,000
Accounts receivable	20,000
Inventories	30,000
Plant and equipment (net)	100,000
Total	$160,000
Accounts payable	$ 15,000
Income taxes payable	5,000
Capital stock	50,000
Retained earnings	90,000
Total	$160,000

Additional information for the first quarter of the new year forecast by the company:

Cash sales	$ 80,000
Credit sales (80% of credit sales are collected in the quarter of the sale; the balance are collected in the following quarter)	120,000
Income tax payable at end of year was paid.	
Operating expenses for the quarter paid in cash	50,000
Depreciation expense	10,000
Dividends declared	15,000

Purchases on account during the quarter are estimated at 40% of sales for the quarter.
50% of purchases during a quarter are paid during the quarter.
The company expects to have $20,000 of inventory on hand at the end of the quarter.
Income tax expense is 30% of net income for the quarter.
Any excess cash at the end of the quarter above $50,000 will be invested in marketable securities.

Required: Prepare a budgeted income statement and balance sheet for the quarter ending March 31, 1978.

P22-6 (Cash forecast)

The following budgeted information is available for the first and second quarters of the next year:

	First Quarter	Second Quarter
Cash sales	$100,000	$125,000
Credit sales	50,000	70,000
Purchases on account	70,000	80,000
Selling expenses	70,000	85,000
General/administrative expenses	10,000	12,000
Taxes	5,000	6,000
Other expenses	10,000	14,000

Additional information:

Cash balance at beginning of year: $20,000.
Purchases for prior December: $50,000.
Purchases are paid for 50% in the month of the purchase and the balance in the following month.
Accounts receivable are collected as follows:
80% in the month of the sale
20% in the month following the sale
Fourth quarter sales last year were $30,000.

Required:

a. Prepare a forecast of collections on accounts receivable for two quarters.
b. Prepare a forecast of payments for purchases for two quarters.
c. Prepare a cash forecast for the two quarters.

P22-7 (Compiling the budget)

Refer to Problem P22-6. In addition to the data in Problem P22-6, assume that the following information is also available.

Cash	$ 20,000	
Accounts receivable	6,000	
Inventory	10,000	
Land	40,000	
Building (20-year life)	100,000	
Accumulated depreciation (8 years)		$ 40,000
Accounts payable		25,000
Common stock		50,000
Retained earnings		61,000
	$176,000	$176,000

It is forecast that the company will declare a $10,000 dividend on June 30 at the end of the second quarter. Ending inventory estimated for June 30 is $60,000.

Required: Prepare a work sheet in the following form that reflects the proposed journal entries resulting from the forecasted data.

Accounts	Trial Balance December 31, 19_5		Transactions		Trial Balance June 30, 19_6	
	Dr.	Cr.	Dr.	Cr.	Dr.	Cr.

Gross margin analysis

23

Chapter 22 introduced the budgeting process as a basic tool of management. We now turn to a discussion of the various measures that management can use to evaluate the actual or budgeted performance of a business. In this chapter we discuss the analysis of the gross margin on sales.

Gross margin (sometimes called gross profit) is the excess of sales over cost of goods sold. Gross margin is a key financial indicator because it represents the dollar amount of financial resources produced by the basic selling activity of the firm. This is the amount available to management for operating expenses and profit.

Because gross margin is so significant for planning and control purposes, management is keenly interested in the reasons for any variance in gross margin from year to year. Similarly, management is eager to know why an actual gross margin differs from a gross margin that was budgeted, or from the gross margin that is typical or desirable for the industry as a whole. *Gross margin analysis* is a technique that develops explanations for any changes in gross margin.

Variances

Exhibit 23-1 summarizes sales, cost of goods sold, and gross margin of the Gross Margin Company for two years. We use gross margin analysis to find out why the gross margin changed from 19_0 to 19_1. (The same technique can be applied for

Exhibit 23-1
Comparative data on gross margin for two years

GROSS MARGIN COMPANY

Partial Comparative Income Statement
For the Years Ended December 31, 19_0 and 19_1

	19_1	19_0	Changes
Sales	$225,000	$100,000	$125,000
Cost of goods sold	90,000	50,000	40,000
Gross margin	$135,000	$ 50,000	$ 85,000
Gross margin as percentage of sales	60%	50%	10%

other kinds of comparisons. For example, suppose that the values labeled "19_0" instead represented budgeted values for 19_1. In that case, the same analysis would provide an explanation of the variances between budgeted and actual gross margins.)

The management of the Gross Margin Company is interested in knowing what caused gross margin to increase from $50,000 last year to $135,000 this year, an increase of $85,000. To help management determine the causes of the variation in gross margin, the company's accountant prepares an analysis of the change in gross margin.

Because the change in gross margin from period to period is influenced by both sales and cost of goods sold, the analysis requires separate consideration of the changes in these two items. The analysis involves two parts—one computational, the other interpretative.

1. Computation of the portions of the change in gross margin that are due, respectively, to changes in sales volume and price and to changes in purchases volume and price.
2. Interpretation of the reasons for the changes that influenced gross margin.

Changes in gross margin from period to period may be due to any one or any combination of the following four variables.

1. Change in sales caused by:
   a. change in selling price (***sales-price variance***);
   b. change in volume of goods sold (***sales-volume variance***).
2. Change in cost of goods sold caused by:
   a. change in unit cost (***cost-price variance***);
   b. change in volume of goods sold (***cost-volume variance***).

The accountant for the Gross Margin Company begins the analysis by accumulating the detailed statistics shown in Exhibit 23-2. The volume of sales and the unit sales price each increased by 50 percent from 19_0 to 19_1. The unit cost increased by 20 percent. Management needs to know how much each of these changes contributed to the overall increase in gross margin.

For purposes of comparison, gross margin often is expressed as a rate, or percentage of sales (see Exhibit 23-1). This makes it possible to compare gross margin rates of different companies (or of the same company in different periods), although dollar amounts may vary greatly. Margin percentages vary widely between different kinds of businesses. For example, supermarkets operate on gross margins of a few

Exhibit 23-2
Detailed statistics supplementing data in Exhibit 23-1

	19_1	19_0
Number of units sold	**150,000**	**100,000**
Sales price per unit	**$1.50**	**$1.00**
Cost per unit	**$0.60**	**$0.50**

percent or less. They depend for their profits on a combination of very high sales volume and low operating expenses. Small grocery stores (with much lower sales volume and proportionately higher operating expenses) must operate on much larger margin percentages.

In the example of the Gross Margin Company, the increase from a gross margin of 50 percent in 19_0 to a margin of 60 percent in 19_1 would be very significant to management. They would want to know just what caused this increase, in order to decide how to maintain (and perhaps improve further) the larger gross margin. Would it be advisable to increase sales volume still more? Would a further increase in sales price be advisable? How much of the increase was due to management policies and how much to external economic factors beyond the control of management?

The computational part of the gross margin analysis provides the basic statistical information that can be interpreted to provide answers to such questions. Although interpretation of gross margin often is based upon percentage figures, the computation of the gross margin analysis is carried out in terms of the dollar amounts. We turn now to the computational part of the analysis.

SALES-PRICE VARIANCE

The sales-price variance reflects the change in sales revenue that is due to the change in sales price from one period to another. It is computed as follows.

1. Current year's units sold at current year's sales prices:

   $a = 150{,}000 \times \$1.50 = \$225{,}000.$

2. Current year's units sold at last year's sales prices:

   $b = 150{,}000 \times \$1.00 = \$150{,}000.$

3. Sales-price variance:

   $a - b = \$225{,}000 - \$150{,}000 = \$75{,}000.$

The increase in sales price (from $1.00 in 19_0 to $1.50 in 19_1) contributed $75,000 to sales revenue, a favorable situation for gross margin. The sales revenue for 19_1 was $75,000 larger than it would have been if the same number of units had been sold at the old price.

Note that the sales-price variance can also be computed in a single step as follows.

Current year's units sold at change in sales price per unit:

$150{,}000 \times \$0.50 = \$75{,}000.$

If the new unit sales price is smaller than the old price, the sales-price variance will have a negative value. If the unit sales price has not changed between the two periods, the sales-price variance will be zero.

SALES-VOLUME VARIANCE

The sales-volume variance shows the change in sales revenue that is due to the change in the number of units sold from one period to another. It is computed as follows.

1. Current year's units sold at last year's price:

   $a = 150{,}000 \times \$1.00 = \$150{,}000.$

2. Last year's units sold at last year's price:

   $b = 100{,}000 \times \$1.00 = \$100{,}000.$

3. Sales-volume variance:

   $a - b = \$150{,}000 - \$100{,}000 = \$50{,}000$

The increase in sales volume from 100,000 units to 150,000 units added $50,000 to sales revenue, a favorable development for gross margin. The sales revenue for 19_1 was $50,000 larger than that of 19_0 simply because of the increase in volume (even if there had been no price increase).

Note that the sales-volume variance can also be computed in a single step as follows.

Change in units sold at last year's prices:

$50{,}000 \times \$1.00 = \$50{,}000.$

If fewer units were sold in the current year, the sales-volume variance would have a negative value. If the sales volume is unchanged from one period to the other, the sales-volume variance is zero.

COST-PRICE VARIANCE

The cost-price variance explains the change in the cost of goods sold from one period to the next that results from the change in the costs the firm had to pay for the goods that it sold. The cost-price variance is computed as follows.

1. Current year's units sold at current year's cost:

   $a = 150{,}000 \times \$0.60 = \$90{,}000.$

2. Current year's units sold at last year's cost:

   $b = 150{,}000 \times \$0.50 = \$75{,}000.$

3. Cost-price variance:

   $a - b = \$90{,}000 - \$75{,}000 = \$15{,}000$

The increase in the unit cost for the goods sold caused the cost of goods sold to increase by $15,000, an unfavorable situation for gross margin. The cost of goods sold was $15,000 higher than it would have been if the goods had been purchased at the old unit cost.

Note that the cost-price variance can also be computed in a single step as follows.

Current year's units sold at change in cost per unit:

$150{,}000 \times \$0.10 = \$15{,}000.$

If the unit cost were lower in the current year than in the past year, the cost-price variance would have a negative value (but representing a favorable contribution to gross margin, because cost of goods sold is subtracted from sales to compute gross margin). If the unit cost is unchanged, the cost-price variance is zero.

COST-VOLUME VARIANCE

The cost-volume variance points out the change in cost of goods sold that results from the change in volume (number of units sold). It is computed as follows.

1. Current year's units sold at last year's cost:

   $a = 150{,}000 \times \$0.50 = \$75{,}000.$

2. Last year's units sold at last year's cost:

   $b = 100{,}000 \times \$0.50 = \$50{,}000.$

3. Cost-volume variance:

   $a - b = \$75{,}000 - \$50{,}000 = \$25{,}000.$

The increase in the number of units sold caused the cost of goods sold to increase by $25,000, an unfavorable development for gross margin. The cost of goods sold would have been $25,000 greater because of the increase in volume, even if there had been no change in unit cost.

Note that the cost-volume variance can also be computed in a single step as follows.

Change in units sold at last year's cost:

$50{,}000 \times \$0.50 = \$25{,}000.$

If the volume of sales decreased, the cost-volume variance would have a negative value (representing a favorable contribution to gross margin). If the volume remained unchanged, the cost-volume variance would be zero.

GROSS MARGIN REPORT

The accountant summarizes the results of his computations for management in a report similar to the one shown in Exhibit 23-3.

Exhibit 22-17 shows another example of a gross margin report, comparing actual results for a current year to budgeted sales for the following year.

Graphic presentation

It may be helpful to use a graphic visualization of the four basic gross margin variances. Using the information from Exhibit 23-2, we can plot this year's sales and last year's sales on a graph of unit price versus sales volume (Exhibit 23-4). The area of the large rectangle represents the 19_1 sales; the shaded area of the smaller rectangle represents the 19_0 sales. The two sales variances can be read from the graph.

Exhibit 23-3 **A gross margin report**

GROSS MARGIN COMPANY

Statement Accounting for Changes in Sales, Cost of Goods Sold, and Gross Margin

For the Years Ended December 31, 19_0 and 19_1

Year	Sales	Cost of Sales	Gross Margin
19_1	$225,000	$90,000	$135,000
19_0	100,000	50,000	50,000
Changes	$125,000	$40,000	$ 85,000
Increases attributable to:			
Sales-volume variance (amount by which revenue increased because more units were sold in 19_1 than in 19_0)	$ 50,000		$ 50,000
Cost-volume variance (amount by which cost of sales increased because more units were sold in 19_1 than in 19_0)		$25,000	(25,000)
Sales-price variance (amount by which revenue increased because sales price was higher in 19_1 than in 19_0)	75,000		75,000
Cost-price variance (amount by which cost of sales increased because unit cost was higher in 19_1 than in 19_0)		15,000	(15,000)
Totals	$125,000	$40,000	$ 85,000

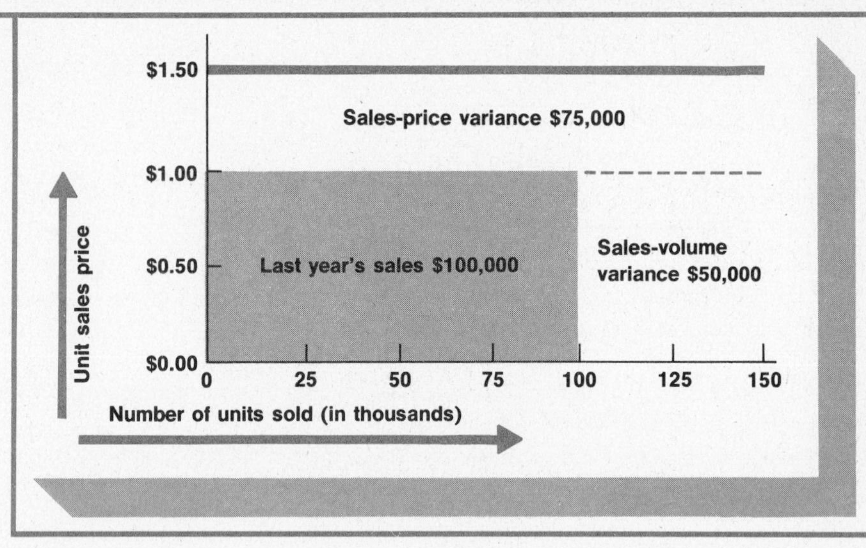

Exhibit 23-4
Sales variances

Note that the sales-volume variance represents the increase in sales that would have occurred if the 19_1 volume of sales had been made at the old unit price. The sales-price variance represents the additional increase in sales due to the increased unit price.

Similarly, we can plot this year's and last year's cost of goods sold (Exhibit 23-5). Here, the area of the large rectangle represents the 19_1 cost of sales; the shaded area of the smaller rectangle represents the 19_0 cost of sales. The two cost variances can be read from the graph.

The cost-volume variance represents the increase in cost of sales that would have occurred if the 19_1 volume had been purchased at the old unit cost. The cost-price variance represents the additional increase in cost due to the increased unit cost.

Finally, we can plot this year's and last year's gross margin (Exhibit 23-6). Here, the vertical axis of the graph represents the contribution of each unit to gross margin (unit sales price less unit cost). The area of the large rectangle represents the 19_1 gross margin; the area of the smaller shaded rectangle represents the 19_0 gross margin. The total price and volume variances can be read from this graph.

The volume variance (sales-volume variance less cost-volume variance) represents the increase in gross margin that would have occurred if the 19_1 volume of merchandise had been purchased and sold at 19_0 prices. The price variance (sales-

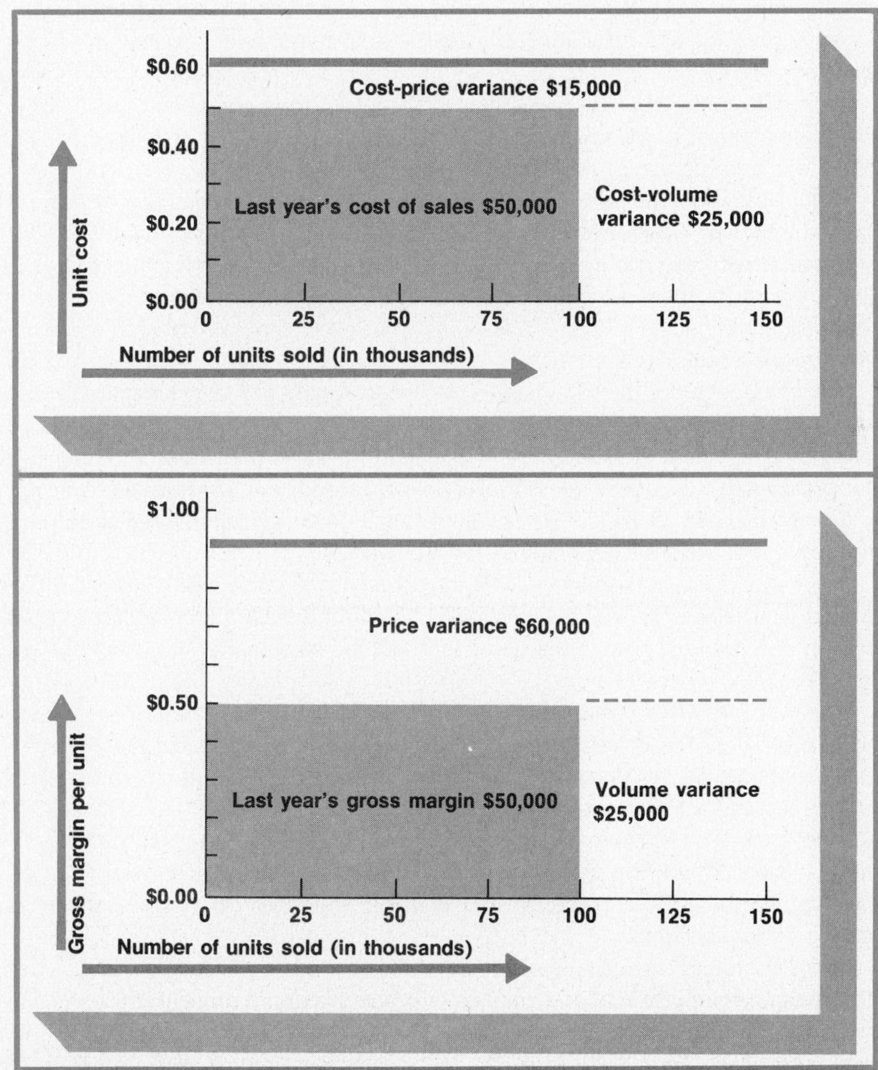

Exhibit 23-5
Cost variances

Exhibit 23-6
Volume and price variances

price variance less cost-price variance) represents the additional increase in gross margin due to the net effects of price changes.

Interpretation

Interpretation of the gross margin analysis involves a study of the reasons for the various components of the change in gross margin, leading to an evaluation of management's options for the future. What factors affect the three components of gross margin (unit cost, unit sales price, and sales volume)?

Unit cost, for the most part, usually is determined by external factors in the case of a merchandising company. The company purchases its inventory at the lowest prices it can find from suppliers. It may be able to reduce cost somewhat by taking advantage of purchase discounts, by making better deals with its suppliers, or by reducing shipping and other incidental costs. For the most part, however, this factor is determined by economic forces outside the control of management. (In the case of a manufacturing company, a larger portion of the unit cost may be subject to management control. Manufacturing costs can be reduced in many cases, and these may be a large portion of the costs of goods sold.)

In our illustration, the rise in unit cost of the merchandise purchased by the Gross Margin Company was beyond the control of the company's management. This cost increase would have occurred no matter what volume of units the company sold in 19_1. Therefore, management will be anxious to know whether similar increases in unit cost are expected in future years—and what effect they will have on the gross margin of the future years.

Unit sales price, for the most part, is under the control of management (although the choices may be restricted by government regulations in some cases). To a large extent, management is free to make changes in the sales price in order to achieve the gross margin that it desires. However, in most cases, changes in sales price also are likely to cause changes in sales volume. As a general rule, a higher sales price will result in a smaller sales volume, and vice versa.

In our illustration, management is free to set any sales price that it desires. It can choose any sales price that it wants for 19_2, and the major purpose of this gross margin analysis is to help in the decision about the sales price that should be set for the coming year.

Sales volume is the most complex of the three factors. Many forces influence the volume of sales. The general level of demand for the kind of product that the company sells may be influenced by population levels, changes in living standards or tastes, passing fads and fancies, changing salary levels and expectations, and so on. The company's advertising and sales efforts may strongly influence the demand for the particular brand sold by the company. The sales price may have a major influence on the demand, particularly if there is competition from other companies selling similar products.

In our illustration, the sales department of the Gross Margin Company concludes that the general demand for the company's product is approximately doubling each year. That is, if the company did not change its price and did not change its sales and advertising efforts, it could expect sales volume to double each year. On the other hand, the sales department estimates that each 50-cent increase in the unit sales price causes sales to decline about 25 percent from what they would have been at an unchanged price. In 19_1, for example, the sales department thinks that the company could have sold 200,000 units at the old $1.00 price. The price increase of 50 cents resulted in a loss of potential sales of 50,000 units.

From the graphical presentation of gross margin (Exhibit 23-6), it is easy to estimate the gross margin that would have resulted if the sales price had not been changed. In that case, the volume variance would have been $50,000 (100,000 additional sales at $0.50 unit gross margin). The price variance would have been $(20,000)—a total of 200,000 units sold at a change of $(0.10) in unit gross margin. The price variance would be negative, because sales price would be unchanged while the unit cost would have increased by $0.10. Therefore, we see that failure to change the sales price would have resulted in a gross margin increase of only $30,000 instead of the $85,000 increase achieved at the higher sales price.

In a similar fashion, management can use the results of the gross margin analysis to evaluate other possible alternatives. In the following chapters we discuss other techniques that help management to choose the best alternative.

Three-way gross margin analysis

Accountants sometimes use a three-way analysis to account for the change in gross margin, instead of the two-way analysis that we have illustrated in this chapter. The three-way analysis of gross margin has a theoretical advantage because it describes, in addition to price and volume variances,

1. a volume/price variance for sales that reflects the changes in sales revenue resulting from the joint change in sales price and volume; and
2. a volume/cost variance that reflects changes in cost of goods sold resulting from the joint change in unit cost and volume.

In other words, the three-way analysis separates each of the two-way price variances into two components—one due solely to the change in price, and the other due to the combined effects of the price and volume changes.

In practice, the two-way analysis is more commonly used than the three-way analysis.

Using the data from the Gross Margin Company example (Exhibits 23-1 and 23-2), the variances for the three-way analysis would be computed as follows. (These variances are represented graphically in Exhibit 23-7.)

1. Causes of changes in sales:
   a. Sales-price variance: last year's volume × change in sales price,

   $a = 100{,}000 \times \$0.50 = \$50{,}000.$

   b. Sales-volume variance: last year's price × change in volume,

   $b = \$1.00 \times 50{,}000 = \$50{,}000.$

Exhibit 23-7
A three-way analysis of the change in gross margin

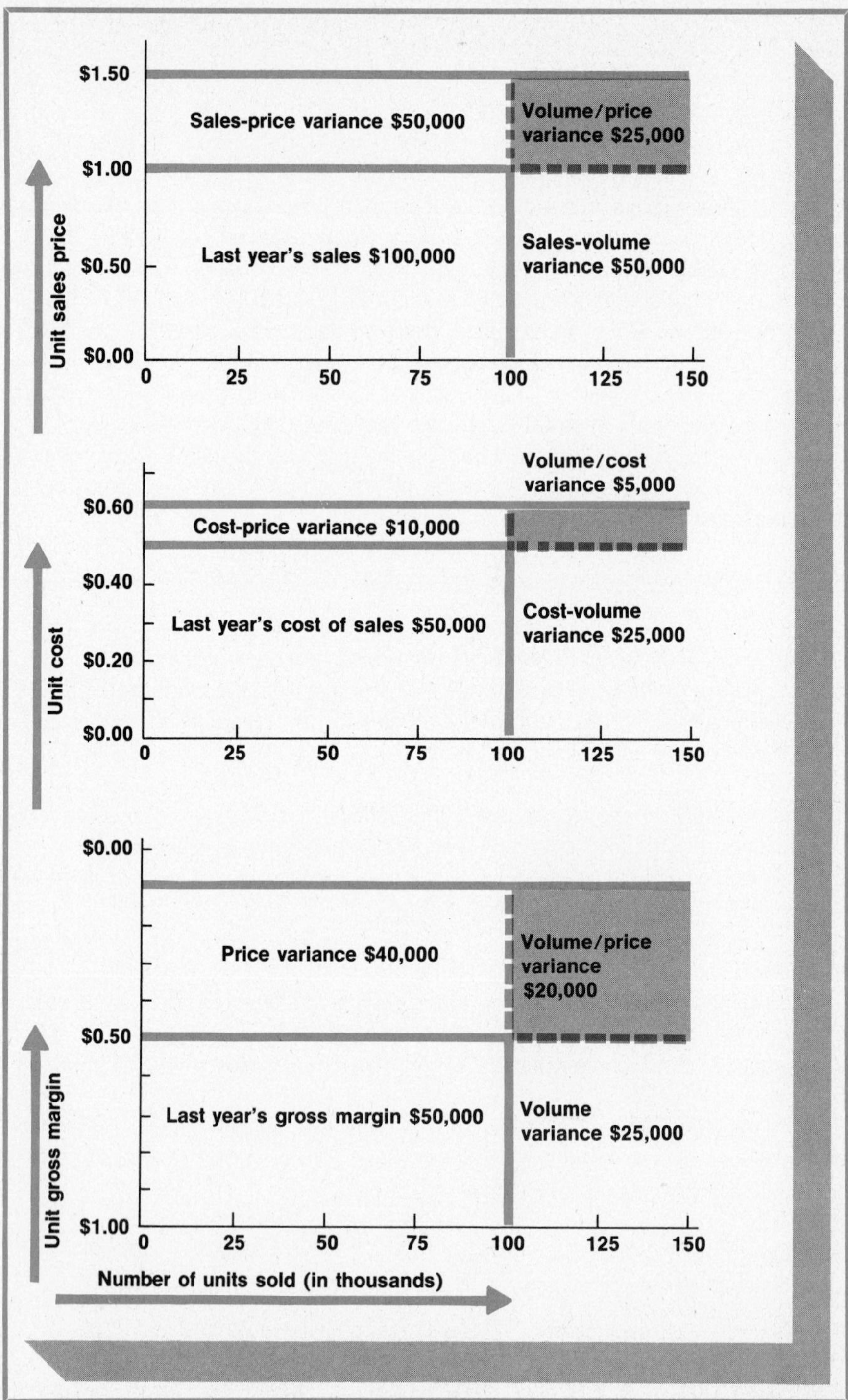

c. Volume/price variance in sales: change in volume × change in price,

$$c = 50{,}000 \times \$0.50 = \$25{,}000$$

d. Sales variance:

$$a + b + c = \$50{,}000 + \$50{,}000 + \$25{,}000 = \$125{,}000$$

2. Causes of changes in cost of goods sold:

a. Cost-price variance: last year's volume × change in unit cost,

$$d = 100{,}000 \times \$0.10 = \$10{,}000$$

b. Cost-volume variance: last year's cost × change in volume,

$$e = \$0.50 \times 50{,}000 = \$25{,}000$$

c. Volume/cost variance in cost of sales: change in volume × change in cost,

$$f = 50{,}000 \times \$0.10 = \$5{,}000$$

d. Cost variance:

$$d + e + f = \$10{,}000 + \$25{,}000 + \$5{,}000 = \$40{,}000$$

As with the two-way analysis, positive values of the sales variances are favorable for gross margin, whereas positive values of the cost variances are unfavorable for gross margin. Note that the three-way analysis yields the same results as the two-way analysis for total sales and cost variances, and also for the volume variances. As the graphs make clear, the only effect of the three-way analysis is to reinterpret each of the price variances as two factors instead of one.

In effect, the three-way analysis answers the following questions.

1. What would have been the effect of changed sales volume if prices had remained unchanged? (Answered by volume variances.)
2. What would have been the effect of changed prices if volume had remained unchanged? (Answered by price variances.)
3. What is the residual change that is due to the combined effects of changes in volume and prices? (Answered by volume/price and volume/cost variances.)

The two-way analysis gives only a single answer to the combination of the final two questions.

Summary

This chapter introduces gross margin analysis as a managerial tool. The computation of variances is demonstrated through an extensive illustration. The variances explain the influences of various factors on the change in gross margin from one period to the next.

Two approaches are available for gross margin analysis. The two-way analysis (most commonly used) identifies four variances contributing to the change in gross margin. The three-way analysis (theoretically preferable) identifies six variances contributing to the change in gross margin.

The computational part of the analysis separates the change in gross margin into various components that can be attributed to changes in sales price, unit cost, and volume of sales. The interpretation of the analysis involves identification of the causes of these component changes and evaluation of management's alternatives in influencing future gross margin results.

In the illustration used in this chapter, gross margin analysis was used to investigate a change in gross margin for a company from one year to the next. The technique can be used in exactly the same way to compare gross margins from two different companies, to compare a budgeted gross margin with an actual gross margin for the same company and the same period, or to compare budgeted gross margins for different budgets based on different assumptions and alternative courses of action.

Appendix

SALES-MIX VARIANCE

In the illustration used in this chapter, the Gross Margin Company sold only a single product. The volume variances computed in the chapter (sales-volume variance and cost-volume variance) are not particularly useful for a multiproduct firm. In such a case, shifts in the selling price, cost, and gross margin for each individual product have separate effects on the total gross margin.

For a multiproduct firm, it is most helpful to represent the merchandise by a combination or ***sales mix.*** The change in gross margin attributable to shifts in the sales mix can be computed; it is called the ***sales-mix variance.*** This variance includes both the changes due to shifts in the gross margins of individual products, and the changes due to shifts in the distribution of total sales among the various products.

Exhibit 23-8 summarizes sales data for the Sales Mix Company over two years. This company sells two products, A and B. In 19_0, the company had a gross margin rate of 41.2 percent of sales. In 19_1, the gross margin rate fell to 38.3 percent of sales. Management wants to evaluate the relative importance of the changes in sales volume and the changes in sales mix in causing this decline in gross margin rate.

1. Volume variance:

a. last year's sales at last year's average gross margin rate,

$$a = \$170{,}000 \times 0.412 = \$70{,}000;$$

b. current year's sales at last year's average gross margin rate,

$$b = \$201{,}000 \times 0.412 = \$82{,}812;$$

c. volume variance,

$$b - a = \$82{,}812 - \$70{,}000 = \$12{,}812.$$

Exhibit 23-8 **Sales data for the Sales Mix Company for 19_0 and 19_1**

	Product A	Product B	Total
19_0 sales:			
Product A, 10,000 units @ $5/unit	**$50,000**		**$ 50,000**
Product B, 20,000 units @ $6/unit		**$120,000**	**120,000**
19_0 cost of goods sold:			
Product A, 10,000 units @ $4/unit	**(40,000)**		**(40,000)**
Product B, 20,000 units @ $3/unit		**(60,000)**	**(60,000)**
19_0 gross margin	$10,000	$ 60,000	$ 70,000
19_0 average gross margin rate ($70,000/$170,000)			41.2%
19_1 sales:			
Product A, 16,000 units @ $6/unit	**$96,000**		**$ 96,000**
Product B, 15,000 units @ $7/unit		**$105,000**	**105,000**
19_1 cost of goods sold:			
Product A, 16,000 units @ $4/unit	**(64,000)**		**(64,000)**
Product B, 15,000 units @ $4/unit		**(60,000)**	**(60,000)**
19_1 gross margin	$30,000	$ 45,000	$ 77,000
19_1 average gross margin rate ($77,000/$201,000)			38.3%

2. Sales-mix variance:
   a. current year's sales at last year's average gross margin rate,

   $b = \$201{,}000 \times 0.412 = \$82{,}812;$

   b. current year's sales at current year's average gross margin rate,

   $c = \$201{,}000 \times 0.383 = \$77{,}000;$

   c. sales-mix variance,

   $c - b = \$77{,}000 - \$82{,}812 = \$(5{,}812).$

In effect, the volume variance measures the change in gross margin that could have been expected if the gross margin rate had remained unchanged. To an approximation, this indicates the effect of the increased dollar volume of sales if the sales mix had remained unchanged. The sales-mix variance measures the change in gross margin that would be expected at the current volume as a result of a shift from the old gross margin rate to the new rate. This approximates the effect of changing the sales mix at a constant volume.

Exhibit 23-9 shows a graphic visualization of the volume and sales-mix variances just computed. The shaded rectangle represents the 19_0 gross margin; the large rectangle represents the 19_1 gross margin. Note that the sales-mix variance is unfavorable for gross margin, so that the height of the 19_1 rectangle is less than that of the 19_0 rectangle. However, the dollar increase in gross margin due to the increased volume is sufficient to offset the dollar decrease due to the change in sales mix, giving a $7,000 increase in gross margin—but a decrease in the gross margin rate.

The results of this analysis suggest that the problem with the sales mix is a serious one. If the increase in sales volume had been smaller, the gross margin might well

Exhibit 23-9
Volume and sales-mix variances

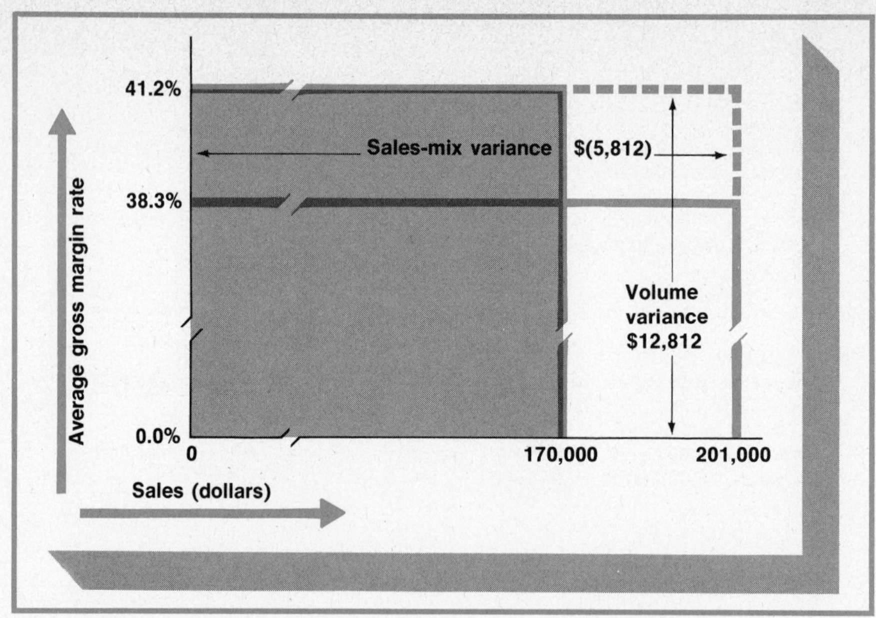

have decreased. In order to decide what could or should be done, the management of the company will need to evaluate the problem with the sales mix.

Questions

1. Define gross margin.
2. Define variance.
3. What are the major causes of variances in sales and in cost of goods sold?
4. In two-way analysis, what are the four major variances in gross margin?
5. Sketch a graphic illustration of the sales variances and the cost variances, using two-way analysis; using three-way analysis.
6. What is the meaning of the sales-mix variance?

Exercises

E23-1 (Gross margin analysis)
From the following data, prepare a statement showing the components of the change in gross margin (use two-way analysis). Also prepare a graphic illustration of the analysis.

	19_6	19_5
Sales	$100	$64
Cost of sales	80	48
Gross margin	$ 20	$16
Units sold	10	8

E23-2 (Gross margin analysis)
The following data are obtained from the records of the Bird Company. Prepare an analysis of change in gross margin, using two-way analysis. Also prepare a graphic illustration of the analysis.

	19_6	19_5
Sales	$240	$210
Cost of sales	120	150
Gross margin	$120	$ 60
Units sold	20	30

E23-3 (Gross margin analysis)
Using the following sales and cost-of-goods-sold data obtained from a company's records, compute the gross margin variances using two-way analysis.

	19_6	19_5
Sales	$375	$260
Cost of sales	250	180
Gross margin	$125	$ 80
Selling price per unit	$7.50	$6.50
Unit cost	$5.00	$4.50

E23-4 (Three-way analysis)
Repeat Exercises E23-1, E23-2, and E23-3, this time using three-way gross margin analysis.

E23-5 (Two-way analysis)
Using the following information, compute the gross margin variances using two-way analysis.

	19_7	19_6
Sales	$11,200	$7,200
Cost of goods sold	8,400	3,600
Gross margin	$ 2,800	$3,600
Units sold	1,400	1,200

E23-6 (Two-way analysis)
Using the following information reported by the Bird Company, compute the gross margin variances using two-way analysis.

	19_7	19_6
Sales	$32,000	$30,000
Cost of goods sold	20,000	20,000
Gross margin	$12,000	$10,000
Units sold	4,000	5,000

Problems

P23-1 (Gross margin analysis)
The Gage Company reports the following data.

	19_7	19_6
Sales	$11,000	$8,000
Cost of goods sold	6,000	4,000
Gross margin	$ 5,000	$4,000

The annual report does not disclose the number of units sold by the company.

However, it does state that average sales prices in 19_7 were 10 percent higher than those in 19_6.

Required: Compute the gross margin variances using two-way analysis. HINT: Prepare a graph from the data, indicating the price increase as 10 percent. Set up a schedule as follows.

	(A) Actual 19_7	(B) This year's volume at last year's price and cost	(C) Actual 19_6
Sales		*a*	
Cost of goods sold		*b*	
Gross margin			

Fill in columns A and C. Note that ***a*** can be computed by dividing this year's sales by the average sales price expressed in percentage of 19_6 price (that is, 110%). How would you explain the difference in sales between columns A and B? Between columns B and C?

Note that b can be computed if the percentage of volume change can be computed for the year. Try this approach:

$$\text{Volume percentage change} = \frac{\text{This year's sales volume at last year's price}}{\text{19\_6 actual sales}}$$

Now, how would you explain the difference in costs between columns A and B on the cost-of-goods-sold line? between columns B and C?

P23-2 (Gross margin analysis)
Refer to Problem P23-1. How would you approach this problem if you knew that the volume had increased 50 percent from one year to the next, instead of knowing the percentage change in selling price?

P23-3 (Gross margin analysis)
Refer to Problem P23-1. How would you approach this problem if you knew the percentage change in cost of goods sold from one year to the next, instead of knowing the percentage change in selling price or volume?

P23-4 (Gross margin analysis)
A financial report prepared for the president of Lems Company provided the following statistics:

	19_8	19_9
Units sold	900	1,000
Sales price per unit	$10	$12
Cost of sales per unit	$ 6	$ 5

Required:

a. Prepare an analysis of the causes of variation in gross margin using two-way analysis.

b. Prepare an analysis of the causes of variation in gross margin using three-way analysis.

c. Explain the differences in the two solutions.

d. Which analysis is theoretically preferable? Why?

The break-even model

24

Profits play a major role in the day-to-day drama of business affairs. Profits provide incentives for owners and managers, act as a measure of performance, and are a guide to the effective allocation of a firm's resources. As indicated in Chapter 22, the first step to profit planning is the preparation of a comprehensive budget. Additional tools for profit planning are available. In this chapter we discuss one such tool —break-even analysis.

Profit is a function of many variables, including selling price, expenses, and volume of sales. We begin by examining these three variables to get some insights into their impact on a business.

RELEVANT RANGE

In gathering data on prices, expenses, and sales volume, we assume that a relevant range of business activity exists for the firm. The ***relevant range*** is that level of activity over which revenue and expense relationships are valid. For example, a firm may assume that it will not operate at less than 50,000 units of sales nor more than 70,000 units. This limited area of activity represents the relevant range for the firm. Data on prices, expenses, and volume below the lower limit or above the higher limit are not considered in the analysis because they fall outside the range of relevancy.

If activity for the year should fall outside this range, conditions probably will be so different from those expected that the assumptions of the analysis would be invalid. Exhibit 24-1 visualizes the concept of relevant range. Graphs used for break-even analysis normally show only the relevant range. In this chapter, we assume a relevant range with a lower limit of zero sales volume. This would be unrealistic in most business situations, but it helps us to see clearly the nature of the factors considered in break-even analysis.

COST BEHAVIOR

The technique of break-even analysis is based on certain basic cost concepts. We must begin with a review of these terms and ideas.

VARIABLE EXPENSES. Variable expenses are those expenses that change in direct proportion to the change in volume of sales over the relevant range of business activity. The total variable expense fluctuates as the sales volume fluctuates. The term ***variable expense*** refers to the variability of the total dollar expense.

Exhibit 24-1
Relevant range

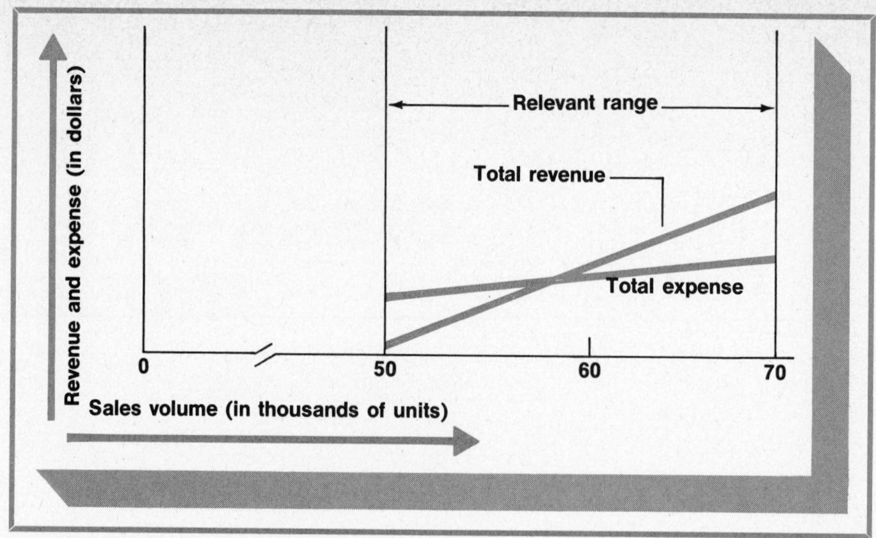

As an example, assume that a firm sells a magazine for $2 per issue. One of the selling expenses is a commission of $1 per issue paid to the salesman. If one unit is sold during the year, the total sales commission is $1. If 1,000 units are sold, the total sales commission is $1,000. The total commission expense varies directly with sales volume; therefore, commission expense is a variable expense. Note that the per-unit commission expense remains unchanged at $1 per unit, regardless of the number of units sold.

Exhibit 24-2 shows the relationship of a typical variable expense to sales volume. Note that, as volume increases, the total variable expense increases.

FIXED EXPENSES. Fixed expenses are those expenses that remain constant at any relevant range of volume within the existing operating capacity of the firm. The term ***fixed expense*** relates to total dollar expense.

As an illustration, assume that the rent expense for a factory is $100,000 per year. If no items are manufactured, the total rent expense remains fixed at $100,000 for the year. If 1,000 items are manufactured and sold, the total rent expense remains at $100,000. Note that the per-unit fixed expense for rent varies inversely with sales. If one unit is produced and sold, the per-unit rent expense is $100,000. If 100 units are produced and sold, the per-unit rent expense is $1,000.

Property taxes, insurance, and executive salaries usually are fixed expenses. Exhibit 24-3 shows the relationship of a typical fixed expense to sales volume. Note that, as volume increases, total fixed expense remains constant.

MIXED EXPENSES. Some expenses do not fall neatly into the pattern of variable versus fixed expenses. Such expenses may contain both a fixed and a variable element. Mixed (or semivariable) expenses are defined as those expenses that change with increases or decreases in sales volume, but do not change in direct proportion to the volume changes.

Telephone expense, maintenance and repair expenses, utilities expenses, and so on, usually are mixed expenses. If sales should drop to zero, these expenses would probably decrease somewhat but they would not decrease as much as the decrease in sales. Exhibit 24-4 shows the behavior of a typical mixed expense. Accountants have devised various methods that can be used to separate the variable and fixed elements of mixed expenses. One such method is described in the appendix to this chapter.

CONTRIBUTION MARGIN. The contribution margin is a significant idea in managerial accounting. *Contribution margin* is defined as sales less variable expense.

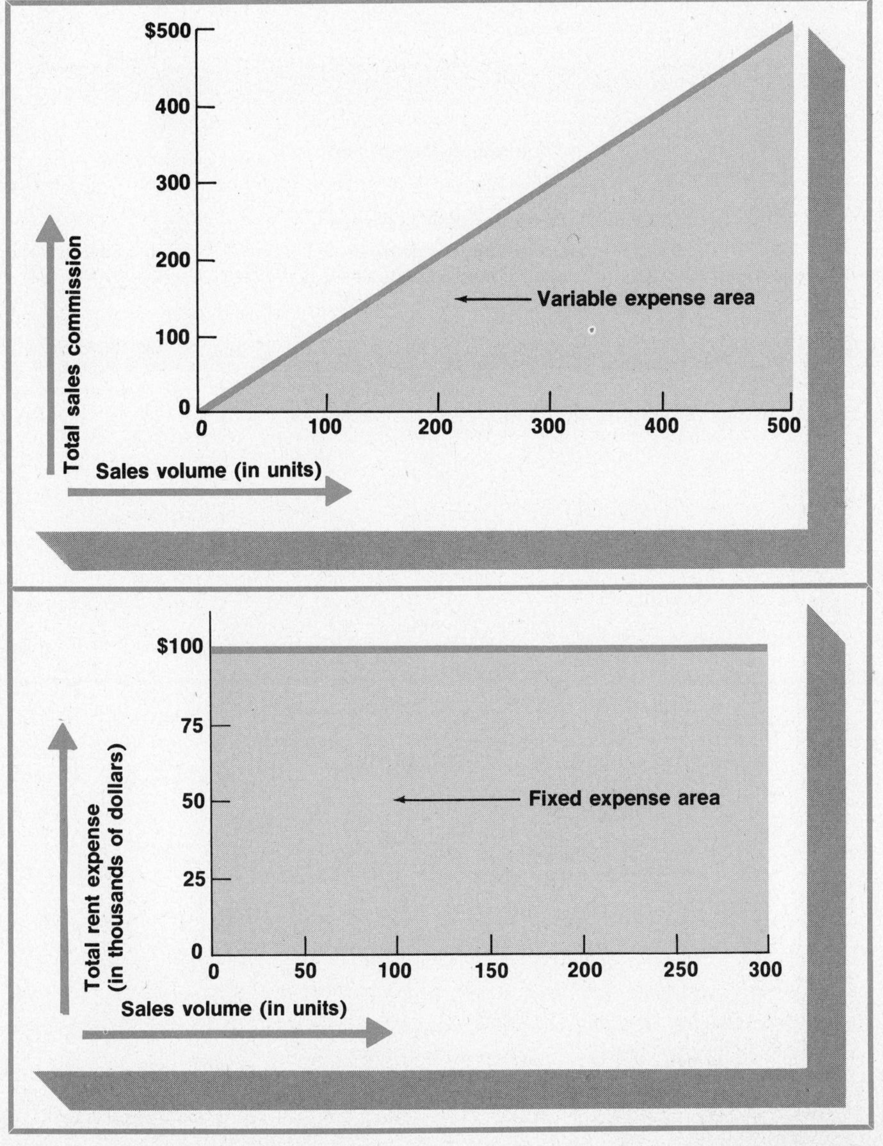

Exhibit 24-2
Viable expense activity

Exhibit 24-3
Fixed expense activity

Exhibit 24-4
Mixed expense activity

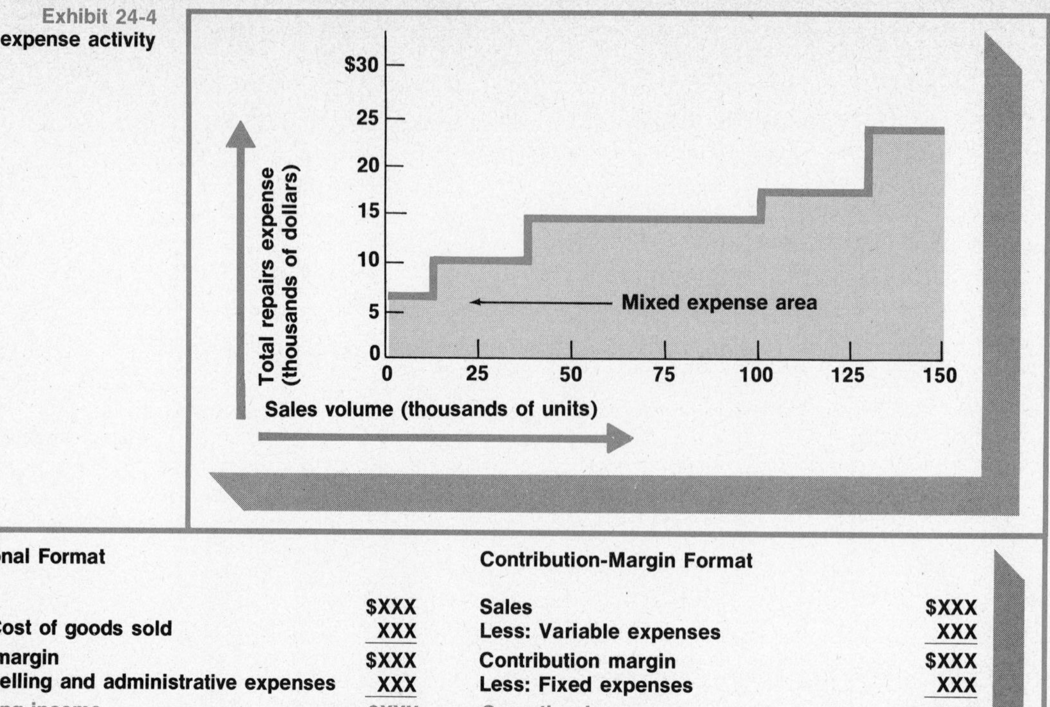

Traditional Format		**Contribution-Margin Format**	
Sales	**$XXX**	**Sales**	**$XXX**
Less: Cost of goods sold	**XXX**	**Less: Variable expenses**	**XXX**
Gross margin	**$XXX**	**Contribution margin**	**$XXX**
Less: Selling and administrative expenses	**XXX**	**Less: Fixed expenses**	**XXX**
Operating income	**$XXX**	**Operating income**	**$XXX**

Exhibit 24-5 **Income statements prepared in traditional and contribution-margin forms**

The traditional income statement (described in earlier chapters) reports expenses on the basis of function—selling, general, administrative, and so on. In managerial accounting, it is often useful to reconstruct the income statement to reflect variable and fixed expenses, thus showing the contribution margin of the firm. Exhibit 24-5 compares income statements in the traditional format and the contribution-margin format.

Contribution-margin dollars are available to meet fixed expenses and to provide a profit for the firm. Obviously, if fixed expenses are the same, then a larger contribution margin will mean a larger profit (or smaller loss) for the company. Exhibit 24-6 visualizes this contribution-margin concept.

Break-even analysis

The term ***break-even point*** refers to a level of operations at which a firm neither makes a profit nor sustains a loss. At the break-even point, the company's revenue equals its expenses. A sales volume below the break-even point results in a loss, whereas a volume above the break-even point results in a profit.

Break-even analysis helps management to evaluate changes in selling prices, variable and fixed expenses, product mix, and similar variables in terms of their effects on earnings. After we show how the break-even point is computed, we demonstrate various applications of break-even analysis.

The break-even point of a business may be computed by mathematical formulas or by graphic techniques. In break-even analysis, we assume that the fixed expense remains constant within the relevant range of activity, that total variable expenses vary in direct proportion to sales volume within the relevant range, and that the selling price per unit is unaffected by any changes in sales volume.

Exhibit 24-7 shows a condensed income statement in the contribution-margin format, with expenses grouped into variable and fixed classifications. In general, note that the income statement reflects the following basic format:

$$\text{Revenue (Sales)} = \text{Variable expense} + \text{Fixed expense} + \text{Profit}$$

At the break-even point, there is no profit or loss. Therefore,

$$\text{Sales at break-even point} = S_{\text{BEP}} = \text{Variable expense} + \text{Fixed expense}$$

Fixed expense is a constant amount, regardless of sales volume. Variable expense, however, is proportional to sales volume. Therefore, we can express variable expense as a percentage of sales, a percentage that remains constant as the sales volume changes. If we call this percentage the ***variable expense rate*** (VER), we have

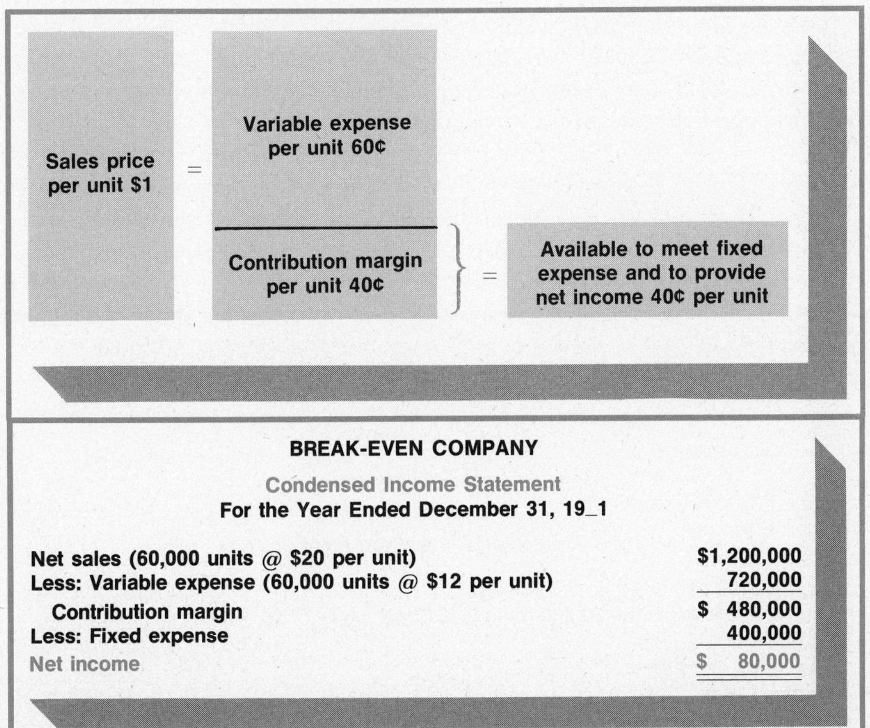

Exhibit 24-6
Contribution margin

BREAK-EVEN COMPANY
Condensed Income Statement
For the Year Ended December 31, 19_1

Net sales (60,000 units @ $20 per unit)	$1,200,000
Less: Variable expense (60,000 units @ $12 per unit)	720,000
Contribution margin	$ 480,000
Less: Fixed expense	400,000
Net income	$ 80,000

Exhibit 24-7
A condensed income statement in contribution-margin format

$$\text{VER} = \frac{\text{Variable expense}}{\text{Total sales}}$$

For any sales volume at which data are available. Then,

$S_{BEP} = (\text{VER} \times S_{BEP}) + \text{Fixed expense}.$

Rearranging the formula,

$(S_{BEP})\,(1 - \text{VER}) = \text{Fixed expense}.$

Therefore,

$$S_{BEP} = \frac{\text{Fixed expense}}{(1 - \text{VER})}$$

Let us use this formula to compute the sales at break-even point for the data in Exhibit 24-7. In this case, fixed expense is $400,000, and

$$\text{VER} = \frac{\$720{,}000}{\$1{,}200{,}000} = 0.60 \text{ (or 60\%)}$$

With this information, we can compute the sales at break-even point:

$$S_{BEP} = \frac{\$400{,}000}{(1 - 0.60)} = \frac{\$400{,}000}{0.40} = \$1{,}000{,}000$$

The Break-Even Company must earn sales revenue of $1,000,000 during a year if it is to break even. At lower sales, it will show a loss; at higher sales, it will show a profit. Exhibit 24-8 shows a hypothetical income statement for the break-even point, confirming the correctness of the computation.

CONTRIBUTION-MARGIN APPROACH

Another approach to break-even analysis makes use of the contribution-margin concept. Recall that the contribution margin is the excess of sales revenue over variable expense. Like the variable expense, the contribution margin can be expressed as a rate (a percentage of sales).

In Exhibit 24-7, the Break-Even Company shows a contribution margin of $480,000 on sales of $1,200,000. This is a ***contribution rate*** of 40 percent. Because the total sales revenue is divided between variable expense and contribution margin, the sum

Exhibit 24-8
Hypothetical income statement for the break-even point

BREAK-EVEN COMPANY
Hypothetical Income Statement
For Computed Break-Even Point

Net sales (50,000 units @ $20 per unit)	**$1,000,000**
Less: Variable expense (50,000 units @ $12 per unit)	**600,000**
Contribution margin	**$ 400,000**
Less: Fixed expense	**400,000**
Net income	**$ 0**

of the variable expense rate and the contribution rate must be 100 percent. In this case, the variable expense rate of 60 percent and the contribution margin of 40 percent do sum to 100 percent.

Therefore, we can rewrite the equation for sales at break-even point as follows:

$$S_{BEP} = \frac{\text{Fixed expense}}{\text{Contribution rate}}$$

In the example, the computation is the same as that used earlier, yielding a break-even point at sales of $1,000,000.

As shown in Exhibit 24-8, the sales of $1,000,000 must represent sales of 50,000 units at the fixed selling price of $20 per unit. If desired, the break-even point in units can be determined directly. From Exhibit 24-7, we find that the contribution margin was $480,000 on sales of 60,000 units. Therefore, the contribution margin per unit is $8. (This figure can also be obtained by subtracting the $12-per-unit variable expense from the $20-per-unit selling price.) In terms of the contribution margin per unit, the basic formula for sales at break-even point can be restated as

$$S_{BEP} = \frac{\text{Fixed expense}}{\text{Contribution margin per unit}}$$

$$= \frac{\$400{,}000}{\$8 \text{ per unit}} = 50{,}000 \text{ units.}$$

The validity of this formula is confirmed by a check with the hypothetical statement of Exhibit 24-8, which shows that the firm does break even on sales of 50,000 units.

SALES NEEDED FOR GIVEN PROFIT

The formulas developed for break-even analysis can be used to provide cost, volume, price, and profit data for management, as shown in the following examples.

Example 1. The management of the Break-Even Company wishes to show a profit of $100,000 in the coming year. It wants to know how many units must be sold during the year to achieve this net income.

Recall the basic formula:

Sales = Variable expense + Fixed expense + Profit.

Let U be the number of units to be sold to produce a profit of $100,000. Then,

$$\begin{aligned} \$20 \times U &= (\$12 \times U) + \$400{,}000 + \$100{,}000; \\ (\$20 \times U) - (\$12 \times U) &= \$500{,}000; \\ \$8 \times U &= \$500{,}000; \\ U &= 62{,}500 \text{ units.} \end{aligned}$$

Exhibit 24-9 shows a budgeted income statement for the coming year, confirming that sales of 62,500 should produce a profit of $100,000.

Example 2. Management asks for an alternative budget for the coming year, based upon sales sufficient to produce a net income equal to 10 percent of sales revenue.

Let S be the sales revenue needed to attain net income equal to 10 percent of sales.

Exhibit 24-9
Budgeted income statement to achieve profit of $100,000

BREAK-EVEN COMPANY	
Budgeted Income Statement	
For the Year Ended December 31, 19_2	
Net sales (62,500 units @ $20 per unit)	**$1,250,000**
Less: Variable expense (62,500 units @ $12 per unit)	**750,000**
Contribution margin	**$ 500,000**
Less: Fixed expense	**400,000**
Net income	$ 100,000

Using the same basic formula as that used in Example 1 (expressed in dollars instead of units),

$$\begin{aligned} S &= (0.60 \times S) + \$400{,}000 + (0.10 \times S); \\ (1.00 - 0.60 - 0.10) \times S &= \$400{,}000; \\ 0.30 \times S &= \$400{,}000; \\ S &= \$1{,}333{,}333. \end{aligned}$$

This value is not quite an even multiple of the sales price. Exhibit 24-10 shows a budgeted income statement based on sales of the nearest possible whole number of units. Note that the budgeted net income is approximately 10 percent of the sales revenue (with the slight difference due to the need to sell a whole number of units).

Break-even chart

Graphic computation of the break-even point is quite simple once you have gathered the basic information and have mastered certain basic charting techniques. The ***break-even chart*** (or graph) gives a visual representation of the sales volume (capacity, or output) at which expense equals revenue. This chart reflects the ***short-run*** relationship of volume to total expense and total revenue. (It may not be valid for the long run, because long-run changes may be expected in sales price, fixed expense, and variable expense rate—all of these factors are regarded as constant in break-even analysis.)

The break-even chart not only permits a visual determination of the break-even point. It also provides a visual summary of all possible budgeted income statements of the kind developed in the preceding section. Its flexible projection of the impact of volume upon expense, revenue, and income makes the break-even chart a useful tool for profit planning and control.

The following steps illustrate the development of a break-even chart (shown in Exhibit 24-13) using the data from the Break-Even Company example (Exhibit 24-7).

1. Prepare the format for the break-even chart.
   a. On the horizontal axis of the graph, mark off a scale in terms of a meaningful measure of volume—for example, dollar sales, unit sales, percentage of capacity. In our illustration, we use dollar sales. Total dollar sales is often the most useful measure of volume because it provides a convenient summary of

volume over various product lines or divisions of a firm for which other measures of volume may differ.

b. On the vertical axis, mark off a scale in terms of dollars for revenue and expense.

2. Plot fixed expense (Exhibit 24-11). The fixed expense line *F* is drawn parallel to the horizontal axis, intersecting the vertical axis at the dollar amount of fixed expense ($400,000 in the illustration), point *A*. (The notation $000 is commonly used in business charts and tables to mean that the figures are expressed in thousands of dollars.) The area between line *F* and the horizontal axis represents the fixed expense incurred at various levels of sales volume. The line is drawn parallel to the horizontal axis because fixed expense remains unchanged at all relevant volume levels.

3. Plot variable expense (Exhibit 24-12).

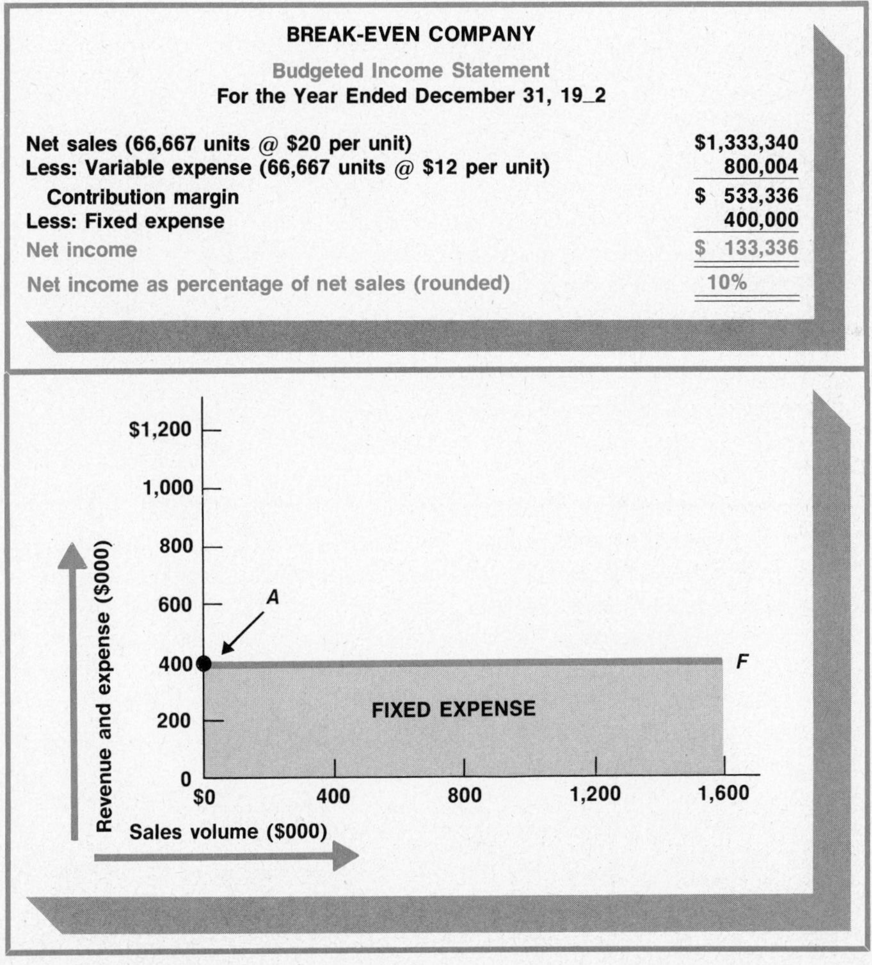

BREAK-EVEN COMPANY
Budgeted Income Statement
For the Year Ended December 31, 19_2

Net sales (66,667 units @ $20 per unit)	$1,333,340
Less: Variable expense (66,667 units @ $12 per unit)	800,004
Contribution margin	$ 533,336
Less: Fixed expense	400,000
Net income	$ 133,336
Net income as percentage of net sales (rounded)	10%

Exhibit 24-10
Budgeted income statement to achieve net income equal to 10 percent of sales revenue

Exhibit 24-11
Plotting the fixed expense line on the break-even chart

Exhibit 24-12
Plotting the total expense line on the break-even chart

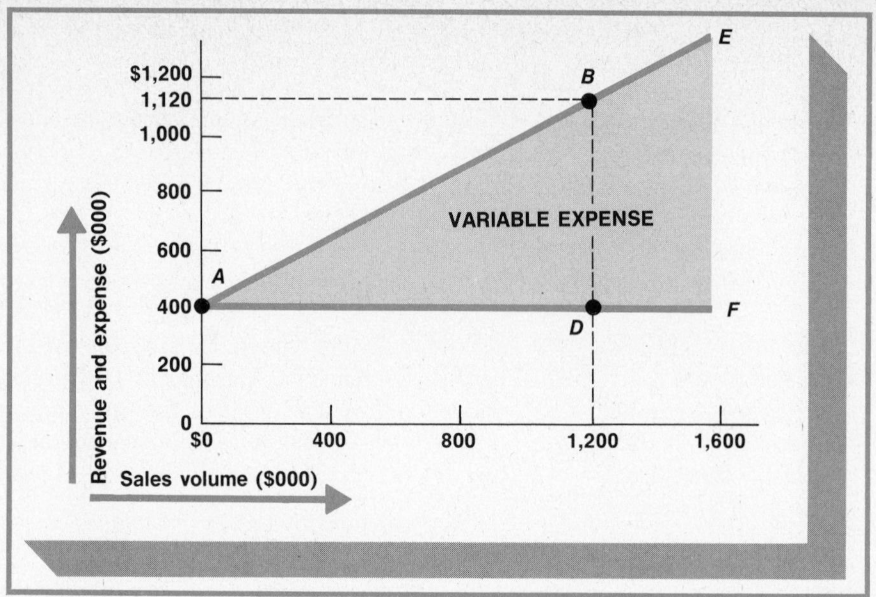

a. The data given in Exhibit 24-7 indicate total expense of $1,120,000 at a sales volume of $1,200,000. This total expense includes $400,000 fixed expense and $720,000 variable expense. Locate the volume of $1,200,000 along the baseline of the graph. The $400,000 fixed expense is already plotted by point *D* on line *F.* Move upward to point *B,* at a height of $1,120,000 as shown on the vertical axis. The distance from point *D* to point *B* ($720,000) represents the variable expense at this sales volume. Mark point *B* on the graph.

b. Because variable expense is proportional to sales volume, variable expense must be $0 when sales volume is $0. Therefore, point *A* can be plotted where the fixed expense line *F* touches the vertical axis, because total expense will equal fixed expense at this sales volume.

c. Draw a straight line *E* connecting points *A* and *B*. The area between line *E* and line *F* discloses the amount of variable expense at different sales volumes. The area between line *E* and the horizontal axis represents the total expense incurred (variable plus fixed expense) at various levels of sales. Line *E* may be considered as a total expense line, because it is plotted at the heights on the vertical axis representing total expenses for each sales volume level.

4. Plot sales revenue (Exhibit 24-13).

a. Plot point *C* to represent the total revenue of $1,200,000 at the sales volume of $1,200,000. (If sales volume were shown in other units than dollars, the values on the two axes would not be identical as they are in this case.)

b. When sales volume is zero (no sales), sales revenue will be $0. Therefore, plot point 0 at the origin of the graph.

c. Draw a straight line connecting points *O* and *C*. This line *R* represents the total revenue at various levels of sales volume.[1]

Mark the break-even point (BEP) where the total expense line *E* intersects the

1. The process of plotting the chart can be summarized briefly as follows. From the available data for a particular sales volume, plot points *B, C,* and *D* along a vertical line. Draw a horizontal line *F* from point *D* to the vertical axis and mark point *A*. Draw line *E* from point *A* through point *B*. Draw line *R* from the origin of the graph through point *C*. Mark BEP where lines *E* and *R* intersect.

total revenue line *R*. The sales volume needed to break even can be read from the horizontal axis; the sales revenue needed to break even can be read from the vertical axis. In this example, because the sales volume is shown in dollars, the two axes yield the same information about the break-even point—that sales of $1,000,000 are needed to break even.

The shaded areas in Exhibit 24-13 represent profit and loss. The profit area in the chart lies to the right of the break-even point—that is, through a range of sales volume where the total revenue line *R* is above the total expense line *E*. Through this range of volume above the break-even point, revenue is greater than expense. The loss area in the chart lies to the left of the break-even point, where the total expense line *E* is above the total revenue line *R*. Through the range of volume below the break-even point, expense exceeds revenue. The expected profit or loss for any sales volume can be read directly from the graph. Conversely, the sales volume needed to obtain a particular profit can quickly be estimated from the graph. (Computations may be needed to determine exact amounts; the graph usually provides only approximate results.)

Case studies

The data for the Break-Even Company (Exhibit 24-7) are used in the following series of cases to illustrate applications of break-even analysis.

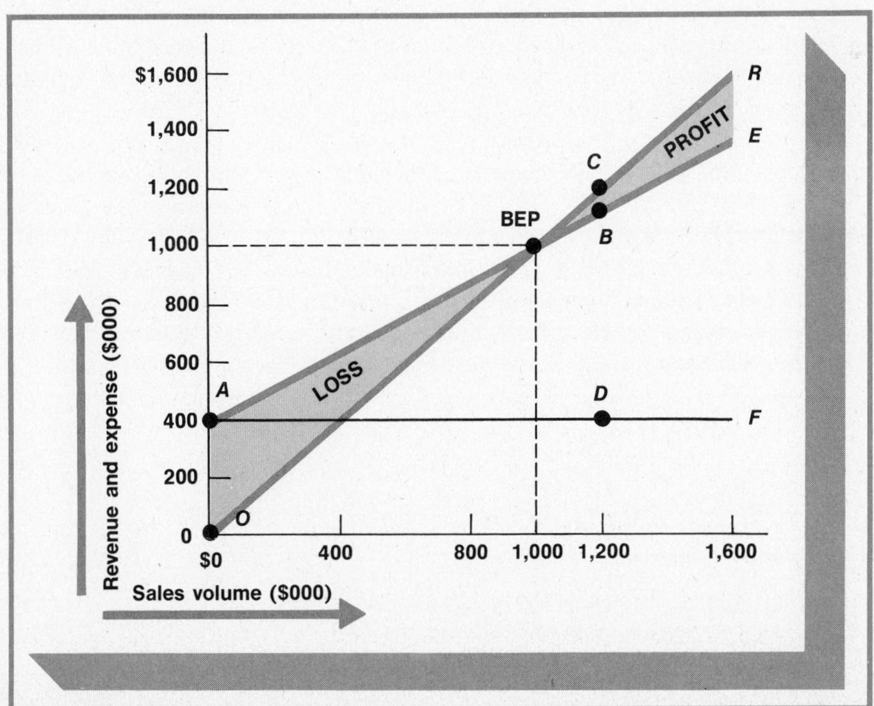

Exhibit 24-13
A conventional break-even chart

Case 1. Management of the Break-Even Company is considering the expansion of its plant facilities. After the expansion, fixed expenses would be $800,000 per year instead of the present $400,000. Variable expenses would remain at 60 percent of sales. The break-even point under present conditions has been computed as $1,000,000. Management wants to know what the break-even point would be after the expansion.

Using the formula given earlier in the chapter,

$$S_{BEP} = (0.60 \times S_{BEP}) + \$800{,}000$$

$$= \frac{\$800{,}000}{0.40} = \$2{,}000{,}000.$$

If the expansion is undertaken, the break-even point in terms of sales dollars will be doubled.

Case 2. Net income for 19_1 was $80,000 on sales of $1,200,000. Management wants to know what volume of sales would be needed after the plant expansion (see case 1) to achieve the same net income.

The solution is similar to that used for example 2 earlier in the chapter.

$$S = (0.60 \times S) + \$800{,}000 + \$80{,}000;$$

$$0.40 \times S = \$880{,}000;$$

$$S = \$2{,}200{,}000.$$

Case 3. Management wants to know the maximum net income that can be achieved with and without the plant expansion described in case 1. The present plant, working at maximum capacity, can produce 75,000 units per year. After plant expansion, the new total plant capacity would be 140,000 units per year.

Maximum net income will be achieved when the firm sells as many units as it can produce. (See Exhibit 24-13; profit is greatest at greatest sales volume.) For the existing plant, the maximum sales volume of 75,000 units at $20 per unit gives a maximum revenue of $1,500,000. For the expanded plant, the maximum volume of 140,000 units at $20 per unit gives a maximum revenue of $2,800,000. We wish to find the net income for these two amounts of sales revenue. (Note that the fixed expense is different at the two maximum volumes, however.)

Maximum revenue = Fixed expense + Variable expense + Profit;

or

Profit = Maximum revenue − (Fixed expense + Variable expense).

For the existing facilities,

$$\text{Profit} = \$1{,}500{,}000 - [\$400{,}000 + (0.60 \times \$1{,}500{,}000)]$$
$$= \$1{,}500{,}000 - (\$400{,}000 + \$900{,}000)$$
$$= \$200{,}000.$$

For the expanded facilities,

$$\begin{aligned}\text{Profit} &= \$2{,}800{,}000 - [\$800{,}000 + (0.60 \times \$2{,}800{,}000)]\\ &= \$2{,}800{,}000 - (\$800{,}000 + \$1{,}680{,}000)\\ &= \$320{,}000.\end{aligned}$$

CONCLUSION. With the information obtained in the three cases, management learns that it can expect the following results if it adopts the proposed plan of plant expansion.

1. The break-even point in sales will increase from $1,000,000 to $2,000,000.
2. The sales volume needed to produce the same net income as that achieved before the expansion will increase from $1,200,000 to $2,200,000.
3. The maximum net income possible for the firm will increase from $200,000 to $320,000.

Margin of safety

The ***margin of safety*** (M/S) is the dollar difference between break-even sales revenue and sales revenue at a certain volume level. Margin of safety may also be expressed as a rate:

$$\text{M/S} = \frac{\text{Sales at given level} - \text{Break-even sales}}{\text{Sales at given level}}$$

For example, in Exhibit 24-7, the Break-Even Company has sales of $1,200,000 when its break-even point is $1,000,000. The margin of safety is $200,000, or 16.7 percent ($200,000 divided by $1,200,000). Generally, a high margin of safety indicates a relatively safe business position. The Break-Even Company could absorb a 16.7 percent decline in sales from the current level before reporting a net loss.

If a firm has relatively large fixed expense, relatively small variable expense rate, and a low margin of safety, it would probably try to improve its profit position by increasing volume or by reducing fixed expense. If the margin of safety for a firm is relatively small and the unit contribution margin is also small, the firm might consider the advisability of increasing selling price or reducing variable expense. Managers should appreciate the fact that, if they operate with a small margin of safety, a small decline in sales is likely to bring net losses.

Summary

Contribution margin is the excess of sales over variable expense. Variable expense includes those expenses that vary directly with sales volume. Fixed expense includes those expenses that do not vary as sales volume changes. Exhibit 24-14 summarizes the behavior of the different kinds of expense.

Exhibit 24-14 **Behavior of variable, fixed, and mixed expenses**

Expense Classification	Behavior of Total Expense	Behavior of Per-Unit Expense
Variable expense	Increases in direct proportion to sales-volume increase	Remains constant as sales volume increases
Fixed expense	Remains constant as sales volume increases	Decreases in inverse proportion to sales-volume increase
Mixed expense	Increases with volume increase, but not in direct proportion to the volume increase	Decreases with volume increase, but not in inverse proportion to the volume increase

Contribution margin is essential to the understanding of break-even analysis. The break-even point is defined as the sales volume at which a firm neither realizes net income nor incurs a net loss. The break-even model provides management with flexible revenue and expense projections under assumed conditions. It enables management to evaluate data about volume, selling prices, expenses, and product mix in an integrated manner. It is especially useful in such marketing decisions as setting pricing policies and forecasting sales.

Break-even analysis assumes that a firm can predict its expenses over a relevant range of sales volumes, and that it can segregate these expenses into fixed and variable classifications. The analysis also assumes that fixed expenses remain fixed over the relevant range, and that variable expenses vary in proportion (a linear relationship) to sales. Such assumptions are not always valid. Many applications of the analysis involve similar questionable assumptions about relationships between selling price and customer demand. However, despite its many limitations, break-even analysis is a useful tool in profit-making activities.

The margin of safety is the dollar excess of sales revenue (at some given level of sales volume) over break-even sales revenue. The margin of safety is a measure of the extent to which a firm's sales could decline without causing a net loss.

Appendix

MIXED EXPENSES

Various methods are available to separate a mixed expense into its fixed and variable elements. Here we use the high-low, two-point method to demonstrate a relatively easy method for making the separation. Other more sophisticated methods (such as the least squares method) often are used in business.

The high-low, two-point method involves the following steps. For purposes of illustration, we suppose that the power expense for a firm varies in relation to machine hours worked during the year, as shown in Exhibit 24-15. We apply the high-low, two-point method to separate the power expense into its fixed and variable elements.

1. Collect data about the mixed expense. Relate each value of the expense to a value of some other related variable, such as direct labor hours, labor costs, units of sales, or percentage of capacity. (The relationship need be valid only over the relevant range of activity being considered in the break-even analysis.)
2. Select the high and low points in expense and activity. In Exhibit 24-15, the high point is period No. 5 and the low point is period No. 1.

3. Compute the variable rate per machine hour (or other variable being used) according to the following formula:

$$\text{Variable rate} = \frac{\text{Change in mixed expense from high to low point}}{\text{Change in activity from high to low point}}$$

$$= \frac{\$17{,}000 - \$7{,}000}{5{,}000 - 1{,}000 \text{ hrs.}} = \frac{\$10{,}000}{4{,}000 \text{ hrs.}} = \$2.50 \text{ per machine hour.}$$

4. Compute the fixed expense at the high (or the low) point of activity, using the following formula:

$$\begin{aligned}\text{Total fixed expense} &= \text{Total mixed expense} - \text{Total variable expense} \\ &= \$17{,}000 - (\$2.50 \times 5{,}000) \\ &= \$17{,}000 - \$12{,}500 = \$4{,}500.\end{aligned}$$

5. To compute the total expected mixed cost of any relevant level of activity, let X be the level of activity. Then,

$$\text{Total mixed expense} = \text{Total fixed expense} + (\$2.50 \times X).$$

For example, the estimated power expense at a level of 2,000 machine hours is:

$$\text{Total power expense} = \$4{,}500 + (\$2.50 \times 2{,}000) = \$9{,}500.$$

The high-low, two-point method of separating a mixed expense into fixed and variable elements can be accomplished graphically as shown in Exhibit 24-16. The graphical computation involves the following steps.

1. Plot the high and low points on a graph of expense versus the other variable.
2. Draw a connecting line through the two points and extend the line to intersect the vertical axis.
3. Read the total fixed-expense element from the vertical axis where the straight line intersects the axis.
4. Compute the variable expense element at either the high or the low point as the dollar difference between the fixed expense and the high or low point, divided by the other variable.

$$\text{Variable rate} = \frac{\text{Total expense} - \text{Fixed expense}}{\text{Level of activity}} = \frac{\$17{,}000 - \$4{,}500}{5{,}000 \text{ hrs.}}$$

$$= \$2.50 \text{ per machine hour.}$$

Time Period	Machine Hours Worked During Period	Power Expense for Period
No. 1	1,000	$ 7,000
No. 2	1,500	9,000
No. 3	3,000	15,000
No. 4	4,200	15,500
No. 5	5,000	17,000

Exhibit 24-15
Variation of power expense over five 10-week periods

Exhibit 24-16
Separating a mixed expense into fixed and variable elements

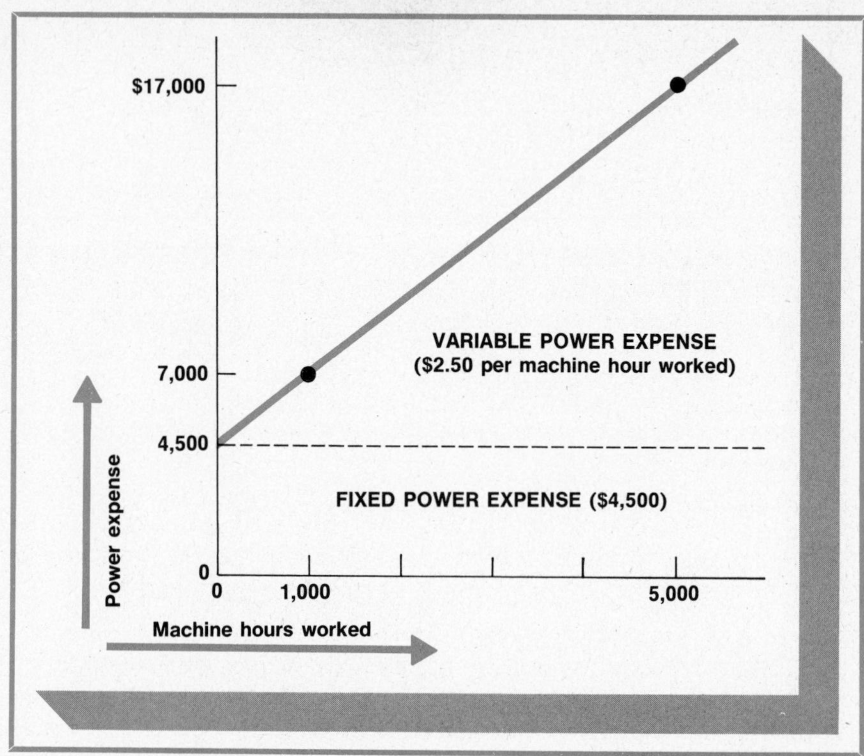

Questions

1. Distinguish between variable, fixed, and mixed expenses.
2. What is contribution margin? Prepare a condensed income statement in contribution-margin format.
3. What is the break-even point? Give the formula for computing the break-even point in dollars; in units.
4. Draw a graph that shows variable and fixed expense, revenue, and the break-even point.
5. What is meant by a relevant range in the context of break-even analysis?
6. What is the margin of safety? How is it computed?
7. How does the behavior of sales-commission expense differ from that of telephone expense?

Exercises

E24-1 (Break-even computation)
Exhibit 24-17 shows a budgeted income statement for the Win Company. Compute the break-even point for the Win Company in (a) dollars and (b) units. Prepare a budgeted income statement for the break-even point to verify your computations.

E24-2 (Break-even chart)
Prepare a break-even chart for the Win Company (Exhibit 24-17).

E24-3 (Margin of safety)
Compute the margin of safety for the Win Company (Exhibit 24-17) (a) in dollars and (b) as a percentage of sales.

E24-4 (Mixed expenses)
A study of the production activity of a firm indicates that light, heat, and power expense is a mixed expense. The company believes that this expense is related to direct labor hours during a period. Data from preceding years indicates that the greatest light, heat, and power expense ($120,000) occurred during a period when direct labor hours amounted to 90,000. The lowest expense ($90,000) occurred in a period with 45,000 direct labor hours. In preparing a break-even study for the firm, the accountant finds it necessary to separate the light, heat, and power expense into its fixed and variable elements.

Required:

a. Compute the variable rate for light, heat, and power expense.
b. Compute the fixed-expense element of light, heat, and power expense.
c. The company expects total direct labor hours to be 135,000 for the next year. What light, heat, and power expense should be budgeted for the year?

E24-5 (Volume of sales to achieve objective)
A firm has fixed expense of $80,000 and variable expense of 40 percent of net sales. The firm wishes to make a net income of $160,000 during the coming year. What dollar volume of sales will be needed? Prepare a budgeted income statement to verify your computation.

E24-6 (Volume of sales to achieve objective)
Estimate the dollar amount of sales needed to attain net income of 25 percent of sales revenue, if fixed expense is $100,000 and variable expense is 60 percent of sales revenue.

WIN COMPANY
Budgeted Income Statement
For the Year Ended December 31, 19_6

Net sales (2,000 units @ $80 per unit)		$160,000
Less: Variable expense:		
Direct materials	$15,000	
Direct labor	50,000	
Factory overhead	10,000	
Selling expense	40,000	
Administrative expense	5,000	120,000
Contribution margin		$ 40,000
Less: Fixed expense:		
Factory overhead	$ 5,000	
Selling expense	9,000	
Administrative expense	6,000	20,000
Net income		$ 20,000

Exhibit 24-17
Budgeted income statement for Exercises E24-1, E24-2, and E24-3

E24-7 (Classification of expenses)
After examining a cost report, the plant manager asks you to classify each of the following expenses as a variable, mixed, or fixed expense.
a. Salaries of inspectors for the assembly line (inspectors are added or laid off with fluctuations in production, but not proportionately).
b. Direct labor.
c. Direct material.
d. Sales commission expense.
e. Depreciation expense (straight-line).
f. Property taxes.
g. Repair and maintenance expense (the firm has its own repair staff, which also maintains the equipment; repairs do not necessarily occur in direct relation to the use of equipment and facilities).
h. Salary of the president.

Problems

P24-1 (Applications of break-even analysis)
Exhibit 24-18 shows a condensed income statement issued by the Control Company. The company is contemplating an investment in additional plant facilities. If the new plant is constructed, fixed expense will increase by $30,000. The maximum potential of the present plant is sufficient to supply sales revenue of $200,000. The expanded plant could provide enough goods to supply sales revenue of $300,000. Variable expense is expected to remain at 20 percent of sales revenue after the new plant is opened.
Required: Compute the following:
a. the break-even point under existing conditions;
b. the break-even point under proposed conditions with the new plant in operation;
c. the sales that would be needed after plant expansion to provide the same net income as that reported in 19_6;
d. maximum net income under present conditions;
e. maximum net income after plant expansion.

P24-2 (Application of variable cost analysis)
In discussing a budget for the next year, the president of the Hardy Firm asks

Exhibit 24-18
Income Statement for Problem P24-1

CONTROL COMPANY
Condensed Income Statement
For the Year Ended December 31, 19_6

Net sales		**$150,000**
Costs and expense:		
Fixed	**$90,000**	
Variable	**30,000**	**120,000**
Net income		**$ 30,000**

her accountant to predict net income for 19_7 if sales for that year are $1,800,000. The following data are available.

	19_5	19_6
Sales	$800,000	$1,300,000
Total expense	600,000	800,000
Net income	$200,000	$ 500,000

HINT: Would it be helpful if you could compute the fixed expense and variable expense rate per dollar of sales? Note that two levels of activity are available.

P24-3 (Application of break-even analysis)
The following production statistics for Able Company and Baker Company are available.

	Able Company	Baker Company
Fixed expense	$60,000	$80,000
Variable expense	$20 per unit	$40 per unit
Selling price	$120 per unit	$80 per unit

Required:

a. What is the break-even point in sales for the Able Company?
b. What is the break-even point in sales for the Baker Company?
c. The sales for the two companies during the past year were $80,000 for Able Company and $240,000 for Baker Company. What is the margin of safety for each company in dollars? in percentage of sales?
d. From the preceding information, which firm appears to be the safer investment risk?

P24-4 (Break-even chart analysis)
In the chart shown in Exhibit 24-19, sales revenue, fixed expense, and variable expense are drawn in a manner different from that illustrated in this chapter. Identify each of the lines, points, distances, and areas labeled in this break-even chart.

P24-5 (Applications of break-even analysis)
The Anxious Publishing Company is considering a decision to publish a book. Estimates indicate that it will cost $30,000 to prepare the manuscript and artwork, and another $50,000 to set type and get the book ready to go to press. If the print order is for 12,000 copies or more, the cost of printing and binding the book will be $6 per copy. Selling expenses will be $2 per copy. From past experience, the firm finds that its general and administrative expense (not related to particular books) is 40 percent of sales revenue. The sales department estimates that it can sell 50,000 copies of the book at a price of $20 per copy.

Required:

a. Compute the break-even point in sales for the publication of this book.
b. Compute the margin of safety in dollars and in copies sold for the predicted level of sales.
c. Company policy is to publish a book only if a profit of 10 percent on sales revenue is expected. Under this policy, should the book be published? What number of copies would have to be sold to attain the required profit rate?

Exhibit 24-19
Graph for Problem P24-4

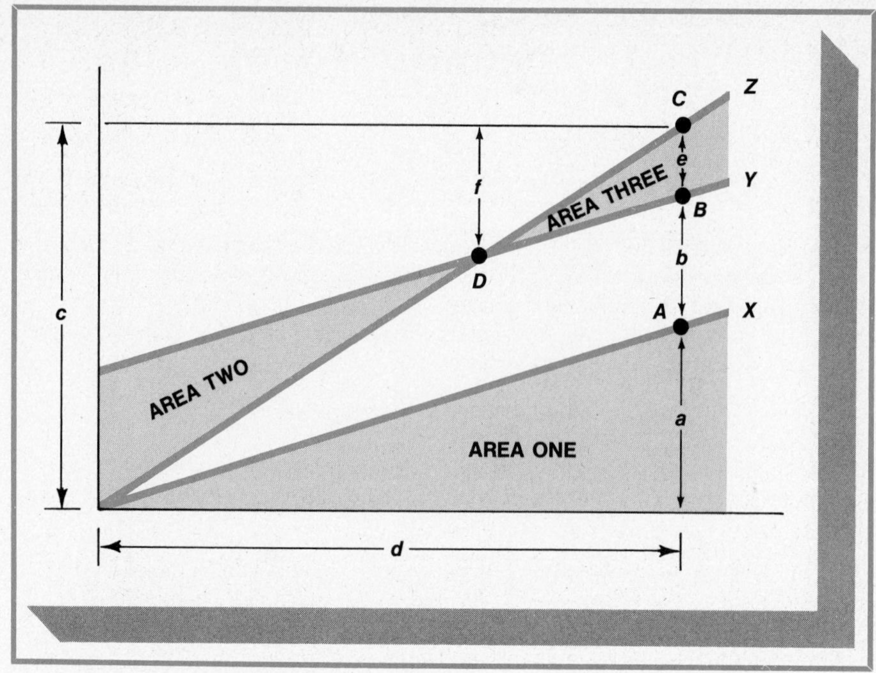

d. The sales department estimates that it could sell 30,000 copies of the book at a price of $25 per copy. Repeat parts a, b, and c for this proposed selling price.

e. Should the book be published? If so, at what selling price? Discuss the reasons for your answer.

P24-6 (Break-even analysis and M/S)

Given the following information, compute the break-even point and the margin of safety for this business:

Net sales		$50,000
Less costs and expense:		
Fixed	$10,000	
Variable	20,000	30,000
Net income		$20,000

P24-7 (Break-even chart)

Refer to Problem P24-6. Prepare a break-even chart for this problem.

Contribution-margin analysis

At any moment, a business firm is faced with many alternative courses of action. The success of the firm requires an understanding and appreciation of the need to evaluate these alternative courses. Decision-making involves choices, and management must have a realistic approach to the analysis of its problems and opportunities. Because of the intricacies and complexities associated with managerial variables, many business situations seem to be unmanageable. Modern management has learned the importance of concentrating on cost-volume-profit relationships to make it possible to cope with such situations. In this chapter we explore the concept of contribution margin. This concept provides an approach to problem solving in situations where alternative courses of action exist.

In Chapter 24, the concept of contribution margin was introduced in connection with break-even analysis. In this chapter we demonstrate the use of contribution margin to assist management in the following situations:

1. profit planning, as influenced by variations in cost, volume, and price;
2. the utilization of scarce resources for profit maximization;
3. acceptance or rejection of additional sales volume;
4. decision about possible shutdown of an operation that is showing a net loss;
5. decisions about allocation of resources among departments;
6. transfer pricing.

Profit planning: Variations in cost, volume, and price

Contribution analysis can help management decide what will happen to profits if

1. fixed expense increases or decreases;
2. selling price per unit is increased or decreased;
3. variable expense increases or decreases;
4. volume of sales increases or decreases; or
5. two or three or four of these factors change simultaneously.

Cost-volume-profit analysis is a very useful tool in applying the contribution-margin approach to such problems. Exhibit 25-1 shows ten independent cases, each representing a certain change from the basic data given in the first line of the table. The basic data represents a situation where a firm is selling 60,000 units per year at a selling price of $20 per unit. Variable expense is $12 per unit, so contribution margin is $8 per unit. From this contribution margin, the firm must meet fixed expense of $400,000. This leaves the firm with net income of $80,000.

Each of the ten cases represents the projected results of a certain change (or set of changes) that management feels might be possible in the coming year. Each case is independent of the others. The cases represent the following changes:

Case A selling price is increased 10 percent;
B selling price is decreased 10 percent;
C variable expense increases 10 percent;
D variable expense decreases 10 percent;
E volume of sales increases 10 percent;
F volume of sales decreases 10 percent;
G fixed expense increases $50,000;
H fixed expense decreases $50,000;
I selling price is decreased 10 percent, variable expense decreases 10 percent, and sales volume increases 5 percent;
J selling price is increased 10 percent, variable expense increases 10 percent, and sales volume decreases 5 percent.

Exhibit 25-1 shows the total contribution margin and the net income (or loss) to be expected in each case. Management can use this kind of cost-volume profit analysis

Exhibit 25-1 Cost-volume-profit analysis of alternative courses of action

Case	Units Sold (*a*)	Selling Price per Unit (*b*)	Variable Expense per Unit (*c*)	Contribution Margin per Unit (*d* = *b* − *c*)	Total Contribution Margin (*e* = *d* × *a*)	Fixed Expense (*f*)	Net Income (*e* − *f*)
Basic	60,000	$20	$12.00	$ 8.00	$480,000	$400,000	$ 80,000
A	60,000	22	12.00	10.00	600,000	400,000	200,000
B	60,000	18	12.00	6.00	360,000	400,000	(40,000)
C	60,000	20	13.20	6.80	408,000	400,000	8,000
D	60,000	20	10.80	9.20	552,000	400,000	152,000
E	66,000	20	12.00	8.00	528,000	400,000	128,000
F	54,000	20	12.00	8.00	432,000	400,000	32,000
G	60,000	20	12.00	8.00	480,000	450,000	30,000
H	60,000	20	12.00	8.00	480,000	350,000	130,000
I	63,000	18	10.80	7.20	453,600	400,000	53,600
J	57,000	22	13.20	8.80	501,600	400,000	101,600

NOTE: Each case is identical to the basic data except for changes in the orange factors, and corresponding changes in the items computed from the changed factors.

as a help in selecting the combination of selling price, sales volume, and expenses (within a relevant range) that can provide the largest net income for the firm.

In the example, suppose that management has control over all factors, so that it can choose which of these cases to aim for in the coming year. Case A offers the most attractive alternative if maximum net income is the only criterion. In other words, if the firm can increase its selling price by 10 percent while holding all other factors constant, it can expect to increase its net income (before taxes) from $80,000 to $200,000. This is an increase of 150 percent in net income.

Or suppose that management has reason to believe that variable expense will increase 10 percent in the coming year (case C). If it holds all other factors constant, it can expect its net income to decrease 90 percent (to $8,000). Case J shows, on the other hand, that the firm might be able to compensate for such an increase in variable expense. If it increases the selling price by 10 percent, and if this increase in price causes only a 5 percent decrease in sales volume, the net income for the coming year could actually increase 27 percent (to $101,600) despite the increase in variable expense.

After evaluating the impact of various expected changes and alternative courses of action, management can select the level of operations needed to achieve a particular objective. It can then proceed to provide the sales force, production facilities, and so on that are needed to reach this level of operations.

Contribution-margin and cost–volume–profit analysis lead to the following general conclusions.

1. Net income can be increased by decreasing fixed expense or by increasing total contribution margin.
2. Total contribution margin can be increased by increasing sales volume or by increasing contribution margin per unit.
3. Contribution margin per unit can be increased by increasing selling price or by decreasing variable expense.

Many other more detailed conclusions can be drawn. For example, if the contribution margin per unit is small and cannot be improved, and if fixed expense cannot be reduced, a large increase in sales volume will be needed to produce a significant increase in net income.

Using data on contribution margin per unit, management can make quick estimates of the impact on net income resulting from changes in sales.

$$\text{Change in net income} = \text{Change in volume} \times \text{Contribution margin per unit.}$$

$$\text{Change in net income} = \text{Change in sales revenue} \times \text{Contribution-margin rate.}$$

Using contribution-margin analysis, management can determine the change in selling price or unit cost that is needed to achieve a desired contribution margin. The required change in selling price or unit cost is given by

$$\frac{\text{Desired change in total contribution margin}}{\text{Number of units to be sold}}$$

Exhibit 25-2
Contribution-margin analysis of three different products

	Product A	Product B	Product C
Sales price per unit	$12	$15	$18
Variable expense per unit	$ 7	$ 9	$10
Contribution margin per unit	$ 5	$ 6	$ 8
Machine hours needed to produce one unit	5	12	10

Utilization of scarce resources

Contribution-margin analysis can help management decide which of several products to produce if restraints (such as scarce resources) limit the total possible production. For example, suppose that a firm can produce and sell three different products as shown in Exhibit 25-2. The products are similar in all respects other than those indicated in the table. Some additional machine time is available in the factory. Management wants to use that time to produce the product that will make the largest contribution to net income.

In solving such problems, don't jump to the conclusion that the firm should produce the product with the largest contribution margin per unit. Such a conclusion would be correct if all products required the same amount of the scarce resource (in this case, machine time). However, in this case, different numbers of units of the different products could be produced with the available machine time.

It takes 5 machine hours to produce one unit of product A. That unit contributes $5 toward fixed expense and net income. Therefore, the contribution margin of product A is $1 per machine hour. The contribution margin of product B is $0.50 per machine hour; that of product C is $0.80 per machine hour. Therefore, the firm can maximize net income for the extra machine time by producing product A.

This example shows the need to give due regard to restricting factors (such as scarce resources) when evaluating possible courses of action. If sales are limited by restraints such as shortages of production facilities or materials, the profitability of different products should be evaluated in terms of the ***margin contribution per unit of the limiting factor,*** rather than per unit of the product.

Possibility of additional sales

Contribution-margin analysis can be used to evaluate the comparative attractiveness of different courses of action, such as the possibility of accepting or rejecting a chance for additional sales volume. As an example, suppose that a firm is capable of producing 50,000 units when operating at capacity. At present, the factory is operating at 90 percent of capacity (that is, 45,000 units). Fixed expense is $100,000; variable expense is $6 per unit. The product is currently selling for $10 per unit.

A customer in a foreign country has offered to buy 5,000 additional units at $7 per unit. Should management accept this offer, thus bringing production up to full capacity? The sales department estimates that the foreign sale would have no effect on domestic sales volume or selling price.

Without contribution-margin analysis, it might seem that the firm should reject the order. At full production of 50,000 units, fixed expense amounts to $2 per unit. Therefore, total expense per unit is $8, and it might seem that the firm will lose money if it sells the 5,000 units at $7 each.

However, contribution-margin analysis shows that this is not the case. No additional fixed expense is incurred if the order is accepted; the fixed expense is already being absorbed by the domestic sales. Therefore, as long as the proposed selling price ($7) of the additional sale exceeds the variable expense ($6) associated with the order, the firm will increase its net income if it accepts the order. The additional order will contribute $1 per unit, or a total of $5,000, toward the net income of the firm. Exhibit 25-3 shows a ***differential revenue and expense analysis*** for this example. Such a schedule is often helpful in analyzing the impact of alternative courses of action.

What should management do if the foreign customer offers to pay only $5.90 per unit for the 5,000 additional units? In this case, variable expense ($6 per unit) exceeds the selling price ($5.90 per unit) for the additional order. Each unit sold at this price would decrease the total contribution margin (and therefore the net income) by $0.10. Acceptance of the order for 5,000 units at this price would reduce the net income by $500. The order should be rejected.

In considering the original $7-per-unit order from the foreign customer, suppose that the sales department reports that the acceptance of the order will have an effect on domestic sales. If the additional 5,000 units are sold to the foreign customer for $7 per unit, the sales department reports that domestic customers will be less willing to buy at the $10-per-unit selling price. They estimate that it will be necessary to lower the domestic selling price to $8 per unit in order to keep domestic sales at the present level of 45,000 units. If the domestic selling price is kept at $10 after accepting the foreign order, the sales department estimates that domestic sales will fall to 35,000 units.

Exhibit 25-3
Differential revenue and expense analysis of possible additional sales order

	Current Volume	Additional Order	Volume if Order Is Accepted
Sales: Current (45,000 units @ $10)	**$450,000**		**$450,000**
Additional (5,000 units @ $7)		**$35,000**	**35,000**
Total			**$485,000**
Less: Variable expense (@ $6 per unit)	**270,000**	**30,000**	**300,000**
Contribution margin	**$180,000**	**$ 5,000**	**$185,000**
Less: Fixed expense	**100,000**		**100,000**
Net income	**$ 80,000**	**$ 5,000**	**$ 85,000**

Exhibit 25-4
Revenue and expense analysis of three courses of action

	Case A	Case B	Case C
Sales: Foreign sales @ \$7 per unit	–	\$ 35,000	\$ 35,000
Domestic sales @ \$8 per unit	–	–	360,000
Domestic sales @ \$10 per unit	\$450,000	350,000	–
Total sales	\$450,000	\$385,000	\$395,000
Less: Variable expense (@ \$6 per unit)	270,000	240,000	300,000
Contribution margin	\$180,000	\$145,000	\$ 95,000
Less: Fixed expense	100,000	100,000	100,000
Net income (net loss)	\$ 80,000	\$ 45,000	\$ (5,000)

Exhibit 25-4 shows an analysis of the impact on net income of the three possible courses of action:

Case A reject the foreign order (sales continue as at present);
Case B accept the foreign order and keep domestic selling price at \$10;
Case C accept the foreign order and reduce domestic selling price to \$8.

In case B, the firm makes the foreign sale of 5,000 units at \$7 and makes domestic sales of 35,000 units at \$10. In case C, it makes the foreign sale of 5,000 units at \$7 and domestic sales of 45,000 units at \$8.

The results of the analysis show that the firm should reject the foreign order under these circumstances. If it accepted the order and reduced its domestic selling price to keep up its domestic sales volume, it would actually show a net loss.

Operation versus shutdown

Suppose that a firm is operating a plant at a loss. The loss is a temporary one, and corrective action can be taken to remedy the loss situation within a short period. Is the firm better off to shut down the plant until the situation is corrected, or to continue to operate? In terms of net income or net loss, the question can be rephrased: Is the loss resulting from continuing operations larger than the loss from a temporary shutdown?

If the loss from temporarily continuing operations is less than the loss from a temporary shutdown, the plant should be operated even though the loss is incurred. If the loss from the shutdown is less than the loss from continued operations, the opposite conclusion would be reached.

Exhibit 25-5 shows a condensed income statement for a plant that is operating at a loss of \$20,000. If the firm decides to keep operating the plant, this loss will continue temporarily. If the firm decides to shut down the plant, volume will be reduced to zero and so will variable expense. However, fixed expense for the plant will be unchanged by the temporary change in volume, so a temporary shutdown would

	Continued Operation	Shutdown
Sales: 1,000,000 units @ $1 per unit	$1,000,000	—
0 units @ $1 per unit	—	$ 0
Less: Variable expense (@ $0.90 per unit)	900,000	0
Contribution margin	$ 100,000	$ 0
Less: Fixed expense	120,000	120,000
Net income (net loss)	$ (20,000)	$(120,000)

Exhibit 25-5
Revenue and expense analysis of operation versus shutdown

result in a loss of $120,000. Obviously, the firm should continue to operate the plant if it expects economic and business conditions to improve in the near future.

The contribution-margin analysis shows that continued operations provide a contribution margin of $100,000 that partially offsets the fixed expense of $120,000. On the other hand, the contribution margin from a shutdown is zero. As a general conclusion, the firm should keep operating the plant if the operations produce a contribution margin greater than zero.

However, note that this contribution-margin analysis is valid only if the relevant range for the analysis of variable and fixed expense extends all the way to zero volume. In most cases, some of the expenses classified as fixed expense at normal levels of operation could be eliminated during a total shutdown. If the shutdown extends over a long period of time, more and more of the fixed expense probably could be eliminated. In the long run, the firm could sell the plant and eliminate the fixed expense entirely. Therefore, in the long run, all expenses become variable expense. If the loss situation is expected to continue for a long time, the shutdown may provide a smaller loss than the continued operation at a loss.

Contribution-margin analysis is basically a technique suitable for short-term problems. If it is to be applied to long-run situations, careful study must be made of the proper classification of fixed and variable expense over the time period being studied.

Comparing profitability of departments

Let us examine another variation of the "operation versus shutdown" decision. The General Department Store operates three departments. The store's accountant presents management with an income statement (Exhibit 25-6) showing that Department A operated at a profit, Department B at a loss, and Department C at its break-even point during the past year.

Management is concerned about Departments B and C. In particular, management is considering the possibility of shutting down Department B. If this is done, the fixed expense of the firm is expected to continue without reduction. The floor space made available by the shutdown of Department B would be divided evenly between Departments A and C. However, this additional floor space is not expected to result in any

Exhibit 25-6 **Income statement for department store (contribution margin format)**

THE GENERAL DEPARTMENT STORE

Income Statement

For the Year Ended December 31, 19_1

	Department A	Department B	Department C	Total
Sales	$100,000	$70,000	$50,000	$220,000
Less: Variable expense	50,000	68,000	40,000	158,000
Contribution margin	$ 50,000	$ 2,000	$10,000	$ 62,000
Less: Fixed expense (Schedule 1)	20,000	10,000	10,000	40,000
Net income (net loss)	$ 30,000	$ (8,000)	$ 0	$ 22,000

Schedule 1
Allocation of Fixed Expense

	Floor Space		Allocated Fixed Expense	
	Square Feet	Percentage	Amount	Percentage
Department A	100,000	50%	$20,000	50%
Department B	50,000	25%	10,000	25%
Department C	50,000	25%	10,000	25%
	200,000	100%	$40,000	100%

NOTE: Total fixed expense of $40,000 is allocated among the departments in proportion to floor space used by the departments, as shown in this schedule.

sales increase for the two surviving departments. Would the shutdown of Department B under these conditions have favorable impact on the store's net income?

Exhibit 25-7 shows a budgeted income statement for the coming year if Department B is discontinued. Note that Department C would now show a loss, and that the firm's net income is reduced $2,000 by the closing of Department B.

We could have predicted this result by contribution-margin analysis of Exhibit 25-6. Note that Department B has a contribution margin of $2,000. If fixed expense and contribution margins of other departments remain the same after Department B is shut down, then the loss of the $2,000 contribution margin from Department B must result in a $2,000 decrease in net income.

The allocation of fixed expense to various departments is somewhat arbitrary. Most of the fixed expense is associated with the entire store operation (as shown by the fact that fixed expense did not change when one department was closed). Therefore, it is more realistic (and less misleading) to prepare an income statement in the form shown in Exhibit 25-8. In this statement, it is clear that each department makes a contribution toward the payment of fixed expense and the net income of the store.

How could contribution-margin analysis be used to deal with additional complications associated with this department store example? Suppose that management is considering replacing Department B with a new rug department that would use the same floor space. The estimated revenue from the rug department would be $90,000, with variable expense of $85,000. Thus the rug department would have a contribution margin of $5,000. Fixed expense for the store would not be changed by the

Exhibit 25-7 Budgeted income statement reflecting shutdown of department that was operating at a loss

THE GENERAL DEPARTMENT STORE
Budgeted Income Statement
For the Year Ended December 31, 19_2

	Department A	Department C	Total
Sales	$100,000	$50,000	$150,000
Less: Variable expense	50,000	40,000	90,000
Contribution margin	$ 50,000	$10,000	$ 60,000
Less: Fixed expense (Note 1)	25,000	15,000	40,000
Net income (net loss)	$ 25,000	$ (5,000)	$ 20,000

NOTE 1: Fixed expense of $40,000 is allocated between Department A (62.5%) and Department C (37.5%) in proportion to the floor space used by each department: Department A 125,000 square feet; Department C 75,000 square feet.

switch in departments. Because the $5,000 contribution margin of the rug department exceeds the $2,000 contribution margin of Department B, it would be profitable to phase out Department B and replace it with the rug department.

Transfer pricing

Businesses that organize themselves into segments can establish profit centers for each segment. A ***profit center*** is a division, department, or other segment of a business that is assigned responsibility for both revenue and expense associated with its operations. Each profit-center manager may be given the responsibility of achieving a certain contribution margin or a certain contribution to net income through the operation of his or her segment of the firm.

Exhibit 25-8 Alternative form of income statement for department store (contribution margin format)

THE GENERAL DEPARTMENT STORE
Income Statement
For the Year Ended December 31, 19_1

	Department A	Department B	Department C	Total
Sales	$100,000	$70,000	$50,000	$220,000
Less: Variable expense	50,000	68,000	40,000	158,000
Contribution margin	$ 50,000	$ 2,000	$10,000	$ 62,000
Less: Fixed expense				40,000
Net income				$ 22,000

In firms with profit centers, one segment of the business may supply parts or services to another. For example, Division A produces radio parts for Division B, which assembles the parts into a finished product. In the separate accounting needed for the profit centers, a problem arises about how to price the intracompany transfers of goods or services. Obviously, a high price for the radio parts would tend to make Division A's profits look good, while a low price for the parts would tend to help the profitability of Division B. How can a fair transfer price be established?

In the past, Division A (Parts) of the Decentralized Company has transferred its output to Division B (Assembly) at a transfer price of $1.50 per part. Division A produces the parts at a variable expense of $1.25 per part. In the coming year, Division B will require 10,000 parts produced by Division A. In planning the next year's operations, the manager of Division B receives a bid from an outside firm, offering to supply the 10,000 needed parts for the coming year at a price of $1.40 per part. The manager of the Assembly Division tells the manager of the Parts Division that he will buy the parts from the outside supplier unless the Parts Division can meet the price of $1.40 per unit. (Top management of the firm has authorized this procedure, and also has stated that the Parts Division should be shut down for the year if it cannot provide the parts more cheaply than the outside supplier.)

The manager of the Parts Division accumulates the data shown in Exhibit 25-9. The fixed expense of $2,000 will be incurred even at zero volume (that is, if the productive facilities of his division are not used for the year). Should the manager of the Parts Division meet the price of the outside competitor and lower the transfer price from $1.50 to $1.40 per part?

The manager of the Parts Division notes that his contribution margin currently is 25 cents per part. If he meets the competition's price, his contribution margin will be 15 cents per part (the $1.40 transfer price, less the variable expense of $1.25). The manager notes that the lower price still provides his division with positive contribution margin. Although the transfer of parts at this price will result in a net loss of $500 for his divisiốn, the complete shutdown of the division would result in a larger net loss of $2,000 (because the fixed expense of $2,000 would still be incurred). If this is a short-term situation, where the loss circumstances can be corrected within a short time, he will show a smaller net loss for his division (a better profitability) if he meets the lower price. Exhibit 25-10 shows a differential revenue and expense analysis justifying his decision. Because the net income for the firm is the sum of the net incomes of its profit centers, this decision will also maximize the net income for the firm.

Exhibit 25-9
Contribution-margin data for Parts Division

	Per Unit	Total
Transfer price (10,000 parts)	$1.50	$15,000
Variable expense	1.25	12,500
Contribution margin	$0.25	$ 2,500
Less: Fixed expense		2,000
Net income		$ 500

Exhibit 25-10
Differential revenue and expense analysis for Parts Division

	Meet Competitor's Price	Don't Meet	Difference
Transfer price (10,000 @ $1.40)	$14,000	—	$14,000
Less: Variable expense	12,500	—	12,500
Contribution margin	$ 1,500	—	$ 1,500
Less: Fixed expense	2,000	$ 2,000	—
Net income (net loss)	$ (500)	$(2,000)	$ 1,500

Suppose that the outside supplier makes a bid of $1.20 per part. In this case, the manager of the Parts Division would note that the variable expense of producing the parts ($1.25 per part) exceeds the transfer price ($1.20 per part). Therefore, the division would have a negative contribution margin if it operated and met this price for the parts. Hence, in this case, the Parts Division should not meet the outside supplier's price, but should shut down for the year. Both the profitability of the division and the net income of the Decentralized Company will be improved by this decision, as shown in the analysis of Exhibit 25-11.

In general, the net income for the entire firm will be maximized if the manager of each profit center behaves as if his division were an independent firm. Competitive bidding against outside suppliers gives the best way of establishing transfer prices between profit centers. When a division cannot improve its profitability by dealing with other divisions, it may improve the profitability of its own operation and the entire firm by dealing with other outside companies or by shutting down its operations.

Summary

This chapter explores at some length the applications of contribution margin. Contribution margin is defined as the excess of revenue over variable expense. In this chapter, contribution-margin analysis is illustrated as a significant managerial tool in six typical business situations that involve special cost-behavior patterns:

1. effect on income of variations in costs, volume, and prices;
2. utilization of scarce resources;
3. acceptance or rejection of additional sales volume;

Exhibit 25-11
Alternative analysis for Parts Division at lower transfer price

	Meet Competitor's Price	Don't Meet	Difference
Transfer price (10,000 @ $1.20)	$12,000	—	$12,000
Less: Variable expense	12,500	—	12,500
Contribution margin	$ (500)	—	$ (500)
Less: Fixed expense	2,000	$ 2,000	—
Net income (net loss)	$ (2,500)	$(2,000)	$ (500)

4. operation versus shutdown;
5. the department-store case;
6. transfer pricing.

In these six cases involving contribution-margin analysis, variable expense proves to be the key to the decision-making process. The student should begin to perceive those situations in which contribution-margin analysis is the proper approach to an intelligent management decision.

The appendices to this chapter deal with cost concepts and linear programming. The student should be familiar with the cost concepts described in Appendix A. Costs usually are involved in managerial decision making; the proper decision can come only from a recognition of the proper cost to consider in analyzing the decision. Appendix B describes linear programming, a mathematical procedure that is useful in planning decisions where a particular factor (such as net income or fixed expense) is to be maximized or minimized.

Appendix A

COST CONCEPTS

Cost is a term used loosely in business language; it has many meanings. In its broadest conceptualization, ***cost*** is an economic sacrifice associated with economic activity. Starting from this very general definition, we make some important distinctions that are useful in understanding more fully the topics discussed in following chapters.

1. Direct and indirect costs.
   a. ***Direct costs*** are outlays that can be identified with a specific product, department, or activity. For example, the costs of materials and labor that are identifiable with a particular physical product are direct costs for that product.
   b. ***Indirect costs*** are those outlays that cannot be identified with a specific product, department, or activity. Taxes, insurance, and telephone expense are common examples of indirect costs.
2. Product and period costs.
   a. ***Product costs*** are outlays that can be associated with production; they are allocated between inventory and cost of goods sold. For example, the direct costs of materials used in the production of an item are product costs.
   b. ***Period costs*** are expenditures that are not directly associated with production, but are associated with the passage of a time period. Period costs usually arise from administrative, selling, and financing functions. The president's salary, advertising expense, interest expense, and rent expense are examples of period costs.
3. Fixed, variable, and mixed costs.
   a. ***Fixed costs*** are costs that remain constant regardless of the volume of ***production,*** over a relevant range of production. Examples include rent and depreciation of building, and real estate taxes. (***Fixed expenses*** are expenses that remain constant and do not vary with the volume of ***sales.*** Recall that an

expense is a cost that has expired and is matched against the revenue of a period.)

b. ***Variable costs*** are costs that fluctuate as the volume of ***production*** fluctuates. They include such items as direct materials and direct labor used in the manufacture of a product, and cost of electric power. (***Variable expenses*** fluctuate as the volume of ***sales*** fluctuates.)

c. ***Mixed costs*** are costs that fluctuate with production, but not in direct proportion to production. Mixed costs contain elements of fixed and variable costs. Examples include the costs of supervision and inspection.

4. Controllable and uncontrollable costs.

a. ***Controllable costs*** are those costs that are identified as a responsibility of an individual or department, and that can be regulated within a given period of time. Advertising, product research and development, and supplies expense are examples of controllable costs. Advertising costs might be controllable by the advertising department but not by a salesperson.

b. ***Uncontrollable costs*** are those costs that cannot be regulated by an individual or department within a given period of time. For example, rent expense is uncontrollable by the factory foreman. Property taxes are uncontrollable by lower-level management. Interest expense may be uncontrollable even by top management over a very short period of time, although top management can control this expense over a longer period.

5. Out-of-pocket and sunk costs.

a. ***Out-of-pocket costs*** are costs that require the use of current economic resources. The factory payroll, president's salary, taxes, insurance, and commission expense are examples of out-of-pocket costs.

b. ***Sunk costs*** are outlays or commitments that have already been incurred. The cost of an asset already purchased is a sunk cost.

6. Incremental, opportunity, and imputed costs.

a. ***Incremental*** (or differential) ***cost*** is the difference in total costs between alternatives. Incremental or differential cost is the total cost added or subtracted by switching from one level or plan of activity to another—for example, by producing an additional group of items. To illustrate, assume that a product can be sold in its present condition, or it can be processed further at costs of $50,000 and then sold. The incremental or differential cost between these two alternatives is $50,000.

b. ***Opportunity cost*** is the maximum alternative benefit that could be obtained if economic resources were applied to an alternative use. For example, suppose that the same machine can be used to produce lawnmowers or lawn furniture. Lawn furniture can be sold for $10,000 and costs directly associated with its production total $4,000. Then the opportunity cost of producing lawnmowers (of ***not*** producing lawn furniture) is $6,000.

c. ***Imputed costs*** are costs that can be associated with an economic event when no exchange transaction has occurred. For example, suppose that the company "rents itself" a building that it might otherwise have rented to an outside party; the rent expense for the building is an imputed cost. Interest and salary payments to a partner are an imputed cost for a partnership.

Appendix B

LINEAR PROGRAMMING

Linear programming is a mathematical procedure designed to assist in planning activities. Most linear programming problems call for the maximization or minimization of some economic objective such as net income, net loss, or costs. These problems often involve the determination of the optimum scheduling routine, product mix, production routing, or transportation route. In such problems, constraints usually exist on available alternatives—for example, constraints on available resources, machine time, manpower, or facilities.

Linear programming problems can be solved by a variety of mathematical approaches, such as the simplex method. Linear programming computer programs are available; business firms normally use such computer programs to solve these types of problems. To demonstrate the concept of linear programming, we develop here a linear programming model for a product-mix problem, and solve the problem graphically. (The student should keep in mind that the determination of a product mix cannot be isolated from the sales capabilities of the firm.)

Problem. A firm has two machines that are used in the production of Products A and B. Machine X has 24 hours of excess capacity; Machine Y has 16 hours of excess capacity. Production of one unit of Product A requires 4 machine hours on each machine; Product B requires 6 machine hours per unit on Machine X and 2 machine hours per unit on Machine Y. Product A has a contribution margin of $5; Product B has a contribution margin of $6. The firm wants to know whether to use the excess capacity of the machines to produce Product A or Product B or a mix of the two. The firm wants to use the excess capacity in a way that will maximize net income.

This problem can be solved through the following steps.

1. ***State the objective.*** Set up an equation that expresses the quantity to be maximized (or minimized) in terms of the factors that can be varied as part of the decision to be made. In this case, the equation should express the contribution to net income (the profit) as a function of the number of units of each product to be produced. We refer to this equation as the profit function. Let x_A be the number of units of Product A to be produced, x_B be the number of units of Product B to be produced, and P be the total contribution margin for the production using the excess machine capacity. Then, the profit function is given by

   $$P = (x_A \times \$5) + (x_B \times \$6).$$

   The problem is to find the values of x_A and x_B that will maximize P.
2. ***Identify limiting factors.*** Establish equations that express the constraints imposed upon the solution. In this case, the constraints are (1) that 24 hours of machine time are available on Machine X and 16 hours on Machine Y; (2) that it takes 4 machine hours to produce a unit of Product A on either machine, 6 machine hours to produce a unit of Product B on Machine X, and 2 hours to produce a unit of Product B on Machine Y; and (3) that no negative production is possible. These constraints can be expressed by the following four inequalities:

$(x_A \times 4 \text{ hrs}) + (x_B \times 6 \text{ hrs}) \leq 24 \text{ hrs};$
$(x_A \times 4 \text{ hrs}) \times (x_B \times 2 \text{ hrs}) \leq 16 \text{ hrs}.$
$x_A \geq 0;$
$x_B \geq 0.$

The first two inequalities express the constraints upon production by Machine X and Machine Y, respectively. The other two inequalities limit production to positive values.

3. *Plot the constraint inequalities on a graph* (Exhibit 25-12). In this case, the third and fourth inequalities limit possible solutions to the area in the upper right quadrant of the graph. The first and second inequalities complete the boundaries of the shaded polygon. This polygon is the area of possible solutions that lie within the constraints imposed by the problem.
4. *Identify possible solutions.* Of the various parts of values for x_A and x_B that lie within the area of possible solutions, which pair of values gives the maximum value for *P* (see step 1)? The optimum solution will always be one of the corner points of the polygon. Exhibit 25-13 shows a list of all the corner points and the value of *P* computed for each point. Each of these points represents a possible solution to the problem. Moving from one corner point to another represents a substitution of units of one product for units of the other. The corner point (3,2) gives the maximum value of *P*. That is, the maximum profit (contribution to net income) can be obtained by using the excess machine capacity to produce 3 units of Product A and 2 units of Product B.

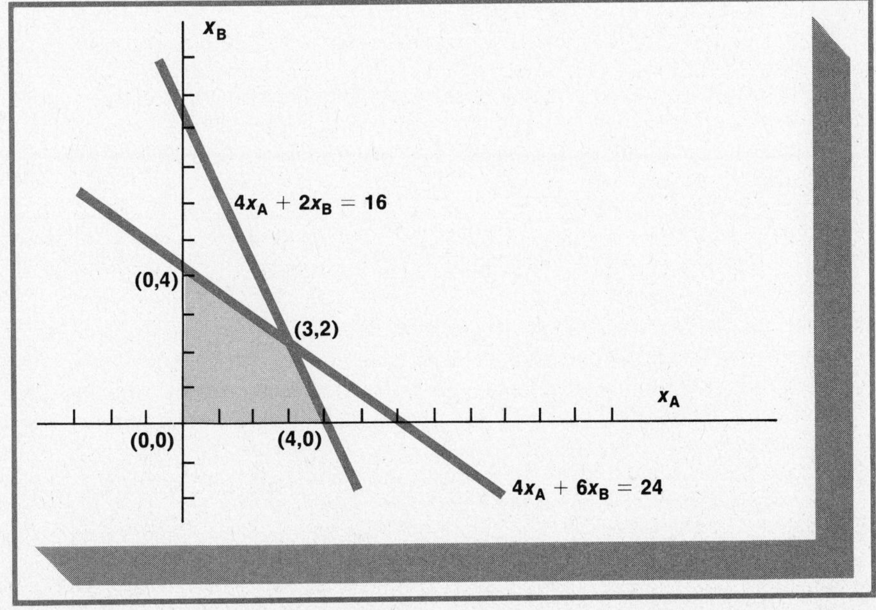

Exhibit 25-12
Graphical identification of possible solutions to problem

Exhibit 25-13
Profit obtained from various possible solutions

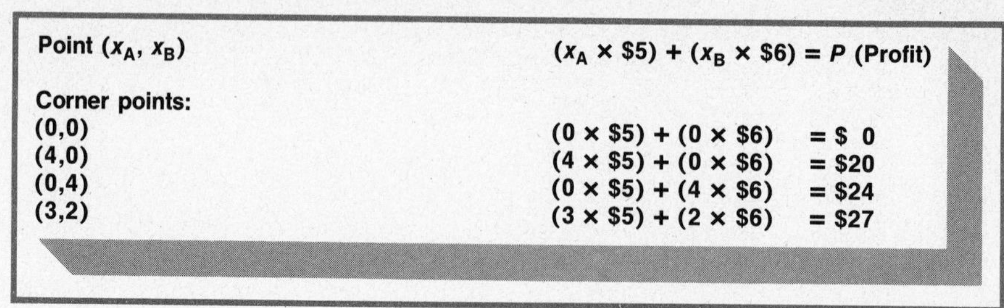

Point (x_A, x_B)	(x_A × \$5) + (x_B × \$6) = P (Profit)	
Corner points:		
(0,0)	(0 × \$5) + (0 × \$6)	= \$ 0
(4,0)	(4 × \$5) + (0 × \$6)	= \$20
(0,4)	(0 × \$5) + (4 × \$6)	= \$24
(3,2)	(3 × \$5) + (2 × \$6)	= \$27

Sensitivity-analysis techniques are available to extend a linear-programming solution to provide answers to questions such as the following:

1. What would happen to the solution of this problem if the contribution margin of Product A were \$4 instead of \$5?
2. What would happen to the solution if 25 hours of excess capacity were available on Machine X instead of 24 hours?
3. What would happen to the solution if Product A required 3 hours of machine time on Machine X instead of 4 hours?

Answers to questions such as these help management to identify the critical constraints on its decisions, and to decide what changes in conditions might be most helpful in maximizing profits. Sensitivity analysis is beyond the scope of this text, but is discussed in more advanced accounting courses.

Questions

1. Is the following statement true or false? Assuming a given plant and sales capacity, to achieve maximum profits the firm should attempt to obtain the largest possible contribution margin per unit of any limiting factor. Give several examples of limiting factors.
2. What is transfer pricing?
3. Is incremental cost the change in total cost resulting from the adoption of a different course of action? Or, is incremental cost the addition to cost from the manufacture or sale of one unit?
4. A businessman has an opportunity to lease one floor of his office building to an outside firm for \$10,000 per year. He chooses not to do so (leaving the space unused) in order to maintain privacy for his own operations. How would you describe this action in terms of one of the cost concepts defined in Appendix A of this chapter?
5. If contribution margin per unit is small and cannot be improved, what major courses of action to improve net income are available to a firm?
6. When fixed expense is high and cannot be reduced, and contribution margin per unit is small and cannot be increased, how can a company attempt to increase its net income?

7. Explain the following terms: (a) product cost; (b) period cost; (c) direct cost; (d) indirect cost; (e) controllable cost; (f) uncontrollable cost; (g) out-of-pocket cost; (h) sunk cost; (i) incremental cost; (j) opportunity cost; (k) imputed cost.

Exercises

E25-1 (Break-even point)
The Contribution Company has fixed expense of $150,000. It sells its product for $24 per unit. Variable expense per unit is $6.

a. Compute the break-even point in dollars, using the contribution-margin approach.
b. Compute the break-even point in units, using the contribution-margin approach.
c. The company has an opportunity to sell some additional units at $9 per unit. This will not change the sales volume at the regular selling price, nor will it change the fixed expense. Should the company accept this order? Explain your answer.

E25-2 (Variations in cost, volume, and price)
In 19_6 the Perry Company sells 120,000 units at a selling price of $150 per unit. Variable expense is $90 per unit; fixed expense is $2,500,000. What would be the net income for 19_7 under each of the following assumptions (consider each case independently):

a. All conditions remain the same as in 19_6.
b. Sales volume increases 15 percent.
c. Variable expense increases 15 percent.
d. Sales price decreases 15 percent.
e. Sales volume increases 15 percent, variable expense increases 15 percent, sales price decreases 15 percent, and fixed expense increases $500,000.

E25-3 (Contribution-margin case)
In 19_6 the Contribution Company has sales revenue of $175,000. It sells a single product at $2.00 per unit, with variable expense of $1.40 per unit. The firm estimates that its sales revenue in 19_7 will be $200,000.

a. Compute the contribution-margin rate in 19_6.
b. Compute the estimated change in net income from 19_6 to 19_7.

E25-4 (Contribution-margin case)
The Growth Company wishes to increase its contribution margin next year by $150,000. It estimates that its volume next year will be 20,000 units.

a. What dollar change should the firm make in the selling price per unit, assuming that other factors remain unchanged?
b. What dollar change must be made in cost per unit, assuming that other factors (including selling price) remain unchanged?

E25-5 (Contribution-margin case)
The Tommy Company produces and sells four products. Product A sells for $120 per unit and has a variable expense of $100 per unit. Product B sells for $100, with variable expense of $90. Product C sells for $35, with variable expense of $20. Product D sells for $40, with variable expense of $30. The company can produce each of the four products on its single machine,

which can operate for 1,500 hours during the year. Production of a single unit on the machine requires 6 hours for Product A, 10 hours for Product B, 3 hours for Product C, and 5 hours for Product D.

Required:

a. How many units of each of the four products can be produced in a year if the company produces only that single product?

b. What is the total contribution margin added by each of the products if total production is devoted to that product?

c. Which product or what mix of products should be produced to achieve the greatest net income for the year? Explain.

E25-6 (Additional order case)

A firm engaged in domestic and foreign trade currently operates as shown in Exhibit 25-14. The firm receives some orders from foreign customers. If it decides to fill these orders, it can do so by additional production without any change in its current level of other sales, its selling price for other customers, or its fixed expense. The firm wishes to accept or reject each sale according to the criterion of maximizing its net income.

a. Should the firm accept an order for 3,000 units at $6 per unit?

b. Should the firm accept an order for 6,000 units at $4.80 per unit?

c. Should the firm accept an order for 2,000 units at $5.01 per unit?

d. If the firm sells 6,000 units at $5.50 per unit, what change in the net income will result?

E25-7 (Continue operations or close down)

A firm has been operating at a loss for several years. Management is hopeful that the loss situation can be reversed, but it is considering the possibility of reducing losses by closing down the plant until economic conditions improve. Management asks your advice about this decision. You are able to gather the following information about the current year, 19_6. The firm has sold 800,000 units at $2 per unit. Variable expense amounts to $1,200,000 for the year, and fixed expense amounts to $500,000. Shutdown of the plant would not change the fixed expense. Management estimates that operations would continue at similar levels of sales, prices, and expense until the economy picks up. Would you advise management to shut down the plant or to continue to operate? Explain.

E25-8 (Contribution margin and selling price)

The One-Time Company is considering how to price its product for the coming year. Various sales prices have been suggested. The sales department has conducted market surveys, and it projects the following sales volumes at the various prices: 130,000 units at $12 per unit; 120,000 units at $13 per unit; 110,000 units at $14 per unit; or 80,000 units at $15 per

Exhibit 25-14
Operating data for Exercise E25-6

Sales (200,000 units @ $8 per unit)	**$1,600,000**
Less: Variable expense (@ $5 per unit)	**1,000,000**
Contribution margin	**600,000**
Less: Fixed expense	**400,000**
Net income	**$ 200,000**

unit. Variable expense is $8 per unit. Fixed cost would remain unchanged over the range of production levels predicted for these prices. The firm's objective is to maximize its net income. Using a contribution-margin approach to pricing, what selling price would you recommend?

E25-9 (Understanding cost behavior)

Expenses reflect a variety of behavior patterns as volume changes. Exhibit 25-15 shows five patterns. The vertical axis of each graph represents total dollars of expense. The horizontal axis represents machine hours (a measure of volume of activity). Indicate the number of the graph that would represent each of the following expenses.

a. Supervisory expense. (Additional supervisors are hired after each additional 10,000 machine hours. If the machine is not in use, several supervisors are kept on the payroll.)

b. Insurance expense on a machine. (The expense is computed at a basic fixed rate when the machine is idle or is used up to a given number of hours. If the machine is used a greater number of hours, the insurance premium increases above the basic rate. The increase is not directly proportional to machine use; the expense for each additional hour of use is smaller than the charge for preceding hours.)

c. Machine-hour depreciation expense on a machine.

d. Straight-line depreciation expense on a machine used in a factory.

e. Factory power expense. (The Utility Company bills the factory at a basic fixed amount plus an additional charge that varies in proportion to machine hours.)

E25-10 (Relationship of concepts)

Compute the missing amounts indicated by letters in Exhibit 25-16.

E25-11 (Linear programming)

A company has two machines with excess capacity: Machine Red has

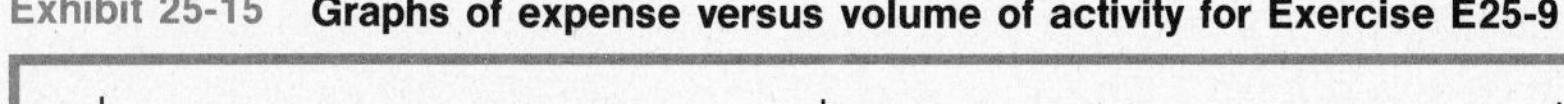

Exhibit 25-15 **Graphs of expense versus volume of activity for Exercise E25-9**

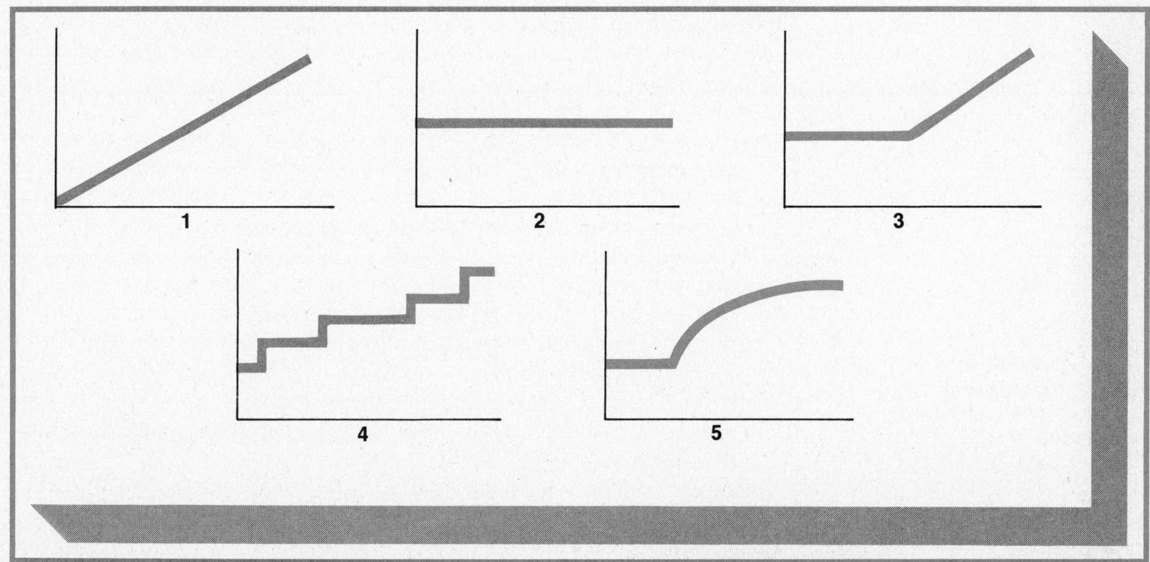

Exhibit 25-16
Data for Exercise E25-10

	Case 1	Case 2	Case 3
Sales	$200,000	$200,000	g
Variable expense	130,000	d	$ 80,000
Fixed expense	40,000	60,000	130,000
Contribution margin	a	e	120,000
Contribution-margin rate	b	30%	h
Net income (net loss)	c	f	i

twelve hours of excess capacity; Machine Blue has eight hours of excess capacity. The company produces products X and Y. The hours required to produce X and Y on the two machines are shown:

	Hours required on Blue	Red
Product X	2	2
Product Y	3	1

The company can make additional profits of $6 per unit of X sold and $7 per unit of Y sold.

Required: Use the graphic method to determine the number of units of X and Y that should be produced and sold in order to maximize profits.

Problems

P25-1 (Accept or reject additional order)

The Two-Part Company manufactures parts that it sells with its main product. Each unit of sales consists of one unit of product and one unit of parts, sold at a combined price of $120. To date, the company has sold 20,000 of these combined units. Fixed expense is $600,000, and this amount is allocated equally between the production of main product and the production of parts. Variable expense for the main product is $50 per unit; variable expense for the part is $30 per unit.

a. The Main Company receives an order for an additional 2,000 combined units; the purchaser is willing to pay $80 per unit. The company has idle capacity that would allow the production of the additional 2,000 products and parts without increasing fixed expense. Should the order be accepted?

b. If the order is accepted, what would the net income of the Main Company be?

c. If the order is rejected, what would the net income be?

d. The management of the company is considering the purchase of 20,000 units of parts from another company. If this purchase is made, the parts division will be closed down; the closed facilities will not be used. The parts can be obtained from the outside supplier for $25 per unit. If the only criterion is maximizing net income, should the company purchase the parts for $25 or continue its parts division? Explain.

e. If the purchase price in part d were $32 per unit, what action would you recommend?

f. If the purchase price were $30 per unit, what would you recommend?

P25-2 (Cost, volume, and profit analysis)

A firm manufactures and sells large toy tractors. Manufacturing costs associated with the toys are $10 per unit of direct materials, $8 per unit of direct labor, and $7 per unit of variable overhead. Selling expense (a variable expense) is $15 per unit. Fixed expense for the firm is $600,000. The firm usually sells 300,000 tractors a year at $60 per tractor.

a. What is the usual net income for the firm?

b. If the sales price is increased 10 percent next year, and volume decreases 10 percent, what is the estimated net income for the firm next year?

c. If the change described in part b does occur, how much additional revenue (if any) is available to the firm for promotional expense (to try to increase sales volume), assuming that the company is willing to show the same net income next year as it had this year?

d. An outside selling agency has offered to handle the selling of the tractors next year for a commission of $20 per tractor. If this arrangement is approved, fixed expense will be reduced by $1,200,000 and the in-house selling expense will be eliminated. The sales agency estimates that it can sell 270,000 units. Should the company approve the proposed selling arrangement? Explain.

P25-3 (Contribution-margin case)

A firm manufactures and sells two products, X and Y, as shown in Exhibit 25-17. The firm can produce X or Y exclusively or in combination. To maximize net income, should the firm produce X, Y, or a combination of the two? Explain.

P25-4 (Discontinuing a department)

The New Land Department Store is undertaking a study to determine the effect on its net income of discontinuing one department, which has been operating at a loss as reported on the income statement in Exhibit 25-18. The study shows that if the Accessories Department is discontinued, all costs assigned to that department would be eliminated except for the following: rent $3,000; depreciation (store equipment) $1,000; heat and light $3,000; office salaries $6,000; insurance expense $1,000. If the Accessories Department is eliminated, management will not add a new department to replace it. *Required:* Should the Accessories Department be eliminated? Explain. (Ignore tax implications of the problem.)

Exhibit 25-17
Operating data for Problem P25-3

	Product X		Product Y
Selling price per unit	**$140**		**$250**
Costs per unit:			
Direct materials	**(60)**		**(90)**
Direct labor	**(30)**		**(60)**
Variable overhead	**(26)**		**(58)**
Contribution margin per unit	**$ 24**		**$ 42**
Fixed expense		**$60,000**	

Exhibit 25-18 **Income statement for Problem P25-4**

NEW LAND DEPARTMENT STORE

Income Statement

For the Year Ended December 31, 19_6

	Furniture Dept.	Rug Dept.	Accessories Dept.	Total
Sales (net)	$600,000	$160,000	$ 70,000	$800,000
Cost of goods sold	350,000	100,000	30,000	560,000
Gross margin (*a*)	$250,000	$ 60,000	$ 40,000	$240,000
Operating expense:				
Advertising expense	$ 35,000	$ 4,000	$ 8,000	$ 25,000
Salesmen's salaries	80,000	21,000	25,000	105,000
Rent expense	8,000	4,000	3,000	15,000
Depreciation expense (display equipment)	7,000	1,000	2,000	9,000
Office salaries	25,000	4,000	4,000	35,000
Insurance expense	3,000	2,500	2,500	5,000
Bad debts expense	2,000	1,000	2,500	1,000
Heat and light expense	10,000	2,500	3,000	10,000
Total operating expense (*b*)	$170,000	$ 40,000	$ 50,000	$205,000
Net operating income (or loss) (a − b)	$ 80,000	$ 20,000	$ (10,000)	$ 35,000

EDGY COMPANY

Budgeted Income Statement

For the Year Ended December 31, 19_6

Sales (120,000 units of Blux @ $50 per unit)		$6,000,000
Variable cost and expense:		
Direct material (Material X, 2 lbs. per unit @ $3 per lb.)	$ 720,000	
Direct labor (3 hrs. per unit @ $3 per hour)	1,080,000	
Manufacturing overhead ($2 per direct labor hour)	720,000	
Selling expense ($4 per unit)	480,000	3,000,000
Contribution margin		$3,000,000
Fixed expense		1,400,000
Net income		$1,600,000

Exhibit 25-19 **Budgeted income statement for Problem P25-5**

P25-5 (Gross margin applications)

The Edgy Company produces a single product, Blux. Exhibit 25-19 shows the company's budget for the coming year.

Required: (Consider each part independently of the others.)

a. If sales in 19_6 actually are 20 percent below the budgeted figure, what net income will result?

b. If actual sales in 19_6 are 20 percent above the budgeted figure, what net income will result?

c. What cost per unit will be incurred if additional sales are made beyond the budgeted figure, assuming that existing capacity is sufficient to handle the transaction?

d. The opening inventory of Blux is 20,000 items; the company wants to have a closing inventory of 25,000 items. How many Bluxes must be produced this year, according to the budget? How many pounds of Material X must be acquired? (There were 6,000 pounds of X on hand at the beginning of the year, and the company wants to have an inventory of 8,000 pounds of X at the end of the year.)

e. The Edgy Company is operating at capacity when it sells 120,000 Bluxes. An additional order for 8,000 Bluxes is received at a sales price of $36 per Blux. If the order is accepted, an additional $75,000 of fixed expense will be incurred. Assuming that the impact on net income is the only criterion in this decision, should the order be accepted?

P25-6 (Contribution-margin applications)

A company has the following income statement for the year:

Sales (10,000 units at $10 per unit)		$100,000
Less:		
Fixed expenses	$ 50,000	
Variable expenses	40,000	90,000
Net income		$ 10,000

Required:

a. Compute the contribution margin per unit.

b. Compute total contribution margin for the year.

c. (1) If the selling price is increased 10 percent and everything else remains unchanged, what is the effect on contribution margin per unit?

(2) What would net income be next year?

d. (1) If variable expenses increase 10 percent next year and everything else remains unchanged, what is the effect on contribution margin per unit?

(2) What would net income be next year?

e. If fixed expenses increase $5,000 next year and everything else remains unchanged, what is the effect on contribution margin per unit?

P25-7 (Additional orders)

A company has the following income statement for the year:

Sales (10,000 at $10 per unit)		$100,000
Less:		
Fixed expenses	$ 10,000	
Variable expenses	80,000	90,000
Net income		$ 10,000

The company has an opportunity to sell abroad at the following prices an additional 1,000 units:

a. $10 per unit
b. $12 per unit
c. $9 per unit
d. $8 per unit
e. $7 per unit

Required: Other things remaining unchanged, which of the opportunities, if any, should the company accept?

P25-8 (Interdepartmental transfers)

A company has two divisions. Division I sells to Division II and to other companies. The following data is available concerning Division I's operations:

	To Division II	To Others
Sales:		
10,000 at $10 per unit	$100,000	
10,000 at $12 per unit		$120,000
Variable expenses ($8 per unit)	(80,000)	(80,000)
Fixed expenses (allocated on unit basis)	(10,000)	(10,000)
Net income	$ 10,000	$ 30,000

Division II learns that it can acquire the item it purchases from Division I at $9.50 per unit from another source. Division I cannot sell any additional products to others if it refuses to accept the lower price asked for by Division II.

Required: Should the manager of Division I accept the lower sales price demanded by Division II?

Control of variable costs: analysis of performance

26

In preceding chapters we have discussed such major profit-planning techniques as the comprehensive budget, gross-margin analysis, and contribution-margin analysis. We now turn to an area that is of considerable significance to management —the control of variable costs.

The primary inputs into a business system are natural, financial, and human resources. To operate successfully, the business must use these resources efficiently and effectively. Efficiency and effectiveness are ***not*** synonyms. An effective action is one that accomplishes an objective. An efficient action is one that accomplishes the objective with a minimum of effort or a minimum of wasted resources. It is possible to be efficient in the sense of wasting few resources, while not being effective in attaining all desired goals. On the other hand, it is possible to be effective without being efficient.

To mow a ten-acre lawn with a hand mower on a hot summer day may (or may not) be effective in eventually getting the lawn mowed. It certainly is not the most efficient way of getting the job done. To attain a target level of production or sales, management might schedule considerable overtime. Such a course of action might be effective, but would it necessarily be efficient?

To measure effectiveness and efficiency, management has developed standard-setting techniques for certain costs and expenses incurred by the firm. In a manufacturing operation, materials, labor, and overhead are major costs.[1] In manufacturing, the ***price*** of these resources and the ***quantities used*** in productive operations are two major cost-control areas. If a manufacturing firm is to maximize its profits, its primary concern must be the control of variable manufacturing costs. One basic method of controlling such costs is through the use of standard costs for analyzing and evaluating performance.

1. Recall that a cost is an economic sacrifice (something given up or foregone, or a liability) incurred in economic activities. An expense is a cost that is expired—a cost that is matched against the revenue of the current period. An unexpired cost is treated as an asset. In the manufacturing process, costs incurred are associated with the units produced. When these units are sold (producing revenue), the corresponding costs are recognized as expenses. Costs associated with unsold merchandise appear as inventory (an asset).

This chapter deals with manufacturing costs. Similar procedures can be used for the control of variable expenses in a merchandising operation.

Standards

Before we can discuss standard costs, we must give a brief description of certain manufacturing terms. (Chapter 30 deals extensively with manufacturing operations.) Manufacturing costs consist of the following three major components.

1. *Direct material:* material costs directly traceable to the product manufactured. The lumber used in the manufacture of a table is direct material; its cost is a direct material cost.
2. *Direct labor:* factory labor directly associated with the product manufactured. The labor used to assemble a table is direct labor.
3. *Manufacturing overhead:* factory costs not directly traceable to particular articles manufactured. Heat and power costs incurred in operating the machines used to manufacture a table are manufacturing overhead. Overhead cost must be allocated in some systematic and rational manner among the products manufactured.

When standard-cost procedures are adopted to control costs, management establishes standards or targets against which to measure actual costs. The standards are ***per-unit*** costs and quantities of direct material, direct labor, and manufacturing overhead projected as desirable through studies and estimates. Any differences or variances between standard costs and actual costs are then evaluated to determine their causes.

The objective of such a standard-cost procedure is to enable management to learn (1) whether there is a difference between actual operations and the desired standards; (2) if there is a difference, how great the difference is; (3) the cause of the difference; and (4) what can be done about it.

To illustrate the standard-cost approach to control of variable manufacturing costs, we use the standard-cost card shown in Exhibit 26-1. This card was prepared by the management of the Standard Cost Company to show the desired standard cost per unit of its Product A. As discussed throughout this chapter, the actual performance of the firm's manufacturing operation will be measured against these predetermined standards to evaluate the efficiency of the operation. (The effectiveness of the

Exhibit 26-1
Standard cost card issued by management of Standard Cost Company for its Product A

STANDARD COST CARD
Product A

Material	
3 pounds of Material X @ $5 per pound	**$15.00**
Direct labor	
2 hours @ $8.50 per hour	**17.00**
Manufacturing overhead	
Variable cost: 2 labor hours at 95¢ per hour	**1.90**
Total variable cost per unit of Product A	**$33.90**

operation would be measured simply in terms of whether or not it produces the number of units of Product A that are required.)

TYPES OF STANDARDS

How should management set standards for the variable costs associated with the production of manufactured items? Should the standards for material, labor, and overhead be set at an ***ideal*** level? That is to say, should the target costs be set at a level that represents the minimum costs attainable under the most favorable operating conditions? Such ideal standards are difficult to impossible to attain in the imperfect real world of day-to-day business. Then, should the standards be set at ***currently attainable*** levels? Such standards represent costs that could be achieved under current, efficient operating conditions.

Currently attainable standards tend to be more realistic targets, and they are used frequently in standard-cost control systems. Employees tend to respond more favorably to situations in which their efforts will be judged by comparison to an attainable guideline or standard. (It is important to begin to think about the impact of accounting procedures on the behavior of people. We discuss behavioral accounting at some length in Chapter 21.)

Material standards

The cost of material for a firm is a function of two factors: (1) the price per unit at which the material is purchased, and (2) the quantity of this material used in the production process. If material costs are to be controlled, standards must be set for the acquisition price per unit of the material and for the number of units of material used in production. The purchasing department has primary responsibility for material purchases.

When the purchasing department sets out to acquire material, it knows that the price it will have to pay is influenced by factors within the control of the firm as well as by factors outside the firm's control. The factors outside the control of the firm include the general economic condition of the country, the degree of competition, the international monetary situation, and the relationship of supply and demand for the material. However, purchase costs are influenced to some extent by the purchasing agent's ability to forecast material needs, the timing of purchases, his knowledge of the market, the transportation means selected, and similar factors within the control of the purchasing department.

PURCHASE PRICE VARIANCE

The ***purchase price*** (or material price) ***standard*** should be set to measure the effectiveness of the material-acquisition process. The ***purchase price variance*** measures the difference between actual prices paid for material and the standard costs established for that material. If the actual price is less than the standard cost, a favorable price variance exists. If the actual cost exceeds the standard cost, an unfavorable price variance develops.

For example, the Standard Cost Company has established a standard price of $5 per pound for Material X, which is used in the production of its Product A (see

Exhibit 26-1). During the current month, the company's purchasing department purchased 35,000 pounds of Material X for $192,500—an average price of $5.50 per pound. The purchase price variance is computed as follows.

Price variance = (Actual per-unit price − Standard per-unit price) × Quantity
= ($5.50 − $5.00) × 35,000
= $17,500.

Note that a positive value of the purchase price variance is unfavorable, because the actual price paid for material exceeded the standard price established for material purchases. This means that the actual purchase price tends to make the cost higher than the standard cost for the product, and therefore to make the contribution margin smaller than what might otherwise be expected.

The purchase price variance can also be computed in terms of actual and standard material costs. The actual cost of the material was $192,500. The standard cost was $5.00 per pound multiplied by 35,000 pounds, or $175,000.

Price variance − Actual material cost = Standard material cost
= $192,500 − $175,000
= $17,500.

After the firm has determined that a price variance exists, it should investigate the situation to determine the cause of the variance—especially if the variance is material (that is, large enough to significantly affect the operations of the firm for the period). As indicated earlier, a favorable or unfavorable purchase price variance could be caused by many factors. An effort should be made to discover the cause(s) of any significant variances, and steps should be taken to prevent their recurrence if the variances are unfavorable.

MATERIAL USAGE (QUANTITY) VARIANCE

The quantity of material used to produce a given product is a measure of the efficiency of the use of materials in the production process. The production department has primary responsibility for the use of materials. Engineering studies often are used to establish the physical quantity of material that should be used in the production process. Other methods of determining quantity standards include studies of past performance and sample analysis under controlled conditions.

A ***material usage variance*** can be computed to control and evaluate the usage of materials in the production process. If the amount of material used in production exceeds the standard amount allowed, an unfavorable usage variance exists. If the standard quantity exceeds the actual quantity used, a favorable usage variance results.

The Standard Cost Company has set a standard of direct material usage for Product A at 3 pounds of Material X per unit of product (Exhibit 26-1). In the current month, the company produced 10,200 units of Product A, using 32,000 pounds of Material X. The standard would require that the company use 10,200 × 3 or 30,600 pounds of Material X in producing the 10,200 units. The material usage variance is computed to show the variance in cost that can be attributed to the variance from standard in direct-material usage. Therefore, this variance is computed using the standard material price (to show the variance that would result from usage alone, if there were no variance in purchase price).

Usage variance = (Actual quantity − Standard quantity) × Standard price
= (32,000 − 30,600) × $5
= $7,000.

Again, a positive value for the variance is unfavorable, because it indicates that the actual material usage tends to cause a variable cost higher than that called for by the standards.

The material usage variance can also be computed in terms of standard costs for the material actually used and the material usage called for by the standards. That is, the actual material usage (32,000 pounds) would cost $160,000 at the standard price of $5 per pound. The standard material usage for the same number of product units is 30,600 pounds, which would cost $153,000 at the standard per-unit price.

Usage variance = Standard cost of actual usage − Standard cost of standard usage
= $160,000 − $153,000
= $7,000.

Material usage variances arise as a result of faulty or good production practices, excessive or minimal waste (scrap), inferior or superior quality of material, inferior or superior quality of workmanship, and so on.

Labor standards

As with direct material cost, we can compute two variances for direct labor costs—one for the wage rate paid to labor and one for labor efficiency. The computation procedures for the labor variances are similar to those for the direct material variances.

The standards set by the management of the Standard Cost Company (Exhibit 26-1) call for the use of 2 hours of direct labor to produce each unit of Product A, and for payment of a labor rate of $8.50 per hour. During the current month, the production department actually used 20,000 hours of direct labor to produce 10,200 units of Product A. The actual wages paid totalled $160,000, an average labor rate of $8.00 per hour.

DIRECT-LABOR RATE VARIANCE

The ***direct-labor rate variance*** measures the difference between actual and standard costs for direct labor for the actual hours worked. The labor-rate variance in many cases has little significance, because labor rates usually are set by union contract or local economic conditions. These factors are outside the control of the production department, which has primary responsibility for control of labor variances. However, some labor-rate variances can be traced to such causes as the improper assignment of a worker to a machine or the use of more workers than necessary. In most cases, the factory foreman has primary responsibility for control of the labor rate variance.

The direct-labor rate variance for the Standard Cost Company can be computed as follows.

Labor rate variance = (Actual labor rate − Standard labor rate) × Actual hours
= ($8.00 − $8.50) × 20,000
= $(10,000).

The negative value of the labor-rate variance is favorable, because the actual direct labor cost is lower than that expected at the standard labor rate. The direct-labor rate variance can also be computed by comparing the actual labor cost (20,000 hours at $8 per hour, or $160,000) to the cost that would have been incurred for the same number of hours at the standard rate (20,000 hours at $8.50 per hour, or $170,000).

Labor rate variance = Actual labor cost − Labor cost at standard rate
= $160,000 − $170,000
= $(10,000).

DIRECT-LABOR EFFICIENCY VARIANCE

The ***direct-labor efficiency variance*** measures the difference between the actual hours used and the standard labor usage for the same production. The dollar amount of the variance is computed using the standard labor rate.

Standards for direct labor efficiency often are established through time-and-motion studies of the production process. Variances from standard labor usage can result from such factors as the efficient or inefficient performance of factory employees, breakdown of machinery, improper training practices, working conditions and hours, or defective materials. The factory foreman has primary responsibility for controlling the labor-efficiency variance.

The direct-labor efficiency variance for the Standard Cost Company is computed as follows.

Labor-efficiency variance = (Actual hours − Standard hours) × Standard rate
= (20,000 − 20,400) × $8.50
= $(3,400).

The negative labor efficiency variance is favorable, because direct labor cost was lower than standard cost due to the use of fewer than standard hours for the month's production. The direct-labor efficiency variance can also be computed by comparing the cost of actual hours at standard rate (20,000 hours at $8.50 per hour, or $170,000) with the cost of standard hours at standard rate (20,400 hours at $8.50 per hour, or $173,400).

Labor-efficiency variance = Standard cost of actual hours − Standard cost of standard hours
= $170,000 − $173,400
= $(3,400).

Exhibit 26-2 shows a graphic illustration of the direct labor variances. (A similar graph cannot be constructed for the direct material variances, because the units of material purchased during the month do not correspond exactly to the units used in production during the month.)

Exhibit 26-2 **Graphic illustration of direct labor variances**

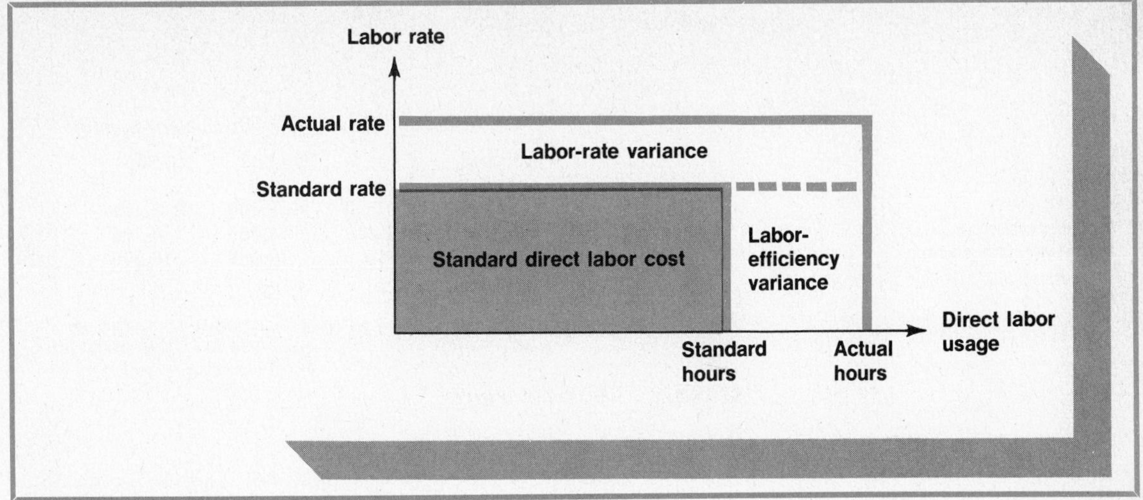

Manufacturing overhead standards

Management can prepare a flexible budget to show the overhead cost that should be incurred for various levels of output. (Here we are dealing only with the ***variable*** costs associated with the manufacturing process.) In such a budget, output level usually is expressed either in terms of units of production or in terms of standard direct labor hours. When the flexible budget is prepared, forecasted financial data are accumulated for a range of activities. Exhibit 26-3 shows the Standard Cost Company's flexible budget for variable overhead cost.

At the end of the budget period, actual overhead cost can be compared with the relevant budget level. A performance report can be assembled to present pertinent evaluations. Exhibit 26-4 shows such a report for the Standard Cost Company for the current month, comparing actual variable overhead cost with the budgeted cost at the actual level of production (10,200 units).

In this example, the performance report shows that variable overhead cost for the month was higher than the standard expense for this level of production. The variable overhead variance is positive (unfavorable), largely as a result of higher than standard indirect labor cost.

As with direct material and direct labor costs, variable overhead cost can be analyzed through two variances—a spending (price or rate) variance and an efficiency (usage or quantity) variance. In a manufacturing firm, variable overhead cost control is ordinarily considered the responsibility of the foreman or manager in charge of the manufacturing department or division.

In computing the overhead variances, overhead cost can be expressed in relation to various measures of activity. On the standard cost card of the Standard Cost Company (Exhibit 26-1), the standard overhead cost is expressed as $1.90 per unit of Product A. However, since 2 hours of direct labor are used as the standard for production of a unit of Product A, the standard overhead cost could also be expressed as $0.95 per hour of direct labor. Similarly, the standard overhead cost might be expressed in terms of machine hours, quantity of material used, labor cost, or sales dollars.

Exhibit 26-3 **Flexible budget of variable overhead cost for Standard Cost Company**

STANDARD COST COMPANY
Flexible Budget: Variable Overhead
For the Year 19_1

	Level of Activity (units of Product A per month)			
	per unit	9,500	10,000	10,500
Indirect labor	$0.50	$ 4,750	$ 5,000	$ 5,250
Indirect material	0.40	3,800	4,000	4,200
Other variable costs	1.00	9,500	10,000	10,500
Total variable overhead costs	$1.90	$18,050	$19,000	$19,950

STANDARD COST COMPANY
Performance Report: Variable Overhead
For the Month Ended July 31, 19_1

	Actual (10,200 units)	*Standard (at 10,200 units)*	*Variance*
Indirect labor	$ 5,630	$ 5,100 (10,200 × $0.50)	$530
Indirect material	4,020	4,080 (10,200 × $0.40)	(60)
Other variable overhead	10,150	10,200 (10,200 × $1.00)	(50)
Total variable overhead	$19,800	$19,380	$420

Exhibit 26-4 **Performance report on overhead cost for the current month**

Direct labor hours often are used as the measure of activity for assigning overhead cost. There are several reasons for this practice: (1) direct labor hours usually are subject to a degree of managerial control; (2) direct labor hours are, at least in part, a cause of variations in variable manufacturing overhead; and (3) variations in direct labor hours are relatively easy to explain to the individuals responsible for controlling overhead costs. The Standard Cost Company uses direct labor hours as the measure of activity in computing overhead variances.

The standard variable overhead rate for the company is $0.95 per direct labor hour. During the current month, the company actually incurred variable overhead cost of $19,800 (see Exhibit 26-4) and used 20,000 direct labor hours. Therefore, the actual variable overhead rate for the month is

$$\frac{\$19{,}800}{20{,}000 \text{ hours}} = \$0.99 \text{ per direct labor hour.}$$

OVERHEAD SPENDING VARIANCE

The ***variable overhead spending variance*** measures the difference between the actual overhead rate and the standard overhead rate. In our example, the two rates are expressed in terms of direct labor hours.

$$\text{Overhead spending variance} = \left(\text{Actual overhead rate} - \text{Standard overhead rate}\right) \times \text{Actual quantity (hours) used}$$

$$= (\$0.99 - \$0.95) \times 20{,}000$$

$$= \$800.$$

The positive value of the overhead spending variance is unfavorable; the actual overhead rate per direct labor hour exceeded the standard rate per direct labor hour. This variance can also be computed by comparing the actual overhead to the overhead that would have been incurred for the same level of activity at the standard overhead rate. At the standard rate of $0.95 per direct labor hour, the actual activity of 20,000 direct labor hours would have led to overhead expense of $19,000.

Overhead spending variance = Actual overhead cost − Overhead cost for actual activity at standard rate
= $19,800 − $19,000
= $800.

The variable overhead spending variance is related to the accuracy of the budget estimates for various variable overhead items, to the degree of control over variable overhead items, to price fluctuations related to individual overhead items, and to other similar factors. In general, this variance is a measure of the degree to which the company succeeded in holding the overhead rate to the desired standard rate in terms of the chosen measure of activity level.

OVERHEAD EFFICIENCY VARIANCE

The ***variable overhead efficiency*** (or usage) ***variance*** is related to the degree to which the manufacturing activity (expressed in terms of the chosen measure of activity level) resulted in production of the standard number of units of product. In our example, the overhead spending variance shows the extent to which actual overhead cost differed from standard overhead cost for the actual direct labor hours used. The overhead efficiency variance shows the extent to which actual overhead cost differed from standard overhead cost because of variations from the standard direct labor hours for the actual production.

During the month, the company produced 10,200 units of Product A. The standard direct labor for this production (2 hours per unit of product) would be 20,400 hours. In fact, the company used 20,000 actual direct labor hours.

Overhead efficiency variance = (Actual direct labor hours − Standard direct labor hours for actual production) × Standard overhead rate
= (20,000 − 20,400) × $0.95
= $(380).

The negative value of this variance is favorable. The actual direct labor hours used were less than the standard direct labor hours allowed for the production attained. The direct labor hours were used efficiently, so overhead cost was somewhat less than that suggested by the overhead spending variance (computed from an overhead rate based on direct labor hours).

The overhead efficiency variance can also be computed by comparing the overhead cost computed for actual activity at the standard rate with the overhead cost computed for standard activity allowed for actual production, also at the standard rate. The overhead cost for the actual 20,000 direct labor hours at the standard rate of $0.95 per direct labor hour is $19,000. The standard allows 2 labor hours for each unit of production, so the standard allows 20,400 direct labor hours for the 10,200 units produced. At the standard overhead rate, the overhead on the standard hours would be $19,380.

Overhead efficiency variance	=	Overhead cost for actual activity at standard rate	−	Overhead cost for standard activity at standard rate
	=	$19,000 − $19,380		
	=	$(380).		

Exhibit 26-5 may be helpful in visualizing the computation of the variable-overhead variances. The shaded rectangle represents the standard overhead cost. The other rectangle represents the actual overhead cost. In this example, the spending variance is unfavorable, while the efficiency variance is favorable.

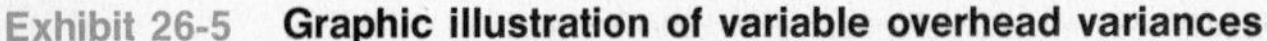

Control of fixed costs

This chapter deals primarily with the control of variable costs. The control of fixed costs is discussed extensively later in the text. However, a brief mention of the topic is appropriate here. Fixed or committed costs are related to a firm's capacity for manufacturing and/or selling. They are costs that relate primarily to property, plant, and equipment—for example, typical fixed costs include depreciation, rent, property taxes, and key administrative salaries.

Exhibit 26-5 Graphic illustration of variable overhead variances

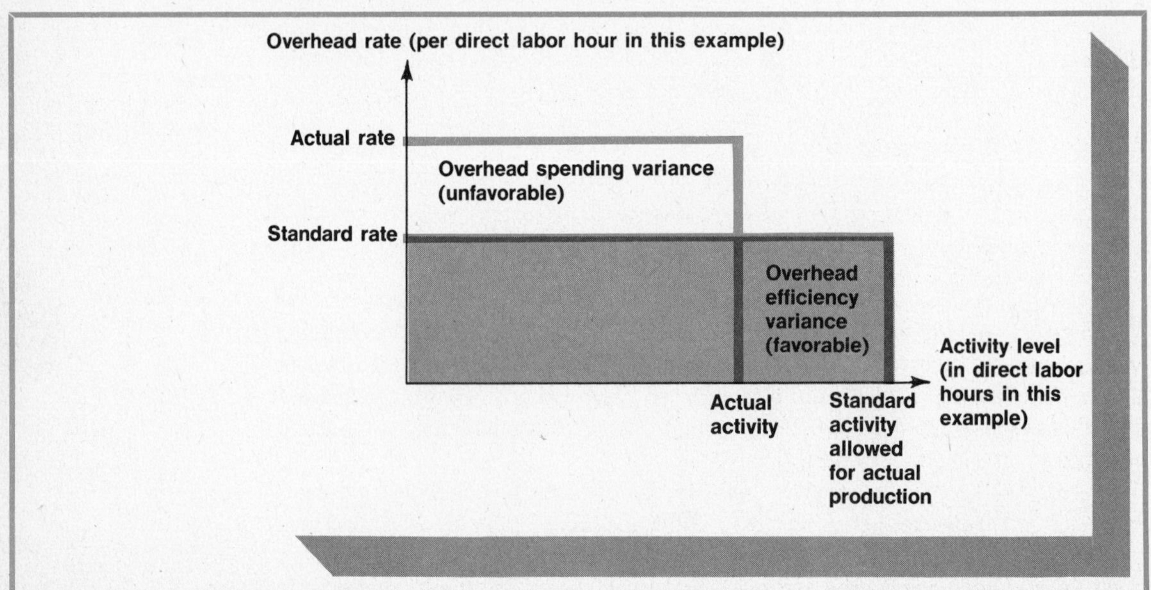

Fixed costs usually are sizeable in amount and are related to long periods of time (they cannot be changed readily in the short run). Because fixed costs are related to the capacity at which a firm operates, control of such costs is essentially a problem of keeping the facilities ***utilized*** as fully as possible.

Because fixed costs do not change as volume changes in the short run, static (rather than flexible) budgets usually are sufficient for controlling fixed costs. Fixed cost data taken from a static budget can be compared with actual fixed costs incurred during a period. Variances should be identified and their causes explained. Chapter 31 (which treats manufacturing operations) discusses a capacity (volume) variance that relates to costs. The acquisition of fixed assets (which are the source of most fixed costs) is controlled primarily by capital budgeting, a technique discussed in Chapter 29.

Summary

Using standards for material specifications and work measurements, management can evaluate performance and control operations. Variances usually exist between predetermined standards and actual performance for a period. These variances typically are associated with price and quantity (or efficiency and usage). The variances are not answers; rather they are questions seeking answers. Where significant in amount, variances should be investigated. If corrective action is possible for an unfavorable variance, such action should be taken.

Exhibit 26-6 summarizes the variances illustrated for the Standard Cost Company in this chapter. Positive variances indicate that actual cost exceeded standard cost (an unfavorable situation). Negative variances indicate that standard cost exceeded actual cost (a favorable situation).

Questions

1. Distinguish between effectiveness and efficiency.
2. What are standards? How can they be used in controlling costs? What is meant by the standard cost per unit?
3. What are ideal and currently attainable standards?
4. Explain how each of the following variances is computed, and explain its significance:
  a. purchase price variance;
  b. material usage variance;
  c. labor rate variance;
  d. labor efficiency variance;
  e. overhead spending variance;
  f. overhead efficiency variance.
5. How does the use of variance analysis relate to the comprehensive budget discussed in Chapter 22?
6. Distinguish between a fixed budget and a flexible budget.

Exhibit 26-6 **Summary of variable cost variances computed in this chapter**

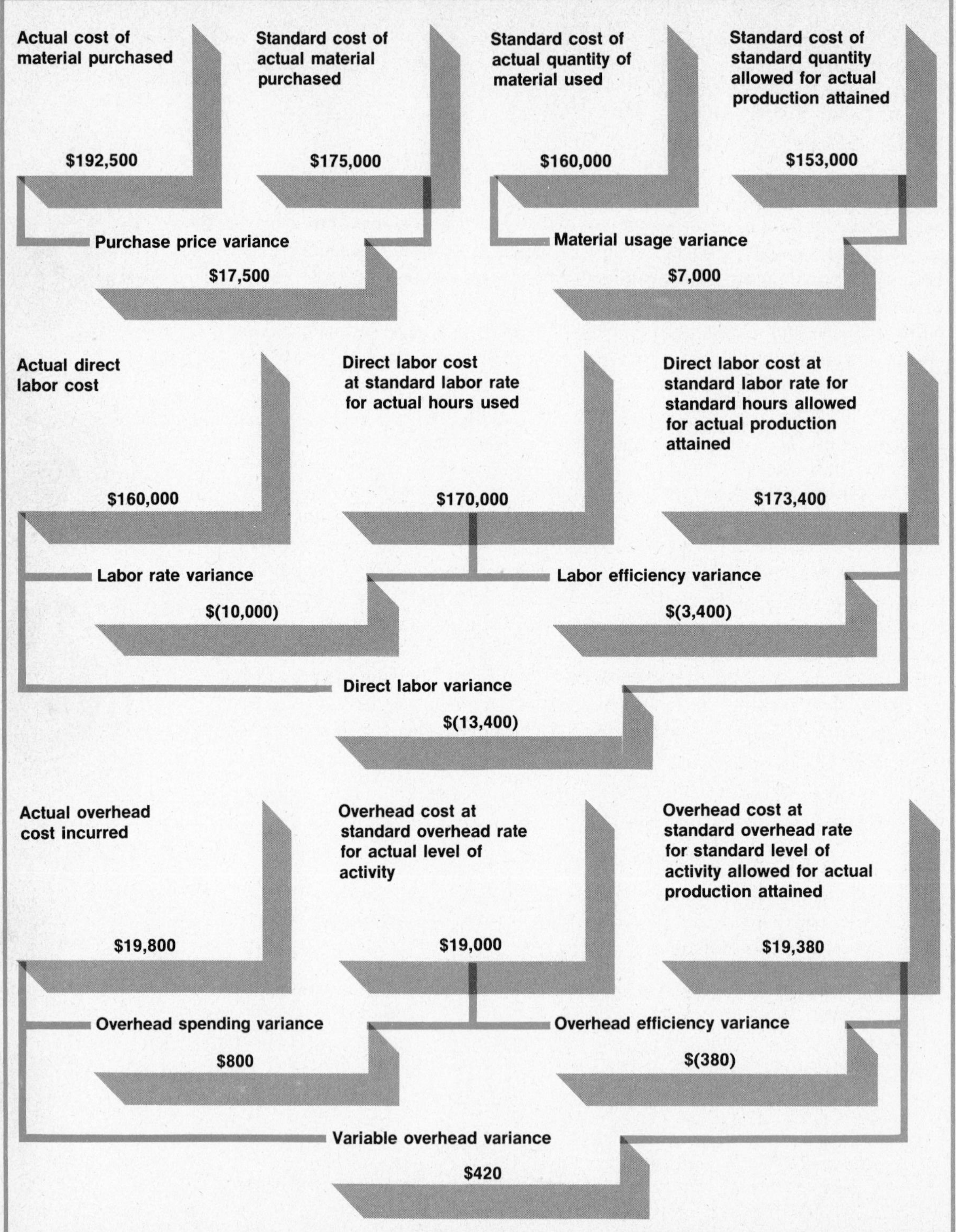

7. Under what conditions may the labor-rate variance be significant to management's decision-making activities?
8. What questions should management ask when examining variances?
9. Why do flexible budgets for manufacturing overhead expenses vary at different levels of production?
10. Distinguish between a cost variance and an expense variance. Which kind of variance would correspond to differences between budgeted and actual income statements?

Exercises

E26-1 (Material and labor variances)

a. The Greer Company established a standard purchasing price of $11 per unit for Material X that it uses in production. During the month, the company purchased 300,000 units of Material X at $14 per unit. Compute the purchase-price variance.

b. The Greer Company manufactures Product Y. The standard usage requirement is set at 3 units of Material X for each unit of Product Y produced. During the month, the company manufactured 55,000 units of Product Y; 175,000 units of Material X were requisitioned and used in the production process during the month. Compute the material-usage variance.

E26-2 (Labor variances)

The Greer Company (see Exercise E26-1) used 410,000 direct labor hours in its production of Product Y during the month. The standard for labor hours allowed is 7.5 hours per unit of Product Y. The standard labor rate is $6.50 per hour of direct labor. The direct labor cost for the month was $3,075,000.

Required: Compute (a) the labor rate variance and (b) the labor efficiency variance.

E26-3 (Overhead variances)

The Greer Company (see Exercises E26-1 and E26-2) incurred $1,400,000 of variable overhead cost during the month. The standard overhead rate is $3.10 per direct labor hour.

Required: Compute (a) the variable overhead spending variance and (b) the variable overhead efficiency variance.

E26-4 (Variable overhead rate)

The Development Company has developed the following budgeted data for its operations at 100 percent of capacity.

Direct labor hours	200,000
Variable overhead costs:	
Indirect labor	$110,000
Indirect material	25,000
Power	130,000
Other costs	60,000
Fixed overhead costs	160,000

Required:

a. Prepare a flexible overhead budget at 90, 95, and 100 percent of capacity.

b. Compute the ***variable*** overhead rate per direct labor hour at 100 percent of capacity.

E26-5 (Variance analysis—six variances)
The Established Company uses a standard cost system, with the following standards:

5 tons of material used per finished unit of product;
10 direct labor hours used per finished unit of product;
$10-per-ton purchase price for material;
$9-per-hour standard cost for direct labor;
variable overhead at $3 per direct labor hour.

The company accumulates the following data on actual performance in June:

5,000 units produced;
30,000 tons of material purchased for $330,000;
24,000 tons of material used in production;
41,000 hours of direct labor used at a cost of $389,000;
$98,000 in variable overhead cost.

Required: Compute the six variances discussed in this chapter.

Problems

P26-1 (Variance analysis—six variances)
The Diverse Company uses standard costs and flexible budgets to control its variable manufacturing expenses. Compute the six cost variances described in this chapter, using the following operating data for the company in March.

Production:	4,600 units.
Materials:	9,000 pounds purchased at $1.60 per pound; standard price is $1.58 per pound; 9,200 pounds used in production; standards allow 2 pounds per unit produced.
Direct labor:	24,000 actual hours at cost of $120,000; standard labor rate $6 per hour; standards allow 4 hours of direct labor per unit produced.
Overhead cost:	$46,000 actual cost; standard overhead rate $2 per direct labor hour.

P26-2 (Variance analysis—six variances)
The standard cost card of the Blanche Company shows the following information for the company's single product.

Direct material: 4 units of material at $12/unit	$48
Direct labor: 3 hours at $5/hour	15

Variable manufacturing overhead cost is budgeted at $225,000 when the plant is operating at a level of 150,500 direct labor hours. The following actual operating data are available for October.

Material:	275,000 units of material purchased at $11.50 per unit; 200,000 units of material used in production; 52,000 units of product produced.
Labor:	142,500 hours of direct labor used at $4.80 per hour.
Overhead:	Variable overhead cost of $230,000.

Required: Compute the six variances described in this chapter. Prepare a brief report for management summarizing the variances and their probable significances.

P26-3 (Variance analysis—six variances)

The following data are available for a company that uses a standard cost system for controlling variable expenses:

Standard cost card—Product Bench	
Material: 5 square feet of lumber at $10/square foot	$50
Direct labor: 4 labor hours at $5/hour	20
Variable expenses: $2 per direct labor hour	8
Total variable cost per bench	$78

During the year, the company produced 1,000 benches. The following actual data are available from the records:

Cost per square foot of lumber	$12
Square feet of lumber purchased and used	4,900
Direct labor cost per hour	$5.50
Direct labor hours used	5,100
Variable overhead	$10,710

Required: Compute six variances associated with direct material, direct labor, and variable overhead and indicate whether each variance is favorable or unfavorable.

P26-4 (Graphic illustration)

Refer to Problem P26-3. Prepare a graphic illustration of the labor variances.

27 Return on investment

Management is responsible to owners for the effective and efficient use of the resources available to the firm. Management's effectiveness is measured by its ability to operate the firm at a profit. Management's efficiency is measured by the size of the net income earned in relation to the amount of assets (financial resources) available for use in earning this income. A comprehensive measure of financial performance called ***return on investment*** (or return on capital) has been designed for use in (1) motivating and evaluating operating performance, (2) evaluating and controlling capital investment projects, and (3) planning profits through pricing, cost, and inventory decisions.

Computing return on investment

The basic formula for computing return on investment (ROI) involves two factors: (1) capital turnover, and (2) margin.

$$\text{Capital turnover} = \frac{\text{Sales}}{\text{Capital employed}}$$

$$\text{Margin} = \frac{\text{Net income}}{\text{Sales}}$$

Capital turnover (ratio of sales to capital employed in generating the sales) is a measure of the movement of assets as a result of sales during the accounting period. For example, a capital turnover of 2 times means that the firm's assets were used to generate an inflow of assets through sales twice as large as the stock of assets held in the business. Capital turnover is a gauge of the general efficiency of management, particularly in relation to its long-run planning and control. The larger the volume of sales that management can generate on a given investment in assets, the more efficient its operations are in creating asset inflow. In general, the capital turnover is only slightly affected by short-run operating decisions, but it is strongly affected by long-run decisions about the use and investment of capital.

Margin (or operating margin percentage on sales) is the ratio of net income to sales, or the earnings expressed as a percentage of sales. The margin is a gauge of the efficiency with which management has generated profit from the volume of sales (asset inflow). In general, margin is most sensitive to the results of short-run decisions about sales activity, costs and expenses, use of current assets, and so on.

The ***rate of return on investment*** (ROI rate) is the product of these two factors:

$$\text{ROI rate} = \text{Capital turnover} \times \text{Margin as percentage of sales}$$

$$= \frac{\text{Sales}}{\text{Capital employed}} \times \frac{\text{Net income}}{\text{Sales}}$$

$$= \frac{\text{Net income}}{\text{Capital employed}} \qquad \text{(Short version)}$$

As simple as this formula appears to be, it takes into account all the items that go into the statement of financial position and the income statement. Exhibit 27-1 shows a structural outline of the relationship of statement items to the rate of return on investment.

Exhibit 27-1 **Relationship of finnancial statement items to ROI formula**

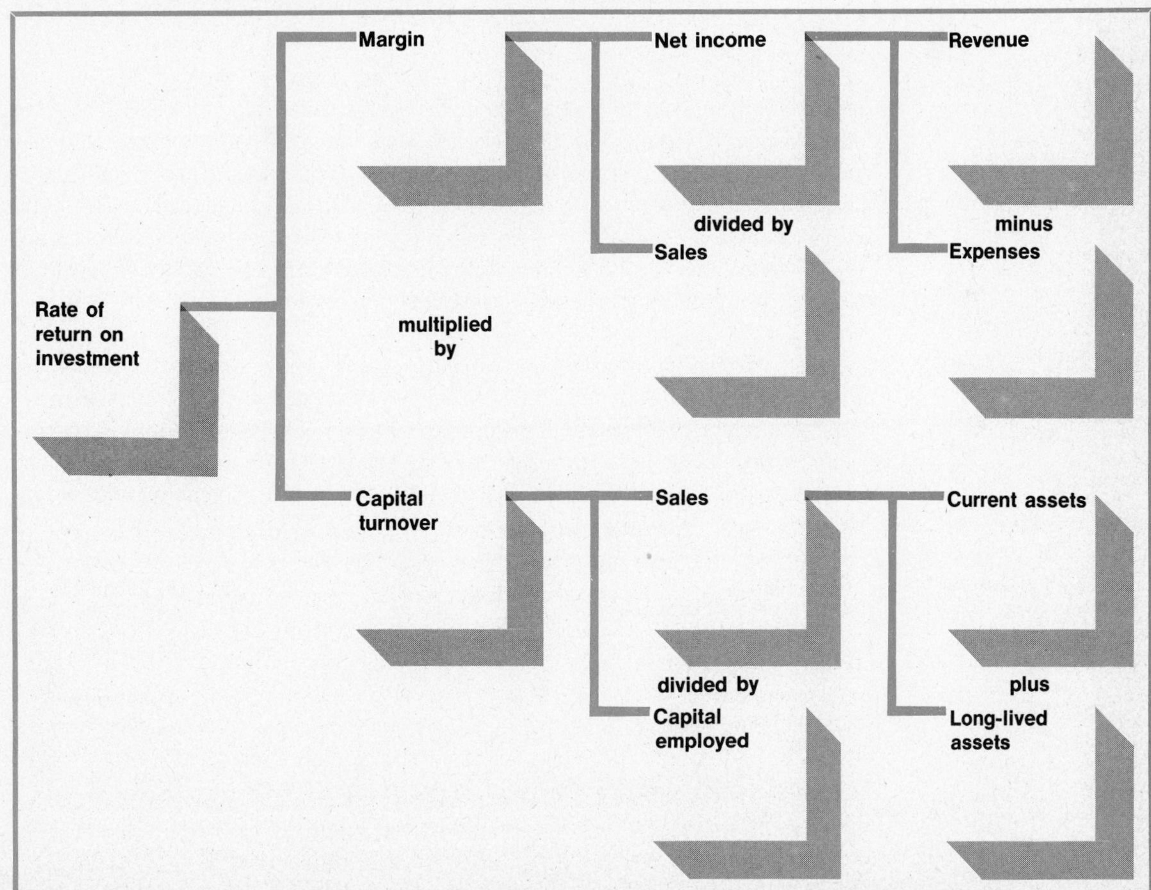

APPLYING THE BASIC ROI FORMULA

As an illustration of the use of ROI analysis, we employ the data for the Break-Even Company shown in Exhibit 27-2. Using this information, we can compute the ROI rate.

$$\begin{aligned}\text{ROI rate} &= \text{Capital turnover} \times \text{Margin}\\ &= \frac{\text{Sales}}{\text{Capital employed}} \times \frac{\text{Net income}}{\text{Sales}}\\ &= \frac{\$1{,}200{,}000}{\$1{,}000{,}000} \times \frac{\$80{,}000}{\$1{,}200{,}000}\\ &= 1.2 \times 6.7\%\\ &= 8.0\%.\end{aligned}$$

It should be noted that the ROI rate can be computed from the shorter version of the basic formula:

$$\begin{aligned}\text{ROI rate} &= \frac{\text{Net income}}{\text{Capital employed}}\\ &= \frac{\$80{,}000}{\$1{,}000{,}000}\\ &= 8.0\%.\end{aligned}$$

Although both versions of the basic formula give the same value for the ROI rate, the longer version is more useful because it reveals the values of the capital turnover and the margin of return on sales. Both of these relationships are important because they localize the sources of change in the return on investment. Ideally, a firm would like to increase its sales while maintaining (or improving) its margin on sales and simultaneously maintaining (or improving) its capital turnover. The longer version of the basic ROI formula emphasizes these dual objectives.

ROI CONCEPTS

The basic formula for return on investment places in proper relationship to one another three items of economic data: sales, net income, and capital employed. No universal agreement exists about the precise meaning of these terms for this computation. However, it is imperative that they be expressed consistently when making comparisons of ROI values (from year to year, company to company, and so on).

Exhibit 27-2
Operating data for the Break-Even Company

Sales (net)	**$1,200,000**
Less: Cost and expense	**1,120,000**
Net income	$ 80,000
Capital employed:	
Working capital	**$ 400,000**
Long-lived assets	**600,000**
Total capital employed	$1,000,000

SALES. The term ***sales*** in the basic formula usually is interpreted as billed sales or net sales (gross sales less discounts, returns, and allowances). Net sales generally is preferred to gross sales. Sales and excise taxes collected by the company usually are excluded.

NET INCOME. ***Net income*** ordinarily is taken to mean net income after taxes. When taxes are deducted in income determination, they are considered an expense of the firm just as any other business expense. The author prefers this interpretation of net income in the general model.

Occasionally, net income before taxes is used in the computations. This definition eliminates the changes in net income from year to year that are due to changes in tax rates (a factor outside the control of the firm).

Other refinements in the use of net income in the ROI formula include (1) net income before depreciation and depletion charges; (2) net income before interest charges; (3) operating income (net income before nonoperating items, extraordinary items, and income taxes); and (4) average net income for a number of accounting periods.

CAPITAL EMPLOYED. The definition of ***capital employed*** in the ROI formula is the area of greatest difference of opinion. The problems arise in deciding (1) which assets are to be considered a part of capital employed, and (2) what valuation should be placed on these assets.

In regard to the first problem, the following are three of the more generally accepted opinions about the assets that should be included in the concept of capital employed.

1. ***Total assets,*** including all current and noncurrent assets.
2. ***Total assets less current liabilities*** (that is, working capital plus noncurrent assets; or gross capital). This definition of capital employed stresses the importance of long-term debt (capital debt) and stockholders' equity (equity capital) as the investment upon which a return is expected. It also eliminates short-term fluctuations in assets due to variations in current assets (working capital is more stable, being unaffected by such changes as short-term loans that create offsetting current assets and liabilities). However, management is expected to employ *all* assets profitably; the deduction of current liabilities from current assets may not be completely justified.
3. ***Stockholders' equity*** (equity capital, or net capital). This definition of capital employed stresses the importance of the owner's investment in the firm.

When ROI analysis is being used to evaluate the performance of management, the measure of capital employed should be one of the first two just listed. Management has total assets (or gross capital) available for use in business operations, and it should be held accountable for their efficient and effective use. If the ROI analysis is being used to evaluate companies as investment opportunities for potential (or existing) owners, the third definition may be appropriate. When stockholders' equity is used as the measure of capital employed, the analysis stresses the long-range ability of the firm to make use of the investments of its owners—including the ability to use that capital to attract other capital from creditors.

The second problem in regard to capital employed is that of valuation of assets. Conclusive criteria are almost impossible to set forth. Many ROI analysts use the following general guidelines.

1. Current assets:
   a. Include only amounts of cash and securities sufficient to satisfy the normal operating requirements of the business; exclude excessive amounts of these assets.
   b. Use either gross amounts or net amounts (after provision for estimated uncollectible accounts receivable) for receivables.
   c. Use financial-statement valuation for inventory.
2. Long-lived assets: Use either original cost, cost less depreciation, or estimated replacement value.

The most important general consideration is to make sure that definitions and valuation standards are consistent within the analysis and are appropriate to the purpose of the analysis. For example, if nonoperating income is excluded from net income, the corresponding assets not used in generating operating income should be excluded from capital employed. If the analysis involves comparisons from year to year or from company to company, definitions should be chosen to make the ROI rates most comparable and meaningful across the range of the study.

Use of ROI analysis in profit planning

We now develop several cases to demonstrate the use of ROI analysis. Each case discusses a particular application of ROI analysis and should be studied carefully.

Case 1. The Planning Corporation sets a desired rate of return of 10 percent on its invested capital of $100,000. Therefore, it wishes to earn net income of $10,000 in the coming year. With fixed expense of $30,000 and variable expense of $1.50 per unit, what sales volume is needed in order to earn the desired ROI for the year if the sales price is set at $2 per unit?

To solve this problem, let V be the sales volume (number of units sold). Then,

$$\begin{aligned}
\text{Sales} &= \text{Variable expense} + \text{Fixed expense} + \text{Net income};\\
V \times \text{Sales price} &= (V \times \text{Variable expense per unit}) + \text{Fixed expense}\\
&\quad + \text{Net income};\\
V \times \$2.00 &= (V \times \$1.50) + \$30{,}000 + \$10{,}000;\\
V \times \$0.50 &= \$40{,}000;\\
V &= 80{,}000 \text{ units}.
\end{aligned}$$

Case 2. Suppose that the Planning Corporation (case 1) instead decides that it expects to sell 80,000 units in the coming year, and it wishes to know the sales price needed to meet its goal of a 10 percent ROI rate.

In this case, we can begin by computing the sales revenue needed to obtain the desired $10,000 net income.

$$\begin{aligned}\text{Sales} &= \text{Variable expense} + \text{Fixed expense} + \text{Net income}\\ &= (80{,}000 \times \$1.50) + \$30{,}000 + \$10{,}000\\ &= \$160{,}000.\end{aligned}$$

In order to generate $160,000 sales revenue on sales of 80,000 units,

$$\begin{aligned}\text{Sales price} &= \frac{\text{Sales revenue}}{\text{Sales volume}} = \frac{\$160{,}000}{80{,}000 \text{ units}}\\ &= \$2 \text{ per unit.}\end{aligned}$$

Case 3. Suppose that the Planning Corporation projects sales of $160,000 for the coming year. What capital turnover is required if the firm is to achieve its goal of a 10 percent ROI rate on $100,000 capital employed?

This problem involves a straightforward use of the basic formula for capital turnover.

$$\begin{aligned}\text{Capital turnover} &= \frac{\text{Sales}}{\text{Capital employed}}\\ &= \frac{\$160{,}000}{\$100{,}000}\\ &= 1.6 \text{ times.}\end{aligned}$$

Case 4. In the situation of case 3, what is the required margin on sales needed to achieve the desired profit objective?

Again, the computation is straightforward.

$$\begin{aligned}\text{Margin} &= \frac{\text{Net income}}{\text{Sales}}\\ &= \frac{\$10{,}000}{\$160{,}000}\\ &= 6.25\%.\end{aligned}$$

Case 5. Confirm that the capital turnover and margin computed in cases 3 and 4 do yield the desired 10 percent ROI rate.

$$\begin{aligned}\text{ROI} &= \text{Capital turnover} \times \text{Margin}\\ &= 1.6 \times 6.25\%\\ &= 10.0\%.\end{aligned}$$

IMPROVING THE RATE OF RETURN

Suppose that a company wishes to plan its operations in a way that will improve its ROI rate. Let us review the factors involved in ROI, as summarized in the basic ROI formula.

$$\text{ROI} = \text{Capital turnover} \times \text{Margin of return on sales}$$
$$= \frac{\text{Sales}}{\text{Capital employed}} \times \frac{\text{Net income}}{\text{Sales}}$$
$$= \frac{\text{Net income}}{\text{Capital employed}}$$

Various alternative courses of action are available to improve ROI.

1. Increase total sales by increasing volume, sales price, or some combination thereof, while maintaining or improving the margin of return on sales.
2. Decrease expenses, thereby increasing net income.
3. Reduce the amount of capital employed (for example, reduce inventory levels, improve collection of accounts receivable, arrange a better use of cash, reduce investment in property, plant, and equipment) without decreasing sales.

Case 6. The board of directors of the Planning Corporation (case 1) decides that it would like to achieve a 15 percent ROI rate in the coming year rather than the current 10 percent rate. How might this increase be obtained?

The basic ROI formula is a tool that can be used to evaluate some possible solutions. In the current situation,

$$\text{ROI} = \frac{\text{Sales}}{\text{Capital employed}} \times \frac{\text{Net income}}{\text{Sales}}$$
$$= \frac{\$160,000}{\$100,000} \times \frac{\$10,000}{\$160,000}$$
$$= 1.6 \times 6.25\%$$
$$= 10.0\%.$$

First, suppose that sales price and sales volume cannot be increased, and that the amount of capital employed cannot be changed. In that case, net income must be modified to attain the desired 15 percent rate of return. Under these circumstances, what net income must be earned to achieve the desired ROI?

$$\text{ROI} = 15.0\% = \frac{\$160,000}{\$100,000} \times \frac{\text{Net income}}{\$160,000}$$
$$15.0\% = \frac{\text{Net income}}{\$100,000}$$
$$\text{Net income} = 15.0\% \times \$100,000 = \$15,000$$

To increase the ROI from 10 to 15 percent, the firm must increase net income from \$10,000 to \$15,000 (without changing sales revenue or capital employed). In this case, management focuses attention on margin rather than turnover (which remains unchanged). The margin must be increased from 6.25% to 9.38%. Since sales revenue cannot be increased, the improvement in net income must come through reduction of expense. A cost-cutting program is needed if the desired ROI is to be achieved. Fixed expense must be reduced by \$5,000, or variable expense reduced by \$0.0625 per unit—or some combination of reductions must be achieved in fixed and variable expense.

Now, let us consider another situation. Suppose that expense cannot be reduced, nor can sales revenue be increased. In that case, the company cannot improve its margin of return on sales. An investigation should be undertaken to determine whether turnover can be increased by reducing the assets invested in the business. What amount of capital employed in the business would provide the desired 15 percent ROI?

$$\text{ROI} = 15.0\% = \frac{\$160{,}000}{\text{Capital employed}} \times \frac{\$10{,}000}{\$160{,}000}$$

$$15.0\% = \frac{\$10{,}000}{\text{Capital employed}}$$

$$\text{Capital employed} = \frac{\$10{,}000}{15.0\%} = \$66{,}667$$

To increase the ROI from 10 to 15 percent, the firm must reduce capital employed from \$100,000 to \$66,667 (without decreasing sales revenue or margin). In this case, management focuses attention on turnover rather than on margin. The turnover must be increased from 1.6 to 2.4. To reduce capital employed in the business, management might reduce the capital invested in cash, inventory, or receivables by improving its control procedures. It should examine ways of reducing the investment in fixed assets. In any event, it should devote its attention primarily to the control of assets, rather than to sales, price, volume, or expense.

In many cases, it is difficult to reduce a firm's investment in assets without harming sales or incurring losses on the sale of assets. For that reason, careful attention to the desired turnover is needed when the firm is planning to make additional investments in assets. It is usually easier to hold the assets down (and the capital turnover up) through careful capital investment than it is to decrease the assets after the turnover has proved to be too low.

Summary

Rate-of-return analysis is one of the most basic tools available for evaluating the effectiveness and efficiency of profit-centered management. The rate of return (ROI) is computed as follows.

$$\begin{aligned}\text{ROI} &= \text{Capital turnover} \times \text{Margin of return on sales} \\ &= \frac{\text{Sales}}{\text{Capital employed}} \times \frac{\text{Net income}}{\text{Sales}} \\ &= \frac{\text{Net income}}{\text{Capital employed}}\end{aligned}$$

The following alternatives summarize the procedures available to manipulate or manage the rate of return on investment.

1. Methods of improving ***margin:***
   a. increase sales revenue more than operating expenses;
   b. reduce operating expenses more than sales revenue.
2. Methods of improving ***capital turnover:***
   a. increase sales revenue relatively more than capital employed;
   b. reduce capital employed relatively more than sales revenue.
3. Methods affecting both ***margin and capital turnover:***
   a. increase selling price;
   b. increase sales volume.

Questions

1. What is the meaning of "return on investment"?
2. What is capital turnover? What is margin? Give the basic formula used in calculating ROI.
3. What is capital employed? Explain and discuss three different definitions of capital employed.
4. Give six suggestions for improving ROI.
5. Under what conditions would it be appropriate to compute the rate of return on stockholders' equity rather than total assets?

Exercises

E27-1 (ROI)

The president of the Lane Company asks her accountant to calculate for her the rate of return on investment for the firm. The accountant assembles the following information: working capital $50,000; fixed assets $450,000; sales revenue $100,000; costs and expenses $80,000.

Required:

a. Calculate the capital turnover for the Lane Company.
b. Calculate the margin for the Lane Company.
c. Calculate the ROI for the Lane Company.

E27-2 (Capital employed concepts)

The following information is made available to you by a client of your management consulting firm: total assets $1,400,000; current liabilities $300,000; noncurrent liabilities $700,000.

Required: Give three interpretations for your client of capital employed, and show the amount of capital employed in this business under each interpretation. Explain circumstances that would warrant the use of each of these three interpretations of capital employed.

E27-3 (ROI)

A client desires to earn a 15 percent return on her invested capital of $200,000. Her firm has fixed expense of $200,000, variable expense of $3 per unit, and a selling price of $8 per unit. She asks you to estimate the dollar sales required to obtain the desired return on her capital. Compute this sales figure.

E27-4 (ROI)

Use the data in Exercise E27-3, except that the selling price per unit is unknown. Management asks you to estimate the selling price per unit needed to earn a 15 percent return on the company's investment from sales of 60,000 units.

E27-5 (Capital turnover and margin applications)

An owner invests $400,000 in a small furniture store. He estimates that sales will average $80,000 per year.

a. What capital turnover is needed to achieve a 25 percent return on his investment?

b. What margin of return on sales is needed?

E27-6 (ROI)

Using data from Exercise E27-5, compute the ROI for the firm.

E27-7 (ROI applications)

The Today Company has capital employed of $150,000 and a rate of return on investment of 20 percent. The company's capital turnover was 4 times.

a. What was the firm's net income?

b. What was the firm's sales revenue?

c. What was the firm's margin on sales?

Problems

P27-1 (ROI concepts and applications)

An accountant computes the ROI for her company, using the long version of the basic ROI formula. The company has sales of $1,250,000, net income of $250,000, and capital employed of $625,000. The accountant computes the ROI as 2.0 × 20.0% = 40.0%.

a. The accountant could have computed the ROI directly, using the short version of the ROI formula, as net income divided by capital employed. Verify that this computation gives the same result as the long version. Conceptually, what is the advantage of the use of the sales data in the long version of the formula?

b. Suggest various possible alternatives available to management to improve ROI.

c. Management desires to obtain a 45 percent return on its investment. Sales prices and volume cannot be changed; capital employed will remain the same. What must be modified to attain the 45 percent ROI, and by how much?

d. Management reports that your solution to part c is impractical. Management then asks what change in capital employed would be needed to attain the desired ROI. What is your answer?

P27-2 (ROI applications)

In evaluating a firm to determine its investment potential, you calculate the following data.

	19_6	19_7
Margin (ratio of net income to sales)	.18	.22
Ratio of net income to total assets	.18	.26
Ratio of net income to owners' equity	.30	.60

Required:

a. Using these statistics, evaluate the firm's operations.

b. How do you account for the fact that the ratio of net income to total assets increased from 18% to 26%, while the ratio of net income to owners' equity increased from 30% to 60%?

P27-3 (ROI applications)

Management of the Renewal Firm is interested in improving its operating performance, as measured by the rate of return on investment, during the coming year. The accountant for the company compiles the following data about current operations: sales $960,000; invested capital $400,000; operating income before taxes $80,000.

Required:

a. What is the current pretax rate of return on investment?

b. The Renewal Company desires to obtain a 25 percent return on its investment. What change in net income must be made if this return is to be attained? How might this be accomplished?

c. If operating income cannot be changed, what change in invested capital would be required to attain the desired rate of return?

P27-4 (ROI applications)

The comptroller (chief financial officer) has assembled the following information about next year's operations.

Assets:	
Accounts receivable	$ 300,000
Merchandise inventory	350,000
Plant and equipment	350,000
Total assets	$1,000,000
Fixed costs	$80,000
Variable costs	$4 per unit
Expected volume	200,000 units

Required:

a. The board of directors wants a 20 percent return on its investment in receivables, merchandise inventory, and plant and equipment. What dollar sales must be made to achieve this objective? What selling price should be set to meet the board's request?

b. What is the budgeted capital turnover?

c. What is the budgeted margin?

d. If the company actually attains a sales volume of only 180,000 units, what will the actual ROI be?

P27-5 (Capital turnover)

The ROI Corporation has a rate of return on its total assets of 12 percent. The rate is discussed at a meeting of the board of directors. One director comments that the firm is doing quite well, because the average rate of return in its industry is 9 percent. However, another director points out that the ROI Corporation has a margin of return on sales of only 9 percent, compared to an industry average margin of 10 percent. The first director responds by saying that this difference in margins is a sign that the company has a good opportunity to do even better on its rate of return.

Required:

a. Compute the capital turnover for the ROI Corporation and for the average of the industry.

b. Discuss the comments of the directors. Explain what steps the firm might take to improve its ROI.

P27-6 (ROI computations)

The following data is available concerning the operations and financial position of a company:

Gross sales	$110,000
Net sales	80,000
Net income	10,000
Total assets	100,000
Current liabilities	20,000
Long-term debt	60,000

Required: Compute return on investment for the company using three different concepts of capital employed.

P27-7 (ROI applications)

The following information is available from a company's records:

Assets		Liabilities and owners' equity	
Cash	$100,000	Current liabilities	$400,000
Accounts receivable	200,000	Owners' equity	400,000
Inventory	200,000		
Property	300,000		

Fixed expenses: $50,000
Variable expenses: $10/unit
Estimated volume for next year: 2,000 units

Required:

a. What sales must the company have if management wants to have a 10 percent return on its investment in total assets? What sales price must be set?

b. What is the budgeted capital turnover?

c. What is the budgeted margin?

d. If the company sells 2,500 units instead of 2,000, what will be the return on capital?

P27-8 (ROI applications)

Refer to Problem P27-7. Assume that the company understands capital employed to mean total assets less current liabilities. What answers would be required for the four questions in the problem?

28 Responsibility accounting and relevant costs

The key figure in any organization is the decision maker. The decision maker may be a person, a committee, or a majority vote. Regardless of where the decision-making authority resides, the site of that authority should be clearly identifiable as a clause in the corporate charter, a section of the bylaws, a name on an organization chart, or elsewhere.

A major role of the accounting system is provision of information useful to those who make the decisions. This information summarizes past economic events, outlines the present financial situation, and estimates possible future consequences of decisions. Responsibility accounting and the relevant-cost approach are two techniques available to the accounting system to help it provide the most useful information for decision makers.

The decision-making process

Decision making ordinarily takes place in an environment of uncertainty. Seldom are all the relevant facts available. Seldom are all the unknowns accounted for, all the alternatives completely explored, or all the side effects carefully identified. Seldom are all the relationships clearly established. Seldom does a solution meet all the restraints imposed by a problem; seldom are decisions unanimously agreed upon. Yet, decisions do get made. And as a result of those decisions, the firm moves forward, is stopped in its tracks, or disintegrates.

Stripped of nonessentials, the decision-making process consists of the following basic steps.

1. Identify the problem.
2. Determine alternative solutions.

3. Evaluate the consequences of the proposed solutions.
4. Select a course of action.

After the problem has been identified and the alternatives isolated and evaluated, the final consideration becomes the making of the decision. If the firm's objectives are known, the selection process requires the selection of that course of action that promises the optimum payoff. The selection of a course of action must be made within a system of values and priorities. Choice is the product of deliberation. The decision maker must avoid two rocks upon which he can founder: (1) excessive caution or irresoluteness, and (2) rashness. The effective decision maker takes the middle path.

Responsibility accounting

Concern with managerial control has led to the development of the budgeting process, contribution analysis, and standard-cost techniques. Planning, control, and feedback are essential elements in any goal-oriented, decision-making enterprise. Once plans have become action programs, the primary concern of management must be with control of operations, which requires the feedback of data about successes and failures. Management must establish reporting procedures that communicate the results of action to the parties with primary responsibility for the efficient and effective attainment of company objectives. Techniques of responsibility reporting have been developed to meet this need for responsive communicative procedures.

A company assembles resources and commits them to operations that it hopes will be profitable. Because the attainment of the company's objectives is a major expectation of the enterprise, it is important that responsibility for goal attainment be fixed within the firm, so that performance can be controlled and evaluated.

Responsibility accounting involves the definition of responsibility centers to motivate and measure performance within the firm. Management has designed three major types of responsibility center.

1. *Expense center:* an organizational unit that is held accountable for the incurring of expense. Expense centers focus attention on the measurement and evaluation of assets used (resources consumed) by the enterprise.
2. *Profit center:* an organizational unit that is held accountable for revenue and expense—that is, for both inputs and outputs of resources.
3. *Investment center:* an organizational unit whose management is held accountable for attaining a satisfactory rate of return on capital employed, as well as for revenue and expense associated with the particular unit. Investment centers focus attention on the relation between capital invested and net increase in capital (revenue less expense).

Responsibility accounting is also called profit-center accounting, or performance reporting. The starting point for this technique is the preparation of an organization chart for the business. The organization chart should reflect a plan of organization

Exhibit 28-1 **A typical business organization chart**

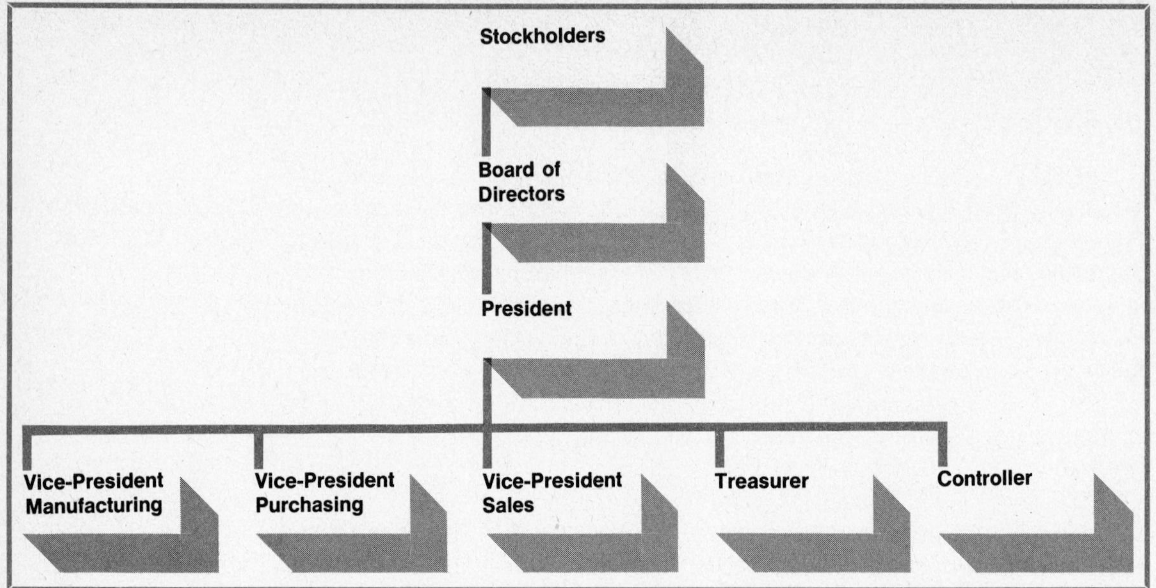

that provides an appropriate segregation of functional responsibilities. Exhibit 28-1 shows, in general terms, a possible organization chart for a business.

The accounting system should reflect the organizational responsibilities described in the organization chart, so that responsibility for results summarized in accounting reports can be traced to particular responsibility centers. Accounting reports should be prepared to summarize the performance of each profit center, expense center, or investment center. Such reports should include only those revenue and/or expense items over which the center has *control.* Also, the responsibility-accounting reports should be designed so that *exceptions* (variances from predetermined standards) are brought to the attention of management.

In this introduction to responsibility accounting, we must know something of controllable costs. *Controllable costs* are those costs that can be regulated or influenced within a stated time interval by the person given responsibility for the center. Suppose that a certain factory is an expense center; the factory foreman or plant supervisor has responsibility for the expense incurred in operation of the factory. The foreman would be responsible for the use of direct labor, direct material, and factory supplies. The costs incurred for these items would be controllable costs within the reporting period. However, insurance on the factory would not ordinarily be under the control of the foreman. Decisions about insurance would be made at a higher level of management. Therefore, insurance expense would not be a controllable cost for the factory expense center. In some cases, the foreman might have responsibility for decisions about purchasing major pieces of factory equipment. However, such decisions involve long-range planning. In short-run (day-to-day or week-to-week) decisions, the equipment cost cannot be altered. Therefore, equipment cost might be considered uncontrollable on monthly reports for the factory expense center, but controllable on annual reports for the same expense center.

In the short run, many costs (such as rent and property taxes) are uncontrollable, because such expenses are fixed over certain time periods by contracts, tax rates, and so on. However, in the long run, all costs are controllable.

Each controllable cost should be assigned to the center that can most readily regulate the cost. In most cases, a controllable cost assigned to a center at a lower managerial level also becomes a controllable cost for higher-level centers with authority over that center. However, the degree of control over the cost may vary at different managerial levels.

Exhibit 28-2 isolates a major responsibility path in a portion of an organization chart. We use this partial chart to conceptualize responsibility accounting for expense centers. The Vice-President Manufacturing is one of several vice-presidents reporting to the President of the company. The Vice-President Manufacturing has responsibility for only those expenses incurred in the manufacturing operations. (The President is responsible to the Board of Directors for all expenses incurred by the company.) Several managers at the supervisory level report to the Vice-President of Manufacturing. The Plant Superintendent of Plant No. 1 has responsibility for controllable costs incurred in operating that plant. The Foreman of Shop A is one of several low-level managers reporting to the superintendent. The foreman has responsibility for controllable costs incurred in running his shop.

The accounting system should provide detailed control information to the foreman. The data on shop expense would be summarized on a ***performance report*** that helps the foreman evaluate the operations for which he is responsible. These data become part of a report to the plant superintendent; his report summarizes data for each factory under his control, and may include other costs controllable at his level

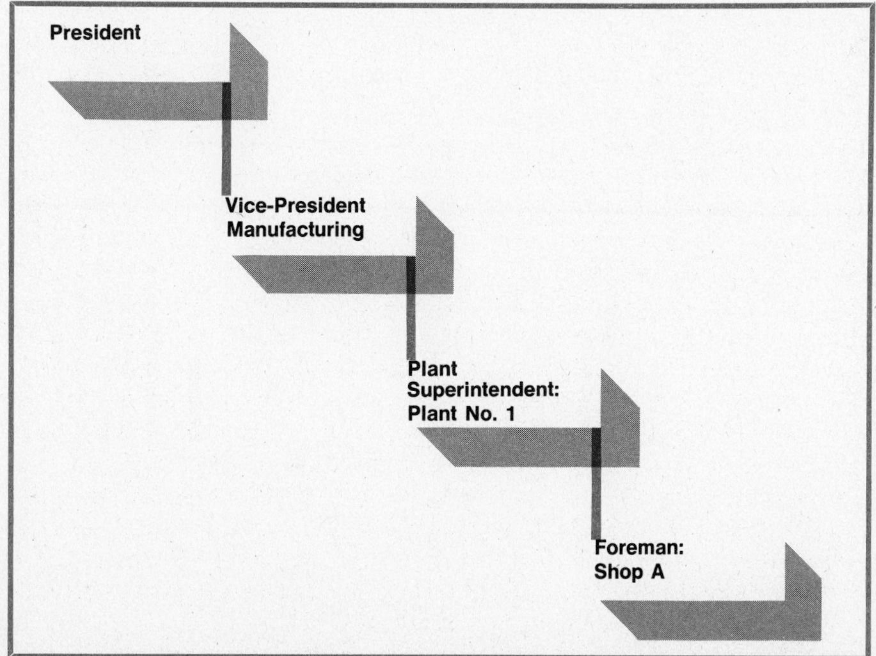

Exhibit 28-2
Partial organization chart showing major line of responsibility

Exhibit 28-3 **Responsibility-accounting reports**

RESPONSIBLE COMPANY
Assembly Shop A
Foreman Report
March 31, 19_1

	Budget		*Actual*		*Variances Favorable / (Unfavorable)*	
Expense	**This Mo.**	**Year to Date**	**This Mo.**	**Year to Date**	**This Mo.**	**Year to Date**
Direct material	$ 15,000	$ 45,000	$ 16,000	$ 50,000	$ (1,000)	$ (5,000)
Direct labor	30,000	90,000	25,000	80,000	5,000	10,000
Supplies	5,000	10,000	5,500	12,000	(500)	(2,000)
Other	100,000	250,000	90,000	295,000	10,000	(45,000)
	$150,000	$395,000	$136,500	$437,000	$13,500	$ (42,000)

RESPONSIBLE COMPANY
Plant Superintendent: Plant 1
Plant Expense Report
March 31, 19_1

	Budget		*Actual*		*Variances Favorable / (Unfavorable)*	
Expense	**This Mo.**	**Year to Date**	**This Mo.**	**Year to Date**	**This Mo.**	**Year to Date**
Assembly Shop A	$150,000	$ 395,000	$136,500	$ 437,000	$13,500	$ (42,000)
Assembly Shop B						
Assembly Shop C			*(Details omitted)*			
Assembly Shop D						
Superintendent's office						
	$500,000	$1,300,000	$490,000	$1,280,000	$10,000	$ 20,000

RESPONSIBLE COMPANY

Vice-President Manufacturing
Expense Report
March 31, 19_1

Expense	*Budget*		*Actual*		*Variances Favorable/(Unfavorable)*	
	This Mo.	Year to Date	This Mo.	Year to Date	This Mo.	Year to Date
Plant No. 1	$ 500,000	$1,300,000	$ 490,000	$1,280,000	$ 10,000	$ 20,000
Plant No. 2						
Plant No. 3			*(Details omitted)*			
Vice-President's office						
	$3,000,000	$9,300,000	$3,100,000	$9,500,000	$(100,000)	$(200,000)

RESPONSIBLE COMPANY

President
Expense Report
March 31, 19_1

Department	*Budget*		*Actual*		*Variances Favorable/(Unfavorable)*	
	This Mo.	Year to Date	This Mo.	Year to Date	This Mo.	Year to Date
Manufacturing	$3,000,000	$ 9,300,000	$3,100,000	$ 9,500,000	$(100,000)	$(200,000)
Purchasing						
Sales						
Treasurer			*(Details omitted)*			
Controller						
President's office						
	$9,000,000	$27,700,000	$9,500,000	$28,300,000	$(500,000)	$(600,000)

Exhibit 28-4 **A profit-center income statement**

PROFIT-CENTER DEPARTMENT STORE
Income Statement
For the Year Ended December 31, 19_1

	Dept. A	*Dept. B*	*Total*
Sales (net)	$1,000,000	$2,000,000	$3,000,000
Cost of goods sold	500,000	1,800,000	2,300,000
Gross margin	$ 500,000	$ 200,000	$ 700,000
Direct departmental expenses	200,000	50,000	250,000
Departmental income	$ 300,000	$ 150,000	$ 450,000
Company expenses not allocated			300,000
Net income			$ 150,000

of authority. The data flow upward in summary fashion to the Vice-President of Manufacturing, and then onward to the President. Exhibit 28-3 illustrates the responsibility-accounting reports for our example. Note that the totals from one report become one item in the report at the next higher level of responsibility. The President's report summarizes all controllable costs for the company's operations during the month.

Income statements that reflect responsibility (or profit-center) accounting have become an accepted form of internal reporting. Exhibit 28-4 shows a typical profit-center income statement for a department store.

Relevant costs

For purposes of decision making involving alternate courses of action, a cost is *relevant* if

1. the cost is an expected future cost, and
2. the cost represents a difference in costs among alternatives.

Sunk costs (costs already incurred) cannot influence decisions involving future action. The past is past; decisions are future oriented. Costs that do not differ among alternate courses of action are not relevant to decision making either.

To demonstrate this concept of relevant costs, consider the following example. Assume that you have purchased an airline ticket from New York City to London on a domestic airline at a cost of $300, and that you have made an unrefundable $75 down payment on the ticket. At the last minute, you discover that you can purchase a similar ticket to London on a foreign airline for $200. Flight time and accommodations are exactly the same on the two flights. Considering that you have already sunk $75 in the nonrefundable down payment, what should you do?

Following the two criteria for relevancy, you should note that only ***future*** and ***different*** costs are relevant to your decision. The alternative courses of action are (1) to complete the purchase of the ticket on which you have made a down payment, or (2) to purchase a ticket from the foreign airline. The future cost of the first alternative is $225; the future cost of the second alternative is $200. Looking at the difference in future costs, you note that the first alternative will cost you $25 more than the second. Therefore, you choose to buy the ticket from the foreign airline for $200. The $75 down payment did not enter into the decision. That was money down the tube. What would your decision be if the foreign airline ticket cost $250? or $225?

With this brief introduction to relevant-cost analysis, you have the basic analytical tools that will enable you to deal with many problems requiring decisions. We now examine three cases in which relevant costing can provide solutions to common business problems. (We exclude tax considerations, which are discussed in a later chapter.)

Case 1: Replacement of equipment. A business manager purchases a computer for $100,000 on January 1, 19_1. The cash cost of operating this computer for the next ten years is expected to be $50,000 per year. At the end of the ten years, the computer will be worthless. On January 2, 19_1, a salesman for a competing computer firm approaches the manager and offers to sell him a computer that can handle the same work at a cash operating cost of only $25,000 per year. This second computer would cost $200,000, would have an expected life of ten years, and would have no expected salvage value at the end of that period. Over the ten years, maintenance and repair expense of $1,000 per year is expected for either machine. The business manager investigates and finds out that he can get only $10,000 in trade-in or resale price for the computer that he already purchased. What should the manager do?

Using a relevant-cost approach to this problem, the manager prepares a schedule of the future costs that differ between the alternate courses of action, as shown in Exhibit 28-5. (Remember that we are ignoring tax considerations.) The analysis shows that the company will obtain cash savings of $60,000 over the ten-year period if it replaces the computer. This $60,000 difference in total costs between the two alternatives is called the ***differential*** (or ***incremental***) ***cost.***

The $100,000 cost of the computer already owned is irrelevant; it is a sunk cost. Only future costs that differ are relevant. (The trade-in value of the old computer *is* a relevant contra cost, because it reduces the costs for one of the alternatives.) The maintenance and repair outlays are irrelevant in this case. Although they are future costs, they do not differ for the two alternatives, and hence are irrelevant.

One further observation. In this case, the carrying value of the old computer was $100,000. Suppose that the old computer had been purchased two years previously

Exhibit 28-5
Analysis of relevant costs in case 1

	Cash Outflows Over 10 Years	
Relevant Costs	***Keep Computer***	***Replace Computer***
Cash operating costs	**$500,000**	**$250,000**
Cash salvage value of computer owned, if traded in today	**—**	**(10,000)**
Cost of new computer	**—**	**200,000**
Total relevant costs	**$500,000**	**$440,000**

and was 20 percent depreciated, so that it had a carrying value of $80,000. Would this make any difference in the cost-relevancy analysis? Not directly, because past costs are irrelevant; the value of the old computer does not enter into the analysis. If anything, that fact might increase the cost of the "keep computer" alternative because the old computer might wear out at the end of its ten-year life, requiring a cost for a replacement. Suppose that the computer already purchased had cost $1,000,000, and all other data in the case remain the same. Would the decision be different? You should answer in the negative. The million dollars are sunk (past) cost and are irrelevant.

Case 2: Sell a product or process it further. A meat-packing firm processes bulk meat to produce Products A and B at a cost of $60,000. Product B is sold immediately for $90,000. The company can also sell Product A immediately for $100,000. Or it can process Product A further to produce Products X, Y, and Z. The additional costs involved in this further processing are $15,000 for Product X, $30,000 for Product Y, and $80,000 for Product Z. The sales revenue obtained from these products is $20,000 from Product X, $60,000 from Product Y, and $120,000 from Product Z. Should the company sell Product A immediately, or should it process the product further and sell Products X, Y, and Z?

This case illustrates a situation that occurs commonly in certain industries such as meat packing, flour milling, and petroleum production. Raw material is processed to produce two or more products. Up to a certain point in the processing (the ***split-off point***), the processing costs cannot be identified with individual products; such costs are called ***joint product costs.*** The question often arises whether the joint products produced at the split-off point should be sold or processed further and then sold. Relevant-cost analysis provides certain insights into such problems.

Exhibit 28-6 diagrams case 2 and shows an analysis of the relevant costs. The alternative of further processing has a differential cost of $25,000. That is, the company will obtain $25,000 greater gross margin if it sells Product A rather than processing it further.

What choice should be made if the selling price of Product A at split off were $80,000? In this case, further processing still has a differential cost of $5,000, so Product A should be sold. What choice should be made if the selling price of Product A were $70,000? Now the alternative of selling Product A has a differential cost of $5,000, so further processing should be undertaken. The point to emphasize in this case is that the joint costs of $60,000 are sunk costs and are irrelevant to the decision about further processing.

Case 3: The make-or-buy decision. A manufacturer of radios purchases certain parts used in producing its radios. The firm has idle capacity sufficient to manufacture these parts. The estimated cost of material, labor, and variable overhead expenses required to manufacture the parts total $100,000. No other use of the idle facilities is feasible. The cost to purchase these items from outside sources totals $90,000. Should the firm make or buy the parts?

This case illustrates a common problem for a manufacturer: should a certain part, product, or piece of equipment be purchased or made? Again, analysis of relevant

Exhibit 28-6 **Analysis of relevant costs in case 2**

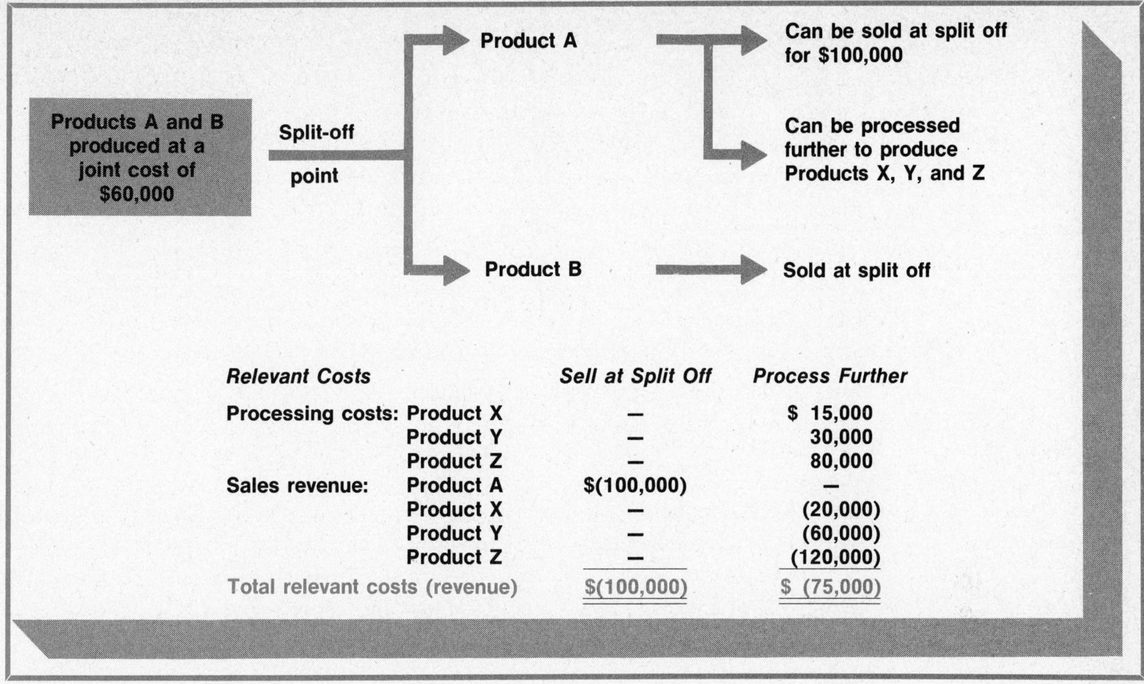

Relevant Costs		*Sell at Split Off*	*Process Further*
Processing costs:	**Product X**	—	**$ 15,000**
	Product Y	—	**30,000**
	Product Z	—	**80,000**
Sales revenue:	**Product A**	**$(100,000)**	—
	Product X	—	**(20,000)**
	Product Y	—	**(60,000)**
	Product Z	—	**(120,000)**
Total relevant costs (revenue)		$(100,000)	$ (75,000)

costs can assist in solving the problem. In case 3, the cost to purchase from outsiders is lower than the variable cost of manufacturing the parts with idle plant capacity, so the parts should be purchased rather than made. The fixed cost of the available plant capacity is a sunk cost and is irrelevant to the decision.

Of course, actual make-or-buy decisions are seldom as simple as this one. The following case illustrates the kinds of complications that can arise.

Case 4: Another make-or-buy decision. A firm currently manufacturing parts used in its main product, and its plant is operating at full capacity. The company learns that it can purchase for $110,000 certain parts that it now makes at a variable cost of $100,000. If it purchases these parts, the plant facilities that become available can be rented to another firm for $15,000. If the firm continues to make the parts, no plant facilities will be available for rental, so the opportunity to earn the rent revenue will be foregone.

Exhibit 28-7 shows the analysis of relevant costs for the make-or-buy decision. The differential cost of making the parts is $5,000. Therefore, the company should purchase the parts and rent out the plant facilities.

In this case, the rental revenue could be regarded as an ***opportunity cost*** associated with the decision to make the parts. That is, it would cost the firm $15,000 ***not*** to rent the plant capacity if it decides to make the parts itself. Using this approach to the analysis, the cost of the "make" decision is $100,000 variable cost for making the parts plus $15,000 opportunity cost for rent given up. The cost of the "buy" decision is only the $110,000 cost of the parts. Again, the differential cost of the "make" decision is $5,000.

An opportunity cost is the monetary sacrifice associated with rejecting an alternative. Treatment of such items as the rent as opportunity costs avoids the need for

Exhibit 28-7
Analysis of relevant costs in case 4

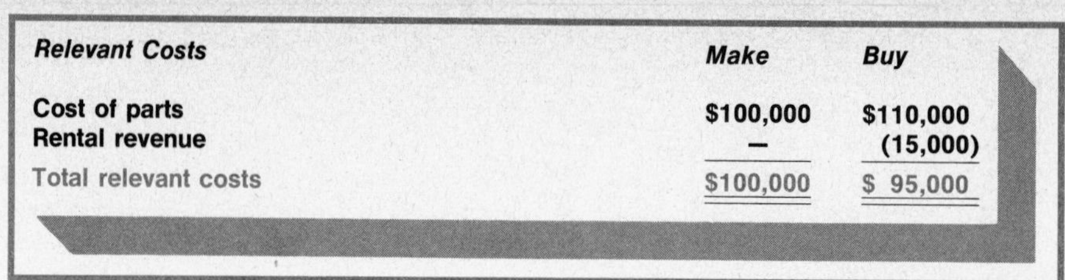

Relevant Costs	*Make*	*Buy*
Cost of parts	$100,000	$110,000
Rental revenue	—	(15,000)
Total relevant costs	$100,000	$ 95,000

"negative cost" items in the analysis. Either approach can be used, but be careful not to list the same item twice. If the "rent given up" is listed as an opportunity cost for the "make" decision, then the rental revenue should *not* be listed as a negative cost for the "buy" decision. Opportunity costs are treated like other relevant costs.

Summary

Responsibility accounting is a procedure designed to measure and evaluate performance by fixing responsibility. Responsibility accounting focuses attention on items that are subject to control by an individual assigned to manage a responsibility center. Responsibility reporting can be structured according to organizational units defined as (1) expense centers, (2) profit centers, or (3) investment centers.

Problem solving implies that alternate courses of action (or choices) exist. Relevant (pertinent) costs are a useful tool for analysis of decision-making problems. To be relevant, a cost must be (1) a future cost, and (2) a cost that differs among alternatives. Past (sunk) costs are irrelevant. All other things being equal, the best alternative is the one with the lowest relevant cost. A differential cost (equal to the difference in relevant costs) can be assigned to all other alternatives with higher relevant costs. Relevant-cost procedures provide a generalized approach to any decision-making problem involving future costs.

Questions

1. What is responsibility accounting?
2. Distinguish among expense, profit, and investment centers.
3. What is a relevant cost?
4. Does responsibility accounting attempt to distinguish between (a) sunk and future costs, (b) fixed and variable costs, or (c) controllable and uncontrollable costs?
5. Are all future costs relevant costs? Explain.
6. Why are past costs irrelevant in a decision-making situation?
7. What is an opportunity cost?

Exercises

E28-1 (Equipment replacement)
A firm is considering the replacement of equipment that cost $90,000. This equipment is 50 percent depreciated and has no salvage value. It has a

remaining expected life of four years. The new equipment would cost $100,000 and is expected to produce a savings in labor and material of $30,000 per year for the four years. Should the equipment be replaced? Explain your answer.

E28-2 (Scrap or reprocess)
The Black Company has $80,000 of obsolete inventory in its warehouse. The firm can sell this as scrap for $25,000, or it can remodel it at an additional cost of $60,000 and then sell it for $80,000.

a. Should the inventory be sold for scrap or reprocessed? Explain.
b. If the reprocessed inventory could be sold for $105,000, what course of action would you recommend?

E28-3 (Keep or replace machine)
A firm is using a machine that cost $150,000, with accumulated depreciation of $80,000 and five years of remaining life. It has a current scrap value of $20,000; at the end of the four years, its scrap value will be zero. A new machine costing $190,000 can be acquired today. This new machine has a five-year life and no resale value at the end of its useful life. Costs to operate the old and new machine are $160,000 and $120,000, respectively. Should the new machine be acquired? Explain.

E28-4 (Joint products)
The Joint-Products Company produces 15,000 gallons of Goff and 25,000 gallons of Zoff from material processed in Department 1 at a cost of $600,000. The Goff is sold without further processing for $1,200,000. The Zoff can also be sold as it comes from Department 1 for $90,000, or it can be processed further at a cost of $10 per gallon and then sold as Super Zoff for $430,000. Should the Zoff be sold at split off or processed further? Explain.

E28-5 (Buy or make)
A firm can purchase the 17,500 parts it needs in its assembly plant for $4 per part. At this time, the company manufactures this part. Cost data associated with the manufacture of the part are $1.25 per unit for direct material, $1.00 per unit for direct labor, and $0.75 per unit for variable manufacturing overhead. The plant is able to manufacture these parts without adding to its fixed overhead of $300,000. The manufacture of parts utilizes one-fourth of the capacity of the plant. If the part is purchased, the idled facilities formerly used to manufacture parts will not be used. Should the firm manufacture or purchase the parts? Explain.

E28-6 (Buy or make)
In the situation described in Exercise E28-5, suppose that the idled facilities can be used to produce $80,000 of a new product with additional costs of $57,000. With this additional information, what would your recommendation be? Explain.

Problems

P28-1 (Joint products)
The South Company produces four joint products at a cost of $3,000,000. The four products can be sold at split off to produce the following sales revenues: Product L $1,400,000; Product M $1,900,000; Product N $2,000,000; Product O $2,500,000. Any of these products can be processed further. The

costs of further processing are $200,000 for Product L; $800,000 for Product M; $500,000 for Product N; and $160,000 for Product O. After further processing, the products can be sold to produce the following revenues: Product L $1,660,000; Product M $2,350,000; Product N $2,200,000; Product O $2,900,000.

Required: Which products should be sold at split off, and which products should be processed further? Explain.

P28-2 (Keep or replace)

Exhibit 28-8 shows the Equipment and Accumulated Depreciation accounts of the Figures Company as they appear on January 1, 19_7. A machine salesperson calls on the Figures Company and explains that a new machine is available to replace the company's present equipment. The new machine would reduce operating costs for the company by $45,000 per year. The new machine costs $175,000, and has no scrap value at the end of its five-year life.

Required:

a. Assuming that the old equipment is scrapped with no disposal value today, what entry would the accountant make to record the disposal of the asset on January 1, 19_7? Why is such a possibility discouraging to management?

b. If the firm's objective is to maximize income over the long run, should the new asset be purchased? Explain.

c. If the management wants to maximize income during 19_7, should the new asset be purchased? Explain.

P28-3 (Continue to operate or close down)

A team of management consultants was retained to determine for management whether a plant should be shut down for a period of time while new markets are being developed for a very profitable new product. The consultants obtained the following data from management about the product currently produced: plant capacity is 125,000 units; total fixed cost when plant is operating at capacity, $350,000; total fixed cost when plant is shut down, $85,000; variable cost per unit, $6; selling price per unit, $8.

Required:

a. What profit or loss is the plant currently making?

b. If you were a member of the consultation team, what would you recommend? (Financial implications are the major consideration.)

P28-4 (Joint products)

The Space Company produces products Sund and Mond at a total cost of $200,000, which can be allocated evenly between the two products. Sund

Exhibit 28-8
Ledger accounts for Problem P28-2

Equipment

Jan. 1, 19_3	**500,000**		

Accumulated Depreciation: Equipment

		Dec. 31, 19_3	**100,000**
		Dec. 31, 19_4	**100,000**
		Dec. 31, 19_5	**100,000**
		Dec. 31, 19_6	**100,000**

and Mond can be sold at split off for $115,000 and $125,000, respectively. Sund can be further processed at a cost of $100,000 and then sold for $180,000. Further processing of Mond at a cost of $70,000 can produce a product that can be sold for $200,000.

Required:

a. If Sund and Mond are sold at split off, what profit results?
b. If Sund and Mond are processed further and then sold, what profit results?
c. Should Sund be sold at split off or processed further?
d. Should Mond be sold at split off or processed further?
e. If your recommendations in parts c and d are both followed, what profit results?

P28-5 (Keep or replace)

A company is trying to decide whether to keep a machine it owns or to replace it with another. The old machine cost the company $50,000 and is 50 percent depreciated. The cash cost of operating the old machine for the next five years is estimated to be $25,000 a year. At the end of the five years, the old machine has no salvage value. A salesman of machinery says that he has a machine that costs $60,000 and has operating costs of $15,000 per year. The machine has an estimated life of five years. The salesman will allow the company $5,000 trade-in on the old machine. Using relevant cost approach, should the company keep the old machine or trade it in for the new one?

P28-6 (Buy or make)

A company is faced with a decision to make or buy a machine. The following information is available:

	Cost of manufacturing the machine
Direct materials	$ 10,000
Direct labor	20,000
Variable overhead	30,000
Fixed expenses that can be identified with the machine and which can be avoided if the machine is not produced	10,000
Joint fixed overhead that can be allocated to the machine (depreciation, insurance, etc.)	30,000
Total estimated cost of manufacturing machine	$100,000

Required: The machine can be purchased for $75,000. Should the machine be purchased or manufactured?

29 Long-range planning: capital budgeting

Businesses constantly face the problem of deciding how to utilize available financial resources. Tomorrow's profits depend to a great extent upon today's investment decisions. Management's investment decisions include answers to such questions as:

Should a new plant be constructed?

Should major improvements in facilities be undertaken?

Should machinery be replaced?

Should bonds be refunded?

The comprehensive budget discussed in Chapter 22 reflects chiefly the results of short-term planning. In contrast, capital investments generally involve long-range projections. Capital-expenditure decisions are critical business decisions—especially in this age of rapid technological change, shorter product life-cycles, and increased competition. Capital-expenditure decisions involve large dollar amounts and long-term commitments.

In the past, capital-investment decisions often were made by intuition and guesswork. Today, we can use techniques that provide a rational approach to long-range planning. This chapter explores several of these dynamic techniques for analyzing and appraising capital expenditures.

Capital budgeting

Capital budgeting is a formal process of long-term planning for relatively large, permanent acquisitions and commitments of a firm's economic resources. Top management has ultimate responsibility for capital-budgeting decisions. Once made and implemented, capital-budgeting decisions often affect the organization for years.

In evaluating capital-budgeting projects, management must consider two major facts:

1. the cost of the investment; and
2. the potential net increase in cash inflows (or reduction in cash outflows) resulting from the proposed investment.

In this chapter we examine three approaches to capital-budgeting decisions:

1. the discounted-cash-flow method, using a net present-value approach;
2. the yield-on-investment approach (also a discounted-cash-flow method); and
3. the payback method.

PRESENT-VALUE CONCEPTS

Money has a time value. That is to say, $1,000 available in cash today is worth more to the firm than a promise of $1,000 in cash available a year from now.

To illustrate this concept, suppose that the firm has a choice of two assets: $1,000 in cash, or a non-interest-bearing note for $1,000 due in one year. If the firm gets $1,000 cash now, it can invest that cash in its own operations or in some other form of investment. During the year, the firm will earn income from its investment. Suppose that the firm can earn 6 percent on the $1,000 during the year. At the end of the year, the $1,000 will have grown to $1,060. Clearly, the cash will then have a greater value than the note, which can only bring in $1,000 (its face value) at its maturity date.

The present-value concept reverses this process of interest computation. The present value of the note should be computed as the amount that will grow to $1,000 in a year, which is about $943. Therefore, the present value of the cash is $1,000 and that of the note is $943. If a longer time period is involved, compound interest computations should be used, because the company would be able to reinvest the money that it earns on the investments. Tables are available to determine the present value of dollars at various compound rates (called ***discounting rates***) over different periods of time. Exhibit 29-1 is an excerpt from a Present Value of $1 Table. This table shows the amounts that must be deposited now at various rates of interest to amount to $1 at the end of a specified number of periods. The appendix to this chapter gives information about the procedures by which such tables are compiled.

Exhibit 29-1
Present value of $1 at various compound rates

	Compound Rate			
Periods	**4%**	**6%**	**8%**	**10%**
1	0.962	0.943	0.926	0.909
2	0.925	0.890	0.857	0.826
3	0.889	0.840	0.794	0.751
4	0.855	0.792	0.735	0.683
5	0.822	0.747	0.681	0.621

NOTE: Let P be the present value, n be the number of periods, and r be the compound rate. Then the entries in the table are obtained by using the formula

$$P = \frac{1}{(1 + r)^n}$$

Exhibit 29-2
Increase in value of a future cash inflow over time

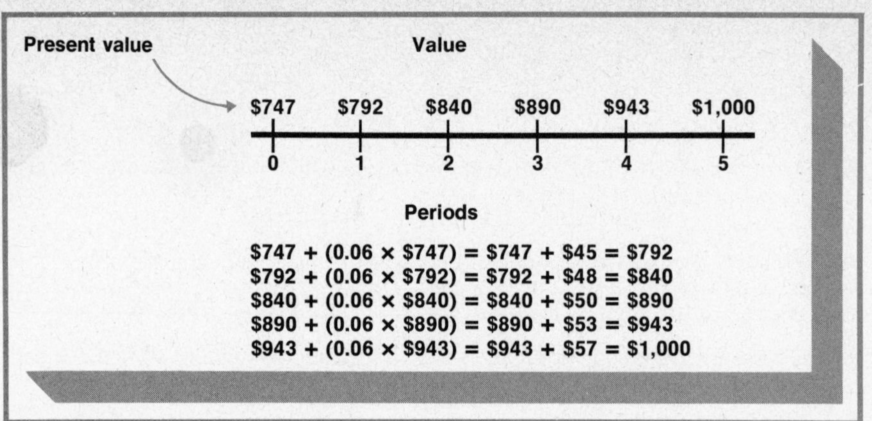

To illustrate the use of this table, suppose that we wish to compute the present value of $1,000 to be received five years in the future, assuming a compound rate of 6 percent. From the table, we find that $1.00 under those conditions has a present value of $0.747. Therefore, $1,000 has a present value of $1,000 × 0.747 = $747. Exhibit 29-2 illustrates this example graphically, showing how the value of the future cash inflow increases over the five years to reach the stated value of $1,000 at maturity.[1]

Another important present-value concept is that of the present value of an annuity. Briefly, an ***annuity*** is a series of equal amounts to be received (or paid) at equal intervals. Exhibit 29-3 is a selection from a Present Value of Annuity of $1 Table. This table shows the amounts that must be deposited now at a specified rate of interest to permit withdrawals of $1 at periodic intervals for various periods. As an illustration, we find the present value of an annuity of $1,000 for five years at 6 percent. Suppose that someone has promised to pay you $1,000 at the end of each of the next five years, and you wish to determine the present value of this promise. The table shows that the present value of a five-year stream of $1 payments at 6 percent is $4.212. Therefore, the present value of the $1,000 annuity is 1,000 times as great, or $4,212. Exhibit 29-4 illustrates this stream of payments and the increasing value over the life of the annuity. Note that the value of each payment increases to $1,000 at the time it is received as $1,000 cash. Then, the value continues to increase because you have the cash available for investment. Therefore, the total value of the annuity is considerably more than $5,000 by the end of the five years.

Discounted-cash-flow method

The discounted-cash-flow method (net-present-value approach) is a tool used in evaluating investment decisions. When this method is used, expected future cash

1. The present value (discounted amount) sometimes is used in the initial recording principle as the exchange price (acquisition cost) for a money claim. In *APB Statement No. 4,* the Accounting Principles Board says that "cash, accounts receivable, and other short-term money claims are usually measured at their face amount. A long-term non-interest-bearing note receivable is measured at its discounted amount" (para. 181 M-1A). *APB Opinion No. 21* (October 1971) amends this principle to indicate that the discounted amount should be used as the exchange price of any money claim bearing an interest rate clearly below a reasonable rate.

Exhibit 29-3
Present value of annuity of $1 at various compound rates

Periods	Compound Rate 6%	8%	10%
1	0.943	0.926	0.909
2	1.833	1.783	1.736
3	2.673	2.577	2.487
4	3.465	3.312	3.170
5	4.212	3.993	3.791

NOTE: Let P be the present value, n be the number of periods, and i be the compound rate. Then the entries in the table are obtained by using the formula

$$P = \frac{1 - \frac{1}{(1 + i)^n}}{i}$$

inflows and outflows associated with the investment are discounted to the present time, using a minimum discounting rate acceptable to management. The *net present value* is the difference between the present value of the cost of the investment and the present value of the cash inflow expected from the investment. If the net present value is positive, the investment is acceptable. If the net present value is negative, the investment is undesirable.

Net present value = Present value of net cash inflows expected − Present value of cost of the investment

Decision rule:
a. All projects with positive or zero net present value are acceptable.
b. All projects with negative net present value are rejected.

Case 1. Management is considering the purchase of a new machine for $11,000. The machine has an expected life of five years and a scrap value of $1,000 at the end of its life. Management assumes a minimum desired rate of return of 10 percent on the investment. The new machine will create cost savings of $4,000 per year for the next five years; the savings are realized at the end of each year. (Ignore income-tax implications.)

Exhibit 29-4 **Increase in value of annuity over time**

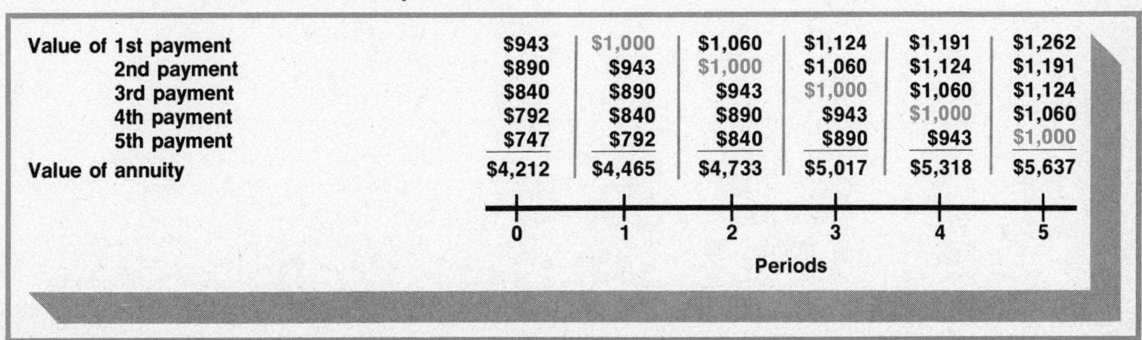

	0	1	2	3	4	5
Value of 1st payment	$943	$1,000	$1,060	$1,124	$1,191	$1,262
2nd payment	$890	$943	$1,000	$1,060	$1,124	$1,191
3rd payment	$840	$890	$943	$1,000	$1,060	$1,124
4th payment	$792	$840	$890	$943	$1,000	$1,060
5th payment	$747	$792	$840	$890	$943	$1,000
Value of annuity	$4,212	$4,465	$4,733	$5,017	$5,318	$5,637

Periods

Exhibit 29-5 **Work sheet for solution to case 1**

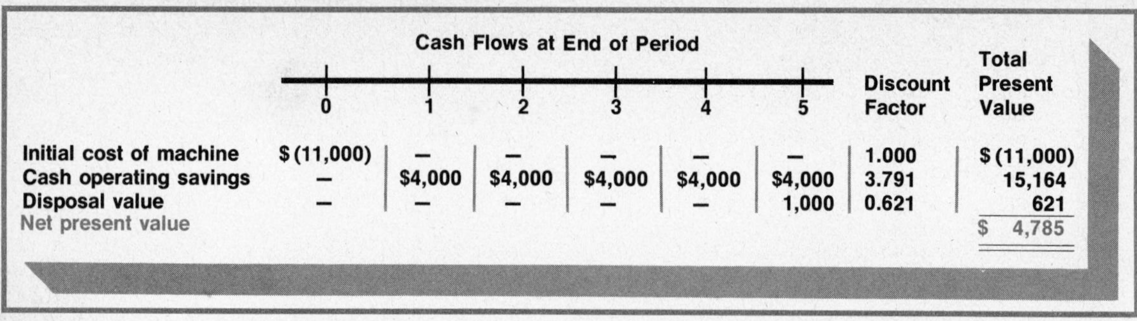

	Cash Flows at End of Period							
	0	1	2	3	4	5	Discount Factor	Total Present Value
Initial cost of machine	$(11,000)	—	—	—	—	—	1.000	$(11,000)
Cash operating savings	—	$4,000	$4,000	$4,000	$4,000	$4,000	3.791	15,164
Disposal value	—	—	—	—	—	1,000	0.621	621
Net present value								$ 4,785

NOTE: The initial cash outflow for purchase of the machine is not discounted, because it is made at the beginning of the first period (present time). The cash inflows due to operating savings are discounted as a $4,000 annuity for five years at 10 percent discount rate (factor from Exhibit 29-3). The disposal value is discounted as a sum of $1,000 to be received 5 years in the future, at 10 percent discount rate (factor from Exhibit 29-1).

Exhibit 29-5 shows a work sheet used to apply the discounted-cashflow method to this decision. The use of the work sheet involves the following steps.

1. Dollar ***amounts*** of cash inflows and outflows are recorded in the columns for the appropriate periods.
   a. The ***direction*** of each flow is indicated. Cash outflows are recorded as negative amounts; cash inflows or cash savings are shown as positive amounts.
   b. The ***timing*** of each flow is indicated by recording it in the appropriate period.
2. Present-value discounting factors are determined from present-value tables and entered in the appropriate column. (Note that the cash operating savings can be treated as an annuity.)
3. Present values of each item are computed and entered in the last column. These values are totalled to determine the net present value of the investment.

Because the net present value of the investment in case 1 is positive, the investment in the new machine is considered desirable. The underlying concept for this method is the idea that the company can earn more by buying the machine than it could by putting the same amount of cash into some other investment that earns a 10 percent rate of return. The effect of the decision rule is to reject any proposed investment that offers less than a 10 percent rate of return.

In the preceding solution for case 1, we have ignored income-tax impacts on the decision-making process. However, income taxes are an important aspect of business life, and their impact on such decisions often is very significant. They must be considered in most capital-budgeting decisions. Therefore, let us reflect for a moment on the income-tax implications of investment decisions.

The payment of income taxes represents a cash outflow; a tax savings represents a cash inflow. If we assume a 48 percent income-tax rate, each dollar of cash revenue equals only $0.52 net (after-tax) cash inflow. Each dollar of cash expense equals only $0.52 net (after-tax) cash outflow. Uncle Sam is a partner in most businesses, sharing in all cash expense and revenue.

In other words,

1. Net cash outflow = Cash expenses × (1 − Income-tax rate);
2. Net cash inflow = Cash revenues × (1 − Income-tax rate);
3. Cash savings on depreciation = Depreciation expenses × Income tax rate.

The meaning of the third point becomes clear in the solution to the next case.

Case 2. The company considering purchase of the machine described in case 1 must pay income tax at a rate of 40 percent of its net income. Taking this fact into consideration, should the company still purchase the machine?

Acquisition of the machine is expected to result in operating savings of $4,000 per year over the five-year life of the machine. These savings would increase taxable income, resulting in a higher tax. The taxable income increases by $4,000 per year as a result of these savings, so 40 percent of this amount (or $1,600 per year) must be paid out in increased income taxes. Therefore, the net cash inflow (after taxes) as a result of the operating savings is only $2,400 per year.

On the other hand, the cost of the machine will be recognized as depreciation expense allocated over the life of the machine. This expense reduces the taxable income and therefore the income tax for each year, resulting in a cash savings. (Recall that depreciation expense results from an adjusting entry; it involves no actual cash outflow at the time the expense is recognized.) If the machine is depreciated over five years on a straight-line basis, depreciation expense of $2,000 per year will be subtracted from the taxable income. Income taxes will be reduced by 40 percent of this amount, or $800 per year.

The $11,000 cash outflow to purchase the machine does not affect income taxes, because this cost is not reported as an expense at the time of the purchase. Similarly, the $1,000 salvage value of the machine has no income-tax impact. After depreciation of $10,000 over the five years, the machine has a book value at the end of its life of $1,000. If it is sold for that amount, there is no gain or loss on the disposal transaction. Therefore, the $1,000 cash inflow resulting from the disposal is not reported as income, and taxes are unaffected.

Exhibit 29-6 shows a work sheet for the decision using the discounted-cash-flow method, this time taking income-tax implications into account. The net present value of the investment project is positive, so the investment in the machine is acceptable. However, note that the net present value of the investment is considerably smaller (the investment less attractive) than it seemed when income taxes were ignored.

Exhibit 29-6 Work sheet for solution to case 2, including income-tax implications

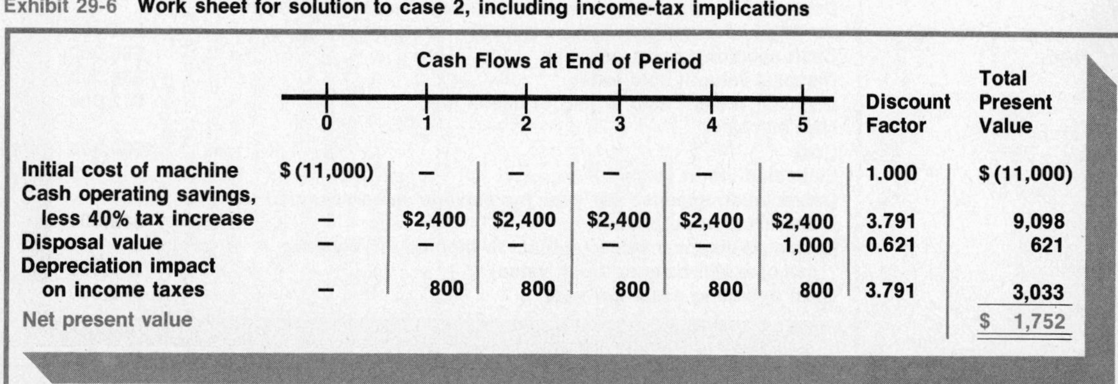

	Cash Flows at End of Period							
	0	1	2	3	4	5	Discount Factor	Total Present Value
Initial cost of machine	$(11,000)	–	–	–	–	–	1.000	$(11,000)
Cash operating savings, less 40% tax increase	–	$2,400	$2,400	$2,400	$2,400	$2,400	3.791	9,098
Disposal value	–	–	–	–	–	1,000	0.621	621
Depreciation impact on income taxes	–	800	800	800	800	800	3.791	3,033
Net present value								$ 1,752

NOTE: Discount factors from Exhibits 29-1 and 29-3, assuming discounting rate of 10 percent.

finds the discounting rate that makes the present value of the expected cash inflow equal to the present value of the cash outflows required by the investment. This rate is the expected rate of return (yield) on the investment project. The discounting rate can be determined through the use of tables and a trial-and-error approach. With this approach, the decision rule takes the following form: If the computed rate of return on the investment exceeds a minimum acceptable rate imposed by management, the investment is considered acceptable.

Case 4. A firm has an opportunity to purchase a machine for $21,060. The machine has an expected five-year life, no scrap value, and will bring a $5,000 cash savings each year for five years. The firm can borrow the money needed to buy the machine at 8 percent interest from its bank. Therefore, management does not wish to buy the machine unless it expects at least an 8 percent rate of return on the investment. (Ignore income-tax implications in the solution.)

Using the yield-on-investment method, the problem can be solved by the following procedure.

1. Determine the expected cash savings from the investment: $5,000 per year for five years.
2. Determine the cash outflow for the initial cost of the investment: $21,060.
3. We wish to find the discount factor (call it F) that will discount the expected cash savings to a present value equal to the initial cash outflow.

   $$\$5{,}000 \times F = \$21{,}060$$
   $$F = 4.212$$

4. We wish to find the discounting rate (X percent) that gives a discount factor of 4.212 for a five-year annuity. (This is the discounting rate for which an annuity of $5,000 for five years has a present value of $21,060.)
5. Refer to the Present Value of Annuity Table (Exhibit 29-3) to find the discounting rate that, at the 5-period row, equals or approximates[2] the computed F factor. The discount factor for a 6 percent rate is 4.212 in the 5-period row. Therefore, the discounting rate X is equal to 6 percent.
6. ***Decision:*** The computed rate of return of 6 percent on the investment is less than the minimum acceptable rate of 8 percent. The investment is rejected.

2. If the computed factor falls between two rates in the table, the approximate rate can be determined by interpolation. For example, suppose that a value of 3.850 is computed for F on a five-year annuity. The table shows that the discount factor at 10 percent is 3.791, and the factor at 8 percent is 3.993. The computed factor is between these two factors in the table, so the computed discounting rate is between 10 percent and 8 percent. The rate X can be estimated by setting up a proportion as follows:

$$\frac{10 - X}{10 - 8} = \frac{3.791 - 3.850}{3.791 - 3.993}$$

$$10 - X = 2 \times (-0.059/-0.202) = 2 \times 0.292 = 0.584$$

$$X = 10 - 0.584 = 9.416.$$

Therefore, the computed discounting rate is about 9.4 percent. This interpolation is based upon the approximation that the discount factor is a straight-line function of the discounting rate between the two values given in the table.

As a general rule, the cost of money may be used as the minimum acceptable discounting rate. The firm must pay 8 percent interest if it borrows money to buy the machine. Therefore, an investment must earn at least 8 percent if the firm is to repay the loan with cash flows from the investment as they occur.

The payback-period method

The payback-period approach to capital-budgeting decisions is often used to measure the value of an investment and to evaluate alternative investments. The ***payback period*** is the time required for the cash inflow from an investment to accumulate to equal the original cash outlay required for the investment. Cash flows are not discounted in this approach.

Case 5. Management is considering two possible investments. A $20,000 investment in Machine A will result in an annual cash savings of $5,000 per year during the six-year life of the machine. A $15,000 investment in Machine B will result in cash savings of $3,000 per year during the ten-year life of the machine. Management wishes to choose the investment with the shortest payback period.

The payback period is calculated as follows.[3]

$$\text{Payback period} = \frac{\text{Initial investment}}{\text{Annual cash savings}}$$

$$\text{Payback period (Machine A)} = \frac{\$20{,}000}{\$5{,}000} = 4 \text{ years}$$

$$\text{Payback period (Machine B)} = \frac{\$15{,}000}{\$3{,}000} = 5 \text{ years}$$

The investment in Machine A has the shorter payback period, and is therefore the more attractive investment because it minimizes the risk in the investment.

If the inflow of cash savings is not the same from year to year, the payoff period is calculated by adding the cash proceeds in successive years until the total equals the original outlay. For example, suppose that a cash investment of $20,000 is expected to produce cash savings of $15,000 in the first year, $10,000 in the second year, $5,000 in the third year, and $4,000 in the fourth year. At the end of the second year, the accumulated cash savings are $25,000—more than the initial investment. The payback period is completed halfway through the second year, when $5,000 in cash savings for the second year are added to the $15,000 savings of the first year. Therefore, the payback period is 1.5 years.

When the payback-period method is used, management chooses the investment

3. Taking income-tax implications into account, the payback-period formula can be expressed as follows for equal annual cash inflows:

$$\text{Payback period} = \frac{\text{Net investment}}{\text{Annual operating saving} - \text{Tax increase} + \text{Depreciation impact}}$$

that provides the quickest payoff (regardless of which investment may give the highest rate of return over the long run). In using this method, management often sets a maximum payback period for acceptable investments. Investments that exceed the maximum payback period are rejected. Research studies have shown that industrial firms often use maximum payback periods of two to five years.

Using this evaluation method, management places full reliance upon the speed of turnover of its investment money. The method has serious drawbacks. It tells nothing of the profitability of the investment,[4] it merely tells how long it takes to recover the initial cash investment. Further the payback method does not take into consideration cash inflows earned after the payoff date. Also, it fails to consider the time value of money.

The payback-period method generally is unreliable as a procedure for evaluating capital investments. Nevertheless, it is used rather widely in business.

Cost of capital

The minimum acceptable rate used in capital-budgeting analysis can be estimated in terms of the cost of capital. Because funds to finance capital may be acquired in a variety of ways (by borrowing from a bank; issuing additional bonds, preferred stock, or common stock; and so on), it is important to have a working definition of the cost of capital. The ***cost of capital*** is a weighted average of the costs of each type of capital.

Case 6. Company A has 1,000,000 shares of common stock outstanding. The stock has a current market value of $100 per share; the company pays an annual dividend of $10 per share. The company also has $25,000,000 of outstanding bonds payable, with a 6 percent effective yield. The company pays income taxes at a 46 percent rate. What is the cost of capital for Company A?

Exhibit 29-10 shows the computation of the average cost of capital for Company A. Note that the income-tax rate affects the cost of the bond capital. The company pays 6 percent interest on the bonds, but the interest expense is deducted from taxable income, so income tax expense is reduced by 46 percent of the interest expense. The cost of the bond capital, then, is 6 percent less ($0.46 \times 6 = 2.8$) percent, or 3.2 percent.

The market value of stock is used in the computation because this is the approximate price that the company could obtain for new shares that it might issue to raise capital. The 10 percent cost of the equity capital is a good measure of the cost of obtaining further capital from owners.

4. The ***payback reciprocal*** can be used as a rough approximation of yield on an investment.

$$\text{Payback reciprocal} = \frac{1}{\text{Payback period}}$$

In case 5, the investment in Machine A has a payback period of 4 years; the payback reciprocal is 1/4. This represents an approximate yield of 25 percent on the investment over the first four years.

Source of Capital	Amount	Proportion of Total Capital (*a*)	Cost (*b*)	Weighted Cost (*a* × *b*)
Common stock	$100,000,000	0.80	0.10	0.08
Bonds	25,000,000	0.20	0.032	0.0064
Total	$125,000,000			
Average cost of capital				0.0864

Exhibit 29-10
Computation of cost of capital for Company A (case 6)

Overall, the cost of capital for Company A is about 8.64 percent. If the company is to make a return on its investments that exceeds the cost of capital, it must earn a higher rate of return than this on its investments of its assets.

Sensitivity analysis

In evaluating the preceding cases of investment decisions, we have arrived at solutions that have the appearance of great precision and accuracy. In the real business world, evaluations seldom achieve such precision. In case 1, we assumed that cash operating savings would be $4,000 per year for five years. In a real business decision, the savings would be known only as an approximate or estimated amount. Suppose that the actual cash savings proved to be $1,000 per year less than had been estimated. What would be the effect upon the investment decision?

If you rework the solution for case 1 using cash savings of $3,000 per year (ignoring taxes), you will find that the net present value of the investment is $1,351 instead of $4,785—the value is still positive, so the investment is still acceptable, but considerably less favorable than before (Exhibit 29-11).

How far can the cash savings drop below the estimated $4,000 per year before the investment ceases to be acceptable? The point at which the investment ceases to be favorable is the point at which the present value of cash outflow equals the present value of cash inflows. The present value of the outflow is $11,000. The present value of the inflows is $621 for the disposal value plus 3.791 times the annual cash savings. Therefore, letting X be the annual cash savings at which the investment becomes unfavorable, we have

$$\$11,000 = \$621 + (3.791 \times X)$$

$$X = \frac{\$11,000 - \$621}{3.791} = \$2,738 \text{ (rounded)}$$

If the cash operating savings drop below $2,738 per year (instead of the $4,000 per year estimated), this investment will become unacceptable by the rate-of-return criterion management has set.

This computation is a simple example of sensitivity analysis. It gives some idea of how sensitive the evaluation of the investment will be to the actual cash operating savings obtained. We find that the investment will have the required rate of return,

Exhibit 29-11 **Revised solution for case 1 with cash savings of $3,000 per year**

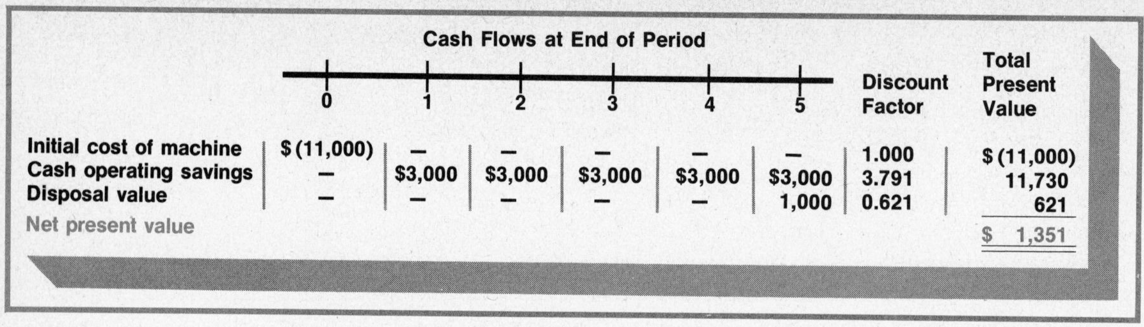

	Cash Flows at End of Period 0	1	2	3	4	5	Discount Factor	Total Present Value
Initial cost of machine	$(11,000)	—	—	—	—	—	1.000	$(11,000)
Cash operating savings	—	$3,000	$3,000	$3,000	$3,000	$3,000	3.791	11,730
Disposal value	—	—	—	—	—	1,000	0.621	621
Net present value								$ 1,351

even if cash operating savings are almost as much as one-third less than the expected savings. More sophisticated techniques of sensitivity analysis are available to give more versatile measures of the reliability of the evaluations.

Sensitivity analysis offers management additional information about capital-budgeting projects. With this tool, management can evaluate proposed projects with varying assumptions about the critical data that enter into the computations. Managerial accountants today are giving increased attention to the use of sensitivity analysis in cash-budgeting problems and elsewhere.

Uncertainty in capital-budgeting analysis

In capital-budgeting analysis, the decision maker often must deal with events that are subject to uncertainty. As we have just seen, the analysis requires assumptions about the amounts of future cash inflows and outflows; the actual amounts may prove to be different from the estimated amounts. Among other uncertainties that can enter into the analysis are such items as the expected life of the asset being considered for acquisition, the salvage value of the asset, and income-tax rates.

Various approaches are currently available to deal with problems of uncertainty. In our previous solutions to the cases in this chapter, we have treated the estimated amounts as if they were certain. If we recognize the uncertainty of the estimates, then we must modify our approach. We might begin to think in terms of an ***expected value*** for a future event, where the expected value is derived from a set of estimates about the probability of various possible outcomes.

Case 7. Company B is evaluating an investment that requires an immediate expenditure of $10,000. Management regards it as certain that the company will earn $20,000 on the investment, but uncertainty exists about when the earnings will be realized. In considering the timing of the receipt of revenue from the investment project, management estimates that there is a 50 percent probability that the $20,000 will be received three years after the initial investment. There is a 30 percent chance that the revenue will be received four years after the investment, and a 20 percent chance that it will not be received until five years after the investment. Management wants to know whether the expected rate of return on this investment exceeds its minimum acceptable rate of 10 percent.

Exhibit 29-12 shows the computation of the expected time of receipt of the revenue. Each of the possible times is multiplied by the probability of that time being the actual time; these values are then summed to give the expected time of 3.7 years. (In effect, the expected time is a weighted average of the possible times, where each possible time is weighted by the probability that the actual time will have this value.)

Now we can treat the computed expected time as the best estimate of the time of receipt of revenue. In other words, we return to our practice of treating this estimate as if it were a certainty. Exhibit 29-13 shows the computation of the net present value of the investment, assuming that the cash inflow will be received 3.7 years after the cash outflow. Because the net present value is positive, the investment would be considered favorable. However, it would be wise to use sensitivity analysis to find out how great the risk may be of making less than 10 percent on the investment if one of the other possible times proves to be the actual time.

The computed expected time is actually the value that would be expected as the average time if this investment could be repeated a great many times, and if the various possible receipt times actually occurred with the distributions that management has predicted. In other words, if this same investment could be repeated many times, management could expect to come out ahead on the average. However, in most cases, an investment will be made only once. Therefore, it is important to know how serious the risk of a loss may be on the single investment. That is why the use of the expected time should be supplemented by sensitivity analysis.

Conditions of uncertainty exist in many business decisions. Probability concepts can be useful in finding solutions to most problems involving uncertainty. The following case demonstrates the use of probability concepts in budgeting problems.

Case 8. A grocer wants to decide how much lettuce to order for tomorrow. Any lettuce ordered but unsold will have to be discarded with no salvage value. The grocer assumes that he suffers no loss in future sales if he runs out of lettuce, so that some customers are unable to get the lettuce they want. The grocer buys lettuce for $10 per crate and sells it for $15 per crate. Over the past 100 days, the grocer has kept records of the amount of lettuce sold (plus any requests for lettuce that he was

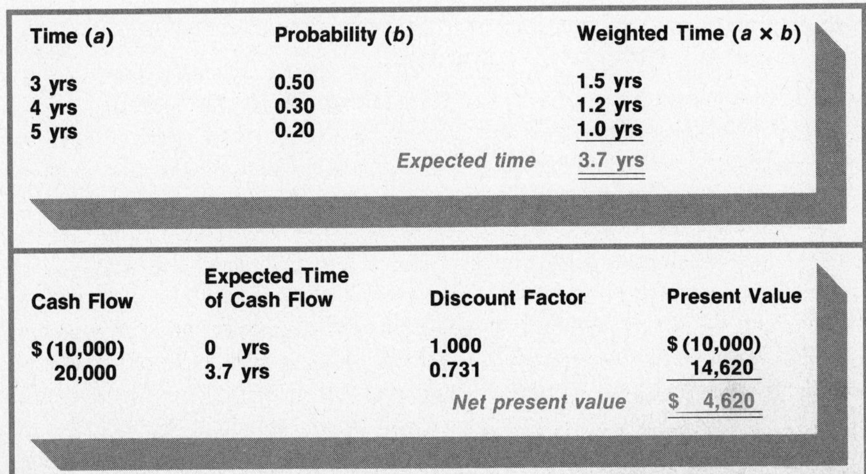

Exhibit 29-12
Computation of expected time of receipt for case 7

Time (*a*)	Probability (*b*)	Weighted Time (*a* × *b*)
3 yrs	0.50	1.5 yrs
4 yrs	0.30	1.2 yrs
5 yrs	0.20	1.0 yrs
	Expected time	3.7 yrs

Exhibit 29-13
Computation of net present value of investment for case 7

Cash Flow	Expected Time of Cash Flow	Discount Factor	Present Value
$ (10,000)	0 yrs	1.000	$ (10,000)
20,000	3.7 yrs	0.731	14,620
		Net present value	$ 4,620

Exhibit 29-14
Past demand for lettuce in case 8

Demand for lettuce (*crates per day*)	Number of days when this demand level occurred	Probability of this event
1	30	0.30 (30/100)
2	40	0.40 (40/100)
3	20	0.20 (20/100)
4	10	0.10 (10/100)
	100	1.00

unable to fill). Exhibit 29-14 shows the number of days on which each level of demand was experienced, and the probability values that the grocer computes from these records. The grocer wants to maximize his probable profit for the day. How many crates of lettuce should he order?

The analysis of this problem involves four possible levels of demand for lettuce and four possible actions by the grocer (ordering 1, 2, 3, or 4 crates of lettuce), so there are sixteen possible actual events (representing each of the possible combinations of a demand level with an order level). To determine the optimum action for the grocer, a table is set up as shown in Exhibit 29-15. To interpret this table, you will need to understand several concepts of probability analysis.

Conditional value is the profit or loss that results from a specific actual event. For example, if the grocer orders four crates of lettuce (at a cost of $40) and demand is only one crate (sales of $15), the grocer has a loss of $25 for the day. The conditional value of this combination of action and demand level is $(25). In Exhibit 29-15, the conditional value (CV) is shown for each of the sixteen possible combinations of action and demand level.

Expected value is the conditional value of an event weighted by the probability that the event will occur. In our illustration, the grocer was able to compute a conditional value for each possible event. From historical records, he was able to determine the probability of each possible demand level. The table shows the computation of an expected value (EV) for each of the possible courses of action. The computation in each action column is similar to that used in Exhibit 29-12. For example, suppose that the grocer orders one crate of lettuce. The first action column shows the conditional value of profit expected for this action at each possible level of demand. Multiplying each conditional value by the probability of that demand level occurring gives the weighted values listed in the EV column. The sum of these weighted values is the expected value of profit for that course of action. (Note that the probabilities sum to 1.00 for each of the action columns.) If the grocer orders one crate of lettuce, his expected profit for the day is $5.00.

The *optimum act* is that act that gives the expected value meeting the decision criterion. In this case, the grocer wants to choose the act that produces the greatest expected profit, so the optimum act is the order of two crates of lettuce, with an expected profit of $5.50. If the grocer performs this optimum act each day (so long as the distribution of demand levels remains the same), he will average $5.50 profit per day over the long run. Ordering four crates of lettuce would offer the chance of making a profit of $20 on those rare days when demand was that high, but over the long run he would average a loss of $8.50 per day if he always ordered four crates. Unless the grocer has some way of predicting more exactly what the next day's demand will be (for example, noting that Saturday is usually a day of high demand), he will do best in the long run by always performing the optimum act.

To summarize, the following procedure is used for dealing with problems of uncertainty.

1. Prepare a conditional value (payoff) listing for each combination of act and event.
2. Assign probabilities to each event.
3. Compute the expected monetary value for each action (multiply each conditional value by the probability of the corresponding event; then sum the weighted values for the action over all possible events).
4. Choose the action whose expected value best meets the decision criterion (usually the maximum expected monetary value).

Summary

Chapter 29 deals primarily with long-range planning, especially as related to project evaluation and decision making in capital budgeting. Two major factors are considered in evaluating capital-budgeting projects:

1. the cost of the investment, and
2. the potential net increase in cash inflow (or reduction in cash outflow) resulting from the proposed investment.

The chapter discusses three approaches to capital-budgeting decisions:

1. the discounted-cash-flow method using a net-present-value approach;
2. the discounted-cash-flow method using a yield-on-investment approach;
3. the payback-period method.

The chapter concludes with a discussion of sensitivity analysis and of procedures for dealing with uncertainty in budgeting decisions.

Exhibit 29-15 **Computation of expected value for each possible action in case 8**

EVENTS Possible Demand *(crates/day)*	**PROBABILITY** *(a)*	**POSSIBLE ACTIONS** *(crates of lettuce ordered)* 1		2		3		4	
		CV *(b)*	**EV** *(a × b)*	**CV** *(c)*	**EV** *(a × c)*	**CV** *(d)*	**EV** *(a × d)*	**CV** *(e)*	**EV** *(a × e)*
1	0.30	$5	$1.50	$(5)	$(1.50)	$(15)	$(4.50)	$(25)	$(7.50)
2	0.40	5	2.00	10	4.00	0	0.00	10	(4.00)
3	0.20	5	1.00	10	2.00	15	3.00	5	1.00
4	0.10	5	0.50	10	1.00	15	1.50	20	2.00
Expected monetary value			$5.00		$ 5.50		$ 0.00		$(8.50)

The appendix to this chapter discusses present-value concepts. The student should be familiar with these valuation concepts because they are relevant to capital budgeting.

Appendix

PRESENT-VALUE COMPUTATIONS

Exhibit 29-1 shows the ***present value of $1*** to be received at the end of a certain number of time periods, discounted at a certain rate. The values in the table are computed from the formula given in the footnote to the table. For example, at a compound discounting rate of 4 percent ($r = 0.04$), the present value of $1 received at the end of one period ($n = 1$) is

$$P = \frac{1}{(1 + r)^n} = \frac{\$1.00}{1.04} = \$0.962$$

The present value of $1 received at the end of two periods ($n = 2$) is

$$P = \frac{\$1.00}{(1.04)^2} = \frac{\$1.00}{1.08} = \$0.925$$

Exhibit 29-2 illustrates another way of proving the validity of the values given in the table. This example uses a discounting rate of 6 percent and shows that an amount of $747 earning 6 percent interest will grow to $1,000 over five periods. Therefore, the present value of $1,000 to be received five periods from now (at 6 percent discounting rate) is $747.

The formula can be used to compute values not shown in the table, for any discounting rate or number of periods.

The ***present value of an annuity*** is the amount which, if invested at compound interest, would provide for the withdrawal of a given number of cash amounts at equal intervals of time. For example, suppose that you deposited $4,212 today in a savings account paying 6 percent interest. At the end of each year after the deposit, you withdraw $1,000 from the account. Over the life of the account, interest earned on the deposit increases the balance of the account, while the withdrawals reduce the balance (Exhibit 29-16). In this example, the balance of the account would be $1,000 just before the withdrawal at the end of the fifth year. That fifth withdrawal would reduce the account balance to zero. Therefore, the present value of an annuity of $1,000 for five years is $4,212. We would use this amount as the present value of cash inflows from an investment expected to return $1,000 at the end of each of the next five years (assuming a compound discounting rate of 6 percent).

Exhibit 29-3 shows the present value of an annuity of $1 for certain discounting rates and certain numbers of periods. The formula given in the footnote to the table can be used to compute the present value for rates or numbers of periods not included in the table.

As an example of the computation of the present value of an annuity, let us consider the present value (at 10 percent discounting rate) of an annuity of $1 received for three periods. From Exhibit 29-1, we can obtain the present value of each of the three payments.

Exhibit 29-16
An annuity of $1,000 for five years

End of Period		Cash Flow	Account Balance
0	Initial deposit (investment)	$ 4,212	$4,212
1	Add interest for 1st year (0.06 × $4,212)	253	4,465
	Deduct one payment ($1,000)	(1,000)	3,465
2	Add interest for 2nd year (0.06 × $3,465)	208	3,673
	Deduct one payment ($1,000)	(1,000)	2,673
3	Add interest for 3rd year (0.06 × $2,673)	160	2,833
	Deduct one payment ($1,000)	(1,000)	1,833
4	Add interest for 4th year (0.06 × $1,833)	110	1,943
	Deduct one payment ($1,000)	(1,000)	943
5	Add interest for 5th year (0.06 × $943)	57	1,000
	Deduct one payment ($1,000)	(1,000)	0

Present value of payment ($1) received after 1 period = $0.909;

Present value of payment ($1) received after 2 periods = $0.826;

Present value of payment ($1) received after 3 periods = $0.751;

Present value of annuity = $9.909 + $0.826 + $0.751 = $2.486.

This agrees (within a difference of $0.001 due to rounding) with the value shown in Exhibit 29-3. You can confirm that this same value is obtained by substituting $i = 0.10$ and $n = 3$ in the formula given in the footnote to Exhibit 29-3.

Note that the table and the equation both assume that the annuity payments are received at the end of each period. More complicated computations would be needed to give an exact computation for cash inflows spread evenly through the years. However, the use of the end-of-the-period approximation is adequate for most purposes of evaluating investments.

Questions

1. Define capital budgeting.
2. What major facts must be considered in evaluating capital-budgeting projects?
3. Why is $1 today worth more than $1 to be received a year in the future?
4. Distinguish between (a) the present value of $1 and (b) the present value of an annuity of $1.
5. List three approaches to the evaluation of capital-budgeting projects, and give a brief description of each.
6. Describe a major advantage of the discounted-cash-flow method of evaluating capital-budgeting decisions.
7. What is the major weakness of the payback-period method?
8. What is meant by sensitivity analysis? How does it relate to capital budgeting?
9. What problems arise when uncertainty is introduced into capital budgeting? What procedures are available to cope with uncertainty in capital budgeting?

Exhibit 29-17 **Present Value of 1, $p = \frac{1}{(1+i)^n}$**

Periods	2%	2½%	3%	4%	5%	6%	7%	8%	9%	10%	11%	12%
1	.98039	.97561	.97087	.96154	.95238	.94340	.93458	.92593	.91743	.90909	.90090	.89286
2	.96117	.95181	.94260	.92456	.90703	.89000	.87344	.85734	.84168	.82645	.81162	.79719
3	.94232	.92860	.91514	.88900	.86384	.83962	.81630	.79383	.77218	.75131	.73119	.71178
4	.92385	.90595	.88849	.85480	.82270	.79209	.76290	.73503	.70843	.68301	.65873	.63552
5	.90573	.88385	.86261	.82193	.78353	.74726	.71299	.68058	.64993	.62092	.59345	.56743
6	.88797	.86230	.83748	.79031	.74622	.70496	.66634	.63017	.59627	.56447	.53464	.50663
7	.87056	.84127	.81309	.75992	.71068	.66506	.62275	.58349	.54703	.51316	.48166	.45235
8	.85349	.82075	.78941	.73069	.67684	.62741	.58201	.54027	.50187	.46651	.43393	.40388
9	.83676	.80073	.76642	.70259	.64461	.59190	.54393	.50025	.46043	.42410	.39092	.36061
10	.82035	.78120	.74409	.67556	.61391	.55839	.50835	.46319	.42241	.38554	.35218	.32197
11	.80426	.76214	.72242	.64958	.58468	.52679	.47509	.42888	.38753	.35049	.31728	.28748
12	.78849	.74356	.70138	.62460	.55684	.49697	.44401	.39711	.35553	.31863	.28584	.25668
13	.77303	.72542	.68095	.60057	.53032	.46884	.41496	.36770	.32618	.28966	.25751	.22917
14	.75788	.70773	.66112	.57748	.50507	.44230	.38782	.34046	.29925	.26333	.23199	.20462
15	.74301	.69047	.64186	.55526	.48102	.41727	.36245	.31524	.27454	.23939	.20900	.18270
16	.72845	.67362	.62317	.53391	.45811	.39365	.33873	.29189	.25187	.21763	.18829	.16312
17	.71416	.65720	.60502	.51337	.43630	.37136	.31657	.27027	.23107	.19784	.16963	.14564
18	.70016	.64117	.58739	.49363	.41552	.35034	.29586	.25025	.21199	.17986	.15282	.13004
19	.68643	.62553	.57029	.47464	.39573	.33051	.27651	.23171	.19449	.16351	.13768	.11611
20	.67297	.61027	.55368	.45639	.37689	.31180	.25842	.21455	.17843	.14864	.12403	.10367
21	.65978	.59539	.53755	.43883	.35894	.29416	.24151	.19866	.16370	.13513	.11174	.09256
22	.64684	.58086	.52189	.42196	.34185	.27751	.22571	.18394	.15018	.12285	.10067	.08264
23	.63416	.56670	.50669	.40573	.32557	.26180	.21095	.17032	.13778	.11168	.09069	.07379
24	.62172	.55288	.49193	.39012	.31007	.24698	.19715	.15770	.12640	.10153	.08170	.06588
25	.60953	.53939	.47761	.37512	.29530	.23300	.18425	.14602	.11597	.09230	.07361	.05882

Exhibit 29-18 **Present Value of Annuity of 1 (Ordinary), $P_o = \frac{1 - \frac{1}{(1+i)^n}}{i}$**

Periodic Rents	2%	2½%	3%	4%	5%	6%	7%	8%	9%	10%	11%	12%
1	.98039	.97561	.97087	.96154	.95238	.94340	.93458	.92593	.91743	.90909	.90090	.89286
2	1.94156	1.92742	1.91347	1.88609	1.85941	1.83339	1.80802	1.78326	1.75911	1.73554	1.71252	1.69005
3	2.88388	2.85602	2.82861	2.77509	2.72325	2.67301	2.62432	2.57710	2.53129	2.48685	2.44371	2.40183
4	3.80773	3.76197	3.71710	3.62990	3.54595	3.46511	3.38721	3.31213	3.23972	3.16987	3.10245	3.03735
5	4.71346	4.64583	4.57971	4.45182	4.32948	4.21236	4.10020	3.99271	3.88965	3.79079	3.69590	3.60478
6	5.60143	5.50813	5.41719	5.24214	5.07569	4.91732	4.76654	4.62288	4.48592	4.35526	4.23054	4.11141
7	6.47199	6.34939	6.23028	6.00205	5.78637	5.58238	5.38929	5.20637	5.03295	4.86842	4.71220	4.56376
8	7.32548	7.17014	7.01969	6.73274	6.46321	6.20979	5.97130	5.74664	5.53482	5.33493	5.14612	4.96764
9	8.16224	7.97087	7.78611	7.43533	7.10782	6.80169	6.51523	6.24689	5.99525	5.75902	5.53705	5.32825
10	8.98259	8.75206	8.53020	8.11090	7.72173	7.36009	7.02358	6.71008	6.41766	6.14457	5.88923	5.65022
11	9.78685	9.51421	9.25262	8.76048	8.30641	7.88687	7.49867	7.13896	6.80519	6.49506	6.20652	5.93770
12	10.57534	10.25776	9.95400	9.38507	8.86325	8.38364	7.94269	7.53608	7.16073	6.81369	6.49236	6.19437
13	11.34837	10.98318	10.63496	9.98565	9.39357	8.85268	8.35765	7.90378	7.48690	7.10336	6.74987	6.42355
14	12.10625	11.69091	11.29607	10.56312	9.89864	9.29498	8.74547	8.24424	7.78615	7.36669	6.98187	6.62817
15	12.84926	12.38138	11.93794	11.11839	10.37966	9.71225	9.10791	8.55948	8.06069	7.60608	7.19087	6.81086
16	13.57771	13.05500	12.56110	11.65230	10.83777	10.10590	9.44665	8.85137	8.31256	7.82371	7.37916	6.97399
17	14.29187	13.71220	13.16612	12.16567	11.27407	10.47726	9.76322	9.12164	8.54363	8.02155	7.54879	7.11963
18	14.99203	14.35336	13.75351	12.65930	11.68959	10.82760	10.05909	9.37189	8.75563	8.20141	7.70162	7.24967
19	15.67846	14.97889	14.32380	13.13394	12.08532	11.15812	10.33560	9.60360	8.95011	8.36492	7.83929	7.36578
20	16.35143	15.58916	14.87747	13.59033	12.46221	11.46992	10.59401	9.81815	9.12855	8.51356	7.96333	7.46944
21	17.01121	16.18455	15.41502	14.02916	12.82115	11.76408	10.83553	10.01680	9.29224	8.64869	8.07507	7.56200
22	17.65805	16.76541	15.93692	14.45112	13.16300	12.04158	11.06124	10.20074	9.44243	8.77154	8.17574	7.64465
23	18.29220	17.33211	16.44361	14.85684	13.48857	12.30338	11.27219	10.37106	9.58021	8.88322	8.26643	7.71843
24	18.91393	17.88499	16.93554	15.24696	13.79864	12.55036	11.46933	10.52876	9.70661	8.98474	8.34814	7.78432
25	19.52346	18.42438	17.41315	15.62208	14.09394	12.78336	11.65358	10.67478	9.82258	9.07704	8.42174	7.84314

Exercises

E29-1 (Present value)
Refer to Exhibit 29-1. What is the present value of $1,000 to be received three years in the future, assuming a discounting rate of 8 percent? What is the present value if the cash is to be received four years in the future? How do you account for the difference?

E29-2 (Present value)
Refer to Exhibit 29-1. What is the present value of $1,000 to be received five years in the future, assuming a discounting rate of 4 percent? assuming a rate of 6 percent? How do you account for the difference?

E29-3 (Present value)
Refer to Exhibit 29-3. What is the present value of an annuity of $1,000 to be received over four periods, at a discounting rate of 6 percent? at a rate of 8 percent? How do you explain the difference?

E29-4 (Present value)
Refer to Exhibit 29-3. What is the present value of an annuity of $1,000 to be received over two periods, at a discounting rate of 10 percent? What is the present value if the annuity is to be received over three periods? How do you explain the difference?

E29-5 (Net-present-value method)
The New Company is evaluating the acquisition of a new machine that sells for $8,500. The machine has a four-year life and $2,000 scrap value. The new machine will provide a cash savings of $2,500 per year during its useful life. The saving occurs at the end of each year. The business considers an investment acceptable if it yields a 10 percent or better return on investment.
Required: Is the new machine an acceptable investment? Ignore tax implications. Show computations, using the net-present-value method of evaluating the project.

E29-6 (Net-present-value method)
The New Company revises its standards to require that all investments yield a return of only 8 percent. Is the investment in the new machine described in Exercise E29-5 an acceptable investment under this new standard?

E29-7 (Net-present-value method)
A manufacturing firm is interested in purchasing a $145,000 candy-twisting machine. The machine has a five-year life and $15,000 scrap value. The machine will reduce costs by $50,000 per year during its useful life. The firm pays income taxes at a rate of 50 percent. The firm desires to earn at least 8 percent on its investments.
Required: Evaluate this proposed investment, using the net-present-value approach. Include tax implications in your evaluation.

E29-8 (Yield-on-investment method)
A firm is considering the acquisition of a highly touted piece of equipment. The equipment costs $31,104, with no scrap value at the end of its four-year life. The equipment will save the firm $9,000 per year over its life. The firm desires a minimum rate of return of 8 percent on the investment.

Required: Evaluate this proposed investment, using the yield-on-investment approach.

E29-9 (Payback method)

A machine costing $27,000 with a useful life of five years will produce cash savings of $4,500 per year. Another machine costing $25,000 with an estimated useful life of six years will produce cash savings of $5,000 per year.

Required:

a. Evaluate the two possible investments, using the payback-period approach. Discuss the value of this approach and the reliability of the evaluation.

b. Using the payback reciprocal for the two projects, estimate the time-adjusted rate of return for each project.

E29-10 (Payback method)

A machine costing $65,000 will result in the following cash savings: $40,000 in the first year; $20,000 in the second year; $10,000 in the third year; and $5,000 in the fourth year. Compute the payback period for this investment.

E29-11 (Investment decision)

Two investments are being considered. Investment A will yield cash operating savings of $1,000 per year for four years. Investment B will yield cash savings of $1,400 for the first year, $1,200 for the second year, $1,000 for the third year, and $800 for the fourth year. Discount rate is 8 percent.

Required:

a. Compute the present value of the cash savings for each investment. Show two different methods to compute the present value for Investment A.

b. Would you prefer to accumulate cash savings as in Investment A or as in Investment B? Explain.

E29-12 (Investment decision—early cash inflows)

Two investments are available, each producing total cash savings of $100,000 over four years. Investment X yields cash savings of $50,000 in the first year, $30,000 in the second year, and $20,000 in the third year. Investment Y yields cash savings of $20,000 in the first year, $30,000 in the second year, and $50,000 in the third year. Using this example as an illustration, discuss the advantage of obtaining relatively large returns from an investment in earlier rather than later years.

E29-13 (Present value and depreciation)

Why may a firm find it more desirable to use an accelerated form of depreciation rather than straight-line depreciation? In your answer, discuss the present value of future cash savings and tax implications.

Problems

P29-1 (Net-present-value method)

A firm accumulates the following data about a new machine and about the old machine that it currently uses in its manufacturing operations.

	Old Machine	New Machine
Carrying value	$45,000	—
Cost	—	$90,000
Depreciation per year	$15,000	30,000
Cash operating cost per year	35,000	12,000
Disposal value if sold today	30,000	—
Disposal value at end of useful life	$0	$0
Remaining years of useful life	3	3

The firm pays income taxes at a rate of 50 percent. It requires a yield of 10 percent on its investments.

Required: Should the firm retain the old machine or purchase the new one? Use the net-present-value approach.

P29-2 (Present value problem)

After you have made your evaluation in Exercise E29-5, management has some second thoughts. They now estimate that cash savings might be only $2,000 per year instead of $2,500 per year. Management wants to know whether your evaluation is altered by this revised estimate.

Required:

a. Respond to management's inquiry.

b. As part of your response, compute the cash operating savings required to have the present value of cash outflow equal the present value of cash inflows. Present this value to management and explain its significance.

P29-3 (Payback and discounted-cash-flow methods)

The Kruz Company has the following policies for evaluating proposed capital expenditures.

(1) The project with the shortest payback period is considered to be the most desirable.

(2) The payback period is not to exceed 60 percent of the estimated life of the project.

(3) Any investment yielding 8 percent or less return (computed by the discounted-cash-flow method) is unacceptable.

The following two investment projects are under consideration.

	Project 1	Project 2
Estimated initial cost	$18,000	$25,000
Estimated life	5 years	7 years
Estimated annual cash inflow:		
Year 1	$ 6,500	$ 7,000
Year 2	6,500	7,000
Year 3	6,500	7,000
Year 4	6,600	7,000
Year 5	6,600	7,000
Year 6	—	7,000
Year 7	—	7,000

Required:

a. Do Projects 1 and 2 meet the standard set by policy (2)?

b. If the payback-period method of evaluation is used, which project is more desirable?

c. Do Projects 1 and 2 meet the standard set by policy (3)? (Ignore tax implications.)

d. Which project offers the larger dollar return on investment in terms of discounted values?

e. What is the approximate yield of each project? (Exhibit 29-19 is an extension of the present value of an annuity table that may be useful.)

P29-4 (Uncertainty)

A merchant sells items for \$30 and purchases them for \$15. The items are perishable; any item not sold on the day that it is purchased is worthless thereafter. In a study of demand over the past 200 days, the merchant finds that he had a demand for 20 items on 90 days, for 40 items on 70 days, and for 60 items on 40 days.

Required:

a. Prepare a conditional value (payoff) schedule reflecting the available alternative daily purchases.

b. Compute the expected monetary values for each alternative.

c. What is the optimum act(s)?

d. Suppose that the merchant were able to predict with certainty the day's demand level before making the purchase for that day. What profit could he expect to make?

e. How much could the merchant afford to pay to a marketing consultant who could predict with certainty the demand for each coming day?

P29-5 (Capital budgeting analysis)

True-False

a. Net cash outflow = Cash revenues × (1 − income tax rate).

b. Net cash inflow = Cash revenues − (1 − income tax rate).

c. Cash savings on depreciation = Depreciation expense × Income tax rate.

d. Net present value (positive) = Present value of net cash inflows expected − Present value of cost of the investment.

e. The present value of an annuity of \$1 can be computed from the following formula:

$$P = \frac{1}{(1 + r)^n}$$

f. The cost of capital can be conceptualized as a weighted average of the costs of each type of capital utilized by a company.

g. The payback period is computed as follows:

$$\text{Payback period} = \frac{\text{Annual cash savings}}{\text{Initial investment}}$$

h. The investment that has the longer payback period is considered a more attractive investment because it minimizes the risk in the investment.

Exhibit 29-19
Extension of table for present value of annuity of \$1

	Compound Rate			
Periods	**8%**	**20%**	**22%**	**24%**
4	**3.312**	**2.589**	**2.494**	**2.404**
5	**3.993**	**2.991**	**2.864**	**2.745**
6	**4.623**	**3.326**	**3.167**	**3.020**
7	**5.206**	**3.605**	**3.416**	**3.242**

P29-6 (Cost of capital)

Two companies have the following sources of capital; the tax rate is 46 percent. Company A pays dividends of $5,000 a year. Company B pays dividends of $15,000 a year.

	Company A	Company B
Common stock (current market value)	$ 50,000	$150,000
Bonds: 6%	150,000	50,000

Required: Compute the average cost of capital for the two companies.

Manufacturing operations

30

In discussing inventory in Chapter 13, our treatment was restricted to accounting for a retail or wholesale merchandising business. Such an enterprise has only one type of inventory—merchandise inventory. We turn now to the special problems of accounting for a manufacturing enterprise that engages in the production of inventory for sale. The major differences in accounting procedures for the manufacturing firm have to do with the treatment of inventory.

Manufacturing costs

In a manufacturing enterprise, workers and machines process materials—transforming raw materials into a finished product, and thereby increasing the value of the material as it passes through the manufacturing process. In a typical factory situation, raw material is purchased and labor is hired to transform the raw material into a finished product. In transforming the raw material, labor is assisted by machinery, plant, power, and similar factors of production. The costs of manufacturing a product consist of three major elements: material, labor, and manufacturing overhead.

1. ***Direct material*** includes materials that are directly traceable to an article being manufactured—for example, raw material that is transformed into a finished product.
2. ***Direct labor*** includes the factory labor directly associated with the manufacture of particular articles.
3. ***Manufacturing*** (factory) ***overhead*** includes those manufacturing (factory) costs that cannot be traced directly to particular articles being manufactured—for example, heat and power used in production; taxes and insurance on factory buildings and equipment; factory repair and maintenance costs; indirect labor (cost of supervisors, foremen, cost accountants, and other employees whose wages cannot be directly identified with particular products manufactured); and indirect material (supplies that are difficult to trace directly into manufacture of particular products).

Because a manufacturing firm purchases raw materials, processes them, and stocks finished goods for sale, it normally has three kinds of inventory on hand at any moment. Its balance sheet usually shows three inventory classifications in the current asset section:

1. *materials*—the basic materials that enter into the production of the finished product;
2. *goods in process* (or *work in process*)—partially completed products that are in the manufacturing process at the end of an accounting period; and
3. *finished goods*—the completed product that remains unsold at the end of an accounting period.

Exhibit 30-1 illustrates the flow of costs through the manufacturing process.

It should be noted that manufacturing costs (material, labor, and overhead) have asset status in the form of materials, goods in process, or finished goods. These expenditures for material, labor, and overhead become expenses when the finished goods are sold. In studying Exhibit 30-1, you should appreciate the importance of proper accounting for product costs. All material, labor, and overhead costs of manufacturing enter into inventory valuations, to appear eventually as cost of goods sold (expense). Therefore, the product costs have direct impact on current assets (inventory) in the balance sheet and on income determination (cost of goods sold) in the income statement.

Exhibit 30-2 shows a typical cost-of-goods-manufactured statement. Exhibit 30-3 shows an income statement for a manufacturing concern. These statements are presented as illustrations of these basic financial statements, and to indicate the relationship that exists between manufacturing costs and inventories. Note that the total cost of goods manufactured during the year as computed on the cost-of-goods-manufactured statement appears as a single item under cost of goods sold in the income statement. Cost of finished goods on hand at the beginning of the year is added to the cost of goods manufactured during the year. Then the cost of finished goods on hand at the end of the year is deducted. The result is the cost of the goods sold during the year.

Cost accounting

Cost accounting is a branch of financial and managerial accounting. As such, it provides management with detailed information about the cost of producing—and, in

Exhibit 30-1 Flow of costs through the manufacturing process

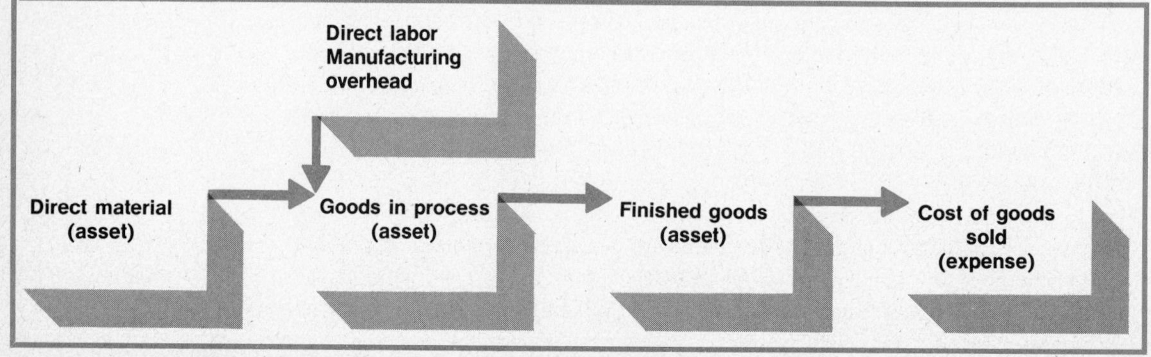

Exhibit 30-2
A typical cost-of-goods-manufactured statement

THE DO-IT-YOURSELF COMPANY

Cost-of-Goods-Manufactured Statement
For the Year Ended December 31, 19_1

Materials used:	
Inventory of raw material, Dec. 31, 19_0	$ 25,000
Purchases (net)	125,000
Total	$150,000
Less: Inventory of raw material, Dec. 31, 19_1	50,000
Cost of materials used	$100,000
Direct labor	200,000
Manufacturing overhead	300,000
Total costs put into process this period	$600,000
Add: Goods-in-process inventory, Dec. 31, 19_0	150,000
Total	$750,000
Less: Goods-in-process inventory, Dec. 31, 19_1	100,000
Cost of goods manufactured	$650,000

Exhibit 30-3
A typical income statement for a manufacturing firm

THE DO-IT-YOURSELF COMPANY

Income Statement
For the Year Ended December 31, 19_1

Sales (net)		$900,000
Less: Cost of goods sold:		
Finish -goods inventory, Dec. 31, 19_0	$125,000	
Add: Goods manufactured during 19_1 (see Exhibit 30-2)	650,000	
Total	$775,000	
Less: Finished-goods inventory, Dec. 31, 19_1	175,000	
Cost of goods sold		600,000
Gross margin		$300,000
Less: Selling and administrative expenses		180,000
Net income		$120,000

some cases, selling—a good or a service. The proper compilation and evaluation of cost data is a major managerial responsibility. A knowledge of product costs has many managerial uses, especially when product costs are used to establish selling prices and to evaluate supervisory performance. Emphasis in the remainder of this chapter is upon (1) control of costs and (2) product costing.

The major cost-accounting systems are used extensively by business to assign costs to manufactured products for purposes of controlling costs and costing products: the job-order cost system, and the process cost system.

1. A *job-order cost system* accumulates costs of material, labor, and manufacturing overhead by specific orders, jobs, batches, or lots. Job-order cost systems are used in the construction, furniture, aircraft, printing, and similar industries, where the cost of a specific job depends on the particular order specifications. In a job-order cost system, costs of material, labor, and overhead for a specific job are accumulated on a job-order cost sheet.

2. A ***process cost system*** accumulates costs by processes or departments (over a certain period of time). Process cost systems are used by firms that manufacture products through continuous-flow systems or on a mass-production basis. Industries that use process cost systems include chemicals, petroleum products, textiles, cement, glass, mining, paints, flour, and rubber. In a process cost system, costs for a department (or process) are accumulated on a departmental (or process) cost sheet. Per-unit costs are obtained by dividing the total departmental costs by the quantity produced during a given period in the department. Unit costs derived in this manner are essentially ***average*** unit costs.

Job-order cost accounting

In this section we develop an illustration of job-order cost accounting. Exhibit 30-4 shows the basic records used in the system. These records are important for purposes of product costing and control. Among the basic records used in a job-order cost-accounting system are the following.

Exhibit 30-4 **Source documents used in a job-order cost system**

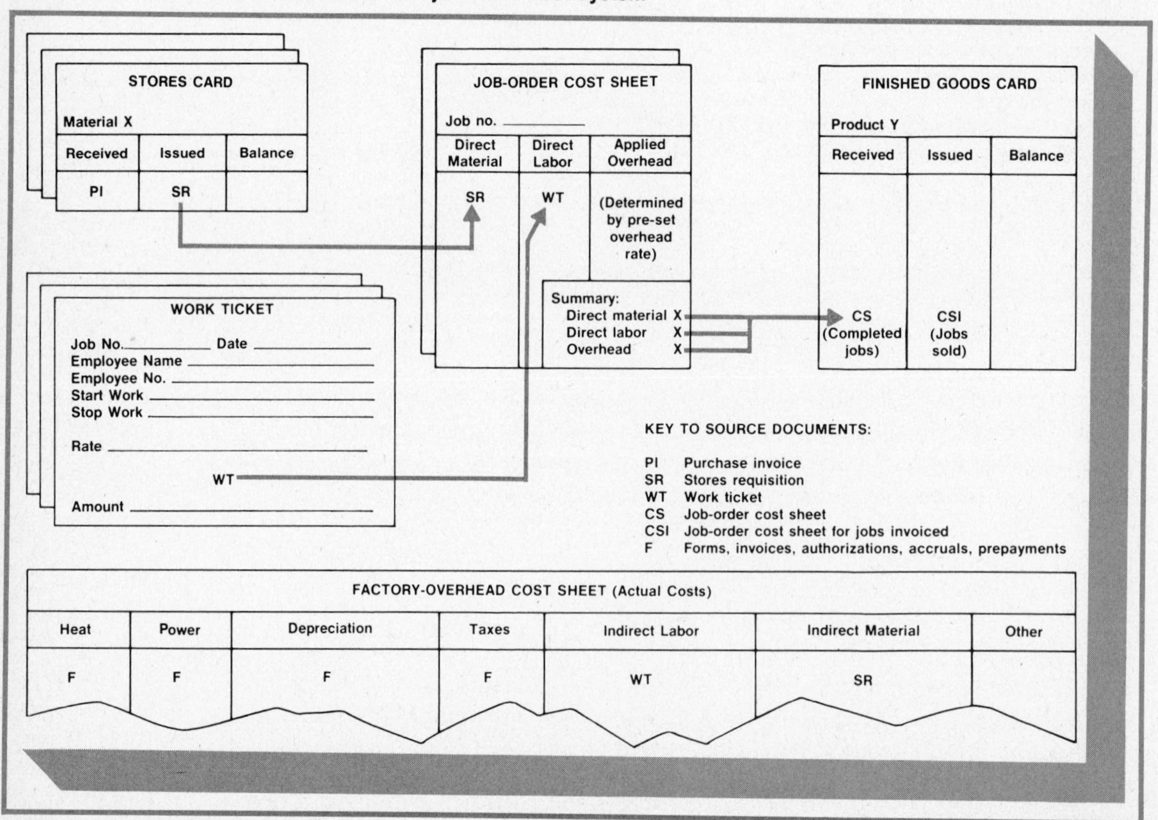

1. The ***stores card*** is a perpetual inventory record for materials purchased and used in production.
2. The ***work*** (or ***job***) ***ticket*** is a record of who worked on what job, for how long, and at what rate.
3. The ***factory-overhead cost sheet*** is a report that summarizes actual manufacturing overhead costs.
4. The ***job-order cost sheet*** is a report that summarizes all costs for a specific job or lot being manufactured.
5. The ***finished goods*** (or parts) ***card*** is a perpetual inventory record for items manufactured.

Exhibit 30-5 illustrates the control accounts used in a job-order cost system and demonstrates the flow of costs through the system. Study this exhibit carefully to obtain an overview of job-order costing.

Now let us look at a specific example to see how a job-order cost system records transactions. The Job-Order Cost Company has received two orders, which are called Job Order No. 1 and Job Order No. 2. Job Order No. 1 was started last year, and is in process at the beginning of the current year. Job 2 was started in the current year. Materials X and Y are used in producing both orders. The following transactions occur during the manufacturing process. The journal entries are shown for each transaction in general journal form. Exhibit 30-6 shows the subsidiary records corresponding to these transactions.

1. The company purchases $50,000 of Material X and $100,000 of Material Y.

Material [or Stores]	150,000	
Accounts Payable		150,000

2. The following materials are requisitioned for production: for Job Order No. 1, $10,000 of Material X and $50,000 of Material Y; for Job Order No. 2, $30,000 of Material X and $20,000 of Material Y; for both jobs, $5,000 of indirect materials.

Goods-in-Process Inventory	110,000	
Manufacturing Overhead: Actual	5,000	
Material [or Stores]		115,000

3. The following labor is used during the period: direct labor on Job Order No. 1, $70,000; direct labor on Job Order No. 2, $80,000; indirect labor, $10,000.

Factory Payroll	160,000	
[Various accounts; wages, withholding]		160,000
To record payroll liability.		
Goods-in-Process Inventory	150,000	
Manufacturing Overhead: Actual	10,000	
Factory Payroll		160,000
To record payroll distribution.		

4. Various costs of $65,000 are incurred as factory overhead during the period.

Manufacturing Overhead: Actual	65,000	
[Various accounts: accounts payable, prepaid insurance, allowance for depreciation]		65,000

Exhibit 30-5 **Control accounts and flow of costs in a job-order cost system**

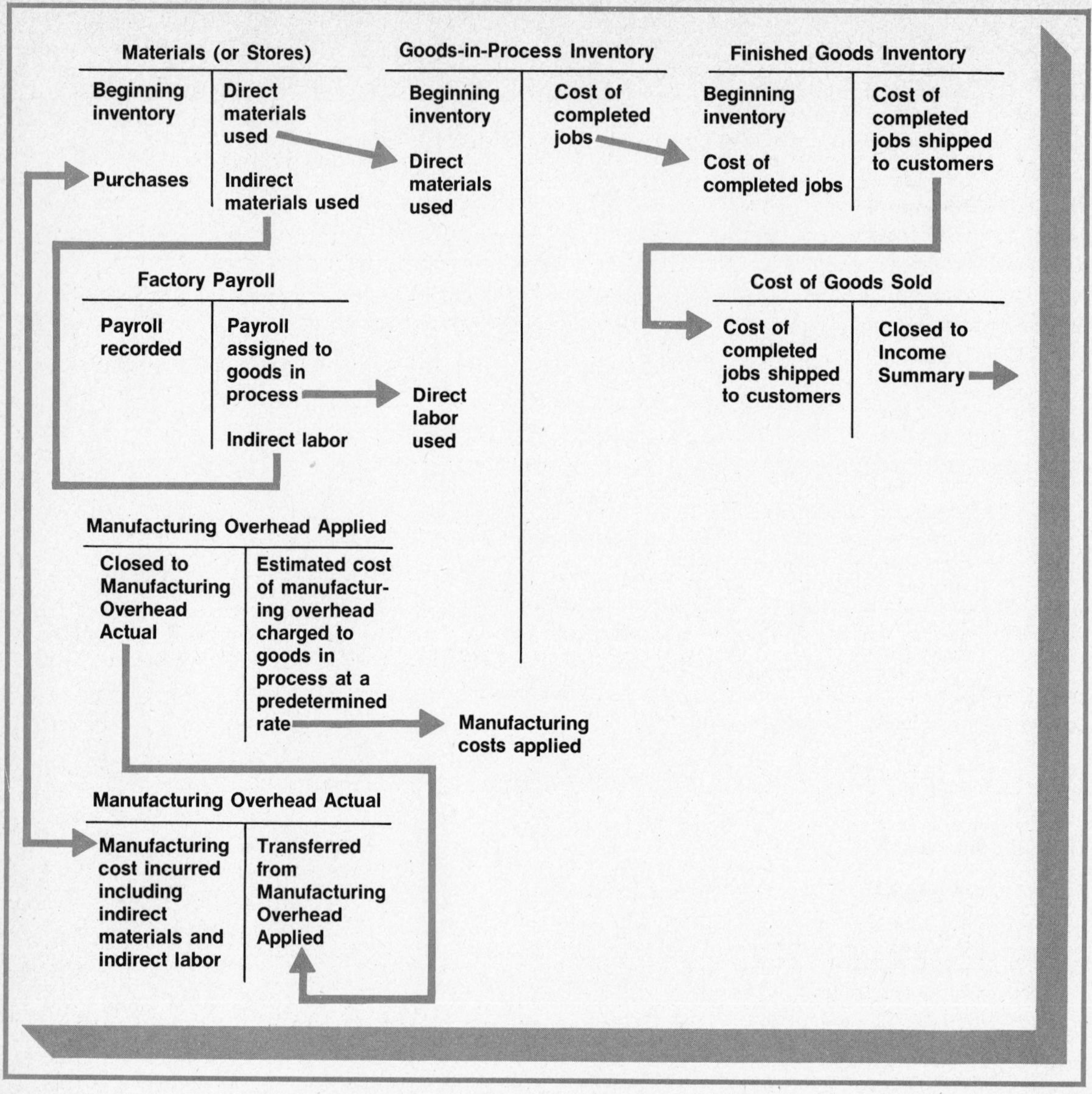

5. Factory overhead is applied to production at a predetermined rate of 50 percent of direct labor cost; $35,000 to Job Order No. 1, and $40,000 to Job Order No. 2.

Goods-in-Process Inventory	75,000	
Manufacturing Overhead: Applied		75,000

6. Job Order No. 2 is completed. Costs associated with the job order are transferred from Goods-in-Process Inventory to Finished Goods Inventory. The costs are listed on the job-order cost sheet.

Finished Goods Inventory	170,000	
Goods-in-Process Inventory		170,000

Exhibit 30-6 **Subsidiary records for job orders no. 1 and 2**

STORES CARD		
Material X		
Received	Issued	Balance
		$15,000
$50,000		65,000
	$10,000	55,000
	30,000	25,000

STORES CARD		
Material Y		
Received	Issued	Balance
		$ 10,000
$100,000		110,000
	$50,000	60,000
	20,000	40,000

JOB-ORDER COST SHEET					
Job No. 1					
Direct Material		Direct Labor		Applied Overhead	
Opening balance	$ 3,000	Opening balance	$ 2,000	Opening balance	$ 1,000
Current period: X	10,000	Current period	70,000	Current period	35,000
Current period: Y	50,000				

JOB-ORDER COST SHEET					
Job No. 2					
Direct Material		Direct Labor		Applied Overhead	
Current period: X	$30,000	Current period	$80,000	Current period	$40,000
Current period: Y	20,000				
	$50,000		$80,000		$40,000
TOTAL: TO FINISHED GOODS:			$170,000		

Job No. 2		
Received	Issued	Balance
$170,000		$170,000
	$170,000	0

7. Job Order No. 2 is shipped to the customer and invoiced for $250,000.

Cost of Goods Sold	170,000	
Finished Goods Inventory		170,000
Accounts Receivable	250,000	
Sales		250,000

In reviewing this illustration, note how total costs are recorded in the control accounts, while the subsidiary records are used to keep track of costs assigned to each job order.

MANUFACTURING OVERHEAD

Manufacturing overhead is somewhat troublesome in cost accounting. Therefore, we give a brief discussion here of the way it is handled in a job-order system.

Although labor and material costs can be known at the time they are applied to a specific job order, this is not the case for most costs treated as manufacturing overhead. Most of the manufacturing overhead costs are not known until the end of an accounting period. For example, heat, power, repair, and similar costs are not known until bills are received—often after a job order is completed and invoiced. Therefore, it is necessary to make an estimate of the overhead costs that are to be assigned to specific orders.

To deal with this difficulty, accountants have devised the following procedure to assign overhead costs to specific jobs.

1. Estimate manufacturing overhead costs at the beginning of the accounting period (on the basis of past experience and knowledge about conditions expected during the period). For example, suppose that overhead costs are estimated at $80,000 for the coming year.
2. Relate the incurring of manufacturing overhead costs to some type of activity. For example, we will assume that the costs incurred for manufacturing overhead are proportional to the direct-labor dollar costs incurred on a specific job. Direct labor costs are estimated at $160,000 for the coming year.
3. Calculate a manufacturing overhead rate based on the information gathered in the first two steps, using the formula,

$$\text{Overhead rate} = \frac{\text{Estimated manufacturing overhead costs}}{\text{Estimated direct-labor dollar costs}}$$

$$= \frac{\$80{,}000}{\$160{,}000}$$

$$= \$0.50 \text{ per direct labor dollar.}$$

4. Use the predetermined overhead rate to apply manufacturing overhead costs to specific jobs. In Exhibit 30-6, direct labor costs on Job Order No. 1 were $70,000. Therefore, overhead costs of 0.50 × $70,000 = $35,000 were applied to Job No. 1. Similarly, overhead costs were applied to Job No. 2 at the rate of $0.50 for each direct labor dollar. The journal entry recording the applied overhead for the two jobs is shown in the fifth transaction for that illustration. When actual overhead costs are incurred, such costs are recorded in a Manufacturing Overhead: Actual account. In the illustration, actual overhead costs incurred were

Exhibit 30-7
Manufacturing overhead accounts before closing

Manufacturing Overhead: Applied

		Job Order No. 1	**35,000**
		Job Order No. 2	**40,000**

Manufacturing Overhead: Actual

Indirect material	**5,000**		
Indirect labor	**10,000**		
Other overhead costs	**65,000**		

$5,000 for indirect material (transaction 2), $10,000 for indirect labor (transaction 3), and $65,000 for other overhead costs (transaction 4)—a total of $80,000 in actual overhead costs. After these costs have been posted in the ledger, the two manufacturing overhead accounts appear as shown in Exhibit 30-7.

5. In the illustration, the original estimate of overhead costs was inaccurate. Overhead costs incurred during the period were $80,000, but only $75,000 of overhead costs have been applied to specific jobs (using the predetermined overhead rate of $0.50 per direct labor dollar). The difference between the Manufacturing Overhead: Applied and the Manufacturing Overhead: Actual account balances represents underapplied (or underabsorbed) overhead. At the end of the accounting period, any under- or overapplied overhead can be closed to Cost of Goods Sold.[1]

   a. Close the Manufacturing Overhead: Applied account to Manufacturing Overhead: Actual.

Manufacturing Overhead: Applied	75,000	
Manufacturing Overhead: Actual		75,000

   b. Close the Manufacturing Overhead: Actual account to the Cost of Goods Sold account.

Cost of Goods Sold	5,000	
Manufacturing Overhead: Actual		5,000

Exhibit 30-8 shows the pertinent overhead ledger accounts after the closing entries have been posted. Both accounts now show zero balances, and all costs have been assigned to costs of goods sold or goods in inventory.

Process cost accounting

In job-order cost accounting, work performed and costs incurred are identified with specific customers' orders. Where the firm manufactures identical units of product

1. In theory, the difference between applied overhead and actual overhead should be prorated among Cost of Goods Sold, Finished Goods, and Goods in Process in proportion to the amount of applied overhead in the ending balances of these accounts. This procedure would have the effect of correcting the predetermined overhead rate to match the actual overhead rate incurred. However, because the variance between applied and actual overhead usually is quite small, this refinement usually is not worth the effort.

Exhibit 30-8
Manufacturing overhead accounts after closing

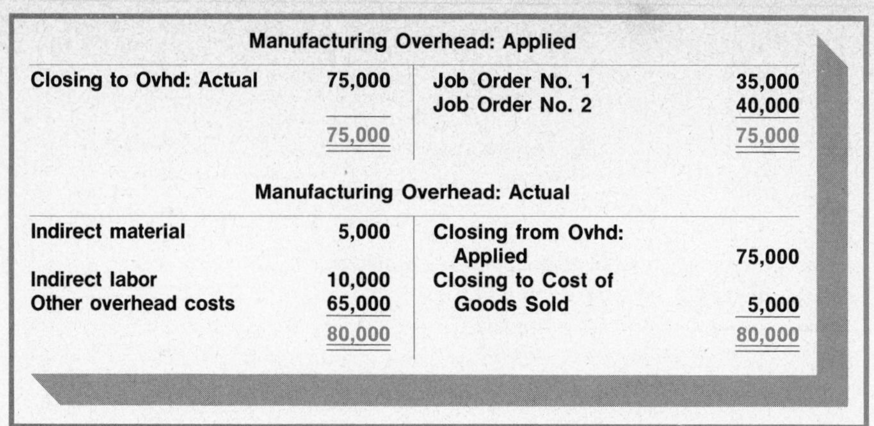

Manufacturing Overhead: Applied

Closing to Ovhd: Actual	75,000	Job Order No. 1	35,000
		Job Order No. 2	40,000
	75,000		75,000

Manufacturing Overhead: Actual

Indirect material	5,000	Closing from Ovhd: Applied	75,000
Indirect labor	10,000	Closing to Cost of	
Other overhead costs	65,000	Goods Sold	5,000
	80,000		80,000

on a continuous basis, it is often impossible to relate specific costs to specific orders. Furthermore, the cost of a particular batch is related to conditions in the factory and general economy—not to the nature of a particular customer's order. For example, suppose that a firm processes milk. Customers place orders for certain quantities of certain grades of milk. The orders are essentially identical, so management cannot adjust selling prices or reject certain orders in order to control its costs and profits on the basis of job-order cost information.

However, in industries where products are similar, a process cost system can be used to assign costs to departments or processes in the production system. Periodically, departmental or process costs are summarized and the number of units of product completed in the department or process is determined. With this information, per-unit departmental or process costs can be computed:

$$\text{Per-unit departmental cost} = \frac{\text{Total departmental cost}}{\text{Number of units completed in department}}$$

The per-unit departmental or process costs can be used in controlling overall pricing policies and in making decisions about internal management.

In a process cost system, three basic schedules are required to accumulate cost and production data.

1. The ***quantity schedule*** is a report that shows physical units in production in a department (or process) during a given period of time.
2. The ***equivalent production schedule*** is a report that converts physical units completed or partially completed into completed units of production. For example, suppose that Department A has completely processed 10,000 gallons of milk during the month. Another 500 gallons are still in process in Department A at the end of the month. The 500 gallons are estimated to be 50 percent completed as to material, labor, and overhead costs. In terms of equivalent production, these 500 partially-completed gallons are equivalent to 250 completed gallons. Equivalent production for Department A is 10,250 gallons for the month.
3. The ***departmental production report*** (prepared for each production department or process) shows quantities of products, total costs, and unit costs. This report summarizes data as visualized in Exhibit 30-9.

THE PROCESS COST COMPANY CASE

We illustrate here a process cost system for the Process Cost Company for the year 19_0. The Process Cost Company manufactures one product, pottery. The production process begins in Department A, where raw material (clay) is molded. When the molding process is completed, the material is transferred to Department B where additional material (glaze) is added and the pottery is baked. When the baking process is completed, the pottery is transferred to the finished goods warehouse.

At the beginning of 19_0, the company had some work in process in Department B, but no work in process in Department A. At the end of the year, both departments have some unfinished pottery in process.

QUANTITY SCHEDULE. A quantity schedule is prepared to show the number of units processed in each department during the year (Exhibit 30-10). The Process Cost Company started 100,000 pots during the year in Department A. Of these units, 20,000 were transferred to Department B, and 80,000 pots were still in process in

Exhibit 30-9
Visualization of the form of the departmental production report

UNITS to be accounted for: Units in process at beginning of period + Units started or transferred in during period	=	UNITS accounted for: Units transferred to next department or to finished goods during period + Units in process at end of period
COSTS to be accounted for: Costs in process at beginning of period + Costs charged to department during period	=	COSTS accounted for: Costs transferred to next department or to finished goods during period + Costs in process at end of period

Exhibit 30-10
Quantity schedule for the Process Cost Company case

PROCESS COST COMPANY
Production Report: Quantities
For the Year Ended December 31, 19_0

	Units	
	Dept. A	**Dept. B**
Quantities to be accounted for:		
Units in process at beginning of year	0	5,000
Units started in process during year	100,000	20,000
Total	100,000	25,000
Quantities accounted for:		
Units in process at end of year	80,000	10,000
Units transferred to:		
Dept. B	20,000	–
Finished goods	–	15,000
Total	100,000	25,000

Department A at the end of the period. In Department B, 5,000 pots were in process at the beginning of the year. During the year, 15,000 pots were completed and transferred to the finished goods warehouse, leaving 10,000 pots still in process in Department B at the end of the period.

EQUIVALENT PRODUCTION SCHEDULE. When some goods in process are only partially completed at the end of the period, it is necessary to compute equivalent production before computing unit costs of production during the period.

In our illustration, the units in process at the end of the period in Departments A and B were about 50 percent completed (in terms of material, labor, and overhead costs). The units in process in the beginning inventory of Department B were 40 percent completed as to all costs. Exhibit 30-11 shows the production of the departments in terms of equivalent production. Note that this schedule is prepared with data taken from the quantity schedule (Exhibit 30-10). Where units are in process at the beginning or end of the period, the number of units in process is multiplied by the appropriate percentage of completion to obtain the equivalent units in process.

The equivalent production schedule indicates that 60,000 equivalent units of pottery were completed in Department A and 18,000 in Department B. These data will be used in preparing the departmental production report (or cost of production schedule).

In the equivalent production schedule shown in Exhibit 30-11, the units in process were assumed to be at the same percentage of completion in terms of all *costs*. In some cases, the percentage of completion may differ for material, labor, and overhead. For example, the work in process in Department A might be 80 percent complete as to material costs, 40 percent as to labor costs, and 30 percent as to overhead costs. In such a case, it would be necessary to prepare separate equivalent production schedules for each element of cost.

Exhibit 30-11 **Equivalent production schedule for the Process Cost Company case**

PROCESS COST COMPANY

Equivalent Production Report: Quantities

For the Year Ended December 31, 19_0

	Equivalent Completed Units	
	Dept. A	**Dept. B**
Units transferred to:		
Dept. B (100% completed in Dept. A)	**20,000**	**—**
Finished goods (100% completed in Dept. B)	**—**	**15,000**
Units in process at end of period:		
Dept. A (80,000 units 50% completed)	**40,000**	**—**
Dept. B (10,000 units 50% completed)	**—**	**5,000**
Total	**60,000**	**20,000**
Less: Units in process at beginning of year:		
Dept. B (5,000 units 40% completed)	**—**	**2,000**
Equivalent production for the year	60,000	18,000

Exhibit 30-12 **Cost of production schedule for Process Cost Company in a form that is convenient for assembling information**

PROCESS COST COMPANY
Cost of Production Schedule
For the Year Ended December 31, 19_0

	Department A			Department B		
	Units	**Unit Cost**	**Costs of Material, Labor, and Overhead**	**Units**	**Unit Cost**	**Costs of Material, Labor, and Overhead**
Units/costs to be accounted for:						
Units/costs in process at beginning of the year	—		—	2,000		$ 25,000
Units/costs started in process:						
Units/costs in department	60,000		$180,000	18,000		115,000
Costs transferred from Dept. A	—		—	—		60,000
Total	60,000	$3	$180,000	20,000	$10	$200,000
Units/costs accounted for:						
Units/costs in process at end of the year	40,000	$3	120,000	5,000	$10	50,000
Units/costs transferred to:						
Dept. B	20,000	$3	$ 60,000	—		—
Finished goods				15,000	$10	$150,000

COST OF PRODUCTION SCHEDULE. Using production data from the equivalent production schedule and cost data obtained from the accounting records, it is now possible to prepare a departmental production report for each department. The *cost of production schedule* is a summary of the departmental reports for the entire company. Exhibit 30-12 shows a convenient form of the schedule for assembling the cost-of-production information. Exhibit 30-13 shows the schedule in a traditional format.

The following cost data were used in preparing the cost of production schedule. For Department A, the costs incurred during the year were $100,000 for material used, $50,000 for direct labor, and $30,000 for manufacturing overhead. For Department B, the costs incurred during the year were $25,000 for material used, $50,000 for direct labor, and $40,000 for manufacturing overhead. In addition, costs of $25,000 were assigned to the units in process in Department B at the beginning of the year.

In the cost of production schedule shown in Exhibit 30-12 (and 30-13), a single per-unit average cost of $3 in Department A was computed by dividing the number of units to be accounted for (60,000) into the departmental costs for material, labor, and overhead ($180,000). This was possible because the three elements of costs were associated with units that were at the same stage of completion (50 percent). If the percent of completion differs for material, labor, and overhead costs, separate schedules must be prepared for the different categories of costs.

For example, suppose that the 80,000 units in process in Department A at the end of the year were 80 percent complete as to material costs, 40 percent as to labor costs, and 30 percent as to overhead costs. Exhibit 30-14 shows a schedule computing the equivalent completed units for these units in process (for each cost

Exhibit 30-13 **Cost of production schedule in traditional format**

PROCESS COST COMPANY

Cost of Production Schedule

For the Year Ended December 31, 19_0

	Dept. A	Dept. B
Units to be accounted for (equivalent production):		
Units in process at beginning of period	—	2,000
Units started during period	60,000	18,000
Total units to be accounted for (*a*)	60,000	20,000
Units accounted for:		
Units in process at end of period	40,000	5,000
Units transferred to Department B	20,000	—
Units transferred to finished goods	—	15,000
Total units accounted for	60,000	20,000
Costs to be accounted for:		
Costs in process at beginning of period	—	$ 25,000
Costs transferred in from Department A	—	60,000
Costs added during period:		
Material, labor, overhead	$180,000	115,000
Total cost to be accounted for (*b*)	$180,000	$200,000
Costs accounted for:		
Costs in process at end of period:		
Material, labor, overhead (40,000 @ $3 per unit)	$120,000	—
Material, labor, overhead, and costs from Dept. A (5,000 @ $10 per unit)	—	$ 50,000
Costs transferred to Department B	60,000	—
Costs transferred to finished goods	—	150,000
Total cost accounted for	$180,000	$200,000

Per-unit costs computed as follows:

In Department A: b/a = $180,000/60,000 units = $3 per unit

In Department B: b/a = $200,000/20,000 units = $10 per unit

category) and a schedule computing the cost of production in the department for each cost category. The per-unit cost of production in the department, the cost of the ending inventory, and the cost of goods transferred to Department B are computed in the exhibit. A similar procedure would be required for any department where goods in process at the beginning or end of the period differed as to percentage of completion of the various costs.

THE PROCESS-COST-ACCOUNTING SYSTEM

Exhibit 30-15 shows the flow of costs through the ledger accounts used in a process cost system. Note that costs of direct material, direct labor, and manufacturing overhead are debited to the Goods in Process accounts of the particular departments as the costs are incurred. When goods are transferred from one department to another, the corresponding costs are credited to the Goods in Process account of the first department and debited to the account of the department receiving the goods. When goods are completed, the corresponding costs are transferred to the Finished Goods account. Finally, when the goods are sold, the costs are transferred to the Cost of Goods Sold account.

The following journal entries summarize the flow of costs reflected in the cost of production schedule of Exhibit 30-13.

Exhibit 30-14 Example of computation of departmental costs when percentage of completion differs for material, labor, and overhead costs

Equivalent Production Schedule: Dept. A

	Material	*Labor*	*Overhead*
Units transferred to Department B (100% completed)	20,000	20,000	20,000
Units in process at end of period (80,000):			
Material costs 80% completed	64,000	—	—
Labor costs 40% completed	—	32,000	—
Overhead costs 30% completed	—	—	24,000
Equivalent units of production for the year	84,000	52,000	44,000

Cost of Production Schedule: Dept A

	Material			*Labor*			*Overhead*		
	Units	Unit Cost	Total Cost	Units	Unit Cost	Total Cost	Units	Unit Cost	Total Cost
Units/costs in process at beginning of year	—		—	—		—	—		—
Units/costs started in process during year	84,000		$100,000	52,000		$50,000	44,000		$30,000
Total	84,000	$1.19	$100,000	52,000	$0.96	$50,000	44,000	$0.68	$30,000
Units/costs in process at end of year	64,000	$1.19	76,160	32,000	$0.96	30,720	24,000	$0.68	16,320
Units/costs transferred to Dept. B	20,000	$1.19	$ 23,840	20,000	$0.96	$19,280	20,000	$0.68	$13,680

Per-unit cost of production in Department A = \$1.19 + \$0.96 + \$0.68 = \$2.83
Cost of goods-in-process inventory at end of year = \$76,160 + \$30,720 + \$16,320 = \$123,200
Cost of goods transferred to Department B = \$23,840 + \$19,280 + \$13,680 = \$56,800

Exhibit 30-15 **Ledger accounts and flow of costs in a process cost system**

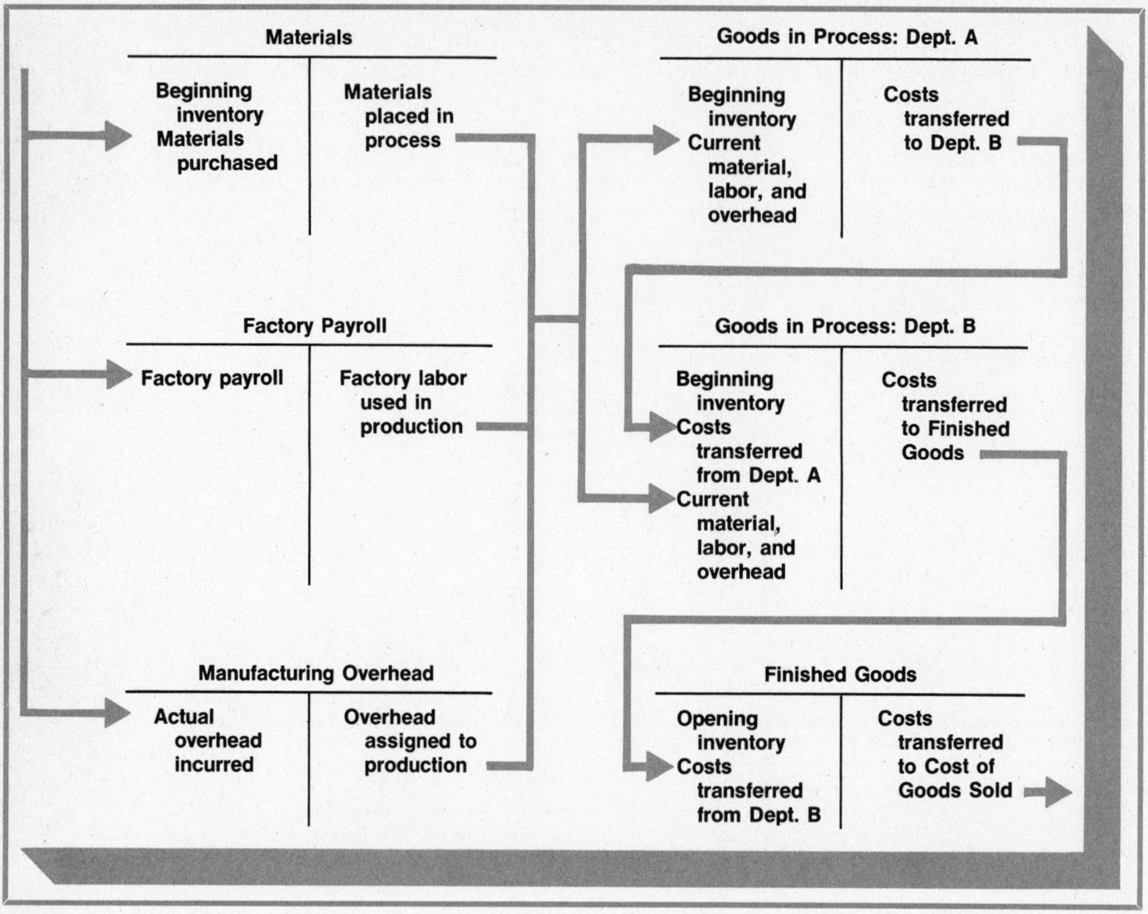

1. To record materials issued to Departments A and B.

Goods in Process: Dept. A	100,000	
Goods in Process: Dept. B	25,000	
Materials		125,000

2. To record $100,000 factory payroll for the period.

Factory Payroll	100,000	
[Wages Payable, Taxes Withheld, etc.]		100,000

3. To record distribution of factory payroll costs to Departments A and B.

Goods in Process: Dept. A	50,000	
Goods in Process: Dept. B	50,000	
Factory Payroll		100,000

4. To record $70,000 manufacturing overhead costs incurred during period.

Manufacturing Overhead	70,000	
[Cash, accruals, etc.]		70,000

5. To record allocation of actual manufacturing overhead to departments.

Goods in Process: Dept. A	30,000	
Goods in Process: Dept. B	40,000	
Manufacturing Overhead		70,000

6. To record cost of goods transferred from Department A to Department B.

Goods in Process: Dept. B	60,000	
Goods in Process: Dept. A		60,000

7. To transfer cost of goods completed in Department B to Finished Goods.

Finished Goods	150,000	
Goods in Process: Dept. B		150,000

After these journal entries are posted to the general ledger, the ledger cost accounts appear as shown in Exhibit 30-16. To complete the illustration, assume that two-thirds of the finished goods inventory is sold for $250,000 on account. The following entries summarize the sale and the flow of cost from Finished Goods to Cost of Goods Sold.

8. Accounts Receivable: Buyer Co.	250,000	
Sales		250,000
9. Cost of Goods Sold	100,000	
Finished Goods		100,000
To record sale of 2/3 of finished goods inventory with total cost of $150,000.		

Exhibit 30-16
Ledger cost accounts after posting entries 1 through 7

Material

Purchased	125,000	(1)	125,000

Factory Payroll

(2)	100,000	(3)	100,000

Manufacturing Overhead

(4)	70,000	(5)	70,000

Goods in Process: Dept. A

(1)	100,000	(6)	60,000
(3)	50,000		
(5)	30,000		

Goods in Process: Dept. B

Bal.	25,000	(7)	150,000
(1)	25,000		
(3)	50,000		
(5)	40,000		
(6)	60,000		

Finished Goods

(7)	150,000		

Exhibit 30-17
Ledger accounts after posting entries 8 and 9

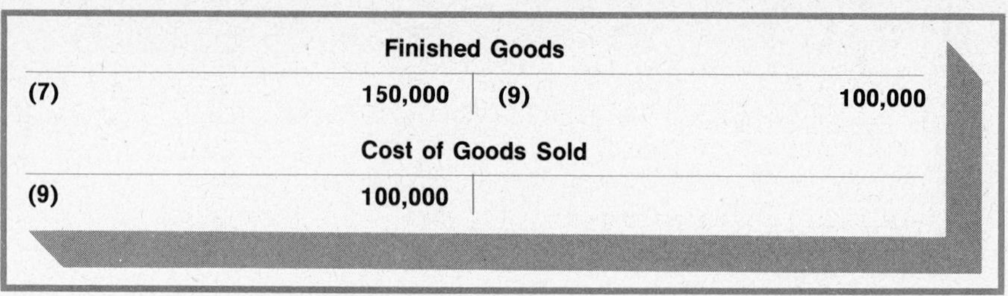

Finished Goods			
(7)	150,000	(9)	100,000

Cost of Goods Sold			
(9)	100,000		

After these entries are posted, the Finished Goods account and the Cost of Goods Sold account appear as shown in Exhibit 30-17.

Summary

The costs of manufacturing a product are direct materials, direct labor, and manufacturing (factory) overhead. Manufacturing operations combine material, labor, and overhead to make goods in process, which when completed is transferred to finished goods. When the product is sold, the cost of the finished goods is transferred to cost of goods sold.

A job order cost system can be used by a company that can identify manufacturing costs with individual products, lots, or orders. A process cost system identifies manufacturing costs with a process or department for a period of time. In computing unit costs, units produced must be expressed as completed units; this may require converting partially completed units to equivalent completed units. A cost production schedule is used to report department production and costs for a period.

Questions

1. What are the three major cost elements associated with manufacturing operations?
2. Distinguish between direct and indirect materials; direct and indirect labor.
3. What three typical types of inventory does a manufacturing firm possess?
4. Distinguish between a job-order cost system and a process cost system. What types of industries may use each kind of system?
5. What are two major objectives of a cost system?
6. What are store cards, job tickets, job-order cost sheets, and finished goods cards? What general ledger accounts control these subsidiary records?
7. Examine Exhibits 30-4 and 30-5 carefully. Describe the flow of costs indicated in these exhibits.
8. Explain the contents of the two accounts shown in Exhibit 30-18.
9. In process cost accounting, what is a quantity schedule? an equivalent production schedule? a departmental production report? Explain the use of each.
10. On a quantity schedule, units to be accounted for include units in process at the beginning of a period plus units started in production during the period. In what two categories are these units accounted for?
11. What is meant by equivalent production?

Exercises

E30-1 (Statements)

From the following 19_6 data, prepare (a) a cost-of-goods-manufactured statement, and (b) an income statement for the Gold Medal Company.

Sales		$1,720,000	
Sales returns and allowances		25,000	
Sales discounts		10,000	
Inventories:	Dec. 31, 19_5		Dec. 31, 19_6
Materials	$ 54,000		$ 59,000
Work in process	175,000		185,000
Finished goods	220,000		135,000
Purchases		$ 515,000	
Direct labor cost		290,000	
Manufacturing overhead cost		225,000	
Selling and administrative expenses		390,000	

E30-2 (Job order)

The Leaves Company uses a job-order cost system. Journalize the following transactions that occur during May 19_6.

a. Direct material purchased on account for $1,100,000.

b. Payment of $900,000 on account for purchases in transaction a.

c. Labor costs incurred during month total $600,000. F.I.C.A. taxes are $35,000; income taxes withheld amount to $60,000.

d. The factory payroll in transaction **c** is distributed to goods in process and manufacturing overhead as follows: direct labor for Job No. 101 of $600,000; direct labor for Job No. 102 of $200,000; indirect labor of $300,000.

e. Other manufacturing overhead costs of $400,000 are incurred. (Credit Cash, Accumulated Depreciation, and so on.)

f. Manufacturing overhead is applied to work in process at a rate of 50 percent of direct labor cost.

g. Raw materials used during the month amount to $80,000 for Job No. 101 and $160,000 for Job No. 102.

h. Job No. 101 was completed during the month.

i. Job No. 101 was sold on account for $1,200,000.

E30-3 (Job order)

Exhibit 30-19 summarizes data from job-order cost sheets of the Coach Company. Jobs No. 1, 2, 3, and 6 were completed during 19_6. Jobs No. 1, 2, and 3 were sold during 19_6. No additional costs were incurred to complete Job No. 1 because of a change in job specifications.

Required: Compute:

a. the goods-in-process inventory at the beginning of 19_6;

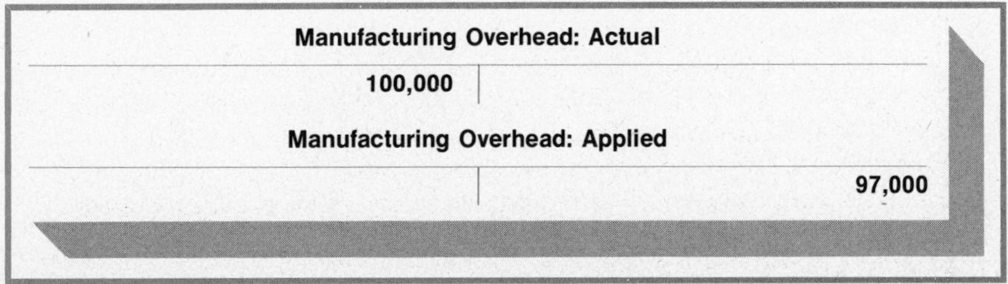

Exhibit 30-18
Ledger accounts for Question 8

Exhibit 30-19
Job-order cost information for Exercise E30-3

Job No.	Balance, Jan. 1, 19_6	Production Costs During 19_6
1	$15,000	—
2	22,000	$5,000
3	13,000	4,000
4	30,000	4,000
5	—	3,000
6	—	6,000

b. the goods-in-process inventory at the end of 19_6;
c. the cost of goods sold in 19_6;
d. the finished goods inventory on December 31, 19_6 (there was no balance in this inventory at the beginning of the year);
e. cost of goods manufactured in 19_6.

E30-4 (Job order)

The predetermined overhead rates for three departments of the Big Time Company are $12 per machine hour for the Cutting Department, 60 percent of direct labor cost for the Assembling Department, and $3 per direct labor hour for the Painting Department. Exhibit 30-20 summarizes cost data for Job No. 73 during the current month. In the Cutting Department, 20 machine hours were used on this job. The job was begun and completed during the month.

Required: Compute the cost of Job No. 73.

E30-5 (Process cost)

The Skoff Company compiles the following data for a single product produced in Process A:

Goods in process, Jan. 1, 19_5	60,000	(75% completed)
Transferred to finished goods	115,000	
Goods in process, Dec. 31, 19_5	55,000	(50% completed)

Required:
a. Prepare a quantity schedule for Process A.
b. Compute the equivalent production for Process A during 19_5.

E30-6 (Process cost)

The Process Cost Corporation compiles the following data for a product produced in a single department: Goods-in-process inventory of 12,000 units on January 1, 19_5 (75% complete as to materials; 40% complete as to direct labor; 40% complete as to manufacturing overhead); 60,000 units transferred to finished goods during 19_5; goods-in-process inventory of 4,000 units on December 31, 19_5 (50% complete as to materials; 30% complete as to direct labor; 20% complete as to manufacturing overhead).

Required:
a. Prepare a quantity report for the department.
b. Compute the equivalent production for material, labor, and overhead for the period.

E30-7 (Process cost)

For the case described in Exercise E30-5, the cost of goods in process at the beginning of the year totaled $85,000; cost of production for the year was $200,000.

Required:
a. Calculate the cost of the ending inventory of work in process, and the cost of goods transferred to finished goods.

	Cutting Dept.	Assembling Dept.	Painting Dept.
Direct material	**$600**	**$100**	**$40**
Actual direct labor rate (per hour)	**$8**	**$6**	**$7**
Direct labor used (hours)	**25**	**15**	**10**

Exhibit 30-20
Cost data for Exercise E30-4

b. Assume that 80 percent of the goods transferred to finished goods were sold during the year. What is the cost of goods sold for 19_6?

E30-8 (Process cost)
For the case described in Exercise E30-6, the following cost data are available. Goods in process on Jan. 1, 19_5: material $27,000; direct labor $28,800; overhead $4,800. Cost during 19_5: material $159,000; direct labor $338,400; overhead $116,800.

Required:

a. Compute the goods-in-process inventory at the end of 19_5.

b. Compute the cost of goods transferred out during the year.

c. What is the per-unit cost of a product in the department?

E30-9 (Equivalent production)
Compute the equivalent production for each of the following two independent cases.

	Case 1	Percent complete	Case 2	Percent complete
Beginning inventory	4,000	75%	30,000	50%
Placed in process	10,000		60,000	
Ending inventory	2,000	25%	12,000	75%
Transferred out	12,000		78,000	

Problems

P30-1 (Job order)
The Printout Company uses a job-order cost system. Journalize the following transactions, which occurred in October 19_6.

a. Direct material purchased on account, $200,000.

b. Labor used during month (factory payroll): $160,000 direct labor on Job No. 10; $60,000 direct labor on Job No. 11; $80,000 indirect labor. (Two entries required.)

c. Other manufacturing overhead costs incurred, $165,000.

d. Manufacturing overhead is applied to work in process at a rate of 80 percent of direct labor cost.

e. Raw materials used during the month: $60,000 on Job No. 10; $25,000 on Job No. 11.

f. Job No. 10 was completed during the period.

g. Job No. 10 was sold on account for $400,000.

P30-2 (Overhead rate)

The Relish Company uses a predetermined manufacturing overhead rate to match overhead expense to work in progress. The management of the Relish Company estimates that the company will operate at a production level of 150,000 direct labor hours in 19_6. Manufacturing overhead is estimated to be $240,000, of which $60,000 is fixed overhead.

At the end of 19_6, records indicate that 140,000 actual direct labor hours were used during the year, and that actual overhead expense incurred was $300,000.

Required:

a. Compute the budgeted overhead rate. How much of this rate is attributed to fixed costs? to variable costs?

b. What amount of overhead did the company apply to the cost of goods produced during the year?

c. Was overhead overapplied or underapplied during the year, and by how much? (This difference is referred to as the total variance.)

d. Calculate the overhead budget at the actual level of production attained. Show the fixed and variable components of this budget.

e. Calculate the overhead budget variances and the volume variance using a format with the following three columns: (A) actual overhead; (B) budgeted overhead at production level attained; and (C) applied overhead.

f. Compute the variable and fixed overhead for actual, budgeted, and applied overhead using a similar three-column format.

g. In the table prepared for part f, compare the Actual Overhead column total with the Budgeted Overhead column total. Did fixed or variable overhead account for the difference? What is this difference called? In general terms, what is the probable cause of this difference?

h. In the table prepared for part f, compare the Budgeted Overhead column total with the Applied Overhead column total. Did fixed or variable overhead account for the difference? What is this difference called? In general terms, what is the probable cause of this difference?

P30-3 (Process cost)

The Falls Manufacturing Company begins production on January 1, 19_1. The company has two departments. Work is started in the Processing Department and transferred to the Assembly Department, from which the finished product is transferred to the company's warehouse. The following transactions occur during January 19_1.

(1) Material purchased on account, $100,000.
(2) Material transferred to the Processing Department for production, $40,000.
(3) Factory payroll amounts to $460,000.
(4) Factory payroll is distributed to the departments as follows: $200,000 to Processing Department; $210,000 to Assembly Department; $50,000 to indirect labor.
(5) Actual manufacturing expense amounts to $700,000.
(6) Manufacturing overhead assigned to production for the year is as follows: $300,000 to Processing Department; $350,000 to Assembly Department.

The two departments report the following production data: 100 units started in production in Processing Department; 80 units transferred to Assembly Department and started in production there; 40 units transferred to Finished

Goods; 20 units in ending inventory of Processing Department (50 percent complete as to all costs); 40 units in ending inventory of Assembly Department (30 percent complete as to all costs).

Required:

a. Prepare journal entries for transactions (1) through (6).
b. Prepare a quantity schedule for the two departments.
c. Prepare an equivalent production schedule for each department.
d. Prepare a report of production costs for each department.
e. Prepare an entry to transfer costs from the Processing Department to the Assembly Department; a second entry is needed to transfer costs from the Assembly Department to Finished Goods.

Additional data:

(7) One-half of the finished goods produced during the period are sold for $1,500,000.
(8) Selling and administrative expenses amount to $600,000.

Required:

f. Journalize transactions (7) and (8). [Two entries are required for transaction (7).]
g. Post all entries to the following accounts: Goods in Process: Processing; Goods in Process: Assembly; Finished Goods; and Cost of Goods Sold.
h. Compute the ending balances in the accounts just set up. Where possible, relate these balances to the reports of production costs prepared earlier.

P30-4 (Job order)

A company uses a job order cost system for controlling costs. At the beginning of June, the company had two jobs in process:

Job 10	$10,000
Job 12	15,000

The following matters occurred during the month.

1. Purchased $100,000 of direct material on account.
2. Paid the account in full.
3. Payroll costs incurred during the month were as follows:

Total payroll	$600,000
F.I.C.A.	30,000
Income taxes withheld	70,000

4. Factory payroll is distributed to indirect labor and goods in process are as follows:

Indirect labor	$100,000
Job 10	10,000
Job 12	90,000
Job 13	200,000
Job 14	100,000
Job 15	100,000

5. The factory payroll is paid.
6. Materials used during the month were as follows:

Indirect materials	$50,000
Job 10	15,000
Job 12	20,000
Job 13	50,000
Job 14	25,000
Job 15	10,000

7. Other manufacturing costs incurred totalled $100,000.
8. Manufacturing overhead is applied to work in process at a rate of 40% of direct labor cost.
9. Jobs 10, 12, and 15 were completed during the month.
10. Jobs 10 and 12 were billed to customers at $50,000 and $250,000, respectively.
11. Administrative expenses and selling expenses of $50,000 and $30,000 were paid during the month.
12. The company transfers any over- or underapplied overhead to cost of goods sold.

Required:

a. Journalize the entries that occurred during the month for the company.
b. Compute the goods-in-process inventory at the end of the month.
c. Prepare an income statement for the month.

P30-5 (Process cost)

The Map Company reports the following departmental data for September.

Department 1:

120,000 tons of material costing $36,000 were put into process.
Payroll for September was $15,000.
Overhead costs for September were $5,000.
90,000 tons were processed and transferred to Department 2.
30,000 tons are still in process. Percents of completion for this work are as follows:

Materials	100%
Labor and overhead	33⅓%

Department 2:

Payroll for the month is $21,000.
Overhead costs are $11,200.
No material was added in Department 2.
The 90,000 tons transferred from Department 1 are accounted for as follows:

Transferred to finished goods	50,000 tons
In Department 2 and finished	10,000 tons
In Department 2 and one-third complete as to labor and overhead in Department 2	30,000 tons

Required: Prepare a Cost of Production Report for Departments 1 and 2. Use the format shown in Exhibit 30-13.

P30-6 (Job order)

A company uses a job order cost system. Record the following transactions:

a. A company purchases $100,000 of material for its manufacturing operations.
b. The company requisitions $50,000 of material for Job Order No. 1 and $25,000 for Job Order No. 2.
c. The factory payroll amounted to $200,000.
d. Direct labor for Job Order No. 1 was $150,000 and $40,000 for Job Order No. 2. Indirect labor charges totalled $10,000.
e. Indirect materials taken from the stores totalled $5,000.
f. Factory overhead is applied to production at a predetermined rate of 50% of direct labor cost.
g. Factory overhead costs were incurred in the amount of $90,000.
h. Job Order No. 1 was completed.
i. Job Order No. 1 is shipped to customer and invoiced for $400,000.

P30-7 (Job order)

Refer to Problem P30-6

a. Post the journal entries to a general journal and to subsidiary records.

b. Take a trial balance of the general journal. Compare control account balances with relevant subsidiary records.

31 Standard cost system and direct costing

Chapter 26 discusses the basic concepts of standard cost accounting. In this section we pick up the thread of that discussion to show the details of accounting procedures in such a system. Review Chapter 26 at this point to refresh your memory on standard cost concepts.

Standard cost systems

In a standard cost system, product costing is achieved by using predetermined standard costs for material, direct labor, and overhead. Control is established by comparing (1) standard costs with actual costs, and (2) standard quantities allowed for production with actual quantities used. Any costs or usages that are out of line are reported to management for evaluation.

We now illustrate the accounting treatment with an example of a standard cost accounting system for the Standard Cost Company, which manufactures one product: quality lawn furniture. Exhibit 31-1 shows a standard cost card for lawn furniture.

Exhibit 31-1
Standard cost card for lawn furniture

STANDARD COST COMPANY
Standard Cost Card: Lawn Furniture

Material:	
5 pieces of Material X at $10 per piece	**$50.00**
Labor:	
2 hours direct labor at $8 per hour	**16.00**
Manufacturing Overhead:	
At rate of $3 per direct labor hour	**6.00**
	$72.00

Recall that such a card shows the standard costs of material, direct labor, and overhead applicable to the production of each unit manufactured.

In a standard cost system, these standard costs are processed into the accounting records. The Material, Goods in Process, and Finished Goods accounts contain ***standard cost*** data that are used for product-costing purposes. Keep this point in mind as we examine the accounting system of this firm that uses standard costs.

MATERIALS

The Standard Cost Company purchased 100,000 units of Material X at $10.20 per unit during the year, to add to its inventory of raw material. According to the standard cost card (Exhibit 31-1), the standard cost per piece of Material X is $10. The standard cost of the purchased materials is recorded in the Materials account (100,000 units @ $10 per unit = $1,000,000). The purchase-price variance (if one exists) is recorded in a special variance account.

Materials	1,000,000	
Purchase Price Variance	20,000	
Accounts Payable		1,020,000

Note that the debit to the variance account represents an unfavorable variance. Also note that the credit to Accounts Payable represents the actual amount of the purchase.

The purchase price variance is developed at the time of purchase in this system. This procedure provides control opportunities because it alerts management to deficiencies or strengths in its purchasing activities as they occur. The ledger accounts shown in Exhibit 31-2 reflect the purchase transaction just journalized. Note that the Materials account contains ***standard*** cost data. The purchase price variance reflects the difference in unit purchase cost from unit standard cost, weighted by the number of units purchased. If actual costs exceed standard cost allowed (as in this situation), the variance is unfavorable and is represented as a debit balance.

Continuing our illustration, we find that 27,000 units of lawn furniture were started in production during the year. For this production, 130,000 pieces of Material X were requisitioned from the inventory of Material X. The standard cost card indicates that the standard quantity of Material X for 27,000 units of lawn furniture is 135,000 pieces (five pieces for each unit of furniture). When materials are issued to production, a material usage variance may develop (as it does in this case). If standard quantity exceeds the actual quantity, the variance is favorable—that is, the firm uses less material than allowed by the standard.

The transfer of Material X from the materials inventory to the goods-in-process inventory is recorded by the following journal entry.

Goods in Process	1,350,000	
Materials		1,300,000
Material Usage Variance		50,000

Again, the entry in the Materials account shows actual quantities at standard cost. The entry in the Goods in Process account shows standard quantities at standard cost. The variance account records the dollar variance due to the difference between standard and actual quantities (Exhibit 31-3). The favorable variance is recorded as a credit.

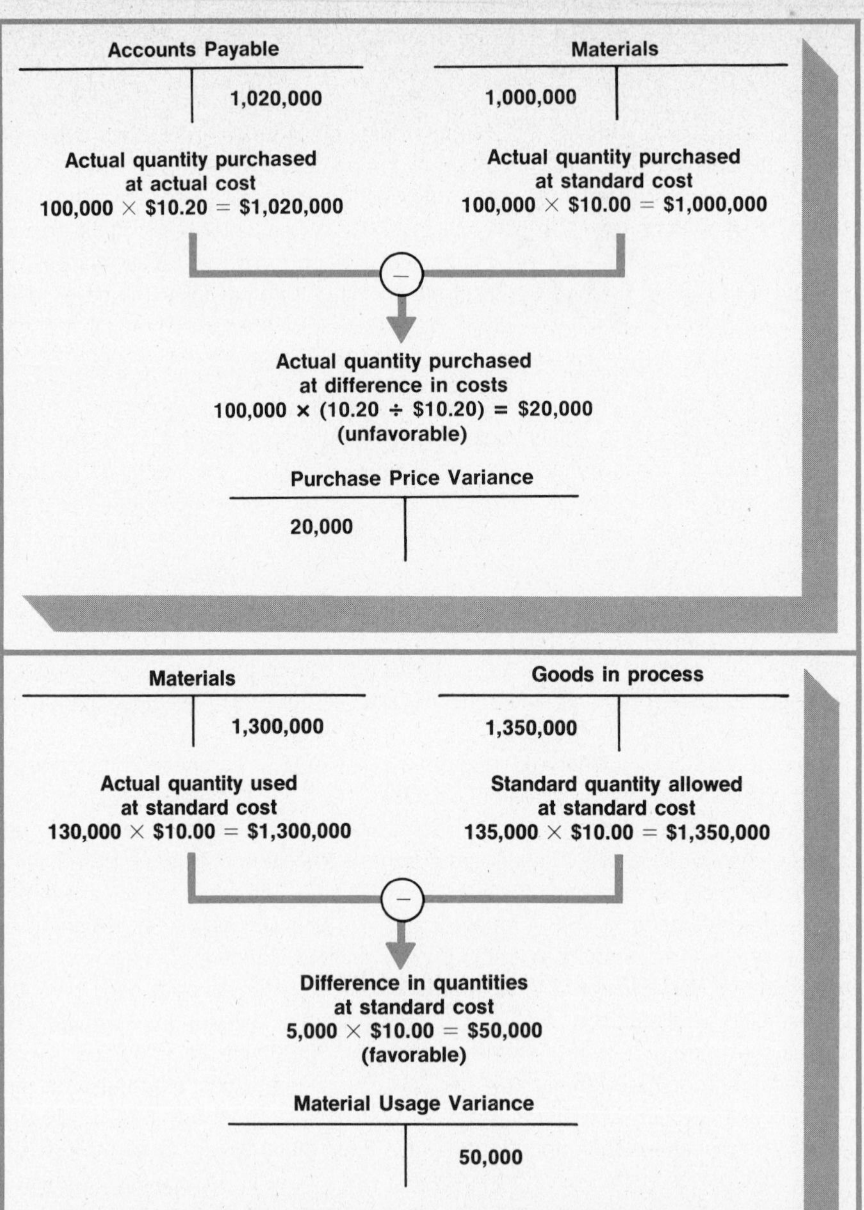

Exhibit 31-2
Development of purchase price variance in ledger accounts

Exhibit 31-3
Development of material usage variance in ledger accounts

DIRECT LABOR In processing the 27,000 units of lawn furniture during the year, the Standard Cost Company used 53,000 direct labor hours at a rate of $9 per hour. The standard calls for two hours of labor per unit of furniture, or 54,000 direct labor hours to produce the 27,000 units, at a standard rate of $8 per hour. The following journal entry summarizes the year's payroll (53,000 hours × $9 per hour = $477,000).

Factory Payroll	477,000	
[Wages Payable, Taxes Payable, etc.]		477,000

The payroll cost should be applied to Goods in Process. When an entry is made for this purpose, a labor rate variance and a labor efficiency variance may develop if the labor rate and labor usage differ from the standards (as they do in this case). These two labor variances are computed as follows.

1. The *labor rate variance* is equal to the actual hours purchased multiplied by the difference between the standard labor rate and the actual labor rate. In this case, the actual labor rate exceeds the standard rate, so an unfavorable labor rate variance occurs—more was paid per labor hour than allowed at standard.
2. The *labor efficiency variance* is equal to the standard labor rate multiplied by the difference between standard hours allowed and actual hours used. In this case, the standard hours allowed exceed the actual hours used, so a favorable labor efficiency variance develops—less labor hours were used than allowed at standard.

In our example, the actual labor rate is $1 higher than the standard, so the labor rate variance is $53,000 unfavorable (53,000 actual hours used × $1). The standard hours allowed are 1,000 hours greater than the actual hours used, so the labor efficiency variance is $8,000 favorable ($8 per hour standard rate × 1,000 hours). Therefore, the following entry summarizes the application of the payroll to Goods in Process and the variance accounts.

Goods in Process	432,000	
Labor Rate Variance	53,000	
Labor Efficiency Variance		8,000
Factory Payroll		477,000

Note that the entry to Goods in Process represents the standard hours allowed at the standard rate (54,000 hours at $8 per hour). Exhibit 31-4 shows the ledger accounts associated with direct labor cost after the posting of the two journal entries dealing with factory payroll.

MANUFACTURING OVERHEAD

The Standard Cost Company had prepared a flexible manufacturing overhead budget (Exhibit 31-5) at the beginning of 19_0. The manufacturing overhead rate was computed at the beginning of the year, based on an expected activity level currently attainable at 60,000 standard direct labor hours. A standard overhead rate of $3 per direct labor hour was established at the expected activity level. A combined fixed and variable overhead rate is required for product costing—such a combined rate must be computed for some assumed level of activity. (In Chapter 26, we used two variable overhead variances to control variable costs and to analyze performance.)

The following data are available concerning manufacturing overhead costs for the year. The standard overhead rate was predetermined at $3 per direct labor hour. The direct-labor standard allowed 54,000 hours for the production actually attained during the year. An actual overhead cost of $150,000 was incurred during the year, and 53,000 direct labor hours were actually used. The following journal entry summarizes the recording of the actual overhead costs during the year.

Manufacturing Overhead	150,000	
[Cash, Accumulated Depreciation, etc.]		150,000

Exhibit 31-4 **Development of labor variances in ledger accounts**

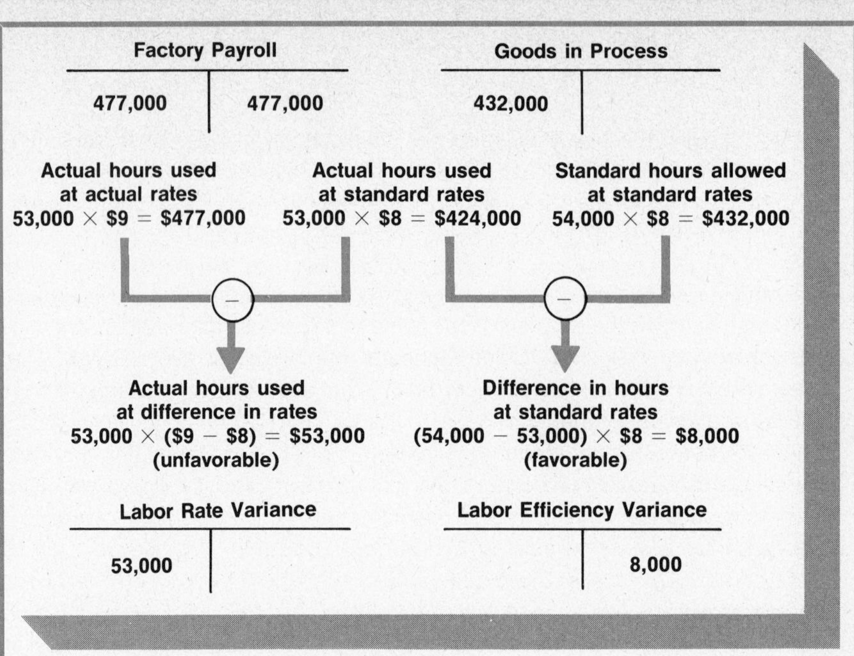

STANDARD COST COMPANY

Flexible Manufacturing Overhead Budget

Percent of capacity	90%	100%	110%
Direct labor hours	54,000	60,000	66,000
Fixed costs:			
Depreciation	$ 25,000	$ 25,000	$ 25,000
Property taxes	50,000	50,000	50,000
Other fixed overhead costs	45,000	45,000	45,000
Total fixed overhead costs (*a*)	$120,000	$120,000	$120,000
Variable costs:			
Supplies	$ 9,000	$ 10,000	$ 11,000
Power	18,000	20,000	22,000
Other variable overhead costs	27,000	30,000	33,000
Total variable overhead costs (*b*)	$ 54,000	$ 60,000	$ 66,000
Total manufacturing overhead costs (*a* + *b*)	$174,000	$180,000	$186,000

Standard overhead rate per direct labor hour (computed at 100% capacity):

$$\text{Variable overhead rate} = \frac{\$60{,}000}{60{,}000 \text{ hrs}} = \$1$$

$$\text{Fixed overhead rate} = \frac{\$120{,}000}{60{,}000 \text{ hrs}} = \$2$$

$$\text{Total manufacturing overhead rate} = \$3$$

Exhibit 31-5 **A flexible manufacturing overhead budget**

The overhead cost is assigned to the year's production at the predetermined rate and using the standard number of direct labor hours allowed (54,000 hours allowed × standard rate of $3 per direct labor hour).

Goods in Process	162,000	
Manufacturing Overhead		162,000

Therefore, at the end of the year (before closing entries), the actual manufacturing overhead cost of $150,000 has been overapplied (by $12,000) to the cost of goods in process (Exhibit 31-6). The Manufacturing Overhead account shows a credit balance of $12,000. The cost charged to Goods in Process (like the other costs charged to that account) represents the standard cost for the volume of goods produced during the year. Two manufacturing overhead variances can be computed.

1. The ***budget variance*** (also called controllable variance, or spending variance) shows the variance that results from operation at a ***performance*** (efficiency) level above or below that expected. It measures the amount by which manufacturing overhead differed from the standard amount allowed for the production level attained. This variance is computed as the difference between (a) the actual manufacturing overhead incurred, and (b) the budgeted overhead based on standard labor hours allowed for actual work completed. If the budgeted overhead exceeds actual overhead, a favorable budget variance develops—less was spent for overhead than was allowed by standards for this level of production.
2. The ***volume variance*** shows the variance that results from operation at an ***activity*** level above or below that expected. The volume variance is a result of fixed overhead cost per unit differing from that allowed in the standard rate (which was computed for expected volume). The volume variance relates to the extent to which plant facilities were used or remained idle. This variance is computed as the difference between (a) the budgeted overhead based on standard labor hours allowed for actual work completed, and (b) the amount of overhead applied to production (standard hours allowed multiplied by standard overhead rate). If applied overhead exceeds budgeted overhead, a favorable variance occurs—the level of activity attained was such as to cause budgeted overhead to be lower than that allowed for in the standard overhead rate.

Exhibit 31-7 shows the computation of these two variances for the illustrated case. Note that the "budgeted overhead based on standard labor hours allowed for actual work completed" is obtained from the flexible manufacturing overhead budget (Exhibit 31-5). The actual level of production (27,000 units of product) requires 54,000 standard direct labor hours (standard of 2 hours per unit). This represents 90 percent of capacity as shown on the flexible budget, with budgeted overhead cost of $174,000 for that level of activity.

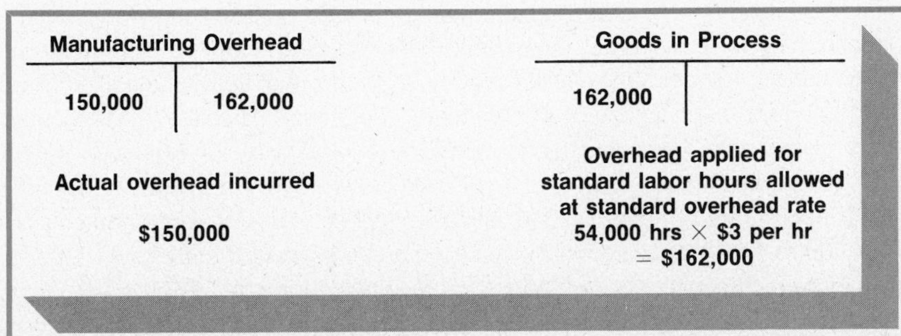

Exhibit 31-6
Ledger accounts for manufacturing overhead before closing

Exhibit 31-7
Development of overhead variances in ledger accounts

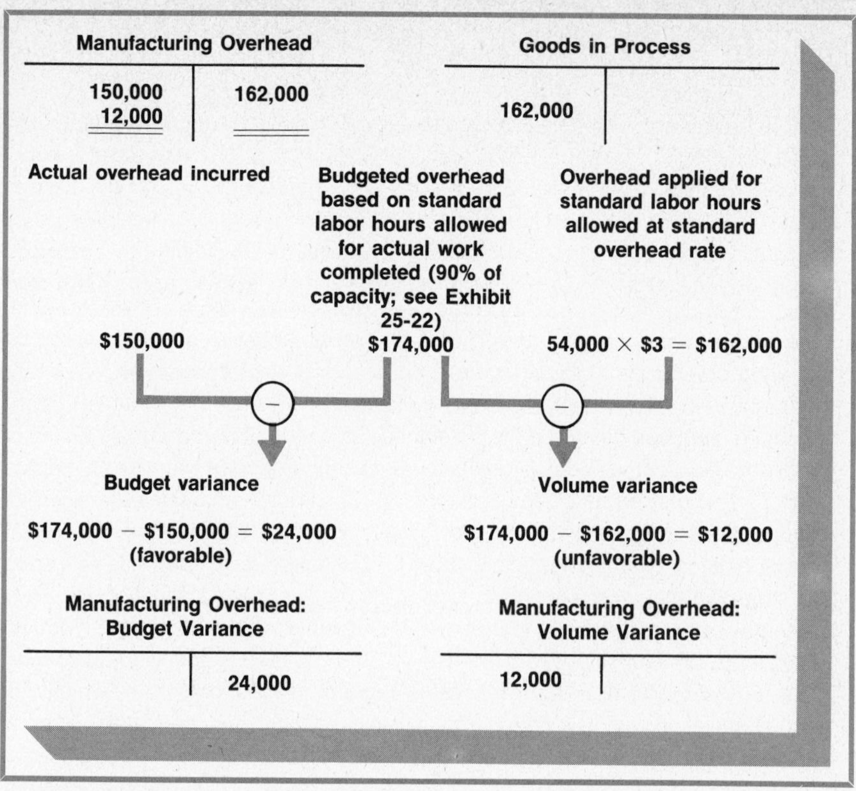

To help clarify the discussion of overhead variances, let us consider the amounts involved in this computation in terms of fixed and variable overhead costs (Exhibit 31-8). Note that the actual overhead involved $120,000 of fixed cost and $30,000 of variable cost. The flexible budget called for use of 54,000 direct labor hours to produce the actual 27,000 units of product (at 90 percent of capacity). This budget called for $120,000 fixed overhead cost and $54,000 variable overhead cost at this level of production. The budget variance ($24,000 favorable) represents the variance between actual and budgeted variable overhead cost. The budget variance is favorable because the actual overhead cost incurred was less than the flexible budget allowed at 90 percent of capacity. If variable cost actually turned out to be the same as that budgeted at the 90 percent level of capacity, there would be no budget variance.

Now consider the volume variance—the difference between budgeted overhead at actual production level and applied overhead (standard hours allowed at standard overhead rate). In Exhibit 31-5, note that the standard overhead rate of $3 per hour is computed for 100 percent level of capacity. At this level of activity, the fixed overhead cost is distributed among 60,000 standard labor hours. When the rate computed for this level of activity is applied to the actual level of activity, the fixed cost will be under- or overapplied (unless the activity level does prove to be exactly that predicted). In our example, the $120,000 of fixed cost should have been distributed over the 54,000 standard labor hours allowed for the actual level of production. That is, if the company had expected to produce 27,000 units during the year, it would have computed its standard overhead rate for this level of activity. In that case, the variable overhead rate would still be $1 per direct labor hour ($54,000/54,000 hours). Therefore, if the company had planned to produce 27,000 units, it would have applied overhead cost to production at a standard rate of $3.22 per standard labor hour. Because it used instead the predetermined rate of $3 per standard labor hour (computed for a higher level of production), the fixed overhead cost has been underapplied. The volume variance is the difference between budgeted fixed overhead for the actual level of production and applied fixed overhead at the standard rate. It is a measure of the cost of not producing at the level originally established when the $3 overhead rate was set. If the actual level of production were the same as that used to compute the standard overhead rate, there would be no volume variance. In our example, the volume variance is unfavorable because available facilities were not used to the full extent planned when the budget was drawn up. Fixed overhead cost must be applied to a smaller volume of production than that originally estimated.

The journal entry that records the two overhead variances closes the Manufacturing Overhead account.

Manufacturing Overhead: Volume Variance	12,000	
Manufacturing Overhead	12,000	
Manufacturing Overhead: Budget Variance		24,000

Exhibit 31-7 includes the ledger accounts as they appear after this entry is posted.

If desired, the budget variance of $24,000 (favorable) could be analyzed further in terms of the two *variable* overhead variances discussed in Chapter 26.

1. The *spending variance* is the difference between actual variable overhead cost and the variable budget overhead allowed for the production attained.
2. The *efficiency variance* is the difference between the direct labor hours used (53,000) and the direct labor hours allowed (54,000), multiplied by the standard variable overhead rate of $1 per hour.

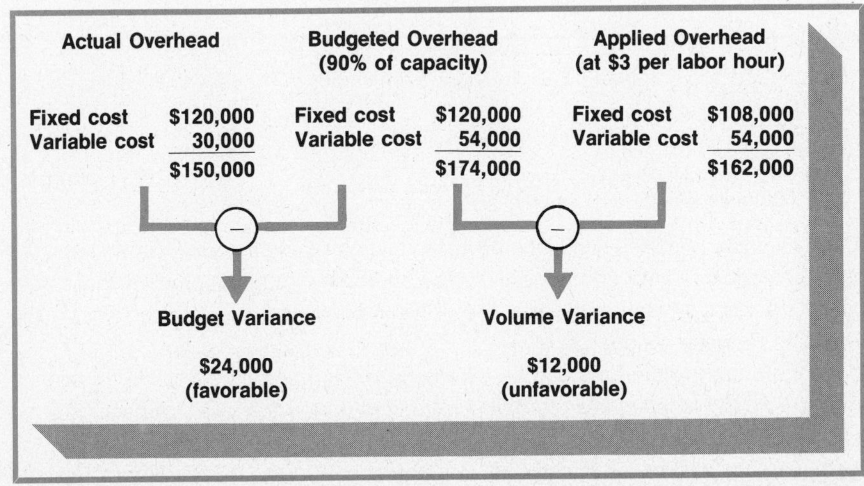

Exhibit 31-8
Overhead variances in terms of fixed and variable overhead costs

Exhibit 31-9
Computation of variable overhead variances

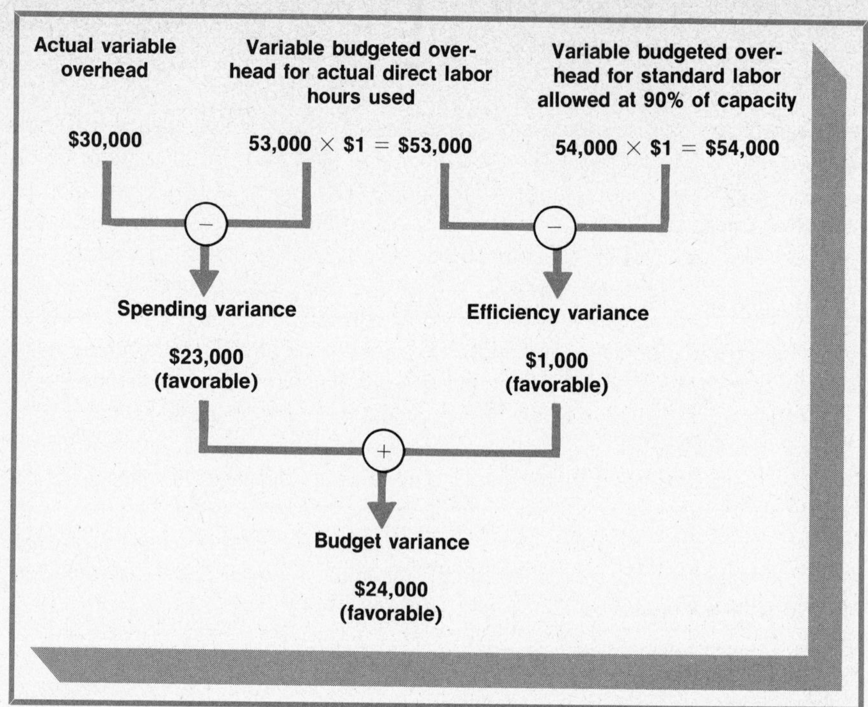

Exhibit 31-9 shows the computation of these variances. The spending variance is favorable because the actual variable overhead was less than the budgeted overhead for the production attained. The efficiency variance is also favorable because less hours were actually worked than the standard allowed at 90 percent of capacity.

FINISHED GOODS

The Goods in Process account accumulates ***standard*** cost data for material, labor, and overhead (see the debit side of the Goods in Process account in Exhibit 31-10, which includes all of the entries made in this account in preceding exhibits). In our illustration, the 27,000 pieces of lawn furniture were completed and transferred to the finished goods warehouse. The standard cost card (Exhibit 31-1) shows that the standard cost of one piece of lawn furniture is $72. Therefore, the entry to record the transfer of the completed lawn furniture from Goods in Process to Finished Goods is the following.

Finished Goods	1,944,000	
Goods in Process		1,944,000
27,000 units @ $72 = $1,944,000.		

In this example, all of the units entered in production during the year were completed and transferred to finished goods. Because all entries in the Goods in Process account are made at standard costs, the transfer entry has the effect of closing the Goods in Process account.

Standard costs often are used as a basis for pricing products for sale. In this example, 20,000 pieces of lawn furniture were sold during the year. The selling price was set at 150 percent of standard cost—that is, at $108 per unit. The following journal entries summarize the sales and the transfer of standard costs from Finished Goods to Cost of Goods Sold.

Accounts Receivable	2,160,000	
Sales		2,160,000
Sale of 20,000 units @ $108 per unit.		
Cost of Goods Sold	1,440,000	
Finished Goods		1,440,000
20,000 units @ $72 standard cost.		

DISPOSITION OF VARIANCE ACCOUNTS

The variance accounts that are developed in a standard cost system should be analyzed carefully to determine the causes of the variances. Where the variances are unfavorable, corrective action should be taken to eliminate their causes. Where the variances are favorable, action may be desirable to ensure recurrence of such conditions in the future.

At the close of an accounting period, the variance accounts can be closed to Cost of Goods Sold, or to the Income Summary account. Where currently attainable standard costs are used for product costing, variances measure efficient or inefficient activities and should be credited or charged to current operations. Where this procedure is used, the inventories of goods in process and finished goods are valued at standard costs. The entry to close the variances to the Cost of Goods Sold account for our illustration is the following.

Material Usage Variance	50,000	
Labor Efficiency Variance	8,000	
Manufacturing Overhead: Budget Variance	24,000	
Cost of Goods Sold	3,000	
Purchase Price Variance		20,000
Labor Rate Variance		53,000
Manufacturing Overhead: Volume Variance		12,000
To close variance accounts to Cost of Goods Sold.		

The effect of this closing entry is to adjust the balance of the Cost of Goods Sold account to reflect the actual cost variances incurred in the manufacturing process during the year. Any balances remaining in Goods in Process and Finished Goods are retained at standard cost valuation.

In theory, it would be correct in some instances to close the variances to Goods in Process, Finished Goods, and Cost of Goods Sold in proportion to the ending balances in these accounts. This would have the effect of valuing all inventories and the cost of goods sold at an approximation of actual costs. In practice, however, the

Exhibit 31-10 Inventory accounts after posting entry for completion of units

Goods in Process

Material (at standard)	**1,350,000**	**Units completed and transferred to Finished Goods (at standard cost)**	**1,944,000**
Labor (at standard)	**432,000**		
Overhead (applied at predetermined rate)	**162,000**		

Finished Goods

Units completed (at standard cost)	**1,944,000**		

variance accounts usually are closed to Cost of Goods Sold as in our illustration. On the income statement, variances can be shown separately after computation of cost of goods sold at standard costs. If the variances are distributed to inventory and cost of goods sold, standard costing produces financial statements identical with those produced by an actual cost accounting system.

Direct costing

In cost-accounting procedures, a distinction is drawn between direct costing and absorption (or conventional) costing. When direct costing procedures are used, all manufacturing costs are separated into product costs and period costs. Costs that change in response to volume are considered product costs; all remaining costs (constant regardless of volume) are period costs. In *direct costing,* the variable costs (direct materials, direct labor, and *variable* manufacturing overhead) make up product costs; these costs are associated with inventory and with cost of goods sold. Fixed manufacturing expenses that reflect the cost of operating plant facilities (regardless of volume of production) are period costs; these costs are not included in computations of inventory and cost of goods sold. They are deducted from gross margin on the income statement for the period in which they are recognized as expenses.

Absorption costing considers *all* manufacturing costs (including fixed manufacturing overhead) as product costs. The only period costs in this approach are those not directly associated with manufacturing (such as selling and administrative expenses). In absorption costing, when production exceeds sales for a period, a portion of fixed cost is included in inventory. Hence, cost of goods sold will be smaller and net income higher than when direct costing procedures are used. (In our example, sales exceeded production because ending inventory was less than beginning inventory.)

Exhibit 31-11 summarizes operating data for a company during a year. Exhibits

Exhibit 31-11 Operating data for income statements in Exhibits 31-12 and 31-13

Sales price per unit **$10**
Normal operating capacity **100,000 units per year**

	Manufacturing Costs at Normal Capacity		Selling and Administrative Expenses	
	Total	Per Unit	Total	Per Unit
Fixed cost/expense	$100,000	$1.00	$ 50,000	$0.50
Variable cost/expense	200,000	2.00	100,000	1.00
Total cost/expense	$300,000	$3.00	$150,000	$1.50

Beginning inventory of finished goods	10,000 units
Production for the year	90,000 units
Sales for the year	95,000 units
Ending inventory of finished goods	5,000 units

Exhibit 31-12 **Income statement based on absorption costing**

INCOME STATEMENT: ABSORPTION COSTING

Sales (*a*)	$950,000	(95,000 units × $10)
Cost of goods sold (standard):		
Beginning inventory	$ 30,000	(10,000 units × $3)
Cost of goods manufactured	270,000	(90,000 units × $3)
Total	$300,000	
Less: Ending inventory	15,000	(5,000 units × $3)
Cost of goods sold (standard) (*b*)	$285,000	
Gross margin (standard) (*a* − *b* = *c*)	$665,000	
Selling and administrative expenses:		
Variable expense	$ 95,000	(95,000 units × $1)
Fixed expense	50,000	
Total (*d*)	$145,000	
Net income (standard) (*c* − *d*)	$520,000	
Less: Underapplied manufacturing overhead	10,000	(See Note)
Net income (actual)	$510,000	

NOTE: Fixed manufacturing overhead was applied to production at the rate of $1 per unit, computed for normal capacity. In fact, production was 10,000 units less than normal capacity, so fixed manufacturing overhead cost was underapplied by $10,000 (the underproduction of 10,000 units multiplied by the $1 per unit fixed manufacturing overhead rate).

31-12 and 31-13 show income statements for this company based upon absorption and direct costing procedures, respectively.

It can be argued that the cost of inventory should include all costs (both variable and fixed) that are associated with the acquisition of the product. Direct costing does not achieve this goal, because it excludes fixed manufacturing overhead from the cost of inventory and goods sold. In the example, net income under direct costing ($515,000) exceeds net income under absorption costing ($510,000) by $5,000. This difference results from the inventory-valuation procedures. Under absorption costing, inventory is valued at $3 per unit (including fixed expense). Therefore, the difference between beginning and ending inventory is—

(10,000 − 5,000 units) × $3 per unit = $15,000.

Under direct costing, inventory is valued at $2 per unit (excluding fixed overhead). Therefore, the difference between beginning and ending inventory is

(10,000 − 5,000 units) × $2 per unit = $10,000.

Thus, direct costing shows a smaller reduction in inventory value and, therefore, cost of goods sold is less and net income is larger by $5,000.

Direct costing procedures are not acceptable for external reporting, although the information that direct costing provides for internal planning and decision-making purposes justifies its limited use. In Exhibit 31-12, note that marginal income is equivalent to contribution margin (discussed in Chapter 25). Direct costing enables management to use a contribution-margin approach in solving many practical business problems.

Exhibit 31-13 **Income statement based on direct costing**

INCOME STATEMENT: DIRECT COSTING		
Sales	$950,000	(95,000 × $10)
Cost of goods sold: Variable manufacturing expense	190,000	(95,000 × $2)
Marginal income: Manufacturing	$760,000	
Selling and administrative expenses: Variable expense	95,000	(95,000 × $1)
Marginal income (Contribution margin) (*a*)	$665,000	
Fixed operating expense (period cost):		
Manufacturing expenses (fixed)	$100,000	
Selling and administrative expense (fixed)	50,000	
Total fixed operating expense (*b*)	$150,000	
Net income (*a* − *b*)	$515,000	

Summary

When a standard cost system is used, a wide variety of accounting procedures are available. The Standard Cost Company case illustrates a typical standard cost system that establishes standard costs in the Materials, Goods in Process, Finished Goods, and Cost of Goods Sold accounts. In this example, a two-way variance analysis is used for manufacturing overhead. When standard costs are used, variances can be computed to identify cases where performance differs from a predetermined standard. Variances may be favorable or unfavorable. Unfavorable variances occur when actual costs (or hours) exceed standard costs (or hours) or budgeted costs. Favorable variances occur when actual costs (or hours) are less than standard costs (or hours) or budgeted costs. Six variances are developed in this chapter.

1. Purchase price variance = Actual quantities purchased *times* (Actual price *less* Standard price).
2. Material usage variance = (Actual quantity used *less* Standard quantity allowed) *times* Standard price.
3. Labor rate variance = Actual hours used *times* (Actual labor rate *less* Standard labor rate).
4. Labor efficiency variance = (Actual hours used *less* Standard hours allowed) *times* Standard labor rate.
5. Overhead budget variance = Actual manufacturing overhead *less* Budgeted overhead based on standard labor hours allowed for production level attained.
6. Overhead volume variance = Budgeted overhead based on standard labor hours allowed for production level attained *less* Overhead applied to production (which is equal to Standard hours allowed *times* Standard overhead rate).

When direct costing is used, only variable costs of production are included in inventories and cost of goods sold; fixed costs are charged off as expenses of the period. Direct costing eliminates income distortions resulting from production for inventories rather than for sales. Direct costing also provides information for special pricing situations where differential cost analysis is required. However, direct costing should not be used in financial statements prepared for external use. Absorption costing is a "full costing" procedure; fixed and variable manufacturing costs are considered costs of the product and are included in inventory and cost of goods sold.

Questions

1. What is a standard cost system?
2. What is direct costing? absorption costing?
3. Accountants refer to cost flows. Explain cost flows in terms of recognition, transference, and expiration.
4. Why is a predetermined overhead rate used in a job-cost system? How is the overhead rate determined?
5. Distinguish between a product cost and an expense. When direct costing procedures are used, are fixed expenses a product cost or a period cost?
6. Are all fixed expenses recognized as expenses during the period?
7. Is direct costing acceptable for external reporting? Explain.

Exercises

E31-1 (Labor and material variances)
The Sea Spray Company uses a standard cost system. The following data for 19__ are available. Expected production (100% of capacity), 10,000 units. Standard direct labor rate, $12 per hour. Standard material price, $6 per bushel. Standard labor hours per unit, 18 hours. Standard material usage per unit, 10 bushels. Actual material purchased, 120,000 bushels at $8 per bushel. Actual material used, 110,000 bushels. Actual direct labor used, 150,000 hours at $10 per hour. Actual units produced, 7,500.

Required: Compute the labor and material variances.

E31-2 (Material variances)
A company purchased 10,000 units of material at $8 per unit. The standard cost of the material was $7.50 per unit. During the month, the company used 9,000 units of material in producing 4,000 targets, the single product manufactured by the company. Standard quantity of material required to produce one target is 2 units.

Required: Prepare journal entries to record the purchase of the material and its issuance out of inventory and into the manufacturing process.

E31-3 (Labor variances)
A company has established standard labor costs per hour of $10. Standard quantities of labor hours per unit of product are 2 hours. The company produced 10,000 products during the month. The company's payroll for direct labor was $209,000. Direct labor cost was $11.00 per hour.

Required: Prepare journal entries to record the labor rate variance and the labor efficiency variance.

E31-4 (T-account analysis for overhead)
The following ledger accounts appear in the records of a company that uses standard costs.

Manufacturing Overhead				Goods in Process		
(a)	500,000	(b)	450,000	(e)	450,000	
		(c)	50,000			

Budget Variance			Volume Variance		
(d)	15,000		(f)	35,000	

Required:

a. Explain the probable transaction or event that resulted in the various entries in the accounts.

b. What was the budgeted overhead amount for the production level attained?

E31-5 (Variances)

The Award Manufacturing Company developed the following standards for a unit of product:

Direct materials	2 lbs. @ $5 per lb.	$10
Direct labor	3 hrs. @ $4 per hour	12
Factory overhead:		
Variable	3 hrs. @ $2 per hour	
Fixed	3 hrs. @ $1 per hour	9
		$41

During November, the company produced 15,000 units. The following costs were incurred during the month:

Direct materials	31,000 lbs. @ $5.10 per pound
Direct labor	44,000 hrs. @ $3.90 per hour
Factory overhead	$142,000 of which $30,000 was fixed overhead

Budgeted overhead based on standard labor hours allowed for production level attained was $118,000.

Required: Compute the following variances and indicate whether the variance is favorable or unfavorable.

a. Purchase price variance
b. Material usage variance
c. Labor rate variance
d. Labor efficiency variance
e. Overhead budget variance
f. Overhead volume variance

E31-6 (Direct and absorption costing)

A firm compiles the following data for its operations during a year.

Direct material used	$ 80,000
Direct labor used	220,000
Variable manufacturing overhead	90,000
Fixed manufacturing overhead	110,000
Selling and administrative expenses	125,000
Units produced during the year	150 units
Units sold during the year	120 units

Required:

a. If the firm uses direct costing procedures, what is the value assigned to the ending finished goods inventory?

b. If the firm uses absorption costing procedures, what is the value assigned to the ending finished goods inventory?

Problems

P31-1 (Recording transactions)

A manufacturing company has established a standard cost system to control its costs. The company has developed the standard cost card shown in Exhibit 31-14 for Wamp, the product produced by the company. During the year 19_6, the following transactions occur. Journalize these transactions.

a. Purchase of 125,000 pieces of lumber at $3.80 per piece on account.
b. During the year, 120,000 pieces of lumber are requisitioned from stores for the production of 46,000 Wamps.
c. During the year, the factory payroll amounts to 180,000 actual hours at an actual rate of $3.50 per hour.
d. The factory payroll is assigned to goods in process.
e. Actual manufacturing overhead during the year amounts to $270,000.
f. Manufacturing overhead is assigned to goods in process on a basis of direct labor hours.
g. The Manufacturing Overhead account is closed; two overhead variances are established. The company uses a flexible budget. The following data are available: budget overhead based on standard labor hours allowed for production attained, $280,000; overhead applied to production (138,000 hours @ $2 per hour), $276,000.
h. Forty thousand Wamps are completed and transferred to finished goods.
i. Twenty thousand Wamps are sold for $1,400,000. (Two entries needed.)
j. The company follows the practice of closing the variance accounts to the Cost of Goods Sold account.

P31-2 (Direct and absorption costing)

The following operating data are available for a manufacturing concern.

Direct labor: 1,200 hours per unit at rate of $4 per hour.
Direct material: $8,000 per unit.
Factory overhead: variable at $10 per direct labor hour; fixed at $600,000 per year.
Selling and administrative expense: variable at $4,500 per unit sold; fixed at $150,000 per year.
Selling price per unit: $40,000 per unit.
Budgeted sales for year: 600 units.
Budgeted production for year: 650 units.
Budgeted production intended for ending inventory: 120 units.

Material:	
3 pieces of lumber at $4 per piece standard cost	**$12**
Labor:	
3 direct labor hours at $3 per hour	**9**
Manufacturing overhead:	
Standard overhead rate of $2 per direct labor hour	**6**
Total standard cost per Wamp	**$27**

Exhibit 31-14
Standard cost card for Problem P31-1

Required:

a. Without showing computations, would the firm's net income be larger if the company used direct costing or absorption costing procedures?

b. Prepare an income statement for the year when direct costing is used.

c. Prepare an income statement for the year when absorption costing is used.

d. How do you account for the difference in net incomes under direct costing and absorption costing?

P31-3 (Variances)

Standard costs for one unit of a company's product are shown:

Material (6 tons @ $10 per ton)	$ 60
Direct labor (6 hours @ $7 per hour)	42
Overhead (6 hours @ $6 per hour)	36
Total standard cost	$138

The current operating level of the company is 80% of capacity. The overhead rate is based on direct labor hours at 80% of capacity. The company's flexible budget is:

	80%	90%
Production in units	1,600	1,800
Direct labor hours	9,600	10,800
Fixed overhead	$32,000	$32,000
Variable overhead	$25,600	$28,800

During June the company operated at 90% of capacity and produced 1,800 units. Actual costs incurred and quantities of materials and labor used during the month were as follows:

Materials purchased and used in production (9,900 tons @ $11 per ton)	$180,900
Direct labor (10,000 @ $6.90 per hour)	69,000
Fixed factory overhead	32,000
Variable overhead	19,000

Required: Compute the following variances:

a. Purchase price variance.

b. Material usage variance.

c. Labor rate variance.

d. Labor efficiency variance.

f. Overhead volume variance.

g. Spending variance.

h. Efficiency variance.

P31-4 (Variances)

A company manufactures a single product. Standard costs per unit for this product are:

Material (10 lbs. @ $1 per lb.)	$10
Direct labor (2 hrs. @ $6 per hour)	12
Factory overhead (2 hrs. @ $32.50 per hr.)	65
Total standard cost	$87

The following budgeted data are available:

	90%	100%
Production in units	1,500	1,800
Standard direct labor hours	2,700	3,000
Factory overhead:		
Fixed costs:		
Rent	$10,000	$10,000
Depreciation	30,000	30,000
Insurance	5,000	5,000
Taxes	5,000	5,000
Supervisory	10,000	10,000
Variable costs:		
Indirect labor	4,500	5,000
Indirect material	9,000	10,000
Power and light	18,000	20,000
Maintenance	2,250	2,500

The company operated at 90% of capacity during May and produced 1,500 units. Actual costs for May were:

Materials purchased and used (17,000 lbs.)	$17,510
Direct labor (2,900 hours)	18,850
Rent	10,000
Depreciation	30,000
Insurance	5,000
Taxes	5,000
Supervisory	10,000
Indirect labor	5,000
Indirect material	10,000
Power and light	15,000
Maintenance	3,000

Required:

a. Compute the price and quantity variances for material and labor.

b. Compute the budget and volume variances for overhead.

P31-5 (Standard cost)

Develop a problem for a company that uses a standard cost system. The system should be designed to produce a total of six variances for material, labor, and overhead. After you have constructed the problem, solve the problem.

P31-6 (Direct costing)

A company sold 1,000 units of its product at $100 per unit. The following operating data are available:

Direct labor	2,000 hours @ $10 per hour
Direct materials	$20 per unit
Factory overhead:	
Variable	$10 per direct labor hour
Fixed	$24,000 per period

Selling and administrative expenses:

Variable	$10 per unit
Fixed	$10,000 per period

Budgeted sales for the year: 1,000 units
Budgeted production for the year: 1,200 units
Budgeted production for ending inventory: 200 units

Required:

a. Prepare an income statement for the year when direct costing is used.

b. Prepare an income statement for the year when absorption costing is used.

32 Income taxes

Like love, income taxes are here to stay. The Sixteenth Amendment to the Constitution of the United States provides the authority for imposing federal income taxes on individuals, corporations, estates, and trusts. The complexities of income-tax legislation are beyond the scope of this introductory text. However, a brief introduction to income taxes will benefit students beginning their study of business subjects.

Individual tax returns

Individuals who keep financial records and pay taxes on a calendar-year basis must file an income-tax return by April 15 (or on the following business day if the fifteenth falls on a Saturday, Sunday, or legal holiday). The return is filed on Form 1040, the U.S. Individual Income Tax Return. Exhibit 32-1 summarizes the basic outline of data reported on this form.

For tax purposes, ***gross income*** means all income except that income exempt from tax, referred to as ***exclusions.*** For example, all salaries earned by an employee are included in gross income. Interest income on most state and municipal bonds is an exclusion from gross income and is not taxed. An item is deductible from gross income for tax purposes only if the taxpayer can refer to a specific provision of the tax statute that authorizes the deduction. Further, a taxpayer must be able to prove that he or she is entitled to the deductions taken. Each taxpayer is required to keep accurate records to support the deductions claimed on the return. To be deductible from gross income, an expense must be:

1. ordinary and necessary; and
2. paid or incurred during the tax year as:
   a. an expense to carry on a trade, business, or profession; or
   b. a ''nonbusiness'' expense associated with the production or collection of income, the management or maintenance of property held for production of income, or the determination or refund of a tax.

Personal income-tax rates are progressive. For 1973 income, the first $500 of taxable income ($1,000 for married taxpayers filing joint returns or for heads of household) was taxed at 14 percent. The rate gradually increases with increasing income, to a maximum rate in 1973 of 70 percent for taxable income over $100,000

Exhibit 32-1 Summary of data reported on Form 1040, the Individual Income Tax Return

1. Gross income (includes all income not specifically excluded by law) Wages, salaries, bonuses, commissions, tips, fees; rents and royalties; pensions, annuities, interest, dividends, endowments; gains on sales or exchanges of property; business income; prizes, awards, alimony or support payments; embezzled or other illegal income; taxpayer's share of income from partnerships, estates, and trusts.	$ XXX
2. Deductible expenses Business and trade expenses; employees' reimbursed expenses; transportation costs of employees; outside salesmen's expenses; expenses attributable to royalties and rent income; employees' moving expenses; losses from sales or exchanges of assets; net operating losses.	(XXX)
3. Adjusted gross income	$ XXX
4. Deductions from adjusted gross income:	
a. Standard deduction or	(XXX)
b. Itemized deductions Charitable contributions; certain personal taxes and interest paid; personal casualty losses; certain medical expenses; investor and professional expenses; child-care expenses; union dues; and other less common expenses.	
c. Deduction for exemptions Personal exemptions for taxpayer and spouse; blindness and old-age exemptions for taxpayer and spouse; exemptions for dependents.	(XXX)
5. Taxable income	$ XXX
6. Tax liability before tax credits	$ XXX
7. Credits against the tax Taxes withheld or prepaid on estimated income; investment tax credit; retirement income credit; and other credits.	(XXX)
8. Net tax payable (or overpayment refundable)	$ XXX

($200,000 for joint returns; $180,000 for heads of household).[1]

A single proprietorship is not taxed as a separate business entity. An individual operating a business as sole owner reports his or her business revenue and expenses on Schedule C accompanying Form 1040, and transfers the net business income to Form 1040 as part of his or her personal gross income. The graduated tax rate applied to personal income can make it very complicated to evaluate the tax impacts of various alternative business investments.

Capital gains and losses

Tax legislation defines certain property as capital assets. For tax purposes, capital gains and losses arise from transactions involving these capital assets, and these gains and losses are subject to special tax rules.

1. Tax legislation is revised frequently. Comments about rates, regulations, and other aspects of tax law in this chapter are updated through mid-1974, with most rates and other specific details drawn from the regulations applying to taxes on 1973 income. To avoid the necessity of constantly emphasizing this fact throughout the chapter, we wish to point it out strongly here. Any specific point about tax law may be revised in the future. Always review pertinent IRS publications for the latest regulations and rulings. Do not assume that any of the specific rates or regulations mentioned in this chapter are still in effect.

According to instructions issued by the Internal Revenue Service, a ***capital asset*** is, "in general, all property you own and use for personal purposes, pleasure, or investment."

Following are some examples: (1) stocks or bonds held in your personal account, (2) a dwelling owned and occupied by an individual and his family, (3) household furnishings used by an individual and his family, (4) an automobile used for pleasure.

In particular, a capital asset as defined by law is any piece of property, held by the taxpayer, except:

(a) stock in trade;

(b) real or personal property includible in inventory;

(c) real or personal property held for sale to customers;

(d) accounts or notes receivable acquired in the ordinary course of a trade or business for services rendered, or from the sale of any of the properties described in (a), (b), or (c), or for services rendered as an employee;

(e) depreciable property used in your trade or business (even though fully depreciated);

(f) real property used in your trade or business;

(g) [a variety of other assets specified in tax legislation].[2]

A sale or exchange of a capital asset will usually result in either a short-term or a long-term capital gain or loss, depending upon the period of time the property is held before the sale or exchange. If held nine months or less for taxable years beginning 1977 and to twelve months for taxable years beginning 1978 and thereafter, the gain or loss resulting from the sale or exchange is classified as short-term. If held more than nine months, the gain or loss resulting from the sale or exchange is long-term.

Short-term capital gains are taxed as regular income. Long-term capital gains are taxed at a maximum rate of 25 percent. However, long-term capital gains are allowed a special deduction equal to 50 percent of the excess of net long-term capital gains over net short-term capital loss. (Net long-term capital gains equal total gains less total losses for all long-term transactions. Net short-term capital loss equals total losses less total gains for all short-term transactions.) Special rules apply where the excess of net long-term capital gains exceeds $50,000.

Short-term capital losses are deducted from ordinary income. Only 50 percent of long-term capital losses are deducted from ordinary income. Further, the total net loss from capital-asset transactions deducted may not exceed $2,000 for taxable years beginning in 1977, and $3,000 in taxable years beginning in 1978 and thereafter. If the deductible net loss is more than $2,000 in 1977, the balance of the loss not deducted may be carried forward indefinitely into the future and used to offset taxable income in future years.

As an illustration, suppose that a taxpayer has a salary of $10,000. He makes a net long-term capital gain of $3,000 during the year, and a net short-term capital loss

2. Internal Revenue Service, ***1973 Instructions for Form 1040*** (Washington, D.C.: U.S. Government Printing Office, 1973), p. 15.

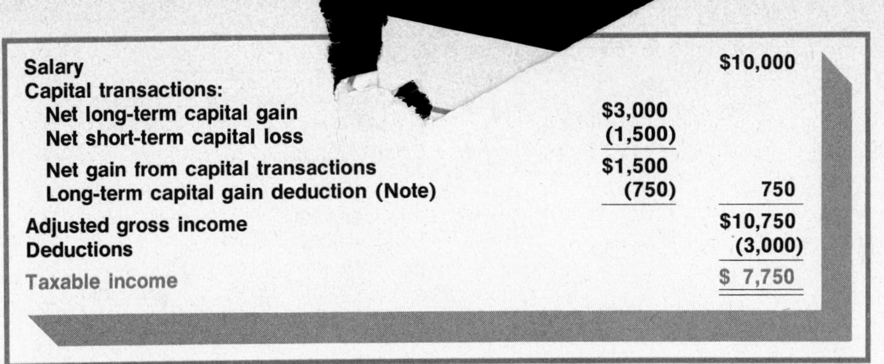

Salary		**$10,000**
Capital transactions:		
Net long-term capital gain	**$3,000**	
Net short-term capital loss	**(1,500)**	
Net gain from capital transactions	**$1,500**	
Long-term capital gain deduction (Note)	**(750)**	**750**
Adjusted gross income		**$10,750**
Deductions		**(3,000)**
Taxable income		**$ 7,750**

Exhibit 32-2
Example of treatment of capital gains and losses

NOTE: This deduction is 50% of the excess of net long-term capital gain over net-short-term capital loss. In other words, the deduction is 50% of the net gain from capital transactions.

of $1,500. His deductions from adjusted gross income total $3,000. Exhibit 32-2 shows the computation of his taxable income.

Taxes on partnership income

A partnership is required to file a tax-information Form 1065, but the partnership itself pays no taxes. Exhibit 32-3 compares the net income of a partnership (as shown in its books and financial statements) with the taxable income of the partnership (as reported on Form 1065).

This partnership shows a net income of $130,000 for the year. However, the taxable income of the partnership for the year is only $10,000. Income from capital gains and dividends is excluded from the partnership taxable income, but each partner reports his share of these capital gains and dividends as part of his own gross income. Salaries and interest on capital paid to the partners are deducted from the partnership taxable income, but are reported as gross income by the partners. Charitable contributions are not deducted from the partnership taxable income, but each partner can deduct his share of the contributions from his own personal adjusted gross income. Finally, each partner pays personal income taxes on his share of the taxable income reported by the partnership.

The details of these computations are fairly complex, but the overall result is that each partner pays personal income taxes on his share of the partnership's net income, much as if this were net income from a single proprietorship owned by him. In both the single proprietorship and the partnership, note that the owner pays personal income taxes on all taxable net income—including both amounts actually withdrawn by him from the business and amounts retained as capital in the business.

Corporation income taxes

Because a corporation is a legal entity separate from its owners, it pays income taxes on its own income. Its owners (stockholders) pay personal income taxes only on the dividends or salaries they receive from the corporation.

The corporation is subject to a normal income tax (a percentage of all taxable income) and a surtax (an additional percentage of income above a certain amount). In 1973, the normal rate was 22 percent (on all taxable income) and the surtax was 26 percent (on all income beyond $25,000). That is, a corporation pays tax at a rate

Exhibit 32-3 **Net income and taxable income f**[illegible]

	Income Statement per Books	Taxable Income
Income:		
Gross profit	$100,000	$100,000
Capital gains (Note)	50,000	—
Tax-exempt interest income	10,000	—
Dividends received (Note)	10,000	—
Other income	20,000	20,000
Total income	$190,000	$120,000
Deductions:		
Partners' salaries (Note)	—	(50,000)
Interest payments on capital to partners (Note)	—	(10,000)
Charitable contributions (Note)	(10,000)	—
Other expenses	(50,000)	(50,000)
Net income per books	$130,000	
Taxable partnership income		$ 10,000

NOTE: Each partner reports in his personal return his share of capital gains and losses, dividends received, charitable contributions, and certain other items that are excluded when figuring the partnership taxable income. Each partner reports as personal income any salaries or interest on capital that he receives from the partnership. *In addition,* each partner reports as income his share of the taxable partnership income.

of 22 percent on the first $25,000 of its taxable annual income, and at a rate of 48 percent on any taxable income beyond the first $25,000. Exhibit 32-4 demonstrates the computation of a corporation's income tax.

In general, the taxable income of a corporation is computed in much the same way as that of an individual. However, exceptions to this statement exist. For example, the corporation is not allowed to take such deductions as those allowed for personal exemptions or the standard deduction. In addition, the tax laws provide for a wide range of special tax deductions and credits that apply to certain kinds of businesses or business activities. These provisions were put into the law to encourage certain kinds of business activities. Their impact varies from corporation to corporation. However, the general effect is that very few of the large corporations actually pay the 48 percent income-tax rate on the net income that they report in their financial statements.

For example, one congressman did a study of 90 large corporations, and found that in 1972, 11 of them (with total reported net incomes of $741.5 million) paid no

Exhibit 32-4
Example of computation of corporate income tax

Gross income	$100,000
Itemized deductions	(60,000)
Difference	$ 40,000
Special deductions	—
Taxable income	$ 40,000
Tax computation:	
Normal tax (22% of $40,000)	$ 8,800
Surtax (26% of $15,000)	3,900
Tax before credits	$ 12,700
Less: Tax credits	—
Net tax payable	$ 12,700

U.S. income taxes; an additional 14 companies (with total reported net incomes of $3.6 billion) paid effective income-tax rates of between 1 and 10 percent on their reported net incomes before taxes. In many cases, a major factor contributing to low U.S. income taxes for international corporations is the fact that amounts paid to foreign governments in income taxes can be deducted from the U.S. income taxes payable.

Corporate income taxes must be filed two and one-half months after the close of the corporation's taxable fiscal year. For example, a corporation that ends its taxable year on December 31 must file its tax return for the year by the following March 15.

Impact of income taxes

The tax laws are a bottomless pit of snares and entanglements. The businessman who ventures into this chasm without expert legal guidance is the proverbial fool. When every dollar of income earned is shared with the government as a partner in profits, management must approach with special deliberation any business decisions that involve risks and expenditures of energy and resources.

We should distinguish at the onset between tax evasion and tax avoidance. ***Tax avoidance*** is the taking of action that prevents the establishment of a tax liability. To avoid a tax when possible is desirable and legal. ***Tax evasion*** is the failure to report legally taxable income or to pay a tax debt that exists. Tax evasion is illegal. The distinction is reflected in the business maxim: Pay every cent of tax owed but not one cent more.

FORM OF BUSINESS ORGANIZATION

In preceding chapters we have discussed the major forms of business organization: the sole proprietorship, partnership, and corporation. We have noted that earnings of the proprietorship and partnership are not taxed to the business entity, but rather are reported as personal income by the proprietor or partners. On the other hand, the corporation is taxed as a separate entity. The corporation pays income tax on its taxable net income (before dividends). The stockholder then pays income tax a second time (with some exclusions) on the dividends that he receives.

To illustrate the tax implications of the form of business ownership, consider two simplified examples. Both businesses have similar revenue and expenses; each is owned and operated by an individual whose personal taxable income is taxed at a rate of 50 percent. One business is organized as a sole proprietorship; the other is organized as a corporation. Exhibit 32-5 compares the income statements of the two businesses. Exhibit 32-6 compares the overall income taxes on the earnings of the two businesses.

In this illustration, all earnings of the two businesses are distributed to the owners. The taxes on earnings of the proprietorship amount to $100,000; taxes on earnings of the corporation amount to $120,650, including both corporate income taxes and personal income taxes of the owner.[3] In this case, the single proprietorship has an obvious tax advantage.

3. This example considers only federal income taxes. It ignores the impact of state income taxes (which may have different relationships between corporate and personal tax rates and procedures). It also ignores certain taxes that states impose upon corporations doing business within the state (but not upon single proprietorships or partnerships).

Exhibit 32-5
Income of comparable single proprietorship and corporation

	Proprietorship	Corporation
Sales	$500,000	$500,000
Operating expenses:		
Owners' salary	—	(100,000)
Other expenses	(300,000)	(300,000)
Taxable income	$200,000	$100,000
Corporate income tax:		
Normal tax (22% of $100,000)	—	(22,000)
Surtax (26% of $75,000)	—	(19,500)
Net income	$200,000	$ 58,500
Cash dividends paid	—	(58,500)
Cash withdrawals by owner	(200,000)	—
Net income retained in business	$ 0	$ 0

Exhibit 32-6
Income taxes on earnings of proprietorship and corporation

	Proprietorship	Corporation
Total taxable income:		
Business entity	$ 0	$100,000
Owner:		
Net income of proprietorship	200,000	—
Salary of corporation owner	—	100,000
Dividends to corporation owner	—	58,500
Total taxable income	$200,000	$258,500
Taxes paid by business entity:		
Corporate income tax (see Exhibit 32-5)	—	$ 41,500
Personal income taxes paid by owner:		
Tax on net income of proprietorship	$100,000	—
Tax on salary of corporation owner	—	50,000
Tax on dividends to corporation owner (Note)	—	29,150
Total income taxes payable	$100,000	$120,650

NOTE: The first $200 of dividend income is excluded from taxable personal income, so the corporation owner pays personal tax of 50% of $58,300, or $29,150, on the $58,500 he receives in dividends. Note that we have assumed that both owners pay personal income tax at a rate of 50%, and that the corporation is not able to take advantage of any special credits or deductions in the corporate tax law.

However, suppose that the corporation did not distribute its $100,000 earnings to its stockholder, but instead reinvested the $100,000 in the business (as retained earnings). In this case, the corporation would still pay $41,500 on its taxable income. However, the stockholder would pay personal income tax of only $50,000 on his salary from the corporation. The proprietorship has to pay the full $100,000 income tax, regardless of whether the owner withdraws the income in cash or reinvests it in the business. Thus, the corporation and its owner would pay only $91,500 in income taxes—less than the amount paid by the proprietor.

This example is oversimplified. Furthermore, we have assumed that the owners pay personal taxes at 50 percent of adjusted gross income, a rate very similar to the corporate income-tax rate. If the income of the business were much smaller, corporate income-tax rates would be considerably higher than personal income-tax rates for the same amounts. However, from this example, we can generalize that—when the owner of a business is in a high income-tax bracket—the corporate form of business may be more attractive than the single proprietorship, *if* a significant portion of the earnings of the business are to be reinvested in the business. If the earnings are relatively small, or if the owner withdraws most of the earnings for personal income, the corporate form of business organization has distinct tax disadvantages.

INVENTORY METHODS

The choice of methods used to account for inventory can influence the amount of taxes paid by a business. In our discussion of LIFO and FIFO inventory procedures in Chapter 13, we note that use of LIFO methods in a period of inflation results in a lower net income and therefore lower income taxes. This occurs because the cost of goods sold reflects the most recent purchases, which are at more recent and therefore higher prices. If the amount of inventory is kept about the same from year to year, a tax advantage tends to be maintained through the use of LIFO during inflationary periods.

Also, if a firm is using LIFO methods during a period of rising prices, it can reduce its taxes by making additional purchases of inventory at the end of the year. The higher priced merchandise will be reflected on the income statement as cost of goods sold, resulting in lower net income and taxable income. Thus, the firm using LIFO during a period of inflation has the opportunity to adjust its taxable income to a desired amount by last-minute purchases of inventory at the close of the year. As a general rule, a firm using FIFO procedures does not have this opportunity.

As an example of the importance of inventory methods, we note that the Department of Commerce estimated that about 14 percent of the profits reported by corporations in 1973 were the result of inflationary effects on inventory valuation.

BORROWING FUNDS

If long-term funds are required in a business, consideration should be given to borrowing these funds rather than obtaining them through an issuance of capital stock. Interest expense on borrowed funds is deductible for tax purposes, whereas dividend expense on stockholder's investments is not deductible. For example, suppose that a corporation's income-tax rate is 40 percent and that it borrows $100,000 at 6 percent interest. Interest expense is $6,000 per year and is tax deductible; the tax saving is $2,400. Hence, the interest expense after taxes is $3,600, representing an after-tax interest rate of only 3.6 percent. When leverage on borrowed funds is taken into consideration, borrowing can be quite attractive. (There is an additional advantage in being a net debtor in a period of inflation, as discussed in Chapter 16.)

MISCELLANEOUS TAX CONSIDERATIONS

A knowledge of tax law offers many opportunities for tax savings or tax deferments. The following examples illustrate a few of the many tax-planning possibilities.

CHANGING TAX RATES. If tax rates are expected to increase in the next year, it may be advantageous to delay incurring expenses such as advertising and repairs until they can be used to offset income that is taxable at the higher rate. If possible, revenue should be increased in the year of lower tax rates. For example, sales orders should be filled in the current year, so that the revenue from sales will be taxed in the year of lower tax rates.

CHARITABLE CONTRIBUTIONS. When charitable contributions are contemplated, the donation of assets other than cash usually is more beneficial both to the donor and the donee. If the business donates property that has appreciated in value, it can deduct from taxable income the fair market value of the property (within limitations). The gain resulting from the appreciation in value is not taxed. If the appreciated property were first sold, and then the cash proceeds of the sale distributed as a charitable contribution, the gain on appreciated property would be taxed, resulting in a smaller donation (and, hence, a smaller tax deduction for the charitable contribution).

TIMING INCOME AND EXPENSE TRANSACTIONS. Generally, it is desirable to avoid situations in which revenue is earned and taxed in one year, while expenses related to that revenue are not incurred until the subsequent year. However, if tax rates are expected to change, this general rule may not apply.

TAX SAVINGS. As a general rule, tax deductions should be taken as soon as available, rather than being deferred to a later year. A tax dollar saved in year 19_1 is worth more than a tax dollar saved in 19_2, because the present value of a dollar received (or saved) today is greater than the present value of a dollar to be received (or saved) in the future. In a period of inflation, the changes in purchasing power make this even more significant.

DEPRECIATION METHODS. The method of depreciation chosen by a business has an impact on taxable income as well as on book income. When a firm uses a faster depreciation method for tax purposes, it reduces the outflow of funds for taxes.[4] In business, the conservation of working capital is a significant matter. To illustrate the impact of tax deductions for depreciation, we present the schedule shown in Exhibit 32-7, in which equipment costing $90,000 with no salvage value and a five-year life is depreciated by two different methods.

In the first year, the extra depreciation taken by using the sum-of-years'-digits method reduces taxable income an extra $12,000. Assuming a tax rate of 40 percent,

Exhibit 32-7
Comparison of annual depreciation expense under two depreciation methods

Year	Straight-Line	Sum-of-Years'-Digits
1	$18,000	$30,000
2	18,000	24,000
3	18,000	18,000
4	18,000	12,000
5	18,000	6,000
Total	$90,000	$90,000

4. Although managers may find accelerated depreciation attractive for tax savings (extra cash) in early years, they may want to use straight-line depreciation for financial statements. Managerial performance often is measured by net income, and straight-line depreciation provides larger net income in early years of the life of newly acquired depreciable assets than does accelerated depreciation. Also, the market price of a corporation's stock often reflects net income. Therefore, management may decide to use straight-line depreciation in its statements, because the net income will be larger on the statements, and the market price of the stock may be favorably influenced. The next section deals with accounting problems that arise when different depreciation methods are used for financial statements and for income-tax returns.

this extra depreciation results in a tax reduction of $4,800. This reduction of tax expense may be important in the year in which the firm must make a large cash outlay for the purchase of the equipment. Also, because of the time value of money, tax savings are worth more when taken as early as possible. In the example, either method results in total tax savings of $36,000 over five years. However, the use of the accelerated depreciation method yields tax savings with a present value (at the time of purchase) of $31,502.40 compared to savings with a present value of $30,326.40 from the straight-line method (assuming a discounting rate of 6 percent).

Income-tax allocation

The high income-tax rate imposed on corporations can create serious problems, especially with regard to reporting taxes on financial statements. One such problem results because of differences in reporting items of revenue and expense for tax purposes and for financial statement purposes.

For example, a corporation may choose to depreciate its tangible fixed assets by the sum-of-years'-digits method for income-tax purposes, while using the straight-line method for its books and financial statements (see footnote 4). In such a situation, the taxable income used to compute tax payments differs from the pretax book income. Exhibit 32-8 illustrates a case where a company purchases for $60,000 a fixed asset with a three-year life and no scrap value. On its books, the firm uses straight-line depreciation. For tax purposes, the firm uses the sum-of-years'-digits method. The tax rate is assumed to be 50 percent of taxable income.

In this simplified illustration, note how pretax book income differs from reported taxable income as a result of the use of the two different depreciation methods. The tax recognition of an expense item differs from the accounting recognition of the item—a timing difference. On the books, depreciation expense and pretax net income are identical for the three years. On the tax returns, $10,000 of the depreciation expense is shifted from the third year to the first. This has the effect of shifting $10,000 of taxable income from the first year to the third. An accounting problem arises because the income-tax expense for a particular year is not properly matched to the net income reported in the books for that year. (Some of the tax expense for net income reported in the first year is not incurred until the third year.)

Other differences arise when income-tax rules and regulations differ from generally accepted accounting principles used in keeping the books. For example, if the owner of an apartment house receives rent for five years in advance, this rent is taxable in the year of the receipt. For accounting purposes, the rental income would be reported as revenue over the five-year term of the lease.

INTERPERIOD ALLOCATION OF INCOME TAXES

To cope with situations like those just described, accountants have adopted as a generally accepted accounting principle the allocation of income taxes between periods.[5] The purpose of interperiod allocation of taxes is to match the tax expense reported in the income statement against the income reported in that statement.

5. Accounting Principles Board, ***Opinion No. 11: Accounting for Income Taxes*** (New York: American Institute of Certified Public Accountants, 1967).

Exhibit 32-8
Example of differing depreciation in books and on tax returns

INCOME STATEMENT

	Year 1	Year 2	Year 3
Revenue	$100,000	$100,000	$100,000
Expenses:			
Depreciation (straight-line)	(20,000)	(20,000)	(20,000)
Other expenses	(40,000)	(40,000)	(40,000)
Pretax net income per books	$ 40,000	$ 40,000	$ 40,000

TAX RETURNS

	Year 1	Year 2	Year 3
Revenue	$100,000	$100,000	$100,000
Expenses:			
Depreciation (sum-of-years'-digits)	(30,000)	(20,000)	(10,000)
Other expenses	(40,000)	(40,000)	(40,000)
Taxable income	$ 30,000	$ 40,000	$ 50,000
Tax liability (50% of taxable income)	$ 15,000	$ 20,000	$ 25,000

Case 1: Pretax income per books exceeds taxable income—deferred income-tax liability. The case illustrated in Exhibit 32-8 presents in the first year an example of the situation where pretax income per books exceeds taxable income for the year. The tax liability incurred for the year reflects payment of taxes on only $30,000 of income; the taxes on the other $10,000 of income reported in the books for this year are deferred until the third year. Allocation of the tax expense is necessary.

The following basic rules describe the allocation of the tax expense.

1. The tax expense to be reported on the income statement is an amount that would be payable if tax rates were applied to net income per books (rather than to taxable income).
2. In a year when the tax expense computed on income per books exceeds the tax liability for the year, the excess expense is credited to a Deferred Income-Tax Liability account. This liability represents the firm's obligation to pay in the future the taxes on income being reported for the current year on the income statement (but not on the tax return).
3. In a year in which the tax liability exceeds the tax expense computed on income per books, the excess tax liability is debited to the Deferred Income-Tax Liability account.

In the first year, pretax net income is reported as $40,000. Taxes on this income would be 50 percent of $40,000, or $20,000. The tax liability for the year is only $15,000. The $5,000 difference is credited to the Deferred Income-Tax Liability account, as specified in rule 2.

Income-Tax Expense	20,000	
Income Taxes Payable		15,000
Deferred Income-Tax Liability		5,000

In the second year, pretax net income and taxable income are each $40,000. The tax liability matches the taxes computed on the net income per books.

Income-Tax Expense	20,000	
Income Taxes Payable		20,000

In the third year, taxes computed on pretax net income per books are again $20,000. Taxable income is $50,000, because of the effect of accelerated depreciation in deferring income from the first year to this year. Tax liability is therefore $25,000. The $5,000 excess tax liability is debited to the deferred tax account.

Income-Tax Expense	20,000	
Deferred Income-Tax Liability	5,000	
Income Taxes Payable		25,000

Observe that the tax expense reported in the books and statements each year relates to the pretax net income per books, thereby providing a good matching of revenue and expense in the accounting system. The Deferred Income-Tax Liability account established in the first year represents the estimated tax liability that must be paid in the third year when taxable income exceeds pretax book income. The deferred income-tax liability is reported as a liability on the balance sheet, either current or noncurrent depending on whether the liability is expected to be paid within the normal operating cycle of the business or within one year, whichever is longer.

Case 2: Pretax income per books is less than taxable income—deferred income tax expense. Suppose that for some reason the situation in Exhibit 32-8 is reversed. That is, straight-line depreciation is used in the tax returns, while sum-of-years'-digits depreciation is used in the books. Then, pretax net income per books is $30,000, $40,000, and $50,000 for years 1, 2, and 3, respectively. Taxable income is $40,000 each year, so tax liability is $20,000 each year.

Again, the necessary tax allocation can be carried out according to three rules.

1. The tax expense to be reported on the income statement is an amount that would be payable if the tax rates were applied to pretax net income per books, rather than to taxable income.
2. In a year when tax expense computed on book income is less than the tax liability for the year (as in year 1 of this modified example), the excess tax liability is debited to a Deferred Income-Tax Expense account.
3. In a year when the tax liability is less than the tax expense computed on book income (as in year 3 of this example), the excess expense is credited to the Deferred Income-Tax Expense account.

These rules are very similar to those used for case 1. However, in this situation, the taxes paid in the first year are ***greater*** than the expense matched against the book income for the year. Therefore, the Deferred Income-Tax Expense account (an asset account) is used to represent an estimated "prepayment" of taxes that will not be recognized as expense until the third year.

The following three journal entries record the tax liability and expense for each of the three years. Computations are similar to those outlined for case 1.

		Debit	Credit
1.	Income-Tax Expense	15,000	
	Deferred Income-Tax Expense	5,000	
	Income Taxes Payable		20,000
2.	Income-Tax Expense	20,000	
	Income Taxes Payable		20,000
3.	Income-Tax Expense	25,000	
	Income Taxes Payable		20,000
	Deferred Income-Tax Expense		5,000

As in case 1, the allocation procedures result in a good matching of tax expense reported each year against net income reported for that year. The deferred income-tax expense appears in the balance sheet as an asset, either current or noncurrent depending on whether the "prepaid taxes" will be written off as expense within the normal operating cycle of the business or within one year, whichever is longer.

INCOME-TAX ALLOCATION WITHIN THE INCOME STATEMENT

We have just discussed income-tax allocation problems that arise because of differences in timing of expense or revenue recognition between the books and the tax returns. In addition, allocation of taxes may be necessary within the income statement for a given year if extraordinary items reported in the income statement have tax consequences. Exhibit 32-9 illustrates an income statement that includes an extraordinary gain of $100,000 on the sale of land. Net operating income before taxes is $500,000. The total net income (including the extraordinary item) is $600,000, and the company pays income tax at a 50 percent rate on this amount. On the income statement, the income tax should be allocated between operating income and the extraordinary item, as illustrated.

Summary

Chapter 32 discusses income taxes from the viewpoints of the individual (single proprietor), partnership, and corporation. The impact of income taxes on a business is demonstrated in a variety of ways. The form of business organization chosen

Exhibit 32-9
An example of intra-statement allocation of income taxes

EXTRAORDINARY COMPANY

Income Statement
For the Year Ended December 31, 19_1

Sales		**$1,000,000**
Less: Expenses		**500,000**
Net operating income before taxes		**$ 500,000**
Less: Income-tax expense on net operating income		**250,000**
Net operating income		**$ 250,000**
Extraordinary item:		
Gain on sale of land	**$100,000**	
Less: Income tax on extraordinary gain	**50,000**	**50,000**
Net income after extraordinary item		$ 300,000

for a business has serious income-tax implications. Matters such as inventory and depreciation methods can affect the amount of taxes payable in a given year. Procedures for acquiring additional funds through borrowing or stock issuances have tax consequences. The student should be aware that tax rules and regulations affect business decisions and cannot be ignored.

Income taxes have created serious reporting problems for businesses. Occasionally, businesses use different reporting procedures for financial statements and for tax returns. In such situations, book income can differ from taxable income. This would result in a mismatching of expense against revenue if tax expenses were reported at the amount of the liability for each year. To provide better matching of expense against revenue, income-tax allocation is recommended. The income-tax expense reported on the financial statements is adjusted to correspond to book income (not to taxable income). In such cases, a deferred income-tax liability or a deferred income-tax expense arises.

Other allocation problems arise within the income statement for a single year if extraordinary items with tax consequences are reported in the statement. The income-tax expense reported in the statement should be allocated appropriately between the operating income and the extraordinary item.

Questions

1. What is the constitutional justification for income taxes?

2. Individuals who pay taxes on a calendar-year basis must file their income-tax returns by what date?

3. Explain the following concepts in relation to income taxes:
   - *a.* gross income;
   - *b.* deductions from gross income;
   - *c.* adjusted gross income;
   - *d.* deductions from adjusted gross income:
     - (1) standard deduction;
     - (2) itemized deductions;
     - (3) exemptions;
   - *e.* taxable income;
   - *f.* tax credits;
   - *g.* tax payable.

4. What is meant by capital gain?

5. Do partnerships pay income taxes? Explain.

6. In a generalized manner, explain how corporate income taxes are computed.

7. If you and several friends were starting a new business, how would income taxes affect your decision about whether to organize as a single proprietorship, a partnership, or a corporation?

8. How can the choice of an inventory method (such as FIFO or LIFO) be influenced by income-tax considerations?

9. How can the choice of depreciation methods be influenced by income-tax considerations?

10. When additional funds are being sought, how may tax implications influence decisions about the acquisition of these funds?

11. Will use of LIFO methods increase or reduce income taxes during a period of rising prices?

12. If prices are rising and income-tax rates are expected to increase, would a firm using LIFO be encouraged to increase the purchase of merchandise at the end of the year? Explain.

13. What is meant by income-tax allocation?

14. Distinguish between interperiod and intraperiod income-tax allocation problems.

15. When income-tax allocation procedures are used, if income per books exceeds taxable income in a certain period, should the accountant record a deferred income-tax liability or a deferred income-tax expense?

Exercises

E32-1 (Individual tax return)

Joe and Maurine Zinx have two children who qualify as dependents for tax purposes. The Zinxes present their tax accountant with the following information.

Salary of Joe	$12,000
Salary of Maurine	9,000
Interest earned on state bonds	6,000 (not taxable)
Interest earned on U.S. Savings Bonds cashed in	500
Gift from Maurine's mother	2,000 (not taxable)
Contributed to church	300
Contributed to League of Women Voters	40 (not deductible)
Life-insurance premiums	510 (not deductible)
Interest on mortgage	1,300
Interest on car loan	720
Sales taxes paid	280
Damage to car in accident	85 (not deductible)
Income taxes withheld:	
Joe	960
Maurine	840

The accountant has added notes about the taxability or deductibility of certain items. Joe and Maurine wish to file a joint return and to itemize their deductions. They are entitled to one exemption (of $750) for each of their children and two exemptions for themselves.

Required:

a. Compute the amount of taxable income for the Zinxes.

b. The taxable income is taxed at the following rates: 14% of the first $1,000; 15% of the second $1,000; 16% of the third $1,000; 17% of the fourth $1,000; 19% of the amount over $4,000 but not more than $8,000; 22% of the amount over $8,000 but not more than $12,000; and 25% of the amount over $12,000 but not more than $16,000. Compute the tax liability of the Zinxes.

c. Compute the tax payable for the Zinxes.

E32-2 (Corporation tax return)

A corporation reports the following tax data on its 19_6 tax return: itemized deductions of $200,000; gross income of $600,000; tax credits of $95,000.

The normal tax rate is 22% of taxable income; the surtax is 26% of income above $25,000.

Required:

a. Compute the corporation's tax liability for 19_6.

b. Prepare a journal entry to record the tax expense.

E32-3 (Leverage)

A corporation decides to raise $350,000 to finance the purchase of major productive assets. The assets will earn $70,000 in a year before taxes (and before interest expense, if money is borrowed). The firm can issue 8% preferred stock or 8% bonds. The income-tax rate is 50%. Should the company issue stock or bonds, assuming that the firm desires to provide the largest possible return to its common stockholders?

E32-4 (Single proprietorship vs. corporate structure)

Carl Careful plans to invest $90,000 in a store. He estimates that the store will have $400,000 revenue during the next year. He will pay himself a salary of $40,000, and he estimates other expenses for the year at $280,000. Careful will withdraw all net income from the business. Corporate income-tax rates are 22% on the first $25,000 of taxable income, and 48% on taxable income beyond the first $25,000. Careful's personal income will be taxed at an average rate of 50 percent. Should Careful incorporate his business or organize it as a single proprietorship? (His decision is to depend upon that alternative that minimizes the income-tax payments. Ignore the dividend-income exclusion.) Explain your answer.

E32-5 (Impact of inventory methods on taxes)

A company has the following purchases and sales during the year.

Jan. 15 Purchase of 120 units @ $90 per unit	$10,800
July 15 Purchase of 130 units @ $100 per unit	$13,000
Total sales for year of 250 units @ $150 per unit	$37,500

The company uses LIFO inventory procedures. The company can purchase units at the end of the year for $110. Cost of merchandise is not expected to decrease next year. The tax rate is 50 percent of taxable income and is not expected to decrease.

Required:

a. The company has an opportunity to acquire 100 more units before the end of the year. Management's objective is to reduce income taxes as much as possible this year. Should the 100 units be purchased? Explain.

b. If the company used FIFO inventory procedures, would the purchase of the 100 extra units reduce, increase, or not affect this year's income taxes? Explain.

E32-6 (Allocation of income taxes)

A corporation reported the following net income and taxable income for three years.

	Book Net Income	Taxable Income
19_5	$140,000	$100,000
19_6	120,000	120,000
19_7	100,000	140,000

The differences between book income and taxable income are due to the use of different depreciation methods. The income-tax rate is 50 percent. *Required:* Prepare journal entries for the end of each year to reflect income-tax expense and allocation.

E32-7 (Allocation of income taxes)
Refer to Exercise E32-6. Suppose that the amounts listed as taxable income were instead the book net income, and vice versa. (That is, interchange the titles on the two columns of figures.) Prepare journal entries for the end of each year to reflect income-tax expense and allocation in this situation.

E32-8 (Intraperiod allocation of income taxes)
Exhibit 32-10 shows two income statements prepared for the same company for the same year. One statement is prepared with intraperiod tax allocations and the other without these allocations. The income-tax rate is 50%.
Required:
a. Which income statement (A or B) reflects intraperiod income-tax allocation procedures?
b. Which income statement is correct? Explain.

E32-9 (Partnership vs. corporation)
Mr. Day and Ms. Nite have decided to operate a dry-cleaning business. They consult you about whether they should organize their business as a corporation or as a partnership. Day and Nite will each invest $100,000. Estimated sales will be $800,000 per year and cash expenses $600,000 per year (not

Exhibit 32-10
Income statements for Exercise E32-8

ONGOING COMPANY
Income Statement A
For the Year Ended December 31, 19_6

Sales		$170,000
Less: Expenses		90,000
Operating income before taxes		$ 80,000
Less: Income-tax expense		40,000
Net income before extraordinary item		$ 40,000
Extraordinary item:		
Fire loss	$(25,000)	
Applicable tax saving	12,500	(12,500)
Net income after extraordinary item		$ 27,500

ONGOING COMPANY
Income Statement B
For the Year Ended December 31, 19_6

Sales	$170,000
Less: Expenses	90,000
Operating income before taxes	$ 80,000
Less: Income-tax expense	27,500
Net income before extraordinary item	$ 52,500
Extraordinary fire loss	(25,000)
Net income after extraordinary item	$ 27,500

including salaries to Day and Nite). Day and Nite will receive salaries of $35,000 each. Any net income will be distributed to the owners at the end of the year as dividends (assume that all dividends are taxable personal income for the owners) or as withdrawals. The personal incomes of Day and Nite are taxed at a rate of 50%. A corporation would be taxed at a rate of 22% on taxable income up to $25,000 and at 48% for taxable income beyond $25,000. *Required:* What cash would the owners obtain beyond their salaries and after personal income taxes if the business is organized as (a) a partnership or (b) a corporation?

Problems

P32-1 (Allocation of income taxes)
The tax liability of the Justin Company was $150,000 in 19_5 and $180,000 in 19_6. There were differences in timing of reporting income on the books and on the tax returns. In 19_5, the pretax income per books exceeded the taxable income by $20,000. In 19_6, the taxable income exceeded net income per books by $20,000. The income-tax rate for the company is 50%. *Required:* Prepare journal entries to record the tax expense and tax allocations for each of the years.

P32-2 (Allocation of income taxes)
Exhibit 32-11 shows figures taken from the income-tax returns of an investment corporation over three years. The rent income shown in 19_5 represented payment received in advance for a two-year lease at $1,250 per month, beginning on July 1, 19_5. In its books, the corporation wishes to recognize this revenue by a rational and systematic allocation over the period of the lease. The income-tax rate for the corporation is 50%.
Required: Prepare journal entries to record the tax expense and tax allocations for each of the three years.

P32-3 (LIFO and income taxes)
A company sold 10,000 units at $10 per unit during the year. It purchased 5,000 units at $4 per unit in January and 5,000 units at $5 in July. There was no inventory at the beginning of the year. It will cost the company $6 to replace inventory sold. The company uses LIFO inventory procedures. Tax rates are 50%. Operating expenses are $20,000 for the year. From a tax point of view, should the company buy 1,000 additional units at $6 before the end of the year? Show supporting data.

	19_5	19_6	19_7
Interest income	$180,000	$180,000	$180,000
Rent income	30,000	—	—
Total income	$210,000	$180,000	$180,000
Deductible expenses	(40,000)	(90,000)	(90,000)
Taxable income	$170,000	$ 90,000	$ 90,000

Exhibit 32-11
Income-tax-return data for Problem P32-2

P32-4 (Intraperiod tax allocation)

A company's records disclose the following data:

Income before income taxes	$40,000
Extraordinary gain before tax, taxed as capital gain	60,000
Prior period adjustment—gain	20,000
Tax rates:	
On ordinary income 40%	
On capital gain 30%	
Retained earnings, January 1, 19_6	75,000

Required:

a. Compute taxes payable for the year.

b. Prepare appropriate sections of an income statement and statement of retained earnings disclosing intraperiod tax allocations.

c. Prepare appropriate sections of an income statement and statement of retained earnings without intraperiod tax allocations.

d. Comment on financial statements prepared with and without income tax allocation.

P32-5 (Interperiod tax allocation)

A company computes depreciation using the straight-line method for accounting purposes and an accelerated depreciation method for tax purposes. Data for three years are shown:

	Accounting net income	Depreciation for accounting	Depreciation for taxes
First year	$100,000	$10,000	$15,000
Second year	120,000	10,000	10,000
Third year	150,000	10,000	5,000

Required: Prepare accounting entries for the three years to reflect the interperiod allocation of income taxes. The tax rate is 50%.

P32-6 (Intraperiod tax allocation)

The following data are available concerning a company's operations:

Retained earnings, January 1, 19_6	$100,000
Dividends for the year	10,000
Sales	100,000
Cost and expenses	60,000
Extraordinary gain subject to 25% income taxes	10,000
Prior period adjustment (a gain) subject to regular income tax rates	60,000

Required:

a. Compute the income tax for the year assuming that the tax rates for the corporation are 22% on the first $25,000 of income and an additional tax of 26% on income above $25,000. Capital gain tax rate is 25%. The company uses an average tax rate when allocating taxes on income other than capital gains.

b. Prepare an income statement and a statement of retained earnings for the company for the year.

Glossary

This glossary of accounting and accounting-related concepts is arranged in logical rather than alphabetical sequence. In this way, each definition is set in context with related terms and concepts. You can read through the glossary as a review and summary of major concepts, or you can use the glossary index on page 796 to find the definition of a particular term.

Accounting terms related to items that appear on the balance sheet and on the income statement are defined in the appendices to Chapters 3 and 4, respectively. Specific financial ratios are defined in Chapter 21, major cost terms in the appendix to Chapter 25, computer-related terms in Chapter 9, and variances in Chapters 23, 26, and 31.

Accounting is the art, discipline, or process of recording, classifying, and summarizing economic transactions and events (in terms of money), and of interpreting the results for users who must make economic or business decisions. *Accountancy* is the profession, occupation, or art of the *accountant,* who is a person proficient in accounting. *Financial accounting* deals with the continuous record of a firm's assets, liabilities, and owners' equity and with changes in these classifications, producing information primarily for the needs of owners, investors, and other external users of accounting information. *Managerial accounting* deals with the collecting, summarizing, reporting, and interpreting of a firm's economic activities, producing information primarily for the internal needs of management. Managerial accounting involves planning, controlling, performance evaluating, and product costing for inventory valuation and income determination. *Internal control* refers to the procedures through which management obtains the information, protection, and control needed for efficient and effective operations. A *private accountant* is employed by a single enterprise. The chief accounting officer of an enterprise is often called the *controller.* The officer in charge of the funds of an organization is called the *treasurer.* A *public accountant* is an independent professional who offers his or her services to the public for a fee. Acting as an *auditor,* an accountant may examine or *audit* an accounting document prepared by someone else and the supporting evidence for that document, in order to reach an informed opinion about the propriety of the document. A *certified public accountant (CPA)* has been licensed by the state to practice public accounting. Professional standards require that the CPA maintain an *independent* attitude that reflects an objectivity and integrity in his or her service to his or her clients.

Accounting functions in an *economic environment,* in which economic conditions and influences affect the development of the firm (or other accounting entity). The *entity* is the unit for which an accounting is made. An economic *event* is an occurrence that changes the resources, obligations, and the residual interests of an enterprise. A ***transaction*** is an activity that changes a balance appearing on the statement of financial position, or in the corresponding detailed accounts. An ***exchange*** is a completed transaction that involves a reciprocal transfer of resources or obligations between the enterprise and another entity. An ***arm's length transaction*** is one in which each of the involved parties is free and willing to promote his or her own best economic interests.

A ***system*** is a method of classifying, coding, and processing. An ***information system*** includes the method and procedures for receiving, processing, and communicating information to users. An ***accounting system*** is an information system that includes the formal and informal records and procedures needed to assemble, record, and report financial information about the economic operations and condition of an enterprise.

The ***accounting cycle*** is the sequence of activities (over a period of time) that terminate in the preparation of financial statements. The ***accounting period*** is the time period whose transactions are reported in a set of financial statements. If this period is twelve months in length, it is called the ***fiscal year*** of the entity, and the statements covering the period are called the ***annual report*** of the entity. The fiscal year may or may not coincide with the ***calendar year,*** the twelve-month period from January 1 through December 31. A ***natural business year*** is a fiscal year whose end coincides with the low point of business activity. The ***operating cycle*** of a business is the average time needed to convert cash into inventory or services, convert those into receivables, and convert the receivables back into cash.

Generally accepted accounting principles represent a concensus at a particular time about the proper way in which the accounting system should treat assets, liabilities, revenue, and expense. Responsibility for the development of authoritative generally accepted accounting principles was given to the ***Accounting Principles Board (APB)*** of the American Institute of Certified Public Accountants (AICPA). The APB has now been replaced by the ***Financial Accounting Standards Board (FASB).***

Accounting information must meet certain criteria. ***Relevance*** requires that financial statements meet the common needs of users in decision-making situations. ***Verifiability*** requires that accounting information be determined objectively, in such a way that the information can be verified by others. ***Freedom from bias*** demands that an impartial approach be used in accumulating, processing, and communicating accounting information. ***Quantifiability*** requires that the accounting system process only those data that can be expressed in numbers.

Accounting statements must meet certain standards. ***Full disclosure*** requires that the statements disclose all the significant information that an informed user needs in a decision-making situation. ***Materiality*** requires that the statements disclose all ***material*** amounts, items, facts, and so on—that is, all those that would be important and useful to an informed user. ***Consistency*** requires that the accounting principles and methods used in one accounting period be used in the next period; exceptions to this concept must be fully disclosed. ***Conservatism*** calls for the earliest recognition of unfavorable possibilities. ***Fairness*** refers to the need for the information in the statements to be substantially correct or equitable.

The accounting system operates under certain basic assumptions. The ***business-entity assumption*** defines the areas of interests and establishes the boundaries of information to be included in the accounting records and reports. The ***going-concern assumption*** stipulates that the accounting entity normally is assumed to have an existence stretching into the indefinite future without likelihood of liquidation. The ***dollar-measurement assumption*** requires that economic events and transactions be measured and reported in terms of money (current dollars in the United States). The ***periodic-and-timely-reporting assumption*** states that financial statements should be prepared at regular intervals to cover relatively short time periods.

Recognition of data occurs when the accounting system accepts the data to be processed. The ***initial recording principle*** is a major accounting principle that determines the date on which an event is recognized and the amounts to be recorded for assets, liabilities, revenue, and expense in recording the event. An asset, liability, revenue, or expense item usually is recorded initially at its ***acquisition cost,*** or ***historical cost,*** which is the exchange price involved in the transaction or event. Revenue is ***realized*** (recognized as a revenue item) when certain criteria are met. The ***realization principle*** states that revenue generally is recognized when (1) the earning process is complete or virtually complete, and (2) an exchange has taken place. The ***matching concept*** is an accounting principle requiring the matching of revenue and expense during an accounting period, so that net income can be calculated properly. The ***expense-recognition principle*** identifies the bases for recognizing which expenses should be deducted from revenue to determine the net income for a period. Depending upon the nature of the expense, it may be recognized by (1) associating cause and effect, (2) systematic and rational allocation, or (3) immediate recognition. ***Accounting procedures*** are methods used to record, classify, summarize, and present in an orderly manner (and by means of accounting records) transactions and events that are, at least in part, of a financial character. Informally, the accounting records of a firm are called its ***books.*** An event is recorded initially by an ***entry*** (record) in a book of original entry, or ***journal,*** in which events are recorded in the order in which they occur. The process of making this entry is called ***journalizing*** the event. A ***ledger*** is a book or group of accounts; each ***account*** is a record of all changes that occur in a particular category of assets, liabilities, or owners' equity. A ***chart of accounts*** is an index or list of ledger accounts. The ***double-entry accounting system*** requires at least two ledger entries—a debit and a credit—to record each event or transaction. The process of making the proper ledger entries from the initial journal entry is called ***posting.*** Each account often is kept as a ***T account,*** a two-column format in which debits are entered on the left side and credits on the right side. The ***accounting equation*** is a mathematical expression of the basic accounting model:

Assets − Liabilities = Owners' equity.

The amount on the left side of this equation measures the ***net assets*** (assets less liabilities). An entry representing an increase in owners' equity or a decrease in net assets is recorded as a ***credit;*** an entry representing a decrease in owners' equity or an increase in net assets is recorded as a ***debit.*** The totals of credits and debits in the ledger must be equal at all times; therefore, the totals of credits and debits posted from a single journal entry must be equal. The net total (difference between debits and credits) of a ledger account at a particular time is called the ***account*** *balance.* A *nominal account* is an account whose balance is closed to a permanent or *real account* at the end of an accounting period; the real accounts remain open after the regular closing of the books, and the balance of a real account appears on the balance sheet.

A *work sheet* is a working paper used to assist the accountant in preparing financial statements and other reports; it also provides a record of the work the accountant has performed. A *trial balance* is a schedule of the ledger account balances as of a particular time. *Adjusting entries* are journal entries made at the end of an accounting period to record changes that have not routinely been journalized during the period. *Closing entries* are journal entries made at the end of an accounting period to transfer nominal account balances to real accounts. A *post-closing trial balance* is a schedule of account balances taken after the closing entries have been posted to make sure that the equality of debits and credits in the ledger has been maintained.

A *special journal* is a subdivision of the general journal in which groups of similar transactions (sales, purchases, cash receipts and disbursements, and so on) are recorded. A *subsidiary ledger* is a group of accounts maintained outside the general ledger; the sum of the balances of the accounts in the subsidiary ledger equals the balance of a related *control account* in the general ledger. The *voucher system* is an accounting system that provides a systematic method of recording and controlling credit purchases, accounts payable, and cash disbursements.

The *book value* of a long-lived asset is its acquisition cost less any accumulated depreciation, depletion, or amortization—that is, the unexpired cost of the asset as shown in the ledger. The book value of a share of stock is the amount of owners' equity assigned to that share. *Fair value* (or *market value*) is the exchange price of a transfer in an arm's length transaction, or an approximation of that price if the transfer does not involve money or money claims. *Current market value* is the price of a good or service at the present time. *Appraisal value* is an estimate of the worth of something. The *price level* is the exchange ratio between money and goods at a given time, as compared with the ratio at some other time.

An *asset* is an economic resource that is expected to benefit the accounting entity and its activities in future accounting periods. An asset is an *unexpired cost*—that is, a cost that is not yet fully recognized as an expense because its benefit has not yet been fully obtained. *Current assets* include cash and other assets that are expected to be sold, consumed, or converted into cash during the next normal operating cycle of the business, whichever is longer. *Working capital* is properly defined as current assets less current liabilities, although the term is sometimes used to refer to the total of current assets alone. *Quick assets* include cash, marketable securities, and accounts receivable—those assets that can readily be converted into cash on short notice. A *marketable security* is an investment that is readily convertible into cash and which management expects to convert within the normal operating cycle of the business. The *liquidity* of a firm refers to the sufficiency of its current assets to meet the day-to-day needs for cash disbursements. The *solvency* of a firm refers to the sufficiency of a firm's total assets to enable it eventually to meet all of its debts; solvency usually is reflected in the excess of total assets over total liabilities.

Long-lived assets (or ***noncurrent assets***) are tangible and intangible assets used in the operations of a business, which have a life longer than the normal operating cycle of the business, and which are not acquired primarily for sale. A ***productive asset*** is an asset held or used in the production of goods or services. Two productive assets are said to be ***similar*** if they are of the same general type, perform the same function, or are employed in the same line of business; if the assets do not meet one of these criteria, they are said to be ***dissimilar. Inventory*** includes the materials and goods held by a firm for purposes of sale as part of the normal business operations of the firm. Inventory is recorded as a current asset; the cost of inventory expires as goods are sold. A problem arises in determining the cost of goods sold, because it is seldom convenient to identify particular items taken out of inventory with their actual individual costs. The ***first-in, first-out (FIFO)*** inventory-valuation procedure assumes that the first item to leave inventory each time is the one that was acquired first; the latest acquisitions are assumed to be still on hand as inventory. The ***last-in, first-out (LIFO)*** procedure assumes that the last item acquired is used or sold first; earliest acquisitions are assumed to be still on hand as inventory at the end of the period.

A ***liability*** is an economic obligation or debt owed to a creditor. A ***current liability*** is a debt that is expected to be paid or settled from current assets or through the creation of another current liability within a year or the normal operating cycle of the business, whichever is longer; a debt that does not meet these criteria is called a ***noncurrent*** (or ***fixed***) ***liability.*** An ***estimated liability*** is an obligation whose amount is not known with precision. A ***contingent liability*** is an obligation that does not exist at the present moment, but is expected to exist if certain possible or probable events occur.

Owners' equity is the residual claim of the owners against the assets of the firm; the amount of owners' equity is equal to the net assets of the firm. ***Paid-in capital*** is the amount contributed by the owners of a corporation. The balance sheet of a corporation normally lists the value of outstanding stock at its par or stated value; any excess paid in by the owners beyond that amount is listed as paid-in capital in excess of par (or stated) value. ***Retained earnings*** represent the cumulative net income of a corporation less losses and dividends; normally, retained earnings equal the excess of owners' equity over paid-in capital. A ***deficit*** is a negative (debit) balance in the Retained Earnings account. A ***reserve*** is a classification or appropriation of a portion of retained earnings; the directors may establish a reserve to indicate that an amount of retained earnings is protected from payment as dividends to owners because the firm expects to need the corresponding amount of net assets for some specific purpose.

Revenue is an inflow of assets (or decrease in liabilities) that increases owners' equity and that results from profit-directed activities of a firm. ***Cost*** is the transfer price assigned in a transaction to an asset, liability, or owners' equity item; in an economic sense, cost is the sacrifice incurred to obtain some benefit in an economic activity. An ***unexpired cost*** (asset) is a cost that is expected to benefit the firm in a future period. An ***expired cost*** (expense or loss) is a cost that is not expected to contribute any discernible benefit to future operations. An ***expense*** is a cost of obtaining revenue during the current period. A ***loss*** is an expired cost that has not assisted in the production of revenue; losses generally are considered a subcategory of expense. A ***casualty*** is a sudden, unexpected, or unusual event that results in a loss. An ***expenditure*** is a payment (or the incurring of an obligation) for a benefit received. A ***capital expenditure*** is an amount expended for the acquisition of a long-lived asset; a ***revenue expenditure*** is an amount expended for a good or service with a useful life less than the normal operating cycle of the business or a year, whichever is longer. ***Gross margin*** is the excess of sales revenue over cost of goods sold. An ***extraordinary item*** is an event or transaction that is both unusual in nature and infrequent in occurrence. A ***prior period adjustment*** is a material adjustment related to a prior period and excluded in the determination of net income; prior period adjustments are reported in the statements as an adjustment of the opening balance of retained earnings.

Earnings per common share, representing the amount of net income assigned to each share of common stock, should be reported on the income statement. A ***common stock equivalent*** is a security that is in substance equivalent to common stock because of the terms or the circumstances associated with its issuance. ***Primary earnings per share*** report the earnings per common share computed using the number of outstanding common shares and common stock equivalents. ***Dilution*** is a reduction in earnings per common share that results from the issuance of additional shares of common stock. ***Fully diluted earnings per share*** report the earnings per common share that would have resulted if all outstanding convertible debentures, preferred stock, options, and warrants were converted or exercised, thus producing the maximum dilution that might be expected in the future.

The ***annual report*** of a firm is an official summary that includes the firm's financial statements for a year, along with related information prepared for stockholders and others with an interest in the firm. ***Financial statements*** are formal reports of an enterprise that summarize the financial position, results of operations, changes in financial position, changes in owners' equity, and other financial activities of the firm over some period. A ***classified financial statement*** is one in which items are arranged in major sets and subsets. A ***comparative financial statement*** presents information covering two or more accounting periods, arranged in parallel columns for easy comparison of the amounts. A ***statement of financial position*** (or ***balance sheet***) summarizes the assets, liabilities, and owners' equity of an accounting entity at a particular point in time. A balance sheet prepared in the ***account form*** lists assets in the left column and lists liabilities and owners' equity in the right column. A balance sheet prepared in the ***report form*** shows assets, liabilities, and owners' equity in a single column. The ***income statement*** reports revenues, expenses, and net income (or loss) for a firm during a particular period of time. The ***multiple-step income statement*** presents operating revenue and expense at the beginning of the statement, with nonoperating items near the end of the statement. The ***single-step income statement*** summarizes all revenue items and then deducts all expense items to arrive at net income or net loss. A ***statement of retained earnings*** is a financial statement that discloses changes in retained earnings during a period. Sometimes the income statement and statement of retained earnings are combined in a single ***statement of income and retained earnings.*** A ***statement of changes in financial position*** discloses the changes that occur between two successive statements of financial position (balance sheets). A ***statement of owners' equity*** discloses the changes that occurred in owners' equity between two dates. ***Pro forma statements*** are forecasts of future balances and results of operations, prepared in the form of financial statements for the future dates. An ***interim statement*** is a financial statement summarizing information for a period ending on any date within the normal reporting year. ***Footnotes*** to financial statements are used to disclose additional information needed for clarity, completeness, and full disclosure; all footnotes are integral parts of the statements.

Accounting on an ***accrual basis*** follows generally accepted accounting principles, recognizing revenue when earned and expense when costs expire. Accounting on a ***cash basis*** recognizes revenue when cash is received and expense when cash is disbursed; cash-basis accounting is not generally accepted for most businesses. To ***accrue*** is to recognize and report an event or transaction in the time period to which its effect relates. ***Accrued revenue*** is revenue earned but not yet received. An ***accrued expense*** is an expense incurred but not yet paid. ***Unearned revenue*** is revenue received but not yet earned. A ***prepaid expense*** is a benefit that has been paid for but not yet received. ***Adjusting entries*** are used at the end of an accounting period to record accruals and prepayments, depreciation, bad debts expense, and similar modifications of account balances.

A ***corporation*** is a legal entity created by a governmental unit, established to accomplish various purposes, and legally separate and distinct from its owners or organizers. The owners of a corporation are the ***stockholders*** (or ***shareholders***), who receive shares of ***capital stock*** issued by the corporation in return for their investment in the corporation. The stockholders elect a ***board of directors,*** a group of individuals (***directors***) who supervise the business affairs of the enterprise. ***Management*** includes officers of the firm who are assigned responsibility for the detailed operations and activities of the firm. An ***equity*** is an owner's interest in a firm; sometimes the interests of creditors such as bondholders are called debt equity. ***Capital*** is the total of funds invested in a business entity by owners and long-term creditors; the term is also used to refer to one of the four factors of production from which income is derived (the other factors are land, labor, and ownership). ***Common stock*** is the basic or ordinary capital stock of a corporation, representing shares in the residual owners' equity of the firm. ***Preferred stock*** is capital stock that has a priority over other shares, especially with regard to dividends and the distribution of assets if the enterprise is liquidated. ***Par value*** is the dollar amount assigned to a share of stock by the charter of a corporation; the term also refers to the face value appearing on a bond, representing the principal amount of the obligation. ***No-par stock*** is common stock that is not assigned a par value in the corporation's charter; the charter usually assigns a ***stated value*** to no-par stock. (The difference between par value and stated value is largely a legal technicality.) A ***premium*** on stock is the excess of its exchange price on issuance over the par value of the stock; the term also refers to the excess of the exchange price when a debt is issued over the principal amount to be repaid at maturity.

In most corporations, stockholders have ***preemptive rights*** to purchase a pro rata (proportionate) share of unissued stock that the corporation issues. A ***stock subscription*** is a contract by which a subscriber agrees to purchase a certain number of shares of stock. ***Stockholders' equity*** refers to the owners' equity of a corporation, which is equal to the net assets. ***Limited liability*** refers to the legal restriction on the liability of shareholders to the amount of their investment. A ***dividend*** is a distribution by a corporation to its shareholders, usually in cash or in its own stock.

Dividends in arrears are undeclared dividends on cumulative preferred stock that arise from failure of the corporation to pay the full specified rate of dividends when due; the dividends in arrears must be paid to preferred stockholders before further dividends can be paid to common stockholders. If the seller of stock retains a declared but not-yet-paid dividend, the stock is said to be sold *ex dividend.* A *stock distribution* or *stock dividend* is a corporate distribution or dividend paid in stock of the corporation issuing the dividend. A *stock split* is the issuance of additional shares of a company's stock to its existing stockholders without additional investment by the stockholders. If a corporation reacquires shares of its own stock and does not cancel them, the shares held by the corporation are called *treasury stock.*

A *parent company* is a company that controls another corporation (the *subsidiary company*) through stock ownership. *Consolidated financial statements* are statements of a parent company with one or more subsidiary companies prepared as if the group of companies were a single entity, with intercompany transactions eliminated. *Minority interest* is the shareholders' interest in a subsidiary company, exclusive of the parent company's interest. An *elimination entry* is made in the working papers for consolidated statements to offset intercompany pairs of accounts that are reciprocal in nature. The *equity method* (or economic method) of accounting for investments in subsidiaries records the investment initially at cost, but then increases the investment account with the parent's share of any increase in the subsidiary's net assets that arises from the subsidiary's earnings, and decreases the investment account with decreases in the subsidiary's net assets that arise from losses and dividend distributions. The *cost method* of accounting for investments in subsidiaries records the investment at cost and retains that balance in the investment account; dividends received from the subsidiary are recorded as revenue by the parent. *Pooling of interests* is a form of business combination in which there has been no substantive change in ownership or control. A *purchase* is a form of business combination in which one business entity is assumed to be purchased by another. A *single proprietorship* (or *sole proprietorship*) is a business owned by one person. A *partnership* is an unincorporated business owned jointly by two or more individuals who share in its profits and losses. A *drawing account* is an account that reflects temporary transactions between a proprietor or partner and the business.

A *bond* is a formal, long-term debt instrument on which interest is paid periodically; the principal is returned at maturity or on call. A *convertible security* is a stock or bond that can be exchanged (at the option of the holder) for a specified amount of other securities of the issuing company. An issue of *serial bonds* has maturity dates at intervals; some of the bonds mature at each of the dates. *Face value* (or par value) is the maturity value (the principal amount) of a security. The *principal* of a loan is the amount borrowed, exclusive of interest charges. *Interest* is the cost of using money. *Yield* is the return on an investment, usually expressed as an interest rate or percentage of the principal. *Cash yield* is the ratio of cash received annually on a security to the market value of the security. *Effective yield* is the rate of interest at which the total present value of payments to be received equals the amount lent or borrowed. *Nominal rate of interest* is the contract interest rate written on a debt instrument. *Maturity date* is the due date of a note, loan, or similar debt—the date on which the principal must be repaid. *Retirement* may refer to the repayment of a debt or the reacquisition of a stock.

Impact analysis is a technique of intensively and extensively probing the effects of events and transactions throughout the accounting system. A *ratio* is the quotient of one quantity divided by another measured in the same units. *Ratio analysis* is a technique of interpreting financial statements by computing *financial ratios* between various amounts shown on the statements. These ratios are compared with *historical standards* (similar ratios from previous statements of the same company) and *industry standards* (similar ratios for other companies in the same industry). *Horizontal analysis* is a technique for analyzing financial statements by comparing data of one period with that of another. *Vertical analysis* is a technique of financial statement analysis that compares data of one period with other data of the same period.

Allocation is the process of assigning costs and revenues to time periods, departments, and so on, according to benefits received, responsibilities assumed, usage, or other rational measures. *Depreciation* is the process of allocating the cost of a tangible fixed asset, less salvage value, over its estimated useful life in a rational and systematic manner. *Depletion* is the process of allocating the acquisition cost of a natural resource to reflect the exhaustion of the resource. *Amortization* is the process of allocating a liability or an intangible asset to revenue or expense over a stated period of time. When an asset is allocated to expense over time, it is often said to be *written off.* A *depreciable asset* is an item of property, plant, or equipment that is used in the normal operations of a business. *Depreciation expense* is the periodic charge that allocates the cost of a tangible fixed asset to expense over its estimated useful life in a rational and systematic manner. *Accumulated depreciation* is the total depreciation recorded for an asset or group of assets since their acquisition; it is the cumulative total of periodic depreciation charges. The *depreciation base* is the acquisition cost of an asset, less salvage value; this is the amount to be written off over the estimated useful life of the asset. *Salvage value* (or *scrap value*) is the residual value of an asset at the end of its useful (service) life. *Straight-line depreciation* (or *amortization*) is a method of allocation that assigns equal amounts of write-off to accounting periods. *Accelerated depreciation* is a depreciation method that provides larger write-offs during the earlier years of the life of an asset than during the later years; this approach is also called a *reducing-charge method* of depreciation. *Composite depreciation* is a depreciation method that establishes a depreciation rate for a group of assets, or for all assets owned, and applies this rate to the group in computing the periodic depreciation charge.

An *invoice* is an itemized statement of merchandise purchased. When merchandise is sold or purchased on credit, the sale or purchase is said to be *on account.* A purchaser may be entitled to deduct a *discount* from the amount due in settling a debt if he or she complies with specific conditions; the term *discount* is also used to describe the amount by which the proceeds received from a debt or stock are less than the principal amount or par value. A *cash discount* is a reduction in an amount owed that results from the payment of the debt within a specified time period. A *trade discount* is a reduction in selling price available to certain classes of business purchasers—for example, to wholesalers or to retailers. *Gross price* is the full invoice cost of merchandise. *Net price* is the gross price less any applicable cash discount.

F.O.B. is a trade term meaning "free on board" and indicating the point to which the seller pays transportation costs for merchandise.

The *perpetual inventory method* is a procedure that maintains a continuous record of units and costs of inventory acquisitions and disposals. The *periodic inventory method* (or physical method) requires that a periodic count of inventory be taken to determine the quantity and valuation of inventory. The *lower-of-cost-or-market inventory method* adjusts the cost of inventory to a lower market value if the utility of the inventory declines. The *gross-profit method* is an inventory procedure that estimates ending inventory by determining the cost of goods sold (as the difference between sales and gross margin on sales) and deducting this amount from goods available for sale. The *retail inventory method* calculates a ratio of cost of inventory to retail price; this ratio is applied to ending inventory at retail to obtain an estimate of the ending inventory at cost.

Bank reconciliation is the process of bringing into agreement the cash balance at the end of a period as shown on the bank statement with the cash balance shown in the depositor's books. *Bad debts* are accounts receivable that are considered uncollectible. *Aging of receivables* is a method of estimating the amount of bad debts by examining individually specific receivables and making a judgment about their collectibility on the basis of the time for which a balance has remained uncollected. *Discounting a note* refers to the practice of using a note receivable as collateral for a loan; the lender deducts interest in advance from the loan, so the amount received is discounted from the amount due on the note; the lender (usually a bank) then obtains repayment of its principal by collecting from the maker of the note. If the maker of a note fails to pay at maturity (or when the note is otherwise duly presented for payment), he or she is said to *dishonor the note.*

Cost accounting refers to the accounting procedures that deal with reporting, processing, and controlling the cost of a process, job, unit, or department of a firm. A *job-order cost system* is a cost-accounting system that accumulates costs for specific jobs or batches of individualized products. A *process cost system* is a cost-accounting system that accumulates costs for departments or processes. A *standard cost* is a predetermined per-unit cost for direct material, direct labor, and manufacturing overhead involved in the production of an item; actual costs are then compared with the standard cost. If the standard costs are considered to be attainable under current, efficient operating conditions (rather than representing unattainable ideal conditions), they are said to be *currently attainable standards.* A *variance* is a difference between actual costs and standard or budgeted costs. A *price* (or *rate*) *variance* is the difference between actual price and standard price, multiplied by the total number of items of direct material or direct labor acquired. A *quantity variance* is the standard price of an item multiplied by the difference between the actual quantities used and the standard quantities allowed for the units produced. *Direct material* is raw material that is directly traceable to usage in manufacturing particular finished goods. *Direct labor* is labor that is clearly identifiable with production of particular goods. *Indirect labor* is that labor not clearly identifiable with production of particular goods, but associated with the general production process. *Overhead* includes factory costs other than direct labor and direct material. A *joint cost* is a cost common to more than one product, department, or other segment of a business operation. A ***transfer price*** is a price charged by one segment of an organization for products or services supplied to another segment. A ***period cost*** is a cost associated with benefits received during a particular accounting period, but not associated with any specific revenue during that period. A ***product cost*** is a cost that is associated directly with a particular item of sales revenue. Normally, relationships of cost and revenue are valid only over a certain spectrum of activity levels called the ***relevant range*** for those relationships. A ***variable cost*** is a cost that changes in total in direct proportion to changes in a related activity level or volume over a relevant range. A ***fixed cost*** is a cost that remains unchanged over a relevant range of activity or volume. A ***mixed cost*** is a cost that includes elements of both variable and fixed costs over a relevant range. ***Contribution margin*** is the excess of revenue over variable expense. The ***break-even point*** is a level of sales where revenue equals expense. The ***margin of safety*** is the percentage or amount of actual revenue in excess of the revenue that would be received at the break-even point. ***Sales mix*** is the combination of products that make up the total sales of a firm. ***Cost-volume-profit analysis*** is an analytical approach that deals with relationships among variations in revenue, expenses, and sales volume. ***Absorption costing*** is a form of product costing that assigns direct labor, direct material, and fixed and variable overhead to inventory cost. ***Direct costing*** is a cost procedure that assigns variable costs to inventory, but assigns fixed manufacturing overhead to the period costs.

A ***budget*** is a forecast of estimated income and expense or financial position for some defined period of future time. A ***comprehensive budget*** is a master budget or forecast that reflects a firm's plans for a period of time. A ***cash budget*** is a forecast of expected cash receipts and disbursements for a period of time. A ***static budget*** is a forecast prepared on the assumption of a single predicted level of activity. A ***flexible budget*** is a forecast prepared with alternative estimates of various items for alternative possible levels of activity. ***Capital budgeting*** is long-term planning for capital expenditures and for the financing of such expenditures. ***Responsibility accounting*** is an accounting approach that establishes organizational centers for controlling revenues and costs. ***Performance reports*** are summaries of actual results and budgeted data. A ***profit center*** is a segment of an enterprise with responsibility for controlling its own revenue and expense to maximize its profit (net income).

When a cost or expenditure is treated as an asset that will benefit a future period, that cost is said to be ***capitalized. Compound interest*** is interest calculated on the principal plus accumulated interest. The ***present value*** of a sum at a future date is the amount that would be invested now at a specified rate of compound interest to accumulate to the given sum at the given future date. The ***discounted-cash-flow method*** is an approach to capital budgeting that discounts expected future cash flows to their present values. The ***net-present-value method*** is a discounted-cash-flow method that discounts expected future cash flows to their present values using a minimum desired rate of return; an investment is rejected if the net present value of the return on the investment is less than the amount of the investment. A ***rate of return*** is the ratio of net income to the capital employed to generate that net income. The ***payback period*** of an investment is the time required for cash flows from an investment to accumulate to an amount equal to the initial investment. ***Trading on*** *the equity* (or *financial leverage*) is an activity that borrows funds at a specified interest rate with the expectation of using these funds to earn a higher rate of return for the benefit of the owners of an enterprise; the term also applies to an activity that obtains funds through the issuance of preferred stock at specified dividend rate with the expectation of earning a higher rate of return through the use of such funds for the benefit of common stockholders.

Linear programming is a method for solving business problems that involve the relationship of variables and limited resources, with the purpose of maximizing profits or minimizing costs. ***Expected value*** is the conditional value of an event weighted by the probability that the event will occur. ***Conditional value*** is the value that is expected to result if a particular event occurs.

A ***capital gain (loss)*** is a gain (loss) resulting from the sale or exchange of a capital asset as defined by tax law; capital gains and losses receive special treatment under provisions of the Internal Revenue Code. The ***allocation of income tax*** is a procedure used to match the tax expense reported in the income statement with the net income before taxes that is reported in the same statement; this procedure is used when accounting methods required or desired for tax purposes do not coincide with accounting methods required or chosen for preparation of financial statements. The ***deferral method of interperiod tax allocation*** is a procedure that defers the tax effect of certain timing differences between tax treatment and book treatment to future periods where the timing differences reverse.

References are to line numbers in the preceding glossary.

Appendix: sample financial statements from annual reports

KELLOGG COMPANY AND SUBSIDIARY COMPANIES

Consolidated Statements of Earnings

	1973	1972
Net Sales	$828,408,328	$699,221,122
Interest and Other Income	7,098,727	5,238,121
	835,507,055	704,459,243
Costs and Expenses:		
Cost of goods sold	539,586,878	436,481,783
Selling, general and administrative expenses	164,385,543	148,565,956
Interest expense	3,387,650	1,498,596
	707,360,071	586,546,335
Earnings before Income Taxes	128,146,984	117,912,908
Estimated Income Taxes:		
United States Federal—		
Current	45,900,000	36,100,000
Net deferred	(500,000)	800,000
Foreign—		
Current	9,700,000	12,300,000
Net deferred	2,500,000	2,000,000
State and Local—Current	5,500,000	6,200,000
	63,100,000	57,400,000
Net Earnings for the Year	$ 65,046,984	$ 60,512,908
Earnings Per Common Share	$ .89	$ .83

See accompanying Notes to Financial Statements.

REPORT OF INDEPENDENT ACCOUNTS

To the Stockholders and
Board of Directors of
Kellogg Company

In our opinion, the accompanying consolidated balance sheets and the related consolidated statements of earnings, stockholders equity and of changes in financial position present fairly the financial position of Kellogg Company and its subsidiaries at December 31, 1973 and 1972, the results of their operations and the changes in financial position for the years then ended, in conformity with generally accepted accounting principles consistently applied. Our examinations of these statements were made in accordance with generally accepted auditing standards and accordingly included such tests of the accounting records and such other auditing procedures as we considered necessary in the circumstances.

Battle Creek, Michigan
February 11, 1974

KELLOGG COMPANY AND SUBSIDIARY COMPANIES

Consolidated Balance Sheets at December 31

	1973	1972
CURRENT ASSETS:		
Cash, including certificates of deposit of $55,084,873 in 1973 and $51,300,000 in 1972	$ 66,329,947	$ 56,037,214
United States Government Securities and Other Short-Term Investments, at cost (approximate market)	4,500,417	2,648,562
Accounts Receivable, less allowances of $550,450 in 1973 and $532,000 in 1972	49,846,514	42,116,922
Inventories:		
Raw Materials and Supplies	61,729,949	42,648,552
Finished Goods and Materials in Process	40,320,150	33,478,825
Prepaid Taxes and Other Expenses	14,823,959	12,565,902
Total Current Assets	$237,550,936	$189,495,977
PROPERTY, PLANT AND EQUIPMENT	208,478,920	191,801,678
OTHER ASSETS:		
Excess of Cost Over Net Assets of Companies Acquired	19,023,385	19,023,385
Other Investments	1,954,109	1,641,280
Patents, Trade-Marks and Goodwill	1	1
	$467,007,351	$401,962,321
CURRENT LIABILITIES:		
Accounts Payable	$ 37,023,569	$ 31,521,090
Foreign and Other Loans	23,258,708	9,755,478
Accrued Salaries and Wages	4,271,631	4,675,000
Other Current Liabilities	33,585,080	24,041,668
Estimated Income Taxes	22,104,476	15,211,098
Total Current Liabilities	$120,243,464	$ 85,204,334
LONG-TERM FOREIGN LOANS	$ 9,041,254	$ 9,186,220
DEFERRED INCOME TAXES	$ 18,278,401	$ 16,032,969
STOCKHOLDERS EQUITY:		
3½% Cumulative Preferred Stock, $100 Par Value— Authorized and issued 85,513 shares, less 61,526 shares in treasury (89,263 less 64,946 in 1972)	$ 2,398,700	$ 2,431,700
Common Stock, $.50 Par Value— Authorized 80,000,000 shares in 1973 and 40,000,000 in 1972; issued 73,105,631 shares in 1973 and 36,432,807 shares in 1972	36,552,816	18,216,404
Capital in Excess of Par Value	14,918,934	12,614,338
Retained Earnings	265,573,782	258,276,356
Total Stockholders Equity	$319,444,232	$291,538,798
	$467,007,351	$401,962,321

See accompanying Notes to Financial Statements.

KELLOGG COMPANY AND SUBSIDIARY COMPANIES

Consolidated Statements of Changes in Financial Position

	1973	1972
FINANCIAL RESOURCES WERE PROVIDED BY:		
Net Earnings for the Year	$ 65,046,984	$ 60,512,908
Depreciation	16,228,374	14,190,806
Non-Current Deferred Income Taxes	2,245,432	2,449,273
Working Capital Provided by Operations	$ 83,520,790	$ 77,152,987
Sale of Properties and Change in Other Assets	2,093,841	4,238,627
Increase in Long-Term Foreign Loans	669,573	3,832,033
Issue of Common Stock	2,389,193	1,130,072
	$ 88,673,397	$ 86,353,719
FINANCIAL RESOURCES WERE USED FOR:		
Additions to Properties	$ 35,312,286	$ 29,110,888
Cash Dividends	39,509,217	37,947,235
Reduction in Long-Term Foreign Loans	814,539	1,413,726
Purchase of Preferred Stock for Treasury	21,526	21,627
	$ 75,657,568	$ 68,493,476
INCREASE IN WORKING CAPITAL	$ 13,015,829	$ 17,860,243
ANALYSIS OF CHANGES IN WORKING CAPITAL		
INCREASE (DECREASE) IN CURRENT ASSETS:		
Cash	$ 10,292,733	$ 8,566,161
United States Government Securities and Other Short-Term Investments	1,851,855	(4,871,975)
Accounts Receivable	7,729,592	4,215,528
Inventories	25,922,722	4,458,984
Prepaid Taxes and Other Expenses	2,258,057	630,222
	$ 48,054,959	$ 12,998,920
(INCREASE) DECREASE IN CURRENT LIABILITIES:		
Accounts Payable	$ (5,502,479)	$ (6,321,048)
Foreign and Other Loans	(13,503,230)	5,709,732
Accrued Salaries and Wages	403,369	(1,758,000)
Other Current Liabilities	(9,543,412)	1,123,186
Estimated Income Taxes	(6,893,378)	6,107,453
	$ (35,039,130)	$ 4,861,323
INCREASE IN WORKING CAPITAL	$ 13,015,829	$ 17,860,243

See accompanying Notes to Financial Statements.

KELLOGG COMPANY AND SUBSIDIARY COMPANIES

Consolidated Statements of Stockholders Equity

	Preferred Stock	Common Stock	Capital in Excess of Par Value	Retained Earnings
Balance, January 1, 1972	$2,464,900	$18,187,116	$11,501,981	$235,710,683
Net earnings for the year 1972				60,512,908
Dividends declared:				
Preferred Stock—$3.50 a share				(85,726)
Common Stock—$ .52 a share				(37,861,509)
Stock options exercised		29,288	1,100,784	
Preferred stock purchased for treasury	(33,200)		11,573	
Balance, December 31, 1972	$2,431,700	$18,216,404	$12,614,338	$258,276,356
Net earnings for the year 1973				65,046,984
Dividends declared:				
Preferred Stock—$3.50 a share				(84,497)
Common Stock—$ .54 a share				(39,424,720)
Stock options exercised		96,071	2,293,122	
Preferred stock purchased for treasury	(33,000)		11,474	
Par value of 36,480,681 common shares issued as a 100% stock distribution		18,240,341		(18,240,341)
Balance, December 31, 1973	$2,398,700	$36,552,816	$14,918,934	$265,573,782

Notes to Financial Statements—1973 and 1972

NOTE 1—SUMMARY OF ACCOUNTING POLICIES: CONSOLIDATION

The consolidated financial statements include the accounts of Kellogg Company and its wholly-owned subsidiaries. Significant intercompany transactions have been eliminated in consolidation.

FOREIGN CURRENCY TRANSLATION

Assets and liabilities of foreign operations are translated into United States dollars at year-end rates of exchange, except property, plant and equipment (and related depreciation) are translated at historical rates. Income and expense accounts, except depreciation, are translated at the monthly average rates prevailing during the year. Net gains and losses from translations are included in current income for the years and are not significant.

INVENTORIES

Inventories are valued at the lower of cost (principally average) or market.

PROPERTY, PLANT AND EQUIPMENT

Fixed assets are stated at cost. The cost of depreciable property, plant and equipment is depreciated over estimated useful lives using straight-line methods at rates averaging 2.7% for buildings and 6.4% for machinery and equipment. Expenditures for maintenance and repairs are charged against income; renewals and betterments are capitalized. The cost of property sold or otherwise retired together with related accumulated depreciation, is eliminated from the accounts and gains or losses on disposition are reflected in income.

INTANGIBLE ASSETS

The "excess of cost over net assets of companies acquired" is not being amortized because, in the opinion of the Company, there has been no diminution in value.

INCOME TAXES

Income taxes have been provided for differences between depreciation, other expenses and income as recorded for financial statement and for tax reporting purposes. Investment tax credits, which amounted to $850,000 in 1973 and $960,000 in 1972, have been used to reduce current income tax provisions.

No provision has been made for additional United States income taxes relating to undistributed earnings of foreign subsidiaries since the Company intends to invest such earnings premanently, or the taxes payable on distribution of foreign earnings are expected to be substantially offset by tax credits. The cumulative amounts of undistributed earnings at December 31, 1973 and 1972 were approximately $72,000,000 and $66,000,000, respectively.

RESEARCH AND DEVELOPMENT

Research and development expenditures applicable to development and improvement of new products, production processes and packaging are expensed in the year incurred.

RETIREMENT PLANS

The Company and its subsidiaries have established various profit-sharing, savings, and pension plans to provide retirement benefits for officers and employees. Expense to the Company and its subsidiaries (and amount funded) under these plans was approximately $14,800,000 in 1973 and $12,100,000 in 1972. The Company's policy is to fund pension costs accrued. Unfunded vested benefits are not significant.

EARNINGS AND DIVIDENDS PER COMMON SHARE

Earnings per common share are computed by dividing net earnings by the monthly weighted average number of shares outstanding, after deducting preferred stock dividends. References in 1973 and 1972 to per share amounts and price per share reflect a 100% common stock distribution in 1973.

NOTE 2—FOREIGN OPERATIONS:

The consolidated financial statements include the following amounts applicable to operations outside North America:

	1973	1972
Assets	$109,627,000	$ 92,996,000
Liabilities	54,195,000	40,284,000
Net sales	201,275,000	165,731,000
Net earnings	7,885,000	7,239,000

NOTE 3—PROPERTY, PLANT AND EQUIPMENT:

	1973	1972
Land	$ 10,521,903	$ 9,591,125
Buildings	97,463,475	90,851,566
Machinery and equipment	220,851,084	205,865,722
Construction in progress	18,900,697	13,548,012
	347,737,159	319,856,425
Less-Accumulated depreciation:		
Buildings	29,487,024	27,234,825
Machinery and equipment	109,771,215	100,819,922
	139,258,239	128,054,747
	$208,478,920	$191,801,678

Depreciation expense amounted to $2,292,647 in 1973 for buildings and $13,935,727 for machinery and equipment. Corresponding amounts for 1972 were $2,404,890 and $11,785,916, respectively.

NOTE 4—FOREIGN LOANS:

Foreign loans at December 31, 1973 are payable in installments from 1974 to 1982 at interest rates from 3½% to 14%. Loans of approximately $4,825,000 in 1973 and $4,880,000 in 1972 are secured by property, plant and equipment. Maturities during the five years ending December 31, 1978 are listed below:

1974	$20,558,708
1975	1,185,327
1976	814,508
1977	1,828,607
1978	4,838,690

NOTE 5—PREFERRED STOCK:

The Company may redeem its outstanding preferred shares at a price of $101.50 currently ($100 after 1985). Each year the Company must offer to purchase 3,750 shares of preferred stock at a current maximum price of $100.50 ($100 after 1975), or apply previously acquired shares (61,526 shares in treasury at December 31, 1973) against this requirement.

NOTE 6—STOCK OPTIONS:

At December 31, 1973, 274,400 shares of common stock were available for granting of options under stock option plans; 831,101 shares were under option at prices from $9.94 to $14.94 a share, of which 649,701 were exercisable. Shares under the various options are exercisable over four years, beginning one year from date of grant. Options granted are at market value of common stock at date of grant.

The following table sets forth certain other information:

	1973	1972
Options granted (shares)	—	291,000
Price per share	—	$ 14.94
Options exercised (shares)	240,017	117,150
Average exercise price	$ 9.95	$ 9.56
Options cancelled (shares)	2,600	24,400

NOTE 7—INCOME TAXES:

Income tax returns filed by the Company have been examined by the Internal Revenue Service and issues have been settled through December 31, 1971. The effect of the settlement on 1973 and 1972 income was not significant.

NOTE 8—FEDERAL TRADE COMMISSION PROCEEDING:

In 1972 the Federal Trade Commission commenced a proceeding against Kellogg Company and three other cereal manufacturers, charging that these companies have maintained a "highly concentrated, non-competitive market structure" in violation of the Federal Trade Commission Act. The complaint seeks such relief as is supported by an adjudicative record, including but not limited to divestiture of assets, licensing of trademarks, prohibition of future acquisitions of competitors, prohibition of any practices found to be anti-competitive, and periodic review of the provisions of any order that may be entered. It is the position of Kellogg Company that it has not violated the Act and the Company, therefore, has contested the charges.

FUQUA INDUSTRIES, INC./1973 ANNUAL REPORT

Financial Highlights (in Thousands Except Earnings Per Share)

	1970	1971	1972	1973	Forecast 1974
Sales and Revenues	$274,151	$309,660	$386,386	$479,188	$541,000
Pre-Tax Income from continuing operations	17,675	21,686	30,531	39,798	47,300
Percent of Sales	6.4%	7.0%	7.9%	8.3%	8.7%
Income From Continuing Operations	8,913	11,102	15,886	20,289	24,000
Earnings Per Share—Continuing Operations					
Primary	$1.02	$1.23	$1.62	$2.10	$2.75
Fully Diluted	1.02	1.13	1.56	2.08	2.75
Average Number of Common Shares and Common Share Equivalents					
Primary	8,281	8,681	9,529	9,449	8,700
Fully Diluted	8,319	9,877	9,928	9,531	8,700
Net Worth (as reported)	$ 97,503	$117,614	$146,803	$141,938	

This data is not intended to be a complete report of the Company's operations and should be read in conjunction with the financial statements on pages 33–37.

Figures are restated for discontinued operations except where indicated.

AVNET, INC. AND SUBSIDIARIES

	Second Quarter Ended		First Half Ended	
	Jan. 2, 1976	Dec. 27, 1974	Jan. 2, 1976	Dec. 27, 1974
Sales	$150,066,000	$139,800,000	$292,934,000	$284,832,000
Income Before Taxes	16,727,000	11,820,000	32,903,000	26,071,000
Taxes on Income	8,634,000	6,026,000	16,945,000	13,341,000
Net Income	8,093,000	5,794,000	15,958,000	12,730,000
Earnings per Common Share:				
Primary	$.59	$.42	$1.16	$.92
Fully Diluted	$.53	$.38	$1.05	$.83
Weighted Average Shares Outstanding:				
Primary	13,413,209	13,330,080	13,422,817	13,329,262
Fully Diluted	15,203,797	15,206,700	15,213,507	15,221,878

Note: During the first half ended January 2, 1976, a total of 29,986 shares of preferred stock (15,791 shares of $1.00 Cumulative Convertible Preferred, 8,095 shares of $3.00 Cumulative Convertible Preferred Series B, and 6,100 shares of $2.50 Cumulative Convertible Preferred, Series C), were converted into a total of 112,230 shares of Common Stock, resulting in an aggregate increase of $82,244 in Avnet's stated capital and a like decrease in Avnet's capital surplus.

AVNET, INC. AND SUBSIDIARIES

Consolidated Balance Sheet

	JUNE 30,	
	1973	1972
Assets		
Current assets:		
Cash	$ 9,711,704	$ 5,590,950
Marketable securities	1,350,000	2,130,800
Receivables, less allowance for doubtful accounts of $3,972,400 in 1973 and $2,559,391 in 1972	75,907,278	67,886,271
Inventories (Note 3)	118,486,082	104,469,473
Prepaid expenses	1,920,884	1,464,865
Total current assets	207,375,948	181,542,359
Property, plant and equipment (Note 4)	30,877,874	30,282,153
Intangibles and other assets (Note 1)	17,712,387	16,573,700
	$255,966,209	$228,398,212
Liabilities and Shareholders' Equity		
Current liabilities:		
Accounts payable	$ 31,409,848	$ 24,920,030
Accrued expenses	15,453,504	14,423,245
Income taxes	6,537,423	5,376,119
Current portion of long-term debt (Note 5)	2,929,691	1,709,778
Total current liabilities	56,330,466	46,429,172
Long-term debt, less current portion (Note 5)	70,795,428	67,861,682
Minority interest in a subsidiary		1,853,884
Commitments and contingent liabilities (Notes 8 and 11)		
Shareholders' equity: (Notes 5, 6 and 7)		
Capital stock:		
Preferred (liquidation preference $13,988,736)	784,932	807,746
Common	11,471,198	11,342,197
Additional paid-in capital	28,181,609	28,180,939
Retained earnings	88,648,857	72,168,873
	129,086,596	112,499,755
Less common stock held in treasury at cost	246,281	246,281
	128,840,315	112,253,474
	$255,966,209	$228,398,212

See notes to consolidated financial statements. (Notes omitted in this appendix.)

AVNET, INC. AND SUBSIDIARIES

Consolidated Statement of Income and Retained Earnings

	YEAR ENDED JUNE 30,	
	1973	1972
Revenues:		
Sales	$440,719,932	$357,552,627
Commissions, royalties and other, net	1,664,349	1,018,013
	442,384,281	358,570,640
Costs and expenses:		
Cost of sales	310,265,922	248,906,208
Selling, general and administrative	82,876,625	73,041,539
Interest	5,199,646	4,768,010
	398,342,193	326,715,757
Income before income taxes	44,042,088	31,854,883
Income taxes:		
Current	22,508,630	16,742,333
Deferred	(187,083)	(900,120)
	22,321,547	15,842,213
Net income	21,720,541	16,012,670
Retained earnings, beginning of year	72,168,873	61,482,347
Cash dividends:		
Preferred (Note 6)	(1,825,216)	(2,052,171)
Common, $.30 per share	(3,415,341)	(3,273,973)
Retained earnings, end of year	$ 88,648,857	$ 72,168,873
Earnings per common share (Note 9):		
Primary	$1.56	$1.15
Fully diluted	$1.43	$1.05
Weighted average shares outstanding:		
Primary	13,269,266	12,917,507
Fully diluted	15,210,290	15,200,939

See notes to consolidated financial statements.

AVNET, INC. AND SUBSIDIARIES

Consolidated Statement of Changes in Financial Position

	YEAR ENDED JUNE 30,	
	1973	1972
Funds generated from:		
Operations:		
Net income	$21,720,541	$16,012,670
Depreciation and amortization	4,130,501	4,028,034
Decrease in deferred income taxes	(187,083)	(900,120)
	25,663,959	19,140,584
Long-term debt incurred	5,667,237	14,635,486
Increase in payables and accruals	12,088,583	3,687,932
Business sold (acquired)	5,000,000	(5,000,000)
Common shares issued in exchange for convertible preferred shares	114,001	781,260
Proceeds from exercise of stock options	106,875	231,860
	$48,640,655	$33,477,122
Funds used for:		
Inventories	$17,620,060	$13,013,004
Receivables	11,613,950	10,445,350
Property, plant and equipment	7,244,008	4,791,187
Cash dividends	5,240,557	5,326,144
Increase (decrease) in cash and marketable securities	3,675,886	(672,470)
Notes received in connection with business sold	2,500,000	
Preferred shares converted into common shares	114,001	781,260
Others, net	632,193	(207,353)
	$48,640,655	$33,477,122

See notes to consolidated financial statements.

INTERNATIONAL BUSINESS MACHINES CORPORATION AND SUBSIDIARY COMPANIES

Consolidated Statement of Earnings and Retained Earnings for the year ended December 31:

	1975		1974	
Gross Income from Sales, Rentals and Services:				
Sales		$ 4,545,358,669		$ 4,281,771,420
Rentals and services		9,891,182,393		8,393,520,412
		14,436,541,062		12,675,291,832
Cost of sales	$1,630,978,001		$1,427,236,901	
Cost of rentals and services	3,717,709,407		3,326,565,294	
Selling, development and engineering, and general and administrative expenses	5,664,897,389		4,758,558,204	
Interest on debt	62,606,484		69,081,417	
		11,076,191,281		9,581,441,816
		3,360,349,781		3,093,850,016
Other income, principally interest		360,527,185		340,789,345
Earnings before income taxes		3,720,876,966		3,434,639,361
Provision for U.S. Federal and non-U.S. income taxes		1,731,000,000		1,597,000,000
Net Earnings for the Year		1,989,876,966		1,837,639,361
Per share		$13.35		$12.47
Average number of shares outstanding: 1975—149,044,427 1974—147,400,733				
Retained Earnings, January 1		6,542,357,821		5,524,387,477
		8,532,234,787		7,362,026,838
Cash dividends		968,988,364		819,669,017
Retained Earnings, December 31		$ 7,563,246,423		$ 6,542,357,821

The notes on pages 23 through 25 are an integral part of this statement.

INTERNATIONAL BUSINESS MACHINES CORPORATION AND SUBSIDIARY COMPANIES

Consolidated Balance Sheet at December 31:

	1975		1974	
Assets				
Current Assets:				
Cash	$ 183,869,340		$ 175,922,776	
Marketable securities, at lower of cost or market	4,584,445,162		3,629,212,884	
Notes and accounts receivable . . . less reserve: 1975, $120,598,674; 1974, $99,320,155	2,300,134,004		2,082,947,955	
Inventories, at lower of average cost or market	740,699,293		688,372,470	
Prepaid expenses	305,595,270		433,567,499	
		$8,114,743,069		$7,010,023,584
Other Investments and Sundry Assets		374,049,143		298,205,622
Plant, Rental Machines and Other Property . . . at cost:				
Land	340,254,618		305,511,464	
Buildings	2,016,970,164		1,702,896,645	
Factory, laboratory and office equipment	2,742,180,563		2,374,276,242	
	5,099,405,345		4,382,684,351	
Less: Accumulated depreciation	2,251,566,028		1,995,581,999	
	2,847,839,317		2,387,102,352	
Rental machines and parts	9,937,925,578		9,634,053,082	
Less: Accumulated depreciation	5,744,080,793		5,302,276,993	
	4,193,844,785		4,331,776,089	
		7,041,684,102		6,718,878,441
		$15,530,476,314		$14,027,107,647

Liabilities and Stockholders' Equity				
Current Liabilities:				
U.S. Federal and non-U.S. income taxes	$1,084,716,052		$1,107,470,802	
Accounts payable and accruals	2,063,931,771		1,861,864,662	
Loans payable	214,266,201		240,585,605	
		$ 3,362,914,024		$ 3,209,921,069
Deferred Investment Tax Credits		44,829,241		36,053,981
Reserves for Employees' Indemnities and Retirement Plans		411,846,782		334,994,760
Long-Term Debt		295,114,802		335,795,878
Stockholders' Equity:				
Capital stock . . . par value $5.00 per share	3,852,525,042		3,567,984,138	
Shares authorized, 156,250,000; issued and outstanding: 1975—149,844,582, 1974—148,259,260				
Retained earnings	7,563,246,423		6,542,357,821	
		11,415,771,465		10,110,341,959
		$15,530,476,314		$14,027,107,647

INTERNATIONAL BUSINESS MACHINES CORPORATION AND SUBSIDIARY COMPANIES

Consolidated Statement of Changes in Financial Position for the Year Ended December 31:

	1975	1974
Source of Working Capital:		
Net earnings	$1,989,876,966	$1,837,639,361
Depreciation and other items not requiring the current use of working capital	2,059,601,675	1,864,579,241
Total from operations	4,049,478,641	3,702,218,602
Capital stock issued under employee plans	284,540,904	280,347,882
Long-term borrowings	29,711,156	53,348,463
	4,363,730,701	4,035,914,947
Application of Working Capital:		
Investment in plant, rental machines and other property	2,438,785,856	2,912,603,050
Less: Depreciation of manufacturing facilities capitalized in rental machines	142,005,802	132,653,331
	2,296,780,054	2,779,949,719
Increase (decrease) in other investments and sundry assets (In 1974, principally securities transferred to current assets, previously held for repayment of long-term debt)	75,843,521	(458,764,397)
Cash dividends	968,988,364	819,669,017
Reduction of long-term debt	70,392,232	369,788,933
	3,412,004,171	3,510,643,272
Increase in Working Capital	$ 951,726,530	$ 525,271,675
Changes in Working Capital:		
Cash and marketable securities	$ 963,178,842	$ 483,071,594
Notes and accounts receivable	217,186,049	237,828,176
Inventories and prepaid expenses	(75,645,406)	458,862,962
U.S. Federal and non-U.S. income taxes	22,754,750	(226,214,659)
Accounts payable and accruals	(202,067,109)	(399,175,585)
Loans payable	26,319,404	(29,100,813)
Increase in working capital	951,726,530	525,271,675
Working Capital at beginning of year	3,800,102,515	3,274,830,340
Working Capital at end of year	$4,751,829,045	$3,800,102,515

NOTES TO CONSOLIDATED FINANCIAL STATEMENTS:

Significant Accounting Policies

Principles of Consolidation: The consolidated financial statements include the accounts of International Business Machines Corporation and its U.S. and non-U.S. subsidiary companies.

Translation of Non-U.S. Currency Amounts: Non-U.S. assets and liabilities are translated to U.S. dollars at year-end exchange rates, except that inventories and plant, rental machines and other property are translated at approximate rates prevailing when acquired. Income and expense items are translated at average rates of exchange prevailing during the year, except that inventories charged to cost of sales and depreciation are translated at historical rates. Exchange adjustments are included in earnings currently and were not material. Statement of Financial Accounting Standards No. 8, "Accounting for the Translation of Foreign Currency Transactions and Foreign Currency Financial Statements" was adopted during the year. The effect of the change in 1975 and prior years was not material and accordingly, prior years have not been restated.

Gross Income: Gross income is recognized from sales when the product is shipped or in certain cases upon customer acceptance, from rentals in the month in which they accrue, and from services over the contractual period or as the services are performed.

Depreciation: With minor exceptions, depreciation of U.S. properties is computed using the sum-of-the-years-digits method. Depreciation of non-U.S. properties is computed using either accelerated methods or the straight-line method.

Retirement Plans: Current service costs are accrued currently. Prior service costs resulting from improvements in the plans are amortized generally over 10 years, except that certain non-U.S. subsidiaries use longer periods not exceeding 25 years.

Expenses: Marketing expenses and development and engineering expenses are charged against income as they are incurred.

Income Taxes: Income tax expense is based on reported earnings before income taxes and thus includes the effects of timing differences between reported and taxable earnings which arise because certain transactions are included in taxable earnings in other years. Investment tax credits are deferred and amortized as a reduction of income tax expense over the average useful life of the applicable classes of property.

Non-U.S. Operations	December 31, 1975	December 31, 1974
Net assets employed in non-U.S. operations are summarized below together with gross income and net earnings from these operations.		
Current assets	$2,813,830,279	$2,320,406,212
Current liabilities	2,101,853,466	1,947,969,428
Working capital	711,976,813	372,436,784
Other investments and sundry assets	216,657,422	177,676,686
Plant, rental machines and other property, net	3,652,608,944	3,388,242,095
	4,581,243,179	3,938,355,565
Reserves for employees' indemnities and retirement plans	411,846,782	334,994,760
Long-term debt	183,364,802	213,295,878
	595,211,584	548,290,638
Net assets employed	$3,986,031,595	$3,390,064,927
	Year 1975	Year 1974
Gross income from sales, rentals and services	$7,271,473,429	$5,946,898,058
Net earnings	$1,105,713,738	$ 919,836,476

Undistributed earnings of non-U.S. subsidiaries included in consolidated retained earnings at December 31, 1975 amounted to approximately $3,046 million. These earnings are indefinitely reinvested in non-U.S. operations. Accordingly, no provision has been made for taxes that might be payable upon their remittance.

Marketable Securities	December 31, 1975	December 31, 1974
U.S. Treasury securities	$2,213,666,502	$1,138,945,915
U.S. Federal agency securities	762,061,269	1,014,027,426
State and municipal securities	451,724,310	300,732,281
Time deposits—non-U.S.	892,801,165	619,251,349
Corporate bonds, notes and other fixed-term obligations	264,191,916	556,255,913
Total	$4,584,445,162	$3,629,212,884
Market value	$4,623,040,556	$3,650,740,295

Long-Term Debt	December 31, 1975	December 31, 1974
International Business Machines Corporation:		
3½% promissory note, due in annual installments, January 1, 1977 to 1985	$ 51,750,000	$ 57,500,000
3½% promissory note, due in annual installments, May 1, 1977 to 1988	60,000,000	65,000,000
	111,750,000	122,500,000
Subsidiaries operating in non-U.S. countries (average interest rate in parentheses) payable in:		
French francs, due 1977 to 1991 (8.3%)	72,473,030	77,493,878
U.S. dollars, due 1977 to 1987 (8.7%)	53,920,759	64,231,539
Canadian dollars, due 1977 to 1991 (8.5%)	21,756,000	22,296,000
Belgian francs, due 1977 to 1983 (7.5%)	19,050,000	18,601,500
Other currencies, due 1977 to 1991 (7.8%)	16,165,013	30,672,961
	183,364,802	213,295,878
Consolidated long-term debt	$ 295,114,802	$ 335,795,878

Consolidated long-term debt at December 31, 1975 was payable:

1977	$ 33,771,483
1978	34,619,092
1979	25,494,162
1980	29,960,359
1981	24,119,987
1982-1986	86,572,688
1987-1991	60,577,031
	$295,114,802

Depreciation

Depreciation of plant, rental machines and other property charged to costs and expenses amounted to $1,680 million in 1975 and $1,575 million in 1974.

Research and Development

Research and development expenses amounted to $946 million in 1975 and $890 million in 1974.

Litigation

In January 1969, the Department of Justice filed a civil antitrust complaint against IBM under Section 2 of the Sherman Antitrust Act, charging the company with monopolizing commerce in general purpose digital computers in the United States.

In January 1975, the Court granted a Department of Justice motion to amend its complaint to add allegations of attempted monopolization of trade in various plug compatible peripheral devices which attach to IBM computer systems.

Trial of the original allegations in the case began in May 1975 and is currently in progress. The allegations added to the complaint in January 1975 will be tried at a later date in the trial.

The government continues to seek divestiture relief, requesting that IBM be reorganized into several independent and competing organizations and that IBM be enjoined from continuing its alleged monopolistic practices.

In April 1970, Xerox Corporation filed a lawsuit against IBM charging patent infringement and misuse of confidential information in connection with the IBM Copier I. In August 1973, Xerox filed a supplemental lawsuit concerning the IBM Copier II. The two lawsuits, which have been consolidated, are in the pre-trial stage. In November 1975, IBM filed an action against Xerox for infringement of an IBM patent relating to office copiers. In that action, Xerox has filed a counterclaim for breach of contract and for patent infringement concerning the IBM Copier II, but involving a different patent from the 1973 action. In its lawsuits and its counterclaim, Xerox seeks injunctive relief and damages in an unspecified amount.

In 1972, the Telex Corporation instituted two lawsuits against IBM alleging violations of the federal antitrust laws and claiming damages, which after trebling aggregated $1,084 million. IBM counterclaimed for theft of trade secrets. In 1973, the District Court found in favor of Telex and awarded damages of $259.5 million. In 1975, the Court of Appeals reversed the lower court decision with directions to enter judgment in favor of IBM. Throughout, IBM was successful in its counterclaim. These cases were settled in October 1975 without any payment of any kind by either party. Telex withdrew, with prejudice, its antitrust claims both in the U.S. and in other countries and IBM released Telex from its trade secret counterclaim.

Eight suits instituted against IBM since 1973 alleging federal antitrust law violations similar to those litigated in the Telex case remain in progress. The plaintiffs, California Computer Products, Inc., Transamerica Computer Company, Hudson General Corporation, Memorex Corporation, Forro Precision, Inc., DPF Incorporated, Memory Technology, Inc. and Sanders Associates, Inc., seek damages which after trebling aggregate $4,515 million (of which $3,150 million is sought by Memorex Corporation and its subsidiaries alone), and in some cases, injunctive relief. Seven of these suits are presently consolidated in the United States District Court for the Northern District of California for the purpose of discovery. The Sanders case is in the United States District Court for New Hampshire. Trial dates have been scheduled in five of these cases for August and November of 1976 and March 1977.

In July 1972, the trial of the Greyhound Computer Corporation lawsuit, filed in October 1969 against IBM, resulted in a directed verdict in favor of IBM. Greyhound had sought an unspecified amount of damages and injunctive relief for alleged violations of the federal antitrust laws and in connection with IBM's 1969 announcement changing the way it charges for and supports its data processing equipment. Greyhound's appeal to the United States Circuit Court of Appeals for the Ninth Circuit was argued in April 1974 and IBM is currently awaiting the decision.

IBM has denied the charges in all of these cases and is vigorously defending each action.

Stock Purchase Plan

At the April 1975 Annual Meeting, stockholders authorized an additional 2,800,000 shares of unissued capital stock for issuance under the IBM Employees 1971 Stock Purchase Plan. Under this Plan, on the annual offering date, each July 1, employees who are not participants in a Stock Option Plan, may purchase IBM's capital stock one share at a time through payroll deductions not exceeding 10% of their compensation. The price an employee pays for a share of stock is equal to 85% of the market price on the annual offering date or on the date the employee has accumulated enough money to buy the share—whichever price is lower.

Employees purchased 1,502,533 shares in 1975, for which $254 million was paid to IBM and credited to the capital stock account. At December 31, 1975, 2,355,469 shares were reserved for sale under the 1971 Plan.

Stock Option Plans

In April 1975, stockholders approved the continuation for a five-year period of a Stock Option Plan for officers and other key employees and 1,800,000 shares of authorized capital stock were reserved for issuance under the 1975 Plan. Under this Plan, as under the 1966 and 1971 Plans, options may be granted for the purchase of IBM's capital stock at not less than 100% of the market price on the day the option is granted.

Qualified options granted have a maximum duration of five years whereas nonqualified options granted have a maximum duration of ten years. Both qualified and nonqualified options become purchasable in four annual installments commencing one year from the date of grant, except for those nonqualified options which were granted simultaneously with qualified options during 1971 and 1972. Shares relating to such nonqualified options cannot be purchased until five years and one day after the date of grant and the number of shares purchasable is reduced on a one-for-one basis as shares are purchased under the related qualified option.

In accordance with the Plans, installments are cumulative and the number of shares that may be purchased and the price per share are adjusted for stock dividends and splits effected after the option is granted.

The following table summarizes stock option transactions during 1975:

	Number of Shares	
	Under Option	Available for Option
Balance at January 1, 1975	1,332,197	1,096
Options granted	522,794	(522,794)
Options terminated	(192,115)	7,866
Options exercised	(82,789)	—
Expired under the 1971 Plan	—	(8,290)
Reserved under the 1975 Plan	—	1,800,000
Balance at December 31, 1975	1,580,087	1,277,878
Exercisable at December 31, 1975	504,674	

IBM received $16.1 million for the 82,789 shares purchased during 1975, which amount was credited to the capital stock account. The 1,580,087 shares under option at December 31, 1975 were held by 849 executives at option prices ranging from $166.38 to $341.60 per share. These prices represent not less than 100% of the market price on the date of each grant from 1971 to date, adjusted for the 25% stock split in 1973. The 1,277,878 shares available for future option grants are all under the 1975 Plan.

Retirement Plans

The company and its U.S. subsidiaries have had for many years a trusteed, noncontributory retirement plan covering substantially all their employees. At December 31, 1975, there were 9,100 individuals receiving benefits under this Plan. Certain subsidiaries outside the United States have retirement plans under which funds are deposited with trustees, reserves are provided, or annuities are purchased under group contracts. The cost of all plans totaled approximately $419 million for the year 1975, compared with $334 million for the year 1974. At December 31, 1975, unfunded or unprovided for prior service costs under all plans amounted to approximately $357 million. The 1974 prepayment of $150 million was applied to the 1975 contribution.

At the latest valuation dates, the actuarially computed value of retirement benefits vested under the terms of certain plans, which included a portion of the above-mentioned prior service costs, approximated the market value of fund assets and balance sheet reserves.

Rental Expense and Lease Commitments

Rental expense amounted to $209 million in 1975 and $182 million in 1974. The approximate minimum rental commitments, in millions of dollars, under noncancellable leases for 1976 and thereafter are as follows: 1976, $164; 1977, $130; 1978, $105; 1979, $87; 1980, $69; 1981 through 1985, $208; 1986 through 1990, $70; 1991 through 1995, $28; after 1995, $22. These leases are principally for the rental of office premises; many contain renewal options and many provide for the company to pay its proportionate share of maintenance, insurance and taxes in addition to the above minimum annual rentals. All of the above amounts are net of minor amounts of sublease income.

INTERNATIONAL BUSINESS MACHINES CORPORATION AND SUBSIDIARY COMPANIES

Five-Year Comparative Consolidated Summary of Operations:

	1975	1974	1973	1972	1971
Gross income from sales, rentals and services:					
Sales	$ 4,545,358,669	$ 4,281,771,420	$ 3,372,239,088	$2,878,863,531	$2,180,140,099
Rentals and services	9,891,182,393	8,393,520,412	7,621,002,865	6,653,729,111	6,093,463,270
	14,436,541,062	12,675,291,832	10,993,241,953	9,532,592,642	8,273,603,369
Cost of sales, rentals and services:					
Sales	1,630,978,001	1,427,236,901	1,242,204,707	1,155,019,098	932,394,287
Rentals and services	3,717,709,407	3,326,565,294	2,952,202,184	2,603,054,950	2,258,706,966
Selling, development and engineering, and general and administrative expenses	5,664,897,389	4,758,558,204	4,025,375,910	3,462,135,097	3,108,475,249
Interest on debt	62,606,484	69,081,417	97,058,119	78,391,959	70,030,856
Other income, principally interest	360,527,185	340,789,345	270,066,022	191,276,017	151,850,896
Earnings before income taxes	3,720,876,966	3,434,639,361	2,946,467,055	2,425,267,555	2,055,846,907
U.S. Federal and non-U.S. income taxes	1,731,000,000	1,597,000,000	1,371,000,000	1,146,000,000	977,000,000
Net earnings	$ 1,989,876,966	$ 1,837,639,361	$ 1,575,467,055	$1,279,267,555	$1,078,846,907
Per share†	$13.35	$12.47	$10.79	$8.83	$7.50
Average number of shares outstanding†	149,044,427	147,400,733	146,061,750	144,953,058	143,811,793
Cash dividends	$ 968,988,364	$ 819,669,017	$ 654,319,289	$ 626,156,605	$ 598,207,496
Per share†	$6.50	$5.56	$4.48	$4.32	$4.16
Stock split:					
Percent	—	—	25%	—	—
Shares issued	—	—	29,182,577	—	—
Shares sold	1,585,322	1,546,572	1,131,116	865,002	947,027
†Adjusted for stock split.					
At end of year:					
Number of shares outstanding	149,844,582	148,259,260	146,712,688	116,398,995	115,533,993
Net investment in plant, rental machines and other property	$ 7,041,684,102	$ 6,718,878,441	$ 5,702,257,928	$5,271,025,074	$5,162,744,738
Long-term debt	$ 295,114,802	$ 335,795,878	$ 652,236,348	$ 772,932,774	$ 676,146,705
Working capital	$ 4,751,829,045	$ 3,800,102,515	$ 3,274,830,840	$2,562,468,943	$1,860,702,787
Number of stockholders	586,470	589,214	574,887	558,332	580,621

REPORT OF INDEPENDENT ACCOUNTANTS

To the Stockholders of International Business Machines Corporation

In our opinion, the accompanying consolidated statement of earnings and retained earnings, balance sheet and statement of changes in financial position present fairly the financial position of International Business Machines Corporation and its subsidiary companies at December 31, 1975 and 1974, and the results of their operations and the changes in their financial position for the years then ended, in conformity with generally accepted accounting principles consistently applied. Also, in our opinion, the five-year comparative consolidated summary of operations presents fairly the financial information included therein. Our examinations of these statements were made in accordance with generally accepted auditing standards and accordingly included such tests of the accounting records and such other auditing procedures as we considered necessary in the circumstances.

January 27, 1976
New York, N.Y.

Price Waterhouse & Co.

Index